W9-CFF-299

ENCYCLOPAEDIA OF
SOUTHERN AFRICA

l

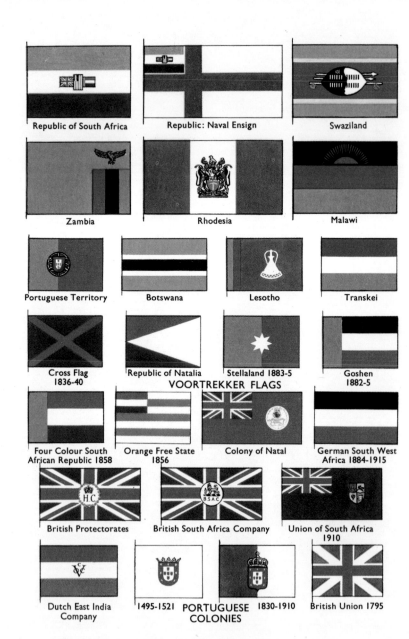

Republic of South Africa

Republic: Naval Ensign

Swaziland

Zambia

Rhodesia

Malawi

Portuguese Territory

Botswana

Lesotho

Transkei

Cross Flag
1836-40

Republic of Natalia

Stellaland 1883-5

Goshen
1882-5

VOORTREKKER FLAGS

Four Colour South
African Republic 1858

Orange Free State
1856

Colony of Natal

German South West
Africa 1884-1915

British Protectorates

British South Africa Company

Union of South Africa
1910

Dutch East India
Company

1495-1521 PORTUGUESE 1830-1910
COLONIES

British Union 1795

PLATE I: NATIONAL AND HISTORICAL FLAGS OF
SOUTHERN AFRICA

Frontispiece

ENCYCLOPAEDIA
OF
SOUTHERN
AFRICA

COMPILED AND EDITED BY

ERIC ROSENTHAL

FIFTH EDITION

FREDERICK WARNE & CO. LTD
LONDON AND NEW YORK

© FREDERICK WARNE & CO. LTD
LONDON, ENGLAND, 1961

© FIFTH EDITION 1970

LIBRARY OF CONGRESS CATALOG CARD No. 75-114791

ISBN 0 7232 1260 0

Made and printed in Great Britain by
William Clowes and Sons, Limited, London and Beccles
1542.170

FOREWORD TO FIRST EDITION

COMPILING and editing the first Encyclopaedia of Southern Africa ever produced, with subjects ranging from History, Biography and Literature on the one side; to Geography, Geology and Natural History on the other, with digressions on Sport, Shipwrecks, Cookery, Local Customs, Political Organisations, Costume and scores of other themes, has been a task requiring more than five years, and even this leaves the writer conscious of unavoidable omissions and deficiencies. To fit over 5,000 items into the compass of a single volume has far surpassed the proverbial problem of the gallon in the pint pot, but the utmost efforts have been made to maintain a balance and an objective point of view, while not overlooking the different races and communities inhabiting this exciting sub-continent.

As the name indicates, this is an Encyclopaedia of *Southern*, not merely of *South*, Africa, so that besides the Republic, it includes Rhodesia, Zambia, Malawi, South West Africa, Mozambique, Lesotho, Swaziland and Botswana.

I have to express my special thanks to the eminent contributors who have in their longer articles—signed and unsigned—so successfully combined learning with readability. Besides these there are a host of other authorities to whom I owe a similar debt—heads of important industries, State Departments in the various countries covered, town clerks, relatives of celebrities, librarians and archivists, university professors and many more. Miss Edith Stephens, the well-known expert on Fungi and Mushrooms, has been particularly helpful.

The illustrations, maps and plates specially drawn by Walter Causton of Cape Town, and by E. Lois Martin of Durban, have required months of intensive work and give much data not elsewhere to be found.

Suggestions will be welcomed for new features and entries in future editions.

FOREWORD TO FIFTH EDITION

Once again an insistent demand from the public has made necessary a new edition of the *Encyclopaedia of Southern Africa*—the fifth in the space of nine years. The opportunity has been taken to amplify and up-date the existing material in this fast-developing sub-continent. Many new facts in Business, Sport, Politics, Defence, Personalities and other fields have been incorporated, and also new sections on mountain heights in Southern Africa, lengths of Southern African Rivers, Heart Transplants, the Metric System, Yachting, the Stock Exchange, Oil Prospecting etc., along with extra maps and illustrations. As before, any corrections will be welcomed.

ERIC ROSENTHAL

Cape Town.

LIST OF MAIN ARTICLES

LIST OF COLOUR PLATES

LIST OF MAPS

KEY TO MAP SYMBOLS

INDUSTRY

Airport	Copper	Lead	Rubber
Antimony	Diamonds	Manganese	Salt
Asbestos	Diamonds, Industrial	Marble	Saw Mills
Canning Fish	Fishing	Motor Assembly	Ship Yards
Canning Fruit	Footwear	Oil Refineries	Sugar
Cement	Gold	Paper Mills	Textiles
Chrome Ore	Hydro-Electric Power	Petrol from Coal (Sasol)	Tobacco
Clothing Manufacture	Industrial Area	Platinum	Tungsten
Coal	Iron & Steel	Railway Workshops	Uranium
			Zinc

AGRICULTURE

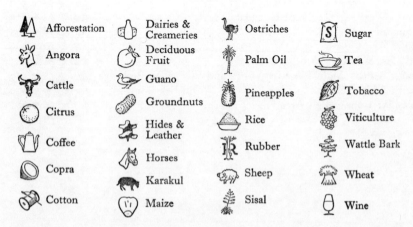

Afforestation	Dairies & Creameries	Ostriches	Sugar
Angora	Deciduous Fruit	Palm Oil	Tea
Cattle	Guano	Pineapples	Tobacco
Citrus	Groundnuts	Rice	Viticulture
Coffee	Hides & Leather	Rubber	Wattle Bark
Copra	Horses	Sheep	Wheat
Cotton	Karakul	Sisal	Wine
	Maize		

A

Aardvark (literally 'Earth-Pig'). *See* ANT BEAR.

Aardwolf. (*Proteles cristatus*). Maanhaar Jakhals or Earthwolf. Distinctive animal with no close relatives, found in many parts of South Africa, especially in bushveld and open treeless country. Nocturnal in habit, it lives in burrows

Aardwolf (Earthwolf)

and is timid of dogs and other animals. It can, however, be easily tamed. Emits a musk smell on being attacked. Its food is largely locusts, termites, eggs and lizards, for which its rudimentary molar teeth and small incisors are adequate. It has a small sharp face and body over 2 feet long. Colouring greyish-yellow, shoulders and body striped with black. *See* MAMMALS.

Aasblom. *See* SUCCULENTS.

Aasvoël. Afrikaans name for Vulture (q.v.), so-called from its habit of eating carrion (aas).

Abakweta. Name applied to native boys at the age of about 13, when they are circumcised. During this time nobody is allowed access to them and they are considered unclean.

Abbotsdale. Village near Malmesbury in the Cape Province. Population: about 800, most of whom are Coloured.

Abdurrahman, Dr. Abdullah. Leader of the Coloured community. Born of

Abakweta Dancers

Malay parentage in Cape Town, he studied medicine at the University of Glasgow, where he qualified in 1893. In 1895 he began practice in the city of his birth, soon acquiring an outstanding reputation. He sat in the Cape Town City Council from 1904 to 1940, and in the Cape Provincial Council from 1914 to 1940. His death occurred on February 2 of that year.

Abercorn. *See* MBALA.

Abercorn Gold Field. North-east o Salisbury and south of Mazoe River, Rhodesia.

Abercorn, James Hamilton, Second Duke of. Associate of Cecil John Rhodes. Born in Scotland on August 24, 1838, and educated at Harrow and Oxford. A close associate of King Edward VII (when Prince of Wales).

Became Chairman of the British South Africa Company (q.v.) upon its foundation in 1888. He died January 3, 1913.

Aberdeen. Town in Camdeboo Mountains, Cape Province, founded as Church village 1856; stock breeding and sheep centre. 2,400 feet above sea-level. Population: 5,140, including 1,300 Whites.

Ablaing, Johannes Cornelis D'. Uncle of Willem Adriaan Van der Stel, whom he succeeded as Acting Governor of the Cape. Began his career in the East Indies, where he was Commander of Palembang. Originally sent to the Cape as 'Secunde'; was made Acting Governor as from June 3, 1707, to February 1, 1708. Later returned to Batavia, where he ended his days as 'Extraordinary Counsellor of India.'

Abraham, Johannes Hendrikus (Hans). First Commissioner-General for Xosa National Unit, covering Transkei and Ciskei Bantu Homeland. Born at Roodebank, Standerton district, 1908, and elected to Parliament in 1948. Appointed Commissioner-General 1960.

Abrahamson, Abraham Eliezer. Rhodesian politician and industrialist. Born at Bulawayo on October 13, 1922, and educated at Milton High School and the University of Cape Town. Saw active service during World War II. As a manufacturer he was elected member of the Bulawayo Chamber of Industries in 1951 and became interested in social questions which ultimately brought him into politics, as member for Bulawayo East, in 1953. From 1958 to 1962 he was Minister of Labour, Social Welfare and Housing in the Territorial Government.

Acacia (Leguminosae). Among the 40 or more South African species of Acacia, occurring mostly in the Lowveld and drier areas, are the following:

Sweet Thorn, Soetdoring (*Acacia karroo*). A small tree, armed with strong 2- to 3-inch thorns, common over most of South Africa, even the Highveld, where the scent of the yellow flowers hangs in the air. The wood makes good fuel but is not durable enough for other uses. The bark can be used for tanning, and the resin for a good quality gum.

Camel-Thorn, Kameeldoring (*A. giraffae*). Is a large tree with spreading crown found widely in Griqualand West. The leaves and pods are browsed by the giraffe and kudu in spite of the fierce stipule thorns at the base of the leaf stalks. The wood makes a hard, heavy timber.

The *Ana Tree* (*A. alkida*) is another large tree, up to 50 feet, with smooth white bark and highly nutritive and almost circular pods. It is common in the Kruger Park, Zululand, South West Africa and elsewhere in the tropics. A fine group of these trees, 9 miles north-west of Potgietersrust, has been proclaimed a National Monument and named 'Livingstone's Trees' (although it is doubtful if he ever saw them).

The *Flame Thorn Tree* (*A. ataxacantha*) is a strong climber or straggly shrub, conspicuous in autumn for its scarlet pods. It belongs to tropical East Africa, the Eastern Transvaal and Natal, and often grows as a dense thicket. The flat-topped, 30-foot *Umbrella Thorn,* Haak-en-Steek (*A. heteracantha*), literally 'Hook-and-Stab,' is the tree most frequently used to illustrate bush-veld vegetation. It has tiny close-packed leaves, both hooks and long slender white thorns, and sweet-scented white flowers.

The *Knob Thorn* (*A. migrescens*), one of the commonest trees in the dry areas, often growing singly in long grass, is a completely deciduous tree, bare of leaves for months at a time. The white flower-spikes appear before the leaves. It has strongly re-curved thorns and may be easily recognised by the thorn-crowned knobs on the trunk. A fine dark slow-growing wood, often used for making jukskeis.

The *Fever Tree* (*A. xanthophloea*) is a tall, deciduous tree bearing scented yellow flowers. Its preference for swampy, unhealthy places won it the name, as did its yellow-green trunk and powdery bark. The most important of the exotic Acacias is the *Black Wattle* (*A. mollissima*), on which the tan-bark industry has been built. A fast-growing tree, doing best in the mist belt, 3,000 feet or more above sea-level.

Achterveld. Portion of Karroo near Victoria West, including Verkeerde Vlei.

Ackermann, Alfred Seabold Eli. Engineer and writer. Born in 1867 and educated at the South African College. From an early age he showed unusual ingenuity, and at 17 displayed a violin of his own design and manufacture at the Industrial Exhibition at Cape Town. Proceeding to England, he was one of the early students at the City and Guilds College in London, where he qualified as both a civil and a mechanical engineer and was later elected a Fellow. He first attracted attention by his writings on coal-cutters in 1902, and in 1907 designed one of the world's first plants utilising the power of the sun, which was actually erected and tried out in Egypt and the U.S.A. He also did remarkable work on investigating the physical properties of clay, deliberately choosing home-made apparatus to show that expensive equipment was not necessary to secure valuable results. Upon the introduction of radio, Ackermann served for a time as consulting engineer to the early British Broadcasting Company and other organisations. For over 30 years he was Secretary of the Society of Engineers, and he held office on other professional bodies. His main fame rests on his book, *Popular Fallacies*, first issued in 1907, and since republished a number of times. He died in London on April 13, 1951.

Acornhoek. Settlement on the Selati Railway, 103 miles from Komatipoort in the Eastern Transvaal, near foothills of the Drakensberg. Important centre for the production of vegetables and sub-tropical fruits.

Acton Homes. Settlement in Natal, near Ladysmith. On January 17, 1900, Lord Dundonald surprised a Boer force there under Commandant C. J. De Villiers.

Adam Kok. *See* KOK.

Adderley, Charles Bowyer (1st Lord Norton). English parliamentary protagonist of Cape Colony. Born in Birmingham, 1814. Large industrialist: interested in early town-planning experiments at Saltley in 1837; helped to start Canterbury settlement in New Zealand. Sat in House of Commons, 1841–78. While there fought for extension of Colonial self-government. Took up cause of Cape colonists in opposing the threatened introduction of convicts in 1849. Out of gratitude the authorities in Cape Town renamed the Heerengracht 'Adderley Street.' After sponsoring much social legislation Mr. Adderley was raised to the peerage as Lord Norton in 1878. He continued his Parliamentary career as President of the Board of Trade and put through Act creating the Dominion of Canada in 1867. He lived to be 91 and died in 1905.

Adders or **Vipers** (Viperidae). A venomous family of snakes, with flat, usually triangular heads, thick, plump bodies and short tails. They are peculiar in having, behind the front pair of large hollow fangs, an indefinite number of embryo reserve fangs, all fixed to a bony hinge. The hinge bends the fangs back to allow the mouth to shut. The Puff-adder (*Bitis arietans*) is the commonest and most widespread in South Africa, its dark body patterned with yellow V-shaped marks. The young are born from eggs incubated in the female (oviparous) and crawl out and away, already poisonous, almost immediately afterwards. Puff-adders eat at perhaps monthly intervals. Their jaws expand easily to swallow a large rat or chicken. They are sluggish movers, but will hiss, puff out their necks and bite, rather than glide away. Average length 2 feet 6 inches. The Night-adder (*Causus rhombeatus*) is also found in most parts of Southern Africa, but although poisonous is not as deadly as the puff adder or mamba. It haunts dwellings at night for its food of frogs and mice, but is not aggressive unless trodden on. It lays a number of eggs and coils round to incubate them. The Hornsman or Horned-adder (*Bitis cornuta*) is so called from the scales above its eyes, and is found in the dry, sandy parts of the Cape. About 18 inches long and a dirty reddish-brown with dark markings. Another variety, the Berg-adder (*Bitis atropos*), also short and thick, about a foot long, with circular markings edged with white, is found in the mountainous parts of the Cape and Natal.

Addison, William. Rhodesian editor and Parliamentary Speaker. Born in Scotland in 1890, he served in World War II and came to Rhodesia in 1923 as editor of the *Bulawayo Chronicle* and later transferred to the *Rhodesia Herald* in Salisbury. After a spell as editor of the *Star* in Johannesburg he returned to Rhodesia, entered politics and was elected Speaker of the Federal Parliament in 1954. He retired in 1959 and died in 1966.

Addo Bush or **Addo National Park.** Scrub forest some 45 miles from Port Elizabeth, covering about 8,000 acres, fenced to contain a special breed of elephants. Formerly there were over 100, but their damage to crops caused the authorities to engage Major P. J. Pretorius (q.v.) to reduce their numbers to 20. They are slowly increasing.

Adelaide. Town in Eastern Cape Province on Koonap River, near Fort

Beaufort. Originally a military post, named after Queen Adelaide, wife of William IV. Established in 1834 as village. Sheep-farming centre. Near Winterberg Mountains. Population: 7,000, including 1,450 Whites.

Adendorp. Village 5 miles from Graaff-Reinet, named after former land-owner, Adendorff. Founded in 1855. Has benefited from Van Ryneveld's Pass Irrigation Scheme, but remains a small community. Population: 1,646, including 320 Whites, 660 Coloureds and 666 Bantu.

Administrative Service Corps. South African military unit, founded February 1, 1923.

Adonis or **Adoons.** Nickname traditionally applied by Afrikaners to the South African baboon.

African Explosives and Chemical Industries. Largest manufacturers of explosives in the world and one of the largest manufacturers of chemicals. Established on March 21, 1924, as a merger of interests of De Beers Consolidated Mines (q.v.) in the Cape Explosives Works and the South African interests then existing of Imperial Chemical Industries Limited. The latter comprised the British South African Explosives Company, with its main plant at Modderfontein, Transvaal, dating back to 1896, and the Kynoch Works at Umbogintwini, Natal, established in 1908. The Cape Explosives Works at Somerset West, Cape Province, were founded by Cecil Rhodes in 1900. Today African Explosives and Chemical Industries has a capital of R71,000,000 and is associated with the Anglo-American group (q.v.). Its works at Modderfontein are the largest single explosives plant in the world, followed by Somerset West. Fertilisers are produced at Umbogintwini and Somerset West, as well as in Rhodesia. A special cyanide plant is operated at Klipspruit and new installations for plastics and other specialities have been erected near Sasolburg (q.v.). Production is more than 5,500,000 cases of explosives yearly, equal to 130,000 tons, and over 125,000 miles of fuse is annually manufactured. The Urea plant at Modderfontein is the largest in the world, providing 110,000 tons yearly of concentrated nitrogenous fertiliser.

African Jabiru. Alternative name for Saddle-Bill (q.v.).

African Jacana. Alternative name for Lily-Trotter (q.v.).

African Metals Corporation Limited. State-backed company associated with the Iscor group (South African Iron and Steel Industrial Corporation Limited, q.v.). Founded July 23, 1937, with an authorised capital of £1,600,000. Mainly engaged in production of pig iron, ferro-alloys and fertilisers, with plants in Natal at Newcastle, (pig iron); in Transvaal at Kookfontein, near Meyerton, and at Vereeniging (ferro-alloys); and at Bellville near Cape Town (rock phosphates) and elsewhere.

In 1962 the Corporation entered into a long-term contract for the delivery to the Yawata Iron and Steel Company of Japan of 5,000,000 tons of South African pig-iron over 10 years, for which a special fleet of freighters was secured. Deliveries began in August 1964.

African National Congress. Political body established by Southern African Bantus in January 1912, under the name South African Native National Congress. The founders were Dr. P. Ka I. Seme, G. P. Montsioa, R. W. Msimang and Alfred Mangena. The first President was the Rev. J. L. Dube (q.v.). In 1914 a deputation was sent by the Congress to England. Annual conferences have been held regularly. In 1944 the African National Congress formed its own Congress Youth League. In recent times a more extreme wing, calling themselves the Pan-African Congress (q.v.), has broken away from the main body of the Congress. Parallel with the development of the African National Congress in the Republic, similar bodies, under the same name, developed in Rhodesia and Malawi. Both A.N.C. and P.A.C. are banned in South Africa.

Afrikaanse Akademie vir Taal, Wetenskap en Kuns (Afrikaans Academy of Language, Science and Art). Established in 1909 by leading scholars, it has played a basic part in encouraging development of the language, by issuing spelling rules, etc. It grants a gold medal for Afrikaans literature and other awards. With the passing of time its activities have been subdivided, each section issuing its own proceedings.

AFRIKAANS—ITS ORIGIN AND DEVELOPMENT
by
J. SMUTS, M.A., PH.D. (Cape Town)
Rhodes University, Grahamstown

AFRIKAANS is the youngest member of the Germanic group of languages and like Dutch, English and Frisian it is Western Germanic. It originated from the Dutch dialects of the 17th century and developed into a separate language during the century and a half of the rule of the Dutch East India Company at the Cape.

This evolution within such a comparatively short time has aroused great interest amongst philologists, and widely different theories as to the origin of Afrikaans have been held. Owing to the absence of written records, these theories were based largely on indirect evidence, such as historical facts and references in travel books to the language spoken in the country districts.

An important fact to remember is that when the settlement at the Cape was founded the Netherlands had no uniform written or spoken language, and that the first Dutch colonists spoke different dialects. The French Huguenots who came to the Cape in 1688 were followed after 1691 by many German settlers. The Dutch also came into contact with the languages of the Hottentots, of slaves from Angola, Guinea, Madagascar and Malaya, and the broken Portuguese of the Eastern slaves. Except for vocabulary, however, there is hardly any trace of direct influence of another language on Afrikaans, and Dutch remained the dominant language, which was in due course adopted by all the foreigners. Some consider evolution to have been spontaneous, and accelerated by the mixing of dialects, remoteness from the mother country and the almost complete absence of conserving influences such as schools and literature. In the main the dropping of inflexions in Afrikaans can be explained, as in English, by the unchecked working of analogy and a few sound laws or tendencies, to some extent already active in the 17th-century Dutch and Low German dialects. The broken Dutch of the foreigners, who outnumbered the Dutch during most of the Company's rule, may also have simplified the language of the Dutch colonists.

It is generally agreed that English cannot be held responsible for the origin of Afrikaans, since the language spoken at the Cape had evidently assumed its modified form before the arrival of the English in 1795. In spite of 150 years of close association since that date and of the higher status of English during so many years, in administration, education and culture, English has had very little influence on the grammatical structure of Afrikaans.

Though the modified form of Dutch spoken at the Cape at the end of the 18th century, particularly by the farmers in the country, was not yet Afrikaans in its present form, it already exhibited the main characteristics of Afrikaans, and in travel books after 1800 we find it referred to as Cape Dutch, Afrikaans-Hollands or 'Boeren-Hollands.'

Although the daughter of Dutch, Afrikaans is a purer Germanic language, few of the French words in Dutch being known to the first colonists, and comparatively few words having been borrowed from other languages with which it came into contact. It is noteworthy that many Afrikaans words of Dutch origin have developed a different meaning.

The phonetic differences between Afrikaans and Dutch are limited to some vowel changes, some changes from voiced to voiceless consonants, and the shortening of words by the loss of a syllable or final consonant.

The distinguishing characteristic of Afrikaans is the simplification of its grammatical structure. Certain attributive adjectives are inflected, while nouns are inflected to form the plural and diminutives. The verb is not inflected to express difference in number or person, and remains unchanged except for the prefixing of *ge-* to form the past participle. Its most remarkable feature is that the regular alternation of the vowel of the verb stem in the imperfect tense and the past participle of strong verbs, characteristic of the Germanic languages, has been abolished in Afrikaans. It has, in fact, discarded the imperfect tense altogether and expressed the past by means of the perfect tense or the present tense in conjunction with an adverb or other word expressing time, aspect or modality. Afrikaans also knows no grammatical gender or case, though in the singular of the personal pronouns there are still different forms for the subject and object. Inflexions have therefore largely been replaced by analytical means of expression in Afrikaans, which is accordingly considered an analytical language.

PLATE II: BIRDS OF SOUTHERN AFRICA

1. Penguin. 2. Cape Turtle Dove. 3. Darter or Snake Bird. 4. Crested Hornbill. 5. Black Sunbird. 6. Knysna Loerie. 7. Paradise Flycatcher. 8. Berghaan. 9. Carmine Bee Eater. 10. Hammerkop or Tekwane. 11. Angola Pitta. 12. Crested Barbett.

Although Afrikaans was already widely spoken, Dutch remained the written and cultural language in the 19th century. Afrikaans was first used as a written language merely to achieve comic or satirical effect, for example by Boniface and by Bain and Rex in their play *Kaatje Kekkelbek* (1834). After 1844 letters in Afrikaans began to appear in *Het Kaapsche Grensblad*, and in 1860 L. H. Meurant published a pamphlet in Afrikaans in the *Cradock News* on the question of the secession of the Eastern Province. A stream of letters and dialogues in Afrikaans followed in various newspapers. No attempt was made, however, to claim any rights for Afrikaans as a written language until 1872, when pleas for Afrikaans began to appear in the newspapers, and in 1875 an association known as *Die Genootskap van Regte Afrikaners* was formed at Paarl to promote the use of Afrikaans, refine the language and advocate its recognition. In 1876 it published the first Afrikaans newspaper known as *Die Afrikaanse Patriot*, which appeared until 1904, and from 1896 to 1906 a monthly magazine known as *Ons Klyntji*. In 1876 an elementary Afrikaans grammar appeared, in 1877 a short history book, in 1878 an Afrikaans spelling-book and reader and in 1902 the first Afrikaans dictionary, the *Patriot Woordeboek*. Specimen translations of several books of the Bible in Afrikaans appeared soon after 1889.

Though Afrikaans as a written language became ever more popular, many influential Afrikaners were strongly opposed to it and advocated the retention of Dutch as the written and cultural language.

The Boer War gave a fresh impetus to the language movement and from 1905 onwards literary work began to appear in Afrikaans. Since then a considerable literature has come into being, including work of lasting merit.

In 1918 Afrikaans was elevated to the status of an official language of the Union and in 1925 it replaced Dutch as one of the languages of Parliament.

In the field of education Afrikaans was recognised in 1914 as a medium of instruction in schools in three of the Provinces of the Union, and was later also introduced in the Universities.

In 1915 the Suid-Afrikaanse Akademie vir Wetenskap en Kuns published the first *Woordelys en Spelreëls* to regulate spelling, which has since been revised several times.

By 1919 Afrikaans had been recognised as an official language of the Church by all the Dutch Reformed Churches, and in 1933 a complete translation of the Bible in Afrikaans was published.

A Standard Dictionary of the Afrikaans language is being compiled with Government support and five volumes comprising the letters A to K have already been published.

Afrikaans is also fast developing into a technical language and during the last fifteen years a number of lists of technical terms have been published by the Akademie, Government departments and other bodies. Technical works in Afrikaans are also beginning to appear.

AFRIKAANS LITERATURE
by
PROFESSOR T. J. HAARHOFF
Cape Town

IN the development of most languages we find a time when the spoken form diverges from the literary form and stakes a claim to recognition as part of the written tradition. Such a time was reached by English in the days of King Alfred and by Italian in the days of Dante. The tendency is for the language to begin shedding its inflexional endings, to simplify its grammar and (as happened in the passage of Latin into the Romance languages and of ancient Greek into modern Greek) to use the diminutives that characterise the speech of the people.

This is what happened when Afrikaans developed from the Dutch of Holland which the first settlers at the Cape brought with them in 1652. Exposed to local influences of the indigenous tribes, of the Malay Portuguese of slaves, of the French of the Huguenots, the language began to diverge from its original form; and as early as 1750 there are written traces of this divergence.

Small wonder, then, that while Dutch sufficed for formal utterances, the spoken language should come to be used for intimate expression.

A decade ago Roy Campbell wrote, in an unpublished letter: 'The Afrikaans language . . . is full of adventure for the bold and daring . . . and unique among contemporary tongues for youth and freshness. . . . Afrikaans is just now in such a state as was the English language when Marlowe first snaffled its jaws with thunder.'

The early writings associated with S. J. du Toit and his friends about 1875 can hardly be called literature, though they demonstrated the potentialities of Afrikaans. It was the War of 1899–1902 that brought the first real Afrikaans literature and roused national feeling. Necessarily, the early poems of the great triumvirate, Jan Celliers, J. D. du Toit ('Totius,' son of the pioneer mentioned above) and C. L. Leipoldt, were largely concerned with the war. Dr. Leipoldt, though often careless as a writer, was by far the most spontaneous—a man of real genius. He was also the writer with the widest range of interest, acquainted with English and European literature and with the Dutch East. Some of his English poems, published after his death, reach a high standard.

Just as the Roman farmer, when he began to develop a literature, was faced with the enormous prestige of an older literature in Greek, the Afrikaner found himself faced with English and European literature, which he feared would swamp his individuality. But the Roman enriched his own tradition by achieving a harmony of cultures. And Leipoldt pointed the way towards an eventual harmonisation, without loss of individuality, of English and Afrikaans cultures in South Africa.

The enormous and genial works of C. J. Langenhoven form a broad foundation for future development. In the novel the theme at first was that of the war, and then, in C. M. van den Heever and others, the degeneration of the Afrikaner who had lost his farm and could not adapt himself to city life. But later the fact that the Afrikaner was definitely established in the big towns brought about a more realistic study of present conditions in South Africa. There have also been notable attempts to deal with situations outside South Africa, for example in the striking dramas of Opperman (*Periandros van Korinthe*) and van Wyk Louw (*Germanicus*) and the novel of F. A. Venter (*Die Man van Cirene*), who also produced a sympathetic study of Native life (*Die Swart Pelgrim*); while Uys Krige has brought home the charm of Spain in prose and in lyrics and above all in his famous drama, *Die Goue Kring*. In the dramatic field G. Beukes and W. A. de Klerk (who made the mountains of S. Africa live for us) have achieved great success. Eugene Marais was outstanding as a poet and rivalled Maeterlinck in his nature-studies. Toon van der Heever, like H. A. Fagan, showed that a judge can be devoted to literary production.

There has been a great advance in character-drawing, where the epigrammatic force of Afrikaans and its humorous potentialities (supremely illustrated in the poet A. G. Visser, the friend of Sir Thomas Holland, the late Principal of the University of Edinburgh, as well as in I. D. du Plessis and in prose writers like C. M. van den Heever and Dirk Mostert) have been used with great effect. Satire is allied to caustic humour, as it was in the Roman, and is seen, for example, in the animal fables of I. D. du Plessis, who is known for his studies of the Coloured people, a sphere in which much good work has been done by C. W. Kuhn ('Mikro') and, recently, by a young writer of much promise, J. S. Rabie.

An interesting development is the emergence of Coloured poets in Afrikaans such as S. V. Petersen and P. J. Philander in whom the pathos of their people is poignantly expressed. There is also the Jewish poetess, Olga Kirsch, who is concerned with the problems of Israel and uses a graceful Afrikaans.

With the widening interest in technique it was inevitable that, in contrast to old and valued stalwarts like D. F. Malherbe, a writer of unexhausted fertility, a new school of poets should have arisen in the thirties. They were influenced by writers like T. S. Eliot and sought new forms of expression and new themes. Turning away from the romantic idea and from rhetoric—though they did not always realise that there is such a thing as good rhetoric—they adapted themselves to the stream-lined world of modern technology and

looked on language with a semantic eye. Much more introspective than the older poets, they flouted the rules of regular rhythm in experiments that are often interesting. Of this school the leaders are Van Wyk Louw, in whom we see a search for the interpretation of life and a return to the Roman conception of the poet as a prophet (Vates); D. Opperman who paid a striking tribute to William Blake and in whom is seen the striving to pierce this veil of external things and reach the truth; Elisabeth Eybers, similarly a seeker for spiritual values who wrestles with the problems of womanhood in tuneful verse; W. E. G. Louw, whose remarkable first volume was the prelude to the movement; Uys Krige, modern in form but in his rich and spontaneous vein of lyrical sentiment mainly romantic, in contrast to the others; C. M. van den Heever, not usually associated with the new group, but like them a seeker and a writer of impressive verse; Ernst van Heerden, a humane poet of great value, who has a fine feeling for language; S. J. Pretorius, largely concerned with social conditions in the city, and a writer of ability; G. A. Watermeyer, who has written an English poem on Atlantis and many ballads of great merit; and others whom there is no space to mention.

Afrikaanse Pers Beperk. Afrikaans publishing house. Established in Pretoria on March 19, 1932, as proprietors of *Die Vaderland*, then a half-weekly paper and successor to *Ons Vaderland* (started in 1915). In 1935 the Afrikaanse Pers was reconstructed and moved its headquarters to Johannesburg where *Die Vaderland* became a daily paper from July 3, 1936. Other journals followed, including the magazine *Die Brandwag* on February 6, 1937, and *Kort en Goed*, the first Afrikaans Digest, in May 1939. *Dagbreek*, the group's Sunday paper, has

been merged with *Landstem*. *See also* NEWSPAPERS. Book publishing, particularly in the educational field, has been extensively developed.

Afrikaanse Verbond Begrafnis Onderneming Beperk. Large South African co-operative burial society, established in Bloemfontein in December 1921 by H. H. van Rooijen. With over 100,000 members and several hundred branches, it maintains its own coffin and other factories. Recently it has also become a life insurance company.

Afrikander Bond. More correctly Afrikaner Bond. Political party, founded in 1879 by the Rev. S. J. du Toit (q.v.), editor of *Di Patriot* of Paarl and founder of the movement for the recognition of the Afrikaans language. It soon amalgamated with the 'Boere Beschermings Vereeniging' (Farmers' Protection Association), formed the previous year in the first instance to oppose a new Excise Act, to which the wine-growers objected. Stimulated by the anti-English feelings brought on by the annexation of the Transvaal and the ensuing Majuba campaign, the Afrikander Bond soon rose to great power, and in 1885 achieved one of its objectives when the use of the Dutch language in the Cape Parliament was legalised. J. H. Hofmeyr (Onse Jan) (q.v.), who soon became the dominant force behind the Bond, though he preferred not to hold office, adopted a policy of friendship and collaboration with Cecil John Rhodes, and of friendliness to the British Commonwealth, even attending a Colonial Conference as a delegate. In 1895 the Jameson Raid put an end to any link between the Afrikander Bond and Rhodes, though it retained, in a large measure, the support of John X. Merriman and other English-speaking leaders. In 1898 the Bond came into power, with W. P. Schreiner (q.v.) as Prime Minister, and remained in office till 1900, the division of loyalties prompted by the South African War confronting its heads with many difficulties. The party continued as the opposition until 1908, when its leaders, J. W. Sauer, N. F. De Waal and others, joined the Merriman Ministry. It finally merged into the South African Party under General Louis Botha at Union.

Afrikander Cattle. Hardy breed of South African cattle, known to the early settlers and already mentioned in the 1850's. Noted for their large horns and resistance to climatic conditions. Successful experiments in introducing Afrikander cattle to the dry regions of the United States, particularly Texas, were carried out in 1930 and after. Now recognised as a breed peculiar to South Africa.

Afrikander Ox

Afrikaner, Large Brown, or **Aandpypie** (*Gladiolus grandis* Thunb.). Bulb with slender stem up to 2 feet. Leaves narrow, ribbed, up to 1½ feet long. Flowers up to three in a spike, 2½–3 inches long, yellowish or red-brown, sweet-scented after sunset. Lower mountain slopes. South-western districts in Cape Province. *See* GLADIOLUS.

Agapanthus or **African Lily.** A strong plant with a showy umbel of blue flowers above a mass of thick sword-shaped leaves, green all the year. The small variety grows on hillsides and the larger under shady trees or by rocky river banks in Natal and the inland districts of the South-Western Cape. Summer flowering. *See* LILY.

Agatha. Centre of former Thabina Gold Field in the Northern Transvaal, about 50 miles from Pietersburg in foothills of Drakensberg. Large plantations and forests near by, also vegetable-growing industry. 4,500 feet above sea-level.

Agriculture. There are approximately 120,000 White-owned farms and small

Afrikaner

holdings in the Republic of South Africa, covering about 220,000,000 acres. Of these, 43,000 farms are in the Cape, 38,000 in the Transvaal, 25,000 in the Orange Free State and 12,000 in Natal. The largest group of farms—16,500—averages between 600 and 1,000 acres, the second largest—16,400—between 200 and 500. About 12,000 are between 1,000 and 1,500 acres and 10,000 are small holdings under 10 acres. There are roughly equal numbers—around 8,500—of farms in the 40 to 100 acre and the 1,500 to 2,000 acre categories. Next come 6,000 farms between 10 and 20 acres, 5,700 of 500 to 600 acres, and slightly fewer between 20 and 40 acres. The total area under cultivation is estimated at 20,000,000 acres.

Maize (mealies) is the largest crop in the Republic, production in record year 1966-67 reaching 109,000,000 bags (equal to about 160,000,000 bushels) and the area planted 8,000,000 acres. The largest production comes from the Transvaal, closely followed by the Orange Free State; these surpass the Cape Province almost threefold and Natal almost fivefold.

The Cape is the chief wheat-growing province, followed by the Orange Free State (less than half the Cape output), the Transvaal (under a fifth), with negligible quantities from Natal.

In Kaffir-corn (sorghum) the largest producer is the Transvaal, its output surpassing the combined yields of the Orange Free State, the Cape and Natal in that order. By far the greater part of the country's barley and rye comes from the South-Western Cape. Oats are grown in the Orange Free State.

Most of the nation's potato output comes from the Transvaal, followed by the Cape, the Orange Free State and Natal. The Transvaal also leads in groundnuts, with the Orange Free State second, Natal third and the Cape fourth. By far the largest output of lucerne is from the Cape, with the Orange Free State second, the Transvaal third and Natal fourth.

In cattle by far the most thickly populated province in the Republic is the Cape, for of the grand total—Black- and White-owned—amounting to about 12,000,000 head, it has approximately 4,000,000, slightly more than one-half in the hands of Whites. The Transvaal, with 3,500,000, comes second (about 250,000 Bantu-owned), then Natal with 2,400,000 (1,100,000 Bantu-owned), and lastly the Orange Free State, with 2,000,000 head (300,000 Bantu-owned).

Nearly half the country's sheep—over 18,000,000 out of 37,000,000—are in the Cape Province, with about 8,000,000 in the Orange Free State, 6,000,000 in the Transvaal and about 1,800,000 in Natal. Of these totals two-thirds are merinos—over 30,000,000—and about 6,500,000 non-woolled, the majority in each case again in the Cape. South Africa, formerly negligible in the karakul field, now has close on 2,000,000 of these animals.

Of the Republic's pigs—about 1,000,000—over one-quarter are in the Cape, followed by the Transvaal, Natal and the Orange Free State. Of close on 400,000 horses the Cape has about 70,000, the Orange Free State about 72,000, the Transvaal 180,000 and Natal 53,000. With mules the order is slightly different, about 100,000 being divided among the Cape, the Transvaal, Natal and the Orange Free State, in that order. Of the 700,000 donkeys the largest number is in the Transvaal, followed by the Cape, Natal and the Orange Free State.

The principal poultry province is the Transvaal, with the Cape close behind, the Orange Free State third and Natal last. (The total for the Republic is about 22,000,000 birds.)

Rhodesia has approximately 6,200 White-operated farms, with some 985,000 acres under cultivation, out of 34,547,000 acres. By far the most valuable crop is tobacco, nearly 100,000 tons of which were grown in the former Federation, most of it in Rhodesia, followed by Malawi. Cotton production has risen 27-fold since 1960, to 54,000,000 lb. in 1966. The largest grain crop in the former Federation was maize, of which Rhodesia accounted for 4,414,000 bags in 1963. There are about 3,500,000 head of cattle in Rhodesia, nearly half owned by Africans.

South West Africa is almost entirely pastoral, the most valuable livestock being the 3,600,000 karakul sheep, in which the territory leads the world. Bechuanaland specialises in cattle ranching; Basutoland, because of its cold climate, in wool and hard wheat; while Swaziland is engaged in forestry and cotton development.

Mozambique is an important exporter of tropical produce, including sugar from the Zambesi valley, cotton, groundnuts and copra. Settlers from Europe have been introduced into the Limpopo valley.

Agterryer. Bantu servants who accompanied Boers travelling and hunting and on their campaigns, to carry their spare guns and stores.

Agtertang. Portion of a wagon holding the back axle to the 'long-wagon'.

Agulhas. Village near Bredasdorp in the Cape Province. Population: 56, including 36 Whites.

Agulhas Bank. A large area extending about 50 miles out to sea from Cape Agulhas, noted for its valuable fishing, the development of which began in the 1890's.

Agulhas, Cape. Southernmost cape in Africa, 26 miles from Bredasdorp. Takes its name from the Portuguese word meaning 'Needles,' on account of the sharpness of its rocks. Because of many wrecks here a lighthouse was built in 1849, and has since been strengthened to 18,000,000 candlepower. A township has been established near by.

Air Force. See SOUTH AFRICAN AIR FORCE.

Air Rhodesia. National airline of Rhodesia, established with effect from November 1, 1967, following the breakup of Central African Airways (q.v.).

Ais-Ais. Hot radio-active spring in South West Africa, much visited by campers. About 100 miles south of Keetmanshoop. Name of Bushman origin.

Alabama. Warship of 1,000 tons used for several years by the Confederate States during the American Civil War of 1861–1865 as a commerce raider against the North. Launched by Laird of Birkenhead on August 24, 1862, she began the famous cruises which brought her into South African waters. After putting in at Saldanha Bay (q.v.) and making repeated captures near Cape Town, she caught the *Sea*

Bride in Table Bay on August 5, 1863. She also took in stores, etc., from Cape Town, received an enthusiastic welcome and successfully evaded the pursuing cruiser *Vanderbilt*. A serious diplomatic crisis arose between the United States and Britain, ultimately settled by arbitration long after the *Alabama* was sunk by the Northern cruiser *Kearsarge* off Cherbourg, France, on June 11, 1864. Her memory is preserved in South Africa in the famous Cape Malay song, 'Daar Kom die Alabama.'

Albacore. *See* YELLOWTAIL.

Albany. District of mixed farming in the Eastern Cape Province of which Grahamstown is the most important centre. Established in 1814 and named after city of Albany, capital of the state of New York, U.S.A.; home of General J. G. Cuyler (q.v.), first Landdrost. Little progress was made until the arrival of the British settlers in 1820. To-day also noted for its pineapple plantations.

Albasini, Joao. Known to the Bantu as 'Juwawa.' White chief of a large group of Bantu under the Transvaal Republic. Of Portuguese (Lourenço Marques) origin, Albasini settled during the 1840's in the Eastern Transvaal in Ohrigstad (q.v.), and later near Schoemansdal. Because of his personality and skill as a hunter, numbers of Bantu sought his protection until the Government appointed him Superintendent of Native Affairs, and then Vice-Consul for Portugal in the Republic. His unfriendly attitude to the authorities lost him his post as Superintendent of Natives in 1868. He died in 1888.

Albatross (*Diomedea exulans*). Huge bird, with 11-foot wing-span, found at sea off the coasts of South Africa. *See* PETRELS and BIRDS.

Albert. District in Northern Cape Province demarcated and named in 1848 after Prince Albert, husband of Queen Victoria. Main town, Burghersdorp (q.v.). Chief industry is wool production.

Albert Falls. Waterfall on Umgeni River, 14 miles from Pietermaritzburg. Village near by.

Albertina (not to be confused with Albertinia (q.v.)). Former name of Orange Free State village now called Swinburne (q.v.).

Albertinia. Town in Cape Province between Mossel Bay and Riversdale. Takes its name from the Rev. J. R. Albertyn of Riversdale, in whose parish it was located. Previously called Fontein Vlei. Village grew early 20th century. Ochre mining near by. Population: 1,600, including 1,011 Whites.

Alberton. Important manufacturing town on the Witwatersrand, 4 miles from Germiston. Established early in present century and proclaimed a municipality in 1939. It was long noted as one of the few 'dry' towns in the Union, owing to the influence of the Dutch Reformed Church. Population: 48,000 including 22,000 Whites.

Albu, Sir George. Gold mining pioneer and magnate. Born in Berlin, Germany, in 1857, he came to S. Africa in 1876, worked for a short time in Cape Town and settled in Kimberley the same year with his brother Leopold (q.v.). He set up in business as a licensed diamond buyer and in 1891 moved to Johannesburg, where in 1895 he consolidated his interests into the General Mining and Finance Corporation (q.v.). He died in 1935.

Albu, Sir George Werner. South African mining industrialist, son of Sir George Albu (q.v.). Born at Johannesburg in 1905, he was educated there and in England. Entering the General Mining and Finance Corporation, he became a manager and on the death of his father succeeded him as chairman. During World War II he served in the Middle East. Committed suicide in 1963 owing to ill-health.

Albu, Leopold. Mining magnate. Born in Berlin in 1860, he came to S. Africa in 1875 and moved to Kimberley in 1876, where he joined his brother George (q.v.). In 1891 he transferred to Johannesburg, and when the General Mining and Finance Corporation was established became the resident partner in London. He died in 1937.

Albuquerque, Alfonso d'. Portuguese navigator and soldier. Second Portuguese Viceroy of India. Possessed of a great reputation gained in the wars against the Moors, he set sail in 1503, accompanied by his brother Francesco, with orders to set up fortresses at Cotchin and elsewhere. In company with Tristao da Cunha (q.v.), he destroyed the towns of Oja and Brava on the coast of East Africa, and succeeded in placing Portuguese authority over Lamu. Albuquerque succeeded Francisco D'Almeida as Viceroy of India on November 5, 1509.

Albuquerque, Captain Mousinho d'. Portuguese soldier. Hero of a famous march, in 1895, of 50 men from Languene Camp on the Limpopo, through the wildest part of Mozambique into the stronghold of Gungunhana (q.v.), who had been defying the Portuguese authorities, and whom he took prisoner.

Alexander Bay. Settlement in Namaqualand, centre of State Alluvial Diggings. Founded in 1925. Population: 2,066, including 1,305 Whites.

Alexander, Morris. South African lawyer and legislator. Born in 1877 at Zlin in East Prussia, he emigrated as a child to the Cape, where he attended the South African College, afterwards qualifying as a barrister at Cambridge. In 1900 he was called to the bar and established himself in Cape Town. He soon became a prominent worker on behalf of the Jewish community, which was still suffering disabilities, and he also became the mouthpiece and champion of the Coloured people. In 1905 he was elected to the Cape Town City Council and in 1908 to the Cape Parliament. He never stopped his work for the oppressed and enjoyed the respect of his opponents. Apart from helping in securing the recognition of Yiddish as a European language, he put the case for the Indians and strongly opposed limiting the entry of strangers into South Africa. He died in 1946.

Alexandra. Bantu township near Johannesburg. Population: 63,233.

Alexandria. Town in Eastern Cape Province, in district of same name. Founded in 1850 and named after Rev. Alexander Smith. Leading area for chicory, pineapple and dairy farming. Population: 2,800, including 830 Whites.

Alfred Ernest Albert, Prince. Second son of Queen Victoria, afterwards Duke of Edinburgh and Duke of Saxe-Coburg and Gotha. Born in 1844, joined the Royal Navy and was sent on a cruise in 1860 aboard H.M.S. *Euryalus*, Captain Tarleton. He sailed from Spithead May 5, 1860, and after touching Brazil arrived in Simon's Bay on July 24, 1860. He then toured the Cape, Orange Free State and Natal, amid enormous enthusiasm, and inaugurated the first work on Table Bay Docks.

Algoa Bay. Large bay in Eastern Cape coast, discovered in 1486 by Bartholomew Diaz on first voyage round the Cape of Good Hope. Port Elizabeth (q.v.) is on the shores of Algoa Bay. Anchorage is good, but south-east winds caused many wrecks until present docks were built. The name was originally applied to Plettenberg Bay on account of its lagoon (alagoa).

Alice. Town in Eastern Cape Province, originally founded in 1836. Defended by the neighbouring Fort Hare (q.v.), it slowly developed. Name derived from that of Queen Victoria's daughter, Princess Alice, Grand Duchess of

Hesse-Darmstadt, and first bestowed by Governor Maitland in 1847. The town stands on the banks of the Tyumie River near the Amatola Mountains. The famous Lovedale Institution is near by. Population: 4,900, including 1,000 Whites.

Alicedale. Railway junction in the Eastern Cape Province, named after Mrs. Alice Slessor (born Dale), wife of the engineer in charge of its construction. Junction of lines to Port Elizabeth, Port Alfred and the Orange Free State. Population: 1,957, including 379 Whites, 512 Coloured and 1,065 Natives.

Alice Mine. Gold mine near Salisbury and scene of a famous rescue during the Matabele Rebellion of 1896. *See* MAZOE PARTY.

Alie. Settlement in Clanwilliam district, in North-Western Province of Cape.

Aliwal North. Chief town of district of same name on northern border of Cape Province, situated on Orange River, here spanned by Frere Bridge. Founded 1849 by Governor Sir Harry Smith, commemorating his victory at Aliwal in India over Sikhs. Convention between Basutos under Moshesh and Orange Free State signed here in 1869. Important strategic point in South African War. Occupied by Boers November 13, 1899, to March 11, 1900. Popular resort on account of sulphur springs. Population: 16,200, including 3,500 Whites, 2,600 Coloureds and 10,000 Bantu.

Aliwal Shoal. Dangerous shoal about 3 miles off Natal south coast, with minimum depth of only 1½ fathoms (9 feet).

Aliwal South. Former name of town of Mossel Bay (q.v.).

Allanridge. Town on Orange Free State gold fields, established 1950 and rapidly growing. It has been laid out on modern town-planning principles

and has a population of 11,000, including 2,700 Whites.

Allard, Bishop Jean Francis. First Catholic bishop in Natal. Born in France, he arrived in Durban in 1852, and built the first Catholic churches in that town and in Pietermaritzburg. In 1861 Bishop Allard entered Basutoland and established the present mission station at Roma. He died at the age of 83 in 1889.

Almeida, Dom Francisco. Explorer, navigator and Portuguese Viceroy of India. Descended from the Counts of Abrantes, he was sent with a fleet of 21 ships and 1,500 soldiers to India, sailing in March 1505. Already enjoying a great reputation for valour, gained in the wars against the Moors, his task was to establish Portuguese authority in Africa and in the New East. He doubled the Cape of Good Hope on June 26, 1505, then captured Kilwa, where he erected a fort. Later he established friendly relations with the chieftain of Malindi, and reached India. There he soon made the name of Portugal feared. He remained until November 1509, when he set forth on his return to Portugal. While in Table Bay, on March 1, 1510, he was involved in a skirmish against Hottentots and was killed.

Aloe. A large genus of succulents of the Lily Family (q.v.), containing stemless plants, bushes and trees. Nearly half the 300 species occur in Southern Africa, notably the Transvaal. While most are drought-resistant the stark and nearly leafless *Aloe pillansii* grows where rain falls only every two or three years—*A. haemanthifolia* grows in the wettest Cape mountains and *A. polyphylla* in snow-clad Lesotho. In Zululand is found the smallest-known *A. saundersiae*, with grass-like leaves a few inches long. *A. cillaris* is a climber among bushes and trees. Among the best-known species are the showy *A. striata* of the Eastern Cape, with its broad, unbarbed leaves; the frequently cultivated *A. arborescem,* the leaves of which have healing properties for burns; and the tall Cape *A. ferox* from which is prepared the drug, Cape Aloes.

In 1685 the Simon van der Stel expedition to Namaqualand found the 15-foot, yellow-flowered Kokerboom or Quivertree (*A. dichotoma*) and noted that its branches were used by Bushmen for carrying poisoned arrows. The largest, *A. bainesii,* is a 50-foot tree with orange flowers growing in the forests from East London district northwards. (*The Aloes of South Africa* by A. W. Reynolds should be further consulted.)

Amaas. *See* AMASI.

Amabele. Railway junction of the line from East London to the north and the branch serving the Transkei. The name, derived from the Xosa word meaning 'breasts,' is that of two hills near by.

Amahlubi. Tribe living near the sources of the Bushmen's River on the slopes of the Drakensberg and descended from remnants of earlier tribes scattered by the wars with Tshaka (q.v.). *See* LANGALIBALELE.

Amajoni. Native nickname for British soldiers, derived from the word 'Johnnie.'

Amajuba. *See* MAJUBA.

Amaleita. Criminal gangs established by Africans during the period of World War I, and noted for their assaults on pedestrians, etc.

Amalia. Village near Schweizer-Reneke in the Western Transvaal. Population: 425, including about 225 Whites.

Amalienstein. Village founded by the Berlin Mission, and named after Frau Amalie von Stein, a benefactress of that body. It is well over a century old and located in the Oudtshoorn district, between Ladismith, C.P., and Calitzdorp.

Amandebele

Amalinda: 1. Suburb of East London, 9 miles distant. It forms part of the municipal area. The railway station formerly called Amalinda is now Arnoldton. **2.** Village near Debe Nek, in the Ciskei. Here, in 1818, was fought the famous battle between the rival chiefs Ndhlambe and Gaika, in which the former was victorious. The battle took place on the so-called 'Kommetje Flats,' which are full of basin-like depressions (kommetjes in Dutch and known as amalinde in Xosa).

Amandebele. Originally a name for the Matabele (q.v.), but now also applied to a small community of Africans living near Pretoria, who are believed to have remained behind in the Transvaal on the historic trek under Moselekatse (q.v.) that led the majority of the tribe to settle in Rhodesia. The Amandebele are noted for their beadwork and a style of house-building characterised by many-coloured paintings.

Amandelboom (literally 'Almond

Tree'). Original name of village of Williston (q.v.).

Amangwane. Alternative native name for the Swazis (q.v.). Also known as Fetcani (q.v.), meaning 'Marauders.'

Amanzi (Zulu for 'The Waters'). Famous farm formerly belonging to the author Sir Percy Fitzpatrick (q.v.), who is buried there. It is near Uitenhage, C.P.

Amanzimtoti ('Sweet Waters' in Zulu). Seaside resort on the Natal south coast, 18 miles from Durban. On river of same name. Population: 28,000 including 9,000 Whites, 5,000 Bantu and 14,000 Indians.

Amaryllis (Amaryllidaceae). Beautiful lily with umbels of pale pink flowers; frequent on lower slopes of Cape mountains. It belongs to an extensive order of bulbous and herbaceous plants, plentiful at the Cape and along Natal coast, and differing from those of the Lily family (q.v.) only in having inferior ovaries. Leaves sword-shaped, flowers showing three sepals coloured like the three petals, six stamens arising from petals and sepals; fruit a many-seeded capsule or a three-seeded berry. Many of the bulbs and other parts are poisonous, as shown by the repeated names, Sore-Eye Flowers (Seeroogblomme) and Gifbol (q.v.). Among the more magnificent members of the family are the Maartblom or Kaffir Almanac (q.v.) (*Haemanthus coccineus*); the Fire Lily, Red Ifafa Lily (*Cyrtanthus*), with its loose umbels of tubular orange and red flowers; the yellow Bush Lily of Natal (one of the wide-open Clivias); and the Nerines, with their curly pink petals and prominent stamens. Kukumakranka (*Gethyllis afra* L.) has a single white flower rising from a tube from the ground before the twisted grassy leaves appear. The fruit, a long transparent berry, is hidden in the soil at the flowering stage and is used medicinally, soaked in brandy, for stomach troubles. Very

similar in growth is the common yellow Autumn Star (*Empodium plicatum*). Common, too, near streams and on the Cape mountain slopes, is the white and yellow Sterretjie (*Spiloxene capensis*), with its dark central pattern.

Amasi (also known as **Maas**). Curdled milk prepared in a calabash and drunk by natives, as well as by a certain number of Europeans. Considered to be extremely health-giving.

Amasoja. Traditional native name for British Tommies.

Amatikulu. Town near Mtunzini in Natal. Sugar-milling centre. Population: approximately 1,508, including 190 Whites.

Amatola Mountains. Range in the Eastern Cape Province, north of King William's Town. Large Government plantations and sawmills. Highest peaks about 6,500 feet.

Amatongaland (also known as **Tongaland**). 600 sq. miles of territory in extreme north of Zululand, adjoining Portuguese territory in Mozambique, and extending from Lebombo mountains to the sea. Despite its unhealthy climate was of great strategic importance both to Natal and to the South African Republic, which, by annexing it, hoped to secure an outlet to the Indian Ocean. Britain's annexation of St. Lucia Bay and the coast in 1884 put an end to these ambitions. Amatongaland, however, continued to be a resort for smugglers and freebooters until its final annexation in 1897. It is now part of the Ingwavuma District and closed to non-official European visitors, owing to its climate. Population: 14,000.

Amatungulu or **Natal Plum** (*Carissa grandiflora* A.D.C.). Shrub with bifurcate spines; very suitable for hedges. Fruit used for jam. Grows along the Natal coast and in eastern Cape.

Amcor. Abbreviation for African Metals Corporation Limited (q.v.).

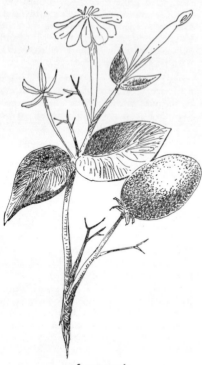

Amatungulu

Amersfoort. Small town in district of Wakkerstroom in Eastern Transvaal. Named after place in Holland. Established in 1867. Maize and wool centre. Population: 3,100, including 1,500 Whites.

Ameshoff, Herman Arnold. Judge of the Transvaal High Court. Born on July 30, 1860, in Amsterdam, and took his law degree at Utrecht in 1887. Began to practise in the Transvaal in 1888, becoming a judge of the Transvaal High Court in 1889, and rising to First Puisne Judge in 1898, which appointment was not at first universally popular. Thanks to his undeniable ability he gained favour, and when Chief Justice Kotze was unfairly dismissed in 1898 he resigned. When the South African War began he returned to Holland, went into business in Paris and died October 19, 1905.

Amsterdam. Village in Eastern Transvaal, which was founded as part of an immigration scheme for Scots by A. McCorkindale (q.v.) in 1867, under name of Roburnia (from Robert Burns). Was later changed by the Volksraad to present designation, but the name 'New Scotland' for the neighbourhood has survived. Amsterdam lies near the Swazi border. Population: 2,400, including 1,030 Whites.

Ana Tree. *See* ACACIA.

Andalusia. Village on Vaal-Hartz irrigation scheme (q.v.) on border of Transvaal, Cape Province and Bechuanaland. During World War II an internment camp for Germans and others was established near by. Population: 656, including 434 Whites.

Andalusite. Refractory mineral, two-thirds of the production in the Republic being exported. Large reserves of andalusite are exploited in the Transvaal.

Anderson, Rev. R. Early explorer at the Cape. Arrived there during the first British occupation and left in 1799, reaching the Orange River at the present-day town of Prieska. Later he encountered Cowan and Donovan (qq.v.) and brought back the only authentic news from them. When W. J. Burchell came to South Africa, Anderson accompanied him on some of his trips. His fate after 1816 is obscure.

Andrews, William Henry. South African labour leader. Born April 28, 1870, in Suffolk, of a working-class family. He became a fitter and turner. In August 1893 he arrived on the Rand, where he soon became active in the incipient Trade Union movement. He took a prominent part in the 1907 miners' strike, and an even more active one in the unrest in 1913. With the rise of the Communist Party, Andrews joined this and was one of the leaders of the 1922 strike. In 1928 he was sent as a South African Workers' Delegate to the Geneva Labour Conference. He died in 1950.

Andries Ohrigstad. Original name of Ohrigstad in the Eastern Transvaal, named after a Voortrekker leader. *See* OHRIGSTAD.

Anemone. *See* CLEMATIS.

Anerley. Village near Port Shepstone in Natal. Seaside resort. Population: approximately 150, including 100 Whites.

Angas, George French. Explorer, artist and zoologist. Born in Durham, England, in 1822, and in 1846 reached South Africa for the first time. There he prepared a large number of drawings which were published in 1849 under the title of 'Kaffirs Illustrated.' He died in England in 1886.

Angas's Bushbuck. *See* INYALA.

Angel Fish (*Holacanthus nicobariensis*). One of the flat Butterfly Fish (q.v.) found off Natal northwards into the Pacific. Pale blue bands stripe the dark body and tail, the markings of which are reputed to resemble the Arabic words, 'There is no God but Allah.'

Angler-Fish (*Lophius piscatorius*). Fish found off Saldanha Bay, Table Bay, west coast of Cape Peninsula, in North Atlantic and Mediterranean. About 4 feet long.

Anglican Church. *See* CHURCH OF THE PROVINCE OF SOUTH AFRICA.

Anglo-American Corporation of South Africa Limited. Mining house established by Sir Ernest Oppenheimer (q.v.) on September 25, 1917, with a capital of £1,000,000. Named from the fact that a certain amount was subscribed by American firms. Its immediate purpose was to develop new gold mines on the East Rand,

but its interests soon expanded in new directions, particularly into the diamond industry, in which it became pre-eminent. Also soon active in developing Zambian copper fields and in South African coal industry. Through association with African Explosives and Chemical Industries (q.v.], became the controlling force in the chemical industry. It also controls the Highveld Steel and Vanadium Works (q.v.). Today is the largest mining group in Africa, and one of the largest in the world, with investments scattered from Cape to Tanzania and West Africa, with offshoots in United States, Canada, Australia and elsewhere. Although nominal capital is only R20,000,000, the value of total interests is over R2,000,000,000, and staff (of all races) numbers over 200,000. Its head office is in Johannesburg.

Angoche. Town in Mozambique, now known as Antonio Enes.

Angoni. Tribe in Zambia and Malawi closely related to the Zulus. Angoniland is the region south-west of Lake Nyasa.

Angora Goats. *See* MOHAIR.

Angra Pequena. Name given by Portuguese navigators to inlet on which Lüderitzbucht is now situated. The words mean 'Little Bay.' Bartholomew Diaz erected a marble cross there in 1486 before reaching the Cape of Good Hope.

Animals. *See* MAMMALS.

Anker. Old Cape measure of capacity, equal to about 8 gallons.

Anreith, Anton. South African sculptor and artist, born in 1755 at Freiburg in Baden, Germany. He was of Hungarian origin, and came to the Cape in 1777 as a soldier in the service of the Dutch East India Company. He won the friendship of Louis-Michel Thibault (q.v.) and developed his powers as a sculptor. Among the earlier works with which he is credited are the two well-known lions now at the top of Government Avenue, Cape Town, and those at the entrance of the Castle, in which he also did certain decorations to the Kat balcony. His best-known works include the beautiful wooden pulpit of the Groote Kerk in Adderley Street, another pulpit in the old Lutheran Church in Strand Street, the organ gallery in the same building, and the pulpit of the Rhenish Church in Stellenbosch. At Groot Constantia he did the pediment of the famous wine cellars, with its classical figures. Many of his designs and models in wax are still in existence. He died on March 4, 1822, at the age of 68.

Antarctic. Although most early Antarctic explorers since Captain James Cook in the 18th century had visited Cape Town going south, serious contacts date from 1910, when Captain R. F. Scott on his last expedition received a £500 grant from the South African Government and further sums from public appeal by Governor-General Lord Gladstone. Thereafter South Africa contributed regularly to the Scott Polar Research Institute, Cambridge, England. In 1919 Professor E. J. Goddard of Stellenbosch University secured support for a South African National Antarctic Expedition; preparations stopped through economic depression. South Africa's importance in whaling and fishing industries and participation in International Geophysical Year revived interest; in 1959 South Africa took part in the first International Conference on the Antarctic in Washington, which recognised South Africa's stake there. Agreement reached with Norway in 1960 by which South Africa may maintain base on Queen Maud Land. First expedition commanded by Hannes Le Grange, a South African meteorologist, who had taken part in 1958 in Sir Vivian Fuchs's famous Transantarctic crossing. Since then other parties have

gone south. Important meteorological research has also been done by South African Weather Bureau at Bouvet Island and elsewhere through South African Navy. In 1963 both these bodies co-operated with United States Government in successful pioneer flight from Cape Town across the Antarctic, in which Professor L. C. King of the University of Natal participated. *See also* MARION ISLAND and SANAE.

Ant Bear or Aardvark (*Orycteropus afer*). A solitary, pig-like mammal, occurring throughout most of Southern Africa, nowhere common and difficult to find on account of its nocturnal habits and its power of rapid burrowing with feet and tail. Harmless to man, it has few teeth, and escapes its enemies by shaking them off its tough, loose skin. Its food consists of thousands of ants and termites, which it fetches out with its very long nose and catches on its sticky tongue.

Anteater, Scaly (or Pangolin) (*Manis temmincki*). Primitive insect-eating mammal found in the Orange Free State, the Kalahari, the Transvaal, South-West Africa and Rhodesia. It is the nearest relative to the Ant Bear (q.v.) and similar in its digging and eating habits, but in appearance more like an armadillo, toothless, with large scales. It is a gentle, harmless creature, confined to ant and termite areas.

Anti-Convict Agitation. A successful campaign to prevent the Cape Colony being converted into a penal settlement. By Order in Council of September 4, 1848, the Cape was designated a colony to which convicts might be deported. The announcement of the news by Governor Sir Harry Smith drew spontaneous resistance throughout the country, mass meetings being held and protests forwarded to England. In spite of this, the transport *Neptune* set sail with a cargo of 288 convicts. She arrived at Simonstown on September 19, 1849. The Anti-Convict Association organised a boycott under which colonists pledged themselves not to supply the *Neptune* with stores or other necessaries. Feeling rose high, suspected supporters of the Government were ostracised and the Governor was warned from London that he might use force to meet official needs. After five months, on February 21, 1850, in consequence of the efforts of Mr. Charles Bowyer Adderley (q.v.) in the House of Commons, the *Neptune* continued her voyage to Tasmania (Van Diemen's Land). This successful resistance was a major factor in the grant, soon after, of the first Parliament to the Cape.

Antimony. Metal used in alloys. 60 per cent concentrate is produced from gold ore in Murchison Range of Transvaal, where are large reserves in the 30-mile belt of altered chloritic quartzites. Less important deposits in Steynsdorp and Barberton districts.

Anvil Bird. *See* TINKER-BIRDS and BIRDS.

Apartheid. Literally 'separateness.' Doctrine enunciated and supported by the National Party in South Africa, and first prominently put before the public in 1949. Although derived from an earlier principle encountered almost throughout South African history, and previously referred to as 'Segregation,' the idea of apartheid aroused worldwide controversy. Its basic idea involves the separate development, settlement, economic existence and government of white and non-white races in South Africa. It is variously distinguished as territorial apartheid, social apartheid, economic apartheid, etc. The doctrine has been violently attacked in the Assembly of the United Nations and elsewhere overseas.

Ape, Blue. *See* VERVET MONKEY.

Apies River (native name **Mbibana** or **Thswane**). Small tributary of the Crocodile River, rises near and flows through Pretoria.

Apples. First grown in Southern Africa by Van Riebeeck, who imported trees from St. Helena in 1654. Since then the industry has attained considerable size, the main producing areas being around Elgin, near Cape Town, developed mainly by the Molteno Brothers and their neighbours since the South African War; on the Highveld, near Johannesburg and Vereeniging; and in the Orange Free State. The Republic has about 3,000,000 apple trees in bearing, and 1,184,000 non-bearing.

Arab. Name formerly used in Natal for Indian, particularly of the trader class.

ARCHAEOLOGY OF SOUTHERN AFRICA
by
the late PROFESSOR A. J. H. GOODWIN
University of Cape Town

WITH the Americas isolated and both Asia and Europe reduced to narrow habitable strips by the Quaternary ice-age, the prehistoric archaeology of Africa assumes immense importance. In South Africa interest began in 1857 when tools were retrieved from the Great Fish River gravels. By 1924 enough was known to make new terminology essential, and lead to eventual (1929) acceptance of an Earlier, Middle and Later Stone Age, corresponding to the Lower Palaeolithic, the Middle Palaeolithic and to subsequent phases defined for Europe (Goodwin and Van Riet Lowe). The Pan-African Congress on Prehistory has met every fourth year since 1947. At the third session (Livingstone, 1955) two 'Transitions' were introduced between the

Earlier and Middle and the Middle and Later Stone Ages, and an Iron Age was added finally.

The *Earlier Stone Age* is best understood from the Vaal River gravels (Zeuner). Semi-conventional tools appear with the Kafuan and Oldowan pebble-cultures, and we may safely date the beginning of recognisable tools at about half a million years ago. Many thousands of sites are known south of Capricorn for the next major phase, the Chelles-Acheul (Stellenbosch). The Vaal River shows a local development in a sequence of five phases. Coastal sites suggest four recognisable phases, covering the same span. Late stages are known from a remarkable site at Kalambo Falls, Zambia, from Montagu Cave in the Cape, and from several important Transvaal caves. This immensely long development probably ended 150,000 years ago. The basic tool was everywhere an almond-shaped hand-axe (some 6″ long, 4″ wide and 1″ thick, or 15 × 10 × 2·5 cm.). This continued into the *First Transition* (Fauresmith Culture), which lasted some 50,000 years to end perhaps 100,000 years ago or later. To the hand-axe were added flake tools, derived from full E.S.A. types, and this complex of scrapers and crude points now dominated, though the refined (4″ or 10 cm. long) hand-axe persisted. Up to this point no human remains survive. This is reasonable when we consider the time and climatic changes involved (Zeuner).

The *Middle Stone Age* occurs stratified above the E.S.A. in the Vaal River alluvia, but at only a few sites in South Africa can a sequence be observed covering even a fraction of this turbulent period. Human remains are known from M.S.A. sites. From earlier phases, perhaps 75,000 years ago, we have 3 humans of species differing markedly from our own. At Hopefield, 80 miles north of Cape Town, a cranium is related to a most important faunal pattern. At Broken Hill mine in Zambia a very similar skull was found in 1919. Both are best considered as *Homo rhodesiensis*. The third, *Homo helmii*, is from deposits left by the ebullient springs at Florisbad, Hagenstad, O.F.S. In no instance is the link between tools and man absolute. The unplaced Boskop (Potchefstroom) skull may belong to a later phase of the M.S.A.

The whole M.S.A. is marked by the victory of points and scraper-tools over the hand-axe. Where a derivative of this last appears it is diminutive and ill-made (perhaps 3″ or 7·5 cm. long). The point, however, progresses. From an awkward but effective triangular shape it achieves an extraordinary precise form in some phases and areas. In other regions this is further streamlined by most careful chipping into a true lance-head, a highly advanced example of stone-working by primitive methods. The longest consistent evolution is known from the Transvaal (Pietersburg culture) in a number of cave and alluvial deposits. The most advanced forms occur in the extreme south (Mossel Bay and Still Bay cultures). Early rock-peckings in the central plateau area may belong to the local M.S.A.

From the M.S.A. we can now date a few late sites by means of Radio-active Carbon, but only where Carbon occurs. This absolute dating does not carry us back beyond some 40,000 years; before then percentage error, low radioactivity and natural contamination make dating valueless. Dates varying from 17,000 to 11,500 years ago (with a 6% error) are known from deposits in the Cave of Hearths (Transvaal). Deposits of possibly contaminated material at Florisbad, O.F.S., show dates from 9,000 to 7,000 years ago. These dates do not by any means cover the whole range of the M.S.A.

The *Second Transition* (Magosian or Howieson's Poort) again shows a blending of old and newer types. Points and lanceheads become smaller and are augmented by blades, generally crescentic in shape. Associated with this phase are a few human skulls, notably one from the Peer's Cave (Fish Hoek valley, Cape Peninsula) showing an early forebear of later small-jawed types. Good stratified sites are known from Rhodesia and Zambia and from Rose Cottage Cave, Modderpoort, O.F.S.

The *Later Stone Age* is a true blade and endscraper phase, typified mainly by the Smithfield and Wilton cultural complexes. These include bored stones, a hunting or coastal strandloper (beach-foods) way of life, a growing tendency to use microlithic tools and to live in rock-shelters, and other characteristics, which began perhaps over 7,000 years ago and persisted up to the time of the first European colonisation of the Cape Peninsula in 1652. The physical remains link clearly with various Bushman and Hottentot types, best grouped as the Khoisan race. Certain S.W. African paintings have been precariously dated at about 3,370 years ago. Finally pottery appears, brought almost certainly with cattle by an advanced Hottentot people, probably related to the Namaqua who also used a little copper. Few polished stone tools are yet known; there is no proof of a full Neolithic phase.

The *Iron Age* is certainly Bantu or African in origin. Carbon dates in Zambia show sites (certainly not the earliest) going back a thousand years. Aligned with the two earlier dates derived from the Zimbabwe ruins, these place structural timbers at 1,505 and 1,360 years ago. A reasonable dating of A.D. 575 may thus be accepted for early phases of this building. Later phases are dated by beads and china derived from outside trade. Similar structures from Mapungubwe and the Libolo area of Angola bring this complex well into recent times, related to known tribes.

Architecture. The characteristically South African style of architecture, commonly referred to as Cape Dutch, is based on the traditional designs of the Netherlands, brought to South Africa by the early settlers and modified to suit conditions there. This applies particularly to the familiar scrolled gables, the counterparts of which are to be found in many cities in the Low Countries. While, however, considerations of space made it necessary there to build several storeys high, the Cape pioneers were able to use one storey, save occasionally in the towns. The climate led to the adoption of the front platform, known as the stoep, where residents could enjoy the cool of the day. For the same reason high ceilings and very thick walls attained popularity, as did shutters closed to keep out the sun.

Most of the builders were non-Whites, ranging from inexperienced Hottentots to skilful Malay slaves who, being obliged to use materials of a cruder nature than was customary overseas, often made shift with mud bricks and roughly finished beams or flooring-boards of native timber.

A characteristic feature of Cape architecture was the 'voorkamer' or front room, opening on to the various living-rooms and giving access to the 'agterhuis,' or main hall. A central courtyard was often shaded by trees or vines. Town houses were frequently of two storeys, with a flat roof, also designed to keep the premises cool.

The coming of the British brought styles from the United Kingdom, of which particularly good examples are to be found in and around Grahamstown, Bathurst and other places settled by the 1820 settlers.

South African architecture underwent a considerable deterioration during the 19th century, when many fine old homes were spoilt by the addition of ugly corrugated iron verandas, or even by the insertion of shop fronts.

Up-country the wanderings of the Voortrekkers (q.v.), and the pioneering conditions generally, led to a vogue for wattle-and-daub structures, as well as the very simple 'hartbeesthuis' found on many early Transvaal and Orange Free State farms. Verandas became an almost universal feature of a South African building, frequently ornamented with 'carpenter's lace.'

Towards the end of the 19th century came steel and later reinforced concrete. The efforts of Sir Herbert Baker (q.v.) brought about a revival of the old Dutch style, and the evolution of a Renaissance type adapted to local conditions, strikingly illustrated in the Union Buildings, Pretoria (q.v.).

Following the establishment of schools of architecture at the universities of Cape Town, Witwatersrand and Pretoria, attention has been given to the use of styles from South and Central America, adapted to South Africa's sub-tropical conditions.

Since the erection of the original Corner House at Johannesburg in 1904, there has been a steady increase in the vogue of American skyscrapers in South African cities, intensified by the lifting of many former height restrictions. One of the tallest buildings in the Republic is the 26-storeyed Sanlam Centre on the Cape Town Foreshore, rising to 306 feet. In 1966 work began on the Carlton Centre, Johannesburg, the highest concrete building in the world, of 51 storeys, reaching 730 feet, also on the Standard Bank head office (445 feet) and the Trust Bank (405 feet). At Cape Town the new Trust Bank Building is 350 feet high.

Arctotis. *See* DAISY.

Arlington. Village near Lindley in the Orange Free State. Population: 1,674, including 251 Whites.

Army. *See* DEFENCE.

Arniston. Village near Bredasdorp in Cape Province, named after wrecked Indiaman. Population: 300, including 30 Whites.

Arnoldton. *See* AMALINDA.

Arnot, David. Law agent and adviser to the Griqua chief Nikolas Waterboer. Born in the Cape. Gaining the friendship and confidence of Waterboer, he became his representative during the complicated negotiations about the ownership of Diamond Fields. He later appeared in 1871 before the Court of Arbitration held in Bloemfontein at which the claims of the Transvaal, Orange Free State and of Waterboer were heard, and was successful in gaining the day for his client.

Arnot, Frederick Stanley. Missionary and explorer. Born in Glasgow on September 12, 1858. Early interested in religious matters, he decided to become a missionary. He reached Natal in 1881, and made his way to Bechuanaland hoping for work. Khama, king of the Bamangwato, gave him a friendly reception and shortly after he proceeded to the present Rhodesia, towards Barotseland. This led to a further journey which in 1884 brought him to Benguela on the coast of Angola. Much of this area was hardly known, and as an explorer he was regarded as the natural successor to David Livingstone. He made no fewer than nine journeys to Africa, during which he wrote successful travel books, notably *Garenganze*. He died in Central Africa in 1914.

Art in Southern Africa. While individual artists, many of great merit, have worked at the Cape from the earliest days, they were nearly all amateurs and visitors, such as Lady Anne Barnard (q.v.). One of the first to attempt professional art was J. C. Poortermans, born in Holland about 1786, who from 1843 to his death in 1870 struggled to make a living. Several of the pioneers were drawing masters, such as W. H. F. Langschmidt and the famous Thomas Bowler, F. T. I'Ons (q.v.) and many others.

Exhibitions of pictures were held from 1850 onwards, but it was not until 1872 that the South African Fine Arts Association made its appearance in Cape Town and, with the aid of £100 from the Cape Colonial Treasury and a few small private contributions, began the collection which today is the National Gallery of South Africa. Housed in the South African Museum in Cape Town for many years, it achieved its own fine building in 1928. Since then many gifts and loans have helped to make it one of the finest south of the equator.

Another outstanding collection came into being in 1913, when Sir Max Michaelis (q.v.) donated several dozen Dutch 17th-century masters, selected by Sir Hugh Lane, to accommodate which the old Town House on Greenmarket Square, Cape Town, was ingeniously reconstructed. Art galleries were set up in many parts of South Africa, including Durban in 1899 and Johannesburg in 1909, the latter largely through the initiative of Lady Florence Phillips, wife of Sir Lionel Phillips. There are art galleries also in Grahamstown, East London, Port Elizabeth, Kimberley, Pretoria and other places. In 1961 the Government acquired the great collection valued at R2,000,000 created by the late Sir J. B. Robinson (q.v.), including works by Tiepolo, Van Dyck, Rubens, Frans Hals, Gainsborough, etc. Salisbury in Rhodesia has a fine modern gallery, to mark the opening of which a large quantity of art treasures was sent out on temporary loan by famous overseas collections.

Regular art exhibitions are held annually in the major centres, the South African Academy in Johannesburg having been started by the Transvaal Institute of Architects. A unique gallery of several hundred historical South African pictures, collected by Mr. W. Fehr, is housed in a section of the Cape Town Castle. South Africa has successfully participated in several overseas art exhibitions at São Paulo in Brazil and in Europe, major participants including Irma Stern, Moses Kottler, Lippy Lipschitz, Gregoire Boonzaier and Terence McCaw (qq.v.). Several non-Whites such as Gerald Sekoto have also gained prominence.

Art schools exist in Cape Town, Grahamstown, Durban, Johannesburg, Pretoria and other South African centres, while some of the universities have departments devoted to the subject.

See also under names of individual artists.

Artificial Diamonds. *See* DIAMONDS, ARTIFICIAL.

Artillery. *See* NATAL FIELD ARTILLERY; REGIMENT, SIXTH FIELD; SOUTH AFRICAN IRISH; TRANSVAAL HORSE ARTILLERY.

Arum or **Pig Lily** (*Zantedescia aethiopica*). Plant of the Araceae family, its large white spathe a familiar ornament to the low, moist parts of the Western Cape Province. The true petals are inconspicuously clustered round the central spadix. The yellow Arum is a protected flower of the Eastern Cape. The small Pink Arum (*Z. rehmannii*), 9–12 inches high, was found first in swampy ground near Dundee and in North Natal, and has become a deeper pink with cultivation.

Asbestos. Important asbestos mines (Chrysotile) in Mashaba and Belingwe districts of Rhodesia, are among the largest in the world. In the Republic four types are now mined: blue crocidolite (North-West Cape and Northern Transvaal), Chrysotile (Transvaal), Amosite (Transvaal) and Tremolite (Natal). Anthophyllite (Northern Transvaal) not lately mined. Since 1939 the Havelock Mine in Swaziland is major producer of Chrysotile, special feature being its cableway across mountains to Barberton. Deposits found in South West Africa.

3—E.S.A.

A.S.C. Abbreviation for Administrative Service Corps (q.v.).

Aschenborn, Hans Anton. German artist. Born February 1, 1888, in Kiel, Germany; trained as a farmer and

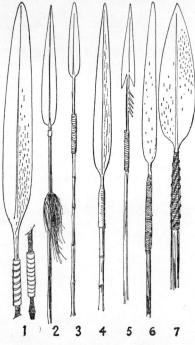

Assegais

1. *Shona.* 2. *Ovambo.* 3. *Tembu.* 4. *Basuto* 5. *Shona.* 6. *Zulu.* 7. *Swazi.*

reached South West Africa early in the present century. Became interested in painting, particularly of wild life of the Colony. He returned to Germany; came back to South West Africa in 1913 and settled on his farm 'Quick-born' (The Spring of Living Water). Fought in World War I and was taken prisoner. Later Aschenborn lived for a while in Stellenbosch, doing commercial and other drawing. Returned to Germany in 1921; died there April 11, 1930.

Ashton. Village in Western Cape, between Worcester and Mossel Bay. Irrigation and fruit-canning centre. Population: 3,600, including 800 Whites, 1,500 Coloureds and 1,337 Bantu.

Askraal. Village near Heidelberg, Cape Province. Population: 750, including 725 White.

Assegai. A native spear. Although described as typically South African, is in name linked with Latin 'Hasta'; became corrupted during Middle Ages. Suggested derivation North Africa, from similar expression, 'zaghayah,' among the Berbers. Geoffrey Chaucer used similar word 'lancegay,' of identical origin. There are two kinds of assegais: the older type, a throwing assegai; and the newer, a stabbing assegai, with broad and extremely sharp blade and short handle. The latter is considered to have been invented by Tshaka (q.v.).

Assegai Bosch. Village on Garden Route in Cape Province.

Assegai Wood or **Assegai Hout** (*Curtisia faginia* Ait.). Tree up to 60 feet. Hard wood used for spokes of wagons. Cape to Natal and Transvaal.

Assenburgh, Louis van. Governor of the Cape of Good Hope. Originally in the service of the Holy Roman Emperor in Austria. Succeeded Willem Adriaan Van der Stel (q.v.). He took office on February 1, 1708. Described as 'fond of pleasures,' he caused puppet shows and bull-baiting displays to be held at the Castle. After an illness of eight months died in Cape Town December 27, 1711, aged 51 years.

Association Football. *See* SOCCER.

Aster, Wild. *See* DAISY.

Atherstone, Dr. William Guybon. South African medical and scientific pioneer. Born in England on May 27, 1814, and came to the Cape with the

1820 settlers. Studied medicine in London and was present at the Sorbonne in Paris in 1839 when Daguerre first demonstrated the principles of photography, and in 1840 when S. F. B. Morse first demonstrated telegraphy. In Grahamstown, where he settled, Atherstone in 1847 carried out the first operation in South African history under anaesthetics. He founded the Albany Museum in 1855 and was one of the first students of South African geology. In 1867 he won immortality by identifying the first diamond found at the Cape. Entering politics he was among the first to propose a Cape to Cairo Railway, long before Cecil John Rhodes. He died in 1898.

Athletics. Athletics in South Africa may be traced to the sporting instincts of the British garrison in Colonial days, but it was the rise of boys' schools in the Cape, Natal and Orange Free State that started serious training. Important clubs, such as the Wanderers in Johannesburg and the Ramblers in Bloemfontein (qq.v.), gave further encouragement. In 1894 the South African Amateur Athletics Association was formed, and the first championship meetings were held. Since then South African athletes have distinguished themselves in local and international events. *See* OLYMPIC GAMES.

Athlone. Large housing estate for Coloureds on the Cape Flats near Cape Town.

Athlone, Earl of (Alexander Augustus Frederick William Alfred George Cambridge). Governor-General of Union of South Africa. Born Kensington Palace April 14, 1874, son of Duke of Teck; original title, Prince Alexander of Teck. Entered Army and served in Matabele Rebellion of 1896, also in South African War, and in World War I, with considerable distinction. In 1923 became Governor-General of Union,

until 1931. In 1940, became Governor-General of Canada until 1946. A man of great charm and popularity, and extremely successful in office. He died on January 16, 1957.

Atlas Aircraft Corporation of South Africa Ltd. First South African aircraft manufacturing corporation. Founded in 1965 with backing from the Industrial Development Corporation (q.v.) and Bonuskor (q.v.), its large works at Kempton Park, Tvl. came into production early in 1967, starting with the Atlas Impala jet trainer 1 (Aermacchi M.B. 326).

Atomic Energy. As one of world's major producers of uranium (q.v.) South Africa is in an advantageous position to develop atomic power, so far prevented by cheapness of local coal. The Atomic Energy Board was established in 1948. Research has begun at the University of the Witwatersrand, which set up a Nuclear Physics Research Unit in 1957 and is now equipped with a Cockcroft-Walton accelerator, while the Council for Scientific and Industrial Research acquired the first cyclotron in the republic. Research reactors were opened in 1965 near Pelindaba, Transvaal, 18 miles west of Pretoria, at a cost of over R10,000,000, and near Faure, Cape Province, the latter operated jointly by the universities of Cape Town and Stellenbosch. Plans have been put forward for atomic power stations in areas far from coalfields, including Western Cape Province and South West Africa. In 1967 approval was given to the building of South Africa's first atomic power station at Melkbosstrand near Cape Town. *See also* SCHONLAND, SIR BASIL.

Auckland. Military village in valley of river Tyumie (q.v.) on former eastern frontier, Cape Colony; established in 1848, named after town in England. Was overwhelmed and destroyed by

Native invaders on Christmas Day, 1850, all the men being killed. Was never rebuilt.

Aughrabies Falls. One of largest waterfalls in South Africa, 25 miles below Kakamas on Orange River. First reported by Dutch explorer Hendrik Wikar in 1778, and called 'The Cataract of King George' by George Thompson in 1824. The name 'Aughrabies' is of Hottentot origin and means 'A Rocky Waterfall.' Recent surveys show a total height of 298 feet, compared with former estimates of 620 feet.

Augsburg. Village near Clanwilliam, Cape Province. Population: 150, including 120 Whites.

Aum (Dutch 'aam'). Old Cape measure of capacity for liquor. Equals 32 gallons.

Aurora. Village near Piketberg, Cape Province. Population: 350, including 300 Whites.

Aus. Village in South-West Africa, 141 miles from Lüderitzbucht. Name of Hottentot origin, means 'Big Snake.' 4,700 feet above sea-level. Used as internment camp after German surrender in 1915. Gold reported near by. Population: 687, including 229 Whites.

Aussenkehr. Oasis on northern side of Orange River. Attempts to develop irrigation of fertile lands were made in 1887 by Petersen Brothers, but failed to because of lack of transport. Since World War II fresh efforts have been defeated by lack of roads and extremely hot climate.

Australian Bug. See DORTHESIA.

Autumn Star. See AMARYLLIS.

A.V.B.O.B. See AFRIKAANSE VERBOND BEGRAFNIS ONDERNEMING BEPERK.

Aviation. Flying in South Africa may be traced to the Napoleonic Wars, when a French prisoner attempted to construct a balloon. Ascents were made during mid-Victorian times, and in 1884 Sir Charles Warren's expedition to Bechuanaland used several balloons for military observation purposes. Balloons were again used during the South African War, and professional balloonists gave displays. In 1906 P. J. Esser of Johannesburg flew 200 yards in a home-made plane, but serious aviation started in 1909, when a Belgian, Albert Kimmerling, gave a successful display from Johannesburg on February 6, 1910. Local enthusiasts continued experimenting, particularly the late Rear-Admiral J. Weston, who built aeroplanes at Brandfort, O.F.S. In 1913 the first Flying School was opened and in 1915 the South African Flying Corps was established by the Union Defence Force. First air mail flown in 1911 from Kenilworth Race Course. Rapid development during World War I, and in 1919 South African Aerial Transports Ltd. first started a regular service. First successful flight from London to Cape Town in 1921 by Sir Pierre van Ryneveld and Sir Quentin Brand. Johannesburg Light Plane Club formed in 1927. In 1929 Union Airways Ltd., with a subsidy from the Government, started regular mail service round the Union. Financial difficulties led to the service being taken over some years later by the South African Railways. The first regular air service between the Union and Britain begun by Imperial Airways on January 20, 1932. In the same year the first autogiro was shown in Durban. In 1969 South Africa had over 2,000 privately owned aircraft, of which over 600 belonged to business firms. *See also* TRANSPORT, JOHN GOODMAN HOUSEHOLD and other individual entries.

HISTORIC FLIGHTS FROM EUROPE TO SOUTH AFRICA

1920 Attempted air race to the Cape. Of four entries three crashed before reaching the Sudan. The fourth, a Vickers-Vimy, sponsored by the London *Times*, reached Tabora, 2,600 miles from London, before crashing. Sir Pierre van Ryneveld and Sir Quentin Brand renewed the attempt. Their first machine, the *Silver Queen*, came down at Korosko, near Khartoum. They continued the journey with *Silver Queen II*, secured in Cairo, and reached Bulawayo on March 6, 1921. There a further machine was secured, the *Voortrekker*, which finally arrived in Pretoria after 44 days of travel.

1926 March. R.A.F. machines flew from Cairo to Cape Town. Sir Alan Cobham flew from London to Cape Town and back in the same machine.

1927 Lieutenant R. R. Bentley flew in 26 days from London to Cape Town, using a Moth machine.

1928 Lady Bailey, wife of Sir Abe Bailey, flew from England to South Africa in 52 days, and succeeded in making the return journey.

1930 Duchess of Bedford flew from Croydon to Cape Town in 10 days. Lieutenant Rheinhold Ferdinand Caspareuthus flew solo from London to Cape Town in 8½ days.

1930 Lieutenant - Commander Glen Kidston flew from England to the Cape in 6 days 10 hours.

Gordon Shore and Peggy Salamon did the journey in 5 days 6½ hours.

1932 J. A. Mollison did the trip in 4 days 17 hours 30 minutes.

1932 André Salet and Captain Joulette of France flew from Le Bourget, near Paris, to the Cape in 3 days 17 hours 15 minutes.

1933 Flight-Lieutenant Nicholetts and Squadron-Commander Gayford of the R.A.F. covered 5,340 miles non-stop in 2 days 9 hours 25 minutes, coming down near Walvis Bay.

1936 February. Flight-Lieutenant T. Rose flew from London to Cape Town in 3 days 17 hours 38 minutes.
C. W. A. Scott in a Percival Vega Gull flew from London to the Rand in 52 hours, 56 minutes and 48 seconds, winning the Schlesinger Air Race.

Since then there has been rapid improvement, though interrupted by World War II, and on July 9, 1959, all records were shattered by a Valiant of the Royal Air Force under Wing-Commander M. J. Beetham, who completed the journey between London and Cape Town in 11 hours 27 minutes.

Avocet (*Recurvirostra avosetta*). Migratory bird belonging to the Waders, found in most parts of South Africa. It has black markings on pure white plumage and a slender, recurved bill. Usually seen in large flocks. *See* WADER.

Avontuur. Small village in Langkloof, Cape Province; terminus of narrow-gauge railway from Port Elizabeth, 177 miles in length. Noted for its fruit and wheat. Named after a farm granted a century ago to Commandant Rademeyer, the word meaning 'Adventure.'

Axe, War of. *See* WAR OF THE AXE.

B

Baardman (*Spropiper squamifrons*) or **Scaly Weaver**. One of the commonest little birds of dry areas, where it can survive without water. Light in colour but with black 'moustache' stripes on throat and white-edged black 'scaly' feathers on forehead and wings. *See* WEAVERS.

Baardman, Cape (*Umbrina capensis*). Fish found in False Bay to Algoa Bay. About 28 inches long.

Baardskeerderbos (from 'Beard Shaver'—a type of spider). Village near Bredasdorp, Cape Province. Population: 170, including 160 Whites.

Babanango. Village and district in Zululand. Founded 1904 near former kraal of Zulu chief Dingaan, and scene of murder of Piet Retief and his Voortrekker companions. Name Babanango is derived from a mist-covered mountain near by and means: 'Father, where are you?' Population: 317, including 149 Whites.

Babbler (family Timaliidae). Tropical birds occurring mainly in the Transvaal and Northern Natal. Varieties include Arrow-marked or Jardine's Babbler and Pied Babbler.

Babe, Jerome. American trader and inventor. He was born in Louisiana, U.S.A., the exact date being unknown; arrived in South Africa about 1865, as representative of Remington Arms Company. Upon discovery of diamonds, he became successful digger, and invented the 'Baby' (q.v.), a popular and successful machine for washing gravel. Worked on the Vaal River and amassed a fair amount of money, most of which, however, he lost again after

his return to United States in 1873. Details of his later years are unknown.

Babiana or **Bobbejaantjie** (Iridaceae). Group of small wiry Cape plants with tubular flowers and grassy leaves. They belong to sandy soil near coast. Winter flowering. *Babiana tubeflora* is a rare whitish variety. The deep pink or mauve *Babiana plicata* is far more plentiful. A lovely little purple *Babiana hiematis* (winter flowering), with broad leaves and resembling a crocus, is also common as far south as Fish Hoek. *See* IRIS.

Baboon, Cape (*Papio porcarius*). Also known to Hottentots as Chacma; Amazosa, Infene; Zulus and Swazis, Imfena; Basuto, Tshweni. Found throughout South Africa to the Zambesi River, in bare, rocky, mountainous country. Feeds on wild fruit, insects, berries, young leaves and sap from certain trees. When driven by hunger, will raid orchards and vegetable gardens. Chief weapons of defence are extremely powerful jaw and well-developed canine teeth. As member of a troop is a formidable fighter. Yellow-brown body, face smoky-black.

Baboon Spider. *See* TARANTULA.

Baboon, Yellow (*Papio cynocephalus*). Found in western coastal regions of Africa, as far south as Mashonaland. Similar habits to those of the Cape Baboon (q.v.), but more aggressive. Yellow-black body, face flesh-coloured.

Baby. Machine invented by Jerome Babe (q.v.) and used for sorting diamondiferous gravel. Was devised about 1871 on the Vaal River Diggings and has remained in use ever since.

Baby

Babylon's Tower (Babylon's Toring): 1. Mountain on edge of Paarl and Stellenbosch districts.
2. Mountain south of Caledon, Cape Province.
3. Mountain near Cradock, Cape Province.

Baca. Tribe originally settled in Natal, but later moved to Pondoland between Tina and Umzimkulu Rivers.

Baden-Powell, Lord Robert Stephenson Smyth. British soldier. Founder of Boy Scout Movement, which brought him lasting fame. Born in England February 22, 1857; educated at Charterhouse. When 19 joined and served with Royal Hussars in India, Afghanistan and, in 1887, in South Africa. He served during unrest in Zululand (1888), in Malta (1893–1897), in Ashanti, West Africa, as Chief Staff Officer during Matabele Rebellion (1896–1897), and then as Colonel of the Irregular Horse in South Africa. By then he was known as artist, writer and secret service expert. During siege of Mafeking his use of schoolboys as messengers and despatchriders inspired his Boy Scout Movement, founded in 1908. He died in 1941.

Badfontein. Small village 14 miles from Machadodorp, Eastern Transvaal.

Badplaas. Mineral baths resort in eastern Transvaal between Carolina and Barberton.

Bafokeng Platinum Mine. Situated on tribal lands of Tswana people in North Western Transvaal and developed by the Union Corporation at a cost of R30,000,000. The Tswana participate in the profits.

Bailey, Sir Abe. South African mine magnate and legislator. Born in Cradock, 1864; son of Thomas Bailey, trader and member of original Cape Parliament. School in Yorkshire, England, and first business post in London. Returned to South Africa aged 20, at beginning of Barberton gold rush. Soon gained considerable wealth and moved to Johannesburg when gold was discovered there. Among the friends who foresaw his possibilities was Cecil John Rhodes. Became involved in Reform Movement at time of Jameson Raid, was imprisoned in 1896 and fined £2,000. During South African War raised several corps of irregulars and served on staff of General Pole-Carew. He succeeded Cecil Rhodes as member for Barkly West from 1902 to 1905. Elected to Transvaal Parliament in 1908. Represented Krugersdorp as staunch Unionist Party member from 1910 to 1924. He was a prominent figure on the Rand Stock Exchange. As member of the firm Ford and Jeppe he developed the Witwatersrand Townships, Mining and Finance Corporation. Registered in 1896, this became the Witwatersrand Townships, Mining and Finance Corporation Ltd. (taken over by the Anglo-American Corporation in 1942). His main interests were on East Rand and in Eastern Transvaal. He developed South African alkali occurrence in North Pretoria. Spent most of later life in England, where known as important racehorse owner and sporting figure. As strong protagonist of better relations between white races in South Africa, he willed large sums for establishment of trust to this end. Died 1940. Buried on hillside overlooking his home in Muizenberg.

Bain, Andrew Geddes. Pioneer of South African geology. Born at Thurso, northern Scotland, in 1796, he reached South Africa in 1820 and began a series of explorations in 1826, during which he already showed his interest in geological matters, especially fossils. Further expeditions followed, and Bain took the opportunity offered by his work as Inspector of Roads to examine excavations made in many parts of the country. One of his major achievements was the construction of Bain's Kloof Pass (q.v.) in the Western Cape Province. His writings were of the greatest importance and certain prehistoric creatures were named after him. Honoured by his colleagues both in South Africa and in England, he died on October 20, 1864. Apart from his achievements as a geologist, he is remembered in South Africa on account of his celebrated ditty, 'Kaatjie Kekkelbek,' creating the figure of a coloured maid which has become proverbial.

Baines, Thomas. Explorer and artist. Born at King's Lynn in 1822, the son of a sea captain, he started painting coats of arms for a coachbuilder, from which he soon passed to landscape and other work. In 1842 he reached Cape Colony, where he taught drawing in Cape Town, until the outbreak of the War of the Axe (q.v.) in 1846 took him to the eastern frontier with the troops. His next headquarters were at Grahamstown. He saw further active service as an artist in 1848 and 1851, gaining a fine reputation for the vividness and liveliness of his drawings. In 1854 he accompanied an expedition to Northern Australia, producing a large number of pictures now preserved by the Royal Geographical Society in London. His home town, King's Lynn, in 1857 presented him with the Freedom of the Borough. Baines was in-

vited to accompany the Livingstone Zambesi Expedition in 1858, but became involved in a number of quarrels, and was badly treated by Livingstone himself. However, he succeeded in visiting the Victoria Falls, of which he made the first paintings, likewise commemorating numerous other scenes in pre-pioneer Rhodesia. His paintings and drawings attracted great interest in London, where he set up a studio and in 1865 published a volume of reproductions of his own work. The success of his book, *Explorations in South West Africa*, resulted in his return to that country, where he visited Lobengula and produced some important early maps. He likewise made valuable discoveries as a naturalist. His 1868 trip to Southern Africa was under the auspices of a new gold-mining company intending to develop the Tati Fields. Baines succeeded in obtaining from Lobengula mining concessions, which acquired great importance when, much later, Cecil Rhodes appeared on the scene. Baines, however, gained no advantage from this, and returned to Natal, where he died in Durban on May 8, 1875. His book, *The Gold Regions of South-Eastern Africa*, with its very fine illustrations and maps, was published posthumously.

Bain's Kloof. Named after Andrew Geddes Bain, famous Colonial engineer. One of the most picturesque passes in South Africa, opened up in 1854, when Bain completed the first highway. The pass begins near Wellington and follows the course of the Wit River. It rises to a height of 2,000 feet above sea-level, and is about 20 miles long.

Baird, Sir David. British general. Born in Newbyth, Scotland, on December 6, 1757; joined army in 1772. Sent to India as Captain in 1779 in the Highland Light Infantry, he won considerable distinction in several campaigns and saw action in the Cape in 1795, when, as a colonel, he helped to take it for the first time. Returning to India he won fresh laurels as a major-general, and led an Indian force against Napoleon in Egypt, making a famous march across the desert to the Nile. In 1806 he commanded the force that took the Cape from the Batavian Republic, after defeating the Dutch troops at Blauwberg. He was ordered to Denmark, where, in 1807, he commanded a division. He died on August 18, 1829.

Bakbos (Baking Bush). Common South African name for *Passerina filiformis.*

Baker, Sir Herbert. Architect. Born in England in 1862, and educated at Tonbridge School. Coming to South Africa in 1892 he was commissioned by Rhodes to rebuild and restore 'Groote Schuur,' and establish a collection of antiques. A long series of jobs followed, including 'The Woolsack,' 'Welgelegen' and 'Rust en Vrede' at Muizenberg (where Rhodes hoped to retire and which after his death was completed for Sir Abe Bailey), the Kimberley Siege Memorial, and the Rhodes Memorial at Groote Schuur. Baker next established himself in Johannesburg, where he built a number of mansions. His most important work in the Transvaal was the Union Buildings in Pretoria, completed in 1913. In that year he returned to England but kept in touch with South Africa by designing many buildings, also South Africa House in London. He gained fame designing, among other things, the new city of Delhi, India, and the new Bank of England in London. To Baker goes most of the credit for the revival of the vogue for old Cape Dutch architecture in Southern Africa. He wrote his reminiscences, *Cecil Rhodes by His Architect.* His death occurred in 1946.

Bakerville. Camp near Lichtenburg, Transvaal. Centre of Alluvial Diamond Rush of 20,000 people in 1926. Population: 1,606, including 336 Whites. The settlement includes the famous Elandsputte Diggings.

Bakwena. Tribe living in Bechuanaland, the name of which means 'People of the Crocodile' after their totem animal. They take their name from an early chief Kwena. Chief Sebele visited England in 1895 and was received by Queen Victoria.

Baldwin, William Charles. Traveller and explorer. Born in England in 1830, he arrived in Natal in 1851, and trekked into the Transvaal, Zululand and into present-day Rhodesia. In 1859 he reached the Makarikari Salt Pan north of the Kalahari. He claimed to be the second white man to see the Victoria Falls, in 1860. Baldwin returned to England in 1861 and died in 1903.

Bale, Sir Henry. Chief Justice of Natal. Born on January 12, 1854, in Pietermaritzburg and educated in England; he practised as an attorney in Natal from 1875, and from 1893 to 1901 represented Pietermaritzburg in the Natal Legislative Assembly. He became Attorney-General and Minister of Education, becoming Chief Justice in 1901. He died on December 1, 1910.

Balfour. 1. Town in the Transvaal, on main railway from Johannesburg to Durban. Established early in 20th century under the name of McHattiesburg and renamed about 1908, after British premier, Arthur Balfour. 22 miles from Heidelberg. New mining developments lately at Winkelhaak. Population: 4,666, including 1,350 Whites.

2. Village below Katberg Mountains in Eastern Cape Province, noted for its beautiful scenery. Orange growing, tobacco and sawmills. Population: 568, including 149 Whites. Named after Secretary of Glasgow Mission Society.

Balgowan. Village in Natal, 105 miles from Durban on Johannesburg main line, near well-known boys' Public School, Michaelhouse (q.v.).

Balla-Balla Gold Field. Situated in Rhodesia, between Bulawayo and Fort Victoria.

Ballantyne, Robert Michael. English author of boys' books. Born in 1825 in Edinburgh, he visited South Africa in 1876, spending some time in the Karroo, Port Elizabeth and the Eastern Province. Two juvenile stories, *The Settler and the Savage* and *The Gorilla Hunters*, were followed by a travel book, *Six Months at the Cape*, published in 1879. He died in 1894.

Ballet. Although occasional visits by dancers were recorded during the 19th century, it was not until 1913 that a serious attempt was made to teach the art locally, much of the credit going to Helen Webb of Cape Town, who began annual performances in the City Hall.

With the backing of the Cape Town Municipal Orchestra, tours were undertaken by the Helen Webb Ballet Company in 1923, while the visit of Anna Pavlova towards the end of 1925 gave further encouragement.

Meanwhile, in Johannesburg, ballet was also being encouraged by Vivienne Tailleur, Marjorie Sturman and others. Visits of overseas companies, including Levitoff's Russian Ballet in 1934, the Ballet de Monte Carlo two years later, the Chauve Souris and others, stimulated interest; but it was mainly owing to the existence of the College of Music that the Cape Town University Ballet came into existence in 1933. Since that time the popularity of the art has grown enormously, and South Africa has produced a number of outstanding dancers, many of whom have gained fame overseas, among them Nadia Nerina, Maud Lloyd, John Cranko, David Poole and Alexis Rassine.

The visit to South Africa of Alicia Markova and Anton Dolin in 1949 provided a fresh stimulus. Thanks to the ability and enthusiasm of Dulcie Howes, the Cape Town University Ballet has gained a popularity beyond the limits of the Republic, and has for years made regular tours as far as Rhodesia and Zambia. In recent times (1964) the Johannesburg School of Art led the way in starting the first High School course in Ballet, and a similar step has been taken in Durban.

Ballinger, Mrs. Margaret Livingstone (Margaret Hodgson). South African Member of Parliament. Born in Glasgow January 11, 1894, came to South Africa in 1904 and studied at Huguenot College, Wellington; Rhodes University College, Grahamstown; and Somerville College, Oxford. After some years lecturing in history at the University of the Witwatersrand she entered Parliament in 1937 as Bantu Representative, remaining until abolition of the system in 1960. A powerful and influential speaker and a founder of the South African Liberal Party, from which she later retired.

Ballinger, William George. South African senator. Born in Birmingham September 21, 1894, educated at Glasgow University and in Denmark. Labour organiser in Scotland, he came to South Africa in 1928 with the I.C.U. (q.v.). He attended International Labour conferences at Geneva, and served as senator to represent the Bantus in the Transvaal from 1948 to 1960.

Balmforth, Rev. Ramsden. Author and clergyman. Born of poor parents at Huddersfield, England, in 1861, he entered the Unitarian ministry in his thirties and in 1897 came to South Africa to take charge of the Free Protestant [Unitarian] Church at Cape Town, with which he remained for over 40 years. Apart from his strong and outspoken views on social reform and pacifism, he was a distinguished writer on literary and theological subjects, his books including *The Ethical and Religious Value of the Novel* and *Jesus the Man*. He died on December 31, 1941.

Balmoral: 1. Village near Knysna, Cape Province, in forest.
2. Village in Eastern Transvaal, between Machadodorp and Pretoria, which figured several times in fights during the South African War. Used for a while by General Louis Botha as his headquarters.

Bam, Sir Peter Canzius Van Blommestein, Stewart-, of Ards. South African industrial propagandist and legislator. Born in Cape Town in 1869 and educated there and in England. Elected as member to the Cape Parliament from 1904 to 1910. In 1907 he became Chairman of the South African Products Exhibition in London and helped to found the South African National Union which encouraged local industries and tradition. Later connected with several other prominent exhibitions overseas. He died in 1928.

Bamangwato. Tribe living in Bechuanaland, part of the Bechuana family. Take their name from a former chief, Ngwato, who settled near Shoshong about 1700. Of peaceful disposition, they held their own against their neighbours, mainly because of the exceptional ability of their chief, Khama (q.v.), who was responsible for placing the tribe under British protection in 1884. Despite much internal quarrelling, a system of Paramount Chiefs has been continued to the present day, under the authority of the High Commissioner. Many of the Bamangwato find work in the Republic. The tribe is estimated at 300,000.

Bambata Rebellion. Rising of the Zulu tribe in 1906 under leadership of Chief Bambata. The cause of the insurrection has never been clearly defined, but is generally ascribed to mistakes made in a new system of taxation and also to a decline in the

authority exercised by the Whites as a result of the recent South African War. Unrest began during January 1906 and on the 30th of that month two policemen were murdered. This was followed by the killing of a magistrate, Mr. M. Stainbank, and of other officials. Troops were mobilised and the murderers of the policemen were publicly executed at Richmond, Natal, on April 2. Bambata, one of the principal leaders, took refuge in the Nkandlha Forest, where he received the support of Dinizulu. By this time the greater part of Zululand was ablaze, and it became necessary to mobilise not only the Natal Volunteer Forces but to call in troops from the Transvaal as well. Bambata was finally killed and Dinizulu captured. Operations were over by August 1906. The whole rebellion cost Natal nearly £1,000,000, besides numerous men killed and wounded. The total losses amongst the rebels are estimated at over 2,000.

Bamboo-Fish (Cape), **Striped Karanteen** (Natal) (*Sarpa salpa*). Fish found off Mossamedes, Saldanha Bay, Table Bay and False Bay to Delagoa Bay, also in Mediterranean and off West Africa. About 18 inches long. *See* BREAM.

Banana. Important crop in Natal, where first settlers found the plant growing wild. Was cultivated in 1850 and flourishes best in the Port Shepstone area. Natal is jocularly referred to as 'Bananaland,' but Mozambique also supplies the rest of Southern Africa.

Banana, Wild. *See* STRELITZIA.

Bancroft. *See* CHILILABOMBWE.

Bancroft, Dr. Joseph Austen. Geologist. Born in Canada in 1882, he came to Southern Africa in 1927 as Consulting Geologist in Zambia for the Anglo-American Corporation. A man of great eminence in his profession overseas, he wrote widely on scientific subjects and was largely responsible for the opening up of the copper deposits of Zambia, particularly of the great mine which now bears his name. He died on December 11, 1957.

Banda, Dr. Hastings Kamuzu. First President of Malawi (Nyasaland) (q.v.). Born near Kazungu in 1902, studied at Lovedale and worked on Rand gold mines. Qualified in medicine at Nashville, U.S.A., and practised in England. Returned to Nyasaland in 1958 implacably opposed to continuance of Central African Federation (*see* RHODESIA AND NYASALAND, FEDERATION OF). In 1960 persuaded British Colonial Office to adopt his views and in 1962 assumed office as as Prime Minister. He became President on July 6, 1966.

Bandolier Kop. Village in the Northern Transvaal, south of Louis Trichardt. Corundum mining centre.

Banket: 1. An almond-studded sweet popular with old Dutch cooks. Name applied to rock containing pebbles, recognised as an indication of gold on the Witwatersrand.
2. Village in Rhodesia.

Banks and Banking. The first bank in the modern sense at the Cape of Good Hope was the 'Lombard Bank,' set up in 1793 under the auspices of the Government, though its facilities, modelled on those of the 'Bank van Lening' in Holland, were very limited. Further development was slow even after the British occupation of the colony. The Cape of Good Hope Savings Bank (q.v.), still flourishing, was launched in 1831, followed in 1837 by the Cape of Good Hope Bank (q.v.), founded by private enterprise. Thereafter a considerable number of small local banks were founded in various country towns, including Beaufort West, Swellendam, Fort Beaufort, Grahamstown and many others, all of which were either merged in the larger institutions that followed or went into liquidation. The only survivors are the

British Kaffrarian Savings Bank at King William's Town, dating from 1860, and the Stellenbosch District Bank (q.v.), founded in 1882.

As settlement spread other colonies followed suit, the Natal Bank, started in 1854, flourishing for many years. Banks were also founded in the Orange Free State—at Bloemfontein in 1862, at Fauresmith in 1863, and elsewhere. The National Bank of the O.F.S. was started in 1877, with funds derived from £90,000 compensation paid by Britain for the Griqualand West Diamond Fields. The first institution in the Transvaal was a branch of the Cape Commercial Bank, opened at Pretoria in 1873. Supported by the Government and by German and Dutch capitalists, the National Bank of the South African Republic was opened at Pretoria in 1890.

Large-scale joint stock banks began with the founding of the Standard Bank of South Africa (q.v.) in 1862, followed by the Oriental Bank, the London and South Africa Bank, and others later withdrawn. The Netherlands Bank of South Africa (q.v.) dates from 1888, and began in the Transvaal. The National Bank of South Africa, so named in 1901, developed from the merger of banks in the Orange Free State, Natal and the Transvaal. It was absorbed into Barclays Bank (Dominion, Colonial and Overseas) (q.v.) in 1926. Youngest among the larger South African banks are Volkskas (q.v.), founded in 1935, and Trust Bank, dating from 1954 (q.v.).

After World War II several overseas institutions, including the National City Bank of New York (which made a previous effort here in 1920), the Chase National Bank, the Bank of Athens, the Bank of Indo-China and the Bank of Lisbon, opened in South Africa, while Grindley's Bank and the Ottoman Bank started in Rhodesia. The oldest bank in that country is the Standard, which opened in a tent at 'Fort Salisbury' in 1892.

During the German régime a number of German banks operated in South West Africa, all of which have given way to the British and South African institutions, which also serve Basutoland, Swaziland and Bechuanaland.

Banking in Mozambique is controlled from Lisbon, through the Banco Nacional Ultramarino, but several British and South African banks have branches there.

Bantom. A corruption of Bandom, a type of pebble found in the river gravel, and often indicating the presence of diamonds. Its name is derived from the fact that it carries a number of stripes (bande).

Bantu. Name literally meaning 'The People,' applied to the aboriginal inhabitants of South Africa, other than the Hottentots and Bushmen. *See* BANTU LANGUAGES and BANTU PEOPLES.

BANTU LANGUAGES OF SOUTHERN AFRICA
by
DR. A. C. JORDAN
Lecturer in Bantu Languages, School of African Studies, University of Cape Town

THE Bantu family of languages —well over 200—covers almost the whole of the southern half of the continent of Africa, from the Gulf of Guinea in the west to the mouth of the Tana River in the east. The term *Bantu* was first used as a linguistic term by Dr. W. H. I. Bleek in the middle of the 19th century for the whole family of languages in which the word for 'people' was 'bantu' or some modification thereof (e.g. *batho, bandu, watu, athu,* etc.), to distinguish it from the Hamitic, Sudanic and Semitic families on the one hand, and from the Khoi-Sen languages on the other. The Khoi-Khoin (so-called 'Hottentots') and the Sen or Thwa (so-called 'Bushmen') constitute enclaves or 'islands' in the southern Bantu-speaking area.

In Southern Africa the Bantu language-family is represented by five different language-groups, each consisting of a number of mutually intelligible dialects, spoken by about 13,000,000 people in all.

(1) The Nguni group includes *Xhosa* (mainly Cape Province), *Zulu* (mainly Natal) and *Rhodesian Ndebele* (radiating from Bulawayo district) as literary dialects. The non-literary dialects of this group include *Swazi* (mainly Swaziland), *Transvaal Ndebele* (Transvaal), *Hlubi, Bhaca, Xesibe, Mpondo,* etc. (north-eastern to south-eastern Cape), *Lala* and *Qwabe* (Natal).

(2) The Sotho group includes *Southern Sotho* (mainly Basutoland), *Tswana* (mainly Bechuanaland, Transvaal and Southern Free State), and *Northern Sotho* (Transvaal) as literary dialects. The non-literary dialects include *Hurutshe* and sub-dialects in Bechuanaland, and *Koni, Tlokwa,* etc., in the Transvaal.

(3) The Venda group has its home in the Transvaal. Its main dialects are *Phani* and *Tsavhatsindi.*

(4) The Tsonga group covers the people commonly known as 'Shangaan' in the Mozambique district of Portuguese East Africa, and is spoken in some parts of the Transvaal as well. It includes *Ronga* (around Lourenço Marques), *Tonga* (Transvaal) and *Tswa* (Transvaal) as literary dialects.

(5) The Shona group has its home in Rhodesia. It has six important sub-groups, viz.: *Karanga* (radiating from Fort Victoria); *Zezuru* (radiating from the vicinity of Salisbury); *Kore-*

kore (south of the Zambesi); *Manyika* (centring in Umtali); *Ndau* (Moçambique and Melsetter); and *Kalanga* (from Plumtree to Wankie). The first two are used as a basis for literary form.

In the sub-classification of the Bantu languages, the first four groups above belong to the south-eastern zone. The Shona group, which does not share the linguistic characteristics that distinguish the south-eastern zone from other Bantu language zones, belongs to the south central zone.

The Bantu languages have a simple, perfectly balanced vowel system. In each language there is a low vowel, *a*. and an equal number of front and back vowels. The vowel phonemes range from five to nine, the average being seven.

There are two semi-vowels, *w* and *y*. The consonants include explosive as well as a few implosives.

A vowel may be short, medium, long or extra-long. In general the vowel in the penultimate syllable is long. Tone may be high, high-falling, high-rising, low, low-falling, low-rising, and has semantic significance, that is, two or more words, consisting of identical phonemes but differing in their intonation-patterns, have entirely different meanings. English *content* (satisfied, or that which is contained) more or less illustrates this.

The noun consists of a stem and a prefix. The nouns fall into a number of classes distinguished by their prefixes. There are classes indicating abstractions, verbal nouns, diminutives, augmentatives, locatives, etc. No less than twenty-three noun-class prefixes have been recorded, but no living Bantu language is known to possess all.

The majority of verb stems are disyllabic, e.g. Nguni *bona*, Sotho *bona*, Tsonga *vona* (see).

The noun is concord-governing. That is, in any expression, any word grammatically related to the noun bears a concord referring to that noun. The concord shows direct relationship to its noun-class prefix.

Since pronouns, qualificatives (i.e. adjectives, demonstratives, etc.) and predicatives are grammatically related to the noun, it follows that there are pronominal, qualificative and predicative concords. The last include subjectival and objectival concords.

In all the moods of the verb, infinitive, imperative, indicative, subjunctive and potential, the negative is formed by affixes and/or modifications of the verb-stem, e.g. Nguni infinitive *u kuhamba* (to go), *u kungahambi* (not to go), subjunctive *ahambe* (that he may go), *angahambi* (that he may not go).

Besides verbs, *copulatives* including no verb at all may be used as predicatives. Copulatives express ideas of 'being.' A copulative consists of a copula and a complement, e.g. Nguni *ndimkhulu*, Sotho *kemoholo* (I am big, but literally 'I big'); Nguni *ngu mntu*, Sotho *ke motho* (it is a person).

There are adjectival, enumerative, demonstrative, quantitative and possessive qualificatives. The adjectives are closely related to the nouns morphologically and semantically. The demonstratives have three or more positional types, indicating something near the speaker, something nearer the hearer than the speaker, and something remote from both speaker and hearer.

A possessive qualificative ordinarily follows the substantive it qualifies, e.g. Nguni *i sandla sam* (my hand, literally 'the hand of me'), Sotho *bana baka* (my children, literally 'the children of me').

The south-eastern Bantu languages are rich in traditional literature, both Prose and Verse. *Narrative Prose* includes Myths and Legends, Fables and Tales, Proverbs and Riddles. Myths tell stories about the origin of things, creation, how animals acquired their tails, how death came into the world, etc. Legends are stories of heroes who championed the cause of man against ogres and other monsters. Fables are animal stories. The animals in these Fables have human attributes. They represent types of people. The Hare is usually the hero. The tales are mainly stories about ordinary folk. *Verse* includes Lyrical and Dramatic verse, Dance-songs, War-songs, Hunting-songs, etc. It also includes that remarkable *genre* known as the *Praise-poem.* Nguni and Sotho are particularly rich in Praise-poems.

Writing began about the middle of the 19th century, with Nguni and Sotho. Both have a fair amount of literature today, including some good translations of English classics. Chief of these is *The Pilgrim's Progress.* The most famous original work so far is the Southern Sotho historical romance, *Chaka*, by Thomas Mofolo. This has been translated into several European languages, including English, French and German. Xhosa writers, in particular, have made a remarkable contribution to Christian worship not only by translations of famous hymns, but by their own compositions. The best-known poets are S. E. K. Mqhayi (Xhosa), who died in 1945, and B. Wallet Vilakazi (Zulu), who died in 1947. Extracts from English translations are included in an anthology of South African poetry edited by Roy McNab and published by Maskew Miller, 1958.

BANTU PEOPLES OF SOUTHERN AFRICA
by
PROFESSOR D. T. COLE
University of the Witwatersrand, Johannesburg

THE aboriginal peoples of Southern Africa, recent European and Asian immigrants excepted, belong to one of two quite distinct ethno-linguistic stocks, the Khoisan (or Bushmen and Hottentots) and the Bantu. A third very small group are the Bergdama of South-West Africa who, like the Bantu, are of Negro stock, but speak a Nama Hottentot dialect.

The Bantu peoples are distributed over most of Africa south of the 'Bantu Line,' an ill-defined boundary which extends, with many irregularities, from Mount Cameroon on the west coast to the north of the Congo River and Lake Victoria, and joins the east coast near the mouth of the Tana River, north of Mombasa. Bantu peoples also occur on adjacent African islands, including the Comoros and the north-west coast of Madagascar. Both numerically and geographically, therefore, the Bantu constitute the most important ethno-linguistic group in Africa.

The term *Bantu* is a linguistic one: it is used of peoples who speak a particular type of language. Altogether there are some 250 Bantu languages, exclusive of dialects, spoken south of the 'Bantu Line.'

Three major divisions of the Bantu peoples of Africa, Western, Eastern and Southern, have been recognised on the basis of geographical distribution and cultural and historical factors. For present purposes, however, an ethno-linguistic classification is more useful, since, with relatively rare exceptions, people of the same ethnic stock speak languages or dialects of the same linguistic grouping.

In South Africa there are four main ethno-linguistic groups of Bantu peoples, Nguni, Sotho (or Suthu), Venda and Shangana-Tsonga. The Nguni group includes the Zulu (Natal), Xhosa (Eastern Cape), Swazi (Swaziland and Eastern Transvaal) and two divisions of Ndebele in the Transvaal (Potgietersrust and Pretoria-Middelburg districts). Also of Nguni stock are the Ndebele (Matabele) of Rhodesia, and the Ngoni tribes in Malawi and Tanzania.

The Sotho group includes the Southern Sotho of Lesotho, eastern and central Orange Free State and southern Transvaal; Northern (Pedi) of central Transvaal; Tswana of Botswana, western Transvaal, western Orange Free State and northern Cape; Kgalagadi of the Kalahari Desert, Botswana; and a number of smaller tribes in the northern and eastern Transvaal, including the Lovedu, Phalaborwa, etc. The Lozi or Rotse of Barotseland, Zambia, are also of Sotho stock and their language fundamentally of Sotho type.

In the Louis Trichardt-Sibasa districts of the northern Transvaal are found the Venda, a small group including the Lemba, but without any other distinctive subdivisions. The Shangana-Tsonga group includes the 'Shangaans' of the eastern Transvaal, and a number of tribes or tribal clusters in southern Portuguese East Africa, the Tsonga, Ronga and Tshwa. Another small group in this area is that of Inhambane, which includes the Chopi and (gi)Tonga.

Apart from the Ndebele referred to above, Rhodesia is the home of the Shona group (Zezuru, Karanga, Korekore, etc.), with offshoots into north-eastern Botswana (Lilima and Kalanga), and into central Portuguese East Africa (Ndau and Manyika). To the north of these in Portuguese East Africa are the Sena, Makua and Yao groups. In Malawi the dominant group are the Nyanja, who extend also into adjacent areas in Zambia and Portuguese East Africa. Other Malawi groups are the Tumbuka-Kamanga and Nyakyusa.

In Zambia the two largest groups are the Bemba, including the Ushi, Bisa, Lala and Lamba; and the Tonga, together with the Ila, Lenje and Soli. Other lesser groups on the eastern and north-eastern borders are the Nsenga and Kunda, the Mambwe and Lungu, the Cewa of Nyanja stock and the Senga of Tumbuka stock, the

last two both extensions into Zambia from Malawi. On the western side, in addition to the Lozi mentioned above we find the Luvale, Luchazi, Chokwe, Lunda and Ndembo in one group which extends into Angola; the Luba group extending southwards from the Belgian Congo and including Kaonde, Mbwela and Nkoya; and the Subiya group, including also Totela, Simaa, Shanjo, Kwangwa, Mashi and Kwandi. This last group—of which our knowledge is quite fragmentary—extends into adjacent areas in Angola, South West Africa (Caprivi Strip) and Botswana.

Finally, South West Africa is populated in the northern half by the Herero, Kwanyama, Ndonga, Kwangali and other tribes, all closely related and allied to the (u)Mbundu, Nyaneka and others of Angola, and to the Yeei, Gcereku and Mbandieru of Botswana.

This short survey is of necessity sketchy and incomplete, as is our knowledge of the Bantu peoples and languages. Even within a few hundred miles of major university centres such as Johannesburg and Pretoria are tribes of whom we know nothing more than the name, and perhaps even that not correctly. A vast field for research awaits the provision of funds and the interest of qualified personnel.

BANTU NAMES FOR CITIES

Cape Town . . .	Khepi ('Cape')
Bloemfontein . .	Mangaung
Durban	Tekweni
East London . .	Istilondon
Grahamstown . . .	Irini
Johannesburg .	Goli; Igoli ('Gold') also Joni and Jozi
Kimberley .	Ndayimani ('Diamond')
Lourenço Marques .	Lolensomaki
Pietermaritzburg .	Umgungunghlovu
Pietersburg . .	Polokwane
Port Elizabeth .	Ibayi ('The Bay')
Pretoria . . .	Pitoli
Rustenburg	Hlabang
Salisbury	Sozibeli

Bantustan. Popular name for 'Separate Development Self-Governing Areas' set up in the Transkei, Zululand, Northern Transvaal and elsewhere in the Republic. Name derived from Pakistan, Hindustan, etc.

Bantu Trade Fair. Non-profit-making organisation established in 1962 by a group of White business men to develop a market and raise living standards among the Bantu population of South Africa. Usually referred to as Batfair, it began in July 1963 at Kwa Mashu near Durban, King William's Town and Hamanskraal near Pretoria, where successful commercial fairs were held by leading manufacturers and business firms, drawing a total attendance of 163,000. Other fixtures were arranged for 1964, the aim being to have six annually in different parts of the Republic. Closed down for financial reasons in 1964.

Bantu Wage and Productivity Association. Founded by White employers in Johannesburg in 1960 to improve the productivity of non-White workers by higher wages. Its activities have spread and have resulted in increases totalling several million Rand.

Baobab (*Adansonia digitata* L.). Also known as 'Cream of Tartar Tree.' Northern Transvaal and Rhodesia. Tree with enormous bole and short branches. Wood spongy. Regarded as the largest of African trees. It was noted by the great German scientist, Alexander von Humbodt, as 'The Oldest Organic Monument of our Planet.' *See* PLANTS, TREES and Colour Plate.

Bapedi. Tribe living in the Northern and Eastern Transvaal. Their early home was in the Lulu Mountains to the east of the Olifants River, and they were linked with the Basuto Moshesh. After being almost decimated by Mosilikatse, survivors were rallied by Sekwati, son of Tulare. He gathered many refugees from other broken-up tribes, who assumed the name of Bapedi. A series of wars with the Boers began in 1846, which resulted in submission to them. Sekwati was succeeded by Sekukuni in September 1861. He rebelled against the authority of the South African Republic and was not brought to submission until 1879, with the assistance of British troops under General Sir Garnet Wolseley. *See also* SEKUKUNI. It is estimated there are 750,000 Bapedi in the Republic.

Baptist Church in South Africa. Ever since the arrival of the 1820 settlers there have been substantial numbers of Baptists in South Africa, the first church being set up in Grahamstown in that year. In 1872 the Baptist Union of South Africa was formed, comprising an association of churches and congregations otherwise self-governed. Mission work was placed on a similar footing in 1892, when the South African Baptist Missionary Society was created. 44,982 members.

Baragwanath Hospital. Bantu hospital in southern suburb of Johannesburg, the largest in the Southern Hemisphere and one of the largest in the world. Erected during World War II for White military patients, especially tuberculosis cases, it was converted to its present purpose in 1945. Baragwanath Hospital has 2,400 beds, 2,100 nurses, 1,500 of them qualified, and 218 doctors. Most of the nurses and many doctors are themselves Bantu. Baragwanath Hospital is an important centre for research and handles 2,000 out-patients a day and 1,000 confinements a month.

Barbel. *See* CATFISH.

Barberspan. Village near Lichtenburg in the Western Transvaal.

Barberton. Town in the Eastern Transvaal, named after the brothers Barber, and formerly a famous gold mining centre and capital of the De Kaap Gold Field (q.v.). It was founded in 1884, and rose to its zenith 2 years later, after the finding of the famous Sheba Reef, when its population passed 8,000 Whites and it had two Stock Exchanges, clubs, etc. Many magnates later prominent on the Rand began their careers at Barberton. Most of the mines were worked out or found unpayable. In recent years Barberton has become an important centre for sub-tropical agriculture. Population: 13,240, including 3,252 Whites.

Barberton. Illegal drink brewed by Africans, the name being derived from that of the town above.

Barberton Daisy. *See* DAISY.

Barberton, Ivan Mitford-. *See* MITFORD-BARBERTON.

Barbet (family Capitonidae). Thickset birds with strong bills, living in the forest and bush, and eating chiefly fruit. Many varieties, most of them nesting in holes of dead trees.

Barclays Bank (Dominion, Colonial and Overseas). Offshoot of the Barclays Bank group of Great Britain. In 1926 this absorbed the National Bank of South Africa Ltd., which had developed from the National Bank of the South African Republic Ltd., founded, largely with German, British and Dutch backing, on April 15, 1891, with its head office in Pretoria. This bank grew rapidly, soon extending its operations to the Cape, Natal and the Orange Free State. In 1910 it absorbed the National Bank of the Orange River Colony, which had been founded on June 27, 1877, and had acquired the original Bloemfontein Bank. The Bank of Africa, founded in August 1879 to take over the operations in this country

of the Oriental Bank, as well as several other local institutions, was merged with the National Bank of South Africa in 1912, while in 1914 the Natal Bank, founded on April 1, 1854, was similarly absorbed. Because of heavy losses sustained by South Africa after World War I, this in its turn was absorbed into Barclays Bank (D.C.O.). The latter has a world-wide chain of branches. Its head office for South Africa is in Johannesburg, and for Rhodesia in Salisbury.

Baring, Sir Evelyn. *See* HOWICK OF GLENDALE, LORD.

Barkly East. Town in north-east Cape Province, on slopes of Drakensberg, south of Basutoland. Laid out in 1874 and named after Governor Sir Henry Barkly (q.v.). Important wool centre. Noted for its fine mountain scenery with peaks up to 11,000 feet. Bushman caves found near by. Population: 5,100, including 1,320 Whites.

Barkly, Sir Henry. Governor of the Cape of Good Hope. Born in London, February 24, 1815, son of Aeneas Barkly, of New Brunswick, Canada. Sat in Parliament for Leominster 1845–1848. Governor of British Guiana 1848–1853, followed by a similar post in Jamaica from 1853 to 1856. From 1856 to 1863 was in Australia as Governor of Victoria. Then went as Governor to Mauritius for 7 years from 1863 to 1870, before being transferred to Cape Colony. There he served for 7 eventful years, during which he had the difficult task of handling the problems created by the discovery of diamonds, including rebellion of diggers on Vaal River. He proclaimed Griqualand West a British dependency in 1871, and was entrusted with the thankless task of persuading an unwilling South Africa to accept Lord Carnarvon's permissive act for the federation of the Cape, Natal, Transvaal and O.F.S., which was far ahead of its time. After retiring on pension in 1878 he became a director of the Standard Bank. Died October 20, 1898.

Barkly West. Town in Griqualand West, 22 miles from Kimberley, on banks of Vaal River. Founded 1870 as diamond diggers' camp under the name of Klipdrift. For a short while was capital of 'Diggers' Republic' of Griqualand West, before its annexation by the Crown. Became the main centre of a line of alluvial 'River Diggings.' Named after Governor Sir Henry Barkly (q.v.). Is acquiring importance as irrigation and farming centre. Population: 4,300, including 840 Whites.

Barnard, Andrew. Colonial Secretary of the Cape of Good Hope. Born in 1762 as the son of the Bishop of Limerick, he joined the government service, and after the first British occupation of the Cape was appointed Colonial Secretary in 1797. Five years earlier he had married Lady Anne Lindsay, better known as Lady Anne Barnard (q.v.). He remained at the Cape till 1802, but revisited the Colony in 1807, without his wife. While there he died at the early age of 45.

Barnard, Lady Anne. Poet and letter-writer. Born in 1750, the eldest daughter of the Earl of Balcarres, in Scotland. As Lady Anne Lindsay she wrote the ballad that gave her literary immortality, 'Auld Robin Gray.' Her authorship remained a secret until 1823, when she admitted it to her friend, Sir Walter Scott. Meanwhile, in 1793, when already 43, she married Andrew Barnard (q.v.), who in 1797 became Colonial Secretary at the Cape. She accompanied him there, and as a pastime wrote a series of letters describing daily life in the Colony, which became a South African classic. She returned to England in 1802, and died in 1825. Her letters did not appear until 1901, when they were edited by Dorothea Fairbridge (q.v.) under the title *South Africa a Century Ago*. She was also an artist of some distinction.

Barnard, Professor Christiaan Neethling. South African surgeon. Born at Beaufort West, Cape Province on November 8, 1922, educated at Beaufort West High School, University of Cape Town and University of Minnesota, U.S.A. Specialised in Cardio-thoracic Surgery and became Director of Surgical Research at Groote Schuur Hospital in 1958. In December 1967 carried out the World's first successful heart transplant. *See* HEART TRANSPLANTS.

Barnato, Barnett (Barney) Isaacs. Mining magnate. Born in 1852 as Barnett Isaacs, son of a publican in the East End of London, he became a part-time vaudeville entertainer and boxer with his brother Henry (q.v.), for which purpose they assumed the name of Barnato. In 1873 Barney followed Henry to Kimberley, where they worked as diggers, diamond buyers and speculators, acquiring great wealth. Through gaining control of several important mines they came in touch with Cecil Rhodes (q.v.). The ensuing struggle resulted in a merger of interests in 1888, Barney Barnato becoming an original Life Governor of De Beers Consolidated Mines (q.v.). From 1889 to 1897 he was member of the Cape Parliament for Kimberley. After the gold discoveries in the Transvaal he moved his headquarters to the Rand, where in 1889 he founded the Johannesburg Consolidated Investment Co. (q.v.), though the firm of Barnato Brothers remained in existence. He was a dominant and colourful figure in the financial, mining, theatrical and sporting worlds, in both South Africa and England. Towards the end his nerves gave way and in 1897 he jumped overboard travelling between Southampton and the Cape and was drowned. His estate was valued at just under £1,000,000.

Barnato, Henry. Mining magnate. Born in London in 1850, came to South Africa with his brother, Barney (q.v.), in 1871. Together they attained great wealth in the Diamond Fields, Henry having by far the larger fortune. He returned to England, became a well-known racehorse owner and died in 1908, leaving £5,800,000.

Barolong. Tribe associated with the Basuto, its name derived from chief Morolong. Said to have emigrated southward from the Great Lakes about A.D. 1400. Settled in what is now Bechuanaland near the Harts River. In 1823, through Wesleyan missionaries, had first contacts with the Cape Government. Having suffered from the attacks of the Matabele, they helped the Voortrekkers against them. This traditional friendship preserved by chief Móroko, who settled later in the present Orange Free State at Thaba Nchu (q.v.). Another section of the Barolong under chief Montsioa, who succeeded to the throne in 1849, fell out with the Transvalers and only concluded peace with them in 1853.

Barosma. *See* BUCHU.

Barotse. Tribe living in Zambia on the upper Zambesi. In 1850 were visited by David Livingstone, who was well received by their chief, Sebitoane. Linyanti, the main kraal, was visited by him and by other Europeans. Later the king, Lewanika (q.v.), came under missionary influence. A stalwart, handsome race, the Barotse are noted for their skill with canoes on the Zambesi and other rivers.

Barreto, Francisco. Portuguese soldier and explorer. With 1,000 troops he was sent in 1570 to contact the legendary Emperor of Monomotapa (q.v.). He penetrated far inland from the Mozambique coast and set up a fort at Sena on the Zambesi, but after several victories was defeated, forced to turn back and lost almost all his men from fever. Died in East Africa in 1573.

Barros. *See* DE BARROS.

Barrow, Sir John. English explorer. Born of poor parents at Ulverston, he began life in an iron-foundry at Liverpool, working his way up from timekeeper to partner. As secretary to Lord Macartney, first British ambassador to China, he went abroad, and in 1797 came with him in that same capacity to the Cape of Good Hope, when Macartney became governor under the first British occupation. Barrow was sent on a combined diplomatic and exploring mission to the frontier, secured a civil service post, married Anna Maria Trüter, a local girl, and returned to England in 1803. His *Travels into the Interior of South Africa* appeared in 1806 and is one of the best-known works of its kind. John Barrow became Secretary of the Admiralty from 1804 to 1845, being created a baronet in 1835. His experience as a young man in a Greenland whaler roused his interest in Polar exploration, and Cape Barrow, Barrow Strait and Point Barrow commemorate his name. In 1830 he founded the Royal Geographical Society. He died in 1848.

Barrydale. Village in mountains 36 miles from Swellendam. Named after the famous merchants of 100 years ago, Barry Brothers. Now noted for fruit and wild flowers. Population: 1,151, including 500 Whites.

Barry, Sir Jacob Dirk. Judge President. Born at Swellendam in 1832 and educated at Swellendam, Cheltenham College and Trinity College, Cambridge. Took a Moral Science Tripos in 1855, and was called to the Bar in London in 1858. Returned to the Cape, and practised there from 1859 to 1865, when he went to Grahamstown. Became Recorder of Griqualand West in 1871, in 1878 Judge of the Eastern Districts and Judge President in 1880. Was interested in education and native welfare. He died on August 14, 1905.

Barry, Dr. James. Military surgeon. Born in Scotland, her parentage unknown. Studied medicine at Edinburgh and joined the British Army as a hospital assistant in 1813. Always wearing men's clothes, she kept her sex a secret and was commissioned as Assistant Surgeon in 1815. Remained at the Cape till 1825, becoming Surgeon Major in 1827. Had a quarrelsome disposition and fought a duel in South Africa. She became Inspector-General in 1859. Only after her death in 1865 was her sex discovered.

Bartolomeu Dias. Settlement and harbour at the mouth of the Sabi River, Mozambique.

Barytes. Mineral used in paint and other industries. Found in Postmasburg, in Eastern Transvaal and near Pietersburg. It is treated commercially at Germiston.

Baseball. Introduced to South Africa about 1892 by Americans working on the Johannesburg gold mines. First matches recorded on Simmer and Jack and City and Suburban Mines in 1895. The efforts of late Dr. Brennan and J. C. Holderness kept the game alive and it gained in popularity. Transvaal Baseball Association founded in 1904. Recently there have been visits by American players with an added stimulus from teams such as the Cumorahs, including members of the local Mormon church.

Bashee River. Enters the Indian Ocean between East London and Port St. Johns. Rises in Tembuland. A village of same name, 105 miles north-east of Kei Road.

Bastard Kudu. *See* INYALA.

Basuto. Tribe inhabiting two parts of South Africa—known respectively as the Transvaal Basuto and the Moshesh Basuto. The former live in the Northern Transvaal, but the majority of the race (totalling about 800,000) come from Lesotho, the mountainous area between the Orange Free

Basuto

State, the Northern Cape Province and Natal. The Basuto originate from remnants of other tribes scattered by the wars and raids of the Zulus under king Tshaka (q.v.). About 1822 Moshesh (q.v.) gathered them together, building a stronghold on the summit of Thaba Bosigo (also written Thaba Bosiu (q.v.)). In 1824 he had an estimated 21,000 followers. This number grew rapidly, but for some time Moshesh still paid nominal allegiance to Tshaka. In the end, however, he grew strong enough to beat off his assaults, and thereafter remained undisturbed. Helped by their impregnable position in the mountains, the Basuto soon developed their own tribe. They stole horses from the frontier settlers and showed themselves considerably more intelligent than most other tribes. Their own customs included the wearing of hats. French Protestant Missionaries arriving in 1831, and later those of Catholic and other churches, were allowed to carry on their work, but without prejudicing the independence of the tribe. The military and diplomatic skill of Moshesh foiled the attempts of the British and of the Boers in the Orange Free State to subdue him. In 1852 the Basuto defeated a British force in the Battle of Berea and in 1858 a campaign by the Orange Free Staters was unsuccessful. After a further war with the latter, Moshesh placed himself under British jurisdiction in 1868. For the next 12 years Basutoland was administered virtually under the Cape Colony, but the injudicious disarmament policy of 1879 led to the Gun War (q.v.) and ultimately, in 1884, to the re-establishment of Basutoland as a territory under a Resident Commissioner, directly administered from Downing Street. The Basuto became a reservoir of labour for the Orange Free State, the gold mines of the Rand, and other parts of the Republic. They continued to live under their Paramount Chief and from 1910 had their own National Council, which received wider powers in 1960. In 1966 the country attained full independence. *See also* LESOTHO and BAPEDI.

Basutoland. *See* LESOTHO.

Bat (Chiroptera). Flying mammal found in profusion all over the world, with a great many specimens in South Africa. Bats have only one young, which clings closely to its mother's chest. There are two main divisions in South Africa: (1) Fruit bats, including the Flying Fox and the Epauletted Fruit Bat, both of which have a wingspan of some 20 inches. Fruit bats have smooth molars for chewing fruit, and both thumb and index finger hooked. They do not hibernate. Great enemies of the farmers from their enormous appetite for fruit. (2) The little Insectivorous Bat by contrast is of great service to man in its diet. It is sensitive of hearing, not only through its ears and by means of the wing-membrane, like all bats, but through the delicate hairs of its 'nose-leaf.' It is cosmopolitan, but especially abundant in the tropics and among trees. Hibernating.

Batavier II. Dutch ship used to convey back to South Africa the body of Presi-

dent Kruger, arriving in Cape Town early in December 1904.

Bateleur. *See* EAGLES and BIRDS.

Batfair. *See* BANTU TRADE FAIR.

Bathoen. Chief of the Bangwaketsi, a sub-tribe of the Bechuana (q.v.), from 1889. He came into prominence in 1895 through visiting England with Khama, king of the Bamangwato (q.v.), and Sebele. He and his companions were received by Queen Victoria, whose sovereignty he agreed to accept. Later, he objected to the control of his territory being made over to the Chartered Company and submitted a protest. During the South African War he furnished wagons to the British military authorities. He died in 1910.

Bathurst. Small town in Eastern Cape Province, founded by 1820 settlers and named after the Colonial Secretary of the day, the Earl of Bathurst. Picturesque old church and houses. Farming centre specialising in pineapples. 34 miles from Grahamstown. Population: 1,140, including 170 Whites.

Battery. Abbreviation for Stamp Battery, used for crushing gold ore. Batteries vary from two stamps upwards, the largest in the world being on the Randfontein Estates, and numbering 600 stamps. Originally stamps were of 400 lb., but were increased about 1905 to 1,250 lb., which facilitated an increase in output. Through the introduction of tube mills (q.v.), stamp batteries gradually declined.

Battiss, Walter. South African artist and expert on Bushman painting. Born at Somerset East, Cape Province, on January 6, 1906, he was educated at Gill College in that town and at the University of the Witwatersrand. He developed a strongly personal style and entered the teaching profession. Among the work that made him prominent was his extensive investigation and critical analysis of Bushman art, on which he wrote several books.

BATTLES IN SOUTHERN AFRICA

Alleman's Nek	June 11, 1900
Amajuba (*see* Majuba)	
Belmont (South African War)	November 23, 1899
Bembesi (Matabele War)	November 1, 1893
Berea (Basuto-English)	December, 1852
Berea (Orange Free State–Basuto)	July 25, 1865
Bergendal (South African War)	August 27, 1900
Blaauwberg (Napoleonic)	January 8, 1806
Blood River (Voortrekker–Zulu)	December 16, 1838
Blouberg (see Blaauwberg)	
Boomah Pass (4th Kaffir War)	December 25, 1850
Boomplaats (Voortrekker–English)	August 29, 1848
Boschberg (Mapoch War)	January 2, 1883
Bothaville (South African War)	November 6, 1900
Brandwater (South African War)	July 15, 1900
Bronkhorstfontein (South African War)	October 28, 1900
Bronkhorst Spruit (1st Boer War)	December 20, 1880
Bushman's Pass (Langalibalele Rebellion)	November 4, 1873
Camdeboo (South African War)	July 14, 1901
Colenso (South African War)	December 15, 1899
Colesberg (South African War)	January 6, 1900
Congella (Voortrekker–British War)	May 23, 1842
Crocodile Pool (South African War)	February 12, 1900
Cyferfontein (South African War)	January 2, 1901
Dewetsdorp (South African War)	April 20, 1900
Diamond Hill (South African War)	June 11, 1900
Doornkop (Jameson Raid)	January 2, 1896
Doornkop (South African War)	May 29, 1900
Driefontein (South African War)	March 10, 1900
Dwarsvlei (South African War)	July 11, 1900
Elandslaagte (South African War)	October 21, 1899
Enslin (Graspan) (South African War)	November 25, 1899
Gibeon (South West Africa) (World War I)	April 27, 1915
Ginginhlovu (Zulu War)	April 2, 1879
Goede Hoop (South African War)	December 2, 1900
Grahamstown (First Kaffir War)	April 22, 1819
Graspan (*see also* Enslin) (South African War)	June 6, 1901
Greylingstad (South African War)	December 26, 1900
Gwandana (9th Kaffir War)	September 26, 1877
Gwanga (War of the Axe)	June 8, 1846
Heilbron (South African War)	June 19, 1900
Helvetia (South African War)	December 29, 1900
Houtnek (South African War)	May 1, 1900
Houwater (South African War)	March 6, 1900
Ibeka (9th Kaffir War)	September 29, 1877
Imbembesi River (*see* Bembesi)	
Ingogo Heights (1st Boer War)	February 8, 1881
Inyezane (Zulu War)	January 22, 1879
Isandhlwana (Zulu War)	January 22, 1879
Italeni (Voortrekker–Zulu)	April 10, 1838

Jacobsdal (South African War)	October 25, 1900
Jagersfontein (South African War)	October 16, 1900
Kaalfontein (South African War)	January 12, 1901
Kambula (Zulu War)	March 29, 1879
Karree Siding (South African War) . . .	March 29, 1900
Kentani (9th Kaffir War)	February 7, 1878
Koedoesberg (South African War) . . .	February 7, 1900
Koranaberg (O.F.S.–Basuto War) . . .	March 25, 1858
Kromspruit (South African War)	January 4, 1901
Labuschagne's Nek (South African War) . .	March 4, 1900
Laing's Nek (1st Boer War)	January 28, 1881
Lake Chrissie (South African War) . . .	February 6, 1901
Lambert's Bay (South African War) . . .	October 29, 1901
Lichtenburg (South African War) . . .	March 3, 1901
Lindley (South African War)	May 31, 1900
Lombard's Kop (South African War) . .	October 30, 1899
Lusizi (9th Kaffir War)	October 21, 1877
Magersfontein (South African War) . . .	December 11, 1899
Majuba (1st Boer War)	February 27, 1881
Mathebi's Kop (Sekukuni War) . . .	July 4, 1876
Modder River (South African War) . . .	November 28, 1899
Mome Gorge (Zulu Rebellion) . . .	June 10, 1906
Morija (Orange Free State–Basuto) . . .	April 25, 1858
Morosi's Mountain (Morosi War) . . .	November 20, 1879
Mosega (Voortrekker–Matabele) . . .	January 17, 1837
Mpukunyoni (Zulu Rebellion) . . .	April 27, 1906
Muizenberg (Napoleonic Wars) . . .	August 8, 1795
Mushroom Valley (1914 Rebellion) . . .	November 12, 1914
Nicholson's Nek (South African War) . .	November 30, 1899
Nooitgedacht (South African War) . . .	August 30, 1900
Nooitgedacht (South African War) . . .	December 13, 1900
Omukaru (Hottentot–Herero War) . . .	September, 1865
Onderstepoort (South African War) . . .	July 11, 1900
Otavi (South West Africa) (World War I) . .	July 1, 1915
Paardeberg (South African War) . . .	February 18, 1900
Pforte (*see* Riet)	
Platberg (O.F.S.–Basuto)	December 6, 1865
Poplar Grove (South African War) . . .	March 7, 1900
Reddersburg (South African War) . . .	April 3, 1900
Rensburg's Drift (South African War) . .	October 27, 1900
Rhenosterkop (South African War) . . .	November 29, 1900
Riet (South West Africa) (World War I) . .	March 20, 1915
Rietfontein (South African War) . . .	October 24, 1899
Rietfontein (South West Africa) (World War I) . .	March 19, 1915
Roodewal (South African War) . . .	June 7, 1900
Rooidam (South African War) . . .	May 5, 1900
Rorke's Drift (Zulu War)	January 22, 1879
Sannah's Post (South African War) . . .	March 31, 1900
Schuins Hoogte (*see* Ingogo Heights)	
Sekukuni's Mountain (Sekukuni War) . .	November 28, 1879
Shangani (Matabele War)	October 24, 1893
Singuesi (Matabele War)	November 2, 1893

Slagter's Nek (Rebellion)	March 6, 1816
Spion Kop (South African War)	January 24, 1900
Sprinkhaan's Nek (South African War) . .	November 16, 1900
Stinkhoutboom (South African War) . . .	June 23, 1900
Stormberg (South African War)	December 10, 1899
Swartbooiskop (*see* Nicholson's Nek)	
Tabaksberg (South African War) . . .	January 29, 1901
Talana (South African War)	October 21, 1899
Tandjesberg (O.F.S.–Basuto)	January 28, 1867
Thaba Bosigo (Matabele–Basuto) . . .	1831
Thaba Bosigo (O.F.S.–Basuto)	August 8, 1865
Trekkoppies (South-West Africa) (World War I) .	April 26, 1915
Tugela (Cetewayo–Umbolazi)	December 2, 1856
Tweebosch (South African War)	March 7, 1902
Tweefontein (South African War) . . .	December 25, 1901
Ulundi (Zulu War)	July 4, 1879
Umzintsani (9th Kaffir War)	December 2, 1877
Van Wyk's Vlei (South African War) . . .	November 2, 1900
Vegkop (Voortrekker–Matabele War) . . .	October 16, 1836
Vegkop (O.F.S.–Basuto War)	March 28, 1858
Ventersburg (South African War) . . .	January 18, 1901
Vet River (South African War)	May 5, 1900
Viervoet (Voortrekker–Basuto)	June 30, 1851
Willow Grange (South African War) . . .	November 23, 1899
Wolwekuil (South African War)	February 14, 1901
Zilikats Nek (South African War) . . .	July 11, 1900
Zuurfontein (South African War) . . .	January 12, 1901
Zwartkoppies (Voortrekker–British) . . .	April 30, 1845

Bauhinia, Rhodesian (*Piliostigma thonningii*). A shrub or 15-foot tree, widespread over the Transvaal Low Veld, Rhodesia and tropical Africa generally. Its leaves are two-lobed and drop early, leaving the tree bare for months in winter. The flowers are white, short-lived and inconspicuous, the fruit a large, heavy pod, 6 by 1½ inches. *See* PEA.

Baumann, Gustav. Surveyor-General of the Orange Free State Republic. Born at Bloemfontein in 1858, son of Isaac Baumann, a German-Jewish pioneer and first mayor of that town, he studied at Grey College and qualified as a surveyor. As Surveyor-General in 1896 he perfected the system of title registration. Fought in the South African War, was taken prisoner and returned to practice,

writing a textbook of land surveying in 1906. He died in 1930.

Bavenda. Tribe living principally in Northern Transvaal, numbering approximately 300,000. Name Venda signifies 'land' or 'world.' The tribe reputedly emigrated from Central Africa towards the end of the 17th or beginning of the 18th century. Bavendas have characteristics representative of almost every African race, practise both cattle-rearing and agriculture and are skilled in the smelting of metals, from which they make implements. Iron and copper smelting were formerly practised, but have gradually died out. Long before the establishment of European mines at Messina the tribe exploited the deposits there. They are also traders and hunters. The crocodile is re-

Bavenda

garded as sacred. The tribe believes in Raluvhimba, a monotheistic deity, and practises an elaborate ritual of rain-making. Most of the Bavenda tribe is concentrated in Zoutpansberg district, north of Louis Trichardt.

Baven-on-Sea. Seaside resort near Port Shepstone, Natal. Population: 500, including 300 Whites.

Baviaanspoort. Settlement near Pretoria, established as Work Colony and reformatory for inebriates. Used, during World War II, as internment centre.

Bax, John (also known as **Van Heerentals**). Early Cape commander. As Second Officer in Ceylon was appointed in November 1674 to succeed Isbrand Goske. Arrived on January 1, 1676. Spent much time establishing friendly relations with the Hottentot tribes, and encouraged farming, especially the sheep industry. Died at the Cape on June 29, 1678.

Baxendale, Major Walter. Rhodesian pioneer and early mayor of Bulawayo. Born in Lancashire in 1870, he came

to Rhodesia in 1890, served in the Matabele Rebellion and the South African War. He died in 1916.

Bay, The. Traditional name applied to Algoa Bay and Port Elizabeth.

Bayete. Traditional Zulu greeting to a great chief. It means literally 'Bring them (our enemies). Give them to us.' First applied as a salute to Dingaan (q.v.) and later restricted to the Supreme Chief in Natal.

Baynes, Joseph. Industrial pioneer and Cabinet Minister in Natal. Born at Settle in Yorkshire, England, in 1842, emigrated to Natal in 1850, where he took up farming, becoming famous as a cattle and horse breeder. Principal achievement, however, was founding of the famous Nelsrust Dairy Farms, near Pietermaritzburg. Introduced the first dipping tank into this area, and established a dairy industry on modern lines. From 1887 to Union he sat in the Natal Parliament, and was Minister of Lands and Works from 1903 to 1904. Upon his death in 1925 his property at Nelsrust was left to the nation as a centre for development and research.

Bayville. Village 8 miles from Blue Cliff Station, founded at end of last century as part of the Sundays River irrigation development, in the Eastern Cape Province.

Bazaruto. Island off the coast of Mozambique, popular seaside and fishing resort. Connected with the mainland by air service and boat. Attracts many Rhodesians.

Beaconsfield. Originally a separate municipality in Griqualand West, but since 1914 part of Kimberley (q.v.). Named after Benjamin Disraeli, Earl of Beaconsfield, British Prime Minister.

Beadle, Sir Thomas Hugh William. Chief Justice of Rhodesia. Born in Salisbury in 1905, and educated at Salisbury High School, Milton High

School and Diocesan College, Ronde-bosch. He studied at Oxford as a Rhodes Scholar and was called to the Bar in England. Practised as an advocate in Bulawayo and served during World War II, being appointed Deputy Judge-Advocate-General for Southern Rhodesia. In 1946 he joined the Rhodesian Cabinet and in 1950 was raised to the Bench. He became Chief Justice in 1961.

Beattie, Sir John Carruthers. Physicist and first Principal of the University of Cape Town. Born in Dumfriesshire, Scotland, in 1866, he was educated at Edinburgh, Glasgow and on the Continent, specialising in physics. In 1897 he came to South Africa to join the staff of the South African College, and while there carried out an important magnetic survey of the whole sub-continent. On the establishment of the University of Cape Town in 1918, he became Principal. He died on September 10, 1946.

Beaufort West. Town in the Karroo, 339 miles from Cape Town, on the main line to the north. Founded in 1820 and named after the Duke of Beaufort, father of Lord Charles Somerset, Governor of the Cape. Beaufort West had the distinction of becoming the first municipality in South Africa, in 1839, earlier even than Cape Town. Important wool and railway centre. Collection of Napoleonic relics in Town Hall, given by the Pritchard family, and brought from St. Helena. Noted for its avenues of pear trees. Population: 16,323, of which 5,297 are Whites.

Beaumont, Sir William Henry. Judge. Born in India on February 24, 1851, and educated in England; military training at Sandhurst. In 1871 he came to South Africa with his regiment and fought against the natives in Natal, becoming private secretary to the Administrator and later, in 1874,

Acting Magistrate in Pinetown. Continuing his military service he went to Ireland, but, retiring from the army, returned to Natal in 1875 to become Clerk of the Executive Council. After serving in the Boer War he was appointed to the Natal Bench in 1902. He died in January 1930.

Bechuana. Group of tribes inhabiting the central part of Southern Africa, particularly Bechuanaland (q.v.). They include the Bakwena, the Baharutsi, the Bamangwato and Bangwaketsi. Originating several hundred years ago in Central Africa, they drove out the Native Bushmen, coming into contact also with the Hottentots. (*See also* BAMANGWATO and BAKWENA.) They number about 600,000. The Bechuana language is associated with Sesuto. *See also* BOTSWANA.

Bechuanaland. *See* BOTSWANA.

Bechuanaland Border Police. Semimilitary force set up in 1885 after the occupation of Bechuanaland by the British, and later absorbed into the B.S.A. Police (q.v.).

Beck, Sir Johannes Henricus Meiring. South African Cabinet Minister and composer. Born in Worcester, Cape Colony, in 1855, he was educated at the South African College, and qualified in medicine in Edinburgh in 1879. He practised in Cape Town and in 1898 was returned as Member of the Legislative Assembly for Worcester. Soon gained prominence through his championship of the 'Beck Act' (q.v.) and in 1908 became a Cape delegate to the National Convention. Upon the founding of Union he was appointed a Senator, and in 1916 Minister of Posts and Telegraphs, a position he held until his death in 1919. Apart from his political work Beck, who for many years lived at the Old Drostdy at Tulbagh, did much to preserve South African monuments, and was a composer of some ability.

Beck Act. Popular name for the Illegal Practices Prevention Act, passed by the Cape Parliament in 1902, mainly at the instance of Sir Meiring Beck (q.v.). Its purpose was to prevent corruption at elections.

Bedford. Town in the Eastern Cape Province. Established by 1820 settlers, and named after the Duke of Bedford, in whose honour the main open space was called Tavistock Square. Leading wool centre. Forested mountains near by. Population: 4,200, including 803 Whites.

Bedfordview. Township east of Johannesburg, originally laid out as small holdings in 1919 but later developed as a residential area. Named after the home town of Sir George Farrar (q.v.) who came from Bedford, England, and who lived near by. Population: 6,800, including 4,200 Whites.

Bee-Eater (family Meropidae). Brightly-coloured bird, with long, slender, curved bill. Catches insects on the wing. Several varieties occur north of the Orange River, but in the south the variety most frequently found is the European Bee-Eater (*Merops apiaster*). Resembles a swallow, apart from pointed tail. A summer migrant from Europe. See BIRDS.

Beira. Seaport in Mozambique at the mouth of the Pungwe River. Takes its name from the former province of Beira in Portugal. It came into existence in 1892, with the railway construction to the new colony of Southern Rhodesia. The site, a mere mud-flat, was fever-stricken and notoriously unhealthy, but the railway building was carried on and successfully completed shortly before the end of the century. Since then Beira has developed into an important seaport, handling a large part of the export and import traffic of Rhodesia, particularly of the Copper Belt, besides being a popular seaside resort for Rhodesians. Population: 85,000, including about 20,000 Whites and 2,000 Asians.

Beit, Alfred. Capitalist and co-founder with Cecil John Rhodes of Southern Rhodesia. Born in Hamburg in the same year as Cecil Rhodes, on February 15, 1853, of an old Jewish family. He learnt the diamond trade under Jules Porges in Amsterdam and elsewhere. In 1875 he went to Port Elizabeth on behalf of his cousins, the Lipperts, who sent him to Kimberley as their representative. There he came into touch with Julius Wernher (q.v.) and with Cecil John Rhodes. Attaining considerable prosperity as a diamond merchant, he became a member of the firm of Jules Porges & Co., and on the retirement of Porges, he and Wernher converted this firm in 1884 to Wernher, Beit & Co. Returning to England he joined forces with Rhodes in his efforts to amalgamate the diamond mines, which resulted in the foundation of De Beers. A Life Governor of De Beers, he was one of the principal figures in the foundation of the Chartered Company and in the first efforts to open up Rhodesia. Wernher, Beit & Co. presently became leaders in Barberton and then in the Witwatersrand gold industry. Beit visited Rhodesia in the very early days, but kept his headquarters in London. Unlike Rhodes, he did his utmost to keep out of politics, though his friendship with him remained undiminished, and he was one of the main trustees and heirs under his will. Upon Alfred Beit's death on July 16, 1906, the Beit Trust (q.v.) came into existence. He also bequeathed enormous gifts for university education and research in South Africa, Rhodesia, Britain and Germany.

Beit, Sir Otto John. Capitalist and philanthropist. Younger brother of Alfred Beit (q.v.), he was born in Hamburg on December 7, 1865, and came to the Rand in 1890 as a member of the firm of Herman Eckstein & Co. In

1896 he returned to London, but maintained his contact with the gold and diamond industries. After his brother's death in 1906 he retired and devoted his efforts mostly to the development of the Rhodes Trust, the Beit Trust and other institutions, to which he gave large sums. He died on December 7, 1930.

Beit Trust. Large endowment set up under the will of Alfred Beit (q.v.) for the development of transportation in Rhodesia and British Central Africa and the general advancement of that region. The original sum left to the Trust in 1906 was £1,200,000, but through sound management it has, despite the disbursement of millions of pounds on bridges, swimming baths for small communities, scholarships and other good causes, grown to several times that amount.

Belfast. Town in the Eastern Transvaal, 6,557 feet above sea-level. 136 miles from Pretoria on main line to Lourenço Marques. Named after Belfast in Ireland, home town of the founder, Mr. O'Brien, in the last century. Severe fighting near here in 1901 during South African War. Chief industry is farming. Fishing resort. Population: 4,568, including 2,000 Whites.

Belingwe. Village and gold field in Rhodesia, between Fort Victoria and Bulawayo. Large cattle ranches near by, established by the Liebig Company and by the Anglo-French Matabeleland Company, also important asbestos workings.

Bell. Village near Peddie, Cape Province. Population 800, including 40 Whites.

Bell, Sir Sydney Smith. Judge of the Cape Supreme Court. Born in London in 1805, and educated in Edinburgh. His law studies interrupted by ill-health, he wrote several books, in-

cluding a *Dictionary of Decisions*. In 1839 he was finally called to the Bar and practised in London. Coming to the Cape, he was appointed a judge of the Supreme Court in 1851, Acting Chief Justice in 1857 and finally Chief Justice in 1868, which position he held until his retirement in 1873. He died in the same year.

Bell, Professor William Henry. South African composer. Born at St. Albans, England, in 1873, he showed musical gifts as a child, and while at St. Albans Grammar School joined the cathedral choir. In 1889 he won the Goss Scholarship at the Royal Academy of Music, where he worked under Sir Charles V. Stanford, and from 1903 to 1912 was Professor of Harmony. In 1912 he became Principal of the South African College of Music at Cape Town. Besides encouraging musical development generally he composed several South African pieces, including a fine Cape Town Symphony. He died in 1946.

Bellair. Suburb of Durban, about 7 miles inland, 223 feet above sea-level. Noted for its pleasant climate.

Bellevue: 1. Village near Alexandria, Eastern Cape Province. Population: 160, including 10 Whites.
2. Township 4 miles outside Bulawayo, administered since 1950 by a Town Management Board. It is mainly residential, with a population of about 900 Europeans and 500 Africans.

Bellville. Industrial town 12 miles from Cape Town and connected by a continuous chain of houses and streets. Developed out of a village named after Charles Bell, Surveyor-General of Cape Colony 1848–1872, and designer of the Cape triangular stamps. Industries include timber, textiles, engineering, etc. Railway junction. Population: 49,000, including 35,000 Whites.

Belmont. Scene of battle during South African War, November 23, 1899. 55 miles south of Kimberley. Heavy losses sustained by British forces. *See also* MAGERSFONTEIN.

Belvidere (not Belvedere). Village near Knysna, Cape Province, founded in 1834 by Charles Duthie, who later built the beautiful little Gothic church, consecrated by Bishop Grey in 1855.

Bembesi. Village 29 miles from Bulawayo, Rhodesia. Scene of battle in Matabele War before final capture and destruction of Lobengula's capital Gubulawayo in 1893. Goldfield near by.

Benjamin, Louis Edmund. Judge. Born in Grahamstown in 1865 and educated at the South African College and Cambridge, where he completed his law studies. He was called to the Bar and practised for a while in London. In 1893 he returned to the Cape, where he lectured to law classes for many years. He was appointed to the Cape Bench in 1920, serving until 1929, and died on December 5, 1935.

Benningfield, Reuben Widdows. Natal pioneer and hunter. Born in 1844, he was the son of Samuel Benningfield, one of the early settlers in Natal. During the 1860's he travelled widely in Rhodesia, and for a while was a trader in Inhambane in Mozambique. Amongst other trophies, he brought back from the interior one tusk stated to have weighed 190 lb. and another weighing 170 lb. Benningfield obtained from the Chief Umtasa of Manicaland a concession of 240 square miles near the Penhalonga Gold Fields, not far from Umtali. Later this was revoked, and the ground given to F. C. Selous as representing the Chartered Company. He returned to Durban, his birthplace, became the head of the firm of Reuben Benningfield & Co. and died in 1912.

Benoni. Town on the Eastern Witwatersrand, 19 miles from Johannesburg, founded in 1904 as a township, and named after the farm on which it was laid out. The name itself occurs in the Bible and means 'Son of Sorrow.' Large gold-mining and industrial centre. Heavy fighting took place here during the Rand Revolt in March 1922. Population: 135,818, including 45,000 Whites.

Berea. Name derived from the New Testament and applied to a number of places in Southern Africa, usually ranges of hills. They include the Berea overlooking Durban, a main residential area; the Berea overlooking Barberton, and the Berea in Basutoland, scene of a battle wherein the warriors of Moshesh defeated the troops of Governor Sir George Cathcart in 1852. Here too a battle took place between the Boers of the O.F.S., under General Fick, and the Basutos in 1865.

Bergbas. Literally Mountain Fibre. *See* PRUIMBAS.

Berg Damaras. Tribe living in South West Africa, the origin of which is largely veiled in mystery. Believed to

Berg Damaras

have lived in South West Africa long before the Hereros migrated. Very much darker in colour than their neighbours. The Berg Damaras' language contains words which appear in tongues spoken in the Sudan, and it is possible that they may have come from North Africa. They are extremely dirty in their habits, regarding water as dangerous. Traditionally the Berg Damaras are classed as servants of the Hereros and of other tribes. A special feature of their religion is the worship of the Holy Fire. Today they number about 40,000.

Berggans. Afrikaans name for Egyptian Goose. *See* GOOSE.

Berghville. Village near Tulbagh, Cape Province. Population: 370, including 90 Whites.

Bergpatrys. Afrikaans name for Greywing Partridge. *See* FRANCOLIN.

Bergpruim (*Pappea capensis* Sond. & Harv.). Shrub or tree up to 20 feet. Wood hard, handsome. Fruit furnishes excellent vinegar. Forests in eastern districts of Cape Province.

Berg River. Rises near Fransch Hoek and flows into St. Helena Bay. Is navigable for small craft for about 30 miles near its mouth. Total length 120 miles. Its chief tributary is the Little Berg River. Velddrift and Laaiplek are important fishing settlements near the mouth. The last hippopotamus shot at the Cape was killed in the Berg River in 1857.

Berg River Scheme. Project prepared in 1962 for development of irrigation along the Berg River in the western Cape Province (q.v.) and opening a fishing harbour at the mouth. Total expenditure is estimated at R22,000,000.

Bergswael. Afrikaans name for European Bee-Eater. *See* BEE-EATER.

Bergtheil, Jonas. Natal pioneer. Born in Bavaria, Germany, in 1819. he was of Jewish origin, and came to the Cape in 1834. Nine years later, Bergtheil settled in Natal, where he intended to establish cotton-growing. A strong protagonist of immigration, he organised several schemes, first attempting to bring colonists from the British Isles and later from Germany. Ultimately, in November 1847, he chartered a ship, which brought from Germany 188 men, women and children to Natal. These were settled near Pinetown in the area now known as New Germany. He was also largely responsible for the construction of the first railway in South Africa, from Durban to the Point, of which he became a director. In 1866 Bergtheil settled in England, where he died in 1902.

Bergville, Natal. Mountain resort in Drakensberg. Population: 1,000, including 500 Whites.

Berg Winds. Name given to unusually dry, hot winds from the interior.

Berlin. Village in the Eastern Cape Province, near King William's Town. Established in 1858 by settlers who came to South Africa with the German Legion after the Crimean War. Farming centre. Population: 2,086, including 579 Whites.

Bertin, Harry. Rhodesian Cabinet Minister. Born in London in 1882, he came to South Africa in 1901 and served in the Boer War, as well as in World War I. Having been called to the Bar in 1931, he was elected to the Rhodesian Parliament and became Minister of Justice, Public Works and Roads. He died on July 24, 1946.

Beryl. Mineral used in manufacture of high-grade alloys, and containing the metal beryllium. Found near Steinkopf and Jackalswater in Namaqualand, also at Ameib and Rossing in South West Africa. There has been a varying production since 1933.

Bethal. Town in the Eastern Transvaal. Contrary to widespread belief the name is not derived from Bethel in the Bible, but is compounded of names of the wives of the owners of the original farms on which it was built, Eliza*beth* Du Plooy and *Ali*da Naude. The town was founded in 1889 and is an important maize producing centre. Population: 16,600, including 6,000 Whites.

Bethanien. Village in South-West Africa. Founded in 1814 as a station of the Rhenish Missionary Society by the Rev. Johann Heinrich Schmelen. Karakul skin-producing centre. About 90 miles inland from Lüderitzbucht. Population: 1,053, including 333 Whites.

Bethany. Village in the Orange Free State, in the Edenburg district, originally a Berlin mission station. Founded in 1834 and named after Bethany in the Bible, meaning 'The House of Unripe Dates.' Sheep breeding centre. Population: 500 Whites.

Bethelsdorp. Mission station near Port Elizabeth, founded for the conversion of the Hottentots by the Rev. Dr. J. Vanderkemp and the Rev. James Read of the London Missionary Society in 1803. Underwent many vicissitudes. Is now mainly a native township. Population: 16,457, including 128 Whites.

Bethesda. Station in Basutoland, founded in 1843 by the Rev. Schrumpf of the Paris Evangelical Mission.

Bethlehem. Town in Eastern Orange Free State; altitude of 5,300 feet. Situated on River Jordan. Important grain, wool and cattle centre. Has creameries and other industrial plants. Tourist centre for Golden Gate and Drakensberg (q.v.). Founded in 1869 and named after its Biblical counterpart. Population: 33,830, including 11,500 Whites.

Bethulie. Town in the south of the Orange Free State, near the Orange River, which is here crossed by a large bridge. Originally started by the Lon-

don Missionary Society in 1883 in an attempt to convert the Bushmen. Abandoned soon after, but restarted by the French Evangelical Mission. Called successively Caledon, Verhuelpolis (after the chairman of the Society), and Bethulia. Renamed Heidelberg in 1863, but called Bethulie again in 1872. Sheep breeding centre. Population: 4,840, including 1,400 Whites.

'Between the Chains.' Famous street market for shares, formerly operated in Simmond Street, Johannesburg, outside the original Stock Exchange. Took its name from the fact that the thoroughfare was closed to traffic by chains at either end. 'Between the Chains' came to an end about the time of the Boer War, and was never revived, because of the new Stock Exchange built in 1903. In its prime the turnover was enormous and business went on during boom times on Sundays as well as holidays.

Beukenhout (*Faurea mcnaughtonii* Phillips). Timber tree up to 60 feet. Knysna and Pondoland. Another variety (*Faurea saligna* Harv.), shrub or tree up to 20 feet, of little commercial use.

Bewaarplaatsen. Pieces of mining ground, mostly on the Witwatersrand, granted by the Government of the South African Republic to mining companies as depositing or storage sites (the word literally means 'Storage Places'), used for the erection of surface machinery, building up dumps of waste rock, etc. In many cases these were later proved to be underlain by valuable gold deposits or they became valuable on account of their proximity to towns. This resulted in prolonged litigation, which was concluded only after the South African War.

Bews, Professor John William. South African botanist. Born at Kirkwall in the Orkney Islands on December 16, 1884, he studied at the

University of Edinburgh and became Lecturer in Botany at the universities first of Manchester and then of Edinburgh. In 1910 he was appointed professor at the Natal University College, where he specialised in grasses. (The genus *Bewsia* is called after him.) In 1912 he was awarded a Carnegie Research Scholarship. He wrote widely in the scientific press and gained an international reputation as an ecologist. He died in 1938. *See* GRASSES.

Beyers, General Christiaan Frederik. Born near Stellenbosch in 1869 and came to the Transvaal in 1889, where he became an attorney and was naturalised as a burger. As such he joined the Boer forces in the South African War and rose to the rank of general. Resuming his practice as an attorney in Pretoria, Beyers became Speaker of the Transvaal Parliament under the Responsible Government. In 1912 he was appointed Commandant-General of the newly-founded Union Defence Force. Next year he visited Europe and there met Kaiser Wilhelm II. Shortly after he came into conflict with General Louis Botha, whom he considered to be too deeply pledged to overseas commitments and he began negotiations with General Delarey (q.v.) and others in disagreement with the Government. The climax came in September 1914, when, after the outbreak of World War I, he resigned his post. General Smuts accused him of high treason. He became involved in the rebellion and was drowned in 1914 while crossing the Vaal River, pursued by Government troops.

Beyers, Frederick William. Judge, Appellate Division. Born in Paarl on October 15, 1867, and educated at the South African College and in Johannesburg, where he qualified as an advocate and practised law, continuing his studies to obtain the LL.B. of the University of Cape of Good Hope in

1901. In 1905 he was admitted both at the Cape and in the Transvaal. Turning to politics, he was a member of the Transvaal Parliament from 1907 until Union. He became Attorney-General of the Transvaal in 1911 and of the Cape in 1914, but returned to politics again to represent Edenburg in the Union Parliament in 1918. In 1924 he became Minister of Mines and Industries in the Nationalist Cabinet. Having practised in Cape Town from 1915 to 1924, he was appointed to the Appellate Division in 1932, retiring in 1937. He died in 1938. One of his major achievements as a Minister was the legislation regulating the diamond industry.

Biermann, Vice-Admiral Hugo Hendrik. Chief of the South African Navy and its first Admiral. Born at Johannesburg on August 6, 1916 and educated at Jan Van Riebeeck High School, Cape Town and on the *General Botha*. Joined S.A. Seaward Defence Force in World War II. Appointed Chief of Staff in 1952.

Biesiesvlei. Village near Lichtenburg, Transvaal. Population: 600, including 200 Whites.

Biggar, Alexander. English settler and soldier. Born in England in 1781, he joined the army and became paymaster of the 85th Regiment of Foot, from which he retired to settle in Hampshire, with the rank of captain. He led a party from that county in the ship *Weymouth*, which arrived in South Africa with the 1820 settlers, and worked in the Kariega Valley, near Theopolis. From there he moved to Durban in 1824, being one of the earliest inhabitants there. When the Voortrekkers arrived he was on excellent terms with them, and was appointed Landdrost. He was killed in a battle with the Zulus on December 23, 1838.

Big Bend. Settlement in Swaziland, near Mozambique border. Population 2,900. Noted for sugar production.

Biggar, Robert. Son of Alexander Biggar (q.v.). As one of the earliest pioneers in Natal, he led a force of 20 English traders, 20 Hottentots and 1,500 native refugees from Zululand against the Zulus. He captured hundreds of cattle on the first expedition, but was killed in an ambush on April 17, 1838. On February 17, his brother George had been slain by Dingaan with the Boer party.

Bignonia. *See* ZIMBABWE CREEPER.

Bilharzia. Parasitic disease occurring over large areas in Southern Africa caused by a flat intestinal worm first discovered at Cairo in 1851 by the German researcher Theodor Bilharz. The worm is largely transmitted by snails occurring in vegetation along and in watercourses. During the present century the infected rivers, originally limited to tropical areas, have spread as far south as the Eastern Cape. Treatment is drastic and difficult.

Biltong (from the Dutch Bil 'Buttock'). Strips of meat, usually game, dried in the air. Game may not be used for this purpose today without special permission.

Bindura. Village in the Mazoe Valley, 56 miles north-east of Salisbury. Established as a mining camp in 1890, Bindura is one of the oldest communities in the country. The Village Management Board was set up only in 1916, and has since been replaced by a Town Management Board. The population is 340 Europeans, 1,480 Africans and 20 of other races. Mining is no longer as prominent as it used to be, and Bindura is important for tobacco growing, flour milling and maize production.

Binns, Sir Henry. Prime Minister of Natal. Born in 1837, he went to Natal in 1858 and in 1860 began sugar farming. From 1868 to 1892 he was manager of the Umhlanga Valley Sugar Estate Co., which he had floated. As early as 1879 Binns was a Government-nominated member of the original Legislative Council of Natal and from 1883 he was an elected member. In 1897 he was appointed Prime Minister, but soon changed over to Colonial Secretary and Minister of Agriculture in the same year. One of his major achievements was to bring Natal into the Convention Customs (q.v.) in 1898. He died in 1899.

Birchenough, Sir Henry. President of the British South Africa Company, and Chairman of the Rhodesia and Mashonaland Railway Company. Born in 1853, he first came to South Africa as Government Special Trade Commissioner for Britain in 1903. He was appointed Chairman of the Committee on Cotton Growing in the British Empire in 1917, and became Government Director of the British Dyestuffs Corporation, Chairman of the Rhodesia Railways in 1925 and President of the B.S.A. Company. He died in 1937.

Bird, William Wilberforce. Early South African writer. Born in England in 1758, he came to the Cape after the second British occupation, and entered the Customs Department, of which he became the head. His reputation rests largely on his book, *State of the Cape of Good Hope in 1822*, published in 1828, which incidentally gives one of the earliest accounts of the 1820 Settlers (q.v.). He died in 1836.

Bird Islands. Group off Port Elizabeth, 5 miles off Woody Cape, consisting of Stag, Seal and Bird Islands the last being the most important, on account of its lighthouse.

BIRDS OF SOUTHERN AFRICA

by

DR. J. M. WINTERBOTTOM

South African Museum, Cape Town

IN considering bird-life, the customary boundaries of South Africa are taken as the Zambesi and Kunene Rivers. The wide variety of climates and environments in this area, from the Namib desert in the west to the mangrove forests of Mozambique in the east, is reflected in the richness of the bird fauna, which, according to the latest list (1952), contains 834 different species. Some of these are peculiar to South Africa and are found nowhere else in the world—examples are the long-billed Sugarbirds (*Promerops*), closely adapted to the Protea flora; the curious Rockjumpers (*Chaetops*); the aberrant Ground Woodpecker (*Geocolaptes*), belying its name in that it is not interested in wood or trees; and the pushful Pied Starling (*Spreo bicolor*) of our fields and open bush.

Others belong to species which, while they extend beyond our borders, are confined to the African continent or, more properly, to the Ethiopian Region (which excludes North Africa but includes Southern Arabia). Examples of these are the Ostrich (*Struthio*), the Secretary-bird (*Sagittarius*), the almost tail-less Bateleur Eagle (*Terathopius*), the tick-eating Oxpeckers (*Buphagus*), the two forms of Guineafowl (*Numida* and *Guttera*), the Colies or Mousebirds (*Colius*) and the beautiful Louries (Musophagidae).

Certain other species, by contrast, are almost cosmopolitan in their distribution, like the Barn Owl (*Tyto alba*), the Arctic-breeding Turnstone (*Arenaria*) and the European Swallow (*Hirundo rustica*). These last two are also examples of birds which breed in Europe and Asia and come to Africa to escape the northern winter. Other well-known birds in this category include the White Stork (*Ciconia ciconia*) and the Euro-

pean Bee-eater (*Merops apiaster*), though the latter also has a breeding population here as well as one in Europe.

In addition to its unique species, South Africa, as compared with other parts of the world, is also particularly rich in certain kinds of birds, such as Larks (Alaudidae—18 species), Grass Warblers (*Cisticola*—17 species) and Shrikes (Laniidae—20 species).

Notwithstanding the anomalous Ostrich and Penguin, the most distinctive feature of birds to the average person is their ability to fly. Three aspects of this are worth mentioning—speed, hovering and gliding. There is no really authentic instance of a bird reaching 100 miles an hour in level flight, though a homing pigeon has been clocked at 94·3 miles an hour; but a Lammergeier (*Gypaetus*) has reached 180 miles an hour in a dive and comparable speeds may be achieved by some of the Falcons (*Falco*) when they swoop. Most birds fly at 20 to 40 miles an hour, Swifts (*Apus*) at 60.

The real hoverers of the bird world are the Hummingbirds, which do not occur in Africa, but our own Pied Kingfisher (*Ceryle rudis*), Black-shouldered Kite (*Elanus*) and Rock Kestrel (*Falco rupicolus*) can all hover in an adequate manner.

If we have no master hoverers in South Africa, we have many master gliders. Of the broad-winged species, which depend on thermal currents in the air for their lift, we have several species of Vultures (Ægypidae) and some of Eagles, especially the Bateleur, while Storks and Pelicans are no mean performers. Off our coasts, there are long-winged birds which use the lift given by wave-action and by differential wind-velocity. The masters here are the magnificent Albatrosses (*Diomedea*), but some of the Petrels and Shearwaters

(Procellariidae) are almost as good and even the Gulls (*Larus*) can do quiet well.

Of the great assemblage of our birds, a few are of direct economic importance —the Gannet (*Morus*), some of the Cormorants (*Phalacrocorax*) and the Penguin (*Spheniscus*) as producers of guano; the Quelea or 'Vink' (*Quelea*) as esa pt of small grain; the White Stork and the Wattled Starling (*Creatophora*) as devourers of locusts; the Red-winged Starling (*Onychognathus*) and some of the Bulbuls (*Pycnonotus*) as enemies of fruit-farmers; and the Barn Owl and Black-shouldered Kite as eaters of rats and mice. The vast tribe of insect-eaters are probably all benefactors of man, though the economic assessment of their value is extremely difficult and complex; while some of the Weaver-birds (*Ploceus*) and Bishops (*Euplectes*) are minor pests of grain but compensate by feeding their young on insects. The beautiful little Sunbirds (Nectariniidae) play a part in the fertilisation of some of our flowers.

For most of our birds, however, it is impossible to state positively whether they are harmful or beneficial, and this may even apply to some of our insecti-vorous species. Do the harmful insects they devour more than offset the harm-ful insects that would have been killed by the predatory and parasitic insects and the spiders which the birds also eat? We have no idea. The drastic reduction in our Eagles has been accompanied by a big increase in dassies, which have a most deleterious effect on our pastures; but we do not know whether this is cause or effect. Certain omnivorous species will be harmless as long as their numbers are so limited that they can subsist on their natural food, but if their numbers increase they may be driven by hunger to become pests.

One of the most fascinating pheno-mena of bird life is the regular migra-tions that occur between the breeding ground and the off-season quarters. We have already referred to some of the birds which breed in Europe and Asia and come to us after breeding in the north. Migrants which do not leave Africa are not so well known, but there are many of them. Most of our Swallows (*Hirundo*) and Swifts fall into this category, and so does the Red-chested Cuckoo or Piet-my-vrou (*Cuculus soli-tarius*). Many of our ducks, too, are long-distance migrants: Ponchards (*Netta*) ringed on the Rand have been recovered in Ovamboland and in Kenya. Sea birds migrate, too, and Giant Petrels (*Macronectes*) ringed on Heard Island, in the Antarctic, have been retaken in South African waters. With the steady increase in the number of our birds that are being marked under the South African Ornithological Society's Ring-ing Scheme we can look forward to a rapid growth of our knowledge in this direction.

It is a popular belief that African birds do not sing so well as birds in Europe. This is completely untrue. Such birds as the Robin-Chats (*Cos-sypha*), Moustache Warbler (*Melo-cichla*), Morning Warbler (*Cichadusa*) and Rock Chat (*Thamnolaea cinnamonei-ventris*) can hold their own with any European bird; and these are only a small selection which might be greatly increased. It is ears to hear, not birds to sing, that we lack in South Africa.

The wealth of strange, beautiful and interesting features in our bird life makes selection very difficult, but no account of our birds would be complete that did not mention the Hamerkop (*Scopus*), to whom many of our native people attribute supernatural powers of a high order and whose huge stick nest is a feature of all that part of our countryside within reach of water. Another large nest is that of the Sociable Weaver (*Philetarius*); it looks like the roof of a native hut and contains the home of many pairs of these birds, each of which has its own private apartment —unless this has been usurped by Love-birds (*Agapornis*), a Pigmy Falcon (*Poli-hierax*) or a snake. A smaller nest of the same sort is built by the Buffalo Weavers (*Bubalornis*).

Odd in quite a different way is the Openbill Stork (*Anastomus*), whose long black beak meets only at either end, perhaps to allow of easy drainage when it crushes the fresh-water snails and mussels on which it feeds. The strange nesting habits of our Hornbills (Bucerotidae), in which the female is walled up in the nest and fed by her mate throughout the incubation period, and in some species until the young are ready to fly, must also be mentioned.

With parasitic birds, which foist their family cares upon other species, South Africa is well supplied. We have nine species of Cuckoo which behave in this way; five species of Honeyguide (Indicatoridae), some of which are also remarkable for their habit of leading men and honey-badgers to bees' nests; and eight species of the Weaverbird family (Ploceidae). Conversely, there are species like the Ostrich, in which several hens may lay in one nest; and others like the Helmet Shrike (*Prionops*), in which a whole flock assist the parents in feeding the young.

Although most species of birds have their defined range, there are some whose range has expanded remarkably in recent years. Among these is the Cattle Egret (*Bubulcus*), which has expanded into the Eastern Cape during the last 50 and into the South-western Cape during the last 30 years and is now a conspicuous bird in both areas.

Birkenhead. Troopship which sank under conditions of great tragedy and heroism on February 26, 1852, off Danger Point (q.v.). She was outward bound from Cork in Ireland, carrying reinforcements for the British forces engaged in the native war. Of a total of 551 passengers, 25 were women and 31 children. Off Danger Point the *Birkenhead* struck an uncharted rock and began to sink. The troops were lined up on deck and, as it was known that insufficient lifeboats were available,

the women and children were first sent ashore, while the men remained standing on deck until they perished under the waves. Perfect discipline was preserved to the very end. Of the total of 638 persons on board, only 184 were saved.

Bishop-Bird (Ploceidae). Brightly coloured bird of Weaver family. Varieties include: Rooi Kaffervink or *Red Bishop-Bird*, the male of which, in the mating season, is a vivid red and black, and rattles his wings as he flies. Polygamous and very pugnacious. *Yellow Bishop-Bird* or Geel Kaffervink of the eastern coastal areas, larger, yellow and black, with similar habits to last. Both prefer marshy habitat. *Golden* or *Toha Bishop-Bird*, yellow and black, found mostly north of Durban. *See* WEAVERS and BIRDS.

Bishops. *See* DIOCESAN COLLEGE.

Biskop, Black, or **Musselcrusher** (*Cymatoceps nasutus*). Fish found off False Bay to Natal. About 40 inches long.

Biskop, White (Cape), or **Brusher** (Natal) (*Sparodon durbanensis*). Fish found off False Bay and Agulhas Bank. About 40 inches long. *See* BREAM.

Bismuth. Metal found near Lydenburg, Pretoria, Pilgrim's Rest, Rooiberg and elsewhere in Republic. The most promising deposits are in Namaqualand and South West Africa. A fluctuating output has been recorded since 1919.

Bisset, Sir Murray. Chief Justice of Southern Rhodesia. Born on April 14, 1876, and educated at Diocesan College. He was admitted to the Cape Bar in 1899 and served in the Boer War, practising in the Cape afterwards until he went to Rhodesia in 1925 to be appointed Senior Judge there, and Chief Justice in 1927. He died on October 24, 1931.

Bitterappel. *See* TOBACCO, WILD.

Bittern (Ardeidae). South African water birds of the Heron family, found in reed beds near vleis and lakes in most parts of the country. They are all long-legged, long-necked and long-billed birds, the adults usually with ornamental plumes. Their strong straight bills are excellent for spearing frogs and fish. Unlike the herons, bitterns nest singly. Usually seen standing on one leg in fresh water or straight up, pretending not to be a bird at all. The *Cape Bittern* or Roerdomp is a large yellow-brown mottled bird, with a ruff that can close down at will, and a booming voice very disturbing at night. The male *Red-necked Little Bittern* is black, with a chestnut back, and has no booming voice. Bitterns are rarely seen until evening.

Bitterwater. Village near Prince Albert, Cape Province. Population: 550, including 160 Whites.

Bizana. Village in Pondoland, near Cape-Natal border and close to Umtamvuma River. Was in independent territory till 1894, and the scene of many tribal battles near by. The name Bizana signifies 'A Small Pot,' and is probably derived from a natural cavity from which a stream rises. Population: 600, including 200 Whites.

Blaasop (family Tetrodon). Variety of South African fish, so called because of its habit of inflating itself when brought to the surface. One variety, the Cape Blaasop (*Tetrodon honckeni*), is found from False Bay to Natal, East Indies, China. About 12 inches long.

Blaauwberg. Village near Cape Town, across Table Bay, noted for its beautiful view of Table Mountain; scene of the landing of the British forces in 1806, and of the ensuing battle which preceded the final defeat of the Dutch forces of the Batavian Republic. Population: 300, including 200 Whites.

Blaauwberg. Also spelt 'Blouberg.' Mountain range in the Northern Transvaal, reputedly rich in diamonds.

Black. Type of ostrich feather, taken from the wing of the male, where it joins the body.

Black, Stephen. South African dramatist, born in Cape Town, 1881. He became a journalist and writer, attaining great success with a series of plays produced about the time of Union, notably *Love and the Hyphen* and *Helena's Hope* (1906). Later he wrote a novel, *The Dorp*, about the 1914 Rebellion. Stephen Black's later years were devoted to polemic journalism. He died in 1932.

Black-and-White (*Plectorhynchus pictus*). Edible fish found off Natal, East Africa, and in Indo-Pacific Ocean. About 15 inches long. *See* GRUNTER.

Black-Bass (Centrarchidae). A family of carnivorous, North American freshwater fish, valuable for food and sport. Black-Bass males build a nest, entice various females to lay in it, then drive them away, and guard the young until they can swim away. Various species have now been introduced into South African rivers and dams: 1. Largemouth Black-Bass. 21 inches, introduced in 1928, and followed within 2 years by Cape-bred fish. Prefers sluggish water. 2. Small-mouth Black-Bass. Likes clear, cool, running water. Introduced into Cape Province in 1937. About 18 inches long. 3. Spotted Black-Bass, introduced in 1939, as being more suited to the peaty floodrivers of South Africa. 20 inches long. At the same time *Blue Gills* (*Lepomis macrochirus*), that breed quickly and are good eating, were introduced to supplement the food of the Black-Bass.

Blackburn, Douglas. South African author. Born in Savoy, France, on August 6, 1857, he was educated at Lowestoft, studied for the Bar, but entered journalism in 1892. Making his home in Johannesburg, he became a successful writer. His best-known book is *Prinsloo of Prinsloosdorp*, a skit on the old type of Boer official. He also wrote *A Burgher Quixote, Richard Hartley, Prospector* and other books. He was a keen yachtsman, and made many long solo voyages. Died in 1916.

Black Circuit. Name given by Cape Colonists to a Circuit Court held in 1812, following charges by the Rev. James Read, Doctor Vanderkemp (q.v.) and other missionaries against the settlers on the Eastern Cape frontier. They were accused of having ill-treated their black servants, and of attacking local tribes, but the majority were acquitted. The Black Circuit caused much ill-feeling, and was regarded as a major cause of the Great Trek.

Black-Fish (*Centrolophus niger*). Found off St. Helena Bay, Saldanha Bay and Table Bay; Mediterranean and North Atlantic. About 46 inches long. Good eating fish.

Black Sash League. 'Women's Defence of the Constitution League.' Established in the Union of South Africa in May 1955 to oppose the policy of the National Government of depriving the non-Whites of their remaining franchise, and of making other changes in the constitution. Its members wear black sashes as a sign of mourning and maintain vigils of 'silent picketing' at places where Cabinet Ministers, Members of Parliament and other prominent personalities are expected to appear.

Black-Tail. South African fish. *See* DASSIE.

Blackwater Fever. Extreme and deadly form of Malaria, so called after colour of patient's urine. Formerly common in parts of Rhodesia and Zambia, but now almost extinct.

Black Week. A period of British defeats early in the South African War. It began on December 10, 1899, with the setback at Stormberg (q.v.), followed by Magersfontein on December 11, with the death of Gen. Wauchope (q.v.)

and the Battle of Colenso (q.v.) on December 15. Two days later the whole of Britain's first-class reserves were called out.

Blaiberg, Dr. Philip Barnett. *See* HEART TRANSPLANTS.

Blanco. Village near George in Cape Province, noted for its scenery. Population: 2,200, including 600 Whites.

Blank, Archbishop Joost de. *See* DE BLANK.

Blanket Vote. Name formerly applied to the vote exercised by uneducated natives in the Eastern Province under the original Cape franchise. At one time it could sway the verdict in several constituencies.

Blantyre. Township in Malawi named after Blantyre in Scotland, where David Livingstone was born in 1813. Situated 3,600 feet above sea-level, the place was founded in 1876 as a station by the Scottish Mission, but only developed into a settlement many years later. It is the seat of the High Court and of other Government offices. Since 1956 Blantyre has been united with the business area of Limbe. Population: 59,000, including 4,000 Whites and 4,000 Asiatics.

Blatjang. A condiment originally made by the Malay slaves, the name being derived from that language. It is composed of peaches, raisins, quinces, dried apricots, vinegar, sugar, etc.

Bleek, Dorothea. Daughter of Dr. W. H. I. Bleek (q.v.), born in Cape Town in 1868. Her life work was to continue the investigation into Bushman culture and language begun by her father. She was responsible for the publication of some magnificent works reproducing their rock paintings, as well as for several books. She completed the dictionary begun by her father (over 1,000 pages of manuscript), which was published shortly after her death on June 27, 1948.

Bleek, Dr. Wilhelm Heinrich Immanuel. South African philologist and authority on the Bushman. Born in Berlin, 1827, he studied oriental languages, for which purpose, in 1851, he first proceeded to England, hoping to find his way to India. Instead he found appointment as an interpreter on the West Coast of Africa, whence in 1852 ill-health forced him to move to the Cape. Through his friendship with Bishop Colenso (q.v.), he became interested in the Zulu language, and afterwards, gaining the support of Governor Sir George Grey (q.v.), he began the almost entirely new study of the Bushmen and their language. Most of the rest of his career was spent in an effort to gain the friendship of this elusive people and to gather material for a dictionary. He held positions first in the Native Affairs Department and later as Librarian of the South African Public Library in Cape Town. Dr. Bleek passed away on August 17, 1875, leaving his dictionary incomplete. Work was continued by his sister-in-law, Lucy Lloyd, and by his daughter, Dorothea Bleek (q.v.).

Blennerhasset, Sister Rose. Pioneer Rhodesian nurse. Born in England, she began her career about 1888 in the Cardiff Union Hospital. In 1890 her health broke down and she emigrated to Johannesburg with a group of other nurses, with one of whom, Lucy Sleeman (q.v.), she established a close friendship. After a while spent on the Rand they moved to Kimberley, and were about to return to England when Bishop Knight Bruce, newly-appointed to Mashonaland, persuaded them to establish the first hospital there. Proceeding by ship to Beira they walked to Umtali, where they set up, under incredible difficulties, what became a successful hospital. Miss Blennerhasset died in 1907.

Blenny. Small, shallow-water, scale-less fish, related to Klip-fish (q.v.). Varieties include *Common Cape Blenny*

(Bifter in Afrikaans), 6 inches long; *Wood's Blenny*, 4 inches long (Algoa Bay to Natal); *Striped Blenny*, with black stripe and silvery body, 5 inches long, found off Natal, East Africa, in the East Indian and Pacific Oceans; and the large 16-inch *Ocean Blenny*, found off Natal and in the Indian Ocean.

Blesbok (*Damaliscus albifrons*). South African antelope, now protected owing to excessive hunting. Stands about 3 feet in height and is a very fast runner. The name 'bles' signifies a white patch, a characteristic feature of its markings. Blesbok are rarely found north of the Limpopo River.

Bleshoender. Afrikaans name for Red-knobbed Coot (q.v.).

Blesmol (Bathyergidae). Small burrowing rodent, differing from Golden Mole (q.v.) in having projecting teeth, small eyes and small tail. It is a dull grey above and whitish below. It lives on juicy roots which are stored in side-tunnels. Although regarded as a curse by the farmers, it does at least usefully break up hard ground. Allied to the Blesmol is the wholly grey Mole Rat and the large, 18-inch-long Sand Mole of the coastal regions.

Blesmol

Blikmanel. Name applied in Afrikaans to wearers of imposing uniforms with many buttons. Literally 'tin coat.'

Blikoor (literally 'tin ear'). Nickname given traditionally to the Orange Free State and Transvaal Boers, but also applied by the Transvalers to the Orange Free Staters.

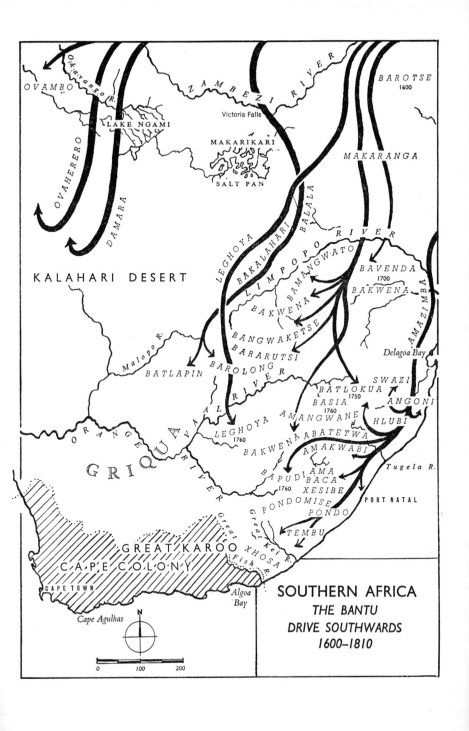

SOUTHERN AFRICA
*THE BANTU
DRIVE SOUTHWARDS
1600–1810*

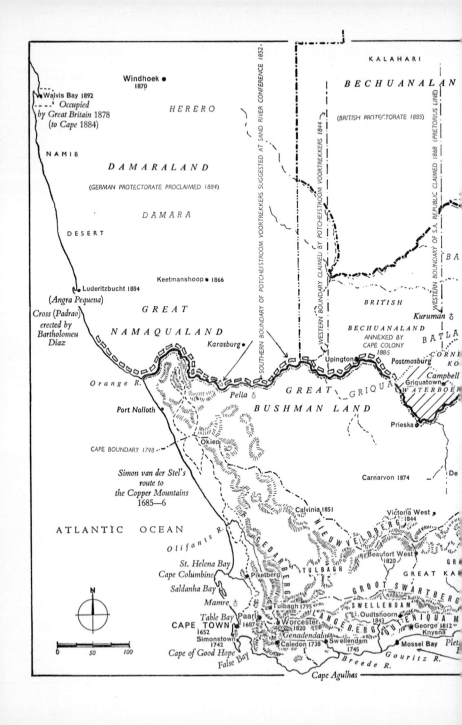

KALAHARI

BECHUANALAN[D]

(BRITISH PROTECTORATE 1885)

Windhoek ●
1870

HERERO

Walvis Bay 1892
Occupied
by Great Britain 1878
(to Cape 1884)

NAMIB

DAMARALAND

(GERMAN PROTECTORATE PROCLAIMED 1884)

DAMARA

DESERT

Keetmanshoop ● 1866

Luderitzbucht 1884
(Angra Pequena)
Cross (Padrao)
erected by
Bartholomeu
Diaz

GREAT

NAMAQUALAND

Karasburg ●

Kuruman ⌗

BRITISH

BECHUANALAND
ANNEXED BY
CAPE COLONY
1885

BATLA

Pella ⌗

Upington

Postmasburg

CORNE
KO

GREAT

Campbell
Griquatown
WATERBOER

GRIQUA

Orange R.

Port Nolloth ●

BUSHMAN LAND

Prieska ●

CAPE BOUNDARY 1798

Okiep

Simon van der Stel's
route to
the Copper Mountains
1685—6

Carnarvon 1874

De

ATLANTIC OCEAN

Olifants R.

St. Helena Bay
Cape Columbine
Saldanha Bay

Piketberg

Calvinia 1851

Victoria West ●
1844

NIEUWVELDBERG

Beaufort West
1820

GREAT KA

TULBAGH

Mamre ⌗

GROOT SWARTBERG

Table Bay Paarl
CAPE TOWN
1652
Simonstown
1742
Cape of Good Hope
False Bay

Tulbagh 1795

Worcester

Genadendal
Caledon 1738

SWELLENDAM

Oudtshoorn
1843

Swellendam
1745

OUTENIQUAM

George 1812
Knysna

Mossel Bay

Plet[t]

Breede R.

Gouritz R.

Cape Agulhas

N

0   50   100

SOUTHERN BOUNDARY OF POTCHEFSTROOM VOORTREKKERS SUGGESTED AT SAND RIVER CONFERENCE 1852

WESTERN BOUNDARY CLAIMED BY POTCHEFSTROOM VOORTREKKERS 1844

WESTERN BOUNDARY OF S.A. REPUBLIC CLAIMED 1868 (PRETORIUS LINE)

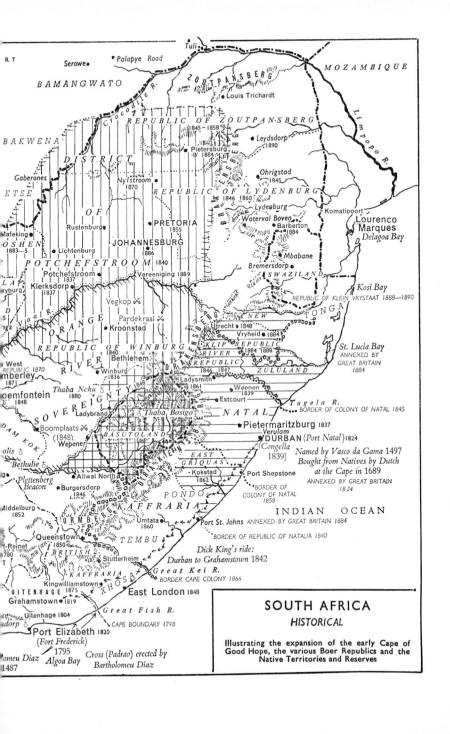

SOUTH AFRICA

HISTORICAL

Illustrating the expansion of the early Cape of Good Hope, the various Boer Republics and the Native Territories and Reserves

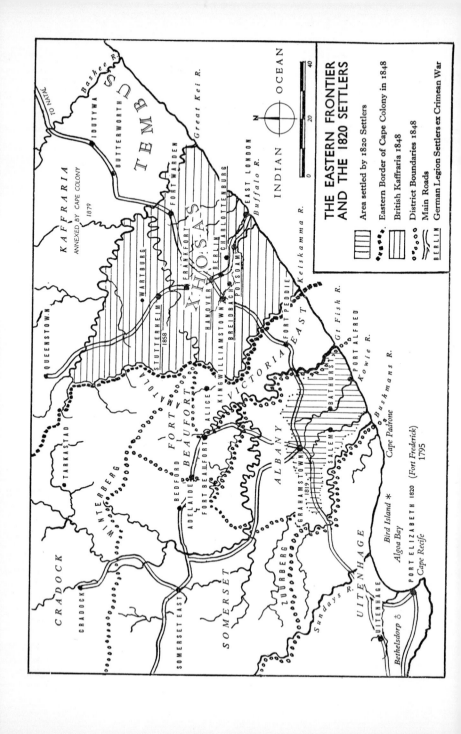

THE EASTERN FRONTIER
AND THE 1820 SETTLERS

Area settled by 1820 Settlers
Eastern Border of Cape Colony in 1848
British Kaffraria 1848
District Boundaries 1848
Main Roads
BERLIN German Legion Settlers ex Crimean War

TEMBUS

KAFFRARIA
ANNEXED BY CAPE COLONY
1879

XHOSAS

IDUTYWA
BUTTERWORTH
FORT WARDEN
WARTBURG
FRANKFORT
HANOVER BERLIN
CHARLOTTENBURG
BREIDBACH POTSDAM
STUTTERHEIM
1858
KING WILLIAMSTOWN
EAST LONDON
Buffalo R.
Keiskamma R.
FORT PEDDIE
Gt Fish R.
BATHURST
PORT ALFRED
Kowie R.
Bushmans R.
Cape Padrone

QUEENSTOWN
KATALA
FORT BEAUFORT
ALICE
VICTORIA EAST
ALBANY
SALEM
GRAHAMSTOWN
1819

TARKASTAD
BEDFORD
ADELAIDE
FORT BEAUFORT
WINTERBERG
ZUURBERG

CRADOCK
CRADOCK

SOMERSET
SOMERSET EAST

ZUURBERG
UITENHAGE
Sundays R.
Bethelsdorp
UITENHAGE
Algoa Bay
Bird Island
PORT ELIZABETH 1820 (Fort Frederick)
Cape Recife   1795

INDIAN OCEAN

Bashee R.
Great Kei R.
TO NATAL

N

0   20   40

Blinkvis. South African fish. *See* SILVIE.

Blinkwater. Village near Fort Beaufort, Cape Province. Population: 1,259, including 39 Whites.

Blockhouse. Fortifications introduced at the Cape during the first British occupation of 1795, a few of them, notably the King's Blockhouse and Queen's Blockhouse on the slopes of Table Mountain, still surviving. Later

Blockhouse

they were widely used on the eastern frontier and in the South African War by Lord Kitchener. Some are as near Cape Town as Wellington and Malmesbury. At first blockhouses were restricted to railway lines, which they were designed to protect, but gradually they became so numerous that some of them were as little as 200 yards apart, interlinked by means of barbed wire and connected by telephone. In spite of the millions of pounds spent on them, the system did not prove particularly effective, as was shown by the success of General de Wet and other guerrilla leaders. Several different types were used, including some of stone, others of corrugated iron and timber.

Cost ranged from £15, turned out by the Royal Engineers, to £70 each.

Bloemfontein. Capital of the Orange Free State and seat of the Appellate Division of the Supreme Court of South Africa. Doubts exist as to the origin of the name, some experts considering it as being derived from a local chief named Jan Bloem, and others from the fact that flowers grew around the spring of an early local farmer named Jan Britz, who settled here about 1840. The town itself dates from 1846, when Major Henry Douglas Warden, Resident of the Orange River Sovereignty (forerunner of the Orange Free State), bought the site for £37 10s. and founded a village. After the withdrawal of the British from the Orange River Sovereignty in 1854, Bloemfontein became the capital of the Orange Free State. Though well administered, it remained a very small town, so that until 1895 the population was only 2,500. The country was so well governed that it was known as 'The Model Republic.' The only outstanding natural feature near Bloemfontein is Naval Hill, which rises from the great Orange Free State plain. The town itself owes its importance to its central position in South Africa, which has stimulated trade and industry. The population today is 146,200, including 63,200 Europeans, 75,300 Bantu and 7,700 Coloureds. The oldest building is the original Fort, erected as early as 1848 by British troops as protection against the Natives. The Raadzaal, where the old Orange River Volksraad used to meet, is now used by the Orange Free State Provincial Council. Near by is the old Presidency, official residence of the First Citizen of the old Republic. Important landmarks include the National Memorial to women and children who died during the South African War, at whose foot a number of famous figures in South African history are buried, including Miss

Emily Hobhouse, President M. T. Steyn, General Christiaan de Wet and the Rev. J. D. Kestell. The University of the Orange Free State, which developed from the original Grey College, set up in 1855 by Sir George Grey, now has about 1,500 students. The President also has a residence at Bloemfontein. There are a number of manufacturing industries and several important magazines are published here.

Bloemhof: 1. Town in the Western Transvaal, believed to be called after a native chief of the 1870's, Jan Bloem. The Vaal River, on which the place is built, has helped to create large alluvial deposits of diamonds, which in bygone times maintained hundreds of diggers; and the Town Lands, proclaimed by the Government, have yielded many fine stones. Population: 7,230, including 2,000 Whites.
2. Large School for Girls at Stellenbosch, established in 1875 by the Rev. J. H. Neethling and Prof. N. J. Brummer, in association with the Dutch Reformed Church.

Blommetjies. Flowers painted on the trek-wagons, a traditional form of ornamentation.

Blood River. Tributary of the Buffalo River in the north of Natal, and famous in South African history as the scene of the final defeat in 1838 of the Zulu chief Dingaan by the Voortrekkers under Andries Pretorius. The Zulus are estimated to have suffered over 3,000 casualties, while the Voortrekkers had hardly any. A monument has been erected near by and thanksgiving services are still held annually.

Bloodwood. See TEAK.

Blouberg. See BLAAUWBERG.

Bloukrans. Hill in Natal, scene of the massacre by the Zulus of a large number of Voortrekkers encamped there. On February 17, 1838, after the murder of Piet Retief (q.v.) and his companions, the chief Dingaan ordered his forces to wipe out the remainder of their party. An impi found them encamped at Bloukrans, and attacked and murdered 41 men, 56 women and 97 children, besides wounding numbers who escaped. In commemoration of the tragedy the neighbouring village was named Weenen (Weeping) (q.v.).

Bloureier. Afrikaans name for Grey Heron. See HERONS.

Blousysie. Afrikaans name for Blue-breasted Waxbill. See WAXBILLS.

Blouvalk. Afrikaans name for Chanting Goshawk. See EAGLES.

Blouvalkie. Afrikaans name for Black-shouldered Kite. See EAGLES and BIRDS.

Blue Ape. See VERVET MONKEY.

Blueback. Note issued by the Transvaal Government in 1865. Altogether £50,000 worth were produced, but their value soon sank to almost nothing. Notes even for denominations as low as 6d. were all signed by the President in person. The name is derived from their colour, but later it was also applied to Orange Free State and other paper money.

Bluebuck. Extinct antelope, formerly found in the Cape Province, but now only to be studied in museum specimens in Europe. A large animal, standing 45 inches high at the shoulder, bluish-grey in colour. Not to be confused with the common little Bluebuck of the Bushveld. Its zoological name was *Hippotragus leucophaeus* and it was related to the Roan Antelope.

Blue Ground. Bluish-grey mineral in which a large percentage of the diamonds of Kimberley are found. Originally it was allowed to weather in the atmosphere on large 'floors,' but in the 1890's the pulsator system of mechanical washing was adopted, since further improved. Blue ground itself is of volcanic origin.

Blue Tongue. Sheep disease, so named after one of its characteristic symptoms. (Bloutong in Afrikaans, also known as Autumn Fever.) A form of influenza closely allied to horse sickness (q.v.). Formerly it afflicted millions of sheep, but since about 1910 a vaccine, developed at Onderstepoort, has almost stamped out the disease.

Blyvooruitzig. Literally 'Joyous Prospect.' Gold mining centre near Potchefstroom, Transvaal. Population: 11,200, including 3,600 Whites.

Board of Executors. Trust company established in Cape Town on August 22, 1838, and still in existence. It is the oldest Trust company in the World.

Boart (also **Bort**). Low grade form of diamond, very poor but useful for drilling, polishing and for other commercial purposes.

Bobotie. Malay dish popular in the Cape. Name probably from a Malay word 'burbur,' meaning potage or pulp. Bobotie is made from minced meat seasoned with curry and spices, and topped with custard.

Boekenhoutsfontein. Large Bantu township north of Pretoria in Sotho Homeland, mostly inhabited by workers employed at Rosslyn (q.v.).

Boerboon, 'Boer Bean' (*Schotia speciosa* Jacq.). Large shrub or small tree up to 15 feet high. The astringent bark has been used medicinally and for tanning. Wood is tough and durable.

Boere-Saamwerk Beperk. Large South African co-operative society. Established 1920 specially to handle the marketing of wool, mohair, skins and other produce. Its headquarters are in Port Elizabeth.

Boer War. *See* SOUTH AFRICAN WAR.

Boesmanskop. Village near Wepener in the Orange Free State. Population: 250, including 60 Whites.

Boetsap. Village near Barkly West, Cape Province. Population: 120, including 100 Whites. The name is of Hottentot origin.

Bogenfels ('Archway Rock' in German). Remarkable rock formation on the coast of South-West Africa, so called after an enormous archway 180 feet high, weathered and worn out of the stone, rising out of the sea some 60 miles south of Lüderitzbucht.

Bok-Bok. Popular name of a game played by boys in South Africa. It is of very great antiquity, and was known under almost the same name among the Romans. One player stands against a wall, while others form a chain, jumping over each other until the whole group collapses.

Bok, Hon. Willem Eduard. Supreme Court judge. Son of Dr. Willem Eduard Bok, born in Pretoria in 1880, educated there and in Holland. Fought in the South African War, and after qualifying for the Bar became private secretary to General Louis Botha in 1907, when the latter became Premier of the Transvaal under Responsible Government. After Union he became Secretary to the Prime Minister, Government Law adviser in 1916 and in 1918 Secretary for Justice. In 1930 he became judge of the High Court of South-West Africa, and in 1933 of the Griqualand West local division. He died in 1956.

Bok, Dr. Willem Eduard. Friend and associate of President Kruger. Born in Holland in 1846, he went to England in 1864 to study the language and in 1876, at the age of 30, after a career in commerce, found his way to the Transvaal. There he gained the friendship of the future President Kruger, accompanying him and the rest of the Independence Delegation to London after the annexation of the country. Later he became Secretary of the National Committee, and joined the staff of *De Volksstem*. After the Majuba

Campaign he was State Secretary from 1884 to 1888. He was Clerk to the Volksraad and Government Commissioner for the newly discovered Witwatersrand Goldfields, where the town of Boksburg was named after him. Cousin of the famous American editor, Edward Bok, of the *Ladies' Home Journal*. W. E. Bok died in Johannesburg in 1904.

Bokkeveld. Area in the Western Cape Province, so named on account of its former wealth in buck. It comprises the Cold Bokkeveld and the Warm Bokkeveld, the former lying at a higher altitude, in the Karroo, east of the Bokkeveld Mountains, while the latter is the fertile fruit-growing region around Ceres.

Bokkum. Dried or smoked fish, its name probably derived from the German Bückling, meaning dried herring. Bokkums are a large item of commerce on the Cape west coast.

Bokmakierie or **Kokkewiet** (*Telophorus zeylonus*). One of the Bush Shrikes, but larger and bolder. Its name is derived from the well-known duet sung between the inseparable male and female. Grey-green, with yellow underpart, black throat and yellow marks on tail. Abundant near Cape Town, but found as far north as Limpopo. *See* SHRIKE.

Boksburg. Town on East Rand established in 1903 and named after the State Secretary of the South African Republic, Dr. W. E. Bok. Noted for its gold mines and for its lake, which is a popular pleasure resort, used for yachting. Population: 108,850, including 44,000 Whites, 54,000 Bantu, 10,000 Coloureds and 850 Asiatics.

Bokwe, The Rev. John Knox. African clergyman and composer of music. Born near Lovedale in 1855, he went to school at that institution and in 1870 found employment there. After working as a telegraphist he took to the composing of music in 1875, and some time after became a minister of the Presbyterian Church. He died in 1922. Bokwe is remembered for his ' Vuka ' and ' Deborah,' and, in addition to his songs and hymns, for a number of plays in Xosa.

Boland (originally **Bovenland**). Official description applied to the Western Cape Province, as distinct from Cape Town itself. The rest of the country was formerly called Onderveld.

Boma. Word used in Malawi and Zambia, but not in Rhodesia to describe District Commissioners Offices. Derived from Chinyanja language and signifies 'Court of a Paramount Chief.'

Bomvanaland. Portion of the Transkei, also known as Elliotdale. It lies on the coast, not far from Umtata.

Bondelswarts. Tribe living in the Warmbad district, which in 1903 rose against the German authorities under the leadership of their chief, Morenga. Of mixed Nama and Herero origin. Under the Peace of Kalkfontein,

Bokmakierie

Governor Leutwein in 1904 granted them a reserve, but Morenga broke the terms, and was finally driven across the Cape frontier, where he was killed in a skirmish with the police. There was further trouble with the Bondelswarts after World War I, when aircraft were used to subdue them.

Bonito, Ocean (*Gymnoscarda pelamys*). Fish found off Cape, in tropical and sub-tropical seas. About 32 inches long. A smaller Bonito or Little Tunny, 17 inches long (*Euthynnus allitterata*), with wavy black stripes, is caught off Natal coast. *See* MACKEREL, CAPE.

Bonnievale. Village and irrigation scheme, near Robertson, Cape Province, established about 1900 by Christopher Forrest Rigg, originally as a settlement scheme for ex-soldiers after the Boer War. The chief crops are grapes and lucerne. Population: 2,540, including 1000 Whites.

Bontebok

Bontebok (*Damaliscus pygarus*). Antelope, interbreeding with and resembling the Blesbok (q.v.). Once common, it is now preserved almost solely in the Bontebok Reserve near Swellendam, where its numbers have increased to about 100.

Bontspan. Oxen of varying colours. The word is also applied to a mixture of meats roasted on a spit.

Bonuskor. Financial company established in 1946 by Dr. M. S. Louw (q.v.) to mobilise capital in Afrikaner hands, particularly through the investment of cash bonuses in life insurance and other companies.

Boomplaats. Farm near Jagersfontein, O.F.S., scene of battle between the emigrant Boers and the British troops under Governor Sir Harry Smith (q.v.) on August 29, 1848. The Boers, under A. W. Pretorius, were defeated, and many of them migrated north of the Vaal River to set up the South African Republic.

Boomslang (*Dispholidus typus*) or **Tree Snake.** Group: Colubridae. Several varieties exist and are usually found in forested areas, often imitating the stiffness of a branch. They grow to a length of nearly 5 feet and vary in colour from black to yellowish-green. Contrary to former belief, Boomslangs are extremely poisonous, although they are usually too timid to attack. A peculiar feature about them is their habit of swallowing each other in fighting. Unlike the Egg-eating Snake (q.v.), they swallow eggs whole and slowly digest shell and all. *See* SNAKES.

Boomvaring. *See* TREE FERN.

Boonzaier, Daniel Cornelis. South African artist and cartoonist, born on November 11, 1865, near Carnarvon, Cape Province. In spite of extreme poverty he managed to give himself an education, secured a post in the Cape Civil Service, and soon began to show an artistic sense that won him appreciation far beyond the boundaries of South Africa, although he never left the country. His fame rests largely on the remarkable series of caricatures and political cartoons which covered nearly 50 years. For 25 of these he was the cartoonist of *Die Burger*, from its foundation in 1915 to 1940, but his work also appeared in a number of other publications, including *The Cape* and *The Owl*. Among his famous creations were the figure of the millionaire, Hoggenheimer, as the incarnation of the Johannesburg mine magnate, and the baboon on a pole (Kees), symbolising South Africa. He died in 1950.

Boonzaier, Gregoire. South African artist. Born at Cape Town on July 31, 1909, the son of the well-known cartoonist D. C. Boonzaier (q.v.), he studied at Cape Town and in London, where from 1934 on he gained a fine reputation, particularly as a landscape painter.

Boos. Type of ostrich feathers taken from the tail.

Border. Name applied to the area around East London, dating back to the time when this was on the frontier of the independent native territories. It is still sometimes used in the sporting world, and has been applied to a Parliamentary constituency.

Border. Village near Warrenton, Cape Province. Population: 950, including 600 Whites. Near northern frontier, hence the name.

Border Industries. System of industrial development encouraged by the South African Government and supported by the Industrial Development Corporation (q.v.) in conjunction with a policy of Bantu "Homelands". Factories are erected near the border of Bantu areas to allow workers to come daily to their employment. Border Industries have been established in the Eastern Cape, in Natal and in the Southern Transvaal. *See also* HA-MARDALE and ROSSLYN.

Borghorst, Jakob. Early Commander of the Cape of Good Hope. Succeeded Cornelis Van Quaelbergen (q.v.) in 1668. Suffered from poor health and left most of the administration to his subordinates. Encouraged exploration of the interior. Returned to Holland in 1670.

Borrow, Captain Henry John. Rhodesian soldier. Born in Cornwall in 1865 and great-nephew of George Borrow, author of *Lavengro*. He began by farming in the Cape; in 1884 joined the Bechuanaland Expedition, and in 1890, along with Major Frank Johnson (q.v.) and Captain Maurice Heany (q.v.), organised the famous Pioneer Column (q.v.). As captain in the local forces he took part in the Matabele War of 1893 and was killed with the Shangani Patrol (q.v.).

Boschetto. Agricultural College for Women near Harrismith in Orange Free State, founded by Miss Norah Miller in 1922. The farm, which measures about 250 acres, previously belonged to her relative, H. R. Wisely, and takes its name from a house in Malta, with which the family was linked. In Italian Boschetto means 'a little wood.' The original building belonged to the Knights of St. John of Jerusalem. Certain support is given by the Government to the college, but it has always remained a private venture. Several hundred students have been trained there. Has closed down.

Boshof. Town in the Orange Free State, between Kimberley and Bloemfontein. Originally known as Van Wyk's Vlei, it was laid out in 1856, and renamed after the early president of the O.F.S., Jacobus Nicolaas Boshof (q.v.). Farming centre. Heavy fighting took place here during the South African War in April 1900, when the French volunteer, Col. de Villebois-Mareuil, was killed. Population: 2,865, including 1,015 Whites.

Boshof, Jacobus Nicolaas. Second President of the Orange Free State. Born in 1808 near Swellendam, and began his career in the Cape Colonial Civil Service. He visited the Voortrekkers in Natal in 1838 and wrote an account of them in the *Grahamstown Journal*. The following year he settled in Natal, where he became Chairman of the Volksraad of the

Republic of Natalia, and, after the British annexation, Registrar and Master of the Supreme Court. In 1854 he was offered the presidency of the O.F.S. in succession to President Hoffman (q.v.). He found himself confronted with many problems, the most serious of which was the threat of war with the Basuto. In addition to this the South African Republic, under President M. W. Pretorius, made efforts to annex the O.F.S. Because of his support for a scheme by Governor Sir George Grey (q.v.) to federate South Africa, he lost popularity with many of his burghers. He resigned in 1858, returned to Natal, sat in the Legislative Council of that colony for several years and died in 1881 near Pietermaritzburg.

Bosman, Daniel (Danie). South African composer. Born at Cape Town on February 7, 1907, he showed early musical ability, but joined the Civil Service, in which he spent his life. His songs, including *Boereseun, In die Skadu van Tafelberg* etc. achieved great popularity but brought him little monetary reward. Died on May 27, 1946.

Bosman, Dr. Frederick Christiaan Ludolph. Afrikaans author. Born at Kuils River, Cape Province, on May 17, 1898 and studied at Cape Town and Amsterdam. He wrote standard works on the South African stage, on Afrikaans philology and history. Appointed Secretary of the Afrikaanse Akademie (q.v.) in 1948 and retired in 1958.

Bosman, Joseph Jacobus. South African banker and founder of Volkskas. Born in Rustenburg in 1895, he began his career working in a small shop and gradually gained experience in a bank. In 1934 he succeeded in establishing the Volkskas Ko-op Bpk., which developed into one of the most important institutions in South Africa, a banking institution mainly under Afrikaner control. He died in June 1952.

Botha, Christiaan Lourens. Judge-President of the Orange Free State. Born at Kroonstad in 1869, he studied at the University of Stellenbosch, Amsterdam and in London, where he was called to the Bar. He began practice in Bloemfontein and entered municipal politics, serving for 4 years as mayor. From 1907 to 1910 he was member of the Orange River Colony Legislative Assembly and after Union sat as member for Bloemfontein from 1910 to 1915. In 1938 he became Judge-President of the Orange Free State and retired in 1939. He died in 1951.

Botha, General Louis. South African statesman and soldier. Born near Greytown, Natal, on September 27, 1862, of a family originally from Germany, also known as Boot. The son of a Voortrekker, he attended a German mission school and went with his parents as a child to the Orange Free State. Beginning his career as a sheep farmer, he took his flocks to Zululand, in the political affairs of which he became involved. After distinguishing himself in the Boer forces which supported the Zulus during the intertribal wars, Botha was one of the founders of the short-lived 'New Republic' (q.v.), which had its headquarters in Vryheid, and which began its existence in 1884. After the demise of the republic he moved to the Transvaal, which remained his home for the rest of his days. In 1895 he was stationed, on behalf of the South African Republic, in Swaziland, to represent the interests of his country, and in 1897 he was elected to the Volksraad. By this time he was already recognised as a man of unusual ability, and when the South African War began in 1899 he joined the forces in Natal, being appointed Assistant General under General Lukas Meyer. There he soon became one of the most prominent figures, playing a leading part in the fighting at Ladysmith, Colenso and Spion Kop. Upon the death of General P. J. Joubert, on March 27, 1900, Botha was appointed Commandant-General of the Transvaal forces. As such he soon displayed outstanding gifts, despite the unfavourable course taken by the fighting. A man of strong will despite his personal charm, he caused the dismissal of several incompetent subordinates, and eluded the efforts of the British forces to trap him. Realising by degrees that the struggle was hopeless, he entered into negotiations with Lord Kitchener in Middelburg on March 7, 1901, but failed to reach agreement. In April 1902 he took the main part in the arrangements that led to the holding of the Peace Conference at Vereeniging, and was one of the signatories to the final treaty. Once this had been settled, he decided as a policy to break with the past and make the best possible use of the new circumstances. This ultimately led to his estrangement from a large part of his own people, but his powers as yet were undiminished, and he took the lead in setting up the party known as Het Volk (q.v.). As the acknowledged leader of the Boer people, he was the almost inevitable choice as the first Prime Minister of the Transvaal in 1907 when Responsible Government was granted, and, after the holding of the National Convention, at which he was a delegate, he was chosen the first Premier of the Union of South Africa. Within a short while the breach occurred with General J. B. M. Hertzog (q.v.), but he continued in office and still enjoyed great prestige. The outbreak of the Rebellion of 1914 (q.v.) was a source of grief and anxiety to General Botha. He successfully suppressed this insurrection and led the attack on German South West Africa, which he brought to a successful conclusion in 1915. Thereafter he went overseas and was treated with great respect. General Botha was present at the Peace Conference at Versailles in 1919, and

signed on behalf of the Union of South Africa. By then his health was already failing, and he died the same year on August 27 in Pretoria at the early age of 57.

Botha's Hill. Village near Valley of a Thousand Hills, Natal. Population: 1,570, including 670 Whites.

Bothaville. Village in the north of the Orange Free State, founded in 1889 by Theunis Botha, who gave the place its name. Located on the banks of the Valsch River, it is the centre of one of the chief grain-producing areas in the Republic, in the heart of the 'Maize Triangle.' During the South African War General Christiaan de Wet suffered here a reverse on November 6, 1900, against troops under Col. Le Gallais, who was killed. Population: 9,300, including 2,000 Whites.

Botletle River. Rises near Lake Ngami and makes its way in an easterly direction towards the Makarikari salt pan. Though it rarely flows, there are brackish pools along its length and sudden floods from time to time.

Botswana (formerly Bechuanaland). Republic in British Commonwealth which received independence on September 30, 1966. It lies between the Northern Cape Province, the Western Transvaal, South West Africa and the Zambesi. Consists of two areas of the Cape Province, and the former Bechuanaland Protectorate. Botswana is occupied by semi-desert country, the Kalahari itself lying within its bounds. No accurate census of the Bantu has been taken since 1946, when the population was given as 292,754 Africans. In addition up to 40,000 work in South Africa. The 1956 Census gave 3,173 Europeans, 700 Coloured and 250 Asiatics. Most of the area has been demarcated into reserves, where the chiefs of the Bamangwato (q.v.), and of other tribes, administer their tribal law. Transport is mainly secured through the railway running from the Republic to Rhodesia, supplemented by a motor service. Cattle-breeding is the principal industry, also a certain amount of hunting and growing of crops such as beans and kaffir corn. Missions are active, but so far no successful work has been done on the Bushmen still to be found in the depths of the Kalahari. Bechuanaland came under European control in 1884, when it was occupied by General Sir Charles Warren, in order to prevent annexation by the Transvaal or the Germans. Of minerals the most important is asbestos, the last return showing 1,562 tons shipped, valued at £165,634. A certain amount of gold is also produced, likewise kyanite, an acid-resisting mineral resembling andalusite. Although situated in the Cape Province, the administration of the Bechuanaland Protectorate was conducted from Mafeking, where a special 'Imperial Reserve' housed the officials. The principal native town is Serowe. Boer settlements, established in late Victorian times, exist in the north, especially in Ngamiland and Ghanzi, now reached by air. Area: 275,000 square miles. The Republic of Botswana has an elected President and a Legislature of 31 members. *See also* GABERONE and BECHUANA.

Botterblom. *See* DAISY.

Botterboom (*Cotyledon fascicularis* Ait.). Erect, branched succulent, 2–3 feet. Sap of leaves applied to blistered soles of feet. *See* CRASSULA.

Bouvet Island. Antarctic island, located 54° 26′ South, 3° 24′ East. Discovered January 1, 1739, by Captain Pierre des Loziers Bouvet, a Frenchman, who was uncertain whether it was an island or part of the Antarctic continent. Not until 1808 did Captain James Lindsay of the sealing vessel *Swan* and Captain Thomas Hopper of the sealing vessel *Otter* again sight this foreland, to which Bouvet had given the name Cape Circumcision. Owing to climatic conditions, it was only in November, 1898, that the *Valdivia*, a German research ship, finally fixed its location. For South Africa Bouvet Island is of great importance as a potential weather-watching station, although the island itself has been annexed by Norway. On April 2, 1964, a South African expedition, conveyed on H.M.S. *Protector* and the South African research ship *R.S.A.*, first put ashore a landing party with the aid of a helicopter and made important observations. Plans are approved for a permanent weather station there.

Bower, Sir Graham John. Statesman and colonial administrator. Born in Ireland on June 15, 1848, son of Admiral James Paterson Bower, he entered the Royal Navy in 1861, rising to the rank of commander. In 1880 he was appointed Private Secretary to Governor Sir Hercules Robinson of the Cape, and in 1884 became 'Imperial Secretary' to the High Commissioner for South Africa. In this capacity he came to hear about the preparations for the Jameson Raid (q.v.), but, having given his word beforehand to say nothing, found himself unable to offer warnings against what he regarded as a disastrous enterprise. After the Jameson Raid much of the blame was quite unjustly placed on Bower's shoulders, with the result that in 1897 he retired from the Imperial Secretaryship. His repeated efforts to have the matter of his dismissal reconsidered were frustrated for political reasons. After holding the post of Colonial Secretary for Mauritius he retired in 1910, devoting the rest of his life to the cause of international peace. The injustice to which he had been subjected was already recognised by many leading personalities in Europe. He died in 1933.

Bowker, Miles. Early agricultural and industrial pioneer in South Africa. Born at Deckham's Hall, near Durham, England, in 1759, he led a party of 1820 settlers in the *Weymouth*, and, after an abortive attempt at Oliveburn, made his home on the estate of Tharfield. A man of great enterprise, he was among the first to attempt the farming of merino sheep on the eastern frontier, and arranged to have wool woven into blankets, a few of which were actually manufactured. He also was among the first to work for the development of the Kowie as a harbour. He died in 1839.

Bowls. Port Elizabeth may claim the credit of having established the first regular Bowling Club in Southern Africa in 1882, when a green was laid out with the assistance of the municipality. Bowls was played soon after in Kimberley, though it was not until 1889 that a club was formed on the Diamond Fields. Cecil John Rhodes incidentally gave considerable encouragement. The first inter-town championship was recorded in 1894 between Kimberley and Port Elizabeth. Cape Town took up bowls in 1898. Johannesburg was comparatively late in the field, making its first entry in the national championships in 1908. Today it is estimated that nearly 100,000 people play bowls in Southern Africa.

Boxing. Professional prize-fighting began in Southern Africa in 1882, when J. R. Couper, having come to Basutoland as a member of the police, fought a certain Bloomfield. From there he soon moved to Kimberley, and thereafter to Johannesburg. In 1889, at Eagle's Nest, outside the town, Couper was pitted against Wolff Bendoff for the World Championship, with a purse of £4,500, the greatest stake till then recorded. Couper won after 27 rounds, a feat doubly remarkable in view of his relatively light weight—10½ stone. Boxing, having been declared illegal in the South African Republic, was faced with many difficulties, but in 1893 the High Court in Pretoria held it permissible. From then on fights were organised with considerable regularity until in modern times fights of world class became possible.

Boydell, Thomas. South African Cabinet Minister and writer. Born in 1882 at Newcastle-upon-Tyne, he trained as a fitter and coming to Natal in 1903 was soon prominent in the Labour Party there. Elected to Parliament in 1902, he became Minister of Posts and Telegraphs in 1924 under the 'Pact' (q.v.), and from 1925 to 1929 was Government Minister of Labour. He later sat in the Senate. After retiring he wrote several books and travelled the world, defending South Africa on lecture platforms. Died July 5, 1966.

Boy Scouts. *See* YOUTH MOVEMENTS.

Brabant, Major-General Sir Edward Yewd. Born in England in 1839, and joined the Derby Militia as an ensign in 1855. The following year he came to the Cape to enlist in the Cape Mounted Rifles, with which he saw active service, finishing in 1870 as captain. He settled in East London and entered politics, being elected to Parliament in 1873. During several native campaigns, against Sandile, Morosi and others, including the Gun War in Basutoland, he gained distinction in the Cape Yeomanry, and rose to be Commandant-General (Acting). Prominent as a farmer, he re-entered politics, served on the Defence Commission and was closely associated with Cecil Rhodes. Upon the outbreak of the South African War, Brabant was asked to form a Colonial Division, of which he was given command. Promoted to general, he made a great name for himself by the successful defence of Jammersberg Drift near Wepener, which lasted nearly a month. He died on December 13, 1914.

Bradley Grass. *See* GRASSES.

Brak (English 'brack'). Term applied to soil or water saturated with salt or soda. Traditionally 'brackish' water is supposed to make good coffee. Methods have now been devised for leaching out the salt from 'brackish' soil to make it suitable for cultivation.

Brakpan. Town on East Rand. Founded in 1919, when it was established as a separate municipality from its neighbour, Benoni, 4 miles away. Important gold-mining and industrial centre. Population: 64,000, including 34,500 Whites.

Brak River. Tributary of Great Fish River (q.v.).

Brak River. Name of two rivers near Mossel Bay—Great Brak and Little Brak.

Brandblaar (*Anemone vesicatoria*). Plant used by the Boer housewife for blistering.

Brand, Sir Christoffel Josephus. First Speaker of the Cape Parliament. Born in Cape Town, 1797, studied law in Holland at the University of Leyden, where he gained his doctorate in 1820, with a thesis on the relations between colonies and their mother country. Returning to the Cape in 1821, he practised as an advocate, and lectured at the South African College. After gaining prominence during the Anti-Convict Agitation (q.v.) in 1849 he helped to draft the constitution of Cape Colony, and became Speaker of the new Parliament in 1854, a position he held until his resignation in 1874. He died in 1875. His son, Sir J. H. Brand (q.v.), became President of the O.F.S.

Brand, Wing-Commander Sir Christopher Joseph Quinton. South African airman. Born in Kimberley on May 25, 1893, and educated in Johannesburg. Served in the Royal Flying Corps in World War I and took part with Sir Pierre van Ryneveld (q.v.) in the famous pioneer flight from London to Cape Town in 1920. He later became Director of Aviation in Egypt.

Brandfort. Town north of Bloemfontein, founded in 1885 and named after

President Sir John Brand of the Orange Free State. (There is an alternative explanation that it was called after a Voortrekker fort burnt down by the Bushmen.) Important wool centre. Battle fought here in South African War on May 3, 1900. Population: 4,800, including 2,000 Whites.

Brand, Sir Johannes Hendricus. President of the Orange Free State. Born at Cape Town in 1823, son of Sir Christoffel Brand (q.v.), and educated at the South African College, he was admitted to the Bar in England in 1849 and settled in the city of his birth. He had established a good practice and was member of the Cape Parliament for Clanwilliam before he received the call to the post in which he was to gain permanent fame, the presidency of the Orange Free State. Arriving at Bloemfontein in 1863 he found the country almost bankrupt and confronted with the threat of another invasion by the Basuto. Undismayed, Brand took charge of the situation and succeeded in securing the arbitration of Governor Sir Philip Wodehouse (q.v.). When this failed he declared war and carried on a long and inconclusive campaign against Moshesh. Scarcely was this ended than the discovery of diamonds on land claimed by the O.F.S. brought him into conflict with the British, and he succeeded in securing a more or less satisfactory settlement. His influence steadily increased and he was three times re-elected President, while the British authorities paid him the unique compliment of persuading Queen Victoria to confer a knighthood upon him. During his administration the Orange Free State, despite its relatively limited resources, gained the nickname of 'The Model Republic,' on account of its excellent administration, prosperity and good educational system. During the First Boer War in 1881 Brand mediated between the Transvaal and the British, and helped to bring about a peace settlement. Full of years and honours he died in 1888, while still in office.

Brand, Pieter. Early traveller in South West Africa. Having accompanied Willem van Reenen (q.v.), he decided to continue on his own account with a few Hottentot servants. He is believed to have reached an area approximately 21½ degrees south, in the Damaraland country.

Brandsolder. Fire-proof floor in a roof as protection against possible flames from the thatch, found in most of the old farmhouses of the Cape.

Brandsolder

Brandvlei. Village near Calvinia, Cape Province. Population: 1,417, including 454 Whites.

Brandvlei. *See* LAKE MARAIS.

Brandwag. Literally a fire guard. Sentries set by the Boers while in the field.

Brandy-Hum. Mixture of brandy and van der Hum (q.v.).

Braunschweig. German settlement near King William's Town, Cape Province. Population: 1,100, including 500 Whites.

Bream. Large family of shallow-water, edible fish, including the *Sea-breams*, which have stout upper jaw-bones, and *Silverfish*, which have more slender jaws and frequent deeper water. Most fish caught by Cape anglers are Breams. (1) *Sea-bream* group includes White Stumpnose; White Biskop or Brusher (projecting teeth, fine sporting fish, 40 inches long); Black Biskop or Mussel Crusher (bulbous snout, good sporting fish, 40 inches long); Red Stumpnose (26 inches long and highly esteemed); White Steenbras (58 inches); John Brown (14 inches, known to rock anglers); Hottentot; Bronze Bream (20 inches, a well-known Natal fish); Roman (red, 20 inches) and Dageraad (red, common on Agulhas Bank); and Karanteen. (2) *Silverfish* group includes Silverfish or Kaapenaar (30 inches, and one of the best-known South African fish, often smoked and sold as haddock); Seventy-four (40 inches); Scotchman (20 inches, deep-water fish caught from Algoa Bay to Natal, characteristic long face); Witvis or Soldier (24 inches); Mudbream (16 inches, Natal and East Africa, deep-water fish, with compressed body); and Red Steenbras (a very large fish, 5 feet or more, False Bay to Natal).

Bredasdorp. Town in Cape Province. Most southerly municipality in the Republic. Founded in 1838 and named after the Hon. Michiel van Breda, Member of the Legislative Council. Farming centre. Population: 5,000, including 2,000 Whites. *See* BONTEBOK.

Bredie. Malay dish of meat and vegetables hashed together. Name comes from Madagascar. It was originally written Breedi.

Breede River ('Broad River' in Afrikaans). Rises in the Warm Bokkeveld, not far from Ceres, and flows through Worcester and Swellendam. Its tributaries include the Hex River and River Zonder Einde (River without End). Of its 200 miles the last 20 are navigable for small ships, a fact which led to the founding, early in the 19th century, of Port Beaufort, from which the Barrys and other merchants exported Swellendam wheat, etc. The traffic is now almost extinct.

Breidbach. Village near King William's Town, Cape. Established by German settlers in 1858. Population: 1,711, including 77 Whites.

Bremer Bread. Bread enriched with tasteless fishmeal to provide a cheap food for the poor, and named after Dr. Karl Bremer (q.v.) who introduced it. It never became popular.

Bremer, Dr. Karl. Cabinet Minister of German descent. Born in Hopefield, Cape Province, on April 27, 1885. Qualified in medicine. An early follower of General Hertzog (q.v.), he entered Parliament as member for Graaff Reinet in 1924. He was Chairman of the South African Medical Council. Interested in social questions, he became Minister of Health in Dr. Malan's (q.v.) National Cabinet, 1951, and did much to combat malnutrition. Introduced Bremer Bread (q.v.). Died July 18, 1953.

Bremersdorp. *See* MANZINI.

Brenthurst Splint. Medical device used in facial and other surgery, developed by South African surgeons at the Brenthurst Military Hospital, Johannesburg, during World War II, and now used throughout the world. Brenthurst was the private residence of the late Sir Ernest Oppenheimer (q.v.), which he lent to the authorities.

Brews, Sydney. South African golf champion. Born at Blackheath, London, May 29, 1899, and educated in Stroud, Gloucestershire. Came to South Africa and between 1925 and 1952 won the South African Open Championship eight times. In 1934 he became a professional at the Houghton Golf Club, Johannesburg. At various times he won the Belgian, French,

Dutch and Philadelphia Open Championships, and was runner-up in the British Open Championship.

Breyten. Village in the Eastern Transvaal, near the source of the Vaal River (q.v.). Founded in 1906 and named after I. J. Breytenbach, the local blacksmith in the early days. Farming centre. Population: 11,100, including 2,000 Whites.

Bristowe, Leonard Syer. Transvaal judge. Born on October 14, 1857, and educated in England, where he took his law degree and was called to the Bar in 1882. After practising in London, during which time he wrote several legal works, he came to the Transvaal. There, in 1903, he was appointed to the Bench. Outside his legal career, he was keenly interested in theosophy and education. In 1922 he returned to England, where he died on April 5, 1935.

Britannia Rock. One of the three huge granite boulders on the Paarl Mountain, whose pearl-like lustre in the sun gave the town its name. *See also* GORDON ROCK.

British Kaffraria. Former separate colony, although under the Governor of the Cape. It was created December 17, 1847, when certain areas west of the Kei River were declared a separate dependency, capital, King William's Town (q.v.). The local chiefs were granted power, later surrendered in return for allowances in money. In 1855 there were only 949 Europeans, apart from troops (but this number grew to 5,895 in 1859, mainly through the coming of the German Legion, q.v.), and about 53,000 natives. East London was the official port. On March 7, 1860, British Kaffraria was proclaimed a separate province, with its own administration under a Lieutenant-Governor, Lieutenant-Colonel John Maclean (q.v.), previously Chief Commissioner. On April 17, 1866, British Kaffraria was incorporated into Cape Colony, and divided into the two districts of King William's Town and East London.

British South Africa Company. Following the grant, on October 29, 1888, of a concession for the mineral rights in Matabeleland by King Lobengula, a charter was issued by Queen Victoria on October 15, 1889, to Cecil John Rhodes, Alfred Beit, Albert Grey, George Cawston, the Duke of Abercorn and the Duke of Fife, authorising them to establish the British South Africa Company, with a capital of £1,000,000 and vast powers, including those to occupy territory, enter into diplomatic relations and carry out military expeditions. As a result the Pioneer Column (q.v.) was sent north to colonise and administer Rhodesia. A supplementary charter was issued on June 8, 1900. After the inquiry by the Cave Commission (q.v.) £4,435,225 was fixed as compensation for rights taken over by the Rhodesian Government from the company. Considerable dissatisfaction having arisen over the system of government by the company, discussions proceeded from 1914 onwards as to Responsible Government, or alternative absorption into the Union. The proposal put forward by General Smuts in 1922, to take over the assets of the B.S.A. Company for £6,836,000, was accepted by the shareholders. The scheme fell through because of the outcome of the Referendum, under which the plan for joining the Union was rejected by the voters. Since the establishment of Responsible Government in 1923, the B.S.A. Company concentrated mainly on the development of its lands and mineral assets, particularly in Zambia. For many years it hardly paid dividends, but in recent times the development of the copper industry, coupled with the ownership of the mineral rights for enormous areas, has more than made up for the shortfalls. Supplementary charters were issued on March 13, 1915, and March 25, 1924. On June 29, 1933, the Southern Rhodesian Government bought the B.S.A. Company's mineral rights in that area for £2,000,000 cash. Following the taking over of its rights in Zambia by the Government the Company was absorbed in 1965 into Charter Investments, in association with Anglo-American Corporation and Central Mining (q.v.).

British South Africa Police. Under its charter, granted in 1889, the British South Africa Company had authority to establish its own police force, which absorbed large numbers of the Bechuanaland Border Police, formed in 1885, soon after the occupation of that country. Units of the British South Africa Police accompanied the Pioneer Column in 1890, and began work immediately after the founding of Fort Salisbury. They did gallant service, not only in normal duties but in the Matabele War, the Mashona Rebellion and in the Boer War, when 300 men took part. During World War I the British South Africa Police gained additional fame in association with the Northern Rhodesian Police. This tradition was maintained in World War II, particularly in the Middle East theatre. Headquarters are in Salisbury, though much recruiting is still conducted in Britain. The force has produced two V.C.s, the late Major R. C. Nesbitt and Captain F. C. Booth.

Brits. Township in the Transvaal, north of Pretoria, centre of the irrigation area served from the famous Haartebeestpoort Dam. Leading tobacco and wheat centre. Founded about 1925 and named after prominent local farmers. Population: 15,500, including 5,500 Whites.

Britstown. Karroo village, founded 1877, and named after its founder. About 30 miles west of De Aar, its importance is mainly as an overnight halt for motorists on the Cape-Rand highway, and as a wheat centre. Population: 2,834, including 847 Whites.

Broadbill (*Smithornis capensis*). Resembling a flycatcher (q.v.). Tropical bird, represented by many local varieties in different parts of Africa. The Natal form is found in dense bush and forest along the coastal belt of that province and Zululand and through Eastern Transvaal. It has a remarkable call uttered while circling at great speed.

Broadcasting. At least one South African made a considerable contribution to the evolution of radio telephony and of broadcasting, through his research work on the thermionic valve. That was Dr. H. J. van der Bijl (q.v.), also author of the standard treatise on the subject. Experimental broadcasting began in South Africa in 1919, but remained in the hands of amateurs until 1922, when a temporary station was set up by the South African Railways to raise funds for the Empire Exhibition at Wembley. The first regular programmes began on July 1, 1924, in Johannesburg, under the auspices of the Associated Scientific and Technical Societies on the roof of Stuttafords' Building, Pritchard Street. This was followed by a similar venture in Cape Town in September 1924 and, on December 10, 1924, in Durban. Financial and technical handicaps led to a temporary shut-down at Johannesburg and progress was so slow that in 1930 there were only 25,121 licences in the Union. At this stage broadcasting was taken over by I. W. Schlesinger (q.v.) who formed the African Broadcasting Company, which incorporated existing stations, installed new equipment, took on extra staff and so increased audiences that when, in 1936, the South African Broadcasting Corporation (q.v.) was formed the licences issued had risen to 120,000, and the figure has since passed 1,800,000. Very High Frequency Modulation was in-

troduced in 1961, when the first of a chain of stations, designed ultimately to cover the whole of South Africa and South-West Africa, came into operation. Bantu broadcasts with a special Bantu staff have become an important part of the organisation in recent years. *See also* RHODESIAN BROADCASTING CORPORATION, TELEVISION and WIRELESS TELEGRAPHY.

Broken Hill. *See* KABWE.

Bronkhorstspruit. Village in the Transvaal, 38 miles from Pretoria, scene of the ambush of the 94th Regiment under Colonel P. Anstruther by the Boers on December 20, 1880. This marked the start of the First Boer War and cost many lives. In 1904 a township was laid out, called Erasmus after its founder C. J. G. Erasmus. It was renamed Bronkhorstspruit in 1929. Flour-milling centre. Population: 2,246, including 1,400 Whites.

Brooke, Brian (originally **Brian Brooke Thompson**). South African actor-producer. Born at Sabie, Transvaal, September 27, 1911, and educated at Grahamstown and the University of the Witwatersrand. Went to England in 1935 to study the stage and served during World War II in the British Army, being present at the Normandy landings and in the campaign through France and Germany. Married the well-known London actress, Petrina Fry. Returned to South Africa in 1946 and started the first professional repertory company in Cape Town, later moving his headquarters to Johannesburg. He brought many stars to the country, including Dame Sybil Thorndike, Sir Lewis Casson, Emlyn Williams, Gwen Ffrangçon-Davies and Claude Hulbert, and has produced more than 200 plays in South Africa. Retired 1969.

Brookes, Dr. Edgar Harry. South African scholar and social worker. Born at Smethwick in 1897, he studied at the University of South Africa and the London School of Economics. In 1923 he became Professor of Public Administration and Political Science at the Transvaal University College, Pretoria, a post he held for 10 years. Meanwhile he entered public life, serving on the South African delegation to the League of Nations in 1927. Deeply interested in the advancement of the non-European in his own country, he was one of the founders of the South African Institute of Race Relations, of which he later became president. From 1933 to 1945 he was principal of the well-known mission foundation, Adams College in Natal. He was elected as a representative of the Bantu in the Union Senate in 1937, sitting there till 1952. In 1947 he served on the Union delegation to the United Nations. From 1959 he was Professor of History in the University of Natal.

Broom, Dr. Robert. Fellow of the Royal Society. South African palaeontologist. Born in Scotland on November 30, 1866, and studied medicine in Glasgow. Appointed Professor of Geology and Zoology at Victoria College, Stellenbosch (now University of Stellenbosch), his study of fossil animals of the sub-continent soon won him a world reputation. From 1897 he produced over 250 scientific papers. Particularly important were his researches on the mammal-like reptiles of South Africa and on early man. He was responsible for the discovery of very early relics in the Sterkfontein Caves and elsewhere. *See* 'MRS. PLES.' In 1920 he was elected a Fellow of the Royal Society, one of the few South Africans to gain this honour. He died in 1951.

Broome, William. Judge, Natal Supreme Court. Born on April 12, 1852, in Greece and educated at Victoria College, Jersey; came to South Africa in 1872, and entered the Natal Civil Service in 1875, in which he held the

offices of Assistant Colonial Secretary, Magistrate of Newcastle and Registrar of the Supreme Court. In 1904 he was appointed to the Natal Supreme Court Bench. He died in August 1930.

Brown, Mrs. John. South African social reformer and worker for women's rights. Born as Mary Solomon on July 20, 1847, she was the daughter of Henry Solomon and the niece of the famous Cape statesman, Saul Solomon (q.v.). At 19 she married Dr. John Brown, and began public work in the Karroo town of Fraserburg. In 1876 they settled in Britain, where for more than 20 years she was famed for her work among the Lancashire working class. In 1905 she returned to South Africa, devoting most of her time to temperance reform, interracial problems, relief of distress arising from the Boer War, and increased privileges for women. She died in 1935.

Brownlee, The Hon. Charles. Native administrator and pioneer. Son of the Rev. John Brownlee (q.v.), he was born at a mission station on the Cape frontier in 1827, and began his career as interpreter for a group of American missionaries in Natal. After farming he took part in the War of the Axe, 1846, and was appointed 'Gaika Commissioner,' an ambassadorial post to the natives, living at Fort Cox, a military outpost. He remained a key man in the Government relations with the frontier tribes. He was wounded during the war of 1852, but later returned to the Gaika country at Döhne. His diplomacy was tested during the Cattle Killing Delusion (q.v.) among the Xosas, and again during the settlement of the German Legion in 1856 and 1857. He later held a magistracy in Somerset East and was promoted to Secretary for Native Affairs. He died in King William's Town in 1890.

Brownlee, The Reverend John. Missionary and founder of King

William's Town. Born near Wishaw, Scotland, on May 1, 1791, he joined the London Missionary Society, who sent him to the Cape in 1817. In 1820 he accepted the joint post of missionary and Government representative in the frontier region of Kaffraria, and made his home in the Tyumie Valley. He soon acquired great influence among the neighbouring tribes, and in 1825 resumed his connection with the London Missionary Society. The station which he established was on the site presently occupied by King William's Town. He died there on December 21, 1871.

Brukkaros, Mount. *See* MOUNT BRUKKAROS.

Brulsande. Literally 'roaring sands.' A strange geological formation in Griqualand West, near Posmasburg, where a peculiarity in the grains of sand produces a roar when the dunes are walked upon.

Brusher or **White Biskop.** *See* BREAM.

Bryant, Father A. T. Catholic missionary and Zulu scholar. Born in London in 1865, he was educated at the University of London and, joining the Catholic priesthood, reached Natal in 1883. He settled at the newly-established mission of Mariannhill (q.v.) and was ordained in 1887. First he worked in the Transkei among the Xosas and Tembus, but in 1896 arrived in Zululand, where he spent the rest of his life. His major fame rests upon his Zulu-English dictionary, which first appeared in 1903 with over 20,000 entries. After this came works on Zulu history and ethnology, now regarded as classics. For 3 years, from 1920 to 1923, Father Bryant was lecturer in Bantu studies at the University of the Witwatersrand. He died in 1953.

Bryden, Henry Anderson. South African hunter, explorer and author. Born in Oxfordshire in 1854, he was educated at Cheltenham College and at Wimbledon. He was a well-known sportsman in his youth, and one of England's early Rugby players. In 1876 he came to South Africa, where he showed an immediate interest in hunting and natural history. After a spell in the eastern part of the Karroo he moved to Bechuanaland, which he explored. Much of the information which he secured while hunting in the northern Kalahari was later used by the British War Office. During the 1880's he was involved in discussions on the political future of Bechuanaland and was a member of the so-called South African Committee which favoured the cause of Paramount Chief Khama (q.v.). It was claimed that because of Bryden's writings Bechuanaland did not come under the control of the British South Africa Company. From 1889, starting with his famous *Kloof and Karroo,* a long series of books came from his pen, including *Gun and Camera in Southern Africa, Tales of South Africa, Nature and Sport in South Africa* and *The Victorian Era in South Africa.* Besides history and travel books he wrote novels and works on natural history and the practical side of hunting. His later years were spent in England where he died in 1937.

B.S.A. Company. *See* BRITISH SOUTH AFRICA COMPANY.

B.S.A. Police. *See* BRITISH SOUTH AFRICA POLICE.

Bubonic Plague. Southern Africa experienced an outbreak of bubonic plague during the South African War, brought to Cape Town by infected linen on ships coming from Asia. Large parts of the slum area known as District Six were demolished. None the less there were several hundred deaths. A revival took place in 1903 among Indian coolies imported to the Rand. Since then fleas and rodents have been carefully watched for infection.

Buchan, John (Lord Tweedsmuir). Author of several South African books and a former Transvaal official. Born in Scotland in 1875, he was educated at Glasgow University and Oxford. In 1901 he became Private Secretary to Lord Milner, High Commissioner for South Africa, and was one of the leading members of his 'Kindergarten,' remaining there until 1903. Among his books one of the most successful is *Prester John*, which is largely based on his experiences in the Transvaal Civil Service. He also wrote in 1920 *The South African Forces in France*. In later years Buchan held many prominent positions in Britain and was Governor-General of Canada. He died in 1940.

Buchanan, Ebenezer John. Senior Puisne Judge, Cape Town. Born on March 8, 1844, at Pietermaritzburg, he was called to the Inner Temple and returned to the Cape where he was admitted to the Bar in 1873. After serving as M.P. for Worcester in the Cape Parliament, he was appointed to the Bench at Grahamstown in 1880, and transferred to Cape Town in 1887. From 1892 to 1920 he served as Senior Puisne Judge. Outside his legal career his interests were mainly centred in freemasonry and education. He died in October 1930.

Buchanan, James. Judge-President of the High Court of Griqualand. Born in Cape Town on September 21, 1841, and educated at the South African College. He was called to the Cape Bar in 1865 and practised there until, in 1872, he became Staats Prokureur of the South African Republic. After serving as judge in the Orange Free State from 1876 to 1880, he was Recorder of Griqualand West and Judge-President in 1882, retiring in 1887. His literary work included translations of Roman-Dutch Law and notes to the Menzies Reports. He died in England in December 1893.

Buchu (Reitraceae). A Hottentot word. Erect, branching shrub up to 6 feet, with small pinkish-white flowers and strongly aromatic leaves, used medicinally—Buchu brandy is an excellent tonic—and for flavouring brandy. Mountain and open kloofs in Western Province, mostly above 1,000 feet. Both *Barosma crenulata* and *Barosma betulina* yield folia buchu. The family includes *China Flower* and *Shepherd's Delight* (Adenandra), little Cape mountain shrubs with pink 5-petalled flowers and aromatic leaves, and the beautiful *Cape Chestnut* (Calodendrum) (*see* CHESTNUT, CAPE).

Bucklands. Village near Herbert, Cape Province. Population: 1,174, including 212 Whites.

Buffalo. Large animal found in the Eastern Cape Province, particularly in the Addo National Park, in Natal, the Kruger National Park, Rhodesia, and beyond. It prefers country where there is plenty of thorn bush, with grazing and sufficient water. Buffalo are extremely dangerous to hunt on account of their unpredictable behaviour and aggressiveness. The larger type averages 5 feet in height at the shoulder, while the Dwarf Congo variety is a foot smaller. Owing to their part in spreading cattle diseases a considerable number of buffalo have been killed off in recent years under supervision.

Buffalo River: 1. River in Eastern Cape Province, rising in Amatola Mountains and entering the sea at East London. King William's Town is also on the Buffalo River. The mouth has been enlarged sufficiently to admit mail-ships, a special feature being the huge 'turning basin' at East London. Length of river 75 miles.

2. River in Natal, a tributary of the Tugela. Played important part in operations during the Zulu War of 1879.

Buffelsbank. Diamond-mining centre in Namaqualand, established 1969 on lease from Coloured Development Corporation in Komaggas Reserve.

Buffels Bay. Small inlet in False Bay near Cape Point, noted for its fishing.

Bukama. Town on the Upper Congo, in the Belgian Congo, where the railhead of the line from South Africa and Rhodesia arrived in 1909.

Bulawayo. Second largest city of Rhodesia. It owes its name to the Matabele kraal, Gubulawayo, some miles outside, where Lobengula (q.v.) originally held court. Bulawayo itself was founded in 1893, immediately after the defeat of Lobengula by the forces of the Chartered Company, and the destruction of his capital. It grew rapidly, and within a year could boast of a Stock Exchange and other amenities, which, however, did not prevent the place from being exposed to considerable danger with the outbreak of the Matabele Rebellion (q.v.), when the inhabitants were obliged to go into laager. The present population (urban area) is estimated at about 248,000, including 51,000 Europeans and 190,000 Africans. The municipal area is 45·8 sq. miles. The arrival of the railway at Bulawayo in 1897 gave it a great impetus, and it became the main centre not only of the administration of the local system but for the supplies to mining industries. Today it has many amenities, including a large park, a Government House, a fine museum, library, the Supreme Court, etc. There are a considerable number of industries, both light and heavy, for which special townships have been laid out. Local manufactures include textiles, pottery, cement, vehicles, engineering, furniture, asbestos.

Bulawayo Chronicle. Daily newspaper issued in Bulawayo, Rhodesia, established on October 12, 1894, and published daily from May 1897. It has been renamed *The Chronicle* in recent years.

Bulbul (family Pycnonotidae). Belongs to a small family of well-known birds, of which the Toppie (*Pycnonotus tricolor layardi*) is the best known. Dark brown with black crest and yellow vent-patch. Very sociable and found everywhere. Usually olive-green. The Cape Bulbul (no black cap) is equally common. All have ringing voices and sing little phrases. A noisy, excitable group and greedy fruit eaters. The Sombre Bulbul or Piet is a bush dweller, more often heard than seen. *See* BIRDS.

Bulhoek. *See* ISRAELITES.

Buller, General Sir Redvers Henry. British soldier. Born in 1839 at Crediton, Devonshire, of a very old West Country family, he went to school at Eton and joined the Army in 1858. After service in India and China he was transferred to Canada, and attracted the notice of General Wolseley (q.v.), who in 1873 took him to West Africa as Intelligence Officer during the Ashanti Campaign. He first saw South Africa during a Native War in 1879, won the V.C. for gallantry during the Zulu War, and was Chief of Staff in the Majuba campaign of 1881 to Sir Evelyn Wood (q.v.). Further service followed in Egypt, the Sudan and Ireland. In 1896 he was promoted to general and in 1898 received a high post at the War Office. On the outbreak of the South African War in 1899, he was sent to the front as commander-in-chief, but found his Colonial war tactics ineffective against the Boers. He was defeated at Colenso, Spion Kop and Vaalkrans, and later superseded by Lord Roberts (q.v.). Despite useful further service, including relief of Ladysmith and victory at Bergendal, he returned to England in 1901, and took command at Aldershot. He died in 1908.

Bultfontein. Village in the Orange Free State, founded in 1870. Not far from Brandfort. Population: 4,200, including 1,800 Whites.

Bultfontein. Famous diamond mine at Kimberley (q.v.).

Bulwer. Township in Natal. Established during term of office of Governor Sir Henry Bulwer (1875–1880) and named after him. Sheep farming and forestry centre, 5,177 feet above sea-level. Population: 500, including 180 Whites.

Bulwer, Sir Henry Ernest Gascoigne. Governor of Natal. Born in England in 1836, a relative of the novelist Bulwer-Lytton (author of *The Last Days of Pompeii*). After studying at Cambridge he entered the diplomatic service, being sent to the Ionian Islands as Official Resident. There he stayed from 1860 to 1864 before being transferred to the embassy staff at Constantinople. After some years in the West Indies he was appointed Governor of Labuan in Borneo in 1871 and in 1875 Governor of Natal, with the extra title of Special Commissioner for Zulu Affairs. During his period of office he had the critical situation of the first British occupation of the Transvaal, the Zulu War and the Majuba Campaign to deal with. In 1886 Bulwer became High Commissioner for Cyprus. He retired in 1892 and for many years lived near Norwich. Died September 30, 1914.

Bunga. The accepted Native name of the United Transkeian Territories General Council, a statutory body of chiefs, magistrates and elected Native representatives, with considerable legislative powers. It was established in 1895 for the districts of Butterworth, Idutywa, Nqamakwe and Tsomo as the Transkei General Council, and extended to cover East Griqualand and Tembuland in 1903 as the Transkeian Territories General Council. In 1931 the Pondoland General Council was added and it became the United Transkeian Territories General Council. The Bunga had its own building in Umtata. *See*

TRANSKEI and CONSTITUTION OF SOUTH AFRICA.

Bunting (family Fringillidae). Small South African singing bird, belonging to Finch family, found in most parts of the country. Buntings are not such songsters as finches (canaries) but still have pretty little chirrups. Except for the Golden-breasted Bunting (abundant near Victoria Falls, and much like a chaffinch) they are quiet little brown birds.

Bunting, Brian. Politician and journalist. Born in Johannesburg, 1920, son of S. P. Bunting (q.v.), a founder of the Communist Party in South Africa, attended Jeppe High School and University of the Witwatersrand. His journalistic career on the *Rand Daily Mail* ended by his joining the Information Section of the South African Air Force during World War II. When peace came he worked for the Springbok Legion (q.v.) and in 1946 joined staff of the *Guardian*, organ of South African Communist Party, and in 1948 became editor. Elected Bantu Parliamentary Representative for Western Cape 1952, but lost his seat through legislation directed against Communism. He left for England in 1963.

Bunting, Sidney Percival. South African Communist leader. Born in England in 1873, the son of Sir Percy Bunting, founder and editor of the well-known *Contemporary Review*, he gave no indication of his political future when young. Educated at St. Paul's School and Oxford he came to South Africa as a volunteer in the South African War, and settled in Johannesburg as a solicitor. There he developed into a champion of the African and after 1913 was deeply interested in the Labour movement. After World War I he went to Russia, became an enthusiastic Communist and helped to establish the movement in South Africa. For his political activities Bunting was repeatedly imprisoned yet he was superseded by others approved in Moscow. He died in 1936.

Burchell, William John. English explorer and traveller at the Cape. Born in 1782 in Fulham, the son of a nurseryman, he joined the English East India Company's service in 1805, in the dual capacity of 'Schoolmaster and Acting Botanist.' After a spell at St. Helena he reached Cape Town in 1810, learnt Afrikaans, and began his treks in 1811 in the north, particularly towards Bechuanaland. He remained in South Africa until 1815, during which he gathered a vast amount of scientific information, a large collection of specimens, and made a number of very fine drawings. Only part of his material was used in his *Travels*, which appeared in 2 volumes in 1822, but much of the additional data, preserved at the University of the Witwatersrand, has been made available in recent times. Burchell went to South America in 1825, and returned to England in 1829 with a mass of other valuable matter. His South African book is a classic of travel. He received an honorary doctorate at Oxford in 1834 and died in 1863. His botanical MSS. are preserved at Kew Gardens, London.

Burger, Die. Afrikaans morning newspaper, established on July 26, 1915, with Dr. D. F. Malan as editor. Its foundation marked the beginning of the Nasionale Pers (q.v.) and it has always remained a strong supporter of the National Party.

Burger, General Schalk. Acting President of the South African Republic. Born in Lydenburg, Transvaal, in 1862, became commandant during the Majuba campaign in 1881, was elected to the Volksraad and in 1896 became member of the Executive Council and later Chairman of the Volksraad. He stood for the Presidency in 1898, but was defeated. In the South African War he commanded the Lydenburg units and on the departure of President

Kruger for Europe in 1900 was made Acting President. As such he signed the Treaty of Vereeniging. After a visit to raise funds for war victims in Europe he became Deputy Leader of 'Het Volk' (q.v.) under Botha and later the South African Party. He died in 1918.

Burgersfort. *See* FORT BURGER.

Burgers, Petrus W. Judge of the Transvaal High Court. Born in Graaff-Reinet in 1854, he was called to the Bar in 1882 and immediately appointed to the Bench of the Transvaal High Court, serving until 1886. He became State Attorney in 1893 and died in 1894.

Burgers, Thomas François. President of the South African Republic. Born on April 15, 1834, near Graaff-Reinet, he studied for the ministry at the University of Utrecht in Holland, and returned to South Africa in 1858. His first congregation was at Hanover in Cape Colony, where he became involved in violent theological controversy on account of his alleged liberalism and disbelief in the literal truth of the Bible. This resulted in litigation. In spite of this he was in 1873 invited by the burghers of the South African Republic to take over the Presidency of the country upon the resignation of President M. W. Pretorius (q.v.). Elected by a large majority over William Robinson, the other candidate, he found himself confronted with a host of difficulties in the Transvaal. A man of great enthusiasm, eloquence and charm, he was none the less recognised as ahead of his time. Head of a country still in a very primitive state and lacking in funds, he attempted an ambitious programme, including the construction of railways. Undertaking a trip overseas he succeeded in raising a certain amount of money on loan in the Netherlands. He purchased material for the railway, which was delivered at Lourenço Marques, where it was left to rust. Upon his return he found the South African Republic involved in a costly and difficult war with the chief Sekukuni in the eastern mountains, and, although he did his best to carry on the campaign, even to going into the field, he found himself unable to cope with the situation. This led in 1877 to the occupation of the Republic by Sir Theophilus Shepstone and his force of 25 policemen, who annexed the country to the British Crown. Unable to secure adequate support from his fellow-citizens, he resigned and went into retirement. He died in 1881. Apart from his political work, he is known as the author of *Sketse uit het Boeren Leven*, which is of literary interest.

Burgersdorp. Town in the Cape Midlands. Founded in 1844 and originally called Klipdrift (not to be confused with the Klipdrift in Griqualand West (q.v.)). Lies near the Stormberg Mountains. In 1861, a theological seminary was started here by the Dutch Reformed Churches, later moved to Potchefstroom. Because of its importance in the early struggle for the rights of the Dutch language a 'Taalmonument' (Language Monument) was erected here in 1893. Scene of fighting during South African War. Population: 10,600, including 3,100 Whites.

Burgerville. Small village 20 miles from De Aar (q.v.). Abandoned about 1910. Because of its water supply the site was later purchased by the town of De Aar.

Burgher Senate. Local authority and Court of Justice established 1796 in Cape Town, with seven members, later reduced to five. Abolished in 1828.

Burnham, Frederick Russell. American soldier and scout. Born in Minnesota, 1862, he spent his youth under conditions of great hardship, and picked up much of his scouting lore in contact with the Red Indians. After an

adventurous youth he found his way to South Africa in 1893. On arrival he was involved in the Matabele War, in which he distinguished himself, and gained the friendship of Cecil Rhodes. He took part in the Matabele Rebellion of 1896 and during the South African War was appointed 'Chief of Scouts' to Lord Roberts. Upon his return to the United States he established the Boy Scout Movement there. Scout Burnham, as he was usually called, died in 1947.

Burton Bread. Introduced during World War I into South Africa by Henry Burton (q.v.). To reduce the importation of wheat, this loaf included mealie flour. Ignorance on the part of the bakers made it a failure.

Burton, Henry. South African politician and statesman. Born in Cape Town, 1866, and educated at St. Andrew's College, Grahamstown. Admitted to the Bar in 1892 and began to practise in Kimberley, where he soon attained success. Because of the Jameson Raid he became a strong supporter of the Afrikander Bond (q.v.), for which he was elected to Parliament in 1902. Almost immediately after entering the House, Burton was responsible for the downfall of the ministry of Sir Gordon Sprigg on the martial law and war losses issues. J. X. Merriman took him into his cabinet in 1908 as Attorney-General, and after Union he became first Minister of Native Affairs and later of Railways. His temperament annoyed the railwaymen and he transferred to the Ministry of Finance in 1920, where he carried out unpopular economies. He retired from Parliament in 1924 and died in 1935.

Burton, Sir William Westbrooke. Judge, Cape Supreme Court. Born in Daventry, Northamptonshire, in 1794, he embarked on a naval career, abandoning which he was called to the Bar in 1824. Coming to the Cape, he was appointed judge of the Cape Supreme Court in 1827. He left South Africa to take up an appointment in New South Wales in 1833 and from there went on to India. He died in London on August 6, 1888.

Burtt-Davy, Dr. Joseph. South African botanist. Born in Derby, 1870, he studied at Cambridge as well as at the University of California and Cornell in the United States. At the early age of 21 he became assistant to the Director of the Royal Botanic Gardens at Kew, near London, and later, from 1893 to 1896, assistant in the Department of Botany at the University of California. Joining the service of the California State Agricultural Experiment Station in 1896, he was their botanist for five years and subsequently held other important posts in the United States. In 1903 he was invited to join the newly-established Department of Agriculture at Pretoria, under the Milner régime, holding the position of Government Agrostologist and Botanist and Chief of the Division of Botany from that year until 1913. He wrote a large number of botanical works on South Africa and organised a botanical survey of the country. In later years Dr. Burtt-Davy settled in England. He died in 1940.

Bushbuck (*Tragelaphus scriptus*). Antelope found in the Knysna Forest and other wooded parts as far as East Africa. It averages about 3 feet at the shoulder and is considered fairly good eating. The males carry short, twisted horns. There are three different varieties: the Harnessed Buschbuck, mostly in Rhodesia; the Cape Bushbuck, in the Cape and Natal; and Gordon-Cumming's Bushbuck, in the Transvaal and Rhodesia.

Bush Cart. Two-wheeled vehicle introduced to South African army in 1936 at the instigation of Oswald Pirow (q.v.) as Minister of Defence. Designed to be manoeuvrable in bush-covered country, it proved a failure and was the subject of much ridicule.

Bushman Paintings. The form of art loosely referred to as Bushman paintings and engravings is encountered over a large part of Southern Africa, and is of the greatest interest both for its inherent excellence and the primitiveness of the artists. Bushman paintings have been found from Rhodesia to South West Africa and from the Cape almost to the Zambesi. Favourite places are the walls of caves, as well as rock shelters and protected natural ledges. Subjects preferred are wild animals, human figures, hunting scenes and, on a more limited scale, domestic animals. How far back many of the Bushmen paintings go is difficult to determine, but many are certainly centuries old. On the other hand there are also paintings showing White men in modern costume. One of the first to study the subject systematically, nearly a century ago, was George W. Stow (q.v.), who succeeded in enlisting the co-operation of Dr. W. H. I. Bleek (q.v.). Many of the most valuable paintings have unfortunately been destroyed through neglect or vandalism, but today there is legislative protection. The retreat of the surviving Bushmen into the desolate parts of the Kalahari desert has helped to reduce the amount of material available for study. A fair number of paintings have been moved from the sites and placed in museums, but today their export is forbidden. The paintings are characterised by strength of draughtsmanship, simplicity of design and unity of colouring, the last being largely due to the limited number of pigments available to the artists. Modern experts compare the bold use of simple colours with present-day poster technique. Theories put forward by Professor Leo Frobenius, ascribing the origin of the Bushman paintings to a hypothetical 'Erythrean Race' of high civilisation which inhabited large parts of Africa in bygone times, have not found much outside support. Besides paintings, Bushmen have been responsible for 'engravings' which have been 'pecked' into the rock with the aid of flint and similar hard substances. Paintings have also been found on ostrich egg shells and even on the walls of buildings. *See also* ARCHAEOLOGY.

Bushman Rice. Name applied to the eggs of certain types of termites, for this reason known to the Boers as 'rysmier.' They closely resemble rice in appearance, and were actually eaten by the Bushmen.

Bushman's River: 1. In Eastern Cape Province. Seaside resort of the same name near its mouth, between Port Elizabeth and Port Alfred. At Kwaai Hoek, near the mouth, Bartholemew Diaz marked the easternmost limit of his voyage round the Cape by erecting a beacon cross of stone, which was rediscovered in 1938 by Dr. E. Axelson of Witwatersrand University.

2. River in Natal, passing town of Estcourt, tributary of Tugela River.

Bushmen. Primitive race regarded as the aboriginal inhabitants of most of Southern Africa. Of very small stature, rarely over 5 feet, they possess a number of physical characteristics peculiar to themselves, notably their wrinkled appearance, extraordinarily keen eyesight, skill as trackers, sense of music and art, and tendency to accumulate vast masses of fat in their buttocks. They show considerable links with the pygmies of Central Africa and are believed to have emigrated from those parts. Their language abounds in clicks, and has only been studied with the greatest difficulty owing to the inability of scholars to make friends with them in the earlier days. They are divided into a number of different groups, notably the Masarwa, who live in the Kalahari. In earlier times there were two types, those who dwelt on hills and those who preferred to live in

caves. None of them possessed the ability to build houses or huts, their accommodation being the most primitive shelters made of branches. Nor did they have tribal organisation in any accepted sense of the word. Upon the advent of the European they were unwilling to make friends, with the result that they were hunted down and almost exterminated. The survivors mostly retired to inaccessible parts, and today the few that are still to be found live in the Kalahari and other barren areas. The number of true Bushmen living today is difficult to estimate, but it is doubtful whether there are more than 1–2,000, most of them in South West Africa. Only in recent times has it become possible to publish a comprehensive dictionary of the Bushman language, mainly as the result of efforts going back to the 1850's on the part of the late Dr. W. H. I. Bleek (q.v.), who continued the efforts of an early missionary, the Rev. Kroenlein, to write down a small vocabulary. Dr. Bleek's work was supplemented by that of Miss L. Lloyd and of his daughter, Miss Dorothea Bleek. To this day the Bushmen are unique in having virtually no missionaries working among them. The country first inhabited by them included not only most of the Cape but also large parts of Lesotho, the Drakensberg and the Transvaal. *See* BUSHMAN PAINTINGS.

Bush Pigs (*Potamochoerus porcus*). Pugnacious animals found in a wide region of Southern Africa, extending from the Eastern Cape Province to Rhodesia and beyond. They prefer thickly-forested country and marshy ground, where they can wallow. They consume a variety of food, including reptiles, insects and eggs. They grow over 2 feet high and usually over 3 feet long, are moderately good eating and are frequently hunted by Europeans and natives. They should not be confused with Wart hogs (q.v.), having smaller tusks, thicker hair, tufts of hair at the tips of their ears and a grunt like that of the domestic pig. They are also noisier and hold up their heads and tails when running, while Wart Hogs hold them down.

Bush Tea, Rooibos Tee, Heuning Tee (*Cyclopia genistoides* and *C. vogelii*). Wild shrubs with small spiky leaves and yellow pea flowers, today cultivated commercially in the Western and North-Western Cape Province. The leafy twigs, fermented and dried, are boiled to make a herb tea, free of tannin. Very similar is *Black Tea* or *Swart Tee* (*Aspalaties tennifolia*). Through the work of Dr. L. Nortier, a method of growing it from seed was discovered near Clanwilliam. Nieuwoudtville (q.v.) is the centre of the Industry. *See* PEA, WILD SWEET.

Bushveld. Term loosely applied to certain lower sub-tropical areas of South Africa, especially in the Transvaal and Swaziland. Bushveld extends northwards from Pretoria to the Limpopo River; altitude up to about 4,000 feet. The name is derived from the dominating thornbush vegetation. *See* VELD.

Bushveld Igneous Complex. Unique geological formation in the central Transvaal, the subject of study by experts not only in South Africa but likewise overseas. Measuring nearly 300 miles from east to west, and several miles in thickness, this 'Lopolith,' as it has been called (from the Greek 'lopos,' a basin), is described by the distinguished geologist, Dr. A. L. Du Toit, as 'one of the most remarkable geological occurrences in the whole world.'

Bustards (Paauws and Korhaans) (family Otidae). Handsome game birds of open plains, well represented in South Africa. Good runners, with long, strong legs. Live mainly on large insects, especially locusts. The largest of

this group, the Gom Pou (40 lb. or more), lives on the Highveld and in Rhodesia. So named from the belief that it eats gum.

Butcher Bird (family Lanius). *See* SHRIKES.

Butha Buthe. Village in Lesotho, the original home of the great chieftain Moshesh before he created the Basuto nation. The name means 'The Place of Lying Down.' Trading centre, with fine mountain scenery near by.

Butler, Lady Elizabeth. Born in 1845 as Elizabeth Thompson at Lausanne in Switzerland. Having studied art in Italy, she soon gained considerable distinction as a painter, specialising in battle scenes, noted for their stirring quality and beautiful finish. In 1877 she married Lt.-Gen. Sir William Francis Butler (q.v.), with whom she spent part of her life in South Africa. Many of her paintings are on South African themes, as, for instance, the Defence of Rorke's Drift, done in 1881. She also wrote about some of her experiences in South Africa. Lady Butler died in 1933.

Butler, Frederick Guy. South African poet and scholar. Born in Cradock, C.P. in 1918 and educated at Rhodes University and Oxford. After a teaching career and service in World War II he became Professor of English at Rhodes University in 1952. He was a founder of the English Academy of South Africa (q.v.). Edited *Standpunte* and *New Coin*. Author of *The Dam*, *Take Root or Die*, *Cape Charade* etc.

Butler, Lt.-General Sir William Francis. Born 1838 in Tipperary, Ireland, and educated in Dublin. At the age of 20 he entered the 69th Regiment and served in the East as well as Canada. His first experience of South Africa was on the staff of General Sir Garnet Wolseley (q.v.) when the latter was sent to Natal in 1875. Wolseley sent Butler on a confidential mission to

Bloemfontein, and later had him on his staff in the Zulu War, 1879–1880. From 1880 to 1898 he held high positions at Aldershot and elsewhere in Britain. Shortly before the outbreak of the South African War, at the end of 1898, he was placed in command of the troops at the Cape, but aroused considerable odium when he warned the authorities that very large forces would be needed to subdue the Boers. For this he was recalled and placed in command of the Western District in England. In his later years he remained in England, although he revisited South Africa in 1906. He wrote a number of excellent books, including several on South Africa, and died on June 7, 1910.

Butterflies. *See* INSECTS.

Butterfly Fish (family Chaetodon). Tropical and sub-tropical East Coast fish, similar to Coral Fish (q.v.). Mostly yellow, with dark markings. 6–8 inches. Several varieties.

Butterworth. Village in the Transkei. Founded as an outpost by the Wesleyan Mission in 1827 and named after its treasurer in London, the Hon. J. Butterworth, M.P. Destroyed during the Native Wars in 1835 and scene of heavy fighting in 1847. Administrative and farming centre. Population: 2,200, including 1,040 Whites.

Button, Edward. Transvaal mining pioneer and founder of the Eersteling Gold Mine (q.v.).

Button Quail (Turnicidae). A smaller bird than the Quail, with no back toe. The female is larger and a more brightly spotted brown than the male. It is he who incubates the eggs, the female mating with several males in succession. Non-migratory and found chiefly in the north of South Africa.

Buxton. Village near Taung, Cape Province. Population: 1,800, including 250 Whites.

Buxton, Lord (Sydney Charles Buxton). Second Governor-General of the Union of South Africa. Born in 1853 in England, the son of Charles Buxton, M.P., he was educated at Clifton and at Cambridge. His political career began when he was elected to Parliament in 1885. After serving on several inquiries he became Under-Secretary for the Colonies from 1892 to 1895. From 1905 to 1910 he was Postmaster-General, the first Post Office wireless station being opened in 1909 during his régime. From 1910 to 1914 he was President of the Board of Trade, during which time he introduced many important measures, including the first legislation for the unemployed under the National Insurance Act, also the Copyright Act, etc. After receiving a peerage, Buxton in 1914 became Governor-General of the Union, as well as High Commissioner for South Africa. As such he had to deal with the difficult period of World War I and the 1914 Rebellion. He received a deputation of Afrikaner women to secure clemency for the leaders of the revolt, notably General de Wet. He returned to England in 1920 and died in 1934.

Buys, Coenraad. Boer outlaw, born in the Cape. (Also known as **Coenraad de Buy** or **Buis**.) Often referred to as 'The First White Transvaler.' Descended from Huguenot stock, he was born near Montagu in 1761. Falling foul of the law, he took refuge among the Xosas on the eastern frontier, was prominent in the Boer rising against the British in 1797, and, moving again into native territory, gained great influence over the famous chief Gaika. For a while he returned to Swellendam under the régime of the Batavian Republic, but he again became restive and trekked to the northern frontier, finally moving into what later became the Transvaal in 1821. There he lived with native women and founded a coloured clan, which became known as the 'Buys Kaffirs.' They settled in the Zoutpansberg, where they were given valuable farms by the later Republican Government, and where they still exist as a separate community. Buys died about 1823.

Buzzard (family Falconidae). *See* EAGLES.

Bwana Mkubwa. Copper mine in Zambia. Original company formed on March 16, 1910, to exploit ancient workings. Operations continued till 1931, when the more promising developments on the Copper Belt further north rendered its future doubtful. The occurrence is mainly of oxide ore, 771 miles north of Bulawayo.

Byocks. Type of ostrich feather, taken from the wing of a male, and of two colours.

Byrne Settlers. Large group of colonists brought to Natal from the United Kingdom in 1849 by a promoter named J. C. Byrne, who had previously visited the Colony. Byrne, an Irishman, had been in Australia and New Zealand. He persuaded the British Government that, against payment of £10 a head for each adult, immigrants should be granted from 20 to 50 acres each. By 1851, 57 shiploads had come, representing about 4,500 souls, including founders of many of the leading families in Natal. They established *inter alia* the villages of Verulam, Richmond, Byrnetown and York.

C

Cabora Bassa. Large electric power project on Zambesi River (q.v.) in Northern Mozambique, designed to supply that country, as well as South Africa, Rhodesia and Malawi. By damming the Zambesi in a narrow gorge (with a wall 510 feet high) 17,000,000,000 kw will be generated, nearly twice the capacity of the Aswan Dam in Egypt, making it the largest in Africa. South Africa has contracted to buy 1,000 megawatts as from 1974 and to participate in construction. Initial cost R165,000,000. Work began in 1969.

Cachalot Whale. *See* WHALE.

Cachet, Rev. Jan Lion. Pioneer of the Afrikaans language. Born in 1838, of Jewish origin. The family name was Stempel (meaning 'seal'), which was later translated into French, Cachet. He reached South Africa at the age of 23, and became a teacher at Cape Town. Moved to Ladysmith in Natal. Here he studied for the Dutch Reformed ministry, in 1868 receiving his first congregation in Rustenburg, Transvaal. A strong supporter of the Gereformeerde (Dopper) movement, he was lecturer to the Theological College, Burghersdorp. In 1875 he again took up a post in Philipstown. Later was minister at Steynsburg in the Cape, before returning for a chair in the Theological College. Interested in social work, in 1879 he joined an expedition to help the Thirstland Boers. A promoter of the Afrikaans language, he contributed to the original issues of *Die Patrioot* and *Ons Kleintjie*. His book, *Die Sewe Duiwels en wat Hulle Gedoen Het*, was one of the first Afrikaans best-sellers. In 1904 he accompanied the Theological College from Burghersdorp to Potchefstroom, remaining in office until 1910, when he retired. He died in 1912.

Calabash

Cadmium. Mineral found at Broken Hill Mine in Zambia.

Cala. Small town in the Transkei, centre of the Xalanga district (q.v.) and capital of Tembuland. Situated on the Tsomo River, a trout stream, in fine mountain scenery. The name means 'Alongside the Mountains.' Altitude: 4,300 feet. Population: 3,550, including 250 Whites.

Calabash. Kind of melon whose shell is used to hold liquid. *See also* MELON.

Caledon, Earl of. Governor of the Cape. Born 1778 in Ireland, son of an Irish Representative Peer in the House of Lords. Appointed Governor of the Cape Colony 1807. Discouraged slavery by selling Government slaves but also dealt with an attempted slave rebellion (1808). A popular Governor; gave a generous gift to the South African Orphanage before returning to Europe in 1811.

Caledon. Town in the Western Cape Province, named after Earl of Caledon (q.v.). Name changed from Zwartberg in 1813. Noted for hot springs, although the sanatorium, destroyed after World War II, has not been rebuilt. There is also a famous Wild Flower Garden. Important wheat-producing centre. Population: 4,323, including 2,214 Whites.

Calitzdorp. Town in the Cape Province, originally a Dutch Reformed Church settlement on land given by Frederick Calitz in 1821. Important irrigation centre, formerly a leading producer of ostrich feathers. Oudtshoorn is 35 miles distant. Population: 2,300, including 1,000 Whites.

Calvinia. Town in North-Western Cape Province at the foot of Hantam Mountains. Founded in 1851 to commemorate John Calvin, the great reformer. Important sheep district. Wheat is grown near by at Zak River. Population: 6,700, including 2,100 Whites.

Cam and Motor Gold Mine. Famous gold mine in Rhodesia, operated by a company floated in 1910 and reconstructed in 1919. The property, 5 miles east of Gatooma, is the most important single producer in the colony.

Cambridge. Suburb of East London, founded as a separate town in 1856, named after Queen Victoria's son, the Duke of Cambridge, Commander-in-Chief of the British forces. Became a separate municipality in 1902, but was merged with East London in 1942.

Camdeboo. Hilly section of the Graaff-Reinet district adjoining the Sneeuberg Range. Name derived from the Camdeboo River, a Hottentot word, signifying Green Heights or Hills.

Area formerly forested and noted for a kind of Stinkwood.

Cam, Diogo. Portuguese navigator and explorer. Details of his life are incomplete, but in the service of King Alfonso V and later King John II he pushed forward the limits of exploration far beyond previous outposts. One of his major discoveries was finding, in 1482, the mouth of the river Congo, where he erected a stone cross rediscovered in 1886. In 1484 he undertook a further journey and in 1486 reached Cape Cross (in what is now South West Africa). The date of his death is uncertain. He was also known by the Latin name of Jacobus Canus and as Diogo Cão.

Camden Power Station. Large installation in Eastern Transvaal, erected for the Electricity Supply Commission (Escom) (q.v.), with an ultimate capacity of 1,600,000 kilowatts and at a cost estimated at R125,000,000.

Camel. The camel is not indigenous to South Africa. Introduced towards the end of the 19th century by the Cape Government for use by police in the Kalahari and Bechuanaland. Also taken to South West Africa, particularly under the German régime. At the beginning of the present century was introduced into Rhodesia. In parts of South Africa was used for the conveyance of mail. A camel-breeding station was maintained in Bechuanaland shortly after World War I.

Camelopard. See GIRAFFE.

Camel-Thorn. See ACACIA.

Caminhos de Ferro de Moçambique. State-controlled railway system operating in Portuguese East Africa and composed of formerly separate lines. They include the sections from Lourenço Marques to the South African border at Ressano Garcia, to Goba on the border of Swaziland, to Vila Luiza and to Malvernia on the borders of Rhodesia, whence a continuation runs to Bulawayo. A section covers the route from Beira to the Rhodesian frontier and others run from Inhambane to Inharrime, from Queliame to Mocuba and from Nacala to Lake Nyasa. The total length is about 1,500 miles.

Camp. Apart from its accepted meaning, this word is used in Lesotho to describe white settlements in native areas.

Campbell (also **Campbelldorp**). Village between Kimberley and Griquatown. Originally a station of the London Missionary Society, called Knoffel Valley or Bulb Valley, established in 1813. It was renamed after the missionary John Campbell. David Livingstone first encountered his future wife, Mary Moffat, under a tree still standing there. Population: 800, including 250 Whites.

Campbell Rand. Range on the Kaap Plateau of the Northern Cape.

Campbell, Rev. John. Traveller and missionary. Born in Scotland in 1766, he worked for the London Missionary Society. In 1812 he inspected their local stations at the Cape and travelled widely for 2 years. Book of travels, including those in the Bechuanaland country, appeared in 1822. He died in 1840.

Campbell, Dr. Killie (Margaret). South African book collector and antiquarian. Daughter of the late Sir Marshall Campbell (q.v.), one of founders of Natal sugar industry, she spent many years building up one of the finest private Africana libraries, with particular emphasis on early Natal and its Bantu tribes. This she made available to students of all kinds and, with her brother William, arranged for its public ownership after her death. She was also largely responsible for the 'Old House Museum' at Durban, devoted to the early history of Natal. Died in 1965.

Campbell, Sir Malcolm. Racing motorist, born in 1885 in Kent. In the course of his various efforts to make records he tested out the possibilities of Verneuk Pan (q.v.) in the North-Western Cape Province. He died in 1948.

Campbell, Sir Marshall. South African sugar industry pioneer. Born in Glasgow July 10, 1848, reached Natal 1850 and became active in cultivating sugar at Tongaat and Mount Edgecombe. Founder of Natal Estates Ltd., one of the largest sugar companies in South Africa. In 1871 he explored what later became Rhodesia. Sat in Natal Parliament, where he was regarded as an expert on Bantu affairs. He died in 1917.

Campbell, Roy (Ignatius Roy Dunnachie). South African poet. Born in Durban on October 2, 1901; educated at Durban High School. Then went to sea. This experience inspired his first famous poem, 'The Flaming Terrapin,' a semi-allegorical work. Together with William Plomer he started *Voorslag*, a controversial South African literary magazine which ran for a short time. Proceeded overseas, spending time in Britain, Southern France and Spain, becoming interested in bullfighting. Fought with revolutionaries in Spanish Civil War. Poetic output increased; was soon recognised as the most eminent South African poet. Among his major works were 'The Wayzegoose,' 'Adamastor,' 'The Georgiad,' and an autobiography. Served in North Africa during World War II until he was disabled. Thereafter he became a Talks Producer in the B.B.C. He died in an accident in April 1957.

Camperdown. Village between Durban and Pietermaritzburg, Natal. Called after a farm, which derived its name from the British naval victory by Admiral Duncan over the Dutch in 1797. Farming centre. Population: 1,000, including 250 Whites.

Camp Fever. Traditional name for enteric, formerly very common at Kimberley and Johannesburg owing to the poor water supplies.

Camps Bay. Suburb of Cape Town and popular seaside resort. Named after Von Camptz, an official of the Dutch East India Company, who owned the farm Ravensteyn, along Kloof Nek. Camps Bay was used as a seaside home for early British Governors. The Round House below Kloof Nek was Lord Charles Somerset's hunting box. Camps Bay was part of Woodstock municipality, and its isolation delayed the introduction of municipal and other services. Its advance began with the building of a tram line in 1902 (since replaced by buses) round Lion's Head. Progressed further since 1913, when various smaller municipalities were united into greater Cape Town.

Canary. Seed-Eater or Sysie (Fringillidae). Singing bird widely distributed through South Africa, belonging to the Finch family. (*See* BUNTING.) The *Cape Canary* (*Serinus canicollis*) has a greenish-yellow back and yellow breast and is always seen in flocks, except when nesting. Its song is less lovely than that of the *Yellow Canary* or *Klein Sysie*, and its colour less bright. The last is a favourite cage bird.

Cane, John. Early Natal settler. Arrived from London at Cape Town in 1813, worked on a farm, qualified as a carpenter, and emigrated to Natal in 1824. There, with Lieutenant Francis George Farewell (q.v.), he settled on the shores of Durban Bay; was sent by Tshaka as his emissary to Cape Town in 1828, with a message for the Governor. For a while recognised as a local chief, in 1830 he was again sent to the Cape by Dingaan, to present ivory to the Governor. Prevented from travelling beyond Grahamstown, and returned to Natal, November 1837. He accompanied Pieter Retief (q.v.) on his first

Cane Rat

visit to Dingaan. Cane was killed in battle with the Zulus on April 17, 1838.

Cane Rat (*Thryonomys swinderenianus*). Nocturnal rodent found in Natal and Eastern Transvaal. Lives on vegetable matter and is highly destructive to crops, especially sugar cane. About 18 inches long and not a rat at all. Chief enemies are pythons.

Cango Caves. Vast limestone caves 17 miles from Oudtshoorn. Discovered in 1780 by J. Van Zyl, a farmer in the Zwartberg Mountains; described by George Thompson in 1824. Extending over 2 miles into the mountains, the exact size is unknown. Are a National Monument. Equipped with electric light where open to the public.

Cannibalism. Practised at various times in Southern Africa. After devastation caused by campaigns of Tshaka (q.v.), certain tribes in the Drakensberg took to cannibalism, particularly under Undara, a leader of the Amadunge. Portions of the human body are sometimes eaten for ritual purposes, but the practice is generally despised by normal Africans.

Canteen Koppie. Hill outside Barkly West (q.v.) noted for geological remains and relics of the Stone Age. Declared a National Monument. Its name derives from the days of the early diamond prospectors.

Cape Argus. Daily newspaper established by Brian Henry Darnell and R. W. Murray on January 3, 1857. Originally a morning paper, it appeared in the evening from 1883. In 1862 was taken over by Saul Solomon & Co., until the firm went insolvent in 1886, when Francis Joseph Dormer founded the Argus Printing and Publishing Company, today the largest newspaper group in South Africa. Renamed *The Argus* Dec. 1, 1969.

Cape Cart. Two-wheeled conveyance of sturdy construction, formerly in universal use in Southern Africa. Drawn by two horses, it could carry half-a-dozen passengers under a canvas or leather hood. Most Cape carts constructed locally, particularly at Paarl, Wellington, Oudtshoorn, King William's Town, Pietermaritzburg and other centres of the wagon-building industry.

Cape Corps. In 1793 a company of Pandours, comprising Coloured men and Hottentots, was raised to defend the Colony against the British. After the first British occupation another Cape Corps, under General Vandeleur, fought in 1799 against the Xosas, and was formed in 1800 into a full-scale regiment, with detachments at Port Elizabeth and Graaff-Reinet. Taken over by the Batavian Republic, they again helped defend the Cape against the British in 1806. The Cape Mounted Riflemen (q.v.), formed about the same time, was originally also a Coloured unit. Coloured men fought in many Frontier and other South African wars during the 19th century, but the tradition had been almost forgotten when during World War I it was decided, on September 20, 1915, to raise a new battalion, once again called Cape Corps. Between October 21 and December 12 the full quota was reached. On February 9, 1916, 32 officers and 1,022 other ranks embarked for East Africa. After a gallant campaign the unit returned to South

Africa in December 1917. In April 1918 it was sent to the Middle East to join General Allenby in breaking the Turkish front. Notable courage was shown at a critical battle at Square Hill in Palestine, September 19, 1918 (q.v.). Battalion demobilised September 1918, but re-formed during World War II, to fight again with much distinction in Middle East; 23,000 men had been recruited by 1942. Later amalgamated with Indian and Malay Corps to form Non-European Services of Union Defence Force. Many served as drivers in the Western Desert. Cape Corps disbanded 1948, but re-established 1963.

Cape False. Former name for Cape Hangklip (q.v.). It took its name from the fact that it lay near the eastern entrance of False Bay.

Cape Flats. Sandy area extending from Cape Peninsula inland and occupying the greater part of the isthmus between Table Bay and False Bay. Stretches roughly to the vicinity of Somerset West. In comparatively recent geological times the flats were covered by the ocean.

Cape Gooseberry (*Physalis peruviana*). Not really a gooseberry at all, but a very popular berry for canning and for making preserves. The scientific name reveals the fact that it was introduced from South America and is not indigenous to South Africa. Belongs to Solanaceae order, like potato, tobacco and petunia. A straggling plant, its berries enclosed in the characteristic dry calyx. *See* TOBACCO, WILD.

Cape Hangklip. Foreland marking the eastern edge of False Bay in the Cape Province, so called on account of its precipitous crags. Formerly known as Cape False.

Cape Hen (*Priocellaria oequinoctialis*). *See* PETREL.

Cape Ivy (*Senecio maxroglossus*). Climbing plant with fleshy, ivy-shaped leaves and clusters of yellow flowers. Common in Western Cape and near East London. *See* DAISY.

Cape Maclear. Foreland on the southern shores of Lake Nyasa, named after Sir Thomas Maclear, Her Majesty's Astronomer at the Cape in the days of David Livingstone.

Cape Malays. *See* MALAYS, CAPE.

Cape Mounted Riflemen (C.M.R.). Semi-military unit developed from the Frontier Armed and Mounted Police (q.v.), established in 1878. Specially organised for rapid movement, members being responsible for their own transport and supplies. It gained much distinction in the Morosi Campaign of 1879, the Gun War of 1881, the Langeberg Campaign and the Boer War. In 1913 became the First Regiment of the South African Mounted Rifles.

Cape Mounted Riflemen (Imperial). Early regiment raised at the Cape in 1806, with British officers and Cape Coloured men. Disbanded in 1817, but was reorganised and continued until 1870. Not to be confused with the Cape Mounted Riflemen (C.M.R.).

Cape Natal. Official Admiralty name for the Durban Bluff.

Cape of Good Hope. Promontory at the end of Cape Peninsula. Does not rise as high as Cape Point, which adjoins it, and which carries a lighthouse. The Cape of Good Hope was supposedly known to oriental navigators even before the discovery of the Cape in 1488 by Bartholomew Diaz (q.v.), its traditional name in the East being Cape Diab. Because of the rough seas encountered here, Diaz called it Cabo Tormentoso, or the Cape of Storms; but the good omen attached to the rounding of the southern extremity of Africa induced King John of Portugal to rename it the Cape of Good Hope.

Cape of Good Hope Bank. Early financial institution, set up in 1837, with a capital of £75,000. It attained considerable prosperity, absorbed several minor institutions, and estab-lished operations in the Transvaal, but closed its doors during the crisis in 1890. Thanks to skilful handling it repaid almost 20 shillings in the pound to creditors, though the shareholders were ruined.

Cape of Good Hope Savings Bank (not to be confused with Cape of Good Hope Bank). South Africa's oldest surviving financial institution. When it was established in 1831, by special ordinance, it originally had numerous branches, but today is concentrated in Cape Town. It accepts savings deposits, does an extensive mortgage business, and has assets of over R23,000,000.

Cape Patriots (Kaapse Patriotte). Movement in the late 18th century in Cape Colony influenced by the American revolt against England and by the French Revolution. It started in 1779, when a deputation was sent to Holland to ask the Dutch East India Company for greater political freedom. Failed to gain redress and gradually faded out, but had considerable indirect results when the Dutch administration collapsed at the end of the century.

Cape Pigeon. *See* PETRELS.

Cape Province. Officially the Province of the Cape of Good Hope. It occupies the territory of the former Cape Colony, being the largest in the Republic, with an area of 277,113 sq. miles, including 374 sq. miles of Walvis Bay and a few sq. miles of Marion Island. Represents nearly 60 per cent of the total area of the Republic of South Africa. The census of 1960 showed a total population of 5,308,839, including 997,377 Europeans, 2,976,827 Natives, 1,314,392 Coloureds and 20,243 Asiatics. White population in 1966, 1,060,000. On March 31, 1957, it had 520,913 European voters, besides 29,273 Coloured voters. The Cape Provincial Council numbers 52 members.

Cape Salmon. *See* GEELBEK.

Cape Smoke. Jocular name applied to cheap Cape brandy.

Cape Times. Morning newspaper established by F. Y. St. Leger on March 27, 1876, as the first daily paper in the country. Among its distinguished editors was F. E. Garrett, friend of Cecil John Rhodes.

Cape Town. Oldest city in South Africa, legislative capital of the Republic, capital of Cape Province, second largest city in the country. Founded by Van Riebeeck on April 6, 1652, when he set up a fort for the Dutch East India Company and a settlement, on the shores of Table Bay at the foot of Table Mountain. The site of this fort is on the present Grand Parade. Near by, under the present Grand Parade Centre (O.K. Bazaars Building), can be traced the steps leading down to the spring from which the early navigators drew their water. The stream, starting at the foot of Platteklip Gorge, ran through the Public Gardens, down Adderley Street and into the sea. For a long time Cape Town was known as De Kaapsche Vlek (the Cape hamlet). By the end of the 17th century it was already referred to as Kaapstad, or, in French, La Ville du Cap. Abraham de Mist in 1803 unsuccessfully attempted to rename it Van Riebeeck Stad, in honour of its founder. Including the neighbouring municipality of Pinelands, the suburb of Bergvliet (administered by the Cape Divisional Council), and sundry other areas, the population at June 1969 was 1,036,700, including 369,000 Whites, 547,000 Coloureds, 110,000 Bantu and 10,700 Asiatics. The municipal area, 102·66 sq. miles, excluding attendant administrative units, covers the greater part of the Cape Peninsula. One of the two principal seaports of the Republic, Cape Town is also the second largest manufacturing centre, industries including engineering, sawmilling, flour-milling, biscuit, garment and furni-

ture manufacturing, printing and many others. Its beautiful situation, many bathing beaches and impressive hinterland have made Cape Town South Africa's principal holiday centre. It attracts approximately 150,000 visitors during the summer season, estimated to spend over £8,000,000. Annual sessions of Parliament bring an influx of officials and legislators. Cape Town started with a few houses around the original fort, which was supplanted in 1685 by the Castle, the oldest surviving building in South Africa. Today the city spreads up the slopes of Table Mountain and Devil's Peak, and towards Green Point and Woodstock. The chief occupation of the inhabitants in the 18th and early 19th centuries was supplying provisions for passing ships, but the opening of the Suez Canal diverted much of the previous traffic to the East. Since the closing of the Suez Canal in 1967 and the development of tankers too big to pass that waterway, the traffic has grown heavier than ever. During the 19th century a number of former villages on the southern side of the city developed into separate municipalities, including Woodstock, Mowbray, Rondebosch, Claremont, Wynberg, etc., as, in the northern area, did Green and Sea Point. Attempts to simplify the provision of water, etc., were successful in 1913, when these units became Greater Cape Town, except for Wynberg, which joined in 1927. Today Fish Hoek and Simonstown, Pinelands and Hout Bay (qq.v.) are separate. Cape Town is spread out round the foot of Table Mountain and adjoining ranges from Kalk Bay to Camps Bay, a distance of more than 25 miles. A railway to Wynberg was begun in 1862 and later carried to Simonstown. This was electrified between 1925 and 1926. An electric line to Sea Point was found unprofitable and removed. The electric railways now also serve the inland suburbs and neighbouring municipalities of Maitland, Vasco, Goodwood, etc. Cape Town had a privately owned system of electric trolley and motor buses. There are over 100,000 motor vehicles. Cape Town has a number of magnificent old buildings, although many have been destroyed for economic reasons. The original Company's garden at the top of Adderley Street still exists as a pleasure resort. Around it are important institutions, including the South African Public Library established in 1818, housing over 500,000 volumes, including the famous Grey Collection of medieval and other manuscripts, the Dessinian Collection, the Fairbridge Africana Collection, etc. Close by are the Houses of Parliament, with the famous Mendelssohn Library (q.v.), the historic Government House, the South African National Gallery, the South African Museum, the Cape Archives, the Supreme Court, the Dutch Reformed Church Synodical Hall and other important buildings. At Groote Schuur, the home of Cecil John Rhodes, who bequeathed the estate for public purposes, is the University of Cape Town, with over 8,000 students, several research institutions and the Medical School. The Royal Observatory, established in 1820, still controlled by the British Admiralty, is the oldest institution of its kind in the Republic. A cableway runs up Table Mountain. The docks, commenced in 1860, have been extended, and today cover nearly 300 acres of protected water. At the cost of nearly R20,000,000 several hundred acres have been reclaimed from the sea at the foot of Adderley Street, where a number of buildings including the new railway station have been constructed.

Cape Tercentenary Foundation. Fund established by Edward and Henry Molteno of Elgin, Cape Province, to commemorate the 300th Anniversary of White Settlement in South Africa in 1952. It makes grants to encourage literary, historic, artistic and other work. Assets over R500,000.

Cape Verde Islands. Portuguese archipelago off north-west African coast comprising 14 volcanic islands, found in 1456 by Alvise Cadamosto for Prince Henry the Navigator. Since its adoption as halt for South African Airways overseas service in 1963, South Africa has contributed largely towards the cost of airfields. Praia is capital of the largest island, Sao Vicente.

Cape Weights and Measures. *See* WEIGHTS AND MEASURES (CAPE).

Caprivi Zipfel (German for 'Caprivi tip.' Also known as Caprivi Strip). Long narrow strip of country, extending from the extreme north-east of South West Africa to the Zambesi River. Measures 300 miles in length and is nowhere more than 50 miles wide. Existence due to the aim of the German authorities at the end of the 19th century to unite their colony in South West Africa with that in East Africa. The name is derived from that of Count Leo de Caprivi who succeeded Prince Bismarck as Imperial Chancellor in 1890. Under his régime the area was ceded by Britain in 1893. The Caprivi Strip is almost dead flat, and, having several large rivers, is of great potential importance to the possible reclamation of the Kalahari Desert. Because of its isolation from South West Africa it was joined to Bechuanaland after World War I, and since 1939 has been administered from Pretoria.

Caracal (*Felis caracal*). Known to the Amaxosa as Incawa and the Bechuanas as Tuane. Commonly called the lynx or 'rooikat,' it is not a true lynx, differing slightly in appearance. It is found throughout South Africa, from the Cape to the extreme north, favouring grassy areas, open kloofs and sparsely-wooded koppies. Its prey consists of rodents and the larger birds. Brick-red in colour, its ears are black, and it varies in size from 3 to 4 feet from nose to root of tail.

Carbonaatje. *See* KARBONAATJE.

Carletonville (not to be confused with Carltonville, q.v.). Gold mining town on Western Witwatersrand. Founded about 1942 and named after Guy Carleton Jones (q.v.). Became a municipality in 1956, merged with the older township of Oberholzer. Population 103,500, with 23,000 Whites.

Carlton Centre. Largest building complex in South Africa. Occupying four city blocks in central Johannesburg, it will cost, when complete in 1971, over R50,000,000. The project includes the World's tallest all-concrete building, 730 feet high, containing 51 floors, a luxury hotel of over 400 rooms, 37 storeys high, two department stores, 150 shops, exhibition halls and parking for 3,000 cars, —also 3½ acres of open space. Work began in April 1966.

Carltonville (not to be confused with Carletonville). Diamond mining camp near Lichtenburg, western Transvaal, which flourished during the alluvial diamond boom from 1924 to 1926.

Carnarvon. Village in the North-Western Cape Province, named after the British Colonial Secretary, Earl of Carnarvon. Originally called Schietfontein, it was founded in 1860, when a large number of native refugees from wars in the Eastern Province were settled here. In 1874, an official township was laid out and the place received its present name. Important sheep centre. Population: 5,000, including 1,400 Whites.

Carolina. Town in the Eastern Transvaal. Established 1882 and named after Mrs. Carolina Coetzee, wife of the founder. Asbestos mines near by, also occurrences of gold and coal. Population: 4,853, including 1,750 Whites.

Carpio Affair. Controversial incident concerning South West Africa. On April 13, 1962, a Special Committee of the United Nations accepted an invitation from the South African Government to allow two of its representatives, Dr. Victorio Carpio of the Philippines and Dr. Salvadore Martinez de Alva, to pay a visit of inspection. They arrived in Pretoria on May 5, had discussions with Dr. H. F. Verwoerd as Prime Minister, Mr. Eric Louw, Minister of Foreign Affairs, and Mr. J. G. H. van der Wath, Deputy Minister for South West African Affairs. From May 9 to May 19 they toured South West Africa and May 21-3 the Transkei. Dr. Carpio was taken ill on May 24, but on May 26 a joint communiqué was issued by the visitors expressing satisfaction with conditions in South West Africa and denying any sight of alleged arms build-up. After their return overseas, Dr. Carpio repudiated the truth of this statement, although he was contradicted by Dr. de Alva.

Carrington, Major-General Sir Frederick. Born in Cheltenham 1844; educated at Cheltenham College. Entered the 24th Regiment in 1864. Came to South Africa in 1875. First campaign in Griqualand West, followed by the Galeka Campaign of 1877, in which he raised and commanded the Frontier Light Horse. Then he went north, and as Commandant of the Transvaal Volunteers stormed Sekukuni's stronghold. In the Gun War he commanded at Mafeteng, which was besieged by the Basuto; later led the Colonial troops in that theatre and was badly wounded. In 1884 commanded the Second Mounted Rifles, and was Commandant of Native Levies in the Zululand troubles of 1888. Became Commandant of the Bechuanaland Border Police in 1893. The same year the Matabele War began and he was Military Adviser to the High Commissioner. In the Matabele

Rebellion of 1896 he was General Officer Commanding. During the South African War he commanded a Rhodesian force designed to invade the Transvaal from the north. He died in 1913.

Carrion Flowers. *See* SUCCULENTS.

Carter, Sydney. South African artist. Born in Enfield, Middlesex, England, on April 2, 1874. Son of artist Richard Carter. Studied at the Royal College of Art, London. A fellow member of the London Sketch Club with Phil May and other artists, he won the Gilbert Garrett Prize in 1898. Exhibited at the Royal Academy, the Paris Salon, etc. After serving in World War I he settled in Exeter. In 1923 he came to South Africa, where he spent the rest of his life. He soon became known locally for his studies of trees and landscapes, and was responsible for the decoration of several important public buildings. He died on December 21, 1945.

Casement, Sir Roger. Irish political leader, born 1864. Although best known for his activities in the Belgian Congo, South America and Ireland, Casement began his career in the British diplomatic service as consul in Lourenço Marques from 1895 to 1898. After a spell in Angola, was transferred to Lourenço Marques. During the Boer War he did special service for 2 years which won him the Queen's South African Medal. Was executed for high treason in World War I in 1916.

Cashan Mountains. Early name for Magaliesberg (q.v.).

Cassia. *See* PEA, WILD SWEET.

Castle Line. Steamship line founded in 1872, when Sir Donald Currie (q.v.) sent the chartered *Iceland* to Cape Town. Name formally adopted in 1876, when the mail contract was divided between Castle and Union Lines (q.v.). Rivalry between two

concerns ended in 1900 with a merging into the Union-Castle Line. At that time the Castle Line had 20 ships, totalling 108,886 tons.

Castle of Good Hope. Fortification erected by the Dutch East India Company to protect the Cape settlement. Oldest historic building in South Africa. Construction approved in 1664, begun under Governor Isbrand Goske in 1665. Progress interrupted from 1667 to 1672, finally completed 1679. Castle has five bastions, known as Oranje, Leerdam, Nassau, Buren and Catzenellenbogen after the titles of the Stadholder of the Netherlands. The castle was seat of the Governor and administration until establishment of British administration, when the Governor took his residence in Government House. Remained military headquarters. Site of the first printing works in South Africa. Although a National Monument, is still officially headquarters of the Union Defence Department at the Cape. Section now devoted to historical pictures and other relics.

Castor Oil, Wild. *See* EUPHORBIA.

Cat, African Wild (*Felis ocreata caffra*). Also known as the Kafir Cat, Wild Cat or Groukat. Found in South Africa wherever there is sufficient bush or forest and where prey is abundant. Prowling by night, the cat lives on rodents and birds, and, being extremely strong and lithe, will even attack the smaller buck. In settled areas it is a pest, preying on poultry and young stock, and is mercilessly trapped and hunted. Similar in size to the domestic cat, it is a speckled grey-brown, paling to yellow on the belly, the upper parts of the legs being black, and the tail striped and ringed in black.

Cat, Black-Footed (*Felis nigripes*). Also known to the Bechuanas as Kakikaan and to the Kalahari natives as Tsipa. Carnivorous animal much like the Serval Cat (q.v.) in appearance and habits, but smaller, with black foot pads. Fawn in colour, it is so covered with irregular black spots in the region of the neck that it appears striped. The tail is short, spotted and striped. The cat measures about 20 inches from nose to tail.

Cat, Serval (*Felis serval*). Also known to the Zulus and Swazis as Indhloti, the Amaxosa as Indhlozi, the Bechuanas as Tali, and the Basuto as Tlodi. Commonly called the 'Tierboskat' or Tiger Bush Cat, it is found all over Africa, but particularly in the south, where it inhabits bushy, wooded or long-grassed areas in the vicinity of water. Prowling by night and extremely timid by day, it hunts all the smaller game, rodents and other wild creatures, many larger birds, and, in more settled areas, the smaller domestic animals. In colour it is reddish-yellow, closely covered with black spots. It stands approximately 2 feet high, measuring about 3 feet from nose to tail.

Catawba Grape. Natal name for a well-known American type, usually called Isabella. Has an unusual flavour, like that of a strawberry.

Catfish or Barbel. (Name catfish is often given to the baby octopus at the Cape.) Large family of river and sea fish, without scales, but with barbels hanging from lips. Spines on back make them dangerous to handle. *Mudbarbel* or *Platkop Barger* the best-known South African river species north of Cape. Buries itself in dry seasons. *Snake Barbel* common on shores and estuaries as far south as East London. *Cape Barger* or *Sea Barbel*, 16 inches long, is common all round the South African coast. Not specially good eating.

Cathcart. Wool centre in Eastern Cape Province. Named after Governor Sir George Cathcart (q.v.). Founded as military outpost 1858. Became a municipality in 1881. Population: 4,700, including 900 Whites.

Cathcart, Sir George. Cape Governor. Son of the first Earl of Cathcart, born 1794, joined the army at 16 years. Appointed Commander-in-Chief in South Africa and Cape Governor in 1852. Fought in Eighth Kaffir War in the Eastern Cape, and against Basuto chief, Moshesh, in the Orange River Sovereignty and Basutoland. Was defeated in battle of Berea (q.v.) by Moshesh, who wisely made peace before retribution could be taken. Killed at the battle of Inkerman, November 5, 1854.

Catholic Church in Southern Africa. The first Catholic service held in South Africa of which there is historical record was the celebration of Mass following the erection of the Padrao of St. Gregory by Bartholomew Diaz on Santa Cruz Island, near Algoa Bay, in 1487. A small chapel built at Mossel Bay by João de Nova in 1501 was the first Catholic place of worship. The oldest existing Catholic church in South Africa is St. Mary's Cathedral, Cape Town, begun in 1840. Until 1805, with the arrival in Cape Town of three priests from the Netherlands, there was no organised Catholic worship, although there were Catholics among the inhabitants of the Cape. Missions to the Bantu began in 1854, when two priests were sent to Zululand by Bishop Allard, O.M.I. The Mariannhill Mission Society developed from the Trappists who founded Mariannhill Mission in 1883. A number of religious orders work in South Africa, notably the Jesuits, Dominicans and Franciscans, as well as others more modern. Two African bishops and six White South African-born bishops belong to the South African hierarchy, with over 200 priests, 100 brothers and 1,000 sisters born in South Africa. The Pope is represented in Southern Africa by an Apostolic Delegate who resides in

Pretoria, and whose post covers the Republic of South Africa, South West Africa, Lesotho, Botswana, Swaziland and Rhodesia. There are five ecclesiastical provinces— Cape Town, Pretoria, Bloemfontein, Durban and Salisbury—with a metropolitan archbishop in each of these sees. The provinces, with dates of foundation, are comprised as follows: *Cape Town.* Archdiocese of Cape Town (1805), Dioceses of Port Elizabeth (1847), Oudtshoorn (1874), Aliwal North (1923), Queenstown (1929), and the Prefecture of De Aar (1953). *Pretoria.* Archdiocese of Pretoria (1948), Dioceses of Pietersburg (1910), Lydenburg (1923), Bremersdorp (1923), and the Prefecture of Volksrust (1958). *Durban.* Archdiocese of Durban (1850), Dioceses of Mariannhill (1921), Eshowe (1921), Umtata (1930), Kokstad (1935), and Umzimkulu (1954). *Bloemfontein.* Archdiocese of Bloemfontein (1951), Dioceses of Keimoes (1882), Kimberley (1886), Maseru (1894), Kroonstad (1924), Bethlehem (1948), Leribe (1952), and the Prefecture of Bechuanaland (1959). *Salisbury.* Archdiocese of Salisbury (1897), Dioceses of Bulawayo (1930), Gwelo (1946), Umtali (1953), and the Prefecture of Wankie (1953). In South-West Africa there are the Vicariates of Windhoek (1892) and Keetmanshoop (1909).

In 1967, there were 2,143,087 Catholics in Southern Africa (excluding Mozambique), comprising 1,751,833 Africans, 217,050 Whites, 162,726 Coloureds, 10,226 Indians, 1,399 Chinese, with 110,694 catechumens, served by 1,837 priests, 900 brothers, 7,194 sisters and 4,136 catechists. In the Republic of South Africa there were 903,609 African Catholics, in Rhodesia 380,583, in South West Africa 79,126 and in the Independent Territories 388,515. White Catholics numbered 188,889 in the Republic of South Africa, 24,115 in Rhodesia, 3,102 in South West Africa

and 944 in the Territories. Coloured Catholics numbered 147,553 in the Republic, 5,826 in Rhodesia, 8,007 in South West Africa and 1,340 in the Territories.

Under the Catholic Church in Southern Africa there were in 1967 2,116 churches, 685 convents, 1,846 schools with 463,555 pupils, 123 hospitals, 286 dispensaries, 62 orphanages, 222 hostels and 98 other institutions.

For historical reasons the organisation of the Church in Portuguese East and West Africa falls under the Sacred Congregation of the Consistory. There are two ecclesiastical provinces: Lourenço Marques in Mozambique with suffragan sees of Beira, Nampula, Porto Amelia and Quelimane; and Luanda in Angola with suffragan sees of Malanje, Nova Lisboa, Sa da Bandeira, São Tomé e Principe and Silva Porto. The Metropolitan of Lourenço Marques, the late Cardinal Teodosio Clemente de Gouveia, was appointed a member of the Sacred College of Cardinals in 1946. He died in 1962 and was succeeded as Metropolitan by Archbishop Alvin.

Cato Ridge. Town near Camperdown, Natal. Population: 420, including 140 Whites. Large metallurgical works.

Cat's Eye. Type of stone called crocidolite found in the wash on Vaal River Diamond Fields, not identical with Cat's Eye found in the Far East.

Cattle Killing Delusion. In 1856 a young Xosa woman, by the name of Nongquase, preached that the day was approaching when Europeans in their country would be driven into the sea. Dead chiefs would arise, kraals would be filled with cattle and grain-pits with new harvests. Upon that day the sun would rise blood-red, fields would stand ready for reaping, illness would disappear, as would old age. All white people and those who had disobeyed orders from the other world would be carried into the sea by a great wind. To make these things possible, it was necessary to kill every head of livestock in the hands of the Xosa nation, and to destroy all grain and garden produce. Despite the efforts of the British authorities, and of the missionaries, the destruction began and could not be stopped. Altogether over 200,000 head of livestock were killed. Special kraals were built for the cattle that would rise from the sea and huts were strengthened to withstand the coming hurricane. February 18, 1857, was the date on which the miracles were to happen. When the sun rose as usual and no sign appeared of anything extraordinary, the Xosas realised that they had been misled. A nightmare of starvation and despair descended upon the people. Official figures show that the population of British Kaffraria fell between January 1, 1857, and July 31, 1857, from 104,721 to 37,229. Further losses were sustained elsewhere. Large sums were given for relief, but the military power of the Xosas was broken for ever.

Cave Commission. Body appointed by the British Government, under Lord Chancellor Cave, to determine the amount of compensation to be paid to the British South Africa Company in return for ceding their powers to the Rhodesian Government. The report, issued on January 15, 1920, fixed the sum at £4,435,225.

Cayzer, Sir William Nicholas. Shipping magnate. Born on January 21, 1910, he joined the Clan Line (q.v.), which under his régime secured control, of the Union-Castle Line (q.v.). Considerable expansion and modernisation of the latter followed soon after.

Cedara. Agricultural college in northern Natal, established by Colonial Government in 1902. Considerable research carried out here.

Cedarberg. Mountain range in the Western Cape Province, so called on account of its cedar trees. Highest points are the Sneeuberg (6,652 feet),

the Sneeukop (6,337 feet), Tafelberg (6,465 feet) and the Krakadouwsberg (5,726 feet). Popular resort for mountaineers.

Cedar, Cape, or Clanwilliam (*Widringtonia juniperoides* Endl.). Tree up to 60 feet, with large spreading branches. It is thought to be the last remnant of that type of vegetation in the south-western area of the Cape Province (Cedarberg).

Cedarville. Village near Matatiele, Cape Province. Population: 930, including 275 Whites.

Celliers, Jan. Early Transvaal journalist. Born at Wellington, Cape, in 1839, went to Paarl, and joined the editorial staff of *Het Volksblad* in 1863. At the request of President T. F. Burgers (q.v.), went to the Transvaal in 1870, and in 1873 settled in Pretoria, where he established *De Volksstem*. Became secretary of the Pretoria branch of the Afrikaner Bond and his writings stimulated Boer resistance against the British annexation. Retired from *De Volksstem* in 1888 and died in 1893. His son was the South African poet, J. F. E. Celliers.

Celliers, Johannes François Elias. Afrikaans poet. Born in 1865 in Wellington, Cape Colony, educated in Cape Town and trekked with his parents to Pretoria in 1873. Then studied land surveying. Upon his return became State Librarian in Pretoria. He fought in the South African War, was associated with the Afrikaans language movement and helped to found the South African Akademie in 1907. Meanwhile he had written in 1905 the poem that made him famous, 'Die Vlakte' (The Plain), still perhaps the best ever produced in the language. Wrote many others of high merit, mostly about the South African countryside, and helped to found the literary journal *Die Brandwag* (not to be confused with its successors). In 1919 was appointed a

PLATE III: BIRDS OF SOUTHERN AFRICA

1. African Hoopoe. 2. Flamingo. 3. Sugarbird. 4. Crimson-breasted Shrike.
5. Lesser Double-collared Sunbird. 6. Cape Vulture. 7. Paradise Whydah.
8. Secretary Bird. 9. Piet My Vrou.

professor at the University of Stellenbosch, where he remained 10 years. He died in 1940.

Cent. Unit of currency adopted in the Union of South Africa under the Decimalisation Act of 1959, with effect from 1961. 100 cents equal one rand (q.v.). Also used in Rhodesia from February 1970. *See* DOLLAR.

Centlivres, Albert van de Sandt. Chief Justice of South Africa. Born at Cape Town on January 13, 1887, and educated at South African College and Oxford. Called to the Cape Bar, he was promoted to the Bench and was Chief Justice from 1950 to 1957. In 1951 he was made Chancellor of the University of Cape Town. Died September 19, 1966.

Central African Airways. State-controlled airline, with headquarters in Salisbury. Not only covered the entire territory of the Federation but maintained links with the Republic, Mozambique, East Africa and London. Split up in 1963 on dissolution of Federation. *See* AIR RHODESIA.

Central African Federation. *See* RHODESIA AND NYASALAND, FEDERATION OF.

Central Mining and Finance Corporation Ltd. *See* CORNER HOUSE.

Central News Agency Limited. South African publishers. Developed from a venture started in 1895 by Michael Davis and Albert Victor Lindbergh (q.v.) for the retail sale of newspapers in Johannesburg. The firm later undertook the distribution of newspapers to private houses and offices on the Witwatersrand and in other parts of South Africa. During the South African War the Agency secured a monopoly for sales of the *Cape Times* and other papers in Cape Town. For years it also ran the railway bookstalls in the Transvaal and Orange Free State. In 1902 it was floated as a limited company with participation of the Argus Printing and Publishing

Company and mining groups, while support of the famous British and Australian firm Gordon & Gotch Ltd. ensured the representation of leading overseas newspapers and magazines. By this time it had also a flourishing bookselling department, published works of many kinds under its own imprint and more recently has handled general merchandise and fancy goods. Today has over 150 branches. In Rhodesia its affiliated company is Kingstons Ltd.

Ceres. Town in the Western Province on Dwars River. Established in 1854, named after the Roman goddess of agriculture, on account of the fertility of the district. Famous for its oaks. Important fruit-growing centre. Population: 6,700, including 2,500 Whites.

Cetewayo (also known as **Ketshewayo**). King of the Zulus. The son of Panda (q.v.). Involved in wars with his brother before succeeding to the throne. Upon the death of Panda in October 1872, he gained unchallenged control of the nation. The British authorities, while recognising Cetewayo's sovereignty, tried to control it. Thus a 'coronation' was carried out in 1873 by Sir Theophilus Shepstone (q.v.). A man of great dignity and ability, but he could not control his military instincts, nor stop his people from 'blooding their spears' on those they regarded as inferior neighbours. Friction continued on the frontier, with the result that in 1879 the Zulu War broke out. After initial victories Cetewayo was defeated, and after the battle of Ulundi was driven into the wilderness, where on August 28, 1879, he was captured. Sent to Cape Town, and held there at the castle as a prisoner of state. Was then moved to the farm, Oude Molen, near by. Because of the chaotic conditions in Zululand, his people asked for his restoration, but this was strongly disapproved by Natal settlers. In 1882 he visited London, where he was welcomed and met Queen

Victoria. The result was his return in 1883 to Zululand, and on January 29, 1883, he was restored as king by Sir Theophilus Shepstone. Soon after, he was defeated in a war against Usibepu. He died on February 8, 1884, and was buried in the Nkhandhla Forest.

C.F.A. Abbreviation for Cape Field Artillery. *See* REGIMENT, FIRST FIELD.

Chacma. *See* BABOON, CAPE.

Chaffinch. Introduced to Groote Schuur, Cape Town, about 1900. Slowly spread round Table Mountain suburbs. Cock bird easily recognised by his pink breast, chestnut back, blue-grey head and flashes of white in wings and tail when in flight. *See* BUNTING and CANARY.

Chai-Chai. Former name of Vila de Joao Belo (q.v.).

Chaka's Kraal. Sugar-growing centre on the north coast of Natal, named after the Zulu king Tshaka (or Chaka). Population: 2,384, including 132 Whites and 1,480 Indians.

Chaka's Rock. Seaside resort on the north coast of Natal, named after the Zulu king who is reputed to have had his subjects thrown over a cliff near by.

Chamber of Mines of South Africa. *See* GOLD MINING INDUSTRY OF SOUTH AFRICA.

Chameleon. Small harmless reptile found in many parts of South Africa, noted for its ability to change colour to match its background. Hence the name, Verkleurmannetjie (q.v.). There are several species in Southern Africa, including the Pigmy Chameleon which measures only 2½ inches. A larger kind in Madagascar grows to 15 inches. Their food consists of insects.

Champion, Allison Wessel George (real name **Mhlongo**). Bantu leader. Born on December 4, 1893, on the Lower Tugela in Natal, and educated at Amanzimtoti Training Institute by the American Board Mission. Began his career as a policeman in Johannes-

burg in 1913 and remained in the force for 2 years. Joined the Crown Mines as a clerk, resigning in 1925 to become organiser for the Industrial and Commercial Workers' Union (I.C.U.), appearing before various Government commissions, becoming a member of the Joint Council of Europeans and Natives and founding the first local Native Advisory Board in Durban. He was exiled from Zululand under the Riotous Assemblies Act in 1930. Mr. Justice De Waal described Champion as 'in many respects a remarkable man.' In later years he lived on his farm at Inanda, Natal.

Chancellor, Sir John Robert. First Governor of Southern Rhodesia. Born in Edinburgh on October 20, 1870, joined the Royal Engineers in 1890 and served in Egypt and India. Was Secretary of the Colonial Defence Committee in 1906, Governor of Mauritius from 1911 to 1916, and of Trinidad and Tobago from 1916 to 1921. Following the grant of Responsible Government to Southern Rhodesia in 1923 he was Governor there until 1928. In later years he was High Commissioner in Palestine. He died in 1952.

Chaplin, Sir Francis Drummond Percy. Administrator of Rhodesia. Born at Twickenham, London, in 1866, studied at Oxford and was called to the Bar in 1891. The following year he emigrated to the Cape, intending to set up as a barrister in Rhodesia, but the outbreak of the Matabele War prevented this. Instead he settled in Johannesburg, and became correspondent to the London *Times*. Met Cecil Rhodes; went to Kimberley. In 1899 he was sent by the *Morning Post* to Russia, where he was stationed at St. Petersburg (now Leningrad). In 1900 he was invited to join the staff of Consolidated Goldfields, Cecil John Rhodes' company. Became Joint Manager in Johannesburg shortly after the British occupation of the city. During the Milner régime he served on the nominated Johannesburg Town Council, and was elected Member for Germiston under Responsible Government. Upon the retirement of Sir William Milton (q.v.), Chaplin was appointed Administrator of Southern Rhodesia. Settled the difficulties arising from the isolation of Rhodesia during World War I, and from the growing unpopularity of the Chartered Company régime. Became Administrator of Northern Rhodesia, holding the two positions jointly until the end of the Chartered Company administration in 1923. Returning to the Union, he settled at the Cape, where he was elected into the Union Parliament in 1924. He died in 1933.

Chapman, James. Explorer and hunter. Born in England in 1831; came to Natal at the age of 11. When he finished his schooling in Cape Town, in 1849, although only 18 he trekked inland from Maritzburg and started work as one of the earliest storekeepers at Potchefstroom. Shortly afterwards he began his first treks inland. In 1851 Chapman came within 70 miles of the Victoria Falls, almost discovering them before David Livingstone. Two years later he undertook another expedition to the north of Bechuanaland and the upper reaches of the Zambesi. He trekked overland to Walvis Bay in 1860, and was one of the first white men to settle in South West Africa, opening a cattle-breeding post at Otjimbingwe. He and Thomas Baines planned a trip from Walvis Bay to the Zambesi below the Victoria Falls, and then on to its mouth, thus crossing Africa. Leaving Cape Town in December 1860, ahead of Baines, James Chapman, with his brother Henry, reached the Zambesi in 1863, but failed to complete the trip to the mouth of the river. Instead they returned to the Victoria Falls, and arrived at Walvis Bay in January 1864. Chapman was a remarkable hunter and also collected natural history specimens. *Travels in the Interior of South Africa* appeared in 1868. He died in Kimberley in 1872.

Charl Celliers. Village near Standerton, Transvaal. Population: 130, including 50 Whites.

Charlestown. Township on the Transvaal border of Natal. Founded in 1889 and named after Governor Sir Charles Mitchell. In its heyday Charlestown was the main trans-shipping point from the railways which ended at the Natal frontier to the ox-wagons and coaches that travelled on to the Rand. Now it is a farming centre. Population: 5,152, including 336 Whites.

Charlesville. Village near Fauresmith, Orange Free State. Population: 750, including 650 Whites.

Chartered Company. See BRITISH SOUTH AFRICA COMPANY.

Charter of Justice. Issued by the British authorities in Cape Colony. Effective on January 1, 1828. The Supreme Court of Cape Colony was established, independent of other branches of government, and comprising a Chief Justice and three Puisne Judges. English court procedure and pleadings were introduced, but the existent Roman-Dutch Law remained in force. Circuits were to be held and the Court of the Vice-Admiralty was abolished. A second Charter of Justice, which introduced certain modifications, took effect on March 1, 1834.

Chat (family Turdidae). Small songster related to Robin and Wheatear. Very soberly coloured. Ground feeder on ants and small beetles. The commonest of several species is the Familiar Chat or Spekvreter, a restless little brown bird that flicks its tail and wings like a Robin. Dull chestnut on rump and tail. The Stonechat or Perdewagter is an attractive, plump little bird, with black head, white collarmarks and reddish breast, seen often on wire fences or low bushes, singing a short little canary-song. See BIRDS.

Chavonnes, Maurits Pasques de. Governor of the Cape. Born at the Hague, in 1654, became a soldier and rose to be lieutenant-colonel in the infantry of the States-General. Was retrenched, but found employment with Dutch East India Company, who appointed him Cape Governor in 1714. Did much for development of the Colony and was promoted to Ordinary Counsellor of India in 1721. Died at the Cape on September 7, 1724.

Cheetah. See LEOPARD, HUNTING.

Chelmsford, Lord (Frederick Augustus Thesiger). British soldier. Born in 1827 and joined the British Army at the age of 17. Served in the Crimea, the Indian Mutiny and under Lord Napier in Abyssinia in 1867. He became adjutant-general in India and major-general in 1877. As such he commanded British troops at the Cape in 1878, and in the Zulu War in 1879. Because of the disaster at Isandhlwana he was superseded by Lord Wolseley, and despite victories at Ulundi and elsewhere he returned to England. Later he was Lieutenant of the Tower of London. He died in 1905.

Chestnut, Cape. A large, deciduous forest tree bearing masses of pink flowers in summer. It is found widely on sloping ground from Swellendam to the Eastern Transvaal. See BUCHU.

Chicory. Mostly cultivated in the eastern Cape Province, near Grahamstown, Alexandria and Bathurst. Production exceeds 14,000 tons yearly. Government supervision has been introduced.

Chililabombwe. (formerly Bancroft). Township in Zambia near the Congo border, serving the Bancroft Copper Mine. It was established in 1955, with an area of 2,579 acres. Shortly afterwards operations were suspended owing to fall in price of copper, but have since been recommenced. According to the 1956 returns had 1,600 Europeans and 7,100 Africans.

Chiloane. Small seaport in Mozambique, near Beira.

Chilvers, Hedley A. South African writer. Born in England in 1879 and educated at Dulwich College, planning a musical career. For reasons of health he came to South Africa in 1901 and worked in a bank, until in 1905 he joined the *Rand Daily Mail* at Johannesburg as music and dramatic critic. Wrote many books, including *Out of the Crucible*, a history of Johannesburg, *The Seven Wonders of South Africa*, *The Yellow Man Looks On*, *The Story of De Beers*, etc. In later years he was Mining Editor of the *Rand Daily Mail* and *Sunday Times*. He died in 1941.

Chimanimani Mountains. Range on border of Rhodesia and Mozambique, reaching a height of 8,000 feet. National Park since 1953.

China Flower. See BUCHU.

Chincherinchee (*Ornithogalum thyrsoides*). Bulbous plant with leaves folded round stem and a spike of white flowers. Flourishes in the Cape Province. Buds exported on a large scale to England. No satisfactory explanation has been given for the name, possibly from the peculiar noise made when two stalks are rubbed together. Like the onion, asparagus, aloe and agapanthus, it belongs to the Liliaceae order, about 800 species of which are in South Africa. See LILY.

Chinde. Seaport in Mozambique, on delta of the Zambesi. Founded as a result of the opening up of Malawi at the beginning of the 1890's. Under a convention between Britain and Portugal in 1891, an area of 25 acres was leased to Britain for 99 years, enjoying territorial privileges. This was abolished by agreement shortly after World War I. A hurricane almost destroyed Chinde early in 1922. The damage has since been made good and Chinde serves as a main centre for the sugar estates on the Zambesi and else-where. Population: 90,000, including 500 Whites.

Chindio. Settlement in Malawi and on the north bank of the Zambesi, terminus of the railway linking Mozambique with Malawi. Notable for the bridge, one of the longest in the world, opened in 1935. Erected by the Cleveland Bridge and Engineering Co. Ltd., it is nearly 2½ miles from end to end.

Chinese. Chinese coins having been found at Zimbabwe and elsewhere, commercial traffic clearly existed here long before white settlement. Van Riebeeck proposed introducing Chinese as servants, but beyond a few stray immigrants numbers remained negligible. After the South African War, the shortage of black labour for the Witwatersrand Gold Mines prompted the authorities to approve the recruiting of Chinese labour. The Transvaal Chamber of Mines set up extensive organisations at Tientsin, etc. During 1904 the first recruits reached the Transvaal, increasing until there were over 50,000 employed on the Reef. Frequent lawlessness subjected the experiment to much criticism, and in 1906 the English Liberal Party won an election on the false reports of 'Chinese Slavery' on the Rand. The improved recruiting of natives made Chinese increasingly unnecessary, and in 1908 repatriation began. By 1910 most labourers had left the country, though a small number of Chinese, about 2,000, live in the Republic, the largest communities being on the Rand (about 1,000) at Port Elizabeth and at Cape Town, where Chinese schools exist.

Chingola. Township in Zambia, adjoining the Nchanga Copper Mine. Established in 1943 and became a full municipality in 1954. Population: 4,600 Europeans and 12,400 Africans. Its area is 3,750 acres.

Chipata (formerly Fort Jameson). Township in Zambia, established in 1899 as headquarters for the British South Africa Company in North-Eastern Rhodesia (now merged with the rest of the country). Here too the North Charterland Exploration Company (q.v.) has its African centre of administration. The main industry is tobacco-growing. Population: 710, including 400 Whites.

Chiperone. Expression used in Malawi, derived from a mountain peak in Mozambique. Refers to cloudy to overcast conditions, with drizzle or rain, from sea air moving into Southern Malawi from the south-east. Chiperone weather is usually preceded by freshening winds and wisps of cloud on Mount Chiperone.

Chipinga. Village in the east of Rhodesia, settled by Boer emigrants over 60 years ago. Near by are extensive plantations of tea and other crops. Population: 1,060, including 280 Whites.

Chipise. Mineral baths resort in northern Transvaal, near the Rhodesian border.

Chiredzi. New town in Rhodesia in Hippo Valley (q.v.).

Chiromo. River port in the south of Malawi, at the junction of the Shire and Ruo Rivers. The British Cotton Growing Association has a depot here.

Chironga Ruins. *See* MATINDERE RUINS.

Chirundu. Gorge of the Zambesi River in the Lomagundi district of Rhodesia, now spanned by the Otto Beit Bridge (not to be confused with the Beit Bridge).

Chobe River. Tributary of the Zambesi. Rises in large swamps; is called the Kwando in its upper reaches, and the Linyanti lower down.

Choma. Township in Zambia, 125 miles to the north of Livingstone and 180 miles south of Lusaka. Established about 1905 as a railway siding, is today centre of an important tobacco and maize growing area. An altitude of 4,703 feet makes the climate reasonably healthy. The population is 490 Europeans, 1,500 Africans and 110 of other races.

Chor-Chor (*Pomadasys bennetti*). South African fish of Grunter family (q.v.).

Chor-Chor, Rooi (*Pagellus natalensis*). Edible fish found off Mossel Bay to Natal, Delagoa Bay and Madagascar. About 14 inches long. *See* BREAM.

Chrissiemeer. Afrikaans name for Lake Chrissie (q.v.).

Christiana. Town on banks of the Vaal River, in the South-West Transvaal. Named after the daughter of the Voortrekker leader Andries Pretorius, who crossed the Vaal at this point. Founded in 1870 as diamond diggings, but its importance today is derived from agriculture and the development of the nearby Vaal-Hartz irrigation areas (q.v.). Population: 6,800, including 3,000 Whites.

Christian Institute of Southern Africa. Inter-religious organisation, established in 1963, aimed at overcoming divisions between denominations. Has about 2,000 members, maintains over 50 Bible study groups, conducts correspondence courses in theology etc. Headquarters are in Johannesburg. Not approved by Dutch Reformed Church.

Christian National Education. Voluntary system of schools established in the former Boer Republics, the Transvaal and the Orange Free State, after the South African War, assisted by the Dutch Reformed Church. Main object was to counteract the policy of 'Anglicisation' introduced by Lord Milner. It was largely successful in this. Following the traditions of the Boers, the schools were conducted mainly in Dutch, and had a strongly

religious element. Proposals to reintroduce the system today have aroused considerable criticism and controversy.

Chromium. Mineral used in steel production, tanning, etc. Rhodesia has large workings and is among the world's chief producers. Chrome ores, with a chrome–iron ratio of up to 1·2 to 1, of which there are reserves exceeding 200 million tons, are being produced in the Rustenburg, Marico and Lydenburg districts of the Transvaal.

Chronicle. *See* BULAWAYO CHRONICLE.

Chronology. *See under* country concerned.

Churchill, Lord Randolph. Father of Sir Winston S. Churchill (q.v.). Visited South Africa in 1891, writing a series of letters for the London *Daily Graphic*, published in book form as *Men, Mines and Animals in South Africa*. Saw the Witwatersrand and was a founder of Rand Mines Ltd., from which he netted a substantial sum. Accompanied by Alfred Beit, Percy Fitzpatrick and others, trekked through newly-occupied Rhodesia, in such luxury as roused Fitzpatrick's sarcasm in his *Through Mashonaland with Pick and Pen*.

Churchill, Sir Winston S. Had several contacts with South Africa in his earlier career. Seven years after the adventures of his father, Lord Randolph Churchill (q.v.), he was in the South African War as a correspondent of the *Morning Post*, was captured near Frere, Natal, taken to Pretoria and escaped from the old Gymnasium School there, making his way to safety via Lourenço Marques. Later he accompanied Sir Ian Hamilton's forces on their march to Johannesburg, which he described.

Church of England in South Africa. So named as a result of the litigation concerning Bishop J. W. Colenso (q.v.) and entirely distinct from the Church of the Province of South Africa (q.v.).

It is a direct continuation of the original Church of England as established at the Cape as far back as 1795, and follows a 'Low Church' doctrine and policy. After a long gap it has again secured its own bishop in recent years. There are approximately 68 churches registered in its name, 15 of which are for Whites. The White membership is around 3,000 and that of the non-Whites served by missions 15,000.

Church of the Province of South Africa. Name given to the Anglican Church in Southern Africa, in communion with the Established Church of England overseas. As a result of the decisions by the Privy Council in the cases concerning Bishop J. W. Colenso (q.v.) in the 1860's, when it was held that the Established Church could not be transplanted to the Colonies, the Church of the Province of South Africa became a voluntary association. At the head of it is the Archbishop of Cape Town, who presides over the Provincial Synod which assembles every five years to legislate on its behalf. Originally the Anglican Church in South Africa fell under the jurisdiction of the Bishop of Calcutta in India, until in 1847 the Bishopric of Cape Town was established. This was followed by those of Grahamstown and Natal in 1853, of St. Helena in 1859, Bloemfontein in 1863, Zululand in 1870, St. John's in 1873 (Eastern Province), Pretoria in 1878, Southern Rhodesia in 1891, Lebombo (Mozambique) in 1893, George, Kimberley and Kuruman in 1911, Johannesburg in 1922 and Damaraland (South-West Africa) in 1924. Since 1954 the Diocese of Rhodesia has been incorporated in the new Province of Central Africa. Apart from its ministrations to several hundred thousand Whites in the Republic, the Church of the Province of South Africa controls a very large network of mission stations, colleges, orphanages and other charitable insti-

tutions. Number of adherents (1969): 420,000 Whites, 268,620 Coloureds, 748,135 Bantu.

Cichlids. Large family of fresh water fish, also found in India and South America. Much prized by Africans as 'Ngege.' Characteristic feature is single nostril on each side. Name Mouth-breeders refers to habit of carrying eggs and young in mouth. Often called Bream in Natal and Rhodesia, and Kurper in Transvaal. Not indigenous at Cape.

Cilliers, Sarel Arnoldus. Voortrekker leader. Born in 1801 near Klein Drakenstein. Grew up near Graaff-Reinet, and joined the Great Trek under A. H. Potgieter in 1837, distinguishing himself in the battle of Vegkop. Was one of a deputation sent back to Cape Colony to help the Voortrekkers. Cilliers distinguished himself in the battle of Blood River, and held a service of thanksgiving after the victory. Settled near Pietermaritzburg, but moved to the O.F.S. after the British occupation of Natal. Helped to draft the O.F.S. constitution in 1854. He died in 1871.

Cinema. *See* FILMS.

Cinnabar. Ore of mercury, found near Ottoshoop, Transvaal, also in the Northern Transvaal, near Gravelotte, where a mine was opened, but closed down in 1946.

Citrus. Oranges have been cultivated at the Cape since the earliest days of settlement, but the industry did not develop until the last years of the 19th century, when the first navel oranges were brought from Brazil and California. Large-scale cultivation began in a number of widely-separated parts of the country, including the Sundays River valley of the Cape, the Kat River area, Citrusdal district of the Western Province and, above all, the Eastern and Northern Transvaal. Thanks to the enterprise of the late I. W. Schlesinger (q.v.), the Zebediela Estate near Potgietersrust developed into the largest single orange orchard in the world, with over 650,000 trees in bearing. The Republic today has nearly 6,000,000 citrus trees, more than half of which are in bearing. Orange orchards have also been established in Rhodesia, particularly in the Mazoe area. Because they are in the Southern Hemisphere, and do not compete with Californian, European and Middle Eastern producers, South African growers have an advantage in the export trade to England and the European continent. Precooling sheds and other installations have been set up in Cape Town and elsewhere. *See* Buchu.

Citrusdal. Citrus centre near Clanwilliam, Cape Province. Population: 1,643, including 800 Whites.

City of the Saints. Traditional nickname for Grahamstown, probably on account of its numerous churches.

Civet Cat (*Vivetta civetta*). Very shy nocturnal animal found in Central Africa, portions of Rhodesia and the Eastern Transvaal, where it prefers to live in thick bush. Measures about 4 feet from head to tail. It is very destructive of small livestock. Two glands near the tail produce a substance known as ' civet,' formerly used in the manufacture of perfumes. Colouring, brown-grey, with dark streaks and blotches. Short ears and legs.

Civil Commissioner. Office in the public service still existing in Rhodesia, but not in South Africa. Established in 1828, the duties being the handling of non-judicial and administrative work of each district. In 1834, the office was united with that of the magistrate, who held the double title. Civil Commissioners were introduced to Rhodesia in the time of Cecil Rhodes. At the Cape they lasted until Union in 1910.

Civil Service. *See* Public Service.

Claim. An area awarded to a qualified citizen, under the Mining Law of

South Africa or Rhodesia. System originated in the United States, was transferred to Australia and brought to South Africa in the 1860's. Claims are of two kinds, Prospectors' and Diggers', their sizes varying according to the nature of the mineral to be exploited. Gold claims in the Transvaal are 150 feet in breadth and 400 feet in length, it being provided that the breadth shall be taken along the strike, and the length across the strike. If possible they should be rectangular in shape, and they should not exceed 60,000 sq. feet. Diamond claims in the Cape measure 30 feet by 30 feet, and in the Orange Free State 90 by 90 feet. In Rhodesia gold claims may not exceed 90,000 sq. feet in area, and no single claim may be more than 150 feet along the strike. Base metal claims in South Africa and Rhodesia are larger than gold claims.

Claim Jumping. The illegal occupation of mining ground, particularly claims, often carried out by fraud or force.

Clan Line. World-wide shipping organisation controlled by the Cayzer, Irvine group of Glasgow, doing a large trade, particularly in cargo, with South Africa. Began operations to the Cape in 1881. *See also* Union-Castle Line.

Clanwilliam. Town in the Western Cape Province. Originally known as Jan Dissels Vlei Dorp, after the owner of the farm, but renamed Clanwilliam in January 1814, when a new township was established by Captain Williams. The Earl of Clanwilliam was father-in-law to the Governor, Sir John Cradock. Efforts were unsuccessfully made to settle groups of Irish-born immigrants here in 1820. Fruit-growing and irrigation centre. Population: 2,500, including 1,000 Whites.

Claremont: 1. Originally a separate municipality, but since 1913 part of the City of Cape Town. Famous for its association with Sir John Herschel (q.v.), who made his historic studies from his observatory at Feldhausen in 1838.

2. Bantu township near Pinetown, Natal. Population: 14,024.

Clarendon, Hyde Villiers (Sixth Earl of). Governor-General of the Union of South Africa. Born June 7, 1877, he was appointed Governor-General and Commander-in-Chief in 1931, remaining until 1937. He proved a popular and well-respected holder of this office, and skilfully handled difficult situations during the great depression, the coalition between General Hertzog and General Smuts, etc. After the completion of his term of office in South Africa in 1937, the Earl of Clarendon became Lord Chamberlain and head of the Royal Household. He died in 1955.

Clarens. Village near Bethlehem, Orange Free State, named after village near Montreux where President Kruger died. Population: 670, including 120 Whites.

Clark, Sir William Henry. Commissioner for the United Kingdom in South Africa. Born in England in 1876. In 1934 was appointed High Commissioner for Basutoland, Bechuanaland and Swaziland in the Union, where he remained till 1939. He retired in 1940, and died in November 1952.

Clarkson, Senator Charles Francis. South African Cabinet Minister. Born in Durban, 1881, he qualified as an attorney in 1905 and in 1911 became Secretary of the Unionist Party (q.v.) for Natal. After serving in the Provincial Council, he became a Union Senator in 1930 and Minister of Posts and Telegraphs in 1933. In 1945 he was Minister of the Interior, until the defeat of General Smuts' Government in 1948. He retired from the Senate in 1957 and died in 1959.

Clayton, Rev. Dr. Geoffrey Hare. Archbishop of Cape Town. Son of the Bishop of Leicester, he was born in that city on December 12, 1884, and educated at Rugby, Cambridge and Cuddeston. In 1934 he came to South Africa as Bishop of Johannesburg, a position he held until 1948, when he was elected archbishop. A man of strong convictions and of considerable self-sacrifice, he resolutely opposed many aspects of Government policy. He died in 1957.

Clayville. Industrial township near Pretoria. Population: 4,310, including 1,049 Whites.

Clematis (Ranunculaceae). The name Traveller's Joy is given to several varieties, including *Clematis glancescens*, a woody climber, growing profusely over bushes in Natal and elsewhere. Clusters of scented white flowers. The Rhodesian Shock-headed Peter (*Clematopsis scabiosifolis*) stands 3–4 feet and is best known by its white feathery fruit heads. To the same family belongs the little yellow *Ranunculus*, about 1 foot, common in damp places at the Cape, and the rare pink and white *Anemone capensis* of the Cape mountain slopes. Ranunculaceae is an order of flowers chiefly distinguished by the indefinite number of stamens. Petals vary in number and size, sometimes replaced altogether by the three or more bright sepals.

Clewer. Township near Witbank, Transvaal. Population: 2,389, including 794 Whites.

Clicks. Sounds peculiar to several South African native languages. They are believed to have come from the Hottentot, being adopted later by the Bantu of the Eastern Coast. The three main forms of click are the X or lateral, the Q or palatal and the C or dental.

CLIMATE OF SOUTHERN AFRICA
by
PROFESSOR STANLEY JACKSON
University of the Witwatersrand, Johannesburg

ALTHOUGH Southern Africa is situated in the tropical and subtropical zones, the altitude of the plateau (3,000–6,000 feet) gives the country a temperate and agreeable climate. Temperatures are moderate; excessive summer heat is accompanied by low humidity and severe winter frosts are uncommon. On the whole, Southern Africa is dry. Only the prominent escarpment on the edge of the plateau, the southern mountain ranges and some parts of the north coast of Natal and of Mozambique receive high rainfall.

The coastal plains bordering the Indian Ocean are hot and moist; these include the broad flat plain of Mozambique and the narrow lowland strip in Natal. The lowlands of Mozambique are hot and humid and, in summer, uncomfortable. The rainy season lasts only from November to April. These seasons are distinguished also by the 'monsoons' or prevailing wind systems. The northern monsoon, an extension of the Asiatic circulation to eastern Africa, begins in September and by December, when it is strongest, blows over central and northern Mozambique and the Channel. In winter the south-east trade provides the southern monsoon. Rainfall is 40–50 inches on the coast near Beira, but decreases to 20 inches on the sheltered part of the Zambesi Valley. Temperature is kept uniform on the coast by the southward-flowing Mozambique current.

The warm region in the east of the Republic—a strip between the coast and the 2,000-foot contour—is cooler and wetter than southern Mozambique; rainfall decreases from 50 inches north of Durban to 30 inches near East London and Port Elizabeth, where the contrast between summer and winter rains disappears. This coast is windy. Along with other parts of the South African coast, the eastern coastal margin experiences short periods of hot 'Bergwinds'—like the Sirocco and Harmattan of North Africa. These Bergwinds, blowing always seaward from the land, conform to the circulation over the whole country, and the high temperatures appear to be due to local divergence and subsidence in a restricted area between an anticyclone and a depression.

The plateau slopes between the coastal plain and the Great Escarpment are of uneven topography and therefore of diverse climates. Rainfall—generally over 30 inches—varies with altitude and exposure. Parts of the Amatola Mountains in the South-Eastern Cape and the exposed slopes of the escarpment in the Eastern Transvaal receive over 70 inches of rain; on the sheltered western side of the Lebombo Mountains the rainfall is below 25 inches.

The plateau has a more uniform climate. The Great Escarpment forms a natural mountainous border in the east, and the surface slopes westwards. The main features of the climate are those that would be expected at this altitude within the sub-tropical belt of high pressure—moderate to low rainfall, decreasing westwards till the country becomes a desert, many cloudless days and large diurnal variations in temperature, wind and rain. Summer is rainy and warm, winter almost rainless and cool.

Zambia, Rhodesia and Malawi have a similar climate to the Republic, but warmer, with more rain in summer and sharper contrast between wet and dry seasons. Only 2–3 per cent of the annual rainfall occurs between May and October. The low valleys are very hot in summer: in the valleys of the Zambesi, Luangwa and Kafue Rivers the mean maximum temperatures just

CLIMATIC STATISTICS FOR PRINCIPAL TOWNS IN SOUTHERN AFRICA

	Mean Annual Rainfall (inches)	Wettest and Driest Months		Mean Daily Max. Temperature in Hottest Month	Mean Daily Min. Temperature in Coldest Month	Greatest and Least Mean Diurnal Range	
Cape Town	24·69	June 4·29	February 0·59	February 80·8	July 47·3	February 19·4	July 15·7
Port Elizabeth	22·68	May 2·40	January 1·18	February 77·9	July 44·8	June 22·7	February 15·5
East London	31·81	March 3·82	June 1·38	February 78·1	July 50·4	July 19·4	March 13·0
Bloemfontein	22·21	January 3·62	June 0·32	January 85·6	July 32·5	August 29·7	February 24·1
Upington	6·14	March 1·65	June/July 0·08	January 95·4	July 40·6	August 29·9	Jan./Feb. 26·5
Durban	39·68	March 5·12	July 1·10	February 80·5	July 51·62	July 20·0	Dec./Jan. 12·1
Pietermaritzburg	36·54	December 5·63	June 0·51	February 81·1	June 42·4	June 28·3	February 18·5
Johannesburg	30·28	January 5·39	June 0·24	January 79·3	June/July 39·4	September 24·7	March 20·7
Pretoria	29·17	January 5·28	June 0·12	January 83·8	July 36·7	August 31·7	Jan./Feb./March 22·3
Lourenço Marques	29·66	March 5·28	August 0·35	February 86·7	July 55·8	July 20·5	Feb./March 15·7
Beira	55·55	January 10·79	September 0·79	February 88·7	July 60·6	June 17·3	March 13·5
Bulawayo	23·64	January 5·49	July/August 0·02	October 84·9	July 44·5	September 27·3	February 18·1
Salisbury	32·63	January 7·71	July 0·03	October 82·7	July 43·8	September 27·1	January 17·4
Luanda	13·23	April 4·76	July 0·00	March 83·8	July/August 64·0	March 12·0	November 9·0
Windhoek	14·25	March 3·11	June/July/August 0·00	December 86·4	July 42·8	August 26·1	March 20·9
Swakopmund	0·7	March 0·2	— 0·04	April 75·0	August 46·4	June 25·0	January 14·0

before the rains begin are over 90° F. South-easterly winds prevail in winter; normally they are dry but occasionally they bring to the south-eastern part of the country misty, cool weather—known as 'guti' weather locally—similar to the drizzle of the Natal mist belt. Zambia is warmer than Rhodesia and has a higher rainfall, but the seasons are similar. January and February are the wettest months and the period from May to September is rainless. October, the month before the rains, is hot.

Over the western part of the interior of Southern Africa is a large region of dry climate extending from the Kalahari to the Karroo and including part of the highlands of South West Africa, Western Orange Free State and Cape Province. Though not dry enough to be called a desert, this area is sparsely settled. The rainfall—between 10 and 20 inches—supports a poor natural vegetation of grass and scrub, and most of the land is suitable only for extensive pastoral farming. This dry region is hot; from October to March day temperatures from 95° F. to 100° F. are usual, but when the air is dry and the ground cools rapidly after sunset the nights may be cold.

Deserts occupy an appreciable part of Southern Africa and climatically the coastal desert is most interesting. Beginning in Angola and extending south-wards through the Namib of South West Africa to the border of the Republic, it spreads inland in the valley of the lower Orange River and the north-western Cape Province. The coastal zone from Angola to the Cape is cool and liable to low cloud and fog—called Cacimbo in Angola—coming in from the sea during the night and dispersing in the forenoon. Winter Bergwinds, remarkable here by contrast with the normal cool weather, cause temperatures above 90° F. and are responsible for the anomaly that the hottest weather is in winter.

Beyond the influence of the cool current the desert is hot and practically rainless, much of it uninhabited and some unexplored.

In the south-western Cape Province is a small region of winter rainfall—the counterpart of the Mediterranean climate of North Africa. Winter is rainy and cool, and summer warm and dry. Both seasons are windy. In winter the gusty north-westers blow, accompanying the frontal barometric depressions from the South Atlantic. As the cold fronts pass, the north-west wind backs to south-west and the colder air arrives, sometimes in a mass deep enough to sweep across the plateau and bring cold snaps. The summer wind is the south-easter, persistent and strong like the trade wind in the ocean a few miles to the west.

Clingstone. *See* TAAIPIT.

Clivia. *See* AMARYLLIS.

Clocolan. Town in the Orange Free State, near Lesotho border. Founded in 1860's, the name being a corruption of the Sesuto word Thlothlolaneng, meaning 'There where we stabbed them.' Farming centre noted for its scenery. Population: 5,900, including 1,360 Whites.

Cloete, Hendrik. Judge of Cape Supreme Court. Born in Cape Town in June 1792, and educated in Holland. After being called to the Bar in England, returned to the Cape to enter the Civil Service in 1813. In 1816 he started legal practice in Cape Town, continuing until 1843, when he moved to Natal, where he was made a judge in 1845. Returning to the Cape, he became a judge of the Cape Supreme Court from 1855 to 1866. He died at Cape Town in December 1870.

Cloete, Stuart. South African author. Born in Paris on July 23, 1897, he was educated at Lancing College and soon after joined the Coldstream Guards, with whom he served in World War I from 1914 to 1918. For a while he carried on cattle ranching in the Bushveld, but becoming interested in writing moved to England in 1935. His world-wide success dated from the issue of *Turning Wheels*, a novel on the Great Trek. He wrote many short stories in the American press and followed these with a series of other books on African subjects, including *The Soldiers' Peaches, The African Giant,* etc.

Close, Ralph William. South African diplomat. Born in Cape Town in 1867 and educated at the South African College, he became a prominent member of the Cape Bar before his appointment as Minister Plenipotentiary for South Africa at Washington in 1934. He remained there until 1943 and died in 1945.

Clydesdale. Colliery centre near Heilbron, Orange Free State. Population: 1,000, including 150 Whites. *See also* COALBROOK.

C.N.E. *See* CHRISTIAN NATIONAL EDUCATION.

Coal. Southern Africa has the largest coal deposits south of the Equator. Exploitation began at the Cape in 1869, but the beds were of poor quality. Later the Natal, Transvaal and Orange Free State fields replaced them. Vast reserves of medium grade in the Republic, mainly in the Transvaal, particularly Witbank, Middelburg and Vereeniging, while in the north of that province big areas still await exploitation. Proved reserves are:

	Million Tons
Transvaal	
Springs-Belfast-Ermelo Triangle	20,000
Waterberg	2,000
Natal	1,000
Orange Free State	1,000
	24,000

There is double this quantity in *probable* reserves. Total output is at the rate of over 55,000,000 tons a year. In Rhodesia coal mining is concentrated at Wankie, which has very large deposits and is equipped to produce about 5,000,000 tons a year.

Coalbrook. Coal-mining centre near Heilbron in the northern Orange Free State on the site of the Coalbrook Colliery, one of the oldest still operating in South Africa. Opened about 1896, belonging to the Clydesdale (Transvaal) Collieries Ltd., associated with the South African and General Investment and Trust Company Ltd. (Sagit). Coalbrook came into worldwide prominence when, on January 21, 1960, a large part of the workings collapsed, entombing those underground. Desperate efforts at rescue extending over several weeks proved unsuccessful. The total death roll of 435 is the heaviest in the history of South African mining.

Cobalt. Mineral found in Zambia and exploited on the Copper Belt. Deposits also exist in the Transvaal.

Cobras (Elapidae). Family of poisonous South African snakes, with deeply-grooved front fangs and highly specialised poison apparatus. They include the Egyptian or Banded Cobra (*Naia haie*), 4 feet long, found in most parts of Southern Africa, up to the Sahara Desert; the Black-necked Cobra, 6 feet, found from Natal northwards; Anchieta's Cobra (*Naia anchietae*), 5 feet, mainly restricted to South-West Africa and Angola; and the Ringhals Cobra (q.v.). By far the commonest is the 5-foot yellow or brown Cape Cobra (*Naia flava*), which is ready to attack all aggressors and is easily recognised by the raised hood (formed over the upper ribs). It frequents farm-houses in search of rats, and climbs trees well. Eggs are laid to incubate in the warmth of holes, manure heaps, roof thatch, etc. *See* SNAKES.

Cock, William. Pioneer of harbour and other developments in the Eastern Cape Province. Born in Oxfordshire, England, in 1794, came to the Cape with the 1820 settlers and recognised the possibilities of a harbour at the mouth of the Kowie River. To this scheme he devoted many years and much capital. A settlement sprang up, called Port Frances, later renamed Port Alfred (q.v.). Cock was elected to the Cape Legislative Council from 1847 to 1853 and again from 1856 to 1868. With the establishment of the first Colonial Parliament, he entered the original House of Assembly. He died in 1876.

Coelacanth (*Latineria chalumna* Smith). Genus of primitive fish, formerly known only in fossil form and considered extinct. In 1939 a trawler near East London netted a 5-foot specimen, bright blue in colour. Although already decomposed, the essential parts were saved by the enterprise of Miss Courtney Latimer of the East London Museum and of Professor J. L. B. Smith of Rhodes University, Grahamstown. A 15-year search by the latter produced a further specimen off the Comoro Islands in the Mozambique Channel. The Prime Minister, Dr. D. F. Malan, sent a special plane to hasten its transport to the Union. Living specimens have since been found and it has been recognised as a fish eaten by local natives. The name coelacanth is derived from two Greek words signifying 'hollow' and 'prickly.'

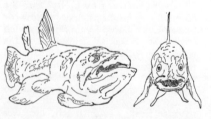

Coelacanth

Coertse, Mimi (Maria Sophia). South African opera singer. Born in Durban in 1933, she grew up in Germiston and began her studies in Johannesburg under Aimee Parkerson and later under Maria Hittorff of the famous Vienna State Academy. In 1953 she joined the permanent staff of the Vienna State Opera, gaining a high reputation all over Europe as a prima donna. In 1961 the Afrikaanse Akademie (q.v.) awarded her a Medal of Honour.

Coetsee, Jacobus. Early South African hunter and explorer. First heard of in 1760, living at Piquetberg in the Western Cape, and making a journey to the north in quest of elephants. Coetsee found the Orange River in 1762, 17 years before its official naming by Colonel Jacob Gordon (q.v.). He followed its course for about 50 miles and brought back the first reliable information.

Coffee. Crop grown in the early days of Natal. Its cultivation was carried on from the 1840's on a small scale, but it was not until 1863 that it came to popularity. By 1872, 3,700 acres were under coffee, the production being 1,680,500 lb. Diseases, however, attacked the plants and the industry has for many years been almost extinct. Thanks to emigrants from Kenya, successful efforts at its revival have begun.

Cofimvaba. Village in the Transkei. Name derived from native words meaning 'squeezing a milk-bag,' because of the excellence of its cattle. Population: 500, including 160 Whites.

Coghlan, Sir Charles Patrick John. First Prime Minister of Southern Rhodesia. Born in King William's Town on June 24, 1863. His father, James Coghlan, had lived at Clocolan in the Orange Free State. Educated at St. Aidan's College, Grahamstown, and qualified as a solicitor, making his home at Kimberley. Built up a large practice, and served in the Town

Guard during the South African War. Moved to Rhodesia where he set up his practice at Bulawayo, and in 1908 was elected to the Legislative Council. He attended the South African National Convention as Rhodesian delegate that year. When Rhodesia failed to enter the Union he concentrated on securing self-government and, after this was granted in 1923, was made the first Prime Minister. He died on August 28, 1927, and was buried at the World's View in the Matopos.

Cogman's Kloof. Pass near Montagu, Cape Province, famed for its scenery and remarkable geological formations. Named after a Hottentot chief, Koekeman.

Cohen, Abner. Jewish South African pioneer, founder of the town of Krugersdorp. Born in London in 1860, and educated in Newcastle-on-Tyne, he emigrated in 1877 to New Zealand, but left again two years later. In 1881, came to the Cape. One of the early arrivals on the Witwatersrand, he established the Homelands Estate near Johannesburg, and in 1887 founded Krugersdorp. He died in 1937.

Cohen, Dr. Emil. Mineralogist, geologist and explorer. Born at Aakjaer in Denmark on October 12, 1842, he came to South Africa for the firm of Lippert and Co. in 1872, to report on the newly-discovered Diamond Fields. He remained for over a year, conducting extensive investigations, not only in Griqualand West but also in the Transvaal, where he made some of the first reports on the Lydenburg Gold Field. Maintained contacts with South Africa after his return to Europe. In 1878 he became Professor of Geology at Strasbourg, Alsace. He was also an authority on meteorites. Died on April 3, 1905.

Coillard, The Rev. François. French Protestant missionary, born at Amiens in 1834. Wished to go to Africa and in 1857 went to Basutoland for the Paris Evangelical Mission. Remained till 1877, when he decided to set up a station in Barotseland, far north of the Zambesi. With his wife he made the long journey, and despite attacks upon his life and imprisonment at the hands of Lobengula, he completed the trek in 2 years. Gained confidence of Lewanika (q.v.) and persuaded him to come under White authority. He wrote a standard book, *On the Threshold of Central Africa.* Died of fever in 1904.

Coinage. *See* CURRENCY.

Cole, Alfred Whaley. Puisne Judge, Cape. Born in London in January 1823, and educated at the London University; was called to the Bar in 1850. Came to the Cape in 1856, practised there, and was four times elected to the Cape Parliament. He became a judge in 1880, and Puisne Judge at the Cape in 1888. He retired in 1891 and died on November 26, 1896. As a young man he was a friend of Charles Dickens. He edited the *Cape Monthly Magazine* for several years and wrote his memoirs.

Cole, Sir Galbraith Lowry. Governor of the Cape of Good Hope. Born in Ireland on May 1, 1772, Cole was Governor of Mauritius from 1823 to 1828 before being transferred to the Cape of Good Hope. During his term of office important developments occurred: the reappearance of the suppressed *South African Commercial Advertiser*, the founding of the South African College, and the building of new roads, including one through Sir Lowry's Pass. Spent much time pacifying the frontier tribes. He retired in August 1833 and died in 1842.

Colenbrander, Colonel Johann William. Rhodesian pioneer. Born at Pinetown, Natal, in 1859, of Dutch ancestors. Went to Zambesia at an early age where he gained the confidence of Lobengula, the Matabele king (q.v.). Became interpreter of the latter and accompanied his envoys to

England in 1889. He played a vital part in sending the Pioneer Column to Rhodesia, and in the 1896 Matabele Rebellion organised his own unit, 'Colenbrander's Boys.' He also accompanied Cecil Rhodes on his famous interview in the Matopos, which put an end to the rising. Fought in the South African War and was accidentally drowned near Johannesburg in 1918, while making a film on the Zulu War.

Colenso. Village in Natal, named after the Right Rev. J. W. Colenso, first Bishop of Natal. 153 miles north of Durban. Originally a wagon halt, established in 1880's, it saw heavy fighting during the South African War, on account of the strategic railway bridge there. In 1924 a large power station was erected, connected with the electrification of the main railway line to Natal. Population: 2,600, including 1,100 Whites.

Colenso, Frances Ellen. Protagonist of the Zulu people. Daughter of Bishop J. W. Colenso (q.v.), was born in England in 1849, and came to Natal in 1855. There she and her sister Harriette helped their father, and wrote widely, pleading the case of the African people. She died in 1887.

Colenso, Harriette Emily. Protagonist of the Zulu people, daughter of Bishop J. W. Colenso (q.v.). Born in England and came to Natal in 1855. As helper to her father and sister, Frances (q.v.), she was active in the political field. After the Zulu Rebellion of 1906 she took a leading part in organising the defence of Dinizulu, the Zulu chief.

Colenso, Bishop John William. First Anglican bishop of Natal, born in Cornwall in 1814. Educated under difficulties, but went to Cambridge where he gained distinction as a mathematician, later writing several standard works on this subject. After being a schoolmaster at Harrow and holding a living in Norfolk, was appointed Bishop of Natal. There he immediately gained the affection of the Zulus, but caused great uproar by refusing to compel polygamous Africans to divorce their surplus wives. In consequence of critical questions on the Bible put to him by converts, Colenso wrote a series of books challenging the literal truth of the Scriptures on many matters. He was charged with heresy and excommunicated by Bishop Robert Gray (q.v.), his Metropolitan, but went to court and was confirmed by the Privy Council in his office as bishop. (Incidentally the court held that the Church of England as a State Church could not be transplanted to the colonies.) Apart from his ecclesiastical activities, Colenso wrote the first Zulu grammar, dictionary and reading books. Was champion of the Zulu people in their dispute with the Colonial Office. He strongly criticised the policy that led to the Zulu War. He died in 1883.

Colesberg. Town in the Northern Cape Province, originally called Toverberg (Magic Mountain). Founded in November 1830, named after Governor Sir Lowry Cole. One of the oldest municipalities in Cape Colony, established 1840. Scene of considerable fighting during the South African War, and held by the Boers for several months. Important wool and horse-breeding area. Population: 7,100, including 1,800 Whites.

Colesberg Koppie. Small hill at New Rush (afterwards Kimberley), so called because a party of diggers from Colesberg made their headquarters there. During the ensuing rush the koppie was literally dug away leaving the Big Hole on its site.

Coligny. Village in the Western Transvaal. Established in 1918 and named after Gaspard de Coligny, famous Huguenot leader in 16th-century France. Important maize-growing area. Diamond digging has occurred at

PLATE IV: TRIBAL BEAD WORK AND ORNAMENTS

1. Zulu 'love letters'. 2, 3 and 4. Bead and wool hair ornaments. 5. Long bead-decorated pipes smoked by Xosa men and women. 6. Basuto 'fertility' doll. 7. Young Zulu woman wearing bead 'love letters'. 8. Bead-decorated calabash snuff box.

intervals in the vicinity. Population: 4,000, including 1,650 Whites.

Colley, General Sir George Pomeroy. British soldier and Governor of Natal. Born of Irish stock in 1835, he was educated at Sandhurst and joined the Army as an ensign in 1852. Was sent to the Cape and was stationed on the frontier as a magistrate, also mapping and surveying for the Army. After serving in China in 1860, holding a professorship at Sandhurst and being promoted to lieutenant-colonel in the Ashanti campaign, Colley paid a short visit to Natal and the Transvaal in 1875. He became Chief of Staff to Lord Chelmsford on the outbreak of the Zulu War in 1879 and major-general in 1880. In the same year he became Governor of Natal, and was confronted with the Boer invasion from the Transvaal. A succession of misfortunes followed. He was defeated at Laing's Nek in January 1881, and in order to make good this set-back occupied the summit of Majuba. The hill was stormed by the Boers on February 26, 1881, and Colley was killed.

Collins, Samuel Vernon. Diamond magnate. Born July 27, 1913, in Beaumont, Texas, where he attended High School. Began work on an oil-field at 16, selling magazines from door to door during the great American Depression. In 1934 he became a driller and in 1944 a contractor, laying submarine pipelines and working for the United States Corps of Engineers. Through these activities he came to South Africa in 1951, where interest in recovering diamonds from the sea floor off South-West Africa led to the founding of Marine Diamonds Ltd. (q.v.), later taken over by De Beers.

Colonial Orphan Chamber. Trust company established in 1856 in Cape Town, and still in existence.

Coloured Affairs. Since October 23, 1958, a separate Department of Coloured Affairs under the South African Government has been in existence, with headquarters in Cape Town and a Commissioner as its permanent head. The first holder of the post was Dr. I. D. du Plessis (q.v.). Amongst the matters it handles are Coloured Education, Land Settlement, Social Services, Reformatories and Child Welfare. Most of the staff are themselves Coloured. Under the Separate Representation of Voters Act, 1951, Coloured voters in the Cape are placed on a separate roll, under which they elect four Whites to represent their interests in the House of Assembly, besides which there are five nominated Senators, and two White members elected by Coloured voters to the Cape Provincial Council. The Union Council for Coloured Affairs, elected by members of the Coloured, Malay and Griqua communities, was the forerunner of the Coloured Persons Representative Council. This numbers 60 members, 20 nominated by the government and 40 elected for the first time on September 24, 1969 by an electorate of 600,000. It has considerable powers in dealing with affairs of the Coloured community. There are 28 seats in the Cape, 6 in the Transvaal, and 3 each in the Orange Free State and Natal. The Coloured Development and Investment Corporation, financed from public funds, has been set up to assist in the financial and business progress of the group. *See also* UNIVERSITY COLLEGE OF THE WESTERN CAPE.

Colvin, Ian Duncan. South African journalist and writer. Born at Inverness in 1877, educated in that city and at Edinburgh University. Shortly after the South African War, Colvin came to South Africa to join the *Cape Times*, where he remained as assistant editor until 1907. He was interested in local history, and wrote extensively, including the *Life of Dr. Jameson, The Cape of Adventure*, a collection of extracts from old travellers, the editorial part of Mendelssohn's (q.v.) *Bibliography*, etc. He died in 1938.

Coly. *See* MOUSEBIRD.

Commando. South African form of military organisation which originated from the need of pursuing native cattle-raiders and other assailants in the early days of white settlement. Soon every able-bodied burgher was obliged, when called upon, to provide his own horse and gun and take part in punitive expeditions. Basically this has remained the feature of the Commando. During the Dutch period at the Cape, Commandos became part of the law of the land. The system was taken over and extended by the Voortrekkers, being most successful in the Transvaal and Orange Free State. At the time of the South African War, Commando duty obliged every common citizen to appear with horse and accoutrements, gun, ammunition and food for a certain number of days. Similar methods were applied in colonies under British jurisdiction under the Volunteer system. With the establishment of the Union Defence Force in 1912, the main features of the Commando system were preserved, so far as the country districts were concerned. Equipment and certain details of organisation have been modernised, but the system still exists. Because of their mobility and success during the South African War, the word Commando was applied to highly trained specialist forces of the Army and the Navy during World War II in Great Britain.

Commerce. *See* TRADE.

Companhia do Mozambique. Chartered company set up by royal decree in 1891, largely modelled on the British South Africa Company (q.v.). It was granted extensive powers of government in the northern portion of Mozambique, having headquarters at Beira (q.v.). Much capital was British. After the expiry of the full period, the Mozambique charter lapsed in 1942.

Companhia do Nyassa. Chartered company established by royal decree in Portugal on September 21, 1891, and March 10, 1893, with powers of administration and exploitation of a large northern portion of the province of Mozambique. Started on March 16, 1893, territory covering approximately 100,000 sq. miles, reaching to the border of German East Africa. The charter lapsed in 1928.

Compassberg. Highest mountain in the Sneeuberg Range, being 8,983 feet. Named in 1778 by Colonel Jacob Gordon and Governor Van Plettenberg, who visited it, because most of the neighbouring country could be surveyed from this point.

Compound. Loosely used to describe premises for housing native and other non-European employees of mines and industrial concerns. Word is derived from the Malay Kompong, still used in Afrikaans. During the 1880's, when the prosperity of the diamond industry at Kimberley was threatened through wholesale thefts, the compound system was introduced by De Beers and other companies. In its strictest form it involved (as it still does) the native employees remaining inside an enclosure during their employment. System was applied on the Rand in a more liberal form. Most compounds are square in shape, with a large courtyard in the centre, and to-day frequently have flowers, lawns and trees. The modern ones hold 5,000 workers or more. Older compounds had large dormitories, but now the inmates are housed in relatively small rooms, with an average of about 8 or 12.

Comrades Marathon. Famous foot race by road from Durban to Pietermaritzburg, a distance of 54 miles. It was established in 1921 by Victor Clapham, on the model of the London to Brighton Stock Exchange Walk. First sponsors were the Comrades of the Great War, forerunner of the British Empire Service League. Trophies were offered by local newspapers, and the race became of national importance. Traditionally held on May 24, it is open to any white male amateur over the age of 18.

Concentration Camps. Settlements established under the auspices of the British military authorities during the South African War to remove the women and children of combatant Republicans from the fighting zones. Although there had been precedents during the Cuban campaign in 1898, the system established towards the end of 1900, by proclamation of Lord Kitchener, was very badly administered. While the motive was a humanitarian one, allegations of callousness and neglect created intense bitterness. Camps were scattered throughout the Transvaal, Natal and the Orange Free State. Overcoming much opposition, Miss Emily Hobhouse (q.v.) had the system re-examined, and secured the adoption of reforms. In October 1901, the concentration camps contained 118,000 Europeans and 43,000 Coloured people. Deaths exceeded 20,000, the numbers being increased by severe outbreaks of measles and other diseases. Later the conditions in the concentration camps improved substantially. A monument to the victims who perished in them has been erected at Bloemfontein.

Concertina Fish. *See* SICKLE-FISH.

Coney. *See* DASSIE.

Congregational Church in South Africa. The birth of the Congregational Church in South Africa may be traced to the activities of the London Missionary Society, particularly to the efforts of Dr. John Philip (q.v.). Congregations are grouped into District Associations, covering Cape Western, South-West Cape, Cape Midlands, Natal, Rhodesia, the Transvaal and the Orange Free State. Adherents (1963): 16,000 White, 137,358 Coloured, 135,167 Bantu.

Connaught, Duke of. Seventh child of Queen Victoria. Born in 1850, he was entered at Woolwich in 1866 and joined the Royal Engineers. Took part in the Egyptian campaign in 1882, served in India, and became Commander-in-Chief in Ireland in 1900. In 1906, with his wife (formerly Princess Louise Marguerite of Prussia) and daughter, Princess Patricia, paid a visit to South Africa. Four years later the duke and duchess returned to open the first Union Parliament, and to inaugurate the new Simonstown docks, etc. He died at the age of 92 in 1942.

Connaught, Prince Arthur. Third Governor-General of the Union of South Africa. Son of the Duke of Connaught (q.v.) and grandson of Queen Victoria. Born at Windsor in 1883 and entered the Army in 1903. In World War I was aide-de-camp to British Expeditionary Force 1914–1916, and with Canadian forces 1917–1918. Was Governor-General of the Union and High Commissioner from 1920 till 1924. Died in 1938.

Connor, Sir Henry. Chief Justice of Natal. Born in Ireland in 1817 and educated at Trinity College, Dublin, where he took his law degree in 1841. After serving as Chief Justice on the Gold Coast, in 1857 was appointed First Puisne Judge of Natal. Spent a short spell at the Cape. Then became Chief Justice of Natal in 1874. His writings on Roman and Roman-Dutch law are in the Natal Provincial Division Library. He died on July 12, 1890.

Conquered Territory. Area in the Eastern Orange Free State, captured from the Basuto by the Boers in 1867 and then farmed. The area, about 3,000 sq. miles, 100 miles in length, includes much of the best wheat country in Southern Africa. Ficksburg (q.v.) is one of its main centres, also Ladybrand, Clocolan and Fouriesburg.

Conradie, Johannes Hendrik. Administrator of the Cape Province.

Born at Prince Albert in 1872; studied at Victoria College, Stellenbosch, and qualified as a teacher. Worked at Christiana in the Transvaal, and later in the Orange Free State, where he became a headmaster. Having served in the South African War, he qualified as a solicitor, and from 1912 to 1921 was Superintendent of the Kakamas Labour Settlement on the Orange River. A foundation member of the Nationalist Party, he was elected to Parliament in 1920. From 1929 to 1938 he was Administrator of Cape Province. He died in 1940.

Consolidated Gold Fields of South Africa, Ltd. Mining group established in 1887 by Cecil John Rhodes and his associates, under the name of the Gold Fields of South Africa. Has large interests on the Witwatersrand as well as in other parts of the world. An associated company is the New Consolidated Gold Fields.

Constantia. Name given to several old wine farms outside Cape Town. The oldest and most famous is Groot Constantia, established in 1684 by Governor Simon van der Stel (q.v.) and named after his wife. He retired and died here. Other farms developed, notably Klein Constantia, High Constantia, etc. Up till 1885 the main farm was in the hands of the Cloete family, its wines internationally renowned. Thereafter it was bought by the Cape Government as a demonstration and experimental wine farm. The mansion Groot Constantia was burnt down in 1925 but has been rebuilt and is now a National Monument.

CONSTITUTION OF THE REPUBLIC OF SOUTH AFRICA
by
H. J. MAY, S.C.

THE four British colonies in South Africa were formed into a union by the South Africa Act, 1909, which came into force on May 31, 1910, and the first Parliament of the Union met on November 4, 1910. On October 5, 1960, a referendum (q.v.) was held on whether the Union was to be a republic, and as the majority of votes cast were in favour of a republic, the Constitution Act of 1961, which came into force on May 31, 1961, gave the Union a Republican form of government, with a State President elected by an electoral college consisting of the members of the Senate and of the House of Assembly. The State President holds office for 7 years, and may not be removed from office save on a resolution passed by a majority of each House of Parliament declaring him to be removed on the ground of misconduct or inability to perform efficiently the duties of his office.

Provision is made for the President of the Senate to be Acting President when necessary. The State President takes the place of the Queen and the Governor-General in the new constitution, and has all the powers formerly held by them.
Parliament. Under the South Africa Act, Parliament consisted of the Queen, a House of Assembly and a Senate. Under the Republican constitution, the State President takes the place of the Queen. The House of Assembly was and is elected in single-member constituencies delimited by a Delimitation Commission of three Supreme Court judges, who perform this duty at intervals of not less than 5 and not more than 10 years, working on the figures of White voters in the latest voters' lists. The Senate used to be constituted on a federal basis, the members of Parliament and the provincial councillors in each of the four provinces electing eight

senators by proportional representation. A further eight were nominated or appointed by the Governor-General-in-Council (the Cabinet), four of them being selected mainly on the ground of their thorough acquaintance with the reasonable wishes of the non-White races of the Union.

The constitution of Parliament was progressively altered from 1910 to 1961, and the House of Assembly now consists of 160 members. The Senate Act, 1955, increased the number of senators for the Union to 89, 65 of them elected by members of Parliament and provincial councillors on a majority vote in each province, 16 of them nominated by the Government, four senators elected in South West Africa and four elected in the Union by Natives. In 1958 one senator was appointed to represent Coloured (as distinct from Native) people in the Cape, and in 1959 representation for Natives was abolished. By the Senate Act, 1960, the number of senators was reduced to 54, of which 11 were elected in the Cape, 14 in the Transvaal, and eight each in the Orange Free State and Natal by proportional representation, two in South West Africa, two nominated by the Government from each province and South West Africa, and one nominated for Coloured voters. These provisions were re-enacted in the Constitution Act, 1961.

Parliament must be dissolved 5 years after its election, but may be dissolved sooner. All members of Parliament must be White persons.

Qualification of Voters. The South Africa Act provided that the qualifications of voters should be the same as those which existed in the four colonies before Union, and that no voter should be disqualified merely by reason of his race or colour without a two-thirds majority in both Houses of Parliament sitting together. This provision and a language equality clause, which could not be altered without a similar majority,

were known as 'the Entrenched Clauses' (q.v.). After a constitutional struggle, Parliament increased the number of senators in 1955 to the number stated above, namely 89, and by the two-thirds majority thus obtained removed the Cape Coloured voters in 1956 from the common roll and placed them on a separate roll, enabling them to elect four members to the House of Assembly. There were thus three separate voters' rolls in the Union: a roll of White voters directly electing 150 members to the House of Assembly for the Union, and six for South West Africa; a roll of special Native voters electing three members of the Assembly for the Cape and four senators for the whole Union; and the roll of Coloured (other than Native) voters in the Cape. Native representation in Parliament was abolished in 1959, and the position now is that all White persons over the age of 18 have the vote, and certain Coloured persons in the Cape Province with the necessary qualifications may elect four White persons to the House of Assembly.

The Cabinet. The Governor-General used to be the representative of the Queen, and the constitution of the Union was modelled on that of a British constitutional monarchy. The State President now takes the place of the Queen and the Governor-General in the constitution, but except for that change the form of government remains the same. The Cabinet consists of 16 ministers who preside over Departments of State. When we speak of the State-President-in-Council, we mean the State President acting on the advice of the Cabinet. The Prime Minister presides over Cabinet meetings, and the doctrine of collective responsibility of the Cabinet applies. Ministers are responsible to Parliament and may sit in either House, and it is compulsory for any person who was not a member of Parliament when he was appointed a Cabinet Minister to find a seat in either

House within 3 months of his appointment. There may be eight deputy ministers.

The Provincial Councils. Each province has a Provincial Council elected by White voters, the numbers being: Cape, 52; Natal, 25; Transvaal, 68; Orange Free State, 25. In addition, the Cape has two White representatives elected by Coloured voters. The Provincial Councils are legislative bodies with limited authority within their territories. They have thirteen subjects of legislative authority, mainly education, hospitals, roads and national parks. They have to act within the ambit of their powers, but within that ambit have full authority. Parliament, however, is supreme. It can at any time restrict or even abolish the powers of the Provincial Councils, which depend to a large extent upon Parliament for finance in the way of subsidies and other revenue. The executive government of the provinces is carried on by an Administrator acting with an executive committee consisting of four members.

The position in South West Africa is similar to that in a province, but the legislature is called the Legislative Assembly and not a Provincial Council, and there are 18 members. South West Africa is not a province of the Republic, but the Parliament of the Republic may, and does, legislate for the territory.

The Courts. There is one Supreme Court for the whole of the country, the former Colonial Courts having become provincial and local divisions of the Supreme Court, with an Appellate Division sitting in Bloemfontein as a last Court of Appeal. The right of appeal to the Privy Council was abolished in 1950. The inferior courts consist in the main of Magistrates' Courts and Native Commissioners' Courts, having civil and criminal jurisdiction, but certain Native chiefs have limited judicial powers. There are also Native Divorce Courts and Native Appeal Courts. Judges of the Supreme Court are appointed by the State-President-in-Council, and may not be removed from office except on an address from both Houses of Parliament, on the ground of misbehaviour or incapacity. *See also* TRANSKEI.

Convicts. *See* ANTI-CONVICT AGITATION.

Convolvulus. *See* POTATO, SWEET.

Coode, Sir John. British harbour engineer, responsible for most of the earlier South African harbour works. Born in Cornwall in 1816, he built Portland breakwater in 1856. Was invited to the Cape to design a 'Harbour of Refuge' in Table Bay, on which work began in 1860. He also designed the original scheme for Port Elizabeth, which, however, did not prove a success. Coode visited South Africa in connection with this work. His scheme for Port Natal was rejected on grounds of expense. Became a member of the Suez Canal Commission in 1888 and died on March 2, 1892.

Cookhouse. Village near Somerset East, Cape Province. Originally a military outpost; was so named by the soldiers on account of its hot climate. Population: 2,100, including 620 Whites.

'Coolie Christmas.' Old-fashioned name applied in Natal to Muharram festival of the Moslem Indians, and to the Diwali of the Hindus, also known as Dipavali, both of which involved a great deal of merry-making.

Coon Carnival. Celebration among the Coloured people in and around

Cape Town, held on the first 2 days of the New Year and marked by hilarious processions of musicians and singers, dressed in fantastic costumes, culminating in several final 'rallies' on sports grounds, etc. The annual event originated in the privileges formerly granted to slaves on 'Second New Year's Day.' It is now regarded as a major attraction for tourists during the Cape summer season, corresponding to Mardi Gras among the Negroes of New Orleans.

Co-operative Societies. After many unsuccessful 19th-century efforts, systematic development began in 1904, when Natal legalised state loans to agricultural co-operatives. Cape Colony imported an expert in 1905 and the Transvaal in 1907. The Co-operative Agricultural Societies Act was adopted in the Transvaal in 1908, followed by the Orange Free State in 1910. Only in 1922 was all South Africa placed on a uniform legal basis. In 1961 the Republic had 322 agricultural co-operatives with 287,319 members and 156 consumer co-operatives with 126,233 members, making a total of 478 co-operatives and a membership of 413,552. Assets exceed R328,000,000 and yearly turnover in 1967 R965,400,000.

Coot, Red-Knobbed (family Turnicidae). Water bird well represented in South Africa. Large and sooty-black, with a white bill and (in older birds) red knobs on the forehead. Very commonly seen. A noisy bird and a strong flier. *See* RAIL and BIRDS.

Cope, Robert Knox, (Jack). South African author. Born at Mooi River, Natal in 1913 and educated at Durban High School. He worked on South African and London newspapers and from 1940 onwards concentrated increasingly on literature, including poetry, short stories and novels. He founded and edited magazine *Contrast* and together with Uys

Krige (q.v.) edited the *Penguin Book of South African Verse* (1969).

Copper. While prehistoric workings exist at Phalaborwa and elsewhere, copper mining began at the Cape in 1685, when Simon van der Stel sent an expedition to Namaqualand, where in 1852 a number of companies began operations, the Cape Copper Company being the most successful. American interests have modernised the plant at Nababeep, etc., in recent years. High-grade blister copper is produced in Namaqualand, an exceptionally pure fire-refined product at Messina, where operations began in 1904, and electrolytic copper at Rustenburg. There are large reserves of sulphidic ores in all three localities, and small deposits occur in the Letaba, Potchefstroom, Zoutpansberg, Warmbaths and Lydenburg districts of Transvaal, and Upington, Kenhardt, Hay, Prieska, Gordonia and Port Elizabeth in the Cape Province. Two deposits of copper associated with nickel and platinum occur near Rustenburg and Mount Ayliff. In Zambia a vast industry has grown up on the 'Copper Belt' (q.v.) and operations are conducted on a smaller scale in Rhodesia at Umkondo. Copper also occurs in South West Africa at Tsumeb (q.v.). *See also* PHALABORWA, MESSINA and NABAPEEB.

Copper Belt. Name applied to area in Zambia, near Congo border, where one of the largest industrial complexes in Africa has developed, based on the vast relatively low-grade copper deposits. Fields had been exploited by natives in Central Africa and were known to David Livingstone; but mining in Zambia was begun at the start of the present century by the Northern Copper Company. Bwana Mkubwa operated from about 1910 until 1931. The Copper Belt proper opened in 1923, when exploitation began, and the town of Ndola (q.v.) was founded. Nkana, Roan

Antelope, Mufulira, Rhokana, Nchanga, Kansanshi, Chibuluma and Bancroft Mines have grown enormously, attracting a large White population. Output in 1961 was about 410,000 tons of electrolytic and 149,000 tons of blister copper, of a total value of £114,000,000 (total for 1962, 603,000 tons) besides cobalt, zinc and other minerals. Nearly 8,000 Whites and 46,000 Africans are employed. The industry was mainly controlled by the Anglo-American Corporation of South Africa and the Rhodesian Selection Trust but in 1969 financial control was taken over by the Zambian government. From Ndola to Bancroft the Copper Belt is about 70 miles in length and about 20 in width.

Coral Fish. Small tropical and subtropical East Coast fish, brightly coloured, having, unlike most fish, one nostril only on each side and deep compressed bodies, like the Butterfly Fish (q.v.). Found among coral reefs and along rocky shores. There are many varieties, including the Angel Fish (q.v.).

Cormorant, Cape (*Phalacrocorax capensis*). *See* DUIKER and BIRDS.

Corncrake (*Crex crex*). Migrant bird recorded in most parts of South Africa. *See* RAILS and BIRDS.

Corner House. Popular name applied to the Central Mining-Rand Mines group of gold mines on the Witwatersrand. Established at Kimberley in 1876 as Jules Porges & Co. (q.v.), moved to Johannesburg in 1887, where the local branch was called Hermann Eckstein & Co. till 1910. Became Wernher, Beit & Co. in 1889, when Porges retired, and the firm was taken over by Julius Wernher (later Sir Julius) (q.v.), Alfred Beit (q.v.) and others. In 1905 the firm became the Central Mining and Finance Corporation. The Corner House group is one of the largest on the Rand, with over

100,000 employees and, besides gold, has important interests including coal, lime, cement, timber, diamonds, base metals, etc. Since 1957 it has been linked closely with the American Engelhart interests. The name is derived from the head office at Johannesburg, the Corner House, a nine-storey block erected in 1904. In 1965 the group moved to a newer and taller building.

Corundum. Mineral found in the Northern Transvaal, used as an abrasive. Exploitation began in 1912, and has undergone many fluctuations. At one time it supported 400 White diggers and 40,000 Africans.

Cory, Sir George Edward. South African historian. Born in London in 1862, educated at Hurstpierpoint in Sussex and King's College, Cambridge, where he studied chemistry. At the age of 29 he came to South Africa as vice-principal at the Government school, Grahamstown. Became lecturer in chemistry and physics at St. Andrew's College, Grahamstown, and, when Rhodes University College was established in 1904, he accepted the Chair of Chemistry, besides being Public Analyst for the Eastern Province. Undertook long tours, and studied ruins and relics of the eastern frontier. Thus began his famous work, *The Rise of South Africa*, the standard history of the Eastern Province, especially of the 1820 settlers (q.v.) and their successors. During his lifetime five large volumes were published, while a sixth was issued years later as part of the Union Archives Yearbook. Also invented the Cory coffee percolator, from which he derived little pecuniary advantage. He died in 1935.

Coryndon, Sir Robert Thorne. South African-born Governor of Kenya. Born at Queenstown, Cape Colony, in 1870, educated at Grahamstown and at Cheltenham College, England. He joined the Bechuanaland

Border Police in 1889, served in the Pioneer Column in Rhodesia, in the Matabele War of 1893, and again in the Matabele Rebellion. Having hunted north of the Zambesi, Coryndon led the expedition of the Chartered Company to Barotseland in 1897, and later became Resident British Commissioner with King Lewanika (q.v.). In 1900 was made Administrator of North-Western Rhodesia, becoming in 1907 Resident Commissioner in Swaziland. In 1914 and 1915 he was Chairman of the Southern Rhodesian Native Reserves Commission, in 1916 Resident Commissioner in Basutoland. In 1917 Coryndon became Governor of Uganda, being promoted to Governor of Kenya and High Commissioner of Zanzibar in 1922. He died on February 10, 1925.

Costume (Bantu). Despite the simplicity of their dress, the various tribes of South Africa have always had very definite styles. Thus the Zulu umutsha, described by Father Bryant (q.v.) as 'a loosely hanging apron of supple hide behind and a bunch of furry tails in front,' was a complete covering for a man's loins, whereas the Hottentots were satisfied to have a covering only in the front. Xosa men were satisfied with an isi-dwaba, or skin blanket, and a goatskin bag to carry their small possessions, particularly tobacco. The Bavenda in the Northern Transvaal preferred a tsindi, or oblong strip of leather made of goatskin, sewn on to a belt, the ludedi, worn round the waist, rather like a loincloth.

Because of the coldness of their country, the Basuto cover themselves with a woollen blanket, or mophoso, sometimes also with one of cotton (or lapae). Basuto are remarkable as being the only African race to wear hats, known as katiba or thloro, which are woven from straw and bear witness to a great deal of artistic ingenuity.

Warriors among the Zulus developed a kind of uniform, the different regi-

ments of Tshaka and other early kings having varying head-dresses and other trappings, such as belts of white cow-hide, cowtails or distinctive shields. Zulu married women traditionally wore a kilt-like skirt of black leather, the details changing according to local fashion; the maidens being content with a tiny fringe of dark-brown string ranging in width from 4 to 12 inches, known as an umkindi. Beadwork was originally worn only by the well-to-do, but through the gradual reduction in price has become almost universal as a decoration.

Among the Xosa, the skirt or isikaka was of oxhide worked until it became soft and then dyed. With this went the um-nweba, or woman's kaross, to which was attached the isi-baca, a kind of hood made of hide. Bracelets and arm-rings were also much in vogue, and a girdle decorated with small brass discs.

Bavenda women formerly wore a cloak of buckskin or cattle skin over their shoulders, but this has in modern times been replaced by an equivalent garment made of cloth, and known as a mwenda. The distinctive sign of the married woman is known as a tshirivha, manufactured from the hide of a goat or sheep, softened by rubbing with cow-dung and water. This is worn round the waist and over the buttocks, with the hair against the skin. By custom it has to be made by the father, husband or betrothed of the woman.

Hottentot women originally wore only a belt, from which dangled leather flaps covering no particular part of the body.

The Herero women are noted for their peculiar head-dress, a kind of helmet made of thick hide, with ear-shaped appendages sticking out at either side and at the back, from which hang long strings of tubing.

Cotts, Sir William Dingwall Mitchell. Industrialist and merchant. Born in Scotland in 1871, established the firm of Mitchell Cotts & Co. of London and South Africa, with world-wide connections, particularly in the colliery trade, as steamship owners and in other fields. He died in 1932.

Cotyledon. *See* CRASSULA.

Coucal (family Cuculidae). Bird allied to Cuckoos (q.v.), but rearing its own young. Burchell's Coucal or Vlei Lourie is most common on river banks or in moist thickets everywhere. Its 'koo-koo-koo'—a gurgling sound—is heard more often than the Coucal is seen. Omnivorous feeder, even on young birds and mice. Black head, chestnut back and broad, dark tail. *See* BIRDS.

Council for Scientific and Industrial Research. Statutory body set up in 1945, in which are centralised the majority of research activities controlled by the State in the Republic. Its headquarters are on a 200-acre site 7 miles outside Pretoria, known as Scientia. Other research establishments are scattered throughout the Republic. Operating in conjunction with the C.S.I.R. is the South African Bureau of Standards. The total annual expenditure is around £2,500,000. Of the European staff of close on 1,000, nearly one-half are qualified scientists or engineers. Research is done in almost every branch of science, including physics, chemistry, building construction, nutrition, engineering, tele-communications, personnel, etc.

Courser (family Cursoriidae). A relative of the Waders, but adapted to open plains and deserts. It has short wings but long legs, and runs with astonishing speed. Eats insects and spiders and snake seeds. Several varieties in the Karroo, Highveld and Kalahari. *See* BIRDS.

Cowan, Dr. Early Cape explorer. Accompanied by Lieutenant Donovan, he left Cape Town in 1808 with a party of Hottentots, penetrating as far as present-day Griquatown. In-

tending to reach Delagoa Bay overland, they went into the neighbourhood of the present Marico River and the Waterberg district, finally striking the Limpopo. The Rev. R. Anderson joined them at Griquatown and brought back the only news ever dispatched by Dr. Cowan. How the travellers died is a mystery, but during the 1850's relics believed to have belonged to Donovan were discovered by settlers. These include regimental buttons of the 83rd Regiment, pocket knives and other trifles.

Cowen, Professor Denis V. South African constitutional lawyer. Born in 1917 and educated at St. George's Grammar School and University of Cape Town. Served as registrar to Mr. Justice Sutton before becoming Professor of Law at U.C.T. in 1945. Served as constitutional adviser to several African states. Became Professor at University of Chicago, 1962. Drafted Constitution of Lesotho (q.v.).

Coxcomb. Mountain near the Uitenhage district in the Winterhoek range, reaching a height of about 6,000 feet.

Cradock. Wool centre in Cape Province. Founded in 1816 and named after Governor Sir John Cradock. Population: 22,000, including 5,580 Whites.

Cradock, Sir John Francis (also known as **Caradoc**). First Lord Howland. Governor of the Cape of Good Hope. Born in Ireland in 1762, son of Archbishop John Cradock of Dublin, he became Governor in 1811. While in South Africa his military ability was of considerable use in the war against the frontier natives. Circuit courts were started under his authority. His land reforms were of permanent importance in establishing the modern system of titles. (*See* QUITRENT.) Promoted to the rank of general in 1812, returned to Britain the following year, assuming the family name of Caradoc, and later received a peerage as Baron Howland.

Craigieburn. Township in Southern Natal, near Umzinto. Population: 1,230, mostly Indians.

Craig, Sir James Henry. British general and Governor of the Cape. Born in Gibraltar in 1748; joined the Army at the age of 15. From 1774 to 1781 served in the Revolutionary Wars against the United States, returning as lieutenant-colonel, having taken part in the Battles of Bunker Hill, Ticonderoga, etc. Next foreign service was in the Low Countries in 1794. Was major-general in charge of the expedition which in 1795 captured the Cape of Good Hope for Britain. From 1795 to 1797 was Governor of the colony, before being transferred to India. Was a fair-minded administrator, respected by Dutch and English. He remained in India until 1802. When war against Napoleon recommenced, he commanded troops in Italy in 1805 and 1806. From 1807 to 1811 he was Governor of Canada. He died in 1812 in London.

Crake (family Rallidae). *See* RAIL.

Crane (family Balearicidae). Ornamental and stately bird, larger relative of Korhaan and Rail (q.v.), found mainly in the Karroo, Highveld, Transkei, Natal and Zululand. All cranes have plumes hanging over on either side of their tails, and are fond of posing and dancing. The *Blue* or *Stanley Crane* belongs to the Highveld and can be easily tamed. Lives on lizards, insects, roots or grain. The magnificent *Crowned Crane* (Mahem), with black head, golden crest and red or gold tail, is a gregarious bird of the vleis of Natal and Zululand.

Cranko, John. Ballet dancer and choreographer. Born in South Africa on August 15, 1927, and educated in Johannesburg, he first came into prominence as a member of the Cape Town Ballet Club and University of Cape Town Ballet. Proceeding to England he soon achieved fame and in 1946, at the age of 19, joined the Sadler's Wells Company. After engagements with the New York City Ballet and the Ballet Rambert he was appointed choreographer at Sadler's Wells in 1951. More recently headed the famous ballet at Stuttgart, Germany.

Crassula (Crassulaceae). Family including trees, shrubs and herbs. Rocheas and Cotyledons, chiefly succulents of Karroo and semi-desert types, have leaves spreading in rosettes over the soil, or rising in fleshy alternate pairs; flowers in one or more umbels. Red Crassula or Klipblom (*Rochea coccinea*) is a showy scarlet summer flower of Western Cape. Cape Snowdrop (*Crassula capensis*) has a delicate umbel of white flowers; a single stem rises from the leaf rosette. A tiny floating *Crassula natans* is common on Cape ponds, only the leaf rosette and hanging flowers rising to the surface.

Craven, Dr. Daniel. South African sportsman. President of South African Rugby Board. Born at Lindley, Orange Free State, October 11, 1910, and educated at University of Stellenbosch and in Europe. Became an outstanding rugby player. In 1931 played for South Africa against Britain, in 1933 and 1937 against Australia, in 1937 against New Zealand and in 1938 captained the South African team against Britain. During World War II served in the South African forces as Lieutenant-Colonel, and later joined the staff of the University of Stellenbosch as Professor of Physical Education. Managed several Springbok teams and has written extensively on rugby.

Crawfish. South African marine shellfish. Also known as Spiny Lobster in England, though, unlike the lobster, it has no claws. Must be distinguished from Crayfish, which is smaller and lives in fresh water. *See also* ROCK LOBSTER *and* MARINE RESOURCES.

Creighton. Village near Ixopo, Natal. Population 270, including 100 Whites.

Cresswell, Colonel Frederick Hugh Page. Labour leader. Born at Gibraltar in 1866, qualified as a mining engineer, in which capacity he first came to South Africa in 1893. Worked in Rhodesia and on the Rand, serving in the South African War in the Imperial Light Horse. Came into prominence as manager of the Village Main Gold Mine at Johannesburg, and protagonist of White Labour in substitution for imported Chinese coolies. Supported Miners' Strike of 1907, became a foundation member of the South African Labour Party in 1910; elected to Parliament in that year, becoming leader of the party. Was arrested during the 1914 strike and served in World War I in South West Africa and East Africa. In 1923 entered into the 'Pact' with General Hertzog (q.v.) and when the latter came into power in 1925 became Minister of Defence and Labour. Later he retired to Cape Town where he died in 1947.

Crewe, Sir Charles Preston. South African soldier and Cabinet Minister. Born in 1858 in England, came to the Cape as a young man. Served in the Cape Mounted Rifles from 1878 to 1881, taking part in several native campaigns. During the South African War, he raised and was in command of the Border Horse. Entering politics, he became Colonial Secretary in 1904, and later Secretary of Agriculture. After Union, was a member of the South African Defence Council and Chief Recruiting Officer during World War I. He died in 1936.

CRICKET IN SOUTH AFRICA
by
R. K. STENT
Cape Times, Cape Town

CRICKET began in South Africa with the formation in 1843 of the Port Elizabeth Cricket Club. The first recorded match was arranged in 1844 in the Trinder Reserve in that city, the players including three 1820 Settlers. In 1864 the Western Province Cricket Club was formed in Cape Town, its earliest match being played at Southey's Field, Wynberg.

No score card was available but a military band was in attendance and such interest was aroused that other matches were quickly arranged, 'Married' playing 'Single,' followed by 'Handsomes' against 'Uglies'!

The ground was described in a newspaper review of the various occasions as being 'undulating, with long grass' and the fielders as having the assistance of large mole-runs, which often stopped balls seemingly destined for the boundary.

The first English side that came to South Africa by C. A. Smith was led (later to achieve stage and film fame as Sir C. Aubrey Smith) and included such top English players as Johnny Briggs, the great Lancashire bowler, F. Hearne of Kent, the Hon. C. J. Coventry of Eton College and Bobbie Abel of Surrey.

Smith's team often met sides that included more than eleven men. Twenty-two batted for Western Province, for instance, so successfully that the home side (helped by W. H. Milton's 36 and 40) won by 17 runs.

The first cricket Test between England and South Africa took place at Port Elizabeth on March 12–13, 1889, with a win for the tourists by 8 wickets.

The team photographs show strange headgear—M. Read sported a 'boater,' F. Hearne a neat panama, the Hon. C. J. Coventry a 'ten-gallon' model and H. Wood a fisherman's sou'wester.

It was not until 1905–1906 that South Africa gained her first cricket victory against England. In a most exciting match, 'Dave' Nourse (father of Dudley, later to captain South Africa) carried his bat for 93 in the second innings to give his side a one-wicket victory.

The Springboks went on to win the rubber against this M.C.C. team, which P. F. (now Sir Pelham) Warner had brought to South Africa, but did not win an international game in England until 1935 when H. F. Wade's team won the rubber in the second Test at Lord's, the only one of the five matches to be decided.

South Africa sent a team to England in 1960 under the captaincy of D. J. McGlew and the managership of Dudley Nourse. A cloud hung over the early stages of the tour owing to a controversy as to whether the action of the Springbok fast bowler Geoff Griffin constituted a throw. He was no-balled on sundry occasions, and after the second Test at Lord's, in which he achieved a hat trick (three wickets with successive balls), it was decided not to use him as a bowler again on the tour. The results achieved by McGlew's side were a little disappointing. They lost the first three Tests and the two remaining ones were drawn.

At home in recent years South Africa shared the rubber with Peter May's strong 1955–1956 side, but could only draw two and lose three against Ian Craig's 1957–1958 Australians.

Again in 1963 T. E. Goddard's touring team shared the honours with Australia, each side winning one match and three being drawn. The South Africans came very close to winning the final Test and the series, being frustrated only by a last-wicket partnership by the Australian tail-enders which left insufficient time for the South Africans to knock off the few runs required. During the tour the 20-year-old Graeme Pollock and E. Barlow developed as aggressive batsmen, and their stand of 341 for the third wicket in South Africa's 1st inn-

ings, out of a total of 595, in the fourth Test Match at Adelaide has gone down as a highlight of South African cricket history.

J. E. Cheetham's side of 1953 achieved cricket world applause by sharing the honours after losing two of the first three matches in Australia. After the fourth one had been drawn, South Africa won the last Test by 6 wickets, McLean and Keith being associated in an unbeaten winning stand of 106.

In 1960–61 the New Zealand cricket team toured South Africa under the captaincy of John Reid. They improved on the record of their predecessors, winning two Tests, drawing one and losing two to square the rubber.

An English team under M. J. K. Smith toured South Africa in 1964–5; one test was won by England, but the rest were all drawn. A South African team under Peter van der Merwe made a short tour of England in 1965. Springboks won one of three tests, the others being drawn.

The tour of South Africa by an Australian team in 1966–67 showed conclusively that South African cricket, again under Peter van der Merwe, was among the World's best, resulting, for the first time ever, in South African Test match victories on her own soil. Of the five Tests South Africa won three, drew one and lost one.

Below is South Africa's full record in international cricket:

	P	W	D	L
v. England				
(in S.A.)	58	13	20	25
(in England)	39	5	16	18
v. Australia				
(in S.A.)	26	3	8	15
(in Australia)	20	4	4	12
(in England)*	3	0	1	2
v. New Zealand				
(in S.A.)	10	6	2	2
(in New Zealand)	6	3	3	0
Total	162	34	54	74

*1912 Triangular tournament. *See also* D'OLIVIERA, BASIL L.

Criminal Law. Unlike the law of England, there is no difference in that of South Africa between felonies and misdemeanours. Crimes are divided into those against the State, property and the person. Some offences, such as adultery, formerly regarded as crimes in the eyes of the law, have lapsed through lack of prosecutions over many years. Crimes peculiar to sections of South Africa's non-White population are witchcraft, pretending to the use of supernatural powers and ritual murder.

While the ultimate power of initiating prosecutions lies in the hands of the Minister of Justice, each province and South West Africa has its own Attorney-General, a permanent official, who has charge of such matters in the Supreme Court, while those in the Magistrate's Court fall under the local Public Prosecutor. Where the State authorities decline to act, private prosecutions may take place.

The Criminal Procedure and Evidence Act of 1917, with its various amendments, regulates the conduct of the courts, prosecutions, the taking of evidence, the summoning of juries, etc. For serious offences there is a preparatory examination, conducted by a magistrate, who may commit the accused for trial or discharge him. The accused had the choice of being tried by a judge and jury or by a judge with two expert assessors, but the former system became defunct as from April 1969.

Supreme Court trials are held both in major centres and on circuit. Sentences in the Magistrate's Court above a certain degree of severity are subject to automatic review by a judge. A special code operates in the Transkeian Territories.

The death penalty by hanging is enforced in the Republic. Criminal law in Rhodesia is mainly based on South African precedent, subject to modifications by local statute, but in Zambia and Malawi the British tradition predominates.

Crocidolite. Ornamental stone found in Griqualand West and other parts of South Africa, in association with asbestos, with which it is geologically linked. It has a golden brown tint, and is popular for ornaments.

Crocodile River. Another name for Limpopo (q.v.).

Cronje, General Pieter Arnoldus. Born about 1835 in the Cape Colony, accompanied his parents on the Great Trek, settling in the South African Republic, where he distinguished himself in several campaigns against the natives. Lived near Potchefstroom, and was commandant of that district when the British occupation of 1877 took place. During the Boer resistance against the new regime, culminating in the Majuba campaign, he led the Republican forces in the successful siege of Potchefstroom. Upon the return of peace, was a close adherent of President Kruger, and was elected into the Volksraad, where he was Superintendent of Native Affairs, and was also appointed to the Executive Council. Took part in several more native campaigns, and came into world prominence when in 1896 his Commando forced the surrender of the Jameson Raiders. Upon the outbreak of the South African War in 1899, he was placed in command of the South African Republic forces on the Western Front and began the siege of Mafeking. Proved less successful than in the past, and was transferred to lead the final attack on Kimberley. Won victories at Modder River and Magersfontein. He was trapped at Paardeberg and on February 22, 1900, capitulated with 4,000 of his men to Lord Roberts. As a prisoner he was sent to St. Helena. He died in 1911.

Cronwright-Schreiner, Samuel. South African writer and husband of Olive Schreiner (q.v.). Born near Bedford, Cape Province, in 1863, descended from an 1820 settler family. Educated at St. Andrew's College, Grahamstown, where he distinguished himself in sport. He presently went farming, met Olive Schreiner in December 1892 on the farm Ganna Hoek, and married her in 1894. He changed his name from Cronwright to Cronwright-Schreiner. Wrote on a variety of subjects, including *The Angora Goat, The Migratory Springboks of South Africa* and political themes. In 1898 he decided to qualify as an attorney, living for a while in Johannesburg. Returning to the Cape, he became interested in politics, and began practising at Hanover, Cape Colony. There he remained until 1907, when he moved to De Aar. In 1903 was elected Member of Cape Parliament for Colesberg, and from 1904 to 1910 he was Member for Beaufort West. In his later years he lived apart from his wife but was reconciled to her, wrote her biography and edited a number of her posthumous books. He died in 1936.

Crow (family Corvidae). Not an important family in South Africa, though the three types are well known. The *White-necked Raven* or *Ringhals* is a common large black bird with a white collar. Nests on rock ledges in the same place year after year. The *Pied Crow*, also a carrion-eater, is best known in South Africa. The *Black Crow* eats grain and insects as well as carrion, often nests in trees and is rarer.

C.S.I.R. *See* COUNCIL FOR SCIENTIFIC AND INDUSTRIAL RESEARCH.

C.T.H. Abbreviation for Cape Town Highlanders. *See* QUEEN'S OWN CAPE TOWN HIGHLANDERS.

Cuama. New port at mouth of Zambesi river, to serve Cabora Bassa (q.v.).

Cuckoo (family Cuculidae). Fairly large bird strongly represented in South Africa in summer. During win-

ter the true cuckoos, as distinct from *Coucals* (q.v.), migrate to Central Africa or further north. Unlike the European cuckoo, the family has many varieties. All have short, strong legs (Coucals have longer ones) and rounded tail. The young are reared in other birds' nests, like European cuckoos, and eject the other fledgelings. Insect eaters, specially fond of hairy caterpillars. The Red-chested Cuckoo (*Piet-my-vrou*) is one of the commonest in wooded parts of South Africa, from Cape Town to Natal. Reaches Cape Town in October, but seldom remains for winter. Sometimes seen in gardens looking for robins' nests. *See* MIETJIE and BIRDS.

Cullinan. Township on the Premier Mine (q.v.) near Pretoria. Founded in 1902, named after Sir Thomas Cullinan, finder of the mine. Used as a military training centre during World War II. Large prisoner-of-war camp for some 80,000 Italians at Sonderwater near by. Population: 4,211, including 1,393 Whites.

Cullinan Diamond. Largest diamond ever found. Recovered in the Premier Mine, near Pretoria (q.v.), by Fred Wells, an official of the company, on January 26, 1905. Weighed 3,106 carats (approximately one and a third pounds), being about 5 inches across. Named after Sir Thomas Cullinan, Chairman of the Premier (Transvaal) Diamond Mining Co. Ltd., was bought by the Transvaal Government for a nominal £150,000 and presented to King Edward VII on his birthday, November 9, 1907. I. J. Ascher and Co. of Amsterdam spent nearly 2 years cutting it up into a number of lesser stones, the largest a drop brilliant, measuring $516\frac{1}{2}$ carats, placed in the Royal Sceptre, and the second largest of $309\frac{3}{16}$ carats, a square brilliant, in the Royal Crown, kept in the Tower of London. The remainder of the 105 stones are also in the Royal regalia, total cut weight being $1,036\frac{1}{2}$ carats.

Cullinan, Sir Thomas. South African industrialist. Born in 1862 in the Eastern Cape Province, entered the building trade, and took part in the native wars during the 1870's. Later went to the Eastern Transvaal and became a Barberton pioneer. Moved to the Witwatersrand, was successful at his trade, but soon entered the field of mining. Became interested in brick and tile production about 1896 and established one of the largest plants in South Africa at Olifantsfontein near Pretoria. After taking part in the South African War, Cullinan secured the right to exploit the still unprospected property of Willem Prinsloo, on which, in 1902, was discovered the Premier Mine. This became the world's largest property of its kind. Later years largely devoted to industrial enterprises, being one of the pioneers in the production of earthenware and similar goods in South Africa. He died in 1936.

Cunene River (also spelt Kunene). On the border of South-West Africa and Angola. Rises in the Benguela tableland of Angola and flows for 720 miles into the Atlantic. Noted for its magnificent but little-known Ruacana Falls (q.v.). In collaboration with the Portuguese authorities in Angola its waters are being developed for irrigation and power production.

Cunha, Tristao da. See DA CUNHA.

Curle, J. H. Author, mining engineer and philatelist. Born in 1870, came to the Witwatersrand during the 1890's and shortly before the South African War conducted a survey which took him to every gold working in the five continents, South Africa included. Became an almost continuous traveller for nearly half a century, covering millions of miles. Curle wrote a large number of books on his experiences, noted for their downright and often unconventional views on matters of the day. Was interested in philately and built up the only collection of early Transvaal postage stamps, which he

left to the Africana Museum in Johannesburg. He died in 1943.

Curlew or **Wulp** (*Numenius arquata*). The largest bird of the Wader family (q.v.) and quite unmistakable for its size, its long curved bill and its wild call. Heavily-streaked, light-brown plumage, showing white when it flies. Commonly found all round the coast and sometimes far inland. Breeds in Europe and Asia, but is sometimes seen in South Africa during the northern breeding season.

Curlew Sandpiper. See SANDPIPER.

Curlewis, Ivan. Judge, Transvaal Bench. Born in Pretoria December 27, 1895, educated at Diocesan College, Cape Town, and R.U.C., Grahamstown. Lost a leg on active service during World War I, continued his studies at Oxford, obtained a B.A. degree in 1920 and was called to the Bar. Returning to the Transvaal, he was admitted in 1921 and practised in Pretoria until he became a judge in 1938. He died on July 16 the same year.

Curlewis, John Stephen. Chief Justice. Born in Paarl on March 31, 1863, educated at the Diocesan College, Cape Town. Taught at Cradock, and became a Civil Servant in 1883. In 1887 was admitted to the Bar, practising in Pretoria, rising to Acting Judge of the Transvaal High Court in 1899. After the South African War resumed his practice in 1902 and was appointed to the Transvaal Bench in 1903, rising to Judge President in 1924, and Chief Justice of the Appellate Division from 1936 to 1938. He died in Pretoria on August 24, 1940.

Currency and Coinage. Right through the régime of the Dutch East India Company to the end of the 18th century, confusion prevailed at the Cape in the matter of currency, coins from almost every part of the world circulating, although the official units were the rixdollars, stuivers and skillings (qq.v.) of Holland. Efforts to regulate matters began after the British occupation, when official rates of exchange were defined, not always with success. British currency became compulsory in 1825, but the expression rixdollar remained in use for many years, even though the founders of the Boer republics were also obliged to use pounds, shillings and pence. In the 1870's attempts were made by President T. F. Burgers (q.v.) of the Transvaal to create a Republican currency, but little eventuated beyond the striking of pattern coins. Because of the Indian labourers, Natal tried the use of rupees in the early 1880's, an experiment soon abandoned. In 1891 the South African Republic established its own mint at Pretoria, from which a local series of coins, identical in value to those of Britain, was issued.

In 1923 the present South African Mint was opened at Pretoria, first as a branch of the Royal Mint in London and later as an independent institution. The year 1961 witnessed a major change when the decimal system was applied to South African currency, based on the rand (q.v.) of 100 cents, equal to 10 shillings. *See* DECIMALISATION.

Bank notes in South Africa date from the early 19th century, the numerous local banks and even important business firms issuing their own. Since 1920 the sole right of issue has been vested in the South African Reserve Bank.

Mozambique currency, comprising contos and escudos, is based on that of Portugal. For Rhodesia: *see* DOLLAR; for Zambia and Malawi: *see* KWACHA and NGWEE; for Swaziland: *see* LILANGENI and LUHLANGA.

Currie Cup. Annual sporting trophy awarded inter-provincially for Rugby, Soccer, Swimming and Cricket. Was presented by Sir Donald Currie (q.v.) in 1889.

Currie, Sir Donald. Shipowner. Born in Greenock, Scotland, on September 17, 1825, educated in Belfast and began work in 1842 with a Liverpool shipping firm. Came in contact with the Cunard Line, and was its agent from 1849 to 1862. Began his own business, sending his first vessels to the East; in 1872 changed to the Cape and established the famous Castle Line. Competing with the older Union Line (q.v.), he soon dominated the trade to South Africa. He became wealthy, helped in settlement of political disputes on the Diamond Fields and was elected to the House of Commons in 1880. In 1900 amalgamated the two rival companies into the Union-Castle Line (q.v.). Chiefly remembered by the public as the founder of the celebrated sporting trophy, the Currie Cup (q.v.). Died on April 13, 1909.

Customs Conventions. In 1889 the first Customs Convention formed between the Orange Free State Republic and Cape Colony. At a conference in Bloemfontein in 1896, President Steyn, of the Orange Free State, attempted to bring in the Transvaal and Natal, as well as Mozambique. No progress made till 1898, when Natal joined. After the war, the Transvaal and Southern Rhodesia were included. The local position was altered in 1910, through the establishment of Union, but periodic renewals of the agreement with Rhodesia took place. In 1930 the first Customs Houses were set up at Beit Bridge and elsewhere. Following the attainment of independence by Botswana, Lesotho and Swaziland, negotiations for revised Customs arrangements have begun. *See also* MOZAMBIQUE CONVENTION. Imperial Preference was introduced in South Africa in 1903, and soon extended to other dominions. Concessions made by the British Government in 1919 for goods produced within the Commonwealth, relations being further clarified at the Ottawa Conference in 1932.

Cutworm (*Agrotis noctuae*). Garden plague in South Africa, actually not a worm at all, but a type of caterpillar. Takes its name from the fact that it eats away the tender plants level with the ground.

Cuyler, General Jacob Glen. Soldier and early British official at the Cape. Born in Albany, New York, in 1775, his father being mayor of that city. Entered the British Army and left the country, since in the American War of Independence his family sided with the British. Came to the Cape as a major at the time of the British occupation in 1806, settling on the eastern frontier. Became Landdrost of the newly-formed district of Uitenhage (q.v.). Officiated during the Slagters Nek Rebellion (q.v.) and supervised the arrival of the 1820 settlers and their colonisation of the frontier region, called Albany after his native town. Cuyler was later promoted general and lived at Cuyler Manor near Uitenhage. He died on April 14, 1854.

Cycads (Cycadaceae). Group of dioecious plants belonging to an ancient type mostly of a small tree-form, usually without branches. Unisexual. About 80 species known throughout the world. The stem averages about 8 feet, stout and rough with scales. Leaves pinnate and resembling those of a large palm. Cones with large leathery scales. Seeds like a large date. North-eastern districts of the Cape Province to Natal and Transvaal. *See* TREE FERN.

Cyphergat. Former colliery centre in the Stormberg mountains of the Cape

Cycad

Province. Opened up in 1860's but now of small importance owing to the superiority of the Transvaal and Natal coal.

Cyprian Bhekuzulu. Senior Chief of the Zulus. (Officially there is no Paramount Chief, only the Chief of the Usutu, the senior tribe of the Zulu nation.) Born on August 26, 1923, and his duties were first carried out by the Regent Mshiyeni who resigned in 1946. Cyprian was formally installed on August 27, 1948.

Cyrtanthus. *See* AMARYLLIS.

D

Dabchick. *See* GREBE.

Dabulamanzi. Famous Zulu chief, half-brother to Cetewayo (q.v.); commanded the attack on the British at Rorke's Drift (q.v.) in the Zulu War. He later surrendered, returned to Zululand, but was involved in fresh unrest. Summoned to Vryheid in 1886, he escaped from arrest, and was shot dead.

Da Cunha, Tristao (also known as **Tristan da Cunha**). Portuguese navigator and soldier. He discovered the group of islands in the South Atlantic, one of which bears his name. Later he explored the coast of Madagascar and in Mozambique destroyed the towns of Oja and Brava. Died in 1520.

Da Gama, Vasco. *See* GAMA, VASCO DA.

Dagbreker. Afrikaans name for Familiar Chat. *See* CHAT.

Dageraad (*Chrysoblephus cristiceps*). Fish found off Table Bay (rare), False Bay to Natal. About 25 inches long. (Name derived from the Afrikaans word for 'Sunrise' because of the colour.) *See* BREAM.

Dagga (*Cannabis sativa*). Wild hemp, identical with the oriental hashish. It possesses strong narcotic properties and from time immemorial has been smoked by many tribes, particularly the Hottentots, from whose language the word is derived. An article of ordinary commerce in South Africa, advertised in the press, until the present century when its cultivation and sale have been made illegal under heavy penalties.

Daily Dispatch. East London morning newspaper, founded September 1872 as the *East London Dispatch.*

Daisy (Compositae). So vast a family—about 10,000 species in the world—that only a few South African types can be mentioned. All are characterised by heads of small-petalled florets surrounded by an involucre of one or more rows of bracts. Fruit a seed often dispersed by a feathery or hooked pappus (extension of the calyx). Nearly all the plants of this family are bitter or astringent, e.g. chicory. Some have only tubular (called discoid) florets, e.g. the many Everlastings (*Helichrysum* and *Phaenocoma*), *Pentzia* and *Athanasia dentata*. Some, like Sowthistle (*Sonchus*) and Wild Lettuce (*Lactuca*), have only flat, ray-like florets (called lingulate). The vast majority have both types of florets (called radiate). Among these are Botterblom (*Gazania*), with its long, showy, loose orange and yellow petals; Wit Botterblom (*Dimorphotheca*), a straggling wall plant with dark centres to its large white flowers; Gousblom (*Arctotis*), dark centres and large golden rays; the many-coloured Barberton Daisies (*Gerbera*); the delicate blue Wild Aster and Felicia; and the several varieties of *Senecio*, with their more widely-spaced florets. *See also* CAPE IVY.

Dale College. Large boys' high school in King William's Town, Cape Province. Founded in 1877, and named after Sir Langham Dale, Superintendent-General of Education of the Cape.

Dale, Sir Langham. Superintendent-General of Education of Cape Colony. Born at Kingsclere, Hampshire, England, on May 22, 1826, he graduated at Oxford in 1848 and secured through Sir John Herschel (q.v.) a professorship at the South African College. In 1858, after its successful reorganisation, he became Superintendent-

General of Education. He played a large part in developing the Board of Public Examinations into the University of the Cape of Good Hope. He was a writer of note and greatly improved the school system of the Colony. Dale died in January 1898.

Daleside. Township near Vereeniging, Transvaal. Population: 1,074, including 783 Whites.

Dalhousie, Simon Ramsey, Earl of. Governor-General of the Central African Federation. Born on October 17, 1914, and educated at Eton and Oxford, he served in the Black Watch in World War II. From 1945 to 1950 he sat in the House of Commons, before receiving his appointment at Salisbury in 1957 in succession to the late Lord Llewellin (q.v.). He continued in office till the dissolution of the Federation in 1963.

Dalindyebo. Chief of the Tembus. Born in 1865, he became a Christian as a boy and succeeded to the leadership of the tribe at the age of 19. Upon the establishment of the Tembuland General Council (Bunga), he played a leading part in its proceedings. He did much for education, was well respected and died in 1923.

Dalling, Bruce Tweedale. South African yachtsman. Born in 1939. Educated at St. John's College and University of Natal. Went to sea, then joined the Hong Kong Police, during which time he took up yachting, and participated in the ' China Race ' from Sydney, and Sydney to Hobart. He served in the crew of *Stormvogel* (q.v.). Became lecturer in Agriculture at Pietermaritzburg. In the single-handed South African yacht *Voortrekker* he participated in the 1968 Transatlantic Race in which he came second, and first on handicap.

Dalton. Village near New Hanover, Natal. Population: 760, including 180 Whites.

Danger Point. Headland on the south coast of the Cape, near Cape Agulhas, and famous as the scene of the wreck of the *Birkenhead* in 1852 (q.v.). It now carries a lighthouse.

Daniell, Samuel. Artist and traveller. Born in 1775, he became secretary and draughtsman of an expedition dispatched from the Cape of Good Hope in 1801 to explore what is now Bechuanaland. He produced a number of strikingly beautiful and accurate pictures, particularly of the native types and settlers in the colony. In 1804 appeared his work, *African Scenery*, one of the most valuable items of Africana. He died 1811 in Ceylon, and his sketch book of South African native tribes was published posthumously in 1820.

Danielskuil (Daniel's Pit). Village near Postmasburg, Cape Province. Population: 1,910, including 700 Whites.

Dannebol. Name used at the Cape for the fruit or cone of Stone Pine tree. The seeds, known as Dannepits, are cracked by children and the kernel eaten. *See* STONE PINE.

Dannhauser. Town near Newcastle, Natal. Population: 1,894, including 405 Whites.

Darling. Town in the Western Cape Province, founded 1854 and named after Lieutenant-Governor Sir George Darling. Farming centre and noted for its annual Wild Flower Show. Population: 2,100, including 700 Whites.

Darnall. Sugar milling centre on the Lower Tugela, Natal. Population: 2,413, including 316 Whites.

Dart, Professor Raymond Arthur. South African anthropologist. Born at Brisbane, Australia, February 4, 1893, studied medicine at the universities of Queensland and of Sydney and served in World War I. After lecturing at

London University and doing research under the Rockefeller Foundation 1921–22, was made Professor of Anatomy at University of the Witwatersrand 1923, and in 1925 Dean of the Faculty of Medicine. Although his main fame rests on his recognition of the revolutionary importance of the Taungs Skull (q.v.), he did much other research and received international honours.

Darter. Common name for Snake-bird (q.v.).

Dartnell, Major-General, Sir John George. South African soldier, born in Canada, 1838. He entered the army in 1855 and served in India during the Mutiny. On taking his discharge in 1869 he came to Natal and served in the Zulu War in 1879, the Basuto War (Gun War) in 1880, and in both the First and Second Boer Wars. In 1874 he established the Natal Mounted Police, which he commanded in various campaigns. He retired 1903 and died in August 1913.

Dassie, Coney or Rock Rabbit. Small mammal found in most parts of Southern Africa. There are two types: the Rock Dassie (*Procavia capensis*) of mountainous country and cliffs, and the Tree Dassie (*Procavia arborea*) which prefers forested country. The Rock Dassie lives in crevices among the stones but does not dig itself in. Owing to the special adhesive quality of the soles of its feet, it is able to climb almost vertical walls of rock. It lives chiefly on vegetation. The Tree Dassie is very similar, except for its colouring, grey instead of brown. Both are completely harmless. *See also* HYRACIUM.

Dassie, Black-Tail (*Diplodus sargus*). Fish found from Walfish Bay to Saldanha Bay, and False Bay to Natal and Zululand. Occurs also in the Mediterranean, West Africa to Angola. About 16 inches long. *See* BREAM.

Dassie Adder. A mythical creature supposed to be a cross between a dassie or rock rabbit and a snake, frequently figuring in old South African folklore.

Dassie Pis. *See* HYRACIUM.

Dassievanger. Afrikaans name for Black Eagle. *See* EAGLES.

Davel. Village in the Eastern Transvaal. Established about 1908 and named after a local farmer, J. Davel. Maize-growing centre. Population: 600, including 160 Whites.

Davidjeswortel. *See* MELON.

Davis, Sir Edmund. Rhodesian and South African capitalist and art connoisseur, born in 1862 near Melbourne, Australia, and educated in Paris and in England. He came to South Africa as a youth of 17 and at an early age made his way to Rhodesia, where he became one of the most successful mining operators, particularly north of the Zambesi. Among the concerns in which he played a leading part were the Rhodesian Broken Hill Development Company, the Wankie Colliery Company and the Loangwa Concessions, of which he became chairman. He was also a prominent figure in the British South Africa Company, the Anglo-American Corporation, the South West Africa Company, Umtali Mines, Turner & Newall and numerous other concerns, not only in Africa. He established his own group of companies, and played a leading part in starting the copper industry in Zambia. He settled in England at Chilham Castle, near Canterbury, where he formed a famous art collection, besides acting as High Sheriff for the County of Kent. In 1915 he presented a collection of modern British paintings to the Luxembourg Gallery in Paris. He died in 1939.

Dawson, Geoffrey. Journalist and newspaper editor. Born in Skipton-in-Craven, Yorkshire, on October 25, 1874, his family name being Robinson.

Educated at Eton and All Souls' College, Oxford, he entered the Colonial Office in 1898, in the South African Department. He became Assistant Private Secretary to Joseph Chamberlain, and in 1901 Private Secretary to Lord Milner, as a member of whose famous 'Kindergarten' (q.v.) he came to South Africa. From 1905 to 1910 he was editor of the *Star* in Johannesburg (q.v.). After his return to England in 1912, he was editor of the London *Times* until he retired in 1941. In 1917, for reasons of inheritance, he changed his name to Dawson. He died in 1944.

Day of the Covenant. *See* DINGAAN'S DAY.

De Aar. Town and railway junction in the Karroo, 500 miles from Cape Town. Founded as a wayside halt in the 1870's by the Friedlander Brothers, on a farm named after an 'Aar' or underground vein of water. Became the junction of lines to the Eastern Province and Orange Free State. During South African War was base of operations for Lord Roberts. In 1914 the link-up with the railways in German South West Africa was carried out from De Aar at the rate of over 1 mile a day. Olive Schreiner lived there for a number of years. Population: 16,700, including 5,650 Whites.

Dealesville. Town near Boshof, Orange Free State. Population: 1,140, including 400 Whites.

De Barros, Joao. Portuguese historian and traveller. He explored the West Coast of Africa before the discovery of the Cape, was stationed on the Gold Coast and held a court position under King John III of Portugal. His greatest work is the *History of the Portuguese Conquest of Asia*, the most reliable account of Bartholemew Diaz at the Cape of Good Hope. De Barros, because of his majestic style, has been called 'The Livy of Portugal.' He was born in 1496 and died in 1570.

De Beer, Diedrich Arnoldus and **Johannes Nicholas.** Two brothers who had since 1860 owned the farm Vooruitzicht on which the diamonds were discovered in 1870 that led to the founding of Kimberley after the great Rush. They sold out for £6,000. Their names have been commemorated in the De Beers Mine and in De Beers Consolidated Mines Ltd., with neither of which had they any further connection.

De Beers Consolidated Mines Ltd. Company formed by Cecil John Rhodes, B. I. Barnato, Alfred Beit and their associates to amalgamate virtually the whole diamond mining industry of South Africa. The company was formed on March 13, 1888, with a nominal capital of £100,000, to take over the De Beers, Kimberley, Bultfontein and Dutoitspan mines. Rhodes, Barnato, F. S. Philipson-Stow and Beit were the original 'Life Governors.' The capital has since been raised to R22,750,000, and its interests widened to cover many other industries.

Debe Nek. Beauty spot and health resort in Amatola Mountains, near King William's Town, Cape Province.

De Blank, Archbishop Joost. Anglican Archbishop of Cape Town. Born in Holland on November 14, 1908, he came to England as a child and was educated at Merchant Taylors' School, London; and at Cambridge, where he studied theology. He took holy orders in 1931 and served in various English parishes. From 1940 to 1946 he was an army chaplain; from 1952 he was Bishop of Stepney, London, before receiving the South African appointment as archbishop in 1957. Retired on grounds of ill-health in 1963. Died in England January 1, 1968.

Decimalisation. Suggestions, going back many years, in favour of the adoption of a Decimal System of currency in South Africa, and sponsored by Mr. P. A. Moore, M.P., in the House of Assembly, were accepted by the Union Government in 1958 upon the report of a special commission. Its recommendation was a system based on the rand (equal to 10 shillings), which was to be divided into 100 cents (q.v.). Methods to facilitate the change, estimated to cost about £9,000,000 in accounting machines, cash registers, petrol pumps, school books, etc., were worked out in collaboration with representatives of industry and commerce, and the switch-over took place on February 14, 1961. The new units of currency also circulate in Lesotho, Botswana, Swaziland and South West Africa, but the old currency will remain in use until it is worn out. Similar measures of decimalisation have been taken in Rhodesia, to which country, as to Australia and New Zealand, South Africa, by special request, furnished advice and information for their own change-over.

De Doorns. Village in the Hex River Mountains, Western Cape Province. Fruit-growing centre. Population: 3,900, including 1,200 Whites.

Defence. The roots of the South African military system go back to the earliest days of White settlement, when levies were called up among the settlers to carry on operations, particularly for the recovery of stolen cattle, against the Hottentots and other local tribes. Out of this grew the famous Commando system (q.v.), which remained in use down to modern times in all four provinces.

Parallel with this developed the Volunteer system, set up in Britain in 1859 and carried to the Cape about 1862. This enjoyed great popularity, both in this colony and in Natal, many regiments still in existence owing their inception to it.

A different military system prevailed in the two Boer Republics, where the main emphasis remained on the Commandos (q.v.) and on the law under which every burgher had, upon receipt of the prescribed notice, to offer himself for service with horse, saddle and provisions for a prescribed number of days. Small standing forces were set up both in the Transvaal and in the Orange Free State as their respective Staatsartillerie (q.v.); they maintained a fairly high standard of efficiency and did good service in the South African War.

Following the establishment of the Union of South Africa in 1910, the entire defence organisation was reviewed, and the citizen militias of several foreign countries, notably of Switzerland, were studied. The South Africa Defence Act No. 13 of 1912 created the Union Defence Force, which embodies the results of these studies. Although amended in 1922 and again in 1932, few fundamental changes have been adopted. Every male citizen of white descent between the ages of 17 and 55 is liable for military service.

The Union Defence Force comprises the South African Permanent Force, with Army, Navy and Marine sections, as well as the South African Military Nursing Service. Attached to it are the South African Military College in Pretoria and several specialised schools, including those devoted to artillery, coastal defence, naval training, air training, etc.

The Active Citizen Force comprises military, air and naval units, which have undergone training in accordance with the law. In addition there are Rifle Commandos, composed of those who do not undergo peacetime training, based on the old Commando system. These receive certain facilities, including free arms and ammunition, from the Defence Department.

Besides the South African Permanent Force and the Active Citizen Force Reserves, there is an Officers' Reserve and a National Reserve, covering all persons not otherwise included.

Cadet corps in schools do not, strictly speaking, form part of the Defence Force but work in close conjunction with it.

The Coloured Corps, which had done excellent service in both World Wars, was revived in 1963.

Non-Europeans are also employed in the Auxiliary Services of the Defence Force, as non-combatants, particularly as drivers, guards, etc.

The Central African Federation had its own military units under the Central Africa Command, besides the Royal Rhodesian Air Force. Since the dissolution of the Federation each state has its own troops. Most of the Royal Rhodesian Air Force has passed under the control of Rhodesia. Africans are not disqualified from service in the Defence Forces, nor from receiving commissions.

In South West Africa the South Africa Defence Act also applies, with the proviso that former German citizens and their children are not liable for compulsory service, though they may volunteer.

See also NAVY, SOUTH AFRICAN, and SOUTH AFRICAN AIR FORCE.

Deferred Pay. Portion of pay due to native workers recruited from Mozambique for the Transvaal gold and coal mines, handed over directly to the Mozambique authorities in terms of the Mozambique Convention (q.v.).

De Hoek. Large cement works near Piketberg. Population: 880, including 200 Whites.

De Kaap Gold Field. In the Eastern Transvaal. Chief centre today is Barberton (q.v.); formerly there were a number of other camps including Eureka City and Jamestown. The field takes its name from a bold promontory among the nearby mountains, which reminded pioneers of the Cape of Good Hope. In its heyday, which lasted from 1882 to 1887, De Kaap produced several millions' worth of gold. Today there are only a few small workings left, but hopes are entertained of reviving some, including the celebrated Sheba Mine.

De Klerk, Senator Johannes. President of the South African Senate. Born at Burghersdorp, Cape Province, on July 22, 1903, and studied at Potchefstroom, qualifying as a teacher in 1926. In 1945 became secretary of European Workers' Protection League and in 1946 Chief Secretary of National Party in Transvaal. After sitting in the Transvaal Provincial Council from 1949 to 1954, entered the Senate and became successively Minister of Labour, Public Works, Mines and Immigration. In 1961 was given portfolios of Interior, Education, Arts and Science. Retired from the Cabinet in 1969.

De Korte, Benedictus. Puisne Judge of the Transvaal High Court. Born in Cape Town on January 28, 1859, and educated at the South African College. He was called to the Inner Temple in 1880 and practised at the Cape from 1880 until 1886, when he went to the Transvaal, rising to Third Puisne Judge of the Transvaal High Court in 1888. In 1889 he became First Puisne Judge and resigned shortly after. After the Boer War he resumed practice in Pretoria, and acted as Librarian of the Supreme Court Library from 1902 to 1922. He died in Pretoria on June 21, 1922.

De la Caille, Abbe Nicholas Louis. French priest and astronomer. Born in 1713, he made some of the first important observations at the Cape. In 1750 De la Caille proposed to the Paris Academy of Science that he visit the Cape of Good Hope to measure a parallel of longitude. Funds were provided from the Royal Treasury, and he arrived on April 19, 1751, setting up his observatory in Strand Street, Cape Town, where a monument to him has since been placed. He remained till 1753, during which time he catalogued 10,035 stars, his results being published in 1763. The Abbe also made important observations of the Moon and of Mars without any assistance, although the Dutch authorities maintained a friendly attitude. Died in 1762.

De la Fontaine, Jan. Governor of the Cape. Came to South Africa in 1710 and was promoted to Secunde under Governor Pasques de Chavonnes (q.v.). Acted as temporary head of the administration upon the death of the latter—from September 1724 to February 1727—and again, after the death of Governor Noodt, from April 1729 to March 1730, when he became Governor. His nickname, 'The Man with the Smiling Face,' gives an indication of his popularity. He remained in office till August 1737, when he retired to Holland.

Delagoa Bay. Inlet on the coast of Mozambique, and one of the finest harbours in Southern Africa. Measuring about 26 miles from north to south and about 22 miles from east to west, it was discovered in 1502 by the Portuguese navigator Antonio do Campo, who was serving under Vasco da Gama. From the earliest days it was recognised as one of the most important trading centres, particularly as fresh water was procurable from the several rivers, including the Rio Espirito Santo and the Maputa. There is an important island, Inhaca (q.v.). Because of its strategic position, several countries attempted to establish settlements there (see LOURENÇO MARQUES), and in 1822, Captain W. F. W. Owen carried out a survey and entered into a treaty with the local chief. Fresh approaches to the natives were made by the commander of H.M.S. *Narcissus* in November 1851, followed in 1869 by the British Corvette *Petrel*, which had instructions to hoist the British flag at Inhaca. The matter of the ownership of Delagoa Bay was finally submitted to the arbitration of the President of the French Republic, Marshal MacMahon, who on July 24, 1875 acknowledged the claims of the Portuguese.

Delalle, Bishop Henri. Catholic bishop. Born in Lorraine, France, in 1869, ordained in Rome in 1894 and sent to Natal in 1896 to join the staff of St. Charles College, Pietermaritzburg. He attracted notice for his services to wounded and suffering during the South African War and in 1903 was appointed Vicar Apostolic and Bishop of a large diocese, covering Natal, Swaziland and the Transkei. Was awarded the Legion of Honour by the French Government. One of his most remarkable experiences was the treatment of two girls 'possessed by evil spirits' at Mariannhill Monastery. He died on February 16, 1949.

De Lange, Johannes, (nicknamed **Hans Dons**). Famous scout of the Voortrekkers, accompanied Gerit Maritz on the Great Trek and rendered service to Pieter Retief and A. W. J. Pretorius as a scout. After the defeat of Dingaan he was appointed official Resident of the Boers with the Zulu King Panda. He later settled near Ladysmith and enjoyed a high reputation. In 1860 he shot and killed a native, for which he was sentenced to death and hanged in 1861 in distressing circumstances.

Delarey, General Jacobus Hercules. Born near Winburg, O.F.S., in 1847. The son of a Voortrekker, he settled with his parents in the Transvaal and made his home near Lichtenburg. He served as a field-cornet in the Majuba Campaign and rose to be Commandant. From 1893 onwards he was a Volksraad member for Lichtenburg, but he first gained prominence by helping to capture the Jameson Raiders. In the South African War he achieved international fame through a series of brilliant victories, notably at Graspan and Two Rivers. In March 1902, at

Tweebosch, he captured Lord Methuen. After the Peace of Vereeniging, Delarey, now a national figure, joined the delegation that went to Europe to collect funds for the Boer War victims. He took part in the National Convention in 1908–1909 and was appointed a Senator in the first Union Parliament. Supporting the views of General Hertzog, he was an early backer of the Nationalist movement, being credited with a wish to restore the Boer republics. His suspected sympathy for the 1914 Rebellion was never proved, for while driving with General C. F. Beyers (q.v.) through Johannesburg on September 15, 1914, the car failed to stop when challenged by a policeman hunting the Foster Gang (q.v.). The policeman fired and killed Delarey.

Delareyville. Village in the Western Transvaal, near Lichtenburg, named after General J. H. Delarey, famous Boer leader, who lived near by. Started as a settlement for Poor Whites, who were to be employed in exploiting a neighbouring saltpan, it developed into a centre for maize-growing and wool-production. Population: 4,640, including 1,100 Whites.

Delegorgue, Adulphe. French traveller and writer. Intended becoming a lawyer, but instead went to sea and in 1838 came to the Cape, from where he proceeded to Natal. His objective account of conditions among the Voortrekkers, Zulus and British was the result of 4 years' stay, and, under the title *Voyage dans l'Afrique Australe, notament dans le territoire de Natal* ... was published in 1847 in Paris.

Delfos, Cornelis Frederick. South African industrial pioneer. Born in Rotterdam, Holland, 1868, he was educated in Amsterdam and came to Pretoria in 1890, where, with his brother, he set up one of the first electrical engineering firms in the Transvaal. Early in the present century he became interested in the possibility of the production of steel and iron from ore in the Pretoria town lands, and erected the first successful blast furnace there in 1918. After many struggles, he was to a large extent responsible for the creation of the South African Iron and Steel Industrial Corporation (*see* Iscor), of which he was a director. He died in 1933.

Delmas. Town near Springs, Transvaal. Population: 6,320, including 1,750 Whites.

Delpoortshoop. Diamond camp, near Barkly West, Cape Province. Population: 1,808, including 386 Whites.

Delville Wood. Scene of a battle in France during World War I. On July 15, 1916, General Sir H. T. Lukin (q.v.), in command of the South African Brigade, received orders to take and hold this position at all costs. The wood was near Longueval, a key position in the Battle of the Somme. The force succeeded in capturing it, but a series of counter-attacks were launched by the Germans. For 5 days these continued almost day and night, the South Africans holding their ground despite fearful losses. Relief came on July 20. Of 121 officers and 3,032 men, the uninjured survivors were 5 officers and 750 men. A national memorial (with a duplicate outside the Union Buildings, Pretoria) was erected there in 1926.

Deneysville. Village near Heilbron, Orange Free State. Population: 260, including 100 Whites.

Dengue Fever. Infectious illness particularly common in Natal during the warm season. The name Dengue is believed to be derived from a Swahili word. It is also common in the West Indies, where it is known as Polka Fever. The symptoms include lassitude, headache, fever, skin eruptions and pain in the joints.

Denyssen, Petrus Johannes. Judge, Cape Supreme Court. Born in Cape Town on August 18, 1811, and educated in Holland. He was called to the Inner Temple in 1836, and admitted at the Cape in 1837. Temporarily abandoning his legal career, he served the Cape Town Municipality as secretary for many years, but in 1856 returned to the Bar and in 1865 was appointed to the eastern district. In 1868 he became a judge of the Cape Supreme Court, retiring in 1877. He died in Germany on November 15, 1883.

D.E.O.R. Abbreviation for Duke of Edinburgh's Own Rifles (q.v.).

Deportees. Name usually given to a group of South African Labour Leaders, who, during the 1914 strike on the Rand, were arrested by order of General J. C. Smuts, and sent down to Durban, where they were placed on a ship bound for England. News of their arrest leaked out and efforts were made by their friends to secure an order of *habeas corpus*. This was granted and a tug hired to intercept the ship off Cape Town, but without success. The deportees reached England, were fêted there by Labour leaders and ultimately returned to South Africa.

D'Erlanger, Baron Emile Beaumont. Banker. Born in Paris, 1866, the son of Baron Frederic Emile d'Erlanger, and succeeded him as head of the banking firm of Erlangers, of Paris and London. During the 1880's he became interested in railway building at the Cape, and in Cecil Rhodes' extensions of the lines into Rhodesia, particularly through his association with George Pauling (q.v.), whose contracts he largely financed. Later he was active in the opening of railways in the Congo and Angola. Baron d'Erlanger died in 1939.

Dernburg, Bernhard. Colonial Secretary of the German Reich. Born on July 17, 1865, at Darmstadt, he began his career in the trust and banking business, but in 1906 became Director of the Colonial Office, and in 1907 Secretary of State. As such he visited German South West Africa in 1908, also the Cape, Transvaal, etc. He remained in the Colonial Office until 1910. During World War I he was sent as a special emissary to the United States and after the revolution in 1919 became Minister of Finance. He died in 1937.

De Rust. Village near Oudtshoorn, Cape Province. Founded in 1900. Population: 1,042, including 458 Whites.

Despatch. Industrial township near Port Elizabeth. Wool-washeries are important. Population: 11,000, including 8,500 Whites.

Dessin, Joachim Nicholas von. South African book collector. Born at Rostock, Germany, came to the Cape in 1727 as a soldier and rose to be Clerk of the High Court of Justice and, from 1737 to 1757, Secretary to the Orphan Chamber. His library of 3,800 printed books and many manuscripts was partly purchased from deceased estates during an outbreak of plague, and on his death on September 18, 1761, was left in trust to Dutch Reformed Church consistory as nucleus of future public library. It was handed over to the South African Public Library on its establishment in 1818 (*see* LIBRARIES) and is still preserved in Cape Town as the Dessinian Collection.

Dett. Hamlet 160 miles from Bulawayo in Rhodesia, on line to Victoria Falls, important as station for the Wankie Game Reserve and for its proximity to Wankie Coal Field.

Devereux, Bishop Aidan. Early Catholic bishop at the Cape. Born in Ireland, he studied there and in Rome and arrived in the Cape in 1839 to take charge of the first Catholic school there. Later he established St. Aidan's College in Grahamstown, and in 1850 founded the first Catholic newspaper in South Africa, *The Colonist*. He became the first Catholic bishop in the

Eastern Province in 1847, and died in 1854.

De Villiers, Lord, of Wynberg. Chief Justice of Cape Colony and of the Union of South Africa. Born in 1842, he was educated at the South African College (1853–1861). Studied law at the Inner Temple, England, as well as in Germany. Returning to Cape Town in 1866, he was admitted as advocate and in 1867 elected as member for Worcester to the House of Assembly. Upon the grant of Responsible Government to the Cape Colony, he became Attorney-General in the original ministry of Sir John Molteno, and excited great criticism by appointing himself Chief Justice in 1873. These protests, however, were soon silenced by the exceptional ability which he displayed, it being acknowledged that he was the ablest lawyer of his time. In 1877 he was knighted as Sir Henry de Villiers. He was frequently invoked as negotiator on important occasions and took his part as member of the Commission that settled the peace with the South African Republic after the Majuba Campaign. De Villiers went to Canada in 1894 as a delegate to the Imperial Conference and again in 1908. He was appointed to the Privy Council and served upon it in his judicial capacity in 1896. In 1899 he arranged the meeting between Lord Milner and President Kruger which was the final attempt to prevent the outbreak of the South African War. For 37 years, from 1873 to 1910, in his capacity as Chief Justice, Lord de Villiers presided over the Legislative Assembly, and in 1908 was chosen as Chairman of the National Convention that settled the terms of Union. He was the inevitable choice as Chief Justice of the Union after its establishment, when he was also created Lord de Villiers of Wynberg. He died in 1914.

De Villiers, Jacob Abraham Jeremy (Japie). Chief Justice of the Union. Born in Fauresmith on Decem-

ber 14, 1868, educated at Grey College, Bloemfontein, he completed his law studies in Amsterdam, and was called to the Bar in 1893. He practised in Johannesburg from 1894 to 1896 and then became State Attorney for the Orange Free State until 1898, when he returned to Johannesburg. After fighting in the Boer War with the Orange Free State burghers, he was deported to Bermuda. When peace returned he travelled on the Continent and in 1903 returned to the Transvaal to resume his practice. After Union he became Attorney-General for the Transvaal, rising to Judge President. In 1920 he was appointed to the Appellate Division and was Chief Justice of the Union from 1929 until he died in 1932.

De Villiers, Marthinus Lourens. South African composer. Born in Paarl, 1885, and showed musical gifts at an early age. Educated in Wellington, he settled as a music teacher in Wepener, O.F.S., where he began composing. Later he studied for the Dutch Reformed Ministry and was stationed at Beaufort West and Simonstown, receiving much encouragement from Professor W. H. Bell (q.v.) of the College of Music at Cape Town University. His most memorable work was the music for 'Die Stem van Suid-Afrika,' by C. J. Langenhoven (q.v.), which he wrote in 1921 and which became the Union National Anthem.

De Villiers, Melius. Chief Justice, O.F.S. Born in Paarl on September 5, 1849, brother of Lord de Villiers (q.v.) and educated at the South African College. Admitted at the Cape in 1872, and 4 years later became a judge in the Orange Free State, rising to Chief Justice in 1889. After the South African War he returned to the Cape to practise there. In 1905 he became professor of Roman-Dutch law at the University of Leiden. He died in Stellenbosch on July 6, 1938.

Devil's Peak. Mountain forming part of the Table Mountain group overlooking Cape Town. Known originally as the 'Windberg.' Height 3,286 feet.

Devil's Snuffbox. Fungus found at the Cape, circular in shape and of a powdery consistency inside. It is also known as Old Maid's Snuff.

Devitt, Harold Napier. South African writer. Born in England 1873, came to South Africa 1889. Did legal work and saw service in the South African War. Joined the Transvaal Civil Service in 1901. Was later appointed magistrate. Wrote widely on South African history and completed books of reminiscences. Died 1954.

Devlin Commission. Inquiry Commission appointed by the British Government on April 6, 1959, under the chairmanship of Mr. Justice Devlin, to report on disturbance in Nyasaland. Its report, which dealt exhaustively with the causes of political and inter-racial friction, and approved the adoption of emergency measures by the authorities, was issued on July 23, 1959.

Devon. Village in the Eastern Transvaal. Notable for occurrence of natural gas coming out of the earth, believed to be connected with possible presence of oil. Named after home county of the surveyor who laid it out. Population: 900, including 150 Whites.

De Waal, Daniel. Judge-President of the Transvaal. Born in Stellenbosch on September 10, 1873, and educated at the Boys' High School there and at Victoria College; completing his law studies at Cambridge. Returning to South Africa, he practised in Pretoria for a short while until the outbreak of the Boer War. After serving with the Boer forces he resumed his practice in Pretoria in 1902. World War I again interrupted his practice, but he took silk in 1919, rising to the Bench in 1920, when he became Judge-President. Retired in 1938. Died in Pretoria on February 19, 1938.

De Waal, Jan Hendrik Hofmeyr. Afrikaans poet and Speaker of Union Parliament. Born near Cape Town in 1871, he studied at Victoria College in Stellenbosch and was called to the Bar in England. From his return in 1897, he became a vigorous worker for the Afrikaans language, in which he wrote extensively. In 1903 De Waal became editor of *De Goede Hoop*, and later one of the founders of the Afrikaanse Taalgenootskap. He entered Parliament in 1915, and was elected speaker in 1929, remaining in office for 4 years. Among De Waal's best-known books is the novel *Johannes van Wyk*. He died in 1937.

De Waal, Sir Nicholas Frederick. First Administrator of the Cape Province. Born in Holland in 1853, came to South Africa in 1880 and settled at Middelburg, Cape, where he practised law. Interested in politics, he became a leading figure in the Afrikander Bond, and in 1898 was elected to the Cape Parliament. Later he was Colonial Secretary in the Cabinet of John X. Merriman in 1908 and, upon the founding of Union, Administrator of the Cape Province. A man of great ability, he was dictatorial, but well respected. He retired in 1926 and died in 1932.

De Wet, Dr. Carel. South African diplomat and Cabinet Minister. Born at Memel, Orange Free State, on May 25, 1924, the grandson of General C. R. De Wet (q.v.), he studied at the University of the Orange Free State and qualified in Medicine at the University of Pretoria. In 1948 he began practice at Vanderbijlpark, Transvaal, of which town he was elected Mayor in 1950. In 1953 he was elected to Parliament, in 1964 became South African Ambassador in London and in 1967 entered the Cabinet as Minister of Mines and Planning.

De Wet, General Christiaan Rudolf. Boer soldier and statesman. Born of Voortrekker parents in the Orange

Free State on October 7, 1854, near Dewetsdorp. He saw action as a boy during the Basuto Wars of the 1860's, and made his living for some time as a transport rider. Moving to the Transvaal, he joined the Republican Forces in the Majuba Campaign of 1880–1881 and fought in that famous battle. After peace, he was elected to the Volksraads both of the Orange Free State and the Transvaal. The outbreak of the South African War saw him in the comparatively modest position as head of an Orange Free State Commando, but his innate ability soon brought him to the fore. A series of raids followed, so well-conceived and successful that his name soon became a byword, not only in South Africa but in countries overseas. On various occasions he made successful escapes under seemingly impossible conditions from great forces mobilised against him. Remaining in the field until the very end, he was present at the final peace negotiations at Vereeniging, and for one day held the position of Acting President of the Orange Free State. As such he signed the peace treaty. Immediately after, accompanied by other Boer leaders, he proceeded overseas to collect funds for the war victims. He then re-entered politics, becoming Minister of Agriculture for the Orange River Colony under the Crown Colony régime. As a member of the National Convention he helped to form the constitution of the Union. He quarrelled with General Botha, and became a founder of the Nationalist Party. Upon the outbreak of World War I, de Wet took charge of a section of the rebels in the Orange Free State, but, after the action at Mushroom Valley, was obliged to take flight, and was finally captured in Bechuanaland. Brought to trial on charge of High Treason, he was sentenced to 6 years' imprisonment and a fine of £2,000. After about a year, however, he was released and lived quietly on his farm, where he died on February 3, 1922. He is buried at the foot of the Concentration Camp Monument in Bloemfontein.

De Wet, Jacobus Petrus. Chief Justice of the Transvaal. Born in 1838 and educated at S.A.C.S. (q.v.), at Leyden and at the University of London; he was called to the Inner Temple in 1863. Returning to the Cape he was admitted there in the same year. In 1873 he became Solicitor-General of the Cape and in 1880 Recorder of Griqualand West. Shortly after, his appointment as Chief Justice was disputed and he went to Ceylon as Acting Chief Justice for a year. He died in England on April 19, 1900.

De Wet, Hon. Nicholas Jacobus. South African statesman, born in 1873 near Aliwal North, Cape Province, and educated at Victoria College, Stellenbosch, and at Cambridge. In 1896 he joined the Cape Bar and practised in Pretoria. He entered Parliament in September 1913 as Member for Wakkerstroom and later sat for Potchefstroom. From 1921 to 1929 he was a senator. From 1923 to 1924 he was Minister for Justice, in 1932 was appointed to the Bench of the Transvaal Supreme Court, and in 1937 was elevated to the Appellate Division at Bloemfontein. From 1939 to 1943 he was Chief Justice, and in that capacity repeatedly acted as Officer Administering the Government. Although more than once offered the position of Governor-General, he refused. He died on February 16, 1960.

Dewetsdorp. Town in the Orange Free State. Founded in 1880 and named after Jacobus Ignatius De Wet, father of the famous Boer general, C. R. de Wet (q.v.), who was heavily engaged there during the South African War in 1900. Scene of an unusual crime in 1927, when the Town Hall was blown up by an official named De Leeuw, who was sentenced to death for killing the Mayor and two Councillors. Wool centre. Population: 3,453, including 985 Whites.

De Wildt. Hamlet in the Transvaal, near Rustenburg, famous in South African history on account of the speech delivered there by General J. B. M. Hertzog (q.v.), on December 7, 1912, which marked the beginning of the process which led to the founding of the Nationalist Party.

Dhlo-Dhlo Ruins. Ancient relics 30 miles from Insiza station in Rhodesia, covering about 3 acres. They are regarded as more recent than the Zimbabwe ruins (q.v.) and of inferior workmanship.

Diamond Fields Advertiser. Morning newspaper established in 1878 as a tri-weekly, but issued daily since May 1882 in Kimberley. It was produced under great difficulties during the siege in the South African War.

Diamonds, Artificial. South Africa's entry into the field of producing Artificial Diamonds began in 1906 when Sir Julius Wernher (q.v.) and other heads of the De Beers investigated the claims of a Frenchman named Lemoine. These proved fraudulent and resulted in a loss to them of £80,000. In February 1955, the news that the General Electric Company in the U.S.A. had manufactured artificial stones of industrial quality prompted the De Beers interests in the same year to set up a Research Centre under Dr. J. F. H. Custers, in Johannesburg. Patent was taken out in 1956. This Adamant Laboratory succeeded in making diamonds in 1958, a fact announced by Mr. Harry Oppenheimer in November 1959. Like the American, the South African product is extremely small and suited only to industrial use. Works for the manufacture of diamonds are operated by De Beers group on the Rand and at Shannon in Ireland. After prolonged litigation a settlement on the use of its patents was reached with General Electric.

DIAMOND INDUSTRY IN SOUTHERN AFRICA

DIAMONDS were discovered in South Africa in 1866, and the Diamond Industry was firmly established with the formation of De Beers Consolidated Mines in 1888. The industry occupies an important place in the economy of Southern Africa and was the foundation of its modern industrialisation. The annual value of the joint output of the South African Republic and South West Africa is higher than that of any other country in the world.

Southern Africa's chief diamond pipes are those in the Kimberley area of the Cape Province, at Premier Mine near Pretoria in the Transvaal, New Jagersfontein Mine in the Orange Free State, the Fincham pipe near Postmasburg in the north-west Cape, and at Orapa (q.v.) in Botswana. The main alluvial diamond area in Southern Africa occurs near the mouth of the Orange River.

Alluvial deposits are exploited north of the Orange River mouth at Oranjemund by Consolidated Diamond Mines of South West Africa; at the State Alluvial Diggings south of the Orange River mouth; at Kleinzee, on the Namaqualand coast of the Cape Province; in the valley of the Orange, below its junction with the Vaal River; and in the Vaal–Hartz River areas. In addition to these sources diamonds have in recent years been recovered from the sea off the South West African coast by mining from barges. Prospecting in the area is being carried out off the coast by De Beers Consolidated Mines' prospecting ship *Rockeater*.

Wesselton, Dutoitspan, Bultfontein and De Beers, the four operating mines in the Kimberley area, produce about 1,200,000 carats a year. The Finsch Mine, which began production in

1966, yielded far more in 1968— 2,215,000 carats.

Operations at Kimberley's famous 'Big Hole', which in its 43-year life yielded nearly R100,000,000 worth of diamonds, ceased in 1914. The old De Beers Mine closed in 1908, but production was resumed at the end of 1963.

Premier Mine, where the world's largest diamond, the 3,106-carat Cullinan Diamond (1·4 lb.) was discovered in 1905, is South Africa's largest diamond pipe mine. In 1968 it was treating approximately 10,500,000 loads (about 1,600 lb. per load) of blueground a year, yielding 2,431,000 carats. Industrial diamonds comprise about 80 per cent of the mine's output.

At Oranjemund, in South West Africa, and northwards along the coast for more than 50 miles, diamondiferous deposits under the desert sands are mined by Consolidated Diamond Mines of South-West Africa. The output, comprising mainly gem stones, was approximately 1,500,000 carats in 1965. The New Jagersfontein Mine, closed in 1933 and reopened in 1949, finally closed down in 1970, but after many years Koffiefontein in the Orange Free State, dating back to 1870, then restarted production.

Mining and recovery methods. Diamonds are recovered from the blueground mined in the pipes at Kimberley, Koffiefontein and Premier after the ground has been crushed and treated in a recovery plant. The treatment plant at Kimberley uses large electrically operated washing pans which work on the same principle as the small hand washing pans used by diggers in the early days. The swirling motion of the liquid in these pans causes the heavy material (or concentrate) in the blueground, including the diamonds, to pass to the outer edge. The light material, or waste, is carried off to the waste disposal dumps while the concentrate is passed over the grease tables. The diamonds adhere to the grease and the rest of the material passes over the table and is disposed of. The grease containing the diamonds is scraped off the tables and boiled, leaving the diamonds to be cleaned in acid and separated from any non-diamond material which might have adhered to the grease.

In other plants a heavy media separation process is used, operating on the principle that diamondiferous concentrates, because of their higher specific gravity, sink to the bottom of the liquid containing the crusher material while the lighter, barren material floats and is carried away as waste. Electrostatic separation is also adopted for the separation of small diamonds, exploiting the fact that diamonds are non-conductive while the waste material is electrically conductive. At all the mines the diamonds are taken to central sorting offices and are sorted into categories based on size, shape, colour and quality in preparation for sale.

Mining methods differ along the South West African coast compared with those adopted in the pipe mines in South Africa. At Consolidated Diamond Mines of South West Africa, the main mining operation is not the breaking of the blueground but the removal of millions of tons of sand overburden. An average of 20 tons of sand and gravels are moved for every carat of diamonds recovered, or a ratio of approximately 100,000,000 parts to one.

Diamond marketing. Until the late 19th century there was no system of co-ordinating diamond sales. In 1892, six years after the formation of the De Beers Consolidated Mines, Limited, came the trade depression, and the competing diamond merchants of Kimberley found themselves in possession of large stocks, the release of which would have resulted in a serious collapse of diamond prices. The scheme succeeded and from it emerged the Diamond Syndicate in the following year, 1893. This was the nucleus of the Central Selling Organisation.

Under the present-day system of

marketing, the principal diamond producers in South Africa and South West Africa, including all the De Beers mines, Consolidated Diamond Mines of South West Africa, Premier Diamond Mine and the State Alluvial Diggings, as well as the Diamond Corporation, are members of the Diamond Producers' Association which co-ordinates the marketing of their gem diamonds. The production of most of the leading diamond mines of the world outside South Africa is handled through the Diamond Corporation. The Diamond Producers' Association has its head office in Kimberley, to which the South African producers send their diamonds for sorting and valuing. The Chief Valuator assesses the value of the cuttable gem stones and they are then sold on a quota principle by which each member of the Diamond Producers' Association is entitled to supply a certain percentage of the diamonds required by the market. First they are sold to the Diamond Purchasing and Trading Company and thence to the Diamond Trading Company, which markets the diamonds by a system of "sights" held ten times a year in London and Johannesburg. Buyers are invited to apply for a "sight", that is, to specify the quantity and quality of the stones they require. Depending on the available supply the diamonds are then made up into individual parcels for the buyers.

The selling companies hold very substantial funds which enable them to buy from the producers even during trade recessions, thereby greatly reducing the risk of being forced to offer diamonds on an unwilling market. Thus an oversupply of diamonds can never bring mining operations to a standstill, a fact which is of prime importance to the mining industry as well as to all those whose livelihood depends upon it.

Industrial diamonds are separated from gem stones by sorters of the Diamond Producers' Association in Kimberley and of the Diamond Corporation in London, and are sent to Johannes-

burg for further division into different industrial categories. The stones received in Johannesburg come not only from the industrial diamond-producing mines of South Africa, but from many parts of the world. After sorting they are marketed through Industrial Distributors (1946) Limited by Industrial Distributors (Sales) Limited, in London and South Africa.

Each gem stone, large or small, must be examined individually and its valuation calls for an expert's extensive knowledge and experience. Diamonds differ from all other mining products in that the final rough product can be divided into more than one thousand categories. The quality of the stone is judged by the absence of flaws and by the colour; the classification aims at giving each separate stone a specific value. Through this classification 'parcels' are made up of clearly defined groups of diamonds.

In 1968 net sales of diamonds made through the De Beers Central Selling Organisation reached the record total of R428,793,000.

Diamond research. On the outskirts of Johannesburg is a unique laboratory, devoted exclusively to diamond research investigations. It conducts research into diamond recovery processes and into methods of improving and adding to the applications of industrial diamonds. It also carries out pure research into all aspects of the diamond.

The Diamond Research Laboratory is one of a complex of laboratories among which is the De Beers Adamant Laboratory, where South African scientists first discovered a method of making synthetic diamond material after three years of research. This synthetic diamond material is now manufactured at plants equipped with South African machinery at Springs on the East Witwatersrand and at Shannon in the Irish Republic. Synthetic diamond material is used extensively in industrial tools.

See also MARINE DIAMOND CORPORA- TION, and FINSCH DIAMOND MINE.

FAMOUS SOUTH AFRICAN DIAMONDS

Date	*Name*	*Size*	*Where found*
1866	'O'Reilly' (also 'Eureka')	21¼	Near Hope Town
1868	'Star of South Africa' (also 'Dudley')	83½	Near Orange River
1872	'Fly'	60	Waldeck's Plant
1872	'Stewart' (also 'Spalding')	288¾	Vaal River
1873	'Tennant'	112	Vaal River
1878	'Tiffany'	125⅜	Kimberley
1878	'Du Toit'	244	Kimberley
1880	'Porter Rhodes'	160	Kimberley
1880	Nameless	428½	Kimberley
1884	'Victoria' (also 'Imperial' and 'Great White')	457½	South Africa
1888	'De Beers'	428½	Kimberley
1889	'Julius Pam'	241½	Jagersfontein
1890	Nameless	258	Kimberley
1891	'Litkie'	205½	Good Hope, Vaal River
1891	'Carns'	107	Vaal River
1891	Nameless	400	Kimberley
1893	'Excelsior'	971¾	Jagersfontein
1895	'Jubilee' (also 'Reitz')	634	Jagersfontein
1895	Nameless	352¾	Kimberley
1896	Nameless	503¼	Kimberley
1896	Nameless	336	Otto's Koppie
1899	Nameless	363	Kimberley
1899	Nameless	337½	Kimberley
1899	Nameless	222	Jagersfontein
1900	Nameless	214½	Kimberley
1901	Nameless	307½	Kimberley
1902	'Brady'	330	Near Fourteen Streams
1902	'Orpin-Palmer'	117¾	Vaal River
1903	Nameless	294½	Jagersfontein
1905	'Cullinan'	3,106	Premier Mine
1905	'Barkly Breakwater'	109¼	Vaal River
1905	Nameless	353	Jagersfontein
1905	Nameless	334	Premier Mine
1905	Nameless	307½	Kimberley
1907	Nameless	523¾	Premier Mine
1907	'Burgess'	220	Vaal River
1907	'Webster'	124	Vaal River
1907	Nameless	335	Jagersfontein
1907	'Otto Borgstrom'	121½	Vaal River
1907	Nameless	373	Premier Mine
1908	Nameless	337	Vaal River
1911	Nameless	514	Premier Mine
1912	Nameless	1,640	Premier Mine
1913	'Van Zyl'	229¼	Vaal River
1913	Nameless	430½	Jagersfontein
1913	Nameless	458	Premier Mine
1913	Nameless	427¼	Kimberley
1914	Nameless	507	Jagersfontein
1916	'Dan Campbell'	192½	Vaal River
1917	'Star of Zion'	85	Vaal River
1919	Nameless	593½	Premier Mine
1919	Nameless	388½	Jagersfontein
1921	'The Arc'	381	Vaal River

Date	Name	Size	Where found
1924	Nameless	1,195½	Premier Mine
1924	Nameless	500¾	Premier Mine
1934	'Jonker'	726	Near Pretoria

Note: this list does not claim to be complete. Many hundreds of large stones are produced by various mines, but the above are among the most famous and spectacular.

Diaz, Bartholomew (more correctly **Bartholomew Dias de Novaes**). Portuguese explorer and navigator. Born in Portugal about 1450. In October 1486 Diaz was appointed commander of an expedition to find its way to India round Africa. He set out in August 1487, accompanied by three small ships, and succeeded in tracing 1,260 miles of hitherto unknown coast. Among the points at which he touched are Port Alexander in Angola, Walvis Bay and Luderitz Bay. He sighted the mountains near Clanwilliam, and rounded the Cape of Good Hope, putting ashore in Mossel Bay. The extreme point of his voyage was near the mouth of the Bushman's River, where he erected a stone cross at Kwaaihoek, rediscovered and preserved by Dr. Eric Axelson in 1938. On his return journey, which was prompted by the mutinous crew, Diaz for the first time saw the Cape of Good Hope, and is believed to have spent about a month in the Cape Peninsula. He arrived back in Lisbon in December 1488, and died in 1500.

Dibeng. Village near Kuruman, Cape Province. Population: 500, including 270 Whites.

Diederichs, Dr. Nicolaas. South African Cabinet Minister. Born at Ladybrand, Orange Free State, in 1903, studied at Grey University College, Bloemfontein, and at universities of Munich, Cologne and Leyden. Joined staff of University of the Orange Free State and wrote extensively, taking a particular interest in the economic rehabilitation of the Afrikaner. Became head of the Reddingsdaadbond (q.v.), Chairman of the Economic Institute of the F.A.K. (q.v.) and of the Decimal Coinage Commission. Elected to Parliament in 1948, he became Minister of Mines and of Economic Affairs in 1958.

Die Erwe. Village near Herbert, Cape Province. Population: 1,200, including 560 Whites.

Dik-Dik. Smallest South African antelope, rarely standing more than 14 inches in height. Lives in particularly barren country, in South-West Africa and elsewhere. A special feature is the strangely-shaped nose. The commonest type is the Damaraland Dik-dik (*Madaqua damarensis*).

Dikkop (Thick Head). Disease of horses, accompanied by the swelling of the tissue under the skin. It may take the form of a swelling of the tongue, for which reason it is also known as Blue Tongue. Also a disease of sheep.

Dikkop (*Burhinus capensis*). Bird with large head and very large eyes; is nocturnal in habit and lives mostly in dry country. Eats small animal food, worms, snails, frogs, tadpoles, insects, etc. Lays two eggs. Less common is the Water Dikkop of river banks.

Dikkop. South African fish. *See* GOBY.

Dimorphotheca. *See* DAISY.

Dingaan. Zulu king, half-brother of Tshaka (q.v.). First came into prominence in 1828, when, with his brother Umhlangana and a servant, Umbopa, he killed that mighty warrior. Dingaan took over the chieftainship and soon became known for his treacherous qualities. At first he maintained amicable relations with the handful of European settlers at Port Natal, and in

1830 sent a mission with presents to the Cape, where Governor Sir Lowry Cole's refusal to receive them offended him. Dingaan allowed Captain Gardiner (q.v.) to establish himself as chief over refugee natives and to begin mission work. When American missionaries arrived, they were also permitted to set up stations. He later came into contact with the Voortrekkers and made a friendly agreement with Pieter Retief (q.v.), whom he treacherously murdered in 1838 with a party of his followers. He failed to wipe out the remaining Voortrekkers, despite the large numbers whom his warriors succeeded in killing. The climax came when he sacked a white settlement in what is now Durban. He was defeated at the Battle of Blood River (q.v.) after which he became a fugitive. His brother, Panda (q.v.), fell out with him, and he was finally driven into Swaziland, where he was assassinated in 1843.

Dingaan's Apricot. *See* KEI APPLE.

Dingaan's Day. Now known as Day of the Covenant. Holiday established on December 16, 1838, in commemoration of the victory of the Voortrekkers over Dingaan and his Zulus at the Battle of Blood River (q.v.).

Dinizulu. King of the Zulus. The son of Cetewayo (q.v.), he became involved in a civil war with his brother Usibepu and in 1884 called in help from among a group of Transvaal Boers. As a result of their assistance, Dinizulu won the struggle and became Supreme Chief. When, however, British authority was extended over the whole of Zululand in 1887, Dinizulu rose in revolt and was sentenced to banishment to the Island of St. Helena. Later he was allowed to return to the country of his birth, but again became involved in a rising in 1906, when the Bambata Rebellion broke out. On this occasion he was again found guilty and banished for life to Middelburg, Tvl. There he died in 1913.

Diocesan College (Bishops). Public school for boys, founded by Bishop Robert Gray in 1849 in Rondebosch and incorporated by Act of the Cape Parliament in 1891. Up to 1912 prepared students for degrees, but discontinued this owing to the development of the University of Cape Town (q.v.). The grounds are among the most beautifully located in South Africa and the buildings, particularly the War Memorial Chapel, are worthy of them. The College is entitled to a Rhodes Scholarship under the will of the statesman.

Dipavali. *See* COOLIE CHRISTMAS.

Disa. *See* ORCHIDS.

Disselboom. The main shaft of an ox-wagon or other animal-drawn vehicle.

Divisional Councils. Institution found only in the Cape Province, originally established in 1855 by the Colonial Government. The whole province is split up into 'Divisions' whose principal duty is the construction of roads. maintenance and other works, including housing in rural areas, for which purpose they have been granted powers to levy an annual rate and to borrow monies. The Civil Commissioner (q.v.) of each Division was until 1910 made the *ex officio* chairman of each Divisional Council. There are 95 Divisional Councils.

Dixie, Lady Florence Caroline. British traveller and author. Youngest daughter of the Marquess of Queensberry, she was born in London on May 24, 1857, as Lady Florence Caroline Sholto-Douglas. At 18 she married Sir Alexander Beaumont Dixie, and in 1878 travelled through South America, reaching South Africa in 1880. During the Majuba Campaign of that year, she was in the field as a war correspondent for the *Morning Post*. In 1882 she wrote on her South African experiences in *The Land of Misfortune*, and supported Cetewayo in her *De-*

fence of Zululand and Its King. She died on November 7, 1905.

Diwali. *See* COOLIE CHRISTMAS.

Dlamini, Prince Makhosini. Prime Minister of Swaziland (q.v.). Born near Hlatikulu in 1914, a member of the Royal family. He trained as a teacher and was headmaster of the Swazi National School at Lobamba until, in 1947, he joined the Swazi National Council. After further study in Europe he led the Independence Delegation in 1963 and in 1964 entered the Legislative Council. He became Premier in 1967.

D.O.A.L. Abbreviation for 'Deutsche Ost Afrika Linie' (German East Africa Line, q.v.).

Doehne (usually written **Dohne**). Village near Stutterheim, in the Eastern Cape Province. Named after the Rev. J. L. Döhne of the Berlin Mission Society and founded in 1857 for members of the German Legion (q.v.). Farming centre.

Doeksteen (literally 'cloth-stone'). Old Afrikaans name for Blue Crocidolite. So called on account of its fibres.

Dog, Hunting (*Lycaon pictus venaticus*). Wild animal found in many parts of South Africa, but now becoming rare. Hunts in packs and can bring down a lion. Because of its danger to cattle, it has been declared vermin and is shot relentlessly. *See* MAMMALS.

D'Oliviera, Basil L. South African Coloured cricketer. Born in Cape Town on October 4, 1934, and educated at Zonnebloem. He showed such exceptional ability at the game of cricket that in 1960 he settled in England, where he became a professional for Worcestershire in 1964. In 1965 he was made captain and in 1966 *Wisden's* ' Cricketer of the Year '. Since then he repeatedly played for England. His exclusion from the M.C.C. team, allegedly on account of his race, led to the cancellation of the 1968 tour of South Africa.

Dollar. Rhodesian coin, equal to 1 Rand, adopted in November 1966, with effect from February 1970. Divided into 100 cents.

Dolly. An early form of stamping machine for breaking up gold-bearing rock on the South African Gold Fields. It originated in Australia, but the name is of South African origin.

Dolos. Method of divination used by native witchdoctors to foretell the future, locate missing property, etc. The name is probably derived from Afrikaans 'dobbel os,' gambling with oxen. Metacarpal and metatarsal bones of goats, sheep, pigs and other animals were used. Later, a game arose among Boer children, known as 'dolosse,' played with bones of sheep or goats.

Dominion Party. Political movement started under the leadership of Colonel C. F. Stallard in 1933, in protest against the fusion of the Nationalist and South African parties (q.v.). Much of its support was derived from Natal. Although at one time it secured several members of parliament, it gradually disintegrated after the retirement of Colonel Stallard.

Donga. A washed-out watercourse. The name is of native origin, and also signifies the side of a house. Today the Government is spending millions on planting vegetation, and constructing catchment dams, in order to combat such soil erosion.

Dönges, Dr. Theophilus Ebenaezer. State President Elect of the Republic of South Africa. Born at Klerksdorp, Transvaal, in March 1898 and studied at Stellenbosch University. Called to the Bar in London, he entered journalism on his return in 1923, editing the *South African Nation,* an English organ of the National Party, later joining the staff of *Die Burger* (q.v.). Entered Parliament in 1941 and in 1948 joined Dr. Malan's first Cabinet as Minister of the Interior.

He attended many overseas conferences, including those of the United Nations, and in 1951 led the South African delegation to the Commonwealth Premiers' Conference. Became Minister of Finance in 1958. He was elected to presidency, but died in 1967 before his inauguration. *See also* J. F. NAUDE.

Donkin, Sir Rufane Shaw. Acting Governor of the Cape of Good Hope and founder of Port Elizabeth. Born in 1773. Joined the Army at 16 years old; served in West Indies and rose to be major-general in the Peninsular War. In 1817 and 1818 was in India, in the Mahratta War. Visited the Cape on his way back to England in 1820 and, in the temporary absence of Lord Charles Somerset, was installed Acting Governor. A new village on Algoa Bay was named Port Elizabeth in honour of his late wife, and a pyramid (still standing in the Donkin Reserve) erected. During his short term of office he reversed a number of military arrangements and, upon his return to England, lodged serious complaints against Lord Charles Somerset. He sat for some years in the House of Commons, was made a Fellow of the Royal Society and Surveyor-General of Ordnance. He died in 1841.

Donnybrook. Dairy centre near Polela, Natal. Population: 470, including 160 Whites.

Donovan, Lieutenant. Early Cape explorer and companion of Dr. Cowan (q.v.).

Dons, Hans. Nickname for **Johannes de Lange** (q.v.).

Doodvoël. Afrikaans name for Barn Owl. *See* OWL.

Doorn River. Tributary of Great Fish River (q.v.).

Dop. Cheap kind of brandy made at the Cape from skins left over after the production of wine. It is notoriously strong and crude to the taste.

Doppers. Popular name for the Gereformeerde Kerk van Zuid Afrika, a section of the older Dutch Reformed Church (Nederduits Gereformeerde Kerk), which seceded from the latter in 1859. It was begun by the Rev. Dirk Postma (q.v.) and follows the Presbyterian usage laid down in 1618–1619 by the Synod of Dordt, as revised in 1913 and 1924. The word 'Dopper' is believed to be a corruption of 'Domper'—one who damps down—in allusion to their Calvinistic principles, even stricter than those of the older Church. President Kruger was a leading supporter. *Inter alia* they prefer psalm singing to hymns. Principal training centre at Potchefstroom. Number of adherents: 120,000 Whites.

Dordrecht. Town in the Cape Province. Founded in 1857, by the Rev. A. Murray of the Dutch Reformed Church and named after a town in Holland famous in the earlier history of that body. Situated in the Stormberg Mountains at a height of 5,370 feet, it is noted for its bracing climate. Occupied in the South African War by the Boers and annexed to the Orange Free State in 1899. Sheep and cattle centre. Population: 4,640, including 1,200 Whites.

Dormouse (Graphiurus). Small rodent found in Southern Africa. There are several varieties, including the Cape Dormouse, the Damaraland Dormouse, the Desert Dormouse, the Grey Dormouse and Darling's Dormouse, the latter peculiar to Rhodesia. Length about $4\frac{1}{2}$ inches; lives chiefly on nuts and other vegetation. *See* MAMMALS.

Dorthesia. Insect pest, also known as **Australian Bug**, introduced into Cape Colony in 1873, where it did immense damage to trees, notably fruit trees. It was ultimately discovered to be the food of a species of Ladybird from California. Large numbers of the latter were imported and successfully wiped out the invader. *See* INSECTS.

Douglas. Village in the Northern Cape Province on the Vaal River, not far from where it joins the Orange River. Established about 1838 as a mission station and named Backhouse, after a Quaker traveller, James Backhouse, who visited those parts at the time. In 1867 it was renamed Douglas after General Sir Percy Douglas, Lieutenant-Governor of Cape Colony. Important irrigation centre. Population: 5,000, including 1,400 Whites.

Dove (family Columbidae). *See* PIGEON.

Dove-Wilson, Sir John Carnegie. Judge-President of Natal. Born in Scotland in 1865, he was called to the Bar in 1888 and practised in Edinburgh until 1894, when he was appointed to the bench of the Natal Supreme Court. In 1911 he became Judge President. He presided over the Treason Trials after the 1922 strike on the Rand. He retired in 1930, and settled in Edinburgh, where he died in April 1935.

Dowling, Dr. Thomas Barrow. South African musician and composer. Born in Hampshire, England, in 1861, he came to Cape Town in April 1888 as organist for St. George's Cathedral. A pioneer in organising choral and other festivals. Died in 1926.

Draai Jackal (literally 'turning jackal'). A Silver Fox. So called because of its habit of turning rapidly on dogs when pursued. *See* FOX and MAMMALS.

Draghoender. *See* MARYDALE.

Drakensberg (also known as **Quath-lamba**). Principal mountain range of Southern Africa. Extends for about 1,000 miles from the Northern Transvaal to the Cape Midlands. The highest point is in the Maluti Range of Lesotho, which forms part of the Drakensberg system. According to recent measurement this is Thaba Tsenyana (11,425 feet), which greatly exceeds Champagne Castle (11,081 feet) and Mont aux Sources (10,769 feet). Other important peaks are Makheke (11,255 feet), Mafadi (11,320 feet), Injasuti (11,315 feet), Hodson's Peak (10,689 feet), Giants Castle (10,878 feet), Cathkin Peak (10,769 feet) and Cathedral Peak (9,856 feet). Important passes across the Drakensberg are the Van Reenen, Olivier's Hoek, Bezuidenhout, Tintwa, De Beers, Sunday's River, Botha's, Laing's Nek, Bushman's Nek and Bushman's River. The name Drakensberg means 'Dragon Mountain' and Quathlamba means 'Piled up rocks.'

Drakenstein. Mountain range in the Western Cape Province, near Paarl and on the southern edge of the Karroo. Groot Drakenstein Peak rises to 4,895 feet.

Drama. *See* THEATRE.

Draper, Dr. David. South African geologist. Born at the Cape in 1859, he was mainly self-taught, and gained his early experience from G. W. Stow. He visited Kimberley, Lydenburg and Natal in the early 70's, finding many facts of fundamental importance. After taking part in the geological exploration of the Witwatersrand, Dr. Draper went overseas at the turn of the century. He also visited Turkey, Borneo and South America, concentrating particularly on diamond mining in Brazil. In 1904 and 1905 he was responsible for the exploration of the tin occurrences in the Bushveld. An honorary doctorate was conferred upon him in 1927 by the University of the Witwatersrand. He died in 1929 and, in his honour, the Draper Medal has been established for outstanding services to South African geology.

Dress. *See* COSTUME (BANTU).

Driemanskap. *See* TRIUMVIRATE.

Drifts Controversy. Diplomatic dispute between the South African Republic and Britain in 1895. The railway line from Vereeniging to the Rand had been completed, providing a link with the Cape, but the rates for the Transvaal section were so high that the

Uitlander business men declared it cheaper to offload at the frontier and send their goods by ox-wagon. In his effort to divert traffic to the Delagoa Bay route, which he favoured, President Kruger on October 1, 1895, issued a proclamation forbidding goods from overseas to be brought into the Transvaal via the Drifts (Fords) over the Vaal River if carried by wagon. This led to a situation so grave that the British Government presented Kruger with an ultimatum on October 16, threatening further action unless the Drifts were reopened. On November 7, 1895, the President withdrew his proclamation.

Drongo (family Dicruridae). Fair-sized bird in many parts of South Africa. Common in wooded districts from Swellendam eastwards, to be seen conspicuously sitting in wait for its insect prey. Fond also of eating bees, which it catches on the wing. Black plumage, broad bill, and usually a forked tail.

Dronkgras. Popular name for several species of grass, including (1) *Melica*

Dronkgras

decumbeus Thunb. and (2) *Equisetum ramosissium*, which have a semi-paralysing effect upon cattle. *See* KLOSSIEGRAS.

Drostdy. Old South African name for the building in which the Landdrost (q.v.) had his home and office. Famous Drostdys are situated at Tulbagh, Worcester and Uitenhage.

Drummond Castle. Steamer of Donald Currie and Co. involved in one of the most disastrous wrecks in South African history. Built in 1881, and measuring 3,663 tons, she was one of the most popular and modern ships of the line, and the first to carry electric light (installed in 1887). On her voyage to England on June 16, 1896, the *Drummond Castle*, off the French coast at Cape Ushant, ripped out her bottom on a reef and sank in less than 4 minutes. Of 245 people on board, three were saved, including a single passenger.

Dubbeltjie. A traditional Cape name for a penny. Originally there was a coin of this name, equal approximately to a stuiver (q.v.).

Dube, Rev. John L. Zulu clergyman and political leader. Born February 22, 1871, in Natal, he qualified for the Methodist Ministry and in 1906 founded *Ilanga Lase Natal*, an influential paper, still in existence. Dube later became a member of the African National Congress (q.v.) and led its deputation to Britain in 1914, protesting against the Native Land Act. He later resigned presidency of the Congress. Known to his countrymen as 'Mafukuzela,' Dube exercised great influence, and was moderate in his views. He attended an international Missionary Congress in Belgium. Dube received an honorary doctorate from the University of South Africa for his services to Bantu education. He aroused the objections of extremists in his later years and died on February 11, 1946.

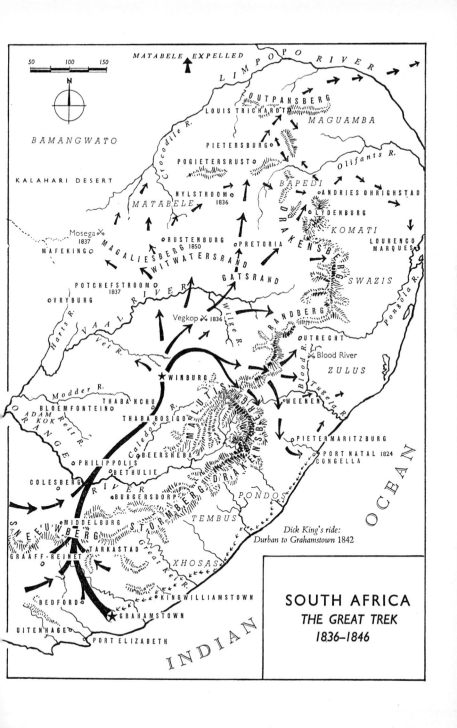

SOUTH AFRICA
THE GREAT TREK
1836–1846

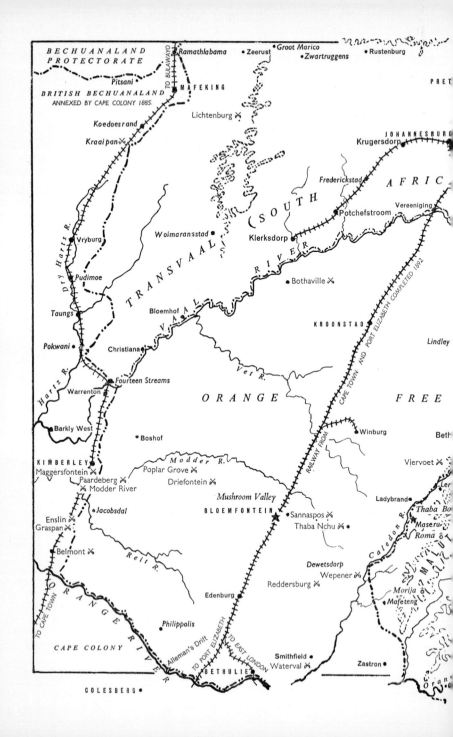

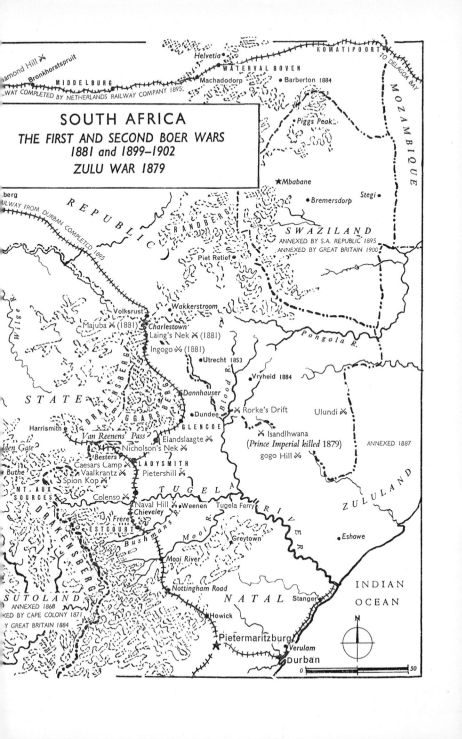

SOUTH AFRICA
THE FIRST AND SECOND BOER WARS
1881 and 1899–1902
ZULU WAR 1879

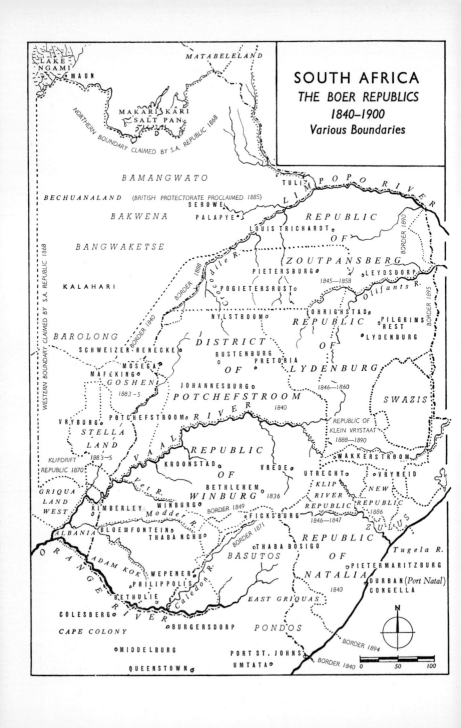

Duck (Anatidae). Water bird well represented in South Africa. Varieties include *Yellowbill* (or *Geelbek* (q.v.)), *Shelduck* (q.v.), *Cape Wigeon* or *Cape Teal*, which resembles *Redbill* (q.v.) but without dark cap and less plentiful; the broad-billed *Cape Shoveller* of the Western Cape and the *Maccoa*, a good diver, with black and chestnut colouring and a tail cocked high when alarmed. *See* BIRDS.

Duckitt, Hildagonda Johanna. South African writer on domestic subjects. Born in 1840, she belonged to one of the earliest English families to settle in the Cape, being a descendant of William Duckitt, who arrived in 1795, as the country's first agricultural expert. Though she led a quiet life, she established her fame through her hobby of collecting traditional Cape recipes, particularly those of the Malays and the pioneer White families. These she incorporated in her *Hilda's Where Is It*, and the *Diary of a Cape Housekeeper*. She died on January 5, 1905.

Duerden, Professor James Edwin. South African zoologist. Born in Lancashire, he studied in London and at Johns Hopkins University in the U.S.A., specialising in corals and marine zoology. Duerden came to South Africa to take the Chair of Zoology at Rhodes University in Grahamstown, and later made important investigations on the natural history of ostriches for the Union Government. He died in 1937.

Dugmore, Rev. Henry Hare. Missionary and writer. Born in England in 1810, he and his family arrived with the 1820 settlers (q.v.) and entered the Methodist ministry. During 45 years of service, he was stationed at Salem, Grahamstown, King William's Town and Mount Coke, after which he settled in Queenstown. Famous as a preacher, who spoke equally well in English and Xosa, he wrote over 100 hymns in that language, equal to one-third of the entire hymn-book. He also wrote *Reminiscences of an Albany Settler*, and a number of other works. Died in 1896.

Duiker. Solitary antelope found in many parts of South Africa and Rhodesia. The name, which signifies 'diver' in Afrikaans, is derived from its habit of suddenly diving into the bush when pursued. Two different types are found, the Red Duiker (*Cephalophus natalensis*), a small and graceful animal, rarely exceeding 2 feet in height, and the Blue Duiker (*Cephalophus monticola*), only 13 inches high.

Duikers (Steganopodes). Family of sea birds with all four toes webbed. Most prolific of guano-producers. Live chiefly on sardines and have a curious habit of holding out their wings to dry after fishing. Largest variety is *White-Breasted Duiker*, seen on Cape Flats. *Trek Duikers* (Cape Cormorant) are black, much smaller and fly in long strings or settle like a mat on the water. Related to Snake Birds (q.v.), Malagas (q.v.), Tropic Birds and Pelicans (q.v.).

Duinebos. *See* SKILPADBESSIE.

Duineveld. Literally 'Dune Country.' Portion of the southern coast of Cape Province in the Riversdale district.

Duin Rat. *See* GERBILLE.

Duivels Kantoor (literally 'The Devil's Office'). Mountain group (Eastern Transvaal) in the Drakensberg, noted for its rugged scenery.

Duiwelskloof (literally 'Devil's Ravine'). Township in the Northern Transvaal, established in 1920 in very picturesque country. Timber-growing centre and producer of sub-tropical fruit and vegetables. Population: 2,809, including 669 Whites.

Duke of Edinburgh's Own Rifles (**Dukes**). South African military unit, founded on November 28, 1855. Served in Ninth Kaffir War 1877–1878, Zulu War 1879, Basutoland

Rebellion, Langeberg Campaign 1897, South African War 1899–1902. German South West African Campaign 1915, and formed part of the First South African Infantry Brigade in Abyssinia and North Africa during World War II.

Dukuza. Principal kraal of the Zulu King, Tshaka (q.v.), established after he secured the throne for himself in 1818. In its prime it had a population of many thousands.

Dullstroom. Town in the Eastern Transvaal, the highest situated in the province, at 6,811 feet above sea-level. Established in 1882 and named after Wolterus Dull, a Hollander who was responsible for its foundation. Farming centre. Population: 1,086, including 340 Whites.

Duncan, Sir Patrick. First South African-appointed Governor-General of the Union. Born at Fortrie, Banffshire in 1870 and educated in Edinburgh and Oxford. He joined the Inland Revenue Department in England and while there attracted the notice of Lord Milner, whose Private Secretary he became and who asked him to come to the Transvaal in 1901. He was appointed Colonial Secretary in 1903 and held the post for 4 years. In 1906 he acted as Lieutenant-Governor. After Union he joined the Unionists and was elected to Parliament in 1911. Upon the Unionist-South African Party merger in 1921, Duncan became Minister of the Interior, of Education and of Public Health, which posts he held till 1924. Under the United Party régime he was Minister of Mines from 1933 to 1936. In that year he was appointed Governor-General of the Union in succession to Lord Clarendon. He died in 1943.

Duncan, Patrick Baker. South African politician and writer. Son of Sir Patrick Duncan (q.v.), he was born in Johannesburg in 1918, and educated at

Diocesan College, Cape Town, Winchester and Oxford. After working as Private Secretary to the High Commissioner, Sir Evelyn Baring, he joined the Basutoland Government Service. In 1952 he gave up his post to take part in the 'Defiance Campaign' of the South African Indian Congress and the African National Congress (q.v.). He served a prison term for entering a Bantu location without a permit. Later he helped to found the Liberal Party (q.v.), editing its organ, *Contact*, which brought him into renewed conflict with the police. He left the A.N.C. to support the Pan-African Congress (q.v.) and in 1961 settled again in Basutoland. He moved to England in 1962. Advocated the use of violence in South Africa to attain his political aims of equality for all races. Died June 4, 1967.

Dundee. Colliery town in Natal. Founded about 1880, 236 miles from Durban. Named after the native town in Scotland of the original farm-owner. Industries include glassworks and brickmaking. Scene of some of the first fighting in South African War, 1899, when General Penn-Symons was killed near the neighbouring Talana Hill. Population: 17,000, including 4,800 Whites.

Dundonald, Major-General Earl (Douglas Mackinnon Baillie Hamilton Cochrane). British soldier. Born in 1852 in Scotland, and entered the Life Guards at the age of 18 in 1870. Served in Egypt and the Sudan and was promoted to Colonel of the Second Life Guards (1895–1899). On the outbreak of the South African War, took command of mounted troops in the South Natal Field Force. Fought at Colenso, on the Tugela, and in the relief of Ladysmith. On account of his gallantry, especially at Bergendal in the Eastern Transvaal, was mentioned in dispatches six times. In later years he served for a while in Canada. He died in 1935.

Dung Roller. Beetle so called on account of its habit of making balls of dung in which to deposit its eggs. These are pushed to a suitable place and covered with sand. It belongs to the Scarab family. *See* INSECTS.

Dunn, John. White chief of the Zulus. Born of English parents about 1836, he lost his father when he was 14 and his mother shortly after, whereupon he began a wandering life as a hunter. After accompanying travellers to the Transvaal, he went to Zululand in 1853, making a living shooting elephants. Later he gained the friendship of the chief Cetewayo (q.v.) and in 1860 killed what was reputedly the last elephant surviving in Natal. Gaining a remarkable knowledge of Zulu psychology he settled for life in their country and received the status of a chief. Many refugees and other tribesmen established themselves at his kraal Emangete, which, after the annexation of the country by the British, was recognised as a native reserve. There his descendants and former subjects continued to live. John Dunn wrote an interesting account of his early experiences, and died in 1895.

Du Plessis, Professor Johannes. Dutch Reformed theologian, central figure in the famous Heresy Case. Born in Cradock, 1868, he was ordained in 1894 and ministered to congregations in Zastron (Orange Free State) in 1894 and Sea Point (Cape Town) in 1899. In 1903 he became Mission Secretary to the Church and in 1910 editor of *Die Kerkbode*, a position he held until 1912. In 1903 Du Plessis undertook a tour of inspection of a number of mission stations started by the Dutch Reformed Church in Malawi and regions beyond, which resulted in the publication of his book, *A Thousand Miles in the Heart of Africa*. In 1911 he wrote a standard work, *The History of Christian Missions in South Africa*. In 1916 he became Professor at the Theological Seminary in Stel-

lenbosch, and while there aroused criticism among a section of his colleagues on account of his alleged liberal views. This resulted in the famous court action, usually referred to as 'Die Kerksaak,' which was heard by the Supreme Court in 1931. It ended in the vindication of Professor du Plessis and the views which he had expressed in the journal *Het Zoeklight*. He died on February 16, 1935.

Du Plessis, Dr. Josias Hendrik Otto. Administrator of Cape Province. Born at Vanrhynsdorp, Cape Province, on February 23, 1907, he was educated at Bredasdorp and at Stellenbosch. After a journalistic career he became Director of the State Information Office, and served in the South African Delegation to the Commonwealth Conference (1949–53) and on the Central Committee of the Van Riebeeck Tercentenary in 1952. In 1953 he was elected to Parliament for Stellenbosch, and in 1958 became Administrator of the Cape Province. His tireless work in this capacity undoubtedly contributed to his early death in 1960.

Dupont, Clifford Walter. Officer Administering the Government in Rhodesia. Born in London on December 6, 1905 and educated at Bishop's Stortford College and Cambridge. He qualified as a solicitor and settled in Rhodesia, but later went farming. Served in World War II and in 1958 was elected to Parliament. He became successively Minister of Justice, Minister of External Affairs, Defence and Deputy Prime Minister. In 1965 he was appointed to succeed Sir Humphrey Gibbs (q.v.) and in 1970 he was made President-Elect.

Durban. Third city of the Republic of South Africa, one of its largest seaports and industrial centres. The name was spelt D'Urban until about 1870, after Governor Sir Benjamin D'Urban of the Cape, under whose régime it was settled in 1824. The city is built around the large, land-locked Bay of Natal, as it was then called, much of the site originally being mangrove swamp. For many years the existence of a bar across the narrow entrance to the harbour prevented the entrance of larger ships, and generally hampered progress. Thanks to dredging and suitable harbour works, this difficulty has been overcome, and, since 1904, large liners have been able to enter the bay. The population of Durban in 1967 was 682,910, including 184,692 Whites, 203,855 Bantu, 30,680 Coloureds and 263,683 Asiatics. The municipal area, exclusive of recent extensions, is 97 sq. miles. Durban witnessed disturbances resulting from the conflicts between the Voortrekkers and the British authorities, including the siege of a party of British soldiers at Congella in 1842. Real growth began in the 1850's; when trade expanded, efforts were made to exploit the harbour, and citizens began to make their homes on the slopes of the hills known as the Berea. In 1855 Durban became a municipality, when most of its buildings were still of wattle and daub. To serve the needs of the traders, shipping and unshipping goods at the Point, the first railway in South Africa was constructed in 1860 to the centre of the town, a distance of about a mile. The same year witnessed the arrival of the first Indians in Natal, who were to give the city its distinctive appearance. The 1870's saw the extension of the railway to Pietermaritzburg and the successful completion of certain harbour works. Durban became a popular seaside resort. The opening up of the Transvaal and the inland areas presently built up an enormous traffic in this respect. The city's growth as an industrial centre has mainly taken place during the present century. Today it is noted for engineering, ship-repairing, motor-tyre manufacture, sugar-milling, flour-milling, sawmilling, chemical manufactures, motor

assembly, etc. Owing to its proximity to the Witwatersrand, the greater part of the requirements of that area are imported through Durban. It is noted for its handsome appearance and well-kept streets, which have a subtropical appearance. Among its most striking attractions are its magnificent sea front, with rows of lofty skyscrapers, also the handsome esplanade along the bay, the large City Hall and beautiful suburbs. Thanks to the building of several bridges over the Umgeni, a very considerable extension has taken place to the north and beyond. A large section of the University of Natal is housed in Durban, developed out of Howard College, established shortly after World War I.

Durban. Hamlet near Peddie, in the Eastern Cape Province, founded by Governor Sir Benjamin D'Urban about 1835.

D'Urban, Sir Benjamin. Governor of the Cape of Good Hope. Born in 1777, of French Protestant ancestry, in Halesworth, near Norwich. On January 16, 1834, he assumed office as Governor of the Cape of Good Hope, where he found the sixth Kaffir War on his hands. This he brought to a successful close, creating the Province of Queen Adelaide. Receiving no support from London in his policy and confronted in the Cape with the problems created by the Great Trek, D'Urban, personally most popular, found his position increasingly difficult. Despite his promotion to Lieutenant-General in 1837, he was dismissed from the post of Governor in 1838. In his military capacity, however, he remained in South Africa until 1846, when he became Commander-in-Chief of the British troops in North America. He died in Montreal, May 1849.

Durbanville. Township near Cape Town, originally known as Pampoenkraal (Pumpkin Kraal or Enclosure) and then as D'Urban, after Governor Sir Benjamin D'Urban (q.v.). To avoid confusion with Durban, Natal, it was renamed Durbanville in 1888. Residential and farming centre in the fertile Koeberg district. Population: 4,600, including 3,100 Whites.

Durnford, Colonel Anthony William. British officer in the Royal Engineers. Born on May 24, 1830, the son of General E. W. Durnford, R.E. Entered the army in 1846, served in the East, and in 1871 came to South Africa, where he was made Colonial Engineer for Natal. After representing the Government at the coronation of Cetewayo in 1873, he attracted attention through his bravery during the Langalibalele campaign in 1875, and was given command of No. 2 Column in the Zulu War in 1879. He was killed fighting gallantly, at Isandhlwana, on January 20, 1879.

Dutch East India Company. Major trading and colonising organisation of the United Netherlands. It was established under a charter granted in The Hague on March 20, 1602. All colonising activities at the Cape were under its jurisdiction.

Dutchman. Name given by diamond diggers to a kind of quartz resembling uncut diamond.

Dutch Reformed Church. *See* NEDER-DUITSCH GEREFORMEERDE KERK.

Du Toit, Dr. Alexander Logie. South African geologist. Born in Cape Town in 1878, he was partly of Afrikaans and partly of Scottish origin. Having passed through the Diocesan College, he was sent to the South African College and then to Glasgow, where in 1899 he qualified as a mining engineer. Specialising in geology, at 23 he became a lecturer at the University of Glasgow. Du Toit returned to South Africa in 1903, to join the Geological Commission in the Cape. He was later geologist to the South African Irrigation Department and to De Beers. He

gained a world-wide reputation by his thorough and comprehensive work. In 1943 he was elected a Fellow of the Royal Society, and received equally important honours in the United States. His fame largely rests on his writings about the drift of continents, on which he put forward several epoch-making ideas. He died in Cape Town in 1948.

Du Toit, Jacob Daniel ('Totius'). Afrikaans poet and theologian. Son of Rev. S. J. du Toit (q.v.), born at Paarl on February 21, 1877. Studied at the theological seminary at Burghersdorp and at the Free University at Amsterdam. Served in the Anglo-Boer War as a chaplain on the Republican side. In 1905 accepted a call to the Dutch Reformed Church at Potchefstroom, where he was appointed professor at the theological seminary in 1911. His first book of poems, *By Die Monument*, appeared in 1908. As one of the best-known Afrikaans writers, he took a major part in translating the Bible and preparing a rhymed version of the Psalms. He died on July 1, 1953.

Du Toit, Rev. Stephanus Jacobus. Founder of the movement for the recognition of the Afrikaans language. Born in 1847 at Daljosafat in the Western Cape, he was educated under Arnoldus Pannevis (q.v.) at the Paarl Gymnasium School, and proceeded to Stellenbosch, where he was ordained in 1874 as a minister of the Dutch Reformed Church. There he became interested in Afrikaans, and, while minister for Noorder-Paarl, in 1875 founded the Genootskap van Regte Afrikaners (q.v.). With this went the launching of *Di Patriot*, the first newspaper in that language, of which he became editor. Besides helping to establish the Afrikander Bond (q.v.) in 1879, Du Toit in 1882 accepted the appointment as Superintendent of Education for the South African Republic, and in 1883 accompanied the

Triumvirate on its Independence mission to England. In 1889 he gave up his educational post and returned to the Cape to resume his connection with *Di Patriot*. This he edited from 1890 to 1904, also starting a children's journal, *Ons Klyntji*, in 1896, and in 1907 *Ons Taal*. Du Toit was among the first to attempt the translation of the Bible into Afrikaans. He wrote many books, including fiction, drama, history and grammar. Early in the 1890's he established a friendship with Cecil John Rhodes, with whom he travelled in Rhodesia. His attitude after the Jameson Raid estranged him from many Afrikaners. None the less his position as a founder of Afrikaans remained unchallenged. He died in 1911.

Dutoitspan. Sheet of water in Griqualand West, which gave its name to a famous diamond mine discovered there in 1869, and to a township adjoining, now part of Kimberley (q.v.). The original mine was taken over by De Beers Consolidated Mines in 1896.

Dwyka River. Tributary of **Gouritz River** (q.v.). Gave its name to well-known geological formation in the Karroo.

Dysselsdorp. Village near Oudtshoorn, Cape Province. Population: 1,225, including 34 Whites.

E

Eagles. Popular name for larger members of Falconidae family, of which the smaller are called hawks. Diurnal birds of prey, characterised by their upright carriage, talons, hooked bill and crop to facilitate swift gorging. Eagles are found in decreasing numbers in South Africa, but are still plentiful and preserved in the game reserves. There are a number of varieties. *Falcons* have streamlined bodies and tails, and pointed wings for great speed. Of these the African Peregrine is common near Table Mountain. The Bateleur (*Terathopius ecaudatus*) —black ruff, chestnut on back and tail, and white under wings—is a remarkable eagle, with immensely long wings, big head and short tail. It lives largely in the air and is capable of terrific speed, killing its prey with a clean stroke. It is plentiful in dry open places. *Kestrels* and *Kites* are more often seen hovering. They are like Falcons in flight, but with longer, broader tails. *Harriers* are loosely built, with long tails, rounded wings, bright yellow eyes and (unlike true eagles) unfeathered whitish legs. *Buzzards* have short, widespread tails and long wings, expanded like fingers. *Sparrow-Hawks* (Goshawks) have short, rounded wings and long, broad tails for darting between trees. *See* BIRDS.

Earthwolf. *See* AARDWOLF.

East Coast Fever (also known as **African Coast Fever**). Serious livestock disease, scientifically known as *Piroplasma parvum,* first discovered in German East Africa by Dr. Robert Koch in 1897. Brought to Beira in 1901 and later to Rhodesia and parts of South Africa. Transmitted by means of brown ticks, it is similar in some but not all respects to Texas fever or Red-

water (q.v.). Thanks to fencing, dipping and other precautions, East Coast fever is no longer the menace it was early in the present century.

Eastern Province Herald. Oldest surviving newspaper in South Africa. Established on May 7, 1845, in Port Elizabeth. It has been appearing daily since January 31, 1898.

East London. South African seaport and city at the mouth of the Buffalo River on the Indian Ocean. It came into existence in 1845 during the War of the Axe (q.v.), when the British military authorities caused troops to be landed at this point, and the rudiments of a settlement sprang up. The oldest section of the town is on the West Bank, today comparatively undeveloped, for it was there that Fort Glamorgan, holding a garrison of 300 men of the 73rd Highlanders, was set up about this time. The famous vessel H.M.S. *Beagle,* in which Charles Darwin made his voyage round the world, was engaged on surveying this area in 1847. The origin of the name East London is obscure, the original name having been Port Rex, in honour of George Rex (q.v.), who brought the first ship into the river. By a Government notice, dated November 28, 1847, the name was changed to East London. The following January, Governor Sir Harry Smith annexed the surrounding country to the Cape. (Parallel to the founding of East London is that of West London (q.v.), situated on the Cape Flats.) At first development was slow, particularly owing to the presence of a bar at the mouth of the Buffalo River, but the arrival in 1858 of 3,150 German settlers greatly stimulated business and prosperity. East London became the outlet for the prosperous and fertile colony of British Kaffraria (q.v.). A railway inland was started in 1874, and in 1886 the first serious efforts were made to improve the harbour. This has culminated in the construction of works costing several million pounds, and a turning basin which allows the entry of vessels up to 38,000 tons. Many other amenities, including electric power and a tramway system, were introduced towards the end of the century. Today East London has a population of 136,750, of whom 51,570 are Europeans, 73,000 Bantu, 1,930 Asiatics and 10,450 Coloureds. Besides being one of the principal ports of shipment for wool and other produce from many parts of South Africa, East London is a favourite holiday resort, not only with South Africans but with Rhodesians, the total number of visitors being close on 60,000 a year. Manufacturing includes motor-car assembly, textiles and confectionery.

East London Dispatch. See DAILY DISPATCH.

Eaton, John Kyer. South African industrial pioneer. Born in Bendigo, Australia, 1871, he emigrated to South Africa as a young man. Convinced of the importance of iron and steel production, particularly through the success of the Broken Hill Proprietary Steel Works in New South Wales, with which he had at one time been associated, he made it his life task to introduce something similar into this country. One of his early efforts was the creation of the engineering firm of Cartweight & Eaton in Benoni, Transvaal, which later developed into the Dunswart Iron and Steel Works. Later he concentrated his attention on the setting up of an iron and steel plant in Newcastle, Natal, which ultimately became part of the Iscor organisation. Eaton settled in Durban, where he established his own firm to manufacture road-making machinery. He died in 1942.

Ebb and Flow. Lagoon near the Wilderness, Knysna, noted for its beautiful scenery.

Ebden, John Bardwell. Cape commercial pioneer and legislator. Born in England, 1787, he spent his early years in China, reaching the Cape of Good Hope in 1805 as clerk in the Victualling Office. Entering commerce he founded a famous commercial house and in 1834 was appointed to the Legislative Council. In 1838 he founded the Cape of Good Hope Bank, of which he remained Chairman until his death. A dominating figure, he was Chairman of the Anti-Convict movement (q.v.). He helped to establish the first local railway company and many other enterprises. One of his early clerks was Sir J. C. Molteno (q.v.), first Prime Minister of the Colony. Ebden died in 1873.

Ecklon, Christian Frederick. South African botanist. Born at Apenrade, in Schleswig-Holstein, then part of Denmark, on December 17, 1795, he studied at Kiel as an apothecary and so became interested in plants. Taken on as an assistant by a Cape Town apothecary named Polemann, who was an amateur botanist, he began making large collections and carried out experiments in a miniature botanical garden of his own. A small pension from the King of Denmark for his researches enabled him to extend his explorations up-country. Although he succeeded in publishing several important works based on his collaboration with K. L. P. Zeyher (q.v.), he suffered many misfortunes, including the destruction by fire of his precious collections. He died in December 1868.

Eckstein, Friedrich. Rand mining magnate. Born in Stuttgart, Germany, in 1857, younger brother of Hermann Eckstein (q.v.). He spent an early period in India, and came to the Rand in 1887. Making his headquarters in London about the time of the Boer War, he became one of the controllers

PLATE I.   Antelopes of Southern Africa
1. Sable antelope. 2. Eland. 3. Kudu. 4. Springbok.
5. Oribi. 6. Waterbuck. 7. Impala.

PLATE 2.   Antelopes of Southern Africa
   1. Blue Wildebeest. 2. Gemsbok. 3. Tsessebe. 4. Nyala antelope.
   5. Klipspringer. 6. Chobe bushbuck. 7. Blue duiker.
   8. Bontebok.

PLATE 3.   University of Cape Town *(top)*
          (by courtesy of the Director of Information, South African Embassy)

          **Old Supreme Court and the 'Groote Kerk', Adderley Street, Cape
          Town** *(bottom)*
          (by courtesy of the State Information Office, Pretoria)

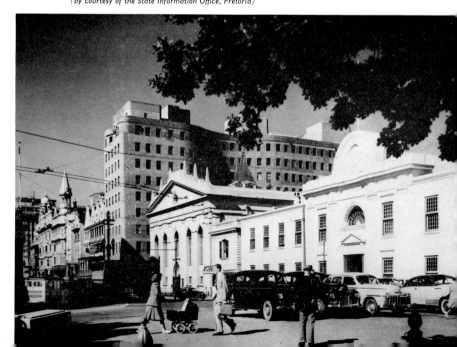

PLATE 4. Boschendal, Groot Drakenstein, one of the Rhodes Fruit Farms *(top)*
(by courtesy of the Dept. of Information, Pretoria)

Bushman Rock Painting (hunting) *(bottom)*

PLATE 5. Radio Telescope for Space Observation,
near Hartebeesthoek, Transvaal *(top)*

Citrus Farm in the Rustenburg Area *(bottom)*
(by courtesy of the Director of Information, South African Embassy)

PLATE 6. Copper Mine, Mufulira *(top)*

Pelindaba Atomic Centre, near Pretoria *(bottom)*

PLATE 7. Gold Mine Headgear, Klerksdorp *(top)*

Oil-from-coal Plant, Sasolburg *(bottom)*
(both photos by courtesy of South African Railways)

Lourenço Marques,
Mozambique *(above)*
*(by courtesy of
the Portuguese State
Office)*

PLATE 8

New Standard Bank
Building,
Johannesburg *(left)*
*(by courtesy of Anglo
American Corp. of S.A. Ltd.)*

of the firm of Wernher, Beit & Co. and succeeded Sir Julius Wernher (q.v.) as Chairman in 1912. Owing to his German origin, he suffered much unpleasantness during World War I, and resigned his position. In his later years he received a knighthood and devoted his energies to cotton-growing in the Sudan. He died in 1930.

Eckstein, Hermann. Diamond and gold mining pioneer and magnate. Born in Stuttgart, Germany, in 1849, the son of a Lutheran pastor, he spent his early years in England with a German firm but came to Kimberley in 1882, to take over the running of the Phoenix Diamond Mining Co. There he gained the friendship of Julius Wernher and Alfred Beit and with them joined Jules Porges & Co. (q.v.). On their behalf he first went to Barberton in 1886 and soon afterwards to Johannesburg to represent the house. He started the firm of H. Eckstein & Co. in 1888, which soon became the leading mining firm on the Rand. Eckstein, a man of great charm, was elected original President of the Chamber of Mines and held office from 1889 to 1891. His health began to fail in 1892 and he died in 1893 in the town of his birth.

Edenburg: 1. Village in Orange Free State. Founded in 1862 as a Kerkdorp (Church Village). The name is sometimes regarded as taken from the Garden of Eden in the Bible and sometimes as a corruption of Edinburgh. Sheep farming centre. Population: 3,000, including 900 Whites. **2.** Original name of Rivonia, Northern suburb of Johannesburg.

Edendale. Settlement near Pietermaritzburg, Natal. Population: 32,356, including 26,387 Bantu, 4,845 Asiatics, 896 Coloured and 228 Whites.

Edenvale. Town near Germiston, Transvaal, established in 1903. Population: 24,720, including 17,500 Whites. Industrial centre.

Edenville. Township near Kroonstad, Orange Free State. Population: 1,300, including 650 Whites.

Education. Present-day South African education is to a large degree modelled on that of Scotland over a century ago. This is due to the fact that the first Superintendent-General of Education, Dr. James Rose-Innes, was a Scot. Prior to 1838 there was no serious attempt at organised education on a national basis in the modern sense, though the first school (attended by the children of both slaves and settlers) was opened in the time of Commander Jan van Riebeeck in 1658, and was followed by a number of others, run in conjunction with the Dutch Reformed Church. After the coming of the British similar schools were opened by English Churches. A milestone was the founding in 1829 of the 'South African Atheneum,' later the South Africa College (q.v.), the first institution of higher education.

In 1838 Sir John Herschel (q.v.), the famous astronomer, while at the Cape, drafted proposals for an Education Department, which became the basis for the present-day system, while the Board of Examiners, established in 1857, was the forerunner of the University of the Cape of Good Hope. (*See* UNIVERSITIES.)

Organised education in Natal started with the Voortrekkers. In the Boer Republics education was largely under Hollander influence, although the generous action of Governor Sir George Grey (q.v.) in setting up, at his own expense, the Grey College in Bloemfontein in 1855, helped to maintain the British tradition in the Orange Free State. The Transvaal began its Education Department, staffed largely from Holland, in 1876, but the Uitlander population of the Rand, dissatisfied at the inadequate facilities on the Gold Fields, formed in 1895 the Witwatersrand Council of Education, which, with funds of £150,000, helped to start a chain of schools, many of which still exist.

Something similar happened after the South African War, when the defeated Boers, with the help of the Dutch Reformed Church, established 'Christian National Schools,' to operate independently of those sponsored by the 'anglicising' departments of Lord Milner's administration.

Since Union in 1910, primary and secondary schools have been in the hands of the provinces, while technical and vocational training, and that of the handicapped, falls under the Department of Education. The country is divided into districts, in each of which a School Board with supervisory powers is elected.

Education for Africans, formerly in the hands of the missions, has since 1958 been under a separate Department of Bantu Education. The Transkei education system is autonomous. There are today over 2,000,000 Bantu children at school in the Republic of South Africa, representing 90 per cent of the potential scholars, but the number in senior classes is relatively low.

Edwards, Samuel H. Trader and explorer. Born in Bethelsdorp near Port Elizabeth in 1827, son of a missionary, who accompanied David Livingstone on some of his earlier journeys into the Bechuana country. After finishing his schooling in Port Elizabeth, Samuel followed them in 1846, and soon began exploring independently. With his friend, J. H. Wilson (q.v.), he made one of the earliest journeys to Lake Ngami. He followed this with numerous other expeditions and entered Matabeleland, where he gained the friendship of Moselikatse. Accompanying Sir John Swinburne on his early expedition to Matabeleland in 1869, he was one of the earliest white men to work for gold in that country, particularly on the Umfuli and Hunyani Rivers. He became a

digger in the 1870's on the Diamond Fields, and then Managing Director of the Monarch Gold Mine in Tati. His last years were spent in Port Elizabeth, where he died at the age of 95 in 1922.

Eerste Fabrieken (literally 'First Factories'). Settlement near Pretoria, on the farm Hatherley, where, in terms of concessions granted in 1882 by the Government of the South African Republic to Alois Hugo Nellmapius, and financed by the firm of Lewis and Marks (Isaac Lewis and Samuel Marks (qq.v.)), factories were erected for the production, as a monopoly, of a variety of goods, including brandy and other liquor, barrels, jams, preserves and glass. Save for the brandy, most of the output was unprofitable, but operations continued on a fluctuating scale until the South African War.

Eersteling. Scene of the first gold mining company's operations in the Northern Transvaal. Situated not far from Potgietersrust, the farm was first worked by Edward Button in 1871 together with William Pigg (q.v.), who in 1872 floated the Transvaal Gold Mining Company. Initially a large rocking boulder was used to crush the ore, but later a proper plant was set up. This was destroyed in the First Boer War in 1880, but the smokestack and a few buildings still survive, and in 1938 were proclaimed National Monuments.

Eerste River. Township near Stellenbosch, Cape Province. Population: 1,834, including 468 Whites.

Egret (family Ardeidae). Bird of small heron type (q.v.), living in flocks near vleis and swamps. The Little Egret (*Egretta garzetta*) has a long black bill and legs, and yellow feet. A handsome bird, to be seen spreading its white plumes (the Ospreys for which thousands of egrets were formerly butchered) over its tree-top nest. The Cattle Egret or Tick Bird (*Bubulcus ibis*) is rather different from the others because of its yellow-brown legs, short yellow bill and brownish-pink breeding plumes. It is more often seen attached to cattle than are other egrets. *See* BIRDS.

Ehrlich, Ludwig. South African mining pioneer. Born in Bavaria in 1863, he began his career in a bank in Frankfurt. Coming to the Witwatersrand in 1890, he became associated with the house of Neumann and director of numerous companies. Later, in 1894, he set up a business and floated various properties. Settling in London in 1896, he was connected with the Modderfontein East Mine, the Luipaardsvlei and many other concerns, also with mining ventures in Australia and Siberia. He died in 1943.

Eiffel Flats. Township 5 miles east of Gatooma in Rhodesia. Chiefly notable on account of its proximity to the well-known Cam and Motor Gold Mine.

Eighteen-Twenty Settlers. Group of British pioneers settled on the Cape Eastern Frontier. The reasons for their coming were twofold, being partly due to the distress prevailing in the British Isles after the Napoleonic Wars, and partly to the desire of the Colonial authorities to provide an effective defence for the still empty regions of the Colony. Discussion of the project began in 1819, although some earlier parties had settled at Clanwilliam (q.v.). Mr. Vansittart, as Chancellor of the Exchequer, secured a grant of £50,000 from Parliament in England to finance the scheme. No fewer than 90,000 people applied for passages, from whom 4,000 were officially selected, comprising 2,415 men and 1,585 women, but a number of independent settlers arrived, bringing the total to approximately 5,000. They were divided into about 60 parties, and provided an enormous addition to the very modest white population of the Cape Colony. This comprised only 47,000, of whom only

4,000 were of British origin. Ships sailed from London, Portsmouth, Liverpool, Bristol and Cork. Most of the settlers were of a very good type, and included members of leading families. The first ship to arrive was the *Chapman,* which reached Algoa Bay on April 9, 1820, while the last was the *Duke of Marlborough,* which arrived towards the end of June. Ground was provided and several new settlements planted, including Bathurst. Many of the early settlers had an extremely difficult time, and a fund was established for their assistance in 1823, but most of them successfully established themselves, if not on the land, then in the towns, and made an incalculable contribution towards the development of Southern Africa.

Eighteen-Twenty Settlers Memorial Association. Established to commemorate the centenary of the 1820 settlers, its object being to encourage the immigration of approved settlers to South Africa, especially farmers. Since its foundation in 1920 it has helped over 100,000 newcomers.

Ei-in-die-Hoed. Children's game played by tossing balls or stones into a hat. (Literally 'Egg-in-the-Hat.')

Eland. The largest antelope, found in the Drakensberg, the Kalahari, Rhodesia and Mozambique, and originally much more widely distributed. It is fond of dry country and also exists in the Kalahari Game Reserve. Eland once occurred in herds of 100, but are now extremely scarce. Carries corkscrew horns, those of the male being shorter and thicker. Experiments have been carried out successfully in crossing with domestic cattle, with which they live happily. Eland bulls grow to a height of almost 6 feet at the withers and their horns to nearly 3 feet in length. The zoological name is *Taurotragus oryx.* The name Eland was bestowed upon the animal by the early settlers because of its imagined resemblance to the Elk (Eland) found in diminishing numbers on the European continent.

Eland's Bay. Fishing harbour on the Cape West Coast, north of St. Helena Bay.

Elandsboontjie or Looiersbossie. Roots used by Bechuana in tanning. Beans used as vegetable.

Elandslaagte. Farming and colliery centre 16 miles north of Ladysmith in Natal. One of the first battles in the South African War was fought here on October 21, 1899, in which heavy losses were sustained by the Boers.

Electricity Supply Commission. Statutory body set up in the Union of South Africa in 1922 by the Electricity Act of that year. By its constitution it operates without Government interference under the supervision of the Electricity Control Board, which is charged with the grant of licences for the construction and operation of power stations. Since then the Electricity Supply Commission, largely through the efforts of the late Dr. H. J. Van der Bijl (q.v.), has built up a vast network of stations and power lines, covering nearly one-third of the area of the Republic. Its total investment is over R1,000,000,000, most of it financed by the issue of its own stocks. Its revenue is at the rate of over R150,000,000 a year, total electricity sales over 30,421,700,000 units, apart from over 22,000,000 units of compressed air and steam sold. The Commission uses approximately 20,000,000 tons of coal yearly and has eight distinct undertakings, of which the largest, covering the Witwatersrand, includes the former network of the Victoria Falls and Transvaal Power Company. Its total installed capacity is approximately 6,000,000 kilowatts. After the present expansion programme, involving the building of the two largest stations in the Southern Hemisphere, at Hendrina and Arnot in the Transvaal, each of 2,000,000 kilowatts, the total capacity will be 14,000,000 kilowatts.

Electric Power. *See also* ESCOM. The first recorded use of an electrical device in the Cape of Good Hope was in about 1809, and the first use of electric light was in September 1879 in Cape Town, shortly after its first demonstration overseas by Edison and Swan. In 1882 the Cape Town docks were first lit by electricity, also the Houses of Parliament, and the first local company was formed. Durban Town Hall was first lit by electricity in 1888, about the same time as its use began on the Witwatersrand. The first permanent power station at Cape Town was inaugurated in 1892, using water power from Table Mountain. The use of electric power in Rhodesia may be traced to the Pioneer Column in 1890, which included in its equipment an electric searchlight. Electric power plants were introduced in Bulawayo and Salisbury during the 1890's (*see also* KARIBA). The Republic has over 600,000 consumers of electricity, of whom nearly 100,000 are other than domestic. The total installed capacity of generating plants in the Republic is approximately 8,000,000 kilowatts, of which 80 per cent is accounted for by the Electricity Supply Commission (q.v.).

Elephant. Largest African land mammal. First found in the environs of Table Bay, but gradually driven north, although a few survive in the Tsitsikama Forest and in the Addo National Park (q.v.). A number have been preserved in the Kruger National Park, in Rhodesia and in Mozambique. The African elephant is smaller than the Asiatic and has conspicuously large ears. The animals reach a height of nearly 11 feet, and reports have been received of specimens of over 12 feet. The tusks of African elephants attain enormous sizes, one of the largest on record being 11 feet 5½ inches in length, over 1½ feet in circumference and weighing close on 300 lb. Elephants are not aggressive, but when aroused can do great damage. Elephant hunting is only allowed under control in Rhodesia, and not at all in the Republic. Elephants found at Addo and in the Tsitsikama Forest differ from the normal African type and are considered to be a special subvariety. See MAMMALS.

Elephant Rock. Traditional name for dolomite, so called on account of the resemblance of its surface to the rough skin of an elephant. Particularly plentiful in the Transvaal.

Elephant's Trunk (*Pachypodium namaquanum*). Popular name for strangely-shaped plant found in Namaqualand, growing about 5 or 6 feet high.

Elf (*Pomatomus saltator*). Carnivorous and voracious fish (40 inches) that feeds in shoals on mackerel, harder and sardines. The elf is wrongly called shad. The true shad is a kind of herring (q.v.).

Elim. Mission station near Bredasdorp, Cape Province. Population: 1,088, including 7 Whites.

Elliot. Town in the Cape Province on the Slang River, founded in 1885 and named after the Chief Magistrate of the Transkei, Sir Henry Elliot. Situated in magnificent scenery, it is a farming centre of importance. Population: 4,500, including 1,300 Whites.

Elliot, Sir Henry George. Chief Magistrate of the Transkeian Territories. Born in Canada on December 25, 1826, he entered the Royal Marines in 1847 and served in the Crimean War. In 1870 he retired and emigrated to Natal, spending some time on the early River Diggings. Thereafter he joined the Cape Colonial Service and in 1877 became Chief Magistrate of Tembuland. His strong personality and many gifts won him enormous influence among the natives. Sir Henry Elliot served in a number

of wars, and was recognised as one of the most distinguished administrators in South Africa. He died in 1912.

Elliotdale. Village in Cape Province. Population: 360, including 110 Whites.

Elliott, Arthur. South African photographer and antiquarian. Born in the United States in 1870, he went as a sailor to the Far East reaching South Africa in 1890. He was engaged in various road shows, and helped to introduce the gramophone into South Africa, being responsible for recording the voice of President Kruger; the disc, unfortunately, has not survived. His chief claim to fame rests on the systematic way in which he photographed historic buildings and preserved pictures of unique importance recording South African development. After many vicissitudes and disputes his collection of 10,000 negatives was finally acquired by the Union Government for the Archives. Arthur Elliott, who held many exhibitions of his work, died in Cape Town in 1938.

Elliott, Sir Charles Bletterman. First General Manager of the Cape Government Railways. Born in Uitenhage on May 8, 1841, he was the son of the Rev. William Elliott. He was educated at the South African College and later in London. At the age of 18 he became a judge's clerk, but was soon transferred to the Colonial Office. For a while he was resident magistrate in Wynberg and in Cape Town, then Chief Clerk to the Minister of Crown Lands and Public Works. This resulted in his promotion in 1876 to Assistant Commissioner of Crown Lands and Public Works, and in December 1880 to General Manager of the Cape Government Railways. During his period of office, the system grew from 700 to over 3,000 miles of track. He was a man of considerable learning, a qualified barrister and an examiner in science for the University of the Cape of Good Hope. He retired in 1902 and died in 1911.

Eloff. Village near Springs, Transvaal. Population: 280, including 230 Whites.

Eloff, Fanie (Stephanus). South African sculptor. Born in 1885 in the Transvaal and related to President Kruger. He studied in Europe, where he developed a characteristic and delicate style, which won him high appreciation both here and overseas. He died in Pretoria in 1947.

Elsburg. Town on Rand, near Germiston, named after a farmer named Els, who owned the original site. Laid out in 1887, it was nearly chosen as the site of the main town of the gold fields, in preference to Johannesburg. Population: 6,800, including 6,300 Whites.

Elsenburg. Famous Cape mansion, originally built by the Secunde Samuel Elsevier, second in authority to Governor Willem Adriaan Van der Stel (q.v.) in 1698. The older house was rebuilt and greatly beautified by Martin Melck in, and after, 1754. Today the estate accommodates the Agricultural Faculty of the nearby University of Stellenbosch and is noted for research on fruit-growing and allied subjects.

Elsie. Afrikaans name for Avocet (q.v.).

Elton, Captain James Frederic. South African explorer, Born in 1840, he joined the army at an early age, taking part in the Indian Mutiny Campaign, and in 1860 fought in China. After a while in Mexico, he came to the Cape in 1871 to report on the gold and diamond occurrences. Settling in Natal, Elton was a member of the Legislative and Executive Council. He explored the course of the Limpopo River in the Transvaal, about 1875, became British consul in Mozambique and helped to suppress the slave trade. After further treks in search of a trade route to Lake Nyasa, he died of fever in 1877,

Ely. Military village established in 1848 near Alice on what was then the Eastern Frontier of the Cape. Abandoned in 1850 as a result of the Native invasion. It is named after one of the towns in England with which Governor Sir Harry Smith (q.v.) was associated as a young man.

Emigrant Tembuland. Portion of the Transkei settled by emigrants from Tembuland proper (q.v.), its principal places being Cala and St. Marks.

Emmer. Literally a bucket. Formerly used as a measure for grain at the Cape.

Empangeni. Town in Zululand and centre of sugar-milling industry. Founded in 1885, but not officially declared a township until 1931. The name Empangeni is derived from a Zulu word signifying to seize or grab. Population: 9,000—4,000 Whites, 4,000 Bantu, 180 Coloureds, 800 Indians.

Engcobo. Village in Transkei. The name means 'a place with long grass and trees along a stream.' Population: 1,158, including 603 Whites.

Engelhart, Charles William. Mining capitalist. Born in New York, February 15, 1917, and educated at Princeton University. Served in the U.S. Air Force during World War II, and succeeded his father in large international interests in the base metal and other industries. Arriving in South Africa in 1950, he became a leading figure in the gold industry, culminating in 1957 with acquisition of control and his election as Chairman of the Central Mining—Rand Mines group (*see* CORNER HOUSE).

English Academy of South Africa. Founded in 1960 to uphold and foster the interests of the English language in South Africa. Its headquarters are in Johannesburg.

ENGLISH LITERATURE IN SOUTH AFRICA
by
PROFESSOR A. C. PARTRIDGE
University of the Witwatersrand, Johannesburg

ENGLISH literature in South Africa commenced with the first occupation of the Cape by the British in 1795, when Andrew Barnard, Secretary to the Governor, Lord Macartney, brought with him his gifted wife, Lady Anne. She was a charming hostess, and endeavoured to be friendly to all sections of the people. Her *Letters* and *Journal* are a lively account of the social life of a gracious colonial period. She had a warmth of natural sympathy unusual in the more austere colonists who made up the band of 1820 settlers. With the latter came another Scot, Thomas Pringle, best described as a Christian Socialist. Pringle made his mark as a poet, educator and polemist, an advocate for the emancipation of slaves and the freedom of the press. His poems, such as *Evening Rambles* and *Afar in the Desert*, are better known than his *Narrative of a Resident in South Africa*. Both poetry and prose are dated in style and of uneven literary merit; abounding in moral sentiments, and 18th-century pictorial felicities of phrase.

The pioneer period of the 19th century terminated with the work of a woman of genius. Olive Schreiner had the advantage of being a child of the soil and of intelligent, if unfortunate, parents. *The Story of an African Farm* grew out of her lonely self-discovery on a Karroo farm where she was employed as a governess at the age of 18. It was happy in its English sponsors, but unfruitful in maturing its author's promise. Her other novels were failures, and her allegorical stories, though often beautiful, too poignantly aimed, and burdened with visionary messages. Olive Schreiner's greatest book is undoubtedly *Thoughts on South Africa*. It is a socio-historical work of immense insight, racial understanding and prophetic fulfilment.

The 20th century saw a new phase in South African literature, in which imagination began to replace observation. Considerable impetus was given to creative activity by the importance to the nation of Union in 1910. South African literary associations arose; but the optimism of this solidarity was rudely broken by political divisions, out of which, however, Afrikaans literature was formed. The first decades produced two books of pioneering altruism in Sir Percy Fitzpatrick's *Jock of the Bushveld* and Kingsley Fairbridge's *Story of Himself*, books with the merits of simplicity, sincerity and manliness, but typical of a nation still adolescent.

The earliest works of fiction born of social observation and human insight came again from two women novelists, Pauline Smith and Sarah Gertrude Millin. The former was the daughter of an Oudtshoorn doctor. Her *Little Karroo* and *The Beadle* offered beautiful and sensitive studies of the country life she had learnt to love with an intimate affection. Sarah Gertrude Millin's was a mind of a different stamp, penetratingly alert, especially for social problems; efficient and masculine in its vigour of style. Novels, based on close study and reflections, such as *God's Stepchildren*, *Mary Glenn*, *The King of the Bastards*, were powerful, moving and uncompromising books, truthful as the observing mind could make them. When she had worked out this phase and assiduously arrived at her later discipline as a diarist, Mrs. Millin became an accomplished biographer and memoir-writer. There are good critics who prefer her *War Diaries* and *The Measure of my Days* to her sociological fiction. The more vigorous prose accompanies the revelation of a remarkable, if somewhat egocentric, personality.

Mrs. Millin pointed the way to the profession of letters for the serious-minded artist, and her followers, both in fiction and poetry, have reaped the harvest, not always of cash, but of genuine critical approval. They are H. C. Bosman, Stuart Cloete, Alan Paton, Lawrence Green, Laurens van der Post, Peter Abrahams, Daphne Rooke, Nadine Gordimer, Dan Jacobson, Francis Carey Slater, Roy Campbell, Uys Krige and Anthony Delius. Even the isolated figures of Frank Brownlee and Guy Butler have been all but professionals, except in the time they have been able to devote to creative writing. Campbell and Bosman were, in their separate ways, the wild men of the thirties. But whereas *The Flaming Terrapin*, *Adamastor*, *Flowering Reeds* and *The Wayzgooze* had the technical accomplishment of the verse to mellow their vaulting ambition and occasional bombast, *Mafeking Road* had to startle awareness alone by the rough-hewn vigour of its prose and its powerful but crude perception of character.

In the years since the conclusion of World War II, South Africa has produced in English a more vital and distinctive literature. Fiction has been largely pre-occupied with the racial question, Paton with its deep tragedy, Abrahams and Jacobson with its inhumanity or injustice. Paton has rightly had the more influential following, not because he is less indignant, but because his profounder spiritual quality gives poise and wisdom to his conception of his task as a creative artist. *Cry, the Beloved Country* must be classed with *The Story of an African Farm* as the most powerful works of fiction to have come from these shores. And Paton might equally have succeeded with *Too Late the Phalarope*, had his public reacted more appreciatively to his theme and his style of presenting the story.

The tribal life of the South African native in his pastoral primitiveness is nowhere so beautifully and sincerely revealed in the novel form as in Frank Brownlee's *Cattle Thief*, described by Richard Garnett as 'a little classic that will live.' The other great book of the post-war decade is Van der Post's *Venture into the Interior*, unique in its blend of descriptive power, philosophical insight, and profound love of what can only be glossed as the 'soul of Africa.' Nadine Gordimer, most accomplished craftsman of the short story, understands and depicts with equal felicity in *Six Feet of Country* and *The Lying Days* the heart of the great metropolis, Johannesburg. One of the unjustly neglected of South Africa's near-masterpieces, however, is Elizabeth Webster's *The Expiring Frog*. Only Paton, in a sympathetic review, has drawn attention to the immense power of its theme of feminine frailty.

Enkeldoorn. Village in Rhodesia, centre of the considerable Afrikaans-speaking community who came here in the days of Cecil Rhodes. Centre for the Charter district. Population: 700, including 200 Whites.

Ennes, Antonio José (also spelt **Enes**). Governor-General of Mozambique, appointed in 1895.

Entrenched Clauses. Legal term applied to those clauses of the constitution of the Union of South Africa which contained special safeguards against alterations by normal Parliamentary procedure. The Entrenched Clauses form Section 152 of the South Africa Act of 1909. This made provision for the qualifications of voters, the number of Members of Parliament to represent the various provinces and the equality of the English and Afrikaans languages. Doubts were thrown in recent years upon the legal efficacy of the safeguards in the Entrenched Clauses.

Eoan Group. Organisation with its headquarters in Cape Town, established in 1934 by Mrs. Southern Holt to encourage cultural activities, particularly music, ballet and the drama, among the Cape Coloured people. Its performances are of a high artistic standard and some very successful tours of classical opera have taken place through most of South Africa.

Erasmus. Township in the Transvaal. *See* BRONKHORSTSPRUIT.

Erf. A plot of ground, the name being derived from the Dutch word meaning an inheritance. There are two kinds in most villages, the dry and water erwe, the latter having irrigation rights. The word erf is not used on the Rand, where the traditional term is Stand (q.v.).

Erica (Ericaceae). Apart from such rare species as Johnstonia in Rhodesia, with its pink globular flowers, the Ericas belong to the Cape, where there are over a hundred varieties—red, pink, green, yellow and white. Among the most common on the mountain slopes is *Erica hirtiflora*, with its small pink bells. Some, like the yellow *Erica jasminiflora* of Caledon, are rare and very local. The Tygershoek Heath has an unusually large variety, long, hanging pink flowers with green tips. *Erica plupenetii* (Hangertjie) is a large sturdy shrub in many colours; and *Erica blenna*, or Lantern Heath, has rather plump orange bells, green-tipped. To the same family belong the cultivated azaleas.

Erlanger. *See* D'ERLANGER.

Ermelo. Town in the Eastern Transvaal, founded in 1880 and named after Ermelo in the Netherlands, home-town of the Rev. Frans Lion Cachet, the first minister. Farming centre. Population: 23,665, including 9,500 Whites.

Erosion. *See* SOIL EROSION.

Erskine, St. Vincent. Early hunter in Rhodesia. He travelled in Mashonaland and Manicaland in the 1860's and 1870's. Originally a surveyor, he took up this occupation and after 1876 settled in what was then known as No-Man's Land, afterwards Griqualand East.

Erwe, die. *See* DIE ERWE.

Escom. *See* ELECTRICITY SUPPLY COMMISSION.

Escombe, Harry. Natal Prime Minister. Born in London in 1838, and educated at St. Paul's School, he came to Natal in 1860, establishing himself as a successful lawyer in Durban. In 1872 he was elected to the Legislative Council, and after serving through the Zulu and First Boer Wars, became Attorney-General in 1893 and Premier in 1897. A man of great foresight, he was responsible for building up the local military forces and started the Natal Naval Volunteers. He was made a Privy Councillor and received an Honorary LL.D. from Cambridge University. He died on December 27, 1899.

Eshowe. Capital of Zululand. Renowned for the beauty of its setting, with a forest in the middle of the municipal area. It was originally a mission station, but became a village in 1880 after suffering a siege during the Zulu War. Administrative and residential centre. Population: 5,350, including 2,500 Whites.

Esperanza. Village near Umzinto, Natal. Population: 1,462, including 140 Whites.

Essenhout (Ash Wood). Common South African name for *Ekebergia capensis*. Used in cabinet-making. There are two kinds—red and white.

Estcourt. Town in Natal, 159 miles from Durban, on main railway to the Transvaal. Originally called Bushman's River Post, it was renamed in

1851 after Mr. T. H. S. S. Estcourt, M.P., who happened to be a friend of the founder, J. B. Wilks. Condensed milk and bacon factories. Trout fishing near by. Population: 13,700 including 4,400 Whites.

Ethiopianism. Movement based on the slogan, 'Africa for the Africans.' It originated in the establishment of Tembu Church of South Africa in 1884 by Nehemiah Tile, a former Wesleyan minister. Other Bantu leaders later seceded to join him, and from this arose a powerful organisation, including a number of churches, loosely linked, notably the African Methodist Episcopal and the African Presbyterian. Entertaining political ambitions at one time, the Ethiopian movement caused considerable anxiety, particularly in the years between 1900 and 1910. In more recent times the name has become almost extinct.

Etosha Pan. Salt pan in north of South-West Africa, covering 2,300 sq. miles, the largest of its kind in Africa. It is fed by a number of rivers, most of the water, however, being lost. Today it is the centre of a reserve, with one of the largest accumulations of big game in the world. The pan lies at a height of 3,400 feet above the sea.

Eucalyptus. *See* GUM and TREES.

Eugenie, Empress of the French. Wife of the Emperor Napoleon III and mother of the Prince Imperial, Louis Napoleon (q.v.). After the death of the latter in the Zulu War in 1879, she paid a visit to South Africa in 1880, spending a night in prayer on the actual spot in Zululand where his body was found.

Eunice Institute. Large school for girls in Bloemfontein, established in 1875 as 'Het Dames Instituut Eunice,' with primary and secondary departments.

Euphorbia or **Anneys** (*Euphorbia gregaria* Marl.). Pineless succulent up to 6 feet, having a gummy exudation.

Great Namaqualand. Family Euphorbiaceae contains many shrubs and trees, as well as semi-desert plants, strangely shaped for water storage. The flowers usually have sepals but no petals. Kaffir Hut (*Euphorbia obesa*) of the Karroo looks like a green-brown football, with ridges of stitching; 12 inches high. Above the 10-inch rough brown cone of *Euphorbia bupleurifolia* grows a head of slender brown and green leaves and flowers. Many of the shrubs and trees contain latex, including Melkboom (*Euphorbia dregeana*) (q.v.). Wild Castor Oil (*Ricinus communis*) is common throughout South Africa. Shrubby plant with palmate leaves. Flower spikes bear male flowers with numerous yellow stamens above, and female below. Fruit, a green capsule from the seeds of which the oil is obtained. *See* PLANTS.

Evander. Mining township near Bethal, Eastern Transvaal. Population: 2,811, including 1,972 Whites.

Evaton. *See* RESIDENSIA.

Everlastings or **Sewejaartjies** (*Helichrysum*). Flowers of the Daisy family (q.v.). They keep their mauve, pink and yellow colours when dried and are popular for funeral wreaths. For a century and a half, large quantities have been exported to France and to other places on the Continent, where they are known as Immortelles.

Excelsior. Village in Orange Free State, founded in 1910. Cheesemaking industry. Population: 2,882, including 657 Whites.

Excelsior Diamond. The largest stone before the discovery of the Cullinan (q.v.) in 1905. It was found in the Jagersfontein Mine in the Orange Free State (q.v.) on June 30, 1893, and weighed 971¾ carats, being 2½ inches long, 2 inches wide and an inch thick. The finder, a native mine worker, received £500 in cash as a reward, besides a horse, saddle and bridle. Apart from its size it was of an exceptionally beautiful colour, bluish-white. It was cut up into 21 brilliants, weighing 364 carats altogether.

Exeter Hall. Building in the Strand, London, erected in 1830, and used mainly for meetings by humanitarian and religious societies, many concerning themselves with colonial affairs. As a result of certain injudicious decisions taken there, Exeter Hall became a by-word in South Africa for sentimental and undiscriminating championship of the native races. The building was demolished to make room for the Strand Palace Hotel, but the phrase has survived.

Exports. *See* TRADE.

F

Factories. *See* MANUFACTURES.

Fagan, Henry Allan. South African judge, Cabinet minister and author. Born at Tulbagh, Cape Province, on April 4, 1889, and educated at Stellenbosch, he was called to the Bar and in due course entered politics under General J. B. M. Hertzog. From 1933 to 1943 he was a Member of Parliament and from 1938 to 1939 Minister of Native Affairs, Education and Social Welfare. He was appointed a judge in 1943 and was Chief Justice of the Union from 1957 till his retirement in 1959. Apart from his public work he became an eminent writer in Afrikaans, winning the Hertzog Prize for Literature. He wrote several successful plays, novels, etc., and invented an improved system of shorthand. Died 1963.

Fairbairn, John. Journalist and statesman. Born in 1794 in Roxburghshire, Scotland, he arrived in South Africa in 1823 and opened a school. He started the short-lived *South African Journal*, from which developed *The South African Commercial Advertiser*, launched in January 1824. He later became its sole owner. It brought him into conflict with Lord Charles Somerset (q.v.) and, after repeated censoring, he succeeded in gaining the right to publish without hindrance and thus established the freedom of the South African press. Fairbairn became a national figure, and worked for many reforms through his paper. His backing of the Anti-Convict Agitation (q.v.) in 1849 won him fresh popularity and he joined the deputation to England in 1850 which ended in the grant of self-government to the Colony. He was elected to the Legislative Council. Served from 1854 as Chairman of the South African Mutual Life Assurance

Society which he helped to found. He died in 1864.

Fairbridge, Dorothea. South African author, born in Cape Town in 1860. She specialised in historical and descriptive writing about the early days of the Cape, edited the letters of Lady Anne Barnard (q.v.) and produced several novels, including *That Which Hath Been*, in 1910, and *Piet of Italy*. She died in 1931.

Fairbridge, Kingsley. Rhodesian pioneer and writer. Born at Grahamstown in 1885 of Scottish ancestry. Worked with his father, a land surveyor on the Vaal River, and in 1896 accompanied his family to Rhodesia. There, his father, Rhys Fairbridge, settled at Umtali, and the youngster spent an adventurous life in primitive surroundings. He made many journeys into extremely wild parts, gathering the material which he later used in his famous autobiography, regarded as a classic in Rhodesian literature. He died on July 19, 1924, and a memorial stands outside the Christmas Pass near Umtali, unveiled in 1953 by the Queen Mother.

F.A.K. Abbreviation for Federasie van Afrikaanse Kultuurvereniginge (q.v.).

Faku. Paramount chief of the Pondos. Born about 1777, he succeeded to the leadership of the tribe in the early 19th century. About 1820 Tshaka (q.v.) defeated him but was unsuccessful in over-running his country. Later Faku placed himself under British protection, and in 1842 agreed to make over part of the present East Griqualand to the Colonial authorities. His permission to the first missionaries to enter his country in 1829 pioneered the establishment of a White settlement at Port St. Johns. He died in 1867.

Falcon (family Falconidae). *See* EAGLES and BIRDS.

False Bay: 1. Large inlet on the southern side of Cape Peninsula, between Cape Point on the western side and Cape Hangklip in the east, which lie approximately 20 miles apart. The name is derived from the fact that early navigators often mistook it for Table Bay. Its water, coming from the Indian Ocean, is several degrees warmer than that of Table Bay, which is on the Atlantic side.

2. Inlet near St. Lucia Bay on the Zululand coast.

Fanagalo. Simplified, artificial mixture of words from various Bantu languages, widely employed as a medium of communication in many parts of Southern Africa. Its use is officially encouraged by the Transvaal and O.F.S. Chamber of Mines and other authorities. The word itself signifies in the Bantu language, 'like this.'

Farewell, Lieutenant Francis George. Early pioneer of Natal. A lieutenant in the Royal Navy, he came to the Cape in 1823, and joined an expedition in the ship *Salisbury* sent to Port Natal. Attracted by the possibilities of the country, he decided to start a settlement, and persuaded 25 other colonists to join him. In June 1824 he built the first houses, but all except four companions left him. In July of the same year he visited Tshaka (q.v.), from whom he received a large grant of land round Durban Bay. During 1828 he went to the Cape to procure trading goods, but on his return was murdered by natives in September 1829.

Farini, Guillarmo Antonio. Stage name of William Leonard Hunt, Canadian showman and explorer. Born at Port Hope, Canada, in 1838, he became prominent in 1859, when he duplicated the feat of the famous tightrope walker, Blondin, in crossing the Niagara Falls. Became an acrobat and specialised in a similar turn in different parts of America. He married Anna Mueller, daughter of an aide-de-camp to Kaiser Wilhelm I, and lived for some years in Germany. A man of much ability as a writer, artist and naturalist, he visited South Africa in 1885 and undertook a journey into the Kalahari Desert in quest of diamonds and to examine the possibilities of cattle ranching. He was accompanied by his adopted son, El Nino Farini (Lulu,) who appeared in female clothes. Farini's claim to have found the ruins of a 'Lost City' caused much controversy and subsequent searching. He wrote a book, *Through the Kalahari*, and exhibited his photographs in London and Berlin. He died, aged 91, at Port Hope in January 1929.

Farrar, Sir George Herbert. Gold-mining magnate and soldier. Born 1859 in Cambridge, England, and educated at Bedford. On leaving school he entered the family firm, Howard Farrar & Co., engineers of Bedford. He came to South Africa and became very wealthy. In partnership with his brother, Sydney Farrar, he played a leading role in opening up the eastern side of the gold fields and in 1893 established the East Rand Proprietary Mines which, by amalgamation and expansion, became one of the largest in the world. A supporter of the Reform Movement, he was regarded as one of the ringleaders of the Jameson Raid and sentenced to death in 1896. However, he was fined £25,000 and reprieved. He served with distinction in the Boer War, became President of the Chamber of Mines, and also took a prominent part in politics under the Crown Colony régime. Farrar was killed in a railway accident while on active service in South West Africa in 1914.

Faure. Village near Somerset West, noted as burial spot of the Moslem saint, Sheik Joseph (q.v.); a place of pilgrimage for the Cape Malays.

Fauresmith. Town in the South-Western Orange Free State. Founded in 1850 and named after the Rev. P. E. Faure of the Dutch Reformed Church and Governor Sir Harry Smith of the Cape, who was in authority over the still existent Orange River Sovereignty, forerunner of the Orange Free State. Centre of much fighting in the South African War. The town has the railway running down its main street. Population: 2,200, including 565 Whites.

F.C.R. Abbreviation for First City Regiment. *See* REGIMENT, FIRST CITY.

Federal Broadcasting Corporation of Rhodesia and Nyasaland (also known as F.B.C.). Statutory body established in the Central African Federation with effect from February 1, 1958, but liquidated in 1963.

Federale Volksbeleggings (literally 'Federal People's Investments'). Afrikaans financial house. Founded July 8, 1940, by Dr. C. R. Louw (q.v.) and others, it has grown into one of the most important institutions of its kind in South Africa, including amongst its subsidiaries companies devoted to mining, industry, etc. In 1963 it established a close link with the Anglo-American Corporation (q.v.) through the establishment of Main Street Investments Ltd. (q.v.), and in 1964 gained control of General Mining and Finance Corporation Ltd. (q.v.).

Federasie van Afrikaanse Kultuurvereniginge (Federation of Afrikaans Cultural Societies). Founded at Bloemfontein in December 1929. Embraces several hundred organisations, covering virtually every branch of social, educational and cultural work. The headquarters are in Johannesburg.

Federation of Rhodesia and Nyasaland. *See* RHODESIA AND NYASALAND, FEDERATION OF.

Fehr, Dr. William. South African art collector and antiquarian. Born in Burgersdorp, Cape Province, in 1894. He became a merchant in Cape Town, but had his collection of early South African pictures as his main interest. Placed on public view at the Castle in Cape Town in 1952, they were ultimately acquired for the Nation by the Government in 1964 at a cost of R310,000. A further collection of 600 water colours was given to the State by Dr. Fehr in 1965 and housed in the old Cape Town mansion 'Rust en Vreugd'. Died on April 2, 1968.

Felicia. *See* DAISY.

Felixton. Sugar centre on Lower Umfolozi River, Natal. Population: 2,089, including 369 Whites.

Felling, Sir Christian Ludolph Neethling. South-African-born manager of the Kenya and Uganda Railways. Born Cape Town, 1880, he went to school in Stellenbosch and later studied law. In 1895 he joined the Cape Government Railways, and rose to be Chief Assistant General Manager of the South African Railways in 1918. Retiring from the service, he took over the post of General Manager of the Kenya and Uganda Railways in 1923. Died on August 19, 1928

Feminas. Long white wing feathers from female ostrich.

Fern, Maidenhair (*Adiantum capillus veneris*). Polypodiaceae family. This well-known delicate fern is protected in the Cape coastal region, as is the Hare's Foot Fern (*Polystichum adiantiforme*) or Seweeksvaring, with its larger, lobed pinnate leaves. *See* TREE FERN.

Ferreira's Camp. Gold Camp named after Captain I. P. Ferreira. *See* JOHANNESBURG.

Fetcani ('Marauders'). Branch of the Zulu people, driven out of Natal by Tshaka (q.v.). Defeated near the present town of Umtata in 1828, and settled among the Xosas. *See* AMANGWANE and SWAZIS.

Fever Tree. *See* ACACIA.

Fezela (Literally 'Finish Off' in Zulu). Name of well-known unofficial Natal cricket team.

Fichardt, Charles Gustav. Nationalist leader. Born at Bloemfontein in 1870, he studied at Grey College and later in Scotland and on the Continent. At the unusually early age of 27 he was elected Mayor of Bloemfontein. In the South African War he distinguished himself at Poplar Grove. After the return of peace he supported General Hertzog, helping to found the National Party in the Orange Free State. He was elected to Parliament as a member for Ladybrand. A man of great personal charm, he was noted as an orator both in Afrikaans and English. He died in 1923.

Ficksburg. Town in the Eastern Orange Free State, near Basutoland border, lying within the Conquered Territory (q.v.). Founded in 1867 and named after Commandant-General J.J. Fick, who led the forces of the Republic against the Basuto in the war of 1865–1868. Its chief importance is as a trading centre for Basutoland, where several industries have been started. Population: 10,900, including 3,000 Whites.

Field Cornet. A military post created in the very early days, to raise Commandos (q.v.). Field Cornets were later entrusted with certain civilian duties, and worked in close collaboration with the magistrates.

Field, Winston Joseph. Prime Minister of Rhodesia. Born at Bromsgrove, England, June 6, 1904. Coming to Rhodesia in June 1921, he took up tobacco farming, and in 1938 was elected President of the Rhodesian Tobacco Association. During World War II served in the Infantry, was elected to Parliament and in December 1962 became Prime Minister. Resigned in 1964. Died 1969.

Fighting Port. Traditional name of East London, on account of its fine military record.

Figtree. Village 23 miles from Bulawayo, Rhodesia, noted in early times as the resort of traders, explorers and missionaries, who had to await the permission of the Matabele king—first Moselekatse and later Lobengula (qq.v.)—before entering Matabeleland. The place takes its name from an ancient fig tree, still growing today and a prominent landmark.

Filabusi. Village in Rhodesia, and centre of gold field.

Films. The first cinematograph projector in the modern sense appears to have been brought to South Africa in 1896 by the illusionist Carl Hertz, and regular shows began soon after, usually in conjunction with variety programmes. Films of news interest were made in Pretoria and elsewhere before the end of the 19th century and professional cameramen operated at the front during the South African War (1899–1902). Cinema houses appeared in Cape Town, Johannesburg and Durban in the early 1900's. The newsreel, *African Mirror*, began about 1912 and is still produced. Independent operators were largely absorbed in the African Films group founded by I. W. Schlesinger (q.v.), who started making films at the first local studios at Killarney, Johannesburg, in 1916, and in 1918 produced a series of major pictures, of which the most outstanding were *The Voortrekkers*, on the Great Trek (q.v.), and *The Symbol of Sacrifice*, on the Zulu War (q.v.). Talking pictures reached South Africa in 1929, though there had been earlier experimental showings. The first Cinerama in the country was opened at Johannesburg in 1961.

Finch (family Ploceidae). *See* CANARY, WEAVER and BUNTING.

Finger grass or **Krulgras** (*Digitaria eriantha* Stend.). Fodder grass of sweet veld, in summer rainfall areas. *See* GRASSES.

Fingoland. Portion of the Transkei, its principal centres including Tsomo, Butterworth and Nqamakwe (qq.v.).

Fingos. Native tribe in the Eastern Province, their official name being Amafengu, which signifies 'Homeless Wanderers.' The tribe came into existence as a result of the wars of Tshaka (q.v.). As landless survivors they wandered across the present Province, and were regarded with great contempt by the older inhabitants. In the War of the Axe in 1846 (q.v.) the Fingos fought on the side of the British, and in return were given considerable areas of land beyond the River Tyumie; also in the district of Victoria East. *See* FINGOLAND.

Finsch Diamond Mine. Situated 40 miles east of Postmasburg in Northern Cape, it was discovered by A. T. Fincham, a local farmer, who with some partners sold their rights in 1963 to De Beers Consolidated Mines (q.v.) for R4,500,000, The diamond pipe covers about 42 acres and is being worked at the outset on the opencast system. The deposits are very rich. *See also* LIMEACRES.

Firgrove. Township outside Somerset West, Cape Province, near Cape Explosive Works. Population: 1,529, including 131 Whites.

First Anti-Tank Regiment, First City Regiment, First Field Regiment. *See* REGIMENT.

Fisant. *See* PHEASANT.

Fiscal. An office of the Dutch East India Company created for the prosecution of criminal cases. It was of comparatively junior rank, but a new grade was created in 1688, when the first Independent Eiscal (q.v.) was appointed. In Afrikaans the word Fiskaal is used jocularly for the Butcher-bird or Shrike (q.v.).

Fischer, Abram. South African Communist leader. Born in Bloemfontein in 1908, the son of Judge P. U. Fischer (q.v.) and grandson of Abraham Fischer (q.v.), he had a brilliant academic career in South Africa and England before being called to the Bar in 1934. He soon built up a large practice and took silk, but became increasingly involved in the work of the Communist Party. This activity continued even after the banning of that organisation, when he was for a long time in hiding. Brought to trial for his part in sabotage and attempted revolutionary activities, he declined to recant and was sentenced in 1966 to life imprisonment.

Fischer, Abraham. Prime Minister of the Orange River Colony. Born 1850 in Cape Town, he was educated at the South African College, and admitted to the Cape Bar. After moving to the Orange Free State, he was elected to the Volksraad in 1878, and became a member of the Executive Council in 1896. His diplomatic skill aroused attention at conferences. During the South African War he went to Europe and the U.S.A. in an effort to secure foreign intervention. After the Peace he helped to found the Orangia Union (q.v.) and became its first President. In 1907, on the establishment of responsible government, he became the first (and only) Prime Minister of the Orange River Colony. He took part in the National Convention, and in 1911 was made a Privy Councillor. In the first Union Cabinet he was Minister of Lands. He died in 1913.

Fischer, Percy Ulrich. Judge-President of the Orange Free State Provincial Division. Born in Bloemfontein 1878, he studied at Cape Town and later at Cambridge. After practising for some years, in 1929 he was promoted to the Orange Free State Bench, and in 1939 became Judge-President. He died in 1957.

Fish Hoek. Town in the south of the Cape Peninsula, 18 miles from Cape Town and on the electric railway to Simonstown. Began as a fishing and whaling station. The word 'Hoek' signifies 'Corner.' Laid out as a township in 1916, became a municipality in 1940. Residential community; and a very popular seaside resort. Under its original title-deed Fish Hoek was to have no 'Wineshops'—a ban still keenly maintained. Population: 7,575, including 7,100 Whites.

Fish Hoek Bay. Original name for Gordon's Bay (q.v.). Not to be confused with the town of Fish Hoek which is on the opposite side of False Bay.

Fishing. *See* MARINE RESOURCES.

Fish River. Tributary of Orange River in South West Africa. Noted for its magnificent canyon, over 2,500 feet deep and 40 miles long.

Fiskaal. Afrikaans name for Shrike (q.v.).

Fitzpatrick, James Coleman. Senior Puisne Judge, Cape Bench. Born in Ireland on January 6, 1816. Father of Sir Percy Fitzpatrick (q.v.). Educated at Trinity College, Dublin, and called to the Irish Bar in 1842. After holding the post of Chief Justice on the Gold Coast, in 1857 he came to South Africa, and became Judge of British Kaffraria in 1861. When this territory was incorporated in the Cape Colony in 1865, he transferred to the Cape Bench, where he rose to senior Puisne Judge. He died in 1880.

Fitzpatrick, Sir James Percy. South African statesman and author. Born in King William's Town on July 24, 1862, the son of Mr. Justice J. C. Fitzpatrick (q.v.). Educated at Downside in England, he began his career as an official in the Standard Bank. He

left this post in order to go prospecting. After a period of transport riding, he made his way to the Eastern Transvaal in 1884. There he enjoyed the experiences which he was later to use in his books. From 1886 to 1889 Fitzpatrick lived in Barberton, after which he came to Johannesburg, and secured a post with the firm of Hermann Eckstein & Co. (q.v.). In 1891 he was employed by Lord Randolph Churchill to help on his expedition through the region that became Rhodesia. This inspired his first book, *Through Mashonaland with Pick and Pen.* He then returned to the mining industry and became a partner in the Corner House. He also engaged in politics and, as Secretary of the Reform Committee, was arrested after the Jameson Raid. Found guilty of high treason, he was fined £2,000. He gave important evidence before the Transvaal Industrial Commission in 1897 and worked for a last-minute settlement between the Transvaal and Britain. During the South African War he wrote *The Transvaal from Within,* which was a best-seller. In 1907 his most famous book, *Jock of the Bushveld,* appeared, which was dedicated to his children. As a stalwart of the Unionist Party, entered the Transvaal Parliament. He was later elected to the Union Parliament. He did a great deal for irrigation in South Africa, particularly along the Sunday's River, where he lived. He died in January 1931.

Fitzsimons, Frederick William. South African zoologist. Born in Ireland in 1871, he came to Natal as a boy and intended studying medicine. When he was 20, he began writing on Natural History, and became an authority on snakes and monkeys. From 1897 to 1906 he was curator of the Pietermaritzburg Museum, which he completely reorganised and catalogued. In 1906 he took charge of the Port Elizabeth Museum, which soon became well known, particularly through the

'Snake Park' which he established. Among his many important books may be mentioned *The Natural History of South Africa* (four volumes); *Snakes of South Africa*; *The Monkeyfolk of South Africa*, and sundry others. Fitzsimons was responsible for the development of an anti-Snake Bite serum bearing his name, which is still used in many countries. In later years he became interested in Anthropology, and excavated ancient sites in the Tsitsikama area. He was responsible for bringing the famous 'Boskop' skull to the notice of the scientific world. He was also keenly interested in Psychic Research. He died in 1938.

Flag Controversy. Name given to the dispute attending the design of the National flag of the Union. The subject had already been ventilated before Union, when a design competition was held, but the country tacitly accepted a modified version of the Red Ensign, with the addition of the South African coat of arms. General J. B. M. Hertzog (q.v.), as Prime Minister, raised the subject afresh. Intense feeling was aroused, especially after it was proposed to give the Union Jack a subordinate position in the design or to eliminate it altogether. Controversy raged for several years, and various commissions were appointed. The final compromise adopted was based on the 'Prinsenvlag' flown by the Netherlands at the time of settlement of the Cape in 1652 (orange, white and blue), with the addition of a central design composed of the Transvaal and Orange Free State Vierkleurs, together with the Union Jack, symbolising the contribution of the various sections to the country's history. The final design was defined in the Nationality and Flag Act of 1927.

Flagstaff. Village in Pondoland, started in 1877 as a trading station, the owners of which hoisted a flag on a tall mast on Sundays, to indicate that the place was closed—hence the name. For many years a station of the Cape Mounted Rifles. Population: 700, including 150 Whites.

Flamboyant (*Poinciana regia*). Flowering tree with brilliant red flowers, largely grown in Durban and other sub-tropical areas, originally from Madagascar.

Flame Lily (*Gloriosa superba*). National flower of Rhodesia. *See* LILY.

Flamingo (family Phoenicopteridae). Bird with compact body and extraordinarily long legs and neck. Structurally, the hooked bill is the most surprising feature. The lower mandible is barely movable and both mandibles are fringed with fine lamellae for straining small particles from the water, as Flamingoes feed largely on the scummy green algae from the bottom of shallow lakes. They breed in colonies, their nests being low mounds of mud.

Flat-Head. Fish with a cylindrical body and a broad flattened head. Dwells at the bottom of shallow and moderately shallow water off Natal, the East Coast and Indian Ocean.

Flemming, Leonard. South African author and humorist. Born in Australia, 1868, he came to the Cape at the age of 15 to learn farming near Queenstown. Later Flemming served in the Boer War and made his home on a farm near Dewetsdorp, O.F.S. The development of this property, which he achieved under the greatest difficulties, became the theme of a whole series of books, which established his reputation in the country. This began in 1915 with *A Settler's Scribblings in South Africa*. His name was made with *A Fool on the Veld* in 1916. Other books followed, all of which enjoyed a considerable vogue. He died in 1946.

Floating Reef. Expression used on the Kimberley Diamond Fields to describe sections of barren ground encountered in the diamond pipes.

Floors. Large pieces of land, mostly outside Kimberley, on which the Blue Ground (q.v.) was formerly placed in order to weather away and allow the recovery of the stones. Their use has today largely been superseded by the pulsator (q.v.) and other methods.

Flora Capensis. Famous botanical work on the plants of South Africa, begun by William Henry Harvey and Otto Wilhelm Sonder in 1859, being later continued by Sir William T. Thiselton-Dyer. The production of the book, which ran into many volumes, was not completed until 1930.

Florida. Township on the Witwatersrand, portion of the municipality of Roodepoort-Maraisburg (q.v.), noted for its attractive lake, created from a natural vlei. Gilwell, the estate where the South African Boy Scout organisations hold its rallies, is near by.

Florisbad. Health resort in the Orange Free State, noted for its warm springs and named after their original owner, Floris Venter. Near here was found the famous Florisbad skull of primitive man.

Floss. Type of ostrich feather secured from the wing covers, and particularly soft.

Flowers. South Africa is rich in flowers and the Cape Peninsula uniquely so. About 178 families, some containing hundreds of species, are represented in this country, many with features distinct from those in other lands. Amongst the oldest in the world are the Cycads (q.v.), which according to Wegener's theory date back to the period before Africa was separated from South America and Australia.

Specially characteristic of the Cape flora on mountain and plain are the Proteas (q.v.) with their vast variety of species. To the Cape also belong the many Ericas (q.v.); further east flourish the Statice and Plumbago, family Plumbaginaceae (q.v.).

The Cape and Natal are specially rich in the great bulb families, Liliaceae (*see* LILY) and Iridaceae (*see* IRIS). The Amaryllis (q.v.) is also well known in South Africa. The strange Strelitzias (q.v.) of the Muraceae family belong chiefly to Natal and northwards. The many orchids (q.v.) grow in sub-tropical coastal and forest areas.

Two enormous flower families, Compositae (*see* DAISY) and Leguminosae (*see* PEA), with their hundreds of groups, are plentiful everywhere. Malvaceae (*see* HIBISCUS) contains chiefly shrubs and trees. Labiatae (*see* SALVIA), the aromatic herb family, is widespread; so too is Scrophulariaceae (*see* NEMESIA).

To the semi-desert Karroo and other sandy areas belong the many succulents (q.v.) of the Aizoaceae family, which includes the vast Mesembryanthemum group; the Crassulaceae family (*see* CRASSULA); and the Euphorbiaceae family, containing the giant Euphorbias (q.v.) and other latex-bearing plants.

Nara (q.v.), that strange desert plant, and the many melons belong to the Convolvulaceae, a family of climbing plants, of which Kaffir Honeysuckle is also a member.

Many thorny shrubs, besides naturalised immigrants such as the Cape Gooseberry (q.v.), belong to the Solanaceae.

Blue is a rare colour among the yellows and oranges of South African flowers, but it occurs frequently in the Campanulaceae family (*see* LOBELIA). One of the Water Lilies (q.v.) (Nymphaeaceae) is also blue.

Among other flowers characteristic of the Cape are the many-coloured little Oxalis (q.v.) and the small white, pink or red Crassulas (q.v.). Space forbids the inclusion of dozens of other families of flowers well known to South Africans.

Fluorspar. Mineral found near Ottoshoop in the Western Transvaal and used in the optical, steel and other industries. Exploitation began in 1918. It also occurs in South West Africa and in Rhodesia.

Fly (*Glossina morsitans*). Popular name for the Tsetse Fly (q.v.). The name 'fly' is also given to the area infested by this insect.

Flycatchers (Muscicapidae). A large family of small birds not easily distinguishable. They live on insects, which they catch on the wing, making short flights from their perch. Bills are wide, flattened and bordered by a few bristles. Many are rather shy and keep near trees.

Flying. *See* AVIATION.

Flying Dutchman. Famous maritime legend of the Cape. According to tradition Captain Hendrik Van der Decken, in the 17th century, encountering hostile winds, swore he would round the Cape of Good Hope, if he had to continue till Doomsday. He was taken at his word, and has been attempting to achieve this ever since. The Flying Dutchman is reported to have been sighted by many seafarers, including the late King George V, as a midshipman in H.M.S. *Bacchante*, in 1880.

Flying-Fish. Belong to the deep sea, and may be seen off the Natal coast and Agulhas Bank, but not in colder seas. They have longish bodies and greatly enlarged pectoral fins. They are really 'gliders,' holding their fins nearly motionless in the air, and propelled by a tail movement underwater. The glide varies from 200 to 300 yards. To change direction, the fish must drop into the water and rise again (*see* SKIPPER). There are both 'monoplane' (*Exocoetus volitans*) (8 inches) and 'biplane' (*Cypsilurus cyanopterus*) (18 inches) types.

Flying Fox. *See* BAT.

Fochville. Village in the Transvaal, near Potchefstroom, founded shortly after World War I and named after Marshal Foch. Farming area. Population: 5,000, including 2,500 Whites.

Football. *See* RUGBY and SOCCER.

Forestal. International company specialising in the production of tannin, established in 1905; started a wattle extract factory in Natal in 1919, and in Rhodesia in 1944.

Forestry. Southern Africa has not many natural forests; the original area thus covered suffered gravely through the need of fuel among the earlier settlers. In the days of the Dutch East India Company, warnings were issued against excessive cutting of wood, but without much effect. Scientific forestry began in Victorian times, but only in 1876 was a Department set up to exercise control over Crown Forests. The first Superintendent of Woods and Forests took office in 1881. Since then systematic and modern protection has spread throughout the country and, since the South African War, also in the Transvaal and the Orange Free State. Natal was slower in starting effective forestry legislation, making two abortive attempts before setting up a Department for this purpose in 1908. After Union the Forestry Departments of the four original colonies were united under a Chief Conservator of Forests. His work was later combined with that of soil conservation. Since 1934 the Forestry Department has operated in conjunction with the Department of Agriculture. Plantings have been carried out on a considerable scale, particularly as a measure to reduce unemployment. Over 2,300,000 acres of plantations have been established in the Republic, of which about 600,000 were planted by the State. In Rhodesia forestry has been encouraged by the Government, notably in the eastern highlands, where large plantations have been laid down, both by public and private enterprise. Large natural forests exist in Malawi, particularly on Mount Mlanje, which is noted for its cedars and other trees. A considerable timber industry has developed. *See also* TREES.

Formosa. Original name given to Plettenberg Bay by the Portuguese navigators, the name signifying 'beautiful.' A neighbouring village now bears the name.

Formosa Peak. Mountain in the Uniondale district overlooking Plettenberg Bay (q.v.). Height 6,000 feet.

Fort Beaufort. Town in Eastern Cape Province, founded as a fort in 1822 to help in safeguarding the Eastern Cape frontier. Named after the Duke of Beaufort, father of the Governor, Lord Charles Somerset, the present township was laid out in 1837. The original fort is still in existence. In 1846 the 'War of the Axe' (q.v.) began through a quarrel in a store at Fort Beaufort. Important wool and citrus centre. Population: 10,800, including 1,600 Whites.

Fort Brown. Village near Grahamstown in the Eastern Cape Province. Established as a military post during the native war of 1835, and named after Lieutenant Brown of the 75th Regiment. Later a police and convict settlement.

Fort Burger (also known as **Burgersfort**). Village in the Eastern Transvaal. Established as a fortified outpost in the Sekukuni War of 1876 and named after President T. F. Burgers (q.v.) of the South African Republic. Captain Von Schlickmann, a German officer, was in charge, who afterwards was killed by the natives. Asbestos and chrome are exploited near by.

Fort Cox. Village on the Keiskama River in the Ciskei built as a military post and named after Major William Cox of the 75th Regiment in 1835. Centre of considerable fighting in several native wars. Today a leading

agricultural college for natives is established there.

Fort Cunynghame. Saw-milling centre between East London and Queenstown. Originally a military post and named after Lieutenant Cunynghame, who was in command. Large plantations surround the place.

Fort England. Fort at Grahamstown, named after Lieutenant-Colonel Richard England of the 75th Regiment, who was commanding officer during the Native War of 1835. The name is now applied to a large hospital.

Fort Frederick. A fort (still standing) erected on the shores of Algoa Bay in 1798, forerunner of the city of Port Elizabeth (q.v.). Named after Frederick, Duke of York, and constructed to keep away French invaders; it is now a National Monument.

Fort Glamorgan. A fort built in 1847 by the British troops on the west bank of the Buffalo River that preceded the founding of East London (q.v.).

Fort Hare. Originally a portion of the Eastern Cape frontier defences and named by Lieutenant-Colonel John Hare, who caused it to be erected in 1847. Involved in many border campaigns, Fort Hare in 1916 became the site of the South African Native College, now the University College of Fort Hare, with over 500 students, mainly Xosas. It adjoins the town of Alice (q.v.).

Fort Jameson. *See* CHIPATA.

Fort Maguire. Early Portuguese frontier outpost on Lake Nyasa in southeast Malawi.

Fort Napier. Military encampment overlooking Pietermaritzburg, named after Governor Sir George Napier of the Cape (q.v.). Laid out in 1844, it remained the headquarters of the Imperial troops in Natal till World War I. From 1914 to 1918 served as an internment camp for several thousand Germans and Austrians from all parts of Southern Africa.

Fort Nottingham. Village near Lion's River, Natal. Population: 80, including 10 Whites.

Fort Rixon. Village in Rhodesia. Established as a military outpost during the Matabele Rebellion of 1896. Farming centre.

Fort Rosebery. *See* MBILA.

Fort Salisbury. Original name of the city of Salisbury (q.v.), Rhodesia.

Fort Selwyn. National Monument in Grahamstown. Portion of original military defences of the city erected in 1835, now in Botanic Gardens. Named after Captain C. J. Selwyn, who com-

manded the Royal Engineers there from 1835 to 1841.

Fort Usher. Settlement in Rhodesia, 10 miles from Matopos Station on the east, originally a military outpost, but now the site of a large hospital, founded by William Lees, for Matabeles suffering from tuberculosis and syphilis. After Lees' death it was placed in the hands of trustees and as the Lees Memorial Hospital was handed over to the Southern Rhodesian Government in 1937.

Fort Victoria. Town in Rhodesia. Founded by Pioneer Column (q.v.) in 1891, some of the original structures still surviving. Important farming and mining centre. Population: 11,700, including 2,400 Whites.

FOSSILS OF SOUTHERN AFRICA

by

DR. A. W. CROMPTON

South African Museum, Cape Town

THE sedimentary rocks and other deposits of Southern Africa often contain the fossilised remains of the hard parts of animals and plants. These date from the following periods of the earth's history: the Devonian, Permian, Triassic, Cretaceous and Pleistocene.

Devonian and Cretaceous fossils are almost exclusively of non-vertebrate marine forms (trilobites, molluscs, shells, etc.) and, as they are well known from other parts of the world, do not deserve the same attention as those of the Permo-Triassic and Pleistocene.

Fossils dating from the middle Permian to the end of the Triassic are found in the upper rock layers of the Karoo System (approximately 240,000 sq. miles, almost half the total area of the Republic) and small outcrops are also found in South West Africa, Botswana, Rhodesia, Zambia and in

East and Central Africa. The System is divided into the Dwyka, the Ecca, the Beaufort and the Stormberg. With one exception fossils are found only in the Beaufort and Stormberg.

Erosion is most active in the Karoo and it is here that fossil remains are commonly found exposed. The length of time involved in the formation of the Karoo System makes it possible to trace the development of certain animal groups that appear to have originated during that period, e.g. the lizards, dinosaurs, birds, crocodiles and mammals.

The dominant animals of Beaufort times, the mammal-like reptiles (Therapsida), are divided into five very different groups. The Deinocephalia (giant-heads)—some the size of modern oxen—had a dome-like thickening of the head and were either carnivorous or herbivorous. The Gorgonopsia

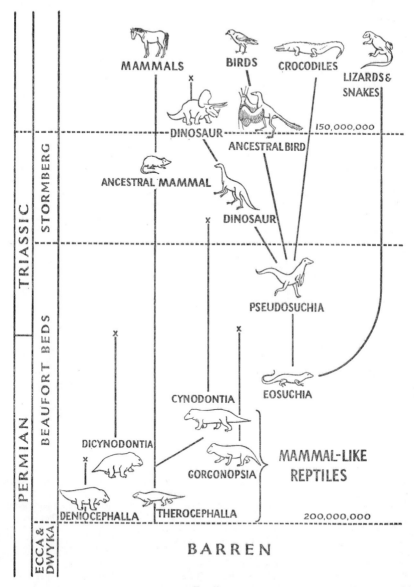

Fossils

(Gorgon-faces), Cynodontia (dog-teeth) and Therocephalia (wild-beast-heads) were smaller, more active and usually carnivorous or necrophagous. The Dicynodontia (two-dog-teeth) were the most abundant of the Therapsida and the most diverse in structure. They were herbivorous and varied in size from that of a rat to that of a cow. In the evolution of Dicynodonts the teeth, except the upper canines, were usually replaced by a horny beak like that of a turtle.

There are few features common to all the Therapsida, but each group tended to develop mammal-like structures.

Small lizard-like forms, the Eosuchia, lived at the same time as the Therapsida in Beaufort times, and the dominant animals, the Archosauria, which replaced the mammal-like reptiles in Stormberg times, were descended from them. Lizards are slightly modified descendants of the Eosuchia.

An early group of the Archosauria are the active, carnivorous Pseudosuchians. Some forms, of extremely light build, began to walk only on their hind legs. Birds are probably their descendants. Other massive forms were similar to the later dinosaurs. The most abundant fossils of the Stormberg are several varieties of dinosaurs, evolved from Pseudosuchians. Although their bony remains are rare, they are also known from footprints preserved in sandstone layers. Some Southern African dinosaurs were lightly built, walked on two legs and were not unlike the modern ostriches; others were massive, up to 20 feet long, and walked on all four legs. These are the forerunners of the gigantic dinosaurs found mainly in East Africa and America.

The Pleistocene was a relatively short span of a million years. Most Pleistocene animals were larger than their living representatives, and some of the extinct types veritable giants. The major feature of this period is the emergence of Man (*Homo sapiens*).

The major fossil-bearing sites of the early Pleistocene are Olduvai Gorge (Tanganyika), Broken Hill (Zambia), Taung (Cape Province), Makapan Valley, Sterkfontein, Kromdraai and Swartkrans (Transvaal), Florisbad (near Bloemfontein, Orange Free State), Cornelia (Orange Free State), the Vaal River Gravels and Hopefield (near Saldanha Bay, Cape Province). Some of these deposits extended over a long period of time and even contain extant mammals. Among the best known fossil-bearing deposits of late Pleistocene and Recent times are Matjies River cave-shelter (near Plettenberg Bay, Cape Province), Wonderwerk cave (near Kuruman, Cape Province), Zitzikama cave (Cape Province), and Fish Hoek cave (Cape Province). Numerous other sites also contain skeletal remains of this period, during the last 30,000 years.

The extinct large animals of the Pleistocene consist of more than 70 species, including animals such as *Sivatherium*, a short-necked, short-legged giraffid with long, knobbly and occasionally twisted, horns; *Stegolophodon* and a number of other huge, extinct elephant forms; *Homoioceras*, a massive buffalo with a 12-foot horn span; *Mesochoerus*, *Tapinochoerus* and other giant bush-pig and warthog forms; various types of sabre-tooth tigers; lion; cave hyaenas; numerous forms of zebrine horses (*Equus*); giant hartebeest and more than 40 other extinct antelope forms.

Southern Africa provides one of the most complete series in the evolution of the Primates (Man, apes, monkeys, lemurs, etc.). Of this group the Pleistocene contains many extinct fossil giant baboons (e.g. *Parapapio*, *Simopithecus*, *Dinopithecus*) and the famous ape-men or Australopithecines ('southern apes'), found hitherto mainly in the Transvaal and in the Cape Province at Taung. These sub-human forms comprise two major groups, *Paranthropus* and *Australopithecus*, differing as much as the gorilla differs from the chimpanzee.

Recently stone ('pebble') tools have been found in association with *Australopithecus*, but it is unlikely that they were manufactured by them. These tools were made by a 'more human' type which probably helped to wipe out the Australopithecines.

Early man is distinguished from the fossil apes not only by such features as larger brain size, a different dentition and the skeletal criteria for erect posture, but also by his ability to manufacture stone implements. Evidence indicates that Man co-existed with the ape-man about 600,000 years ago. The Australopithecines averaged about 4 feet 6 inches and walked erect, so freeing their hands, and were a side-branch of, though close to, the direct line of ancestry of Man. Some scientists consider that another Transvaal form, *Telanthropus*, fills the transition between the Australopithecines and the true Hominids.

Foster Gang. Band of criminals who carried out a successful series of robberies in South Africa between 1912 and 1914. The founder, William Foster, an Irish immigrant, grew up in Johannesburg and became a popular footballer. He was joined by a younger brother, by an American John Maxim, and by Carl Mezar of mixed Dutch and German descent. Their chief claim to prominence is that, after holding up a jeweller's shop in Cape Town in 1912, they terrorised the Rand in 1914. A police cordon was set for them, which led to the unfortunate death of General J. H. Delarey (q.v.) who was shot while ignoring a police challenge. The gang, brought to bay in Kensington, Johannesburg, committed suicide on September 18, 1914.

Fouche, Jacobus Johannes. State-President of the Republic of South Africa since 1968. Born at Wepener, Orange Free State, on June 6, 1898, and educated at Stellenbosch University. Went farming and sat as National member for Smithfield from 1941 to 1950. In 1951 became Administrator of Orange Free State and in 1959 was appointed Minister of Defence.

Founders' Day. Holiday in Rhodesia, celebrated on the first Tuesday in July, following Rhodes Day (q.v.). So named in honour of Pioneer Column (q.v.) which crossed the Tuli River on that day in 1890.

Fourie, Jopie (Josef). South African rebel. Born August 27, 1878, near Pretoria; educated at Grey College, Bloemfontein, took part in the suppression of the Jameson Raid and fought in the South African War. In 1912 he joined the newly-established Union Defence Force, in which he received an officer's commission. Upon the outbreak of World War I, he identified himself with the 'Armed Protest Movement,' which culminated in the Rebellion (q.v.). He was taken prisoner in an action near Pretoria and placed before a court martial, was found guilty of high treason and shot on Sunday morning, December 20, 1914. The circumstances at the trial and execution caused great bitterness, and there were widespread political demonstrations at his funeral and afterwards.

Fouriesburg. Town in the Eastern Orange Free State, named after the owner of the original farm Christoffel Fourie. Founded in 1892. Noted for its beautiful mountain scenery. Was the last formally proclaimed capital of the Orange Free State Republic during the South African War in 1901. Near by heavy fighting took place and the town was almost wiped out. Important centre for wheat and cattle farming. Population: 1,900, including 550 Whites.

Fourteen Streams. Village on the Vaal River, near the Transvaal-Cape border. Already known as Fourteen Streams in the 1880's, when the Rev. John Mackenzie explained the name as derived from 'a series of falls in the Vaal River in the neighbourhood.' The place saw some of the first fighting in the South African War. For some years Fourteen Streams was the terminus of the railway from the Cape but this was extended, at the expense of De Beers Consolidated Mines, to Johannesburg. For this purpose the Klerksdorp-Fourteen Streams Railway Co. was formed in 1905, with a capital of £200,000 and £800,000 in debentures. The line was opened in April 1906, and the company expropriated in 1911 for £813,746.

Fox. A more slender and graceful nocturnal mammal than the Jackal; greyish yellow; quite inoffensive to stock. The Silver Fox or Vaal Jakkals (Vaalpens) belongs to the thorny scrub of South Africa. Not common. Delalander's Fox (*Otocyon megalotis*) runs in the dry western parts. Both species live on insects, rats and mice, eggs and fruit. *See* MAMMALS.

Francistown. Capital of Tati (q.v.). Named after Daniel Francis, an early miner and prospector of the Tati goldfields in 1870. It is now a trading and administrative centre of Botswana. Population: 10,000.

François, Auguste Leo. South African artist. Born in Chemnitz, Germany, of Huguenot descent, in 1870. Educated in Dresden and in Rome, he came to South Africa at the instigation of Cecil Rhodes in the early 90's. He settled in Durban, where he became a well-known painter and chairman of the Natal Society of Artists. In 1925 founded the South African Institute of Art, of which he was elected first president. He wrote copiously on art subjects. Died in 1938.

François, Captain Hugo von. Soldier in German South West Africa. Brother of Major Kurt von François (q.v.), he

was born in 1859 at Reichenbach in Silesia, Germany, entered the Prussian army and was posted to South West Africa. There he wrote a standard book, *Deutsch Suedwestafrika* in 1899. He was killed in the Herero War near Ovikokorero in September 1904.

François, Major Kurt von. Explorer and soldier in German South West Africa. Born in Luxemburg in 1853, he joined the Prussian army and accompanied the German explorer von Wissman in 1883 on a trip up the river Aasai in the Congo. Later he explored other parts of that country with Grenfell and explored Togoland on the West Coast in 1887. After the establishment of German authority in South West Africa he was appointed commander of the troops (1889 to 1894). From 1895 to 1896 he travelled in the Cape, East Africa, Tunis and Tripoli. He died in 1931.

Francolin (family Phasianidae). Game bird well represented in South Africa, of which the larger is popularly called Pheasant and the smaller Partridge. Many are such determined runners and hiders as to be poor sporting birds. Varieties include Swempi, a sporting little partridge in Natal, Transvaal and Kruger Park; Greywing, the common partridge of the Cape, the covey rising with shrill squawks; Redwing, fonder of marshy places than Greywing, but resembling it; and the Guineafowl (q.v.). *See also* PHEASANT.

Franke, Colonel Victor. Last German military commander in South-West Africa. Born at Zuckmantel in Silesia, Germany, in 1866, and joined the army as a youth. He was sent to South West Africa in 1896 and soon attracted attention by his courage and competence. In the Herero War he gained fame by saving the German forces from defeat at Grootberg, and on other occasions. On the outbreak of World War I, after the unexpected death of the official commander,

Franke found himself at the head of the German forces, facing the South African troops under General Louis Botha. He capitulated at Khorab on July 9, 1915, after a lengthy campaign and died in Hamburg, Germany, 1937.

Frankel, Professor Sally Herbert. South African economist. Born at Johannesburg on November 22, 1903 and educated at St. John's College, University of the Witwatersrand, and the London School of Economics. From 1931 to 1946 he was Professor of Economics at the University of the Witwatersrand, after which he took over the Chair of Economics of Under-developed Countries at Oxford. He acted as adviser and arbitrator to various governments on numerous occasions, and wrote extensively on his science.

Frankenwald. Large estate between Johannesburg and Pretoria, named by Alfred Beit (q.v.) after a district in Germany. He acquired the property in the 1890's and employed a forester named Genth, who had worked for Prince Bismarck, to lay out the gardens and plantations. On his death in 1906, Beit bequeathed the estate as the site for a university serving both the Rand and Pretoria. This idea proved impracticable, but the University of the Witwatersrand has since developed the estate as a botanical research station.

Frankfort: 1. Village in the Eastern Cape Province founded by the German military settlers in 1858. Population: 1,639, including 287 Whites.

2. Town in the Orange Free State, founded in 1868 by a German named von Gordon, an official of the old Republic. It lies on the picturesque Wilge River, and has several flour mills, and a trade in agricultural produce. Considerable fighting took place here during the South African War, and for a short while in 1900 Frankfort was the seat of the Republican Government. Population: 7,000, including 2,100 Whites.

Franklin Game Reserve. Area of 479 acres outside Bloemfontein, including Naval Hill as the chief local landmark. Large numbers of buck, birds and other species are preserved here by the Provincial Administration of the Orange Free State, which set up the Reserve in 1930.

Fransch Hoek (literally 'French Corner'). Town in Western Cape Province so named because it was originally settled by Huguenot refugees in 1688. Noted for its beautiful setting among the mountains, it is still a wine-producing and fruit-growing centre. A noble monument was erected to commemorate the 250th anniversary of the Huguenots, in 1938. Population: 1,624, including 820 Whites.

Fraser, Sir John George. South African statesman. Born in Beaufort West on December 17, 1840, the son of the Rev. Colin Mackenzie Fraser and thus the uncle of Mrs. (President) M. T. Steyn. Educated in Scotland, he returned to the Orange Free State in 1861, fought against the Basutos, and was appointed Secretary to President Sir Johannes Brand (q.v.). Thereafter he became Registrar of the O.F.S. High Court, Secretary to the Volksraad, and Master of the Orphan Chamber. In 1877 he retired from the service of the Republic to enter the Volksraad as Member for Bloemfontein, which he held for 19 years, from 1880 to 1899. Fraser stood, unsuccessfully, for President in 1896. After the Boer War he was appointed to the Orange River Colony Legislative Council, in 1902, and later to the Inter-Colonial Council. Under responsible government he was elected to Parliament and led the opposition. Upon the establishment of Union he became a Senator (1910–1920). He died in June 1927.

Fraserburg. Town in the Karroo. Established in 1850 and named after the Rev. Colin Fraser, father of President Steyn's wife. Wool-growing centre. Noted for its cold climate. Population: 2,500, including 1,000 Whites.

Fraser Falls. Waterfall near Lusikisiki in the Transkei, dropping 350 feet in three leaps.

Fraser of Lonsdale (Lord William Jocelyn Ian). Born in Eastbourne, England, August 30, 1897, son of a well-known Basutoland trader, educated in South Africa and England, and in due course called to the Bar. Blinded during World War I, he none the less became head of the family firm, D. & D. H. Fraser, and of other important concerns. From 1922 to 1925 was a member of the London County Council and in 1924 was elected to the House of Commons. From 1937 to 1939 was Governor of the British Broadcasting Corporation and from 1947 to 1958 President of the British Legion. Received a Life Peerage on August 1, 1958.

Frederikstad. Settlement in the South-Western Transvaal, named after Frederick Wolmarans, in 1885. Scene of fighting during South African War.

Freemasonry. The oldest surviving Masonic establishment south of the equator is the Lodge de Goede Hoop, the constitution of which was issued at The Hague in Holland on November 1, 1772. A site adjoining the present Government House in Cape Town was secured in 1800, on which the temple was erected at the then considerable cost of £9,000 and dedicated by the Commissary-General, Jacob Abraham de Mist in his capacity as Deputy Grand Master National, on July 7, 1803. An indication of the popularity of Freemasonry even in those days is afforded by the fact that some 200 members of the craft were present at the ceremony. The building, an architectural masterpiece by L. M. Thibault (q.v.), was burnt down in 1892, but has been rebuilt. For many years—from 1854 to 1885—the adjoining refectory was used

to accommodate the Parliament of Cape Colony, until the present House was opened. Freemasonry spread steadily through Southern Africa, including Rhodesia and South-West Africa. Today there are lodges in most towns, the Netherlandic, Scottish, English and Irish constitutions being widely represented.

Freesia or **Aandblom** (Iridaceae). Small bulbous plant of the Western Cape, much exported to Europe. The white spike of beautifully scented flowers faces upwards from the bent stem. *F. elimensis* has long slender sessile leaves and belongs to moister soil than *F. middlemosti*, which has leaves of the gladiolus type and grows on stony hillsides. *See* IRIS.

Free State Coal. Jocular name for dried manure, used for heating in the days before development of coal.

Frelimo. Revolutionary organisation in Mozambique, its name was derived from the first syllables of the Portugese words 'Frente de Liberacao de Mozambique' (Liberation Front of Mozambique). Founded at Dar-es-Salaam, Tanzania, in 1962 by Eduardo Mondlane and assisted by the Organisation of African Unity in 1963. Attempted an invasion of Mozambique from the north but failed. *See* EDUARDO MONDLANE and MOZAMBIQUE.

Fremantle, Professor Henry Eardley Stephen. South African scholar, editor and politician. Born in England in 1874; educated at Eton and Oxford. After serving in Wales and Oxford, became Professor of English and Philosophy at the South African College in 1899. Fremantle later was editor of the *South African News*, from 1903 to 1908, following a strongly pro-Afrikaans policy. A close friend of General Hertzog, he was one of the few English-speaking founders of the Nationalist Party; he died in 1932.

French Hoek. *See* FRANSCH HOEK.

Frere, Sir Bartle (more fully **Sir Henry Bartle Edward Frere**). Born in England in 1815, he became Governor of Cape Colony and High Commissioner for South Africa in 1877. Frere's policy, both towards the Natives and the Boers, gave rise to much criticism, especially after his initial conciliatory moves towards the Zulus were followed in 1879 by the Zulu War; when he countenanced the occupation of the Transvaal by Sir Theophilus Shepstone (q.v.) for Britain, and later promised redress of Boer grievances. Among colonists Frere was extremely popular and his recall in 1880 created a storm of angry comment. He wrote and published a detailed defence of his policy in 1881, and tried to forestall trouble, due to the mishandling of the political situation with the Transvaal, which he correctly foresaw. Highly regarded by Queen Victoria, the Prince of Wales and many leading personalities, he died in 1884.

Friend, The. Daily morning paper published in Bloemfontein, established as *The Friend of the Sovereignty and Bloemfontein Gazette* in June, 1850. First appeared daily in 1896 and was suspended from 1900 to 1902 during the South African War. Early in 1900 it was run by a group of war correspondents, including Rudyard Kipling.

Frijkenius, Simon Hendrik. Dutch Commissioner-General at the Cape; he was born in 1747. With S. C. Nederburgh (q.v.) he went to the Cape in 1791 to examine affairs of the Dutch East India Company, but, having failed to raise the taxes needed to restore solvency in the Colony, continued to Java. He died in Batavia on June 6, 1797.

Frontier Armed Mounted Police. Semi-military force established in Cape Colony, 1855, for the purpose of securing and maintaining the border against Native attack. Organised by Governor Sir George Cathcart (q.v.), it attained much distinction under Sir Walter Currie. In 1878 became known as the Cape Mounted Riflemen (q.v.).

Froude, James Anthony. English historian. Born in Dartington, Devonshire, in 1818, he was sent to South Africa in 1875 by Lord Carnarvon to report on the prospects of his unification scheme (his remedy for the troubles of the country being a benevolent dictatorship). His two-volume account of his journey is still one of the best-known books on South Africa. He touched again at the Cape in 1885, on his way to Australia, and paid high tribute to the beauties of the Cape in his book, *Oceana*. Died in England on October 20, 1894.

Fruit. Although the suitability of the Cape for the cultivation of many kinds of fruit had already been noted by Jan van Riebeeck and other early settlers, it was not until the latter part of the 19th century that serious efforts were made to place the industry on a scientific basis and to develop an export trade. Grapes, peaches, plums and other deciduous fruit, as well as citrus, were known to flourish, but it was the advent of refrigeration on ships in the late 1880's that made possible the first experimental shipments. Difficulties of transport, particularly from the growers to the dockside, delayed advance, yet the excellence of certain shipments which survived made a deep impression in London and encouraged Cecil John Rhodes, John X. Merriman and other leading personalities to give practical help. At this stage individual growers had to make their own arrangements with the steamship companies, pre-cooling was as yet unknown and, because of the heavy wastage, prices were erratic and the risks very heavy. The foundation of the famous Cape Orchard Company was followed by a notable development in the Stellenbosch and Paarl areas between 1896 and 1898. On the eve of the Boer War in 1899 shipments from the Western Cape Province came to 10,817 cases, mostly deciduous fruit. Citrus began to play a rôle about 1907, when 3,000 boxes were shipped, a number which on the eve of World War I had risen to 40,000. Standard packing, regular spraying and Government inspection improved the general level of quality, and stressed the need for pre-cooling. Associations of farmers in various parts of the country helped to improve methods of handling and transport, and a growing number of ships, particularly of the Union Castle Line, were equipped with refrigeration. A total of 309 tons of South African fruit exported in 1900 had grown by 1910 to 2,705 tons, and to-day is close on 850,000 tons. The Western Cape Province, within a radius of approximately 150 miles of Cape Town, is the principal area for deciduous fruit, including grapes, peaches, plums, prunes, nectarines, etc. Apple cultivation is largely concentrated in the Elgin area, and in the Langkloof. Citrus flourishes mainly in the Northern and Eastern Transvaal, in parts of Natal, in the Sundays River Valley near Port Elizabeth, the Kat River area of the Eastern Cape Province, and Citrusdal in the Western Cape. Sub-tropical fruits, including pawpaws, avocado pears, mangoes and litchies, are mainly grown in the Northern and Eastern Transvaal and in the Natal coastal region. The main pineapple area is in the Eastern Cape Province, particularly near Bathurst. Research is concentrated at the Western Province Fruit Research Station at Stellenbosch, the Horticultural Research Station in Pretoria and the Citrus and Sub-tropical Research Station at Nelspruit, Transvaal. Pre-cooling plants on a very large scale have been constructed in Cape Town, Port Elizabeth, East London and Durban, while a certain amount of South African fruit is also shipped

through Lourenço Marques. Closely associated with the operation of the orchards is the production of dried fruit, mainly in the Western Cape Province. Canneries and jam factories are found mainly in the Western Cape Province, on the Witwatersrand, in Port Elizabeth and in Durban. The Deciduous Fruit Board and the South African Co-operative Citrus Exchange are the two principal bodies exercising authority over the producers, while marketing is regulated by the Perishable Products Control Act. Owing to the fact that its seasons are the reverse of those in the northern hemisphere, South Africa has become one of the main exporters of fresh fruit overseas, not only to Britain but also to large parts of the Continent of Europe, particularly Sweden, Holland and Germany. The number of citrus trees in bearing in the Republic is about 6,000,000, while deciduous orchards account for about 3,000,000 apple trees, 5,000,000 pear trees and smaller numbers of other fruits.

Fugard, Athol. South African dramatist. Born at Middelburg, Cape Province, in 1932, he studied at the University of Cape Town, but gave it up to become a sailor and later a reporter. Settling near Port Elizabeth, he made his name with the play, *The Blood Knot*, successfully produced in South Africa, Britain and the U.S.A., followed by *People are Living There*, *Boesman and Lena* and others.

Fugitives' Drift. A crossing on the Buffalo River, Natal, near Isandhlwana, where, during the Zulu War of 1879, a handful of British survivors managed to cross.

Funduzi. *See* LAKE FUNDUZI.

Fungi. *See* MUSHROOMS.

Fynn, Henry Francis. Pioneer of Natal. Born in England, he came to the Cape in 1818 and settled on the Eastern Border, where he remained for 4 years until 1822, when he returned as supercargo of a ship. He came to know the East Coast, saw Delagoa Bay, travelled inland, and in 1824 was sent by a syndicate of Cape Town merchants to establish a trading post in Natal. On their behalf he explored that country and negotiated both with Tshaka and Dingaan. In 1825 Fynn became a minor chief for the districts of Bellair and Umbilo and, despite a quarrel with Dingaan, was in 1831 recognised as a 'Great Chief.' Three years later, in 1834, he returned to the Cape to assist the authorities as a native expert in their negotiations on the frontier. In 1859 he was back in Natal as a magistrate. He died in 1861. His diary, long missing, was published in 1950, edited by James Stuart and D. McK. Malcolm.

G

Gaberone. Capital of Botswana (q.v.), on railway to Bulawayo, named after the Chief, Gaberone Matlapin, who reigned there when the place was founded in the 1890's. Following South Africa's secession from the British Commonwealth in 1961 it was developed as administrative capital of Bechuanaland Protectorate in replacement of Mafeking (q.v.). The 'stad' at Gaberones is the headquarters of the Bamatele tribe, the village being centre for the Gaberones Block, a large area of ground earmarked for white settlement in the days of Cecil Rhodes, and today used mostly for ranching. As a result of the grant of independence to Botswana in 1966 many modern Government buildings were erected in the town. Population: 18,000.

Gaika. Xosa chief. Son of Mlawu, born near the Eastern Frontier about 1779. When his father died in 1797, after the British occupation of the Cape, he laid claim to the chieftainship of the Rarabe clans of the Xosas, but was opposed by Ndlambe, his uncle. Later Gaika made an agreement with Governor-General Janssens of the Batavian Republic. After the British occupation he arranged a similar agreement with Lord Charles Somerset. Thus British help was given to him when Ndlambe attacked him at Grahamstown in 1819. Ndlambe was defeated and Gaika became the chief. Gaika agreed to allow certain ground to be used as a buffer state, but continued to give trouble. He died in 1829.

Galago. Animal belonging to the Lemur family, commonly known as the Bush Baby or Nag Apie, and found in forests from Natal northwards. It has huge eyes, soft, thick fur and a long tail. A night animal, feeding on fruit, young plants, buds, lizards, insects and birds' eggs. Awkward on the ground, it is extremely agile and graceful among the branches of trees. The several varieties differ only in size, from 7 inches to about 18 inches. They are quick to hide from view, but can easily be tamed. *See* MAMMALS.

Galekaland. Portion of the Transkei, main centres including Willowvale and Kentani (qq.v.).

Gallamsiekte. Disease of livestock formerly prevalent in Transvaal, Orange Free State and Bechuanaland. Effective treatment discovered by Sir Arnold Theiler (q.v.) at Onderstepoort. *See* LAMSIEKTE.

Gallwey, Sir Michael Henry. Chief Justice of Natal Supreme Court. Born in County Cork, Ireland, on October 30, 1826, educated at Trinity College, Dublin, and called to the Irish Bar in 1853. Coming to Natal in 1854, he practised in Pietermaritzburg until 1857, when he was appointed Attorney-General. In 1890 became Chief Justice of the Natal Supreme Court and retired in 1891. He died in Pietermaritzburg on July 25, 1912.

Galsworthy, John. English novelist. Born in 1867 at Coombe in Surrey. His father, John Galsworthy senior, was a director of the Cape Copper Co. As a young man John junior was sent to Namaqualand as Mine Secretary at O'okiep. He presented copies of his books to the mine staff library years later. In 1929 he revisited South Africa. He died in 1933.

Gama, Vasco da. Portuguese explorer and navigator. In January 1497 King Emanuel appointed him to command a new expedition to attempt to reach India by sea round Africa. Da Gama studied reports by Bartholomew Diaz

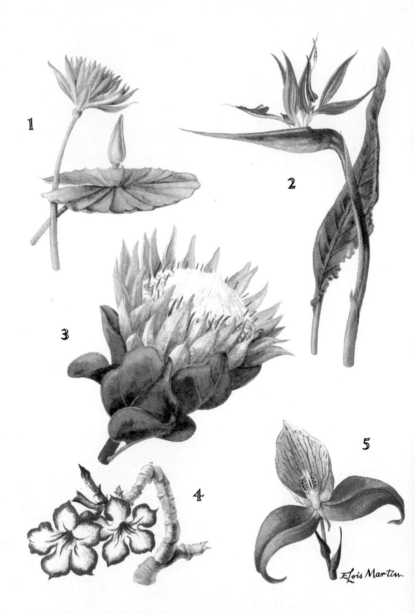

PLATE V: FLOWERS OF SOUTHERN AFRICA
1. *Nymphaea capensis* (blue water-lily).   2. *Strelitzia reginae* (crane flower).
3. *Protea cynaroides* (giant protea).   4. *Adenium multiflorum* (impala lily).
5. *Disa uniflora* (red disa: Pride of Table Mountain).

(q.v.) and by his chief steersman, Pero d'Alenquer, and set forth with 4 ships on July 8, 1497, from the River Tagus. Four months later the flagship, *San Gabriel*, with its companions, reached St. Helena Bay, near the present Velddrift. Passed the Cape of Good Hope and reached Mossel Bay on November 25, 1497. On Christmas Day he passed the coast of Pondoland and Natal. (The latter means 'Christmas' in Portuguese.) On January 11, 1498, Da Gama entered the Inharrime River, near Delagoa Bay, continuing to Quelimane and Sofala. Gained much information from local natives, and embarked near Malindi, with local pilots. May 18, 1498, saw India, thereby realising the hopes of many generations. The Portuguese spent about 4 months near Calicut before leaving on September 20, 1498. Stopped, amongst other places, at Zanzibar, off the coast of Mozambique, and at Mossel Bay, rounding the Cape on March 20, 1499. Da Gama's official diary ends on April 25 of the same year, near Senegambia, but he is known to have arrived on July 10 in Lisbon. In 1524 Da Gama returned to India, to investigate atrocities committed by some of his countrymen. Restored good relations, but never returned to Portugal. Died at Cochin in 1524.

Game Protection. The first attempt at game protection in South Africa dates from July 29, 1814, when Governor Lord Charles Somerset ordered that certain species be preserved from shooting between July 1 and November 30 of every year. This was extended, in March 1822, to cover other species, which were added to from time to time. Then, as now, beasts of prey, including lions, were classified as 'vermin' and not subject to protection.

Beginning in 1825 a system of licences for shooting game was introduced, though a landowner was allowed to hunt freely on his own

property. Because of the enormous amount of game throughout South Africa in earlier days there was little call for further measures, but in 1846 the Republic of Ohrigstad (q.v.) in the Northern Transvaal introduced certain prohibitions, and in 1858 the newly established government of the South African Republic strictly limited the opportunities for hunting elephant.

Game rangers were introduced into the Transvaal under a Volksraad resolution of 1870; the use of traps and snares was prohibited and close seasons were defined. Additional restrictions came into effect in 1891 and 1893. A year later the Pongola area became the first Game Reserve in the Transvaal, to be followed on March 26, 1898, by the proclamation of the famous Sabie Game Reserve, for which President Kruger personally may largely claim the credit. A further area, on the Shingwedzi River in the north, was added in 1903.

Game preservation was introduced into Natal in 1866, and considerably extended in 1884, when close seasons and licences were adopted. Similar precautions were incorporated in the 'Wetboek' or Code of Laws in the Orange Free State in 1891.

Thanks largely to the patience and enthusiasm of the late Lieutenant-Colonel J. Stevenson-Hamilton, who became Warden of the Sabie Game Reserve, provision was made for the establishment of National Parks under an Act passed in May, 1926. The most important result was the conversion of the Sabie and Shingwedzi Game Reserves into the Kruger National Park. Many others followed, including the Kalahari National Park, the Addo National Park, the Mountain Zebra National Park (qq.v.), etc.

In addition, nature reserves and game reserves have been established by the four provinces of the Republic, each of which has a special ordinance dealing with the subject. The oldest of these, the Game Ordinance No. 2

of 1912 in Natal, was followed by Ordinance No. 6 of 1937 in the Orange Free State, the Game Ordinance of the Transvaal in 1949 and the Wild Life Protection Ordinance of the Cape in 1950.

Measures for the protection of game have been introduced in South West Africa, at its famous sanctuary at the Etosha Pan and elsewhere, in the High Commission Territories and in Mozambique, the last being particularly renowned for its Gorongoza Reserve (q.v.) near Beira. Rhodesia, Zambia and Malawi require the issue of licences to hunt, enforce close seasons and have maintained a number of game reserves, the most famous of which is at Wankie.

Through these measures many species formerly in danger of extinction have been saved, including the Mountain Zebra, the Bontebok, the Knysna Elephant, the White Rhinoceros, etc. The Wild Life Protection Society in the Republic and the Rhodesian Hunters and Game Preservation Association both aim to stimulate interest in protecting animals and birds.

Gamka Kloof (*see also* HEL, DIE). Inaccessible valley in upper reaches of Gamka River, inhabited by White settlers for generations. Cannot be reached by wheeled vehicles. Fertile but suffers from lack of communications. Road authorised in 1959.

Gamka River. Tributary of the Gouritz River (q.v.).

Gamtoos River. Hottentot word meaning water. Rises in the Sneeuberg. Upper reaches known as the Kariega; near Winterhoek the Groot River; and below that the Gamtoos. 350 miles from its source it enters the sea near Humansdorp at St. Francis Bay.

Gandhi, Mohandas Karamchand. Indian leader. Born in Porbandar on October 2, 1869, qualified as a barrister in London, arrived in South Africa, 1893, to appear for Indian clients in Durban. His treatment as an Indian inspired his campaign for Indian rights. During the South African War, he organised a corps of Indian stretcher-bearers and again during an outbreak of plague on the Rand, and during the Bambata Rebellion in Natal in 1906. After the South African War, Gandhi practised as an attorney in Johannesburg, coming into conflict with the existing legislation. Supported by a number of Europeans, he organised his famous Passive Resistance Campaign, which led to numerous arrests and to his own imprisonment. After various demonstrations, and a defiance of the ban on travel by Indians between the Transvaal and Natal, Gandhi made a settlement with General J. C. Smuts, as Minister of the Interior, embodied in the Indian Relief Act of 1914. Thereafter Gandhi returned to India, world-famous as a nationalist leader. Maintained contact with South Africa to a certain extent. After witnessing the triumph of the Indian Nationalist cause, Gandhi was murdered on January 30, 1948.

Gangelizwe. Chief of Tembus (q.v.). Threatened with war for killing a Galeka woman, he submitted to the British in December 1875, remaining loyal through the Gaika-Galeka War of 1877–1878. Died in December 1884.

Ganna. Common South African name for *Salsola aphylla*. Plant used by early Boers in making soap, the ashes being a valuable ingredient. Also known as 'Kanna.'

Gannet or Malagas (family Sulidae). Semi-oceanic birds, much less bound to the shore than gulls, terns or cormorants. They feed by plunging headlong from a height on to fish swimming near the surface, and from a distance appear gleaming white. Are chief inhabitants of the Cape Guano Islands. *See* DUIKER and BIRDS.

Gansbaai. Fishing village near Caledon, Cape Province. Population: 1,215, including 908 Whites.

Ganspan. Village near Warrenton, Cape Province. Large naval ammunition store established near by during World War II. Population: 1,900, including 1,250 Whites.

Ga Rankuwa. Large Bantu township north of Pretoria, in Sotho Homeland, inhabited by workers employed at Rosslyn (q.v.).

Garcia, Frederico Ressano. Portuguese statesman and Colonial Minister. Born in 1847, he studied Engineering in Paris, entered the Portuguese parliament and held a chair at the University of Lisbon. Brought in touch with the Transvaal during the building of the Lourenço Marques–Pretoria Railway around 1890, the border town of Ressano Garcia (q.v.) was named after him. Died in 1911.

Garden Route. Name commonly given to the railway and road route between Cape Town and Port Elizabeth, more especially to the stretch between Swellendam and Oudtshoorn, on account of its vegetation, fertile farms and beautiful scenery.

Gardiner, Captain Allen Francis. Sailor and missionary. Born 1794 in Oxfordshire, entered the Royal Navy and fought in the Napoleonic Wars, from 1810 to 1826, finishing as Commander. Always interested in religion, he took his discharge to set up the first mission station in Natal. Tried to win over Dingaan (q.v.) and his Zulus, became discouraged and finally withdrew to South America. He wrote the best early account of Natal, the *Narrative of a Journey to the Zoolu Country of South Africa in 1835 and 1836*. Worked in Bolivia, tried converting the Indians of Tierra del Fuego, and in 1851 died there of starvation.

Gardiner, Frederick George. Judge President of the Cape. Born on April 19, 1874, in London, came to South Africa as a child, educated at Mossel Bay, Diocesan College and Keble College, Oxford. Returning to the Cape,

was admitted to the Bar on April 12, 1897. This was followed by his appointment as Attorney-General of the Cape Province in 1910. In 1912 he took silk and, after being Acting-Judge three times, was appointed permanent in 1914, becoming Judge President of the Cape in August 1926. He died on August 22, 1935.

Gariep. Hottentot name for the Orange River.

Garies. Town in Namaqualand, about 30 miles from the coast, centre of a wheat-growing area. Hottentot name derived from a species of local grass. There was fighting near by in the later stages of the South African War. Population: 1,103, including 569 Whites.

Garraway, Sir Edward Charles Frederick. Resident Commissioner of Basutoland. Born in Ireland in 1856, qualified in medicine at Dublin, and came to South Africa as District Surgeon at Millwood near Knysna in 1888. Served in Bechuanaland Police and, after the South African War, entered the South African Constabulary, becoming Chief Medical Officer. Was Military Secretary to Lord Gladstone after the establishment of Union, and became Resident Commissioner of Bechuanaland Protectorate from 1916 to 1917, followed by a similar appointment in Basutoland. He died in 1932.

Garrett, Fydell Edmund. Newspaper editor. Born in Derbyshire in 1865; he always suffered from poor health. Entered Cambridge in 1884, where he attracted attention by his literary gifts. Became a follower and friend of W. T. Stead, editor of the *Pall Mall Gazette*, who sent him in 1889 on a tour of South Africa. Upon his return he became assistant editor of the *Pall Mall Gazette* at the time when it was the most sensational and abused paper in England. Among his friends was Alfred Milner, afterwards Lord Milner (q.v.). Stayed on the Continent and Egypt on account of his health, joined the

Westminster Gazette from 1893 to 1895. Became editor of the *Cape Times* on the eve of the Jameson Raid. Arriving at the Cape, he immediately plunged into local affairs, as a friend and supporter of Cecil John Rhodes. Made a trip to Johannesburg and Pretoria, and set down his experiences and views in *The Story of an African Crisis*. The *Cape Times* acquired through him a large circulation and great influence. Garrett was a member of the Cape Parliament from 1897 until 1899. His health became worse, and in 1900 he returned to England. Knowing that his days were numbered, he continued to work and to write some fine poetry. He died in 1907.

Gatacre, Major-General Sir William Forbes. British soldier. Born in Shropshire in 1843 and entered 77th Regiment of Foot in 1862. Served in India and the Sudan, was appointed to the command of the Third Division, South Africa Field Force, in 1899. As such, had to protect the railway from East London inland, but was defeated at Stormberg in December 1899. Later he took Dewetsdorp, but a British force at Reddersburg, O.F.S., was obliged to surrender owing to Gatacre's inability to relieve it. For this was removed from command in South Africa and given charge of Colchester district. In later life he explored Abyssinia and died of fever in 1905.

Gates of St. John. Famous landmark at the mouth of the Umzimvubu (St. John's River) near Port St. Johns in the Transkei. They are two great crags rising above the estuary.

Gatjeponder. Derisive term applied by members of the Dopper (q.v.) section of the Dutch Reformed Church to the less conservative members of that denomination. Literally a wearer of a 'gat-japon' or frock-coat, as distinguished from the Dopper's short jacket.

Gatooma. Town in Rhodesia, between Salisbury and Bulawayo, 3,184 feet above sea-level. Founded in 1907 and became a municipality in 1917. Name is derived from a local Chief, Katuma. Apart from farming and gold mining, there is a considerable textile industry, based on the local cotton production, and the two spinning mills have over 35,000 spindles. The population is 17,342, comprising 2,650 Whites, 14,442 Africans and 250 Asiatics and Coloureds.

Gatsrand. Range of hills in Western Transvaal, north of Potchefstroom, where military operations occurred in the South African War, and the famous Boer leader, Commandant Danie Theron, was killed. A monument has been erected to his memory.

Gaul, Dr. William Thomas. Bishop of Mashonaland. Educated at Trinity College, and ordained in 1873. Came to South Africa as Vicar of Bloemfontein where he remained until 1880, followed by 15 years as Archdeacon of Kimberley. Through his friendship with Cecil John Rhodes, he became Bishop of Mashonaland from 1895 to 1907. His later years were spent as honorary Canon of Cape Town Cathedral. He died on May 17, 1928.

Gaunt, John. Rhodesian diplomat. Born at Portsmouth, England, on April 28, 1905, he studied at Oxford and entered the Northern Rhodesian service in 1928. On his retirement in 1948 he entered politics and was successively leader of the Confederate Party (1953) and the Dominion Party in 1955. Under Federation he was Minister of Mines from 1962 to 1964, and of Local Government and Housing. In 1965 was appointed Accredited Diplomatic Representative of Rhodesia in Pretoria. Retired in 1969.

Gazania. *See* DAISY.

Geelbek: 1. (*Anas undulata*). The best-known and most generally distributed duck in South Africa. Also known as Yellow-bill. *See* DUCK.

2. (Cape Salmon) (*Atractoscion aequidens*). Fish found in Table Bay and from False Bay to Natal. Also found in Australian waters. About 40 inches long, and a valuable food-fish.

Geelgat. Afrikaans name for the Cape Bulbul. *See* BULBUL.

Geelslang (literally 'Yellow Snake'). Popular name for the Cape Cobra. *See* COBRA.

Geelvink. Afrikaans name for Cape Weaver. *See* WEAVER.

Geilsiekte. Disease of sheep, due to eating unsuitable grass.

Gelderland. Dutch cruiser sent by Queen Wilhelmina of the Netherlands to Lourenço Marques during the South African War, to bring President Kruger and his entourage to Europe. The ship sailed on October 19, 1900, and arrived at Marseilles on November 22.

Gem of the Karoo. Nickname given to Graaff-Reinet.

Gemsbuck (Dutch for chamois, from its fancied resemblance to that animal). Large antelope, standing nearly 4 feet at the shoulder, occurring in the Kalahari Desert, particularly in the Gemsbuck National Park, South-West Africa and Rhodesia. The Gemsbuck prefers dry country and is specially adapted to exist on very scanty vegetation. Its symmetrical horns, seen sideways, are believed to have given rise to the legend of the unicorn in the Middle Ages. It is particularly good eating, but now protected. The zoological name is *Oryx gazella*. *See* MAMMALS.

Genadendal. Moravian mission station, the oldest in South Africa, founded in 1737 by George Schmidt, *The Apostle of the Hottentots*. It lies near the Zonderend Mountains, not far from Caledon, and is known for its beautiful old buildings and picturesque situation, which attracts many artists. Name means 'The Valley of Grace.' Population: 2,788, including 4 Whites.

'General Botha.' South African naval training station. Established through the gift of the former cruiser H.M.S. *Thames*, which was moored outside Simonstown in 1921, and designed for the training of boys for the Merchant and Royal Navies. In 1947 the establishment was moved to Gordon's Bay and in 1964 it came under the control of the South African Navy, which transferred it to Saldanha Bay. *See* NAVY, SOUTH AFRICAN and SOUTH AFRICAN NAUTICAL COLLEGE.

General Estate and Orphan Chamber. Trust Company established at Cape Town in 1856 and still in existence.

General Mining & Finance Corporation Ltd. Gold-mining group. Established in Johannesburg by the brothers George and Leopold Albu in 1895. They controlled many important properties, including the Meyer and Charlton, in those days the richest property on the Rand. Prior to World War I it had backing from Germany through the Dresdner Bank. Most important Company is the West Rand Consolidated, one of the largest producers in the world. The General Mining restarted the first gold mine after the South African War (the Meyer and Charlton) in 1902 and was the first uranium producer on the Rand after World War II, on the West Rand Consolidated. In recent years it became closely linked with the Strathmore Investment Group.

Genet or **Musk Cat.** Nocturnal animal related to the Civet (q.v.), found throughout South Africa, particularly in thick bush. It is very shy and silent in its movements and feeds on poultry and small animals. About 8 inches in height and length, with a tail twice as long. *See* MAMMALS.

Genootskap van Regte Afrikaners (Association of True Afrikaners). Formed in Paarl in 1875 by a group, comprising the Rev. S. J. Du Toit (q.v.), D. F. Du Toit, C. P. Hoogenhout, S. G. Du Toit, A. Ahrbeck, G. Malherbe, P. J. Malherbe. Its purpose was to encourage the use of Afrikaans as a language, issue a newspaper in that tongue, promote publication of a dictionary and

grammar, and encourage religion and patriotism. Fought against the influence of Nederlands Dutch as well as of English, and lasted till the end of the 19th century, when it was replaced by other bodies.

GEOLOGY OF SOUTHERN AFRICA

by

PROFESSOR M. S. TALJAARD
University of Stellenbosch

SOUTHERN Africa, excluding Tanganyika, the Congo and Angola, has an ancient geological history, a fascinating array of mineral deposits and a great variety of climates and landscape. It has also provided some very famous fossils of plants, animals and earliest man.

Just about a hundred years ago the first reports of minerals and rocks in this vast area began appearing—but long before that ancient metal hunters mined gold and copper and tin in Rhodesia and Zambia (Kitwe and Zimbabwe), in the Limpopo valley—at Mapungubwe, at Zaaiplaats and Palaborwa in the Eastern Transvaal Lowveld. Early finds of gold at Barberton and Pilgrims Rest, coal at Indwe and later in Natal, the Transvaal and Wankie gave a great boost to the study of rocks in Southern Africa, while the discoveries of diamonds at Kimberley and gold on the Witwatersrand, and later iron, platinum and manganese, accelerated the process of rock examination. We know now that our rock foundation is cooled and crystalline granite—much compressed and changed, and in places covered by layers of ancient lavas, muds, sands and limestones. Into these upper covers later molten materials were injected as great pools, sheets, thin wall-like masses and in chimney-shaped vents.

Such world-renowned intrusions as the Bushveld Igneous Complex, the Great Dyke of Rhodesia, the swarms of dykes and sheets of Karroo

Dolerite, the diamondiferous Kimberlites (pipe-like) and the great lava sheets of the Maluti Mountains, the Lebombos and the Kaokoveld of South West Africa, can be mentioned. They differ widely in age, appearance, form, size and composition; and from them came, as vapours and solutions, enormously varied minerals, some of great economic importance. They include the ores of tin, copper, mica, corundum, gold, platinum, vanadium, zinc, lead, antimony and arsenic; of beryllium, lithium, tungsten, columbium and tantalum; and not least the ores of uranium. Our vast gold, coal, manganese and asbestos deposits had different origins, mostly waterborne and deposited or infiltrated into bedded deposits of lime, sands, muds and pebble beds.

The diamond—born of great heat and pressure—occurs in its birthplace, tightly embedded in the rare Kimberlite rock which occurs in pipe-like vents. There are many such chimneys blown through our crust by long dead volcanoes.

For great distances in Zambia, Rhodesia, Malawi, the Northern and Eastern Transvaal, South-West Africa and the Northern Cape Province in the Republic, the plateau is built of these ancient granites, including in narrow belts even more ancient sedimentary rocks and lavas, now much changed by heat, compression and faulting.

The younger covering layers are preserved in older basins of folding, representing as they do old lava flows and the deposits of ancient continental landlocked seas, into which glaciers, ice sheets, rivers and winds shed great loads of sand, mud, lime and gravels—since turned to sandstones, shales, limestones and conglomerates. This process was repeated many times and for many millions of years, and so were born our great systems of rocks. Southern Africa was then part of a vast continent (Gondwanaland) and only later became a drifted-off portion (the whole of Africa) bordered by ocean waters. Its edges for varying distances were dipped below sea-level by earth movements, and received at such times marine deposits which were later uplifted.

When animals and plants came to inhabit our lands, some were preserved after death as fossils, which help to tell us how cold or warm or dry the climates were. Most have become extinct, but our younger marine fossils in the Cape, Cretaceous and Tertiary marine rock beds tell of marine life and the borders of land and sea.

The more recent deposits are those of the interior Kalahari desert basin, filled by wind-blown sands, temporary lake muds and desert limestones. Our older stream terraces are in places diamond-bearing, washed down from the sites of Kimberlite pipes; and along our western shores the marine terraces of Namaqualand and Pomona bear witness to similar actions. Some diamonds could have come from off-shore submarine volcanic vents but many of them came from the hinterland, via the Orange River drainage system.

Zambia offers us copper, zinc, lead and coal, the last of the same age as that found at Wankie (Rhodesia), Vereeniging, Witbank (Transvaal) and the Natal Coalfields. Coal originated from washed-in plants, collecting in great continental lakes on the shores of which a 'giant-lizard fauna' lived and died, leaving us the skeletal remains of the Karroo Reptiles. They became extinct when the climate changed from wet to dry and the great lakes were filled by wind-blown sands and later covered by vast sheets of lava.

The Karroo System of the Republic is found in northern South West Africa, Rhodesia (Wankie) and in the down-shifted portions of Zambia and Malawi. The copper, lead and zinc ores occur as infiltrates in much older systems of layered rocks invaded by younger granites as at N'Kana and Broken Hill. The copper and gold of Rhodesia and the Northern Transvaal occur in much older rocks (more than 2,000 million years ago).

The asbestos and manganese ores are of mysterious origins, seemingly formed as infiltrates from crustal waters which migrated into porous horizons of folded sedimentary rocks.

The gold of the Witwatersrand is an ancient placer deposit much changed by pressure and the effects of solutions, emanating from invading igneous dykes and sheets of igneous rocks.

The great copper deposits of Messina and Namaqualand are of igneous origin and occur in the basement granites of great antiquity. The mountains and valleys of Southern Africa have a dual origin. Some are remnants of erosion left high by crustal uplift, as remnants of eroded highlands. Of such origin are the Table Mountains of the Kaokoveld in northern South West Africa and the Drakensberg of Lesotho.

The great scarp mountains of eastern Rhodesia, facing west across the Sabi Valley, have their form and altitude due to faulting and stream erosion. So also were the great highlands of western Malawi born, the Livingstone Mountains and the Nyika Scarplands.

The fold ranges of the famed Garden Route in the Cape Province are mountains formed by folding of the crustal layers, etched by river sculpture. Such are also the older ranges of Barberton, the Murchison Range and the Windhoek Highlands of South West Africa.

Because flat-lying, cover layers of rock occupy great areas of the interior plateau, a mesa-and-butte landscape has resulted in regions of semi-arid climate. These are the features of the Great Karroo and the Fish River Valley lands of southern South West Africa.

Much of Mozambique is featureless and low-lying, being a plain but recently emerged from the sea. It is badly drained and its surface studded by shallow lakes near the present shore. It is well wooded and its soils productive of maize, manioc, sugar-cane and sisal.

George. Town in the Western Cape Province originally known as 'George Town,' the first to be established under the British régime in South Africa. Founded in 1812 and named after George III, who presented a Bible to the church, which became a Cathedral in 1911. Picturesquely situated below Cradock Peak, George enjoys an English-type climate—hence it is one of the few places in South Africa where hops can be grown. Industries include shoe manufacture. Population: 22,360, including 11,000 Whites.

Geranium. *See* PELARGONIUM.

Gerard, Father Joseph. Catholic missionary and saint, born near Nancy, France, of peasant stock, on March 12, 1831. He joined the Oblate Order and on May 10, 1852, was admitted to the priesthood. Along with two other Oblates he arrived in Durban on January 21, 1854, and commenced his mission work in Natal. Because of discouraging conditions he moved to Basutoland in 1862, and gained the confidence of Moshesh (q.v.). Under great difficulties he introduced the Catholic faith to a largely hostile community, and built his first church in 1863. Living an extremely ascetic life, he gained great influence, among both converts and pagans, being known to the Basuto as Ramehlolo (Father of Miracles). Many stories were circulated about his sanctity. His later years were spent at Roma. He died on May 29, 1914. Since March, 1955, proceedings have been in progress for his beatification and canonisation.

Gerbille (Muridae). Small South African rodent about 6 inches long, with large eyes, short front and long back legs. It flourishes particularly in dry veld. There are several varieties, of which the Cape Gerbille is known in Afrikaans as the Duinrot. It inhabits an underground burrow and lives on vegetation and insects. Classed as vermin because of its liability to pick up rabies. *See* MAMMALS.

Gereformeerde Kerk van Suid Afrika. Official name for Doppers (q.v.).

German East Africa Line. In 1837, Carl Woermann, a Hamburg merchant, started sending ships to West Africa. His son, Adolf Woermann, continued this and in 1879 began trading with East Africa, and the trading outposts of the house ultimately became the nucleus of the German colony. The establishment of German control in East Africa induced the German Colonial Office to back the launching in May, 1890, of a new steamship company, the Deutsche Ost-Afrika Linie, with which it signed a mail contract. Adolf Woermann was on its original board. German East Africa Line traded down the East Coast only as far as Lourenço Marques until 1892, when the *Kaiser* was sent to South Africa. A West Coast service followed, and ultimately a round-Africa service. Adolf Woermann & Sons in 1898 started their own direct service from Hamburg to Cape Town and beyond, paying particular attention to the needs of German South West Africa. Operations continued on a steadily growing scale till World War I ended them. After the return of peace, the interests of the two enterprises were more closely merged, and a considerable fleet was established before the Second World War once again interrupted services. Since 1945, the German East Africa Line has concentrated largely on cargo and a limited amount of passenger traffic.

German Legion (Deutsche Legion). Group of German volunteers who served with the British Army in the Crimean War. After peace was signed in 1857, they were brought as settlers to the frontier of the Cape of Good Hope and given land in British Kaffraria, along with certain cash benefits. Altogether over 2,400 men, women and children arrived, under Baron von Stutterheim. A number of villages with German names, including Berlin, Hamburg, Stutterheim, Döhne, etc., were established. Many well-known South African families are descended from these colonists.

Germiston. Town east of Johannesburg. Leading gold-mining and industrial centre, largest railway junction in South Africa. Manufactures include engineering, textiles, furniture, chemicals, etc. Lake near by used for yachting. Named after the birthplace near Glasgow of John Jack (of the Simmer and Jack Mine). In its earlier days Germiston was known as Elandsfontein Junction. Founded in 1887. The Rand Refinery, where all gold recovered on the fields is treated, stands there. Population: 204,605, of which 84,419 are Whites, 113,620 Bantu, 4,256 Coloureds and 2,310 Asiatics.

Geysdorp. Village near Delareyville, Transvaal. Scene of South African War action. Population: 250, including 170 Whites.

Ghanzi. Settlement in North of Botswana established in 1898, as a result of Cecil Rhodes' encouragement, by Boer trekkers led by Adrian Hofmeyr. Still existent and mainly engaged in ranching.

Ghoen. Name given by South African children to a stone used for playing hopscotch. The name is of Hottentot origin. Also name for large marble.

Giant's Castle. Mountain in the Drakensberg, near Estcourt, noted for its scenery and resort near by. Height 10,878 feet. Large game reserve maintained here, covering 50,000 acres, and containing many species of antelopes, birds, etc.

Giant Snake. See PYTHON.

Gibbs, Sir Humphrey Vicary. Last Governor of Rhodesia. Born in London on November 22, 1902 and educated at Eton and Trinity College, Cambridge. He emigrated to Rhodesia in 1928 and went farming. In 1959 he was appointed Governor. Refusing to relinquish his authority after U.D.I. (q.v.) in 1965, he remained in Government House, Salisbury, despite the appointment of a successor by the Government, until the Referendum result in favour of a Republic in 1969, when he resigned.

Gibeon. Village in South West Africa, south of Windhoek. Founded as a station by the Rhenish Mission Society in Germany in 1862, destroyed in 1870 in the wars between Hottentot tribes, was scene of fighting during the South-West Africa Campaign in 1915. Farming centre. Population: 485, including 102 Whites.

Giesenskraal. Village near Britstown, Cape Province. Population: 750, including 90 Whites.

Gifbol or Seeroog-blom (Buphane toxicaria. Gaive). Plant widespread in northern Cape Province. Bulb contains latex used for poisoning arrows. The dry scales used as bedding. See AMARYLLIS.

Gijlswijk, Archbishop Bernard Jordan. Catholic prelate and first

Apostolic Delegate to South Africa. Born in Delft, Holland, in 1870, he entered the priesthood as a young man and rose to be Archbishop. In 1923 came to South Africa, and worked for development of Catholic institutions of every kind. He died there in 1944.

Gill College. Founded in 1867 by Dr. William Gill at Somerset East, Cape Province, as a high school and university training centre for boys. Since 1904 the graduate side has disappeared, but the school continues. Many well-known South Africans have studied there, including Chief Justice Sir James Rose-Innes (q.v.).

Gill, Sir David. Astronomer. Born in 1843 in Aberdeen, Scotland, educated at Dollar Academy. Trained as a watchmaker, which proved of great value in his work. Developing an early liking for science, he attended lectures at Marischal College, and, through his researches in time-keeping, began to concentrate on astronomy. Lord Crawford (the Earl of Lindsay) placed him in charge of his private observatory at Dun Echt in 1872. In 1877 he went to the island of Ascension with his wife, to observe the transit of Venus. In 1879 was appointed Her Majesty's Astronomer at the Cape, a position he held for nearly 30 years. Under him the Cape Observatory became world-famous, attracting a succession of celebrated visitors. Amongst Gill's major work was the survey of the Southern Heavens (*Durchmusterung*), the photographing of the moon, the commencement of the Cape Geodetic Survey, the measuring of star distances, the attempted building of the 'Perfect Clock' to measure the earth's rotation, etc. Gill left the Cape in 1907, and died in England in 1914.

Gill, Dr. William. Medical and educational pioneer of the Eastern Cape Province. Born in Scotland, studied medicine at Glasgow University, settled at Somerset East in 1829, and

died there in 1863, leaving his money for the foundation of Gill College (q.v.).

Gillitts (Emberton). Village near Pinetown, Natal. Population: 1,773, including 420 Whites.

Gim. Rhodesian alluvial gold stored by the natives in birds' quills and used for barter.

Gingindlovu. Village near Mtunzini, Natal. Sugar centre. Population: 190, including 150 Whites.

Ginsberg, Franz. South African pioneer industrialist. Born at Beuthen, Germany, in 1862, came to the Cape in 1880 and settled at King William's Town. Working first as a photographer, he began manufacturing matches in 1886, and candles in 1888. Elected mayor, he took a leading part in developing the town. Was a pioneer in opening the South-West African diamond fields in 1908. From 1910 to 1927 Ginsberg was a Senator in the Union Parliament. He died in 1936.

Giraffe (Arabic 'Zaret') (*Giraffa cameleopardalis*). The traditional name Camelopard arose from the legend that it was a cross between a camel and a leopard. Hence the Afrikaans Kameelperd. Giraffes, once common from Orange River to Zambesi, are now found (in Southern Africa) only in Botswana, the Kruger National Park, Western Rhodesia and Mozambique. Of a number of varieties the common South African species is *Giraffa cameleopardalis capensis*. The animal likes open country, where the leaves of the Kameeldoorn (Acacia) are plentiful. The male stands about 18 feet 6 inches and the female about 16 feet. It has two small horns and a rudimentary third horn. It has no weapons but its heels, its speed and its keen senses, and is quite harmless. Research has recently been carried out at the University of Cape Town on the circulation of its blood, in connection with the prevention of blackouts among airmen. *See* MAMMALS.

Girl Guides. *See* YOUTH MOVEMENTS.

Girouard, Colonel Sir Edouard Percy Cranwill. Canadian engineer and soldier. Born at Montreal in 1867, educated at the Royal Military College, Kingston, Canada; joined the army in 1888, serving in the Sudan, where he distinguished himself in the construction and organisation of railways. On the outbreak of the South African War, was made Director of Railways for the British forces from 1899 to 1902, and organised the Imperial Military Railways (q.v.). Later settled in England and in 1907 became High Commissioner for Northern Nigeria, Governor from 1908 to 1909 and Governor of East African Protectorate 1909–1912. In World War I was Director-General of Munitions. He died in 1932.

Gladiolus (Iridaceae). A genus of plants growing from corms, containing many lovely varieties—today protected all over the Cape. The delicate pink and blue Sandpypie (*G. gracilis*), with its grass-like leaves, is a winter flower of the West and South-West Cape. A larger gladiolus with sword leaves and more frilly petals, marked with deep pink, is the Painted Lady (*G. debilis* and *G. blandus*). The large (and small) speckled Brown Afrikaner (*G. grandis* and *G. maculatus*) grow in many shades of reddish-yellow and reddish-brown. Other varieties are to be found throughout Southern Africa on dry veld and along the coast. *See* IRIS.

Gladstone. Suburb of Kimberley, named after British Prime Minister, William Ewart Gladstone.

Gladstone, Lord (Herbert John Gladstone). First Governor-General of the Union of South Africa. Son of the English Prime Minister, W. E. Gladstone. Born in 1854, educated at Eton and Oxford. Was Private Secretary to his father, and in 1880 was elected to Parliament. From 1881 to 1885 he was a Lord of the Treasury, Financial Secretary at the War Office in 1886, Under Secretary, Home Office, 1892–1894 and Commissioner of Works, 1894–1895. From 1899 Gladstone was Chief Whip of the Liberal Party, and Home Secretary from 1905–1910, when he was appointed Governor-General of the Union. During his term he aroused much criticism through his action in the Umtali Murder Case (q.v.). He returned to England in 1914 and died in 1930.

Glanville, Ernest. South African writer and journalist. Born at Wynberg in 1856, educated at St. Andrew's College, Grahamstown. As a boy he helped his father, T. B. Glanville (q.v.), to take the first printing press to Kimberley by ox-wagon. Correspondent in the Zulu War of 1879 for the London *Daily Chronicle*, went to England and became assistant editor of the *Daily Telegraph*. On his return he was editor of the *Cape Argus* from 1908 to 1910, and thereafter of the *Bulawayo Chronicle*. He wrote a number of books, the best known of which is *Claw and Fang*; was an authority on farming. He died in 1925.

Glanville, Thomas Burt. Early Cape writer and Immigration Commissioner for the Cape Government. Born in Devonshire, he spent his earlier career in the East, with 9 years in India, before coming to the Cape in 1850. In 1866 was elected to Parliament for Somerset East, and in 1872 for Grahamstown. Became interested in journalism, helping to establish the first newspaper at Kimberley in 1870. In 1875 he published one of the first guide books to South Africa, retired to England about the same time and died in 1878. A collection of his essays entitled *At Home and Abroad* appeared posthumously.

Glasogie or **Witogie.** Afrikaans names for Cape White-Eye. *See* WHITE-EYE.

Glenashley. Township near Inanda, Natal. Population: 1,054, including 771 Whites.

Glencoe. Town near Dundee, Natal. Scene of South African War battle. Population: 9,130, including 3,200 Whites.

Glenelg, Lord (Charles Grant). British Colonial Secretary, son of the Chairman of the East India Co. Born 1778 in Kidderpore, Bengal; was called to the English Bar, entered Parliament in 1811 and the Cabinet in 1813, as First Lord of the Treasury. In 1835, having been made Lord Glenelg and Colonial Secretary, he inaugurated a vacillating policy in South African affairs. Disgust at his return to the frontier tribes in the Eastern Cape of the newly conquered buffer zone, 'The Province of Queen Adelaide,' was a major cause of the Great Trek. He resigned office in 1839 and died in Cannes 1866.

Glen Grey. Native reserve near Lady Frere in the Eastern Cape Province (Tembuland). Glen Grey Act, introduced in 1894 as an experiment in Native self-government, by Cecil John Rhodes, Prime Minister of the Cape. The Glen Grey Act authorised the setting up of Native Councils, which led to the creation of the Transkei Bunga (q.v.).

Gliding. Attempts at gliding were first made in South Africa by Goodman Household (q.v.) in Natal in the 1870's, and were repeated in a different form by S. V. Vine near Pretoria in 1912. After that came a long lull until, thanks to the experience gained in Germany after World War I, fresh efforts were made by a group of amateurs on the Witwatersrand in the late 1920's. Some of these pioneers themselves came from Germany and in August 1930 the Germiston Flying Club launched the first training glider in the country. Thereafter further gliding experiments took place in other parts of the Union, some of them under the auspices of the South African Air Force near Pretoria. The outbreak of World War II brought a further break in amateur gliding, but there has been a gratifying revival since 1945. Apart from the Witwatersrand, gliding is carried on near Cape Town, in Natal and elsewhere.

Globe and Phoenix Gold Mine. Famous property in Rhodesia, near Que Que (q.v.), established in 1895 and still in operation. Involved in a court case against the Amalgamated Properties of Rhodesia. The issue involved was whether, under the Rhodesian Gold Law, a reef might be followed by a claim-holder into an adjoining property, in accordance with the principle already established in the United States. The case, one of the longest and costliest on record in Southern Africa, began in 1913, and was decided in April, 1919 in the House of Commons. Hearing had taken 171 days, cost to shareholders being over £200,000.

Glossopteris. A genus of fossil plant found widely in the coal measures of the southern hemisphere, including South Africa, and recognised as the most important member of the Glossopteris flora which clothed the ancient continent of Gondwanaland in Permo-Carboniferous times, and formed its chief constituent of its coals. The plant was known for well over a century by many species of leaves only, but in 1952 the first fructifications (organs of reproduction) were identified by Dr. Edna Plumstead of the University of the Witwatersrand. The finding gave rise to international excitement in botanical circles, for the structures were unique, necessitating the creation of a new class of plants—the Glossopteridae—and so advanced for their time that they may well prove to be missing links in the century-old search for the origin of flowering plants. The original fructifications were found by

S. F. le Roux in quarries near Vereeniging, Transvaal.

Gluck, Mrs. Sarah. Postmistress of the village of Lady Grey (q.v.), who during the South African War refused to haul down the Union Jack when the Boers occupied the place.

Gnu. See WILDEBEEST.

Go-Away Bird. Common name for Grey Lourie. See LOURIE.

Goba. Village in Mozambique, 43 miles from Lourenço Marques, terminus of the railway agreed to early in the present century, from Lourenço Marques to Swaziland. The line to Goba was completed in 1912. See SWAZILAND RAILWAY.

Gobabis. Village in South West Africa founded by the Rev. Cook for the Rhenish Mission in 1840, abandoned from 1846 to 1875, owing to native wars, and then re-established. Scene of fighting in the Herero War in 1904 (q.v.). Centre of Karakul skin industry. Population: 5,560, including 2,600 Whites.

Goby. A large group of small fish, some marine, others found in streams and rivers. Low, nearly cylindrical body and well-developed fins. Its eggs are attached to the under surface of stones and are sometimes guarded by the male.

Godlonton, Robert. Cape newspaper pioneer and legislator. Born in 1794 in England, he qualified as a printer and in 1820 became one of the settlers on the Eastern Frontier. His first South African post was as magistrate's clerk but in 1834 he joined the *Grahamstown Journal* and raised it to great influence. Godlonton was one of the original representatives in the Cape Parliament in 1854. He died in 1884.

Goedemoed. Village near Rouxville, Orange Free State. Population: 350, including 130 Whites.

Goedgegun. Village in Southern Swaziland. Settled by Afrikaners and established in 1923. Farming centre. Population: 1,700, including 250 Whites.

Goedverwag. Village near Piquetberg, Cape Province. Population: 1,455, including 6 Whites.

Goering, Dr. Heinrich. First German Administrator of South-West Africa. Born in Emmerich in Germany on October 31, 1839, he was appointed 'Reich Commissioner' for the newly-acquired territory of South-West Africa in 1884. Landed at Angra Pequena, went inland to Okahandja and persuaded local chiefs to sign a series of treaties, placing themselves under the protection of the Kaiser. In 1888 became Consul at Port-au-Prince, Hayti, retiring in 1895. His son, Field-marshal Hermann Goering, was born in 1893, while his father was on home leave. Dr. Goering died in 1913.

Goerz, Adolf. South African mining magnate. Born in Germany in 1857, a brother-in-law of George von Siemens, head of the Deutsche Bank, who induced him to come to the Transvaal in 1888. Established the Goerz Syndicate in 1889, and in 1892 the Rand Central Ore Reduction Company. In October 1895 interests were amalgamated into A. Goerz & Co. Ltd., which later became the Union Corporation. He died in 1900.

Gogga. Word of Hottentot origin, used in South Africa to signify all crawling creatures. Also used figuratively of a bogey.

Goldberg, Benjamin Disraeli. Former Rhodesian Cabinet Minister. Born in Dublin, Ireland, May 12, 1902, came to Rhodesia aged 10 and was educated at Salisbury and the University of Cape Town. Began practice at Umtali as a solicitor and was elected to the Federal Parliament as Member for Border, December 1953. In 1956 became Minister for Home Affairs in the Federal Cabinet under Sir Roy Welensky and in 1962 Minister of Health.

Golden Gate National Park. Situated in Eastern Orange Free State in beautiful mountain scenery and opened in 1964. Called after characteristically shaped and coloured rock formation.

Golden Valley: 1. Area in the Eastern Cape Province along the Great Fish River, south of Cookhouse. Noted irrigation and fruit-growing district. **2.** Settlement near Gatooma in Rhodesia, so called from former gold mining.

Golding, George John. South African Coloured leader. Born at Ladismith, Cape Province, May 28, 1906. Associated as a teacher with work of Dr. A. Abdurrahman (q.v.). A strong supporter of moderation, he was elected President of Coloured People's National Union in 1944 and a member of the Coloured Affairs Council. Died in 1965.

Gold Law. This was formed gradually by experience. Traditionally, the right of mining precious metals in South Africa is vested in the State. The owner of the ground is granted a mynpacht (q.v.). Ground believed to contain gold must first be thrown open to prospecting by the Department of Mines, and after that to pegging. Elaborate provisions exist under which the mineral seekers may establish their rights. Since about 1908 a system of mining leases has developed, particularly in the Transvaal and O.F.S., under which the State grants rights of exploitation to approved companies. It is thus possible to operate on a large and economical scale.

GOLD-MINING INDUSTRY OF SOUTH AFRICA

ALTHOUGH searches for gold in South Africa date back to the early Dutch settlement, the first finds of real importance were not made until the 1870's. These resulted in a gold field being established in the Pilgrim's Rest-Lydenburg area of the North-Western Transvaal to mine deposits on or near the surface. In 1883, prospecting was started on the Witwatersrand by H. W. Struben (1840–1915) and his brother F. P. T. Struben (1851–1931) which led to the discovery of the Confidence Reef on the farm Wilgespruit in September 1884.

The Main Reef gold-bearing series was discovered on the farm Langlaagte, near present-day Johannesburg, in February 1886. Although the discovery was to prove momentous in South Africa's history, it is not known precisely how the find was made and there have been several claimants to the honour.

Discoverer's rights were, however, granted by the Government to George Walker and an Australian, George Harrison, one of whom is reputed to have tripped over the Main Reef outcrop and dislodged a piece of ore which he panned and found to be auriferous. Some authorities state that the work of the Strubens made this discovery inevitable.

There is controversy, too, over the geological history of this reef and others discovered later. These reefs are part, or extensions, of the Witwatersrand Basin, a system of layers of sedimentary rocks about 25,000 feet thick. At first these layers may have been deposited more or less horizontally but subsequent earth movements and contractions moulded them into the shape of a saucer. One theory is that gold, in the form of finely-divided particles, was carried down by rivers and deposited on the bed of a great inland lake which formed in the saucer.

Settling on the bottom of the great lake, these relatively heavy particles collected around pebbles and gravel and were covered by muds and sands which eventually became shales and quartzites. After periods when other rock layers, barren of gold, were laid down, still further narrow reef bands were deposited in the System, like occasional gold leaves in a very large book. Then the whole system was tilted and sundered by great upheavals of the earth's crust and the System gradually covered and abutted by younger sedimentary deposits. When some of these younger sediments were partially eroded, a portion of the saucer's gold-bearing rim lay exposed as an outcrop along the central Witwatersrand.

The Gold Mining Industry was developed from this outcrop, first in a series of shallow workings and incline shafts. Later it was necessary to follow the ore bodies deep below the surface.

To reach these reefs, shafts are sunk through the barren 'country rock,' and tunnels called 'cross-cuts' are blasted horizontally at various levels to meet the inclined plane of its reefs. Then from the cross-cuts, other tunnels, or drives, are cut—again horizontally, along the line of the reef. Drives on succeeding levels are then connected by yet other tunnels driven upwards on the plane of the reef, when they are called 'raises,' and downwards, when they are called 'winzes,' so as to cut the reef into large blocks. The ore is then taken out by continuously widening the raises and winzes, the low-roofed chambers thus formed being called 'stopes.'

Rock-breaking in the gold mines—in shaft-sinking, tunnelling and stoping—is done by explosive charges placed in machine-drilled holes. The broken ore is transported to the shafts and hoisted to the surface where, in reduction works, it is crushed and milled to the fineness of face powder and mixed with water to form a pulp.

The mining engineer and metallurgist in fact recover the gold by first returning the ore to a condition closely resembling its fluid prehistoric state. The pulp is then agitated in a cyanide solution and the finer particles dissolved by the cyanide.

The next step is to separate, by filtration, the barren slime from the gold-bearing solution and then precipitate the gold-bearing solution with zinc dust. The gold precipitates as a black slime which is treated with acid, filtered, calcined, smelted in crucibles in large furnaces and formed into bars of gold. These bars are delivered for refining by the gold mines to the Rand Refinery, Germiston, the largest gold refinery in the world, where silver and base metals still present in the bullion bar are extracted and fine gold bars, each weighing about 400 oz. are produced. It is in this form that the gold is marketed.

Organisation of the Industry. From the earliest days it was recognised that the common interest of the gold mines could best be advanced by a central, co-operative organisation. Hence the establishment of the Transvaal Chamber of Mines in 1889.

The Chamber of Mines of South Africa is an organisation whose members are gold, coal, uranium, diamond, platinum, antimony, copper and asbestos producing companies, and its existence enables the members' representatives to discuss all matters of common interest. The Chamber acts on behalf of its members in matters concerning the mining industry as a whole, such as negotiations with trade unions, the attraction to the industry of White and Bantu labour, the prevention of accidents, technical research, the refining of gold and the preparation of uranium for sale abroad.

The Chamber forms a link, too, between the major mining-financial corporations or groups, thus extending the sphere of co-operation between the producers. Soon after the discovery of the Witwatersrand gold reefs, it became obvious that mining from ever greater depths below the surface would demand far more money and far more complex technical operations than had ever before been needed in gold mining.

In the Group System, groups of

mines are associated under a single corporation or company and, by pooling ideas and certain services, get, at a reasonable cost, valuable technical assistance which they might otherwise have been unable to afford. These corporations employ managerial and secretarial staffs; consulting, mining, mechanical and electrical engineers; metallurgists; geologists; chemists and advisers on Bantu affairs and other matters.

In practice, each of the seven principal mining groups has a representative on the Gold Producers' Committee of the Chamber of Mines. This body is delegated authority by the Executive Committee of the Chamber to deal with matters affecting the interests of the gold and uranium mining industry. The Gold Producers' Committee consists of the President of the Chamber, two Vice-Presidents and four other members.

The Gold-mining Areas. Gold-producing mines, members of the Chamber of Mines, stretch in an arc of about 300 miles from Evander on the Far East Rand to the Orange Free State. The arc stretches from Evander, the newest goldfield on the Far East Rand, north-westwards to Springs and then westwards, through the West Rand to Randfontein. After a short gap the mines begin again on the Far West Witwatersrand (the West Wits Line) which runs roughly south-westwards towards Potchefstroom. Then there is another gap before it links up with the mines of the Klerksdorp district. After crossing the Vaal, the arc swings southwards through the Orange Free State goldfields to Virginia.

Along this arc are about 50 gold-producing mines, members of the Chamber, and a few smaller mines.

In 1968 the main operating statistics for gold mines, members of the Chamber, were: total production 30,759,269 ounces fine; working revenue R771,945,417 and dividends R117,823,705, (including repayment of capital R1,250,939 and R4,383,908 inter-company dividends).

The labour force was composed of 40,491 Whites and 368,135 Non-Whites and annual wages totalled R225,116,706. The mines also spent more than R320,083,845 on food and stores, of which 95½% were of South African origin.

Since World War II working costs of the gold mines have jumped from an average R2·38 per ton milled (1945) to R4·04 per ton in 1955 and R6·29 per ton in 1969.

Golf. Introduced to South Africa officially in 1882, when the first club was formed at Cape Town under the Chairmanship of General Sir H. D'O. Torrens, in command of the British Garrison, and supported by Sir David Gill and a number of other well-known citizens. The first course was laid out at Wynberg, and a golf-house constructed. In 1886 this Cape Golf Club held its first competition. Golf then spread early to Kimberley, Grahamstown, King William's Town, Port Elizabeth, Uitenhage, Aliwal North, Mafeking, Paarl, Bedford, Johannesburg and Klerksdorp. The first club on the Rand was in 1890. There are approximately 350 golf courses in Southern Africa, of which over 300 are in the Republic.

Gom Pou (*Choriotis kori*). *See* BUSTARDS.

Gonakudzingwa. Detention camp in Rhodesia, near southern border.

Gonubie. Seaside resort on the Indian Ocean, north of East London, at the mouth of the Gonubie River. Population: 1,300, including 900 Whites.

Good Hope, **H.M.S.** British cruiser built in 1902 and so named because the cost was mainly borne by the Cape Colonial Government as a voluntary gift to the Imperial Treasury. She was of 14,000 tons and carried two 9·2-inch guns and sixteen 6-inch guns.

PLATE VI: FLOWERS OF SOUTHERN AFRICA

1. *Gladiolus psittacinus* (parrot gladiolus).   2. *Gloriosa virescens* (flame lily).
3. *Erythrina lysistemon* (Kaffir boom).   4. *Stapelia nobilis* (carrion flower).
5. *Zantedeschia oculata* (yellow arum).

H.M.S. *Good Hope* was the flagship of Admiral Sir Christopher Craddock in the Battle of Coronel off South America and was sunk on November 1, 1914.

Goodman, Robert Gwelo. South African artist. Born at Taplow on the Thames in England, on July 1, 1871. Arrived at Cape Town with his parents in 1886. Like his father, he joined the Cape Government Railways and was stationed at Paarl. As a young man he began painting, and made his first appearance at the Royal Academy in 1900, followed by exhibitions in the Paris Salon, etc. His work attracted attention on account of its strong and characteristic colouring and style. After painting scenes in the South African War, Goodman returned to England in 1901, and in 1903 went for a spell to India. From 1904 to 1915 he lived in Britain most of the time. There he gained a great reputation and sold pictures to famous galleries, to royalty and to well-known collectors. Thereafter he lived at the Cape, and, apart from his landscapes, became noted for flower paintings. He died in 1939.

Goodwood. Town in the Cape Province, 7 miles from Cape Town. Important manufacturing and residential centre. Established in 1905. Called after the race course in England because the township owners planned a course in this vicinity. Project abandoned after a single meeting, but the community developed rapidly until in 1938 it became a municipality. Today its population is 100,000, of whom about 18,000 are Whites. Among the many industries are furniture manufacturing, printing, shirt-making and engineering.

Goold-Adams, Sir Hamilton John. Lieutenant-Governor of the Orange River Colony. Born in 1858, the son of L. R. W. Goold-Adams, joined the British Army, and in 1878 was commissioned a Lieutenant. First served in South Africa with General Sir Charles Warren's expedition against

the Bechuanas in 1884, and as a Major commanded the Field Force in the Matabele War of 1893. In 1895 he became a Major in the 1st Battalion of the Royal Scots and Resident Commissioner for Bechuanaland. There he was respected by all races for his ability and tact. During the siege of Mafeking in the South African War he further distinguished himself, and thus in 1901 became Lieutenant-Governor of the newly-annexed Orange River Colony. He remained there till 1910, seeing the introduction of Responsible Government and the preliminaries to the National Convention and Union. Was transferred as High Commissioner to Cyprus, where he was till 1914. He died on April 12, 1920.

Goose (family Anatidae). Occurs plentifully in well-watered areas. Varieties include: the Dwarf Goose, a pretty little bird, smaller than a duck and unlike a goose in habits, feeds under water, white face, green and chestnut body; Spur-winged, a giant goose sometimes nesting in trees; Egyptian (the commonest goose), white, red and black wings, conspicuous in flight, sometimes builds in trees in pairs, or in colonies on rock ledges.

Gorah. Bushman musical instrument, played by the mouth. Made of reeds, across which is stretched a length of sinew.

Gordimer, Nadine. South African author, born at Springs November 20, 1923, and educated at Witwatersrand University. Gained early distinction as short story writer and novelist in South Africa, England and United States, and became contributor to the *New Yorker* and other leading journals.

Gordon, General Charles George (Chinese Gordon). British soldier. Born in 1833 at Woolwich, and trained in the Royal Engineers. Gained nickname for success in quelling the Taiping Rebellion for the Emperor of China (1863–1864). Administered the Egyptian Sudan, where he suppressed

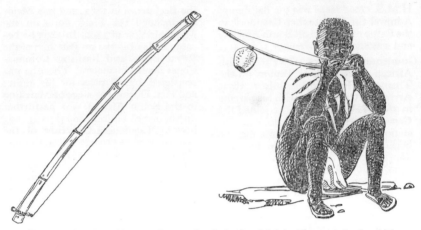

Type of Gorah (left); showing mode of playing (right). Note calabash which acts as resonator.

the slave trade in the 1870's. Contact with South Africa arose after he fell out temporarily with his employer, the Khedive of Egypt while on a visit to India, and took charge of the Royal Engineers in Mauritius. In 1882 he accepted command over the Colonial forces at the Cape. Arrived in June of that year and was confronted with the rising of the Basuto, the Gun War (q.v.). Gordon went unarmed to meet the chief Masupha in his kraal to effect a settlement. His views did not coincide with those of the Colonial Government and on October 16, 1882, he resigned. Soon after, Gordon returned to the Sudan and died on January 26, 1885, at Khartoum.

Gordon, Colonel Robert Jacob. Soldier, explorer and founder of the South African merino sheep industry. Was born in Holland of Scottish emigrants, and served in a Scottish regiment under Colonel Dundas. He reached the Cape on June 1, 1777, as second in command of the garrison. Soon after his arrival he began his travels and in August 1779, having discovered a river in the north of the

Colony, he hoisted the Dutch flag, and named it the Orange River, after the stadholder of the Netherlands. Later, with Governor Van Plettenberg, visited the Eastern Frontier and, in 1780, became Commander of the Cape Garrison. Imported to the Cape from overseas the first merino stock. In 1795, the British attacked the Cape, Colonel Gordon had a breakdown, and after the surrender, he committed suicide on October 5, 1795.

Gordon-Cumming, Roualeyn George. Traveller and hunter. Born in Scotland in 1820, the son of Sir William Gordon-Cumming of Altyre, joined the Madras Cavalry as a cornet in 1838, and served in India for 2 years. In 1843 he came to South Africa to join the Cape Mounted Rifles, but soon became a professional hunter. Made four hunting trips into the interior. Killed chiefly elephants and lions, penetrating across the Limpopo River to the vicinity of the Macloutsie in 1847 and 1848. He embodied his findings in the book that made him famous, *Five Years of a Hunter's Life in the Far Interior of South Africa,* published in 1850. Later he lost most of his money and died at the age of 46 in 1866.

Gordon Rock. Huge boulder of granite on the hill overlooking Paarl, one of the group whose glistening surface gave the place its name (meaning Pearl in Dutch). Gordon Rock is called after Colonel Jacob Gordon (q.v.).

Gordon's Bay. Seaside resort on the northern side of False Bay in the Cape Province, near the Strand. Originally a fishing village, was named after Colonel Jacob Gordon (q.v.). Population: 1,200, including 1,000 Whites.

Goromonzi. Village in Rhodesia. Name first applied to the district of Salisbury. It is important as containing the first secondary school for Africans to be set up in the Colony.

Gorongoza National Park. Large game reserve in Mozambique, noted for its wealth of royal game. Approximately 100 miles from Beira.

Goshawk (family Falconidae). *See* EAGLES.

Goshen. More correctly 'Het Land Goosen.' Miniature Boer republic, set up by a group of Transvaal burgers under N. C. Gey van Pittius on October 24, 1882. Founded on land ceded to them by the Bechuana chief Moshete, as a reward for their help in an inter-tribal war. Name is derived from the Bible, the area previously being called the Rooigrond (Red Ground). Attempted to unite with Stellaland (q.v.). President Kruger placed both states under Transvaal protection, but they ceased to exist after the British occupation of Bechuanaland in 1884.

Goske, Isbrand. Governor of the Cape of Good Hope. Came there as Commissioner in 1665, instructed to select a site for the Castle. In 1671 he returned, again as Commissioner, but immediately after was made Governor, arriving in October 1672. He remained 4 years, and started social legislation, through the founding of the Orphan Chamber, etc. The Castle was completed and the opening of the Hottentots Holland district begun. He returned to the Netherlands in 1676.

Goudini. Health resort in the Western Cape Province, noted for hot springs, and fruit and wine farms. The name is believed to be a Hottentot corruption.

Gouldsbury, Henry Cullen. Rhodesian poet. Born in 1881, the son of an officer in the Indian Police, he joined the British Army and came to Rhodesia in 1902 as a civil servant. Impressed by the beauty and romance of the country, he began writing prose and verse, and acquired the nickname of the 'Kipling of Rhodesia.' In 1908 he moved from Southern to Northern Rhodesia, where he remained as a Native Commissioner until 1914, when he enlisted in the Royal Berkshire Regiment. He was later transferred to the King's African Rifles, and distinguished himself in the East African campaign. He died of a tropical illness in August 1916, leaving a fine reputation as a novelist and poet. He was also joint author of a standard work, *The Great Plateau of Northern Rhodesia.*

Gouph. Area of the Gamka River in the Karroo, noted for its fertility. The name is of Hottentot origin.

Gouritz River. 400 miles long. Rises near Beaufort West, flows through gorges in the Swartberg Mountains and enters the sea west of Mossel Bay. Tributaries include Gamka, Olifants and Dwyka Rivers. Is crossed by two remarkable bridges, 200 feet above the river, the first built in 1892 (road) and the second (railway), 720 feet long, built recently.

Gousblom. *See* DAISY.

Gouveia. Popular name given to Manuel Antonio de Sousa, Goanese-born chief in Mozambique. Emigrated to the colony about 1850, and established himself as a leader among the local tribes. Was friendly with the Government, and relieved the settlers living at Sena, who were besieged by the Shangaans (q.v.). He therefore received official recognition, and for 20 years maintained his own army, the only effective one in the country. Supported the chief Umtasa in Manicaland who fought for control of the tribe in 1874 and secured his influence. Was killed in 1892 during a war with Chief Makombi.

Government. *See* CONSTITUTION.

Government, Local. Under the Constitution of the Republic of South Africa, local authorities fall under the jurisdiction of the Provincial Councils, though each province has its own characteristic institutions, many with roots going far back into the past. Of these the most distinctive is the system of Divisional Councils (q.v.), brought into existence in 1855 in Cape Colony, and still limited to that province.

The first form of local administration at the Cape was the system of Heemraden (q.v.), established in the 17th century in conjunction with the Landdrosts (q.v.). A hundred years later in 1796 the British authorities, during the first British occupation of the colony, set up the Burgher Senate at Cape Town as its first distinctively municipal administration.

Municipalities in the modern sense date from 1836, when an ordinance was passed authorising the election of councils on the requisition of not less than 25 property owners. The first community to take advantage of this was Beaufort West, which in January 1837 became the earliest municipality in South Africa. Somerset East followed a month later, and soon after George, Grahamstown and Cradock. Not until 1840 did Cape Town itself attain this dignity. Municipal government has since been defined in many enactments, the most recent being the Provincial Ordinance No. 19 of 1951.

Inferior in status and adapted to the needs of smaller communities are Village Management Boards, while for still more restricted areas the Cape Province recognises Local Boards.

Natal has a local government system dating back to the founding of Pietermaritzburg in 1838, though conditions were so primitive that the running of the town and of the Republic of Natalia could both be attended to by the Volksraad. True municipal government, however, began under the British régime in 1848, when the Cape ordinance was applied in Natal, then still regarded as a 'dependency.'

Towns in Natal became the subject of individual enactments, but in 1862 a 'Municipal Corporations Law' was adopted and has been frequently modified down to the present day. Major urban communities in the province are divided into boroughs (the only ones in South Africa) governed by Town or City Councils, townships administered by Town Boards, with Health Committees for still smaller villages.

In the Transvaal 'Regulations for Villages' (Dorpsbestuur), introduced by the Volksraad in 1858, served as a basis of local administration for many years. The discovery of gold and the founding of digger communities, first in the Eastern Transvaal and later on the Rand, prompted the introduction of Diggers' Committees and Sanitary Boards, the latter remaining the sole authority even in Johannesburg, until 1895, when the town had over 100,000 people and a Stadsraad, elected by the inhabitants under a Burgomaster, took its place. One restriction, incidentally, was that half of the representatives must be burghers. This arrangement continued until the end of the South African Republic. After the Peace of Vereeniging in 1902, the Milner administration introduced municipal government based on the British tradition, with Mayor and Town Council, chosen on the ward system. Subordinate to the City and Town Councils in the larger centres are

Village Councils, and in lesser places Health Committees. A distinctively Transvaal form of administration are the Peri-Urban Areas Health Boards, created in 1943 specially to deal with the extensive and populous communities on the edges of the larger towns, and not provided by them with services.

The Orange Free State system of local government dating from 1850 was also changed after the South African War to comply with the British model. Here the lesser authorities are the Village Boards of Management. Mention should also be made of the Malaria Committees and local Health Commissions in Natal, whose purposes are indicated by their titles.

All local authorities in South Africa have to comply strictly with the powers conferred upon them by law, particularly in the matter of finance, the enactment of by-laws, etc. According to the latest available figures the largest number of local authorities was in the Cape Province, with 254, followed by the Transvaal with 111, by Natal with 88 and by the Orange Free State with 74. (This is apart from the 96 Divisional Councils in the Cape.)

The first municipal legislation in Rhodesia was the adoption, immediately after the occupation, of the Municipal Act of 1882 of the Cape of Good Hope. Upon its foundation in 1890 a Board of Management was established at Fort Salisbury, to be replaced by a Sanitary Board in 1895. Meanwhile Bulawayo, upon its foundation, also received a Board of Management in 1894. The first comprehensive purely Rhodesian enactment was the Towns Management Ordinance of 1894, which was followed by the Municipalities Ordinance of 1897, later amended in many respects. To-day local government in Rhodesia includes Municipalities, Town Management Boards and Village Management Boards.

In South West Africa the system is identical with that of the Republic. Mozambique possesses both Municipalities and Local Boards, the latter nominated by the Government.

Graaff, Cornelis Jacob van de. *See* VAN DE GRAAFF.

Graaff, Sir David Pieter de Villiers. South African Cabinet Minister and industrialist. Born in 1859 in Villiersdorp, Cape. When his father died he was employed by his uncle, J. Anthony Combrinck, a leading Cape Town butcher. Became manager at an early age. Upon Combrinck's entering politics, he and his brother, Jacobus Graaff (q.v.), developed the business, introducing the first modern cold storage installations to South Africa. The concern became the Imperial Cold Storage and Supply Company, ultimately gaining the support of Cecil John Rhodes and of the late Samuel Marks (q.v.). During the South African War, the Imperial Cold Storage attained the importance which it has today. Sir David Graaff played a leading part in local politics, and in 1891 became Mayor of Cape Town. During this period he introduced the first electric lighting installation. A strong supporter of the Afrikaner Bond, he was elected to the Cape Parliament and from 1908 to 1910 was Minister without Portfolio under John X. Merriman. After Union, from 1910 to 1912 he was Minister of Public Works, Posts and Telegraphs, Minister without Portfolio from 1912 to 1913, Minister of Finance from 1915 to 1916. He died in 1931.

Graaff, Sir de Villiers. Leader of the South African parliamentary opposition. Born on December 8, 1913, the son of the late Sir David De Villiers Graaff (q.v.), he succeeded to the title in 1931. He served in World War II, being taken prisoner by the enemy. Elected to Parliament he rapidly gained prominence, and was chosen as successor to J. G. Strauss as head of the United Party in 1956.

Graaff, Senator The Hon. Sir Jacobus Arnoldus. South African Cabinet Minister. Born in Villiersdorp in 1863, joined the firm of his uncle, J. A. Combrinck, and was in partnership with his brother, Sir David Graaff (q.v.). In 1903 was elected to Parliament for the Afrikaner Bond, and in 1913 joined General Botha's Cabinet as Minister without Portfolio. He was a protagonist of South African industry. He died in 1927.

Graaff-Reinet. Town in the Cape Province on the Sundays River, nicknamed 'The Gem of the Karroo' on account of its fertility. Founded in 1786 and named after Governor van de Graaff (q.v.) and his wife, Reinet van de Graaff. There was a rebellion in 1795 and the foundation of a short-lived Boer republic. Noted for old Dutch houses, streets with their irrigation channels and general prosperity. Formerly a centre of the ostrich-feather industry, Graaff-Reinet now draws its main prosperity from wool, fruit and the produce of irrigation schemes. Population: 17,800, including 5,700 Whites.

Graafwater. Village near Clanwilliam, Cape Province. Population: 620, including 450 Whites.

Grabouw. Town in the Western Cape Province, on the Palmiet River, which separates it from Elgin. Founded by a trader named E. L. Langschmidt about 1850, who came from Grabow in Mecklenburg, Germany. Government forestry estates and deciduous fruit orchards make it an important centre. Has developed chiefly in the present century. Population: 5,100, including 1,400 Whites.

Graeme College (formerly Victoria Boys' High School). Public school at Grahamstown, established in 1873 by Robert Templeton.

Graham, Sir John James. Secretary to the Law Department of the Cape of Good Hope. Born at Cape Town in 1847, descendant of Robert Burns' friend, Graham of Fintry. Educated at St. Andrew's College, Grahamstown, entered the Cape Civil Service in 1864. Was an outstanding administrator, laying the foundations of the South African Public Service. He introduced reforms in the Prison System. Died in 1928.

Graham, Sir Thomas Lynedoch. Judge-President, Eastern Districts Court. Born at Grahamstown on May 5, 1860, educated at St. Andrew's College, the South African College and Clare College, Cambridge. Called to the Inner Temple in 1885; returned to Cape Town and commenced practice there the same year. Specialised in criminal practice for 4 years, becoming Attorney-General in 1898. Entered the Cape Cabinet in 1898. In 1904 was appointed to the Eastern Districts Bench and was Judge-President from 1913 to 1937, when he retired. Keenly interested in public affairs, he became chairman of the Cape Civil Service Commission from 1904 to 1906, and from 1918 to 1920 presided over the Union Public Service Commission of Enquiry. He died at Grahamstown on May 7, 1940.

Graham-Little, Sir Ernest Gordon. South African member of the House of Commons and medical authority. Born in Cape Town and educated at the South African College, he studied medicine in Dublin, London and Paris, specialising in dermatology, in which he gained prominence. He was chairman of several professional bodies, became member of the Senate of London University in 1906 and was elected as its representative in the House of Commons in 1924. He continued to hold office until his death in 1950.

Grahamstown. In the Eastern Cape Province. Founded 1819 by Colonel John Graham, troop commander and son of Robert Burns' patron, Graham of Fintry. Became the centre of the area where the 1820 settlers were established. Was nearly captured by a Native army, but progressed steadily and became a recognised centre for churches and schools. Considerable fighting took place there in the 1835 and 1846 Native Wars, Fort Selwyn and Fort England being relics of those days. Soon Grahamstown was one of the most important towns in the Colony. Hence in 1853 it secured the second bishopric in South Africa. St. Andrew's College, founded in 1855, grew into one of the leading public schools, its higher classes being forerunners of Rhodes University College, now Rhodes University. Few industries exist, but the local pottery is popular and is exported. Population: 40,900, including 11,800 Whites. *See also* UNIVERSITIES.

Grahamstown Journal. Daily newspaper at Grahamstown from December 1831 till 1919, when it was merged in *Grocott's Daily Mail* (q.v.). Was nicknamed the 'Settler's Bible.'

Grain Elevators. Although a grain elevator was erected in Johannesburg in 1907 and plans for the construction of a chain, under the auspices of the South African Railways, were discussed in 1914, it was not until 1922 that work began on a system designed to cover most of the producing districts and export points of the country. Thirty-five elevators were installed, including one of 42,000 tons' capacity at Congella, Durban, and another of 30,000 tons' capacity at Cape Town Docks; the remaining 33 were between 1,750 and 5,800 tons. The total cost was £2,560,302 and the combined capacity 182,950 tons. Since then private installations include the first one in Rhodesia at Bulawayo in 1930. A chain of 35 new grain elevators, costing R7,000,000, was commenced in 1964 by the North-Western Maize Growers' Co-operative covering the Transvaal, Northern Cape and Orange Free State.

The largest grain elevator in the Republic, with a capacity of 60,000 tons, was built in 1964 at East London.

Granger Bay. Inlet on Table Bay, adjoining Cape Town Docks, and site of training college for South African Merchant Navy established in consequence of the transfer to naval control of the *General Botha* (q.v.). New buildings at Granger Bay, put into use in 1965 at a cost of R1,000,000, provide training facilities for 30 students, which can be extended to 60. It is officially known as the South African Nautical College, Granger Bay.

Grangetown. Village near Inanda, Natal. Population: 800, including 5 Whites.

Grape Mildew. *See* OIDIUM.

Graphite. Mineral also known as Black Lead and Plumbago. Although widely distributed, the only workable mine in the Republic is in the Zoutpansberg. There is another small mine near Bethanie in South West Africa.

Grasfontein. Farm near Lichtenburg, Transvaal. Scene of great Diamond Rush, 1925. Population: 1,026, including 47 Whites.

Graskop. Township in the Eastern Transvaal, picturesquely located in the Drakensberg. Originally a gold mining camp, now mainly engaged in timber growing. Noted as being the best place to see 'The Edge of the Low Veld,' with a 2,000 feet sudden drop. Established in 1880's. Population: 2,133, including 401 Whites.

Grass, Bradley (*Cynodon bradleyi*). One of the most popular lawn grasses on the Witwatersrand. A drought-resistant perennial, increasing by means, not of seed, but of surface stems. Named after William Bradley, a Rand pioneer, who first found and cultivated it soon after the Boer War.

Grass, Rhodes (*Chloris gayana*). Originally imported from India in the Queenstown district by French Moravian missionaries about the middle of the 19th century. Cultivated by Cecil John Rhodes (q.v.) at Groote Schuur and later identified as the Indian *Chloris compressa*. Seeds profusely and is a valuable perennial grass for hay and summer pasturage wherever there is sufficient rain. It has been unsuccessful in Rhodesia and in other areas of high altitude.

Grass Ridge Dam. Large irrigation works on Great Fish River in Eastern Cape Province. Built in 1921 to supplement supplies from Lake Arthur (q.v.). Dam wall of 1,530 feet is of earth, with a concrete core, and rises to a height of 80 feet (96 feet above foundations). Suffered from silting and is being superseded by the Commandodrift Dam.

Grass Snakes. *See* SKAAPSTEKERS.

Grasses. Much of the South African veld is not, strictly speaking, grassland at all, but open, bushy country where tufty (not mat) grass grows sparsely. In the Karroo these tufts are chiefly annuals. Permanent short stubby grass grows more plentifully on the Highveld, green in summer and brown in winter. The scrub and bush of the Lowveld are surrounded by thick, long grass. The comparatively fertile Western Cape is today an area of mixed farming, where grassland plays a small part. Van Riebeeck found the Table Mountain slopes green with grass and the Hottentots moving their sheep and cattle seasonally from place to place. During the 18th century the settlers, pressing eastwards with their own increasing stock, entered still richer pasturage. The Orange Free State, into which the Voortrekkers penetrated about 1836, was covered with luxuriant grass. The native practice of spring burning—of negligible harm among migratory tribes—killed the primary grass, *Themeda triandra*

(Rooigras), which the Voortrekkers early learnt to be the best grazing of all, and which was dominant at that time over most of the grassland in smooth, close tufts. Permanent settlement, ploughing, fires and continuous grazing produced secondary and less nutritious grasses, annuals and perennials, of the Aristida, Eragrostis and Sporobolus types. Side by side with this change has come the disastrous change in soil erosion (q.v.). The vegetation maps prepared by the Union Botanical Survey Advisory Committee in the last few years have shown clearly indifferent grassland expanding at the expense of forest, thorn scrub invading grassland and, most serious of all, the eastward spread of Karroo flora. Today bush and savannah occupy 33 per cent of South Africa, grassland 25 per cent and desert scrub 35 per cent—the last an encroachment of mainly Rhenoster-Bush (q.v.) and Macchia (Fynbos) of perhaps 13 per cent during three centuries.

Interest in South African flora by individual botanists goes back to the superintendents of the East India Company's garden. The 18th century produced great collectors, such as William Burchell, C. F. Ecklon and K. L. Zeyher (qq.v.). But the scientific study of grass did not begin until 1858, when Dr. Ludwig Pappe (q.v.) was appointed to the new post of Colonial Botanist. He and his successor, the Rev. John Croumbie Brown, first drew attention to the serious effects of veld burning on the water resources of the Karroo. The post of Colonial Botanist was abolished in 1866, and not until the last decade of the century do we hear of experiments in burning and resting veld by Dr. Selmar Schönland (q.v.) of Rhodes University College, and of the work of such botanists as Dr. J. M. Wood and the great Dr. R. Marloth (qq.v.). Dr. E. E. Galpin was a fascinated collector, who gave his name to a grass genus. To

Cecil John Rhodes (q.v.) we owe the popularity of the Rhodes Grass (*see* GRASS, RHODES) and the interest aroused among experimental farmers. One of these was Sir Percy Fitzpatrick (q.v.), who tried out many tons of imported seed to find a winter pasture grass. Pasculum and New Zealand Tail Fescue (Tussock Grass) were both popularised by him. In 1905 Dr. I. B. Pole-Evans, appointed to the Transvaal Agricultural Department, began studying the rôle of indigenous grasses in the national economy. His intensive research resulted in the formation in 1918 of the Botanical Survey Advisory Committee. In 1910 Dr. J. W. Bews (q.v.) was given the Chair of Botany at the Natal University College. The keen experiments of General J. C. Smuts at his farm near Irene must also be mentioned. One of the Finger Grasses (*Digitaria*) is called after him and he wrote the introduction to the great compendium *The Grasses and Pastures of South Africa*, which came out in 1955, after his death. Owing to the differences in temperature, rainfall and altitude in South Africa, research in fodder grasses, turf and soil binders yields a wide variety of results.

Gravelotte. Village in the North-Eastern Transvaal. Established 1916. Mining centre. Named after a farm belonging to the Rev. Winter, a German missionary, who had fought as a Prussian officer in the battle of Gravelotte in the war against France in 1870–71.

Gray, Bishop Robert. First Anglican Bishop of Cape Town. Born near Sunderland, England, in 1809, studied at Oxford and was ordained at Wells in 1834. After holding various livings, including that of Stockton, was appointed Bishop of the newly-created diocese of Cape Town, which previously fell under the jurisdiction of Calcutta. He built up the Church of England in South Africa, also founding many ecclesiastical institutions, including the Diocesan College (Bishops) (q.v.) at Cape Town. In 1853 Gray was appointed Metropolitan of South Africa. Coming into conflict in doctrinal matters with Bishop J. W. Colenso of Natal (q.v.), his authority as such was challenged. In a series of court cases, ranging up to the Privy Council, it was finally laid down that the Anglican Church was not 'by law established' outside England. The result was the founding of the Church of the Province of South Africa. Established five new South African dioceses, and largely on his suggestion, the Universities Mission to Central Africa was launched. Bishop Gray died in 1872.

Grease Tables. Device used on South African diamond mines, based on the fact that diamonds will adhere to grease, remaining blue ground being washed away by water. The apparatus was built by George Labram (q.v.) and F. B. Kirsten at Kimberley and patented in 1897. De Beers Consolidated Mines used it under royalty, but ultimately bought it outright, as also the Labram automatic sorter.

Greasy Slip. Mineral found in diamond pipes, in conjunction with Blue Ground (q.v.). Geologically described as a crystalline carbonate of lime. Name acquired on account of its soapy feel.

Great Brak River. Village near Mossel Bay, at the mouth of the Brak River, headquarters of large leather and shoe manufacturing works, controlled by Searles Limited. Enterprise was started in the 1860's by Charles Searle, who occupied the toll house at Great Brak River. Almost the entire community is employed and housed by the firm, which has traditionally enforced a policy of total prohibition of liquor. Population: 2,340, including 666 Whites.

Great Fish River. In Eastern Cape Province. Famous in Cape history as marking the frontier between colonists and Xosa tribes. Rises in Sneeuberg and flows for 300 miles, reaching the Indian Ocean north of Port Alfred. Tributaries include Tarka River, Little Fish River, Brak River, Doorn River, Koonap River and Kat River. Cradock, Somerset East and Fort Beaufort are on the Fish River or its tributaries. The Fish River Bush is noted for its wild life.

Greathead, James Henry. South African engineer, inventor of Greathead Shield, used throughout the world in tunnelling through soft ground. Born in 1844 at Grahamstown, son of an 1820 settler. Educated at St. Andrew's College in that city and in England, articled to a London engineer and thereafter lived in Britain. The Greathead Shield was the result of work with Peter Barlow, F.R.S., in building the Tower Subway in 1868. Greathead was entrusted with the construction of the first London Tube railway in 1890. He died in 1896.

Great Riet River. Tributary of Sundays River (q.v.).

Great Trek. Mass emigration of colonists, mostly of Dutch origin, from the Cape of Good Hope in the 1830's. Isolated treks had been in progress almost since the beginning of European settlement in South Africa. Causes of the Great Trek were manifold, including the lack of understanding by the British Colonial Office and their representatives of the problems of the Frontier farmers, the inadequate compensation received for slaves liberated under the Emancipation Law, the return to the neighbouring tribes of the 'Province of Queen Adelaide,' which had been set up as a buffer territory, also an inborn dislike of tax-paying and centralised administration by many of the earlier colonists. Generally speaking, British settlers sympathised with the protests of the Voortrekkers, as was indicated in Grahamstown when a Bible was presented to Pieter Retief. Among the first organised parties to leave the Cape was that of Louis Trichardt, who in 1835 led Boers, mostly from the Albany district, across the Frontier to the north. Were joined by a party of about the same size, under Jan van Rensburg, making 30 wagons. Reached the Zoutpansberg area, the present Northern Transvaal. Van Rensburg's party went east, and disappeared. In 1867, a white man and a woman were found living among the local Bantu, and were believed to be the only survivors, captured as children, from the group. Trichardt's party, after many hardships, reached Lourenço Marques, where they were decimated by fever, the survivors being brought to Natal by ship. Meanwhile further groups had left the Cape Colony, despite the warnings of the Dutch Reformed clergy and of the Government officials. Among their chief leaders was Andries Hendrik Potgieter, whose followers reached present-day Potchefstroom. Other groups settled in what is now the Orange Free State, where they came into conflict with Moselekatze (q.v.) and established the town of Winburg. The most important groups were under Pieter Retief and Gerrit Maritz. Retief reached Thaba N'chu in 1837, and was elected Commandant-General of 1,000 emigrants in April. In October 1837, Retief and an advance party crossed the Drakensberg and entered Natal, where they signed a treaty with the Zulu chief, Dingaan (q.v.) This resulted in murder of the party at his kraal, and an attempt to kill the survivors at Blaauwkrans. On December 16, 1838, the Voortrekkers were vindicated in the Battle of Blood River, where Andries Pretorius with 460 Boers defeated 10,000 Zulus, of whom 3,000 were killed. The Great Trek had virtually ended, but the British authorities still regarded the Trekkers as under their jurisdiction, which was extended by proclamation to the empty lands of the north. Despite the establishment of the Republic of Natalia by the Boers, a force under Captain J. C. Smith was despatched from the Cape to Port Natal, where they were besieged. British authority was asserted, resulting in further treks from Natal into the Transvaal or back into the Orange Free State. In 1843 the Republic of Natalia finally submitted to the authority of Queen Victoria. The establishment of independent republics in the Orange Free State and the Transvaal, coupled with the setting up of the British Colony of Natal, marked the end of the Great Trek.

Grebe (family Podicipidae). Protected fresh water bird found throughout South Africa, and much like the European species. The legs are placed so far back as nearly to prevent its walking. Webbed toes but not closely joined. Excellent underwater swimmer and diver for crabs and fish. Can fly heavily. Plumage very silky. The Great Crested Grebe has a fine ruff and double crest, but is less known than the little Cape Dabchick, which moves in large flocks and is a dark little bird, with chestnut on cheeks and neck in breeding season. Its breeding call sounds like a rippling laugh. *See* BIRDS.

Green, Frederick. Early hunter and traveller. Left Grahamstown about 1852, and penetrated into modern Rhodesia. Lived permanently 125 miles from the Victoria Falls and made numerous trips to Lake Ngami, Walvis Bay and other remote points. He worked in close collaboration with Charles John Andersson.

Green, Lawrence George. South African author. Born at Kimberley in 1900, he was educated at the South African College, Cape Town. He served in World War I in the R.A.F. and in the S.A.A.F. in the Middle East in World War II. He worked as a journalist in Fleet Street and for many years on the *Cape Argus*. He gained a remarkable knowledge of the less familiar aspects of Africa which he embodied in over 30 books on travel,

history and reminiscence, total sales of which exceed 450,000. Among the best known are *Grow Lovely, Growing Old*; *Tavern of the Seas* (over 50,000 sold); *Lords of the Last Frontier*; and *To the River's End*.

Greendale. Township 6 miles east of Salisbury, mainly residential, established in 1950. The population is 3,400 Europeans and 3,800 Africans. There are a number of factories.

Greene, Sir Conyngham. English diplomat, born in Ireland in 1854. From 1896 to 1899, during the critical period when relations between Britain and the South African Republic deteriorated, Conyngham Greene was Her Majesty's Agent at Pretoria, with the rank of Chargé d'Affaires. He died on June 30, 1934.

Greene, Colonel Edward Mackenzie. Natal soldier and Cabinet Minister. Born at Pietermaritzburg in 1857, educated at Lancing, England. Fought in the Zulu War and commanded Natal Carbineers in South African War. Elected to the Natal Parliament, was Minister of Railways and Harbours, and Colonial Treasurer in the ministry of Sir F. Moor (q.v.). At the National Convention he was a delegate from Natal, and after Union a member of the Railway Board. He died in 1931.

Greenshank (*Tringa nebularia*). Large, migrant wading bird, generally distributed on every kind of fresh and brackish water in South Africa. Olive-grey, with grey-green legs and long bill, slightly upturned. Usually seen among smaller waders. *See* WADER and RUFF.

Gregorowski, Reinhold. Judge of Transvaal. Born at Somerset East on April 12, 1856, he was educated at Gill College and the University of the Cape of Good Hope, where he was awarded the Porter Scholarship to enter Gray's Inn. Having won a studentship, he was called to the Bar in 1878 and returned to the Cape in the same year to commence practice. In 1881, at the age of only 25 years, he became a judge in the Orange Free State and in 1892 State Attorney. He continued to practise in Bloemfontein until he became a judge of the Transvaal High Court in May 1896, his most famous trial being that of the Jameson Raiders. A year later, however, he resigned to become State Attorney of the Transvaal, and soon afterwards Chief Justice. In 1902 he set up a practice in Pretoria, and in 1913 was appointed to the Transvaal Bench. He died in Pretoria on November 19, 1922.

Grey College, Bloemfontein. Founded in 1855 for boys; named after Governor Sir George Grey, who took a great interest in the progress of education in the O.F.S. Republic, contributing several thousand pounds to its funds. Many leading Free Staters, including President M. T. Steyn, were pupils of Grey College. Its degree classes have been merged in the University of the Orange Free State.

Grey, Sir George. Governor of Cape Colony. Born in 1812 in Lisbon, son of Colonel Grey, killed at Badajos in the Peninsular War. From 1841 to 1845 was Governor of South Australia, and from 1845 held a similar office in New Zealand, greatly helping the progress of that colony. Grey's next post was at the Cape, where he arrived in 1854. Was liked by English, Boer and Native, and had the reputation of being the best governor of all time. He travelled through the Cape Colony, the Orange Free State and Natal, making peaceful settlements with Moshesh and with Adam Kok. Encouraged the commencement of the first railway at the Cape, gave large sums towards the founding of Grey College at Bloemfontein, erected hospitals for the Natives to combat the influence of witch-doctors, and presented his library to the people of Cape Colony. He was recalled in 1859 for having encouraged a scheme for the unification of the whole of South Africa without authority. Was restored to office, and then sent to New Zealand in 1861. He entered the New Zealand Parliament, and from 1877 to 1879 was Prime Minister. In 1894 he returned to England and he died there in 1898, being buried in St. Paul's Cathedral, London.

Grey High School (originally Grey Institute). Established at Port Elizabeth in 1856, named after Sir George Grey, Governor of the Cape, who took a personal interest in it. The first headmaster was J. R. Macleish, who was succeeded by a number of other able men, notably the poet W. A. Way (q.v.).

Greylingstad. Township in the Transvaal. Established in 1910 and named after the founder, a farmer named Greyling. In 1913, another township was established, 3 miles off near the railway, and named Willemsdal, after the owner of the site, Willem Bezuidenhout. Greylingstad was deproclaimed, and the name transferred to Willemsdal. Much gold mining development has taken place near by. Population: 1,342, including 313 Whites.

Grey Shirts. Anti-Semitic and anti-foreign Fascist organisation started in South Africa by Louis T. Weichardt about 1933. After several of its leaders had been convicted by the Supreme Court in Grahamstown, it gradually lapsed into obscurity.

Greyton. Village near Caledon named after Governor Sir George Grey (q.v.). Prosperous area, engaged in vegetable and fruit growing. Population: 1,000, including 500 Whites.

Greytown. Town in Natal, founded in 1854, on the Umvoti River and named after Governor Sir George Grey of the Cape. Centre of wattle-growing industry. During the Bambata Rebellion of 1906 Greytown was a main centre of military operations, and later the scene of the trial of the Zulu chief, Dinizulu. Population: 9,800, including 2,200 Whites.

Griffith. Paramount Chief of the Basutos. Son of Lerotholi, called after the famous Colonel C. D. Griffith, Governor's Agent for many years in Basutoland. Succeeded Letsie the Second in 1913. In contrast to his early restiveness, he was strongly loyal during World War I. He died in 1939.

Griffith, Bishop Patrick Raymund. First Catholic bishop in South Africa Born in Ireland in 1798, studied in Lisbon and Rome, became a well-known preacher and Prior of Dublin. In 1837 he was appointed the first Vicar Apostolic of the Cape of Good Hope by Pope Gregory XVI. He arrived in Cape Town in 1838, and during the next 25 years raised the number of Catholics at the Cape from 700 to over 30,000. He died in 1862.

Grimley, Bishop Thomas. Early Catholic Bishop of Cape Town. He arrived from Ireland in 1861. Introduced the Marist Brothers and their schools to the Cape and built St. Mary's Cathedral. He died in 1871.

Grimm, Hans. German writer on South African and South-West African subjects. Born in Wiesbaden March 22, 1875, was in business in East London as a young man, but later returned to Germany. There his short stories on the former German colonies, and his novel *Volk ohne Raum* (1925), embodying expansionist tendencies sympathetic to the Nazis, sold in millions. He died in 1959.

Griqualand East (formerly known as **No-Man's-Land**). District in the Eastern Cape Province. Settled in 1862 by about 2,000 emigrant Griquas under Adam Kok III. They came from Griquatown (q.v.), lived at Philippolis in the Orange Free State (q.v.) and trekked through Basutoland, bringing

most of their 20,000 head of stock and 300 wagons to this empty but fertile highland area. With headquarters at Kokstad (q.v.), the Griquas were semi-independent, issuing paper money (now very rare) in 1868, and also currency, but pressure from the nearby Native tribes and from the approaching White men was too strong. In 1878 Griqualand East became part of the Cape, being placed under magistrates, who restored order. A rebellion occurred in 1880, but since then the country has flourished and is today one of the Republic's most important dairy and cattle areas.

Griqualand West. Area north of the Orange River, extending into Southern Bechuanaland. Settled by Griqua tribes (q.v.) towards the end of the 18th and the beginning of the 19th centuries, principal settlement being Klaarwater, later renamed Griquatown (q.v.). Territory embraced present-day Kimberley. At the close of the 1860's, diamonds were discovered, and the sovereignty over the area became politically important. Three claims were made to Griqualand West —by the Orange Free State, the South African Republic and the Griqua chief Waterboer, who had succeeded Adam Kok (q.v.) when the latter emigrated to Griqualand East (q.v.). The Keate Award (q.v.) decided that Griqualand West was under Nicholas Waterboer. Fact disputed by diamond diggers, along the Vaal River, who in 1870 set up a Republic of Griqualand West, annexed to the British Empire in October, 1871. A separate British Colony was established in July 1873, annexed to Cape Colony by act of Parliament in 1877. The final merger completed in 1880. Today the High Court of Griqualand West at Kimberley and the local Deeds Office are reminders of its erstwhile independence.

Griquas. Race of mixed origin, European and Hottentot. Migrated early 19th century to northern frontier of the Cape near the Orange River. Under the Rev. J. Campbell and other missionaries their settlement Klaarwater became Griquatown. Name derived from a Hottentot tribe settled near Saldanha Bay, known in 17th century as Grigriquas. Later they threw off missionary influence and established their independence under the successive leadership of Adam Kok (q.v.), his son Cornelius and grandson Adam Kok the Second. Most of the tribe later emigrated into the present Orange Free State, near Philippolis. In 1862 they trekked once more, suffering fearful hardships, crossing the Drakensberg and Basutoland. In No-Man's-Land, the present Griqualand East, they set up a capital at Kokstad. Despite having a Volksraad, they failed to establish an efficient community and became involved in Native wars. Griqualand East came under British authority in 1878 and was divided up into magistracies. Europeans have settled, but the Griquas retain certain rights and still have an annual meeting. Unlike other local races, their language is Afrikaans, enriched by a number of expressions peculiar to themselves.

Griquatown. Town in Griqualand West, founded as a mission station in 1802 by the London Mission Society. Called Klaarwater (Clear Water) on account of the spring discovered by the Rev. Kramer and the Rev. Anderson. Rev. John Campbell renamed it Griquatown in 1813. Became capital of the tribe under Adam Kok the First (q.v.), who emigrated with his followers in 1820, and was replaced by Nicholas Waterboer, who lived there when diamonds were found and who was buried there. Population: 2,000, including 800 Whites.

Grobler, Senator Esias Reinier. Boer leader and Administrator of the Orange Free State. Born 1861. Member of O.F.S. Volksraad from 1886 till the end of the Republic. During the

South African War, commanded troops on the Cape border, and opposed General Gatacre in the Battle of Stormberg. Was interested in farming, became President of the Legislative Council of the Orange Free State under the Crown Colony régime from 1907 to 1910, and, after Union, became a Senator. From 1924 to 1929, Grobler was Administrator of the Orange Free State. He died in 1937.

Grobler, Piet Gert Wessels. Cabinet Minister. Born in 1873 near Rustenburg, Transvaal, in the house of his uncle, President Kruger; educated at the Pretoria Gymnasium. Became Under-Secretary for Foreign Affairs, and accompanied President Kruger into exile, as his secretary. Returning to South Africa after the South African War, became a supporter of General Louis Botha, who made him chairman of the Land Bank in the Transvaal. In 1910 was elected M.P. for Rustenburg, and when Hertzog split with Botha he supported the latter. He became Minister of Lands in the first Nationalist Cabinet in 1924 and from 1933 to 1938 was Minister of Native Affairs. He died in 1942.

Groblersdal. Village in the Transvaal, centre of the irrigation area served by the Loskop Dam (q.v.). Population: 4,000, including 1,850 Whites.

Grocott's Daily Mail. Grahamstown daily newspaper, established in January 1872 as *Grocott's Penny Mail.*

Grootfontein: 1. Agricultural College near Middelburg, Cape Province. Farm where a military cantonment was set up during the South African War. Handed over by the War Office to the Union Government in 1911, and became an agricultural college. Internationally known for wool research and the training of wool farmers, technicians, etc.
2. Village in South ｜West Africa, founded by Boer emigrants in 1885 as capital of the Republic of

Upingtonia. Under German regimé became the headquarters of the South West Africa Company Ltd., a British ranching concern. Now an important cattle centre, with base metal (vanadium and other) workings in the vicinity. Population: 4,825, including 2,150 Whites.

Grootfontein Meteorite. One of the largest meteorites known, found on the farm Hoba West near Grootfontein, South-West Africa, first scientifically examined by the American astronomer Dr. W. J. Luyten in 1929. The mass of nickel-iron is estimated to weigh about 60 tons.

Groot Marico. Village near Marico, Western Transvaal. Population: 780, including 160 Whites.

Grosvenor. English East Indiaman wrecked on August 4, 1782, on the coast of Pondoland, on a return voyage from the East. Most of the ship's company and passengers, including a number of English aristocrats, gained the shore, and began a march to the Cape. Out of 150 only nine reached civilisation. Relief expeditions saved four more, but the others died. Certain lighter-coloured natives in the Transkei are supposed to be descended from white women taken as wives by natives. The *Grosvenor* carried cargo estimated at about £1,500,000, including gold, precious stones, etc., some of the coins being washed ashore. Efforts made to recover the treasure by diving and tunnelling from below, notably in 1906 and 1920. More recent attempts have been made, but doubts have been cast on the correctness of the site selected.

Grosvenor Beads. Red beads, carved from carnelian, occasionally washed ashore on the coast of Pondoland and traditionally associated by settlers with the treasure of the *Grosvenor* (q.v.). Beads are, however, of far earlier manufacture, probably of Eastern origin. Varying from about half an inch to 2 inches in diameter, they are crudely drilled for threading.

Groundnuts. South African name for peanuts.

Group Areas. System of land distribution in South Africa based on the principle of Apartheid (q.v.), first introduced under Act No. 41 of 1950. This Act was repeatedly altered and was re-enacted as the Group Areas Act of 1957. Varying provisions have been made for the different provinces. The Act is administered under the Group Areas Board of 12 members from its head office in Pretoria. Regional offices are in Cape Town, Port Elizabeth and Pietermaritzburg. From time to time various areas, mostly urban, are proclaimed and reserved for members of particular groups—white, Coloured, Asiatic or Bantu. Provision is made for gradual change-over and for the payment of compensation, also for the prevention of speculation.

Groutville. Mission station on the Natal North Coast, founded by and named after the Reverend Aldin Grout of the American Board of Mission in 1836.

Growth Funds. *See* UNIT TRUSTS.

Grünau. Small village in south of South West Africa.

Grunberg, Leon. French engineer, sent out in 1895 by the firm of Schneider of Le Creusot to introduce improved ordnance to the Staatsartillerie (q.v.) of the Transvaal. With his companion, Leon, he greatly increased efficiency and, upon the outbreak of the South African War, supervised the manufacture of munitions in Begbie's Foundry, Johannesburg, and in the Railway Workshops, Pretoria.

Grunter, Spotted Steenbras, Tiger (*Pomadasys operculare*). Edible fish found off Agulhas Bank to Natal, East Africa and Indian Seas. About 15 inches long. The name Grunter comes from the noise it makes and 'Tiger' from its resemblance to the South African spotted leopard, miscalled 'tiger' by the early settlers. *See* CHOR-CHOR and BLACK-AND-WHITE.

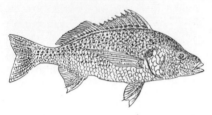

Grunter

Grysbok (*Nototragus melanotis*). Small shy antelope common in Southern Africa, the name meaning 'grey buck' in Afrikaans. A hardy animal which can last a long time without water. Grysbok average about 1 foot 8 inches at the shoulder. *See* MAMMALS.

Guano Islands. Group of small islands scattered along the West Coast of the Republic and the coast of South-West Africa. The existence of vast deposits of guano led to the exploitation of these islands in the 1830's and 1840's, but no attempt was made to bring them under control till 1866, when they were annexed to Cape Colony. They now come under a special Superintendent, attached to the Department of Agriculture, who regulates the exploitation of the deposits. The average recovery is about 5,000 tons a year. The best-known Guano Islands are Plumpudding, Ichaboe, Roastbeef, Halifax, Possession, etc. They have no permanent population.

Guardians' Fund. Funds deposited with the Public Debt Commissioners, administered by the Masters of the Supreme Court in South Africa (q.v.) and containing unclaimed money. At prescribed intervals of several years the unclaimed moneys are advertised in the *Government Gazette*, and after 50 years such funds revert to the Government. In addition the Guardians' Fund contains certain moneys belonging to minors or those otherwise under tutelage.

Guarrieko (*Fockea crispa*). Extremely rare plant found at the Cape in the 18th century, when specimens were brought to Europe. One of these, planted in the gardens of the Imperial Austrian palace of Schönbrunn in 1798, is still flourishing. Believed to be entirely extinct in South Africa itself, it was rediscovered by Dr. R. Marloth near Barrydale and Willowmore in 1906.

Gubbins, John Gaspard. South African book collector and antiquarian. Born in England in 1877, he came to South Africa as a young man and accumulated a fortune by successful mining of base metals near Ottoshoop, in the Eastern Transvaal. Collected Africana, which he housed at his homestead, until the establishment of the University of the Witwatersrand, when he decided to give it his collection. In addition a large number of antiquarian treasures were handed over to the Johannesburg Public Library, for which a special Africana Museum was established. Gubbins died in 1935.

Guineafowl (family Phasianidae). Common game bird found in thick bush, from Eastern Cape Province northwards. The nearly-bare neck and plump, speckled body are well known. A wary bird, running in flocks and flying well. Scratches for its food of grubs, roots and insects, in bush country. The Crested Guinea Fowl is a tropical dweller of Natal and Kruger Park. *See* FRANCOLIN.

Gulls and **Skuas** (Laridae). Sea birds related to the Waders and found on the coasts of South Africa, never flying far out. They are scavengers and pirates, not fishers, except of shell fish, which they will carry to a height and drop on the rocks. The Black-backed Gull is the most common. *See* TERN and BIRDS.

Gum, Flowering. One of many Eucalyptus trees imported from Australia; most successfully grown in south-western Cape. The many shades of pink and red flowers are a glory in summer.

Gungunhana. Paramount Chief of Gazaland, Mozambique, in the second half of the 19th century, hostile to the Portuguese authorities at Lourenço Marques and elsewhere. Towards the end of September 1894, a military force was sent against him, under Colonel Mousinho d'Albuquerque. Gungunhana was defeated and exiled to Angola, where he died in 1907.

Gungunhlovu. Principal kraal of the Zulu king, Dingaan (q.v.), built to commemorate his murder of Tshaka (q.v.). Name signifies 'The Kraal of the Elephant.'

Gun War. Name given to the campaign resulting from the rising of the Basuto tribe. They refused to surrender guns to the Cape Government, under whose jurisdiction they had been since 1868. Hostilities began in December 1879, continuing for several years. Repeated efforts at a settlement failed, and the Colony spent over £3,000,000 on the campaign. In 1883 the Cape handed Basutoland to the Imperial Government.

Gurnard. Well-known shallow and deep-water fish of both temperate and warm seas, somewhat under 12 inches long. All varieties characterised by mailed head and pectorals, with finger-like rays that support the fish as it 'walks' over the bottom, and help it search out crabs and other prey. A projecting bony snout also ploughs through the sand.

Guti. Cloudy to overcast weather occurring throughout the year, with drizzle and moderate to fresh south-westerly winds, associated with the invasion of maritime air into Rhodesia. Can occur intermittently throughout the year. *See also* CHIPERONE.

Gwaai Forest. *See* TEAK.

Gwanda. Township in Rhodesia, between Bulawayo and Beit Bridge. Mining and ranching centre, founded in the 1890's. Name from Majahunda tribe. Near spot where Cecil Rhodes had his famous indaba with the rebellious Matabele chiefs in 1896.

Gwebi. Agricultural college in Rhodesia, near Salisbury.

Gwelo. Town in Rhodesia, centre of the Midlands area. Founded in 1894; used as a camp for settlers and their families during the Matabele Rebellion of 1896. Originally dependent on gold mining; now an important manufacturing town, where the Czech firm, Bata, produces footwear. Name derived from the Gweilo River near by, connected with the native word Kwela, to climb. Population: 43,150, including 9,500 Whites.

Gymnasium. Educational institution, used in two senses in South Africa (apart from its conventional meaning as a place for physical training): (*a*) boys' high school established at Pretoria and Paarl at the end of the 19th century on the Dutch model; (*b*) military college established at Pretoria (Voortrekkerhoogte) in 1949. Its naval counterpart at Saldanha Bay dates from 1951, as does the Air Force Gymnasium at Lyttelton near Pretoria.

HAAK-EN-STEEK

Haak-en-Steek. *See* ACACIA.

Haarlem. Village near Uniondale, Cape Province. Population: 820, including 100 Whites.

Haartebeestpoort. Large irrigation scheme west of Pretoria. Gap in the mountains and the Crocodile River, dammed up by a concrete wall 460 feet long, 161 feet high above the river bed and 193 feet above the foundations. Work began in August 1916 and was completed about 1921. When full the dam covers 6½ sq. miles and can irrigate 40,000 acres. The townships of Schoemanville and Kosmos have been laid out on its shores and yachting is a popular sport.

Hackius, Pieter. Early Dutch Commander of Cape of Good Hope. Ruined his health through long service in the Indies for the Dutch East India Company, when chosen to replace Jakob Borghorst (q.v.), who was recalled as an invalid. Efforts were made to stimulate immigration from Holland during his régime. Died at the Cape on November 30, 1671, and was buried in the newly-built Castle.

Hadada (*Hagedashia hagedash*) or Green Ibis. *See* IBIS.

Haden, Francis Seymour. Natal official. Born in England in 1850, he came to South Africa in 1876 as Assistant Private Secretary to Governor Sir Henry Bulwer of Natal. There he rose to be Chief Clerk in the Colonial Secretary's office at Pietermaritzburg and in 1885 to Colonial Secretary. Several times Seymour Haden acted as Deputy Governor of Natal and Zululand, as well as President of the Natal Trade Commission. He was frequently used in negotiations with the South

HAGGARD

African Republic and the Cape in matters of commerce. When Natal received Responsible Government in 1893 he retired to England. Died 1918.

Haemanthus. *See* AMARYLLIS.

Haenertsburg. Village in the Northern Transvaal, centre of the former Woodbush Gold Fields, and named in 1894 after the discoverer, C. F. Haenert. Near Magoeba's Kloof. Population: 250, including 170 Whites.

Haga-Haga. Seaside resort near Komgha, Eastern Province. Population: 210, including 140 Whites.

Haggard, Sir Henry Rider. Novelist. Born in Norfolk, 1856. Secretary to Governor Sir Henry Bulwer of Natal, 1875. He joined the staff of Sir Theophilus Shepstone (q.v.) when the latter occupied the Transvaal, and helped General Brooke to hoist the British flag in Pretoria, on the Queen's Birthday, 1877. In the Government Service, was Secretary to the 'Sekukuni Commission,' appointed to settle the disputes with this chief, and then Master of the Supreme Court, in 1878. While in the Transvaal, he gained experience which was to be of unique value to him in writing his books. In 1882 came his first work, *Cetewayo and his White Neighbours*, dealing with the problems arising from the Zulu War. Then followed his first novels, *Dawn*, in 1884, *The Witch's Head* and *King Solomon's Mines* in 1885. Three of his best works appeared in 1887—*She, Jess* and the immortal *Allan Quartermain*, whose adventures were based on those of F. C. Selous (q.v.). By this time Rider Haggard was world famous and was pouring out a stream of books, mostly South African historical romances. He became interested in agriculture, and in land settlement. During 1916 he revisited South Africa on behalf of the resettlement scheme for ex-service-men. He died on May 14, 1925.

Hake. *See* STOCKFISH.

Half-Aum. Old Cape measure of capacity, equal to about 16 gallons.

Halfmense (Half Men, *Adenium namaquanum*). Namaqualand plant, 6–8 feet high, topped by a crown of leaves giving it a strange resemblance to a human being at a distance. *See* PLANTS.

Hall, Dr. Elsie. South African pianist. Born in Australia in 1880, she showed musical gifts at the age of four, and at ten years old attracted the notice, while in London, of Bernard Shaw, then a leading musical critic. He mentioned her in one of his books and fore-told a great future for her. During her studies in Germany she was allowed to play before Johannes Brahms and received further encouragement. In her very long and successful career as a concert pianist she received honours all over the world, including both Europe and the United States. Amongst her other distinctions was that of teaching music to members of the British Royal

Halfmense

Family, including Princess Mary (later the Princess Royal). Married to Dr. Stohr, she lived for some time in Zambia, but ultimately settled at the Cape.

Hamanskraal. Village north of Pre-toria, named after a former Native Commissioner, Mr. Haman, of the nearby reserve. Salt-producing centre.

Hamardale. Industrial township, be-tween Pietermaritzburg and Durban, founded in 1960, with the backing of the Industrial Development Corpora-tion (q.v.), as part of the Border Industries policy (q.v.). Contains a substantial number of factories.

Hamburg. Village founded by German settlers, near Peddie, Cape Province. Population: 1,100, including 150 Whites.

Hamel. South African name for a wether or castrated ram.

Hamelberg, Hendrik Antonie Lodewijk. Diplomat and official in Orange Free State Republic. Born in Zalt-Bommel on May 2, 1826, quali-fied as an advocate and in 1855 emi-grated to South Africa, where he found his way to the newly-founded Orange Free State Republic. There he played a leading rôle in guiding the country's relations with the Cape, the Basutos and the Transvaal. He returned to Holland in 1871 and became O.F.S. consul. Hamelberg kept an interesting diary (published by the Van Riebeeck Society in 1952) and made sundry contributions to the press in South Africa and in the Netherlands, be-sides writing the words of the Orange Free State 'Volkslied' (q.v.) adopted officially in 1866. He died in 1896.

Hamerkop (*Scopus umbretta*). Bird allied to the Herons (q.v.), but dif-ferent in appearance. Its plumage is brownish, the bill deep, flattened side-ways, ridged and hooked at the tip. The name is derived from the crest projecting backward from its small head. Common wherever there are frogs to be caught. Its gigantic tree-nest is made of sticks and grass bound with mud, and has a side entrance. *See* BIRDS.

Hamilton. Former name of Trompsburg, O.F.S. (q.v.).

Hamilton, Sir Frederick. South African journalist. Born in London in 1865, he came to South Africa in 1889 and first edited the *Zoutpansberg Review* at Pietersburg, becoming editor of the *Star* in Johannesburg in 1894. During the Jameson Raid period he was a member of the Reform Committee, for which he was found guilty and fined £2,000. He returned to England in 1896, where he edited the *African Review*. In 1899 he retired and concentrated on finance. Died 1940.

Hamilton, General Sir Ian Standish Monteith. British soldier. Born in 1853 in Corfu, his first active service was in Afghanistan in 1878, followed in 1880 by the Majuba campaign. After lengthy duty in the East he returned in 1899 to South Africa, where he fought at Elandslaagte, Wagon Hill near Ladysmith, Diamond Hill, etc. and was promoted Major-General. Becoming Chief of Staff to Lord Kitchener, he led mobile columns in the Western Transvaal, one of which occupied Johannesburg. Hamilton wrote a number of books, containing South African memories, and died at the age of 94 in 1947.

Hamilton, Lieutenant - Colonel James Stevenson. *See* STEVENSON-HAMILTON, LIEUTENANT-COLONEL JAMES.

Hamiltons. Oldest Rugby Football Club in South Africa. Founded in Cape Town in 1875, and named after a club in Scotland. Most of the original members lived in Sea Point; the first captain was W. Y. Philip. It is still flourishing.

Hammarskjöld, Dag Hjalmar Agne Carl. Secretary-General of the United Nations. Born in 1905, and educated at the universities of Uppsala and Stockholm. Assistant Professor at University of Stockholm in 1933, Under-Secretary for Finance in 1936 and Chairman of the Bank of Sweden in 1941. After holding posts as Financial Adviser and Cabinet Minister in Sweden, became delegate to U.N. General Assembly in 1949 and Secretary-General in 1953. Visited South Africa January 6–12, 1961, and while on a mediatory mission in the Congo was killed in an air crash in Zambia on the night of September 17, 1961.

Hammond, John Hays. Mining engineer. Born in San Francisco on March 31, 1855; educated at Yale University and at Freiberg in Germany. In 1893 he was retained by Barnato Brothers (q.v.) to report on certain of their properties; then joined the service of Cecil John Rhodes, and was appointed Consulting Engineer of the Consolidated Gold Fields of South Africa (q.v.). Settling on the Rand, Hammond was one of the four main leaders on the Reform Committee, and was arrested and tried after the failure of the Jameson Raid. He was sentenced to death, but later released against payment of a fine of £25,000. Hammond represented President Taft at the coronation of George V in 1911. Died 1936.

Handsupper. Term of contempt used of members of the Republican forces who surrendered to the British during the South African War.

Hanepoot. Type of South African grape, originally from the Mediterranean, considered to be one of the best for flavour.

Hankey. Village on the Gamtoos River, Cape Province. A station of the London Missionary Society, named after its secretary, the Rev. William Alers Hankey. Founded in 1826. Fruit-growing is the main industry of the neighbourhood. Population: 3,057, including 338 Whites.

Hanover: 1. Town in the Karroo. Founded in 1876 and named after the home town, in Germany, of the original farm owner, Mr. Gous. Wool centre. From there the Rev. T. F. Burgers (q.v.) was summoned to become President of the South African Republic. Population: 1,900, including 450 Whites.
2. Village near King William's Town, established by German military settlers in 1858. Population: 400, including 120 Whites.

Hardap Dam. Irrigation dam near Mariental, South West Africa, third largest in Africa, 27 miles long and four miles wide. Completed 1963.

Harder (or Springer, from its habit of leaping out of water) (*Mugil cephalus*). Silvery fish caught around the Cape Peninsula and noted for its excellent flavour. *See* MARINE RESOURCES.

Harding. Village in South Natal, named after Sir Walter Harding (q.v.). Established in 1877 as a military outpost, and occupied a strategic position in the Griqua Rebellion of 1878 under Smith Pommer (q.v.). Proclaimed a township in 1911; is today an important dairy and forestry centre. Population: 2,925, including 461 Whites.

Harding, Walter. First Chief Justice of Natal. Born in 1813, he was appointed clerk to a puisne judge at the Cape in 1829. Held various posts and in 1836 prepared a précis of the records of Supreme Court criminal trials dating back to 1736 for the clarification of Roman-Dutch law. The following year he collected and published the laws in force in the Cape Colony. After serving as Clerk of the Peace in Swellendam, he became Crown Prosecutor in Natal in 1846. In 1846 he created, as Lieutenant-Colonel, the Volunteer Yeomanry Cavalry Corps. In 1856 he became Recorder of Natal and in 1858 the first Chief Justice of Natal. He died on April 19, 1874.

Hare (Leporidae). Surface-dwelling rodent widely found in South Africa. Differs from rabbit in larger size, longer legs and browner fur. Produces its young fully furred and with eyes open. The flesh is red. There are several species, including the Cape Hare (*Lepus capensis*); the Rock Hare (*Pronolagus ruddi*), which lives in mountainous country particularly in Natal; the small Red Hare (*Pronolagus crassicaudatus*), found between the Cape, the Midlands and Rhodesia, and the Kol Haas or South African Hare (*Lepus saxitilis*) of the Bush-veld. Hares grow about 2 feet long. There is little evidence that hares suffer from Myxomatosis, the disease which has affected rabbits, and it certainly has not appeared in the hares of South Africa. *See* SPRING HARE and MAMMALS.

Harpuisbossie (*Euryops multifidus*). Medicinal plant found in the Eastern Cape Province, the resin of which is used for home remedies. Its name is derived from the old Dutch word 'harpuis' meaning pitch or resin.

Harris, Colonel Sir David. South African diamond magnate, soldier and legislator. Born in London on July 12, 1852, he emigrated to the Cape in 1871. From Durban he walked to Kimberley, a distance of about 600 miles, and began work as a digger. Within 2 years he was prosperous, and had gained the friendship of Cecil John Rhodes, with whom he remained on intimate terms for many years. Harris's career as a soldier began in 1876 when he joined Du Toit's Pan Horse and fought in the Gaika-Galeka War, Eastern Cape. Several other native campaigns followed, including the Langeberg, in which he distinguished himself, and became Lieutenant-Colonel. In 1897 he succeeded as member of the Cape Parliament on the death of his relative Barney Barnato. He retained his seat for 32 years and gained wide respect on account of his great knowledge of the diamond industry. In 1897 he became a director of De Beer's Consolidated Mines, until September 1931, when he resigned. He commanded the Town Guard during the siege of Kimberley, and was mentioned in dispatches. He died in 1942.

Harris, Dr. Frederick Rutherfoord. First Secretary of the British South Africa Company (Chartered Company 1888). Born in 1856 in England, he studied medicine at Edinburgh and came to South Africa in 1882. Became friend and confidential agent of Cecil John Rhodes. In 1894 was elected to Parliament for Kimberley and, despite implication in the Jameson Raid preparations, was re-elected in 1898. He was a leader of the Cape Progressive Party, but later retired to Wales, where he died on September 1, 1920.

Harris, Lord (George Robert Canning). Chairman of the Consolidated Gold Fields of South Africa. Born in England on February 3, 1851; educated at Eton and Oxford; succeeding to the family title in 1872 and entered the Government Service in 1885 as Under-Secretary for India. After holding posts, including that of Governor of Bombay from 1890 to 1895, he served in the South African War and became Chairman of the Consolidated Gold Fields in 1899, a position he held for 30 years, until his death in 1929. Lord Harris was a celebrated cricketer and captained the English team against Australia in 1878, 1880 and 1884.

Harris, Sir William Cornwallis. South African explorer and author. Born 1807. He visited South Africa in 1835 and trekked to the Matabele chief Moselekatse, returning in 1837. Wrote three famous books, *Narrative of an Expedition into Southern Africa*, first published in Bombay, 1838, *Wild Sports of Southern Africa* in 1839, and *Portraits of Game and Wild Animals of Southern Africa* in 1840. He died in 1848.

Harrismith. Town in the Eastern Orange Free State, named after Governor Sir Harry Smith of the Cape (q.v.);

founded in May 1849. It lies at the base of the Platberg Mountain, and is noted for its beautiful setting and bracing climate; altitude 5,321 feet. It saw fighting in the wars against the neighbouring Basuto tribe, and again in the South African War, when its strategic position was important. Is now an industrial centre, with large woollen mills started soon after World War I, and handles much trade with Basutoland. Population: 15,600, including 4,600 Whites.

Harrison, George. Alleged discoverer of the Witwatersrand Gold Field. A friend of George Walker and George Honeyball (q.v.), his earlier career is shrouded in mystery, but, according to researches of James Grey, there is documentary evidence to prove that he received the first claims as discoverer of the Main Reef series in 1886. He left the Rand afterwards but his later career is unknown.

Hartebeesfontein. Village near Klerksdorp, Transvaal. Population: 2,000, including 600 Whites.

Hartebeest. Antelope found in most parts of South Africa, but now becoming very rare. Both male and female grow horns. Of the two varieties, the Cape (*Bubalis caama*), commonly known as the Red Hartebeest, is now almost confined to the Kalahari region, certain parts of Natal, Cape Province and Orange Free State. Lichtenstein's Hartebeest (*Bubalis lichtensteini*) lives in Rhodesia and further north. Hartebeest range in height up to 4 feet at the shoulder. They are extremely fast runners and are fairly easily tamed. *See* MAMMALS.

Hartebeesthoek. Site of South African Radio Space Research Station near Krugersdorp, Transvaal, set up by Council for Scientific and Industrial Research (q.v.), in collaboration with the United States National Aeronautic and Space Administration, and placed in official use on September 8, 1961. Used for tracking satellites and making radio-telescope observations. *See also* SPACE RESEARCH.

Hartebeest Hut. Primitive dwelling erected by the Voortrekkers and early settlers in the Transvaal and Orange Free State, usually made of wattle and daub. The origin of the name is in doubt.

Hartingsburg. Original name for Warmbaths, Transvaal. Named after Professor Harting, a pro-Boer spokesman in Holland at the time of the First Boer War.

Hartley. Town in Rhodesia, between Bulawayo and Salisbury. Founded about 1890 as Hartley Hill, a mining camp named after Henry Hartley, famous early hunter and explorer (q.v.). The original village was heavily engaged in the Mashona Rising of 1896. Owing to its unsuitable position, Cecil Rhodes had it moved to its present site, in 1901, shortly before his death. Is now a mining, farming and industrial centre. Population: 2,100, including 450 Whites.

Hartley, Frida. South African social worker. Born of wealthy parents in 1878 near Bassenthwaite, Cumberland, she lost her hearing through illness and began working in the London slums, being appointed Official Visitor at Holloway Prison. During World War I she served in the Women's Land Army and extended her social work. In 1920 she came to South Africa, taking up the post of Official Visitor at Pretoria Prison. Finding no facilities for homeless and friendless women she started a home in 1922 which was named after her. She died in November, 1943.

Hartley, Henry. Rhodesian hunter and explorer. Born in England, 1815, and came to the Eastern Cape with the 1820 settlers. As a hunter, in the 1840's, he made his way to the Transvaal beyond the Limpopo. There he won the friendship of the chief Moselekatse. He found some of the first-known gold in

Rhodesia in the 1860's and acted as guide to the German explorer Carl Mauch (q.v.). He died in 1876 on his farm in the Magaliesberg, Transvaal.

Hartswater. Village near Warrenton, Cape Province. Population: 4,900, including 1,000 Whites.

Harveya. *See* NEMESIA.

Hatfield. Township 5 miles south of Salisbury, mainly residential. Population: 400 Europeans and 4,500 Africans. Established 1952.

Hatherley. Village near Pretoria, Transvaal. Population: 140, including 135 Whites. *See* EERSTE FABRIEKEN.

Hathorn, Kenneth Howard. Judge, Natal bench. Born in Salford, England, on June 2, 1849, he came to Natal with his parents in 1850 and attended the Pietermaritzburg High School. After serving his articles he was admitted as attorney in 1871 and as advocate in 1877. He represented Maritzburg in the Natal Parliament from 1901 to 1906. In 1901 he was called to the Inner Temple, and on May 28, 1910, was appointed to the Natal bench. He retired in 1926 and died in Pietermaritzburg, March 1933.

Hattingspruit. Village near Dundee, Natal. Colliery centre. Population: 650, including 190 Whites.

Havelock, Sir Arthur Elibank. Governor of Natal. Born in 1844, son of Lieutenant-Colonel W. H. Havelock. Joined the 32nd Regiment in 1862, and reached the rank of captain. From 1874 to 1875 and again from 1879 to 1880 was Chief Civil Commissioner in the Seychelles Islands, with a term as Colonial Secretary of the Fiji Islands from 1875 to 1876. Then transferred to the West Indies and to West Africa; as consul to Liberia in 1881. Became Governor of Natal in 1885 and remained until 1889, during the unsettled period when the future of Zululand and Swaziland was being decided. Left before the expiry of his

5-year term. Thereafter he was Governor of Ceylon (1890–1895), of Madras (1895–1900) and of Tasmania (1901–1904). He died on June 25, 1908.

Havelock Mine. One of the largest Asbestos Mines in the World, on Swaziland side of Transvaal border, across which runs the 13-mile cableway to Barberton (q.v.). Output about 6,000 tons a year. Population 4,500.

Havenga, Nicolaas Christiaan. Cabinet Minister. Born in Fauresmith, O.F.S., 1882; educated at Grey College, Bloemfontein and, at the age of 17, joined the Boer forces in the South African War, as secretary to General J. B. M. Hertzog (q.v.). He was wounded and suffered from the after-effects all his life. After the Peace of Vereeniging he became an attorney in Fauresmith and in 1910 was elected to the first O.F.S. Provincial Council. From the start he supported General Hertzog in the Nationalist Party and in 1915 was elected to Parliament. Upon Hertzog's accession to power in 1924, Havenga became Minister of Finance, a position he continued to hold for 15 years until the resignation of the Hertzog government in 1939. He became leader of the new Afrikaner Party. When the latter rejoined the Nationalists in 1948 he again became Minister of Finance until 1953. He died in 1957.

Hawk. *See* EAGLES.

Haworthia. *See* LILY.

Hawston. Village near Hermanus, Cape Province. Population: 1,209, including 12 Whites.

Healdtown. Mission station near Fort Beaufort in the Eastern Cape Province, belonging to the Wesleyan Methodist Church. Specialised in the training of teachers. Established in 1867 with the assistance of a Mr. and Miss Heald of Manchester, who gave £1,000 towards its launching. The first principal was the Rev. W. Impey. Present population: 1,500, including 100 Whites.

Heany, Captain Maurice. Rhodesian pioneer and soldier. Born in the United States, he came to South Africa in the 1870's; took part in the occupation of Bechuanaland in 1884 and became associated with Major Frank Johnson and Captain H. J. Borrow (q.v.) in organising the Pioneer Column in 1890. He secured mining concessions as founder and General Manager of the Bechuanaland Trading Company and took a distinguished part in the Matebele War of 1893. Captain Heany died in 1927.

Heart Transplants. World attention was aroused by the feat of Professor Christiaan N. Barnard (q.v.) in successfully transplanting the first human heart on December 3, 1967 at Groote Schuur Hospital, Cape Town. The heart of Denise Darvall, aged 25, and killed in a motor accident, was transplanted to Louis Washkansky, aged 53. He died on December 21, 1967, but on January 2, 1968, Professor Barnard transplanted the heart of Clive Haupt, a young coloured man aged 24, who had died suddenly to Dr. Philip B. Blaiberg, a Cape Town dentist, aged 58 who survived until August 17, 1969. Pieter Smith of Johannesburg, aged 52, received a new heart on September 7, 1968.

Heartwater. Disease of cattle and sheep, only found in Africa. Thanks to research at Onderstepoort Laboratory (q.v.), a treatment, involving sulphonamide therapy, has proved effective in immunising calves.

Heath. *See* ERICA.

Hectare. Metric land measure still used in South West Africa, where, with the Metric System, it was introduced during the German régime. One hectare equals 2·471 acres or 1·1675 morgen.

Hedgehog (*Erinaceus frontalis*). Small spiky mammal once common in South Africa, now rare except in the Karroo.

It lives chiefly on insects, snails and small reptiles. *See* MAMMALS.

Heemraad. Old Dutch title, originally applied in the Netherlands to officials charged with the care of dikes ('Dike-Reeve'). At the Cape Heemraden were appointed to sit with the Landdrost as assessors in hearing cases and dealing with local affairs. The first four, appointed in Stellenbosch, 1685, were Henning Huising, Jan Mostert, Gerrit Van der Bijl and Hermanus Smit. The title was abolished in 1828, with the introduction of the present system of Magistrates. Under the 1858 Constitution, Heemraden was recognised in the Transvaal, but later fell into disuse.

Heerenlogement. Famous cave, northwest of Clanwilliam in the Western Cape Province, district Van Rhynsdorp. The name means in Dutch 'Gentlemen's Lodgings' and was given because for nearly 300 years it was used as a shelter by travellers. Was first recorded in 1661 by Pieter van Meerhoff, the explorer who stayed there. Simon van der Stel (q.v.) stopped there on his way to seek copper in Namaqualand. Inscriptions by callers date from 1712. The cave was proclaimed a National Monument in 1939.

Heidelberg: 1. Town in the Cape Province between Swellendam and Riversdale, on the Duivenhoeks River. Formerly an important ostrich farming centre, but now mainly engaged in the fruit, wool and wheat trade. Aloes, used for medical purposes, grow on neighbouring hills. The name is derived from the Heidelberg Catechism used by the Dutch Reformed Church. Because of confusion with its namesake in the Transvaal, vain efforts were made to rename it Dewaalville, after Sir Frederick de Waal (q.v.). Population: 3,711, including 1,347 Whites. **2.** Town in the Southern Transvaal, established in 1866, proclaimed a municipality in 1903. For a short while in 1880 was the capital of the

Transvaal, at the start of the First South African War. The Peace Treaty that ended the campaign was signed there in 1881. Noted for its beautiful kloof and for its many schools. Population: 12,200, including 5,500 Whites. **3.** Original name of Bethulie, O.F.S. (q.v.).

Heilbron. Town in the Northern Orange Free State, laid out in 1874. Named after an ancient city in Germany. Maize and milling centre. Was for a short while the seat of the Orange Free State Republican Government after the fall of Bloemfontein in 1900 and saw considerable fighting during the South African War. Figured prominently in the beginning of the 1914 Rebellion. Population: 8,900, including 2,500 Whites.

Hel, Die (The Hell). *See* GAMKA KLOOF.

Helderberg College. Co-educational institution near Somerset West, Cape Province. Controlled by the Seventh Day Adventist Church, and the first of its kind outside America. Started as the Claremont Union College in the Cape Town suburb of Claremont. In 1918 was replaced by the South African Training School, 18 miles from Ladysmith, Natal. Renamed Spionkop in 1922. Three years later became a Native mission training school, and the European institution was transferred to its present site. About 100 of its 400 acres are under cultivation. The college offers a practical training in trades and agriculture, as well as the usual school subjects.

Helpmekaar ('Help Each Other'): **1.** Organisation established in 1915 after the Rebellion (q.v.) for the purpose of enabling Afrikaners to assist each other. Its immediate purpose was to help pay the fines imposed on those convicted and to provide financial aid for their families, but soon became much wider in scope, and collected over £150,000. Used in recent years mainly to provide bursaries for deserving students.

2. Village in Natal. Population 100, including 20 Whites.

Helvetia. Village near Machadodorp in the Eastern Transvaal, scene of important fighting during the South African War.

Hely-Hutchinson, Sir Walter Francis. Governor of Natal (1893–1901) and of the Cape Colony (1901–1910). Born in Dublin, son of the Earl of Donoughmore. Educated Harrow and Cambridge. Was appointed attaché to Sir Hercules Robinson (q.v.) on a mission to the Fiji Islands and Australia. Appointed Colonial Secretary for Barbados, West Indies (1877–1883). Became, first, Secretary to the Government and then Lieutenant-Governor of Malta (1884–1889), Governor of the Windward Islands, West Indies (1889–1893). First Governor of Natal (1893–1901) under Responsible Government. There he handled delicate problems and annexed the 'Trans-Pongola' territories of Amatongaland, thus forestalling President Kruger. During South African War appointed to the responsible post of Governor of Cape Colony. Noted for his tact and popularity. Returned to England, where he settled in Kent. Died September 23, 1913.

Hendrina. Village near Middelburg, Transvaal. Population: 2,047, including 720 Whites.

Henkries. Small settlement in Northern Namaqualand, noted for date-growing.

Henley-on-Klip. Village in the Transvaal, near Johannesburg, and popular fishing resort on the Klip River. Established about 1916. Population: 700, including 300 Whites.

Hennenman. Town near Ventersburg, Orange Free State. Population: 7,000, including 2,500 Whites.

Herald Snake. *See* SNAKE-HERALD.

Herbert, Sir Thomas. English traveller. Born in 1606, studied at Oxford and Cambridge. In 1627 he accompanied an early English mission to Persia, and saw 'The Road Worthily cald Good Hope,' of which he left one of the earliest accounts in his book, *Some Yeares Travels into Divers Parts of Asia and Afrique*, published in 1638. Herbert was involved in the troubles of Charles I, whose good friend he became, and who gave him a copy of Shakespeare's Second Folio, now kept at Windsor Castle. He died 1682.

Hercules. Village north of Pretoria, notable for large cement works. The name is derived from an early trade mark used by the Pretoria Portland Cement Company.

Hereeniging. Political term in Afrikaans, meaning 'reunion.' Applied to attempts to reunite the old National Party, under General J. B. M. Hertzog, and the South African Party, under General J. C. Smuts, for which purpose a special Hereeniging Congress met in 1929 in Bloemfontein, but failed. In 1933 a similar attempt brought about the 'Herenigde Party,' the present United Party.

Herero. Tribe in South West Africa. They are tall, dignified and light in colour; believed to have emigrated from Central, or possibly North, Africa. They indulge in ancestor-worship and are chiefly engaged in cattle breeding. The women wear an unusual headdress, vaguely reminiscent of that of the Vikings. The Hereros were first encountered in 1760 by Jacobus Coetsee. In 1830 the German missionary Schmelen, followed in 1842 by the Rev. Hugo Hahn, tried to convert them to Christianity. The Germans colonised the country and came into repeated conflict with the Hereros under Chief Samuel Maherero. Main Herero War (1904–1907) (q.v.) led to complete defeat of tribe, with a large number of deaths, many of them due to thirst. Hereros now number about 40,000 and are found mainly on South West African farms.

Herero War. Campaign in German South West Africa which began with a rising of local Herero and other tribes in 1904 and soon spread throughout the country. The Hereros were joined by the Bondelswarts, Namas and other groups. For a long time the German authorities were on the defensive and it was not until over 20,000 white troops had been mobilised and over £60,000,000 spent that the revolt collapsed in 1907. German losses were 179 officers and 2,169 men killed. The numbers of the Hereros dropped from 97,000 to 20,000.

Hermannsburg. German village in Natal, 15 miles from Greytown. Established as a Lutheran Mission Station in 1854, it included a school for European boys, at which a number of eminent men, including General Louis Botha (q.v.), were educated. The area still has a pronounced German element.

Hermanus. Seaside resort on Walker Bay, about 75 miles from Cape Town. Began in 1855 as a fishing village named Hermanuspietersfontein, after its headman, Hermanus Pieters. Since 1904 a popular resort with excellent fishing, bracing climate, beautiful scenery, yachting and golf. Sir William Hoy (q.v.) was life-long champion of Hermanus and established one of the first road motor services in 1912. Government Magnetic Observatory built there. Population: 5,180, including 2,570 Whites.

Hermon. Village in the Western Cape Province. Cement factory and wheat trading are its main interests. Population: 400, including 100 Whites.

Herons (Ardeidae). Long-legged, long-necked and long-billed birds well represented in South Africa near vleis and swamps. Most birds of this family have ornamental plumes, live mainly near fresh water and use their straight bills for spearing fish or frogs. They fly slowly, their long wings down-curved. The Cape has several large heronries, both in reeds and on treetops inland. For the smaller herons *see* EGRETS and HAMERKOP.

Herring (family Clupeidae). The true herring does not occur in South Africa, but the name is applied to another fish, the Caranx or King Fish, which is found off Natal. *See* MARINE RESOURCES.

Herrman, Dr. Louis. South African historian and educationist. Born at Southampton in 1883, and studied there, at the University of London and University of Cape Town. Having qualified as a teacher he came to Cape Town in 1907, but maintained his original interest in science, specialising in Social Biology, on which he did research in London. He became principal of Cape Town High School in 1933. His best-known work is *The History of the Jews in South Africa*, originally published in 1930. He wrote extensively on Jewish South African history and in 1935 *In the Sealed Cave, a Scientific Fantasy*.

Herschel. Village in the Cape Province, near the Lesotho border, laid out in 1873, and named after the great astronomer Sir J. F. W. Herschel (q.v.). The village is 6,000 feet above sea-level, has beautiful mountain scenery and very cold winters. Population: 100, including 50 Whites.

Herschel, Sir John Frederick William. Astronomer. Born 1792; son of the great astronomer Sir William Herschel. His astronomical researches led to his visiting the Cape of Good Hope in 1834. He remained for 4 years, with his observatory at Feldhausen, Claremont, Cape Town. There he discovered 1,708 nebulae and clusters, besides 1,202 pairs of double stars. He broke new ground in regard to measurements of radiation from the

Sun, indicated the link between outbursts on the Sun and the Auroras on Earth, and made many far-reaching discoveries. By request of the Cape Government, he worked out the Colony's school system, still followed. His Cape Astronomical Observations were published in 1847 at the expense of the Duke of Northumberland. He died in 1871.

Herschel School. Well-known school for girls at Feldhausen, Claremont, where Sir John Frederick William Herschel (q.v.) carried out his research. The school, which is run on public school lines, was founded in 1920.

Hertzog. Village in Cape Province. Population: 110, including 60 Whites.

Hertzog, Dr. Albert. Former South African Minister of Posts and Telegraphs and of Health. Son of the late General J. B. M. Hertzog (q.v.). Born at Bloemfontein July 4, 1899, and educated at Grey College there and universities of Stellenbosch, Oxford, Leyden and Amsterdam. After qualifying for the Bar he entered Parliament in 1948 and joined the Cabinet in 1958. He left the Ministry in 1968 and started his own party.

Hertzog, General James Barry Munnik. Prime Minister of the Union of South Africa. Born near Wellington on April 3, 1866, son of a farmer, Albertus Munnik Hertzog; spent part of his boyhood in Kimberley when still a mining camp; moved to the Orange Free State. 1881 went to Victoria College, Stellenbosch, intending to study for the ministry, but changed to law. He graduated in 1889 and went to the University of Amsterdam, where he gained a doctorate in law. Practised in Pretoria 1893–1895; Judge of the Supreme Court of the Orange Free State Republic 1895–1899. During the South African War rose to prominence as one of the most audacious generals of the Orange Free State, carrying out bold raids into the

Cape Province, and fighting a number of successful actions against the British. He took part in peace negotiations. Later became the unchallenged political leader of the Orange Free State and one of the founders of the Orangia Union Party. Elected to the Cabinet under the Crown Colony régime in 1907, he put into effect his controversial views about the equality of the English and Dutch languages, dismissing certain school inspectors who opposed him. He took part in the National Convention and became a member of the first Union Cabinet under General Louis Botha (q.v.). In opposition to Botha he made a speech at De Wildt in 1912 laying down the principle of 'South Africa First,' and the 'Two Streams Policy' (English and Afrikaans). He resigned from the Botha Cabinet and established the National Party. This he built up until in 1924, by agreement with the Labour leader, Colonel F. H. P. Cresswell (q.v.), he became Prime Minister, a post he held for 15 years. The Gold Standard Crisis in 1932 brought unity between him and General Smuts (q.v.). Together they established the United South African National Party. Hertzog achieved the full equality of the English and Afrikaans languages and the recognition by Britain of the equality of the Dominions, including the right of secession and allied privileges (Statute of Westminster, 1931). His cautious dealing with Nazi Germany caused friction with General Smuts. In September 1939 he refused to follow Britain in declaring war against Hitler, was defeated in Parliament and resigned office. He retired to his farm, where he died on November 21, 1942.

Hertzog Prize. Award established on May 27, 1914, for outstanding literary works in Afrikaans. It was created by General J. B. M. Hertzog (q.v.) out of moneys collected by admirers to cover damages for which he had been adjudged liable in a court case.

Now administered by the Afrikaanse Akademie (q.v.).

Hertzog Tower. Highest man-made structure in the Republic of South Africa, named after Dr. Albert Hertzog, Minister of Posts and Telegraphs, and erected on Brixton Ridge, Johannesburg, in 1961. It rises to a height of 750 feet and is designed for Very High Frequency radio transmissions and television. Equipped with a lift and a viewing platform for sightseers.

Hertzogville. Village in the Orange Free State, named after the Prime Minister, General J. B. M. Hertzog. Maize farming centre. Population: 1,784, including 600 Whites.

Het Volk. Party in the Transvaal under Crown Colony régime. *See under* VOLK.

Hex River. Tributary of Breede River (q.v.). Also a tributary of the Limpopo, in the Transvaal. (Name is Dutch for 'Witch.')

Heyman, Colonel Sir Herman Melville. Rhodesian soldier and pioneer. Born Gibraltar 1859; educated in London and came to South Africa in 1877. Joined the Cape Mounted Rifles and served in the Gaika-Galeka War 1877-1878, the campaign against Morosi in 1879, the Basuto Gun War 1880-1881. Gained prominence in the British South Africa Company's Police in 1890, when he prevented the Portuguese from gaining a foothold in Rhodesia, through military action at Macequece (q.v.). Heyman served in the Matabele War of 1893 and held important positions in the Rhodesian service. Retired in 1896 to become resident director for Willoughby's Consolidated (q.v.). From 1901 to 1907 and again from 1907 to 1920 he sat in the Legislative Council. Presided over the Imperial Land Commission in 1894. During World War I he commanded the Rhodesian Reserve Regiment. He died in 1935.

Hibiscus (Malvaceae). One of a group of shrubs and herbs widely spread in Southern Africa, liking sunshine and moisture. Five sepals united at the base, five petals, and numerous stamens united into a tube round the pistil. Flowers axillary. Yellow and pink predominate. Deccan Hemp (*Hibiscus cannabinus*) common all over Rhodesia, has fine yellow flowers with a dark centre. The beautiful crimson *Hibiscus praeteritus* grows at the Victoria Falls. Many varieties in Natal, including the Orange Trailing Hibiscus (*H. surattensis*), a coastal climber, with hooked prickles. To the same family belong Wild Cotton (5-6 feet, a perennial on banks of spruits), Wild Hollyhock and the Pink Mallow. The golden or dwarf *Hibiscus Aethiopicus* is common as far south as the Cape, especially after veld fires. Under shelter in the Cape Peninsula grows the sticky little pink-flowered shrub, *Malvastrum scabriosum*.

Hiemstra, Commandant-General Rudolph Christian. South African soldier. Born March 10, 1912 at Lydenburg, Transvaal. He joined the Permanent Force as a cadet in 1931, being posted to the S.A. Air Force in 1936. He became Inspector of Transport in 1941. After service as Military Attaché to Embassies in several European countries, he returned to become Adjutant-General and in 1955 attended the Imperial Defence College in London. After reaching the rank of Combat-General in 1959, he was made Commandant-General and Secretary for Defence on October 17, 1966.

Highlands. Township north-east of Salisbury, with its own Town Management Board, established in 1943. It is mainly residential and has a population of 8,457 Europeans and 9,425 Africans.

Highveld Steel and Vanadium Works. Large plant near Witbank erected by Anglo-American Corporation of South Africa (q.v.) with initial output at capacity of 480,000 tons of steel per year. Cost is estimated at over R100,000,000. Production began in 1968. *See also* STEELPORT.

Hillcrest. Township near Pinetown, Natal. Population: 1,640, including 983 Whites.

Hilton College. Boys' public school in Natal. Founded in 1868 by the Rev. W. C. Newnham in Pietermaritzburg, but in 1872 moved 4 miles north from Hilton Road, on main line to the Rand.

Hilton Road. Village near Pietermaritzburg, Natal. Population: 1,250, including 700 Whites.

Hime, Lieutenant-Colonel, the Right Hon. Sir Albert Henry. Prime Minister of Natal. Born at Kilcool, Ireland, on August 29, 1842, son of the Rev. M. C. Hime. Went to school at Enniskillen and studied at Trinity College, Dublin, before entering the Royal Military College in Woolwich. He joined the Royal Engineers in 1861, did excellent work as an engineer in the West Indies and was promoted to Colonial Engineer of Natal, arriving there with the rank of captain in 1875. Appointed member both of the Executive and the Legislative Councils of the Colony, he took part in the Zulu War, and surveyed the boundary with the O.F.S. He continued as Colonial Engineer until 1893, when Natal received Responsible Government. In 1897 he was elected to Parliament, becoming Minister of Lands, Works and Defence until 1899, when he became Prime Minister. He resigned in 1903. His home was in Pietermaritzburg where he died in 1919.

Himeville. Village in Natal, near Drakensberg; altitude 5,200 feet, founded in 1905. It takes its name from Sir Albert Hime, Prime Minister of Natal (q.v.). Trout fishing resort and farming centre. Population: 200, including 100 Whites.

Hindon, Captain Oliver John (Jack). Boer scout. Born in England on April 20, 1874, he joined the British Army as a drummer boy and at the age of 14 came to South Africa when his regiment was transferred to Zululand. Because of ill-treatment by his sergeant-major, he and some other lads deserted to the Transvaal. For a while he worked on the Rand Goldfields, before becoming a successful builder and contractor in Middelburg. As a reward for the support he gave to the authorities during the Jameson Raid, he was naturalised as a burgher and entered the Republican Mounted Police. On the outbreak of the South African War he joined the Boer forces and became a legend for dash and daring, largely in association with Captain Daniel Theron (q.v.). One of his most famous feats occurred at Spion Kop, where with De Roos and Henri Slegtkamp he managed to hold up General Buller's force for several hours. Later, at the head of his own corps, he did great damage in blowing up British railway lines. He died in Pretoria on March 19, 1919.

Hintsa. Chief of the Xosa people. Born early in the 19th century, he came into prominence during the war against the Cape in 1835. He finally sued for peace and offered to help the British to collect the cattle. In doing so he tried to escape and was shot. He was succeeded by his son, Kreli (q.v.).

Hippopotamus (*Hippopotamus amphibious*) **or See Koei** (Sea Cow). These animals, once found throughout South Africa, even on the shores of Table Bay, by van Riebeeck's settlers, are today limited to the northern parts of the Transvaal, the Kruger Park, Zululand, Rhodesia and Mozambique. A small herd of about 30 is known to live in the Orange River below the Aughrabies Falls. They are related to the pig. So-called Seekoegats, where hippos formerly wallowed, are not uncommon. Extremely good swimmers, they can remain underwater for minutes. Although shooting is today prohibited, the hippo's meat is excellent. A bull is about 4 feet high and 14 feet long. See HUBERTA and MAMMALS.

Hippo Valley. Irrigation settlement on Lundi River, Rhodesia, with large sugar and citrus production.

Historical Monuments Council (formerly **Commission**). Statutory body in South Africa, set up in 1934. Appointed and financed by the Government, it can recommend natural and historical monuments which it considers suitable for preservation, under proclamation. Several hundred in every part of the Republic have been so dealt with. Renamed and reorganised in July 1969.

History. See countries concerned, also under individual events.

Hlabisa. Village near St. Lucia Bay in Zululand, established in 1892. Population: 100, including 50 Whites.

Hlobane. Colliery village in Northern Natal, pronounced 'Shlobane.' Founded in 1904, when the coal-fields were opened, but already known in the last century as a kraal, near which heavy fighting took place during the Zulu War of 1879. The name means 'A Beautiful Place.'

Hlonipa. A native custom by which certain words may not be used by certain persons, particularly in relation to their families. A form of taboo.

Hluhluwe (pronounced 'Shlooshloo-way'). Game Reserve in the north of Zululand covering approximately 40,000 acres and noted for its white rhinoceros herd, rediscovered there after the animal had long been thought extinct. There are many other species of game and a rest camp for visitors is maintained. Unlike some reserves, this one is notable for its fine scenery.

Hobby. Bird of prey, member of the Falcon family, visiting South Africa as a migrant. See EAGLES.

Hobhouse. Village in the Orange Free State, named after the famous reformer of the Boer War Concentration Camps, Miss Emily Hobhouse. Founded about 1904. Population: 1,110, including 430 Whites.

Hobhouse, Emily. English social worker and reformer. Born 1860 in Cornwall, daughter of the Rev. Reginald Hobhouse and member of an influential political family. After a sheltered girlhood, she went as a temperance worker to a mining camp in Minnesota, U.S.A., and later attempted ranching in Mexico. On the outbreak of the South African War she became interested in the South African Women and Children's Distress Fund, and learning of alleged abuses in the Concentration Camps went to South Africa to see for herself. She soon discovered that all was not well, overcame serious opposition, including arrest and deportation, but finally was allowed to reveal the facts. The abuses, mainly due to inexperience and administrative ignorance, raised a national outcry in England. Through the appointment of a 'Ladies' Committee,' with influential backing, reforms in the camps brought the disgraceful mortality rate for women and children to normal. After the war Miss Hobhouse, now a national figure, started home industries for Boer girls in Philippolis, O.F.S. (q.v.). She did further outstanding relief work in Europe during World War I. Died in 1926, given a state funeral and was buried at the foot of the Women and Children's Memorial in Bloemfontein, the greatest honour the Afrikaner people could bestow.

Hockey. The earliest recorded organised hockey matches in South Africa were arranged at Newlands, Cape Town, in 1899 by V. A. van der Byl, who was also the organiser and first

President of the Western Province Hockey Union, founded in 1902. Largely on account of the presence of the British garrison, a start was made up-country, the game being organised in the Orange Free State in 1904 and in the Transvaal in 1906, under rules of the Hockey Association of England. Progress remained slow but in 1919 steps were taken to set up a National League. Not until August 1924 was the South African Hockey Union launched. It includes the four provinces of the Republic, as well as Rhodesia and South West Africa. The first tour of an English team took place in 1925 and in 1927 the first South African team went to Britain and Belgium. Since then there have been a number of others, including South Africa in Europe (1953), England in South Africa (1954), America and Scotland in South Africa (1958) and South Africa in Europe (1959).

Hodges, Sir William. Chief Justice, Cape Supreme Court. Born in Melcome Regis in Dorset, England, on August 29, 1808, he was educated at Salisbury and London University and called to the Inner Temple on May 3, 1833. He was made Chief Justice of the Cape Supreme Court in 1858 and died in 1868.

Hoernle, Agnes Winifred. South African ethnologist and social worker. Born in Kimberley in 1890, daughter of Senator W. K. Tucker, she had a brilliant scholastic career, at the South African College, Cape Town, at Newnham College, Cambridge, at Leipzig and Bonn in Germany and in Paris. On her return to South Africa she undertook a research project in the Richterveld (q.v.) to study the local tribes and followed this with further work in South West Africa. She married Professor R. F. A. Hoernle (q.v.) and continued her own work for many years as a prominent writer on Social Anthropology and allied subjects. She died in 1960.

Hoernle, Professor R. F. Alfred. South African philosopher. Born in Germany, he studied in that country and at Oxford, beginning his career as a lecturer at the University of St. Andrew's. In 1908 he was appointed Professor of Philosophy at the South African College in Cape Town, until 1911. He went to Newcastle-on-Tyne, where he remained from 1912 to 1914 and again from 1920 to 1923. From 1914 to 1920 Hoernle was Assistant Professor of Philosophy at Harvard. He moved to Johannesburg, where he held the Chair of Philosophy at the University of the Witwatersrand, until his death. Apart from many books on his own subject, he was a pioneer in his endeavours to improve race relations in South Africa, and noted for his liberal outlook. He died in 1943.

Hoetjes Bay. Inlet in Saldanha Bay, on its northern side, good natural harbour. Believed to be called after the family of Oetgens van Wavern in Amsterdam.

Hoffa, Dr. Albert. South African-born scientist. Born in Richmond, Cape Colony, on March 31, 1859, the son of a local doctor; studied medicine in Germany. In 1886 was appointed lecturer (Dozent) at the University of Wuerzburg; promoted to Professor in 1896. In 1902 he moved in a similar capacity to Berlin. Is regarded as the 'Founder of Modern Orthopaedics,' to use the description of *Brockhaus' Encyclopedia*. Died on December 31, 1907. Author of textbooks on orthopaedic surgery, bandaging, etc.

Hoffman, Josias Philippus. First President of the Orange Free State. Born in Stellenbosch, 1807. Little is known of his earlier career, except that he was a man of standing in the Orange Free State Sovereignty, who helped to sign the Bloemfontein Convention as representative of Smithfield, where he lived. President in 1854, troubled by lack of money and bad officials. To placate the Basuto chief Moshesh he presented him with a barrel of gunpowder. Protest to this led to his resignation in 1855. He went farming near the Caledon River. Died 1879.

Hofmeyr. Town in the Eastern Cape Province, founded in 1873 and first called Maraisburg. Because of another Maraisburg in the Transvaal, now part of Roodepoort (q.v.), it was renamed in honour of Jan Hendrik Hofmeyr (Onze Jan), in 1911. Among the local industries is salt production. Population: 2,430, including 600 Whites.

Hofmeyr, Jan Hendrik. Generally known as 'Onze Jan.' Born in Cape Town, 1845; educated at the institute 'Tot Nut van Het Algemeen' and the South African College. He acquired fame as the editor of the paper *Zuid Afrikaan*, renamed *Ons Land*; became the political champion of the farmer and merged his own organisation with the Afrikaner Bond (q.v.), of which he was the unchallenged chief. His efforts for Afrikaans-speaking South Africa included both Republics, and from 1890 until the Jameson Raid he collaborated closely with Cecil John Rhodes. Accepting the value of South Africa's connection with the British Commonwealth, he attended Colonial conferences in England. His major achievement was the recognition of the equality of the Dutch and English languages. He also sought to prevent the outbreak of the South African War and very nearly succeeded. Because of his enormous influence with the Afrikaner people, he was called in to assist in the drafting of the South African Constitution and served as a member of the delegation that brought the final draft to London. While there in 1909, he died. His life was written by his nephew, J. H. Hofmeyr (q.v.).

Hofmeyr, The Rt. Hon. Jan Hendrik. Deputy Prime Minister of the Union of South Africa. Born in Cape

Town, March 1894, he was recognised as the most brilliant student on record at the South African College, where he matriculated at the age of 13. Proceeding to Oxford as a Rhodes Scholar (while still wearing short trousers), he came first in Classical Moderations and first in Greats. At the age of 23 he became Professor of Classics at the Johannesburg School of Mines and in 1919, its principal, a position he continued to hold after its conversion to the University of the Witwatersrand. From 1924 to 1929 he was Administrator of the Transvaal. Elected to Parliament, he was successively Minister of the Interior, Minister of Health and Education from 1933 to 1936, Minister of Finance and Deputy Premier under General Smuts. An outstanding orator and author of several books, he was regarded as Smuts' inevitable successor but he predeceased him in 1948, aged 54.

Hole-in-the-Wall

Hole-in-the-Wall. Remarkable rock formation on coast of Transkei, near mouth of Bashee River. Two large and wall-shaped rocks joined by a narrow ridge form well-known landmark for navigators. Height 210 feet.

Holkrans. Farm near Vryheid, Natal, scene of a tragic incident during the South African War, when a group of 56 Republican burghers were surrounded by a force of Zulus, and killed.

Hollam's Bird Island. Part of the Guano Islands off South West Africa, annexed to the Cape of Good Hope in 1867.

Holland-Africa Line. Established shortly after World War I, operating from Amsterdam. The first vessel to arrive at the Cape was the *Rijndijk*, in December 1919. Beginning with chartered vessels, the Company presently started its own fleet, which was always noted for its punctuality and efficient running. Reconstruction has repeatedly taken place and the Line has merged with several independent Dutch enterprises.

Hollyhock. *See* HIBISCUS.

Hondeklip Bay. Inlet on coast of Namaqualand, used as minor port. Takes its name from a curious dog-shaped rock. Used as fishing centre and has a crayfish cannery.

Honeyball, George. Alleged discoverer of the Witwatersrand Gold Fields. Born 1855, he came out as a young man to stay with his aunt, Mrs. Oosthuizen, at Langlaagte, near the present Johannesburg. There, working as a blacksmith, he claimed to have found the Main Reef. His later poverty was relieved by a pension from the Transvaal Chamber of Mines. He died on March 19, 1949.

Honey-Guide (family Indicatoridae). Plain-coloured bird remarkable in two ways: for the habit of acting as guide to bees' nests, and for parasitic breeding habits. Found chiefly from the Cape Peninsula eastward round the coastal belt to Natal and the Transvaal. *See* BIRDS.

Honeysuckle, Cape. *See* ZIMBABWE CREEPER.

Hoogenhout, Casparus Petrus. Early Afrikaans writer. Born in Amsterdam, 1843, he came to South Africa in the 1860's as clerk to the Netherlands Consulate in Cape Town.

Honey-Guide

There he met Arnoldus Pannevis (q.v.) and through him, in 1870, became a teacher. He was a loyal supporter of the Afrikaans language movement, and began writing in that medium as far back as 1873, producing, probably, one of the first specimens of translations from the Bible. He also wrote frequently for *Die Patriot* (q.v.) under the name of 'Oom Jan wat Versies Maak.' (Uncle Jan Who Writes Verses.) He retired from his teaching post in 1908 and died in 1922.

Hoopoe (family Upupidae). Handsome bird generally distributed over South Africa, and differing from the European type only in darker brick-red colour. Conspicuous crest can be shut down at will. Long, curved bill to extricate insects. The Kakelaar (or Wood Hoopoe) is black, not crested but decorated with a long tail. Usually in chattering groups of five or six, hunting insects on the trees. *See* BIRDS.

Hoopstad. Town in the Orange Free State. (Not to be confused with Hopetown (q.v.).) Founded in 1876, named after its surveyor, a Mr. Haupt. In his honour it was called 'Hauptstad,' German for 'Capital City.' This it was not, so the name was altered to Hoopstad, the 'Town of Hope.' Considerable fighting took place there in the South African War. Population: 3,950, including 950 Whites.

Hop, Hendrik. Early hunter and traveller in the Cape. First heard of in Paarl, 1761, as a member of the Burgher Militia. Hop went, in 1761, as leader of 61 hunters on the trail of Jacobus Coetsee (q.v.) in quest of the Orange River, about which the latter had brought the first reliable information. Hop succeeded in reaching his goal and crossed into what is now South-West Africa, from whence he returned in April 1762, with useful data about trading possibilities.

Hopana. Illegal drink brewed widely by Africans, particularly in the Transvaal.

Hopefield. Village in the Western Cape Province, not far from Saldanha Bay. Established in 1852 and named after the two promoters, Major Hope, then Auditor-General, and a local resident, Mr. Field. Wheat growing and honey producing centre. Population: 2,480, including 800 Whites.

Hopetown. (Not to be confused with Hoopstad (q.v.).) Town in Northern Cape Province, near the Orange River, famous in South African history as the place near which, in 1867, the first diamonds were found, and where the first large purchases of diamonds were made by the local traders, Lilienfeld Brothers. The town again experienced a slight diamond boom in 1917, but its prosperity depends mainly on the wool growers of the district, and on the products of irrigated lands. The name of Hopetown is derived from an ornament (still existent) belonging to an early settler's wife. It was in the shape of an anchor, symbolising hope, and a coloured servant was so impressed by

it that he made a copy in tin, which he gave to his mistress. She nailed it over her house door, where it may still be seen. Shortly after, a village was laid out here, in 1854, and the incident was commemorated in the name of the town. Population: 3,050, including 1,100 Whites.

Hopley, William Musgrave. Judge, Southern Rhodesia. Born at Cradock June 13, 1853, he was educated at St. Andrew's, Grahamstown, and Diocesan College, Cape Town. Proceeding to Cambridge he took a first class in the Law Tripos and was called to the Middle Temple in 1878. Settled down to practise in Cape Town, going on to Grahamstown and then to Kimberley. In 1885 he became Crown Prosecutor and took silk in 1890. In 1892 he was appointed Judge of the High Court of Griqualand, and in 1914 Judge in Southern Rhodesia. He died in Johannesburg on March 10, 1919.

Hornbill (family Bucerotidae). Large, ungainly bird, commonly miscalled Toucan, after a tropical South American bird of different family. Enormous bill, surmounted by equally large casque. Hornbills feed largely on the ground, off insects, lizards and fruit. Several varieties found from Knysna north into Zululand. The Crowned Hornbill of the Eastern Province often leaves the bush in winter to seek food in gardens. The huge Ground Hornbills live, like Secretary Birds, off mice and snakes, and can be tamed. They are social birds, the females laying in a common nest where the eggs are brooded by one male. The strange habit of cementing up the female while she broods is common to all the other varieties. *See* BIRDS.

Horse-Racing. Introduced to the Cape of Good Hope during the First British Occupation. On September 27, 1797, the first race meeting was held under a newly-established Turf Club, the stewards being Brigadier-General

Fraser, Major Bell and Major Sharpe. The present South African Turf Club dates from 1802, and is among the oldest in the British Commonwealth. Until 1874 races took place on the Green Point Common, Cape Town, after which a move was made to Kenilworth. Earliest racing began in the Eastern Province, in Grahamstown, 1820. Important racing centres were Durban, Pietermaritzburg and later Kimberley and Johannesburg, meetings in the latter city dating from 1887. The South African Jockey Club was set up in Port Elizabeth in 1882. Although racing in Durban took place as far back as 1852, the Durban July Handicap, today recognised as South Africa's most important race, dates back to the reconstitution of the Durban Turf Club, 1897, the Gold Fields Handicap in Johannesburg to December 1887 and the South African Derby to 1885. In Rhodesia horse-racing started almost simultaneously with the occupation by the Pioneer Column in 1890.

Horses. Horses are not indigenous to Southern Africa and were indeed so unknown to the Zulus and other tribes that on first seeing mounted men they believed that rider and animal formed a single creature. They were introduced at a very early stage, the first shipment to the Cape from Batavia taking place in 1653, within a year of the landing of van Riebeeck. As the local conditions had a deteriorating effect on the animals from Java, better stock was brought to South Africa in 1689, which laid the foundation of the famous Cape breed soon known throughout the world. In 1769 the first exports opened a market for remounts, particularly in India, which continued into modern times. The arrival of the horse-loving British garrison at the end of the 18th century gave a great stimulus to breeding and some magnificent pedigree animals were introduced. The farms of the Hantam area of the Cape

were particularly famous. Governor Lord Charles Somerset not only encouraged horse-racing but at his own expense introduced many excellent stallions. Some of the local tribes developed a liking for horses and stole animals of quality from farms near the frontier. This accounted largely for the evolution of the high-grade Basuto pony, which became noted for its hardiness and strength. The Basuto today are themselves a nation of horsemen. Despite the triumph of the motor-car and the disappearance of cavalry, South Africa still has well over a million horses, more than half in the Cape Province, while Basutoland has approximately 100,000. Encouragement is given to the improvement of the breed in that country by the provision of stallions at purely nominal prices. *See also* HORSE-RACING and HORSE SICKNESS.

Horse Sickness. Serious disease, scientifically known as *Oedema Mycosis*, and in Afrikaans, as Perde Siekte. Reported in Southern Africa since 1719. In Victorian times it was found in most warmer parts of the sub-continent in an epizootic form, particularly between December and May. The death rate was high and animals which recovered, called 'salted,' commanded a high price, on account of their resistance to reinfection. During a single outbreak in the Cape over 70,000 horses died. Research was first carried out on Horse Sickness in the 1890's by Dr. Alexander Edington, Director of the Colonial Bacteriological Institute, who reported that the disease was 'due to the presence in the blood of the vegetative spores of a micro-organism of a fungoid character.' In recent times Horse Sickness was combated, first by the serum-virus method of inoculation, and after 1930 by the 'neurotropic' mouse-brain vaccine developed at Onderstepoort Laboratories (q.v.), which has been most successful.

Horse-Whim

Horse-Whim. Large, wooden wheel, used in early diamond-mining for hauling up buckets containing diamondiferous soil.

Hospitals. Control of hospitals in South Africa falls under the Department of Public Health, but their administration is normally vested in the various Provincial Councils.

The first hospital in the country was established by Jan van Riebeeck in 1652 for the treatment of scurvy-stricken sailors and travellers from passing ships bound for the Indies. The oldest existing institution is the New Somerset Hospital in Cape Town, founded in 1859, while the largest single institution is the Baragwanath Native Hospital in Johannesburg, with over 2,000 beds. Other large hospitals are the Johannesburg General (1,200 beds) and Groote Schuur with over 800 beds, which are used for teaching by the universities of the Witwatersrand and of Cape Town. Other well-known hospitals are the Addington Hospital in Durban, founded in 1878, Grey's Hospital (over 800 beds) in Pietermaritzburg, the Provincial Hospital at Port Elizabeth, the Grey Hospital at King William's Town, the Kimberley Hospital, the Pretoria Hospital and, in recent years, the Karl

Bremer Hospital, erected to serve the northern suburbs of Cape Town, and to provide a teaching hospital for the medical faculty of the University of Stellenbosch. The new Tygerberg Hospital took over this function and has 1,500 beds.

A chain of special hospitals has also been provided for the treatment of tuberculosis, one of the best known being the Nelspoort Sanatorium in the Karroo. The largest institution for lepers is outside Pretoria, patients formerly on Robben Island and at other centres having been transferred there. There are mental hospitals at Valkenberg in the Cape Town suburb of Observatory, at Fort England, Grahamstown, Port Alfred, Fort Beaufort, Queenstown, Pietermaritzburg, Krugersdorp, Pretoria, Bloemfontein, Maitland and Potchefstroom.

In Rhodesia hospitals fall under the Ministry of Health. The best-known institutions are in Salisbury and Bulawayo, both of them originally conducted by nuns.

Hotagterklip. Village near Bredasdorp, Cape Province. Population: 220, including 10 Whites.

Hottentot. One of the aboriginal races in the Cape. The origin of the name is believed to be a corruption of their clicking sounds. A yellow race of Mongolian appearance, with high cheekbones, they were fond of cattle and were nomads by instinct. Pure Hottentots have now become extremely scarce, having been decimated by outbreaks of smallpox in the 18th century and later by interbreeding with their neighbours.

Hottentot (*Pachymetopon blochi*). Fish often found off South-West Africa to Table Bay, False Bay and Agulhas Bank, occasionally as far as Algoa Bay. About 18 inches long. One of the Breams (q.v.).

Hottentot Fig. *See* SOUR FIG.

Hottentot God or Mantis (Mantidae). Insect of which there are over 100 South African species, simulating flowers, dry leaves and sticks. Related to grasshopper.

Hottentots Holland. Range of mountains on the northern side of False Bay, near Cape Town. Rises to a height of 5,000 feet.

Houhoek. Hamlet near Elgin in the Western Cape Province. Leading fruit-growing area. The name is explained—either as 'The Corner where Chopping is done,' or 'The Corner where one Halts.'

Household, John Goodman. South African pioneer of aviation. Born in England on December 9, 1845, he emigrated to Natal in 1864 and settled at Karkloof, where, in addition to farming, he carried out experiments on gliders. These culminated (1871) in the construction of a machine with which he succeeded in taking off from the top of the kloof, flying the full width of the valley, approximately three-quarters of a mile. This was remarkable owing to the fact that it preceded by many years the feat of Lilienthal in Germany. Portions of Household's machine, which was constructed of bamboo and silk, were preserved long after, but, owing to lack of encouragement, he never continued his experiments. Household died in Pietermaritzburg on March 13, 1906.

Housing. Organised housing schemes in South Africa date from the period immediately after World War I, when money from public funds was made available for the first time. The original Housing Act, No. 35 of 1920, gave local authorities permission to borrow funds from the Treasury at low rates of interest, restrictions being applied to the size and cost of the residences to be put up. Operations were carried on under a Central Housing Board, and large projects, combined with slum clearance, were completed in Bloemfontein and Cape Town. As the development of the country caught up with the needs of householders, the demand dwindled, but it never died away completely, the needs of non-Europeans remaining urgent.

One highly successful project, the Citizen's Housing League, was also started about the same time by Bishop S. H. Lavis of Cape Town. By erecting thousands of homes in the suburbs of Epping, Thornton and elsewhere, it became one of the largest and most successful property owners in the country, all profits going back into fresh development.

Renewed demands for houses developed throughout South Africa during World War II, with the result that in 1944 the Central Housing Board was replaced by the National Housing and Planning Commission, to which large funds were made available at very low rates of interest. Use was also made of the existing Building Societies and persons in fixed employment could secure almost the entire cost of their future homes at purely nominal rates of interest. Further provision was made for the poorer community through sub-economic schemes and long-term periods for repayment of up to 40 years. Housing schemes for ex-volunteers received particular attention from the authorities, including the use of several former army camps.

Recent years have witnessed an intensified housing problem for the black and coloured races. Because of the industrial revolution through which the Union was passing, hundreds of thousands of Africans found their way to the cities, where enormous squatters' camps grew at an alarming rate. After 1955 a concerted attack upon this problem, in which over 100,000 houses were built (notably in and around Johannesburg), greatly relieved the situation. Apart from simple houses for Africans, built on mass-production principles and costing about £200 apiece, large numbers of rather more pretentious homes have been constructed, as well as blocks of flats, etc.

In Rhodesia the wave of immigration after World War I also produced an acute housing crisis, which the Government strove temporarily to remedy by permitting the construction of homes from pisé de terre, a material with only a limited life but of low cost. More recently this gave way to an ambitious loan programme, largely earmarked for the African races.

Hout Bay. Inlet on the Atlantic side of the Cape Peninsula; noted in the first days of Dutch settlement for the wealth of natural timber growing on neighbouring hills, which inspired its name 'Hout,' meaning 'wood' in Dutch. The place was fortified by the Dutch East India Company on account of its strategic importance. In recent years it has attained prominence as a fishing harbour, while manganese was for a while mined near by. Famous for its beautiful scenery, Hout Bay is a popular resort for holiday-makers and artists. Population: 3,787, including 1,106 Whites.

Houtperd (Wooden Horse). Invented by the Hottentots to help them cross rivers in flood. It comprised a block of wood about 6 feet long, with a peg at each end, and was used as a raft.

Howes, Dulcie (Mrs. Dulcie Cronwright). South African ballet producer and teacher. Born in Cape Town in 1909, studied in London under Margaret Craske and worked with Pavlova, Karsavina and Ninette de Valois. In 1934 she established the Cape Town University Ballet, of which she remained the director. She achieved outstanding successes down the years, training many dancers who later gained fame abroad.

Howick. Township in Natal, 18 miles from Pietermaritzburg, noted for its magnificent waterfall, on the Umgeni River, which drops 364 feet in a single leap. A rubber factory operates near by. The village was established in the 1880's. Population: 10,900, including 2,100 Whites.

Howick of Glendale, Lord (formerly **Sir Evelyn Baring**). British administrator. Born in England September 29, 1903, and educated at Winchester and Oxford. Entered the British Civil Service in 1926 and from 1929 to 1932 was Secretary to the Agent-General for India in South Africa. After retiring from the Indian Civil Service through ill-health in 1934, was Governor of Southern Rhodesia from 1942 until 1944. From 1944 to 1951 he was High Commissioner for the United Kingdom in South Africa and Administrator of the High Commission Territories. In 1961–1962 he was Chairman of the Colonial Development Corporation.

Hoy, Sir William Wilson. First General Manager of the South African Railways. Born in Kinrosshire, Scotland, in 1868, he entered the service of the North British Railway Company at the early age of 12 in 1880, and 9 years later emigrated to South Africa to join the Cape Government Railways. There he rose to be Chief Traffic Manager in 1895 and representative of the Cape Government Railways in Johannesburg in the following year. Upon the extension of the line to Bulawayo, he was stationed in that town for a while, and later served in Kimberley, Port Elizabeth and Bloemfontein. During the South African War he worked for the Imperial Military Railways and, after the setting up of the civil administration in 1902, became General Manager for the Central South African Railways. In 1910 Hoy became first General Manager of the unified system covering the whole country. During World War I he was Director of Military Railways in the South West African campaign, holding the rank of colonel. He retited to Hermanus, for the advancement of which town he was largely responsible, and where he died in 1930.

Huberta. Celebrated hippopotamus which suddenly appeared in Zululand towards the end of 1928, and made its way across the Tugela into Natal. For 2½ years it wandered round that area, appearing also in the middle of Durban, and running into many entertaining adventures reported in detail in the press. At first the animal, considered to be a male, was jocularly given the name of Hubert. After travelling south, with deviations, for nearly 1,000 miles, the hippo was accidentally shot near King William's Town by a farmer in April 1931. It was then discovered to be a female and she was posthumously rechristened Huberta. Her adventures were reported not only throughout South Africa but in the overseas press.

Huddleston, Father Trevor (Bishop of Masasi). Anglican priest and writer. Born on June 15, 1913, he studied at Lancing, Oxford and Wells, taking Holy Orders in 1937. He joined the Community of the Resurrection in 1941, for whom he came to South Africa. Working mainly in the Johannesburg slum suburb of Sophiatown and in the Anglican mission at Orlando, he became an outspoken objector to many steps taken by the authorities, notably the removal of Sophiatown's black residents to new quarters, which led him to write the best-selling book *Naught for your Comfort*. In 1949 he became Provincial in South Africa for the Community of the Resurrection, and remained till 1955. Returning to the English headquarters of the Community at Mirfield, he was appointed Prior in 1958 and Bishop of Masasi in Tanganyika in 1960. Became Bishop of Stepney October 1968.

Huggard, Sir Walter Clarence. Judge of the South African High Commission Territories, and Legal Adviser

to the High Commissioner. Born in Ireland, 1883, he was educated in Belfast and at Dublin University, where he was called to the Bar in 1907. Entering the Colonial Service, he was stationed in Nigeria, West Indies, Kenya and Malaya. There he rose to be Chief Justice of the Strait Settlements. In 1937, a year after his retirement, he was appointed Judge of the High Courts of Basutoland, Bechuanaland and Swaziland. Died June 21, 1957.

Huggins, Sir Godfrey. *See* MALVERN.

Huguenot. Originally a separate village, named Lady Grey Bridge, established in the 1850's and named after the wife of Governor Sir George Grey (q.v.); it is now absorbed into the town of Paarl, with a railway station also called Huguenot. Important industries, including distilleries, are located there.

Huguenot College. Established 1873 in Wellington, Cape Province, as Huguenot Seminary, institution for higher education of girls, by Miss Anna Bliss and Miss Abby Ferguson, who came to the Cape from Mt. Holyoke College, U.S.A. The school, encouraged by the Rev. Andrew Murray (q.v.) and the Dutch Reformed Church, was patronised by leading families; became the only Women's College in South Africa and later part of the University of South Africa. In recent years has been turned into a Training College for Social Workers by the Dutch Reformed Church.

Huguenot Memorial. Erected in 1948 near French Hoek, Cape Province, to commemorate the immigration of the Huguenots to the Cape in the late 17th century. Designed by J. C. Jongens, it is built of Paarl granite, with figures by Coert Steynberg (q.v.).

Huguenots. Although a number of French Protestant refugees, obliged to leave their native land through persecution, had entered the service of the Dutch East India Company as early as

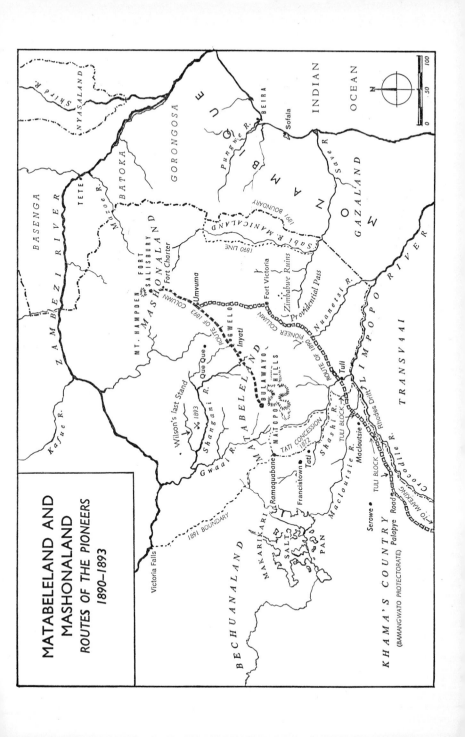

MATABELELAND AND MASHONALAND
ROUTES OF THE PIONEERS
1890–1893

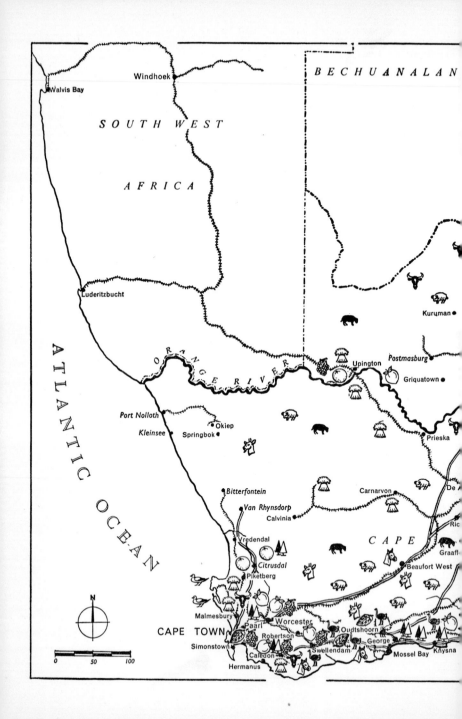

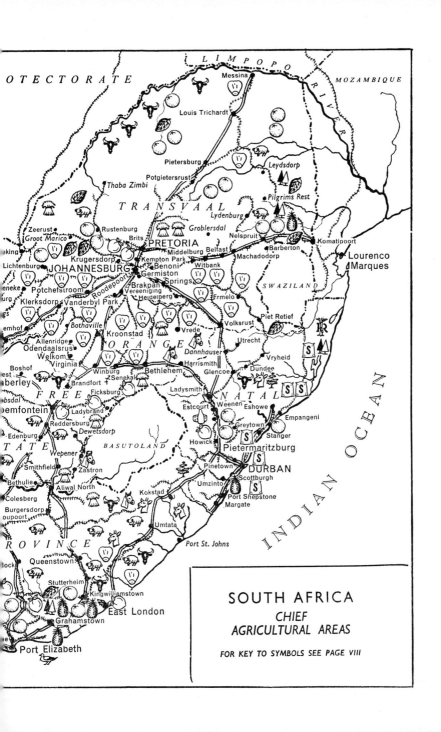

SOUTH AFRICA
*CHIEF
AGRICULTURAL AREAS*

FOR KEY TO SYMBOLS SEE PAGE VIII

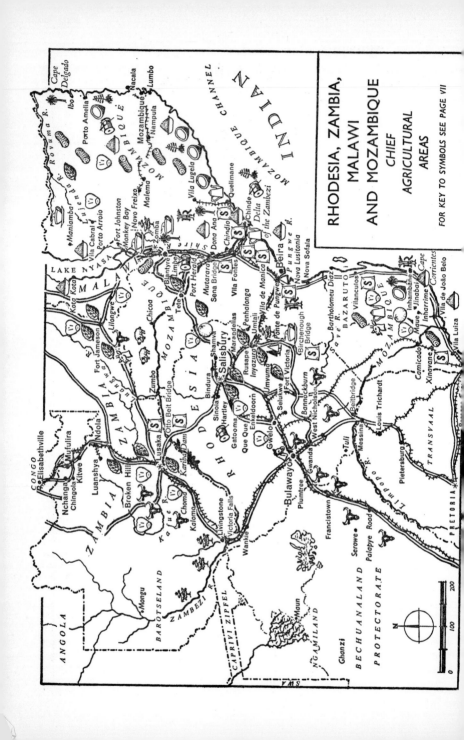

RHODESIA, ZAMBIA, MALAWI AND MOZAMBIQUE

CHIEF AGRICULTURAL AREAS

FOR KEY TO SYMBOLS SEE PAGE VII

1607 and had found their way to the Cape of Good Hope, the real immigration took place only after the revocation by Louis XIV of the Edict of Nantes, which had for about a century guaranteed religious freedom to this community. More than 500,000 fled. Only a very small percentage—about 176—came to South Africa, but their contribution to its development was great. The first refugees sailed on December 31, 1687, and the last in the following April. The Dutch East India Company had approved of giving them help and Governor Simon van der Stel (q.v.), anxious to build up the white population at the Cape, welcomed them warmly. Accustomed to wine-growing and intensive agriculture, they were given land in the area now known as Fransch Hoek, where they worshipped under their own pastor, Simond. The French language, discouraged by the authorities, died out within a generation or two. By that time the Huguenots had intermarried with the local Dutch and German families. Many of the best-known names in South Africa, including Malan, De Villiers, Du Plessis, Du Preez, Theron, Joubert, Retief, Marais, Roux and Lombard, etc., came to the Cape in this way.

Huilbos or Kajatehout, African Wattle (*Peltophorum africanum* Sond.). Tall ornamental tree with yellow flowers and acacia-like leaves. The wood is used for handles and the bark medicinally. Northern Transvaal. *See* PEA, WILD SWEET.

Huilebalken. Professional mourners (literally weepers) engaged in the early days in the Cape to attend funerals. The last important occasion when this happened was at the burial of Lady Somerset, wife of Lord Charles Somerset in 1815. *See also* TROP-SLUITERS.

Hukweveld. Name applied to the western half of the Caprivi Zipfel (q.v.).

Hulett, Sir James Liege. Natal industrialist, pioneer and statesman.

Born in England, May 17, 1838, and emigrated to Natal in 1857; began farming near Nonoti, experimenting with arrowroot, cotton, coffee and maize, finally concentrating on the production of sugar, in which he soon took the lead. At Kearsney (q.v.) he also pioneered the growing of tea. Elected to the Legislative Council in 1883, he rose to be Speaker of the House and Minister of Native Affairs under Responsible Government. He established the firm, J. L. Hulett & Sons Ltd., in 1892 for the production of tea, but soon included sugar growing and manufacturing. Since the first mill was opened in 1903 at Tinley Manor, operations have expanded enormously. One of Hulett's major claims to fame is the opening up of Zululand to sugar production, which he began, by agreement with the Natal Government in 1905. The first large refinery in South Africa was set up at Rossburgh, near Durban in 1911, and ultimately taken over by a separate concern. Upon the establishment of Union, Sir Liege Hulett, who had meanwhile moved to Durban, became a Senator. He died in 1928.

Hull, Henry Charles. South African Cabinet Minister. Born in 1860; qualified as a solicitor and settled on the Witwatersrand. Was a member of the Reform Committee and found guilty of treason after the Jameson Raid. During the South African War he served in the forces, and later entered the Transvaal Legislative Council, strongly opposing the introduction of Chinese labour. Under Responsible Government, Hull served as Treasurer in the Transvaal Cabinet, being one of the delegates to the South African National Convention. In the first Union Cabinet Hull became Minister of Finance. He died in 1932.

Humansdorp. Town in the Cape Province, founded in 1845 and named after the owner of the original farm, Mr. Human. Fruit-growing centre.

Population: 4,000, including 2,000 Whites.

Hume, David. Early Cape traveller. Born in Scotland, 1796, he reached the Cape in 1817. As a trader, he found his way to Bechuanaland in 1825 and made his headquarters in the present village of Kuruman. He enjoyed the high respect of the natives and when in 1829 the Rev. J. Archbell arrived, intending to call on Moselekatze, it was Hume who brought him there safely. Inspired by reports of gold inland, Hume trekked on beyond the Limpopo into what is now Rhodesia. Occasionally he went down to the Cape and in 1834 brought a consignment of ivory to Grahamstown. Upon his return he acted as guide to Sir Andrew Smith (q.v.) when he went to the Magaliesberg, into the country of Moselekatze. He died in 1863 and his son, William Hume, became a prominent citizen of Port Elizabeth, the suburb of Humewood being named after him.

Humpata. Official name San Januario de Humpata. Settlement in the south of Angola, formed by the Thirstland Boers who trekked from the Transvaal and arrived about 1877. Most of the settlement was abandoned about 1926, when the survivors and their descendants moved to South West Africa. *See* THIRSTLAND TREK.

Hurley, Archbishop Denis Eugene. Catholic Archbishop of Durban. Born at Cape Town, November 9, 1915, and educated at St. Thomas's Boys School, Newcastle, and St. Charles' College, Pietermaritzburg. On entering the priesthood, he took his degree at the Gregorian University in Rome. In 1940 he became curate at Emmanuel Cathedral in Durban, and in 1951 Archbishop.

Huss, Father Bernard. Catholic missionary and social worker. Born in Germany and came to Natal in 1894. After service in the Drakensberg, became deeply interested in Africans.

Established and built up St. Francis College, Mariannhill Monastery (q.v.), where he was principal for 15 years and trained converts in agriculture. He wrote several books, was a pioneer of co-operative societies for black farmers and took a firm stand against communism by setting up Catholic African Unions. He was highly respected by all communities and was often consulted by the Government. Died August 5, 1948.

Hutchinson. Village in the Karroo, founded, in 1885, as Victoria, West Road, but renamed in honour of Governor Sir Walter Hely-Hutchinson (q.v.) in 1901. It is a junction for branch lines running towards the wheat areas of Zak River and Calvinia. Population: 800, including 300 Whites.

Hutton, Frederick Augustus. Judge of Eastern Districts Bench. Born in Bedford, Cape, on June 15, 1862, educated in his home town and at Victoria College, Stellenbosch, where he took his B.A. in 1883. He joined the Civil Service and in 1885 became registrar to Judge C. G. Maasdorp. After taking his LL.B. in 1892, he was admitted and practised in Grahamstown until he rose to the Bench there in 1913. In 1922 he was transferred to Kimberley and retired in 1932. He died on February 15, 1940.

Hyaena. Nocturnal and carnivorous mammal related to the wolf. Coarse, spotted or striped fur; the shorter hind-legs add to its ungainliness. A scavenger and a coward; now probably extinct in the Cape. *See* MAMMALS.

Hyobanche. *See* NEMESIA.

Hyracium. Substance made from the excreta of Dassies (q.v.) found on the edges of cliffs inhabited by these animals. It has valuable medicinal qualities and is used in the preparation of drugs for certain kidney complaints. This was known to the early Boer settlers who referred to it as Dassie Pis.

I

Ibis (Plegadidae). Bird related to the Storks, but smaller, with shorter legs and long down-curved bill. Only two species are common in South Africa. The Sacred Ibis (of Ancient Egypt, where its mummies have been found in tombs) has a bare head and shiny black, bare neck, in sharp contrast to the white body and black plumes over the tail. A scavenger of muddy and sandy shores, common all down the coast of the continent, though rare in Egypt today. The Green Ibis or Hadada is a veld, not a water bird, hunting insects in small parties, with loud cries, from which the second name is derived. Nests in trees, usually overlooking a stream. Dull olive-grey, with bronze and pink sheen.

Ibo. Seaport and settlement near Mozambique. Situated on an island in the Cape Delgado archipelago, the name was already known in the 17th century; it was formerly the centre of slave trade, to suppress which, forts were erected in the 18th century. Today Ibo is an administrative and trading centre. Population: 4,500 (about 40 Whites).

Ichaboe Island. Small island off the coast of South West Africa, exploited for its guano deposits. It was annexed to the Cape in 1867.

I.C.U. Popular abbreviation for Industrial and Commercial Workers Union. An organisation of Bantu labour, formed in Cape Town, 1919, by Clements Kadalie. It aimed 'to do for the African labourer what the South African Trades Union Congress did for the European worker.' Beginning with 24 members, it soon spread throughout the country and by 1924 numbered over 100,000. Its main organiser was Allison Wessel George Champion (q.v.). Affiliated to the International Trades Union Congress

in Amsterdam, the I.C.U. enjoyed such prestige abroad that Kadalie in 1927 paid an official visit to Britain to study Trades Unionism there. One result was the importation of a professional organiser, Mr. (later Senator) W. G. Ballinger from Scotland. By this time dissension had set in, and both Champion and Kadalie started independent movements. The I.C.U. gradually disintegrated, and, save for the Natal offshoot, disappeared after 1930.

I.D.B. Abbreviation for 'Illicit Diamond Buying.' The name came about largely as a result of the adoption, in 1882, of the Diamond Trade Act, which made it illegal for anybody except a licensed buyer to trade in precious stones. Its provisions have become increasingly severe, so that today it is an offence to be in possession of uncut stones without proper explanation. At one time as much as a quarter of all the stones found at Kimberley were stolen and passed through the hands of the illicit diamond buyers. In recent years I.D.B. has had a considerable revival on the alluvial diggings and in Namaqualand. The traditional place of punishment for an I.D.B. convict was the breakwater in Cape Town.

Idutywa. Town in Transkei. Population: 1,299, including 384 Whites.

Igusi. Variety of timber found in Rhodesia, particularly in the Gwaai Forest (q.v.) and noted for its resistance to ants, for which reason it is largely used in building.

Ila. *See* MASHUKULUMBWE.

I.L.H. Abbreviation for Imperial Light Horse (q.v.).

Ilibandhla. Swazi tribal council advising the Paramount Chief.

Illicit Diamond Buying. *See* I.D.B.

Illovo. Sugar milling centre and sea-side resort about 23 miles south of Durban. It consists of two distinct settlements—Illovo Beach, where the bathing beach is located, and Illovo River, near the large sugar mill. The name 'Illovo' means 'Welcome' in Zulu.

Illovo River. Rises in the Byrne Forests and enters the Indian Ocean south of Durban. Tributary is the Umquahumbi.

Ilmenite. Ore of Titanium found near Umgababa, Natal. *See* RUTILE and URANIUM.

Imbokodvo. Pro-Government party in Swaziland, supporting Sobhuza II (q.v.).

Immelmann, Max. German air ace. Born in Dresden on September 21, 1890, he came to South Africa as a child and grew up in Uitenhage, Cape Province. He returned to Germany to join the Air Force there and became a national figure after 15 victories on the Western Front. By an extraordinary coincidence, he was shot down in July, 1916, by a South African, Captain G. R. McCubbin, serving with the Royal Flying Corps. Major Allister Miller (q.v.) was selected to drop a wreath on the grave of a gallant opponent.

Immigration. Organised immigration to South Africa began with the landing of Jan van Riebeeck's (q.v.) party in 1652. To supplement the shortage of women, groups of young girls were brought from orphanages in Amsterdam. In 1687 and 1688 came the Huguenot (q.v.) colonists. Further large-scale projects had to wait for the British régime, which witnessed the immigration of the Moodie parties to Swellendam, Clanwilliam, etc., in 1817 (*see* BENJAMIN MOODIE). In the 1840's German settlers were brought to Natal by Jonas Bergtheil (q.v.) and by Thomas Byrne (*see* BYRNE SETTLERS). Later groups included the German Legion (q.v.) on

the Eastern Cape frontier after the Crimean War, and other German immigrants in 1858 and 1874. Hundreds of settlers came to South Africa to recover from lung affections in Victorian times, among them Cecil John Rhodes (q.v.). This led indirectly to the adoption of immigration laws and health restrictions. In the present century immigration to South Africa has fluctuated considerably. The Union Immigration Act unified the restrictions on entry to the country from 1913. It was modified by the Quota Act, heavily reducing the inflow from Eastern Europe, in 1930. In 1935, when Nazi persecution broke out in Germany, an Immigration Board with wide powers of selection was established. After World War II encouragement was given to immigration by General Smuts (q.v.), special ships being chartered to convey newcomers, until his resignation from the premiership brought a reversal of policy. In recent times fresh encouragement has been given to settlers from Britain and the Continent of Europe, where selection commissions have been sent. South Africa has also become a member of an international body dealing with these matters. Free passages are provided for approved applicants. A welcome is also offered to Whites displaced in Tropical and Central Africa by the advent of Black Governments there. In its earlier days Rhodesia made repeated efforts to encourage immigration, including some by the Salvation Army, but was handicapped by lack of funds and opportunities. Since World War II a vigorous policy has brought a spectacular rise in the population, though for political reasons the number of arrivals has declined in recent years.

Impala or **Rooibok** (*Aepyceros melampus*). South African antelope, now protected and mostly limited to the Eastern Transvaal, Rhodesia and Mozambique. A graceful animal, it stands about 3 feet at the shoulder. Its agility is famous, and leaps of 28 feet have been noted. The male alone bears beautiful curly horns. Coat bright chestnut red, white underneath. *See* MAMMALS.

Impala Line. Established in 1964 jointly by West German and South African interests to operate a regular service between South Africa and the Far East. It began operations with three new refrigerated vessels belonging to the Hansa Line, trading with Japan.

Imparani, Treaty of. Signed in March 1866, making peace between the Orange Free State and the Basuto chief Molapo.

Impendle. Village in Natal. Population: 150, including 40 Whites.

Imperial Light Horse. South African military unit, founded on September 21, 1899. Equipment of original force largely paid for by Alfred Beit (q.v.). Fought in South African War, in Zulu War 1906, World War I (South West Africa), Rand Revolt 1922, World War II (Abyssinia and North Africa).

Imperial Military Railways. Official name given, during the South African War, to the railway system captured from the South African Republic and Orange Free State in the course of hostilities (Netherlands South African Railway Company and the Orange Free State Railways). They were placed under the control of Col. Sir E. Percy Girouard (q.v.) and later absorbed into the Central South African Railways.

Imports. *See* TRADE.

Impumbe. Long tuft of hair, often growing to a height of 3 or 4 feet, worn by the Mashukulumbwe in Rhodesia (q.v.).

Inboeking. Custom formerly followed in the Transvaal, by which children captured from the local tribes were apprenticed to burghers. This gave rise to considerable criticism, to the effect that it was a form of slavery. It was ultimately abandoned.

Incomati. Settlement in Mozambique near Lourenço Marques, noted for its large sugar estates. *See* XINAVANE.

Indaba. Meeting of native councillors with the chief. The word signifies 'news.' Has become a South African idiom.

Independence Delegation. Name given to a group of Nationalists who were despatched by their followers in 1919 to the Peace Conference to ask for the grant of republican independence to the Union. It was led by General J. B. M. Hertzog and comprised Dr. Hjalmar Reitz, Dr. E. G. Jansen, N. C. Havenga, Senator A. D. W. Wolmarans, Dr. D. F. Malan, A. T. Spies and F. W. Beyers, with Dr. Gey van Pittius as Secretary. Owing to shipping difficulties the delegation had to travel via the U.S.A., where they were entertained by members of Congress, then to England, where they failed to meet Mr. Lloyd George, the Premier. They therefore went to Paris but were equally unsuccessful. The return journey was accomplished only by travelling first from Europe to Java, and then back to South Africa. The delegates were absent for about 7 months.

Independent Fiscal. Post in the service of the Dutch East India Company created in March, 1688, to supervise the work of their servants, and responsible solely to the supreme authorities in Amsterdam. They sat on the Council of Policy in each colony, had direct access to all records and accounts and were charged with the task of preventing corruption. First holder of the post at the Cape was Cornelis Johan Simons, appointed in 1689. They were not very successful in their work, but the post was not abolished until 1793.

Indians. The importation of Indians into South Africa was due to the labour shortages on the sugar plantations of

Natal, which became acute during the 1850's. Owing to the unwillingness of the local Zulus and other tribes to work there, the Government of the Colony of Natal began negotiations with the authorities in India, and after an enabling law had been passed in 1859, the first indentured workers arrived in 1860. Their numbers increased comparatively slowly, the total up to 1874 being barely 5,000, but the obvious improvement in the prospects of the sugar industry led to a steady increase in demand and to a corresponding rise in the number of arrivals. By 1876 there were 6,787 Indians in Natal, but by 1884 there were 27,206 and by 1891 there were 35,763.

Although the first imported labourers were meant to stay for only 3 years, this period was later increased to 5 years. Wages were fixed at 10s. a month, rising at the rate of 1s. per month for each year, besides free rations and housing, estimated to cost about 8s. a month.

After the expiry of the indentures, most of the immigrants preferred to remain in Natal, which produced the nucleus of the so-called 'Free Indians,' reinforced by the importation of women, and by an extremely high birth rate. By degrees the Indians made their appearance in other provinces, particularly in the Transvaal, where they arrived about 1881. A substantial immigration began also to the Cape. In the Orange Free State, because of a strict ban, there are virtually none.

While the majority of Indians continued to work in agriculture, others became prominent as traders towards the end of the 19th century. Their modest standards of living and money-making abilities aroused antagonism, and led to the imposition of restrictive legislation, which in the Transvaal, under the Kruger government, took the form of a prohibition on the ownership of land. Litigation on some of these issues led to the arrival in 1895 of M. K. Gandhi (q.v.), who,

on making his home in South Africa, began the struggle for greater freedom, in which the support of the Indian as well as of the Imperial Government was invoked, the dispute acquiring an interest extending far beyond the limits of this country.

The visit of the well-known Indian nationalist leader Gokhale in 1909 strengthened the opposition to restrictive laws, and from 1911 onwards a passive resistance campaign, inspired by Gandhi, took effect. Importations came to an end in the same year, when the last shipment of 500 labourers was despatched to Natal. Thenceforward encouragement was given to repatriation, though the numbers of those returning to Asia never became impressive, and the vast majority of the population were of South African birth. In 1911 the number of Indians in Natal was 149,791. Thirty years later, in 1941, this had grown to 239,000. The 1951 census gave 366,664 in the Union, while the 1960 census showed no less than 477,414, of whom 394,237 were in Natal (as against 274,240 Whites), 20,243 in the Cape Province, 62,918 in the Transvaal and 16 in the Orange Free State. The Indian population is mainly of Hindu origin, though large numbers of Moslems are also to be found.

The imposition of fresh restrictions, notably the Class Areas Bill introduced in 1924, aggravated ill-feeling, but repeated efforts were made to provide a friendly settlement. In 1926 a deputation from India arrived to investigate the question at first hand, and the following year the Hon. Srinavasa Sastri became the first Indian Agent-General in the Union. Efforts were also made to improve educational facilities and to encourage a movement away from purely trading activities. The Indians themselves have been organised into several different groups (the most important being the South African Indian Congress), among whom dissension and rivalry exist.

Serious riots, which involved considerable loss of life, occurred in Durban in January 1949, when Africans attacked local Indians. A large number of houses were burnt and over a hundred killed. A Government Commission endeavoured to find the cause, but its report was inconclusive. Fresh protests were aroused in India through the introduction in 1950 of the Group Areas Act, in consequence of which the diplomatic representation of India in the Union was withdrawn in June, 1954.

The number of Indians in Rhodesia, Malawi and Zambia is estimated at about 35,000, of whom about 15,000 are in Rhodesia and about 12,000 in Malawi. *See* NATIONAL INDIAN COUNCIL, UNIVERSITY COLLEGE FOR INDIANS and SOUTH AFRICAN INDIAN COUNCIL.

Induna. Senior Councillor in a native tribe, particularly among the Zulus and Xosas.

Industrial and Commercial Workers Union. Bantu Trades Union. *See* I.C.U.

Industrial Development Corporation. Government-sponsored organisation set up in the Union under the Industrial Development Act No. 22 of 1940, with the purpose of encouraging and financing manufacturing and similar undertakings. Its original capital was R10,000,000, of which only R1,000,000 was issued; the first Chairman was Dr. H. J. van der Bijl (q.v.), with Dr. H. J. van Eck as Deputy Chairman and Managing Director. Since then the capital has grown until its total investment is over R300,000,000, including many of the most important concerns in the country.

Industries. *See* MANUFACTURES.

Indwe. Town in the Cape Province. Founded in 1867 as a coal mining centre, exploiting the low-grade local deposits which could not compete against those of Natal and the Transvaal. Now chiefly engaged in dairying and farming. The name is derived from the native name for the crane, a species of bird which flourished there. Population: 3,120, including 820 Whites.

Ingogo. Heights on the frontier of Natal and the Transvaal, and scene of a battle in the First Boer War, also known as Schuin's Hoogte, fought on February 8, 1881. The British troops were under Lieutenant-Colonel Ashburnham, and those of the South African Republic under Commandant Nicolaas Smit. The British lost 7 officers and 69 men, besides 3 officers and 64 wounded. The Boer casualties were 8 killed and 6 wounded.

Ingubu. Name used by Africans in Natal for second-hand garments. The word was derived from an expression meaning 'skin.'

Ingwavuma. Village in Northern Natal, near Mozambique border. Administrative centre. Population: 340, including 70 Whites.

Inhaca (also known as **Inyack**). Island in Delagoa Bay, 8 miles long and 3 miles wide. Chosen for its isolation from hostile natives as the earliest Portuguese settlement in Delagoa Bay. Today it is used by fishermen and also as a site for a Biological Research Station, operated by the University of the Witwatersrand in conjunction with the Portuguese authorities.

Inhambane. Seaport in Mozambique and principal harbour of Gazaland. Centre of important agricultural district. The bay has been known since 1498, when it was discovered by Vasco da Gama. Development, however, only began in 1890. Population: 70,000, including 900 Whites.

Inkblom. *See* NEMESIA.

Inkosi. Zulu name for a chief; used as a term of respect to a European and to a superior of his own race.

Inkosikazi. Zulu term of respect to a woman, applied to the wife of a chief or to a white woman.

Inkruip Plaas (literally 'Creeping-in Farm'). A farm established in the early days on a piece of ground, the neighbouring owners of which were in dispute about their boundaries. In this way valuable properties were often secured. Compare Uitvalgrond (q.v.).

Innes, Dr. Robert Thorburn Aytoun. South African astronomer. Born in Edinburgh, 1861, he was educated at Inverness. He took up astronomy as a boy and, despite great handicaps, rose to international distinction. Originally in the liquor trade, he settled in Australia, where he gave up a flourishing business in order to concentrate on science. He arrived in South Africa in 1896 as an assistant at the Royal Observatory, Cape Town, to Sir David Gill. Upon the establishment of the Transvaal Observatory, 1903, in Johannesburg, he was appointed Director, and was responsible for the installation of the famous 26" telescope there. He discovered the star nearest to the earth, known as Proxima Centauri, and did important research on star-streaming, the structure of the universe and mathematical astronomy. Innes died in 1933.

Innesdale. An independent municipality north of Pretoria, founded soon after the South African War and named after Sir James Rose-Innes, then Chief Justice of the Transvaal and later of the Union. It was incorporated in Pretoria, October 1931.

INSECTS OF SOUTHERN AFRICA
by
DR. S. H. SKAIFE
Cape Town

ALL the major orders of insects are well represented in South Africa. Among the Orthoptera (cockroaches, grasshoppers, crickets and their kin) the most important species is the brown locust, *Locustana pardalina*. Formerly this was a very serious pest, sweeping across the country in huge swarms that did great damage, but nowadays a close watch is kept on its breeding areas in the north-west of the Cape Province, and incipient swarms are attacked and destroyed. Occasionally the red locust, *Nomadacris septemfasciata*, invades the Republic from Central Africa, but this species is also kept more or less under control by an international organisation with its headquarters in the Lake Tanganyika region.

There are about 150 species of termites found in South Africa, belonging to the order Isoptera, of which some 1,800 species are known to the world. Two species of primitive, wood-inhabiting termites have been accidentally introduced into the country—the West Indian dry-wood termite, *Cryptotermes brevis*, is a pest in Durban and Port Elizabeth, and the Oriental damp-wood termite, *Coptotermes formosanus*, has established itself in Simonstown. The most harmful native species are the fungus-growing termites, such as *Macrotermes natalensis*, which are found in the warmer areas and do great damage to timber in buildings. The grass-eating termites, *Hodotermes* species and *Trinervitermes* species, are very common and destructive in the grassveld regions.

The large order that includes plant bugs, scale insects and aphides, Hemiptera, includes many serious pests. A number of these are not indigenous but have been introduced from overseas and are now widely spread and well established: these include the Australian bug, *Icerya purchasi*, several scale insects such as the red scale, *Aonidiella aurantii*, and the pernicious scale, *Aspidiotus perniciosus*, some aphides, mealie bugs and others. The aphides, or plant lice, that have been introduced, differ from their relatives in Europe and America in that no males are found among them in South Africa: the more congenial climate here enables the parthenogenetic females to breed continuously throughout the year. Cicadas are common and the shrill song of the males is characteristic of the hot weather.

Among the butterflies and moths, Lepidoptera, there are very many striking and handsome species, such as the Silver-spotted Ghost Moth, *Leto venus*, found in the Knynsa forests, the large Hawk Moths and Emperor Moths, the Swallow-tail, Mother-o'-pearl and Charaxes butterflies, and so on. From an agricultural point of view, however, some of the smaller kinds are far more important because of the damage they do. There is, for example, the army worm, a small dark-coloured caterpillar about an inch long that sometimes appears in countless thousands and devours all the pasturage in large areas. The moth that develops from this caterpillar, *Laphygma exempta*, is about $1\frac{1}{2}$ inches across the outspread wings, with dark brown fore-wings and pale hind-wings. Because the caterpillars appear suddenly in vast numbers and then disappear, they are sometimes spoken of as mystery worms. The Codling Moth, *Cydia pomonella*, is only one of many introduced species that have become serious pests: these include moths (three species), the diamond-back moth, *Plutella maculipennis* (a pest of cabbage plants), the Mediterranean flour moth, *Ephestia kuhniella*, the wax moth, *Galeria mellonella*, the American bollworm, *Chloridea obsoleta*, and many others. The prickly pear moth, *Cactoblastis cactorum*, was deliberately introduced and spread some years ago in the hope that it would control the pest prickly pears, but parasites, diseases and baboons have prevented it

from multiplying sufficiently. Some native moths have turned their attention to cultivated plants and become pests: these include the wattle bagworm, *Acanthopsyche junodi*, the maize stalk borer, *Calamistis fusca*, the fruit-piercing moths, such as *Achaea lienardi*, and others.

Among our butterflies perhaps the most striking phenomenon is that known as Mimicry. Some species, such as the African Monarch, *Danaus chrysippus*, are protected from birds, lizards, frogs and other enemies that might be tempted to eat them by their unpleasant taste and smell. Other species, such as the Mocker Swallowtail, *Papilio dardanus*, are not protected in this way—they are edible. But the Female Mocker Swallowtail resembles the distasteful species so closely that only a trained entomologist can distinguish them. Apparently this close resemblance deceives the insect-eaters into leaving the edible mockers alone. There are no less than five different forms of female Mocker Swallowtails, each of which is similar in colouring, markings and size to a distasteful species. The male mockers are all alike, black and yellow, and are not protected as the females are, because they are not so important.

Beetles, Coleoptera, form an enormous group of several thousand species, with some very large and handsome species among them, our biggest wood-borers, Cerambycidae, reaching a length of nearly 4 inches. The Scarabaeidae, the family that includes the dung beetles, is very well represented because of the great herds of herbivorous mammals that formerly roamed the veld. The numerous pests include the wood-borers, such as the powder-post beetles, *Lyctus* species, and the European house borer, *Hylotrupes bajulus*, the grain weevils, *Sitophilus* species, the leaf-eating beetles, *Lema* species and many others.

Among the flies, Diptera, are many species of great economic importance. The tsetse flies and malaria-carrying mosquitoes, that were mainly responsible for Africa remaining the Dark Continent for so long, are now under control in South Africa. The three species of tsetse flies formerly found in Zululand and the low-veld of the Transvaal have now been almost if not quite eliminated, and the two worst malaria carriers, *Anopheles funestus* and *A. gambiae*, are no longer the menace they were.

Fleas, *Aphaniptera*, are not as abundant as might be expected because our climate is too dry for them. Nevertheless, plague, carried by rat fleas, is endemic over a large part of the country because rodents are so common and their fleas can breed in the sheltered burrows. But this dangerous disease is also well under control nowadays. The jigger flea, *Tunga penetrans*, is found in subtropical areas but is not a serious pest.

Ants, bees and wasps, Hymenoptera, are very numerous. We have something like 400 species of ants in South Africa, more than ten times as many as are found in Britain. The worst pest, however, is not a native ant, but the introduced species, the Argentine ant, *Iridomyrmex humilis*, which found its way to the Cape from South America about 60 years ago and is now widely spread along our south coast. There are no bumble bees in Africa south of the Sahara: their place is taken by the large black and yellow carpenter bees, Xylocopidae, which are solitary and which make their homes in dead logs and branches of trees. Our honey bees consist of races of the common honey bee found elsewhere. The two commonest and most important are known as *Apis mellifica adansoni*, a yellow-banded variety, and *Apis mellifica unicolour*, a black variety that is said to be remarkable in that laying workers among them can produce queens as well as drones.

See also SPIDERS.

Intombi. Bantu name for a young girl or virgin.

Intonga. Bantu name for a fighting stick.

Inyala or **Bastard Kudu** (*Tragelaphus angasi*). Antelope found in the subtropical parts of Southern Africa, particularly from Zululand to Malawi. It is fond of dense and swampy country. A handsome animal, with fairly long, slightly-twisted horns; about 42 inches high at the shoulder; rich brown colour, with a white stripe down the back and others round the barrel. The meat is excellent. *See* MAMMALS.

Inyanga. Holiday resort in the eastern mountains of Rhodesia, noted for its beautiful situation, near the Rhodes Inyanga Estate, now a National Playground and National Park. Cecil Rhodes personally opened up the estate, where he grew apples and many other crops. Close by is the famous Pungwe Gorge, a spectacular canyon through which breaks the Pungwe River. Many relics of ancient civilisations, including the mysterious 'Slave Pits' (q.v.) and the miles of irrigation terracing are to be found in the vicinity.

Inyangani. Highest mountain in Rhodesia, in the Inyanga range on the Eastern border. Height 8,250 feet.

Inyati. Mission Station in Rhodesia, 42 miles from Bulawayo in the Bubi district, of which it is the headquarters. Originally a Matabele kraal, it was opened in 1859 by the Rev. Robert Moffat for the London Missionary Society. Scene of fighting in the Matabele War.

Inyazura. Village in Rhodesia between Salisbury and Umtali. Largely settled by Afrikaans-speaking immigrants from the south. Tobacco and other crops. Population: 200 Whites.

I'Ons, Frederick Timpson. South African artist. Born in Islington, London, in 1802, he showed early gifts as a draughtsman and became a teacher. In 1834 he reached the Cape and settled in Grahamstown, where he made it his task to record the life of the early settlers and of the Natives with whom he came in contact. Although his quarrelsome temperament brought him difficulties and although his work was not of high artistic quality, his vigorous style of painting won him many admirers and he kept going by such devices as teaching drawing and painting theatrical scenery. He went to Kimberley after the discovery of diamonds but failed to make his fortune. He died on December 18, 1887. Today his paintings are in considerable demand.

Ipomoea. *See* POTATO, SWEET.

Irene. Village near Pretoria, founded by Alois Hugo Nellmapius and named by him after his daughter Irene. The place was originally an estate, where Nellmapius carried out numerous experiments with foreign plants and crops, from 1890 onwards. Later it was bought as a model farm by the Republican Government. The village developed after the Boer War, and was notable as the home of General J. C. Smuts, who lived just outside on his farm, Doornkloof. Population: 1,259, including 1,007 Whites.

Iridium. Precious metal found in association with osmium and gold, especially in the Black Reef on the Rand, and sold on a considerable scale. It is used for fountain-pen nibs.

Iris (Iridaceae). A very large and varied family of plants in South Africa, including Watsonia, Babiana, Gladiolus, Ixia, Tulp (Homeria) and Freesia (*see under separate heads*). Chiefly herbaceous plants, with food storage in corms and rhyzomes; leaves swordlike and sheathing; flowers of great beauty of form and colour; perianth six-cleft, often partly tubular, or irregular but symmetrical to a central line; three stamens, ovary inferior, fruit a capsule of three divisions. Plentiful in Cape coastal region where first Europeans found the Hottentots eating many roots of this family. The real Iris type (Moraea) has six, nearly-separate 'petals,' three of which have usually clear guide marks; stigma divided into three, and petal-like, e.g. the tall yellow *Moraea ramosissima* growing in moist places up to 2,500 feet, Western Cape to Humansdorp, and in Natal along the coast. In dense clumps along the river banks in Natal grows also the large White Iris (*Moraea iridoides*), and the Yellow Iris (*Moraea spathaceae*), the flowers of which appear before the leaves and often after a grass fire. The Peacock Flower or Uiltjie (*Moraea villosa*), in its many variegated colours, belongs to the Stellenbosch and Ceres districts.

Iron. Important deposits of haematitic ore (60–63 per cent Fe) of the Lake Superior type are being exploited at Thabazimbi, near Rustenburg, Transvaal, and in the Postmasburg area, by the Iscor group (q.v.). The following table gives approximate reserves by grades:

	% Fe	*million tons*
Straight ores	over 55	1,300
Straight ores	40–55	6,000
Siliceous ores	25–40	2,000
Titaniferous ores	45–55	2,200

Ferro-alloys are being manufactured near Vereeniging, some being available for export. Iron is found both in Rhodesia and Zambia, but only mined on a limited scale.

Ironwood, Black or **Swart Ysterhout** (*Olea laurifolia* Lam.). Shapely tree up to 70 feet. Wood close-grained and heavy. Knysna and Eastern Divisions of Cape Province. *See* PLANTS.

Ironwood, Red (*Rhamnus Leyheri* Sond.). Tree about 20 feet. Fruit edible, wood strong. Magaliesberg.

Ironwood, Rhodesian. *See* MOPANE.

Irrigation. The Inyanga District of Rhodesia contains the most ancient system of irrigation in Southern Africa, comprising a system of furrows, channels and terraces covering many miles of hill country, and built by an unknown race centuries before the coming of the White Man. Irrigation by furrows from rivers was practised on a limited scale by many early colonists and even in the Eastern Cape by missionaries over 100 years ago, but it was not until 1866 that the Rev. Dr. John Croumbie Brown, Colonial Botanist and Professor of Botany at the South African College, Cape Town, was asked to prepare a report, 'The Hydrology of South Africa,' on the water reserves of the country, which was followed by an official memorandum on the irrigation possibilities. The Cape passed the first Irrigation Act, making Government help available and establishing a system of Irrigation Boards, in 1877. Natal followed in 1886, the Orange Free State in 1891 and the Transvaal in 1908, much of the later policy being based on the advice of the British engineer Sir William Wilcox, of Egyptian and Indian fame, who in 1901 visited South Africa and prepared a report for Lord Milner. In 1912 a Union Irrigation Act replaced the earlier laws, extending the system of Boards to cover the entire country and setting up a Union Irrigation Department in Pretoria. To reduce litigation, special Water Courts were established. Besides designing and building dams, weirs, canals and other installations, the Department is responsible for sinking boreholes on farms at nominal charges. The total area in the Republic today under irrigation is about 700,000 acres. See under individual projects, including Vaaldam, Buchuberg, Haartebeest-poort, Mazoe, Kariba, Zak, the Kalahari Scheme, etc. South-West Africa has a similar irrigation law

to the Republic. Rhodesia has over 50,000 acres under irrigation, with further large projects under the Kyle Dam Scheme (30,000 acres), near Fort Victoria, and the Sabi Valley Scheme (possibly 250,000 acres). Very large plans in Zambia include the Kafue Flats (possibly 120,000 acres). The Rhodesian Water Laws date back to 1913, and have since been amplified. Large irrigation works covering over 50,000 acres have been constructed near Villa de João Belo in the Limpopo Valley in Mozambique, designed for European settlement.

Isaacs, Nathaniel. Pioneer of early Natal. Born in Canterbury in 1808, he belonged to an old Jewish family in England. In 1822, having lost his father, he joined his uncle, father of the famous South African statesman, Saul Solomon (q.v.), then still living in St. Helena. In 1825 a post in the brig *Mary* under Lieutenant King, R.N., began a series of adventures that took him to Natal, where he was shipwrecked. He gained the friendship of the Zulu king Tshaka, secured concessions which might have made Natal a British colony many years before this came to pass, but failed to interest the authorities. He set down his experiences in his book *Travels and Adventures in Eastern Africa,* which appeared in London in 1836, and told the story from 1825 to 1832. Later he settled in West Africa, near Sierra Leone, where he was last heard of in 1858.

Isandhlwana. Mountain in Natal. The name in Zulu means 'The Little Hand,' alternatively 'The Third Stomach of a Cow,' because of its alleged resemblance in shape to that organ. Here on January 22, 1879, occurred one of the worst disasters in British military history, an entire army being encircled and wiped out by the Zulu forces of Cetewayo. Casualties amounted to over 770 Europeans killed, also several hundred Natives, the full figures never being ascertained.

Iscor (Afrikaans: Yskor). Popular abbreviation for the South African Iron and Steel Industrial Corporation Ltd. (q.v.).

Isibongo. Professional praiser employed by Zulu chiefs.

Isipingo. Seaside resort on the Natal South Coast, some 11 miles out of Durban. The name is derived from that of a wild fruit growing there. Population: 7,936, including 1,379 Whites.

Israelites. Bantu sect which established itself in 1921, under a leader named Enoch, at Bulhoek, on ground outside Queenstown, C.P. Efforts were made to remove them from their squatters' camp, but they ignored any requests and the authorities finally sent down a patrol of 400 police. Even then they refused to move. In the end force was used and a considerable number of the Israelites were killed and injured.

Italian Line (Navigazione Libera Triestina of Trieste). First regular service of this Line—cargo and passenger—established with the encouragement of General J. B. M. Hertzog

in 1925. Extended later by the addition of several large liners, including the *Giulio Cesare*. Since World War II a number of fine new vessels have been added.

Iwa. Language spoken in Zambia, mainly by members of the Mashukulumbwe race (q.v.).

Ixia (Iridaceae). Slender wiry bulbous plant, spring flowering in the Cape Peninsula. It has a small loose spike of bright flowers with tubular petals and grassy leaves. The one most generally found on damp mountain slopes is the White *Ixia polystachya*. Among other varieties are the Yellow and Pink Kalossies (*Ixia maculata* and *I. paniculata*); the Red Ixia (*Schizostylis coccinea*); and the Pink-to-purple *Ixia incarnata* of the dry Ceres, Montagu and Western Karroo areas. *See* IRIS.

Ixopo. Village in the south of Natal. Founded in 1878 under the name of Stuartstown, called after J. Stuart, a leading old-time magistrate. Dairy centre. The story of *Cry, the Beloved Country* begins in this area. Population: 1,918, including 802 Whites.

J

Jabavu, John Tengo. Bantu journalist and statesman. Born 1859, in Heald-town, of a poor family; qualified as a teacher and found his first post in Somerset East. At the age of 22, in 1881, *Isigidimi Sama Xosa*, a paper issued at Lovedale, needed an editor and he was appointed to the post. Moving to King William's Town he started his own journal, *Imvo Zabant-sundu* in 1886, the first newspaper ever to be owned and run solely by Bantu. It soon acquired great influence and is still in existence. He enjoyed the friend-ship of many leading Europeans, in-cluding Sir James Rose-Innes, Chief Justice of the Union. A strong sup-porter of the Wesleyan Church, he was largely responsible for the founding, in 1916, of the South African Native College at Fort Hare. He had a vigorous and persuasive literary style and was moderate in his views. He died in 1921 at Fort Hare.

Jabs. Long ostrich feathers taken from the wing of the female bird, where it joins the body.

Jacaranda (*Jacaranda acutifolia*). Family Bignoniaceae. South American tree with clusters of mauve flowers and delicate pinnate leaves. The streets of Pretoria and parts of Johannesburg are adorned with beauty in early summer. *See* ZIMBABWE CREEPER. The former Town Engineer of Pretoria, J. J. Jameson, who planted it there on a large scale 50 years ago, was nicknamed 'Jacaranda Jim.'

Jackal (*Canis aurens*). A nocturnal mammal with foxy face and bushy tail, greyish-yellow in colour. Hunts in packs. So widespread in South Africa and so destructive to stock that the Government pays a reward for each animal killed. *See* MAMMALS.

Jacky Hangman. Popular name for the Butcher bird. *See* SHRIKE.

Jacobs, Simeon. Attorney-General and judge. Born in England in 1830. He was called to the Inner Temple in 1852 and came to the Cape under the auspices of Sir George Grey in 1860. From 1860 to 1866 he was Attorney-General of British Kaffraria and in the latter year Solicitor-General for the Eastern Province. He then became Member of Parliament for Queens-town and in 1874 Attorney-General for the Cape Colony. In 1877 he re-tired on account of ill health. In 1880 he was raised to the Eastern Districts Bench, but for health reasons went overseas soon after, and died in Eng-land on June 15, 1883.

Jacobsdal. Small town on the Modder River not far from Kimberley, but in Orange Free State. Noted for its salt-pans. It takes its name from the original farm-owner, C. J. Jacobs, and was laid out in 1858. Population : 2,600, includ-ing 545 Whites.

Jagersfontein. Diamond-mining town in the Orange Free State. Originally the name of a farm belonging to Evert Jager, a Griqua, who in 1856 sold it to C. J. Visser. The finding of diamonds in 1870 led to the founding of a town, which soon rivalled Kimberley in the high quality of its stones. The Jagers-fontein Mine, though closed in 1933, was reopened after World War II but closed down in 1970. Here, in 1893, the Excelsior, the second largest stone on record, was found (q.v.). Population: 4,015, including 665 Whites.

Jagersfontein Road. Former name of Trompsburg, O.F.S. (q.v.).

Jagger, John William. Merchant and Cabinet Minister. Born in Yorkshire in 1859, he was educated at a grammar school and came to the Cape in 1880. Three years later he founded the firm that still bears his name and which soon grew into one of the largest houses in South Africa. A keen student of economics, he became the mouthpiece of Commerce and in 1903 was elected to the Cape Parliament. There he remained a strong upholder of Free Trade. He took part in the National Convention and in 1921 became Minister of Railways under General Smuts, with the onus of carrying out an unpopular policy of retrenchment. He gave generously to the cause of education. He died in 1930.

Jakobs, Petrus. Boer elephant hunter. First mentioned near Lake Ngami in 1851; he hunted in Mashonaland during the 1860's, in company with Jan Viljoen (q.v.). He finally settled near the Waterberg and died in the 1870's.

Jameson, Sir Leander Starr. South African and Rhodesian statesman. Born in Edinburgh in 1853, the same year as his two lifelong collaborators, Cecil John Rhodes and Alfred Beit (qq.v.), he was the son of a lawyer with literary gifts, and the youngest of a family of ten. After going to school in Scotland and England, in 1872 he entered University College, London, where his sensitivity to suffering made him faint at the sight of his first operation. None the less he was a brilliant student, and when in 1878 Dr. Prince of Kimberley wrote to University College asking for a partner, Jameson was recommended. By this time he had added to his qualifications in Vienna, and was in practice as a specialist.

In Kimberley Jameson was soon recognised as the ablest doctor on the Diamond Fields. He was immensely popular and gained the close friendship of Cecil John Rhodes. From an interest in finance they turned to the development of Mashonaland and

Matabeleland. On Rhodes's behalf Jameson undertook three successive missions to Lobengula in 1889 and 1890, the outcome of which was the confirmation by the Matabele king of the concession to the British South Africa Company (q.v.). Although Jameson accompanied the Pioneer Column (q.v.) he held no official position save as 'Rhodes's representative,' but in 1891 he succeeded Archibald R. Colquhoun as Administrator of Mashonaland, further establishing his popularity with the settlers. Under his régime the war against the Matabele broke out in 1893 which resulted in the occupation of Gubuluwayo and the downfall of Lobengula. In 1894 Matabeleland also came under the administration of 'Dr. Jim.' The following year he became deeply involved as leader in the Jameson Raid (q.v.). After his surrender to the Boers he was handed over to the British Government and placed on trial in London. The hearing before Lord Russell of Kilowen, Baron Pollock and Sir Henry Hawkins, with a jury, began on July 20, 1896, and lasted 7 days. He was sentenced to 15 months' imprisonment, and sent first to Wormwood Scrubs and then to Holloway Gaol, but was released in December 1896 on account of ill-health. Returning to Rhodesia in 1898, he made an extensive trek over the route of the future telegraph lines and railways.

Upon the outbreak of the Boer War he offered his services to the Imperial Government, reached Ladysmith during the siege, but broke down in health. In 1900 he was elected to the Cape Parliament, where his personality brought him rapid advancement. In 1902, upon the death of Cecil John Rhodes, he became leader of the Progressive Party, and in 1904 was made Prime Minister. The severe depression upon which the Cape Colony had now entered confronted him with many problems. In 1907 he attended the Imperial Conference in London and in 1908 became a member of the National Convention which drafted the constitution for the Union. Here his charm won over many of his Afrikaner political opponents. To the surprise of many he was not in the original Union Cabinet, but was elected to Parliament in 1910 and became leader of the Unionist opposition. In 1912 he retired to London, where he died in 1917.

Jameson Raid. Armed invasion of the Transvaal carried out by Dr. L. S. Jameson (q.v.) with the avowed object of remedying the grievances of the Uitlanders (q.v.). Ever since the discovery of gold on the Witwatersrand in 1886, the newer inhabitants of the country, who settled in Johannesburg and near by, had been accumulating grievances as to political rights, the inadequacy of public services, taxation, manufacturing monopolies and a number of other subjects. These became more acute as the Boer authorities showed little sympathy for the complainants. In 1892 the Transvaal National Union was formed to find a remedy, but by degrees its moderate programme became more extreme. Cecil John Rhodes gave the movement his strong support. Many of the best-known figures on the Rand became interested in the idea of securing help from outside. Gradually the plan took shape, of starting a rising in Johannesburg, and large quantities of arms and ammunition were smuggled in. The aims of the movement were uncertain, but seemed to have been to preserve the Republic under a leader other than Paul Kruger. Secret preparations were made for military action. Dr. Jameson, who was Administrator of Rhodesia, assembled a force of Police and volunteers at Pitsani, on the frontier of Bechuanaland and the Transvaal. Impatient of delay, he started off on December 29, 1895, without the approval of his collaborators in Johannesburg or of Cecil John Rhodes in Cape Town. The Boer authorities received warning and immediately mobilised commandos. Great confusion prevailed in Johannesburg. Jameson's force, commanded by Sir John Willoughby (q.v.), comprised 511 Europeans, about 150 Native drivers, with maxims, three guns, 640 horses and 158 mules. At Doornkop, near Krugersdorp, the invaders were met by the Boers, forced to capitulate and later handed over by President Kruger to Britain for trial. Meanwhile a 'Reform Committee' of prominent citizens had been set up in Johannesburg. With the collapse of the Raid, they were arrested and imprisoned in Pretoria. On April 27, 1896, the trial of the Reformers began at Pretoria, four of the leaders being sentenced to death, Sir Lionel Philips, Frank Rhodes, George Farrar and John Hays Hammond, while the remainder were each given 2 years' imprisonment and a fine of £2,000. The death sentences were each commuted by President Kruger to a fine of £25,000, and banishment from the Transvaal, while the 2-year sentences were also remitted. Dr. Jameson was tried in England on July 20, 1896, and sentenced to 15 months' imprisonment, while his fellow-raiders, who were also tried there, received sentences varying from 3 to 10 months. The increased political friction which resulted from the raid made the South African War almost inevitable.

Jamestown. Town near Aliwal North, Cape Province. Population: 1,600 including 700 Whites.

Jan Frederick. Afrikaans name for Cape Robin. *See* ROBIN.

Jan Groentjie. Afrikaans name for Malachite Sunbird. *See* SUNBIRD.

Jan Kempdorp. Township near Christiana, Transvaal, named after General Jan Kemp. Population: 1,944, including 1,304 Whites.

Jannasch, Professor Friederich Wilhelm. South African musician and composer. Born in Mamre, near Malmesbury, in 1853, of missionary parentage; he showed early talent, and was sent to Germany and to the Conservatoire in Stockholm where he studied under the great Norwegian composer Edvard Grieg. On his return to the Cape he was appointed organist of the Dutch Reformed church in Stellenbosch and became a successful composer. His major achievement, however, was in the field of teaching, culminating in 1905 in the establishment in Stellenbosch of the first Conservatoire in South Africa. He died on April 19, 1930.

Jansen, Dr. Ernest George. Governor-General of the Union of South Africa. Born in Dundee, Natal, August 7, 1881, and studied law at the University of Cape Town. Began practice as an attorney in Pietermaritzburg and later as an advocate. Entered politics shortly before Union as Secretary of 'Het Kongres,' an Afrikaaner organisation, and was a foundation member, in 1909, of the Afrikaanse Akademie. After Union held office in the South African Party as Secretary for its Natal branch until 1915, when he became one of the original members of the National Party. After serving as a member of General Hertzog's 'Independence Delegation' (q.v.), he was elected M.P. for Vryheid in 1921 and in 1924 became Speaker, an office he discharged with much success. From 1929 to 1933 he was Minister of Native Affairs until, on the establishment of the United Party (q.v.), he became Speaker a second time. He retired from Parliament in 1943, re-entered it in 1947 and in 1948 again became Minister of Native Affairs under Dr. D. F. Malan. After playing a leading part in the inauguration of the Voortrekker Movement, he became Governor-General of the Union on January 1, 1951. He died on November 25, 1959.

Janssens, Lieutenant-General Jan Willem. Last Dutch governor of the Cape. Born in Holland in 1762 he became a military engineer, specialising in fortification. When the Cape of Good Hope was restored by Britain to Holland under the Peace of Amiens in 1802 he was appointed Governor. A man of ability, he applied a progressive policy but after four years, war was resumed. Defeated in the Battle of Blaauwberg in 1806, he surrendered to the British and returned to Holland. Died in 1838.

Jansenville. Town on the Sundays River, not far from Graaff-Reinet in the Cape Province. Founded in 1854. The last Dutch Governor under Batavian Republic, General J. W. Janssens, is generally believed to have given his name to the place, though it is not clear why it should be spelt with a single 's.' Prosperous wool centre. Population: 3,120, including 850 Whites.

Jardine, Major William. South African book collector and antiquarian. Born in Cape Town, 1867, was educated at the South African College and in England. After retiring from business, he built up one of the finest libraries of Africana in existence, which was ultimately purchased by the Union Government, and embodied in the Library of Parliament. He then started a second library, equal to the first one, which was housed at his famous estate Applegarth, near Sir Lowry's Pass. He died in 1948.

Jarvis, Hercules Crosse. Early South African commercial magnate and legislator. Born in Britain in 1803, he reached the Cape at the age of 14, with Colonel Brown, who was on the staff of Lord Charles Somerset. Returning to England to complete his education, he came back to South Africa in 1822 to join a local firm of wine exporters and merchants. Soon he became interested in public affairs and was one of the first champions for an artificial harbour in Table Bay. Elected a Commissioner of Cape Town Municipality in 1845, he became Chairman in 1848, a position corresponding to Mayor, which office he held until 1860. Largely because of him, Table Bay Docks were begun in the latter year. He was a founder of the South African College in 1829, and helped to lead the Opposition against the importation of convicts in 1849. He died in 1889.

Jay, Blue. Common name for European Roller. A migrant from Europe and Mediterreanean lands, not breeding in South Africa, but found in the Northern Transvaal and sometimes in the Eastern Cape. A large blue bird, green below, with a brown mantle. *See* ROLLER.

effreys Bay. Seaside resort near Port Elizabeth. Named after an early trader in those parts in the 1850's. Noted for its beautiful sea-shells. Fishing industry. Population: 1,500, including 430 Whites.

Jeppe High School. Name applied to separate schools for boys and girls in Johannesburg suburb of that name, opened as a single unit in 1897 as Jeppestown Grammar School. Moved to present site in 1915 and divided in 1924. It made a South African record about this time by providing from its cricket team five Springboks in one year and four in another.

Jessievale. Large timber-growing estate in Eastern Transvaal, near Lake Chrissie (q.v.), with over 8,000,000 trees.

Jews. Apart from the Jewish mapmakers on the island of Majorca, who supplied the charts used by the early navigators to round the Cape of Good Hope, and the Jewish pilots who guided Vasco da Gama (q.v.) from the East African coast to India, Jews were among the founders of the Dutch East India Company and baptised Jews were among van Riebeeck's first colonists at the Cape. Several of the well-known figures in the early days, including Adam Tas (q.v.), were of Jewish origin. Until the end of the 18th century, however, their numbers were few and there was no organised observance of their religion. After the first British occupation a certain number arrived as soldiers and in other capacities. Several Jews were also among the 1820 settlers, notably the Norden, Sloman and Norton families. Immigration from Germany began to grow from the arrival of the Mosenthals in the 1830's and continued steadily through the Victorian age, being considerably stimulated by the discovery of diamonds and of gold. The first Jewish congregation was established in Cape Town in 1841, followed by others in Grahamstown, Port Elizabeth and elsewhere. From the 1870's substantial numbers of Jews from Eastern Europe reached South Africa, many of them settling on the Diamond and Gold Fields. Before the end of the 19th century they greatly surpassed the numbers of Jewish immigrants from Britain, Germany and Western Europe. In every field of activity, from introducing Angora goats to the Cape to opening coal mines in the Transvaal, pioneering manufactures, etc., Jews played a prominent part. Several were elected into the early Colonial legislatures. Important milestones were the establishment of the Transvaal (later the South African) Jewish Board of Deputies in 1903, and the recognition of Yiddish as a European language for immigration purposes. A large percentage of South African Jews could trace their origins to a group of small villages in Lithuania, particularly around Ponevez. World War I greatly reduced immigration from this area, and the adoption of the Quota Law in 1930 practically terminated it. There was a further revival of Jewish immigration owing to Nazi persecutions after 1933, but this too was heavily reduced after 1935. Of about 130,000

Jews in South Africa, more than half live on the Witwatersrand, about 50,000 of them in Johannesburg. Jews have also been connected with the history of Rhodesia from the earliest times, including traders long before the occupation. Several Jews were in the Pioneer Column, and others lost their lives in the Shangani Patrol. The largest community in Rhodesia today is in Bulawayo. Altogether there are about 5,000 in Rhodesia, Zambia and Malawi.

Jigger Flea. Insect found in the subtropical regions of Africa, imported from the West Indies, where it is known as the Chigoe. Natives are clever at removing the flea when it burrows under toenails, and the skin of the feet.

Joel, Jack Barnato. Mine magnate. Brother of S. B. Joel, born in London, 1862. He entered the firm of Barnato Bros., but soon returned to England. Was a well-known racehorse owner and sportsman, and won the Derby in 1911 with 'Sunstar.' He died in 1940.

Joel, Solomon Barnato. Mine magnate. Born in 1866 in London, the brother of Jack Joel, and a nephew of B. I. Barnato (q.v.). Coming to South Africa as a young man, he settled in Johannesburg and soon became a prominent figure. During the Reform Movement, he was imprisoned and fined. Upon the death of B. I. Barnato and his brother Wolf, S. B. Joel became head of the firm of Barnato Bros. and of the Johannesburg Consolidated Investment. He settled in England, where he was also known as a leading racehorse owner. In 1915 he won the Derby with his horse 'Pommern.' He died on May 22, 1931.

Joel, Wolf. Mining magnate. Nephew of Barney Barnato (q.v.), and brother of S. B. Joel (q.v.). Born in London, 1864, he came to South Africa in 1889, and was a popular figure in early Johannesburg. In 1898 the German adventurer, von Veltheim (q.v.), tried forcing him into a plot to kidnap President Kruger and when Joel refused, shot him dead in his office. He left over £2,000,000.

Johannesburg. Largest city in Southern Africa and third largest in Africa. (Cairo has a population of over 2,000,000 and Alexandria of nearly 2,000,000). Population 1,364,520, including 476,712 Whites, 773,415 Bantu, 76,331 Coloureds and 38,000 Asiatics. Johannesburg came into existence early in 1886, when the first tents were pitched in Ferreira's Camp. The first township was laid out on the farm, Randjeslaagte, between October 19, 1886, and November 3, 1886, and on November 18, 1886, the sale of the new 'standsdorp,' took place. The city was called after Field Cornet Johannes Petrus Meyer, according to the researches of the late James Gray. The growth of the new community proceeded at a fantastic rate, and within a year the population was estimated at 10,000. Between Natal Camp (now Jeppestown) and Ferreira's Camp was laid out the central township of Johannesburg. Extensions were soon proclaimed in Marshall's to the south, Braamfontein to the north and elsewhere. By 1889 the city already had horse-trams, and in 1890 the first electric light installations appeared. Joubert Park became the first official lung, and in the early 1890's fashionable suburbs developed on Hospital Hill and in Parktown. By 1895 Johannesburg had 100,000 people of all races, about half of whom were European. Notwithstanding this spectacular growth, the Boer authorities declined to give it municipal status, and administration continued with an inadequate Sanitary Committee, dating back to the very beginning of the community. In 1897 a modified form of municipal administration was adopted, under a Boer-appointed burgomaster. This condition continued until the South African War. On May 31st, 1900, Johannesburg was occupied by the British and was placed under military rule, which continued until 1901. Lord Milner, who believed in the great future of the city, made his headquarters there. Although the administration was later transferred to Pretoria, that of the Railways and of the Mines remained. In 1904 Johannesburg received its first elected Town Council, and a system of government was adopted which still exists. Numerous outlying suburbs were amalgamated and the area of the city extended from 8 to over 80 sq. miles. Tram lines were laid out to the north and south, and in 1906 the system was electrified. Spectacular growth continued, and the population rose to 237,000 in 1911 and to 381,000 in 1931. The foundation stone of the present City Hall was laid in 1910 by the Duke of Connaught, and the building completed in 1915. In 1922 the Transvaal University College, which had become the South African School of Mines, became the University of the Witwatersrand, which today has over 7,000 students. The total area of Johannesburg has grown to 180 sq. miles, over 100 sq. miles on the south being added in 1969. The highest point of the city is Observatory Hill, 5,925 feet above sea-level, and the lowest, near the Zoo Lake, nearly 1,000 feet less. Over 5,690 acres are devoted to open spaces and parks. The streets cover 1,549 miles. Transport is maintained by motor buses and trolley-buses, the last tramcars being scrapped in 1961. The net municipal income of the Johannesburg municipality for the year ending 1969 was R84,953,000. Apart from the gold mines, which still employ a major part of the city's activities, Johannesburg is by far the largest manufacturing centre in South Africa, and accounts for more than half the bank clearings. Its industries include engineering, brewing, flour milling, clothing and chemicals. It is one of the principal educational centres of South Africa, with numerous institutions, including an Art School and a Technical College. The total number of motor vehicles in the city today is approaching 200,000. Owing to the grave congestion of traffic, a series of bridges has been built over the city, and preparations made for skyways and other trunk routes. The new main railway station cost over R20,000,000. The municipal valuation exceeds R1,148,724,000 and there are nearly 30,000 municipal employees, about 9,000 being Whites.

Johannesburg Consolidated Investment Co. Ltd. Mining group, established by B. I. Barnato (q.v.) in September 1889. In 1905 it took over the Barnato Consolidated Mines Ltd. It has large holdings in the gold, coal, brewing and other industries.

John Brown (*Gymnocrotaphus curvidens*). Fish found off False Bay to East London. About 14 inches long. *See* BREAM.

Johnny (*Lutianus fulviflamma*). Fish found off Natal, East Africa to S. Pacific. About 12 inches long. *See* SNAPPER.

Johnson, Charles. English missionary and Anglican Archdeacon of Zululand. Born in 1850, he came to Natal as a young man, and in 1880 took over the establishment of St. Augustine's Mission (q.v.), where he spent the rest of his days. With hardly any money he developed the station until it had 35 churches (including one at St. Augustine's, holding 2,000 people), 34 schools and a hospital. In 1900 he became Archdeacon of Zululand. Revered by the Zulus, he died in 1927 and was buried at St. Augustine's.

Johnson, Major Frank. Rhodesian soldier and pioneer. Born in Norfolk, England, in 1866, he was educated at King's Lynn, and arrived in South Africa at the age of 16. After 2 years in the Cape Colonial Civil Service he joined the forces under General Sir Charles Warren occupying Bechuanaland in 1884, and then the Bechuanaland Border Police. In 1886 he formed a mining syndicate in Cape Town to prospect Matabeleland, which resulted in the founding of the Bechuanaland Exploration Company. He made the acquaintance of Lobengula and in 1890, in partnership with his friends, Captain M. Heany and Captain H. J. Borrow, entered into a unique contract with Cecil Rhodes to organise the Pioneer Column (q.v.) that occupied Mashonaland. Afterwards Johnson settled in Cape Town, where he took an interest in military affairs. He fought in the Langeberg Campaign of 1897 and returned to Rhodesia in 1898. He died in the Channel Islands during the German occupation in 1940.

Johnson, Dr. George Lindsay. South African authority on the eyesight of animals and on colour photography. Born in England, 1854, he studied in Manchester, Cambridge and in Germany, specialising in ophthalmic surgery. A scientist of outstanding ability, he not only wrote many important books, including a treatise on glaucoma, but produced in 1909 *Photographic Optics and Colour Photography*, followed in 1910 by *Photography in Natural Colours*, both of which were among the first of their kind. Johnson, who came to South Africa at the beginning of the present century, invented a number of new optical instruments, including an improved ophthalmoscope. He died in Natal in 1943.

Johnston, Sir Harry Hamilton. Writer, explorer, administrator and artist. Born in London, 1858, and educated at Stockwell Grammar School, and King's College, London. As a young man he studied art, in which he acquired distinction. His opportunity for reaching Africa came in 1879, when he travelled extensively

in the north, in Angola and up the River Congo in the early 80's. He later commanded an expedition sent by the Royal Society to Mount Kilimanjaro in 1884, became Vice-Consul in the Cameroons in the following year and Acting Consul for the Niger Coast Protectorate in 1887. Appointed British Consul for the Province of Mozambique in 1888, he took an expedition to Lake Nyasa and afterwards to Lake Tanganyika, for the establishment of the British Central Africa Protectorate in 1889, now known as Malawi. Here Johnston headed a force which suppressed the slave trade. His versatility included the discovery of an entirely new animal in the Central African jungles, the okapi, the authorship of many books, such as a continuation of Dickens' *Dombey & Son*, treatises on Bantu languages and a collection of short stories, and the composing of music. Sir Harry Johnston enjoyed the high respect of the British Foreign Office. He died in 1927.

Jolivet, Bishop Charles Constant. Catholic Bishop of Natal. Born in France, he came to South Africa in 1874 and made his headquarters in Durban. He was the first to celebrate Mass in Pretoria. During the quarter of a century of his service, he raised the number of churches in his diocese from five to 81, and schools from less than half a dozen to 46. He died in 1903.

Jonathan, Chief Leabua. First Prime Minister of Lesotho (q.v.). Born of Basuto Royal stock in 1914 near Leribe, the son of Chief Tsikoane, he had little schooling, but worked for the Paramount Chief and rose to preside over his Tribal Court. Elected to the Basutoland National Council, he helped to redraft the country's constitution. He founded the Basutoland Congress Party in 1959 and despite initial set-backs in 1960 recovered influence, played a leading part in achieving Independence. Became Premier in 1966.

Jones, Guy Carleton. Mining engineer and geologist. Born in Halifax, Canada, June 30, 1888, and educated at McGill University, Montreal. Came to South Africa in 1914, where, except for War service, he spent the rest of his life with the Consolidated Goldfields of South Africa (q.v.), contributing largely to the development of the gold industry beyond the previously accepted limits at Randfontein, as well as to the platinum industry. Awarded the Gold Medal of the Institute of Mining and Metallurgy in London, he died on December 3, 1948. *See* CARLETONVILLE.

Jones, Senator John David Rheinallt. Born, 1884, in Wales and educated at Bangor and Beaumaris. He came to South Africa in 1905 and joined the staff of the former South African School of Mines and Technology in Johannesburg, later the University of the Witwatersrand. Interested in the welfare of non-Europeans, he helped to establish the South African Institute of Race Relations in 1929, of which he became the first Director, and in 1937 was elected to the Union Senate as Native Representative. He was also Secretary of the Witwatersrand Council of Education, and editor of *Bantu Studies*. He wrote a great deal and died in 1953.

Jones, Sydney Twentyman. Judge President, Eastern Districts Court. Born in Cape Town on January 20, 1849, and educated at the South African College and Cambridge, where he had a distinguished career and attained the LL.M. degree in 1876. After being called to the Middle Temple in 1873 he returned to the Cape and was admitted in 1874, practising in Cape Town until his appointment to the Bench of the High Court of Griqualand in 1882. In 1887 he was transferred to

the Eastern Districts Court and became Judge President in 1901. His outside interests included education and sport, and he founded the Villagers' Football Club. He retired in 1904 and died in 1913.

Jonker Diamond. Fourth largest stone on record (726 carats in the rough), found by Jacobus Jonker, a digger, on the farm Elandsfontein, near Pretoria, January 17, 1934. Cut into 12 magnificent stones from 5·3 to 142·9 carats in the rough.

Jorissen, Eduard Johan Pieter. Judge and statesman in the South African Republic. Born in Zwolle, Holland, 1829. Gave up his career as a minister in 1868 to become a journalist. Accompanied T. F. Burgers, President of the South African Republic, to Holland in 1875. Returning next year, he began to study law, and in 1878 became State Attorney. He accompanied the Independence Delegation to England in 1879, took part in the peace negotiations after Majuba and from 1888 to 1900 was a judge. He died in 1912.

Josini Dam. Largest dam in South Africa, forming part of Pongola Poort –Makatini Flats Irrigation Scheme, erected where the Pongola River cuts through the Lebombo Mountains. Construction begun in 1963. The dam wall required 750,000 tons of cement, measured 1,800 feet along the crest and 293 feet above the lowest foundation. The area to be irrigated is over 150,000 acres, requiring 1,000 miles of irrigation canals, the largest of which is 75 feet wide and 10 feet deep. *See also* MAKATINI FLATS and PONGOLA.

Joubert, General François Gerhardus. Born in the Cape Colony, 1827, emigrated to the Transvaal as a follower of A. W. J. Pretorius and was elected to the Volksraad. Became a leader in the First Boer War, and was in command of the ambush into which

Col. Anstruther led his men at Bronkhorstspruit on December 17, 1880. He died in 1903.

Joubert, General Petrus Jacobus. Born in the Cape Colony, 1831, he entered the Volksraad and came into prominence as Acting President in 1875 during the term of office of President Burgers. Upon the First British Occupation of the Transvaal, he played a leading part in opposing the new régime, visiting the Cape in company with President Kruger and also becoming a member of the Independence Delegation to Europe. During the First South African War, he was a member of the Triumvirate, and was appointed Commander-in-Chief of the Republican Forces. He was a signatory to the peace settlement in Pretoria. As a member of the Executive Council, Joubert came more and more into conflict with President Kruger, representing, as he did, the less conservative element in the population. He was appointed Superintendent of Native Affairs for the South African Republic, and in 1896, Vice-President. Joubert stood repeatedly for election against President Kruger but was defeated. In the South African War he was appointed Commander-in-Chief of the Boer Forces in Natal, and played a gallant part in the earlier operations, until he was attacked by sickness and died in March 1900.

Joubertina. Village near Humansdorp in the Cape Province, named after the Joubert family, which was prominent there. Founded in 1907. Fruit-growing centre.

Juanasburg. Village on the Eastern Cape Frontier, established for military settlers in 1848, but destroyed on Christmas Day 1850 by a sudden Native invasion. Named after Lady Juana Smith, the Spanish-born wife of Governor Sir Harry Smith.

Jukskei. Originally a yoke used for oxen and draught animals, applied by the Boers to a game now widely played throughout South Africa. Jukskei originated in the Western Province, and in 1938 was placed on an organised basis. Jukskei is a team game played on special courses and an elaborate code has developed. The sport is controlled by a Central Council and annual tournaments are held.

July Handicap. Premier South African horse-race originally established in 1894. The stakes amount to R25,760 and the turnover on the Totalisator exceeds R600,000. Held annually in Durban.

Jumping Beans. Seeds and plants which contain the larva of a small moth, usually the *Carpocapsa saltitans.* These exercise a strong tension from within, causing the bean or seed to hop about in a surprising manner.

Juta, Sir Henricus Hubertus. Speaker and Judge. Son of J. C. Juta (q.v.), he was born in Cape Town, 1857, educated at the South African College and the University of London. He was called to the Inner Temple on January 26, 1880, and practised at the Cape in the same year. In 1894 he became Attorney-General and from 1896 to 1898 was Speaker of the Cape House of Assembly. He took silk in 1893 and became Judge-President of the Cape Provincial Division in 1913. He was appointed to the Appellate Division in 1920, retired in 1923 and died on May 16, 1930.

Juta, Jan Carel. Publisher. Born at Zaltbommel, Holland, in 1824, of a family from Stralsund in Germany; married Louise Marx, sister of Karl Marx, the author of *Das Kapital*, and in 1853 emigrated to the Cape, where he established himself as a bookseller and publisher. Handling a wide range of subjects, he specialised in legal and educational works, and started the first regular series of law reports in the 1860's, which continue to appear. He was also responsible for many famous books on South Africa, including Thomas Bowler's *Album of Cape Town*, in 1866, and works on Bantu languages. In later years Juta's health deteriorated and he went to England, where he died in 1886.

Juta, René (more correctly, **Henriette Irene Louise Juta**). Born in Cape Town, the daughter of Jan Carel Juta (q.v.), she wrote *The Cape Peninsula*, published in 1910, and in 1920 a novel on the early Cape, *The Tavern*, based on the story of Dr. James Barry. She later married a British diplomat, Luke H. Hansard, and lived in Europe, where she wrote a book about Corsica. She died on June 22, 1940.

K

Kaalfontein. Township near Kempton Park, Transvaal. Staff training centre for South African Railways. Population: 1,287, including 1,134 Whites.

Kaap. *See* DE KAAP.

Kaapmuiden. Village in the Eastern Transvaal; the name means 'The Mouth of the Kaap,' because the Kaap River here joins the Crocodile. Founded in 1895, when the railway was completed from Lourenço Marques to Pretoria, it is now a farming and mining centre. In the latter part of the South African War there was a considerable amount of fighting near here, and the bridge was blown up.

Kaapsche Hoop. Village in the De Kaap Valley (q.v.) of the Eastern Transvaal, established as a gold camp in 1884 by alluvial diggers, now an important forestry centre, and noted for its beautiful scenery. Population: 400, including 80 Whites.

Kabwe (formerly **Broken Hill**). Mining township in Zambia. Started in 1904, and named after Broken Hill in Australia. The original company was reconstructed in 1910 and again in 1916. The mines produce lead, zinc and bismuth and a certain amount of copper and other minerals. In 1920 one of the earliest known human remains, the skull of the Broken Hill Man, was found in a cave near by. Population: 36,000, including 5,000 Whites.

Kadake. Village in Swaziland, terminus of Swaziland Railway (q.v.) near Oshoek, on Transvaal border.

Kadalie, Clements. Bantu trade union leader, born in Malawi at the end of the last century. He came to the Union, and settled in Cape Town, where in 1919 he became interested in a strike of black dockers. Out of this developed the I.C.U. (q.v.), of which he remained the leader until the decline of this powerful body. Kadalie showed great ability and collaborated with both Coloured and Indian organisations. He was repeatedly in trouble with the Police. In later years he retired to East London, where he died in 1951.

Kaffervink. Afrikaans name for Long-tailed Widow-bird. *See* WEAVER.

Kaffir. Originally a term applied to all black aboriginal inhabitants of Southern Africa other than Hottentots and Bushmen. The term is derived from the Arabic, and signified a nonbeliever, but has gradually acquired a significance objectionable in the mind of the African. None the less the expressions Kaffirland and Kaffraria are still in use. In the early days it was often written Caffre.

Kaffir Almanac (*Haemanthus*). Bulbus Cape and Natal plant with a single red tulip-like flower and fleshy spotted stem rising from two prostrate leaves. Its blossoming time was considered by the Zulus as right for mealie planting, hence the name. *See* AMARYLLIS.

Kaffir Beer. Alcoholic liquor made from Kaffir corn (q.v.) and also known as Utshuala. It contains certain vitamins and has medicinal properties.

Kaffirboom (*Erythrina caffra*). Beautiful flowering tree, also known as Coral Tree, which flourishes particularly in the Eastern Province and Natal. The scarlet blossoms come out before the leaves. *See* PEA, WILD SWEET.

Kaffir Circus. Expression for the section of the London Stock Exchange specialising in South African gold shares.

Kaffir Corn. Traditional name for sorghum or millet. It is grown in South Africa for the production of Kaffir beer (q.v.) as well as for meal.

Kaffir Piano or **Marimba.** Musical instrument used by many African

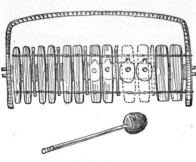

Kaffir Piano

tribes. Like the Xylophone, it is made of strips of wood varying in length, but strung along a series of calabashes which serve as a sounding board, It is played with a hammer and can produce complicated melodies. Kaffir pianos are used for native dancing.

Kaffir Plum or **Kafferpruim** (*Harpephyllum caffra* Bernh.*). Tree up to 50 feet, ornamental as street tree. Wood hard. Fruit edible. North-eastern coastal areas in Natal.

Kaffirs. Name for South African gold shares on the London Stock Exchange.

Kaffir Wars. Name given to a series of campaigns on the Eastern Frontier of the Cape Colony between the British (soldiers and settlers), and the Xosa and other tribes. The First Kaffir War took place in 1811–1812. The Second followed in 1818, the Third in 1819, the Fourth in 1834–1835. The War of the Axe (1846–1848) is usually not included in the 'numbered' series, so that the Fifth Kaffir War is known as that extending from 1850 to 1853. The Sixth Kaffir War was in 1858, Seventh from 1877 to 1878 (also known

as the Galeka War), while the Eighth, known as the Tamboekie War, was fought in 1879. This was the last of the Frontier Kaffir Wars.

Kaffraria. *See* BRITISH KAFFRARIA.

Kaffrarian Pea. The seed of the Kaffirboom (q.v.).

Kaffrarian Rifles. South African Military Unit, raised in East London on December 20, 1883. Served in the Langeberg Campaign, 1897; Siege of Mafeking, 1899, Siege of Wepener and throughout South African War; German South West African Campaign, 1915; formed part of 4th South African Infantry Brigade garrisoning Tobruk when it was captured in 1942. Motto: *Nunc Animis.*

Kafue. Township in Zambia, 20 miles to the south of Lusaka on the banks of the Kafue River. Established about 1905 as a halt on the railway line to the North, 3,241 feet above sea-level. Industries have been set up and it is expected that the development of Kariba (q.v.) will give a considerable stimulus to the town. Population: 310 Europeans, 820 Africans and 50 of other races.

Kaiser Matanzima, Chief. *See* MATANZIMA, CHIEF KAISER.

Kaiser Wilhelm Gold Field. Northeast of Salisbury, Rhodesia, and near Mozambique border.

Kajatehout. *See* TEAK.

Kakamas. Successful irrigation settlement on the Orange River below Upington; started by the Dutch Reformed Church as a means of reclaiming the Poor Whites during the 1880's. The ground is exceedingly fertile and the products include sultanas, vegetables and lucerne. The total population today amounts to over 2,500 Whites. The village of Kakamas has 3,400 people, of whom 900 are white.

Kakelaar. *See* HOOPOE.

Kalahari Desert. Huge dry area in the centre of Southern Africa, abutting on the Cape Province, the Transvaal, Rhodesia, South West Africa and Angola. Most of it falls within Botswana. Its total extent is approximately 350,000 sq. miles, but not all of this is desert in the accepted sense. Rivers which flow occasionally and large salt pans are to be found. After rain vast stretches are excellent cattle country. In the sandy zone, particularly in the south, the tsamma melon flourishes, and helps to maintain clans of hunting Bushmen who remain uncontrolled. Waterholes exist in places and there is much game.

Kalahari National Park. About 250 miles north of Upington, and 2,386,429 acres in area (nearly 4,000 sq. miles). Noted for its large numbers of antelopes, including gemsbok in thousands, also lions, wild ostriches and many other species. Roads and other facilities for tourists are being developed.

Kalahari Scheme. Project put forward by Professor E. H. L. Schwartz (q.v.) of Grahamstown for changing the conditions in the Kalahari Desert by diverting the Okavango River in the extreme north into its former bed. He envisaged restoring water, at a comparatively low cost, to a system of rivers which for many years had ceased to flow, thus improving the rainfall and making large areas of desert habitable. The strong support given to the idea by farmers and others persuaded the Union Government after World War II to appoint a commission of experts to investigate its feasibility on the spot. Their report, however, was not encouraging and little has been heard of the Kalahari Scheme in recent years.

Kalkfontein. *See* KARASBURG.

Kalkfontein Dam. Large irrigation works near Fauresmith, Orange Free State, with a stretch of water, when full, 15 miles in length.

Kalkoentjie: 1. Name given to a wild flower in the Western Cape and in Namaqualand, known as *Gladiolus*

alatus. The name, 'small turkey,' is presumably from its shape.

2. Cape Longclaw (*Macronyx capensis*). A brown bird of the Pipit and Wagtail family (q.v.), with a red throat, yellow under-parts and very long claws. It lives in grassy ground and long, damp grass.

Kalomo. Township in Zambia, between Livingstone and Lusaka. It lies 4,057 feet above sea-level, and has a population of 80 Europeans, 700 Africans and 40 Asiatics. The chief activity is tobacco growing and cattle breeding.

Kalulushi. Township in Zambia, established in 1953, located at a height of 4,200 feet above sea-level. It is used as the residential area for the nearby Chibuluma Copper and Cobalt mine, and is situated some miles from Kitwe. The population is 840 Europeans, 1,220 Africans.

Kamaherero. *See* MAHERERO.

Kamanassie Dam. Large irrigation work on the Kamanassie River near Oudtshoorn, Cape Province. The concrete dam wall is 1,265 feet long and 115 feet high above the river bed (145 feet above foundations). When full the dam covers 1¼ sq. miles, and is 9 miles long. The area irrigated is about 25,000 acres.

Kameel. Name frequently and mistakenly given by the early Boer settlers to the giraffe. Knowing camels only from descriptions and from the illustrations in the early Bibles, they confused the two creatures. An alternative explanation derives it from the medieval Camelopard, the naturalists of those days believing that it was a cross between a camel and a leopard.

Kamieskroon. Village in Namaqualand. Mission Station. Population: 750, including 310 Whites.

Kannaland. Portion of the Cape Province between Touws River and the Swartberg. The name is derived from the fact that it used to be inhabited by many Eland (Kanna in Hottentot language).

Kannetjies. *See* SUCCULENTS.

Kannon Island. Irrigation settlement on the Orange River, on an island of the same name. It was started about 1940 by a group of Afrikaans settlers from Kakamas, who established themselves in what they recognised to be a wild but very fertile spot. Population today is over 2,000 Whites.

Kanye. Settlement and administrative centre in Botswana, headquarters of the Bangwaketse tribe. Population: 34,045.

Kaokoveld. Area in the north of South West Africa, most of it earmarked for native reserves and not open for European occupation. It is extremely wild country, well watered and full of game. Reports have been received that certain species, like the Quagga (q.v.), may still survive there.

Kaparings. Wooden sandals worn by the Cape Malays, and held to

Kaparings

the foot by means of a knob between two toes. They are also referred to as Kaproens.

Kapenaar. *See* SILVERFISH.

Kapepwe, Simon. Cabinet Minister in Zambia. Born in 1922 at Chinsala, he qualified as a teacher and joined the African National Congress and spent some time in India, returning to Zambia in 1955. As an office-bearer of the A.N.C., he came into conflict with the authorities. He became a leader of the United National Independence Party (U.N.I.P.) and helped to negotiate with London on Independence. Was appointed Foreign Minister.

Kapiri Mposhi. Village and administrative centre in Zambia, 40 miles north of Kabwe.

Kapokbossie. *See* ROSEMARY, WILD.

Kapokvoël. Afrikaans name for Penduline Tit. *See* TIT.

Karakul. Species of black sheep introduced into South West Africa in 1907, by the German Colonial authorities, from the near East, notably Persia, because of its similarity of climate. Karakul farming is most profitable and is now the major source of income for South West Africa. It is also successfully carried on in North-Western Cape Province, Namaqualand, Gordonia and elsewhere. Many leading buyers have their offices in Windhoek, where sales are regularly held, one of the major purchasers being the famous Hudson Bay Company of Canada.

Karanteen. South African fish. *See* BREAM.

Karasburg. Village in the south of South West Africa, Karakul breeding centre. Formerly known as Kalkfontein. Population: 2,275, including 1,200 Whites.

Karbonaatje. Old Cape dish, comprising slices of meat cut thinly and roasted over the fire.

Kareeboom (*Rhus Gueinzii* Sond.). Large shrub or small tree. Flowers very small. Wood tough and light, suitable only for hoe handles. Eastern districts of Cape Province and Natal. *See* KRAAIBOS, SUUR KAREE, and PLANTS.

Kareiga River. Tributary of Gamtoos River (q.v.). Another river of the same name rises near Grahamstown and enters the sea south of Port Alfred.

Kariba. Gorge on the Zambesi River below the Victoria Falls, the site of the largest dam and hydro-electric scheme in Africa and one of the largest in the world. The works, which were started in 1955, after careful investigation by local and overseas experts, are estimated to cost up to £80,000,000. They have been financed partly through the World Bank, through Government grants and through advances from Zambian copper mining groups, whose needs, along with those of a large part of Rhodesia generally, are to be met from this source. The main installation, which will be about 250 miles from Salisbury, includes an artificial lake, damming up the Zambesi for about 180 miles by means of a wall, 420 feet high, and a power plant inside a mountain, rushing through which, the river will generate 600,000 KW. The scheme involved the resettlement of thousands of natives, whose lands were flooded, and the construction of a network of power-lines extending to the Copperbelt and far across Rhodesia.

Karibib. Village in South West Africa, noted for its marble quarries. The name is derived from the Hottentot name of a local bush. The marble, which is of good quality, was in German times exported to South America and elsewhere. Population: 1,395, including 477 Whites.

Karino. Village in the Eastern Transvaal, near White River, and noted for its orange plantations.

Kaross. Prepared skins, made into a blanket. The word is derived from the Hottentot. The manufacture of karosses is an industry of some importance in Bechuanaland.

Karree. Honey beer, prepared by the Coloured people and allowed to ferment. Considered to be very nourishing and refreshing. The word is derived from the Hottentot. The sediment is often used by housewives as yeast.

Karreedoring (*Lycium arenicolum* Miers). Shrub up to 9 feet. Cape Province and Griqualand West.

Karreedouw. Village in Cape Province in the Langkloof, near Humansdorp. Population: 600, including 450 Whites. It was established about 1905. The name is of Hottentot origin.

Karridene. Seaside resort on the South Coast of Natal, founded by and named after Lieutenant-Colonel Walter Karri-Davies, pioneer of the Rand, who came from Karridale in Western Australia, and started the import of Karri timber to South Africa. The village came into existence during World War I.

Karroo. There are two Karroos in South Africa, the Great and Little Karroo. The latter lies in the south-western part of the Cape Province, adjoining Oudtshoorn and the Swartberg, while the former extends over the greater part of the northern area, right to the Orange River. The word Karroo itself is derived from the Hottentot. It is characterised by small flat-topped koppies, dry climate and sparse vegetation, although much of it is extremely fertile when irrigation is possible. It includes some of the best sheep country in the world.

Karroo Bush, Bitter or **Bitterbossie** (*Chrysocoma tennifolia* Berg.). South-east coastal area to Natal. Shrubby. Leaves short, narrow. Flowers small yellow, in compact heads.

Karroo Bush, Sweet or **Skaapbos** (Pentzia). Low, much-branched shrub.

Eaten by goats and sheep. Karroid areas.

Kasama. Township in Zambia and capital of the Northern Province. It lies between Mpika, Abercorn and Fort Rosebery, at a height of 4,370 feet. Founded in 1898, its growth has been slow. The population is 210 Europeans, 1,580 Africans.

Kasane. Village on Chobe River in Northern Botswana. Population 600, including about 15 Whites. Of strategic importance to Caprivi Zipfel (q.v.).

Katel. Portable bedstead used in ox-wagons. Name derived from the Hindustani.

Katima Mulilo. Administrative headquarters of Caprivi Zipfel (q.v.).

Katjiepiering (*Gardenia thunbergia*). Small bushy tree occurring in most forests of Eastern Cape and Natal. It bears strongly scented, snow-white flowers. The name is of Malay origin and really refers to *Gardenia florida*.

Katonkel, Cape (*Sarda sarda*). Scaly fish found from Walvis Bay to Mossel Bay and Atlantic Ocean. About 30 inches long. Poor as a food fish. The Eastern Province Katonkel or Commerson's King-Fish, by contrast, is a fine sporting fish, about 4 feet long, well known in Australia and sometimes called Snoek in Natal. *See* TUNNY and MACKEREL.

Kat River. Tributary of the Great Fish River (q.v.). Rises in the Katberg in the Eastern Cape Province.

Kat River Settlement. Established in 1829 by the Rev. Robert Read of the London Missionary Society, to teach habits of industry to a large group of vagrant Hottentots. By 1833 there were 2,185 Hottentot and Coloured residents and 731 Natives. Although a fair amount of progress was made the inhabitants joined a rebellion in 1851, whereupon the settlement was broken up and most of it given to white farmers. Some of the original mission

communities still exist. The soil is unusually fertile, much of it being irrigated, and producing oranges.

Kaunda, Dr. Kenneth David. African leader. Born near Chinsali, Zambia, in 1924. As a teacher he became interested in the African National Congress and took a lead in opposing the continuance of the Central African Federation. Despite a prison sentence his power steadily grew, and he extended his work overseas, still upholding methods of comparative moderation. In 1961 he entered the Cabinet of Zambia. In 1964 became Prime Minister. Following the establishment of the Republic, he was appointed President.

Kazungula. Settlement at the point where the Chobe River flows into the Zambesi. It is popular as a centre for hunting and fishing.

Kearsney. Settlement in Natal, near Stanger, on the North Coast. Originally the home of Sir James Liege Hulett, pioneer of the sugar industry, who built his mansion there in the 1880's, calling it after his birthplace in Kent. Because of its suitable climate he began tea plantations and a tea factory, but they have been given up in recent years. After Sir Liege Hulett's death his house became a boys' school, later removed to another part of Natal, but still called Kearsney College (q.v.). The House is now used as a 'Home of Healing,' under church auspices.

Kearsney College. Large public school for boys, run under the auspices of the Methodist Church at Botha's Hill, but originally at Kearsney on the Natal North Coast (q.v.) where in 1928 it occupied the former home of Sir Liege Hulett.

Keate Award. Arbitration on the ownership of the Griqualand West Diamond Fields carried out by Lieutenant-Governor Robert Keate of Natal. In 1870 his determination of the boundary between the South African Republic and the Orange Free

State went in favour of the Republic. Called in a year later as a final arbitrator in a similar dispute between the South African Republic and the Griqua chiefs Waterboer and others, Keate gave his award against the Republic.

Keate, Robert William. Lieutenant-Governor of Natal. A barrister of Lincoln's Inn, where he was called in 1844. Became Civil Commissioner in the Seychelles Islands in 1849, and Lieutenant-Governor of Granada in the West Indies in 1853, followed 3 years later by a similar appointment in Trinidad. In 1867 Keate became Lieutenant-Governor of Natal, where he found a bad depression. He was often in opposition to the views of the Legislative Council. He played an important rôle as arbitrator (*see* KEATE AWARD) in boundary disputes. In 1872 he retired.

Keetmanshoop. Town in South West Africa. Founded in 1866 as a station of the Rhenish Missionary Society of Barmen, Germany, and named after its President, Johann Keetman. The present township was built in 1898 on a site granted by the local native chief. Important sheep farming and railway centre. Population: 10,300, including 5,000 Whites.

Keg. Old Cape measure of capacity applied to liquor, equal to 4 gallons.

Kehla. Headring worn by the married Zulu as a sign of status. It is usually made of resin worked into the hair.

Kei Apple (*Dovyalis caffra*). Small, spiny tree, indigenous to the hot, dry ridges of the Transkeian coastal belt. Bears a sour fruit, called Dingaan's Apple in Natal.

Keimoes. Village on the Orange River below Upington, originally a Hottentot kraal, but now the centre of a flourishing irrigation settlement dating back to the 1880's. Population: 3,050, including 950 Whites.

Kehla

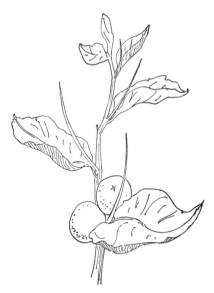

Kei Apple

Kei Mouth. Seaside resort near Komgha, Cape Province. Population: 320, including 160 Whites.

Kei River (strictly speaking the Great Kei). Important river in the Eastern Cape Province. Rises in the Stormberg and flows about 200 miles. Enters the sea north of East London. Chief tributaries are the White Kei, Indwe and Tsomo Rivers. The Kei River was chosen as the southern boundary of the native reserve known as the Transkei, thus separated from what became known as the Ciskei.

Keiskama River. Rises in the Amatola Mountains and enters the Indian Ocean south of East London. Its length is approximately 100 miles. The village of Hamburg is located near its mouth. The name Keiskama in Hottentot means 'Sweet Waters.' In 1847 the Keiskama became the Eastern boundary of Cape Colony. Chief tributary is the Tyumie River.

Keiskammahoek. Town in Cape Province, former frontier post. Population: 2,221, including 262 Whites.

Keiweg (Kei Road). Village near King William's Town, Cape Province. Population 500, including 150 Whites.

Kekewich, Major-General Robert George. British soldier. Born in Devonshire, 1854, educated at Marlborough and joined the Army in 1874. After service in Malaya, Egypt and the Sudan, he was posted to South Africa on the outbreak of the South African War, and was in command of the troops defending Kimberley. During the siege he came into violent conflict with Cecil Rhodes who insisted on making his own arrangements with civilians for defence, etc. After the relief Colonel Kekewich was promoted to Major-General. He died in 1914.

Kelly-Kenny, General Sir Thomas. British soldier. Born in 1840, in Ireland. Joined the Army at the age of 18 and served in China in 1860. His chief claim to prominence was his rôle in the South African War in which he commanded the Sixth Division in 1900. Later he engaged in battles at Paardeberg, Poplar Grove, Driefontein and elsewhere, being placed in command of the newly-captured Orange Free State in the same year. After serving as Adjutant-General from 1901 to 1904 he retired in 1907 and died on December 26, 1914.

Kelvin Grove. Large country club at Newlands, Cape Town, with wide range of sporting sections. Housed in former estate and mansion of Rimer family. Founded in 1924. Official name is Western Province Sporting Club. Membership over 3,000.

Kemp, General Christoffel Greyling. Born in the Transvaal, 1872, he attended the State Gymnasium School, Pretoria, and in 1889 qualified as a teacher. Two years later he took a post in the Education Department of the S.A. Republic, also becoming a lieutenant in the Volunteers for the Krugersdorp District. Served in native campaigns and against the Jameson Raiders. He distinguished himself in the S.A. War and rose to be General. Upon the formation of the Union Defence Force in 1912 he became an officer and joined the 1914 Rebellion, making an historic trek across the Kalahari desert with his unit, after the defeat of the insurgents, reaching German territory. Later he surrendered to the S.A. authorities and was sentenced to imprisonment but was released in 1916. In 1920 Kemp became member of parliament for Wolmaranstad, and in 1924 Minister of Agriculture under General Hertzog, becoming Minister of Lands in 1936–1939. He died in 1946. His memoirs appeared under the name of *Vir Vryheid en vir Reg.*

Kempton Park. Town on railway between Johannesburg and Pretoria, named after Kempten in Germany, though mis-spelt. Manufacturing industries, including the Modderfontein Dynamite Factory near by (q.v.), also Jan Smuts Airport, the largest in

Africa. Population: 58,214, including 30,000 Whites.

Kendal. Colliery centre near Witbank, Transvaal. Population: 2,735, including 545 Whites.

Kenhardt. Village in North-Western Cape Province. Founded in 1889 and named after an early trader. The main products of the district include wool and wheat. Population: 2,832, including 764 Whites.

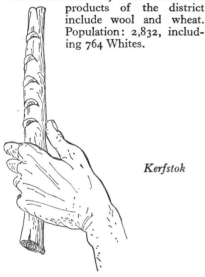

Kerfstok

Kentani. Village in Transkei. Population: 280, including 100 Whites.

Kenton-on-Sea. Village near Bathurst, Eastern Cape Province. Population: 170, including 60 Whites.

Kerfstok. Notched tally stick. Used on old South African farms to keep check of lost cattle and sheep.

Kerr, Philip Henry (Marquis of Lothian). Statesman, writer and official. Born in London, 1882, he studied at Oxford and came to South Africa in January 1905 as a member of Lord Milner's famous 'Kindergarten' (q.v.). He held important posts, including that of Assistant Secretary to the Inter-Colonial Council and of the Committee of the Central South African Railways, as well as of the Transvaal Indigency Commission. In 1908 he became editor of *The State*. Upon his return to England, he was editor of *The Round Table*, with which he remained from 1910 to 1916. During World War I, Lord Lothian was Secretary to the Prime Minister, Mr. Lloyd George, and in 1931 he became Chancellor of the Duchy of Lancaster. He died in 1940.

Kersebos 'Candle Bush' (*Euclea racemosa* Murr.). Shrub up to 8 feet. Wood hard and heavy, used by turners and formerly burnt instead of candles by settlers. Southern and Eastern divisions of Cape Province.

Kestell. Town in the Orange Free State, named after the Rev. J. D. Kestell, a well-known leader of the Dutch Reformed Church and one of the secretaries at the peace discussions that ended the South African War. It was founded in 1905 and is a prosperous farming centre. Population: 1,820, including 595 Whites.

Kestell, Rev. John Daniel. Born in 1854 in Natal, studied in Holland and in 1882 became Dutch Reformed Minister in Kimberley, where he remained till 1894, before moving to Harrismith. Upon the outbreak of the South African War he joined the O.F.S. forces as chaplain and after being in the field for several years, served as Secretary to the Peace Conference at Vereeniging along with D. van Velden. He later wrote what is the recognised account of the proceedings, his experiences of the war and a biography of General de Wet in Afrikaans. In later years he was repeatedly moderator, also editor of *Die Kerkbode* and a translator of the Bible into Afrikaans. Thanks to him the Reddingsdaad (q.v.) movement was begun to help the poorer Afrikaner. He died in 1941 and was buried at the foot of the Bloemfontein monument to the Women and Children who died in the South African War.

Kestrel (family Falconidae). *See* EAGLES and BIRDS.

Ketshwayo. *See* CETEWAYO.

Khaki Bush (*Althernarathera achyrantha*). Weed found very widely in South Africa. It was imported from Argentine as fodder during the South African War, and became a plague round the country soon after. The law enforces the removal of this weed from lands.

Khalifa. Moslem celebration widely popular among the Cape Malays. Under the influence of music and the monotonous beating of drums they work themselves into a frenzy and—without any loss of blood—pierce themselves with swords, cut their limbs and run pins and sharp objects through their flesh. The practice is frowned on by the Moslem religious leaders, but continues and is carried out as a form of entertainment at the Cape.

Khama. King of the Bamangwato, and one of the greatest men the black races have produced. According to recent researches, he was born about 1837. He became involved in tribal quarrels and in 1860 was baptised. At an early stage he decided to ban the use of liquor in all territories under his control. He put this into effect after his accession to the chieftainship in 1872. Successfully beating off attacks by the neighbouring Matabele, he held his own against all efforts made by the Boers to extend their power into his territory. Later he became friendly with the British and gave assistance to the Pioneer Column of Cecil John Rhodes. Khama visited England in 1895 and was received by Queen Victoria. He enjoyed enormous prestige both with Europeans and Africans; died in 1922.

Khama, Sir Seretse. First President of Botswana (q.v.). Grandson of Khama (q.v.), he was born in 1921 and succeeded his father Segkoma as Paramount Chief at the age of four. After studying at the Mission Institutions of Tiger Kloof and Lovedale, he continued at Fort Hare, Witwatersrand University, Oxford and London. Called to the Bar, he aroused great protest in his own country by his marriage to an English girl, Ruth Williams. For some time he lived in exile, but returned with his wife and family in 1956 and was restored to the chieftaincy. Became President in 1966.

Khami Ruins. Extensive ancient buildings near Bulawayo, scattered over nearly 3 sq. miles. In size and in general importance they are regarded as second only to Zimbabwe. Large numbers of relics have been found in the debris, though the workmanship is not as good as that of Zimbabwe (*see* MAPUNGUBWE and MATINDERE.)

Khoi-Khoin. Name used by the Hottentots of themselves. It means 'a man.'

Kierrie or **Knobkierrie.** Stick with a large knob at the end of it, used as a weapon by most natives in Southern Africa.

Kiewiet. Afrikaans name for Crowned Lapwing. *See* PLOVER.

Kijaat (also **Kiaat**). Common South African name for *Pterocarpus Angolensis*. Also known as Cape Teak. Used for furniture.

Kimberley. City in the north of the Cape Province, and centre of the diamond industry. Named after the Earl of Kimberley, who was Colonial Secretary of Britain at the time of its foundation, in 1871, when an exodus occurred from the earlier River Diggings on the Vaal River to the Dry Diggings, referred to as 'New Rush.' In 1873 these camps were converted into a township named Kimberley, near which developed another community, Beaconsfield. Digging was concentrated at Colesberg Koppie, named after the large number of miners from that Cape village. The

Koppie was literally dug away, and the gigantic pit, now referred to as the 'Big Hole,' came into existence. No longer used, it is still a most impressive landmark. By 1878 Kimberley had over 40,000 inhabitants, most of whom lived in great discomfort, under canvas and tin. Municipal Government was granted in 1878 and vigorous efforts made to improve health and living conditions. A successful Stock Exchange, the forerunner of the larger one in Johannesburg, was formed. The railway arrived in 1885, and 3 years later the numerous rival concerns, operating in and around the Big Hole where extensive collapses of reef had occurred, were amalgamated by Cecil John Rhodes and his supporters into De Beers Consolidated Mines (q.v.). On the city the immediate results were unfortunate, for the individual digger disappeared and, with the reorganisation of the industry on an economic basis, there was a depression. This was overcome, and Kimberley entered on a period of fairly steady growth, varied by occasional setbacks, chiefly due to the fall in the diamond market. During the South African War Kimberley was besieged by the Boers for 124 days from October 1899 to February 1900, those cooped up in the town including Cecil John Rhodes. In recent years, Kimberley, apart from the activity of its diamond mines, has developed certain industries, notably engineering, clothing manufacture and diamond cutting. It is also a business centre for irrigation areas in the Northern Cape. The population is 96,200, of whom 30,000 are Whites, 45,000 Bantu, 1,200 Asiatics and 20,000 Coloureds.

Kimberley Reefs. Original name of Bindura (q.v.).

Kinderbewys. Literally 'Child Proof.' A mortgage bond passed by a parent under Roman-Dutch law in South Africa, securing the inheritance for his or her minor child, due to it from a predeceased spouse.

King Edward VII School. Originally known as Johannesburg College; began its existence in 1894, occupying the mansion of B. I. Barnato (q.v.) in Berea for a while and then, about 1911, moved to Houghton Estate. Large preparatory, high school and boarding departments for boys.

Kingfishers or **Visvangers** (family Alcedinidae). Thickset, short-tailed birds, with long, sharp bills. Usually brightly coloured, although one, the Pied Kingfisher, is black and white. He is the commonest of the 'water' kingfishers. The beautiful red, green and orange Malachite Kingfisher is a tiny crested bird. The 'bush' (Halcyon) Kingfishers feed on insects. *See* BIRDS.

Kingklip (*Genypterus capensis*). Fish found off west coast from St. Helena Bay to Cape Point, and Agulhas Bank to Algoa Bay. About 5–6 feet long. A fairly deep-water fish and one of the finest for eating. *See* MARINE RESOURCES.

King, Richard (Dick) Philip. Natal pioneer and hero of a ride famous in South African history. Son of Philip King, he was born in Chatham, England, on November 28, 1813, one of 13 children, and came to South Africa with his parents who were 1820 settlers. He reached Natal about 1828 and worked for Captain Allan Gardiner as a wagon driver and thus came to know the road through unsubdued Native territories back to Grahamstown, which proved of great importance to him later. After the arrival of the Voortrekkers in Natal in 1838 the British Government sent troops under Captain Smith to establish fortifications at Congella. These were besieged by the Boers, and the garrison was in a serious plight when on May 26, 1842, Richard King, who was with the British force, undertook to ride to Grahamstown for help. Having been brought by boat across Durban Bay, by G. C. Cato and his brother C. J.

Cato, King, accompanied by a Zulu, Ndongeni, began his ride through wild country full of hostile tribes, completing the journey of 600 miles on his horse 'Somerset.' He arrived in the record time of 10 days, delivered the message that the garrison was in urgent need and enabled relief to be sent by ship from Port Elizabeth. King received £15 reward. He returned to Natal, farmed near Isipingo, and died there in 1871. Ndongeni, his native companion, was still living at an immense age in 1911.

King's African Rifles. British Colonial regiment designed for service in several parts of Africa. Originated as far back as 1893 when a force of Askaris (African soldiers) was established. Separate battalions were found as far afield as British Somaliland, Kenya, Uganda, Tanganyika and Nyasaland. From the start a high standard of efficiency and discipline was maintained and under their British officers the K.A.R. were soon recognised as an outstanding fighting force. They took part in the campaign against the 'Mad Mullah' in Somaliland in 1898 and again in 1903. During World War I they were prominent in the East African campaign against General von Lettow-Vorbeck and his German Colonial army. In World War II they won even greater laurels on the frontiers of Italian Somaliland (where they operated with the Northern Rhodesia Corps) and later in Burma. Disbanded in 1963.

Kingsburgh. Municipality on the South Coast of Natal, formed by the amalgamation of Doonside, Warner Beach, St. Winifreds, Winklespruit, Karridene and Illovo Beach. It extends for several miles along the coast and covers a total area of 2,400 acres. The original Health Committee became a Health Board in 1931, a Town Board in 1942, and a Borough in October 1952. Kingsburgh lies about 20 miles south of Durban on the main south coast road,

and each village has its own railway station. The majority of the population is European, numbering 5,400, as against 1,780 Bantu and 30 Asiatics. The municipal valuation is nearly R7,534,000.

Kingsley. Village near Glencoe in Natal, established in 1903. Farming centre. Population: 1,064, including 63 Whites.

Kingswood College. Public school for boys established in Grahamstown by the Methodist Church in 1894. Has a fine record for sport.

King William's Town. Named after William IV of England; on the Buffalo River in the Eastern Cape. The Rev. John Brownlee established a mission station in 1825, at Tsatsoe's Kraal. There was no white community until 1835, when Sir Benjamin D'Urban, Governor of the Cape Colony, laid out the village of King William's Town, as capital of the Province of Queen Adelaide. The following year this Province, by order of the Colonial Secretary, Lord Glenelg, was handed back to the Natives, who destroyed the village. In 1847 it was re-established by Governor Sir Harry Smith (q.v.) who made it the capital of what became British Kaffraria (q.v.). The town prospered as a military, administrative and trading centre, which supported wagon-building and other works. To-day there is a considerable textile plant at Zwelitsha (q.v.). Population: 16,000, including 7,100 Whites, 2,190 Coloureds, 5,700 Bantu and 150 Asiatics.

Kinross. Township in the Transvaal, founded in 1910 and named after the home town of its surveyor. Important maize-growing and farming centre. Population: 2,100, including 1,000 Whites.

Kipling, Joseph Rudyard. English poet and novelist. Born in India in 1865 and educated in England, he attained fame by his verses and stories while editor and contributor to the

Civil and Military Gazette at Lahore.
Travelling widely in Asia and America,
he owed his contacts with Southern
Africa mainly to Cecil John Rhodes
(q.v.) who invited him to the Cape.
Rhodes placed the house known as
'The Woolsack' at his disposal on his
several visits, the first during the South
African War. In that campaign Kipling played a rôle as temporary editor
of *The Friend* (q.v.) in Bloemfontein
after the British occupation in 1900.
He wrote a number of well-known
poems and stories on Southern Africa,
as well as the inscription on the
Rhodes Memorial at Groote Schuur.
He died in England in 1936, having
maintained his contacts with South
Africa to the end.

Kippersol (also **Kiepersol**). Popular
name of Indian origin for a tree widely
found in South Africa. It is sometimes
referred to as the 'parasol tree' on
account of its shape.

Kirkwood. Town in the Sundays
River Valley near Port Elizabeth and
first called Bayville (1885). Re-
established (1913) under its present
name in honour of John Somers Kirkwood, as the centre of the irrigation
settlement of Strathsomers Estate.
This has proved successful in the considerable production of citrus and
other fruits. Population: 6,500, including 1,250 Whites.

Kippersol

Kirstenbosch. Estate near Cape Town,
which belonged to the Kirsten family.
It was bought by Cecil John Rhodes
and incorporated in the Groote
Schuur Estate, at the end of the last
century, but in 1913, was, by unani-
mous vote of Parliament, chosen as the
site of the National Botanic Garden,
with an area of about 1,200 acres on a
slope of Table Mountain. Thanks to the
work of the late Prof. Pearson, who is
buried there, and of his successors, it
is today recognised as one of the finest
and most beautiful botanic gardens in
the world.

**Kitchener, Earl of Khartoum (Hora-
tio Herbert Kitchener).** British
soldier. Born in Ireland at Ballylong-
ford in 1850 and trained for the Royal
Engineers at the Royal Military Academy, Woolwich, which he entered in
1867. Commissioned at the age of 21,
he was lent to the Palestine Exploration
Fund for archaeological work in 1874;
did surveying in Cyprus in 1878, and
in 1882 began his long career in Egypt
and the Sudan that was to make him
famous. He rose to be Governor-
General of the Eastern Sudan in 1886
and Sirdar or Commander-in-Chief of
the Egyptian forces in 1892. This led,
6 years later, to the conquest of the
Sudan in 1898, and to the avenging
of General Gordon's death at Khartoum. The next year he was called to
South Africa as Chief-of-Staff to Lord
Roberts (q.v.) and in 1900 he succeeded
the latter as Commander-in-Chief.
Kitchener's main ability lay in the field
of organisation. He created the blockhouse system, suppressed rebellion in
the North-west Cape, and despite
many setbacks brought the war to an
end with the Treaty of Vereeniging in
1902. He spent the ensuing years in
India and the East, became Secretary of
State for War in 1914, raised 3,000,000
men by voluntary enlistment before
the adoption of conscription and
protested against the continuance of
the Dardanelles expedition. Sent to

Russia on the eve of the Revolution he was drowned off Northern Scotland in H.M.S. *Hampshire* in 1916.

Kite (family Falconidae). Bird of prey of hawk-type found throughout South Africa. Varieties include the African, Black-shouldered and Yellow-billed Kite. *See* EAGLES and BIRDS.

Kittermaster, Sir Harold Baxter. Governor of Nyasaland. Born in May 1879, near Coventry, educated at Shrewsbury and at Oxford. Shortly after the South African War he entered the Transvaal Education Department, where he served from 1903 to 1907. He was Governor of Somaliland Protectorate from 1926 to 1931, after serving in East Africa. Went to British Honduras, and in 1934 became Governor of Nyasaland. He died on January 14, 1939.

Kitwe. Town in Zambia and business centre of the Copperbelt. Laid out in 1935 as a Government township adjoining the Nkana Mine. It is one of the fastest-growing communities in the country. Population: 115,000, including 12,500 Whites.

Klaarstroom. Village near Prince Albert, Cape Province. Population 190, including 50 Whites.

Klapbroek. Trousers, usually made of skin, worn by the early Boers and folding downwards like those of a sailor.

Klawer. Village near Vanrhynsdorp, Cape Province. Population: 1,784, including 771 Whites.

Klein-Brakrivier (Little Brak River). Village near Mossel Bay. Population: 260, including 140 Whites.

Klein Majuba. *See* NICHOLSON'S NEK.

Kleinmond. Seaside resort near Hermanus, Cape Province. Population: 830, including 400 Whites.

Klein Vrystaat. Miniature Boer republic, established on the eastern frontier of the Transvaal. It came into

Klapbroek

existence on March 10, 1886, on territory which had been granted to F. I. Maritz and J. F. Ferreira in 1877 by the Paramount Chief of Swaziland, Umbandine. The whole republic covered about 15,000 morgen, or less than 50 sq. miles, and had a population of 72. It lasted for 5 years, during which it was governed by a 'Driemanskap' or Triumvirate. On May 2, 1891, it was incorporated as Ward I of the district of Piet Retief in the South African Republic.

Kleinzee. Alluvial diamond diggings on the coast of Namaqualand discovered in 1925, taken over by the Cape Coast Exploration Company Ltd. and afterwards exploited on a restricted scale by De Beers Consolidated Mines. The labour is mostly European. Population: 500, including 140 Whites.

Klerksdorp. Oldest town in the Transvaal. Established on the Schoonspruit by the Voortrekkers in 1837 and named after one of them, J. De Clerq (J's. son). The first township consisted of only 25 plots and was known as the Oude Dorp (Old Village). In 1886 gold was found near by, and a new township started, which soon overshadowed the other on the opposite side of the river, attaining such prosperity that it supported a Stock Exchange (still standing, though no longer in use). Vast sums were spent on gold properties near by, including the Buffelsdoorn and Machavie. Erratic deposits and metallurgical troubles put an end to most of these operations. During the South African War fighting took place near here and also, on April 9, 1901, the first discussions about a possible peace settlement between the representatives of the two Republics. It then became a leading grain-producing area. Its mining fortunes had a spectacular revival after the discovery of the Rand gold reef extensions beyond Randfontein in 1932. Since 1933 large developments have taken place, including the opening of the Stilfontein and other wealthy gold mines. The town is now a manufacturing centre and growing rapidly. Population: 60,000, including 27,500 Whites.

Klipblom. *See* CRASSULA.

Klip-Fish (Clinus). Large family of shallow-water fish, abundant in cold Cape seas.

Klipfontein. Township near Kempton Park, Transvaal. Population: 1,312, including 480 Whites.

Klipheuvel. Site of large overseas beam wireless station, erected by the Marconi Company in 1923–1924; later taken over by the Union Post Office. The masts, 820 feet high, were the tallest man-made structures in the Union, but have since been replaced.

Klipplaat. Railway junction near Jansenville, Cape Province. Population: 2,077, including 740 Whites.

Klipspringer (*Oreotragus oreotragus*). Small, stocky antelope, the name meaning 'rock jumper' in Afrikaans,

from its habit of living in dry, mountainous parts. It is usually under 2 feet in height and has very small horns. It is famous for its sure-footedness and, like the Swiss chamois, can leap immense distances. The coarse, bristly, yellow-brown hair is in demand for stuffing saddles.

Kloof. Town near Durban, on the road to Pietermaritzburg, noted for its rolling country, cool climate and beautiful views. Population: 8,000, including 4,500 Whites.

Klops. Nickname for Coloured and Malay participants in fancy dress, taking part in the Coon Carnival (q.v.).

Klossiegras (*Melica decumbens* Thunb.). Tufted, up to 1½ feet. Leaves very rough. Intoxicating to stock. Oxen are reported to die from eating it. Eastern divisions of Cape Province, also in Orange Free State and Griqualand West. *See* DRONKGRAS.

Kluit. Afrikaans name for Avocet (q.v.).

Knersvlakte. Barren but highly mineralised area north of Vanrhynsdorp in the Western Cape Province, where, since World War II, important occurrences of radioactive minerals have been developed.

Knobnoses. Branch of the Baraputse tribe in Northern Transvaal who scarify the bridges of their noses with small knobs.

Knysna. Minor port of the Republic of South Africa, between Cape Town and Port Elizabeth, situated on a picturesque lagoon, entered through a narrow portal of rock known as The Heads. First visited by H.M.S. *Podargus*, a sloop, in 1817; a trade in timber from the magnificent forests surrounding the bay gradually grew up. George Rex (q.v.), who settled near by at Melkhoutkraal in 1816, helped to develop the port and had a ship built there. Sawmills were later set up by the Thesen and Parkes families, and a line built into the forest by the South-Western Railway Company. From 1818 a pilot was stationed at Knysna. The rise of other ports gradually drew traffic away and despite the use of the place for the building of naval launches in World War I, and for air patrols, it was given up by the South African Railways and Harbours administration some years later. Its prosperity now depends on the timber and tourist trades, both of which are flourishing. Population: 14,000, including 4,230 Whites.

Koch, Dr. Robert. German bacteriologist and discoverer of method of treating Rinderpest (q.v.). Born at Clausthal, Germany, in 1843; after gaining experience as Public Health official, and taking part in German Cholera Research expeditions to Egypt and India in 1883, became Professor at the University of Berlin in 1885, and from 1891 to 1904 was Director of the Institute for Infectious Diseases. Recognised as the founder of Bacteriology, he made a series of epoch-making discoveries, including the Tuberculosis bacillus in 1882, the Cholera bacillus and a method of treating anthrax. Invited by the Cape Government in 1896 to find a treatment and preventative for Rinderpest. He was given a free hand and, working mostly in Kimberley and in Bechuanaland, evolved a method of injecting serum from infected cattle which had recovered. This was found to afford protection for a limited period, if given in large doses. Later he proved that better results were obtained by using the bile of sick animals. Koch's efforts started South Africa's expanding veterinary research. He won the Nobel Prize for medicine in 1905 and died in 1910.

Kock, General Johannes Hermanus Michiel. Boer leader and soldier. Born at the Cape in 1836, he joined the Great Trek and took part in the Battle of Boomplaats. In the South African Republic, he became Landdrost of Potchefstroom and was elected as member of the Volksraad for that area. Interested in church matters, he was largely responsible for the adoption in the Republic of paying all Protestant ministers from State funds. In 1891 he became Member of the Executive Council and in 1899 was placed in charge of certain Boer forces in Northern Natal. Wounded in the Battle of Elandslaagte he died a few days later, in 1899.

Kocksoord. Township near Johannesburg, established during the 1890's. It was named after Servaas de Kock, a surveyor of Pretoria; later Assistant Surveyor-General of the South African Republic.

Koegas Atrocities. Name given to an incident in 1879, on the North-Western Frontier of Cape Colony. It occurred during a rising of Korannas and other tribes, against whom a commando of burghers was despatched. Several prisoners were found to have been shot down by their escort. On another occasion an encampment, including a number of women and children, was attacked at a place called Koegas, and its defenders mercilessly slain. Details leaked out and resulted in the arrest of five of the White men for murder. They were brought to Victoria West for trial, but racial feelings ran high and a jury acquitted them. Violent controversy resulted, culminating in a libel action, in which the Attorney-General of Cape Colony, Mr. (afterwards Sir) Thomas Upington (q.v.) sued the editor of the *Cape Argus* for £10,000 damages. He was awarded £5 and costs. The matter came up for discussion in the House of Commons, and drew the attention of influential circles in Europe.

Koekemakranka. *See* AMARYLLIS.

Koffiefontein. Diamond-mining town on the Riet River in the Orange Free State. A camp of sorts had existed there since 1870, when the first stones were picked up, but no township was laid out till 1892. The name has been explained in various ways—that the original Griqua owner of the area, Klaas Kok, found some coffee seeds in a nearby fountain or that two farmers, du Toit and Scholtz, exchanged two fat ewes there for a quantity of coffee. The diamond mine is noted for its high-quality stones and was of the open-cast type. During the South African War there was considerable fighting near by. The mine, which came under the control of De Beers in 1911, was later closed down owing to a slump and during World War II the buildings were used by the Government as an Internment Camp. In 1950 the mine was reopened. Koffiefontein is also an agricultural centre. Population: 2,985, including 841 Whites.

Koggelaar. Afrikaans name for Capped Wheatear (q.v.).

Koggelmander. South African name for a lizard and sometimes also for a chameleon.

Kok (Afrikaans for 'Cook'). Name of a succession of coloured rulers of Griqua people (q.v.). *Adam Kok*, a cook, bought his freedom from slavery and settled near Piquetberg in the early 18th century. He became headman of neighbouring families and moved them to the Namaqua country, where they became the Griqua people. *Cornelius Kok* (his son) succeeded and reigned until about 1816. *Adam Kok II* gained friendship of missionaries. Abdicated in favour of Waterboer (q.v.) in 1819. Died 1837. *Adam Kok III* led historic trek of his people from Philippolis in the Orange Free State (where they had settled), over the Drakensberg into No-Man's-Land (q.v.), which became known as Griqualand East; laid out Kokstad. In October, 1874, he brought his people under Cape Colonial Government and died December 30, 1875. His grave is a place of pilgrimage for the Griquas.

Kokerboom (*Aloe dichotoma* L.f.). Namaqualand and southern parts of South-West Africa. Stem thick, up to 12 feet, branched above the middle. Portions of the stems were hollowed and used by Bushmen as quivers.

Kokkewiet. Alternative name for Bokmakierie (q.v.).

Kokstad. Town in the Eastern Province, and capital of the former independent territory of Griqualand East. Established by Adam Kok III (q.v.) in 1862 after he led his tribe, the Griquas, there, on their historic trek across the Drakensberg from Philippolis in the Orange Free State. The town lies below Mount Currie, and is the centre of a flourishing cattle district, with a dairy industry. It contains buildings and monuments dating back to the days of the Griqua state. Population: 10,000, including 3,050 Whites. Altitude: 4,210 feet.

Kolbe, Monsignor Frederick Charles. Catholic scholar, author and priest. Born in George, Cape Province, 1854, and son of a well-known Protestant minister of the London Missionary Society. Intending to take Law, he studied at the School for the Sons of Missionaries in Blackheath, London, and at the South African College. Had entered the Inner Temple when he was converted to the Catholic faith and entered the priesthood. After taking his Doctorate of Divinity in Rome he returned in 1882 to South Africa. Of great intellectual brilliance, he was not only eminent in his Church, but, despite deafness, was a leading figure in University circles, author of several books on philosophical and religious subjects, a mountaineer and scientist. He was created a Monsignor and died in 1936.

Kolbe, Peter (more correctly Kolb). Early German traveller at the Cape. Born near Marktredwitz in Franconia in 1675. The son of a blacksmith, he grew up in great poverty but managed to attend the University of Halle, where he secured his doctorate for a thesis on the nature of Comets, in 1701. Becoming secretary to Baron Ferdinand von Krosigk (ancestor of Count Schwern-Krosigk, the Nazi Minister of Finance), Kolbe was made tutor to his sons and sent abroad, when he acquired a taste for travel. He came to the Cape in 1705, where he was well received by Governor William Adriaan van der Stel, and began a scientific study on every aspect of life in the Colony and among its people—black and white. He remained until 1712, when an attack of temporary blindness caused him to return to Europe. There his famous book, *Caput Bonae Spei Hodiernum*, appeared in Nuremberg as a folio in 1719 and was repeatedly reprinted. A classic, many of its once disputed statements are to-day confirmed. Later a headmaster, he died in Germany in 1726.

Komatipoort. Border station near Barberton, Transvaal. Population: 2,031, including 674 Whites.

Komgha. Town near King William's Town in the Eastern Cape Province; originally an army camp during the 1847 Native War. The town was established in 1877, during the Galeka War. Wool and farming centre. Population: 2,273, including 513 Whites.

Kommadagga. Village near Somerset East, Cape Province. Population: 1,880, including 990 Whites.

Kommetjie. Village near Fish Hoek, Cape Province. Population: 310, including 240 Whites.

Konya. Native word for 'unknown and unlucky voice at night' and also for the kind of grasshopper (*Pneumorus*) that makes a chirruping noise in the dark.

Konza. Zulu custom of paying respects to a chief.

Kookfontein. Large metallurgical works near Vereeniging, Transvaal. Population: 2,201, including 2,039 Whites.

Koonap River. Tributary of the Great Fish River. For a time part of the Cape frontier. In 1830 farms were given out between the Koonap and Kat River (q.v.) on 'Military Tenure,' i.e. occupants had to help defend the border in case of war.

Ko-operatieve Wijnbouwers Vereeniging van Zuid Afrika Beperkt (*Co-operative Wine Farmers' Association of South Africa Ltd.*). (The spelling of this name is in Dutch, not Afrikaans, owing to the fact that in 1917 the latter language was still in its beginnings.) Established in 1917 and placed by Act of Parliament in complete control of the Union's wine growers. It owes its existence largely to the initiative of the late Dr. C. W. H. Kohler, who, realising the inadequacy of earlier measures to rehabilitate the once flourishing Cape wine and spirit industry, convinced the Government of the need of co-operatives and supervision. Under the law, membership of the K.W.V. (as it is usually called) is compulsory for growers, who are obliged to sell to it that part of their grape crop not needed as fruit for raisin-making, etc. The K.W.V. possesses its own large cellarage, wineries and distilleries in Paarl (where its head office is located), Stellenbosch, Worcester, Montagu and Robertson. It operates research and testing laboratories, negotiates export agreements, fixes the prices for distilling wine and renders the official returns. The aim of rehabilitating the industry has been fully achieved and, thanks to a conservative financial policy, the Association has assets running into millions. It produces wine, brandy, liqueurs, eau de Cologne, grape juice and moskonfyt (must), vermouth, cocktails, spirits, etc. For export it treats, blends and matures wines grown by local farmers. Virtually all the wines and spirits marketed in the Republic and sold by individual firms have passed through the control of the K.W.V., one of whose main purposes is the maintenance of quality. *See also* WINE.

Koopmans-De Wet, Mrs. Marie.
Born in Cape Town, 1834, as Marie de Wet, she began life in the same house in Strand Street with which her name is permanently associated, her father being a well-known advocate in the city. In 1864 she married J. C. Koopmans, a Hollander, Usher of the Black Rod in the first Cape Parliament. Furnished in great style, her home soon became a centre of hospitality known throughout the Colony. She gathered treasures, particularly of early Cape art and furniture, from many parts She was also a leader in the revival of the rights of the Afrikaner. During the South African War, Mrs. Koopmans-de Wet allowed her house to be used as a depot for the collection of goods for the relief of women and children. After her death in 1906, her original collection was dispersed, but the house was later bought and re-established as a museum of South African national antiques, many of the early treasures finding their way back again. Today it is a national monument.

Kopersbond Beperk ("Buyers' Association"). Large Afrikaans co-operative society established in Johannesburg in March 1940.

Koppies (originally written **Kopjes**). Village in the Northern Orange Free State, and a centre of large farming district. Founded about 1908, and notable in South African history as one of the places where the 1914 Rebellion began. General Christiaan de Wet lived near by. Population: 4,178, including 830 Whites.

Koppie Walloper. Early name used in Kimberley for diamond buyers who travelled from claim to claim.

Korana. Hottentot tribe living on the Northern Frontier of Cape Province, divided into a number of clans, includ-

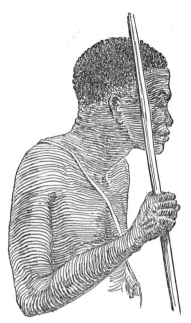

Korana

ing the Springbokke, the Towenaars (magicians) and Regshande (right hands). Believed to have originated near the Great Lakes in Central Africa, from which they were driven south by the Bantu. Many settled along the valley of the Orange River. Taller than the other Hottentots, they were more aggressive and less honest. One of their customs was to expose their old people to be devoured by wild animals. Many of them settled at Klaarwater and Campbell, where they came under the influence of a famous pioneer missionary, the Rev. John Campbell. After about 1820 their power declined and they mixed with the Bushmen and other tribes. Today pure Koranas are almost extinct.

Korhaan. *See* BUSTARD.

Kornet Spruit. Tributary of the Orange River (q.v.).

Korsten, Georg (Ge). South African singer (tenor). Born on December 6, 1929 in Rotterdam, Holland, the youngest of a family of eight. He came to South Africa in 1936. From boyhood he had shown exceptional vocal qualities and though he took up the profession of electrical engineer at Pretoria, from 1957 onwards he gained a high reputation in opera. In 1963 he was awarded a special State bursary to gain experience overseas, in which course he was highly successful. He has appeared in over thirty operas.

Kos. Old Cape measure of capacity, applied to liquor, equal to $7\frac{1}{2}$ gallons.

Kosi Bay. Inlet on the coast of Zululand, with nearby lagoon. The Government have considered developing this as a harbour by cutting a channel into the lagoon. In 1923 Sir George Buchanan, a leading overseas expert, visited the site and worked out plans, in conjunction with adjacent Sordwana Bay. Though technical problems are not insurmountable the project has not been followed up, but the increasing load on the Rand-Durban line, coupled with the growth in the coal exports, has revived the idea in recent times.

Koster. Town in the Transvaal Bushveld, founded in 1913 and named after its surveyor. Prosperous citrus and farming centre. Population: 4,500, including 1,300 Whites.

Kottler, Moses. South African sculptor. Born in Europe in 1896, he came to the Cape very young. He studied in Palestine, at Munich and in Paris. As a young man he showed exceptional gifts and became known internationally for his sensitive work in various media, including wood, stone and bronze. Among his best-known sculptures are the statues of 'Meidjie,' a young African girl, of General Christiaan de Wet, whom he knew personally, and of President T. F. Burgers, and the

carvings on the Johannesburg Public Library, etc.

Kotze, The Rev. Johannes Jacobus. Dutch Reformed Minister and central figure in a heresy case. Born in Cape Town in 1832, he was ordained in 1858, and took over the congregation in Darling. There he came into conflict with the Church authorities in 1862 on account of his alleged liberal views. This resulted in a case heard in Cape Town on August 23, 1864, in which Kotze was justified. He remained in office until his retirement in 1894. He died in March 1902.

Kotze, Sir John Gilbert. Chief Justice of the South African Republic. Judge, Appellate Division. Born in Cape Town on November 5, 1849, and educated at the South African College and London University. He was called to the Inner Temple in 1874 and returned to the Cape the same year to begin practice, but in 1876 moved to Grahamstown. In 1877 he was appointed Judge of the High Court of the Transvaal and was raised to Chief Justice in 1881. In 1897 he fell out with President Kruger and in 1899 went to the Cape. A year later he was appointed Attorney-General of Rhodesia. He took silk in 1902 and in 1903 was appointed to the bench of the Eastern Districts Court, where he became Judge-President in 1904. In 1913 he was appointed Puisne Judge at the Cape and Judge-President there in 1920. In 1922 he joined the Appellate Division, and retired in 1927. Died in Cape Town on April 1, 1940.

Kotze, Sir Robert Nelson. Government Mining Engineer and inventor. Born in 1870, and educated at the South African College and at Clausthal, Germany. Began mining career in 1895, in the Transvaal. There he was appointed Government Mining Engineer under Crown Colony régime in 1908, until he retired in 1927. From 1929 to 1930 he sat as a Member of Parliament. He was director of De

Beers and many other companies. Among his important achievements was the invention of the Konimeter, used for counting dust particles in mines, of great value in solving ventilation problems. He died in 1953.

Kougadam. Village near Humansdorp in the Cape Province. Population: 1,123, including 249 Whites.

Kousbandjie (*Elaps hygae*) (group Elapidae). A very poisonous small snake found in the Cape. The name means a garter, on account of its characteristic stripes of black and scarlet. *See* SNAKES.

Kowie River. Small but picturesque river in Eastern Cape Province. Rises near Grahamstown and enters Indian Ocean at Port Alfred. Length 45 miles. Large sums were spent in Victorian times on developing the mouth of the Kowie as a harbour. *See* PORT ALFRED.

K.R. Abbreviation for Kaffrarian Rifles (q.v.).

Kraaibos 'Crow Bush' (*Rhus crenata* Thunb.). Low shrub with purplish shiny berries. Port Elizabeth. *See* KAREEBOOM and SUURKAREE.

Kraaifontein. Township near Bellville, Cape Province. Population: 7,690, including 4,000 Whites.

Kraaipan. Village between Mafeking and Vryburg in Bechuanaland, notable in history as being the scene of the first fighting in the South African War. After the declaration of hostilities, on October 12, 1899, the Boers captured an armoured train at Kraaipan.

Kraal. Word used throughout Southern Africa for both a Bantu or other black tribal village of huts and also an enclosure used for livestock. The word is derived from the Portuguese *curral*, a paddock or cattle pen. The equivalent Spanish expression is *corral*, an enclosure or courtyard. Taken over by the early Dutch settlers, it was used in the writings of Peter Kolben as far back as 1705, and probably earlier.

Krakeelrivier. Village near Uniondale, Cape Province. Population: 1,593, including 341 Whites.

Kramat. Word used among the Cape Malays to describe the tombs of Moslem saints and holy men buried in and

Kramat

near the Cape Peninsula. More correctly written Karamat. There are five such tombs: near Faure (Sheikh Joseph (q.v.)), on Signal Hill, at Oudekraal, Constantia and on Robben Island; some contain more than one individual grave. Pious Moslems regard as an act of special merit making the circuit of the kramats, sacrificing and praying at each.

Krantzkop (now officially spelt **Kranskop**). Village in Natal, near Greytown in the heart of the wattle-growing country. Its main feature is the famous peak, from which it takes its name, the almost vertical faces of which have been scaled only three times, first, in 1879, by Captain A. M. Montgomery of the Natal Native Contingent. The native name is Ntunjambili, which means 'The Two Holes' because of two characteristic gaps near the summit. Near by are the former Umsinga Gold Fields.

Krause, Albert Edward Jacobus.
State Attorney, Transvaal. Born in
Bloemfontein, September 1856, he
became State Attorney of the Orange
Free State in 1883. In 1889 he was
appointed judge. In that year he
resigned to become State Attorney of
the Transvaal. He died in Bloemfontein on July 31, 1900.

**Krause, Frederick (Friedrich) Ed-
ward Traugott.** Judge-President of
the Orange Free State. Born in Bloemfontein on April 29, 1868, and educated
at Grey College in that city, as well
as at Victoria College, Stellenbosch,
and then at Amsterdam, where he
secured his Doctorate of Law in 1893.
Later in the same year he was called
to the Bar in London, and, returning
to South Africa, began to practise at
Pretoria. Krause was noted as an outstanding criminal lawyer, and in 1896
became First State Prosecutor in
Johannesburg, where he appeared at
the famous trial of von Veltheim
(q.v.). Upon the outbreak of the South
African War he was appointed 'Special
Commandant' for the Witwatersrand,
in which capacity he later surrendered
the city of Johannesburg to Lord
Roberts. He was arrested for a
political offence and sentenced to 2
years' imprisonment. Resuming practice in Johannesburg in 1904, he soon
became one of the leaders of the
Johannesburg Bar, appearing in most
of the important trials. In 1923 he was
appointed to the Bench in the Transvaal, and 10 years later became Judge-
President of the Orange Free State. In
1938 he retired, but continued to
figure prominently in the fields of
penal reform and historical research
(particularly on the early history of the
Witwatersrand). He died at the age of
91 in 1959.

Kreef. Traditional Cape name for
crayfish. *See* MARINE RESOURCES.

Kreli. Paramount chief of the Xosas.
Born about 1818, son of Hintsa (q.v.),
he attained prominence in 1854 when
he defeated the Tembus by skilful
action. Four years later, in 1858, he
was again at war with them, and a
third time in 1873. Against the British,
Kreli showed himself a remarkably
skilled diplomat, and in 1846 he gained
the better of Sir Andries Stockenstrom
at a peace conference. This was finally
concluded in 1848, and paved the way
for a friendly meeting with Governor
Sir Harry Smith near King William's
Town. From 1850 to 1852 he was
again at war with the British and was
heavily defeated. He agreed to a peace
in 1853, and his power was finally
broken after the Cattle-Killing Delusion (q.v.). From 1877 to 1888 Kreli
was again involved in war with the
Cape Colony, in which he was beaten
and driven into Bomvanaland, where
he died in February 1893.

Kreupelhout 'Cripple Wood' (*Leuco-
spernum conocarpum R.Br.*). Shrub up
to 8 feet. Stems softly hairy. Bark
astringent, used in tanning. Cape and
Caledon divisions.

Krige, Christman Joel. Speaker of
Union Parliament. Born in Stellenbosch, 1868, he qualified as an attorney
and settled in Caledon, Cape Province,
where he entered politics on the Afrikander Bond side and was deported
during the South African War. After
becoming mayor he was elected to the
first Union Parliament in 1910 as a
follower of General Louis Botha, became Chief Whip of the South African
Party, and, upon the retirement of Sir
John Moltene in 1915, Speaker of the
House. This post he held until 1924.
He died in 1933.

Krige, Uys. South African poet and
author. Born at Bontebokkloof near
Swellendam in 1910 and educated at
Cape Town and the University of
Stellenbosch. Became a journalist and
gained distinction in 1938 with his
Afrikaans play *Magdalena Retief*.
Lived for a while in France and Spain.
During World War II served in

Abyssinia and Egypt, being taken prisoner in 1941 and sent to Italy, where he escaped in 1943. This gave him material for his book *The Way Out*, written in English, which aroused much attention. Wrote *Die Wit Muur*, *Die Palmboom*, and displayed remarkable gifts as a poet. Edited literary magazine *Vandag* and translated Shakespeare's *Twelfth Night* into Afrikaans. Won several literary awards, including prize in World's Short Story Competition. Made translations into Afrikaans from Spanish and French literature.

Kritzinger, General Pieter Hendrik. Boer leader. Born near Port Elizabeth in 1870, and migrated in 1882 to the Orange Free State. In 1887 he began farming near Rouxville and joined that commando during the South African War. He distinguished himself under the command of General C. R. de Wet (q.v.) and carried out a long and daring raid into Cape Colony 1900–1901, which tied down many British troops. He became a member of the Cape Provincial Council in 1930 and sat in it until his death in 1935.

Krombek (*Sylvietta rufescens*). Small Warbler (q.v.) found commonly in most parts of the country, but abundant in the Kruger Park. It has a very short tail, flits a yard or two, then creeps up and down the branches, hunting for insects. *See* BIRDS.

Kromdraai. Township near Witbank, Transvaal. Population: 2,601, including 231 Whites.

Kroonstad. Town in the Northern Orange Free State, on the Valsch River. Its name has been variously explained by allusion to the Russian fortress of Kronstadt, near Leningrad, which was in the news at the time of its foundation in 1859, and to a horse, named Kroon, belonging to a local official. During 1900 it was for several months capital of the fugitive Republican Government. A leading maize-growing and farming centre, it has

acquired added prosperity in recent years through the rise of the Orange Free State gold fields. Population: 50,700, including 16,500 Whites.

Kruger Millions. Treasure allegedly hidden by or on behalf of President Paul Kruger (q.v.) in the later stages of the South African War. Details as to the size of the hoard vary widely. Many expeditions have attempted to find it, but without success. The basis of the tradition is the fact that gold mining was continued by the Boer Government on a limited scale before they evacuated the Rand. This bullion was brought to the Pretoria Mint, and removed, some of it in half-minted form. Most of it was used for war expenses, some possibly hidden by individual commandos in the field, but the amounts involved are wildly exaggerated.

Kruger National Park. Largest National Park in the Republic of South Africa, approximately 8,000 square miles. Bounded on the east by Mozambique, it extends about 200 miles from Komatipoort to the Limpopo River, 20 to 50 miles wide. Mostly level, with Bushveld flora. Opened in 1898 as Sabi Game Reserve, to which were later added the Shingwedzi Game Reserve in the north and gifts of individual farms. In its present form the National Park came into existence in 1926, named after President Paul Kruger (q.v.). It contains most major species of South African wild life, including elephants in the north, lions, leopards, giraffes and many antelopes. Efforts are afoot to replace the rhinoceros, which is now extinct. The earlier development was largely due to Lt.-Col. James Stevenson-Hamilton (q.v.). Traversing the Park is a section of the Selati Railway and a network of roads to serve the rest camps—Pretoriuskop, Lower Sabi and Skukuza in the south, Satara, Tshokwane, Orpen and Letaba in the middle, and Shingwedzi and Punda

Maria in the north. The main visiting season is winter. It sees over 150,000 visitors annually, only a section being open throughout the year.

In 1969 it was estimated that the Park contained 8,000 elephants, 15,000 buffalo, 16,000 wildebeest and 18,000 zebras. As these numbers were considered excessive, a system of culling was adopted.

Krugersdorp. Town on West Rand, named after President Kruger. Founded in 1887 by Abner Cohen. One of its chief landmarks is the famous Paardekraal Monument, to commemorate the gathering at which the Boers decided in 1880 to rise against the British, who then occupied the Transvaal. Krugersdorp is an important gold mining and industrial centre. Dr. L. S. Jameson (q.v.) and his followers surrendered to the Boers in January 1896 just outside Krugersdorp. Population: 100,325, including 35,300 Whites, 62,000 Bantu, 2,300 Coloureds and 725 Indians.

Kruger Statue. Bronze monument to President Kruger in Church Square, Pretoria, modelled by Anton von Wouw (q.v.) and presented in 1899 by Samuel Marks (q.v.) to the Transvaal Republican Government. During the Boer War the statue was taken by the Royal Engineers and re-erected at Broome Park, England, while the four accompanying statues of burgers were put in the Drill Square of the Royal Engineers. At the request of General J. C. Smuts the statues were re-erected in Pretoria, first outside the railway station and later in Church Square.

Kruger, Stephanus Johannes Paulus. Last President of the South African Republic, and generally recognised as the greatest figure Afrikanderdom has produced. Of German origin, his family came from the Uckermark, north of Berlin, where the name is not uncommon. He himself wrote it with the 'Umlaut' (two dots), after the German fashion. Recent research by Professor C. J. Uys of the University of the Orange Free State shows that he was born not at Steynsburg, Eastern Cape Province, but on the farm Zoutpansdrift, near Venterstad. His birth date, October 10, 1825, may also be incorrect. His father, Kasper Jan Hendrik Kruger, and his mother, Elsie Fransina Steyn, joined the Great Trek (q.v.) and Paul experienced all the hardships of the time. At 15 he was recognised as a burgher. He married at 17 and settled on his farm, Waterkloof, near Rustenburg in the Transvaal. One of his hunting experiences was amputating his own thumb. He became a strong protagonist of the Dopper sect (q.v.) in whose churches he remained a lay preacher to the end of his life. He participated in several native wars, and in 1854 showed outstanding bravery in rescuing the body of Commandant Potgieter from the besieged mountain stronghold of Chief Makapan. Unsuccessfully, he worked for the unification of the Transvaal with the Orange Free State. During the ensuing Civil War he backed van Rensburg and seized the town of Potchefstroom (q.v.). After the failure of President Burger's over-ambitious programme, he became one of the mainstays of the national resistance to the British annexation policy. After Shepstone had hoisted the British flag in 1877, he joined the protesting deputation to London, impressing all by his innate skill as a negotiator. Failing, he concentrated on anti-British propaganda among his own people in the Transvaal, and, as Vice-President of the South African Republic, accompanied another fruitless deputation to London and the Continent in 1878. From now on he built up resistance to British administration, and when the real revolt began in 1880 he became a member of the Triumvirate (q.v.). He attended peace negotiations and, as Vice-President, summoned the extraordinary session of the Volksraad that confirmed the

Convention of Pretoria. In 1883 he was first elected President of the South African Republic and became its dominating personality. Following the Barberton and Witwatersrand gold discoveries, the enormous increase of foreigners confronted him with his life's problem, that of reconciling the supremacy of the Boers with justice to the immigrants. He failed to obtain a sea coast near St. Lucia Bay and had continued frontier skirmishes in Swaziland and in the area adjoining Bechuanaland, where British sovereignty clashed with the power of the Transvaal. Moreover, he had to restrain his burghers from crossing the Limpopo, in order to prevent friction with Cecil Rhodes. In 1888, elected President for the second time, he came into even stronger conflict with Rhodes. Certain Uitlanders were friendly, while others were extremely hostile. To counterbalance British influence, he introduced many Dutch officials, headed by the State Secretary, Dr. W. J. Leyds, and favoured the construction of a railway line to Lourenço Marques before the completion of any through British territory. In this he was unsuccessful. In Europe, however, he evoked sympathy and admiration for his diplomatic skill, and particularly impressed Prince Bismarck. In the Transvaal, amid overwhelming difficulties, he was charged with deliberately obstructing the development of the Rand, with nepotism, with corruption and many other offences. On the other hand his own people venerated him increasingly. Efforts to ease the situation between the Uitlanders and the Government were nullified by the occurrence of the Jameson Raid (q.v.) at the end of 1895. The leaders of the British cause, notably Cecil John Rhodes, Joseph Chamberlain and Lord Milner, were insistent that the Uitlanders be given the franchise, but Kruger refused more than a token concession, because they outnumbered his burghers. By the time he was ready to compromise the South African War had become inevitable. Although very moderate in his treatment of the Jameson Raiders, whom he handed over for trial to the British, and in that of the Reformers, whose sentences he commuted to fines and banishment, he was unable any longer to cope with the position. He was re-elected by a large majority in 1898 and war broke out in October 1899. Being over 74, in bad health and unable to stand the campaigning, he paid several visits to the commandos in the field and remained in Pretoria until May 29, 1900, only a few days before its occupation by the British. On October 21, 1900, he boarded the warship *Gelderland* sent out by Queen Wilhelmina to Lourenço Marques. He proceeded first to France and then to Holland, where he remained until the end of the war, doing his utmost to rally assistance for the Boer Republics, and where he began dictating his memoirs. He moved to Switzerland and there, on July 10, 1904, he died. He was buried in the Old Cemetery in Pretoria on December 16, 1904.

Kruger Rand. South African gold coin, struck in November 1967. Weighing 1 ounce and equivalent in size to half a crown, it carries a portrait of President S. J. P. Kruger. 10,000 were struck and sold to collectors at R31 each.

Kruger Telegram. Name usually applied to a message sent by Kaiser Wilhelm II, the German Emperor, to President Kruger immediately after the Jameson Raid. It was despatched on January 3, 1896, and read: 'I express to you my sincere congratulations, that, without appealing for the help of friendly powers, you and your people have succeeded in repelling with your own forces the armed bands which had broken into your country, and in maintaining the independence of your country against foreign aggression.' The telegram gave great offence in England and led to the cooling of relations with Germany.

Kruidjie-roer-my-nie. 'Little plant, touch-me-not' (*Melianthus comosus* Vahl.). Shrub up to 4 feet, unpleasantly scented. Flowers secrete much nectar. Eastern districts of Cape Province.

Kruisfontein. Village near Humansdorp, Cape Province. Population: 3,062, including 5 Whites.

Krulgras. *See* FINGER GRASS.

Kubusie. Village near Stutterheim in the Eastern Cape Province, noted for its forests. It has lost some of its former importance as a wool-washing, timber and trading centre, through the relaying of the main railway line.

Kudu (*Strepsiceros capensis*). Antelope found in reserves in the Eastern Province, also in the Northern Cape,

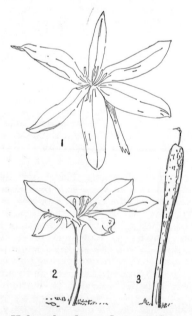

Kukumakranka: 1 *flower;* 2 *flower rising from a tube before the leaves appear;* 3 *fruit after flowering*

the Kalahari, South West Africa, the Kruger National Park, Zululand, Mozambique and Rhodesia. An impressive animal, standing 5 feet at the shoulder, it is famous for the great spiral horns, peculiar to the bull. Kudus are fond of thickly wooded country and river beds. Inclined to be timid, they provide excellent meat, but are now strictly protected. Not until 1834 was the first complete specimen of a Kudu secured for study.

Kuifkop. Afrikaans name for Cape Bulbul. *See* BULBUL.

Kuils River. Town near Bellville, Cape Province. Population: 7,510, including 3,000 Whites.

Kuisip River. Intermittent stream in South West Africa. Rises in mountains beyond Windhoek, crosses Namib plain, and occasionally reaches Atlantic Ocean. Usually only recognisable by vegetation growing along its bed.

Kukumakranka. Cape Flower. *See* AMARYLLIS.

Kunene River. *See* CUNENE.

Kupugani ('Help Yourself'). Voluntary organisation established in South Africa in 1962 to buy surpluses of bulk quantities of farm produce and distribute them just above cost price among the under-privileged, particularly Bantu.

Kurper. South African fresh-water fish. *See* CICHLID.

Kuruman. Town in the Northern Cape Province in Bechuanaland. Founded in 1821, by the Rev. Robert Moffat of the London Missionary Society. In 1885, after the expedition of Sir Charles Warren to occupy Bechuanaland (q.v.), a village was established about 3 miles off. One of the famous landmarks is the 'Eye' of Kuruman, a spring yielding no less than 4,500,000 gallons a day in the middle of the semi-desert. Population: 7,000, including 3,700 Whites.

Kushlick, Taubie. South African theatrical producer. Born Taubie Braun, May 7, 1910, in Port Elizabeth, where she studied elocution at the Holy Rosary Convent, continuing at the Royal Academy of Music, London. Both as actress and producer she has gained a considerable reputation over a wide range of plays.

Kustingbrief. Mortgage bond passed under Roman-Dutch law in favour of the seller of immovable property to cover the unpaid portion of its purchase price. ('Kusting' is an old Dutch word for Mortgage, while 'Brief' is a letter.)

Kwaai Hoek. See BUSHMAN'S RIVER.

Kwacha ('Dawn'). Zambian and Malawi coin (equal to 1 Rand) and comprising 100 Ngwee (q.v.).

Kwa-Mashu. Large Bantu housing scheme in Durban. Its ultimate population is estimated at 100,000.

Kwambonambi. Village on Lower Umfolozi, Natal. Sugar Centre. Population: 270, including 100 Whites.

Kwartel. Afrikaans name for Cape Quail (q.v.).

Kwashiorkor. Nutritional disease found among African natives and elsewhere.

Kweek. See QUICK GRASS.

Kwikstertjie. Afrikaans name for Cape Wagtail. See WAGTAIL.

K.W.V. See KO-OPERATIEVE WIJN-BOUWERS VEREENIGING.

Kya. Name for native hut, or (popularly) servants' quarters.

Kyle Dam. Large irrigation scheme near Fort Victoria, Rhodesia.

Kylemore. Coloured township near Stellenbosch, Cape Province. Population: 1,035.

Kylsant, Lord (Sir Owen Philips). Shipping magnate, born in 1863. In his capacity as head of the Union-Castle Line, he negotiated various agreements with the Union Government. Died in 1937.

L

Laager. Characteristic South African defensive fortification established by the early settlers and used with great success by the Voortrekkers (q.v.) Wagons were drawn closely into a circle, and the intervening spaces closed with thornbush. In the centre were placed the women, children and cattle. The men defended the position against enemy attack while the women loaded guns and attended to the wounded.

Laaiplek. *See* VELDDRIF.

Labram, George. American engineer. Born in the U.S.A., he came to South Africa in 1894, being appointed Chief Mechanical Engineer for De Beers Consolidated Mines on October 8, 1896. He soon attracted attention by devising the very successful grease-table for catching diamonds in sorting, his fellow-inventor being F. B. Kirsten. The device, patented in 1897, was taken over by De Beers. During the siege of Kimberley Labram built Long Cecil (q.v.), but he was killed by a Boer shell on February 9, 1900.

Ladismith. Town in the Western Cape Province, in the Little Swartberg Mountains, founded in 1852 and named after the wife of Governor Sir Harry Smith (q.v.). To distinguish it from its counterpart in Natal the name is spelt with an 'i' instead of a 'y.' Formerly an important ostrich feather centre, it is now noted for other types of farming, including fruit and dairy produce. Population: 2,332, including 1,116 Whites.

Ladybrand. Town in the Eastern Orange Free State, named after the wife of Sir Christoffel Brand, Speaker of the Cape House of Assembly, and mother of President Sir Johannes Brand (q.v.). It was founded in 1867 at the foot of the picturesque Platberg. Situated in the heart of the Conquered Territory (q.v.), it is famous for its wheat production, and there are flour mills in the town. During the South African War, on September 2, 1900, a battle was fought there. Population: 8,100, including 2,200 Whites.

Lady Frere. Village in the Eastern Cape Province named after the wife of Governor Sir Bartle Frere (q.v.). It was founded in 1879 and is a centre for a large native area. Population: 1,000, including 200 Whites.

Lady Grey. Village in the Cape Province, near the Basutoland border, noted for its beautiful mountain scenery in the Wittebergen. It was established in 1858 and named after the wife of Governor Sir George Grey. The place acquired world-wide prominence during the South African War, when the postmistress, Mrs. Sarah Gluck, defied an invading Boer commando and refused to haul down the Union Jack, which the invaders good naturedly allowed her to retain for the entire period of their stay. Population: 2,500, including 641 Whites.

Ladysmith. Town in Northern Natal, founded in 1861, and originally named Windsor. Its present name is derived from the wife of Governor Sir Harry Smith of the Cape (q.v.), whom he rescued in romantic circumstances at the storming of Badajos in the Peninsular War, and later married. For long the railhead for traffic to the Transvaal. It gained world fame during the South African War when besieged by the Boers. The siege began on October 27, 1899, and lasted till February 28, 1900. Heavy fighting occurred. Farming and industrial centre. Population: 32,750, including 10,000 Whites.

Lagden, Sir Godfrey Yeatman.
Expert on native affairs and administrator of native territories. Born 1851, in England, he entered the British Post Office in 1869, and first came to South Africa as Chief Clerk to the State Secretary of the Transvaal under the First British Occupation in 1878. Later he became Private Secretary to Sir Owen Lanyon (q.v.) and Secretary to the Executive Council. During the Majuba Campaign he was besieged in Pretoria. He later served on several commissions. Lagden was War Correspondent during the Egyptian Campaign of 1882–1883, and served for a while in the Colonial Service in Sierra Leone and the Gold Coast. From there he went to Basutoland in 1884, where he distinguished himself and became Resident Commissioner in 1890. In 1892, he was Commissioner in Swaziland, and again in Basutoland from 1893 to 1901. As Chairman of the Inter-Colonial South African Native Affairs Commission in 1902–1904, he produced the classic report on the colour problems. Lagden served during the South African War and was repeatedly mentioned in despatches. He wrote a standard book on the Basutos in 1909, and was a distinguished hunter. Died in 1934.

Laing's Nek. Pass in Northern Natal; scene of a battle in First Boer War, on January 28, 1881, when General Sir Pomeroy Colley tried to force a way for his troops against the Boers under Commandant-General Piet Joubert. He was defeated with a loss of 83 men (including seven officers) killed and 111 wounded, almost one-sixth of his force.

Laingsburg. Village in the Karroo founded in 1881 and named after a Cabinet Minister, T. Laing. A health resort for lung complaints, now chiefly noted as a wool centre. Population: 2,815, including 1,042 Whites.

Lake Arthur. Name of large irrigation dam 18 miles south of Cradock, Cape Province. Named after Prince Arthur of Connaught, Governor-General of the Union, and begun under his régime in 1921. The wall was 1,640 feet long, on the Tarka River, and 107 feet above the river bed (124 feet above foundations). Suffered severely from silting; a new dam at Commandodrift is to make good these losses.

Lake Chrissie. Large semi-permanent sheet of water in the Eastern Transvaal, also village adjoining, named after Christina (Chrissie) Pretorius, daughter of President A. W. J. Pretorius (q.v.). Normally the lake measures 2 miles in width by about 6 in length with a circumference of about 16 miles, and a depth of up to 20 feet. Since the great rains of 1918 it has increased in size and average depth. Near by are large forestry plantations.

Lake Funduzi. Natural lake in the Zoutpansberg district of the Northern Transvaal; considered the only true lake in the Republic. It was caused by a landslide in the mountains and is about 3 miles long. The Bavenda, in whose reserve the sacred lake is situated, used formerly to cast their dead into its waters to be devoured by crocodiles.

Lake Macilwaine. Large dam near Salisbury, Rhodesia, 9 miles long, proclaimed as a National Park and Nature Reserve.

Lake Malawi (formerly Lake Nyasa). Large Central African lake, first visited by a Portuguese, Gaspar Bocarro, in 1616, but forgotten until it was rediscovered by David Livingstone in 1859. It covers nearly 12,000 sq. miles. Of a long narrow shape, it is 360 miles from north to south, while its width varies from 20 to 50 miles. There are several steamers on the lake, serving bathing resorts, notably Monkey Bay, much patronised by Rhodesians.

Lake Marais. Large irrigation scheme on the Breede River, in the Cape Province, 6 miles south of Worcester.

The earthwork dam is 3,252 feet long and 28½ feet high, creating a water-area, when full, of 6 sq. miles. Total irrigable area is about 20,000 acres and is being added to by the construction of other works in the region. Lake Marais is also called the Brandvlei Dam, on account of the hot springs which feed it (temperature 145° F.).

Lake Mentz. Large irrigation dam on the Sundays River (q.v.), in the Eastern Cape Province, 1,260 feet long, 94 feet high above the river bed (114 feet above lowest foundation). Situated 42 miles below Jansenville, the area when full is 7½ sq. miles. Works were begun in 1918 and completed about 1921. Owing to silting the dam has had to be raised.

Lake Ngami. *See* NGAMI.

Lake Nyasa. *See* LAKE MALAWI.

Lambert's Bay. Inlet on the coast of the Western Cape Province and a minor port of South Africa. Known to early Dutch navigators and settlers, and first colonised about 1800. The name is derived from Admiral Sir Robert Lambert, commander of the Cape Station from 1820 to 1821. During the year 1901 what was jocularly described as 'The Only Naval Action of the South African War' was fought here, when members of General J.B.M. Hertzog's commando fired at H.M.S. *Sybille* as she lay at anchor. Today Lambert's Bay is an important fishing and crayfish canning centre. Population: 3,500, including 1,000 Whites.

Lammergeier (*Gypaetus barbatus meridionalis*). Huge bird of prey once common in the Southern Cape mountains and the Drakensberg range, from Natal to the Transvaal. Rare today. *See* BIRDS and EAGLES.

Lammervanger. Afrikaans name for Martial Eagle. *See* EAGLE.

Lamsiekte (misnamed). Cattle disease known medically as Olsteoma. According to Sir Arnold Theiler (q.v.), a disease of the muscular system caused

Lammergeier

by a toxin which accumulates in the muscle and is derived from grasses or certain weeds. He did not consider it to be infectious.

Landau, Dr. Judah Leo. South African Jewish scholar, poet and Rabbi. Born on May 4, 1866, near Brody, Galicia, in former Austria-Hungary, and descended from a long line of scholars, he became interested at an early age in the revival of Hebrew as a spoken and written language. After studying at the University of Vienna he gained his degree as Doctor of Philosophy in 1898 and soon after joined the Zionist movement, which had been founded by Dr. Theodor

Herzl. In 1901 he took up the post of Rabbi in Manchester, and in 1903 came to Johannesburg in a similar capacity. There he remained for the rest of his life as Chief Rabbi, as well as Professor of Hebrew at the University of the Witwatersrand and the holder of many other offices. His work as a writer began at the age of 15, when a long epic in Hebrew was published, followed by many books and dramas in the same language. He died in 1942.

Landdrost. Title now applied in Afrikaans to Magistrates, but derived from a medieval German word 'Drost,' meaning governor of a province. It was introduced into South Africa under the Dutch East India Company, the first appointment being in 1685, when Jan Mulder became Landdrost of Stellenbosch, where he presided over a local court assisted by four 'heemraden' (q.v.). The title of Landdrost disappeared in the Cape in 1828 and was replaced by that of Magistrate and Civil Commissioner (q.v.); was revived in the Boer Republics, and in 1957 restored in Afrikaans as an official equivalent of Magistrate.

Langa. Bantu township on the Cape Flats, outside Cape Town. Scene of disturbances during March 1960.

Langalibalele. Chief of the Amahlubi tribe in Natal, and leader of a rebellion in 1873. Langalibalele, with his followers, lived between Cathkin Peak and Giant's Castle in the Drakensberg, near the source of the Bushmen's River. Following the establishment of Kimberley, many of his young braves found work on the diamond mines and used their earnings to buy guns. The local magistrate called upon him to have these returned, but, despite repeated summoning, Langalibalele refused to attend. In October, 1873, a force was mobilised to bring him to submission, comprising 200 regulars, 300 Natal volunteers and about 6,000 loyal natives, accompanied by two guns. Sir Theophilus Shepstone and Sir Benjamin Pine, the Lieutenant-Governor, were with the force. After a laborious ascent a detachment of Natal Carbineers and Royal Engineers reached the Chief's kraal, but found he had escaped to Basutoland. He was finally run to earth near Leribe and brought for trial to Pietermaritzburg. Langalibalele was sentenced to banishment for life and heavy sentences were imposed upon his followers. Bishop Colenso (q.v.) interposed on their behalf, whereupon the sentence of banishment to Robben Island was modified. Langalibalele returned to Natal in 1886, where he died 3 years later.

Langasem (Literally 'Long Breath'). Afrikaans name for European Nightjar. See NIGHTJAR.

Lange, Sir Johannes Henricus. Judge, High Court of Griqualand. Born in Uitenhage on April 1, 1852, and educated in that town and at Cambridge. He was called to the Inner Temple in 1876 and returned to practise in Kimberley in 1877. From 1878 to 1880 he was Parliamentary Draughtsman and Clerk to the Legislative Council of Griqualand West. From 1881 he practised in Kimberley, combining this with service as Member of Parliament between 1888–1892. In the latter year, Lange became Crown Prosecutor in Kimberley and was raised to the High Court of Griqualand Bench in 1896. He died at the Cape on January 5, 1923.

Langebaan. Village on Saldanha Bay, the name meaning in Dutch 'Long Course,' being derived from the long stretch of fine beach. Founded about 1870, and formerly a whaling station. Fishing is today the chief industry. Population: 600, including 200 Whites.

Langenhoven, Cornelis Jacob. Afrikaans poet. Perhaps the most popular of all writers in that language, he was born in 1873 near Ladismith, Cape, and was brought up by relatives. He early became interested in literature, helping to edit a school magazine and to start an English debating society. Having taken his degree at Stellenbosch, he was called to the Bar in 1900, and began writing. He did not come into prominence until comparatively late. In 1911 he wrote *Stukkies and Brokkies* (Bits and Pieces), and in 1912 took over the editorship of *Het Zuid-Westen* in Oudtshoorn, with which town he was ever after linked. Elected into the Cape Provincial Council, he succeeded, in 1914, in having Afrikaans instead of Dutch adopted as the second language for schools in that province, an epoch-making event. In that year appeared his first best-seller, *Ons Weg deur die Wereld* (Our Way through the World), followed by more than 50 books, all showing a sharp wit, keen observation and a startlingly wide range of subjects, from political pamphlets to the tenderest poetry. His most famous single work was *Die Stem van Suid-Afrika*, which being set to music by M. L. De Villiers (q.v.) became the official national anthem of the Union. Elected to Parliament in 1920, and in 1925 to the Senate. His works were among the first to be issued in a collected edition in Afrikaans. For many years he ran a feature in *Die Burger*, of which he was a founder, called *Aan Stille Waters*. He died in 1932.

Langholm. Large pineapple-growing estate in the Bathurst district of the Eastern Cape Province, established in 1916 through the efforts of I. W. Schlesinger (q.v.). At one time it had several thousand acres under cultivation, and ranked as the largest single pineapple plantation in the world. In recent years it has reverted to individual cultivation.

Langley, Noel Aubrey. South African dramatist, film writer and novelist. Born in Natal on December 25, 1911, and educated at Durban High School and the University of Natal, he went overseas and soon made his mark both in England and the United States. His successes include *Cage me a Peacock*, *Queer Cargo*, *Little Lambs Eat Ivy* and *There's a Porpoise Close Behind Me*. One of the films with which he was associated in Hollywood was *The Wizard of Oz* in 1938. He also provided the script for a screen version of Dickens' *Pickwick Papers* in 1952.

Lanner (*Falco biarmicus*). Bird of prey, resembling peregrine falcon, but with cinnamon colouring on head and breast, found in mountain districts nesting in rock faces. *See* EAGLES.

Lansdown, Charles William Henry. Judge and legal writer. Born near Bristol, England, in 1874; he came to South Africa in 1884, and in 1889, at the age of 15, joined the Cape Civil Service. Qualified for the Bar in 1905, and joined the Department of Justice; in 1908 was appointed Law Adviser to the Union Government. He soon attracted attention, both on account of his legal ability and as joint author of well-known legal standard works on Criminal Law and the Liquor Law. In 1931 Lansdown became a judge of the Natal Provincial Division and in 1937 Judge-President of the Eastern Districts Local Division. He died in 1957.

Lanyon, Sir William Owen. Soldier and colonial administrator. Born in Ireland in 1842, the son of Sir Charles Lanyon, a distinguished civil engineer, he joined the British Army and was sent to the West Indies, where in 1865 he saw active service during a rising in Jamaica. During the First British Occupation of the Transvaal he was appointed Administrator in 1879. He suffered poor health and his unfriendly manner excited the hostility of the burghers, contributing to the outbreak of the First Boer War, which began under his régime in 1880. Later, in 1882 and 1884–1885, he served in Egyptian campaigns. Lanyon died in New York, 1887.

Lapwing, Crowned (*Stephanibyx coronatus*). *See* PLOVER.

Large Mouth Black Bass (*Micropterus* (*Huro*) *salmoides*). Fish found in North America and introduced into South Africa in 1928, preferring lakes and sluggish water. About 21 inches long.

Lark (Alaudidae). Family of smallish brown or mottled birds, not easily distinguishable. They feed on the ground on insects and grain, and perch high up to sing. No variety sings with the consistency or strength of the European lark. *See* BIRDS.

Latrobe, Rev. Christian Ignatius. Moravian missionary. Born in England in 1758, became known as a composer of hymns, for which he is still remembered. Was sent to South Africa in 1815 to inspect the settlements of the Moravians in Genadendal and elsewhere. He left a valuable account of the country and of events including the Slagters Nek Rebellion, which appeared in 1818 as *Narrative of a Visit to South Africa.* . . . Latrobe died in 1836.

Lattakoo. Name used by early travellers and settlers for the chief kraal of the Batlapin tribe in Bechuanaland. Among its early visitors was Robert Moffat.

Laurence, Sir Percival Maitland. Judge-President, High Court of Griqualand. Born at Walesby in England and educated at Cambridge, where he had a distinguished career. He was called to the Bar at Lincoln's Inn in 1878, but indifferent health sent him to the Cape, where he was admitted in 1880. In 1881 he went to Kimberley and soon became Second Puisne Judge of the High Court of Griqualand rising to Judge-President in 1888. He retired in 1913 and died in England on February 28, 1930.

Lauts, Professor Ulrich. First Boer representative in Europe and first writer on the Voortrekkers. Born in Amsterdam, 1787, the son of a merchant, became a lecturer in Science and Letters. While on the staff of the Naval College, Lauts became interested in the Voortrekkers and met J. A. Smellekamp (q.v.). As a result he wrote *De Kaapsche Landverhuizers* (Cape Emigrants) in 1847. Later he helped to arrange for the despatch of the first clergyman to the Transvaal, of which he became consul in 1857. He died in 1865.

Law. The foundation of the Law of South Africa—the Common Law—is Roman Dutch (q.v.) (Romeins-Hollands Recht). Unless abrogated by disuse or repealed by statute, the old Placaats of the States of Holland, passed before 1652, are binding even today. Those passed between 1652 and 1806 are not binding, unless promulgated in South Africa, as, for example, the Placaat of 1658 relating to Lessees. When in 1806 the Cape was ceded to Great Britain, the Common Law remained unaltered, despite the efforts of certain English judges to introduce English Law. Nevertheless, in certain fields, e.g. interpretation, the Law of England, being more developed and not often in conflict with Roman-Dutch Law, was gradually absorbed into the South African system. Prior to Union, each of the Colonies and States had separate legislative bodies, and the South Africa Act provided that the law of each Province should continue in force until repealed by Parliament. Since 1910 the supreme legislative authority has been Parliament, though Provincial Councils have sovereign powers within defined limits (*see* CONSTITUTION).

Although in certain fields, e.g. Bills of Exchange, each Province still retains independent legislation, Parliament has passed numerous 'Consolidating' Acts unifying the law in force throughout South Africa (e.g. Administration of Estates, Magistrates' Courts, Criminal Procedure, Registration of Deeds, etc.). In other fields Parliament has taken over, or closely copied, legislation of other countries, notably England (Evidence, Insolvency, Companies, etc.). Similarly Income Tax legislation is largely derived from that of Australia. Nevertheless there is a vast mass of legislation which is original and often in advance of that in other parts of the world. Appeals from South African Courts lay to the Privy Council until 1950, when, by virtue of the repeal of Section 106 of the South Africa Act, the Appellate Division of the Supreme Court became the highest Court of Appeal. Following the doctrine of *stare decisis*, a court will always follow its own decision unless clearly wrong, but subordinate courts are obliged to follow a decision of a superior court, irrespective of such considerations. The decisions of foreign courts are never binding, but are of persuasive authority, especially in those fields where legislation and common law is similar.

In Rhodesia, the Roman-Dutch Law, as existing in the Cape Colony at the time of the original occupation in 1890, was introduced at the outset and, save where modified by statute, still holds good. Until 1955, appeals from the High Court of Southern Rhodesia lay to the Appellate Division of the Supreme Court of South Africa at Bloemfontein, but this practice has now been abolished.

The law of Zambia and Malawi is based on that of England, as modified by statute.

Since the occupation of South West Africa in 1915 its law has been assimilated to that of South Africa, unless modified by local ordinances. Roman law still applies in respect of certain older land titles and mining rights.

The law of Mozambique is basically that of Portugal, in addition to local enactments. *See also* CRIMINAL LAW and ROMAN-DUTCH LAW.

Lawn Tennis. Was introduced into South Africa in the early 1880's, and

in 1884 the first South African inter-town contest took place between Port Elizabeth (for long the centre of the game in the country) and Grahamstown. By 1888 the Cape Association of Tennis Clubs could be established, and a start had already been made in Natal, along with a tennis section at the Wanderers Club, Johannesburg. In 1891 the first South African Tennis Championships took place. The first international games were played in 1908, when a British team under G. W. Hillyard toured the country. At the Olympic Games in Stockholm in 1912, a South African player, C. L. Winslow, won the singles, with H. A. Kitson, also from South Africa, as the runner-up, and in 1913 for the first time the South African team comprising V. R. Gauntlett, C. Leach and R. F. le Sueur took part in the Davis Cup Tournament. After World War II the name of E. W. Sturgess achieved international prominence at Wimbledon and elsewhere, and in 1960 Sandra Reynolds reached the final of the Ladies' Singles at Wimbledon.

In 1966 Robert Hewitt and F. Macmillan won the Men's Doubles, while in the Inter-Zone Finals for 1967 South Africa beat Brazil, though she lost to Spain. Cliff Drysdale beat the World player Rod Laver in 1969.

Lawrence, Harry Gordon. South African Cabinet minister, and political leader. Born at Rondebosch, Cape Town, on October 17, 1901, he was educated in that city, read for the Bar and began legal practice. He entered politics under General Smuts, being elected member for Salt River in 1929. In 1938 he became Minister of Labour, Social Welfare and Public Health. He served as Union delegate to the United Nations in 1947. Later he was a prominent opposition leader and became a founder and outstanding figure of the Progressive Party when its members seceded from the United Party (q.v.).

Lazarus, Ezrael. Largest grain farmer in South Africa, usually referred to as the 'Mealie King.' Born near Kovno in Lithuania in 1880, he came to the Transvaal in 1896 and began life with a few shillings in Johannesburg. Having lost all his possessions through the Boer War, he started again near Kinross in the Transvaal, by planting potatoes. In 1906 he bought the farm Langsloot, covering about 1,800 acres, and followed this later by the more famous Bombardie and Cologne, on the edge of the districts of Middelburg and Bethal, covering altogether about 8,000 acres. There he developed maize production on an unheard-of scale, until he averaged 150,000 bags of mealies a year, besides 150,000 bags of potatoes, 3,000 bags of wheat, 2,000 bags of pumpkins, 1,000 bags of groundnuts and large quantities of other produce. Lazarus used over 2,500 tons of fertilisers a year, and had over 20,000 acres under cultivation, approximately 32 sq. miles. He owned altogether about 60,000 acres in the Transvaal, with about 10,000 head of cattle. His staff numbered about 40 Europeans and over 2,000 natives. He died in 1946.

Leabua Jonathan, Chief. *See* JONATHAN, CHIEF LEABUA.

Lead. Owing to its usefulness in casting bullets, attempts to exploit this metal were made near the present town of Uitenhage as early as 1792, and were reported on in 1805 by Heinrich Lichtenstein. Repeated efforts were made to open the so-called 'Maitland Mines,' down to modern times. In the Transvaal the Voortrekkers exploited Galena ores near Ottoshoop and near Pretoria. Lead also occurs in Natal. Large deposits are found at the Tsumeb Mine in South West Africa and at Broken Hill in Zambia.

Leaguer. South African measure for liquor, 126 gallons.

Leask, Thomas. Traveller and hunter. Born in the Orkney Islands in 1839, he reached Natal in 1862 and began his travels in Mashonaland in 1866. Accompanied by Dr. Calderley, he went to the Zambesi in 1869, and the two were among the earliest Europeans to see the Victoria Falls. Leask was a personal friend of both Moselekatse and of Lobengula. He retired in 1870 and went into partnership with J. Taylor, as Thomas Leask & Co. in Klerksdorp. There he played a leading part in the discovery of the first gold and was elected the first President of the Klerksdorp Chamber of Mines in 1887. He died in Scotland in 1912.

Lechwe (*Cobus lechi*). Large Southern African antelope, flourishing particularly in the Kalahari region and in Rhodesia. It reaches a height of over 3 feet at the shoulder, the male having a handsome set of horns. David Livingstone was among the first to see the Lechwe on his trip to Lake Ngami in 1849.

Leeudoringstad. Village near Wolmaranstad, Transvaal. Population: 2,715, including 1,000 Whites. A record explosion took place near by in 1932, when a train carrying 1,200 tons of dynamite blew up.

Lehfeldt, Professor Robert Alfred. South African economist. Born in Birmingham, 1868, and educated at Cambridge, he began his career as Professor of Physics, in which capacity he came to the South African School of Mines and Technology in 1906. He retained this post until 1917, but became increasingly interested in the subject of economics, on which he became a world authority. He wrote a number of books, both on chemistry and economics. Lehfeldt died in mysterious circumstances in 1927.

Leibbrandt, Rev. Hendrik Carel Vos. First Cape archivist. Born 1837 in Cape Town, he studied for the Dutch Reformed ministry in Holland, where he was a contemporary of

President T. F. Burgers (q.v.). In 1859 he became a minister of the Dutch Reformed Church in Victoria West, Cape Colony, but, involved in disputes, gave up the ministry in 1877, his attitude being strongly on the side of modernism. Some time after, in 1881, Leibbrandt was appointed archivist for the Cape Colony and, in addition to producing order out of chaotic sets of unclassified records, published a long and valuable series of books on his own researches. He died on January 2, 1911, in Cape Town.

Leipoldt, Dr. Christian Frederick Louis. Afrikaans poet. Born in Worcester, Cape, 1880, the son of a German missionary. He grew up near Clanwilliam, was educated at the S.A. College, and passed his Civil Service examination, but in 1897 joined the staff of *Het Dagblad* in Cape Town, and then of the *South African News*. From boyhood he had shown an almost equal ability as a writer in English and Afrikaans. During the S.A. War he contributed to many overseas papers, but changed afterwards to shorthand reporting for the Cape Circuit Court. Going to Europe in 1902, after the *South African News* had been closed under Martial Law for its pro-Boer sentiments, Leipoldt decided to study medicine, but continued his travels, which took him over much of Europe, including Russia. He graduated at Guy's Hospital, London, in 1907, became Assistant M.O.H. for Hampstead, began writing on medical themes and specialising in pediatrics (children). For health reasons he went on a long trip to the East, returned to England, took a post as Medical Inspector of Schools in Hampstead, from which he was called in a similar capacity to the Transvaal in 1914, this being the first appointment of its kind in S.A. Meanwhile he had begun his career as a writer of Afrikaans books and in 1911 became a national figure with *Oom Gert Vertel*, a collection of poems.

Others followed, all of high quality, and including drama, essays, children's stories, etc. Becoming M.O.H. for Cape Schools in 1919, he spent a short while on the editorial staff of *Die Volkstem* in Pretoria, practised as a children's specialist in Cape Town, and from 1926 was editor of the *South African Medical Journal*. After his retirement in 1940 he devoted all his time to writing. Among his works was an excellent life of Jan van Riebeeck (1936) and *Bushveld Doctor*, his own experiences in the Transvaal, both in English. Leipoldt's downright and unconventional views often brought him into the news, including his championing of wine as a remedy for certain childhood ailments. He died in 1947 and was buried on the Pakhuis Pass near Clanwilliam.

Leipoldtville. Village near Clanwilliam, Cape Province. Population 40, entirely White.

Lelspreeu. Afrikaans name for Wattled Starling. *See* STARLING.

Lemon. *See* CITRUS.

Lemonwood or **Wild Lemon, Boriehout, Bog-a-Bi** (*Xymalos monospora* Baill.). Large tree in Eastern Cape Province and northwards, in mountain forests of Natal and Transvaal. Wood yellowish, suitable for ornamental furniture, but needs many years for drying.

Lenshina, Alice. *See* LUMPA.

Leonard, Bishop John. Early Catholic Bishop at the Cape. Born in 1829, he became Bishop in 1872 and was amongst other things responsible for the establishment of a school for the deaf and dumb and many institutions in the Western Province. Bishop Leonard died in 1908.

Leonotis. *See* SALVIA.

Leopard (*Felis pardus*). Known to the Zulus, Swazis and Amaxosa as Ingwe and the Basuto as Inkwi. Carnivorous animal, fallaciously called a tiger ('tier' or 'vlakte tier') by the Boers. Found in kloofs, bushy koppies and forests from the Cape to North Africa. While differing considerably in size and markings, the colour of a typical leopard is yellow, closely covered with black spots. Black leopards have been found in South Africa, but are comparatively rare. Their natural prey are baboons and monkeys, rabbits, dassies and other rodents, the smaller buck and larger game fowl, but when hunger drives they will attack, even in broad daylight, sheep, goats, calves and other domestic animals. As a result they are mercilessly hunted and are fast being exterminated in South Africa.

Leopard, Hunting (*Cynoelurus jubatus*). Commonly known as the Cheetah, Luipard or Vlakte Tier; differs from the true leopard in having one part canine to three parts feline, the claws being blunt and visible, like those of a dog. Slender and lithe, it is built for speed, with long legs and narrow chest. In colouring it is very similar to the Leopard (q.v.). Formerly found all over Africa on grassy plains and in scattered bush, it has been driven by stock farmers from all but the most inaccessible fastnesses in the Kalahari and Rhodesia.

Leribe. Village in Lesotho, near the Orange Free State border, formerly known as Thlotse Heights. The original fort, erected in 1879, is still standing, also the hut where General C. G. (Chinese) Gordon lived in 1882. Today it is a tourist and native trading centre. The name Leribe means 'Undulating,' because of the configuration of the neighbourhood.

Lerotholi. Paramount Chief of the Basuto. Born in 1840, he was the son of Letsie the First (q.v.), whom he succeeded in 1891. A man of great ability, he was largely responsible for the establishment of a National Council for the Basuto. He died in 1905.

Le Roux, Le Roux Smith. South African artist and broadcaster. Born at Cape Town in 1914, he studied at the Michaelis School of Art in that city, at the Slade School in London, and in Rome. At an early age he gained distinction, particularly as a decorative painter, and in 1949 was appointed Director of the Art Centre in Pretoria. He was Assistant Director of the Tate Gallery for a while, but later became a consultant for leading collectors in America and elsewhere. He attained great popularity as a broadcaster on the B.B.C. with his series with a South African flavour. Died in 1963.

Leslie. Village near Bethal, Transvaal. Population: 2,757, including 325 Whites.

Lesotho (formerly Basutoland). Bantu kingdom in the British Commonwealth, which received its independence in 1966. The ruler is of the House of Moshesh (q.v.) There is an elected Parliament and Cabinet. Situated between the Cape, Natal, the Orange Free State and the Transvaal. Covering 11,716 square miles, it has a population of 859,000. including 2,000 Europeans, 1,000 Asiatic and Coloured. In addition about 160,000 are working in the Republic, particularly on the Rand. Basutoland is the most elevated part of the sub-continent, having some of the highest peaks, which reach nearly 11,000 feet. A single railway line operates, running from the Orange Free State to the capital, Maseru. Europeans live there by special permission, as Civil Servants, traders or officials. Principal industries are wool-growing, cattle breeding and the production of hard wheat, to which the country, with its cold climate, is particularly well suited. Concessions have lately been granted for the opening up of diamond deposits. Missions are very active, and a university has been set up at Roma, under the auspices of the Roman Catholic Church, which draws students from the Republic and neighbouring territories. There are few roads, but a main highway has been begun through the mountains, which will open up magnificent scenery, and give access to areas hitherto reached only by pack-horse. One of the major attractions is the falls of the Maletsunyane, over 600 feet high.

Lesseyton. Wesleyan Methodist Mission Station in the Eastern Cape Province, established in 1851 to train natives for the Ministry.

Letcher, Owen. South African writer, hunter and mining expert. Born in England in 1884, he studied mining in Cornwall and travelled extensively as a young man in Zambia, writing several books on the subject. He distinguished himself in World War I, particularly in Central and East Africa. In later life, became editor of the *South African Mining Journal* in Johannesburg, and produced a number of books, devoting particular attention to the great copper possibilities of the Congo. He died in 1943.

Letsie the First. Paramount Chief of the Basutos. Eldest son of Moshesh, whom he succeeded in 1870. He was considered as weak and unsatisfactory, and was much overshadowed by his son, Lerotholi, who succeeded him in 1891.

Letsima. Basuto custom, by which the people were forced to work in the gardens of the chief. It gave rise to considerable difficulties in administration, and was forbidden in 1872, but the allied custom of Maboela (q.v.) was recognised.

Lettow-Vorbeck, General Paul Emil von. *See* VON LETTOW-VORBECK.

Leutwein, Theodor. Governor of German South West Africa. Born in 1849 in Struempfelbronn, Baden, Germany; came to South West Africa as Commander of the military forces in 1894 in the campaign against the Chief

Hendrik Witbooi (q.v.). Was appointed Administrator (Landeshauptmann) in 1895 and Governor in 1898. In 1904, as a result of the Herero troubles, he was replaced by General von Trotha (q.v.) and retired from the Colonial Service in 1905. He died in Germany on April 13, 1921.

Le Vaillant, François. French naturalist and explorer of the Cape. Born in 1753 in Paramaribo, Dutch Guiana, of French parentage, the story of his coloured ancestry being lately disproved. Specialising in birds, he travelled widely in Europe and in 1781 arrived at the Cape. He remained 3 years, visiting the Karroo, Namaqualand, the Kalahari and the Eastern Province. His account is full of exaggerations and inventions, but he made a noted contribution to early South African ornithology. His travels soon acquired great popularity, were translated into many languages, and his *Birds of Africa* remained a standard work. He died in 1824.

Levy, Joseph Langley. South African editor and author. Born in Liverpool in 1870, he originally studied art, in which he retained an interest all his life, and later became an authority on the English stage. As a young man he travelled in Australia and to other parts, working for a while in Fleet Street, and publishing several novels and plays. In 1910 Langley Levy came to Johannesburg to become editor of the *Sunday Times*, from which he retired shortly before his death in 1945. His valuable collections of early children's books and works on the drama have been acquired by the Johannesburg Public Library.

Lewanika. King of Barotseland, Zambia. Born about 1843 he was known as Robosi and attracted attention because of his bravery in a rising against the tyrannical Makololo, rulers of the Barotse in 1866. In 1876 he was made chief and set up his main kraal at Lealui. Coming under the influence of the famous French missionary, the Rev. François Coillard (q.v.), in 1885, Lewanika, as he renamed himself, adopted a policy of moderation, in striking contrast to the barbarity prevailing previously, although he never formally became a Christian. On Coillard's advice he offered in 1890 to place himself under the régime of the Chartered Co., and abolished slavery. Lewanika died in 1916.

Lewis, Ethelreda. South African author. Born as Ethel Howe, at Matlock in Derbyshire, England, in 1875, she assumed the name of Ethelreda and, coming to South Africa, married Dr. Joseph Lewis of Cape Town. She wrote a number of novels, of which one of the most outstanding, *The Harp*, published in 1925, is an account of life in a small town on the Cape coast. Her main claim to prominence, however, is as the discoverer and editor of *Trader Horn* (q.v.). The series of books which resulted, brought her considerable reflected fame in South Africa and overseas. She died in Port Alfred on July 31, 1946.

Lewis, Isaac. South African industrialist. Cousin of Senator Samuel Marks (q.v.). Born in Russia in 1849, he came to South Africa in 1870 and joined in founding the firm of Lewis & Marks, which became one of the largest landowning and industrial concerns in the sub-continent. His rôle, however, was less active than that of Marks, and he was less familiar to the public. He died in 1925.

Lewis, Neville. South African artist. Born at Cape Town on October 8, 1895, and educated at the South African College and in London, he became one of the country's most eminent portrait painters, his sitters including the late King of Spain, Alphonso XII, Sir Winston Churchill, the Earl of Athlone, General J. C.

Smuts, Field-Marshal Lord Montgomery, Field-Marshal Lord Alexander and many others. During World War II he served as an official artist at the front.

Leydsdorp. Village in the Northern Transvaal, formerly the centre of an important gold field, proclaimed in 1887. The township itself, named after the State Secretary of the South African Republic, Dr. W. J. Leyds, was founded in 1890.

Leyds, Dr. Willem Johannes. Boer statesman. Of Dutch origin, he was born in Java in 1859, and educated in Holland, securing his doctorate in law in Amsterdam, 1884, when President Kruger was visiting Europe. A meeting resulted in the offer to Leyds of the post of State Attorney, which he accepted in 1888, at the age of 29. During the difficult period of the early Rand, and the rising hostility with the Uitlanders, Leyds became the close associate of Kruger, whose policy he interpreted, incurring the hearty dislike of the Johannesburgers. In spite of this his ability was acknowledged, especially in non-controversial matters of administration. In 1897 he was sent as Ambassador-at-Large for the Republic to Europe, with his headquarters in Brussels, and he remained the mouthpiece of the Boer cause through the South African War. After the Peace of Vereeniging he retired to Holland, where he wrote extensively on Transvaal history and arranged his archives (now in Pretoria). He died in 1940.

Liberal Party. Established May 9, 1953, at Cape Town, and developed from the earlier South African Liberal Association. Its original president was Mrs. V. M. L. Ballinger, with Alan Paton and Leo Marquard as joint vice-presidents, Dr. O. D. Wolheim as national chairman, and Leslie Rubin as national vice-chairman. It was non-racial and opposed to both Fascism and Communism. Under legislation forbidding multi-racial political parties it ceased to exist in 1968.

Libode. Village in the Transkei, noted for its scenery, and for nearby 'Execution Rock' (Emiangana) used by the former chiefs of the Pondos. Population: 400, including 120 Whites.

Libraries. The first traceable library in the modern sense is believed to be that of Johannes Nicolaas von Dessin who as secretary of the Orphan Chamber had particularly good opportunities to buy up books during the outbreak of smallpox. Upon his death in 1761 he left this library, which consisted largely of works on theology and similar subjects, to the Public Authorities, who stored it away in a Dutch Reformed church. When in 1818 Lord Charles Somerset founded the South African Public Library, the 'Dessinian Collection,' as it is called, became part of it, and it is still in existence. To furnish revenue the Governor assigned to the library the tax on each cask of wine brought for sale into the Cape, a state of affairs which continued until 1829. Thanks to many other gifts, including the remarkable collection of medieval manuscripts and early books from Sir George Grey (q.v.), the South African Public Library, which today has about 350,000 volumes, has probably the most valuable, if not the largest, collection in the southern hemisphere. As settlement in the Cape advanced, libraries were started in most other colonial towns, particularly Grahamstown, Port Elizabeth and Kimberley, parallel development taking place in Natal, where the Natal Society built up a fine collection in Pietermaritzburg. Libraries were also set up in the Orange Free State and the Transvaal. Today the largest individual institution in the country is the Johannesburg Public Library, with its many branches, which has over a million books and a very fine technical section known as the Seymour Memorial Library. Other important collections are the State Library in Pretoria, the Parliamentary Library in Cape Town, including the Mendelssohn Library (q.v.), as well as those of the various universities. In recent years the Government policy of providing free library services has resulted in the enrolment of a very high percentage of the population as readers, among them increasing numbers of non-Whites. The largest provincial service is that of the Cape, with about 2,000 distribution points, a staff of 350 and a stock of over two million books. Expansion is taking place in other parts of the Republic at a great rate. Encouragement has also been given to the building of libraries in Rhodesia, Zambia and Malawi in South West Africa and in Native territories. Training in librarianship is given at the Universities of Cape Town and the Witwatersrand, the profession being organised into the South African Library Association.

Licente. Coin issued in Lesotho (q.v.). 100 equal 1 Maloti (q.v.). They have been struck in 5, 10, 20 and 50 Licente pieces. One Licente equals 1 South African cent.

Lichtenburg. Town in the Western Transvaal, founded in 1885 by H. G. Greef, and so called because, at the original outspan, the lights (Lichten) of the trekkers' wagons could be seen from afar. The place was notable as the home of the famous Boer leader, General Delarey, and of the 'Seer' Nicholaas van Rensburg (q.v.). There was considerable fighting near the town in the South African War. Later it acquired fame as a centre of the alluvial diamond diggings, which brought a population of over 25,000 to Elandsputte and other camps near by in 1925–1926. Today it is a maize-growing and farming centre. Population: 15,750, including 7,000 Whites.

Lichtenstein, Dr. Martin Karl Heinrich. German explorer and traveller at the Cape, born in Hamburg, 1780. When Great Britain returned the Cape of Good Hope to the Batavian Republic in 1801 he offered his services and became -medical officer to the Governor, General Janssens, and his son's tutor. Lichtenstein arrived in Cape Town in 1802, travelled widely to the eastern frontier and elsewhere, and later was appointed medical officer to the Hottentot Light Infantry. In 1805 he was sent by Janssens to visit the Bechuana tribes as Government Commissioner. He returned to Germany after the recapture of the Cape by the British in 1806. His *Travels in Southern Africa* appeared in 1810 and 1812 and became a standard work. He died in 1857.

Lidgetton. Village near Lions River, Natal. Population: 260, including 10 Whites.

Liebig Ranch. Large cattle ranch in the south of Rhodesia, near West Nicholson (q.v.), acquired in 1910 by the Liebig Extract of Meat Company in England. It covers over 1,250,000 acres and supports thousands of cattle, from which various meat products are made in Rhodesia.

Liebig's Drift. Crossing over the Limpopo River, recognised as an official port of entry to the Republic, and giving access to Liebig's Ranch in Rhodesia (q.v.).

Lilangeni. Swaziland gold coin, worth R25, divided into 50 Luhlanga (q.v.).

Lilongwe. Capital of Malawi since August 23, 1966. Established in 1947. Centre of the farming industry. Altitude 3,500 feet. Population: 390 Europeans, 3,980 Africans, 300 of other races.

Lily (Liliaceae). One of a large family of bulbous and tuberous plants and Karroo succulents. Flowers usually brightly coloured, consisting of a perianth of 6 segments, sometimes free and sometimes tubular, 6 stamens, superior ovary of 3 united carpels. Among the members are: *Agapanthus* (q.v.); the beautiful pink scented Belladonna Lily (*Amaryllis belladonna*), abundant in Eastern Cape scrub, bulbous, winter leaves that die in summer, March flowering; Chincherinchees and a group of aloes (*Haworthia*) showing many adaptations to droughty conditions. Of these, *Haworthia pilifera* has a white spike of flowers, brown leaves barbed and tipped with blue, spread wide over the ground in a whorl like a Jerusalem Artichoke; autumn and winter; Eastern Cape. *Haworthia vicosa*, an autumn and winter Karroo plant, with a similar but more delicate inflorescence has leaves folded sheath-like up the stem. The Rhodesian Flame Lily (*Gloriosa superba*) is another member of this family, climbing many feet high in damp soil by means of its hooked leaves; 'petals' frilly. *See* AMARYLLIS for Fire Lily, Bush Lily, etc., *and also* ALOE.

Lily-Trotter (family Jacanidae). Bird specialised for running on floating water-weeds, having enormously lengthened toes and an extremely long, very

Lily-Trotter

sharp, hind claw. The legs are also very long, the greater part of the 'thigh' being covered with scales. Food is mainly insects and seeds of grasses and water-plants. Fairly common in Natal.

Lilyvale. Village near Tulbagh, Cape Province. Population: 140, including 20 Whites.

Limeacres. Village near Finsch Diamond Mine (q.v.), 4½ miles distant. It was founded in 1964 and already has a population of several hundred whites.

Limehill. Bantu resettlement scheme near Newcastle, Natal, the subject of controversy, in 1968, owing to alleged lack of amenities.

Limpopo River. Large Southern African river. Rises in the Magaliesberg near Pretoria and flows for 900 miles to enter the Indian Ocean in Mozambique, near the port of Chai-Chai (q.v.). Also known as the Crocodile River, its major tributaries are the Olifants in the Transvaal (360 miles long, not to be confused with the Olifants River in the Cape Western Province), the Sand River (145 miles), Marico (140 miles), Pongola (120 miles) and the Nuanetsi, Shashi and Magalagwen.

Lindbergh, Albert Victor. South African capitalist. Born at Penarth, Wales, 1874, he came to the Transvaal in 1892 and found work with the *Star* in Johannesburg, for which he organised house-to-house distribution. In this way met with Michael Davis, and in partnership with him established the Central News Agency Limited (q.v.). He was also one of the financial backers of the *Rand Daily Mail* (q.v.) and *Sunday Times* (q.v.), with which he retained a lifelong connection. He died in 1939.

Lindequist, Friedrich von. Governor of German South West Africa. Born on the German island of Ruegen in the Baltic in 1862, he entered the Government Service, was Consul-General in

Cape Town, and in 1905 became Governor of German South-West Africa, where he remained until 1907. He died in 1945.

Lindley. Town in the Orange Free State, named after the American missionary, the Rev. Daniel Lindley, who ministered to the Voortrekkers. It was founded in 1876 and was almost completely destroyed in the South African War, but later rebuilt. Today it is an important agricultural centre. Population: 3,930, including 1,100 Whites.

Lindley, Rev. Daniel. Missionary and pioneer minister. Born in Ohio, U.S.A., in 1801, he was ordained as a minister of the Presbyterian Church and selected by the American Board of Foreign Missions to work among the Matabele. He arrived in Natal in 1837, where, amid much discouragement, he set up missions to the Zulus. The arrival of the Voortrekkers led to his appointment as their pastor and for years he was virtually the only ordained minister in the O.F.S. and Transvaal, travelling vast distances and baptising, marrying and confirming thousands. He resumed his mission work to the Zulus in 1847 and continued until 1858. Returned to the U.S.A. (1858–1862), then spent another 8 years in the South African mission field. From 1873 to his death in 1880, he again lived in America.

Lion (*Felis leo*). Known to the Zulus and Swazis as Ingonyama, Imbubesi or Imbubi; to the Amaxosa as Ingonyama; and to the Basuto and Bechuana as Tau. Carnivorous animal, now mainly confined (outside the game reserves) to the wilder parts of Central Africa, with a few stragglers in Zululand and Rhodesia. Varying greatly in size, colour and profusion of mane, the average weight is about 500 lb. The lion has no fixed abode, but will move on, hunting by night and sleeping by day. The last lion recorded in the Cape Colony was killed in 1842, and in Natal in 1865.

Lions River. Village in Natal. Population: 460, including 10 Whites.

Lippert, Edward Amandus. Mining concessionnaire. Born in Hamburg, 1853, of a Jewish family originally named Lipman. His father, David Lippert, was head of a commercial house trading with the Cape. With his brother William he settled, first in Port Elizabeth and then in Kimberley, where they were joined by their cousin, Alfred Beit (q.v.). Moving to Johannesburg, Edward Lippert secured valuable industrial concessions from President Kruger, including a monopoly for manufacturing dynamite, which led to his founding the famous works at Modderfontein (q.v.), but aroused great opposition from the gold producers. He also obtained a concession to plant mining timber north of Johannesburg, the plantation, Saxonwold, later becoming a fashionable suburb. From Lobengula (q.v.), Lippert secured a land concession in Matabeleland, so valuable that Cecil Rhodes had to come to terms with him to exploit his own mining rights in that country. He returned to Germany after the South African War, ran a successful dairy business in Hamburg, but lost his money in the inflation after World War I. He died on December 8, 1925.

Lipschitz, Lippy. South African artist and sculptor. Born in Lithuania in 1903, he came to South Africa in 1908. A Capetonian, he favours the modern approach and is widely admired both for his powerful carvings and for his original ideas in graphic art, notably his 'Monotypes,' the technique of which he largely developed himself.

Literature. *See* AFRIKAANS LITERATURE and ENGLISH LITERATURE.

Little Berg River. Tributary of the Berg River (q.v.).

Little Fish River. *See* GREAT FISH RIVER.

Litunga. Title of the Hereditary Ruler of Barotseland, Zambia.

Livingstone. Town in Zambia on banks of Zambesi six miles from Victoria Falls (q.v.). Founded 1905 and until 1935 capital of Northern Rhodesia. Population: 37,330 including 4,000 Whites.

Livingstone, Dr. David. African explorer and missionary. Born in Blantyre, Scotland, on March 19, 1813, at 10 he began work in a cotton mill, educating himself and qualifying in medicine at Glasgow and London. In 1838 he joined the London Missionary Society and he came to South Africa in 1840. From his headquarters at Kuruman he worked among the Bechuanas and neighbouring tribes, and in 1849 undertook his first journey of exploration to Lake Ngami (q.v.), in company with Mungo Murray and William Cotton Oswell (q.v.). Crossing the Kalahari Desert, they reached Lake Ngami on August 1, 1849. While at Kuruman Livingstone became involved in a frontier dispute between the Boers and the tribes under Sechele, in which his mission station was destroyed. Resuming his travels into the interior, he reached the Upper Zambesi, where tsetse fly stopped his scheme of setting up a mission station. During a 2½-year trek he found the Victoria Falls (q.v.) in 1855, returned to England the next year and in 1857 published his *Missionary Travels and Researches in South Africa*. His later career was mostly in Central Africa, commencing in 1858 as British Consul at Quilimane (q.v.) in command of an expedition that discovered Lake Nyasa. Tracing the sources of the Nile, he reached Lake Mweru and Lake Bangweolu. Sent to bring news of him, Henry M. Stanley met him in 1872. Livingstone, however, refused to return, and died on May 1, 1873.

Llewellin, Lord (John Jestyn Llewellin). First Governor-General of the Central African Federation, born near Sevenoaks, Kent, England, on February 6, 1893. He died soon after his arrival in Rhodesia to take up the appointment in January 1957.

Load. Measure of weight used for diamond-bearing ground, equal to four-fifths of a ton.

Loan Farm. Form of title granted to many of the early settlers in South Africa. Originally they were held under yearly leases against payment of a rent.

Lobamba. Seat of Swaziland parliament, 10 miles from Mbabane.

Lobatsi. Village in Botswana, north of Mafeking, on the line to Rhodesia. Sechuana name meaning 'Large Wooden Chips.' Creamery plant and meat packing works were erected here after World War I. Population: 8,000.

Lobelia (Campanulaceae). Delicate little plant of the Harebell variety, found all over South Africa. Wiry stem; petals, sepals and stamens 5, ovary inferior, fruit a capsule. The usual variety (*Lobelia pinifolia*) is blue. *Lobelia coronopifolia* is less fragile and blue or pink. *Lobelia parcastranthus* is yellow, and the Natal *Lobelia scabra* is a brown, semi-prostrate variety. The many *Wahlenbergias* have blue hairbell-shaped flowers. *Roella ciliata* is a common little Cape shrublet a few inches high, with large open white, blue or mauve bells.

Lobengula. King of the Matabele (q.v.). Son of Moselekatze (q.v.) by an inferior wife, born about 1836. As a result of an attempt on the throne by Nkulumane (his elder half-brother, also called Kuruman), the boy, Lobengula, was nearly killed by his father, and escaped by being smuggled away. He succeeded Moselekatze in 1868, put an end to a rebellion and set up his capital at Gubulawayo near the present city of Bulawayo. Despite many barbaric traits, Lobengula was not without virtue, and showed considerable friendship to hunters, traders and such

Europeans who found their way to his kraal. Following a visit by the Rev. J. S. Moffat, he entered into a treaty in 1886, giving certain rights to the British authorities, followed in 1888 by the grant of the famous Concession to C. D. Rudd (q.v.). Coming into conflict with the forces of the Chartered Company, he tried later to reassert his authority over the Mashonas, resulting, in 1893, in the Matabele War, when he was defeated and driven from his capital. He died in 1894, somewhere in the bush, near the River Zambesi.

Lobola. Native custom by which a bridegroom pays a price in cattle to the parents of his future wife. Although it is a form of compensation for the pain which the mother has undergone in bearing and in bringing up her daughter, it is actually handed to the father. The practice is still observed on a considerable scale in the Native Reserves, but the cattle are often replaced by payment in cash. Lobola is not regarded as purchase.

Local Government. *See* GOVERNMENT, LOCAL.

Location. Large Native Reserves as well as small areas in municipalities ear-marked for residence by Africans.

Loch Athlone. Large dam near Bethlehem, Orange Free State (q.v.).

Loch, Lord (Henry Brougham Loch). Governor of Cape Colony. Born in 1827, he was Governor from 1889 to 1895, through the period of increasingly bitter relations between the British and Transvaal Governments. He did his best to maintain friendly relations with President Kruger. Received a peerage in 1895. During the South African War was responsible for raising 'Loch's Horse.' He died in 1900.

Lochiel. Forestry centre near the Swaziland border, in the Transvaal.

Locke, Arthur D'Arcy ('Bobby'). South African golf champion. Born in Germiston, Transvaal, November 20, 1917. Took up golf as a boy, and at 18, in 1935, won the Natal, Transvaal, South African Open and South African Amateur Championships, followed next year by the Natal Open and the Amateur British Open. From 1938 he won the South African Professional Championship 17 times. Apart from winning the Canadian, French, Egyptian, German, Irish, Swiss, Dutch, Mexican, Australian, New Zealand and other championships, Locke won the British Open Championship four times, in 1949, 1952, 1957 and 1959, being the only player to do so except the famous Walter Hagen and Peter Thomson. Following a serious motor accident he retired from international play.

Lock-Shoe. A device locked into the side of a wheel to prevent wagons skidding downhill.

Locust-Bird. Common name for Wattled Starling. *See* STARLING.

Locusts. Major insect pest in Southern Africa almost since the beginnings of White farming. Several distinct species exist. The most common are Brown Locusts (*Locustana pardalina*) which are permanently present in semi-desert areas, and periodically swarm elsewhere. Red Locusts (*Nomadacris septemfasciata*) originate from Central Africa, where the International Red Locust Control Service checks incipient swarms in the breeding grounds. The Republic, a member of this organisation, today feels safe from invasion. Desert Locusts (*Schistocerca flaviventris*) inhabit the sandy parts of the Kalahari, and seldom reach the swarming stage. The Tropical or African Migratory Locusts (*Lucusta migratoria migratorioides*) are scattered and relatively harmless visitors. Other types, formerly considered distinct, are now known to be different stages of growth. Locusts hatch from eggs into 'Voetgangers,' normally behaving like grasshoppers for generations. Swarming occurs under certain conditions of overcrowding, and is comparable, according to Dr. Malcolm Burr, to the swarming of ants or bees, or to human migrations. Why these phenomenal increases occur periodically is unknown, but suddenly the locust army advances, devouring everything green, and finally takes to the wing. In Johannesburg in 1907 the sky was darkened for hours and the countryside laid bare. In the anti-locust campaign in Cyprus, 1881, 1,300 tons of egg clusters were dug up and burnt. The first systematic attempt at their extermination was the passing of a law in Natal in 1895. Efforts were also made to propagate a fungus fatal to the insects. After the South African War a Locust Officer was imported to the Transvaal from Cyprus, and before Union both the Cape and Orange Free State followed suit. Conservatism among farmers remained a handicap. Serious outbreaks after World War I led to the adoption of the arsenic solution spray pump, manufactured on the Rand. Research was undertaken by the Department of Agriculture, and the Union joined the International Locust Control Service. By timely application of poison to known breeding areas, the damage has in recent years been greatly reduced.

Loeriesfontein. Village near Calvinia, Cape Province. Population: 2,192, including 682 Whites.

Lombardy. Township near Kempton Park, Transvaal. Population: 1,229, including 992 Whites.

London and Rhodesian Mining and Land Company Limited. Mining group established in May 1909 with very large holdings of land, at one time over 1,655,000 acres, as well as gold and other workings in Rhodesia, Zambia and Malawi. Usually referred to as LONRHO.

Long Cecil. Nickname given to gun manufactured in De Beers workshops in Kimberley, during the siege of that city by the Boers during the South African War. It was a 28-pounder and made from a piece of steel shafting by men without any artillery experience, rifled, mounted, tested and put in service within the space of 24 days. It fired its first shell against the besiegers on January 19, 1900, and was named in honour of Cecil John Rhodes, who was in Kimberley at the time. The man mainly responsible for the achievement was George Labram, Mechanical Engineer of De Beers Consolidated Mines (q.v.). Altogether the gun fired 225 shells. It is preserved as a monument at Kimberley.

Longlands. Diamond digging centre near Barkly West, Cape Province. Population: 100, including 80 Whites.

Long Tom. Nickname given to a French breech-loading gun, manufactured by Schneider of Le Creuzot and used by the Boer artillery in the South African War. It fired a 94-pound shell and had a range up to 10,000 yards. Used extensively at the sieges of Mafeking, Ladysmith and Kimberley.

Long Tom Pass. Pass in the Eastern Transvaal near Sabie. So called because, during the later stages of the South African War (q.v.), the famous Boer siege gun, 'Long Tom' (q.v.), was finally brought there and abandoned.

Lonrho. See LONDON and RHODESIAN MINING AND LAND COMPANY LIMITED.

Loskop Dam. Large irrigation scheme 36 miles north of Middelburg, Transvaal. The wall across the Olifants River is 1,420 feet long, and 120 feet high. Work was begun in 1934. Irrigable area is about 40,000 acres. The centre of the district is Groblersdal. Large output of sub-tropical fruit, vegetables and other crops.

Lothian, Lord. See KERR.

Lottery. See RHODESIAN STATE LOTTERY and LOURENÇO MARQUES LOTTERY.

Louis Napoleon. Prince Imperial of France. Son of the Emperor Napoleon III and the Empress Eugenie, he was born in Paris on March 16, 1856. To secure experience on active service he joined the forces during the Zulu War and was killed in an ambush on the Ityotyozi River in Zululand on June 1, 1879. His mother, the Empress Eugenie, paid a special visit to South Africa. His remains are buried in England.

Louis Rood. Village near Van Rhynsdorp in Cape Province. Population: 1,624, including 142 Whites.

Louis Trichardt. Town in the Northern Transvaal, named after the famous Voortrekker (q.v.). Founded in 1898, it is noted for the beautiful scenery in the neighbouring Zoutpansberg mountains and for its farming activities. Population: 15,220, including 4,500 Whites.

Lourenço Marques. Capital of Portuguese East Africa, officially known as the Province of Mozambique. Population: 200,000, including about 70,000 Whites and 5,000 Indians. Situated on the shores of Delagoa Bay and near the mouth of the River Espirito Santo, it takes its name from an early Portuguese trader, Lourenço Marques (q.v.). Like Cape Town, it began as a watering station for ships travelling between the Far East and Europe. The first attempt at permanent settlement was in 1721, when a Dutch expedition from the Cape set up a trading post at Catembe. About 50 years later an Austrian trading factory was begun. After 10 years of existence this was wiped out by a Portuguese party sent over from Goa, and the present town of Lourenço Marques came into existence. It remained for many years one of the most unhealthy settlements in Africa, notorious for fever and bad climate, besides being exposed to attacks from natives. After the rival claims of several nations had finally been disposed of (*see* DELAGOA BAY), the real growth of the community began, being stimulated by the construction of the first railway to the Transvaal in 1894, the frontier being only 55 miles distant. Since the completion of the railway to Pretoria in 1895, Lourenço Marques has secured an increasing proportion of the traffic of the Witwatersrand Gold Fields, and today ranks as one of the major ports of Southern Africa. On account of its nearness to Johannesburg, closer than is Durban, Lourenço Marques has always had a large number of South African commercial houses. There are a number of manufacturing industries, and its harbour is noted for its modern and efficient equipment, including particularly its coaling appliances. Several railways have been built from Lourenço Marques to other points, including the frontier of Swaziland at Goba in 1912, to Xinavane in 1914, to Marracuene, and, most recently of all, to Southern Rhodesia, with which it now has a direct link. Lourenço Marques is a popular holiday resort for South Africans; it has a University and operates a large commercial broadcasting station, run by the Radio Club of Mozambique, providing coverage for large parts of the Republic.

Lourenço Marques Lottery. Established in 1917 by the Central Commission for Social Assistance for the Colony of Mozambique, and leased out by that Government authority. By law a fixed percentage of the receipts must be used for benevolent purposes.

Lourie (family Musophagidae). A purely African bird; a fruit eater found mainly in Natal, Zululand and the Eastern Transvaal, also in forests from George and Knysna round the coastal belt. Large, crested, long-tailed and brightly coloured from the presence of copper on the quills. The crimson wings are beautiful in flight,

against the dull green of the body. Heavy rain sometimes washes out the colour. Louries run gracefully along branches. The Grey Lourie (Go-Away Bird) of bush country gives a warning cry when disturbed by hunters, and is seen in small groups. *See* BIRDS.

Louw, Dr. Charles Robert. South African financier. Born at Murraysburg, Cape, in 1875 and educated at the Paarl Gymnasium and Victoria College, Stellenbosch, he qualified as an attorney and practised for many years at Ermelo, Transvaal. In 1918 Dr. Louw became one of the original founders of the Suid-Afrikaanse Nasionale Trust en Assuransie Maatskappy (Santam) and the Suid-Afrikaanse Lewens-Assuransie Maatskappy (Sanlam), of which he was made Chairman. Retiring from legal practice, he settled at Somerset West in the Cape, where he acquired a wide range of other interests and established the Federale Volksbeleggings group, of which he became Chairman. Other interests included the African Homes Trust, Macmanus Brothers, Ltd. and the Trust Bank of Africa.

Louw, Dr. Eric Hendrik. South African Cabinet minister. Born at Jacobsdal, Orange Free State, on November 21, 1890, he studied at Victoria College, Stellenbosch, and Rhodes University College, Grahamstown. In 1917 he was called to the Bar and practised in the latter city. His political career began with his election as Nationalist member for Beaufort West in 1924; in the following year he became South African Trade Commissioner for the United States and Canada. There followed a term in 1929 as High Commissioner in London. From 1929 to 1932 he was South African minister in Washington, followed by similar posts in 1933 in Rome and in 1934 in Paris. He also represented the Union at various sittings of the League of Nations at Geneva and from 1948 was with the United Nations. In 1948 and again in 1961 he attended the Commonwealth Conference in London. He retired from active politics in 1963. Died on June 24, 1968.

Louw, Dr. Marthinus Smuts ('Tinie'). South African financier. Born at Ladismith, Cape Province, August 15, 1888, and educated at Stellenbosch University and Edinburgh. After teaching in the Orange Free State he joined Sanlam (q.v.), the first Afrikaner to be a qualified actuary. He established many important financial institutions, notably Bonuskor, which, by a new method, mobilised capital in millions.

Louw, N. P. van Wyk. Afrikaans scholar and poet. Born June 11, 1906, at Sutherland, Cape Province, he studied at the University of Cape Town, where in 1929 he became a lecturer on Education. From 1950 to 1957 he held the chair of Afrikaans at the University at Amsterdam, Holland, and since 1958 at the University of Witwatersrand. His fame rests mainly on his poetry and drama which have repeatedly gained him the Hertzog Prize (q.v.) and other awards. *See* AFRIKAANS LITERATURE.

Louw, William Ewart Gladstone. Afrikaans scholar and poet. Born May 31, 1913, at Sutherland, Cape, and educated at the universities of Cape Town and Amsterdam. Well known as a critic, poet and essayist.

Louwrens, Hilligard Muller. Judge, Cape Bench. Born in Riversdale, Cape, on July 11, 1868, and educated at Victoria College, Stellenbosch. Beginning his career as a teacher in 1886, he switched to law and from 1892 to 1903 practised at the Side Bar in Riversdale and Mossel Bay respectively. In 1903 he entered the Middle Temple and was called in 1906, returning to the Cape in the same year. After years of successful practice he took silk in 1921 and was appointed to the Cape Bench in 1924. He died on October 1, 1934.

Louwsburg. Village in Northern Natal, named after David Louw, a local pioneer. Cattle trading centre. Population: 1,191, including 190 Whites.

Lovebird, Rosy-Faced (*Agapornis roseicollis*). Small parrot, and the only South African Lovebird. Lives in the dry country and is regarded by natives as a guide to water. *See* BIRDS.

Lovedale Missionary Institution. Large educational institution for Bantu at Alice, Cape Province, founded in 1826 under the name of Incehra and later renamed Lovedale in honour of Dr. John Love, Secretary of the Glasgow Missionary Society. Abandoned in 1836 on account of frontier troubles, Lovedale was restarted the following year on a new site. Thanks to the efforts of the Free Church of Scotland, which took over in 1844, Lovedale soon acquired great importance, particularly owing to Dr. James Stewart (q.v.). Apart from the religious side, work was largely concentrated on education, and several famous white South Africans, including Sir James Rose-Innes (q.v.), studied here in the early days. But its chief distinction was gained as a training centre in trades for the Bantu. With the development of the neighbouring University College of Fort Hare (*see* FORT HARE), Lovedale's activities on that side have been reduced.

Loxton. Wool centre near Victoria West, founded in 1899. Population: 1,300, including 230 Whites.

Luanshya. Township in Zambia, on the Copperbelt, established in 1931, close to the Roan Antelope Copper Mine, many of whose employees live there. Population: 44,000, including 4,300 Whites.

Luckhoff. Town in the Orange Free State, named after the Rev. H. J. Lückhoff, the first Dutch Reformed minister there. The settlement was founded in 1892, and is a flourishing farming community. Population: 900, including 250 Whites.

Lucky Bean (*Abrus precatorius* L.). Slender, woody creeper, stems ¾ inch thick and fernlike leaves with narrow leaflets. Mauve pea-flowers, black pods containing the red and black poisonous seeds used as charms and ornaments. Flourishes in north-eastern Transvaal. The roots are used medicinally in India as a liquorice substitute.

Lüderitz (also known as **Lüderitz-bucht**). Town in South-West Africa, named after Adolf Lüderitz (q.v.), founder of the original German colony, who landed here in 1883. The place was originally called Angra Pequena (q.v.) but was renamed in his honour after his disappearance and death. Although a German military station was set up here in 1894, and it was used as a harbour, it was not till 1909 that the discovery of diamonds and the resulting boom led to the founding of a municipality. At that time it maintained a stock exchange, but today its importance, apart from the port, lies in trade with the diamond fields and in fisheries and canning. Population: 7,410, including 2,450 Whites.

Lüderitz, Adolf. German coloniser, born in Bremen on July 16, 1834. He made the acquaintance of Heinrich Vogelsang, who had schemes for establishing a German settlement on the West Coast of Africa. Lüderitz secured the support of the German Foreign Office, and, when Vogelsang reported, in 1883, the purchase of land at Angra Pequena from local chiefs, he took ship there and arrived in September of that year. Diplomatic disputes followed, but Bismarck upheld Lüderitz's claims, and the foundations were laid of the colony, which became German South West Africa in 1884. In that year Lüderitz also attempted to secure concessions in what was then still unoccupied Pondoland, through August Einwald. He returned to South West Africa in 1886, and,

while coasting in a small vessel near the mouth of the Orange River, was carried out to sea and never heard of again.

Lüderitzland. Early name given to South West Africa, in honour of Adolf Lüderitz (q.v.).

Lugard, Lady. *See* SHAW, FLORA LOUISE.

Luhlanga. Swaziland silver coin, equal to one Rand. *See* LILANGENI.

Lukin, Major-General Sir Henry Timson. South African soldier. Born in Fulham, London, on May 24, 1860, educated at Merchant Taylors' School and in 1879, came to South Africa where he took part in the Zulu War. After a brief return to England, he came back and in 1880 joined the Cape Mounted Rifles as a lieutenant. He fought in Basutoland, spent years in the Eastern Cape, participated in operations against the Chief Galishwe in Bechuanaland and in the Langeberg Campaign of 1897. During the South African War he commanded the artillery in the Colonial Division and took part in the siege of Wepener, as well as in many other actions, which brought him promotion to Lieutenant-Colonel, and the D.S.O. After the war he became Colonel commanding the Cape Mounted Rifles and later Commandant-General of the Colonial Forces at the Cape. He attended King George V Coronation in 1911, and on the founding of the Union Defence Force in 1912 became Inspector-General. During World War I he fought in German South West Africa, Egypt and France, in command of the South African force at Delville Wood (q.v.), and was gassed. He rose to Major-General and died in 1925.

Lumbo. Settlement on the mainland of Mozambique, close to the island of Mozambique; trading centre.

Lumpa. African religious movement based on a distorted form of Christianity, started in Zambia (Northern

Rhodesia) by Alice Lenshina, who gained thousands of followers in the remote districts. Refusals to acknowledge Government rights or to pay taxes led to police and later military action during 1964. About 500 members of the sect were killed during the disturbances.

Lundi Ruins. *See* RUNDI RUINS.

Luneburg. Station of the Hermannsburg Mission founded in 1854, in Northern Natal, and named after the town in Germany.

Lung-Sickness (Longsiekte in Afrikaans). Highly-infectious form of pleuro-pneumonia occurring in cattle.

Lusaka. Capital of Zambia. Replaced Livingstone in 1935. It is the seat of the Governor and of the administration; supports a number of industries. Its altitude, about 4,200 feet, gives it a relatively cool climate. Population: 114,000, including 12,000 Whites.

Lusikisiki. Village in Pondoland, founded in 1894, and deriving its name from the noise made by the reeds that grew near by in former times. Trading centre. Population: 750, including 200 Whites.

Lutheran Church (Evangelical Lutheran). Group of churches originally established by German colonists at the Cape in the 18th century and still largely supported in the German community, especially in South West Africa. Extensive missionary activity. Total number of adherents 800,000.

Luthuli, Chief Albert John. Bantu leader and Nobel Prize winner. A Zulu, born at Groutville, Natal, in 1898 and educated at Adams College, he qualified as a teacher and served on the Native Representative Council until its abolition in 1946. Became President of the African National Congress (q.v.). His opposition to the

South African Government and his part in the public burning of passes after the disturbances at Sharpeville (q.v.) left him confined to his home near Stanger in Natal. In 1961 the Swedish authorities nominated him for the Nobel Peace Prize, which he received in the same year. He was elected Rector of Glasgow University in 1962. Died on July 21, 1967.

Lydenburg. Town in the Eastern Transvaal, founded in 1847 by the Voortrekkers, who set up an independent republic which was soon merged into the rest of the Transvaal. The name is derived from the sufferings (Lyden) undergone there by the pioneers, which led to the abandonment of the earlier Andries Orighstad (q.v.). Gold and other minerals were discovered near by in the 1870's and fighting took place there in several Native wars. In the South African War it saw fresh hostilities. In 1924-1925 it became the centre of a new platinum field. Today it is a trout fishing, mining and farming town. Population: 8,000, including 3,500 Whites.

Lynx. *See* CARACAL.

Lyttelton. *See* VERWOERDBURG.

Lyttelton, Alfred. British statesman and Secretary of State for the Colonies. Born in England, 1857, and educated at Eton and Cambridge, he took up a legal career, and in 1903 joined the Balfour Cabinet as Secretary of State for the Colonies. As such he was responsible, against many protests, for allowing the introduction to the Rand of Chinese coolie labourers. He put forward the first version of the Transvaal constitution in 1905 under the Crown Colony régime, which was named after him, the Lyttelton Constitution. It was altered owing to the advent to power of the Liberals soon after and superseded. He died on July 4, 1913.

Lyttelton, General Sir Neville Gerald. Born in Worcestershire, England, 1845. During the South African War he commanded the Fourth Brigade (2nd and 4th Division) in Natal, at Spion Kop and elsewhere. In the Transvaal Lyttelton fought along the Delagoa Bay Railway, and in Lydenburg, at Helvetia. From 1902 to 1904 he was Commander-in-Chief of the British forces in South Africa and returned to become Chief of the General Staff (1904–1908). He died in 1931.

M

Maag Bomme (literally Stomach Bombs). Indigestible type of dumplings eaten by the Boers in the field.

Maartblom. *See* AMARYLLIS *and* KAFFIR ALMANAC.

Maasbanker or Horse-Mackerel (*Trachurus trachurus*). A very well-known Cape fish related to the Yellowtail (q.v.), caught from St. Helena Bay to Natal, and in the North Atlantic. Twenty inches; greenish or bluish above and silvery below. Rather a coarse texture, as the name Horse-Mackerel suggests. *See* MARINE RESOURCES.

Maasdorp, Sir Andries Ferdinand Stockenstroom. Chief Justice, Orange River Colony. Born in Malmesbury in the Cape on January 14, 1847, and educated at Graaff-Reinet and London, where he took his B.A. in 1869, and was called by the Inner Temple in 1871. Returning to the Cape, he began practice in 1872 and represented Graaff-Reinet in the Cape Parliament from 1874 to 1878. In that year he was appointed Solicitor-General at Grahamstown, combining this with a lucrative private practice for nearly 19 years, until he was admitted to the Transvaal Bar in 1897. Shortly before the Boer War he returned to practice in Grahamstown, and in 1900 became a member of the Special Treason Court of the Cape Colony. In 1902 he was appointed Chief Justice of the Orange River Colony. He retired in 1919 and died in Rondebosch on March 18, 1931. His *Institutes of South African Law* in 4 volumes is still a standard work.

Maasdorp, Christian George. Judge-President of the Cape. Born in Malmesbury, Cape, brother of Sir Andries Ferdinand Stockenstroom Maasdorp (q.v.) and educated at Graaff-Reinet and London. He was called by the Inner Temple in 1871 and returned to the Cape, to be admitted there in the same year. After practising in Griqualand West and for 3 years in the Eastern District Court, he was appointed Attorney-General of the Transvaal in 1877, but resigned in 1880 and moved to Cape Town. In 1885 he became a judge of the Eastern Districts Court and in 1896 was transferred to the Cape Bench. After Union he was appointed Judge-President of the Cape and Judge of Appeal. He retired in 1922 and died in May 1926.

Mabelreign. Township 5 miles northwest of Salisbury, established in 1950 and laid out as a garden city. It has a population of 4,400 Europeans and 2,600 Africans.

Maboela. Basuto custom under which certain tracts of land are set aside for the cattle of chiefs. *See* LETSIMA.

Mabopane. Self-contained Bantu city established 20 miles north of Pretoria, adjoining Garankuwa (q.v.) on a 13,000-acre site, planned for population of over 300,000.

Macala. Seaport in Mozambique, situated beside a large natural harbour, linked by rail with Rhodesia and the border of Malawi.

Macartney, George, First Earl. Governor of the Cape of Good Hope, born on May 14, 1737, at Lissanoore, County Antrim, Ireland. In 1796 Macartney became the first regular civilian Governor, remaining until 1798. Confronted with colonists of republican leanings, he was inclined to strong reaction, but he helped to adopt improvements of permanent value, such as the establishment of a Post

Office. He resigned in 1798 and died in Ireland in 1806.

McCabe, Joseph. Early trader and hunter. Little is known of his young days, except that he emigrated from the Cape in 1850 and settled in the Transvaal. He was one of the first White men to cross the Kalahari. He became a trader in Matabeleland, and in 1860 settled in the present Bechuanaland at Molepolele, where in 1865 he died. Apart from his hunting achievements, he was a pioneer collector of botanical specimens, many of which he sent to Kew Gardens.

McCann, Cardinal Owen. Catholic Archbishop of Cape Town. Born at Cape Town on June 24, 1907, he was educated there at the Marist Brothers College and in Rome, entering the priesthood in 1935. For some time he edited the Catholic newspaper *Southern Cross*. He became archbishop in 1951 and cardinal in 1965.

McCaw, Terence. South African artist. Born in 1913 at Pilgrim's Rest, he studied at Johannesburg under Sidney Carter, but soon developed his own style. Though he has spent much time in Europe, particularly in Italy, he has retained his contact with South Africa, being specially noted for his landscapes.

McCorkindale, Alexander. Scottish-born concessionnaire and pioneer of the Eastern Transvaal. He came to South Africa in the 1850's and was a well-known hunter. In 1864 he approached the Volksraad in Pretoria with a scheme for establishing a settlement in the Eastern Transvaal, and in return offered to provide the Government with postage stamps, ammunition and banking facilities. The outcome was the grant of an area of about 500,000 acres, which he endeavoured to develop by means of a company formed in Glasgow. Plans were drafted for the establishment of a settlement to be known as New Scot-

land, with a village called Roburnia (after Robert Burns) as its capital. The scheme was a failure but a certain number of settlers actually came to the Transvaal. Roburnia survived and is today known as Amsterdam. McCorkindale died in 1871.

McCubbin, Captain George Reynolds, D.S.O. South African air ace. Born in Cape Town on January 18, 1898, and educated in Johannesburg. He joined the Royal Flying Corps in 1916 and shot down Captain Max Immelmann (q.v.), the famous German air ace. He died on May 8, 1944.

Macdonald, Sir Hector Archibald. British soldier. He was born in Scotland in 1853, and enlisted at the age of 17 as a private in the Gordon Highlanders. Distinguished himself in India, where he was commissioned as Second Lieutenant and won further fame for gallantry at Majuba in 1881. After service in Egypt and the Sudan, was promoted to Major-General and sent to South Africa in 1900 after the outbreak of war. Among his successes were the preliminaries to the relief of Kimberley, also those actions which led to the surrender of General Cronje at Paardeberg and of General Prinsloo at Tabaksberg. He returned to India, but fell a victim to libellous accusations and committed suicide in Paris in 1903.

MacDonald, James Ramsay. British Prime Minister. Born in 1866, he helped to found the British Labour Party. As one of its leaders he gained a place in South African history through his championship of the Boer Cause during the South African War, which brought him great unpopularity. In September and October, 1902, immediately after the Peace, MacDonald visited the Transvaal and O.F.S., embodying his findings in a book *What I saw in South Africa*, issued that year. It won him much respect among the Boers.

Macequece (also known as **Villa de Manica** and **Massekessi**). Town in

Mozambique near the Rhodesian border, on the railway to Beira. It was established in 1888, in an effort by the Portuguese to safeguard their claim to Manicaland. Macequece became the centre of international diplomatic friction when the Portuguese forces were driven out by Colonel Sir L. H. Melville Heyman (q.v.). Today it is a frontier post and also centre of prospecting activities. Of the population of 9,000, about 450 are White. *See* MASSEKESSI INCIDENT.

McGregor. Village in the Robertson district of the Cape Province. Established in 1861 as Lady Grey, but renamed in honour of the Rev. Andrew McGregor of Robertson (who also officiated here), because of the existence of another Lady Grey (q.v.) in the Wittebergen. The district is noted for the production of fruit and raisins, also for the growing of whipsticks. Population: 1,300, including 220 Whites.

McGregor, Alexander John. Judge of the Supreme Court. Born in 1864 in Robertson, Cape Province, he studied at the South African College and qualified in law at Oxford, being called to the Bar in 1889. His first post was as State Attorney of the Orange Free State in the same year, and in 1892 he received a judgeship, from which he resigned in 1895. He practised at the Cape Bar for many years, before joining the Eastern Districts Court in 1913, returning to the Orange Free State in 1915. Retired in 1929 and died on November 28, 1946.

Machado, General Sir Jorge. Portuguese engineer and Governor General of Mozambique. First came into prominence in 1880, when he visited Pretoria in connection with the construction of the original railway line from Mozambique to the Transvaal under the McMurdo Concession. He took a leading part in the survey of the route ultimately followed by the Netherlands-South Africa Railway

Company, and in his honour an Eastern Transvaal village was called Machadodorp (q.v.). Machado himself was Governor-General of the Province of Mozambique during the South African War, where he followed a pro-British policy, for which reason he received a knighthood on the King's Birthday, 1902, as K.C.M.G. Died 1925.

Machadodorp. Village in the Eastern Transvaal on the main line to Lourenço Marques. Established in 1895, when the railway was built, and named after the Portuguese General J. J. Machado, who played a part in realising the project. During the South African War Machadodorp was the seat of the Government of the Republic after the evacuation of Pretoria, from May 30 to August 27, 1900. It saw considerable fighting. In more recent times the warm springs have made the village a health resort. Population: 1,305, including 440 Whites.

Machilla. Portable hammock suspended from a pole, carried by native bearers, and formerly used on a wide scale in Mozambique and elsewhere. It was, however, forbidden by the authorities early in the present century, and is now almost unknown.

Mackenzie, Lieutenant-Colonel Sir Duncan. South African soldier. Born in Natal on August 19, 1859, he was educated at Hilton College and served in the South African War, the Natal Native Rebellion and other campaigns, becoming commander of the Natal Carbineers. He died in 1932.

Mackerel, Cape (*Scomber colias*). Fish found in Table Bay and from False Bay to Natal. About 16 inches long. Similar to the European variety and extensively canned. This economic importance applies equally to two other types, the Striped (12 inches) and the Frigate Mackerel (14 inches long) both found in tropical and sub-tropical seas from Natal eastwards. All mackerels have firm, oily flesh, reddish in colour. The family includes more widely Tunny, Bonito and Katonkel (q.v.). *See* MARINE RESOURCES.

Maclean, Colonel John. Lieutenant-Governor of Natal. Began his career in the British Army but in November 1845 was appointed Government Agent at Fort Peddie, Commissioner to the T'Sambie tribe in 1847 and Chief Commissioner of British Kaffraria in 1852. When this area became a separate Colony in December 1860, Maclean became the first Lieutenant-Governor. Because of his skill in handling natives he was promoted to Natal in 1864, but through ill-health was obliged to retire in July 1865.

Macleantown. Village near East London, Cape Province. Population: 610, including 150 Whites.

Maclear. Town in the Northern Cape, in the foothills of the Drakensberg. Founded in 1876 and named after Her Majesty's Astronomer at the Cape, Sir Thomas Maclear. A famous trout-fishing resort, it lies in beautiful country. Population: 3,542, including 818 Whites.

Macloutsie. Village in Bechuanaland, used as a base by the Pioneer Column that occupied Mashonaland in 1890.

Macmac. Mining camp in the Eastern Transvaal, founded in 1872, and so called because of the large number of diggers of Scottish descent. Today it is chiefly noted for its waterfall, 185 feet in height.

MacMahon Award. Award made by Marshal MacMahon, President of the French Republic, on July 24, 1875, as arbitrator in a dispute between Britain and Portugal on the ownership of Delagoa Bay (q.v.).

Macowen, Professor Peter. South African botanist. Born, 1830, in Hull, he was a schoolmaster, then specialised in botany. On account of his health he came to South Africa in 1861 and set-tled in Grahamstown. Later he taught science at Gill College, Somerset East, and in 1881 became Director of the Cape Town Botanic Gardens, as well as Curator of the Cape Government Herbarium and Professor of Botany at the South African College. He attained international distinction in his science, particularly in connection with economic botany. Died in 1909.

Macsherry, Bishop Hugh. Catholic Bishop in South Africa. Born in Ireland, 1852, he entered the priesthood in France, 1876, and worked in Ireland for many years before arriving in South Africa in 1896. He was particularly active in the setting up of schools and the development of Catholic nursing services. Died in 1940.

Macuse. River in Mozambique. *See also* PORTO BELO.

Madeley, Walter Bayley. Labour leader. Born in Woolwich, England, in 1873, and educated in India, where his father, a soldier, was stationed. In 1889 he was apprenticed at Woolwich Arsenal and in 1896, as a qualified fitter, he reached Kimberley. He first came into prominence in the 1907 Rand Strike on the mines and was elected into Parliament as Labour member for Benoni. From 1925 to 1928 was Minister of Posts and Telegraphs and of Public Works in the Hertzog Cabinet, under the 'Pact' of the Nationalists with the Labour Party. Aroused attention through his objection to automatic telephones, which he claimed would displace labour. He died in 1947.

Mafeking. Town in Northern Cape, originally a kraal of the Baralong tribe, who gave it the name meaning 'Among the Stones.' It became a European settlement after the occupation of the country by the forces under Sir Charles Warren in 1884. Apart from its importance as an administrative centre, Mafeking gained world fame through its successful defence under General Sir Robert (later Lord) Baden-Powell in the South African War. The siege by the Boers lasted from October 16, 1899, to May 17, 1900, and the delirious scenes accompanying receipt of its relief gave a new word to the English language, 'to Maffick.' Today Mafeking owes its importance mainly to dairying and cattle-breeding. Population: 6,400, including 5,000 Whites. Until 1961 the 'Imperial Reserve' at Mafeking was the administrative capital of the Bechuanaland Protectorate, the only capital in the world outside the country it governed. *See* GABERONE.

Mafeteng. Village in the south-west of Lesotho, the name meaning 'The Place of Unmarried Women.' Scene of fighting in the 1880 'Gun War.'

Magaliesberg. Range in the Southern Transvaal, named after an early native chief (Mogali). The area is chiefly noted for its tobacco and fruit production, of which the Hartley family were pioneers. A fictional resident was the celebrated hunter, Alan Quatermain, in the novels of Sir Henry Rider Haggard. During the South African War General Christiaan de Wet made a famous escape across a seemingly impassable section of the mountains.

Magersfontein. Farm near Modder River and scene of battle during South African War on December 11, 1899, resulting in a heavy defeat of the British by the Boers. Major-General A. J. Wauchope was killed and with him a large part of the Highland Brigade. Altogether the British lost over 1,000 men, including 244 killed and 651 wounded. The Boers suffered considerably, particularly the Scandinavian unit, which was nearly wiped out.

Maguire, James Rochfort. Rhodesian pioneer. Born in England, 1855. Educated at Oxford, where he made the acquaintance of Cecil John Rhodes. Later he came to South Africa and together with C. D. Rudd (q.v.) took a leading part in securing the concession from Lobengula. He remained a close friend of Rhodes. Helped to found the Chartered Company, being a member of the Board and of its main subsidiaries. He specialised in Railway construction in Rhodesia. Died in 1925.

Magut. Village in the north of Zululand, near the Pongola River, the name of which means 'Bewitched.' It is important as an irrigation centre and for the production of sub-tropical crops. Population: 200, including 50 Whites.

Magwa Falls. Beautiful waterfall in the Transkei, 15 miles from Lusikisiki, 450 feet high, in narrow gorge. Magwa means 'marvellous.'

Mahalapye. Native township in Bechuanaland, 45 miles south of Palapye.

Mahashini. Kraal of the Paramount Chief of Zululand, 18 miles from Nongoma (q.v.).

Mahem. Alternative name for Crowned Crane. *See* CRANE.

Maherero. Chief of the Herero tribe (q.v.) in South West Africa. The son of Jonker Afrikaner, upon whose death in 1863 he became one of the most feared leaders in the country. He freed his people from the rule of the Namas after a 7 years' war and by 1870 was settled at Okahandja in considerable prosperity. There he became involved in another war against the Nama, which lasted 10 years, from 1880 to 1890. White settlement was now beginning and Maherero realised that he could not withstand the white man's power. He died in 1890, and was succeeded by his son, Samuel Maherero.

Mahlabatini. Village in Natal. Population 340, including 60 Whites.

Mahogany Bean Tree (*Afzelia quanzensis* Welw.). Northern Transvaal and Delagoa Bay. Medium to large tree. Timber valuable.

Mahogany, Cape, or Rooi Essenhout (*Trichilia emetica*). Splendid forest

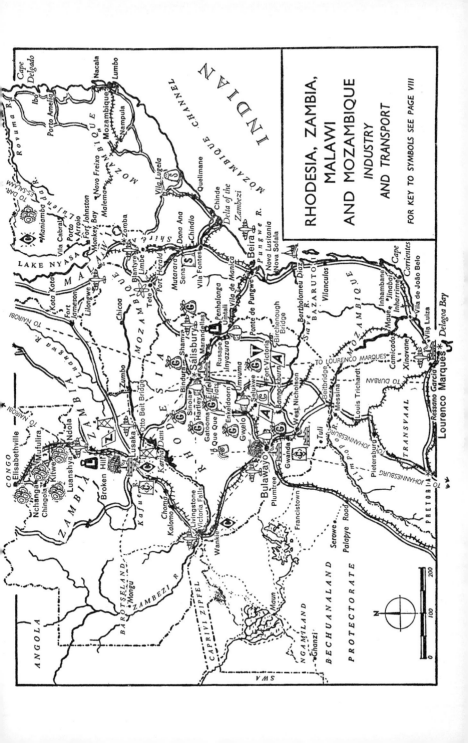

RHODESIA, ZAMBIA,
MALAWI
AND MOZAMBIQUE

INDUSTRY
AND TRANSPORT

FOR KEY TO SYMBOLS SEE PAGE VIII

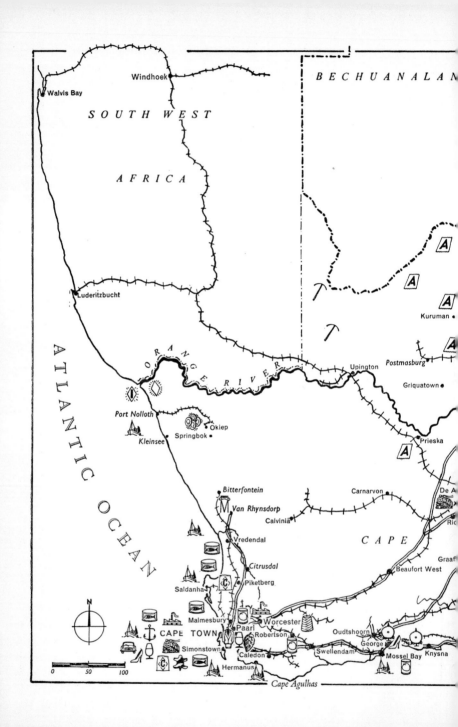

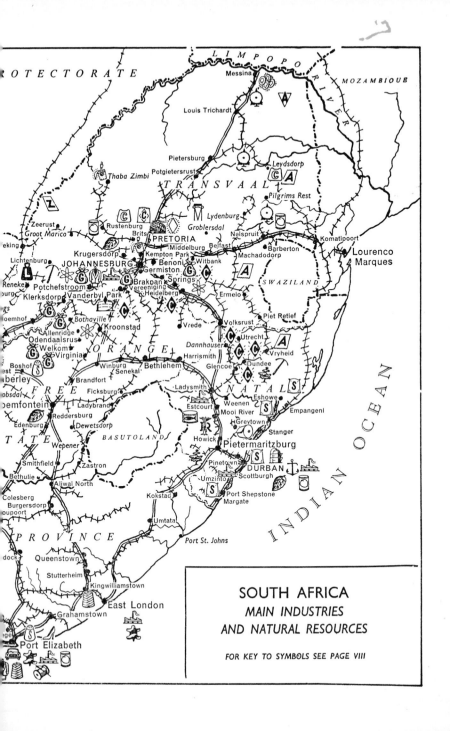

SOUTH AFRICA
*MAIN INDUSTRIES
AND NATURAL RESOURCES*

FOR KEY TO SYMBOLS SEE PAGE VIII

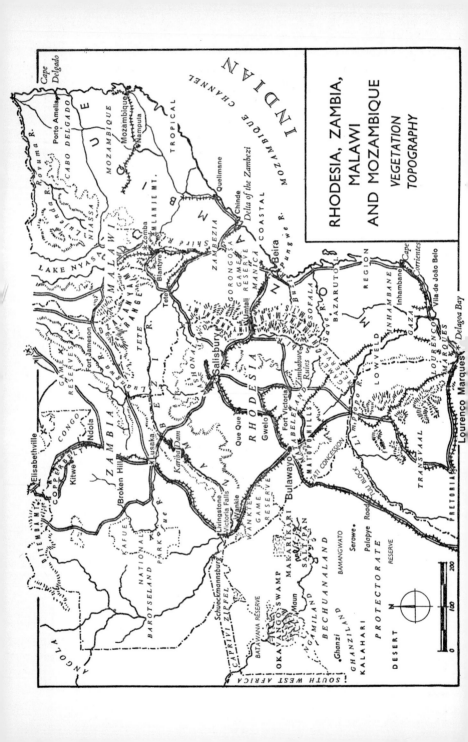

RHODESIA, ZAMBIA,
MALAWI
AND MOZAMBIQUE

VEGETATION
TOPOGRAPHY

tree with wide, spreading crown. Only occurs in the moist forests of coastal belt of the Transkei, Natal and Zululand, also the Eastern Transvaal. Timber is light yet suitable for furniture.

Maidenhair. See FERN, MAIDENHAIR.

Maitland, Sir Peregrine. Governor of Cape Colony, born in 1777, and becoming Governor in 1844. Honest but slow in his methods, he relied too much on his subordinates, spending much of his time in vain attempts to ensure a permanent peace settlement with the frontier native chiefs. He came into conflict with the Voortrekkers in Natal, over whom he was expected to enforce British authority. In 1847 he was recalled to England. He died in 1852.

Majuba (also **Amajuba**) 'The Hill of Doves.' Hill near Charlestown on the border of Natal and the Transvaal (q.v.) and scene of a British defeat in the First Boer War, on February 27, 1881. The summit of the hill had been occupied by British troops under General Sir Pomeroy Colley (q.v.), when, under cover of darkness, a storming party of Boers, under Commandant Piet Joubert, climbed Majuba, surprised and killed Colley and 92 of his men and wounded 134. Boer casualties were negligible.

Makana. Prophet and leader of the Xosa people. Born towards the end of the 18th century, the son of Balala. Of comparatively low rank but by personality and by his doctrines (not officially a Christian but acknowledging the existence of a God) succeeded in gaining great authority over the Xosas, to whom he introduced the habit of burying corpses. He was known to the Europeans as Links, on account of his lefthandedness. Supporting the cause of Ndlambe (q.v.) he sent him a large number of warriors and in 1819 helped to lead the attack on Grahamstown. On being defeated, he surrendered to Landdrost (afterwards Sir Andries) Stockenstrom, and was sent to Robben Island for internment. Trying to escape on August 9, 1820, he was drowned in the surf, but such was his influence that for more than 50 years the Xosas refused to believe that he was dead.

Makapan's Gat. Cave near Potgietersrust in the Northern Transvaal, used as a hiding place by the chief Mokopane (Makapan) in his wars against the early Boer settlers. Following his murdering of a group of colonists under Commandant Hermanus Potgieter in 1854, a punitive expedition was led against him by Commandant J. P. Potgieter (q.v.) and the future President, Paul Kruger (q.v.), who virtually wiped out the tribe after a 25-day siege of the cave.

Makarikari. Large salt pan in Kalahari Desert (q.v.) in the north of Botswana. Area about 5,000 square miles.

Makatini Flats. Tract of level country between Lebombo Mountains and Indian Ocean in northern Zululand; 150,000 acres will ultimately be irrigated from the Pongola River (q.v.) under a government scheme.

Makolololand. Part of the Shire Highlands of Malawi. Possessing a considerable population, a fertile soil and a good climate, at a height of about 3,500 feet, it attracted the attention of the Portuguese who in 1888 and 1889, through their explorer Serpa Pinto, repeatedly tried to take possession of it. They failed and in 1891 it became a part of the British Central Africa Protectorate, which became Nyasaland Protectorate in 1907.

Malagas (*Morus capensis*). Popular name for gannet (q.v.).

Malan, Group-Captain ('Sailor') Adolf Gysbert. South African airman. Born at Wellington, Cape Province, on October 3, 1910. After the training ship *General Botha* he served in the Union-Castle Line until 1936. During the Depression he transferred to the Royal Air Force, where he won international fame. 'Sailor' Malan was one of the principal commanders of the fighter force in the Battle of Britain in September 1940. Returning to South Africa, he worked for ex-servicemen, and in 1951 held office in the War Veterans' Torch Commando. Wartime hardships undermined his health, and he died on September 17, 1963.

Malan, Charles Wynand. Cabinet Minister. Born in Paarl, 1884, he became interested in politics at a very early age, his brother being F. S. Malan (q.v.) and his father the local chairman of the Afrikander Bond. Qualifying as an attorney he set up practice in Humansdorp, and became a follower of General Hertzog almost from the start of the Nationalist Party. He was elected to Parliament in 1915 and became Minister of Railways in the first Hertzog Cabinet. He proved an unusually able administrator. He died suddenly in 1933 at the age of 49.

Malan, Dr. Daniel François. Prime Minister of the Union of South Africa. Born near Riebeek West, Cape Province, on May 22, 1874, he had his lifelong rival General J. C. Smuts (q.v.) as a childhood companion and for a while even attended the same school. Entering Victoria College, Stellenbosch, he studied for the Dutch Reformed Church ministry and in 1905 received his Doctorate in Divinity at the University of Utrecht in Holland for a thesis on the philosophy of Bishop Berkeley. He served as minister at Montagu and Graaff-Reinet, making a tour of Dutch Reformed missions in Rhodesia and the Belgian Congo in 1913, on which he wrote a short book, *Na Congoland.* A strong supporter of Afrikaner aspirations, Dr. Malan was one of General Hertzog's earliest followers,

and was appointed editor of *Die Burger* in 1915, when the latter became the first official newspaper of the National Party. Entering Parliament, he soon made his mark as a logical and powerful speaker, and when General Hertzog came into power in 1924 he took over the Ministry of the Interior. In the Cabinet he proved a powerful force, his department being particularly well run. He refused, however, to support General Hertzog when in 1933 the latter decided to fuse his party with that of General Smuts, and soon after helped to start his own 'purified' National organisation, which grew in power until in 1948 it defeated the United Party. Dr. Malan became Prime Minister and Minister of External Affairs, in which capacity he visited London and took part in the Commonwealth Conference. He retired from office in 1954 and spent his last years writing an account of his work for Afrikanerdom and of his political ideas. He died on February 7, 1959.

Malan, François Stephanus. South African statesman. Born near Wellington, Cape, in 1871, and attended school in Paarl. In 1892 he secured his degree at Victoria College, Stellenbosch, before proceeding to Cambridge to read for the Bar. He began to practise in Cape Town in 1895, became editor of *Ons Land,* an opponent of Rhodes and a supporter of the Afrikander Bond. In 1900 he was elected member for Malmesbury but was sent to prison for allegedly seditious articles in his paper. Increasingly identified with the cause of the Afrikaner. Malan refused the offer of the Cape Premiership in 1908, but became Minister of Agriculture. He took a leading part at the National Convention, and repeatedly served in the Union Cabinet. A sponsor of the National Monuments Commission, the Afrikaans Akademie and other important bodies, he enjoyed great prestige. He wrote a diary of the National Convention published by the Van Riebeeck Society (q.v.). He died in 1941.

Malaria. In Southern Africa this disease is rapidly being exterminated, due to new medical preparations, but precautions should still be taken in certain portions of the Lowveld, Northern and Eastern Transvaal, as well as in low-lying parts of Rhodesia, such as the Sabi Valley. It is also common in certain areas of Zambia and Malawi. Supplies of medical preparations are distributed free by the Government. In the Republic, the Health Department has conducted much research. Some years ago it borrowed the services of the overseas expert, Professor Swellengrebel, and is carrying out a systematic process of oiling and eradicating pools where malaria-bearing mosquitoes breed. Similar measures are being applied in Zambia and Rhodesia. The progress made is indicated by the last available returns, the total number of yearly deaths due to malaria in the Republic being only 15 Europeans and 4 non-Europeans.

Malawi (formerly Nyasaland). Republic in Central Africa. Of its area of 45,747 sq. miles, more than a quarter, 12,298 sq. miles, is accounted for by Lake Malawi (q.v.). The land itself is 520 miles long and varies in width from 50 to 100 miles. Its altitude varies from 200 feet above sea level in the Shire Valley to 1,500 feet at Lake Malawi, 3,500 to 4,000 feet on the plateaux, and 9,843 feet at Mlanje (q.v.). The present population is about 2,900,000, of whom 8,900 are white and 10,700 Asian. The capital is Zomba (q.v.). Originally ravaged by slave traders, Malawi was pioneered for white settlement by missionaries of the Scottish Presbyterian and Roman Catholic Churches. During the 1890's Mr. (later Sir) Harry Johnston succeeded in putting an end to the slave trade,

with a force composed partly of Indian troops. After disputes with the Portuguese authorities had been settled, Malawi became a British protectorate in 1891, under the name of British Central Africa. Colonial Office authority was adopted in 1904 since when there has been steady development, including the construction of the Shire Highlands Railway, etc. In 1965 work began on the extension of the Mozambique railway connection to Vila Cabral near Lake Malawi. The principal industries are the production of tobacco, tea and cotton and tropical and semi-tropical products. Revenue is also derived from tourists, who are attracted by the picturesque waters of Lake Malawi, and by the beauties of the Mlanje Mountain Range, the central feature of the lofty Malawi plateau. Under the independence constitution of 1964 Malawi was a monarchy, with Queen Elizabeth II as its head, but on July 6, 1966 it became a republic with Dr. H. K. Banda (q.v.) as President. There is a National Assembly or Parliament of 53 members, three of which are chosen by White voters. Following an exchange of diplomatic representatives with South Africa in 1968 large sums were invested in Malawi development including the building of a new capital at Lilongwe. There are 289 miles of railway. From 1953 to 1963 Malawi belonged to the Central African Federation (*see* RHODESIA AND NYASALAND, FEDERATION OF).

Malay-Portuguese. Mixed patois, akin to pidgin English, spoken in the East and derived from these two languages. At one time thought to have been ingredient of Afrikaans, but this theory has been disproved.

Malays, Cape. Community of Eastern, mostly Malay, origin, in and around Cape Town, where a large section occupies the 'Malay Quarter' on the slopes of Signal Hill. Their ancestors were brought to the Cape as slaves by the Dutch East India Company, the first arrivals being recorded in 1667. Later came a number of political exiles from Malaya, notably Sheikh Joseph (q.v.). Comparatively little admixture by other races has taken place and they remain devout Moslems, noted for their law-abiding character and high standard of morals. As artisans they specialise as horse-grooms, coachmen, fishermen, tailors, cabinet-makers and coopers. They still practise many old customs and sing their melodious songs—almost the only form in which their language is preserved. Today they speak Afrikaans. Professor Van Selms of Pretoria has found religious books printed for them as early as the 18th century in Constantinople in Arabic characters! Pure Cape Malays today number about 35,000.

Malcolm, Sir Dougal Orme. President of the British South Africa Company (Chartered Company). Born on August 6, 1877, in Scotland and educated at Eton and Oxford, he entered the Colonial Office in 1900 and from 1905 to 1910 was Private Secretary to Lord Selborne, while High Commissioner in South Africa. From 1910 to 1911 he held a similar post with Lord Grey in Canada and in 1912 joined the staff of the British Treasury. Malcolm was elected a director of the Chartered Co. in 1913, of which he later became President. He was also Vice-President of the British Borneo Co. and held several honorary posts. He died in 1955.

Malfa, Wild (*Pelargonium cucullatum* Ait.). Low shrub from which many garden hybrids are derived. South-Western districts of Cape Province. *See* PELARGONIUM.

Malherbe, Daniel Francois. Afrikaans poet and novelist. Born at Paarl on May 28, 1881, the son of one of the founders of Die Genootskap van Regte Afrikaners (q.v.). After studying at Stellenbosch and in Germany, he

taught at Carnarvon, Cape Province, and in 1909 was appointed Professor of Modern Languages at Bloemfontein. In 1918 he became the first Professor of Afrikaans anywhere. As one of its strongest protagonists, he collected vocabularies, proverbs and much other material, and edited the *Tydskrif Vir Wetenskap en Kuns*. He has written dramas and historical novels.

Mali Dyke. Geological dyke in the Eastern Transvaal, noted among early prospectors for its high gold content. Hence the name 'Mali,' signifying 'Money' in the Bantu language.

Mallow, Tree (*Hibiscus tiliaceus* L.). Tree up to 30 feet. Bark has strong fibre suitable for textile purposes. Natal coast. *See* HIBISCUS.

Malmesbury. Town in the Western Cape Province, centre of the district known popularly as the Zwartland (Black Country), by which the original settlement was long known. It attracted attention in the days of the early Dutch settlement because of its warm sulphur springs, still used, and of its fertile soil, the Zwartland being one of the best wheat districts in South Africa. The first church and bath-house were erected in 1745, but the real growth began after Governor Sir Lowry Cole, in November 1828, laid out a new village and in 1829 renamed it in honour of his father-in-law, the Earl of Malmesbury. Population: 8,540, including 3,590 Whites.

Malmesbury Accent. Pronunciation of Afrikaans ascribed to inhabitants of the Malmesbury district (q.v.), of which the main feature is the guttural 'r' (gebreide 'r'). It is found in other parts of South Africa today, and is used not only by Whites but by many Coloured people. General J. C. Smuts, who came from the area, always spoke with a Malmesbury accent.

Maloti. Gold coin issued by Lesotho (q.v.) in 1966. It equals one Rand (10 shillings) in value and is divided into 100 Licente (q.v.). Pieces of 4, 2 and 1 Maloti are struck.

Maltahöhe. Village in South-West Africa, between Lüderitz and Windhoek. It is called after Frau von Burgsdorff (born Malta), wife of a local official, the word 'Höhe' being German for 'Height.' Karakul-breeding centre. Population: 1,044, including 315 Whites.

Maluti Mountains. Large range in eastern Lesotho (q.v.), forming part of Drakensberg. Highest point over 11,000 feet.

Malvern, Viscount (Sir Godfrey Huggins). Prime Minister of Southern Rhodesia and of the Central African Federation. Born in England in 1883 and educated at Malvern College, he took up medicine and qualified at St. Thomas's Hospital, London. He emigrated in 1911 to Southern Rhodesia, where he soon attained distinction as a surgeon, continuing in practice even after entering political life. In 1923 he was elected to the Legislative Council, and in 1933 became Prime Minister and Minister of Native Affairs, positions he continued to hold for record periods, the former till 1953 and the latter till 1949. Upon the establishment of the Central African Federation he became the first Prime Minister. He retired in 1956 simultaneously with his elevation to the peerage.

Mamba (*Dendraspis angusticeps*) Group: Elapidae. Highly poisonous snake, found in dense vegetation throughout Natal, Zululand, the Eastern Transvaal and Rhodesia. *Green Mambas* reach a length of about 9 feet, and belong to the creeper-covered bush, those in sunny areas being of darker hue; mating takes place between green and black varieties and the young hatch sometimes green and sometimes black. The Black Mamba belongs to more open country and grows to 12 feet and more. Colour in snakes generally is puzzling and seems connected with diet, sunlight and surrounding colours, the same species being variable. Another variety, 8 feet long, named Gough's Mamba (*Dendraspis mamba*) was discovered in the Transvaal in 1910. The venom of these snakes is recognised as the most terrible of any in South Africa, death being likely to take place within a few minutes. *See* SNAKES.

Mambone. Small trading centre in Mozambique on Sabi River.

MAMMALS OF SOUTHERN AFRICA

by

C. J. SKEAD

Kaffrarian Museum, King William's Town

SOUTH of about 10° latitude there are some 350 species, of which 315 are on land and 35 in the seas. Land mammals range from the pigmy shrew of a few ounces in weight to the 6-ton elephant, while marine mammals include whales, dolphins, dugongs and seals.

Although Africa's rich antelope fauna of 39 species, and its 38 species of large carnivores, have stolen the popular limelight, their respective numbers are far less than the 88 species of rodents (rats, mice, squirrels, porcupines, etc.) and the 89 of bats. There are about 14 species of whales and many dolphins, while Cape fur seals of the west and south-west coasts are occasionally joined by vagrant elephant-seals (and in one instance the crab-eating seal) from Antarctica.

In the highest order of Primates, the

Chacma and yellow baboons, the grey and Samango monkeys are well known. Bush-babies of Rhodesia and Zambia make fascinating pets when tamed.

The Insectivores include the tiny pointed-nosed, mouse-like shrews, seldom seen by humans. The rat-sized elephant-shrew hops, kangaroo-like, in dry rocky places. Hedgehogs, despite their use as *muti* in witchcraft, are still fairly numerous. Bats sleep in natural caves in their thousands, or inhabit house-roofs and churches. The large dog-faced fruit-bats damage fruit; otherwise bats are valuable in insect control. Golden moles, with their raised surface tunnels, known to gardeners, are widespread. These must not be confused with the destructive mole-rats, also common inhabitants of gardens. Interesting among them is the giant forest mole of the south-east Cape.

Carnivores such as jackals, dogs, foxes, cats and mongooses fell heavily before Man's expansion in Africa. Lions, cheetahs, hyaenas and wild dogs are now found in reserves. Civets, genets, grey cats, the small mongooses, the tough-skinned honey-badgers or ratels the small foxes and the otters still persist, while the maanhaar-jakkals, or maned jackals, live almost entirely on termites, a strange diet for an animal allied to the dogs.

Elephants, rhinoceroses, hippopotami, pigs, giraffes and zebras need no comment. The nocturnal antbear, which thrusts its long sticky tongue into the galleries of termite mounds when gathering food, is rarely seen. The scaly ant-eater, with its heavily-plated tortoise-like shields in place of hair, is now very scarce. The diurnal dassie or rock-rabbit is a major pest in areas where predatory cats and foxes have been reduced. Its nocturnal relative, the bush dassie, is best known for the horrid stridency of its voice.

Now mostly confined to reserves or protected on farms are the antelopes, which were once so plentiful that early chroniclers referred to the veld as being 'covered with game as far as the eye can see.' Two species have been exterminated, the blue antelope of the Southern Cape, a relative of the roan and the sable; and the quagga of the Cape and inland plateaux. The bontbok, the mountain zebra and the Cape hartebeest have been saved from the same fate. Otherwise wildebeest, waterbuck, eland, nyala, rietbok, kudu, etc. persist. The smaller duiker, steenbok, bushbuck, dik-dik, etc. hold on precariously. Interesting among these is the klipspringer, which has a coarse 'spiny' covering of hair instead of the normal soft hair.

While the large mammals have decreased, the insignificant rodents flourish. Porcupines are common; cane-rats, as large as guinea-pigs, occupy eastern coastlands; spring-hares emerge from burrows at night to hop about on their long back legs; ground-squirrels, often miscalled mongooses, abound on the inner dry plateaux; flying squirrels glide between trees in tropical forests, supported by a membrane of skin between fore-leg and flank. Water-rats, tree-rats, striped mice, gerbilles, dormice, rock-rats, pouched-rats, fat mice, field mice, each in its natural niche, are not all inimical to Man. The mole-rat ravages garden vegetables and bulbs. One of its kin, the Cape sand mole-rat of the Cape coastal plain, grows to the size of a guinea-pig. Red hares, Cape hares, veld hares and river hares are surface dwellers, unlike the burrowing rabbits of Europe.

Mammals are adaptable to many climatic and geographical variations. Some are restricted in habitat, e.g. to forests or the vicinity of water, but many a species ranges from the dry Kalahari to sub-tropical and tropical coastal areas in Zululand and northwards, and/or to the elevated coldness of Basutoland. Those in the dry parts are generally paler than those in the moist areas.

Mammals are drab in colour except the zebras and cats, where stripes and spots relieve the monotony. The senses of smell, hearing and sight are acute in a world of keen competition. Horns vary from straight points in duikers to the wide spirals of kudus or the heavy bosses of buffaloes. Sometimes both sexes have horns, sometimes only the males possess these secondary sexual characters, which are not primarily defence weapons. The mechanism of the stink muishond, or pole-cat, is a nauseating fluid ejected voluntarily from glands under the tail. The insignificant shrews often possess a musky scent which cats avoid.

Alien mammals which have become part of the 'wild' fauna are the destructive house rats and house mice; the tree squirrels of the Cape, attractive but troublesome; fallow deer which are so adaptable that their resistance to drought is often superior to many indigenous antelopes; and the European rabbit which fortunately is confined to coastal islands, e.g. Robben Island in Table Bay and Bird Island in Algoa Bay.

Mamre. Mission station near Malmesbury, Cape Province. Population: 2,355, including 8 Whites. Originally known as Groenkloof, it was founded by the Moravian Brethren in 1808.

Manatoka (*Myoporum insulare*). A small exotic tree with fleshy leaves and inconspicuous white flowers. Grows well by the sea as a hedge or for shade.

Mandela, Nelson Rolihlahla. Bantu political leader. Born in the Transkei, 1918, son of Chief Henry Mandela, he qualified in Law in 1942. Joining the African National Congress in 1944 (q.v.), he took a leading part in the resistance movement against Government policy, and in 1952, under the Suppression of Communism Act, was restricted to the Magisterial District of Johannesburg. He was charged with high treason in 1956, but acquitted. In 1964 he was one of the accused in the Rivonia Trial (q.v.). Pleading guilty to an attempt to start civil war and insurrection, he was sentenced to life imprisonment on Robben Island. In 1969 he was allowed to settle at Kimberley.

Mandini. Village near Mtuzini in Natal. Large paper mill. Population: 2,284, including 681 Whites.

Manganese. Mineral used in manufacture of steel, etc. The Postmasburg-Kuruman area of the Northern Cape, containing several hundred million tons of ore, is the most important

source in Southern Africa. In general, the ores are hard and capable of being handled and transported without crumbling. The manganese content varies from 30 to 50 per cent, with from 5 to 30 per cent iron, about 8 per cent silica and low phosphorus. In the Transvaal and Southern Cape alluvial and fissure replacement deposits have been exploited, the former deposits for the low grade requirements of the uranium recovery plants. A small amount of 40–50 Mn grade is exported from both areas.

Manica. Tribe in Rhodesia, near Umtali. *See* UMTASA *and* MASSEKESSI. Their country is highly mineralised and lies partly on the Portuguese and partly on the Rhodesian side.

Mannikin (family Ploceidae). Small weaver bird common in Natal, parts of the Transvaal and in the Eastern Province. *See* WEAVER.

Manson, Harley William Daniel. South African dramatist and poet. Born in Tanganyika on January 29, 1926, he went to St. Andrew's School in Grahamstown and served in Italy in World War II. Continuing his studies at the University of the Witwatersrand he spent some time in the British Colonial Service before becoming a lecturer in English at the University of Natal. Meanwhile he won high acclaim with his plays, including *The Magnolia Tree, The*

Green Knight, The Festival etc., which were performed not only in South Africa but by the BBC and elsewhere overseas. He won several literary awards and was reaching new heights when he was killed in a motor accident on May 29, 1969.

Mansvelt, Doctor Nicolaas. First Superintendent-General of Education in the Transvaal. Born in Wassenaar, Holland, in 1852, qualified as a school teacher, and in 1874 met the famous Dutch Reformed minister from South Africa, J. Lion Cachet (q.v.) who was revisiting the land of his birth. As a result he was appointed to the staff of the Gymnasium Boys' School in Stellenbosch. He became interested in and wrote about Afrikaans, and was appointed Secretary of the new S.A. Taalbond (q.v.) in 1890. Called to Pretoria the following year as Superintendent-General of Education, he reorganised the whole system, and began local training of teachers. Upon the occupation of the Transvaal in the South African War he resigned and returned to Holland, where he died in 1933.

Mantatisi. Chieftainess and African conqueror. She came into prominence about 1823 as the leader of the Batlokua tribe. Possessed of great military gifts, she organised a vast horde of warriors, who descended upon the neighbouring tribes, most of whom they wiped out. Her name was one of terror, rivalling that of Tshaka (q.v.) She was responsible for depopulating the greater part of the present Transvaal and Orange Free State. In her honour the tribe was known as Mantaties. Little is known about her personally; she was the mother of the Chief Sikonyela, with whom Pieter Retief (q.v.) came into contact. She died about 1830.

Mantis (*Mantis masta*). Insect also known as Hottentot God (q.v.).

Manufactures. While manufactures in South Africa began with the advent of the first settlers, their true start may be reckoned from the installation in the 1820's of the first steam engines at the Cape. This allowed operations on a more than purely manual scale. Lack of population, the indifference of Government and the hostility of importers held up progress for many years, South Africa being sarcastically referred to as 'the Land of Samples.' Exhibitions in Cape Town in 1877 and 1884, in Port Elizabeth in 1885, in Grahamstown in 1887 and in Kimberley in 1892 gave enterprising local pioneers a chance of showing their wares, but at the close of the century the country could offer little except velskoens and similar roughly made footwear, wagons and other vehicles, simple furniture, beer and brandy and attempts at canning and confectionery. The first Industrial Census in the Cape Colony was held in 1891. The growth of nationalism, as expressed in the Afrikander Bond (q.v.), brought the first demands for protective tariffs, which gained support from Cecil Rhodes (q.v.). The opening up of the Diamond and Gold Fields, with their resultant demand for machinery, laid the foundations for an engineering industry in Cape Town, Durban, Kimberley, Port Elizabeth and Johannesburg. At Modderfontein (q.v.) a large explosives plant was built. The South African War gave a stimulus to the use of Begbie's Foundry in Johannesburg (destroyed by explosion) and the Netherlands Railway Company's workshops in Pretoria for the production on a modest scale of munitions for the Republics, while the making in besieged Kimberley of the gun 'Long Cecil' (q.v.) was another sign of the country's possibilities. At Sweetwater, near Pietermaritzburg, S. L. Green attempted to smelt local iron ores. Despite the post-Boer War slump progress was made, including the building of the Rhodes-sponsored De Beers Explosives Works near Somerset West in 1902, the opening of a similar plant at Umbogintwini by Kynochs in 1908 and the start of Lever Brothers' Soap Works in Durban in 1910; but in spite of slight tariff concessions the country still lagged far behind the other dominions. In 1911 the Industrial Census showed a gross output worth £17,249,000. World War I, which cut off supplies from abroad, gave South African industry its first big chance; by 1916 the output figure had risen to £40,435,000 and in 1921 to £98,308,000. The Hertzog Government's policy of protecting tariffs gave useful help. Then came a sharp drop due to a slump, and not until 1928 was the latter figure passed, at £106,770,000; but the world depression sent the output back to £90,948,000 in 1932. By 1934, however, all past records were left behind at £131,597,000, and the rise has continued since then without a break. On the eve of World War II in 1939 South Africa's manufacturing output stood at £199,617,000. When the struggle ended in 1945 and fresh shortages had stimulated enterprise even more than in 1914–18, the total was £417,438,000. Post-war development put this far in the shade, and the yearly output of South Africa's factories is today over R5,500,000,000. Together they employ about 1,007,000 people, of whom nearly 260,000 are White. The chief manufacturing area is the Witwatersrand, with Johannesburg as its centre, including as its outliers Vereeniging, Vanderbijlpark, etc. Next come the Western Province, Durban and Port Elizabeth. Equally impressive in proportion is the rise in manufacturing in Rhodesia, which, from almost negligible totals before World War II, now produces goods worth about £150,000,000 and employs about 120,000 people, including 16,000 Whites.

Manzini (formerly **Bremersdorp**). Original European capital of Swaziland. Named after A. Bremer of the trading firm of Wallenstein and Bremer, who helped to found it in 1890, and renamed Manzini in 1962. Being only a few miles from the Swazi king's kraal it became the centre of white settlement, and, after 1894, of such white administration as existed. Looted and destroyed during South African War, but later rebuilt, Bremersdorp became a road transport centre; was proclaimed a township in 1918, but was superseded as official capital by Mbabane. Population: 16,000, including 650 Whites.

Mapumulo. Village in Natal. Population: 110, including 40 Whites.

Mapungubwe. A group of ruins in the Northern Transvaal on the summit of an isolated hill near the Limpopo River. The word Mapungubwe itself signifies the 'Hill of Jackals.' On December 31, 1932, a farmer, E. S. J. van Graan, accompanied by his son, discovered a way to the summit of the hill, where, in addition to a number of structures, he found a considerable quantity of gold ornaments of great beauty and value. This led to further expeditions, which prompted the Government to place the whole area under official protection. Mapungubwe is believed to be associated in its origins with Zimbabwe (q.v.).

Maquassi. Village in the South-Western Transvaal on the main line to Kimberley. As a White settlement it is the oldest in the Transvaal, founded as a Wesleyan mission station by the Rev. Samuel Broadbent in 1823 and abandoned 3 years later. During that time the first White child in the Transvaal was born there, and the first printing done. The present township was laid out in 1910. The name is derived from a Bushman word meaning an aromatic plant, *Croton gratissiumum*. Population: 1,850, including 620 Whites.

Marabastad. Village on the railway from Pretoria to Pietersburg, named after a native chief. Established about 1880 as a result of gold discoveries—

found to be disappointing—and used as the site of a fort by the British during the First South African War. The ruins of this structure are now a National Monument.

Marabou (*Leptoptilos crumeniferus*). Large bird found in the northern part of South Africa, occasionally visiting the Kruger Park. It is a scavenger, like the vultures, and has a similar ugliness, with dark, slaty back, whitish rump, huge bill and bare neck drawn down between its shoulders. A pink pouch beneath the bill completes its unsightly appearance. *See* STORK.

Maraisburg: 1. Original name of Hofmeyr, Cape Province (q.v.).
2. Town on the Witwatersrand named after an early mining magnate Piet Marais. Now part of Roodepoort, with which it was united in 1905. *See* ROODEPOORT-MARAISBURG.

Marais, Eugene Nielen. Afrikaans author. Born near Pretoria in 1872, he was educated in Paarl, and became a contributor to *De Volksstem*. After serving in the editorial departments of the pro-Kruger English paper *The Press* in Pretoria and of *The Observer*, he was appointed editor of *Land en Volk* in 1892. Here and as correspondent for the London *Times* he showed exceptional gifts as a writer, but in 1898 he decided to change his career. Proceeding to England, he studied medicine and then changed to the law. After exciting adventures in the South African War he settled for some years in the wilds of the Waterberg where he developed outstanding ability as a student of animal life, particularly of baboons and ants. In 1917 he returned to Pretoria to practise as an advocate until, in 1921, poor health made him settle as an attorney, first in the Transvaal village of Erasmus, and then, until 1927, in Heidelberg. During this time he had been writing a great variety of works in classical Afrikaans—poetry, drama and natural history. His *Burgers van die Berge* was translated into Eng-

lish as *My Friends the Baboons* and, like his *Soul of a White Ant* (originally *Die Siel van 'n Mier*), received an excellent press. The latter incidentally was largely taken over by Maurice Maeterlinck in his similar Flemish book on ants. Marais died in 1936.

Marais, Johannes Henoch. South African magnate and philanthropist. Born at Coetzenberg, near Stellenbosch on September 8, 1851, he began his career as a farmer, but, following the discovery of diamonds on the Vaal River, went north and made a large fortune in Kimberley. In 1892 he returned to Coetzenberg, which he very successfully developed, and in 1899 was elected to the Cape Parliament as representative for the Afrikander Bond. Thereafter he remained a strong supporter of Nationalist aspirations and helped the Afrikaner cause by leaving £100,000 for higher education in Stellenbosch. This was turned to account by the University in that town, which came into existence on April 2, 1918. Marais died in 1915.

Marais, Johannes Stephanus. South African financier. Born in Fraserburg, Cape Province, April 23, 1919, and educated at the University of Stellenbosch, he became associated in January 1943 with the Federale Volksbeleggings group (q.v.) and in 1954 established the Trust Bank of Africa (q.v.).

Marandellas. Township in Rhodesia, 45 miles east of Salisbury. It lies at a height of 5,440 feet above sea-level and has a population of 1,680 Whites and 5,000 Africans. The name is derived from that of a local chief who lived there at the time of the first European occupation, Marandellas being one of the first townships in Mashonaland. Much of its importance is derived from the fact that there are three large private schools for boys, namely Ruzawi, Peterhouse and Springvale. Nearly an eighth of the entire tobacco production of Rhodesia comes from this area, and there are a number of factories in the township.

Marble. Large deposits of this stone are exploited at Marble Hall in the Transvaal. While under the German régime the Karibib quarries in South-West Africa maintained an export trade. Valuable marble deposits also exist near Port Shepstone on the Natal South Coast.

Marble Hall. Marble quarries near Groblerstad, Transvaal. Population: 1,218, including 382 Whites.

Marburg. Norwegian settlement near Port Shepstone, on the South Coast of Natal, established in 1882 by a group of emigrants from Bergen and elsewhere. It still maintains its character including a Norwegian church and other institutions. Population: 4,067, including 658 Whites.

Marematlu. Freedom Party political organisation in Lesotho (q.v.), pro-Royalist in policy.

Marengo. *See* MORENGA.

Margate. Seaside resort on the Natal South Coast, which has undergone spectacular growth since its foundation in 1930, until it is now one of the largest towns in Natal, with many hotels. The traffic is mainly due to the excellence of the bathing. Population: 2,000 including 1,392 Whites.

Mariannhill. Large Catholic mission station near Durban, founded by Abbot Franz Pfanner in 1882. It is run by the Trappist order and includes workshops for many trades, a hospital, guest house, etc. Population: 11,504, including 326 Whites.

Mariental. Founded in the last century by German missionaries as a station, in South West Africa, it has developed into a village on its own. Karakul-breeding centre. Population: 6,350, including 2,150 Whites.

Marikana. Village near Rustenburg, Transvaal. Population: 1,995, including 387 Whites.

Marimba. Native name for Kaffir piano (q.v.).

Marine Diamond Corporation Limited. Company formed in South West Africa on June 15, 1961, with a capital of R10,000,000, for recovering diamonds from the sea bottom. Operations began in October 1961 under S. V. Collins (q.v.) and certain companies controlled by him and other interests. A sea-going tug of 759 tons, equipped for prospecting and processing, recovered the first stones in Wolf Bay, south of Lüderitz, November 15, and on December 9 brought 45 gem diamonds, representing 8·96 carats, to Cape Town. Further prospecting along the South-West African coast met with success. In August 1962 Barge No. 77 was put to use in the Chameis area. Measuring 165 by 45 by 10 feet, and equipped with 12-inch airlift, this "floating mine unit" accommodated a staff of 56. By June 1963 she had recovered nearly 52,000 carats, representing 116,369 diamonds, but on July 1, 1963, was driven ashore by gales and lost. A new unit, Barge III, started within 80 days and continued the successful programme. A self-propelled unit, "*Diamantkus*," arrived from the United States August 1, 1963, with larger equipment, and started work January 8, 1964. By January 31, 1964, production value was R1,435,000. The Marine Diamond Corporation was ultimately taken over by the De Beers group, whose vessel *Rockeater* carried out extensive prospecting, with the barge *Pomona* engaged in mining. Underwater output however has been on the downgrade in recent years, falling from 134,514 carats in 1967 to 82,421 in 1968. Among other companies operating near the same coast is one controlled by the international oil magnate, Paul Getty. *See also* DIAMOND INDUSTRY IN SOUTHERN AFRICA.

MARINE RESOURCES OF SOUTHERN AFRICA
by
DR. C. J. MOLTENO

THE southern half of the African Continent has on its west coast a rich marine life which is being fairly intensively exploited by Angola, the Mandated Territory of South West Africa and the Republic of South Africa, Japanese refrigerated tuna boats continuing to fish the high seas off the South African coast, transshipping their catches in Cape Town. Russian, Spanish and other fishing craft are much in evidence.

Of the total annual landings on the African Continent of approximately 2,000,000 metric tons of fish, Angola, South West Africa and the Republic of South Africa account for over 1,500,000 tons.

The reason for the abundant fish life in the waters of the west coast is the northward-moving Benguela current which in the zones of offshore winds causes upwelling of cold, nutrient rich water, which provides the basis for a prolific growth of plankton. On the east coast the waters are influenced by warm southward-moving currents of tropical origin and deficient in essential salts, with the result that no fisheries of any importance have been developed along this seaboard. The west coast, besides having hydrological conditions conducive to an abundance of marine life, has a fairly wide continental shelf stretching from Cape Town to near the border of Angola. This has made possible a flourishing fishery based on the bottom trawling of various species of demersal fish such as the Cape Hake, *Merluccius capensis* (Castlenau), Kingklip, *Genypterus capensis* (Smith) and Soles, *Austroglossus* species.

North of South West Africa the cold Benguela current starts moving away from the land and is replaced by warmer waters along most of the Angola coastline. In these mixed waters a prolific fish life is being intensively exploited by the Portuguese. Still further north the Benguela current flows westward to form the south equatorial current.

The Republic of South Africa and the mandated territory of South West Africa was in 1968 catching some 1,206,500 short tons of fish per year. Of this total the deep sea trawlers, based chiefly at Cape Town and operating as far north as Walvis Bay, accounted for about 121,000 tons, of which about 65 per cent consisted of Cape Hake.

The trawling industry was started in South Africa towards the end of the last century and today is without doubt the most highly organised and efficiently run branch of the fishing industry. Trawled fish is processed into a wide range of products while the waste material is used to make annually some 6,000 to 7,000 tons of white fish meal and 200,000 gallons of liver oil, containing Vitamin A.

The inshore fishery in the Republic and South West Africa has, since World War II, expanded so much that today it far surpasses the trawling industry, both in total landings and value of catch. The reason for this rapid growth of the fishery is very largely the result of the development of the fish meal and oil and canning industry based on pilchards, *Sardinops ocellata* (Pappe), maasbankers, *Trachurus trachurus* (Linnaeus) and mackerel, *Scomber colias* (Lowe). The 1968 landings of these species in the Republic and South West Africa were of the order of 1,046,000 tons, of which about 1,000 tons were maasbankers; 99,000 tons mackerel; and the rest pilchards. These fish accounted for 250,000 tons of fishmeal and 50,000 tons of canned fish, which with the fish oil included has a total value of from R35,000,000.

Another extremely important section of inshore fishery in the Republic and South West Africa is the freezing and canning of the rock lobster, *Jasus lalandii* (Milne Edwards (Ortmann)). This crustacean is fished from Cape Town to about 40 miles north of Luderitzbucht; while the beds surrounding the islands of the Tristan da Cunha group, some 1,500 miles west of Cape Town, are fished during the summer months by South African refrigerated boats. The total production of frozen and canned rock lobster tails, for the Republic and South West Africa, ranges up to 6,000 tons per annum.

Very large rock lobster breeding grounds discovered on Seamount Vema, in 1959, some 1,500 miles north-west of Cape Town were visited by ships of many nations and temporarily exhausted.

Apart from the rock lobster fishery, the crustacean and mollusc resources of Southern Africa have hardly been developed at all. Shrimps are found in the warmer waters of the Indian and Atlantic oceans and are fished on a small scale in the Portuguese territories of Mozambique and Angola, but landings are small. Oysters are fairly plentiful along many parts of the coast, but have never been fully exploited along scientific lines. Recently, however, at Knysna in the Cape Province an attempt has been made with government assistance to build up an Oyster-farming industry.

Abalones *Haliotis* or perlemoen—as they are known locally—are abundant in many areas of the Cape coastal waters

and the canning of them for export to the Orient has, after many vicissitudes, developed into a small but stable industry.

Line fishing, although a poorly organised section of the South African inshore fishery, accounts for a considerable volume of fish, which in some years has been estimated to reach as high as 33,000 tons.

At Gansbaai in the Cape Western Province, the line fisherman, with the assistance of the government-sponsored Fisheries Development Corporation of South Africa Ltd., have formed themselves into a successful Fishermen's Co-operative.

The most important of the line fish is the Snoek, *Thyrsites atun* (Euphrasen), which usually represents about one-third of the total landings. Tuna fish are found in the warmer waters between Mossel Bay and St. Helena Bay, and provide game fishing for sport anglers, although the Division of Fisheries is continuing experimental fishing in this field. During 1964 some 4,000 tons of frozen tuna were exported but by 1968 this enterprise had disappeared.

A fairly large shark fishery exists in the Cape, based on the Vaalhaai or Soupfin shark, *Galeorhinus galeus* (Linnaeus). This species, of which the carcase is salted and dried for consumption by Africans, has a liver rich in Vitamin A.

Whaling has for many years been carried out from shore stations in South Africa. At present there is one station at Durban and another on the West Coast near Saldanha Bay.

Marion Island. Small island lying approximately 1,200 miles south-east of Cape Town in the Antarctic Ocean, and annexed to the Union on January 4, 1948, by an expedition carried by H.M. South African Ship *Transvaal*. This was followed by the similar occupation of Prince Edward Island,

13 miles off. Although the islands had been previously visited, and had been mapped in 1873 by the famous survey vessel H.M.S. *Challenger*, they had never been put to permanent use. The purpose of the South African occupation was to set up a meteorological station, maintained on Marion Island

ever since and relieved at approximately yearly intervals.

Maritzburg. *See* PIETERMARITZBURG.

Maritz, Gerhardus Marthinus. Voortrekker leader after whom Pietermaritzburg is named. Born near Graaff-Reinet in 1798, and after receiving a good education, practised the trade of a wagon-builder. He joined the party of Graaff-Reinet emigrants in 1836, entered the present Orange Free State, and on December 2, 1836, was elected President of the Burger Council. The following year he shared with A. Hendrik Potgieter (q.v.) command of the punitive commando sent against Moselekatse and his Matabele warriors. Though the venture was successful, differences arose, and Maritz joined Pieter Retief on his trek across the Drakensberg into Natal. After the murder of Pieter Retief, he was selected to lead the commando against the Zulus, but stood back in favour of Potgieter. As a result of the hardships which he sustained in the war Maritz fell ill and died in 1839. In his honour and in that of Pieter Retief (q.v.) the newly-founded capital of the republic of Natalia was named Pietermaritzburg.

Maritz, General Salomon Gerhardus (Manie). South African soldier and rebel. Born in 1876, he fought with the Republican forces in the South African War, distinguishing himself by his gallantry in Natal. Later he served under General de Wet in his raids into the Cape Colony in 1900, and received charge of a commando of his own. Towards the end of the campaign he was active in the North-West Cape, organising the rising in the district of Kenhardt, and capturing the town of Springbok just before the signing of peace. Thereafter he went to Europe, and returned after the establishment of Union. When the Union Defence Force was founded in 1912 he was granted a

commission, and stationed as District Staff Officer near Upington. As such he refused in 1914 to take part in the campaign against German South West Africa, began a rebellion, and later, on October 9, 1914, joined the Germans. When the Union forces, under General Botha, took South West, he crossed over the border into Angola and later went to Portugal and Spain. For a number of years he remained in Europe, until in 1923 he returned and was tried for his participation in the Rebellion, for which he was sentenced in 1924. The advent to power of General Hertzog resulted in his liberation. He then went farming in South West Africa, but resumed interest in politics after the advent of the Nazis, starting an anti-Semitic and pro-Fascist movement of his own. In December 1940 he was killed in a motor accident near Pretoria.

Marks, Senator Samuel. South African industrial and agricultural pioneer. Born in Neustad, Russia, in 1850, he emigrated to England as a young man, where his first industrial efforts comprised the finishing of certain types of knives in Sheffield. In 1868 Marks reached the Cape where he spent his earlier years as a 'smous.' In Kimberley he attained early success and at one stage financed Cecil John Rhodes. With his cousin, Isaac Lewis (q.v.), who followed him to South Africa, he set up the firm of Lewis & Marks in Barberton, and then moved over to Pretoria. With his headquarters at the famous Zwartkoppies Estate (q.v.) he gained the lasting friendship of President Kruger. He not only set up a model farm at Zwartkoppies, but began, at Hatherley near by, the first experiments in manufacturing, the place being appropriately known as Eerste Fabrieken. Possessed of enormous vision, he tried his hand at projects as varied as brandy, jam, glass and canning. He opened up the first coal mines near

Viljoen's Drift and with Isaac Lewis established the town of Vereeniging. At Maccauvlei he created one of the largest plantations of trees in South Africa. Following the South African War, he became heavily interested in the cold storage industry at the Cape, to supply the needs of the Rand mine compounds. As early as 1896 he had been attracted by the possibility of establishing a steel industry in the Transvaal, but did not achieve success until 1913, when the Union Steel Corporation of South Africa (q.v.) started its first blast furnaces at Vereeniging. Other industries established by Samuel Marks included the production of bricks and tiles and flour milling. Appointed a senator after Union, he became famous for the shrewdness of his political judgment. He died on February 18, 1920.

Marlborough. Township six miles north of Salisbury, established in 1947. It has a population of 1,900 Europeans and 1,500 Africans. Mainly residential.

Marlin, Herschel's (*Makaira herscheli*). Ocean fish, with a bony, marlin-spiked 'nose.' The British Museum specimen, 11 feet long, was named after the astronomer, Sir John Herschel, who was at the Cape in the 1830's when it was found. Other records have been made since then: False Bay (1929), Algoa Bay (1939), Flesh Bay, near Mossel Bay (1940). About 13½ feet long is the maximum caught.

Marloth, Dr. Rudolf. South African botanist. Born in Luebben, Germany, on December 28, 1855, he studied at the University of Berlin and came to South Africa in 1883, being appointed soon after to the Chair of Chemistry at Victoria College, Stellenbosch. Later he lectured on Botany and other sciences, and soon acquired a world reputation. His monumental works include *The Flora of South Africa*, which now realises high prices. He died in 1932.

Maroela (*Sclerocarya caffra* Sond.). Tree or shrub. Leaves half to one foot long. Flowers in spikes. Drupe almost orbicular, size of a small walnut. Transvaal and Natal.

Marquard. Town in Orange Free State, founded in 1905. Population 3,232, including 973 whites. Named after the Rev. J. J. T. Marquard.

Marques, Captain Lourenço. Portuguese trader and explorer. He accompanied João da Nova in 1501 on the expedition in which he discovered Delagoa Bay (q.v.). Later, in 1545, he was sent by Dom George Teles de Meneses, Governor of the Fortress of Mozambique, in a pinnace to investigate the coast beyond Cape Corrientes. The settlement which ultimately became the city of Lourenço Marques (q.v.) was named after him.

Marracuene. Popular pleasure resort for the inhabitants of Lourenço Marques. It is also known as Vila Luiza.

Marshall-Hole, Hugh. Rhodesian pioneer and official. Born in Tiverton, Devonshire, England, 1865, and educated at Blundell's School and at Oxford. He graduated in law, 1887, and in 1890 joined the service of the Chartered Company, reaching Rhodesia in 1891. He served in the Matabele Rebellion of 1896 and in the South African War. After being sent to recruit labour for Rhodesia in Arabia in 1901, which venture proved a failure, he became Administrator of North-Western Rhodesia (1903 and 1904). Later he became Civil Commissioner in Bulawayo, which post he held until 1908. After several other appointments he retired in 1913. He served in World War I; wrote several books and died in 1941.

Marsh Rose (*Orothamnus zeyheri* Meisn.). Erect sparsely branched shrub, about 6 feet. Moist mountain slopes. Flower-heads up to 3 inches long, consisting of rose-red spatulate bracts,

Marsh Rose

surrounding the much shorter cluster of lemon-yellow flowers. Caledon Division. Very rare. Flowers April–October. *See* PROTEA.

Martin (Family Hirundinidae). Small, long-winged bird, very strongly represented in South Africa, some species being migratory. It differs from a swallow (q.v.) in being more stocky in build, more brown-and-white in colour and in having an ordinary tail. Sand Martins nest in the holes of banks, the South African Sand Martin in small colonies, the Banded Sand Martin (a migrant to warmer parts) in pairs. Hundreds of Rock Martins sit in lines along the Cape Town Houses of Parliament ledges, and nest on rock faces or house walls.

Martinus Wesselstroom. Original name for Wakkerstroom (q.v.).

Marydale. Formerly Draghoender. Village in North-West Cape Province. Trading and asbestos mining centre. The original name, signifying 'Dragoon' in Dutch, was that of a Hottentot chief. Population 1,150, including 300 Whites.

Maseru. Capital of Lesotho (q.v.). Founded 1880. Population: 6,000 including 600 Whites.

Mashona. African tribe in Rhodesia. Their origin is little known, but they are believed to have occupied much of their present territory as far back as the 16th century. Of peaceful disposition, they were noted for their skill in iron-working as well as in trade. They washed for gold in the rivers and manufactured mats, which they sold to other races. About 1840 the country was invaded by the Matabele (q.v.) who killed the Mashona on a very large scale and drove the survivors into the hills, where they lived in strongholds among the rocks. Many of them were made slaves by the Matabele. Upon the arrival of the Pioneer Column in 1890, the Mashona submitted without much trouble, but raids against them by the Matabele continued. In 1895 they joined in the Matabele rising against the Whites. Today they are mainly engaged in agriculture and industry.

Mashona

Mashonaland Herald and Zambesi Times. *See* RHODESIA HERALD.

Mashukulumbwe. Tribe in Zambia, living on the Kafue River and

Mashukulumbwe

Lukanga Swamp, west of Broken Hill. Of Bantu origin, they are of two different types, tall and handsome, and short and bull-necked. They are known chiefly for their strange head-dress, the hair growing nearly 4 feet into a long tuft. Formerly extremely warlike, they have been peaceful under European control. Also known as Ila.

Mason, Sir Arthur Weir. Judge-President of the Transvaal. Born in Palmerton, Pondoland, and educated at Bath and at London University. Returning to South Africa in 1880, he qualified as an attorney and was admitted as an advocate in 1881. After practising in Durban he joined Hathorn & Mason of Maritzburg, and in 1896 was appointed judge in Natal, being transferred to the Transvaal Bench in 1902. He became Judge President in 1923 and died on June 8, 1924.

Massekessi (also spelt Macequece and Masse-Kasse) **Incident.** Diplo-matic crisis which arose between the British and Portuguese authorities in regard to the Portuguese frontier between Mozambique and what became Southern Rhodesia. Basing their claims on the travels of early Portuguese explorers and missionaries, the authorities at Lisbon declared Manicaland within the jurisdiction of the Portuguese Crown. This was disputed by the British South Africa Company, and when, early in 1891, a British force established a fort at Massekessi on the eastern border, Portuguese troops drove them out and hauled down the British flag. This caused great offence and military action was promptly taken, under Captain, afterwards Sir, Melville Heyman (q.v.). The Portuguese finally withdrew and on May 14 the Union Jack was again hoisted. *See* MACEQUECE.

Master of the Supreme Court. Official charged with the supervision and, if necessary, custody of deceased and insolvent estates. There are four Masters of the Supreme Court in South Africa, one for each province, with their seats in the respective Provincial capitals. There is an Assistant Master in Kimberley, and, since 1956, in Grahamstown. The Master has powers of control over Executors, Trustees of Insolvent Estates, guardians and tutors of minors and lunatics. Unclaimed moneys are paid over to him and kept by him in the Guardians' Fund.

Masupha. Basuto chief. Third son of Moshesh (q.v.). He first came into prominence in 1853, when he attacked the chief Sikonyela. Of a warlike and restless disposition, he invaded the country of the Pondos in 1858, but was defeated. His father lost control over him, and he carried out various raids on his own account. When Moshesh died, his son, Letsie, was not able to keep his hold on the seat of government at Thaba Bosiu, where his place was taken by his brother

Masupha. In the Gun War (q.v.) in 1880, Masupha was one of the main leaders of Basuto resistance, and made an attack on British Government headquarters at Maseru. He continued his resistance but was finally persuaded to accept the jurisdiction of a magistrate. Becoming involved in frequent disputes with his neighbouring chieftains, he defied the Colonial government. In 1897 he again went to war with Lerotholi (q.v.), who sided with the authorities. He was defeated and died a few months later.

Matabele. African tribe living principally in Rhodesia. More correctly Amandebele, the name meaning 'Those who disappear.' Originally a branch of the Zulu people (q.v.), their origin is traced to the revolt of their leader, Moselekatse (Umsiligaas, also known as Silkaats to the Voortrekkers). Having been given command in 1817 by Tshaka (q.v.) he failed, after a successful raiding expedition, to send the due tribute to his overlord. Tshaka immediately sent a punitive expedition to wipe out him and his followers, whereupon Moselekatze fled across the Drakensberg. There he began to exterminate the inhabitants of what is now the Orange Free State and the Transvaal. Coming into conflict with the Voortrekkers in 1836, he was defeated at Vegkop and Mosega, and finally trekked north across the Limpopo to settle as the Matabele. Henceforth they were recognised as the paramount military power in this part of Central Africa, with the Mashonas (q.v.) as their servants. After the death of Moselekatse in 1868, power passed to his son, Lobengula (q.v.). Their military power was finally broken after the Matabele War of 1893, despite an attempt at revival in the Matabele Rebellion in 1896–1897. Since then the nation has dwelt in peace. Lobengula's family still exists, but there is no recognised Paramount

Chief. There are approximately half a million Matabele today.

Matabele Rebellion. As the 1890's advanced, progress in the colonisation of Rhodesia was so satisfactory that the outbreak of a revolt took the majority of the colonists by surprise. On March 20, 1896, no fewer than 141 Europeans were murdered in Matabeleland, while by June 14 another 103 were killed in Mashonaland. Many acts of great heroism took place, notably the drama at the Alice Mine of the Mazoe Party (q.v.). Both in Bulawayo and in Salisbury and in most other centres the inhabitants went into laager, and the position continued precarious for months. Owing to their elusiveness the suppression of the rebels proved exceptionally difficult, even after troops under Colonel Plumer (later Field-Marshal Plumer) were sent from the Cape, along with others under Sir Frederick Carrington. Fighting continued after the withdrawal of the Matabele to the stronghold of the Matopos, and might have gone on indefinitely, but for the courage of Cecil John Rhodes, who, accompanied by Dr. Hans Sauer, Johann Colenbrander, Vere Stent and two natives, Jan Grootboom and Makunga, walked unarmed into the enemy stronghold, and, after long discussions, finally persuaded the Matabele to lay down their arms. The fighting ended in October, 1897, having lasted over a year. Some 62 Europeans were killed and 139 wounded in the fighting.

Matabele Thompson (nickname for **Francis Robert Thompson**). Rhodesian pioneer and concessionnaire. Born in Port Elizabeth, 1857, he began his life on the Diamond Fields, settled on a farm on the northern frontier, but gave it up after his father was killed by natives. He was living in Bechuanaland when Rhodes asked him to organise the compound system in Kimberley. While working in early

Johannesburg, he was chosen by Rhodes, on account of his influence with the natives, to visit Lobengula, from whom he secured the historic concession on which the Charter was based. He lived in Bulawayo for two years, sat in the Cape Parliament from 1895 to 1903 and died in 1927.

Matabele War. For a long time the hostilities between the Matabele and their former slaves, the Mashona, produced friction on the frontiers of Mashonaland, which was already under European occupation, and Matabeleland, where Lobengula still held sway. Warnings were sent by the British authorities to curb the restless warriors. Matters came to a head in July 1893, when an impi of Matabele attacked a group of Mashonas near Fort Victoria. This led to the mobilisation of the British forces, and, although further delays took place, it was recognised by September that hostilities were inevitable. On the 5th of that month a column left Salisbury to join another one from Victoria. War began officially on October 3, when a force left Iron Mine Hill for Matabeleland. A battle was fought at Shangani on October 24, and a further victory was gained on November 1, when 7,000 Matabele were defeated near the banks of the Bembesi River. Lobengula, realising that his impis could make no further effective resistance, abandoned his capital, Gubulawayo, which he set on fire, and which was occupied by the forces of the Chartered Company on November 4, 1893. Through the misjudgment of the position, however, a serious setback was suffered by the British on December 4, when a patrol under Major Allan Wilson was wiped out near the Shangani River, 100 miles to the north-west. (*See* WILSON, MAJOR ALLAN.) On January 23, the death of Lobengula put a virtual end to the campaign. British troops were commanded by Major P.

W. Forbes. Fifty-three Europeans and 38 natives were killed on the European side. The Matabele losses were impossible to estimate, but ran into several thousands.

Matabele Wilson (nickname for **Benjamin Wilson**). Rhodesian pioneer. Born in Cumberland, England, 1861, he reached the Cape in 1881, settled in Kimberley and in 1883 joined Sir Charles Warren when he occupied Bechuanaland. After exploring the Kalahari, including the Makarikari Salt Pan in 1886, he went in 1888 to Gubulawayo, one of the first white men to go there. He served in the Matabele War and Rebellion, and later became manager of part of the famous Rhodesdale Ranch. Matabele Wilson died in Cape Town, where he had retired, in 1959.

Matanzima, Chief Kaiser Daliwonga. Bantu leader in the Transkei (q.v.). Born 1915, he became Chief of the Emigrant Tembu in 1943. Educated at Lovedale (q.v.) and Fort Hare (q.v.), he graduated in Law and joined Transkeian General Council. In 1956 he served on the committee for integrating the existing Bantu authorities into the Transkeian General Council and in 1962 was unanimously elected Chairman of the Transkei Territorial Authority. He was elected First Minister of the Transkei in 1963.

Matatiele. Town in the Transkei, founded in 1874 and situated near the Drakensberg. The name in the native language means 'The Ducks have Flown,' referring to a dried-out vlei. Important dairying and wool centre. Population: 3,500, including 1,100 Whites.

Matie. Traditional nickname for a Stellenbosch university student. Derived from the Afrikaans 'Tamatie' (tomato) on account of the red blazers formerly worn.

Matindere Ruins. Ancient relics in Rhodesia, located near Gutu in the Charter district. They are on bare granite, rising about 100 feet above the veld and are elliptical in shape. Altogether they measure about 250 feet by 180 feet. Adjoining them are the Chironga Ruins. (*See* ZIMBABWE, KHAMI and MAPUNGUBWE.)

Matjesfontein. Township in the Karroo, established by J. D. Logan in the 1880's as a health resort for those suffering from lung complaints. It acquired widespread popularity and was used as a base hospital in the South African War. It now also boasts a famous 'Karroo Garden.' J. D. Logan was nicknamed 'The Laird of Matjesfontein.' Population: 250 including 110 Whites.

Matola. Settlement and industrial township near Lourenço Marques, six miles from the railway. Site of a number of important factories and warehouses.

Matopos. Range of granite hills, near Bulawayo in Rhodesia, measuring about 50 miles in length and 25 miles in width, from north to south. Sotjia, the highest point, is 5,100 feet above sea-level. To the Matabele the Matopos were a sacred area, and a stronghold. The famous indaba of the Matabele Rebellion (q.v.) took place there. In 1902 Cecil Rhodes was laid to rest at World's View in the Matopos, where today other famous Rhodesians, including Jameson, Coghlan, the Shangani Patrol, etc., lie buried.

Matopos Dam. Built by direction of Cecil John Rhodes on the Matopos Estate near Bulawayo. The water extends for nearly a mile and is used for irrigation. The wall is an earth embankment, 80 feet high, 1,200 feet long, 390 feet wide at the base, and 15 feet at the top. About 700 acres are irrigable. Completed in 1903.

Matsieng. Village in the west of Lesotho, seat of the Paramount Chief. *See* MORIJA.

Matthews, Ernest Lewis. Judge and Legal Adviser to Union Government. Born in Gloucester, England, on April 12, 1871, and educated at King's College, London, and Oxford. He was called to the Inner Temple in 1895 and practised in London for a few years. Coming to the Transvaal, he was admitted in 1902 and became Legal Adviser to the Transvaal Government. After Union he became Senior Legal Adviser to the Union Government. He took silk in 1912, became a Natal judge in 1926 and retired in 1938. He died in Johannesburg on December 23, 1941.

Matubatuba. Village near Hlabisa, Northern Zululand. Population: 540, including 200 Whites.

Mauch, Dr. Carl. German explorer. Born at Stetten in Württemberg, he began his career as a school teacher, having also studied geology. He first reached South Africa in 1858 as an ordinary sailor. He visited the Transvaal and foresaw the mining of gold in the Lydenburg area. In 1864 he found gold in Tati in the corner where Bechuanaland, the Transvaal and Matabeleland meet. He trekked through the present-day Rhodesia and reported the presence of gold. His most remarkable forecast was made in 1867 when he declared that an enormous gold field would be discovered, some day, on the Witwatersrand. Mauch was one of the first white men to visit the Zimbabwe Ruins. Hardships in South Africa ruined his health and he died at the early age of 38 in 1875 through accidentally falling out of a window in Stuttgart, Germany.

Maun. Village in the north of Botswana, important as hunting and trading centre.

Mauser, Wilhelm. German gunsmith and manufacturer, born at Oberndorf on the Neckar in Germany on May 2, 1834. He was responsible for the invention of the well-known Mauser rifles which he manufactured with his brother, Paul (1838-1914). Wilhelm set up large works in Württemberg, which supplied thousands of weapons used by the Republican forces in the South African War, including both rifles and pistols. He died on January 13, 1882.

Maynardville. Open-air theatre in Wynberg, Cape Town in the grounds of an old mansion owned by William Maynard Farmer. Established in 1957 and specialising in annual Shakespeare season. Its unique beauty has won its fame even overseas.

Mazabuka. Village in Zambia, 231 miles from Livingstone, on railway to the Congo. Administrative and farming centre. Population: 1,900, including 250 Whites.

Mazoe Dam. Large irrigation dam 25 miles north of Salisbury, built in 1920 by the British South Africa Company for its citrus orchards on the Mazoe Estate. The dam wall is 100 feet high and the water is impounded for 12 miles, while the irrigable area is estimated at 10,000 acres, not all exploited. Cost about £120,000.

Mazoe Party. Famous episode in Rhodesian history. During the Matabele Rebellion of 1896 a number of settlers and officials, men and women, mostly belonging to the Alice Mine, near Mazoe, 27 miles from Salisbury, found themselves cut off. A wagonette had been sent out from Salisbury to bring in the women, but could no longer make its way through the enemy lines. Two telegraphists, J. L. Blakiston and Routledge, heroically stayed behind to send messages for help, until the wires were cut and they were slain, while the remainder,

having covered the wagonette with sheets of iron to protect the women, fought their way through the rebels, a number of them being killed. After many hours the Mazoe party ultimately managed to reach help, and were brought into Salisbury.

Mbabane. Capital of Swaziland. Established about 1909. Noted for its good climate and picturesque situation in the Mdimba Mountains. Population 14,000. The name means ' The thing that digs and crushes out hollows ' from the local rapid stream.

Mbala (formerly Abercorn). Township in the extreme north of Zambia (Northern Rhodesia), close to Lake Tanganyika. It was established in 1893 and named after Cecil Rhodes' friend and fellow-director of the Chartered Company, the Duke of Abercorn. Mainly an administrative centre, headquarters of the International Red Locust Control, the district is noted for cattle-ranching. The population is 1,140, of which 140 are Europeans. 5,400 feet above sea-level. General von Lettow-Vorbeck, commander of German troops in East Africa, surrendered at Abercorn on November 14, 1918, after signing of the Armistice in Europe. Renamed in 1968.

Mbila (formerly Fort Rosebery). Township in the north of Zambia. Established towards the end of the last century and originally named after the Earl of Rosebery, Prime Minister of England. Is near a manganese mine at Behati, and near Lake Bangweolu, which exports fish. The population is 120 Europeans and 1,140 Africans.

Mchopi. African tribe in Mozambique, supplying many recruits to the Witwatersrand gold mines; noted for the excellence of its dancers and musicians who specialise in playing a kind of Xylophone (Native piano).

Meadowlands. Bantu township near Johannesburg, Transvaal. Population: 58,959.

Meadowridge. Garden city established in 1954 in association with Pinelands (q.v.) and opened March 23, 1955. Situated south of Cape Town, near Constantia. Population: 1,063, including 1,005 Whites.

Mebos. Apricots preserved in salt according to an old Cape recipe, believed to have originated in the Dutch East Indies. The name is a corruption of the Arabic 'mush-mush,' meaning 'apricot.'

Medicine. Jan van Riebeeck, first Commander of the Cape of Good Hope in 1652 and a ship's surgeon, established the medical tradition in South Africa. One of his first tasks was the setting up of a hospital for seafarers suffering from scurvy. (*See* HOSPITALS.) Most of the medical practitioners at the outset were in the employ of the Dutch East India Company, but the Huguenot settlers (q.v.) who arrived in 1688 included several surgeons, who were among the first local private practitioners. The first record of a South African qualifying in medicine is that of Diedericus Weitner, who entered the University of Leyden in Holland in 1748.

Outbreaks of smallpox and other epidemics led to attempts at primitive public health legislation and measures for the control of leprosy. After the British occupation in 1795 stricter measures were adopted to raise professional standards, and in 1807 a 'Supreme Medical Committee' was set up, with powers to license physicians, surgeons and apothecaries. For a long time effective control of medical work in South Africa remained in the hands of the Army authorities, among whom Dr. James Barry (q.v.), the mysterious woman who masqueraded as a man, enjoyed particular prominence as Colonial Medical Inspector. To her goes the credit for improving the quality of the examinations and of the local hospitals.

Scientific combating of disease may be traced to the setting up in 1803, by the authorities of the Batavian Republic, of a 'Vaccine Committee' as a precaution against smallpox, converted by the British in 1811 into the 'Vaccine Institution.' The founding of a School for Midwives in 1810 in charge of Dr. Wehr, a German, was the first serious effort in the direction of medical education.

In 1827, or possibly even earlier, the first Medical Society was organised at Cape Town, being engaged in active discussion and in the promotion of research. In 1830 the Colonial Medical Committee was created by ordinance to control the operations of the profession, while in 1847 the *Cape Town Medical Gazette* made its appearance. The same year marked the earliest operation in South Africa under an anaesthetic. Performed by Dr. W. G. Atherstone (q.v.), District Surgeon of Grahamstown, with Dr. Haddaway of the 91st Regiment and Dr. Irwin of the 27th Regiment, on June 16, this was 'its first use out of America and Europe.' The preparation used was 'vapour of sulphuric ether.' About 3 years later, in 1850, Dr. F. L. C. Biccard first used chloroform at Cape Town.

Increasing numbers of South Africans were now going to Europe to study medicine, particularly to Edinburgh and Leyden. Various local societies were established, but over large areas the conditions remained primitive, and the traditional dependence on home remedies continued.

A Natal Medical Committee was established in 1856, but there was still little control in the Boer Republics until 1864, when the Orange Free State introduced its first legislation concerning licences. The Transvaal only followed suit in 1881.

The South African Medical Association, which took no account of political boundaries, was founded in 1883, at the same time as the *South African Medical Journal*, which still flourishes, while in 1887 the British Medical Association set up a local branch in Griqualand West (Kimberley), followed by Cape Town in 1888, Grahamstown in 1893 and Natal in 1896. The first South African Medical Congress took place at Kimberley in 1893.

Demands for medical education may be traced back more than a century, to 1858, when proposals were made for a Medical School in conjunction with the South African College, Cape Town. In 1890 the University of Edinburgh agreed to recognise certain courses in chemistry, etc., taken at the South African College by students duly proceeding to study medicine there. Similar credits were later given by other universities, including Glasgow and St. Andrews. First-year medicine was taught at Cape Town from 1904 onwards, but long delays occurred and it was not until the establishment of the University of Cape Town in 1918 that the full course was established. The first medical graduate qualified in South Africa in 1920. After the University of Cape Town, courses were instituted at the University of the Witwatersrand, which also led the way in providing facilities for dentistry. Since then the universities of Pretoria and Stellenbosch have set up medical faculties.

Practice in South Africa is today regulated by the Medical, Dental and Pharmacy Act No. 13 of 1928, with its amendments, under which the South African Medical and Dental Council was constituted as the supreme authority, with its counterpart, the South African Nursing Council. Both these have disciplinary powers and the right to accept or refuse registration.

Already in the early days of settlement a Medical Committee was set up in Rhodesia, and in 1906 a system of registration for doctors and dentists was adopted. *See also* HEART TRANSPLANTS and HOSPITALS.

Meelbol. Traditional food for infants among the Boers, composed of finely-ground maize or flour, baked while held tightly in a cloth and afterwards crushed and mixed with milk. It is of great nutritive value.

Meerkat (literally Sea Cat). Small mammal found in many parts of South Africa, including the Eastern Province, Namaqualand, Griqualand East and other areas. It usually lives in burrows and eats insects, reptiles and other small creatures. There are two varieties, the Bushy-tailed Meerkat (*Cynictis penicillata typicus*), and the Slender-tailed Meerkat (*Suricata suricatta*). Both are popular as pets.

Mees. Afrikaans name for Tit (q.v.).

Meintjes, Lourens. World Champion cyclist. Born in Aberdeen, Cape Province, on June 9, 1868, he became noted as a cyclist while still at school in Queenstown, and successively captured most South African titles at an early age. This culminated in 1893 with his winning the 100-kilometre Cycle Championship of the world at at the Chicago World's Fair, followed by a succession of similar victories in other events. During the South African War he served as captain in the Cape Town Highlanders. He later went farming in Bechuanaland and died in 1941.

Meiring's Poort. Pass through the Swartberg Mountains in the Cape Province, noted for its spectacular scenery, 2,400 feet above sea-level.

Melkboom (*Euphorbia dregeana* E. Mey.). Succulent bush up to 6 feet. Attempts have been made to use the sap for rubber production. Found in Namaqualand and South West Africa. *See* EUPHORBIA.

Melkhoutkraal. Mansion and estate near Knysna, Cape Province, home of George Rex (q.v.).

Melmoth. Village in Zululand, named after Sir Melmoth Osborne, British

Resident, who was in charge at the time of its foundation in 1879. A tourist centre. Population: 1,160, including 364 Whites.

Melon (Cucurbitaceae). Among the many cucumbers, gourds and other tendril climbers of this family are: Kaffir Watermelon (*Citrullus vulgaris*) a ground plant of the Eastern Cape; David Jieswortel (*Melothria punctata*), a climber well known all over South Africa, with red berries, small white flowers and nearly heart-shaped leaves; the Calabash of the drier areas used when dried by all South African tribes for strong beverages and souring milk; and 'Naras or Bitterpit (*Acanthosicyos hotrida* Welw.), perennial thorny wild melon endemic in coastal desert of South West Africa. Seeds eaten by Bushmen and others.

Melsetter. Township in the eastern part of Rhodesia, established in 1893 by Thomas and Dunbar Moodie, who brought the first group of trekkers there. The name is derived from the original Moodie estate in the Orkney Islands off Northern Scotland. Despite the richness of the country and the fine mountain scenery among the Chimanimani range, the place has grown very slowly. Farming is the main occupation and forestry is progressing. Population: 350, including 150 Whites.

Melton Wold. Large estate in the Karroo, about 25 miles from Victoria West, established about 1880, and today a well-known health resort.

Memel. Village near Vrede, Orange Free State. Population: 1,146, including 418 Whites.

Mendelssohn Library. *See next article.*

Mendelssohn, Sydney. South African bibliographer and book collector. Born 1861, in Bristol, the son of a rabbi, he came to Kimberley as a young man in the late 1870's and accumulated a substantial fortune, first as an employee and then as head of the New Vaal River Diamond Company. Upon retiring from business he started the finest private collection of books on Southern Africa. In addition he compiled his famous *South African Bibliography*, which appeared in two large volumes in 1911, to mark the establishment of the Union. It gave details of over 9,000 books on the sub-continent, commencing with early Portuguese publications and bringing the subject well into the 20th century. This remains the most important work of its kind. Mendelssohn died on September 26, 1917, and left his library to the Parliament of the Union, with certain moneys designed to finance the continuation of his work.

Mendi. Troopship belonging to the Elder-Dempster Line, lost through striking a mine in the English Channel. She was carrying a large number of the Native Labour Corps from South Africa. The disaster took place on February 21, 1917, nearly 700 Africans losing their lives in circumstances of considerable gallantry. A remarkable feature of the incident was that news of the loss of the *Mendi* reached remote kraals in the Native Territories of South Africa days before the official report came through by cable.

Mennell, Frederic Philip. Rhodesian geologist. Born in Victoria, Australia, 1880, educated at University College, London, and on the Continent. In 1901 he came to Rhodesia to start the Museum in Bulawayo, of which he was the first curator. He became interested in the syndicate that established the Asbestos industry, which grew into the Rhodesian and General Asbestos Corporation. Besides doing outstanding work in determining the mineral resources of the Colony, he sat in the first Parliament under Responsible Government as member for Bulawayo District and was the author of several scientific books. Died 1932.

Mentz, Colonel Hendrik. Cabinet Minister. Born in 1877 in the Wittebergen, O.F.S., he went to the Transvaal in 1887 and qualified as an attorney. He fought in the South African War under General Beyers, and established himself in practice in Pretoria. During World War I he fought in South West Africa. He was elected to Parliament as a supporter of General Smuts in 1915 and became Minister of Lands in 1920. He died in 1938.

Menzies, William. Judge, Cape Supreme Court. Born in Edinburgh on April 27, 1795, and educated there. He was a great authority on Roman-Dutch Law, prepared the first set of Cape Law Reports and became one of the first judges of the Cape Supreme Court, established in 1828. He died in Colesberg on November 1, 1850. A personal friend of Sir Walter Scott.

Mercer, Cecil William. British novelist, better known under his pen name of Dornford Yates. Born in England on August 7, 1885, he read for the Bar and during World War I served in Egypt and elsewhere in the Middle East. He became known for his humorous stories as well as for his longer books. He died at Umtali, Rhodesia, in June 1959.

Merchant (Koopman in Dutch)— Rank in the service of the Dutch East India Company. There were two grades—Senior and Junior—both being concerned with the trading activities of the Company. A Senior Merchant ranked immediately below a Secunde (q.v.).

Mercury. *See* CINNABAR.

Merriman, John Xavier. South African statesman and Prime Minister of Cape Colony. Born in Street, Somerset, England, 1841, son of Bishop N. J. Merriman of Grahamstown (q.v.). He came to South Africa in 1849, and qualified as a land surveyor. In 1869 he entered politics and joined the ministry of Sir John Molteno in 1875. He served in the government of Sir Thomas Scanlan and other premiers, holding the position of Commissioner for Crown Lands from 1875 to 1878, and from 1881 to 1884. For a while he was on the Witwatersrand, engaged in mining. From 1890 to 1893 he was Treasurer-General, and again from 1898 to 1900. He became a member of the Government Enquiry into the Jameson Raid in 1896, and drew up its report. From 1908 to 1910 he was Prime Minister and Colonial Treasurer, during which time he also became a member of the National Convention. After Union he was a private member in the Union Parliament, noted for his outspoken views and fundamental conservatism. He was a successful wine farmer at Schoongezicht near Stellenbosch. Deeply respected by the entire country, including his political opponents, he died on August 2, 1926.

Merriman, Bishop Nathaniel James. Anglican Bishop of Grahamstown. Descended from one of Oliver Cromwell's commanders, he was born in London, 1111, educated at Winchester and at Brasenose College, Oxford. Upon entering the Church, he first worked in Lancashire, where he became a close friend of W. E. Gladstone, and later in Street, Somerset, where his son, John X. Merriman (q.v.) was born. He came to the Cape in 1848 as Archdeacon of Grahamstown, and for a while was engaged in mission work, being famous throughout the country for his very long walks. In the controversy against Bishop Colenso, he sided with Bishop Gray (q.v.). Appointed Bishop of Grahamstown in 1871, he remained there until his death in 1882. Apart from his ecclesiastical work, he was a writer of some merit.

Merrivale. Village near Lions River, Natal. Population: 510, including 230 Whites.

Merweville. Village near Beaufort West, Cape Province. Population: 730, including 380 Whites.

Messina. Mining town in the Northern Transvaal, near the Limpopo River, founded in 1904 after the discovery there of large copper deposits by Colonel John Grenfell and his associates. The place depends for its prosperity on the Messina (Transvaal) Development Co. Ltd., which operates the largest copper mine in the Republic. The name Messina is a corruption of the native 'Musina,' meaning copper. Population: 12,500, including 3,500 Whites.

Metcalfe, Sir Charles Herbert Theophilus. Railway engineer and Rhodesian pioneer. Born in 1853, he was educated at Harrow and at Oxford; he entered the firm of Sir Douglas Fox, Consulting Engineer to the B.S.A. Company and to Cecil John Rhodes. As such he was connected with the survey and construction of a large part of the Rhodesia Railways, as well as their extensions through the Congo. He supervised the building of the Victoria Falls Bridge, for the design of which he was largely responsible. He was an intimate friend of Cecil Rhodes, became a Director of the Rhodesia Railways, and of the Victoria Falls and Transvaal Power Company. He died on December 29, 1928.

Methodist Church. *See* WESLEYAN METHODIST CHURCH.

Methuen, General Lord (Paul Sanford Methuen). British soldier and Governor of Natal. Born in Somerset, England, 1845, he was educated at Eton and joined the Scots Guards in 1864. He saw service on the Gold Coast in 1873, and against the Ashantis, was stationed in Ireland and from 1877 to 1881 was Military Attaché to the British Embassy in Berlin. Again served in Egypt and the Sudan and in 1884 took charge of a unit called Methuen's Horse in operations in Bechuanaland. Promoted in 1888 as Deputy Adjutant-General in South Africa, he returned to Britain, but on the outbreak of the South African War was put in command of the First Division Army Corps in South Africa. General Cronje defeated him heavily at Magersfontein. In 1902 he was wounded and taken prisoner at Tweebosch by General Delarey, who treated him with great chivalry. After holding commands in England from 1903 to 1906, Methuen became Commander-in-Chief of British troops in South Africa, where he remained from 1907 to 1909, being Governor of Natal from 1909 until Union. From 1915-1919 he was Governor of Malta and thereafter Governor of the Tower of London. He died in 1932.

Metric System in South Africa. Under the Weights and Measures Amendment Act of 1969 the gradual adoption of the Metric System was authorised in South Africa. A special ' Metrication Department ' was set up by the South African Bureau of Standards, supported by thirteen specialist committees. Following the earlier use of the Centigrade temperature scale for weather reports, came the change over to the Kilogram and Metre in retail trade from 1969. Industries and universities followed in 1970, also land surveyors. It is intended to have the conversion complete by 1973. *See also* WEIGHTS and MEASURES (CAPE).

Meurant, Louis Henri. Pioneer of the Afrikaans language, born in 1812 at the Cape, of a French-speaking father and an English mother who had immigrated in 1808. In return for financing his purchase of a press, George Greig promised Meurant's father to teach the young man printing. In this way he became involved in the disputes concerning the original appearance of the *South African*

Commercial Advertiser. After a spell as a hunter up-country, Meurant established himself as a printer in Grahamstown, where he produced the *Grahamstown Journal* and several other publications in English and Dutch. Joining the Civil Service, he became Magistrate of Cradock, and in 1860 produced what is generally regarded as the first real book in Afrikaans, *Zamenspraak Tusschen Klaas Waarzegger en Jan Twyfelaar* (*Conversation Between Klaas Truthsayer and Jan Doubter*). Although the political issues discussed have long been forgotten, the little book was of great importance as marking the recognition of Afrikaans as a language. In 1885 Meurant wrote his reminiscences under the title of *Sixty Years Ago*. He died in Riversdale, Cape Colony, in 1893.

Meyer, Dr. Frederik. South African engineer and industrialist. Born at Griquatown, Cape Province, on January 28, 1898, he was educated at the De Villiers Graaff Institute and in Berlin. He joined the South African Iron and Steel Industrial Corporation (ISCOR) soon after its foundation, and became chairman after holding key positions in the works.

Meyer, General Lucas Johannes. Boer soldier. Born in the Orange Free State in 1846, grew up in Natal and later settled in the South African Republic. Strongly opposed to the British annexation of the country, he fought in the Majuba Campaign in 1880–81. First came into prominence in 1884 by leading a Boer contingent, who backed Dinizulu (q.v.) in an intertribal war against Usibepu. In return an area of land was given to the Boers on which they established the New Republic with Meyer as President. When this was merged in the Transvaal, 1887, he was elected to the Volksraad. He held a command in the Boer forces in Natal in the South African War, signed the Peace of Vereeniging in his capacity as a

member of the Executive Council of the South African Republic, and died, while on a visit to Europe, on August 2, 1902.

Meyerton. Industrial town near Vereeniging, Transvaal. Population: 17,100, including 9,000 Whites.

Meyerton Farms. Settlement near Vereeniging, Transvaal. Population: 1,539, including 796 Whites.

Meyrick Park. Township west of Salisbury, established in 1941, with its own Town Management Board, chiefly residential. It has a population of 400 Europeans and 300 Africans.

Mhlatuzana. Settlement near Pinetown, Natal. Population: 7,260, including 20 Whites.

Mhlumeni. Settlement in Eastern Swaziland. Population 2,200.

Michaelhouse. Well-known public school for boys in Natal. Founded in Pietermaritzburg by Canon J. C. Todd in 1896, but was removed to Balgowan, its present site, north of Pietermaritzburg on the main line to the Rand, in 1901. Its preparatory school, Cordwalles, however, remained in Pietermaritzburg. Michaelhouse is the official Diocesan school for Natal, and the Bishop is at the head of the Governors.

Michaelis Collection. Art collection in Cape Town, comprising valuable Dutch and Flemish Old Masters, presented by Sir Max Michaelis (q.v.). The gift numbered 59 pictures to which additions have since been made. The collection is housed in the old Town House on Greenmarket Square, built in 1755 and skilfully rearranged in keeping with the original style by the architect J. M. Solomon.

Michaelis, Sir Max. South African mine magnate. Born in Germany in 1860, he came to Kimberley in 1878, where he entered the diamond trade. Shortly after he went into partnership with Sir Sigismund Neumann and later entered the firm of Wernher, Beit & Co. (q.v.). He retired and devoted a large part of his time to his interest in the fine arts. One of his benefactions was the foundation of the Michaelis School of Arts at the University of Cape Town, and the establishment of the famous Michaelis Collection (q.v.). Michaelis also gave liberally to the Art Gallery in Johannesburg. He died in England on January 26, 1932.

Michell's Pass. Famous road opened in 1848, giving access through the mountains to the district of Ceres. It is called after Colonel Charles Michell, Surveyor-General of Cape Colony, who was also the engineer responsible. At its highest point the pass is 1,800 feet above sea-level.

Middelburg: 1. Town in the Cape Province, founded in 1852, and named after a town in the Netherlands. Important wool and general farming centre. Near by is Grootfontein Agricultural College (q.v.). Population: 11,700, including 2,300 Whites.
2. Town in the Transvaal on the railway to Lourenço Marques, founded in 1866 under the name of Nazareth, and renamed Middelburg in 1874, also after the Dutch city. Farming centre, with collieries near by and growing industries. During the South African War the first attempts at peace negotiations took place there in February 1902. Population: 25,050, including 10,000 Whites.

Middeldrift. Village in the Eastern Cape Province, on the Keiskama River, originally a frontier outpost, but now the centre of important irrigation works. It was laid out in 1882 and given its present name to distinguish it from other fords across the river. Population: 200, including 80 Whites.

Middelmannetjie (literally 'Little Middle-Man'). Colloquial expression for strip of grass-grown earth between the wheel-tracks on a veld road.

Mietjie. Afrikaans name for Klaas's Cuckoo (*Lampromorpha klaasi*). It is green-backed, with white rump and white bands on its tail. Found from the Cape Peninsula over most of South Africa, except dry veld. The Afrikaans name gives the sound of its call. Sometimes a migrant. Its hosts are often kingfishers, sunbirds and warblers. *See* CUCKOO.

Miller, Major Allister MacIntosh. South African airman. Born in Swaziland on September 10, 1892, he was the first European born in that country. Educated at the South African College in Cape Town and at Rhodes University, he went to England in 1913 to study engineering, but when World War I broke out enlisted in the Cavalry. In February 1915 he changed over to the Royal Flying Corps, forerunner of the R.A.F., distinguished himself in France, and rose to be Flight Commander. Returning to South Africa, Major Miller carried out a series of flights round the Union, in order to stimulate enlistments for the Royal Flying Corps. Immediately after the war ended he began his efforts to start civilian flying in South Africa, but encountered many difficulties. In 1924 he was elected to Parliament. In 1925 he succeeded in persuading the Government to start an experimental service between Durban and Cape Town. Continuing his efforts to stimulate flying, he succeeded in 1929 in establishing Union Airways, which began with a fleet of 5 machines on August 26, operating between Cape Town, Durban, Port Elizabeth, Bloemfontein and Johannesburg. Many financial difficulties were encountered, and in 1934 Union Airways were taken over by the State as South African Airways. Major Miller's later years were crowded with many troubles, but he never gave up his efforts in the cause of flying. He died October 14, 1951.

Millin, Sarah Gertrude. South African author. Born in Russia in 1889, she came to the Cape as a small child, her parents settling near Barkly West. She spent much of her youth in Kimberley, where she soon showed signs of literary ability and began writing as a young girl in the magazine *The State*, set up to popularise the idea of Union. Her first novel, *The Dark River*, appeared in 1920, to be followed by *Middle Class* in 1921, *Adam's Rest* (1922) and *The Jordans* in 1923. The books that made her famous were *God's Stepchildren*, issued in 1924, and *Mary Glenn* in 1925. Many of her stories take place on the diamond diggings and deal with the problem of colour in South Africa, being noted for their sharp psychological insight. In a different field were her biographies of Cecil John Rhodes (1933) and General Smuts (1936). Mrs. Millin, who married the late Mr. Justice Philip Millin, has also written her own life (*The Night is Long* and *The Measure of My Days*) and an extensive series of books on World War II. Died July 6, 1968.

Milner, Lord. Born as Alfred Milner on March 23, 1852, in Bonn on the Rhine, he was partly of German origin. An exceptionally able administrator, he was appointed Governor of Cape Colony in 1897, and took charge of the negotiations with President Kruger, meant to avoid the outbreak of the South African War (q.v.). Unfortunately his uncompromising views led to the breakdown of last-minute discussions in Bloemfontein, 1899. After the annexation of the two Boer Republics, Lord Milner was made Governor of both the Transvaal and the Orange River Colony in 1901. His admitted aim of overcoming the power of the Afrikaner by the importation of English settlers aroused the antagonism of the Boers, but it was acknowledged that the Civil Service and other departments which he established were extremely efficient, and he undoubtedly did a great deal for the development of the country. He returned to Britain in 1905 after much of the war damage had been repaired. During World War I Lord Milner was one of the principal members of the British Cabinet. He died on May 13, 1925.

Milner's Kindergarten. Jocular nickname given to a group of exceptionally gifted young men who were brought to South Africa by Lord Milner at the end of the South African War in 1902, in order to occupy key positions in the Transvaal. Most of them came from Oxford, Cambridge and other British universities. They included John Buchan (Lord Tweedsmuir), the future Sir Patrick Duncan, Philip Kerr (later Lord Lothian), Lionel Curtis, R. H. Brand (later Lord Brand) and others, all of whom attained great distinction, either in South Africa or on the world scene.

Milnerton. Town in Cape Province, adjoining Cape Town on Table Bay. Founded in 1902. Racing and manufacturing centre. Population: 8,000, including 7,000 Whites.

Milton, Sir William Henry. Administrator of Southern Rhodesia. Born at Newbury, Berkshire, England, in 1854, the son of the Rev. William Milton, he was educated at Marlborough and in 1878 entered the Cape Civil Service. There he rose in 1885 to be Clerk of the Executive Council and in 1891 became Secretary to the Prime Minister, Cecil John Rhodes. In 1896 Milton was transferred to Southern Rhodesia as Chief Secretary and Secretary for Native Affairs, being present during the difficult period of the Matabele Rebellion. After serving as Acting Administrator in 1897 he became Senior Administrator in 1898 and Administrator proper in 1902. This post he held until 1914. He died in 1930.

Milton School. Founded in Bulawayo, 1910, and named after Administrator of Southern Rhodesia, Sir William Milton. School for boys, with preparatory and senior sections. Removed to large new buildings outside city in 1925. One of its Old Boys was the late Dr. H. F. Verwoerd, Prime Minister of the Republic of South Africa.

Mimosa. *See* PEA, WILD SWEET, and ACACIA.

Minerals. *See* individual minerals.

Mist Belt. Term used in several parts of South Africa for mountainous regions noted for their cool misty climate, particularly in Northern Transvaal and Natal.

Mitchell, Sir Charles Bullen Hugh. Governor of Natal. Son of Colonel Hugh Mitchell, originally trained for the Royal Navy, entered Royal Marines in 1852 and fought in the Crimean War, retiring with the rank of Lieutenant-Colonel. His career in the Colonial Service began in 1868 in British Honduras, followed in 1874 by British Guiana. In 1877 he first saw Natal as Colonial Secretary, being promoted in 1886 to Governor of the Fiji Islands and High Commissioner of the Western Pacific. For a while he was Governor of the Leeward Islands, 1887, and Governor of Natal, 1889, during the period of change-over to Responsible Government. His last appointment was as Governor of the Straits Settlements and High Commissioner of Borneo in 1893. He died in Singapore, December 1899.

Mitford-Barberton, Ivan. South African sculptor. Born at Somerset East, Cape Province, in 1896, educated at St. Andrew's College, Grahamstown. Served in two world wars and spent 15 years coffee planting in Kenya. After studying art in England, France and Italy, he joined the staff of the Michaelis Art School at the University of Cape Town.

Mixed Commission. Tribunal established by agreement between Britain and the United States under a treaty dated 1862, as part of their efforts to stamp out the African slave trade. It sat at Cape Town and comprised British and American judges, who were empowered to condemn as prizes slave ships captured by British or American naval patrols. Similar courts sat at Sierra Leone and in New York, and there was an equivalent agreement with Portugal. The arrangement came to an end in 1870.

Mizeki, Bernard. Bantu Christian martyr in Rhodesia. Born about 1860 in Mozambique, he was of the Shangaan tribe. Coming to Cape Town in 1886, he became a Christian and trained as a catechist at Zonnebloem College. Accompanying Bishop W. Knight Bruce to Mashonaland in 1888 he worked among his own race. He died for his faith in 1896.

Mlanje. Mountain group and plateau in Malawi, the highest point of which reaches 9,843 feet, while over 100 sq. miles average 6,000 feet. The summit is usually veiled in clouds. Famous as a health resort and for tea growing. Many settlers are established there.

M'Limo. Oracle obeyed by the natives of Matabeleland during the Rebellion of 1896, and said to have lived in the fastnesses of the Matopo hills. The African has always been uncommunicative about this subject.

Mochudi. Seat of Bakgatla tribe in Botswana. Population 17,712.

Modderfontein Dynamite Factory. The largest in the world; belongs to African Explosives and Chemical Industries. It was established in 1894, north-east of Johannesburg on a site covering several thousand acres. Besides manufacturing over 3,000,000 cases of explosives yearly, there are very large installations for the fixation of nitrogen from the atmosphere, for the manufacture of ammonia and other chemicals and for basic scientific research. Staff numbers over 4,000 of all races. Population: 7,578, including 2,379 Whites.

Modder River (Muddy River). Battlefield near Kimberley, scene of heavy fighting during the South African War early in 1900. *See* MAGERSFONTEIN.

Moederkappie. *See* ORCHIDS.

Moewe Bay. Harbour on north coast of South West Africa, 170 miles south of Cunene River (q.v.). Development began in 1969 to encourage fishing industry and mining.

Moffat, Howard Unwin. Second Prime Minister of Southern Rhodesia. Born on January 13, 1869, in Kuruman, Bechuanaland, where his father, the Reverend J. S. Moffat, brother-in-law of David Livingstone, was stationed. He was educated at St. Andrew's College, Grahamstown, and qualified as a mining engineer. Settling in Rhodesia, he was elected to the Legislative Council. Succeeded Sir Charles Coghlan (q.v.) as Prime Minister upon his death in 1927, and held office until 1933. He died in 1951.

Moffat, Robert. South African missionary. Born in Scotland in 1795, he joined the London Missionary Society in 1816, and was sent by them to Namaqualand. His first great success was the conversion of the local chief, Afrikaner. In 1820 Moffat settled at Lattakoo (q.v.), but, finding that this station was likely to be destroyed, moved to Griqua Town in 1824. The following year he went to Kuruman, where he remained. One of his major works was a translation of the New Testament into Sechuana, which he completed in 1830. Thereafter he visited England and met David Livingstone, who married his daughter. In 1859 Moffat moved to the Matabele country, where he set up the first

mission station, but had to give it up in 1870. He died in 1883.

Moggel. South African freshwater fish, also known as Mud-Mullet.

Mohair. Animal fibre shorn from Angora goats. The introduction of these animals is largely due to the enterprise of the firm of Mosenthal Brothers of Port Elizabeth, who, during the 1860's, succeeded in importing the foundation stock from Turkey, which until then had jealously maintained a monopoly. Later additional pedigree animals were brought from Asia Minor to the Cape with the help of Cecil John Rhodes (q.v.). The industry has been subject to many fluctuations, and is mainly concentrated in the Karroo and the Eastern Province. At one time, in 1895, there were over 3,000,000 Angora goats in Cape Colony alone, but today the number for the entire Republic is about 600,000. Annual exports amount to about 6,500,000 lb., and are being promoted by a co-operative society.

Mohale's Hoek. Village in the south of Lesotho, named after an old-time chief. It was the scene of an ambush in 1858, in which the Basuto inflicted losses on the Boers.

Mokhotlong. Village on the eastern side of Lesotho, famed for its inaccessibility, once reached by a difficult horseback journey from Natal, but now connected with civilisation by a jeep service and by air. Administrative post.

Mole, Giant Golden (*Chrysospalax trevelyani*). A small burrowing rodent found only in the Eastern Cape, between King William's Town and Port St. John's. Insect-eating and completely harmless. Both this and the Smaller Golden Mole (*Amblysomus hottentotus*) are without tails and are shorter, with blunter snout and deeper head, than the European mole. They have only rudimentary eyes but an acute sense of smell. Although alleged to harm farmers' crops, research shows that they live almost exclusively on insects and grubs, which they catch a few inches to a foot underground. Their only damage is therefore in disturbing young plants, while they usefully dig up the subsoil. The Golden Mole is often confused with the destructive Blesmol (q.v.).

Molepolole. Headquarters of Bakwena tribe in Botswana. Population 29,625.

Mole Rat. *See* BLESMOL.

Mole Snake (*Pseudaspis cana*). Group Colubridae. Non-poisonous species found in sandy scrub in all parts of South Africa. It lives on rats, moles and lizards, round which (as does every non-poisonous snake) it coils its body before swallowing them. The fur usually is cast out some hours later, but the bones are often digested by powerful juices. The Mole Snake is one of the few uninterested in climbing trees. It gives birth to its young alive—40 or more at a time. The colour varies—shiny black, brick red or brown with black spots. *See* SNAKES.

Mollymauk. *See* PETRELS.

Molopo River. Watercourse in Botswana, which forms the southern boundary of the Republic. It formerly flowed far more frequently than it does now and the scheme for reclaiming the Kalahari Desert put forward by Professor E. H. L. Schwartz (q.v.) provides for restoration of its waters. When flowing it ultimately enters the Orange River.

Molteno. Town in the Eastern Cape Province, formerly noted for coal mining, but now for wool. The coal was found in the neighbouring Stormberg in 1859. While no other sources were available it sold readily, but when better qualities came on the market, in the Transvaal and Natal, it could not compete. The town was established in 1884 and named after Sir

John Molteno, first Premier of the Cape. Population: 6,500, including 900 Whites.

Molteno, Percy Alport. Financier and philanthropist. Son of Sir J. C. Molteno (q.v.), he was born in Edinburgh, 1861, and was called to the Bar in 1886. Making his home in Scotland, he was elected to the House of Commons as member for Dumfriesshire (1906–1908). During the South African War he was a strong champion of the Republicans, and afterwards worked vigorously for relief. A partner in the firm of Donald Currie and Co., he had large shipping interests, established with his wife the Molteno Institute for Parasitology at Cambridge and raised over £500,000 for the relief of Vienna in 1919. He helped to found the Royal Institute of International Affairs, and died in 1937.

Molteno, Sir James Tennant. Speaker of the Union Parliament. Son of Sir J. C. Molteno (q.v.), he was born in Cape Town in 1865, read for the Bar at Cambridge and was admitted in 1889. He was Member for Namaqualand (1890–1898). From 1910 to 1918 he was Speaker. He wrote several books, and died in 1936.

Molteno, Sir John Charles. First Premier of Cape Colony. Born in 1814 in England, he emigrated to the Cape in 1831, finding his first post in the South African Public Library. In 1837, he became a trader in wool in the Karroo, fought in the War of the Axe in 1846 and continued in business until 1854, when he was elected to the first Cape Parliament. There he became known as 'The Lion of Beaufort.' A strong champion of Responsible Government, he was appointed Prime Minister in 1872. He remained in office until 1878, when he resigned because of differences with Governor Sir Bartle Frere. He was Colonial Secretary from 1881 to 1882, and died in 1886.

Molteno, Vice-Admiral Vincent Barkly. Son of the first Cape Premier, Sir J. C. Molteno (q.v.). Born in Cape Town, 1872, and entered the Royal Navy, served in the Vitu Expedition in Zanzibar, 1893, was promoted Flag Captain, 1913, and commanded several important ships in World War I, including H.M.S. *Revenge* and *King George V*. Appointed Aide-de-Camp to the King, he retired as Vice-Admiral in 1926. He died in 1952.

Moma. Harbour on the coast of Mozambique; used for the export of tropical produce. The large population of 100,000 includes about 100 Whites.

Monckton Commission. Appointed by the British Government in 1959, under the chairmanship of Lord Monckton and including representatives of many parts of the Commonwealth, to review the constitutional position of the Central African Federation and to prepare recommendations. The Commission heard several hundred witnesses and travelled great distances throughout the area concerned. Its report was issued to the public on October 11, 1960. Among its recommendations were a general loosening of the structure of the Federation, including larger representation for the African inhabitants of Northern Rhodesia and Nyasaland, the entrenchment of a Bill of Rights in the Federal Constitution, the establishment of a Council of State to prevent discriminatory legislation, and the grant of the right of secession after a term of years to individual territories in the Federation. Numerous other suggestions were put forward, notably in regard to the franchise, Civil Service, etc. In Southern Rhodesia an assembly of 60 members was envisaged with equal numerical representation for Black and White. The report was the precursor of the break-up of the Federation in 1963.

Mondlane, Eduardo. Bantu revolutionary leader in Mozambique. Born in 1921 in Gazaland, he was educated by missionaries, at the University of the Witwatersrand, in Lisbon and the U.S.A. After working for U.N.O. he founded Frelimo (q.v.) in 1962 and started a rising. He was assassinated by his own people in 1969.

Money. *See* CURRENCY.

Mongoose. Carnivorous mammal, belonging to the Civet family, and found widely in South Africa. Its ability to kill snakes is well known, but rats, mice, eggs and insects, roots and berries are all items in its diet, and it should be regarded much more as a friend than an enemy of man. There are a number of varieties, all with slim, tapering bodies and faces, long, hairy fur and bushy tails. They are shy and unaggressive, and can be easily tamed.

Monkey Bay. Pleasure resort on Lake Nyasa, and headquarters of the local steamer service. Noted for its bathing, fishing and beautiful scenery.

Monkey Rope. Lianas of various types found growing as tree-parasites in the sub-tropical forests of Southern Africa.

Monkeys. There are only three families of these Primates in South Africa: the Arboreal monkeys (Cercopithecidae) of which the Vervet (q.v.) or Blue Ape is most common; the rock-climbing Baboons (q.v.); and the Lemurs. *See* GALAGO and MAMMALS.

Monomotapa. Ancient empire, believed by early travellers to exist in the interior of Southern Africa, and shown on many maps. Its capital was the imaginary Vigiti Magna. Commander Jan van Riebeeck actually sent an expedition to find the place in 1660, but it returned empty-handed. Monomotapa was said to be ruled by an Emperor who had a 'treasure city' Davagul. The legend is said to derive from distorted accounts of native tribes.

Montagu. Town in the Western Cape Province, founded in 1850, and named after Sir John Montagu, Colonial Secretary, under whose auspices the area was opened up in 1848 after the construction of the famous Montagu Pass. Valuable mineral springs near by have helped to develop the place as a health resort. It is noted for the production of wine and fruit. Dr. D. F. Malan, before entering politics, was Dutch Reformed Minister at Montagu. Population: 6,400, including 2,700 Whites.

Montagu, John. Colonial Secretary of the Cape of Good Hope. Born in 1797, he was descended from the Earls of Manchester, a famous naval and military family. He joined the army at 17, and fought in the Battle of Waterloo, being appointed to a post in the Colonial Service in Van Diemen's Land (later Tasmania). In 1843 Montagu became Colonial Secretary of the Cape. One of his first achievements was the reorganisation of the Colony's finances and the settlement of its public debt, followed by reforms in the convict labour system, in the provision of health services and hospitals, and, above all, in improvements to the roads on which the country's transport mainly depended. He also did fine work in establishing schools and improving the administration of the courts. During the Anti-Convict Agitation of 1849, he endured considerable odium, but found his views vindicated. He died in 1852, his name being commemorated in the famous Montagu Pass, for the opening of which he was responsible, as well as in the town of Montagu, Cape.

Mont-Aux-Sources. Mountain set in the magnificent scenery of the Drakensberg (q.v.) range, commonly but not correctly believed to be the highest peak in Southern Africa. It rises to a height of 10,769 feet, but although it presents an exceedingly steep face on the Natal side, the ascent from the Orange Free State is comparatively easy. Known to the natives as Pofung (Eland), it received its present name from the early French Protestant missionaries Arbousset and Daumas, who visited it in 1836. In recent years it has become a National Park, and one of the most popular tourist and mountaineering resorts in South Africa.

Monypenny, William Flavelle. Irish journalist. Born near Armagh; studied at Dublin and at Balliol College, Oxford; became a contributor to the *Spectator* from 1891 to 1893 and assistant editor of the London *Times* from 1894 to 1899. In February 1899 he was appointed editor of the *Star* in Johannesburg. Soon after his arrival he was assaulted by the well-known Boer scout Daniel Theron, who objected to certain remarks he made about Boer women. On the outbreak of the South African War, Monypenny joined the Imperial Light Horse as an officer, served through the siege of Ladysmith and was later appointed Director of Civil Supplies under the Military Governor of Johannesburg. When the *Star* reopened in 1902 he resumed the editorship, but resigned in 1903 as he disagreed with its support of the importation of Chinese labour. His later years were devoted to writing what became a standard life of Benjamin Disraeli. It was incomplete when he died on November 23, 1912, and was finished by G. E. Buckle.

Monze. Township in Zambia, between Lusaka and Livingstone. It was established in 1938 and has a population of 110 Whites, 740 Africans and 100 Asiatics. It is chiefly a farming centre for tobacco and maize.

Moochi. Loin-cloth made of skins and worn by Zulu men. Sometimes also made of the tail hair of animals.

Moodie, Captain Benjamin. Soldier and South African pioneer. Born at Melsetter in the Orkney Islands,

Scotland, in 1789, he served in the Ross and Caithness Militia and, having lost his family property, decided to bring 200 Scottish emigrants to the Cape. Assisted by the British Government, the party arrived in 1817, three-quarters of them mechanics and the rest labourers. For each Moodie paid £20 passage money. Most of them soon found employment at Cape Town and elsewhere, while Moodie himself settled on the farm Grootvadersbosch, near Swellendam. After the arrival of the 1820 settlers (q.v.) he spent some time on the eastern frontier, but owing to the unsettled conditions returned to his estate. He died on April 2, 1856.

Moodie, Lieutenant Donald. South African historian. Born at Melsetter, Scotland, on June 25, 1794, he entered the Royal Navy in 1808 and served through the Napoleonic Wars in the Mediterranean and elsewhere. Retiring with the rank of lieutenant in 1816, he emigrated in 1820 to the Cape, where he joined his brothers, Benjamin (q.v.) and John. Having unsuccessfully tried farming, he joined the Cape Colonial Civil Service and was for a while in charge of the Cape of Good Hope Bank. From 1845 to 1849 he was Colonial Secretary of Natal, and in 1857 Speaker of the Legislative Assembly at Pietermaritzburg. To him goes the credit of having made the first serious effort to safeguard and publish early Cape archives, in which connection he issued a series, called *The Record*, now extremely rare, giving reprints of items going back as far as Jan van Riebeeck. *The Record*, although never completed, is still regarded as a classic of its kind. Donald Moodie was responsible for several other rare early historical pamphlets, some of which were issued in Natal. He died near Pietermaritzburg on August 27, 1861.

Moodie, Duncan Campbell Francis. South African poet and historian. Son of Lieutenant Donald Moodie (q.v.)

and born in Cape Town on January 24, 1838. His interest in history began while helping his father in the preparation of his *Record*. During the 1870's he went to Australia, where he settled in Adelaide and issued a newspaper, besides writing history and poetry. His most famous work was the two-volume *History of the Battles and Adventures of the British, the Boers and the Zulus in Southern Africa*, usually referred to as *History of the Battles*. It originally appeared in Sydney, was later republished at the Cape and is today scarce. It contains a mass of material not easily found elsewhere. D. C. F. Moodie died at sea in March, 1891.

Moodie, George Pigot. Mining pioneer of the Transvaal. Second son of Lieutenant Donald Moodie (q.v.), he was born in Grahamstown on January 22, 1829, and qualified as a land surveyor. Emigrating up-country, he became Surveyor-General of the Transvaal from 1881 to 1884. While living there he found gold in the Eastern Transvaal, and secured the famous Moodie Concession, on which much of the wealth of Barberton (q.v.) was later discovered. He retired to Cape Town and died at Westbrooke, near Rondebosch, on November 2, 1891.

Moodie Trek. Emigration of South African settlers to Rhodesia organised and led by Thomas Moodie, son of James Moodie, who had settled in the Orange Free State. Inspired by his cousin, Dunbar Moodie, who had gone to Mashonaland with the Pioneers, and was mining in the Penhalonga Valley, he decided to bring a party of Boers and their families by wagon to the fertile Eastern District, now known as Melsetter. The trek began at Bethlehem, O.F.S., on May 5, 1892, and after 1,000 miles of the greatest danger and hardship was completed eight months later. The trekkers established the village of Chipinga (q.v.), where their descendants are still living. Thomas Moodie died in 1894.

Mooi River (Beautiful River): **1.** Farming and trout-fishing centre in Natal, so called because of the attractiveness of its position. Creameries and other industries operate. Population: 5,700, including 1,200 Whites.
2. River in the Western Transvaal on which Potchefstroom is situated; used for irrigation.

Moolman. Village near Piet Retief, Transvaal. Population: 190, including 80 Whites.

Moor, Sir Frederick Robert. Prime Minister of Natal. Born in 1853 and educated at Hermannsburg Mission School, Natal. When 19 went as a digger to Kimberley, where he was elected to the Mining Board. In 1880 settled down as a farmer in Natal, and in 1886 was first elected to the Legislative Assembly, in which he sat until Union. From 1893 to 1897 he was Minister of Native Affairs, and again from 1899 to 1906. From 1906 until Union he was Prime Minister. In the first Union Cabinet he was Minister of Commerce and Industries and sat in the Senate until 1920. He died on March 18, 1927.

Moorddrift. Scene of the murder of a party of Boers and their families in 1854 by Makapan and his followers. *See* MAKAPAN'S GAT.

Moore, Sir Leopold Frank. Northern Rhodesian pioneer and journalist. Born in London, 1868, he qualified as a chemist and in 1892 joined the firm of Lennon in Cape Town. In 1893 he became a chemist in Mafeking, moving 5 years later to Bulawayo. He interested himself in politics between 1898 and 1902, when he proposed the importation of Chinese into Southern Rhodesia. In 1904 he went to Northern Rhodesia, opening as a chemist at 'The Old Drift,' forerunner of the town of Livingstone.

Two years later, in 1906, the town was shifted to its present site, and Moore established the *Livingstone Mail*, which he continued to edit for nearly 40 years. He was elected to the Advisory Council for Northern Rhodesia in 1918 and in 1924 to the Legislative Council. He took part in negotiations for the proposal to incorporate Rhodesia in the Union in 1922. Died in 1945.

Moorreesburg. Village in the Western Cape Province, named after the Reverend A. Moorrees, who once officiated there. It was founded in 1879, and is noted for the milling of wheat and other grain grown near by. Population: 4,500, including 2,300 Whites.

Mopane or Rhodesian Ironwood, Turpentine Tree (*Copaifera mopane* Kirk). Stout forest tree. Wood very durable, dark. Zambesi forests. *See* PEA, WILD SWEET, and PLANTS.

Moran, Bishop Patrick. Early Catholic Bishop of the Eastern Province. Born in Ireland, he came to Grahamstown in 1856 in succession to Bishop Devereux (q.v.). Bishop Moran was transferred to New Zealand in 1869 and died in 1895.

Moravian Brethren. German mission organisation, founded in 1722 in Herrnhut, Saxony, under the protection of the pious Count Zinzendorf. Emigrating through religious persecution, they adopted the still existent constitution in 1727. Apart from their work in Europe, they soon established mission stations overseas, starting at the Cape in 1737, when George Schmidt, one of the Brethren, who gained the name of 'The Apostle of the Hottentots' founded Genadendal (q.v.). Other stations followed, including Mamre near Malmesbury.

Morenga. Chief of the Bondelswarts tribe. Took a prominent part in the Herero War in South West Africa between 1904 and 1907. Finally driven over the Cape frontier, he was killed in a fight with the Cape Mounted Police in 1907. The officer responsible, Major Elliott, received a decoration from Kaiser Wilhelm II. Morenga's death marked the end of the campaign.

Morgan Bay. Seaside resort near Komgha, Cape Province. Population: 110, including 70 Whites.

Morgen. Measure of land, derived from the Rhenish system introduced by the first Dutch settlers. It equals 2·11654 acres, while an English square mile equals 302·38 morgen. According to the Rhenish system (still in official use for surveying), 144 Cape square feet equal 1 Cape square rood, and 600 Cape square roods equal 1 morgen.

Morgenzon. Village in the Eastern Transvaal, founded in 1912, the name signifying 'Morning Sun.' Farming centre. Population: 1,616, including 510 Whites.

Morice, George Thomas. South African Judge. Born in Aberdeen, Scotland, on September 18, 1858, and educated at Aberdeen University and Oxford. He was called to the Middle Temple in 1883 and, after a visit to Holland, came to Pretoria to practise, 1884. He was appointed a judge of the Transvaal High Court in 1890. After the Boer War he practised in Pretoria and took silk, holding several appointments, including President of the Swaziland Court and President of the Income Tax Court. He died in Johannesburg on November 1, 1930.

Morija. French Protestant mission station in Lesotho, founded in 1833, picturesquely situated in the west of that country. It was the scene of fighting during the war between the Orange Free State and the Basutos in 1858. Name derived from the Bible, the English version being Moriah. Near by is Matsieng, seat of the Paramount Chief of Basutoland. Morija is noted for its excellent mission press, which draws its customers from the Republic and elsewhere.

Morning Glory. See POTATO, SWEET.

Moroko. Chief of the Barolong tribe in the Orange Free State. Originally on friendly terms with British authorities, he declared himself independent when the Sovereignty was given up in 1850, and established friendly relations with the Republic. Because of the help he gave in the campaign of 1858 against the Basutos, Moroko enjoyed the confidence of the Boers, and had his lands guaranteed to him. His headquarters were at Thaba N'chu, almost the only native reserve in the Orange Free State. He entered into a treaty with the O.F.S. in 1865 and again fought for that country against the Basutos in their campaign of 1865–1866. He died in April 1880, and in July 1884 his territory was annexed to the Republic, though acknowledged as a reserve for the Barolong. See also THABA N'CHU.

Morosi. Chief of the Baphuti clan of the Basuto people. He first came into notice in the 1830's on account of his association with Moshesh (q.v.). Of warlike disposition, he held his own against the Colonial forces during the 1850's, and was left undisturbed at his stronghold in the head waters of the Orange River. In 1879 his refusal to obey the demobilisation laws of the Cape Government led to a full-dress campaign which involved the mobilisation of a considerable White force. Morosi was killed on November 20, 1878, when his mountain was successfully stormed.

Mortimer. Village on the Fish River in the Eastern Cape, centre of irrigation settlements. Near by, on Schreiner's Kop, lie the remains of the writer Olive Schreiner (q.v.).

Mos. The juice of the unfermented or partly fermented grape used at the Cape. Compare English 'must.'

Mosbolletjie. A delicious bun made with mos (q.v.) instead of yeast, according to an old Cape recipe.

Moselekatse (also known as **Umsili-gasi** and **Silkaats**). First king of the Matabele (q.v.). Born in Zululand, towards the end of the 18th century, became a general under Tshaka (q.v.), distinguishing himself in many raiding expeditions. About 1824, after a quarrel with Tshaka, he fled across the Drakensberg with several thousand followers, the nucleus of a future nation. Making his headquarters at Mosega in the present Marico district of the Transvaal, Moselekatse wiped out most of the tribes between the Orange and the Limpopo rivers. As a result of his defeat by the Voortrekkers, he finally decided to emigrate across the Limpopo. Establishing his rule over a wide area, he almost completely subdued the Mashona (q.v.). He died in 1868. *See also* MATABELE.

Mosenthal Brothers. South African commercial house. Founded by Adolph Mosenthal and his brother Joseph, who came to South Africa in 1839, and opened in Graaff-Reinet. Later branches and subsidiaries were set up in Port Elizabeth, East London and in many other places. Through their associations with Cecil John Rhodes and other leading figures, the house of Mosenthal played an important rôle in the beginnings of the diamond industry of Kimberley, and on the goldfields of the Rand. The firm is still largely occupied in produce and many other branches of commerce.

Moshesh. Paramount Chief and founder of the Basuto nation. The son of Mokachane, he was born in the late 1790's near the village of Butha-Buthe in Northern Lesotho. Possessing tact and skill, he gained the support of disorganised refugees from many other races (*see* BASUTO). After establishing himself on the summit of Thaba Bosigo in 1832, he gave a cordial welcome to the French missionaries who arrived the following year, but never allowed himself to be converted to Christianity. By an occasional submission to seemingly overwhelming force, and gradual reassertion of his power, he managed to maintain himself against both the British and the Boers, even successfully beating off a final attempt by the Orange Free State forces to storm Thaba Bosigo in 1865. He enjoyed prestige among both black and white, and died in 1870, one of the greatest men the Bantu races have yet produced.

Moshesh's Day. Public holiday in Lesotho, in honour of the famous Basuto chief, and celebrated on March 12.

Mosi-oa-tunya. Bantu name for Victoria Falls (q.v.), literally ' Smoke that Thunders '. Now also applied to the neighbouring town of Livingstone (q.v.).

Moskonfyt. Grape juice syrup prepared on Cape farms. In recent years it has been produced commercially and sold on a large scale.

Mossel Bay. Seaport and seaside resort between Cape Town and Port Elizabeth. Portuguese seafarers, including both Bartholemew Diaz and Vasco da Gama, touched there, and in 1500 Pedro d'Ataide went ashore, leaving a note of his visit in an ancient melkhout tree, now a National Monument. The present town was founded in 1848; the district was Mossel Bay, but the settlement was called Aliwal South, in honour of a recent victory gained in India by Governor Sir Harry Smith. Later this was changed to Mossel Bay. Industries include canning, paint manufacture, etc. Population: 15,800, including 5,000 Whites.

Mossel River. Seaside resort on Walker Bay, now part of Hermanus (q.v.).

Mossie. *See* SPARROW.

Moths. *See* INSECTS.

Motor Cars. The first 'horseless carriage' in Southern Africa was introduced by J. P. Hess of Pretoria in December, 1896. It was a Benz, 1½ horse-power, built in Mannheim in Germany. Besides being demonstrated on the Wanderers Ground, Johannesburg, on January 4, 1897, it was shown at Berea Park, Pretoria, to President Kruger, who awarded a special medal to Mr. Hess on that account. Shortly after, the first motor cars in Durban and in Cape Town made their appearance. Motor transport was used on a small scale during the Boer War and increasingly after peace was signed. Rhodesia secured its first motor car in 1902, through the efforts of Major Charles Duly of Bulawayo, and in the same year the first motor bus appeared in Johannesburg. Large-scale importations of motor cars began in 1913, when 4,000 vehicles were brought into South Africa. Motor-car assembly began in Port Elizabeth in 1924. The Republic today has about 2,000,000 motor vehicles, of which about 1,250,000 are passenger cars, while Rhodesia has approximately 60,000. In 1963 the Ford Company, General Motors and other leading makers began engine manufacture at Port Elizabeth and elsewhere.

MOUNTAIN HEIGHTS OF SOUTHERN AFRICA

Name	Height above sea-level	Area
Amajuba	7,000	Natal
Anderson (*see Mount Anderson*)		
Aus	5,249	South West Africa
Avoca Peak	9,090	Barkly East
Babilonstoring	3,835	Caledon
Belingwe Peak	4,937	Rhodesia
Ben Macdhui	9,846	Barkly East
Ben Nevis	8,599	Barkly East
Bilthouers Bank	6,267	Nuweveld Mountains
Blouberg (Geodetic Beacon)	6,177	Riversdale
Bonnyvale Peak	9,638	Barkly East
Brandberg	8,276	South West Africa
Brandwag Peak	5,945	Hex River
Breslin's Kop	9,286	Barkly East
Bruintje's Hoogte	5,764	Somerset East
Buffels Peak	6,765	Hex River
Buffelshoek Twins	6,230	Hex River
Cango Berg	6,639	Groot Swartberg
Cathkin Peak	10,438	Drakensberg
Cedarberg	6,340	East Griqualand
Cockscomb	5,772	Eastern Cape
Compassberg (Kompasberg)	8,214	Sneeuberg
Constantia Berg	3,048	Constantia
Darwin (Mt.) (*see* Mount Darwin)		
Devil's Peak	3,282	French Hoek
Elandsberg	6,363	Wakkerstroom
Erongo	7,666	South West Africa
Etjo	6,953	South West Africa
Fonteintjiesberg	6,533	Hex River

Name	Height above sea-level	Area
Formosa Peak	5,500	Plettenberg Bay
Gadzema Kop	4,221	Rhodesia
Gaika's Kop	6,439	Seymour
Gansberg	7,770	South West Africa
Gatberg	6,204	Griqualand East
Giant's Castle	10,868	Drakensberg
Governor's Kop	2,780	Albany
Great Brukkaros	5,800	South West Africa
Groot Wellington Sneeukop (*see* Wellington Sneeukop)		
Hampden (Mt.)	5,247	Salisbury
Hang Klip	6,842	Queenstown
Hangklip	1,489	False Bay
Hanglip (The Dome)	5,640	Zoutpanskop
Helderberg	3,732	Somerset West
Hoëberg	4,673	Knysna
Hogsback	6,355	Amatola Mountains
Ingeli	7,447	Natal
Inyangani (Mt.)	8,250	Inyanga, Rhodesia
Iron Crown	6,976	Haenertsberg, Transvaal
Job's Kop	5,696	Natal
Jumble Peak	7,517	Griqualand East
Kamiesberg (Sittensberg)	5,130	Namaqualand
Karasberg	6,561	South West Africa
Katberg	6,007	Fort Beaufort
Keeromsberg (Geodetic Beacon)	6,808	Hex River
Kogelberg (Geodetic Beacon)	4,161	Gordon's Bay
Kolkop (Geodetic Beacon)	4,487	Griqualand West
Kwa-Mandlangampisi (Slangapiesberg)	7,435	Wakkerstroom
Lady Kok (Ku-Nolamgeni)	6,611	East Griqualand
Lion's Head	2,194	Cape Town
Lord Hill	7,240	South West Africa
Ludendorff	7,166	South West Africa
Machache	9,471	Maluti Mountains
Majuba (*see* Amajuba)		
Matroosberg	7,386	Hex River
Mauchberg	8,700	Lydenberg
Meiring's Poort Peak	6,988	Groot Zwartberg
Menisi Peak	5,000	Rhodesia
Milner Peak	6,546	Hex River
Mlembe	6,109	Transvaal-Swaziland Border
Moltkeblick	8,276	South West Africa
Mont aux Sources	10,822	Drakensberg
Mostert's Hoek Twins	6,664	Mitchell's Pass
Mount Anderson	7,494	Lydenburg, Transvaal
Mount Currie	7,297	Griqualand East
Mount Darwin	4,850	Rhodesia
Mount Joel	6,982	Griqualand East
Nauchas	6,900	South West Africa

PLATE VII: MOTHS OF SOUTHERN AFRICA

1. *Xanthospilopteryx superba* (S.A.).   2. *Egybolis vaillantina* (S.A.).   3. *Ophideres salaminia* (S.A.).   4. *Miniodes discolor* (S.A.).   5. *Euchloron megaera* (S.A. and Rhodesia).   6. *Euchroma amoena* (S.A.).

Name	Height above sea level	Area
Naudeberg	5,402	Robertson
Naukluft	6,583	South West Africa
Nooitgedacht	6,078	Magaliesberg
Ntabamhope	6,509	Natal
Okonjenje	6,240	South West Africa
Omatako	7,630	South West Africa
Ombotozu	7,300	South West Africa
Omotayo	8,800	South West Africa
Otjihanamapero	6,700	South West Africa
Ouberg	5,618	Graaff-Reinet
Paarlberg (Geodetic Beacon)	2,396	Paarl
Paresis	6,283	South West Africa
Platberg (Mtabazwe)	7,856	Harrismith
Pilanesberg	5,535	Rustenburg
Riebeek's Kasteel (Kasteelberg)	3,195	Malmesbury
Roodeberg	7,244	Hex River
Schnellskop	6,244	Woodbush Mountains, N. Transvaal
Selukwe Peak	5,073	Rhodesia
Selinda (Mt.)	3,500	Melsetter, Rhodesia
Seweweeks Poort Peak	7,632	Swellendam
Sneeukop (Cedarberg)	6,333	Cedarberg
Sneeuwkop (Geodetic Beacon)	5,221	Somerset West
Snowdon	8,926	Barkly East
Stettynspiek	5,983	Worcester
Stormberg (Vaalkop)	7,081	Molteno
Suurberg	3,238	Port Elizabeth
Table Hill	8,961	Barkly East
Table Mountain (Maclears Beacon)	3,563	Cape Town
Table Mountain	3,151	Pietermaritzburg
Tafelberg	5,431	Middelburg, Cape
Thaba 'Nchu	7,014	Orange Free State
Thaba Putsoa	10,154	Lesotho
Thabentsonyane	11,425	Lesotho
Thule	8,322	Griqualand East
Toorkop	7,222	Klein Zwartberg
Toringberg (Geodetic Beacon)	6,980	Klein Zwartberg
Twins	4,905	Jonkershoek
Umvukwe Peak	5,731	Rhodesia
Victoria (Mt.)	4,600	Rhodesia
Waterberg	6,333	South West Africa
Watershed (Geodetic Beacon)	8,184	Griqualand East
Wedza (Mt.)	4,379	Rhodesia
Wellington Sneeukop (Groot)	5,528	Wellington
Wemmershoek Peak (Geodetic Beacon)	5,793	French Hoek
Winterberg, Great	7,772	Bedford
Winterhoek Berg (Groot Winterhoekkop)	6,815	Tulbagh Road
Wolkberg	6,428	Pietersburg
Zonder Einde Berg (Pilaarkop)	5,430	Zonder Einde Mountains

Mountain Rose

Mountain Rose (*Protea rosacea* L.). Shrub 2 to 3 feet, much branched. Leaves very narrow, pungent. Flowerheads up to 2 inches long, pendulous, consisting of bright red or crimson ovate-oblong bracts surrounding the much shorter crimson flowers. Divisions of Ceres, Paarl, Tulbagh and Worcester. Mountainsides. June–November. *See* PROTEA.

Mountain Zebra National Park. Area of about 3,700 acres on the farm Babylonstoren in the district of Cradock, Cape Province, where this rare species, in danger of dying out, has been preserved, and increased in numbers. The National Park was proclaimed in 1937. *See also* ZEBRA.

Mount Ayliff. Village in Griqualand East, named after the Rev. J. Ayliff, an early missionary. Founded in 1878, it lies near the Insiza Mountains, where deposits of nickel are being opened up. Population: 700, including 175 Whites.

Mount Brukkaros. Extinct crater near Keetmanshoop in South West Africa, in desolate surroundings, for which reason it was chosen in 1929 by the Smithsonian Institution in Washington, U.S.A., for the making of observations on solar radiation. The station, organised by Dr. C. G. Abbott, was dismantled in 1931.

Mount Darwin. Mountain in the north of Rhodesia, so named in honour of the naturalist Charles Darwin by the hunter F. C. Selous. It reaches a height of 4,850 feet. Near by is a township and administrative centre of the same name, where the Magistrate is stationed. Mount Darwin acquired international prominence shortly after World War I, when a local chief, a witch-doctor and others were found to have carried out a human sacrifice to break a drought. The killing of the victim was followed by heavy rains, but those responsible were severely punished.

Mount Edgecombe. Sugar-growing settlement on the north coast of Natal, 13 miles from Durban, named after a famous estate in the West of England. Site of both the large sugar mill of the Natal Estates Ltd. and the research establishment of the Natal Sugar Association.

Mount Fletcher. Village in the Transkei founded in 1882 and named after a Captain Fletcher, who was stationed there. Population: 700, including 200 Whites.

Mount Frere. Village in the Transkei, founded in 1876 and named after Governor Sir Bartle Frere. It is at the foot of a mountain of the same name. Fighting took place near by in 1880, during the Baca Rebellion. Population: 1,322, including 350 Whites.

Mount Pleasant. Township north of Salisbury, established in 1954, with a population of 500 Europeans and 600 Africans.

Mount Selinda. Mission station of the American Board in the east of Rhodesia, noted for its tract of virgin forest, almost the last surviving there. Founded in 1890 with the encouragement of Cecil Rhodes the mission is still flourishing.

Mousebird or **Coly** (Family Coliidae). Smallish bird found only in Africa. The name is derived from the soft, rather hairy plumage as well as the way in which it creeps about among twigs. It has a tall crest, stiff, pointed tail and flies straight as an arrow, alighting upright against a tree, and often sleeping in that position. Colies are sociable birds, flying in small groups and are great fruit devourers. See BIRDS.

Mouth-Breeder. *See* CICHLID.

Mozambique. Also known as Portuguese East Africa. Officially defined as an 'Overseas Province,' this important and wealthy country covers 297,654 sq. miles (771,000 sq. kilometres) and has a population of approximately 6,600,000, of whom about 163,000 are White. Extending from 10° to 26° latitude south, it varies in width from 50 miles near Lourenço Marques, to 718 miles at its widest point. The administration is headed by a Governor-General, whose seat is at Lourenço Marques, the capital (q.v.). Mozambique is divided into nine districts, Lourenço Marques, Gaza, Inhambane, Manice, Sofala, Tete, Zambezia, Mozambique, Cabo Delgado and Nyasa. Each district is subdivided into so-called Concelhos. The Governor-General holds office for a spell of four years, renewable, and is assisted by a Secretary-General, as well as by two Provincial Secretaries. Of the European population, approximately 3,000 are foreigners, the 600 British subjects being the largest group, followed by about 340 Italians and approximately equal numbers of Ger-

mans and South Africans. The main non-European races belong to the Tonga group, who live south of the river Save, while between the Save and the Zambesi is the Karanga group. The Nyanja inhabit the north-western part of Mozambique. The principal rivers are the Zambesi, which flows for about 600 miles through the Colony, the Limpopo, the Pungwe, the Rovuma, the Maputa, the Incomati, the Lurio and the Licungo. The highest point in the province is Binga Peak in the Chimanimani range on the Rhodesian border, which reaches approximately 7,600 feet. Among the main mineral products are coal, which occurs near Tete at Moatize; gold, found in the same area, as well as near Vila de Manica; graphite, radio-active minerals and bauxite. Prospecting for petroleum has been in progress for many years. Sugar is one of the largest agricultural products, particularly at the Sena Estates on the Zambesi. Mozambique also has the largest single coconut plantation in the world, of over 2,000,000 palms, covering nearly 40,000 acres. Cotton, tea, coffee, rice and rubber are cultivated. There is a large export of fruit to the Republic, particularly bananas. Railways run from Lourenço Marques to Pretoria, as well as to Rhodesia. There is also a line from Beira to Umtali, and several shorter lengths from minor ports. Air lines and shipping services operate to the most important centres.

MOZAMBIQUE—CHRONOLOGY

498 Vasco da Gama, on his way back from India, visits Inhambane and Quelimane, and on March 1 lands at Mozambique.

1500 Foundation of Quelimane.

1502 Vasco da Gama visits Sofala.

1505 Portuguese Fort built at Sofala.

1507 Fortress built on Mozambique Island by the Portuguese.

1515 Antonio Fernandez explores present-day Rhodesia.

1530 Town of Sena founded on the Zambesi.

1544 First fortifications built near present site of Lourenço Marques.

1545 Foundation of the town of Tete.

1561 Martyrdom of Gonsalo da Silveira in present-day Rhodesia.

1569 Expedition to avenge Silveira ed by Francisco Baretto.
Baptism of the King of the Monomotapa.

1629 Treaty between the Portuguese and Monomotapa.

1721 Attempt by Dutch East India Company to set up a trading station at Lourenço Marques.

1752 Administration of Mozambique separated from that of Portuguese India.

1771 Attempt by Austrian Asiatic Company to establish a colony at Delagoa Bay, under an Englishman, Colonel William Bolt.

1781 Fortress built at Lourenço Marques and first Governor appointed.

1798 Dr. F. J. de Lacerda explores interior of Mozambique.

1802–1811 Pedro Baptista and Amaro José cross from Angola to Mozambique.

1822 Captain W. F. W. Owen surveys and annexes Delagoa Bay.

1875 Arbitration between Britain and Portugal by Marshal MacMahon awards Delagoa Bay to Portugal. First attempt at railway line from Lourenço Marques to the Transvaal.

1888 Construction of line from Lourenço Marques to Pretoria.

1895 Opening of railway from Lourenço Marques to Pretoria.

1897 Lourenço Marques becomes capital of Mozambique in place of the town of Mozambique.

1898 Railway from Beira to Umtali completed.

1909 Mozambique Convention signed with Transvaal.

1927 Portuguese Marconi Company establishes radio station.

1928 Charter of the Nyasaland Company expires.

1933 Broadcasting begun from Lourenço Marques.

1942 Charter of Mozambique Company expires.

1943 Portuguese East Africa divided into four districts.

1946 Archbishop of Lourenço Marques raised to dignity of Cardinal.

1948 Telephone service opened from Beira to Rhodesia.
Prospecting contract between Government and Mozambique Gulf Oil Co.

1950 Marshall Aid for Beira expansion. Convention between Portugal and Britain on the port of Beira.

1951 New port at Nacala opened, 50 miles south of Mozambique.

1952 State visit by Governor-General of Mozambique to Southern Rhodesia.
Mineral Survey of Mozambique with American aid—62,000 sq. miles.

1953 Production of Uranium ore begun.
Telephone link-up, Nyasaland to Beira.

1954 Mozambique becomes a province of Metropolitan Portugal.

1955 Railway from Rhodesia to Lourenço Marques opened.

1961 Portuguese citizenship conferred on all inhabitants of overseas provinces.

1962 Gradual abolition of Customs duties on trade with Portugal.

1964 President Tomaz of Portugal visits Mozambique.

1966 Frelimo (q.v.) began guerilla warfare across northern boundary.

1968 Territorial claims by Malawi rejected.

1969 Murder of Frelimo leader Eduardo Mondlane, succeeded by Uria Simango.

Mozambique. One of the oldest cities and original capital of Portuguese East Africa, where Vasco da Gama landed on March 1, 1498. The island on which it is situated was occupied by the Portuguese in October 1507. Shortly after, the castle, which is still in existence, was erected there, mostly from materials brought out in tiny caravels from Portugal. Mozambique underwent repeated sieges by Arabs and others, and was the subject of an unsuccessful attack from the Cape in 1662. Though subordinate to the Portuguese administration in Goa, India, it remained the centre of administration for the whole of Portuguese East Africa until towards the end of the 19th century. For very many years, almost until modern times, Mozambique was a convict settlement. It is now famous for its tourist attractions, notably the Fort, built between 1508 and 1511, the Governor's Palace, etc. Population: 13,000, including about 1,000 Whites.

Mozambique Company. *See* COMPANHIA DO MOZAMBIQUE.

Mozambique Convention. Agreement between the Republic of South Africa and the Portuguese Government, regulating traffic between the two countries, particularly with the Witwatersrand Gold Fields. At the end of the 19th century the steadily-growing percentage of African workers who found employment on the gold fields became a major economic factor. After the South African War the Transvaal Government made efforts to regulate the traffic, the Portuguese endeavouring to draw the maximum financial and other advantages from the position. The first Mozambique Convention was concluded in 1909 and operated until 1919. In return for authority to recruit native labour in Mozambique, the port of Lourenço Marques was guaranteed a defined rail traffic proportion of the overseas imports to the Transvaal, not below 50 per cent and not more than 55 per cent. This applied to a so-called 'Competitive Area,' covering most of the Rand, as well as Klerksdorp, Vereeniging and Pretoria. After it had been temporarily renewed, the original Convention came to an end in March 1923, and a provisional arrangement continued until

1928. Under the previous agreement the number of natives who could be recruited had been given as 105,000, but this was now reduced to 80,000. The Portuguese authorities were allowed to take over directly half their earnings, to be repaid upon their return to their homes in Mozambique (known as 'Deferred Pay'). With the growing percentage of natives on the Transvaal gold and coal mines (to which the Convention was restricted), derived from the Union of South Africa and other territories, particularly Rhodesia and areas further north, the Union's dependence on Mozambique diminished, and the agreement has since been varied several times. The Convention is still in operation, but subject to one year's notice by either party.

Mpolweni. Bantu settlement near New Hanover, Natal. Population: 2,272.

Mpulungu. Port on the Zambian side of Lake Tanganyika, centre of the fishing industry. A service of steamers operates every three weeks to Kigoma on the Tanganyika side of the lake.

Mqanduli. Village in Eastern Cape Province. Population: 420, including 130 Whites.

'Mrs. Ples.' Jocular name given to a set of bones of a semi-human ape found by Dr. Robert Broom (q.v.) near Krugersdorp.

Msinga. Village and administrative centre in Zululand, the name meaning 'to spy.' It was a centre of disaffection in the 1906 Rising.

Mtunzini. Settlement in Zululand, formerly the seat of the White Chief of the Zulus, John Dunn (q.v.). Sugar-growing centre. Population: 700, including 170 Whites.

Muden. Mission station and village near Greytown, Natal, noted for its large citrus orchards, laid out and developed by the late I. W. Schlesinger (q.v.).

Mud-fish (*Tilapia mossambica*). Fresh-water fish found near East London and Glen Grey areas, Natal, Transvaal, Ngamiland, Rhodesia, Mozambique, East Africa to Abyssinia. About 14 inches long.

Mud-Skipper (*Periophthalmus kolreuteri*). Fish found off Port St. Johns, Natal, East Africa, in Indo-Pacific. About 5 inches long. Remarkable for its amphibious habit of clinging to rocks and stems above the water, then jumping back and skimming the surface with a series of jumps, to hide in the mud or swim away. Feeds on crabs and insects.

Mufulira. Mining town on the Zambian Copperbelt, 49 miles from Ndola. Founded in 1924. The Mufulira Copper Mine, which adjoins it, is one of the largest in Africa. Its growth has been spectacular and the population is now 28,700, including 3,500 Whites.

Muid. Old Cape measure of capacity, also known as a sack and equal to 3 bushels or 4 schepels (q.v.).

Muir, Karin Yvette. South African champion swimmer and the youngest world record holder of any kind. Born at Kimberley in 1953 she broke all local records as a school-girl, and in 1965 at Blackpool, England made a World record by covering 110 yards backstroke in 68 seconds, which she further improved on March 1, 1966 by another 0·3 of a second. In August 1966 at Lincoln, Nebraska, and Vancouver, Canada, she again set new World records for the 200 metres backstroke (2 minutes 26·4 seconds) and 220 yards backstroke (2 minutes 28·2 seconds).

Muir, Sir Thomas. Mathematician and Superintendent-General of Education for the Cape. Born at Stonbyres in Scotland in August 1845, he studied at Glasgow University and in Germany, being the top Greek and mathematical student of his year. After teaching mathematics at St. Andrews and Glasgow, he was appointed Superintendent-General of Education at the Cape of Good Hope in 1892, and was twice awarded the Keith Medal of the Royal Society of Edinburgh for mathematical research. He became Vice-Chancellor of the University of the Cape of Good Hope, and President of the South African Association for the Advancement of Science in 1910. He wrote several books on mathematics, especially on the Theory of Quaternions, on which he was a world authority. Muir died in 1934, leaving his mathematical library, one of the finest in existence, to the South African Public Library in Cape Town.

Muishond (*Ictonyx capensis*). South African variety of polecat, noted for its evil smell. Of nocturnal habits, and equipped with long teeth and claws; kills snakes and other dangerous creatures such as its relative the weasel.

Muizenberg. One of the best-known South African seaside resorts. Its name is derived from Wynand Muys, an early official of the Dutch East India Company, who lived in this neighbourhood. Muizenberg was a fishing village which first came into the news in 1795, when a small action was fought there against the Dutch by the British troops advancing from Simonstown on Cape Town. The redoubts were in existence until recently near the site of the present bowling green. The railway came to Muizenberg in 1885, when its real advance began. The first pavilion was built in 1910 and replaced in 1928. A new programme of beach improvements is under way. Muizenberg is on False Bay and 14 miles from Cape Town, of which it is a suburb.

Muller, General Hendrik. Boer leader. Born in Cape Colony in 1865, he grew up in the O.F.S. and later the Transvaal, where he went through several native campaigns. Entering the South African War as a corporal in the Boksburg Commando, he rose to generalship by reason of his dashing feats of arms, one of the best known being his capture of a heavy British gun, the 'Lady Roberts,' at Helvetia in the Eastern Transvaal. He took part in the peace negotiations at Vereeniging. In later years he was a director of the Land Bank. He joined in the 1914 Rebellion, sat in Parliament for some years and died in Johannesburg in 1945.

Muller, Dr. Hilgard. Foreign Minister of the Republic of South Africa. Born at Potchefstroom, Transvaal, 1914 and attended school there. Studied at University of Pretoria and in 1937 went to Oxford as a Rhodes Scholar, also becoming a Rugby Blue. After qualifying as a barrister, returned and became Senior Lecturer in Latin at University of Pretoria. Wrote several books on ancient history in English and Afrikaans. Entered Pretoria City Council 1951 and from 1953 to 1955 was Mayor. Elected as Member of Parliament for Pretoria East, he became South African Ambassador in London in 1961 and Foreign Minister of the Republic in 1964.

Mullet, Red. *See* SURMULLET.

Munnik, Senator George Glaeser. Pioneer of the Northern Transvaal and writer. Born in Worcester, Cape Colony, 1846, he entered the Civil Service and became Civil Commissioner of Barkly East. He fought in the Basuto, Tamboekie and other wars, and went to the Transvaal after the discovery of gold. Joining the Republican Civil Service, he became Landdrost and Mining Commissioner in the Northern Transvaal. He fought in the South African War, was taken prisoner and became one of the first Transvaal M.P.s under Responsible Government. After Union he became a Senator. A noted expert on horses, he succeeded in improving opportunities for the importation of pedigree stock. He wrote several books, including novels and reminiscences. Senator Munnik died in 1935.

Murchison Range. Outlier of the Drakensberg in the North-Eastern Transvaal, named after the great Victorian geologist, Sir Roderick Murchison, and known for its gold deposits, mostly refractory. The peaks reach a height of over 6,000 feet.

Murray, Rev. Andrew. Born at Graaff-Reinet, son of the Rev. Andrew Murray, Snr., in 1828. At an early age he was sent, in company with his brother John, to Scotland to study theology, and obtained his degree at 17 years in 1845 at the University of Aberdeen. After further training he returned to South Africa and was appointed to the Dutch Reformed Congregation in Bloemfontein, being for a considerable period almost the only minister in the Orange Free State. Single-handed, he built up an effective church organisation to cover the Republic, in whose affairs he took a considerable part by helping to protest against the retrocession of the sovereignty in 1854. After 6 years he accepted a call to Worcester, Cape Colony, where he became involved in a violent theological controversy arising from the alleged liberal tendencies of the Rev. A. J. Kotze and the Rev. T. Burgers. This led him to write a series of books, the production of which was to continue almost to the end of his life. After a spell in Cape Town he moved to Wellington in 1871, having in the meantime become Moderator. He continued to play a leading part in the affairs of his Church, and gave notable support to the founding of the Huguenot Seminary at Wellington. His writings gained him a large audience particularly in England and the United States, where his books to this day sell in English translations. He died at the age of nearly 90 in 1917.

Murray of Lintrose. Early South African traveller. Born in Scotland of a noble family, he visited the Cape in 1845 and accompanied William Cotton Oswell (q.v.) on his trip to the Limpopo. He was a friend of David Livingstone and of Robert Moffat.

Murraysburg. Town in the Cape Midlands, near Graaff-Reinet, founded in 1859, and named after the famous Dutch reformer minister, the Reverend Andrew Murray. Well known as a horse-breeding centre, and for farming generally. Population: 2,840, including 800 Whites.

Museums in Southern Africa. The South African Museum in Cape Town is the oldest in the subcontinent, and still the most important. Opened on June 10, 1825, it had as its original curator Dr. Andrew Smith (later Sir Andrew), a famous naturalist and explorer, the first of a long line of distinguished holders of the office. Accommodated for many years with the South African Public Library, it secured its own building in 1897, which has since then been repeatedly enlarged. Its main collections are in the fields of natural history and anthropology, but it also has many other treasures.

The Albany Museum in Grahamstown dates from 1855, and is specially noted for its herbarium, the largest in South Africa. Port Elizabeth began its museum in the 'seventies, but not until 1905 did it receive serious encouragement from the municipality. Under its curator, F. W. Fitzsimons (q.v.), it gained world fame through its Snake Park. The National Museum in Bloemfontein was started by the former Orange Free State Republic in 1877, and has done important work in archaeology and other fields. Durban Museum was begun in 1887 by the town council, one of its most famous exhibits being the most nearly perfect skeleton of that extinct bird, the dodo. The Kaffrarian Museum in King

William's Town, opened in 1889, is noted for its outstanding work on mammals, particularly under the late Captain Shortridge. Pretoria has the Transvaal Museum, opened in 1893, with its large scientific collections, and separate premises in different parts of the city, besides the Kruger Museum, the President's former home.

Dating from the present century are the Natal Museum in Pietermaritzburg (mainly scientific collections), set up in 1903, the Voortrekker Museum in the same city (1912), the McGregor Museum in Kimberley (1907), the East London Museum, famous for its Coelacanth (q.v.) (1921), the Boer War Museum in Bloemfontein and the splendid Africana Museum in Johannesburg (1935). Numbers of smaller museums exist. In Rhodesia there are museums in Salisbury, Bulawayo and Umtali, also at Livingstone in Zambia and elsewhere. There is also a fine museum at Lourenço Marques.

Musgrave, Sir Anthony, Lieutenant-Governor of Natal. Began his career as Governor's secretary in the Leeward Islands (West Indies) in 1850. In the following year decided to read for the Bar at the Inner Temple, only to be called to a fresh appointment in the West Indies, where he rose to be Lieutenant-Governor of the island of St. Vincent in 1862. Went as Governor to Newfoundland in 1864, to British Columbia in 1869 and, as Lieutenant-Governor to Natal in May 1872. Involved with the Langalibalele Rebellion he did not remain long and in 1873 became Governor of South Australia. His later appointments were in Jamaica in 1877 and in Queensland in 1883. His son Anthony Musgrave (Junior) served as his secretary in Natal, and rose to distinction in the Colonial service, dying in 1912.

Musgrave, William. Attorney-General of the Cape and Judge of the

Supreme Court. Born in England, 1792, he was called to the Bar at the age of 22, began practice in London and in 1818 joined the Colonial Service as Solicitor-General of several West Indian islands. In 1823 he was appointed Attorney-General for the colonies of Montserrat, Barbuda and Antigua. A friend of Governor Sir Benjamin Durban, he came to the Cape in 1836 where he was admitted to practice at the Bar. Three years later he became Attorney-General for a short period and in 1843 was appointed a Judge of the Supreme Court. He died in Cape Town on October 6, 1854.

Mushrooms and Fungi. South Africa produces hundreds of kinds of mushrooms, toadstools and other large fungi, poisonous and otherwise. About 90 of these are worth cooking, perhaps the most palatable being the Field Mushroom, the Cep and some of the young Puffballs. Only nine are known to be poisonous to all human beings, but four more are poisonous to some. The rest are described as 'harmless, but not worth eating,' or species not yet tested. Much research on the subject remains to be done.

One of the most poisonous is the Death Cup (*Amanita phalloides*), known in Afrikaans as Duiwelsbrood, nearly always encountered under oak trees and believed originally to have been imported with them to South Africa. It is commonest between May and the end of July. The Cape Death Cup (*Amanita capensis*) is equally fatal. The Fly Agaric (*Amanita muscaria*), also poisonous, usually grows under pine trees, though at times it is also met with under oaks. The name (Vlieeswam in Afrikaans) is derived from the fact that it is widely used as fly poison. The Panther (*Amanita pantherina*) closely resembles an edible species and is also known in America and Europe. A family of seven people died from eating it in 1927. The

Copper Trumpet (*Clitocybe olearia*), so called from its curious colour and shape, is poisonous, though not so deadly as some other species, and is also found in Mediterranean countries.

A large genus of Fungi is the Inocybe, but of the 150 species known only nine have been found in South Africa, eight near Cape Town and one near Pretoria. Despite their harmless appearance, some are dangerous. The most poisonous is *Inocybe eutheles*, found under pine trees, as is *Inocybe obscura*, which smells of radishes. Lastly there is *Inocybe hirtella*, shaped like a child's hat and curling at the edges. Patients eating it usually recover after 24 hours.

The Yellow-Staining Mushroom (*Psalliota xanthoderma*) causes digestive upsets only to some people. The Green-lined Parasol (*Lepiota morganii*), which often grows on lawns in the Transvaal and Natal, is not necessarily fatal, but produces very unpleasant effects. Poison Pie (*Hebeloma crustulini forme*) occurs in Europe and America as well as in South Africa, and is so called from its resemblance to a miniature pasty. Neither poisonous nor edible are the Purple-Stemmed Russula (*Russula drimeia*), found in pine forests, and the Orange Tuft (*Pholiota spectabilis*), which grows on living or dead timber, as does the Sulphur Tuft (*Hypholoma fasciculare*). The Dye Balls (*Pisolithus tinctorius*) are found growing under eucalyptus trees. Their Greek name, meaning 'peastone,' comes from their resemblance to a stone packed with tiny peas. They are used by French peasants as a dye.

Edible fungi in South Africa include the Field Mushroom (*Psalliota campestris*), the Horse Mushroom (*Psalliota arvensis*), of a rather strong flavour, the Forest Mushroom (*Psalliota silvicola*), the Noble Mushroom (*Psalliota nobilis*), the Shaggy Ink-cap (*Coprinus comatus*), the Lactarius or Pine Ring (*Lactarius deliciosus*), the Cape Russula (*Russula capensis*), the

White Parasol (*Lepiota zeyheri*), the Blusher (*Amanita rubescens*), the Volvaria (*Volvaria speciosa*), the Cep or Edible Boletus (*Boletus edulis*), the Poplar Boletus (*Boletus duriusculus*) and several other members of the family, the Little Puffball (*Lycoperdon hiemale*) and the Sulphur Shelf (*Polyporus sulphureus*).

Note. The reader is referred to *Some South African Poisonous and Inedible Fungi* by E. L. Stephens, illustrated by Mary Maytham Kidd, and to *Some South African Edible Fungi*, by the same author and artist, published by Longmans Green & Co., Cape Town, 1953.

Plate IX shows four poisonous toadstools; a young one is shown beside each fully developed one. These young ones are at first entirely enclosed in a white membrane, and it will be seen that the remains of this membrane have stuck as a lot of little white patches on the top of the cap in the Panther and the Fly Agaric. In the Death Cup, however, the cap has broken clean through the membrane, which remains round the base of the stem as the 'cup,' from which this toadstool derives one of its popular names. The Cape Death Cup (*Amanita capensis*), which has so far only been found in the Cape Peninsula in spring, has a whitish buff or creamy cap, which makes it very dangerous, as people have died through mistaking it for a field mushroom; but, like the three other toadstools shown, it has white gills (the gills are the plates hanging down from the cap), whereas the Field Mushroom has dark gills when mature. Avoid all fungi with white gills till you learn which are good eating, and you will avoid the risk of eating these four poisonous kinds. The two Death Cups are both deadly poisonous, the most poisonous of all fungi, and the Panther is also very poisonous. The Fly Agaric is not deadly, but causes delirium and hallucinations.

Music. The survival of 18th-century musical instruments and other relics in South Africa bears witness to the interest shown by the more cultured and wealthy early settlers. Several compositions with local references survive, including an anonymous collection of Dutch sailors' songs on the 'Voyage to the Cape' and two others by C. Schubarth for the Würtemburg Cape Regiment. Music teachers, including E. K. Green and E. Logier, began their work in Cape Town in Napoleonic days, and the first locally printed composition appeared there in 1840. An organ was installed in the Groote Kerk, Cape Town, in 1828. Musical societies, amateur orchestras and military bands flourished throughout the 19th century, even in villages. Occasional tours by virtuosi such as Edward Remenyi (q.v.) helped to maintain interest. Although music was taught at most schools and colleges and there were several small privately owned institutions in various parts of the country, it was not until 1905 that the Stellenbosch Conservatoire came into being, mainly through the initiative and enthusiasm of Professor F. W. Jannasch (q.v.). This was followed in 1912 by the foundation of the South African College of Music in Cape Town, under Professor W. H. Bell (q.v.). Since then Faculties of Music have been set up at most South African universities. Another major development was the establishment of the Cape Town Municipal Orchestra in 1914, under Theophil Wendt (q.v.). Orchestras followed in Durban and Johannesburg. The Johannesburg Musical Society, which claims to be the oldest in South Africa, was founded in 1902, while the Johannesburg Philharmonic Society dates from 1910. The first attempt at opera in South Africa goes back to 1815. Since the arrival of Sefton Parry in 1854 many visiting companies have toured the country. Among the many musical artists who have visited South Africa are Ignaz Paderewski, Jascha Heifetz, Yehudi Menuhin, Fritz Kreisler, John McCormack, Amelita Galli-Curci, Rafael Kubelik, Beniamino Gigli and Mark Hambourg.

In recent years South Africa has produced composers of some standing, including Arnold van Wyk, Stefanus Grové, Stephen Eyssen, Jan Joubert and others. Earlier in the present century Bosman de Ravelli, a pupil of de Pachman, was a virtuoso of distinction, and among singers Friedrich Dalberg (Frederick Dalrymple) and Mimi Coertse have starred not only on English but on continental operatic stages.

Musselcrusher. South African fish. *See* BISHOP, BLACK.

Mutasa. *See* UMTASA.

Muti. Zulu name for medicine, from a word meaning a tree or a herb. It can be curative or magical. Some of the most powerful varieties of muti are reputedly from human bodies and a result of ritual murders. The traffic in muti is today largely supervised by the police, particularly in the cities.

Mynpacht. Portion of a gold-bearing farm, particularly in the Transvaal, which, under the law, is awarded to the owner of the ground. It represented a fixed percentage of the surface area. The title under which it was held was known as a 'Mynpachtbrief.' The word means 'hire of a mine.'

N

Naartjie (derived probably from Indian Tamie Nartei, a citron). South African name for tangerine, a member of the citrus family, with an easily-peeled skin.

Naauwpoort: 1. Railway Junction in the Cape Midlands, 570 miles from Cape Town, 270 miles from Port Elizabeth and 331 miles from East London. Used as important military base in South African War. The name means 'Narrow Gate' in Afrikaans. Population: 7,230, including 2,418 Whites.
2. Pass between the Witwatersberg and Magaliesberg, scene of fighting in South African War, in January 1901.

Nababeep. Mining village in Namaqualand with large plant for the production of copper, originally established in 1860's by Cape Copper Company. During World War II the United States Government financed a new installation for the O'Okiep Copper Co. there. Population: 6,418, including 2,027 Whites.

Naboomspruit. Village in the Transvaal, north of Pretoria, established 1923, originally a centre for platinum fields, and noteworthy as the site of the first practical use of the Dutton 'Road-Rail' system, a South African invention to provide cheap transport. Its name is derived from a species of Euphorbia that flourishes there. Farming centre. Population: 3,800, including 1,400 Whites.

Nagana. Cattle disease transmitted by the Tsetse Fly (*Glossina morsitans*) and allied to Sleeping Sickness. Found in Zambia and Zululand. Combated by aerial spraying with D.D.T. and in other ways which have much reduced the menace.

Nag Apie. *See* GALAGO.

Nagreier. Afrikaans name for Night Heron.

Naguil. Afrikaans name for Rufous-cheeked Nightjar.

Nama. Tribe living in South West Africa, closely allied to the Hottentots, although slightly taller. They are very light-skinned and probably came from North Africa. Unlike most South African tribes in the territory, they are slowly increasing, numbering about 40,000. They worship a Supreme Being. Cattle-breeding is their main occupation.

Namaacha. Hill village in the Lebombo Mountains in Mozambique, 55 miles from Lourenço Marques, noted for its healthy climate and for its medicinal springs.

Namib. Desert region along the coast of South West Africa. Varying in width from 30 to 80 miles, it consists in the main of sand dunes, from which hills of rock and gravel occasionally emerge. The Namib extends with few interruptions for almost a thousand miles along the borders of Angola to near the mouth of the Orange River, but in the area north of the Swakop River (q.v.) the dunes are lower and less continuous, while occasional watercourses break through to the sea. Despite its barrenness the Namib has a certain amount of vegetation and wild life. (*See* WELWITSCHIA MIRABILIS.) The discovery of diamonds in the Namib in 1904 led to the establishment in certain areas of important workings. Boreholes in the river valleys have at times produced considerable supplies of water.

Namibia. Name given by some members of the United Nations to South West Africa—not recognised by Government.

Namutoni. Fort established by the German authorities in the north of South West Africa, as a stronghold against local tribes. It stands on the edge of the Etosha Pan (q.v.) and resembles a medieval castle. During the 1904 Herero rising it was successfully held by eight men against a force of 500 Ovambos. It was captured by the South African troops in 1915, after which it was used as a police post. It is now an historic monument.

Nancefield. Bantu township near Johannesburg, Transvaal. Population: 2,257.

Napier. Village in the Western Cape Province, near Bredasdorp, established in 1840 and named after Governor Sir George Napier. The 'Bontebok National Park' is near by. Farming centre. Population: 1,460, including 918 Whites.

Napier, Sir George Thomas. Governor of the Cape of Good Hope. Son of Colonel George Napier, and elder brother of the famous soldier-author of *History of the Peninsular War*, he was born in 1784. He became Governor in 1837, during the Great Trek period. Annexed Natal in 1843 and made alliances with Adam Kok and Moshesh (q.v.). Returned to England in 1844 and died at Geneva in 1855.

'Naras. *See* MELON and PLANTS.

Narina Trogon (*Apaloderma narina*). Resplendent tropical bird inhabiting forest country in South Africa, from the Transvaal through Zululand and Natal to Eastern Cape Province and Knysna. A rarely-seen insect-eater, with a deep cooing voice at breeding times. Its head and back are dark green, the rump crimson.

Nasionale Pers. Publishing house established in 1915 with the object of popularising the use of the Afrikaans language. Its directors included most of the early leaders of the Nationalist Party. Among its first tasks was the issue of the newspaper *Die Burger*, edited by Dr. D. F. Malan and *Die Huisgenoot*, edited by Prof. J. J. Smith. Beginning with a capital of £30,000, it has issued several thousand Afrikaans books of every description. Its headquarters are in Cape Town, but its ramifications extend throughout the Republic.

Natal. Province of the Republic of South Africa, covering an area of 34,000 sq. miles. So called because early Portuguese navigators first sighted it on Christmas Day (Natal). Since 1897 Zululand has formed part of Natal. The total population of Natal was 2,933,447 in 1960, of whom 340,293 were White, Bantu 2,155,824, Asiatic 394,237 and Coloured 43,093. White population in 1966 was 388,000. Natal had 155,760 voters in 1955.

Natal Advertiser. Now known as the *Natal Daily News*. Established in 1878, it was renamed in August 1937. It appears as an evening paper in Durban.

Natal Carbineers. *See* ROYAL NATAL CARBINEERS.

Natal Daily News. *See* NATAL ADVERTISER.

Natal Field Artillery. South African military unit, now part of Third Field Regiment, South African Artillery, founded as Natal Field Artillery on June 3, 1870. Fought in South African War 1899–1902, in World War I (South West Africa) and in World War II.

Natal Land and Colonisation Company. Founded in England in December 1860 with a capital of £225,000, it acquired large areas to encourage settlement in Natal. It received Government support in its emigration proposals, but became in the main a property-holding concern. Finally disappeared after World War II.

Natal Mercury. Morning paper in Durban, established on November 25,

1852. Since January 1878 it has been published daily.

Natal Mounted Police. Semi-military unit established in 1874, under Major (afterwards Major-General) Sir J. G. Dartnell. It gained distinction in local native campaigns, in the Zulu War, in the South African War, and in the 1906 Zulu Rebellion. Upon the establishment of the South African Police in 1913, it was merged in that body.

Natal Mounted Rifles. South African Military Unit, founded on December 29, 1862. Served in South African War 1899–1902, Zulu Rebellion 1906, World War I (South West Africa), and World War II (Abyssinia, North Africa and Italy).

Natal Rock Snake. *See* PYTHON.

Natal Witness. Daily morning paper issued in Pietermaritzburg. Established on February 27, 1846, by David D. Buchanan, it is one of the oldest surviving journals in South Africa. It has appeared daily since January 1881.

Nathan, Dr. Manfred. South African writer on legal and general subjects. Judge of the Income Tax Court. Born in Hanover, Cape Province, 1875, came to the Rand as a young man in Republican times and, after working on a newspaper, qualified for the Bar. He became one of the most prolific writers on legal subjects in the country, his largest work being *The Common Law of South Africa*, issued between 1904 and 1907. He also wrote a biography of President Kruger, and works on the Great Trek. He served on various public bodies and was an acting judge of the Supreme Court. He died in 1945.

Nathan, Sir Matthew. Governor of Natal. Born of an Anglo-Jewish family in 1862, he entered the Royal Engineers in 1880, and served in the Nile Expedition of 1885, and elsewhere. He became Governor of Natal in 1907 and remained there until 1909. He was Governor of Queensland, Australia, from 1920–1926, and died in 1939.

National Anthem. *See* 'STEM VAN SUID-AFRIKA, DIE.'

National Bank of South Africa. *See* BARCLAYS BANK (DOMINION, COLONIAL AND OVERSEAS).

National Convention. Body set up by the various colonies to work out the details of the Union Constitution. It comprised 12 delegates from Cape Colony, 8 from the Transvaal, 5 each from Natal and the Orange River Colony, and 3 from Southern Rhodesia, the latter having the right to speak, but not to vote. The meetings, presided over by Sir Henry (later Lord) De Villiers, Chief Justice of the Cape, began in Durban on October 12, 1908, and went on until November 5. They continued in Cape Town between November 23, 1908, and February 3, 1909, were resumed at Bloemfontein on May 3, and ended there on May 11, 1909.

National Finance Corporation of South Africa. Statutory body set up on September 20, 1949, for the purpose of providing a money market in the Union. Its shareholders are leading financial concerns and banks. It takes short-term deposits, discounts bills, etc.

National Indian Council. Interim body of 25 members approved in 1963 to act as mouthpiece of the Indian community in South Africa, pending the establishment of an elected body. Approved as a stopgap by a conference of Indians held at Pretoria in December 1963. *See* SOUTH AFRICAN INDIAN COUNCIL.

National Parks. Under Act No. 56 of 1926, the National Parks Board was created in South Africa, with its headquarters at Pretoria. Under its control are over 12,000 square miles, representing six National Parks including Kruger (q.v.), Kalahari (q.v.), Addo (q.v.), Bontebok (q.v.), Mountain Zebra (q.v.) and Golden Gate (q.v.). In addition there are numerous Provincial Reserves in the Cape, Transvaal, Natal and Orange Free State. Rhodesia has 14 National Parks: at Inyanga, Victoria Falls, Wankie, Matopos, Zimbabwe, Vumba, Sinoia, Chimanimani, Sebakwe and elsewhere. Zambia has one at Kafue, besides game reserves.

National Party (officially **Nasionale Party**). Founded in 1913 by General J. B. M. Hertzog after his secession from General Louis Botha's South African Party (q.v.). This party name had been used in the pre-Union Cape Parliament under General Botha, but the Hertzog National Party began with 6 members in the House of Assembly, growing to 27 after the election of 1915. In 1924 Hertzog concluded the Pact (q.v.) with the Labour Party, which brought him into office that year. This National Party ceased to exist in 1933, when it merged in the present United Party. Upon the secession of Dr. D. F. Malan (q.v.), it again came into being and in its new form has lasted to the present day.

National Scouts. Unit formed by the British military forces authorities during the latter stages of the South African War, composed of members of the Republican forces who had changed sides. They were regarded with such dislike by their fellow burghers that the words 'National Scout' became a term of abuse. Official returns in May 1902 show 1,480 members. After the return of peace they were largely ostracised and a number of them formed their own church in the Transvaal.

National Theatre Organisation. Established in 1948 with Government assistance to bring the drama, both in English and in Afrikaans, to all parts of South Africa, especially to the country districts. Under the guidance of several eminent actors and producers, among whom Leontine Sagan deserves special mention, it built up companies of actors and a system of portable stage sets capable of being used even in small village halls. Since 1962 the original organisation has been placed on a provincial basis, with sections devoted to drama, ballet, opera and other music. Provision is also made for the Bantu and Coloured communities.

National Veld Trust. Non-profit-making organisation set up in South Africa in 1942, largely at the instigation of the late Louis Esselen, to enlist public support for the Government's campaign against soil erosion (q.v.), to carry on educative propaganda and to demonstrate methods of improvement. Its headquarters are in Johannesburg. Its symbol is the Green Cross.

Native Recruiting Corporation. Large organisation associated with Transvaal and O.F.S. Chamber of Mines for the recruiting, in South Africa itself, of Bantu workers for the mines. Founded 1896. *See* WITWATERSRAND NATIVE LABOUR ASSOCIATION, *and also* GOLD-MINING INDUSTRY.

Naude, Hugo. South African artist. Born at the Cape in 1869, he studied painting and soon became known for his vivid and pleasing pictures of Western Province scenery. He made his home at Worcester and enjoyed national popularity. After he died in 1941 an art centre in this town was named after him.

Naude, Jozua Francois (Tom). Former South African Cabinet Minister, Parliamentary Speaker and President of the Senate. Born at Middelburg, Cape Province, April 15, 1889, he qualified in Law and in 1920 became Member of Parliament for Pietersburg. At different times he was Minister of Posts and Telegraphs,

Health, Finance and Interior. Appointed Speaker of the House of Assembly in 1948 and in 1960 President of the Senate. Acting State President 1967. Died May 31, 1969. *See* DR. T. E. DÖNGES.

Navy, South African. The first step towards the creation of local naval tradition was taken by the Natal Colonial Government on April 30, 1885, when the Natal Naval Volunteers were established in Durban, under the command of Harry Escombe (q.v.). In 1905 the Royal Naval Volunteer Reserve was established in Cape Town, and in 1913 the two were merged into a South African division of the R.N.V.R. The latter did service during World War I, many of its members being posted to the Royal Navy. Although individual South Africans had done extremely well overseas, where several had risen to high rank, including Admiral Sir Neville Syfret and Vice-Admiral V. B. Molteno (q.v.), the need was felt for a more distinctive local organisation and in 1922 the South African Naval Service came into existence. Its original ships included H.M.S. *Protea*, a survey vessel, and the *Immortelle*, and *Sonnebloem*, given by the Admiralty. Further facilities for training were made available through the provision of the training vessel, *General Botha*. For reasons of economy, however, the South African Naval Service went out of existence in 1934, and it was not until 1939, under threat of World War II, that the South African Seaward Defence Force was established. Merged with the Royal Naval Volunteer Reserve in 1942, into the South African Naval Forces, the Volunteers distinguished themselves in the Mediterranean and elsewhere, particularly with little ships taken from their peacetime duties. After the return of peace, the South African Naval Service, with which was associated the Seaward Defence Force, became officially the South African Navy, and a programme of expansion was approved. The taking over by the Union Defence Department of the Naval Dockyard at Simonstown in 1957 provided a fresh impetus for expansion, and several frigates, corvettes, etc., were secured. The South African Navy today maintains a training Gymnasium near Saldanha Bay as well as a base at Salisbury Island, Durban. Close liaison continues with the Royal Navy though the last British ship was withdrawn in 1966. The first submarines were ordered from France in 1968.

Nazareth. Original name for the Transvaal town of Middelburg (q.v.).

Nchanga. Copper-mining town in Zambia, near the Congo frontier. Adjoins Chingola (q.v.).

Ndlambe. Chief of the Rarabe clan of the Xosa, and uncle of Gaika (q.v.) with whom he was engaged in a long-drawn contest for the control of the tribe. In 1818 at the Battle of Kommetje Flats outside Grahamstown, Ndlambe was defeated. He died in 1829, only a few months before his rival, Gaika.

Ndola. Copper-mining town in Zambia established 1924. Apart from copper and cobalt treatment plants, there are a number of industries and the amenities are rapidly growing in number. Population: 100,100, including 12,400 Whites.

Ndube. White Zulu Chief. A Swiss by the name of N. Duby, from the village of Schupfer in Switzerland. He emigrated to South Africa in 1893 and settled in Zululand, where he gained the rank of a chief. During the South African War he fought on the side of the Boers and in the Bambata Rebellion (q.v.) of 1906 he was on the side of the Zulus.

Ndumu Game Reserve. Situated in the north of Zululand, this covers 24,000 acres, near the Portuguese border. The animals include many

E.Lois Martin.

PLATE VIII: BUTTERFLIES OF SOUTHERN AFRICA

1. *Myrina ficedula* (S.A. and Rhodesia). 2. *Precis cebrene* (S.A. and Rhodesia). 3. *Danais chrysippus* (S.A.). 4. *Terias desjardinsii* (S.A.). 5. *Eronia leda* (S.A. and Rhodesia). 6. *Papilio antheus* (S.A. and Rhodesia).

species of antelopes as well as hippopotami, and the fresh-water lake contains black bass.

Ndwedwe. Native reserve in Natal, near Verulam, noted among the followers of the Shembe sect (q.v.) as a place of pilgrimage (Ndhlanga-gazi Mountain). Near by is the Valley of a Thousand Hills.

Nederburgh, Sebastian Cornelis. Dutch Commissioner-General at the Cape of Good Hope, born in The Hague on March 7, 1762. On November 4, 1791, he left, in company with Simon Hendrik Frijkenius (q.v.) as Commissioner-General, to investigate affairs of the Dutch East India Company, which were in a perilous plight. They arrived in Simonstown in the *Amazone* frigate, on June 12, 1792. Finding the position almost hopeless, they proceeded to Batavia, where Nederburgh remained until 1799, when he returned to Holland via the Cape. He was taken prisoner by H.M.S. *Anson* on March 11, 1800, but was allowed to continue to Holland. There he became Chief of the Department for East Indies under the Batavian Republic in 1806. He died on August 3, 1841, at Graven Zande.

Nederduitsch Gereformeerde Kerk (Dutch Reformed Church). By far the largest church of the white population in South Africa. The original settlers under Jan van Riebeeck in 1652 were accompanied by a 'Ziekentrooster' (Sick Comforter) who, not officially qualified, was expected to carry out certain ministrations. The first ordained minister, the Rev. J. van Arckel, arrived in 1665. In 1683 a church was begun in Stellenbosch and in 1700 the corner-stone of the Groote Kerk in Cape Town was laid. The affairs of the Church were regulated by the Church Ordinance of De Mist in 1804. During the earlier part of the 19th century, a shortage was overcome by the importation of large numbers of

Presbyterian ministers from Scotland, who were of a very high standard and founded many of the best-known South African families, such as the Murrays, McGregors, Robertsons and Rose-Innes. In 1824 the first Synod of the Dutch Reformed Church was held in Cape Town, and its first missions were begun in 1826 by the Rev. L. Marquard. Considerable disorganisation, which took many years to rectify, followed the departure of about 10,000 members of the Church in the Great Trek. Apart from the partly-qualified Erasmus Smit (q.v.) the needs of the emigrants were met by the Rev. Daniel Lindley (q.v.) and other missionaries, but the Rev. Dr. Abraham Faure was specially deputed in 1843 to visit them and make new arrangements. In 1859 the first Theological Seminary was opened in Stellenbosch. Cases of Liberalism brought litigation in the 60's and 70's involving the Rev. J. J. Kotze and the Rev. T. F. Burgers (q.v.). In recent years the Church has concentrated largely on missions and social work. Number of adherents: 1,326,344 Whites, 442,944 Coloureds and 556,898 Bantu.

Nederduitsch Hervormde Kerk. Associated with the body of the same name in the Netherlands. The Rev. van der Hoff, who arrived in the Transvaal from that country in 1853, was the first minister stationed in South Africa. The Constitution of the South African Republic in 1858 recognised this as its official Church, its doctrines differing in certain respects from those of the other Dutch Reformed Churches. According to the 1963 figures there are 190,342 White members, largely in the Transvaal.

Nehlovukazi. Literally Cow Elephant. Title given to the Queen Mother of Swaziland.

Nel, Michael Daniel Christian de Wet. Minister of Bantu Administration and Development in the South

African Government. Born 1901 in the eastern Cape and studied at the University of Pretoria. Joining the National Party in 1937, he soon acquired prominence and was elected first to the Transvaal Provincial Council and in 1943 to Parliament. Appointed Minister of Education, Arts and Science in 1958, but soon after took over his present portfolio, in which he played a leading part in applying the Bantu policy of the National Government.

Nelly. Common name for Giant Petrel. *See* PETREL.

Nelspoort. Village in the Karroo, near Beaufort West, where in 1920 the Union Government established a tuberculosis sanatorium, generously endowed by Mr. John Garlick of Cape Town.

Nelspruit. Town in the Eastern Transvaal, founded in 1889 and named after the original farm owner. Leading centre for the production of citrus and other sub-tropical crops. The Department of Agriculture maintains a research station there. During the South African War it was for a short while the seat of the Transvaal Government. Population: 22,914, including 7,900 Whites.

Nelsrust. Estate in Natal, near Pietermaritzburg, established in 1880's by Joseph Baynes (q.v.) and in his honour also known as Baynesfield. The estate was one of the first modern farms in the Colony and included one of the original dipping tanks. Its main speciality was dairying and the production of pedigree cattle. Under his will Mr. Baynes left Nelsrust to the South African nation for research and other purposes. Nelsrust Dairies Ltd. is a large commercial concern originally associated with the estate, and now operating in Johannesburg and elsewhere.

Nemesia or Weeskindertjies (Scrophulariaceae). Common and delicate little plant, in a variety of pastel shades of flower. This snapdragon family has tubular flowers opening usually into 2 lips, 4 stamens and 4/5 sepals. It contains many root parasites: *Hyobanche sanguinea* or Soetkop is a stout, fleshy Cape parasite 4 to 6 inches, with a scarlet mass of flowers. *Harveya* is a semi-parasitic group with large, attractive flowers, white, pink or orange, tubular but opening wide into 5 petals that turn black when touched. (Hence the name Inkblom for the white variety.) Stout, yellowish stem with small leaves pressed against it. As with many parasites, green is absent in the plant. Witchwood (*Striga asiatica*), the bane of Rhodesian mealie lands, is a slender grassy plant with small scarlet flowers (a mauve variety in Natal). Partly parasitic on grass roots.

Nerina, Nadia (Nadine Judd). South African ballet dancer. Born in Cape Town, she made her first stage appearance as a child in Bloemfontein but began her dancing career in Durban. In 1946 she went to Sadlers Wells in London, where she gained distinction and became a prima ballerina of fame. Also appeared at Covent Garden, London, in Europe and the U.S.A.

Nerine. *See* AMARYLLIS.

Nesbitt, Murrogh De B. South African writer and pioneer of cripple self-rehabilitation. Born in 1898, he grew up in the Orange Free State; at the age of 13 lost both legs under a truck on the Jagersfontein Diamond Mine. By sheer willpower and persistence he succeeded, not merely in rebuilding his own life and becoming an athlete, swimmer, rider, etc., but in teaching numbers of disabled persons to lead a normal existence. The ideas set down in his best-seller, *The Road to Avalon*, resulted in the establishment of a self-rehabilitation centre near Tulbagh, of that name. For reasons outside his control this enterprise later closed down, but Nesbitt continued his work in the

Orange Free State, and wrote a second book, *Avalon Adventure*. He died near Port Elizabeth in 1959.

Netherlands Bank of South Africa Ltd. Founded in 1888 under the name of the Nederlandsche Bank en Crediet Vereeniging, with its head office in Amsterdam and its South African head office in Pretoria. Developing more slowly than some of its rivals, it specialised in Continental commerce and, through affiliated concerns, in mortgage business. In 1925 it took over the Transvaal Commercial Bank. As a result of the German occupation of Holland during World War II, control of operations was transferred from Amsterdam to Pretoria and then to Johannesburg, which in recent years has become the head office.

Netherlands South African Railway Company. Private company established in Holland in 1884 to exploit the concession from the South African Republic for a railway from Lourenço Marques to Pretoria. The capital was 15,000,000 guilders (£1,250,000), not all of which was immediately subscribed. In 1889 the Netherlands South African Railway Company completed its first line from Johannesburg to Boksburg, popularly known as the 'Rand Tram.' Other lines followed, but the major efforts were concentrated on the completion of the link with Delagoa Bay, which, after many delays and much loss of life, due to the bad climate, was completed in 1895. At the time of the South African War the company controlled 688 miles of line. The company was liquidated after the Peace of Vereeniging.

New Bethesda. Village near Graaff-Reinet, established as a mission station. Became a municipality in 1886. Population: 3,000, including 280 Whites.

New Cape Central Railway Ltd. Privately-owned railway company, formerly operating in South Africa. Formed in London, 1883, as the Cape Central Railway, with powers granted by the Colonial Government to build a line from Worcester to a place near Montagu, then known as Roodewal, but renamed Ashton by the Company. The first 30 miles came into use in April 1887, as far as Robertson, and reached Ashton, 42½ miles away, in October. The Company found itself in difficulties in 1889, was liquidated and reconstructed. In 1893 the New Cape Central Railway Company was formed, again in London, and an extension authorised to Swellendam. This was later continued to George, giving the company 233 miles of route. Under its grant, the Cape Government had the right to take over the New Cape Central Railway as from 1907, a right not exercised until 1925, when the enterprise was merged in the South African Railways.

Newcastle. Town in Natal at the foot of the Drakensberg, founded in 1854 and named after the British Secretary for the Colonies, the Duke of Newcastle. Its main importance is as a coal mining centre, and through the large metallurgical plant operated there by Amcor (q.v.), as associate of Iscor (q.v.). For many years J. K. Eaton tried to establish steelworks there, but, despite a certain amount of success, the present activities are concentrated on pig iron. In 1969 it was announced that the Amcor plant had been taken over by Iscor, which would erect its third steel plant at Newcastle. (*See* SOUTH AFRICAN IRON AND STEEL INDUSTRIAL CORPORATION.) There are other industries. Fighting took place during the South African War, and from October 1899 to May 1900 Newcastle was occupied by the Boers, and renamed Viljoensdorp. Population: 17,418, including 4,700 Whites.

New Consolidated Goldfields. *See* CONSOLIDATED GOLDFIELDS.

New Douglas Colliery. Township near Middelburg, Transvaal. Population: 1,822, including 342 Whites.

New England. Sheep-breeding area in Northern Cape, near Barkly East, colonised in 1860 by descendants of 1820 settlers. Cold but bracing climate in Drakensberg Mountains.

New Germany. Village near Pinetown, Natal. Population: 2,750, including 2,000 Whites.

New Guelderland. Settlement on the north coast of Natal, 55 miles from Durban, established by a Dutch syndicate in the 1860's with the object of bringing out colonists from Holland, and now a sugar-growing area.

New Hanover. German settlement in Natal, founded in 1850 and close to the Noodsberg Range. The descendants of the original colonists have largely maintained their language and traditions. Wattle-growing is the main industry. Population: 1,500, including 350 Whites.

Newnham, Rev. W. O. Founder and first Headmaster of Hilton College, Natal (q.v.). Born in Farnham, Surrey, 1825, came to Natal 1855. Associated with Bishop J. W. Colenso. Returned to England but was back in Natal in 1863. Founded College in Pietermaritzburg in 1868, and moved to Hilton in 1872. His later years, 1877–1893, were spent in England, where he died.

New Republic. Community established in Northern Natal in August, 1884, on a territory covering approximately 3,000,000 acres, ceded by the Zulus to a group of Boers who had supported the Chief Dinizulu (q.v.) in his struggle for supremacy against Usibepu. The settlement was established in Vryheid, which became the capital, and a simple form of administration, headed by General Lukas Meyer, came into operation. At first the New Republic claimed a protec-torate over Zululand, but on October 22, 1886, it agreed to relinquish this under an agreement with Governor Havelock of Natal, who acknowledged their independence on this condition. The most distinguished citizen of the New Republic was General Louis Botha (q.v.). Finally, on September 11, 1887, after a difficult existence, the New Republic became part of the South African Republic, and was formed into the district of Vryheid.

New Scotland. Farming area in the Eastern Transvaal, originally settled by Scottish emigrants brought out by Alexander McCorkindale (q.v.) in 1867. The centre was first called Roburnia, in honour of Robert Burns, but was renamed Amsterdam (q.v.).

Newspapers. Many difficulties attended the establishment of the newspaper press in South Africa. Although H. H. Smith, a master printer, who arrived at the Cape soon after the British occupation in 1795, petitioned for the right to set up a press, it was another firm, Walker & Robertson, who received the first authority to start a newspaper. On August 1, 1800, the pending publication of the *Kaapsche Stads Courant*, with its English equivalent, the *Cape Town Gazette and African Advertiser*, was made known. The first number, printed on August 16, 1800, is the lineal ancestor of the present *Government Gazette*. Within a short time the Government took over the journal, paid out £2,000 compensation to Walker & Robertson and moved the press to the Castle, Cape Town.

For the next 24 years, until 1824, printing remained a Government monopoly. Efforts were made in 1823 by Thomas Pringle (q.v.) and Abraham Faure to start a monthly magazine, of which they issued a prospectus, but the plan was given up and instead, on January 7, 1824, with the approval of the Colonial Secretary in London and against the wishes of Governor

Lord Charles Somerset, the first number of the *South African Commercial Advertiser* was issued. Its early career was very stormy, being marred by actions for libel, demands for security in cash and finally by its bodily suppression at the instance of the Governor. George Greig, the printer, not only had his press sealed up but was ordered to leave the colony within a month. The circumstances were, however, brought to the notice of the authorities in London, and on August 31, 1825, the *Advertiser* started again, this time with John Fairbairn (q.v.) as editor. This overruling of an arbitrary governor is generally recognised as marking the birth of a free press in South Africa.

Thenceforward the number of newspapers and magazines steadily grew, including the *Zuid-Afrikaansche Tijdschrift*, the pioneer magazine in Dutch, started in 1824, and the ambitious *Cape of Good Hope Literary Gazette* in 1830. In the same year printing began in Grahamstown, and the famous *Grahamstown Journal* (q.v.), nicknamed *The Settlers' Bible*, made its début in December 1831, the lineal ancestor of the present *Grocott's Daily Mail*. Printed by L. M. Meurant, it enjoyed the distinction of being the first South African newspaper published outside Cape Town.

Of the many newspapers and magazines that followed, the vast majority have disappeared, but a few still flourish, including the *Eastern Province Herald* (q.v.) begun in 1845, the *Natal Witness* (q.v.), in 1846 (only 2 years younger than the pioneer Voortrekker paper *De Natalier*, started at Pietermaritzburg in 1844), and the *Friend of the Sovereignty and Bloemfontein Gazette* (now *The Friend*, q.v.), on June 10, 1852.

In 1857 the *Cape Argus* (q.v.) was established, in the same year as the first newspaper in the Transvaal, the *Staats Courant*. At Potchefstroom, on October 15, 1859, appeared *De Oude Emigrant* (*The Old Emigrant*), the first local journal in private hands, published by J. P. Borrius. Early newspapers in Dutch included *Het Volksblad*, issued in Cape Town in 1849, but it was not until 1875 that the first Afrikaans paper was launched, the famous *Patriot* (q.v.).

With the discovery of diamonds and gold came a rapid increase in the scale of the local press, not only on the fields themselves but in the older settlements. From this period dates the *Diamond Fields Advertiser*, started in 1875 at Kimberley, and the transfer of the *Eastern Star* by ox-wagon from Grahamstown to Johannesburg in 1887, where it was renamed the *Star* (q.v.).

Towards the end of the 19th century came the development of chains of newspapers, the most important being controlled by the Argus Printing and Publishing Company. This body also started the first papers in Rhodesia, headed by the handwritten and duplicated *Mashonaland Times*, which became the present *Rhodesia Herald* (q.v.). The *Cape Times* (q.v.) dates from 1876 and was soon acknowledged one of the most influential journals in the country. Although there were a number of smaller mission journals, the real beginning of the Bantu press was in 1884, when John Tengo Jabavu (q.v.) founded *Imvo Zabantsundu* at King William's Town.

The present century has been marked by the development of the popular newspaper, of which Edgar Wallace, as first editor of the *Rand Daily Mail* in 1902, and George Kingswell, founder of the Johannesburg *Sunday Times* in 1906, may be regarded as the pioneers. Higher technical standards, brighter presentation and the widespread use of illustrations and cartoons expanded the popularity of the South African press. The largest circulation today is that of the *Sunday Times*, which is approximately 430,000 a week. Among the dailies the *Star* averages around 167,000 and the *Rand Daily Mail* 112,000. The largest circulation among the Afrikaans weeklies is that of *Dagbreek-Landstem*, over 377,000. *Die Burger* (q.v.), founded in 1915, is the original newspaper of the Nasionale Pers, and was first edited by Dr. D. F. Malan (q.v.).

A notable feature of the South African press in recent years is the rapid development of a Black reading public. *Drum*, which has separate editions for East and West Africa, as well as its local version produced in Johannesburg, claims sales totalling over 300,000 in the continent. Other successful magazines of the same type are *Zonk* and *Bona*. *See also* PRESS COMMISSION.

The press in Rhodesia is largely controlled by the Rhodesia Printing and Publishing Company, an offshoot of the Argus Company. Altogether the Republic has 20 daily papers and Rhodesia 2. There are about 550 registered periodicals of which nearly half are issued in the Transvaal, those serving the non-European community numbering about 50. Approximately 60 journals of all kinds are issued in Rhodesia, Zambia and Malawi.

Newton, Arthur. South African runner. Born in 1881, he became a farmer, and as a young man showed exceptional ability on the running track. He came into national prominence when he was over 50, after he broke records for cross-country running. His main purpose in seeking this prominence was to draw attention to grievances about the ownership of his farm. His unconventional methods failed to bring him success in this field, but his fame was soon established. Later Newton withdrew from South Africa and went overseas, one of his achievements being to run across the United States from Atlantic to Pacific. He died in 1959.

Newtown: 1. Coloured settlement near Wellington, Cape Province. Population: 1,272

2. Suburb of Johannesburg.

N.F.A. Abbreviation for Natal Field Artillery (q.v.).

Ngami. Lake in the north of the Kalahari Desert, which has greatly dwindled in extent since first sighted in 1849 by David Livingstone. Its area, originally about 300 sq. miles, is now to a large extent mere swamp. Professor E. H. L. Schwartz (q.v.) incorporated Lake Ngami in his scheme for the reclamation of the Kalahari. Owing to the flatness of the country it may be possible to restore the flow of the rivers feeding the Okavango marshes, which have become choked up. Several Government inquiries have examined the plan.

Ngodwana. Village founded in 1965 in Eastern Transvaal for workers of the new R13,000,000 paper mill.

Ngoya. University College in Zululand, established for Bantu students in 1959. *See also* UNIVERSITIES.

Ngqeleni. Village in Eastern Cape Province. Population: 460, including 150 Whites.

Ngwane. Alternative name for Swaziland (q.v.).

Ngwee ('Brightness'). Zambian coin in circulation from 1968. 100 Ngwees equal 1 Kwacha (equal to 1 Rand).

Ngwenya Iron Ore Mine. Large workings in north-western Swaziland worked by Anglo-American Corporation of South Africa. *See* SWAZILAND RAILWAY.

Ngwenyama ('King'). Title bestowed by the Swazi people upon Sobhuza II (q.v.).

Nibmar. Word coined to describe British Labour Government's conditions for recognition of independence of Rhodesia (q.v.). It comprises the initial letters of 'No Independence Before Majority African Rule'.

Nicholls, George Heaton. South African legislator and diplomat. Born in London, 1876, he joined the Army in India and fought in Burma and Tirah. During the South African War he came to South Africa, enlisted in the Northern Rhodesian Police and accompanied Chief Lewanika on his visit to London for the coronation of King Edward VII. After working in the Northern Rhodesian Civil Service, Heaton Nicholls spent some time in British New Guinea, where he commanded the local Native Constabulary before settling as a farmer in Natal. He became prominent as President of the Zululand Sugar Planters' Union and of the South African Sugar Planters' Union, besides founding the Umfulozi Co-operative Sugar Planters. In 1920 Heaton Nicholls was elected to Parliament as Member for Zululand, and showed himself as a strong supporter of the British cause. He joined the South African Delegation on a Parliamentary tour of Canada in 1928, attended the Imperial Conference in London in 1931 as an adviser, took part in the Indian Round Table Conference and many other important events. He was later appointed a permanent member of the Native Affairs Commission. He served successively as Union High Commissioner in London and as Administrator of Natal. At an advanced age he was leader of the Union Federal Party in Natal. Heaton Nicholls wrote extensively, and was the author of a novel called *Bayete*, on the Bantu threat to white civilisation. He died in 1959.

Nicholson's Nek. Elevation near Ladysmith, Natal, and scene of a battle on October 30, 1899, in which heavy casualties were sustained by the British, including the loss of 850 prisoners. General Christiaan de Wet (q.v.), in seizing the northern end of the hill, began the series of victories that was to bring him world fame.

The action is also referred to as 'Klein Majuba.'

Nickel. Metal recovered in South Africa near Rustenburg, and also found near Mount Ayliff, Cape Province, in Zululand, in the Waterberg, near Barberton, etc. So far the output has been small. In recent years production has been developed in Rhodesia, where three mines have been opened.

Niekerkshoop. Village near Hay, Cape Province. Population: 820, including 220 Whites.

Nieshout. *See* SNEEZEWOOD.

Nieuwoudtville. Village in the Cape Province, founded in 1897, between Calvinia and Van Rhynsdorp, and named after the original farm owners. Centre for the production of rooibos tea (*see* BUSH TEA). Population: 900, including 450 Whites.

Nigel. Mining town on the Eastern Witwatersrand, named after Nigel MacLeish, finder of the Nigel Gold Mine. Founded in 1909. Rising industrial centre. Population: 38,350, including 12,000 Whites.

Nightjars (Caprimulgidae). A most interesting family of night birds found in the Cape, Natal and Zululand, related to the Swifts but larger. They are insect-feeders that conceal themselves as bark and leaves all day, and fly openly or sit on the roads by night. They sing a lovely whistling song.

Ninevites. Criminal gangs which flourished among Africans, particularly after World War I on the Witwatersrand. They indulged in housebreaking, murder and other offences. After a considerable number of capital sentences they passed into obscurity.

Nkana. Large copper mine in Zambia. Discovered in 1910 by Moffat Thompson, its serious development began after 1924, when it had come under the control of Chester Beatty, and of what became the Rhodesian Selection Trust, under Sir R. L. Prain. It is now one of the leading producers in the world. The mine adjoins the town of Kitwe (q.v.).

Nkhandla Forest. Large area of natural forest in Zululand, burial place of the Zulu king Cetewayo (q.v.). During the 1906 Zulu Rebellion this region was a centre of the fighting. Large wattle plantations have been established and there is also cattle farming. The village of Nkhandla has a population of 280, including 80 Whites.

N.M.R. Abbreviation for Natal Mounted Rifles (q.v.).

Nobel Prizes. *See* THEILER, DR. MAX and LUTHULI, ALBERT.

Nofal, Emil. South African film producer. Born in 1926 of a poor family, he started at fourteen in the Killarney (Johannesburg) film studios of I. W. Schlesinger (q.v.), and worked there many years. In 1958 he produced his first picture, *Rip Van Wyk*, a South African adaptation of *Rip Van Winkel*, and was associated with Jamie Uys (q.v.) until 1964, when he started on his own account. Among his controversial but successful pictures are *Die Kandidaat* (Afrikaans) and in 1969 *Katrina*.

Noki. *See* ROCK RAT.

No-Man's-Land. Original name for Griqualand East (q.v.).

Nondweni. Former gold mining camp in Zululand, now almost abandoned. During the Zulu War in 1879 Louis Napoleon of France (q.v.) was killed near by.

Nongoma. Village in Zululand and administrative centre, scene of a battle between the rival chieftains Dinizulu and Usibepu in 1888, and situated near Mahashini (q.v.) seat of the Paramount Chief of Zululand today. The name Nongoma is derived from a

word meaning 'Wizard.' Population: 1,650, including 485 Whites.

Nonquase. *See* CATTLE KILLING DELUSION.

Noodhulpliga. *See* SUID-AFRIKAANSE NOODHULPLIGA.

Noodsberg. Farming area near the Valley of the Thousand Hills in Natal, so called by the Voortrekkers on account of the distress (Nood) in which they found themselves at the time. There are two ranges, the Great and Little Noodsberg, and the highest point is about 4,000 feet. Wattle bark is the principal product.

Noodt, Pieter Gysbert. Dutch Governor of the Cape. Previously employed by the Dutch East India Company as Director of Fortifications in India, he first visited the Colony in 1718 and remained for nearly a year. He showed himself as a disagreeable and quarrelsome character, but it was only upon his return, in 1727, as Governor that his unsuitability was manifested fully. He explored some forests of the interior, but his name is chiefly associated with the barbarous treatment of a number of soldiers, who were driven to mutiny by his behaviour. His sudden death, while sitting in his chair, was regarded as a judgment from Heaven. Later research has, however, shown that his part in the affair was not as bad as tradition alleges. Noodt was buried in the Groote Kerk in April 1729.

Nooi. A term of respect by natives for a young European woman. It is believed to have been derived from a Portuguese word 'Noiva' meaning bride.

Nooiensuil. Afrikaans name for Barn Owl. *See* OWL.

Noordgesig. Coloured township near Johannesburg, Transvaal. Population: 7,775.

Noorsveld. Name given to area around Jansenville in the Eastern Province, derived from species of bush, the

Noors, allied to the Euphorbia. The plant is eaten by sheep and other small stock.

Norfolk Island Pine (*Araucaria excelsa*). One of the exotic trees from Norfolk Island near Australia, which stands unmoved by the Cape winds. Grown for ornament along the coast from Cape Town eastwards. Tall and symmetrical, with branches in regular whorls.

North Charterland Exploration Company Ltd. Land and mining company in Zambia, registered on May 17, 1895, to acquire from the British South Africa Company Ltd. an area of 10,000 square miles, between the Anglo-Portuguese (Mozambique) frontier, Nyasaland and the Loangwa River. The original capital was £1,000,000. It was reconstructed in 1910 and in 1937, with a smaller capital, and is now mainly engaged in tobacco growing, transport, ranching and land development.

Northern Rhodesia. *See* ZAMBIA.

Northey, Major-General Sir Edward. British soldier. Born in England in 1868, and educated at Eton and Sandhurst. First distinguished himself in several Indian Frontier wars followed by service in the South African War. In World War I he commanded the King's Royal Rifles in France and Belgium, before being placed in charge of the Nyasa-Rhodesian Field Force in 1916, which gained considerable success in the East African Campaign. In 1918 he was appointed Governor of Kenya. He died on December 25, 1953.

Norton. Township in Rhodesia, 25 miles west of Salisbury. Although its history goes back to the early days of the Colony, its growth is comparatively recent, stimulated by the construction of the great dam, Lake Macilwaine (q.v.). The present population is only 160 Europeans and 660 Africans, but plans have been laid for the development of a large factory and housing area, with accommodation for 30,000 people.

Nottingham Road. Village in Natal, in the Drakensberg foothills, called after the Nottinghamshire Regiment stationed there. Founded in 1850. It is famed for its trout-fishing, as well as for the magnificent dairying and farming country. Population: 1,062, including 324 Whites.

Noupoort. *See* NAAUWPOORT.

Nqamakwe. Village in Eastern Cape Province. Population: 310, including 140 Whites.

Nqutu (meaning a 'vessel with a flat top'). Village in North-Eastern Zululand, so named because of the shape of the neighbouring mountain. Population: 360, including 90 Whites.

N.R.C. Abbreviation for Native Recruiting Corporation (q.v.).

Ntsikana. First convert to Christianity among the Africans of the Eastern Cape Province, now commonly accepted by them as a saint. Born at the end of the 18th century, of the Gaika tribe, he met Dr. J. T. Vanderkemp (q.v.), the pioneer missionary on a visit to Gaikaland in September 1799. Thus began his earliest interest in Christianity. He had visions foreshadowing the establishment of the new creed, taking a stand against a distorted version, composed of Christian and pagan ideas, put forward by a leader named Nxele. Ntsikana soon acquired great influence in the whole countryside and began to compose religious songs which are still sung by his compatriots. He had many fresh visions and made prophecies which were fulfilled. Many came to consult him at his home near Fort Beaufort. While it does not appear that he was ever formally converted, Ntsikana preached the doctrines of the Gospel to his neighbours and enjoyed the friendship of many missionaries. He died in 1876, since when he has been held in increasing veneration by the Xosas, who hold an annual ceremony in his memory and refer to him as St. Ntsikana.

Num-Num (*Carissa arduina* Lam.). Very spiny shrub bearing edible scarlet berries and bright green leaves. It grows generally on the forest edge in areas of summer rainfall, from George to Zululand.

Nuwerus. Village near Vanrhynsdorp, Cape Province. Population: 420, including 330 Whites.

Nyanga. Bantu township on the Cape Flats outside Cape Town. Scene of disturbances during March 1960.

Nyasaland. *See* MALAWI.

Nylstroom. Town in the Transvaal, north of Pretoria. Its name is derived from the fact that the early trekkers mistook a local stream for the unknown source of the Nile. It was founded in 1864 and is today the centre of a large and prosperous farming area, specialising in groundnuts and tobacco. Population: 7,665, including 4,000 Whites.

O

Oak (*Quercus*). Many varieties grow well in South Africa wherever there is deep, rich soil. The Common Oak (*Q. robur*) was introduced by Simon van der Stel (q.v.) and has been one of the beauties of the Cape Peninsula and the South-Western Cape ever since. Both the Pin Oak (*Q. palustris*) and the evergreen Holm Oak (*Q. ilex*) grow successfully also in the Transvaal and Orange Free State. The evergreen Cork Oak (*Q. suber*) grows best in the South-Western Cape.

Oats, Francis. Leader of the Diamond Industry. Born in Cornwall, 1848. He interested himself in Trade Unionism as a youth and at the age of 19 attended the first Miners' Congress in Paris in 1867. Later he became a mining engineer and as such was imported by the Kimberley Mining Board in 1875. As manager of the Victoria Mine he came into contact with Cecil John Rhodes and was made one of the Life Governors of De Beers Mines upon its foundation. In 1905 was elected Chairman and remained in office until his death in 1918.

Odendaal Report. Memorandum prepared by Commission under the Hon. Frans Hendrik Odendaal, Administrator of the Transvaal. Appointed in September 1962 to examine the position in South West Africa and make recommendations. The Report, issued in 1964, proposed the extension of the area occupied by non-White peoples in the territory by 24,000,000 acres—an additional 50 per cent, most of which is owned by White farmers or by the State, and which is valued at R38,000,000. Homelands are proposed for various groups in Ovamboland (population 240,000), Okavangoland (28,000), Kaokoveld (9,000), East Caprivi (16,000), Damaraland (44,000),

Namaland (35,000), Hereroland (35,000), Rehoboth Gebiet (11,000), Bushmanland (12,000) and Tswanaland adjoining Botswana. Proposals for the expenditure of R236,000,000 over a period of 10 years, include the development of hydro-electric power on the Cunene River, with a 100,000 kilowatt station at the Ruacana Falls, construction of hundreds of dams, 700 miles of roads and many other major works.

Odendaalsrus (formerly written **Odendaalsrust**). Town on the Orange Free State gold fields, named after the original owners of the farm on which it is laid out. Established in 1905, it remained a village until the spectacular gold discoveries near by in the 1940's. Today Odendaalsrus has a population of 19,000, including 7,000 Whites.

Oerder, Frans David. South African artist. Born in Rotterdam, Holland, 1867, he showed his artistic gifts as a child and at 13 began his training, which included study in Italy and in Belgium. At the age of 23, in 1890, he came to the Transvaal to take up work with the Netherlands South African Railway Company, which included painting signposts! Fortunately he found a position as an art teacher and was sent into the field as an official artist on the Boer side in the South African War. His sense of colour and beauty won him reputation as a landscape and a flower painter. From 1908 to 1938 he lived in Holland. He died in Pretoria in 1944.

Ofcolaco. Settlement in the Eastern Transvaal, its name being an abbreviation of the sponsors, the Officers' Colonial Land Company. It was started soon after World War I by a group of retired ex-officers, largely from India, who, after many struggles, succeeded in attaining substantial prosperity, mainly through growing citrus and other sub-tropical crops.

Off-Colour. Diamond slightly tinted with yellow.

Ogilvie, Canon George. Founder of Rugby Football in Southern Africa. Born in Calne, Wiltshire, England, on June 30, 1826, he went to school at Winchester, and took his degree at Oxford, where he took Holy Orders. His early years, from 1855 to 1858, were spent in South America, at Buenos Aires, whence he came to Cape Town as Precentor of St. George's Cathedral and first headmaster of St. George's Grammar School. From there he went to Diocesan Collegiate School in Cape Town, 1861, renamed Diocesan College (Bishops) six years later. He introduced the Winchester version of Rugby football, and became an original supporter of local scratch teams. In 1875 the two first clubs (Western Province and Hamiltons) were founded with Ogilvie's help and in the following year the change from the Winchester to the 'Carrying Code' of the Rugby Union was brought about. Canon Ogilvie died in Cape Town on May 1, 1915.

Ohrigstad. Village in the Eastern Transvaal, established under the name of Andries Ohrigstad in 1845, but abandoned two years later, when most of the residents migrated to Lydenburg (q.v.) because of the fever prevailing in the older settlement. In recent years the village, which had fallen into ruins, has gradually come to life again. Population: 1,100, including 300 Whites.

Oidium. Also known as Grape Mildew. Disease of the vine, caused by a parasitic fungus of the Erysipheae family. It made its appearance at the Cape in October 1859 and quickly spread through the entire Western Province, doing great damage. The matter was referred to Dr. L. Pappe, Colonial botanist, who was unable to find a remedy for a long time. Indeed, Oidium had very nearly wiped out the vine in the Cape Colony, before the plague was stopped by large shipments of sulphur from abroad, which were applied by a simple apparatus. This is still used in South African vineyards to prevent a recurrence.

Oil in South Africa. Efforts to discover mineral oil go back to the 1890's when syndicates were formed to follow up alleged strikes in the Cape, Transvaal and Orange Free State. These were renewed in the early 1900's when several boreholes were sunk. In 1913 an overseas expert retained by the Government gave it as his view that, despite oil seepages in coal formations, the country had no payable deposits. In 1964 the State took over control of oil prospecting leases and established the Soekor (Southern Oil Exploration Corporation) (q.v.). Most of South Africa and its adjoining off-shore shelf is under grant to large overseas prospecting groups. Two large drills capable of reaching depths of 20,000 feet were imported in 1966 and began work in the Karroo. On March 26, 1969 it was announced officially that petroleum gas had been struck on the continental shelf, 40 miles offshore from Plettenberg Bay (q.v.) in water 400 feet deep. The strike, yielding 35,000,000 cubic feet a day, including 'volatile petroleum products', was made by the research ship *Glomar Syrte* of the Superior Oil Company. For the time being the discovery was sealed off.

Okahandja. Village in South West Africa and former seat of a Herero chief. It became a Rhenish Mission Station in 1840, and saw much fighting in native wars. The signing of the original treaty between the Germans under Dr. Heinrich Goering (father of the Nazi leader) and the Hereros took place there in 1885. The Germans erected a fort, in which they were besieged during the Herero War of 1904. More recently the canning plant of the Liebig Company was erected there, but closed down again. Dr. Heinrich Vedder, the famous missionary and historian, lived there for many years. The name means 'a ridge' in the native language. Population: 3,739, including 1,174 Whites.

O'Kiep. *See* O'OKIEP.

Old Bunting. Trading post on Wild Coast of Pondoland, so called after a former Buntingville mission station.

Old Maid's Snuff. *See* DEVIL'S SNUFFBOX.

Old Umtali. Mission station about 14 miles from Umtali (q.v.) in the east of Rhodesia. Here in 1890 the village, designed to be the capital of Manicaland, was established, but removed some years later to the site of modern Umtali, most of the first buildings being allowed to fall into decay. Chief reason for the change was that the railway passed through the other site.

Olifantshoek. Village near Postmasburg, Cape Province. Population: 1,459, including 561 Whites.

Olifants Nek Dam. Large irrigation project in the Magaliesberg, nine miles South of Rustenburg, Transvaal. Built in 1926–7, the concrete wall is 440 feet long and 80 feet high, the irrigable area being 4,290 acres.

Olifants River: 1. River in Western Cape Province, rising in the Great Winterhoek and for 80 miles flowing through narrow valleys in the Olifants River Mountains and Cedarberg. Used for irrigation. Chief tributary Doorn River. Length 200 miles. Enters sea on west coast.
2. River in the Transvaal. Rises east of Pretoria, flows north-east to the Limpopo. Length 360 miles.

Olive, Wild or **Olywehout** (*Olea verrucosa* Link). Tree up to 30 feet, resembling the European olive. Wood slow-growing and hard. Occurs in most parts of the Republic of South Africa.

Oliviera, Basil L. D'. *See* D'OLIVIERA, BASIL L.

Olympic Games. The first occasion on which South Africans took part in the international Olympic Games was in London, 1908, when R. E. Walker won the 100 metres final in 10·45 seconds, while C. A. Hefferon came second in the Marathon race. At Stockholm in 1912, K. K. McArthur won the Marathon race, with another South African, C. W. Gitsham, second. Len Richardson, the only representative of the British Commonwealth, came fourth in the cross-country race, while C. Winslow not only won the singles, but partnered by H. A. Kitson, won the doubles at tennis. The next Olympic Games in which South Africa took part after World War I were in 1920, when Bevil Rudd won the 400 metres track race, C. Walker won the bantam-weight boxing and L. Raymond the singles at tennis. In 1924 Willie Smith was the winner of the bantam-weight boxing, S. J. M. Atkinson came second in the 110 metres hurdles, C. C. McMaster was third in the 10,000 metres walk and H. Kaltenbrun second in the road cycling race. In Amsterdam, 1928, S. J. M. Atkinson won the 100 metres hurdles, and in Los Angeles, 1932, Miss M. Clark won the high jump, Laurie Stevens the light-weight boxing and D. Carstens the light-heavy-weight. Since then the record of the South African teams at Olympic Games included fewer winners, owing to the increasing severity of competition.

In 1963 the International Olympic Games Committee confronted the South African Olympic Games Committee with the demand that no Apartheid (q.v.) be applied as far as the

South African representative team was concerned. The South African Committee accepted this, provided the non-Whites reached the necessary standard of performance. Representatives of Whites and non-Whites were accordingly to attend the 1964 Olympic Games at Tokyo. The International Committee, however, demanded that the South African Committee also formally and publicly express its disapproval of Apartheid. When the South African Committee protested that this signified the introduction of politics into the Olympic Games, the International Committee withdrew its invitation to Tokyo, where accordingly South Africa went unrepresented in 1964. A few Rhodesian entrants were present. After lengthy negotiations the International Olympic Committee agreed to allow South Africa to send teams, including both white and non-white competitors, to the games held in 1968 in Mexico City, but at the last moment the authorities succumbed to political pressure and the invitation was withdrawn.

Olyvenhouts Drift. Original name for Upington (q.v.). Dutch for olive wood.

Omaruru. Town in South-West Africa, between Windhoek and Swakopmund. It began as a station of the Rhenish Mission in 1864, and in 1870 was given the first church and school. Although the name signifies in Herero 'bitter water,' the area is not without a sweet water supply. During the Herero War the local fort was besieged by the insurgents. More recently gold was discovered near by. The place has a flourishing creamery, and is a centre of the karakul trade. Population: 2,750, including 900 Whites.

Onderstedorings. Village near Williston, Cape Province. Population: 40, including 10 Whites.

Onderstepoort. Veterinary Research Station near Pretoria, established, as a result of the Rinderpest outbreak of 1896, by the late Sir Arnold Theiler (q.v.), under whom it developed into one of the largest and most successful institutions of its kind in the world. Apart from the research and routine (vaccine production, etc.) which fall under the Department of Agriculture, Onderstepoort houses the Veterinary Faculty of the University of Pretoria. The township is laid out on Garden City principles.

Onrus. Seaside resort near Hermanus, Cape Province, on Walker Bay, much favoured by campers in the summer season. Population: 400, including 250 Whites.

Onseepkans. Village near Kenhardt, Cape Province. Population: 1,086, including 271 Whites.

'Onze Jan.' Nickname for Jan Hendrik Hofmeyr (q.v.).

Oogies. Colliery village in the Transvaal. Named after the 'oog,' or 'eye,' formation in which springs occur. Laid out on the farm Oogiesfontein in 1928. Near by is the Oogies Navigation Colliery. Population: 2,310, including 429 Whites.

O'okiep. Copper mining village in Namaqualand. Founded in 1852, and developed by the Cape Copper Company and its successors. The name is derived from the Hottentot and means 'very brackish.' The surrounding country is desolate. As a young man John Galsworthy, the novelist, was stationed as mine secretary at O'okiep. Population: 2,967, including 827 Whites.

Oorlams. A name applied to Hottentots in South West Africa, who were able to speak Dutch or English, also used as an adjective to mean 'shrewd.' Origin obscure, one theory being that it is derived from the name of an early settler in Namaqualand, another that it comes from the Malay 'Orang Lama' (old man).

Oortjie. Traditional Afrikaans expression for a farthing, signifying a little order (i.e. decoration) from the fact that their Dutch equivalent was broken off a larger coin stamped deeply with a cross.

Oosthuizen, Marthinus Jacobus. Boer hero. Born in 1819 near Uitenhage, and joined the Great Trek. His claim to permanent fame lies in his behaviour on February 16, 1838, when, after the massacre of Pieter Retief and his companions, Oosthuizen brought his own family into safety and then returned to an exposed position, where he barricaded himself as best he could and awaited the enemy attack. Single-handed he kept them at bay for a while, and then dashed through 1,500 Zulus, bringing ammunition to a number of his comrades. In after years he was a farmer in Natal, and died in 1897.

Opgaaf. Certain taxes or tax-lists, levied in former times by the Government.

Oppenheimer, Sir Bernard. Mining magnate. Brother of Sir Ernest Oppenheimer (q.v.). Born in Germany, 1866, he came to Kimberley as a young man and was a successful diamond merchant and share operator. Returning to England, he attracted attention through his ambitious but unsuccessful efforts after World War I to establish large Diamond Cutting Works, employing ex-servicemen, in Brighton, Cambridge, Durham and Fort William. He died on June 13, 1921.

Oppenheimer, Sir Ernest. South African mining and industrial magnate. Born at Friedberg in Hesse, Germany, 1880, he came to London as a young man to join the staff of his relative, the well-known diamond merchant, Dunkelsbuhler, who in 1902 sent him to Kimberley as his representative. He came to be recognised as one of the soundest experts among the buyers. Upon the discovery of diamonds in what was then German South West Africa, he made a journey there on behalf of the interests he represented

and produced an unusually wise and far-seeing report on the possibilities, as early as 1910. He was elected to the Kimberley Town Council and in 1912 became mayor, a position he held for three years. During this time he achieved the long-sought amalgamation of Kimberley with the neighbouring town of Beaconsfield. Upon the outbreak of World War I, he moved to Johannesburg. Securing backing from the United States, he took over large German and other interests and established the Anglo-American Corporation of South Africa. It soon became one of the largest mining groups in South Africa, particularly on account of its development on the East Rand. Oppenheimer had noticed the possibilities offered by the occupation of German South West Africa by the Union troops in 1915, and at the earliest opportunity he secured control of the existing German interests there, which resulted in the formation of the Consolidated Diamond Mines of South West Africa. He became a leading figure in the affairs of the De Beers Consolidated Mines, of which he was elected Chairman in 1929. He reorganised the diamond industry, creating new bodies to handle sales and generally to stabilise production. Within a short while virtually the whole of the industry was under his control, including the Premier (Transvaal) Diamond Mining Company Ltd. and Jagersfontein. The menace to the stability of the market created by the enormous discoveries in Namaqualand was overcome by him through the buying out of the interests of Dr. Hans Merensky. He became interested in Rhodesia, where the Anglo-American established a subsidiary, and in the early 1930's he began large-scale investments in the Rhodesian Copper Belt, of which he was one of the first to realise the possibilities. The Anglo-American thus became a major factor. Sir Ernest Oppenheimer realised the possibilities of gold occurrences in the Orange Free State and encouraged drilling operations in the Odendaalsrust area. The outcome was the discovery of an entirely new goldfield shortly before World War II. Sir Ernest Oppenheimer was now one of the principal figures, if not *the* principal figure, in South African mining, and his industrial empire dominated the country. He continued to expand his interests into many new fields, and exercised great influence in South Africa, London and the United States. Later he placed a great part of his authority in the hands of his son, Mr. Harry Oppenheimer. From 1924 to 1938 he was member for Kimberley in the Union Parliament. Sir Ernest Oppenheimer died in Johannesburg, 1957, leaving an estate valued at over three and a half million pounds, of which a million was earmarked for public purposes.

Oppenheimer, Harry Frederick. South African financier and industrialist. Born at Kimberley on October 28, 1908, he was educated at Charterhouse and Oxford before joining the mining groups created by his father, Sir Ernest Oppenheimer (q.v.). During World War II he served with the 4th South African Armoured Cars from 1940 to 1945. From 1947 to 1958 he was Member of Parliament for Kimberley, but resigned in order to concentrate on the vast interests passing under his control on the death of his father, which led to his appointment as Chairman of the Anglo-American Corporation of South Africa, De Beers Consolidated Mines, etc.

Opsitting. Literally 'to sit up.' Old Boer custom by which a young man courting was allowed to sit up with the girl of his choice while the rest of the family retired. A candle was left burning on the table, its length an indication of the degree of favour which he had attained—a long candle showing that he was well liked.

Opstal. Farm buildings. Under the old Cape law, settlers securing a Loan Farm were entitled to the ownership of improvements which they added, including vineyards and orchards.

Orange Free State. Province of the Republic of South Africa, occupying the territory of the old Orange River Republic. After the South African War it was known as the Orange River Colony, but its original name was restored after Union. It comprises 11 per cent of the total area of the country, and in 1960 its total population was 1,373,790, of whom 274,596 were Europeans, 1,073,613 Bantu, 25,565 Coloureds. The number of Asiatics was negligible, namely 16. White population in 1966 was 312,000. The area of the Orange Free State is 49,838 sq. miles. The Orange Free State had 134,670 voters in 1955.

Orange River. First discovered by Europeans in 1760. Named by Colonel Jacob Gordon after Stadholders of Holland in 1779. One of the great rivers of Africa. Rises in Basutoland, where it comprises the Sinqua and the Sinquanyane. Later it is joined by the Kornet Spruit, the Kraai River and the Caledon (near Bethulie, O.F.S.). Its largest tributary is the Vaal (500 miles long), followed by the Hygap and Haartebeest Rivers. Below Upington the Orange River takes its mighty plunge in the Aughrabies Falls (q.v.) before continuing its course through 300 miles of wilderness in Namaqualand and the Richtersveld. Its course ends in the Atlantic, near Alexander Bay. The total length of the Orange River is about 1,200 miles and the towns on its banks include Aliwal North, Prieska and Upington. Much of its soil is very fertile, particularly near Kakamas, where it has gained the name of 'The Nile of South Africa.' The original Dutch name of the Orange was the 'Groot Rivier,' and to the natives it was the Gariep, a Hottentot word of similar significance. There are important bridges across the Orange at Aliwal North (Frere Bridge), near Hope Town (1,230 feet long) and near Alexander Bay (Oppenheimer Bridge—3,000 feet long). Area drained by the Orange River is estimated at 400,000 sq. miles.

Orange River Scheme. Very large project, estimated at R540,000,000, for the economic development, over some 30 years, of the Orange River, its tributaries and several other South African waterways. The survey was made in 1956, the scheme adopted by Parliament in 1962 and work begun in 1963. Larger than the Tennessee Valley Scheme, on which it is partly based, it includes irrigation development, the production of electric power and the diversion of existing rivers, by means of tunnels and canals, into new areas. Irrigation is planned of 760,000 acres from a series of major dams, including Ruigte Vallei (q.v.), near Norval's Pont; Van der Kloof (q.v.), near Petrusville, Cape Province; and Torquay (q.v.), between Hopetown and Douglas. Hydro-electric power stations with total capacity of 177,000 kilowatts are to be erected. (*See* ELECTRICITY SUPPLY COMMISSION.) A mountain tunnel, 51 miles long and 16 feet in diameter, will lead the Orange into the Fish River, while another 32-mile tunnel, 8 feet in diameter, will link and stabilise the Fish River and the Sundays River basins. Domestic needs for many towns, such as Bloemfontein and De Aar, will also be provided for.

Oranges. *See* CITRUS.

Orangeville. Village on the Wilge River, near Heilbron in the northern Orange Free State. Farming centre. Population: 485, including 135 Whites.

Orangia Union. Party formed by the Afrikaans-speaking and ex-Republican population of the Orange Free State, during the Crown Colony régime, by General J. B. M. Hertzog, General

Christiaan de Wet, Abraham Fischer (qq.v.) and others. It came into power in the 1907 Election and remained in office until Union in 1910, when it merged in the South African Party.

Oranje Vrystaatse Veld Artillerie. Original name of Sixth Field Regiment, South African Artillery (*see* REGIMENT, SIXTH FIELD).

Oranjekrag ('Orange Power'). Village established in connection with Orange River Scheme (q.v.) near the site of the large power station on Hendrik Verwoerd Dam.

Orapa. Diamond-mining centre in north of Botswana established by De Beers Consolidated Mines in 1968. Population about 350, including 50 Whites.

Orchids (Orchidaceae). A most curious and interesting family of plants, many of them growing (but not feeding) on trees and other plants. Strikingly lovely or complex flowers form three sepals, often as large and bright as the three petals. One petal often is a lip or hood, one sepal often a spur. Ovary inferior. Fruit a capsule. Among the beauties of the Cape Peninsula are the delicate Blue Disa (*Herschelia gramini*) and the larger Rooi Disa or Pride of Table Mountain (*Disa uniflora*). Less lovely but more strange is the little Mammakappie (*Pterygodium catholicum*) of the West and South-West Cape, with its dark, spotted leaves and the greenish-yellow and pink flowers, to which it owes its name. Not unlike these is the Rhodesian *Disa welwitschii*, in which the odd sepal forms a hood with a long spur; the stem reddish, clasped by the leaves; flowers a dense pink spike. On the stony hillsides of Western Cape grows the little Spider Orchid (*Batholina burmanniane*), the long hairy stem rising out of the small leaf flat on the ground; petals mauve and feathery. In the forested areas of Eastern Cape, and the bush of Griqualand East is the

Tree Disa (*Mystacidium filicorne*), its spike of white flowers and long spurred white sepals hanging from its tree host.

O'Rell, Max. French humorist and traveller. His real name was Paul Blouet and he was born in Brittany on March 2, 1848. After some years in England as a journalist and school-master, he began a series of travels and lectures, which were to make him famous. He visited South Africa in 1893 and embodied his experiences in *John Bull & Co.*, dealing with a tour round the British Empire as it then was. He met President Kruger and made pungent remarks about South African politics. He died in 1903.

Oribi (*Ourebia ourebi*). Small graceful antelope, 26 inches high, found from the Cape to Rhodesia and Mozambique. It prefers open country, or flat mountain tops, and goes about in pairs or small parties. The male alone has short, straight horns. Tawny-yellow coat with white underparts.

Oribi Gorge. Spectacular gorge in southern Natal, near Port Shepstone, cut by the Umzimkulu River, with sides in many places almost vertical and hundreds of feet deep. A motor road through the gorge is a favourite run for tourists. One of the most remarkable sights is the 'Baboon's Castle,' with its virtually unclimbable precipices.

Orioles (Oriolidae). Moderate-sized birds of starling build, usually with bright yellow plumage and black markings. All have rich singing voices. The European Golden Oriole comes to South Africa as a migrant in very small numbers, and keeps to the wooded country. A more frequent visitor is the larger South African Golden Oriole, which nests as far south as the Northern Transvaal. The Black-Headed Oriole is a resident. It is less shy and readier to make known its song. Common in woods north of Cape Town.

Orkney. Town in the Western Transvaal, near Klerksdorp; important mining centre, serving the Vaal Reefs Gold Mine, the Western Reefs, etc. There is a large cement factory and a uranium treatment plant. Situated on the Vaal River, it is much frequented by sportsmen and holidaymakers. Seven miles away is the great new Vierfontein Power Station of the Electricity Supply Commission, serving a large part of the new goldfields. Population: 36,000, including 12,000 Whites.

Orphan Masters. Officers appointed under the government of the Dutch East India Company for the administration of deceased and insolvent estates. They were usually leading officials or merchants, and acted jointly as a group. Later, after the establishment of the British régime, the system of Orphan Masters, who together formed the Orphan Chamber, was abandoned, and a Master of the Supreme Court (q.v.) took their place.

Orr, Thomas. South African Cabinet Minister. Born in 1857 in Armagh, Ireland, he joined the British Civil Service in the Exchequer Department, and became Auditor-General for Natal in 1902. Retiring on pension on foundation of Union in 1910, he became Member for Pietermaritzburg North, and was Minister of Finance from 1917–1920. He died in 1937.

Osmiridium. *See* IRIDIUM.

Oshakati. Capital of Ovamboland. *See* OVAMBO and SOUTH WEST AFRICA.

Osprey (*Pandion haliaetus*). A fair-sized bird of prey resembling the Peregrine and other fishing owls, and found in most parts where fresh-water fish—its exclusive diet—can be caught in its prickly, padded claws. A hoverer with slow flapping wings, brown back, white underparts, whitish head and small ear tufts. Not certainly known to breed in South Africa. For 'osprey' of of the milliner, *see* EGRET.

Ossewabrandwag. Movement started in South Africa by Colonel J. C. Laas about 1938. It was partially modelled on the Nazi Storm Troopers, and used an emblem closely resembling that of its German counterpart. The Ossewa Brandwag had a semi-military organisation, its more active group being represented by the Stormjaers. During World War II it was declared illegal. After undergoing various vicissitudes and finally incurring the condemnation of the National Party as well as of the United Party, it gradually disintegrated. *See also* DR. J. F. J. VAN RENSBURG.

Ostrich (*Struthio camelus*). Indigenous bird connected with an important industry. Of the five local varieties, the predominating one is the Southern Ostrich. From the earliest days of white settlement, ostriches were hunted for their plumes, for the European market. By 1860 their number had been so much reduced, despite their natural fleetness of foot, that several farmers attempted their domestication. The earliest efforts were recorded about 1853. In 1865 80 birds were in captivity and the exports came to 17,522 lb., worth £65,736. From then on the industry grew rapidly, being concentrated in the vicinity of Graaff-Reinet and the Eastern Province. Profits were immense and prices rose until over £1,000 was paid for a pair of breeding birds. The first great boom began in 1880 and lasted until about 1885. An even greater one set in from 1910 to 1913, when from 746,736 birds, nearly all in the Cape, some £3,000,000 worth of feathers were exported. The onset of World War I caused a crash, both in prices and production, from which the industry has never recovered. Most of the birds were slaughtered to produce leather instead of feathers. In recent times there has been a gradual revival, but there are only about 50,000 birds left to produce less than 100,000 lb. of feathers yearly. Nearly all of these birds are in the Oudtshoorn district. The development of the industry has been largely responsible for the intensive farming practice in this part of the world. The ostrich is peculiar in that its flight apparatus (wings, keeled breastbone and muscles) is so rudimentary as almost to have disappeared. The breastbone, for example, is flat, unlike that of such other birds as flightless pigeons and parrots. To compensate, the ostrich has developed a speed and strength adequate for wild South African life. Feathers are drawn only from the males. A few wild birds survive in the Kalahari and Bushveld. *See* BIRDS.

Oswell, William Cotton. Explorer and hunter. Born in England, 1818, he was educated at Rugby and at Haileybury. As a young man he spent 10 years in India in the Civil Service of Madras, where he did a great deal of elephant hunting. In 1844 he first came to South Africa, where he was attracted by the big game and empty spaces. On his first trek he accompanied the Scottish explorer, Murray of Lintrose (q.v.), and later, in 1849, he gained the friendship of David Livingstone and accompanied him on his famous trip to Lake Ngami, and again on his first journey to the Zambesi in 1851. Shortly after, he left South Africa for Britain and took part in the Crimean War as a secret service agent. He wrote a standard book on his travels and died in 1893.

Otavi. Village in South West Africa, formerly noted for its copper mines. Population: 2,800, including 1,000 Whites.

Otavi Mine. Established in 1888 as the Otavi Minen und Eisenbahn-Gesellschaft with a capital of £200,000 as a subsidiary of the South West Africa Company (q.v.). In 1906 it built the 300 mile narrow-gauge railway line from Swakopmund to Tsumeb, where a considerable copper industry was established. More recently the concern has been taken over by the O'okiep Copper Company and is known as the Tsumeb Mine (q.v.).

Otjikoto. Lake in the north of South West Africa, extremely deep (over 600 feet), formed in an old crater, and measuring 820 feet by 650 feet. The level of the water varies slightly with the rise and fall of tides. The lake was discovered by Francis Galton in 1851, and regarded as a holy place by the natives. About 20 miles distant, at Guinas, is a larger, but lesser-known sheet of water. During World War I the Germans, before surrendering, threw quantities of arms and ammunition into Otjikoto.

Otjiwarongo. Village in South West Africa, noted for its dairying and sheep farming. It serves as a centre for the Waterberg district to the east, with a number of smaller holdings. Since 1933 a number of returned Angola Boers have settled near there. Population: 6,377, including 3,000 Whites.

Otomys (Vlei Muis) (Otomyinae), Small rodent, six or eight inches long, resembling the rat, but stouter, with a shorter, bristly tail. There are several varieties, all found in the Karroo and Rhodesia, where they live in burrows and breed rapidly.

Otterford. Village near Humansdorp, Cape Province. Population: 210, including 50 Whites.

Otto Beit Bridge (not to be confused with Beit Bridge built across the Chirundu Gorge of the Zambesi River (q.v.)), 1,080 feet long and linking Rhodesia and Zambia. The bridge is 103 miles from Lusaka and 230 miles from Salisbury. It was built in 1939, at the expense of the Beit Trust (q.v.). Construction carried out by Dorman Long & Co., cost over £186,000.

Ottosdal. Village near Lichtenburg, Transvaal. Population: 1,629, including 556 Whites.

Ottoshoop. Town in the Western Transvaal, founded in 1886 as centre for the Malmani Goldfield. Noted for the fertility of its surroundings, which are watered by the Malmani River. A curiosity is the 'Vanished Lake,' which is known to have existed there in 1825, and to have measured several miles in length. It has been drained and the site is now a thickly-cultivated agricultural area. The name of the place is derived from the first landdrost, C. B. Otto, who was stationed near by at Zeerust. Population: 800, including 200 Whites.

Ouderling. Elder of the Dutch Reformed Church.

Oudstrydersbond (Old Fighters Association). Organisation started in 1920 in the Orange Free State and the Transvaal, to safeguard the interests of ex-burghers of the former Boer Republics, and of those who fought for them in the South African War. It has paid particular attention to securing pensions for veterans.

Oudtshoorn. Town in the Cape Province, famed for its association with the ostrich feather industry. Founded in 1843 in the Zwartberg on the Grobbelaars River, and named after the early Dutch dignitary, Adriaan van Rheede van Oudtshoorn. Rose to great prosperity in the 1880's and again in the early 1900's as a result of the ostrich feather boom, when many mansions were built there. Other industries, including the successful cultivation of tobacco and lucerne, have helped to restore the fortunes of the town. Near by are the Cango Caves (q.v.). Population: 25,400, including 10,400 Whites.

Ou Grietjie (Little Old Greta). Nickname for historic ship's cannon used by Voortrekkers in campaigns against Zulus and Matabele.

Ouklip. Literally old rock. A type of decomposed dolomite, typical of many parts of the Transvaal.

Oulap. Colloquial Afrikaans for a penny. Literally 'an old rag.' Its origin is obscure.

Outjo. Village in the north of South-West Africa. Centre of a large stock-raising territory. Population: 3,330, including 1,510 Whites.

Outspan. Area marked off by law on every South African farm, available for passing travellers without charge. Anyone is allowed access to an outspan provided he does not do any damage to the farm itself. He may also make use of a reasonable quantity of grazing and water.

Ovambo. Tribe living in the north of South West Africa, comprising the Ondonga, the Ombalantu, the Onkolonkathi, the Ukuanyama, the Ukuambi, the Ukualuthi, the Ongandjera and Eunda. They are of Bantu origin, worship the spirits of their ancestors and attach much importance to the wearing of charms. Most of them live in reserves in the area of Ovamboland, which lies between Etosha Pan, Angola and the Kaokoveld. They number about 200,000. Since 1968 the Ovambo have their own Legislative Council of 42 members and a large measure of self-government.

Oviston. Village established near Orange River in connection with Orange River Scheme (q.v.) near entrance to Fish River Tunnel.

O.V.S.V.A. Abbreviation for Oranje Vrystaatse Veld Artillerie. *See* REGIMENT, SIXTH FIELD.

Owen, Reverend Francis. English missionary. Studied at Cambridge and graduated in 1826. While acting as curate at Normanton, Yorkshire, he heard an appeal for missionaries in Natal made by Captain Allen Francis Gardiner (q.v.) and volunteered for service. He arrived in Cape Town in 1837 and opened a station for the Church Missionary Society in Dingaan's country. While there he was the unwilling eye-witness of the massacre of Pieter Retief and his followers (q.v.) of which he wrote the only first-hand account. As a missionary he made little progress. He returned to England in 1841, settled near Sheffield and died in Alexandria, 1854. His diary, recovered by Sir George Cory, was published in 1926.

Owl (family Strigidae). Nocturnal bird of prey, splendidly adapted to night hunting. All varieties are light in body, with fluffy plumage and fluffy edges to their long wings. Their eyes see forward and sideways at the same time, and they have very large ear-openings behind their feathers. The beak and talons are hooked for catching mice, fish, small birds and rodents. They swallow their prey whole and deposit pellets of fur below the roost. Among many varieties, the Eagle Owls, as elsewhere, are the largest and most formidable, even to hares and guinea fowl. Barn Owls are found most commonly here as in every part of the world except New Zealand. One South African type, the Marsh Owl, hunts in small parties. In the Bush Country the smaller owlets are most common. *See* BIRDS.

Oxalis (Oxalidaceae). Belongs to the Sorrel family and is a very large South African group (sometimes classified with Pelargonium (q.v.)). Mainly in South-West Cape. Small herbs with bulbous storage and brightly-coloured delicate spring and winter flowers. The leaves vary greatly, but have three leaflets. Plant contains Oxalic acid. Yellow Sorrel (9–12 inches, leaves on long stem) was eaten by first settlers to cure scurvy. Dozens of smaller varieties, white, pink, purple and orange-red, decorate the sandy Cape hill slopes.

Oxbow Scheme. Water supply project agreed to between South African and Lesotho Governments, to supply 250,000,000 gallons a day from a point on Upper Orange River, mainly to the Witwatersrand. To be completed in 1974.

Oxpecker or Tick-bird (Sturnidae). Tropical bird of starling family (q.v.), the name derived from its habit of climbing all over wild game and domestic animals, removing ticks. (No connection with the White Tick Bird. *See* EGRET.) Colour brownish yellow, with a red or yellow bill. *See* BIRDS.

Oystercatcher, Black (*Hoematopus moquini*). Bird of wader family found in South Africa on the coast. Black plumage with vermilion bill and pink legs. *See* BIRDS.

Oysters. *See* MARINE RESOURCES.

Paardekraal. Farm near Krugersdorp, famous for the gathering held there on December 16, 1880, which marked the commencement of the First Boer War. On this occasion thousands of Transvaal burghers, dissatisfied with the British annexation under Sir Theophilus Shepstone, assembled there and, casting stones on a symbolic heap, pledged themselves to recover their independence. A monument has been erected over the heap of stones, and Paardekraal has remained a rallying place for the Afrikaner.

Paarl. Town in the Western Cape Province, on the Berg River, established in 1657 by Abraham Gabbema. It takes its name from the great smooth granite rocks, which crown the ridge overlooking the town, and which were thought to resemble a Pearl (Paarl, in Dutch). Today Paarl is a leading centre of the wine industry, with distilleries, canning and jam factories, cigarette factory and other important industries. It stretches for over seven miles, mostly along an endless main street, and is noted for its beautiful old Dutch houses, its oak avenues, vineyards and gardens. In the history of Afrikaans, Paarl occupies a unique position, as it was there, in 1875, that the famous 'Genootskap van Regte Afrikaners' was established, whose efforts ultimately brought about the creation of a new literature and the recognition of a new official language. Population: 50,000, including 15,200 Whites.

Pacaltsdorp. Village near George, Cape Province, established in 1813 as a station of the London Missionary Society by the Rev. Charles Pacalt. Today the picturesque little place is chiefly inhabited by Coloured people. Population: 2,019, including 10 Whites.

Packer, Joy. South African author. Born at Cape Town as Joy Petersen in 1905, she began writing as a young girl. She married Admiral Sir Herbert Packer when the latter was still a young officer, a fact that gave her material for her first book, *Pack and Follow*, about the experiences of a naval wife. This attained great success and was followed by *Grey Mistress*. She also wrote a series of novels with a South African setting which achieved worldwide popularity, some of them being filmed. One of the best known is *The Valley of the Vines*.

Pact. Term applied to the political agreement made between the National Party under General J. B. M. Hertzog and the Labour Party under Colonel F. H. P. Cresswell, in 1924, by which they combined their efforts to unseat the South African Party government of General J. C. Smuts. It resulted in the accession to power of a new government under General Hertzog, in whose Cabinet several Labour ministers held portfolios.

P.A.G. Abbreviation for Prince Alfred's Guard (q.v.).

Page, Gertrude (Mrs. Alec Dobbin). Rhodesian novelist and dramatist. Born as Gertrude Page, daughter of John E. Page of Bedford, she married Captain George Alexander Dobbin and went to Rhodesia at the beginning of the present century. She made her name with a book of an almost entirely new type, on the Rhodesian bush, beginning with *Love in the Wilderness* and following it up with *The Edge of Beyond*, which became a best-seller. Among her other well-known works was *Silent Rancher*, in 1909, and *Jill's Rhodesian Philosophy*, in 1910. Returning to England, she wrote *Paddy, the Next Best Thing*, which was a great success on the stage, as was a version of *The Edge of Beyond*. She died on April 1, 1922.

Painted Lady. Popular name for two rare, much-prized Cape flowers: (1) *Gladiolus debilis*—white with red marking; (2) *Gladiolus macowanianus*—pink with deeper pink marking. Both are slim, delicate-looking plants, belonging to the vast Iridaceae family, and grow in the Cape Peninsula, from Constantia southwards.

Painting. See ART and BUSHMAN PAINTINGS.

Palabora. See PHALABORWA.

Paladins. See YOUTH MOVEMENTS.

Palapye. Native town in Botswana and seat of the Paramount Chiefs. It was founded by the famous Khama (q.v.). Its importance has, however, declined through the rise of Serowe. Also written Palapwe and Palachwe.

Palgrave, William Coates. South African diplomatist. He joined the Cape Police in 1869, but after the discovery of the diamond fields became magistrate in Du Toit's Pan and in Kimberley. In 1876 he was sent on a special mission to Damaraland, to examine the prospects of that country. This resulted in the annexation to Cape Colony of Walvis Bay and surrounding territory (q.v.). Palgrave's advice to the Cape Government to annex the whole of what is now South-West Africa was unfortunately not acted upon. Later, in 1884 and 1885, he was again sent to Damaraland on a special mission.

Palmiet (*Prionium serratum* Drege). Reed up to 6 feet high with sword-shaped leaves used for thatching out-buildings. Found on margins of rivers and marshes in the Cape Division to Uitenhage.

Pan-African Congress. Organisation which broke away from the African National Congress (q.v.) in 1959, upholding the policy of 'Africa for

Africans, ' but accepting the existence of ' White Africans ' as well as Black. Banned in South Africa.

Panda (also Umpanda). Zulu king, son of Senzangakona and brother of Dingaan. Also known as Umpande. Falling out with Dingaan, he led a large party of his adherents from Zululand across the river Tugela into Natal, where he received protection from the Voortrekker settlers in 1839. The Boers decided to recognise him as head of the emigrant Zulus, and, accompanied by a commando of burghers, he fought against Dingaan in 1840. Following a final battle at Magongo, on the Umkuzi river, Dingaan's power was completely broken and on February 10, 1840, Commandant-General M. W. Pretorius installed Panda as King of the Zulus, though he maintained his fealty to the Volksraad of Natalia. While he indulged in occasional barbarities, his general attitude towards the Europeans was friendly, and in 1843 he agreed to cede the strategically situated Santa Lucia Bay, at the boundary of Mozambique, to Queen Victoria. In return the British recognised him as an independent king. In his later years he quarrelled with his son, Cetewayo (q.v.). He died in 1872.

Pandours. See CAPE CORPS.

Pangolin. See ANT-EATER.

Pannevis, Arnoldus. Pioneer of Afrikaans. Born in Holland in 1838 in Oudekerk, he began his career in the Dutch Navy, but owing to poor health, studied for the ministry. Having heard of chances in South Africa, he decided to emigrate there and in 1866 arrived in Cape Town to take up a position as teacher of Latin and Greek at the Paarl Gymnasium. Here the future founder of the Afrikaans language, the Rev. S. J. du Toit, was one of his pupils. He became interested in what was known as the 'Taal,' and in 1872 published a plea for the translation of the Bible into that language. His letter in the *Zuid Afrikaan* led, three years later, to the establishment of the Genootskap Van Regte Afrikaners (q.v.) which was to start the movement for the admission of Afrikaans as a language. He started writing in Afrikaans and died in 1884.

Paper. *See* SAPPI.

Pappe, Dr. Karl Wilhelm Ludwig. South African botanist. Born at Hamburg in 1803, he qualified in medicine, but made botany his life study at the Cape, where he specialised, *inter alia*, in medicinal plants, timber trees and ferns, on each of which he wrote authoritative treatises. He died in Cape Town in 1862.

Paradise Island. *See* BAZARUTO.

Paradys. South African National Short-Wave Centre, 12 miles from Bloemfontein, established in 1956. Of nine powerful short-wave transmitters, two are specially used for the South African Broadcasting Corporation's International Service.

Paris Evangelical Society. French Protestant Mission. It began its work in Wellington in the Cape, 1829, but soon spread to Bechuanaland and Moselekatse's country, and, in 1833, settled in Basutoland, where it has played a prominent rôle ever since, particularly through the famous station at Morija.

Park Rynie. Seaside resort on the Natal South Coast. Originally an estate called Park Rainy by a Mrs. Rethman, because of the wet weather she experienced there. It was first referred to as Park Rynie in 1861. Population: 2,179, including 334 Whites.

Parliament. *See* CONSTITUTION.

Parow. Town near Cape Town, established in 1910 by Captain Ferdinand Parrow, a German skipper trading on the South African coast in Victorian times. Its advantageous position on the railway, as well as other attractions, has led to very rapid growth. The industries include printing, timber, engineering. Population: 52,100, including 32,000 Whites.

Parrot (family Psittacidae). Tropical bird commonly found from Knysna in the Cape to Natal and Zululand and the Transvaal Bushveld. A number of varieties exist, but none has the gorgeousness of tropical American parrots. The Cape or Levaillant's Parrot is the only large one, and may be seen and heard flying in flocks among high trees, its green rump and red wing-edges visible. The South African Brown (or Meyer's) Parrot, with blue rump, belongs to the Transvaal Bushveld. Further east, in the Kruger Park and in Zululand, is a similar type, the Brown-Headed Parrot, with a green rump. *See* LOVEBIRD.

Partridge. *See* FRANCOLIN.

Parys. Town in the Northern Orange Free State on the Vaal River. It was established in 1881, and so called by the surveyor, a German named Schilbach, who had taken part in the siege of Paris (Parys in Dutch) during the Franco-German War of 1870–1871. For a short while, during the South African War, Parys was the seat of the Orange Free State Government. Contains a number of industries and is today a popular holiday resort for visitors from the Rand. Population: 15,060, including 6,700 Whites.

Pasipas. Hill near Bulawayo, noted for its quarries of pink and red freestone. much used for buildings in that city. The top of the koppie is 4,178 feet above sea-level.

Patensie. Village near Humansdorp, Cape Province. Population: 1,623, including 586 Whites.

Paternoster. Village near Hopefield, Cape Province. Population: 430, including 50 Whites. Large lighthouse near by.

Paterson. Village near Port Elizabeth, established in 1879 by John Paterson, (q.v.). Farming centre. Population: 1,868, including 169 Whites.

Paterson, John. Statesman and commercial pioneer. Born in Aberdeen, Scotland, in 1821, he came to the Cape in 1840 as a schoolteacher and settled in Port Elizabeth where he acquired considerable prominence. A man of great enterprise, he was interested in industry, and helped to establish the *Eastern Province Herald*, as well as insurance and trust companies. In 1854 he was elected a Member for Port Elizabeth in the first Cape Parliament, and in 1862 he succeeded in establishing the Standard Bank of South Africa. Notwithstanding the success which attended this venture, Paterson himself suffered severe losses and finally went insolvent. He rebuilt his fortunes and was mentioned as a possible premier of the Cape when Responsible Government was established in 1870. He died in 1880 while returning to the Cape from England in the mail steamer *American*.

Paterson, William. British traveller. Born in 1755, he joined the army, but soon became an eminent botanist, for which reason he visited the Cape in 1777. During the two years spent there he made four expeditions, on one of which he accompanied Col. Jacob Gordon (q.v.), when the latter gave the Orange River its name. He also widely explored the present Eastern Province. He died in 1810.

Pathfinders. *See* YOUTH MOVEMENTS.

Paton, Alan Stewart. South African novelist and political leader. Born at Pietermaritzburg on January 11, 1903, he studied at Pietermaritzburg College and the University of Natal. Becoming interested in social work he was appointed principal of Diepkloof Reformatory, where he secured remarkable results in the rehabilitation of young delinquents. His world fame, however, dates from 1948, when the novel *Cry, the Beloved Country* won acclaim in every continent. This was followed by *Too Late the Phalarope* and other works. He helped to found the Liberal Party in South Africa, was elected its president, and lectured widely in the United States and elsewhere. His passport was withdrawn in 1960 on account of some of the sentiments he expressed.

'Patriot, Die.' First newspaper in the Afrikaans language, and original organ of the movement for its recognition. Established by the Rev. S. J. du Toit (q.v.), the first issue appeared on January 15, 1876, at Paarl, and continued as a weekly until 1904, when it was renamed the *Paarl Post*, which is still in existence. In its latter stages it became involved in considerable political controversy on account of its alleged association with Cecil John Rhodes.

Patriot. *See* CAPE PATRIOTS.

Patrys. Afrikaans name for partridge. *See* FRANCOLIN.

Pauling, George. South African engineer and contracting magnate. Born in 1853, he was articled and worked on the construction of early London local railways, and on other lines in Britain. In 1875 he came to South Africa as an assistant engineer on the Cape Government Railways in the Eastern Province. He soon discovered that independent contracting was more profitable and set up on his own. From 1882 to 1885 he built the line from Sterkstroom to Aliwal North, and, in 1884, secured the contract for extension from Beaufort West to Kimberley. As this proved unprofitable, he joined the gold rush to Barberton in 1886 and worked for a while as a mining engineer. Returning to England he gained the support of Baron Emile Beaumont d'Erlanger (q.v.) and did some work in the East, but in 1888 d'Erlanger sent him to the Transvaal to report on mining properties. He met President Kruger and secured the contract to build the 'Rand Tram,' the first line in the Transvaal. In 1892 Cecil Rhodes engaged him to build the line to Rhodesia from Vryburg, and soon after from Beira as well. From then on Pauling was kept busy in Africa, though he did certain outside contracts as well. He built the lines to Salisbury from Umtali, and from the south to Bulawayo, also, the Bulawayo–Salisbury section, the extension to the Victoria Falls and beyond. In the Union he built the line to Caledon over Sir Lowry's Pass and sundry others. One of his later contracts was for most of the Benguela Railway in Angola. He died in 1919.

Paulpietersburg. Village in Northern Natal, originally in the New Republic (q.v.), laid out in 1888 and named in honour of President Paul Kruger and General Pieter Joubert. It saw heavy fighting in the South African War, and was almost completely destroyed. Near by a colliery is operating. Population: 3,700, including 750 Whites.

Paul Roux. Town in the Eastern Orange Free State, named after the Reverend Paul Roux, and founded about 1914. Farming centre. Population: 1,658, including 450 Whites.

Pea, Wild Sweet (*Podalyria calyptrata*) (Leguminoseae). Ertjiebos. Belongs to one of the largest of flowering-plant families, including trees, shrubs, climbers and herbs, all over Southern Africa. Many have great economic, medicinal or nutritional value. Fruit is in all cases a pod, or legume. Flower varies widely. Roots grow nodules inhabited by bacteria that gather nitrogen from the air and enrich poor soil. Three sub-families, according to petal arrangement: Mimosoidae, including Mimosas, Acacias (q.v.) and Dichrostachys (Sicklebush)

—all with 'powder-puff' or catkin-like flowers. Caesalpinioideae, including the Bauhinias of Rhodesia, Cassias, Mopane tree (q.v.), African Wattle or Huilbos (q.v.) and the Natal Tree Fusia. Flowers irregular but not butterfly-shaped, uppermost petal innermost in bud. Papilionatae, including all the smaller shrubs and herbs with butterfly-shaped flowers, the uppermost large petal being outermost in the bud, the two side ones forming a pair of wings, and the two lowest joined into a keel. Rhodesia grows many kinds of Yellow Crotalaria, shrubs, herbs and creepers, all with three leaflets; some 300 species of Indigo flowers (formerly used in India to produce the dye which today is a bi-product of tar), the flower-keel spurred and the leaves herring-boned up a short stem, with the odd leaflet at the top (imparipinnate); and many species of Vetch (Tephrosia). At the Cape pink and yellow flowers predominate. There is the Pink Keurboom (*Virgilia oroboides*), several varieties of Kaffirboom (q.v.) (*Erythrina caffra*) and pink shrublets of the Podalyria and Indigofera varieties, Bush Tea (q.v.) (Cyclopia) and wayside veld flowers too many to be mentioned.

Peach Brandy. A crude strong spirit made from yellow peaches and drunk in the country districts.

Pearl Fish (*Fierasfer gracilis*). Species of Klip Fish (q.v.) found off Natal, East Indies. About 6 inches long. It has a long, slim body and no scales. The name comes from its habit of living inside oysters, starfish, etc.

Pearston. Town in the Eastern Cape Province, established in 1859 and named after the Reverend John Pears, who ministered to the 1820 settlers in Albany, and later to the Dutch Reformed Congregation in Cradock. Sheep-farming is one of the major industries. Population: 2,667, including 443 Whites.

Pebane. Port and holiday resort in Mozambique. Population: 60,000, including about 100 Whites.

Peddie. Town in the Eastern Province, originally founded as a British frontier post under the name of Fort Peddie, in 1835, and named after Lt.-Colonel John Peddie of the 72nd Highlanders who was stationed there. The place saw much fighting in a number of native wars, and was once actually captured by the Xosas, but they were driven out again. Farming centre. Population: 1,300, including 430 Whites.

Peers, Charles E. South African artist. Born in Lancashire in 1874, he studied in Liverpool and came to South Africa in 1904. He is known in particular for his delicate and beautiful water colours. He died in 1944.

Pekelaar. The Dutch word means Pickled Herring, but the name is given to any fish preserved in salt or dried in the sun. It is particularly used of snoek (q.v.).

Pelargonium (Geraniaceae). Group of larger pink or red flowered perennial herbaceous plants, of which the smaller variety is a Geranium or Cranesbill. From the Pelargoniums have been produced the many garden Geraniums of Europe. Five sepals, five petals, the fruit beaked and tapering into five capsules, each of which terminates in a hardened style which separates when ripe and curls up with the capsule. Found throughout South Africa, but most commonly in the Cape.

Pelican (family Steganopodes). A curious bird belonging to the Duiker family (q.v.) with a long neck, heavy body, short legs and enormous bill, beneath which hangs the pouch for its spare fish. Like other large birds, the pelican is a study in attitudinising until it flies, when the long wings, black-tipped, give it balance and grace. Down by the vleis it is often seen fishing as one of a group. *See* BIRDS.

Pellissier, Reverend Jean Pierre. French Protestant missionary. Born in St. Arey, near Grenoble, 1808; ordained in 1831 and in the same year sent to South Africa by the Paris Evangelical Mission. He took part in the opening of a mission station in Motito, Bechuanaland, in 1832, but moved to the present Orange Free State in the following year. There he built up the mission station at Bethulie (q.v.) gaining the respect of the early Boer settlers and the approval of the Dutch Reformed Church. He died in 1867.

Penal System. *See* PRISONS.

Penguins (family Spheniscidae). Sea birds breeding in large numbers on Dassen Island and other guano islands off the coasts of the South-Western Cape, where they nest in sand burrows or crevices. Ungainly on land, with their paddle-shaped wings, stiff movements and scaly feathers, once in the water they are expert divers for fish. *See* BIRDS.

Penhalonga. Township in the east of Rhodesia, 11 miles north of Umtali. The name, of Portuguese origin, means 'Long Rocks.' Established soon after the occupation in 1890, it has some of the oldest gold workings in the country, including the famous Rezende Mine near by. Population: 500, including 150 Whites.

Penn-Symons, General Sir William. *See* SYMONS.

Penstone, Constance. South African artist and one of the very few women cartoonists on record. She was born in Chesterfield, Derbyshire, England, and after studying art, went to Australia, where she taught in several institutions, later spending some years in America. There she designed stained-glass windows for the famous jewellers' firm of Tiffany & Co., New York. In 1896 she came to South Africa and took up the post of cartoonist first on the *Owl*, and some years later on the *Cape Times*, where she used the nom de plume 'Scalpel.' She later married Crosland Robinson, the artist and died in Cape Town in 1928.

Penvaan. Hamlet in Natal, near Vryheid. The name is derived from a Zulu word meaning 'Waterbuck.' The place is notable for a remarkable echo from its surrounding heights.

Pepper Tree (*Schinus molle*). Exotic tree grown very successfully for shade and ornament under drought and frost conditions. It has drooping foliage and branches of small red berries, the male and female organs being borne on separate trees. Was widely planted in early Johannesburg and Bulawayo.

Perceval, Captain Robert. English traveller and writer. Born in England in 1765. A relative of Spencer Perceval, the British Prime Minister who was murdered, he joined the army, and as captain in the 18th Regiment of Infantry took part in the first British Occupation of the Cape in 1795. Under General Craig he led the attack on the fortifications at Muizenberg, and was the first officer to reach Cape Town. His book, *An Account of the Cape of Good Hope*, is based on his experiences during a two-year stay, and gives close-up pictures of everyday existence. He went to the East, wrote a book on Ceylon and died in 1826.

Perdekop. Village near Volksrust, Transvaal. Population: 1,372, including 591 Whites.

Perdewagter. Afrikaans name for Stonechat. *See* CHAT.

Peregrine. *See* EAGLES.

Perestrello, Manuel de Mesquita. Portuguese navigator and writer, who was wrecked on the east coast of South Africa in 1554. He prepared a chart and detailed account of the loss of his ship, the *St. Benedict*, for King Sebastian of Portugal.

Peripatus. Unique creature of great antiquity forming a link between jointed animals or arthropoda (which include shrimps, lobsters, centipedes, butterflies, bees, spiders, scorpions, etc.), on the one side, and worms on the other. It was discovered in 1826 in the East Indies, and has since been found in several parts of the Southern Hemisphere, including South America, Australia, New Zealand and South Africa. *Peripatus capensis* is the best known of all. It resembles a slug, but has a soft, velvety skin, red, blue or dark green in colour, has antennae and can eject a sticky substance for several inches to catch its prey of tiny insects. Its mode of breathing resembles that of insects, but its internal structure is that of worms. The peripatus grows to a length of about 4 inches, and—another surprise—produces its young fully formed. It lives in the dark, under stones or among dead leaves.

Perlemoen. A large Venus' Ear shellfish lined with mother-of-pearl and found on the coast of the Western Cape Province. Has become a favourite dish both as a salad and in other forms, and in recent years has been largely canned for export. *See* MARINE RESOURCES.

Persoon, Christian Hendrik. Early South African botanist. Born at the Cape of Good Hope on December 31, 1761, son of an immigrant from Germany, he was sent to Europe as a boy of 12. Having studied at Leyden and Goettingen, he qualified in medicine, then began to specialise in botany, concentrating his attention on cryptogamic plants, notably mushrooms. His work was of such importance that he is remembered as 'The Father of Mycology.' Elected a member of the Linnean Societies of London and of Philadelphia, as well as the Society of Naturalists of Berlin, he enjoyed international fame. Towards the end of his life he settled in Paris, where he died in November, 1836. His most celebrated work is *Observationes Mycologicae*, published in 1796, and, the *Commentatio de Fungis Clavae Formibus*, published in 1797.

Peruvians. Derogatory name applied to lower class Jews, particularly those who came to the early diamond and gold fields. Various explanations have been given of this word, but the correct one appears to be that, in the pioneer days of Kimberley, they formed a body calling themselves the Polish and Russian Union, the initial letters of which formed the word PRU.

Petrels. Family name Tubinares, from the fact that their nostrils are carried in horny tubes projecting from the bill. Sea birds nesting in the far south during the Antarctic summer. They include the tiny Storm Petrels, commonest of all the little wave-skimmers; the medium-sized Cape Hens (Bassions), black, with a white bill and throat; Cape Pigeons (Pintados), with their chequered body and white-patched wings; great yellow-beaked Mollymawks (small albatrosses) with

Petrels or Mollymawks

black wings, that follow the travellers in thousands and the Wandering Albatross itself, its black-tipped wings spread over an 11-foot span. *See* BIRDS.

Petrusburg. Town in the Western Orange Free State, named after the farm-owner, Petrus Venter, and established in 1892. Noted as a centre for potato-growing. Population: 2,300, including 1,100 Whites.

Petrus Steyn. Town in the Northern Orange Free State, named after the original farm-owner. It was founded in 1914, and was noted for its wool-washery. Today it is mainly a grain centre. Population: 2,300, including 700 Whites.

Petrusville. Village near Philipstown, Cape Province. Population: 1,430, including 268 Whites.

Pettman, Rev. Charles. South African philologist. Born at Whitstable, Kent, in the year 1851, he qualified for the Wesleyan ministry and came to the Cape in 1876, to become the first minister of any denomination in East London. He held posts at many other places in the Eastern Province and elsewhere, but became best known on account of his writings about South African place names and South African words generally, the latter embodied in his treatise *Afrikanderisms*. He died in 1935.

Phalaborwa (formerly spelt Palabora). Mining centre noted for its wide variety of products, including phosphates, copper and vermiculite. Ancient workings show early mining of copper. In 1932 modern development began, backed by the Industrial Development Corporation (q.v.) which set up the Phosphate Development Corporation (Foskor). Output at 500,000 tons a year covers most of South Africa's needs. The Industrial Development Corporation was largely responsible for the opening up of vast low-grade copper deposits through the Palabora Mining Company, backed by

American, German and British interests, the last including the Rio Tinto group. Phalaborwa aims at turning out 80,000 tons of copper yearly. Other deposits are being examined. Total investment estimated at over R74,000,000.

Phalarope (*Phalaropus fulicarius*). Rare sea-bird, breeding in the Arctic and seen in False Bay only once in 1931, after a heavy storm, and once off the coast of South-West Africa. It lives like a Wader (q.v.) during the breeding season, and then, as a member of a flock, becomes an Ocean Petrel and flies off into the blue.

Phalarope

Pheasant. The larger game bird of the Phasianidae family, darker and heavier than the Partridge, its blacker plumage lined with white. Varieties include the Cape Pheasant (Fisant in Afrikaans), found near Cape Town and in the Western Cape; the Natal Francolin, smaller and with more white in plumage; and the Red-billed Francolin, common north of the Vaal. *See* FRANCOLIN.

Philadelphia. Village near Bellville, Cape Province. Population: 150, including 80 Whites.

Philip, Dr. John. Missionary and author. Born in 1775 at Kirkcaldy in Scotland, he joined the London Missionary Society, which, in 1819, sent him on a visit of inspection with a delegation to South Africa. In 1822 he was made Superintendent of all the Society's stations at the Cape. He immediately became a champion of the non-Europeans, secured the grant of equal rights to free 'persons of colour' in 1828, the same year in which he published *Researches in South Africa*, and aroused strong opposition from colonists for his opposition to Sir Benjamin D'Urban's policy of annexation, proposing instead Bantu states. He had much influence in Downing Street and died in 1851.

Philippolis. Town in the Southern Orange Free State, named after Dr. John Philip, who in 1821 started a station there for the London Missionary Society. Frequent wars occurred until the emigration of the Griquas under Adam Kok III in 1862, when a European village was laid out. It was again in the fighting zone during the South African War, the small British garrison of 41 men successfully holding out while besieged for six days in October 1900. After the return of peace Miss Emily Hobhouse (q.v.) established a school at Philippolis to train Boer girls in home industries, especially in lace-making, which flourished for some years. Wool production and general farming are the main sources of prosperity today. Population: 2,400, including 710 Whites.

Philipstown. Village in the Northern Karroo, named after Governor Sir Philip Wodehouse; established in the 1860's. The township of Willemsmit controlled by the Dutch Reformed Church adjoins it, but is separately administered. Population: 2,122, including 476 Whites.

Phillips, George Arthur (nicknamed 'Elephant'). Early hunter and trader in Rhodesia. Born in England about 1837, he came to Natal in 1862, and moved on to the Transvaal shortly after. He started his trek in Matabeleland in 1864, and became a noted hunter. Together with George West-beech he began trading near the Victoria Falls. Retired in 1890 and died in 1896.

Phillips, Sir Henry Lushington. Judge of the Natal Supreme Court. Born in England about 1825, he was called to the Bar at the Middle Temple in November, 1850, and in 1858 was appointed Puisne Judge in the Supreme Court of Natal. There he remained until 1877, when he became Acting Chief Justice in the Barbados, followed by a similar post in the Straits Settlements. In 1878 he was back again in Natal as Senior Puisne Judge, but was soon after transferred to Cyprus. In 1880 he retired on pension and died about 1885.

Phillips, Lady. Art connoisseur and champion of women's rights in South Africa. Born Dorothea Sarah Florence Alexandra Ortlepp in Colesberg, Cape Province, she was married in 1885 to Mr. (later Sir) Lionel Phillips (q.v.), with whom she came to the Rand. There she was a prominent hostess and wrote several political books. She organised exhibitions and was largely responsible for the foundation of the Johannesburg Art Gallery. Much of her life was spent in England, but her later years were passed in her home at Vergelegen, near Somerset West, Cape Province. She died in 1940.

Phillips, Sir Lionel. South African mining magnate. Born in London, 1855, he was educated in England and came to South Africa at the age of 20 in 1875, spending his early years running diamond mines in Kimberley. He gained the friendship and confidence of Alfred Beit and of Cecil John Rhodes. In 1889 he moved to Johannesburg, where he became a leading figure in the firm of Hermann Eckstein & Co., which represented the interests of Alfred Beit in the Transvaal. He was recognised as largely responsible for the advance of the gold mines, on both the technical and financial

sides. Greatly concerned with politics, he was one of the main figures on the Reform Committee, and, after the failure of the Jameson Raid, was arrested and tried on a charge of high treason. Phillips was amongst those sentenced to death, a penalty later commuted to a fine of £25,000. In 1913 he narrowly escaped assassination in Johannesburg. Shortly after, he moved to England, where, during World War I, he became one of the principal advisers and helpers of the Government in the control of essential metals. He returned to South Africa after the restoration of peace, and retired from business, making his home at Vergelegen, a famous farm near Somerset West. He was prominent in stimulating art and educational developments in the Transvaal, and was among the founders of the 1820 Settlers Association. He died in 1936.

Phoenix. Village near Durban, mainly inhabited by Indians and notable as the former residence of Mahatma Gandhi (q.v.). There he issued the journal *Indian Opinion* which was continued by his son Manilal.

Phosphates. Mineral used for fertiliser, found in the Northern Transvaal, in the Western Cape Province and in Natal. With state assistance large works have been established at Phalaborwa, and also near Cape Town, for treating the product.

Photography. Introduced into the Cape of Good Hope at an early stage. At the original demonstration at the Sorbonne in 1839 by Daguerre, Dr. W. G. Atherstone of Grahamstown, then a medical student, was present. The first daguerreotypist was operating in Grahamstown in 1845. A number of other pioneers followed in the 1850's, and by 1860 the first recorded press photograph was taken, when Prince Alfred formally started the construction of Table Bay Docks. Photographic history was made at the

Cape in 1872, when Sir David Gill took the first successful photographs of the moon from the Royal Observatory in Cape Town. The first photographs of the Victoria Falls were taken by Ellerton Fry, who accompanied the Pioneer Column into Rhodesia in 1890. In South African photography Howard Coster attained considerable distinction as a Court photographer in London, while Dr. George Lindsay Johnson (q.v.) became an international authority on colour photography.

Phylloxera. Insect pest of the vine introduced into the Cape of Good Hope in 1873, after ravaging most vineyards of France and other producing countries overseas. Despite all efforts it spread through South Africa in the 'eighties and 'nineties, bringing ruin to many farmers. In the end it was found necessary to cut down and burn the older stocks and replant them with phylloxera-resistant strains from California. Since then it has ceased to be a menace.

Picannin. A small African child. Despite its association with Africa, the word is derived from the Spanish 'pequeno' signifying 'small' and 'hino' meaning 'a child.' Compare Angra Pequena (q.v.).

Pienaar, Andries Albertus ('Sangiro'). Afrikaans writer. Born at Broederstroom, near Pretoria, in 1894, educated at Heidelberg, Transvaal, and at Stellenbosch University. Became a journalist and spent much of his early life in East Africa. *Uit Oerwoud en Vlakte* is translated into English as *The Adventures of a Lion Family*, published in 1924. He later became interested in making films on African wild life.

Pienaar, Major-General Daniel Hermanus. South African soldier. Born in Ladybrand on August 7, 1893; was in a concentration camp with his mother during the South African War;

joined the Natal Police in 1911 and then the Artillery the following year. In 1913 he enlisted in the South African Mounted Riflemen as a gunner. During World War I he served in the South African Field Artillery in East Africa as well as in Palestine and Syria, finishing as Second Lieutenant. Upon the return of peace he started his career in the South African Permanent Force and on the outbreak of World War II held the rank of Colonel-in-Command at Voortrekkerhoogte. When the First South African Brigade was sent to East Africa in 1940, Pienaar was appointed Brigade Commander. His élan and brilliant application of traditional Boer tactics to modern conditions of warfare, particularly after his transfer to the Western Desert in 1942, soon won him renown far beyond the limits of Southern Africa. He took an important part in all the fighting on the Egyptian frontier and the final triumph at El Alamein. His personality and ability made him enormously popular with South African and other troops. Returning from 'up north' to the Union on December 19, 1942, he was killed in an aeroplane crash on the shores of Lake Victoria.

Pienaars River. Village north of Pretoria, named after a local pioneer, and founded in 1908.

Pierneef, Jacob Hendrik. South African painter. Born in Pretoria, 1886, of Dutch parents, he accompanied them to Holland in 1901, where he studied art in Rotterdam. Returned to South Africa, to become Librarian at State Library in Pretoria, but began painting and in 1914 undertook a special study trip to Europe. He soon became known through his simple and striking interpretation of the Bushveld and other local scenes in paintings and woodcuts. Among his most important works is the series of paintings in Johannesburg station concourse. He died in 1957.

Piet. Afrikaans name for Sombre Bulbul. *See* BULBUL.

Pietermaritzburg. Capital of Natal and second largest city of the province. The name commemorates Pieter Retief, the Voortrekker leader, and Gert Maritz, President of the Voortrekker's Council. Although approval was given to its foundation on October 23, 1838, it was not until after the Battle of Blood River, on December 16 of the same year, that the first steps were taken in laying out the village, and not until 1840 was house-building commenced on a systematic scale. During the existence of the Voortrekker Republic of Natalia, the Volksraad met there, and after this experiment terminated, the British kept it as their administrative centre, erecting Fort Napier in order to house the Garrison. Municipal government was introduced in 1854, and in 1856 the first Legislative Council of the Colony of Natal met there. The city was linked by rail with Durban in 1880 and with Johannesburg 15 years later, in 1895. The population is 112,693, consisting of 45,930 Whites, 34,000 Bantu, 26,770 Asiatics, 6,000 Coloureds, while the municipal area is slightly under 50 sq. miles, or 31,948 acres. Altitude above sea-level is 2,160 feet. Besides being the seat of the Provincial Administration, containing the Education and other departments, the University of Natal, and a museum and other institutions, Pietermaritzburg has a number of industries, including dairying, wattle bark extraction and the rolling of aluminium.

Pietersburg: 1. Town in the Northern Transvaal, founded in 1884 and named after General Piet Joubert. Important business centre. During the South African War it was for a short while in 1900 the seat both of the Transvaal and Orange Free State Republican governments. It was occupied by Plumer on April 8, 1901. Today it handles a great deal of agricultural produce, as well as traffic to the Kruger National Park and other scenic centres. Population: 36,274, including 15,000 Whites.
2. Village in the Northern Cape Province, scene of considerable fighting in South African War, in September 1901.

Pietjie Kanarie. *See* SISKIN.

Piet-My-Vrou. Afrikaans name for both the Red-chested Cuckoo (q.v.) and the Noisy Robin (q.v.). *See* BIRDS.

Piet Potgietersrust. *See* POTGIETERSRUST.

Piet Retief. Town in the Eastern Transvaal, on the borders of Swaziland, with which it has always been closely linked. Founded in 1885, it was named after the Voortrekker leader. The area is noted for forestry and tobacco. Portion of the Piet Retief district was the independent Klein Vrystaat (Little Free State) q.v. During the South African War in 1901 it was for a short while the seat of the Transvaal Republican government. Population: 8,100, including 3,500 Whites.

Pigeons (family Columbidae). Pigeons and Doves are well represented in South Africa. The best known is the Cape Turtle Dove (*Streptopelia capicolia*), found everywhere among trees. It is grey-brown, with a black half-collar round its neck. A striking member of this group is the large Delalande's Green Pigeon or Natal Green Pigeon (*Treron calva*), a fruit eater of the sub-tropical Eastern Cape.

Pigg, William. Pioneer of Swaziland and founder of Pigg's Peak village, as well as of the Eersteling Gold Mine (q.v.).

Pigg's Peak. Township in Swaziland, a trading centre, but now also noted for large forestry developments. Population 1,400.

Pig Lily. Common name for the Arum (q.v.).

Piketberg. *See* PIQUETBERG.

Pilansberg. Range of mountains in the Transvaal, named after a Bechuana chieftain Pilane, chiefly notable on account of its unique geological formation—a volcanic centre associated with the Bushveld Igneous Complex (q.v.).

Pilchards (*Sardina ocellata*). Members of the Clupeidae family appear under various names, e.g. Cape Sardine, Whitebait, Pilchard and Herring. Small, shallow-water fishes, of economic importance lately to South Africa through the extension of the canning and fish-oil industries. (*See* MARINE RESOURCES.) These fishes move in vast shoals, often coming into river estuaries along the east and south-east coasts. The eggs are floating. The young are tinned as 'sardines' and the adults, of 6–9 inches, as 'pilchards.'

Pilgrims Rest. Mining town in the Eastern Transvaal. Established as a gold diggers' camp in 1870. During the alluvial boom it had a population of some thousands, but this dwindled with the rise of Barberton and the Rand. Considerable mining activity in the neighbourhood followed the founding, in 1895, of the Transvaal Gold Mining Estates, the largest gold property in the Republic outside the Rand. In recent years its operations have declined and been replaced by one of the largest privately-owned forests in the country. Population: 1,000, including 350 Whites.

Pim, Howard. Art collector and pioneer of native welfare. Born in Dublin in 1862, he qualified in accountancy and first came to South Africa in 1890 to organise the accounting system for the B.S.A. Company. Settling in Johannesburg in 1894, he took part in the South African War and later served on the nominated Town Council of Johannesburg in 1903, becoming Deputy Mayor. In later years he did much towards providing recreational and educational facilities for natives on the Rand, besides building up a fine art collection, which he left to the city of Johannesburg. He died in 1934.

Pine, Sir Benjamin Chilley Campbell. Governor of Natal. Born in Devonshire in 1813, studied at Trinity College, Cambridge, and was called to the Bar in 1841. The following year he joined the Colonial Service in Sierra Leone, being promoted to Governor in 1848. He was transferred to Natal in 1849 as Lieutenant-Governor, remaining till 1856 and gaining considerable popularity. After further service on the Gold Coast, in the West Indies and in Western Australia, he was again appointed to Natal, this time as Governor, in 1873, where he stayed two years before retiring on pension. He contributed the article on 'African Colonies' to the *Encyclopaedia Britannica*.

Pinelands. Garden city near Cape Town. Established at the instigation of Richard Stuttaford (q.v.) in 1920, who gave a sum of £10,000, to be used as a basic fund for development. The enterprise soon paid for itself and, being operated by a company not for profit, was able to return all its earnings for the benefit of its inhabitants. The site of Pinelands was the former forestry estate of Uitvlugt on the Cape Flats. Great pains were taken to maintain high standards of architecture and maximum safety precautions for traffic. In 1948 Pinelands became a municipality, with a growing population now over 15,200, nearly all White. Owing to the exhaustion of available land, a further settlement has been started in recent years near Constantia, under the name of Meadowridge (q.v.).

Pinetown. Town in Natal, 13 miles from Durban, named after Governor Sir Benjamin Pine (q.v.). Established in 1850 as a health resort, it earned the nickname of 'The Cheltenham of Natal.' In the Zulu War of 1879 it became a military base camp, and afterwards an important manufacturing centre. Population: 23,000, including 14,000 Whites.

Pinto. *See* SERPA PINTO.

Pioneer Column. Force formed under the leadership of Major Frank Johnson at the instance of Cecil John Rhodes in 1890, to put into effect the concession granted by Lobengula for the occupation of Mashonaland. For a sum of £88,285 10s. a corps was raised of 180 men. Accompanied by 300 police and guided by the famous hunter F. C. Selous (q.v.), they began their march from Macloutsie on June 28, 1890, reached Tuli on July 1 and, after crossing Providential Pass, hoisted the British flag on September 13 on a small hill that became Salisbury. They were disbanded on October 1, each member of the force being entitled to a free farm, and other privileges.

Pipe. Geological expression used in South Africa to describe a crater of extinct volcanoes in which diamonds are frequently to be found. The most famous pipes are those of Kimberley, but there are many others, barren of precious stones.

Pipelines. *See* TRANSPORT IN REPUBLIC OF SOUTH AFRICA.

Pipit (family Motacillidae). Lark-like bird, soberly coloured and spotted or streaked. Many of the varieties live in open, rocky country. Both the Longclaws and the Wagtails (q.v.) belong to the family.

Piquetberg. Town in the Western Cape Province, founded in 1840, and named after a nearby mountain, on which the early Dutch Governor Isbrand Goske had caused an outpost (piquet) to be placed. Today it is a flourishing grain and general farming centre, with an important cement industry. Population: 4,505, including 2,000 Whites.

Pirie Bush. Large natural forest near King William's Town. Near it are trout-hatcheries.

Pirow, Oswald. South African Cabinet Minister. Of German descent he was born at Aberdeen, Cape Province, in 1890. After his studies in South Africa, Germany and the Inner Temple, London, he was called to the Bar. In 1924 he was elected to Parliament where his drive and ability gained him the posts of Minister of Justice and Minister of Defence under General J. B. M. Hertzog. Though he did much to improve military efficiency, his alleged pro-German leanings and particularly his visit to Adolf Hitler roused much criticism. He wrote books on Bantu life and a life of General Hertzog. Died 1959.

Pitsani Potluko. Trading post in Bechuanaland near the Transvaal border, used in 1895 by Dr. L. S. Jameson and his followers as a base from which their raid into the South African Republic was launched. *See* JAMESON RAID.

Pitso. A Basuto name for a gathering of councillors.

Plaatje, Sol T. Bantu author. Born in 1878 in Boshof, O.F.S., he went to school at the Lutheran Mission at Pniel and then became court interpreter. During the South African War he worked for the defenders in the siege of Mafeking. Founded Sechuana newspapers in Kimberley and became first General Secretary of the African National Congress in 1912. Twice he took part in deputations overseas—1914 and 1919. He wrote copiously, including a number of books, notably *Mhudi*, a Sechuana novel, *Sechuana Proverbs* and translations of Shakespeare's plays into that language. He died in 1932.

Plague. *See* BUBONIC PLAGUE.

PLANTS OF SOUTHERN AFRICA

by

M. LEVYNS

University of Cape Town

IN a broad survey the vegetation of South Africa may be divided into three main classes, the first widespread and the other two relatively localised. These are: (1) the main African flora; (2) the belt of semi-desert scrub running obliquely from the Namib in South West Africa to the Karroo in the south; and (3) the small-leafed bush, known as Cape Flora, or technically as sclerophyll, which is most highly developed on the mountains and along the coastal strip of the south-west.

The main African flora extends over the whole of tropical Africa and south to all provinces of the Republic. In the Cape Province, however, it is confined to the eastern part and peters out a little south of East London. The most characteristic aspects of this extensive flora are found in the tropics.

Climate, especially rainfall but also the presence or absence of frost, and the type of soil, determines vegetation. The optimum conditions under which forest develops are infrequent in South Africa. Parkland, with grass or low shrubs between the trees, is most prevalent in the tropical parts. With diminishing and often erratic rainfall, trees become smaller and are finally replaced by bushes, often of a thorny nature. These are found over large stretches of the Kalahari, much of which, far from being the desert of popular fiction, makes excellent ranching country.

A great variety of trees and shrubs is to be found. Sometimes one particular kind dominates the landscape, such as species of Brachystegia in Zambia, Angola and Tanganyika. The northern parts of the Kruger National Park are covered with mopane forest (*Colophospermum mopane*), or in the drier parts, with mopane bush. Some of the trees are very striking, such as the grotesque baobabs (*Adansonia digitata*), where the girth of the trunk may exceed the height of the tree. Another which cannot fail to attract attention is the graceful fever tree (*Acacia xanthophloea*), its trunk and branches coloured a sickly yellow. As the popular name suggests, it inhabits swampy places where malarial mosquitoes abound. In drier areas grow those curiosities, the tree Euphorbias. At the south-eastern limit of this flora, tree Euphorbias often grow socially, giving a nightmarish quality to the landscape.

In the Highveld of the Transvaal and in parts of the Orange Free State where severe frosts occur, trees and bushes give place to grassland, of which a more luxuriant type occurs in Natal on the seaward side of the Drakensberg. Both these types are derived from the main African flora and are related to those occurring further north.

The region of semi-desert scrub starts in South West Africa as a coastal strip of varying width and crosses the Orange River into the Western Cape Province, continuing on the landward side of the mountain ranges of the south-west. The Langeberg and Outeniqua Mountains form its southern boundary. In other places, especially in the east, the boundaries are ill-defined between this and the main African flora.

The lowest rainfall is along the western coastal belt where it is 5 inches or less a year, and where none may sometimes fall for several years. Some remarkable plants have their home there, perhaps the most celebrated being *Welwitschia mirabilis*, northwards from Walvis Bay, the only place in the world where this member of the lower seed-bearing plants occurs. Strict protection came only just in time to save it from extinction. In the same region grows the 'Naras, a spiny and seemingly leafless member of the pumpkin family, the fruit of which is eaten by the natives.

The southern part of the region, the Karroo (a Hottentot word meaning bare), has a higher rainfall, though it seldom exceeds 10 inches a year. The vegetation consists of low bushes, separated by bare earth. In the Ceres-Calvinia-Karroo and the Little Karroo, succulents abound, but with increasing altitude and severe frosts the succulents tend to disappear. Their place is taken by small, gnarled bushes which, lacking the capacity of succulents to store water, enter into a period of dormancy and to a casual observer appear to be dead. Restored to vigorous life after heavy rain, they burst into leaf and flower. Numerous annuals and dormant bulbs add their share to the upsurging life, turning the Karroo for a short time into a brilliantly coloured flower garden. Among the very few plants able to remain green when rain is withheld for months on end, are the doornboom (*Acacia karroo*) and the kareeboom (*Rhus lancea*), which are confined to water courses and send down roots for great distances to hidden supplies.

The Cape sclerophyll is characterised by proteas, heaths, pelargoniums, certain reeds and numerous genera and even families peculiar to this region. All the higher mountains of the south-west and south have a covering of Cape plants, as also the coastal strip from St. Helena Bay to Port Elizabeth. Not only is the Cape flora quite unlike any other in Africa, but it is one of the richest, if not the richest, in the world. The massing of species in the south-western corner, with its winter rain, has long intrigued scientists. Greatest in the Caledon Division, the numbers of species diminish in an orderly fashion northwards and eastwards. Curiously enough, traces of this flora are to be found on mountains throughout Africa south of the Sahara. Frequently some species may be found on the upper slopes of any of the higher mountains

of tropical East Africa, without a trace of them on the lowlands in between. One must assume these isolated islands to be relics of a flora once covering Africa, and that the mountains with their great variety of climates have afforded it a refuge. The Cape flora is essentially montane and older than those of the Karroo and tropical Africa. Some botanists suggest it to be the remnant of an old Austral flora, thus accounting for its real though distant affinities with that of western Australia. Others think that it had a northern origin and that the isolated patches on mountains in Central Africa give clues to its southward migration.

Forests, rare in Southern Africa, and of an evergreen type quite different from that of the tropics, occur in the Knysna and Humansdorp divisions where the rainfall is evenly distributed throughout the year. The principal trees are Yellowwoods (*Podocarpus*), Ironwoods (*Olea*), Stinkwood (*Ocotea*), etc. The same type of forest grows in sheltered mountain ravines in the south-west and also on the mountains of eastern Africa. Its origin is as much a mystery as that of the Cape flora.

Flowering plants are relatively recent arrivals on the earth's surface. There is no trace of them in the older sedimentary rocks in which fossilised remains of more primitive types of plants abound. At the time that the Karroo rocks were being laid down, a cold temperate flora, known as Glossopteris, flourished. This was composed of primitive seed-bearing plants, ferns and their allies, but no flowering plants. Fossils of this flora have been found in most lands of the southern hemisphere, now widely separated by sea. Ferns still make up a part of our modern flora but Glossopteris and its allies have vanished.

Lower forms of plant life, such as mosses, liverworts, algae, fungi and lichens abound in South Africa as elsewhere but do not show to any marked extent the peculiar endemic features of the more highly evolved plants.

Platanna (*Xenopus laevis*). A species of South African frog, which through research at the Cape Town University has achieved considerable importance in science. Injected with fluid drawn from women, it is a quicker indication of pregnancy than any other test. For this reason these frogs are collected and exported to all parts of the world. The word 'Platanna' is believed to be a corruption of the word 'Plathander' meaning 'flat-handed.'

Platinum. Noble metal mined in Rustenburg district, and also recovered as a by-product on Rand gold fields. In 1923–1924 extensive reefs were found in Lydenburg, Waterberg and Potgietersrust district and a platinum boom swept the country. South Africa is the world's second largest platinum producer.

Platteland. Literally flat country. Colloquial term for the country district.

Player, Gary Jim. South African golf champion. Born in Johannesburg November 1, 1935, and educated at King Edward VII School, he began his sporting career with rugby and cricket, but at 14 took up golf. Even a serious accident in 1950 failed to hamper him, and by 1954 he had already undertaken his first tour as a professional in Britain. In every country where he appeared he made a sensation. His debut in 1958 in the United States almost immediately placed him in the top class. He won the British Open Championship in 1959, the U.S. Open in 1965, the 'Tournament of Champions' in America in 1969 and has since continued his triumphs.

Plettenberg, Joachim Ammema, Baron van. Governor of the Cape of Good Hope. Born in Leeuwarden, Netherlands, on March 8, 1739, son of Colonel Hendrik Casimir van Plettenberg, of the Dutch cavalry, and his wife, born van Ammema. Having studied law at Utrecht, he joined the service of the Dutch East India Company, which in 1764 sent him to Batavia. Two years later he was posted as Independent Fiscal to the Cape, being promoted to Secunde in 1772 and to Governor in 1774. His term of office coincided with war against the British, and a French force was sent out to reinforce the garrison. Plettenberg took a considerable interest in exploring the Colony (*see* PLETTENBERG BAY). Discontent arose about his administration and from 1779–1781 an inquiry was held in Holland. In 1785 he retired, making his home at Zwolle. He died on August 18, 1793.

Plettenberg Bay. Township on the coast of the Cape Province, between Cape Town and Port Elizabeth, situated on the shores of an inlet of the same name. It is called after the Dutch Governor Joachim van Plettenberg (q.v.) who visited it in 1778, and left a famous beacon carrying his coat of arms, still to be seen there. The neighbouring forests were used for shipbuilding in former times and a whaling station was set up, which operated until about 1913. Since then Plettenberg Bay has become a flourishing holiday resort and residential centre. Population: 900, including 500 Whites.

Ploegbreker (**Plough-breaker**). Plant. Common South African name for *Erythrina zeyheri*. So called because the tough roots interfere with cultivation.

Plomer, William Charles Franklyn. South African author. Born in South Africa on December 10, 1903, he was a close friend in his younger days of Roy Campbell (q.v.), and with him started the magazine *Voorslag* in Natal, scandalising large sections of the public with their views on the colour and other questions. His first novel, *Turbott Wolfe*, appeared in 1926, followed in 1927 by *I Speak of*

Africa. An appointment as a university lecturer in English in Japan resulted in *Paper Houses* (1929). After a spell in the Far East he settled in England, where his works included *Cecil Rhodes* (1933) and *Museum Pieces* (1952). Apart from this he became associated with the publishing firm of Jonathan Cape.

Plover (Limicolae). Bird of the Wader family, found on the coasts of South Africa and in many varieties, on freshwater or on dry ground. Most Plovers have short, light bills, and feathers that stand up like a forehead. Some are indigenous, like the small White-fronted Sand-Plover, which is often seen on sandy shores. Others breed in the Arctic and Sub-Arctic and then come south. Among these is the Crowned Lapwing, the commonest of the dry-land plovers in South Africa, which lives in scattered flocks and has a grating cry. Dark breast band and black-and-white banded cap are conspicuous.

Plowman, Sir George Thomas. Administrator of Natal. Born in 1858 in England, he emigrated to Natal as a young man and entered the Civil Service. From 1901 to 1910 he was Secretary to the Prime Minister, and Secretary for Lands and Work. During the South African National Convention he served as Joint Secretary. Upon the establishment of Union, he became the first Provincial Secretary of Natal (1910 to 1917), then Deputy Administrator and from 1918 to 1928 Administrator of Natal. He died in 1943.

Plumbago capensis (Plumbaginaceae). Straggling evergreen shrub 7 to 8 feet, on edge of bushy country, Eastern Cape and Natal. Periwinkle-blue flowers. Much cultivated as a hedge.

Plumpudding Island. Small island off the coast of South-West Africa, exploited for its guano deposits, and annexed to the Cape in 1867. Its name is derived from the alleged resemblance in shape to this dainty.

Plumtree. Village in Rhodesia, 65 miles south of Bulawayo. Population: 1,000, including 300 Whites. *See* PLUMTREE SCHOOL.

Plumtree School. Boys' school at Plumtree (q.v.), founded for the children of railwaymen by Bishop Gaul (q.v.) in 1902. Has developed into a leading public school which draws boys from distant places. Up to 1914 it was also attended by girls.

Pniel: 1. Mission station and diamond-digging centre near Barkly West, Cape Province. Population: 1,150, including 20 Whites.
2. Coloured settlement near Paarl, Cape Colony. Population: 1,308.

Pofadder. Village near Kenhardt, Cape Province. Population: 2,030, including 453 Whites.

Police. *See* SOUTH AFRICAN POLICE, CAPE MOUNTED RIFLEMEN, FRONTIER ARMED MOUNTED POLICE, SOUTH AFRICAN CONSTABULARY, BRITISH SOUTH AFRICA POLICE.

Polo. Introduced into South Africa by officers of the British garrison, polo was first played at King William's Town and in 1876 the first match took place in Natal. In 1885 the first polo club in Southern Africa was established in Cape Town, under the auspices of the British Garrison. It used part of the racecourse at Kenilworth. Early players included the late Lord Baden-Powell, of Mafeking fame, who was an active local organiser. In 1885 another club was started in Port Elizabeth, and by degrees polo spread round the country. It has attained particular popularity in Lesotho, owing to the widespread use of horses there. Lord Patrick Beresford (later the Marquis of Waterford) then stationed in South Africa, presented the Beresford Cup in 1915, since that time the chief trophy. More than 20

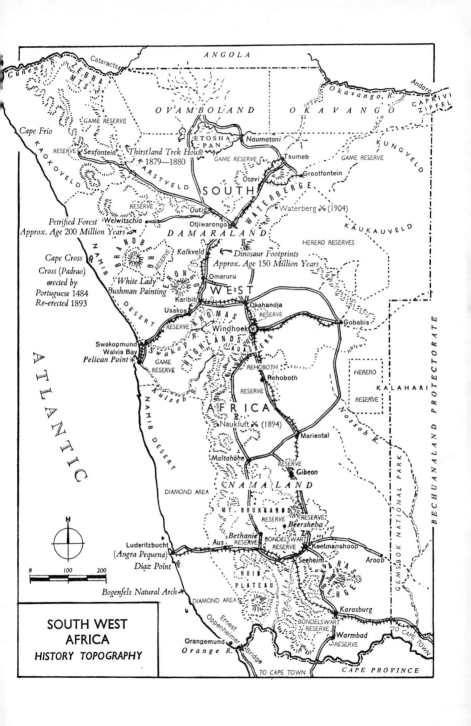

ANGOLA

Cunene R.
Cataracts
ZEBRA MTS

Cape Frio

OVAMBOLAND

OKAVANGO

Okavango, R.

Andara

CAPRIVI ZIPFEL

KAOKOVELD

GAME RESERVE

ETOSHA PAN

Naumatoni

KUNGVELD

RESERVE Sesfontein

Thirstland Trek House
1879—1880

Tsumeb

GAME RESERVE

GAME RESERVE

KARSTVELD

SOUTH

Otavi

Grootfontein

WATERBERGE

RESERVE Outjo

Waterberg (1904)

KAUKAUVELD

Petrified Forest
Approx. Age 200 Million Years

Welwitschia

Otjiwarongo

DAMARALAND

HERERO RESERVES

Cape Cross
Cross (Padrao)
erected by
Portuguese 1484
Re-erected 1893

NAMIB

BRANDBERG

ERONGO

RESERVE

Kalkveld

Dinosaur Footprints
Approx. Age 150 Million Years

"White Lady"
Bushman Painting

Omaruru

WEST

Karibib

Usakos

RESERVE

Swakopmund
Walvis Bay
Pelican Point

KHOMAS HIGHLANDS

Okahandja

RESERVE

Gobabis

Windhoek

AUASBERG

DESERT

Swakop R.

GAME RESERVE

REHOBOTH

Rehoboth

HERERO

RESERVE

KALAHARI

Kuiseb

AFRICA

RESERVE

BECHUANALAND PROTECTORATE

ATLANTIC

NAMIB DESERT

Naukluft (1894)

Mariental

Maltahöhe

Nossob R.

RESERVE

Gibeon

NAMALAND

DIAMOND AREA

MT. BRUKKAROS

RESERVE

RESERVE

Beersheba

N

Bethanie RESERVE

0   100   200

Luderitzbucht
(Angra Pequena)
Diaz Point

Aus

BONDELSWART
RESERVE

Koetmanshoop

Seeheim

KARAS BERGE

Aroab

HUIB
PLATEAU

Bogenfels Natural Arch

DIAMOND AREA

Karasburg

BONDELSWART
RESERVE

SOUTH WEST
AFRICA
HISTORY TOPOGRAPHY

Ernest
Oppenheimer
Bridge

Orangemund
Orange R.

Warmbad

RESERVE

TO CAPE TOWN

GEMSBOK NATIONAL PARK

TO CAPE TOWN

CAPE PROVINCE

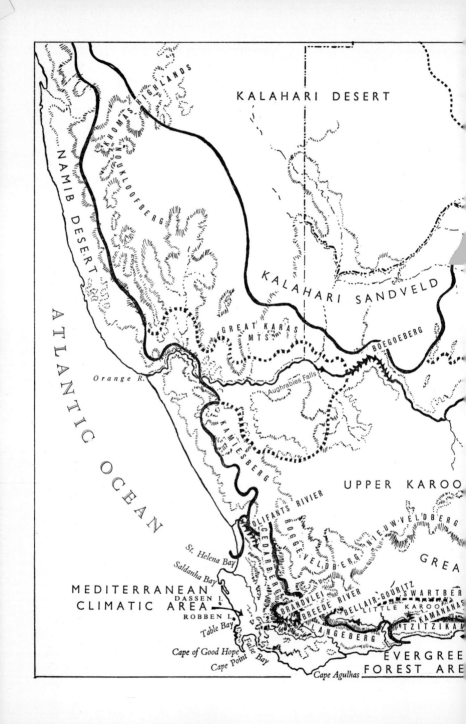

KALAHARI

THORNVELD

N'JELELE

ZOUTPANSBERG

KRUGER

NATIONAL

LOW

VELD

PARK

BUSH VELD

LEBOMBO HILLS

Limpopo R.

BOSVELD

MARICO

MAGALIESBERG

LOSKOP

HIGHVELD

HARTEBEESPOORT

DRAKENSBERG

WITWAT'ERS'RAND

SKOONSPRUIT

BOSKOP

GRASSVELD

VAALDAM

HIGH VELD

PONGOLA

EASTERN LITTORAL

VAALHARTZ

BOTHAVILLE

MIDDLE VELD

MALUTIS

St. Lucia Bay

RUSTFONTEIN

DRAKENSBERG

KALKFONTEIN

DRAKENSBERG

GRASS LANDS

Tugela R.

SUB-TROPICAL COASTAL AREA

DRAKENSBERG

MASSIF

EASTERN

INDIAN

STORMBERG

WATERDOWN

OCEAN

KAROO

WINTERBERG

LAKE ARTHUR

N

SOUTH-EASTERN LITTORAL

BIRD

Algoa Bay

0   100   200

SOUTH AFRICA
IRRIGATION SCHEMES
TOPOGRAPHY   VEGETATION

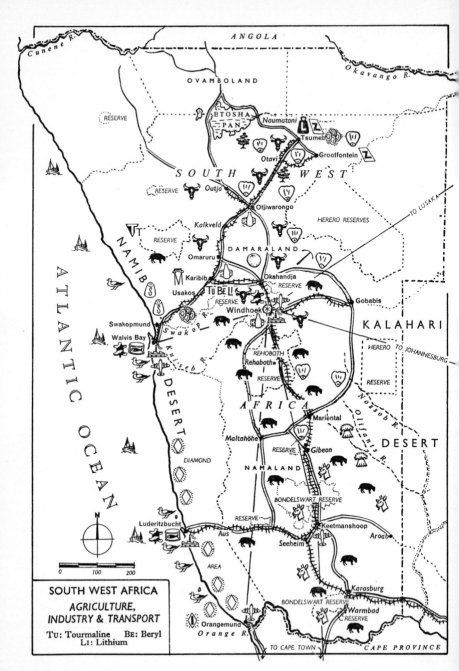

ANGOLA

Cunene R.

Okavango R.

OVAMBOLAND

RESERVE

ETOSHA PAN

Naumatoni

Tsumeb

Grootfontein

Otavi

S O U T H   W E S T

Outjo

RESERVE

Otjiwarongo

HERERO RESERVES

TO LUSAKA

Kalkveld

RESERVE

DAMARALAND

Omaruru

Karibib

Okahandja

RESERVE

N A M I B

Usakos

TU BE LI

RESERVE

Windhoek

Gobabis

K A L A H A R I

Swakopmund

Walvis Bay

Swakop R.

Kuiseb R.

HERERO   TO JOHANNESBURG

REHOBOTH

Rehoboth

RESERVE

RESERVE

A T L A N T I C   O C E A N

D E S E R T

A F R I C A

Mariental

Olifants R.

Nossob R.

D E S E R T

Maltahöhe

RESERVE

Gibeon

DIAMOND

N A M A L A N D

BONDELSWART RESERVE

Luderitzbucht

RESERVE

Aus

Seeheim

Keetmanshoop

Aroab

N

AREA

0   100   200

Karasburg

BONDELSWART RESERVE

Warmbad

RESERVE

Orangemund

Orange R.

TO CAPE TOWN

C A P E   P R O V I N C E

SOUTH WEST AFRICA
*AGRICULTURE,
INDUSTRY & TRANSPORT*

Tu: Tourmaline   Be: Beryl
Li: Lithium

FOR KEY TO SYMBOLS SEE PAGE VIII

official tournaments have been held, visiting teams having come from Britain, Rhodesia and Argentina.

Pomeroy. Village in Natal in the Biggarsberg, between Dundee and Greytown, noted for its scenery, called after the late Governor Sir Pomeroy Colley, and founded about 1880. There was fighting near by in the Zulu Rebellion of 1906. Population: 350, including 20 Whites.

Pondok. Primitive house used by natives, particularly Hottentots in South West Africa. The word is derived from the Malay and means 'a house made of leaves.' In South Africa it is very often made of pieces of tin, reeds, etc.

Pondoland Coconut Palm. Common South African name for *Jubaeopsis caffra*. Peculiar species believed to have been brought to Pondoland by early slave traders.

Pondomisi. Tribe living in the Eastern Cape Province, and not to be confused with the Pondos (q.v.). Although of similar origin, they were independent, and in the early 19th century ruled by two rival chiefs, Umhlonhlo and Umditshwa. In 1872 Umhlonhlo asked to be taken under the authority of the Cape Colony, and was followed in 1873 by Umditshwa with a similar request. Both went into rebellion in 1880; Umditshwa surrendered and was sentenced to three years' imprisonment, but Umhlonhlo escaped capture until 1903. The area was subsequently placed under a magistrate.

Pondos. Tribe of the Xosa family in the Eastern Cape Province, also known as the Aba-Mbo. First encountered on the west bank of the Umzimvubu, where they suffered greatly through the invasions at the beginning of the 19th century by Zulu impis under Tshaka (q.v.). In 1828 they were visited by a British officer, Major Dundas, who found them in great poverty. Their chief, Faku (q.v.), finally offered to submit to Tshaka as a vassal, but his ambassadors arrived at the Zulu King's headquarters on the very day when he was assassinated. In 1829 the Rev. William Shaw, a Methodist, went to convert the Pondos to Christianity. During the war in 1835 between the Cape Colonists and the Xosas, the Pondos sided with the Europeans. In 1844 Faku entered into a treaty with Sir Peregrine Maitland, under which, in return for his collaboration, he received all the territory south of the Umzimkulu River, down to the Umzimvubu. With the downfall of the Xosas, the Pondos remained the only independent tribe in the Eastern Province, though they were in a very primitive state, and rent by civil wars. Faku's son, Umqikela, succeeded him on his death, in October 1867, as Paramount Chief of the Pondos, but proved unfriendly to the Cape Government, and was involved in internecine wars with his brother, Umhlangaso. In 1878 Governor Sir Bartle Frere withdrew the recognition of Umqikela as Paramount Chief. To prevent gun-running and foreign infiltration, the mouth of the Umzimvubu River was taken over by the Cape Colony in 1878 and a settlement established under the name of Port St. John (q.v.). Umhlangaso tried to introduce German agents, headed by August Einwald in 1886, to counteract British influence, but was unsuccessful. In February, 1888, Umqikela's son, Sigcau (also known as Sigcawu), succeeded as Paramount Chief of the Pondos, and adopted a friendly policy to the Cape Government. Chaotic conditions continued, however, and in September, 1894, after Sigcau had voluntarily submitted, Pondoland was annexed to Cape Colony. The origin of the Pondo tribe is obscure, but it is known to have been made up of fragments of other tribes in the 17th century. Today many Pondos serve as mine workers on the goldfields of the Rand.

Pongola River. Rises in Swaziland, follows northern border of Zululand, joins the Usutu and, as the Maputa, enters Delagoa Bay. Large irrigation schemes have been developed on its lower reaches.

Pont. A corruption of the word Pontoon. A floating bridge used on many South African rivers. Formerly pontoons were owned largely by local companies and some of them, particularly in important positions, became well known throughout the country. Among the best known was Norvals Pont, belonging to a Scotchman of that name, which operated across the Orange River and gave its name to a village.

Pontac. A dark heavy Cape wine. The name is derived from a town in the south of France the product of which it is believed to resemble.

Poole, David. South African ballet dancer. Born in Cape Town on September 7, 1925. Trained by Dulcie Howes and Cecily Robertson and danced with Cape Town Ballet Club. In 1947 he went to London where he became leading dramatic dancer at Sadler's Wells. Returned to Cape Town in 1958 to teach at University Drama School.

Poor Whites. Mainly as a result of the poverty caused by the Rinderpest (q.v.) a very large group of Europeans in South Africa found themselves unable to earn an adequate living in rural districts. They came into the towns to re-establish themselves. Early attempts to help included founding the Johannesburg suburb of Vrededorp. The Poor Whites increased in such numbers that in 1930 they were estimated at 150,000. An inquiry was held by the Dutch Reformed Church in collaboration with the Carnegie Corporation, as to the best methods of helping them. Among the most successful efforts was the founding of irrigation and forestry settlements and the employment of Whites in semi-skilled work on railways, roads and elsewhere. Thanks to the general increase in prosperity and the industrialisation of South Africa, the Poor White of the old type is almost extinct.

Poppadums. Cape Malay dish of flour, water, spice and curry. Made in thin wafers.

Poqo (Bantu word meaning 'pure' or 'completely'). Illegal movement discovered among South African Bantus in 1962 to drive out White inhabitants by terrorism.

Porcupine (*Hystrix africao-australis*). Rodent known for its characteristic defensive quills. Upon being driven into the flesh of attackers, they are difficult to remove. Porcupines live on vegetable food and do considerable damage to crops, though they also destroy certain poisonous plants which are a danger to cattle. They are about 28 inches long, live in burrows and are common to most parts of Southern Africa. *See* MAMMALS.

Porges, Jules (originally JULIUS). Mining magnate. Born 1838 in Prague, settled in Paris in the 60's and became a leading diamond merchant. Both Alfred Beit (q.v.) and Sir Julius Wernher (q.v.) worked for him and were sent by him to Kimberley. He himself arrived there in 1875 and became a successful operator in shares, claims and stones, later extending operations to the Witwatersrand. In 1880 he returned to Europe. Although he retired from business in 1889, he died only in 1921, having long outlived both Beit and Wernher.

Porpoises (Delphinidae). Members of the Whale (Cetacean) family. Schools of them have appeared in False Bay,

Cape, from time to time, leaping and playing among the bathers. *See* WHALE.

Port Alfred. Seaside resort and former seaport at the mouth of the Kowie River in the Eastern Cape Province. Its use as a harbour was first attempted by the 1820 settlers, who brought cargoes ashore there. In 1855 the first systematic attempts at improvement began, with the formal opening of the place as Port Frances, named after the wife of Governor Sir Lowry Cole. William Cock formed the Kowie Harbour Improvement Co. which in 1857 began embankments to increase the depth of the river entrance. In 1860, Port Frances was renamed Port Alfred, in honour of Prince Alfred (q.v.) who was visiting South Africa at the time. Attempts at developing the harbour continued for many years, the expenditure totalling £800,000. At one time lines of sailing ships and steamers could be seen at anchor in the Kowie, but the silting up of the entrance proved too costly and the port was abandoned in the present century. Now a leading seaside resort, with a famous golf course. Population: 6,600, including 1,500 Whites.

Port Beaufort. Former seaport at the mouth of the Breede River in the Cape Province, serving the Swellendam district. It was called after the family name of the Governor Lord Charles Somerset, and established by the well-known mercantile house of Barry and Nephews of Swellendam, who put up warehouses and other buildings. Development began in 1816 and continued until the 1870's, small steamers as well as sailing ships entering the river. Gradually it fell into neglect and today it is solely a seaside and fishing resort

Port Durnford. Anchorage off the coast of Zululand, used during the Zulu War of 1879 for putting ashore British troops and their supplies. Here, too, Cetewayo (q.v.) was landed upon his return to Zululand, on being restored to the throne in 1883. The place takes its name from Colonel A. W. Durnford (q.v.) of the Royal Engineers who was killed at the battle of Isandhlwana in 1879.

Port Edward. Seaside resort on the south coast of Natal, on the border of the Cape, 35 miles below Port Shepstone, established in 1924, and named after the then Prince of Wales (Duke of Windsor). Population: 300, including 120 Whites.

Port Elizabeth. Seaport and manufacturing city in the Eastern Cape Province, named after Lady Elizabeth Donkin, wife of Sir Rufane Shaw Donkin, who was Lieutenant-Governor of the Cape at that time. Although Fort Frederick, which is still standing, was erected on the shores of Algoa Bay as early as 1799, the real birth of Port Elizabeth did not take place until 1820, when the arrival of the British settlers in the Eastern Province created the need for a harbour and community there. From the beginning the place was noted for its enterprise, and soon established itself as the principal exporting port of the Colony. Efforts to develop the harbour in Algoa Bay were greatly hampered by the turbulence of the sea, and a basin, constructed on the advice of Sir John Coode in 1870, had ultimately to be abandoned. Towards the end of the 19th century Port Elizabeth began to develop the manufacture of leather goods and footwear, in which it is still pre-eminent in South Africa. The first harbour was completed in 1928. Because of its convenient situation, Port Elizabeth, called the 'Liverpool of Cape Colony' in Victorian days, is favoured by important overseas firms for the erection of assembly and other manufacturing plants. Among these the motor industry is particularly important. Manufactures for which it is today noteworthy are footwear, engineering, confectionery, timber and many others. The municipality has an outstanding record for the manner in which it has overcome the housing problem, both for black and white. Population: 381,230, including 119,000 Whites, 107,000 Coloureds, 152,000 Bantu and 5,200 Asiatics. The municipality of Walmer (q.v.) was merged in Port Elizabeth on January 1, 1967.

Porterville. Village in the Western Cape Province, named after the Hon. William Porter, Attorney-General of Cape Colony in Victorian times. It was founded in 1877. Wheat and fruit producing centre. Population: 2,900, including 1,310 Whites.

Port Grosvenor. Harbour established by Captain Sidney Turner on the coast of Pondoland in 1878, and so called on account of its proximity to the scene of the wreck of the famous Indiaman the *Grosvenor* (q.v.). Because it was impossible to control the traffic there and from fear of alleged arms smuggling it was closed down by the British authorities in 1885. The traffic was always small.

Port Herald. Small town on Malawi frontier with Mozambique. Situated on the Shire River, it formerly enjoyed a special importance as the limit of navigation, prior to the building of the railway. It was founded about 1890.

Port Matola. *See* MATOLA.

Port Natal. *See* DURBAN.

Port Nolloth. Town on the northwestern coast of the Cape Province, serving Namaqualand. Established in 1855 on a roadstead previously known as Robbe Bay (Seal Bay), and called after Commander M. S. Nolloth, who surveyed the coast in H.M.S. *Frolic*, it was meant to serve the needs of the new copper mines in Namaqualand. In 1869 a railway was built for 100 miles inland by the Cape Copper Co. to O'okiep (q.v.). This has been replaced in recent years by a road-motor service. There is a small

jetty. Canning factories have been established. Population: 3,050, including 800 Whites.

Porto Amelia. Seaport in Mozambique. Noted for its magnificent natural harbour, covering nearly 40 sq. miles. Development has been pushed ahead since World War II, and ships of up to 12,000 tons can enter. Population 50,000, including 500 Whites.

Porto Belo. Harbour in Mozambique on the mouth of the Macuse. Also known as Macuse.

Port Rex. Original name of East London (q.v.) after George Rex, who first took a ship into the Buffalo River.

Port Shepstone. Town in Natal, on the south coast 80 miles from Durban, named after Sir Theophilus Shepstone (q.v.), the Natal statesman of Victorian days. Situated at the mouth of the picturesque Umzimkulu River (1877), it was hoped to develop it as a harbour, and substantial sums were expended on works, but the obstacles proved too great. Port Shepstone has become a popular seaside resort, as well as the centre of a rich farming area—sugar, bananas, etc. Near by are important marble deposits. Population: 4,238, including 1,755 Whites.

Port St. John. Small seaport and holiday resort at the mouth of the St. John or Umzimvubu (Elephant) River in the Transkei, established as a White enclave in native territories not annexed by the Cape Colony. In 1870 it was ceded to the latter by the local chief, Nquiliso, and in 1884 it was formally occupied. While its commercial importance, which tempted German authorities to try annexation, has dwindled, its magnificent scenery—particularly the 'Gates' through which the river breaks—have made it famous as a tourist resort. Since the grant of self-government to the Transkei proposals have been revived for its redevelopment as a port. Population: 1,280, including 313 Whites.

Postma, Reverend Dirk. Founder of the 'Dopper' Section of the Dutch Reformed Church in South Africa (q.v.). Born in 1818, Holland, studied at the Theological College in Kampen as a minister of the Gereformeerde Kerk, which in 1857, by special request, sent him to the South African Republic. Here dissatisfaction, going back many years, had arisen about certain tendencies in the older Church. In 1859 Postma, who had become minister in Rustenburg, founded the new offshoot of his own Church, and held the first service under an old tree. He moved to Burghersdorp, Cape Colony, in 1869, when he took charge of a new theological seminary, forerunner of Potchefstroom University. He died in 1890.

Postmasburg. Town in the Northern Cape Province, named after the Rev. D. Postma, and established 1890. It saw fighting during the South African War. Its progress after the discovery of diamonds in 1919 was followed in 1926 by important finds of manganese, from which a very large industry has developed, the product of which is partly used by the Iscor steel works and partly exported. To carry the output a special branch railway has been built. Population: 9,500, including 3,000 Whites.

Post Retief. Village in the Eastern Cape Province, in the Little Winterberg, home of Pieter Retief (q.v.) before he joined the Great Trek (q.v.). Here he held the post of Field-Cornet.

Potato, Sweet (*Ipomoea batalas*) (Convolvulaceae). One of many climbers with trumpet flowers, belonging to Rhodesia, where genus *Ipomoea* is most plentiful. Purple Morning Glory (*Ipomoea purpurea*) is found widely in Natal. Members of the Convolvulaceae family are rare at the Cape. All these climbers twist anticlockwise in South Africa and clockwise in Europe.

Potchefstroom. Original capital of the Transvaal and one of its two oldest towns. One explanation of the name is that it is derived from the Voortrekker Andries Hendrik Potgieter who, being the Chef, or Chief, of the Voortrekkers, settled beside the Mooi River (Afrikaans 'stroom'). This rather far-fetched idea has been lately countered by a much simpler theory that the name is derived from a collection of pot-sherds found near the stream, in Dutch, 'potscherf' (a name which appears on several old maps). Potchefstroom, founded in 1838, was recognised as the capital of the local Voortrekker community. Even the foundation of Pretoria in 1855, and the proclamation of the newer town as the 'seat of Government,' did not affect the status of the older centre, which has continued to be known as 'The Old Capital' down to the present day. Hollow though this honour might be, there is no reason to doubt that Potchefstroom remained the 'capital' of the Transvaal until the end of the Boer régime. During the First Boer War, in 1880, a British force was besieged in a tiny local fort, although it held out until the signing of peace. During the South African War, Potchefstroom was occupied by the British in June 1900. After the return of peace, a British garrison was stationed there, and brought into existence the famous military camp, later taken over by the Union Defence Force and used as a training centre in both World Wars. Since 1933 Potchefstroom has acquired importance as a gold mining centre, through the discovery of an extension of the Witwatersrand beyond Randfontein in this direction. It is the seat of a university, established in 1951, and developed from the old Theological Seminary, founded in the

1860's, of the well-known Agricultural College and of other institutions. The population is 52,780, including 25,000 Whites, 2,400 Coloured, 380 Indians and 25,000 Bantu.

Potgieter, Andries Hendrik. Voortrekker leader. Born in 1792, farmed near Tarkastad before the Great Trek, and in 1835 took a party of emigrants from those parts to the north. In the present Orange Free State he was joined by others, led by Sarel Cilliers (q.v.). He soon showed great gifts as a military leader, and led Boer forces against the Matabele and other hostile tribes, gaining victories at Mosega, Vegkop and elsewhere. In 1836 he crossed the Vaal and helped to found Potchefstroom in 1838. He was followed in 1845 by Andries Orighstad. He died in 1852.

Potgieter, Pieter Johannes. Commandant-General of the South African Republic. The date of his birth is uncertain and so are many details of his life. His father was the well-known Voortrekker leader Andries Hendrik Potgieter (q.v.). In 1853 he was appointed successor to his father as Commandant-General. As such his chief claim to fame was in leading the attack on the stronghold of chief Makapan in the Northern Transvaal, in which he was killed, in 1854.

Potgietersrus (originally Piet Potgietersrust). Town in the Northern Transvaal. Established in 1854 and named after the Voortrekker leader Commandant Piet Potgieter, who was killed by the natives under Chief Makapan not far away, at Moorddrift (q.v.). The outbreak of fever caused the earlier settlement to be abandoned in 1870 and it was not re-established until 1890, since when it has attained a high degree of prosperity. The town became a centre of prospecting and mining activity during the 1925 platinum boom, but is now noted chiefly for its trade in sub-tropical produce, particularly in oranges from the nearby

Zebediela Estate (q.v.), and from other properties, also in groundnuts. Population: 12,893, including 6,500 Whites.

Poto, Victor. Paramount Chief of Western Pondo tribe. Born August 1, 1898, and educated at Buntingville Institution, Clarkebury, Healdtown and Fort Hare. Succeeded his uncle, Paramount Chief Dalindyebo, in 1918 and became member of the Pondoland General Council, the Native Representative Council and other administrative bodies. Well known as a Methodist churchman and as a Bantu leader in Transkei (q.v.).

Pottinger, Sir Henry. Governor of Cape Colony, born in 1789. In 1840 he was sent to China, becoming the first Governor of the new colony of Hong Kong. From 1846 to 1847 he was Governor of the Cape, where he spent most of his time on the eastern frontier. He retired to Malta, where he died in 1856.

Poultry. The Republic of South Africa has about 11,000,000 head of poultry, of which 10,300,000 are fowls. Of these the largest number are in the Transvaal, about 3,700,000, followed by the Cape with about 3,300,000, the Orange Free State with 1,900,000 and Natal with about 1,400,000. Of the 200,000 ducks, about one-third or 66,000 are in the Transvaal, 61,000 in the Cape, 44,000 in Natal and 28,000 in the Orange Free State. Of approximately 240,000 turkeys to be found in the Republic, again the largest number are in the Transvaal—82,000, with 68,000 in the Cape, 64,000 in the Orange Free State and 24,000 in Natal. Of the 74,000 geese, however, the largest number are in the Cape, about 32,000, with 19,000 in the Transvaal, 17,000 in the Orange Free State and 6,000 in Natal.

With the approval of the Egg Control Board, a substantial percentage of the 30,000,000 dozen eggs produced in the Republic is shipped abroad. Over 5,400 farmers belong to the South

African Poultry Association, the principal body in the industry.

Rhodesia, Zambia and Malawi are almost self-supporting in the matter of poultry, but still import turkeys and other birds for the table.

Power Stations. *See* ELECTRIC POWER.

Prain, Sir Ronald Lindsay. Rhodesian capitalist. Born in Chile, South America, September 3, 1907. Educated at Cheltenham and became active as London financier. In 1953 came to Rhodesia, where he became Chairman of the Rhodesian Selection Trust Limited (q.v.).

Prazo. System of land tenure prevailing in Mozambique in former times. The word means a lease, but was applied to grants of estates by the Portuguese Crown, the white occupants having to pay a yearly sum on behalf of the local natives as taxes. In return they were granted a monopoly of trade in the area and the right to recover the taxes paid from the natives themselves, either in the form of work or produce or cash. It proved very unsatisfactory and was ultimately abolished.

Prehistory. *See* ARCHAEOLOGY.

Preller, Dr. Gustav Schoeman. South African historian and pioneer of the Afrikaans language. Born in Pretoria, 1875, he began as a shop assistant, changed over to lawyer's clerk and finally entered the Civil Service of the South African Republic. For 10 years he was in the Department of Mines. During the South African War he distinguished himself on the front. Meanwhile he had become interested in the advancement of the Afrikaans language and literature, to which he was one of the most important contributors. For a while he edited *Land en Volk*, and later *Die Volkstem* and *Ons Vaderland* (renamed *Die Vaderland*). Among his many important books is the standard biography of Pieter Retief and a series *Voortrekker*

Mense in six volumes. Preller edited the diary of Louis Trichardt (q.v.), wrote on early Pretoria and on many other subjects, a certain amount of it in English. He died in 1943.

Premier Estate. Owned by the British South Africa Company, which has established large citrus orchards there. It is located in the Umtali district, in the east of Rhodesia.

Premier Mine. World's largest single diamond mine. Found in 1902 near Pretoria on the farm Zonderwater (q.v.) belonging to Willem Prinsloo and opened up by Sir Thomas Cullinan, through the Premier (Transvaal) Diamond Mining Co. Ltd., so called to distinguish it from the older Premier Diamond Mining Company, which operated the Wesselton Mine (q.v.) at Kimberley. The Premier Mine measures 2,900 feet across in one direction and 1,400 feet in the other, with an average depth of over 500 feet. Here in 1905 was found the Cullinan Diamond (q.v.).

Presbyterian Church of South Africa. Through its close similarity in organisation and doctrine to the Dutch Reformed Church, a strong link has existed between them from the earliest days. Although a Presbyterian church was established by the Rev. George Thom at Cape Town in 1813, it was the decision to call the Rev. Dr. John Philip (q.v.) as the minister that led to its conversion to a Congregational basis. Hence a new start was made in 1827, when the Church of St. Andrew in Somerset Road, Cape Town, was begun, with the Rev. Dr. James Adamson as minister. This is now the oldest congregation in South Africa. In 1838 a Presbyterian congregation was started in St. Stephen's Church, Riebeeck Square, Cape Town, specially for the recently liberated slaves. Many pulpits of the Dutch Reformed Church were filled by Presbyterian ministers of great distinction, while large numbers of early

Dutch Reformed ministers received their training under Presbyterian auspices at the University of Edinburgh and elsewhere. Since 1897 the various congregations in the country have formed part of the Presbyterian Church of South Africa, which is closely allied with that of Rhodesia. The General Assembly meets annually under an elected Moderator. There are eight Presbyteries, namely Cape Town, King William's Town, Natal, Orange River, Orange River Native, Port Elizabeth, Transvaal and Rhodesia. The ministers are trained at Rhodes University, Grahamstown. Adherents in South Africa (1963): 110,873 Whites, 204,585 Bantu.

Press. *See* NEWSPAPERS.

Press Commission. Inquiry carried out in South Africa into the activities, ownership and policy of the South African press, with particular reference to the correspondents of overseas journals and news agencies. The inquiry was set up in 1950 under Mr. Justice J. W. van Zyl (q.v.) and completed its labours in 1964. The report, issued in nine large volumes, contains strong criticism of the distortions of news transmitted from South Africa to other countries.

Pretoria. Administrative capital of the Republic of South Africa, capital of the province of the Transvaal. Founded in the year 1855 as Pretoria Philadelphia, and named after President A. W. J. Pretorius. The population in 1967 was 484,700, including 260,400 Whites, 205,000 Bantu, 9,200 Coloureds and 10,100 Asiatics. The city lies in a valley, through which flows the Apies River, and is dominated by the Union Buildings. It is noted for its handsome streets and for its famous Jacaranda avenues. The heart of Pretoria is Church Square, with its statue of President Kruger, surrounded by the former Volksraad Building, the South African Reserve Bank, the Gen-

eral Post Office and other important structures. Although a large section of the inhabitants is employed in Government service, including the great Railway Workshops at Koodoospoort, Pretoria has considerable industries, the most important being the Iscor Steel Works. There are also flour mills, engineering shops and other manufactures. The University of Pretoria, originally the Transvaal University College, has today the largest number of students in the Republic. Near by is the famous Veterinary Research Laboratory at Onderstepoort (q.v.). Until the discovery of gold on the Witwatersrand, Pretoria was almost rural in its conditions, but electric light, trams and other conveniences came in the 1890's. The city was evacuated by the Boer authorities within a few days of the arrival of the British, in June, 1900. After the return of peace, it became the seat of the Milner Administration, which moved there from Johannesburg in 1905. A large number of research laboratories and other institutions of the Council of Scientific and Industrial Research are today located in Pretoria. The Radcliffe Observatory also operates in this city. The Union Buildings were erected between 1910 and 1913, to the designs of the late Sir Herbert Baker, and house a large number of Government Departments, including that of the Prime Minister. Outside the city stands the Voortrekker Monument, erected at a cost of about £340,000, inaugurated formally on December 16, 1949. It stands on the summit of a hill, its central features being the symbolic grave of Pieter Retief and his followers, on which a ray of sunlight falls on the 16th of December every year. In 1964 the area of Pretoria was extended from 70 to 220 square miles, making it the largest municipality in South Africa.

Pretoria Highlanders. Original name of First Anti-Tank Regiment, South

African Artillery (*see* REGIMENT, FIRST ANTI-TANK).

Pretoria News. Established on June 11, 1898. It ceased publication during the South African War, but has appeared as a daily ever since.

Pretoria North. Township near Pretoria, Transvaal. Population: 12,589, including 11,137 Whites.

Pretorius, Andries Wilhelmus Jacobus. Voortrekker leader and General. Born in Graaff-Reinet, 1798, took part in several frontier campaigns and in 1837 undertook a preliminary trek to the north. He fought against Moselekatse with A. H. Potgieter and then settled in Natal. After the murder of Pieter Retief, was appointed Commandant-General and defeated the forces of the Zulu King Dingaan at the battle of Blood River in 1838. For some years after the occupation of Natal by the British Pretorius remained in that Colony, maintaining friendly relations with the authorities. In 1847 he moved about among the emigrants organising a protest against the pending British annexation of the Orange River Sovereignty. This brought him into conflict with Governor Sir Harry Smith and in 1848 he led the Boer force that was defeated at Boomplaats. Pretorius emigrated to the Transvaal, where he settled near Potchefstroom. In 1852 he took the lead in concluding the Sand River Convention (q.v.), recognising the independence of the South African Republic. He died in 1853.

Pretorius, Marthinus Wessel. First President of the South African Republic. Born near Graaff-Reinet in 1819, he joined the Great Trek under his father A. W. J. Pretorius. He accompanied him to Natal, where he fought against the Zulus, and then to the Transvaal, where he was elected Commandant-General—one of four—and drafted the first constitution—the '33 Articles' in Rustenburg. In 1857 he

was elected President of the South African Republic, and made it his task to amalgamate the smaller republics, including Lydenburg and the O.F.S. He succeeded with the former, but although he received the unique honour, in 1860, of also being elected President of the O.F.S., he failed in his plan. In that same year he resigned as President of the South African Republic, to negotiate with Moshesh, and to visit Cetewayo and the Governor in Cape Town, in a further effort to pacify the whole country. Civil War meanwhile began in the Transvaal and he did his best to mediate, resigning the O.F.S. Presidency in 1863. In 1864 he was elected a second time as President of the South African Republic. He led a punitive force against the Basuto in 1865 and in the same year went to the Zoutpansberg to restore peace in the north. Three years later he formally extended the authority of the South African Republic north of the Limpopo into the area now known as Rhodesia, a claim afterwards contested by the British. He laid claim to the Diamond Fields on the Vaal River, but was forced to withdraw. Re-elected President in 1868, he resigned in 1871, worked vigorously against the British authorities after the annexation and was imprisoned as a trouble-maker. When the Boer revolt began Pretorius was elected a member of the Triumvirate and signed the Convention of Pretoria, re-establishing the country's independence. He died in Potchefstroom, during the South African War, on May 19, 1901.

Pretorius, Major P. J. Professional big game hunter and military guide. Born in the Transvaal in 1883, became transport rider for British South Africa Co. and others in Rhodesia in 1899, professional hunter in Northern Rhodesia, Tanganyika and elsewhere. During World War I served with South African forces in German East Africa and succeeded in locating

German cruiser *Koenigsberg*, while hidden in waterways in Rufiji River delta. Later employed by Government to thin out wild elephants in Addo Bush (q.v.) and helped to make films on South African wild life. Died 1945.

Pretorius Kop. Rest camp in the Kruger National Park. The name is thought to be derived from the fact that President M. W. Pretorius halted there on one of his treks. The camp is near the site of the headquarters of the 'White Cheif' Joao Albasini (q.v.). Pretorius Kop was first a farm, and later the home of the famous old-time ranger of the Sabi Game Reserve, Harry Wolhuter (q.v.). Since the Kruger National Park was established accommodation for several hundred tourists has been provided there. It lies in the south, near White River.

Price, Dr. Bernard. Engineer and physicist. Born in London, 1877, and educated at the Central Technical College, Kensington. He began his career with the famous consulting engineers, Merz & McLellan, and was the inventor of the Merz-Price Differential System of Automatic Discriminating Cut-outs. In November, 1909, he came to South Africa to become Chief Engineer for the recently-established Victoria Falls and Transvaal Power Company Ltd. (q.v.), of which in 1927 he became General Manager. During this time he held many leading positions, including the presidency of the South African Institute of Electrical Engineers and was a member of the Council of University of the Witwatersrand. He retired in December 1936. The Government appointed him a member of the Social and Economic Planning Council and of other important bodies. He was responsible for the foundation and endowment of the Bernard Price Institute for Geophysical Research and for the enormous advancement of

power production in the Union. He died in 1948.

Prickly Pear (*Opuntia tuna*). A plant which has become a very serious weed over thousands of square miles, particularly in the Eastern Cape Province. Methods of exterminating it have been developed in recent years, by means of cactoblastis insects, and of turning it into fodder after burning off the prickly hairs.

Prieska. Town on the Orange River, originally called Priskab, a Hottentot name meaning a she-goat. The village dates from 1878, though the place was known at the beginning of the 19th century. Fighting took place there during the South African War. Population: 9,000, including 2,000 Whites.

Prime Bloods. The best grade of ostrich feathers secured from wild birds.

Prince Albert. Town in the Cape Province, established in 1855 and named after Queen Victoria's husband. Located near the majestic Swartberg Mountains, it is noted for its beautiful scenery and for the excellence of its farm produce, including tobacco, fruit and other crops. Population: 4,500, including 1,150 Whites.

Prince Alfred. Son of Queen Victoria, who visited South Africa. *See* ALFRED ERNEST ALBERT.

Prince Alfred Hamlet. Village in the Western Cape Province, near Ceres, named after Prince Alfred, son of Queen Victoria, and established in 1867. Fruit-growing centre. Population: 1,182, including 356 Whites.

Prince Alfred's Guard. South African Military unit, founded on September 19, 1856. Fought in the 9th Kaffir War in 1877, in the Gun War in Basutoland in 1880–1881, the Langeberg Campaign, 1897, the South African War (1899–1902), also the First and Second World Wars, as part of the 6th South African Armoured Division.

Prince Alfred's Own Cape Field Artillery. Original name of First Field Regiment, South African Artillery (*see* REGIMENT, FIRST FIELD).

Prince Edward School, Salisbury. Founded in 1902 and named after the son of the then Duke of Cornwall (later King George V), who became Prince of Wales (now Duke of Windsor). It is one of the largest schools for boys in the Rhodesian capital, with Junior and Senior divisions.

Prince Imperial. *See* LOUIS NAPOLEON.

Princess Alice's Own. Name of Pretoria Regiment (*see* REGIMENT PRETORIA).

Pringle, Thomas. South Africa's first poet in English. Born in 1789 in Blaiklaw, Scotland. Went to Edinburgh University in 1806, where he met many famous men, including Sir Walter Scott, and his future associate, John Fairbairn. After attempting a Civil Service career, he became editor of *Blackwood's Magazine*, but found the reward so poor that he joined the 1820 settlers and settled at Glen Lynden in the Eastern Province. Driven off the land by bad times, Pringle became librarian in Cape Town, 1822, and, in collaboration with Fairbairn (q.v.), received permission to start a paper, which made its appearance early in 1824. It was called *The South African Journal* and promptly roused the displeasure of Governor Lord Charles Somerset (q.v.). Pringle refused to allow his writing to be controlled but the journal died with the second number, and so did an academy which he and Fairbairn started. Pringle returned to the eastern frontier and began to write on the sufferings of the settlers, helping to start an appeal for help. He went back to Britain in 1826 and the result of his appeal was a sum of £10,000 for the distressed colonists. His last years were spent in England, where he became Secretary of the Anti-Slavery Society, and exposed the misdeeds of Somerset. Pringle's main fame, however, rests on his poems, the first on South African themes, notably *Afar in the Desert, The Lion Hunt* and many others, which caught the attention of critics by their felicity of phrase and novel theme. He died in 1834. Several editions of his collected works appeared, the first in 1837.

Prinsloo, Willem. Boer pioneer. Born in the Cape in 1818, he joined the Vootrekkers in 1836 and fought against the Matabele. He became a hunter and settled on the East Rand, where he occupied the farm Modderfontein. This he sold for £40,000, and then moved to Kaalfontein near Pretoria in 1888. Once again mineral wealth was discovered there and he moved on to the farm Sonderwater near by, where Sir Thomas Cullinan (q.v.) discovered the Premier Mine. He died in 1908.

Prior, Melton. War artist and illustrator. Born in London on September 12, 1845, the son of William Henry Prior, landscape artist, he joined the staff of the *Illustrated London News* at an early age, and was present on their behalf at more than 24 campaigns and revolutions all over the world. He first visited Africa during the Ashanti War in 1873, and later saw the Tambuki Campaign of 1878, the Zulu War of 1879, the Gun War in Basutoland in 1880, the Majuba Campaign, the Jameson Raid, the Matabele War and the Boer War. His vivid and rapid draughtsmanship provided a unique pictorial record of the major events on these occasions. He died on November 2, 1910.

Prisons. Apart from reformatories and similar institutions which fall under the Social Welfare Department, places of detention for offenders in the Republic of South Africa comprise convict prisons, gaols, farm colonies, inebriate reformatories, labour outstations and prison farms. The largest single prison in the Republic is at

Pretoria, where are kept the majority of persons sentenced to long terms.

Attached to the Ministry of Justice is the Director of Prisons, his duties being officially 'to build up and supplement in the criminal elements necessary to prevent a recurrence of the crime.' As an alternative, in the case of habitual criminals, a system of indeterminate sentences has been in use since 1910. Offenders can rehabilitate themselves by good behaviour, their records being examined at regular intervals. Apart from encouraging education and useful work, this system enables the ordinary South African prisoner, by a system of marks, to show the progress he is making towards becoming a useful member of society. The Prison Visitors' Board, having studied the record, decides when the time has come to authorise a reduction in his sentence. In addition the Social Services Association of South Africa has as its aim the preparation of the offender for his return to normal life, and the maintenance of a link between him and his family. It also gives help in finding employment after release. Trades are taught in the prison workshops, and inmates are allowed to make savings on a limited scale. All products of prison workshops are used by the Government and not resold.

The former World War II internment camp at Baviaanspoort has been turned into a prison camp for White first offenders under less severe restraint than other prisoners. Even more advanced 'open' methods of detention exist at Sonderwater, also in the Transvaal. Farm prisons, the subject of much discussion and criticism, are designed to keep offenders, particularly Bantu, employed on agricultural work, away from the demoralising atmosphere of an ordinary gaol. Approved buildings have to be erected by farmers' associations, which are also responsible for the payment of departmental staff. To raise standards

of education in officials, a special Prison Service Training Depot has been set up in Pretoria in conjunction with the Police Training College, the courses lasting 6 months.

In the former Central African Federation each of the three constituent states, Southern Rhodesia, Northern Rhodesia and Nyasaland, maintained its own prison services, associated with its respective police force. *See also* SOUTH AFRICAN POLICE.

Progressive Party. Political organisation set up in South Africa by a group which in 1959 seceded from the United Party (q.v.) with the aim of granting constitutional powers and privileges to the Black population greater than the United Party were willing to concede. It does not, however, go as far as the Liberal Party in striving for a non-racial society.

Pronkbok. *See* SPRINGBOK.

Pronking. An Afrikaans word meaning 'showing off,' cf. German 'prunk.' Habit of many antelopes, particularly Springbok, of making peculiar bounds at certain seasons.

Pronking

Protea. Name given to a considerable group of shrubs and trees found mainly in the Cape Peninsula and the South-Western Cape Province, although a few species also occur in the Transvaal and Orange Free State. The Proteaceae,

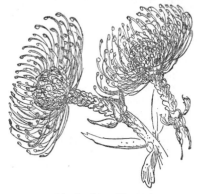

Pin Cushion (Protea)

deriving their name from the many-shaped Greek god, Proteus, boast of some 300 species. Famed for their beauty and richness in honey, Proteas flower mostly at the beginning of winter in the Western Cape Province. Although claims have been made for other plants, the Protea is generally recognised as the South African national flower. The individual flowers are all of similar structure but grouped in so many ways as to make a wide range of species. Flower generally a head surrounded by a cup-like involucre of leathery bracts, as in the Suikerbos or Sugar Bush (*Protea mellifera*); or a spike, as in the Wild Almond (*Brabeium stellatifolium*). Four sepals, bearing the four stamens, petal modified into a pappus of hairs, often golden-brown. Superior ovary. Very large and persistent stigma and style, especially noticeable in Kreupelhout (*Leucospermum Bolusii*). Fruit, a nut dispersed by wind or, as in the Wild Almond, by wind and water. Pollinated by bees and long-billed birds, e.g. Sunbirds

(q.v.). The plentiful nectar of the Sugar Bush is used medicinally. Among many magnificent species are the rarer Giant Protea (*P. cynaroides*) and the fine-leaved Blushing Bride (*Serruria florida*), the Mountain Rose (q.v.), Marsh Rose (q.v.) and the Silver Tree (q.v.), of which the flowers are less ornamental than the shimmering leaves.

Protem. Hamlet in the Western Cape Province, near Bredasdorp, so called because it was originally meant to be a temporary terminus for the branch railway there. Wheat and general farming centre.

Providential Pass. Defile near Fort Victoria in Rhodesia. So called because, at the time of the occupation of the Pioneer Column (q.v.) in 1890, the latter believed themselves to be in a cul-de-sac and in danger of being ambushed by the natives. Although they were mistaken, the name testifies to the relief they felt after emerging from it. Altogether the pass measures about 9 miles in length.

Province of Queen Adelaide. Buffer territory established by Governor Sir Benjamin D'Urban on the eastern border of the Cape, on ground taken in the recently-concluded campaign against the neighbouring tribes. It comprised the region between the old frontier up to the River Kei, between the Stormberg and the ocean. Most of it was given out to loyal native occupants, but the action was disapproved by the Colonial Office and perforce abandoned. It was established on May 10 and given up on December 5, 1835.

Pruimbas (*Colpoon compressum*). Wild plant found in the Western Cape, the berries of which were dried and eaten and the rind used by the Boers for tanning.

Prynnsburg. Estate in the Orange Free State, between Ficksburg and Clocolan, established by Charles Newbury, Diamond Fields pioneer, in

Victorian times, and noted for its plantations and its collection of wild game.

Public Service. Under the Constitution of the Republic of South Africa, control of its Public Service falls under the Public Service Commission, a permanent body with headquarters at Pretoria. Its duties include the creation of new posts, their classification and grading, the definition of scales of salaries and pensions, retirement benefits, etc. The Public Service does not, however, include the President and his staff, judges of the Supreme Court or employees of the South African Railways, Harbours and Airways, provincial administrations and the administration of South West Africa. Members of the Permanent Armed Forces, the South African Police, Post Office and other State departments are included. The total number of Public Servants in 1967 was 212,788.

Pudimoe. Village in Bechuanaland, between Vryburg and Kimberley, noted as a centre of the cattle-breeding industry. It is the junction between the main line and the branch to Schweizer-Renecke in the Western Transvaal.

Puku (*Cobus vardoni*). Large antelope found in Rhodesia, particularly in the valley of the Zambesi and towards the boundary of the Belgian Congo. The Puku prefers swampy areas and the banks of rivers. Due to excessive hunting it has become extremely rare and is now protected. It stands about 3 feet high at the shoulder, and has an orange-yellow coat. The male bears twisted horns.

Pulsator. Machine devised on the diamond mines of Kimberley towards the end of the 19th century for the mechanical treatment of blue ground (q.v.). Its design was largely the work of the late A. M. Robeson of De Beers. The pulsator is used as the last stage of sorting, when concentration is already largely achieved.

Punda Maria. (Also written **Punda Milia**). Rest camp in the north of the Kruger National Park, near its northern gateway. It has accommodation for 120 tourists, besides other facilities.

Putfontein. Settlement near Benoni, Transvaal. Population: 2,798, including 1,284 Whites.

Putsonderwater (literally Well Without Water). Settlement near Kenhardt in the North-Western Cape Province.

Pypertjie. Afrikaans name for Bar-Breasted Weaver Finch. *See* WEAVERS.

Python (family Boidae) or **Natal Rock Snake.** Species of non-poisonous snake found in Southern Africa, which disposes of its prey by crushing it in its folds. The longest recorded is 25 feet. Despite its size the Python is comparatively harmless, contenting itself with eating cane rats, hares and even small buck. It is found in the thick bush country of Natal, Rhodesia, Eastern Transvaal and (another variety) in South West Africa. Pythons are interesting anatomically: two horny spurs near the vent, and the remains of a pelvis, showing their connection with the legged lizards. They love to wallow in water and are excellent climbers. The female, unlike most snakes, sits coiled above her batch of leathery eggs (40 or more) to incubate them. When hatched, they scatter independently. Pythons will show fight if wounded, using their sharp teeth as well as constrictive power. *See* SNAKES.

Q

Quacha's Nek. Village in the south of Lesotho, with very fine mountain scenery. Administrative post. The name means 'One Who Hides.'

Quaelbergen, Cornelis Van. Early Commander of the Cape of Good Hope. Began his career with Dutch East India Company at Masulipatam, where he became Commander, and was transferred to the Cape in 1666. Fell into disfavour and was dismissed in 1668 for helping a French fleet, not knowing it was hostile, owing to the slowness with which news of the outbreak of war then travelled. Was rehabilitated later and rose to Governor of Banda in the East Indies.

Quagga (*Equus quagga*). Extinct animal, striped like the Zebra on head and neck, plain brown elsewhere, formerly widespread, especially in the Karroo and Orange Free State, and shot by Voortrekkers for their servants' food. Last Quagga believed to have died in the Orange Free State about 1878, although a few may survive in

the Kaokoveld (q.v.), South West Africa. A live Quagga, given by the Cape Governor Sir George Grey (q.v.), was on view in the London Zoo from 1858 to 1864. Museum specimens are to be found in Cape Town, Bloemfontein and in Europe. Height, 4 feet 6 inches at the shoulder.

Quail (family Phasianidae). Game bird related to the Francolin and Guineafowl (qq.v.). Most varieties are migrants from the tropics, and appear irregularly. The Cape Quail or Kwartel is very similar to the European kind. Speckled brown, a low, compact figure and small down-turned tail. *See* BUTTON-QUAIL.

Quatermain, Allan. Hero of a number of romances by Sir Henry Rider Haggard (q.v.), believed to be based on Frederick Courtney Selous (q.v.).

Quathlamba. *See* DRAKENSBERG.

Queen Adelaide, Province of. *See* PROVINCE OF QUEEN ADELAIDE.

Queensburgh. Natal municipality, adjoining Durban, established in 1924 and including Northdene, Malvern, Cavendish, Escombe and Moseley. Population 16,100, including 11,200 Whites, 1,500 Indians and 3,000 Bantu.

Queen's College. Large school for boys in Queenstown, Cape Province. Founded in 1858 by C. E. Ham as 'Prospect House Academy.' During the 1870's was a co-educational school, but soon reverted to its original status. Renamed Queen's College in honour of Queen Victoria in 1910.

Queen's Own Cape Town Highlanders. South African Military unit, founded on April 24, 1855. Served in Langeberg Campaign 1897, South African War 1899–1902, German West Africa 1915, and with Sixth Armoured

Quagga

Division in North Africa and Italy during World War II. Renamed Cape Town Highlanders June 1, 1961.

Queenstown. Town in the Eastern Cape Province, founded in 1850 and named after Queen Victoria. It lies near the Katberg mountains and, because of the risk of native attack, was laid out in an unusual hexagon pattern to allow the approaches to be commanded by artillery. The main open space lies in the centre of this hexagon. Important centre for the wool and general farming industries. Population: 43,000, including 11,300 Whites, 3,500 Coloureds, and 28,000 Bantu.

Quelea. Bird related to the Pink-billed Weaver (q.v.). Whole head is crimson. This is a major pest of grain in the Orange Free State and Transvaal, as well as Rhodesia and East and West Africa. *See* BIRDS.

Quelimane. Seaport on the northern coast of Mozambique, one of the oldest towns in Southern Africa, having been established as a municipality in 1763. It serves as an important trading and export centre for the sugar and other tropical crops, including sisal, cotton, tobacco, tea and mealies. Its outer harbour is known as Tangalane. Population: about 12,000, including 3,000 Whites.

Que Que. Town in Rhodesia, founded in 1900, after the discovery of the famous Globe and Phoenix Gold Mine, which adjoins it. The name is derived from a curious 'three-pronged' headgear worn in olden times by the inhabitants of the district. Numerous small gold mines in the neighbourhood used the town as their centre. In more recent times prosperity has received a fresh stimulus through the

establishment of the works of the Rhodesian Iron and Steel Company (RISCO) near by at Redcliff. Population (including Redcliff): 18,000, including 3,500 Whites.

Quick Grass. Name given to a fine grass which is widely grown in South Africa, known botanically as *Cynodon dactylon*. The name is probably derived from the Dutch Kweek, meaning to cultivate.

Quitrent. System of land title at the Cape introduced with the earliest Free Burghers, by which property-holders paid an annual rent in lieu of services. At first this took the form of tithes of the grain harvest, but after July 3, 1714, a monetary tariff was substituted for 'Loan Places.' Governor Sir John Cradock, on August 6, 1813, introduced 'Perpetual Quitrent,' to which the title of any Loan Place could be converted. This system is still largely in operation.

Qumbu. Village in the Transkei, between Kokstad and Umtata. Established in 1876, it was annexed, with the surrounding country, to the Cape Colony in 1879. A rebellion broke out the following year among the Pondomisi, the neighbouring tribe, in which Hamilton Hope, who conducted himself with great bravery, was killed. A monument has been erected to his memory. Population: 800, including 200 Whites.

Quolora (pronounced Kwelegha). Seaside resort on the 'Wild Coast' of Pondoland, in the Eastern Cape Province.

Quthing. Village in the south of Lesotho, noted for its fine scenery. The name is of Bushman origin, though its meaning is uncertain.

R

Raaff, Commandant Pieter Johannes. Boer pioneer of Rhodesia. Born in 1850's, he first came into prominence as commandant of Raaff's Rangers in the Zulu War of 1879, winning the C.M.G. Later he settled in Pretoria, went prospecting and became Magistrate at Fort Tuli, after the occupation of Mashonaland. In the Matabele War of 1893 Raaff again raised his force of 'Rangers' in Johannesburg and did fine service. He died on January 26, 1894.

Racing. *See* HORSE-RACING.

Radio. *See* BROADCASTING.

Rail (family Rallidae). Bird family including the Crakes, Reed-Hens, Moorhens and Coots. As a rule they have long legs and long toes. Most of the Rallidae live in marshes or long grass. They have loud call-notes and nest among marsh vegetation. Their downy chicks can run and swim as soon as they are hatched. Most of the family are poor fliers.

Railways. *See* TRANSPORT and RHODESIA RAILWAYS.

Ramathlabama. Village in Bechuanaland, on frontier of Cape and Bechuanaland Protectorate, headquarters of Protectorate Regiment at outbreak of South African War and sacked by the Boers in an unexpected attack. The name is derived from an incident in which the Chief Montsioa killed a lion at close quarters, and means 'to straddle over.'

Ramblers Club. Founded 1896 in Bloemfontein. Large sporting club, with sections for rugby, hockey, cricket, bowls, tennis, etc. Has its own golf course.

Ramkie. Musical instrument, made by the Hottentots and Bushmen by stretching half-a-dozen strings over a thin board or portion of a calabash.

Ramoutsa. Village in Botswana, used as base by the Pioneer Column before moving into Mashonaland in 1890. Headquarters of the Bamelete tribe. Now a trading centre. *See also* MACLOUTSIE.

Ramsbottom, Dr. Alfred Ernest William. First Administrator of the Orange Free State. Born in Grahamstown on August 1, 1860, he was educated at Grey College, Bloemfontein, and then proceeded to Dublin, where he qualified in Medicine, 1884. Established as a doctor, first in Fauresmith, Orange Free State, and later in Bloemfontein and Heilbron, he became interested in politics and was appointed Colonial Treasurer under the Crown Colony régime after the South African War. He was made the first Administrator of the O.F.S. after Union, holding office from 1910 to 1915. He died in 1921.

Ramsgate. Seaside resort on the Natal South Coast, south of Margate. Population: 1,400, including 800 Whites.

Rand. Unit of currency, adopted in Union of South Africa, South West Africa and High Commission Territories as the basis of its coinage under the Decimalisation Act of 1959, with effect from February 14, 1961, at that time equivalent to 10 shillings. It is subdivided into 100 cents. The word 'Rand' is derived from 'Witwatersrand,' to emphasise its gold backing. The abbreviation is R (singular and plural) written before the numeral. *See* CENT, and KRUGER RAND.

Randburg. Municipality formed from group of outlying north-western suburbs of Johannesburg, established

July 1, 1959. Population: 46,150, including 32,000 Whites.

Rand Daily Mail. Daily morning paper established in Johannesburg in 1902 by Henry Freeman Cohen, with Edgar Wallace as its first editor. It has continued to appear ever since.

Randfontein. Town on the Western Witwatersrand, part of Krugersdorp (q.v.) but since 1929 a municipality on its own. It is 27 miles from Johannesburg, and has grown around the famous Randfontein Estates Gold Mine, established in the earliest days of the fields by Sir J. B. Robinson (q.v.). Randfontein Estates has the largest stamp battery in the world—600 stamps. A pretty sheet of water, the Homestead Lake, is among the attractions of the town. Population: 46,370, including 17,000 Whites, 1,300 Coloureds, 70 Asiatics, 28,000 Bantu.

Rand Mines Ltd. Mining group associated with Corner House (q.v.), formed in 1893 to develop the deep level gold workings on the Witwatersrand.

Rand Revolt. Name commonly applied to industrial disturbances on the Witwatersrand in 1922. The immediate cause of the trouble was the disappearance of the Gold Premium, which, in the later stages of World War I, and immediately after, had made good the heavy rise in mining costs, and had allowed the grant of large increases in pay to the White miners. When this windfall vanished, the miners refused to agree to reductions. Sporadic strikes began in 1921, but did not become widespread till 1922. The New Year marked a strike on the collieries of the Transvaal, which soon spread to the gold mines of the Rand. Miners organised themselves into 'commandos' and began to terrorise and 'pull out' other workers. Efforts at a settlement failed and early in March, 1922, an orgy of violence began, which necessitated the calling out of the Union Defence Force, the use of air-craft of the S.A.A.F. as well as of artillery. General J. C. Smuts, as premier, was widely blamed for letting the position get out of hand. After nearly a week of fighting the Revolt was crushed. Casualties were estimated at over 200 killed and about 1,200 injured. Several of the strikers were sentenced to death for murder, and some were executed.

Rand Tram. Name given to the first railway in the Transvaal, which ran from Johannesburg to Boksburg, a distance of 14 miles. It was begun in 1889 and completed the following year. Unlike most inland railways, it joined no line to the coast, so that all the material and rolling stock had to be brought to the site by ox-wagon! The line belonged to the Netherlands South African Railway Company (q.v.) and the name Rand Tram was given to it to spare the feelings of conservative Volksraad members, who feared that railways might ruin transport-riding with ox-wagons.

Rand Water Board. Corporation established by ordinance of the Milner Government in 1903, charged with supplying the needs of the Witwatersrand area. It took over the assets of the earlier private companies and was granted borrowing and other powers. The various municipalities of the Rand, the city of Pretoria, Vereeniging, the mining industry and the South African Railways are represented on the Board, whose area of supply covers 6,074 sq. miles with a population of about 3,000,000. Supplies of water are mainly drawn from the Vaal River, across which the Board first constructed a large barrage, completed in 1923, followed in more recent years by works utilising the water impounded by the Vaaldam (q.v.). Daily sales of water exceed 200,000,000 gallons.

Ranunculus. *See* CLEMATIS.

Rat (Murinae). A number of varieties of these rodents are to be found in

Southern Africa, the most notorious being the imported Brown Rat, also known as the Sewer Rat, which came in early ships from Europe. This animal does damage to the tune of millions every year in the Republic alone. Some specimens grow to a length of over a foot, excluding the tail. Rats are particularly dangerous because their fleas carry the Bubonic plague organism.

Rathenau, Walter. German industrialist and statesman. Born in 1867, son of the famous industrialist Emil Rathenau, who founded the Allgemeine Elektrizitaets-Gesellschaft (A.E.G.). After completing his studies Walter Rathenau also became a director in 1899, and was brought into contact with South Africa through the interest of the A.E.G. in a project to develop power from the Victoria Falls. This led to the foundation of the Victoria Falls and Transvaal Power Company in 1906. In 1908 Rathenau accompanied Bernhard Dernburg (q.v.), the German Colonial Secretary, on his trip to South West Africa and South Africa. During World War I he controlled the provision of raw materials for the German war effort. He took part in the peace negotiations in 1919 and entered the Cabinet in 1921. A man of outstanding ability, whose assassination by political gangsters in 1922 was an international loss.

Raven. *See* CROW.

Rawsonville. Village in the Western Cape Province near Worcester (q.v.). Named after Rawson W. Rawson, Colonial Secretary. Population: 1,040, including 497 Whites.

Raylton. Suburb of Bulawayo, so called because it is chiefly inhabited by railwaymen.

Rayne, Leonard. South African actor and theatrical producer. Real name William Hannay Watts Cowie. Born in Blyth, England, in 1870, he came to South Africa in the 1890's and for many years ran the Standard Theatre in Johannesburg and toured the country. Particularly noted for his productions of *A Royal Divorce*, in which he took the leading part, *The Rosary*, and others. He died in 1925.

Rayton: 1. Village near Pretoria in the Transvaal, founded 1904, and named after Mrs. Ray Wollaston, wife of the General Manager, Colonel Wollaston, of the Montrose Diamond Mine near by. Farming centre. Population: 700, including 600 Whites.

2. Village near Bloemfontein. Population: 500, including 160 Whites.

R.B. Abbreviation for Regiment Botha (q.v.).

R.C.B. Abbreviation for Regiment Christiaan Beyers (q.v.).

R.D.L.I. Abbreviation for Royal Durban Light Infantry (q.v.).

R.D.L.R. Abbreviation for Regiment de la Rey (q.v.).

Rds. Abbreviation for Rixdollar (q.v.).

R.D.T. Abbreviation for Regiment Danie Theron (q.v.).

R.D.W. Abbreviation for Regiment De Wet (q.v.).

Reader, H. Early Rhodesian trader and hunter. First mentioned in the travels of James Chapman in 1852, he lived near Lake Ngami, also hunted in the vicinity of the Chobe River. In 1862 he visited the Victoria Falls after their discovery by David Livingstone. Little is known about his later years.

Rebellion. Name given to the South African insurrection in 1914. Despite the establishment of the Union of South Africa, there was still considerable bitterness resulting from the South African War, which had ended in 1902. When, in 1914, war broke out between Britain and Germany, many former Republicans felt disinclined to fight on the Allied side. Stimulated by stories of the visions of the alleged 'prophet,' Niklaas van Rensberg (q.v.), who foretold the collapse of the

British Empire, opposition against any military commitments began to take shape. Matters came to a head when, in September 1914, General Louis Botha, as Prime Minister, announced the intention of the Union to invade German South-West Africa. Protests were made in different parts of the country, but there was little if any direct co-ordination between the leaders, who included General Solomon Gerhardus (Manie) Maritz in the North-West, General C. F. Beyers, Commander of the Union Defence Force in the Transvaal, Captain Jopie Fourie (q.v.) and General Christiaan de Wet (q.v.). Strong efforts, made by the Dutch Reformed Church, by President M. T. Steyn (q.v.) and other powerful forces to prevent hostilities, were a failure, and fighting began almost simultaneously in the Transvaal, near Upington in the Cape, and in the Orange Free State. General Louis Botha mobilised the newly-established Defence Force, and called upon loyal burghers to support the Government. Large numbers of motor cars were commandeered. At Mushroom Valley in the Orange Free State General de Wet was defeated and took refuge in Bechuanaland, where he was caught. General Beyers was drowned while crossing the Vaal River, General Maritz was driven into exile in South West Africa and Jopie Fourie was captured and shot under military law. The last Rebels surrendered early in 1915, many of them being sentenced to terms of imprisonment. Efforts were made by the German authorities in South West Africa to encourage the Rebellion by means of a so-called 'treaty' with General Maritz, guaranteeing the re-establishment of a Republic in the Union.

Redbill (*Anas erythrorhyncha*) or **Red-billed Teal.** One of the most commonly found ducks on open water. Dark cap clearly separated from white cheek. Pink bill. Nests of down, in thick grass. *See* DUCK.

Redcliff. Township near Que Que (q.v.) in Rhodesia, and site of the Rhodesian Iron and Steel Company (RISCO) Works.

Reddersburg. Town in the Orange Free State, founded in 1857, and named after the Saviour (Redder in Dutch), by the Dopper section of the Dutch Reformed Church, to which most of the pioneers there belonged. General Christiaan De Wet captured an entire British column there in the South African War. Today it is mainly a wool-producing centre. Population: 2,600, including 700 Whites.

Reddingsdaadbond (Association for an Act of Rescue). Movement started in 1939 at the instigation of the Rev. Dr. J. D. Kestell (q.v.) for the economic rehabilitation of the poorer Afrikaner. It is Christian-National in tone, and associated with the Federation of Afrikaans Cultural Societies (F.A.K.) (q.v.). There are a number of divisions—for Trade, Employment, Bursaries, Agriculture, Women, etc.

Redelinghuys. Village near Piketberg, Cape Province. Population: 260, including 170 Whites.

Red Hot Poker (*Kniphofia uvaria*). Popular name for a plant about 2 feet high with tubular bells of flowers, red above and yellow below, on a long stalk. Like others of this large family, including some aloes and the hyacinth, the sword-shaped leaves rise out of the soil. It likes damp, shady places and has become an ornamental garden plant.

Red Kaffir. Term used for members of the Xosa tribe, owing to their habit of smearing themselves with red clay and wearing red blankets.

Red-Lipped Snake. *See* HERALD SNAKE.

Red Spider (*Tetrarhynchus*). A red mite which attacks fruit and other cultivated trees in many parts of South Africa.

Redwater (also known as **Texas Fever** or **Bovine Piroplasmosis**). Identified in the United States by Dr. T. Smith in 1889, this cattle disease was found by Dr. Robert Koch at Kimberley in 1896 to correspond to a local disease called Redwater, first reported near the mouth of the Tugela, Natal, in 1870. The cause is the Blue Tick (*Rhipicephalus decoloratus*). It spread into the Transvaal, Orange Free State and Transkei, no fewer than 100,000 head dying from this cause in 1885 in the last-named area alone. It is now successfully combated by dipping and inoculation.

Reedbuck or **Rietbok** (*Redunca arundinum*). Antelope found wherever there is thick vegetation, along the river banks—eastern side of South Africa, Zambesi and Nqami districts and northern part of South West Africa. Stands about 3 feet high at the shoulder, has a speckled brown and yellow coat and—male only—short, twisted horns. *See* MAMMALS.

Reed-Hen (family Rallidae). The King Reed-Hen, common in Cape vleis, is the largest and most handsome of the Rails (q.v.), green and purple, with an orange bill and forehead, and blue throat. It walks elegantly, using its foot, like a hand, to feed itself. It eats snails, seeds and young shoots, and does not easily appear on view.

Reef. Popular name for the Witwatersrand Goldfields, as distinct from Johannesburg proper.

Reeves, Bishop Ambrose. Anglican Bishop of Johannesburg. Born at Norwich on December 6, 1899, he studied at Cambridge, Mirfield and elsewhere, took Holy Orders in 1927, and served as rector in Liverpool before receiving a call to the see of Johannesburg in 1949. In South Africa he came into prominence on account of his interest in the position of the non-European population, which brought him into conflict with the Union Government. He lectured widely on South African subjects in Britain and the United States. In 1960 he moved from Johannesburg to Swaziland and then to Europe. Upon his return to Johannesburg he was deported and shortly after resigned his see.

Referendum. The first Referendum, in the modern sense, held in South Africa took place in Natal on June 10, 1909, to determine whether the Colony should join the Union of South Africa. Out of a Voters' Roll of approximately 24,000 (all male), 14,822 votes were cast, namely 11,121 in favour of Union and 3,701 against it. Another Referendum took place in Southern Rhodesia on October 27, 1922, to decide whether the Colony should join the Union of South Africa or assume Responsible Government. The results were 8,774 votes for Responsible Government, 5,989 votes for Union, 93 spoilt papers.

On October 5, 1960, the Union of South Africa held a Referendum to decide whether its form of government should be changed to that of a Republic. Of the 1,800,748 voters on the Roll, 1,633,772 polled. There were 850,458 votes in favour of a Republic and 775,878 against. Apart from this there were a few hundred rejected votes.

Province	Total Voters	For	Against
Transvaal	818,047	406,632	325,041
Cape	591,378	271,418	269,784
Natal	193,103	42,299	135,598
O.F.S.	160,843	110,171	33,438
Total	1,763,371	830,520	763,861
S.W.A.	37,377	19,938	12,017
Grand Total	1,800,748	850,458	775,878

Majority in favour of Republic	74,580
Number of voters who did not vote	166,676
Percentage poll	90·7

Regiment Botha. South African military unit, founded on April 1, 1934. In World War II formed part of the 5th South African Infantry Brigade and served in the Abyssinian Campaign. In 1941 the regiment went to Egypt and in the same year was badly depleted at Sidi Rezegh. As part of the 1st South African Division it took part in the battle of El Alamein. With the 6th South African Division it also served in Italy.

Regiment Christiaan Beyers. South African military unit, founded on April 1, 1934. During World War II amalgamated with the Regiment Botha (q.v.).

Regiment Danie Theron. South African military unit, founded on January 1, 1954.

Regiment de la Rey. South African military unit, founded on April 1, 1934. During World War II served at various stations in the Transvaal. In 1945, as part of the 6th South African Armoured Division served throughout the Italian campaign. Motto: 'Ons Waarsku' (We Warn).

Regiment De Wet. South African military unit, founded on April 1, 1934. Headquarters in Kroonstad, O.F.S. During World War II amalgamated with the President Steyn Regiment (q.v.).

Regiment, First Anti-Tank. South African military unit, officially, 'First Anti-Tank Regiment, South African Artillery.' Founded as Pretoria Highlanders on September 21, 1939.

Regiment, First City. South African military unit, founded in Grahamstown on October 7, 1875. Served in Ninth Kaffir War, 1877; Basutoland Rebellion, 1880; South African War, 1899; German South West African Campaign, 1915; Madagascar Campaign and with Sixth Armoured Division in Italy during World War II. Motto: 'Virtute et opera.'

Regiment, First Field. South African military unit, officially 'First Field Regiment, South African Artillery.' Formed originally as Volunteers, with the title 'Cape Volunteer Artillery' on August 26, 1857, by Lieutenant-Colonel the Chevalier du Prat. In 1867 the title 'Prince Alfred's Own Cape Town Volunteer Artillery' was granted. Served in 9th Kaffir War, 1878; Basutoland Rebellion, 1880; South African War, 1899; German South West Africa, 1915 and throughout North African Campaign in World War II.

Regiment Gideon Scheepers. South African military unit, founded on April 1, 1934.

Regiment Hertzog. South African military unit, founded on July 1, 1952.

Regiment Kemp. South African military unit, founded on January 1, 1954.

Regiment Louw Wepener. South African military unit, founded on April 1, 1934. Headquarters at Ladybrand, O.F.S. Volunteers from this unit joined the President Steyn Regiment and fought in North Africa and Italy during World War II.

Regiment Onze Jan. South African military unit, founded on April 1, 1934.

Regiment President Kruger. South African military unit, founded on January 1, 1954.

Regiment President Steyn. South African military unit founded in Bloemfontein, O.F.S., in 1934. Mobilised in June 1940, with volunteers from the De Wet and Louw Wepener (qq.v.) Regiments and the O.V.S. Veld Artillerie, it arrived in Egypt in 1941 for service in the desert with the 5th South African Infantry Brigade.

Regiment Pretoria. South African military unit, founded as Princess Alice's Own on July 1, 1913. Served in German South West Africa Campaign in 1914 and in World War II served with 7th South African Infantry Brigade in Madagascar, and 6th South African Armoured Division in Italy. Motto 'Second to None.'

Regiment, Seventh Medium. South African military unit, officially 7th Medium Regiment, South African Artillery. Founded as 3rd Transvaal Scottish on October 16, 1939.

Regiment, Sixth Field. South African military unit, officially 6th Field Regiment, South African Artillery. Founded as Oranje Vrystaatse Veld Artillerie on July 1, 1926. Stationed in Bloemfontein and Bethlehem. Served with the President Steyn Regiment during World War II.

Regiment Smuts. South African military unit, founded on July 1, 1951.

Regiment Suid-Westelike Distrikte. South African military unit, founded on April 1, 1934, in Oudtshoorn, Cape. Volunteers from this regiment were drafted to the 5th Armoured Car Regiment and served in North Africa in 1941.

Regiment Tobie Muller. South African military unit, founded on January 1, 1954.

Regiment, Twenty-Second Field. *See* SOUTH AFRICAN IRISH.

Rehoboth. Town in South West Africa, established as a station by the Rhenish Mission in 1845 and named after a place mentioned in the Bible. Chiefly noted now because of its association with the Rehoboth Bastards, a colourep tribe living near by in their own reservation, and possessing their own 'Volksraad,' which enjoys certain powers of self-government. Population: 2,954, including 99 Whites.

Reinhardt's Deep-Sea Angler (*Himantolophus reinhardti*). Fish found North Atlantic and Japan. Only record of this in South African waters is a specimen cast up on the west coast of the Cape Peninsula in 1923. About 14 inches long.

Reitz. Town in the Northern Orange Free State, named after President F. W. Reitz, and established in 1891. There was a large wool-washery, operated by water-power, but this was later given up. During the South African War fighting occurred there, and the Orange Free State Government was very nearly captured by the British on July 10, 1901, escaping at the last moment. Today it is a leading farming centre. Population: 7,012, including 2,700 Whites.

Reitzburg. Village in the Orange Free State (not to be confused with Reitz), in the Vredefort District, originally known as Lindequesfontein.

Reitz, Colonel Deneys. South African writer and statesman. The son of President F. W. Reitz (q.v.), he was born in Bloemfontein, 1882, and moved to Pretoria when, in 1898, his father became State Secretary there. As a boy of 17 he joined the Boer forces in the South African War, gaining the experiences he set down on paper, but did not publish for many years. After the Peace he was an irreconcilable and lived as a transport rider in Madagascar, returning in 1904. His lifelong friendship with General Smuts enabled him to make a fresh start. He qualified as an attorney and practised in Heilbron, O.F.S. During World War I he joined the Army, went to German South-West and German East Africa, and then to France, where he rose to command the Scots Fusiliers. Upon his return to South Africa he entered Parliament in 1920, began practice in Johannesburg, and served repeatedly in General Smuts' cabinets, holding the portfolios of Lands (1923–1924), Mines and Native Affairs. His real claim to fame, however, arises from his memoirs of the South African War which he published under the title of *Commando*. This was immediately recognised as of outstanding quality and has become a South African classic. Later he wrote *Trekking On* and *No Outspan*, continuing the story of his career, but he never wrote his planned biography of President Kruger. In 1942 he was appointed Union High Commissioner in London, and died there in 1944.

Reitz, Francis William. President of the Orange Free State. Born in 1844, Swellendam, member of a family well known in that district. He was educated at the South African College and was called to the Bar at the Inner Temple in 1867. Upon his return to the Cape he began practice and continued until 1874, when, at the request of President Sir Johannes Brand, he accepted the post of Chief Justice of the Orange Free State. Apart from his legal work, he was interested in the Afrikaans language, and wrote poems, which attained great popularity, including the celebrated *Klaas Geswint en Syn Perd* (a rendering of Burns' *Tam O' Shanter*), also *Die Boer se Saterdag Aand* (The Cotter's Saturday Night). He continued to hold his position as Chief Justice until 1888, and gave support to the Afrikander Bond when this came into existence. Upon the death of President Brand, in 1888, he was elected his successor, and held the post of State President until 1895, when, because of poor health, he resigned. His public career was not ended. In 1897 he moved to Pretoria, where he was admitted as an advocate, and soon after appointed Judge of the Supreme Court. Upon the departure in 1898 of Dr. W. J. Leyds (q.v.) to Europe, he became his successor as State Secretary and as such drafted the famous ultimatum to Great Britain which led to the outbreak of the South African War. During hostilities he remained in the field and signed the Peace Treaty under protest. In 1910 he became President of the new Senate of the Union of South Africa, a position which he continued to hold until 1929, when he retired to the Cape. He died in 1934.

Reivilo. Agricultural village in the Northern Cape Province, important dairy centre. The name Reivilo is 'Olivier' written backwards. The original settlement goes back to 1883, but the present industry has grown since World War I. The population is 2,123, including 900 Whites.

Religion. *See* individual Churches.

Rembrandt Tobacco Corporation. Large industrial group established in 1941 by Dr. A. E. Rupert (q.v.) with its official S.A. headquarters at Paarl and Stellenbosch. Today it is a worldwide enterprise with assets of close on R400,000,000. It has control of the Carreras, Rothman and Dunhill organisations in England and others in Ireland, Holland, Germany, the U.S.A., Canada, Australia, New Zealand, Malaya and many other countries. With 30 factories in several continents it produces over 70,000,000,000 cigarettes yearly.

Remskoen. A brake wagon-lock used in the early days before the modern screw-operated brake. It is also used figuratively, for anyone who holds back progress, hence the expression, 'a Remskoen Party,' in early Cape politics.

Renault, Mary (real name **Mary Challans**). Novelist. Born in London, 1905. After nursing during World War II she emigrated in 1948 to Durban and in 1958 settled in Cape Town. Her fame rests mainly on a series of novels based on a detailed study of life in Ancient Greece; *The Last of the Wine* (1956) was followed by *The King Must Die, The Bull from the Sea*, etc.

Renders, Adam. Rhodesian explorer and discoverer of Zimbabwe Ruins. Born in Germany, 1822, he emigrated as a boy to the United States, and reached the Cape in the 1840's in a trading ship. Making his way to Natal, he joined the Voortrekkers, fought at Boomplaats (q.v.) under Andries Pretorius (q.v.), whose daughter he married. Later he settled in the Zoutpansberg, and went hunting in what is now Rhodesia. On one of these trips in 1867 (not 1868 as usually stated) he discovered Zimbabwe. He died about 1880.

Renosterbos (*Elytropappus rhinocerotis* Less). Dense bush, usually 2 to 3 feet high; weed on fallow grain lands. Found throughout southern half of Cape Province. *See* GRASSES.

Rensburg. Village near Heidelberg, Transvaal, founded 1932. Population: 2,710, including 2,015 Whites.

Republic Day. National holiday in South Africa, formerly known as Union Day, May 31. Coincides with the anniversary of the Treaty of Vereeniging, 1902, the establishment of the Union of South Africa, 1910, and the proclamation of the Republic of South Africa, 1961.

Republic of South Africa. Title since May 31, 1961, of the former Union of South Africa (q.v.). Its total area is 472,359 sq. miles, of which the Cape Province represents 277,113 sq. miles, plus 374 sq. miles of Walvis Bay (q.v.) administered as part of South-West Africa; the Transvaal 110,450 sq. miles; the Orange Free State 49,866 sq. miles; and Natal 33,578 sq. miles. Marion Island and Prince Edward Island in the southern Indian Ocean also form part of the Republic and are administered with the Cape Province. In addition, the territory of South-West Africa (q.v.) (317,887 sq. miles) is administered by the Republic. Its ocean currents, plateau formation and distance from the Equator give most of the Republic a fairly temperate climate, suitable for White settlement. (*See* CLIMATE OF SOUTHERN AFRICA.) For details of constitution *see* CONSTITUTION. Pretoria is the administrative capital of the

Republic and Cape Town the legislative capital. The population in 1966 was 18,298,000, of whom 3,481,000 were White. According to the last census covering all races, in 1960, the largest White population, 1,455,372 was in the Transvaal, with 997,377 in the Cape, 340,293 in Natal and 274,596 in the Orange Free State. Population by provinces (all races) (1960):

Cape

White	.	.	.	997,377
Coloured	.	.	.	1,314,392
Asiatic	.	.	.	20,243
Bantu	.	.	.	2,976,827
				5,308,839

Transvaal

White	.	.	.	1,455,372
Coloured	.	.	.	105,217
Asiatic	.	.	.	62,918
Bantu	.	.	.	4,601,545
				6,225,052

Natal

White	.	.	.	340,293
Coloured	.	.	.	43,093
Asiatic	.	.	.	394,237
Bantu	.	.	.	2,155,824
				2,933,447

Orange Free State

White	.	.	.	274,596
Coloured	.	.	.	25,565
Asiatic	.	.	.	16
Bantu	.	.	.	1,073,613
				1,373,790

Republic

White	.	.	.	3,067,638
Coloured	.	.	.	1,488,267
Asiatic	.	.	.	477,414
Bantu	.	.	.	10,807,809
				15,841,128

(Estimate for June 1968: White 3,639,000, Bantu 13,042,000, Coloured 1,912,000 and Asiatic 574,000. Total 19,167,000.) There are over 17,000 factories, employing more than 900,000 people, of whom nearly 300,000 are white. The number of farms occupied by Whites is nearly 100,000, represent-

ing an area of about 220,000,000 acres. About 23,000,000 acres are under cultivation, about one half of this being under maize. *See also* FORESTRY, TRANSPORT, ROMAN-DUTCH LAW, BANTU PEOPLES, as well as individual entries.

Republic of South Africa

ECONOMIC DEVELOPMENT IN FIGURES

	1953	1965	1968
Gross domestic product (R million)[1] . . .	3,401	7,514	Not available
*Gross domestic capital formation (R million) . . .	857	2,315	Not available
Financial Institutions (R million):			
Commercial banks[2]:			
Demand deposits . .	682	984	1,416
Fixed deposits . .	74	727	941
Savings deposits . .	68	287	415
Building societies[3]:			
Share capital . . .	276	955	997
Deposits . . .	312	729	981
Post Office Savings Bank[3]:			
Deposits . . .	173	136	152
National Savings certificates[3]	35	106	101
National Finance Corpn.[2]:			
Deposits . . .	128	110	148
Money in circulation[2] . .	888	1,471[6]	2,061[6]
External transactions (R million):			
Imports[4]	860	1,753	1,878
Exports (excluding gold)[5] .	599	1,056	1,503
Trade balance (exclud'g gold)	−261	−697	−375
Balance of payments . . (Balance on current A/c.) .	−172	−294	83
Gold and Foreign exchange reserves[2] . . .	223	455	1,100

* Includes Botswana, Lesotho and Swaziland
[1] Year ended 31st December   [2] As at 31st December   [3] As at 31st March
[4] Immigrants' effects excluded from 1965
[5] Excluding gold bullion and gold coin. Re-exports (imported goods exported) included from 1965. Emigrants' effects excluded from 1965.
[6] Coin and bank notes in circulation outside the banking sector and demand deposits with the banking sector, excluding foreign deposits and government deposits.
Due to the revision of this statistical series, figures for 1953 are not comparable with those for 1965 and 1968.

	1953	1965	1968
Mineral sales			
(R million)[2]:			
Total	432	1,153	1,366
Gold	295	767	784
Uranium . . .	8	Not available	—
Diamonds . . .	28	50	76
Chrome ore . . .	5	7	9
Copper ore . . .	19	40	101
Iron ore	2	18	29
Coal	33	81	97
Manganese . . .	9	18	24
Other		172	246
Mineral production (volume)			
Gold—million ounces . .	11·9	30·6	31·1
Diamonds—million carats .	2·7	5	7·4
Coal—million tons . .	31·4	53·4	56·9
Copper ore—1,000 tons .	39·8	66·6	141·4
Manufacturing industry			
Contribution to gross domestic product (R million)[1] .	629	1,644	Not available
Per cent of gross domestic product	18·5	21·9	Not available
Cement production (million tons).	2·3	4·3	4·9
Index of electric current generated (1948=100) . .	144·2	Not calculated by the Bureau	
Employment indexes[1]			
(1953/54=100)			
Manufacturing . .	142	149·1	174·2
Mining	112	120·0	118·9
Construction . . .	129	145·9	237·7
Price indexes			
Agricultural products (basis 1947/48 to 1949/50=100 July to June) . .	147·2	164·6	173·8
Wholesale (November 1960=100) .		108·3	116·6
Consumer (October 1958=100) .	87	113·2	123·3
Preliminary			
Agriculture			
Total production (R millions) .	641·8	1,016·2	1,190·8
Index of volume of production (1947/48–1949/50=100)	117	179	196
Sugar production (1,000 tons)	670·2	1,395·4	2,008·7
Groundnut crop (1,000 tons, shelled)	101·9	146·3	166·0
Wheat (million bags of 200 lb.)	6·2	11·8	12·0
Mealies (million bags) .	37·9	49·5	57·7

[1] The annual index numbers refer to the averages for the twelve months July to June.
[2] Sales.

	1953	1965	1968
S.A. Railways and Harbours			
Revenue			
Grand total (R millions) . .	249·8	587	754
Railways	220	493	594
Harbours	11·6	29	41
Airways	9·2	34	55
Other	—	31	64
Public debt (R million)[1]			
Internal	1,684	3,076	4,123
External	97	147	95
Central Government			
(R million)[2]			
Revenue collections on revenue account:			
Total . . .	451	1,087	1,492
Posts, Telegraphs and Telephones . . .	41	106	141
Customs and Excise . .	98	294	387
Expenditure from revenue account (R millions):			
Total	434	1,008	1,421
Agriculture . . .	44	65	118
Defence . . .	44	189	242
Public Works . . .	12	26	33
Posts, Telegraphs and Telephones . . .	32	76	100
Bantu Administration and Development . .	9	22	32
Bantu Education[3] . .	15	14	30
Education, Arts and Science .	10	32	48[4]

[1] As at 31st March   [2] Year ended 31st March

[3] Up to and including 1965 the amount shown for Bantu Education comprises the fixed statutory appropriation only.

For 1968 the total expenditure on the Bantu Education Account is shown.

[4] Includes Schools of Industries and Reform Schools.

Request Farm. Former title found in the Orange Free State and South African Republic, when any qualified burgher was allowed to make a request to the nearest Field Cornet for the grant of a piece of land. Once these requests were approved and entered up, the applicant was entitled to an area of 3,000 morgen (about 6,300 acres). A considerable number of these Request Farms are still in existence.

Residensia. Township near Vereeniging, Transvaal, laid out in 1904 under the name of Evaton. In 1962 it was given its present name, a large number of Bantu being removed from slums and rehoused. Population 2,420, including 2,000 Whites.

Ressano Garcia. Village in Mozambique, a frontier post on the railway to Pretoria and Lourenço Marques. Named after Frederico Ressano Garcia (q.v.).

Retief, Pieter. Voortrekker leader. Of French descent, he was born near the present town of Wellington in 1780, and as a young man moved to the eastern frontier, where he settled on the farm Mooimeisjiesfontein in 1814. He experienced many vicissitudes, both in farming and in business, being engaged as a building contractor. He fought in the Frontier Wars and in 1822 was appointed Commandant. With the approach of the crisis that culminated in the Great Trek, Retief became a spokesman for the emigrants, and later was elected one of their leaders. Before the final departure in 1837 he issued an historic manifesto, explaining the purpose of the emigration. After helping to establish the first system of government at Winburg, Pieter Retief led the expedition across the Drakensberg into Natal, and went to interview the chief Dingaan (q.v.) about the grant of an area for settlement. Dingaan demanded that before making any arrangements, the Trekkers should help him to recover certain cattle which had been stolen from him. This Retief carried out, but upon his return he and his party, while enjoying Dingaan's hospitality early in February, 1838, were treacherously attacked and slain.

Rex, George. Mysterious personality and pioneer associated with the opening up of Knysna (q.v.). He is reputed to have been the son of George III of England, who while Prince of Wales, married Hannah Lightfoot, known as 'The Fair Quakeress.' The marriage is stated to have been performed by a clergyman at Kew, near London, but the page of the register for the day in question has been removed. Hannah Lightfoot afterwards married a Mr. Axford. It is certain that George Rex (whose name implies a royal origin) came to the Cape in 1795 and was treated with great respect by the authorities there. He was appointed Marshal of the Admiralty Court and later, in 1817, settled at Melkhoutkraal, near Knysna, where he lived in great state and affluence. He died in 1839 and his grave is still to be

seen. His son John Rex was also a prominent colonist, and was reponsible for the opening up of the Buffalo River (now East London) to shipping. A noteworthy fact is that on a number of occasions members of the British Royal family have shown a more than usual interest in the Rex family, starting with the hunting expeditions of Prince Alfred in the 1860's and continuing into the 20th century, when Princess Beatrice visited them, as did the Prince of Wales (now Duke of Windsor).

Reyersbach, Louis Julius. Mining magnate and pioneer of early South African motoring. Born in Germany, 1869, he joined the London office of Wernher, Beit & Co. in 1891, was sent to Kimberley in 1894 and to Johannesburg in 1901. There he became a senior executive of the Rand Mines group, and was largely responsible for the Crown Mines amalgamation. He retired in 1914 and died in England in 1927.

Reynolds, Sir Frank. Natal sugar pioneer and legislator. Born in 1852, he was educated in England and entered the sugar industry as a young man. He sat in the first Natal Parliament and served in its military forces. After the establishment of Union he was a member for Umzimkulu. He died in 1930.

R.G.S. Abbreviation for Regiment Gideon Scheepers (q.v.).

R.H. Abbreviation for Regiment Hertzog (q.v.).

Rhebok (*Pelea capreolus*). A slight, graceful antelope found in most parts of Southern Africa south of the Limpopo, standing 2 feet 6 inches at the shoulder. Fond of rough country. The male carries small twisted horns. Its flesh is not considered good eating.

Rheinallt. Jones, Senator John David. *See* JONES, SENATOR JOHN DAVID RHEINALLT.

Rhenish Institute. Girls' High School at Stellenbosch, founded by the Rhenish Mission Society in 1860.

Rhenostervoel. Afrikaans name for Red-billed Oxpecker. *See* OXPECKER.

Rhinoceros. Largest land mammal in Southern Africa after the elephant. There are two species. The Black Rhinoceros (*R. bicornis*), once found all over Southern Africa, is now confined to the Bushveld, the Eastern Transvaal and Rhodesia, while the White Rhinoceros (*R. simus*), never seen south of the Orange River, is now only found in the Hluhluwe (q.v.) and other National Parks, in Zululand and in certain corners of Rhodesia. At one time believed to be extinct, it was rediscovered towards the end of the 19th century. The Black Rhinoceros stands about 5 feet at the shoulders, the body measuring about 10 feet round. The occasional White Rhinoceros has been found nearly 7 feet at the shoulder, and close on 14 feet round. Both types suffer from poor eyesight and are low in intelligence, but have a keen sense of smell and hearing. The White Rhinoceros has a straight, not a prehensile upper lip. Both have two horns, and cases have been reported of the larger front one reaching nearly 5 feet. The last Black Rhinoceros in the Cape was shot not far from Port Elizabeth in 1853.

Rhodes. Village in the Northern Cape, in the foothills of the Drakensberg, near Barkly East. Named after Cecil John Rhodes. Noted for its cold climate. Farming centre. Population: 450, including 150 Whites.

Rhodes, Cecil John. Statesman and Empire-Builder, and of all English-speaking people the man who has had the greatest influence on the history of the African continent. Rhodes was born in the English town of Bishop's Stortford, son of a minister, the Rev. Francis Rhodes, on July 5, 1853. Educated at a local school, he was sent at the age of 17, on account of his weak lungs, to Natal, where his brother, Herbert Rhodes, had already commenced farming in the Umkomaas Valley. The venture was not a success, and the discovery of diamonds, coupled with that of the founding of New Rush (Kimberley) caused Cecil Rhodes in 1871 to move to that centre. His first attempts at money-making included digging, pumping water from claims and the manufacture of ice. These enterprises prospered, and by the time he was 20, Rhodes was able to carry out one of his main ambitions, to study at Oxford. He remained there for a year, until 1873, but was forced to return to Kimberley because of the renewal of his tubercular trouble. He was back at Oxford again in 1876, as a member of Oriel College and kept terms until 1878. In 1877 he made his first will, already designed to encourage the expansion of British power over the world. Returning to Kimberley, his financial genius made him one of its wealthiest men, and in 1880 he not only founded the De Beers Diamond Mining Company (not to be confused with De Beers Consolidated Mines), but was elected to the Cape Parliament for Barkly West. He alternated this work with his studies at Oxford, where he secured a pass degree in 1881. Already noted in Parliament for his strong British ideas, Rhodes none the less had a high regard for the Dutch-speaking Afrikaner, and in 1882 took part in the efforts to control Boer freebooters on the frontiers of Bechuanaland, Stellaland and Goshen (qq.v.). His first appointment to the Cape Cabinet came in 1884, when he was, for a short while, Treasurer of the Colony. Already his thoughts were turning towards the expansion of British authority into the north, beyond the Limpopo River. He recognised that Kruger was his principal opponent, and made it his life's work to frustrate Boer attempts to obstruct him. One of his first major successes was the proclamation of British authority over Bechuanaland. The discovery of gold on the Rand and at Barberton led Rhodes to invest in these fields, and in 1887 he established the Goldfields of South Africa, forerunner of the Consolidated Goldfields of South Africa (q.v.). By this time he was hard at work amalgamating the diamond mines of Kimberley, winning over his opponent, Barney Barnato (q.v.), and securing the wholehearted support of Alfred Beit (q.v.). He also obtained the financial backing of the Rothschild interests in London. Having established contact with various traders and adventurers in the far north, Rhodes in 1888 sent his Kimberley partner, Charles Dunell Rudd (q.v.), to Gubulawayo to secure a concession for the mineral rights in Matabeleland from Lobengula (q.v.). The amalgamation of the diamond interests was now completed, through the establishment in the same year of De Beers Consolidated Mines Ltd. He had made two more wills, in each of which his plan for the safeguarding of British power over the world was more explicitly set out. The grant of the concession by Lobengula gave a justification for the founding of the British South Africa Company (q.v.) in 1889, and Rhodes began plans for the occupation of Mashonaland. The following year he was elected Prime Minister of Cape Colony. With the news that the Pioneer Column had reached Fort Salisbury, he pushed ahead with the plan for carrying the railway from the Cape to Cairo. In England Rhodes was already regarded as one of the most important figures of the day, and his emissaries were working far north of the Zambesi, while he was preparing to buy Lourenço Marques from the impoverished Portuguese. As Prime Minister he succeeded in securing the occupation and annexation of Pondoland, in the Eastern Cape. Scores of

ambitious plans were not merely taking shape, but carried out by him. He helped to have the Cape Railways extended to Johannesburg, through the Orange Free State. He bought up large tracts of land outside Cape Town, where he built his mansion, Groote Schuur. He laid plans for the construction of a Cape-to-Cairo telegraph line, he worked for the setting up of large-scale new industries in South Africa, poured enormous sums into the country which soon after was called Rhodesia in his honour. Aware of the fact that the native problem was supreme in South Africa, he took a long step towards finding a solution by the introduction of the Glen Gray Act (q.v.). He also had a considerable share in the opening up of British East Africa. In 1895 he became a Privy Councillor. The intransigence of President Kruger in refusing concessions to Uitlanders led Rhodes in 1895 to identify himself with the movement which culminated in the Jameson Raid (q.v.). The failure of this expedition, led by Dr. Jameson, who was one of his closest friends, caused a permanent breach with the Afrikaner in the Cape, and his resignation as Prime Minister of the Colony and as Managing Director of the Chartered Company. A serious rebellion broke out in Rhodesia, which Rhodes, manifesting the greatest personal courage, finally ended by walking unarmed into the Matopos and discussing matters with the insurgent natives. In 1897 the railway reached Bulawayo, an added triumph to him. He met with much hostility both in Britain and in South Africa on account of his share in the Raid, and though, in 1898, he resumed his position as Managing Director of the Chartered Company, the South African War cut across all his ambitions for the establishment of a South African Union. He had caused the building of a large dynamite factory outside Cape Town, and the laying out of the famous Rhodes Fruit

Farms near Groot Drakenstein. Upon the outbreak of the South African War in 1899, he found himself in Kimberley, where he remained during the siege, at loggerheads with the military commander, Colonel Kekewich (q.v.). For several years his health had been failing, and on March 26, 1902, he died in Muizenberg, and was buried at 'The World's View' in the Matopo Hills in Rhodesia. For the provisions of his will, *see* RHODES SCHOLARSHIPS.

Rhodes Clause. Provision introduced by Cecil John Rhodes in 1894 and adopted in 1898 in the constitution of Rhodesia, whereby Customs duties on British goods imported into Rhodesia were in no case to exceed those then in force in the Cape Colony. After the establishment of Responsible Government in 1923 the Rhodes Clause was abolished.

Rhodes, Colonel Francis (Frank) William. British soldier and elder brother of Cecil John Rhodes. Born at Bishop's Stortford in 1850. He went to South Africa earlier than his brother, spent a short time in Kimberley, but fell ill and returned in 1873 to enter the Royal Dragoons. Served in Egypt and the Sudan in the 1880's and later in Ireland and India before being attached in 1893 to Sir Gerald Portal on a mission in Uganda. Retiring from the Army in 1894, he went to Rhodesia, where he deputised as Administrator for Dr. L. S. Jameson. From there he moved to Johannesburg, became involved in the Reform Movement and in the Jameson Raid, for which he was imprisoned by the Kruger Government and fined £2,000. Returning to Rhodesia he fought in the Matabele Rebellion of 1896, before being appointed correspondent of *The Times* in the Sudan campaign of 1898. On the outbreak of the South African War he served in Ladysmith, Mafeking and elsewhere with much distinction. After some years on the family estate of Dalham

in England, he returned to South Africa and died in Cape Town on September 25, 1905.

Rhodes Day. Public holiday in Rhodesia, in honour of Cecil John Rhodes, celebrated on the first Monday in July, and followed by Founder's Day (q.v.).

Rhodes Grass. *See* GRASS, RHODES.

Rhodesia (formerly **Southern Rhodesia**). Area 150,333 square miles, of which 79,533 square miles constitute Mashonaland and 70,800 square miles Matabeleland. The capital is Salisbury (q.v.). Population (December 1968): 4,700,000, including 4,480,000 Africans, 241,000 Whites, 9,000 Asians and 15,000 Coloureds. The national income in 1963 was £313,400,000, compared with £170,200,000 in 1954. Principal mineral products: gold, asbestos, chrome ore, coal, iron ore, tin and copper. Building construction in 1962 was valued at £5,489,000. Exports in 1967 were valued at £100,600,000 and imports at £93,500,000. Owing to the efforts of Britain and the United Nations to enforce a blockade, further details are not published.

Manufacturing has made great progress in Rhodesia. From 1946 to 1961 the output rose from £7·6 million to £148,737,000. From 1946 to 1961 the number of factories increased from 435 to 1,279, while employees of all races rose from 39,958 in 1946 to 91,797 in 1961. Communications are by road, rail and, increasingly, air. Tarmac is replacing 'strip' surfaces on the main roads. *See* RHODESIA RAILWAYS. The most important source of electric power is the Kariba Scheme (q.v.) controlled by the Rhodesia Electricity Supply Commission, the Zambia copper mines being by far the largest consumers.

There are three daily newspapers, including an African daily, published in Salisbury and Bulawayo; two Sunday newspapers and 22 other newspapers, two of them published three times a week, one twice weekly and the rest once a week or once a fortnight. Eight of these are for Africans, printed in the vernacular and in English.

Agriculture is advancing in Rhodesia, much experimental work being undertaken. Large irrigation schemes are operating in the Sabi Valley. Maize production has risen to 4,037,000 bags of 200 lb. each. The most important crop, from the revenue point of view, is tobacco, which enjoys a large overseas market. Virginia flue-cured tobacco output rose to 216 million lb. in 1962. Exports before U.D.I. (q.v.) were nearly all to the United Kingdom, amounting to £40 million in 1962. As a result of Britain's Sanctions Policy the trade since 1965 is in Government hands and conducted secretly. Sugar is successfully grown on the Triangle Sugar Estates, about 67,000 tons a year. Plans are afoot to cultivate 16,000 acres. Rhodesia produced 1·4 million lb. of tea from the Eastern Highlands. There, too, large softwood plantations have been established.

Rhodesia and Nyasaland, Federation of (1953–63). The Federation comprised the self-governing colony of Southern Rhodesia and the Protectorates of Northern Rhodesia and Nyasaland. Its total area, over 484,000 sq. miles, of which Northern Rhodesia (now Zambia) occupied more than half, was larger than that of the Republic of South Africa.

Rhodesia, Northern. *See* ZAMBIA.

RHODESIA—CHRONOLOGY

1505 Occupation of Sofala by Vasco da Gama and establishment of first Portuguese fort.

1817– Moselekatse, Kumalo Chief, flees
1840 from Tshaka and settles in Matabeleland, about 12 miles from Bulawayo, founding the Matabele nation.

1853 Birth of Cecil John Rhodes at Bishop's Stortford, England.
Birth of Leander Starr Jameson at Edinburgh.
Birth of Alfred Beit at Hamburg, Germany.

1855 Victoria Falls discovered by David Livingstone.

1858 Royal Geographical Society appoint Thomas Baines artist to Zambesi expedition under Livingstone.

1859 London Missionary Society establish Inyati Mission Station under Dr. Robert Moffat.

1861 Survey by Baines and Chapman on expedition to Victoria Falls.

1868 Death of Moselekatse.
Zimbabwe Ruins discovered by Adam Renders.

1870 Lobengula succeeds Moselekatse as King of the Matabele.
Hope Fountain Mission founded by Rev. J. B. Thomson.

1871 Cecil John Rhodes arrives in Natal.
Karl Mauch writes an account of Zimbabwe Ruins.
Concession granted to Thomas Baines by Lobengula to prospect for gold in his territory.

1888 Rudd Concession signed at Umvutcha, near Bulawayo, granting mineral rights to Rhodes and associates.

1889 Chartered Company formed.

1890 Pioneer Column under Colonel Pennefather marches north.
British flag hoisted at Fort Salisbury.
Railway extension from Kimberley to Vryburg opened.

1891 British Protectorate over Bechuanaland, Matabeleland and Mashonaland.
President McMahon arbitrates on Anglo-Portuguese boundary. Dr. L. S. Jameson becomes Chief

Magistrate and Administrator of Mashonaland.

1892 Telegraph reaches Fort Salisbury.

Beira Railway Company established, and first 75 miles opened.

First school for European children at Salisbury.

1893 The Moodie Trek reaches Chipinga.

Work begun on railway from Vryburg to Mafeking.

Matabele and Mashonas clash at Victoria.

Matabele War. Lobengula's kraal occupied.

1894 Death of Lobengula.

Railway from Vryburg to Mafeking opened.

1895 Territory named 'Rhodesia' by proclamation of Dr. L. S. Jameson.

1896 Dr. Jameson resigns as Administrator.

Matabele Rebellion breaks out.

Mashonaland Rebellion breaks out.

Rhodes visits Matopos to make peace with Matabele chiefs.

1897 Umtali moved to new site.

Municipalities of Salisbury and Bulawayo created.

End of Mashona Rebellion.

Opening of railway from Vryburg to Bulawayo.

1898 Railway reaches Umtali from Beira.

1899 Legislative Council for Southern Rhodesia established.

Beira–Salisbury Railway opened.

1902 Death of Cecil Rhodes.

Railway from Bulawayo to Salisbury completed.

1904 Interment of Major Allan Wilson and his patrol in Matopos.

Railway to Victoria Falls completed.

Victoria Falls Bridge opened.

1906 Death of Alfred Beit.

1910 Duke of Connaught tours Rhodesia.

1913 Appointment of Dr. Starr Jame-

son as President of British South Africa Company.

1915 Supplemental Charter issued.

1917 Death of Sir Starr Jameson.

1920 Cave Commission award B.S.A. Company a sum of £4,435,225, for assets taken over by the Government.

1922 Referendum of voters decide on Responsible Government.

1923 Southern Rhodesia annexed to Great Britain.

Responsible Government established in Southern Rhodesia.

1924 First elections to Legislative Assembly.

1925 Visit of His Royal Highness the Prince of Wales to Southern Rhodesia.

1926 Cairo to Cape Town flight of R.A.F. broken at Bulawayo.

1927 Death of Sir Charles Coghlan, first Premier of Southern Rhodesia, and succession of the Hon. H. U. Moffat.

1928 Sir Cecil Hunter Rodwell, K.C.M.G., becomes Governor of Southern Rhodesia.

1929 Beit Bridge over Limpopo opened.

1930 Customs Conference at Cape Town reaches agreement.

1932 Imperial Airways plane *City of Basra* reaches Bulawayo on Cape–London service.

1933 Moffat Government offer £2,000,000 for mineral rights accepted by Chartered Company.

Reform Party win General Election. Hon. G. M. Huggins becomes Prime Minister.

1935 Trade Agreement with Union.

Incorporation of Salisbury.

First State Lottery draw.

Birchenough Bridge across the Sabi River opened.

1940 Empire Training School (R.A.F.) opened at Salisbury.

Celebration of Jubilee at Bulawayo.

1941 De Beers abandon diamond rights concession.

1943 Gatooma Cotton Mills opened.
Bulawayo celebrates 50th anniversary of occupation of Matabeleland.

1944 British Government rejects proposal for amalgamation between Southern and Northern Rhodesia and Nyasaland.

1945 First meeting of Central African Council for Rhodesia and Nyasaland in Salisbury.

1946 Parliament accepts motion to establish University.

1949 Agreement reached in Federation talks at Victoria Falls.
Colony's £53,000,000 Four-Year Plan presented in Parliament.

1950 Rhodesian Premier attends Commonwealth Conference in London.
Direct railway to Lourenço Marques proposed.

1951 Census shows 65 per cent increase in White Population since 1946.

1952 28,000,000 Dollar Loan received from International Bank. Immigration restrictions adopted.

1953 Rhodes Centenary Exhibition at Bulawayo.
Visit by Queen Mother and Princess Margaret.
Establishment of Federation of Rhodesia and Nyasaland. Lord Llewellin, first Governor-General of Federation, appointed.

1954 University College of Rhodesia and Nyasaland founded.
Railway from Bannockburn to Lourenço Marques opened.

1955 Anglican Church Province of Central Africa established.
Federal Supreme Court appointed.
Start of work on Kariba Dam.

1956 Retirement of Lord Malvern as Premier. Succeeded by Sir Roy Welensky.

1957 Death of Lord Llewellin. Succeeded by Lord Dalhousie.
University College of Rhodesia opened.

1958 Rhodesian Iron and Steel Commission denationalised and works at Que Que restored to private ownership.

1959 Disturbances in Nyasaland.
Campaign to save game from areas flooded by Kariba Dam.

1960 Opening of Kariba Dam.
Monckton Commission report on Rhodesian constitutional development.

1961 London conference on future constitutional changes.

1962 Oil refinery at Umtali begun.

1963 Break-up of Federation.

1964 Ian Smith Prime Minister.
Name changed from Southern Rhodesia to Rhodesia. Referendum held on independence.

1965 After lengthy negotiations the Government on November 11 issued Unilateral Declaration of Independence.

1966 Imposition of Oil Sanctions by Great Britain, not supported by South Africa. Start of terrorist activity from Zambia.

1967 Commission drafts new Constitution. Rhodesia Railways separated from those of Zambia.

1968 New Rhodesian flag adopted.
Visit by Sir Alec Douglas-Home.
Meeting on H.M.S. *Fearless* of Messrs. Harold Wilson and Ian Smith.

1969 Republic declared in Rhodesia.

Rhodesia Herald. Daily morning newspaper issued in Salisbury, Rhodesia, founded originally by W. E. Fairbridge on June 27, 1891, as the *Mashonaland Herald* and renamed in 1892. Since 1898 it has been appearing daily.

Rhodesian Broadcasting Corporation. Statutory body. Headquarters are at Salisbury and it runs commercial and non-commercial programmes, in English and in various African languages. There are stations at Salisbury, Bulawayo, Gwelo, Que Que, Gatooma and Umtali in Rhodesia. Rhodesia Television (Private) Ltd., which operates a television service, began in November 1960. Zambia has stations at Lusaka and Kitwe. *See also* BROADCASTING, SOUTH AFRICAN BROADCASTING CORPORATION and WIRELESS TELEGRAPHY.

Rhodesian Dollar. *See* DOLLAR.

Rhodesian Iron and Steel Commission. Statutory body, popularly known as RISCOM, established in 1942, for the purpose of meeting, as far as possible from local sources, the needs of the colony in iron and steel. It built works near Que Que, with an initial capacity of 30,000 tons a year, but met with many difficulties, owing to the smallness of the market, high costs, etc., and passed in October 1957 into the hands of a group of British industrialists.

Rhodesian Selection Trust Limited. Mining group established May 22, 1928, with very large interests in the copper industry of Zambia (Northern Rhodesia). Its original capital of £500,000 has since been raised to £22,000,000. Its headquarters are in Lusaka and it includes the Mufulira Copper Mines, Roan Antelope and others.

Rhodesian State Lottery. Established in 1935, the first draw taking place on December 20 of that year.

Rhodesian Teak. *See* TEAK.

Rhodesia Railways. Transportation system operating in Zambia and Rhodesia, and to a limited extent beyond their frontiers. Its origin may be traced to the Bechuanaland Railway Company Ltd., established in London in 1893, with a nominal capital of £8,000, later enlarged,

its object being to construct a line northwards from the existing terminal at Vryburg. Construction began in May, 1893, and within 17 months had reached Mafeking. In October, 1897, the railway reached Bulawayo. Meanwhile work had begun on another line from the coast, by the Beira Railway Co. Ltd., formed in 1892, with a capital of £250,000, under the Chairmanship of Alfred Beit. Despite tremendous difficulties, construction was started in the same year, Umtali being reached in 1898. The remaining section, from Umtali to Salisbury, was constructed by the Mashonaland Railway Company Ltd., registered in 1897, with a capital of £450,000, the link being completed on May 1, 1899, and running powers being secured with the Beira and Beira Junction Railway Company. The Bechuanaland Railway Company changed its name to Rhodesia Railways Limited in 1899, and became the dominating concern in the territory, with a capital of £2,000,000, and a large debenture issue. It was responsible for linking up Beira with Salisbury and Bulawayo, and for carrying the main line to the Victoria Falls and ultimately to the Congo boundary. A special subsidiary was later formed, called the Rhodesia-Katanga Junction Railway and Mineral Company Ltd., while another concern, the Blinkwater Railway Company Limited was responsible for the branch from Gwelo to Fort Victoria. More recently the Rhodesia Railways built a direct line from Bannockburn in Rhodesia through Mozambique to Lourenço Marques. After lengthy discussions, and the passing of the necessary legislation, Rhodesia Railways were purchased by the State in 1947 for £30,000,000, transfer being carried out two years later. In 1959 an agreement was reached with the South African Railways under which Rhodesia took over the operation of the section of the old Bechuanaland Railway from Vryburg to Bulawayo, which had hitherto been in the hands of the South African Railways. In 1967 the section of the Rhodesia Railways north of the Zambesi, covering 706 miles, passed into the separate control of Zambia, though certain operating arrangements continued. The remaining mileage of the Rhodesia Railways is 2,029.

Rhodes Scholarships. Under the will of Cecil John Rhodes (q.v.) about one-third of Rhodes' estate, amounting to about £2,000,000 out of about £6,500,000, was vested in trustees. He asked to be buried in the Matopos and that the neighbouring country be developed as a public pleasure ground and farm. His residence at Cape Town, Groote Schuur, was to become the home of the Prime Minister of the United South Africa. £100,000 was left to his old college, Oriel at Oxford, and 60 scholarships, each of a value of £250 a year, tenable for three years, were awarded to a carefully-selected group of young men, mostly from the English-speaking world, including 24 from South Africa, 21 from Australia, six from Canada, three from New-foundland, three from the Bermudas, three from Jamaica and a number, later to be determined, from the United States. Rhodes laid down that not merely educational qualities but those of character and sportsmanship were to be taken into account. The number of scholarships was later raised to 160, and the value to £600 a year. Fifteen scholarships were also placed at the disposal of the German Emperor, and later transferred to German students. All were tenable at Oxford, where Rhodes House is the headquarters of the Trust. Other provisions of Rhodes' will include the preservation of the family estate, Dalham Hall, in England.

Rhokana Corporation. Large copper mining company in Zambia, belonging to the Anglo-American group.

Founded in 1923. Its holdings include the Bwana Mkubwa, Nkana and Bancroft Mines.

Ricards, Bishop James David. Catholic bishop in Grahamstown. Born, 1828, in Ireland, he came to Grahamstown in 1849, bringing with him the first nuns to reach this country. He worked on the eastern frontier as a military chaplain, teacher and writer. While there he helped to identify the first diamond discovered at the Cape. In 1871 he was consecrated as a bishop in Grahamstown. He died in 1893.

Richards Bay. Inlet in the Zululand Coast, with fishing resort and game reserve. Proposals to develop it as a harbour were examined by an overseas expert, Sir George Buchanan, in 1923, in conjunction with the Kosi Bay scheme. Work began on a new port in 1968, including facilities for handling large oil tankers, a 520-mile pipeline to the Rand, a railway to coalfields, and large Aluminium smelter. *See* Kosi Bay.

Richardson, Sir Lewis. South African commercial pioneer. Born in Birmingham, 1873, he came to South Africa as a child in 1881 and settled in Port Elizabeth, where he became one of the leaders of the ostrich feather and wool trade. After World War I he helped considerably in gifts for the resettlement of returned soldiers. He died in 1934.

Richmond: 1. Town in the Karroo, named after the Duke of Richmond, father-in-law of Governor Sir Peregrine Maitland. Founded in 1844. Noted as the birthplace of the great South African-born medical pioneer, Dr. Emil Hoffa (q.v.), founder of the modern sciences of Orthopaedics. Scene of fighting in South African War. Wool-growing centre. Population: 3,030, including 1,000 Whites.

2. Town in Natal, founded in 1850 by the Byrne Settlers (q.v.) near Pietermaritzburg. Wattle-growing and farming centre. Population: 2,570, including 550 Whites.

Richterveld. North-western part of Little Namaqualand. Area to the south of the Orange River, in its major loop before reaching the sea. Noted for its extensive mineralisation, including deposits of copper, tin, etc. still undeveloped. Explored between 1907 and 1914 by Fred. C. Cornell. Named after the Rev. W. Richter, Inspector of the Seminary of the Rhenish Mission Society at Barmen, Germany, in 19th century. The name is often wrongly spelt Richtersveld (with an 's').

Rickshas. Vehicles introduced about 1893 from Japan mainly through Sir Marshall Campbell (q.v.). In 1903 Durban had over 1,000 rickshas, whose use soon spread to Pietermaritzburg, Johannesburg, Pretoria, Bulawayo, Salisbury and other centres. They are mainly used today by tourists and for parcels delivery purposes.

Riebeeck, Abraham van. Governor-General of Netherlands East Indies. Son of Jan van Riebeeck (q.v.), born at the Cape of Good Hope on October 18, 1653. Went to Holland at age of seven, studied Law at Leyden, and joined services of Dutch East India Company, who sent him as Under-Merchant to Batavia in 1677. He rose steadily in importance and in 1709 became Governor-General. He died in Batavia, 1713.

Riebeeck, Jan (Johann) van. *See* VAN RIEBEECK.

Riebeeckstad. Town on the Orange Free State Goldfields, founded in 1955. Population: 1,009, including 801 Whites.

Riebeek East. Town in the Eastern Cape Province, founded in 1840 and abandoned temporarily in 1846 during the native wars. The Voortrekker leader Pieter Retief (q.v.) lived near by at Mooimeisjesfontein. Under its original title deeds Riebeek East, like Fish Hoek (q.v.), is 'dry.' Farming centre. Population: 900, including 400 Whites.

Riebeek Kasteel. Mountain in the Western Cape Province, so called on account of its resemblance to a castle. It was first sighted by a party under Corporal Cruythoff Colony, sent out by the first Commander of the Colony, in whose honour the name was given. The present village near by dates from the 1860's. Population: 1,000, including 400 Whites.

Riebeek West. Village in the Western Cape Province, established in 1858, and notable as the place where both General J. C. Smuts and Dr. D. F. Malan went to school. Farming centre. It is named after Jan van Riebeeck. Population: 1,265, including 544 Whites.

Rietvink. Afrikaans name for Masked Weaver.

Rimington, Major-General Sir Michael Frederic. British soldier. Born in Wales in 1858, and entered Inniskilling Dragoons in 1881. After service in the Bechuanaland Expedition in 1884 and 1885, as well as in Zululand in 1888, he saw active service in the South African War, where as commander of 'Rimington's Scouts' (also known as Rimington's Guides), he won distinction at Magersfontein, at Thaba Nchu, the Brandwater Basin and elsewhere. In his later career he was Inspector-General of Cavalry in India. He died in 1928.

Rinderpest. Cattle plague known in Europe and Asia in the days of antiquity. Endemic in Central Africa, and known in Somaliland in 1889, it began to spread southward, reaching

Uganda in 1890, Nyasaland in 1892 and Bulawayo in March, 1896. It then spread with lightning speed, and crossed the Orange River in March, 1897, despite special cordons and fences. Bovine cattle died like flies and by the time the epidemic subsided, the losses in Southern Africa were estimated at over 4,500,000 head. The disease takes the form of a fever attended by inflammation of all the membranes, pus discharge from nose, followed rapidly by death. Dr. Robert Koch (q.v.) evolved a method of inoculation with a serum that proved successful.

Ringhals (*Sepidon haemachates*) or **Spitting Snake.** Group: Elapidae. Also known as Ringhals Cobra. Very poisonous snake, found in most parts of Southern Africa. About 5 feet long. The Afrikaans name means 'ring collar,' and refers to the yellow markings on most varieties. The Ringhals is one of the most aggressive of snakes, and will chase on sight, rearing its hood and hissing out its venom in the victim's eye before it bites. Even its 30 or more young are ready to spray poison from birth. They are born alive (Viviparous). *See* COBRAS and SNAKES.

Riscom. Popular name for the Rhodesian Iron and Steel Commission (q.v.).

Rissik, Johann Friedrich Bernhard. First Administrator of the Transvaal. Born in Holland, 1857, and qualified as a land-surveyor. He was Acting Surveyor-General of the South African Republic, responsible for the laying-out of Johannesburg. For this reason he is thought by some authorities to be the godfather of the city. In 1907 he became Minister of Lands and Native Affairs under the Crown Colony Government. Upon the establishment of Union Rissik became the first Administrator of the Transvaal, from which post he retired in 1917. He died in 1925.

Ritchie. Village near Kimberley. Population: 1,722, including 235 Whites.

River or **Mud Bream** (*Acanthopagrus berda*). Fish found off Algoa Bay (rare), Natal, East Coast of Africa, Indian Seas to East Indies. About 16 inches in South Africa, but up to 30 in other regions. *See* BREAM.

River Horse. *See* HOUTPERD.

Rivers. Of the river systems of South Africa, only a comparatively small number flow into the Atlantic Ocean. Indeed in South West Africa (with the exception of the important northern boundary river of the Cunene) most rivers hardly flow at all, including the principal one, the Swakop. In the Republic the largest river is the Orange, which, like the Olifants and the Berg, empties itself into the Atlantic. On the south coast of the Republic are the Breede, the Gouritz, the Gamtoos and the Sundays Rivers, while the Kowie, the Great Fish, the Keiskama, the Buffalo, the Great Kei, the Bashee, the St. Johns (or Umzimvubu), the Umzimkulu, the Umgeni, the Tugela, the Umfulozi and the Pongola are only a few of those which feed the Indian Ocean. Rising in the Republic and flowing beyond its borders into the Indian Ocean are the Maputa, the Komati and the Limpopo (or the Crocodile). Rhodesia's contributions include the Sabi, the Buzi, the Pungwe and the Zambesi.

Unfortunately the tableland formation of Southern Africa has prevented the development of navigable rivers, the only usable stretches being along the Berg River, the Buffalo (which possesses South Africa's sole major river port, East London), and near the mouth of the Maputa. All these stretches are very limited and of little economic importance. The Lower Zambesi, however, is used by sternwheelers of the type familiarised on the Mississippi River. *See also* under names of individual rivers.

RIVERS OF SOUTHERN AFRICA

Name	Length in miles	Flows into
Bashee	200	Indian Ocean
Berg	120	Atlantic Ocean
Breede	200	South Atlantic Ocean
Buffalo (Cape)	100	Indian Ocean
Caledon	200	Orange River
Crocodile	120	Limpopo River
Cunene (see Kunene)		
Fish (see Great Fish)		
Fish (Aub) (South West Africa)	250	Orange River
Gamtoos	350	Indian Ocean
Gouritz	400	South Atlantic Ocean
Great Fish	300	Indian Ocean
Kei (Great)	200	Indian Ocean
Keiskamma	100	Indian Ocean
Komati (Incomati)	180	Indian Ocean
Kowie	45	Indian Ocean
Kuisib	200	Atlantic Ocean
Kunene	600	Atlantic Ocean
Letaba (Great)	120	Olifants River (Transvaal)
Limpopo	900	Indian Ocean
Magalakwen	330	Limpopo River
Maputa	180	Indian Ocean
Nyl	120	Magalakwen River
Okavango	610	Okavango Swamps
Olifants (Transvaal)	360	Limpopo River
Olifants (Cape)	200	Atlantic Ocean
Orange	1,360	Atlantic Ocean
Pongola	120	Maputa River
Pungwe	150	Indian Ocean
Sabie	95	Komati River
Sabi (Save)	380	Indian Ocean
Shire	250	Zambesi River
St. John's (see Umzimvubu)		
Sundays	300	Indian Ocean
Swakop	250	Atlantic Ocean
Tugela	200	Indian Ocean
Umfulosi (White)	160	Indian Ocean
Umgeni	100	Indian Ocean
Umkomaas	150	Indian Ocean
Umtamvuma	70	Indian Ocean
Umtata	120	Indian Ocean
Umzimkulu	120	Indian Ocean
Umzimvubu	150	Indian Ocean
Vaal	500	Orange River
Zambesi	1,600	Indian Ocean

PLATE 9. Kariba Dam *(top)*
Kitwe, Zambia *(bottom)*
(by courtesy of Anglo American Corporation (C.A.) Ltd.)

The Big Hole,
Kimberley
*(by courtesy of
South African Railways)*

PLATE 10

Parliament House of
the Transkei at
Umtata

*(by courtesy of the
Dept. of Information,
Pretoria)*

PLATE 11.   S.A.S. *President Steyn* *(top)*
            (by courtesy of R. Pabst)

            Fishing Harbour, Lamberts Bay, Cape Province *(bottom)*
            (by courtesy of South African Railways)

PLATE 12.   On Malanje Plateau, Malawi *(top)*

Valley of a Thousand Hills, Natal *(bottom)*
(by courtesy of the Dept. of Information, Pretoria)

PLATE 13.   Union Buildings, Pretoria *(top)*   Aerial View of Salisbury *(bottom)*
(by courtesy of South African Railways)   *(by courtesy of the Rhodesia Government)*

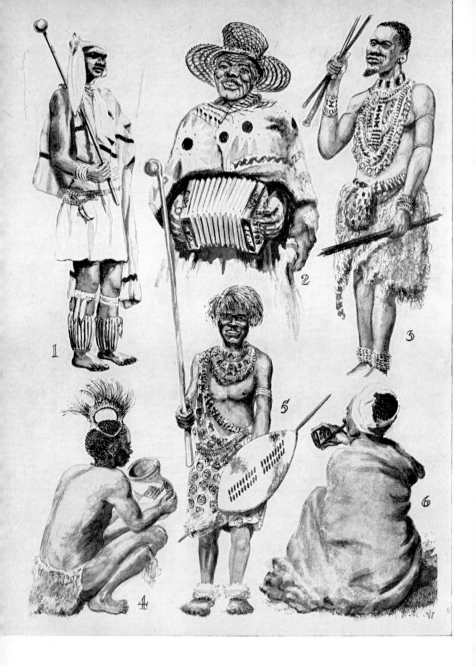

PLATE 14. Tribal Dress (Men)
1. Young M'pondo. 2. Basuto with characteristic woven hat.
3. Zulu with bead ornaments. 4. Ovambo man. 5. Swazi youth.
6. Xosa tribesman in red blanket.

PLATE 15. Tribal Dress (Women)
   1. Xosa woman and her baby. 2. Zulu married woman.
   3. Herero (South West Africa). Her dress takes 12 yards of material.
   4. M'pondo woman (East Pondoland).
   5. N'debele woman with 'sausage' ornaments.
   6. Venda girl (North-East Transvaal).

PLATE 16.   Conveyor for the Swaziland Iron Ore Development Company *(top)*
(by courtesy of Anglo American Corp. of S.A. Ltd., Johannesburg)

Victoria Falls *(bottom)*

Riversdale: 1. Town in the Cape Province, established in 1838 beside the Langeberg range. It is named after the Hon. Harry Rivers, then the local magistrate and later Colonial Secretary. Important wool, grain and cattle centre. During the South African War General Christiaan de Wet passed near there. Population: 5,071, including 2,270 Whites.
2. Township near Vereeniging, Transvaal. Population: 1,378, including 1,168 Whites.

Riverton. Hamlet on the Vaal River, and site of the pumping station for the Kimberley waterworks. Popular weekend resort. Diamond diggings formerly operated near by.

River View. Township near Hlabisa in Zululand. Population: 1,483, including 390 Whites.

River Zonder Eind. Tributary of Breede River (q.v.).

Riviersonderend. Village near Caledon, Cape Province. Population: 1,560, including 860 Whites.

Rivonia Trial. Named after fashionable northern suburb of Johannesburg, where in June and July 1963 quantities of equipment were found, designed for attempted civil war in South Africa. Of the ten men prosecuted three were white—Denis Goldberg, Lionel Bernstein and James Kantor; one Indian—Ahmed Mohamed Kathrada; and six Bantu—Nelson Mandela (q.v.), Walter Sisulu, Goban Mbeki, Raymond Mhlaba, Elias Molsoaledi and Andrew Mhlangeni. The case was tried by Mr. Justice Quartus de Wet, Judge President of the Transvaal Provincial Division of the Supreme Court of South Africa; 173 witnesses were called by the prosecution, and six of the accused gave evidence under oath. Mandela, Sisulu, Goldberg, Mbeki, Molsoaledi and Mhlangeni admitted their guilt and Mandela was sentenced on June 11, 1964, to life imprisonment, with lesser sentences for the

others, except Kantor, who was discharged.

Rixdollar. A coin used at the Cape under the Dutch régime. The word is a corruption of Ryks daaler, meaning a dollar of the 'ryk' or empire (compare Reich formerly used in Germany). The value of a Rixdollar was approximately 1s. 3d. The Rixdollar was finally abolished on March 31, 1841, at the Cape of Good Hope, but in the Boer Republics it continued for some time after. As late as 1862 the denomination, though not the coin, was still in official use in the O.F.S., and it was not until 1868 that the conversion of the Rixdollar to the system now in use was finally laid down. The rate at that time, incidentally, was four Rixdollars to 10s.

R.K. Abbreviation for Regiment Kemp (q.v.).

R.L.W. Abbreviation of Regiment Louw Wepener (q.v.).

R.N.C. Abbreviation for Royal Natal Carbineers (q.v.).

Roan Antelope (*Hippotragus equinus*) or **Bastard Eland.** Large antelope, standing 4 feet 6 inches at the shoulder. Both sexes carry tall, sweeping horns, rather shorter and less robust than those of the Sable Antelope. The head is dark brown, with white patches and white muzzle. Roan makes excellent meat, but today is protected and found only in the Eastern Transvaal and Rhodesia.

Roan Antelope Mine. Large copper mine in Zambia, adjoining the township of Luanshya (q.v.). The company was established in 1927 to take over the development of earlier discoveries, going back to the finding of the original ore-body by William Collier in 1902. Coming under the control of the Rhodesian Selection Trust group, first under Alfred Chester Beatty and later under Sir R. L. Prain, the mine developed into one of the most important undertakings of its kind in Africa.

Roast Beef Island. Small island off the coast of South West Africa, exploited for its guano deposits. It was annexed in 1867, to Cape Colony.

Robben Island. Island in Table Bay, 5 miles from the mainland, covering about 3 sq. miles. It takes its name from the numerous seals (robben in Dutch) originally found there. As early as 1591 it was visited by the English Admiral Raymond, and in 1601 by the Dutch navigator Joris van Spilbergen. When white settlement began, sheep were placed on the island and efforts made to develop a sealing and fishing industry. Because of its isolation it came to be used as a place of banishment, both for political prisoners, including the famous Xosa leader and prophet Makana (q.v.), and for the incurably ill, particularly lepers and lunatics. From 1846 onwards it was used as a station for these unfortunates, and this continued until 1931. More recently Robben Island has been a key point in the defence of Cape Town, large installations being placed there in World War II. Because of its bad record for shipwrecks there is a lighthouse on the island. Its reconversion to a convict prison was announced in 1959.

Roberts, Earl (Frederick Sleigh Roberts). British soldier, born in Cawnpore, India, in 1832. Both in the Indian Mutiny and after he had an outstanding career, being awarded the V.C. in 1858. He rose to be Commander-in-Chief in India in 1885. Promoted Field Marshal in 1895, he took command in South Africa at the end of 1899. Drawing on troops from every part of the British Empire, he reorganised the transport and supply arrangements. His first great success was the capture of General Cronje at Paardeberg with 4,000 men in February, 1900. Shortly after he took Bloemfontein, Johannesburg and Pre-

toria. After defeating General Louis Botha at Diamond Hill and driving him into the Eastern Transvaal, Roberts returned to England in October 1900. From 1900 to 1905 he was Commander-in-Chief of the British Army and took great pains to warn against German militarism. He died in 1914.

Roberts Heights. *See* VOORTREKKER-HOOGTE.

Robertson. Town in the Western Cape Province. Established in 1853 and named after the well-known minister of the Dutch Reformed Church, the Reverend Dr. William Robertson. It lies below the Langeberg, and is noted as an irrigation centre, with a large production of fruit and wine. Population: 8,166, including 3,510 Whites.

Robertson, Alfred George. Administrator of the Transvaal. Born in Natal, 1867, he was educated at Hilton College, and began his career by running a coach service to Barberton. In 1895 he settled in the Wakkerstroom district where he became a leading sheep farmer and pioneered improved methods. Elected to the Transvaal Parliament in 1907 under the Crown Colony régime, he sat in the Transvaal Provincial Council after Union and was Administrator from 1917–24. He died in 1929.

Robin (Turdidae). Belongs to a family of well-known singing birds, all ground feeders. Of these, the Cape Robin or Jan Frederick (*Cossypha caffra caffra*) is most familiar everywhere, with his white eyebrows and reddish-orange chest. As he jerks his tail up, one sees the dark central bar against the orange. The Noisy Robin or Piet-my-vrou (*Cossypha dichroa*) is brighter coloured, shyer, but sings in mimicry of many other birds. The Cape Ground Robin (*Erythropygia coryphaeus*) is a brown-grey little bird of the drier bush between Cape Town and Bloemfontein. He has white feathers in his fan tail. The Capped Wheatear (q.v.), the Chats (q.v.) and the Thrushes (q.v.) belong to the same family.

Robins, Lord (Ellis Robins). Rhodesian financier and soldier. Born at Philadelphia, U.S.A., on October 31, 1884, he studied at the University of Pennsylvania and came to Oxford as one of the original American Rhodes Scholars. In 1907 he entered journalism as assistant editor of *Everybody's* magazine, a post he retained till 1909. After a spell in politics he joined the City of London Yeomanry on the outbreak of World War I, doing military service in various theatres till 1921. He came to Rhodesia for the B.S.A. Company and made his home in that country, rising to the post of resident director and ultimately as president. During World War II he served in the East African campaign and attended the Eastern Group Conference. Acquiring British nationality, he received a knighthood in 1954 for his public service in Rhodesia and was raised to the peerage in 1958. Died July 21, 1962.

Robinson, Sir Hercules George Robert. Governor of Cape Colony. Born in 1824 in England, the son of Admiral Hercules Robinson. Went as a cadet to Sandhurst and received a commission as a lieutenant in 1844, but left the Army two years later to enter the Colonial service. His first senior post was in the West Indies in 1854, whence he was transferred in 1859 to become Governor of Hong Kong, remaining until 1865. Ceylon (1865 to 1872) and New South Wales (1872 to 1880) followed. In 1880 he became Governor of Cape Colony and High Commissioner for South Africa. Almost immediately after he was confronted with the First Boer War and the defeat at Majuba. He went to England to settle the terms of the new Convention with the South African Republic after the restoration of its independence. After this came

the scramble for Bechuanaland in 1884, when he authorised the despatch of Sir Charles Warren's occupation force. During his term of office the occupation of Mashonaland by Cecil Rhodes and his associates raised fresh diplomatic problems which were successfully dealt with. After the end of his term in 1889 he went back to England but, six years later, in 1895, was sent for a second time to the Cape as Governor, mainly to deal with the growing crisis in relations with the Boer republics. He secured the release of Dr. L. S. Jameson after the Raid in 1896, although expressing disapproval of his actions. In appreciation of his handling of the situation he was created Lord Rosmead in the same year. He died in 1897.

Robinson, Sir John. Prime Minister of Natal. Born in England in 1839, he came to Natal with his family in 1850, and in 1852 helped his father to start the *Natal Mercury* (q.v.) which is still flourishing. He continued his journalistic work, both in Natal and elsewhere, for most of his life. Entering local politics, he soon rose to prominence, and was elected to the Legislative Council, besides which he served as delegate to several Colonial conferences. For many years he worked for the grant of Responsible Government to the Colony, and when this was achieved in 1893, was appointed Premier, continuing to hold office until 1897. He died in Durban on November 4, 1903.

Robinson, Sir Joseph Benjamin. Mining magnate. Born in Cradock, Cape, in 1840, son of an 1820 settler, he began trading at Dordrecht and fought in the Basuto War of 1865. After the discovery of diamonds, he was among the first to reach the River Diggings. Attaining great wealth on the Diamond Fields, jointly with his partner, Marcus, he became a leading personality in early Kimberley, of which city he was elected Mayor in

1880, and Member of the Legislative Assembly in 1882. He was among the first to realise the possibilities of the gold discoveries in the Transvaal, first in Barberton and later on the Witwatersrand, although his claims to be the actual discoverer are unsubstantiated. His boldness in buying the farm Langlaagte for £6,000 at a time when many of his fellow-capitalists were hesitating, led him to still further prosperity and he soon attained the rank of millionaire. Among the major properties with which he was associated may be mentioned the Robinson Mine, as well as the Robinson Deep, likewise the Randfontein Estates Mine (q.v.). Throughout his life he preferred to take the Boer side, and cultivated the friendship of President Kruger. He also established his own financial concern, the Robinson South African Banking Corporation, which lasted for a number of years. Towards the end of the 19th century he settled in England, where at Dudley House, he built up a great gallery of pictures. The proposal of the Labour Government under Mr. Ramsay MacDonald to confer a peerage upon him created so much criticism that it was later withdrawn. He died in 1929. In recent years his picture collection was brought to Cape Town and displayed for a time in the South African National Gallery.

Robinson, William. Hunter and explorer. Brother of Sir J. B. Robinson (q.v.) he was born in Kent in 1820 and accompanied his parents as a settler in South Africa. Finding the life near Grahamstown uncongenial, he moved to Cradock and in 1840 trekked into the far interior. Beginning as a schoolmaster, he presently changed to elephant-hunting, and, having a very powerful physique, proved successful. Many of his trips took him into unknown areas, and he reached Lake Ngami almost immediately after David Livingstone, in 1851 and 1852. His boldest undertaking was to stand as

President for the Transvaal in 1872, when he was defeated by the Rev. T. F. Burgers. William Robinson lived to an immense age, and died as recently as 1915, when he was 95.

Rochea. *See* CRASSULA.

Rock Grunter, Chor-Chor (*Pomadasys bennetti*). Fish found in Mediterranean and on west coast of Africa southwards to Angola, and from False Bay to Natal. About 22 inches long. *See* GRUNTER.

Rock-Jumper (*Chaetops frenatus*). A striking and lively bird, belonging to the South-Western Cape Province (including the Cape Peninsula), not unlike a thrush in habits but smartly dressed in black and white coat, with deep chestnut rump. It has short wings and prefers to hop from rock to rock on its strong legs, flicking aside the leaves for insects. It nests in a hole in a rock.

Rock Lobster. South African shellfish. Differs from crayfish and crawfish (q.v.) in having three pairs of legs terminating in hooks and in being larger. Its familiar red colour comes from boiling. *See* MARINE RESOURCES.

Rock Rat (Octodentidae). Rodent about 6 inches long, found in Namaqualand, and adapted to a very dry climate. It lives on stunted vegetation, and can be easily tamed.

Rock Snake. *See* PYTHON.

Roedean School. Well-known school for girls in Parktown, Johannesburg, established in 1903 by Miss T. Lawrence and Miss K. M. Earle, who came to the Transvaal from the Roedean School in Brighton, England, with which the South African counterpart has always maintained a link.

Roella. *See* LOBELIA.

Roer. Literally a tube in Dutch. Heavy old-fashioned gun used by the Voortrekkers in hunting elephants.

Roerdomp. Afrikaans name for Cape Bittern. *See* BITTERN.

Roggeveld. Literally Rye Veld. A portion of the Karroo, particularly around Sutherland and Fraserburg, once noted for the good quality of the rye grown there. A cold bracing area.

R.O.J. Abbreviation for Regiment Onze Jan (q.v.).

Rollers (family Coraciidae). Stout, short-legged birds with strong, hooked bill and beautiful plumage of blue and lilac. Feed on insects, which they catch on the wing. Nest in holes in trees. Seldom found south of the Orange River. Name derived from habit of the European Roller (Blue Jay) of turning over in its flight.

Roman (*Chrysoblephus laticeps*). Fish found off False Bay to Natal, and also Zanzibar and Mauritius. About 20 inches long. A well-known anglers' fish. Name originally 'Rooi Man' (Red Man) on account of colour. *See* BREAM.

Roman Catholic Church. *See* CATHO-LIC CHURCH IN SOUTHERN AFRICA.

Roman-Dutch Law. The common law of South Africa; derived from the 17th century law of the Netherlands. This had developed on the foundation of Roman Law (particularly the Corpus Juris of the Emperor Justinian) introduced into the Low Countries in the days of the Caesars, but to some extent modified, especially in the fields of procedure, interpretation and contract, by local Germanic custom. In the hands of great jurists such as Voet, Grotius and others it became eminently suitable for the needs of an advancing civilisation. Introduced into Rhodesia by the pioneers, under one of the earliest proclamations; it has also replaced German Law in South West Africa. Outside South Africa, it has survived to a limited extent in the former Dutch colonies of British Guiana and Ceylon. In Holland it was replaced by the Code Napoléon, introduced at the beginning of the 19th century. *See* LAW.

Roman Rock. Isolated rock outside Simonstown in False Bay, now carry-ing a lighthouse, erected about 1860.

Rondavel. Characteristic form of South African house. Its plan is derived from that of the native hut, being circular in sections, with a thatched roof. Owing to the cheapness of its con-struction, coolness and general suit-ability to the climate, the rondavel has become a popular form of architecture and has been considerably elaborated. Its first use by Europeans was in the form of wattle and daub construction, but about 1860 the British military authorities began to build rondavels for housing troops.

Rood, Colonel Karel. South African industrialist. Born October 15, 1893, at Van Rhynsdorp, Cape Province, studied at the South African College and qualified in Law. After service in World War I he settled at Vereeniging, where in 1918 he was elected to the Town Council and later Member of Parliament. Soon afterwards he be-came interested in the Union Steel Corporation, and was made Chair-man. He played a leading part in the South African steel industry generally and in the establishment of many subsidiary enterprises.

Roodepoort-Maraisburg. Town on the western Witwatersrand, estab-lished as Roodepoort mining camp in 1888, on a farm of that name (Red Gate in Dutch), about 13 miles from Johannesburg. The progress of neigh-bouring gold mines stimulated its growth and after the South African War, in 1902, a Health Board was set up, embracing Roodepoort, Marais-burg, Florida, Delarey and Greymont, the latter being excised in 1916. The surrender of Dr. L. S. Jameson and his raiders in 1896 was the most dramatic incident in its early history, taking place at Doornkop, just south of the Durban-Roodepoort mine. In 1904 the town became a municipality. Florida, noted for its artificial lake, developed as a popular holiday and residential resort. Considerable manufacturing and general industrial activity now exists in the Roodepoort-Maraisburg area, apart from the still flourishing gold-mines. Population: 116,800, including 62,500 Whites, 1,550 Coloureds, 1,750 Asiatics, 51,000 Bantu.

Rooi Baadjie. Afrikaans name for a British soldier, literally a Red Coat. It has also been applied to a locust.

Rooibekkie. Afrikaans name for Common Waxbill. *See* WAXBILLS.

Rooibostee. *See* BUSH TEA.

Rooi-Els or **Red Alder** (*Cunonia capensis* L.). Tree up to 50 feet. Superior timber for cabinet-making. Coastal areas, Cape Province to Natal.

Rooi Fisantjie. Afrikaans name for Ruddy Waxbill. *See* WAXBILLS.

Rooi Gras or **Red Grass** (*Anthistiria imberis*). Native grass, much valued for cattle, found most plentifully in the Eastern Cape Province.

Rooigrond (Red Ground). Area in Bechuanaland, ceded over by the Bechuana chiefs in 1880's, to Boer freebooters under Adriaan de la Rey and by him converted partly into the Republic of Stellaland (q.v.) and of Goshen (q.v.). Cecil Rhodes finally secured the annexation of the territory to the British Empire in 1885.

Rooiklossiegras (*Fingerhuthia africana* Lehm.). Fodder grass. Griqualand West and Karroo.

Rooikrantz. Popular name for one of the Australian wattles, with small Mimosa flowers. Imported to bind the sand of the Cape Flats, it is today unfortunately ousting much of the indigenous mountain vegetation. A straggling barky tree, often twisted but seldom growing tall.

Rooinek. Jocular name for an Englishman, used in early times in South Africa. Supposed to be derived from the allegedly red complexion of English immigrants. On the same basis the English are sometimes referred to as Rooibaard (Red Beard) or Rooibaadjies (Red Coats) from the old military uniforms.

Rooivalk. Afrikaans name for South African Kestrel. *See* EAGLES.

Rooke, Daphne. South African author. Born at Boksburg, Transvaal, as Daphne Pizzey, she attended Durban Girls' High School and in 1946 settled for a while in Australia, where she married, but returned to Natal in 1954. She wrote *Mittee*, a novel which became a worldwide success, also *Rattoons* and other stories, several of which were translated into foreign languages. Her themes are largely derived from life in Natal and Zululand.

Rooney, Bishop John. Catholic prelate in South Africa. Born in Ireland in 1844, he came to the Cape in 1867, and in 1886 became a bishop. He was noted for his vigorous activity in the mission field. He died in 1927.

Roos, Gideon Daniel. Director-General of the South African Broadcasting Corporation. Born at Worcester, Cape Province, on October 28, 1909, and educated at Stellenbosch, he went to Oxford as a Rhodes Scholar and also studied at Leyden in Holland. Like his father, Paul Roos (q.v.), he was a distinguished rugby player, gaining his 'blue' for Oxford. Although called to the Bar in 1933 he preferred to join the original African Broadcasting Company, and when in 1936 this became the S.A.B.C. (q.v.) he continued in its service. In 1937 he helped to organise the Afrikaans programme and in 1942 was made Secretary of the Corporation, of which he became Director-General in 1948. He resigned in 1961 to become South African director of the Performing Rights Society.

Roos, Paul Johannes. Captain of first South African international rugby team. Born near Stellenbosch in 1880, and educated at Wellington and Stellenbosch. Having qualified as a teacher, he found his first post at Rustenberg, Transvaal, in 1902. Ever since 1897, in his college days, he had been an outstanding rugby player, and when, in 1903, he returned to Stellenbosch, he was soon one of the best-known men in the game. In 1906 he captained the first South African overseas rugby team, the 'Spring-Bokken' or Springboks, and gained an almost unbroken series of victories in Britain and France. He became head-master of a boys school, was a leading rugby administrator, was elected to Parliament and died in 1948.

Roos, Tielman Johannes de Villiers. Deputy-Premier and Nationalist Leader. Born in Cape Town, 1879, he was educated at the South African College and qualified for the Bar. In 1902 he reached Pretoria, where he built up a good practice. Although interested in Het Volk (q.v.) his rise to prominence came after Union, when he became one of the first supporters of General J. B. M. Hertzog, and in 1915 was elected to Parliament for Lichtenburg, Transvaal. He helped to defend General Christiaan de Wet at his trial after the 1914 Rebellion. By virtue of his eloquence, extremism and humour, Tielman Roos became one of the best-known figures in South Africa, with the nickname of 'The Lion of the North,' the chief lieutenant and in-evitable successor of General Hertzog. When the latter came to power in 1924 Roos was Deputy-Premier and Minis-ter of Justice. As such he did good work in reforming the Liquor Act, the Companies Act and other important legislation. Owing to failing health he retired from politics, 1929, and accep-ted a seat on the Appellate Division bench in Bloemfontein. During the Gold Standard crisis of 1932 and ensuing political deadlock he decided to return to politics, resigned his seat as a judge, and started a new political party. This resulted in the reconcilia-tion of General Smuts with General Hertzog and the foundation of the United South African National Party. Tielman Roos found himself left 'out in the cold.' His health deteriorated still further and he died on March 28, 1935.

Rorke's Drift. Trading post in Natal, on the Buffalo River, famous in South African history on account of its defence during the Zulu War. After their defeat of the British forces at Isandhlwana, the Zulu armies descen-ded upon Rorke's Drift on January 22, 1879. They found the buildings forti-fied and held by 130 men of the 24th Regiment, commanded by Lieutenant Chard and Lieutenant Bromhead. Attacked by 4,000 Zulus, the tiny force, taking shelter behind biscuit boxes and bags of mealies, held firm, and despite the fact that the hospital, with 35 wounded, caught fire, they saved the inmates and beat off the attack. The Zulus lost over 350 dead and many more wounded, while the defenders' casualties came to 17 dead and 10 wounded. Several V.C.s were awarded to the garrison of Rorke's Drift.

Rose-Innes, Sir James. Chief Jus-tice of the Union of South Africa. Born in Grahamstown in January 1855, he was educated at Gill College, Somerset East, and passed his legal examinations at the University of the Cape of Good Hope in 1877. The following year he was admitted to the Bar and, combining practice with journalism, soon became well known. Entering the Cape Parliament in 1884 as member for Victoria East, he was elected for the Cape Division in 1888, took silk in 1889, and became Attorney-General in Cecil Rhodes' ministry in 1890. Three years later he resigned, in order to become President of the Political Association, and held a watching brief on behalf of the Imperial Government during the trial of the Reform prisoners in the Transvaal. After serving as Attorney-General of Cape Colony from 1900 to 1902, he was appointed Chief Justice of the Transvaal, which position he held until Union. Upon the founding of the Appellate Division in 1910, he became Senior Puisne Judge, and, upon the death of Lord De Villiers in 1914, Chief Justice. He retired in 1927, and died in 1942. Apart from his legal eminence, he was known as a strong Liberal and negrophile in politics.

Rosemary, Wild or **Kapokbossie** (*Eriocephalus umbellatus* D.C.). Low shrub. Flower-heads becoming very woolly with age.

Rosendal. Village in the Orange Free State, founded in 1911 in the Wittebergen Range near Basutoland. Population: 730, including 286 Whites.

Rosetta. Mountain resort in Natal, near the Drakensberg, noted for trout fishing. Population: 650, including 100 Whites.

Rosmead, Lord *See* SIR HERCULES GEORGE ROBERT ROBINSON.

Rosmead Junction. Originally known as Middelburg Road, established in 1880 and named after Lord Rosmead (Sir Hercules Robinson), Governor of Cape Colony. Population: 1,340, including 388 Whites.

Ross, The Hon. Hamilton. South African mercantile pioneer. Born in Scotland in 1775, he came to South Africa as an officer in the Scots Guards at the time of the first British occupation, and won the distinction of hoisting the Union Jack upon the capture of the Cape. Having married a South African girl, he spent some time in India, but made his home in Cape Town in 1803. Three years later he opened the famous firm of Hamilton Ross & Co., soon one of the most important in the country. As one of the founders of the Commercial

Exchange, as a pioneer in the export of wine, as a sponsor of one of the earliest banks, as a Member of the Legislative Council from 1834 to 1849, and as a leader in the Anti-Convict Agitation (q.v.) of 1849, he was one of the leading public figures in the Colony. His manifold efforts at stimulating development included road-building, an active share in the foundation of the South African College, the founding of the Cape Town Chamber of Commerce, the ownership of his own merchantmen and many other achievements. He died on February 16, 1853.

Rosslyn. Industrial township near Pretoria, established near the 'Border Industries' programme (q.v.).

Rossouw. Village in Cape Province. Population 450, including 100 Whites.

Rotary Clubs. The first Rotary Club on the African continent was formed in Johannesburg in 1920 and received its charter in May, 1921. During the first 3 years clubs were formed in Durban, Port Elizabeth, Pretoria and Cape Town, in that order. By 1960 there were over 80 clubs in South Africa and some 40 in Rhodesia, Kenya and Uganda; total membership in South Africa, Rhodesia, Zambia and South-West Africa is about 3,000. There is no club in Mozambique, but clubs have been formed in Luanda, Angola and in Madagascar. Only one member can represent his classification, but classifications can be subdivided. The object of the clubs is to encourage the principle of service in all trades and occupations, and to maintain high ethical standards. Each club is autonomous in its governance.

Roteiro. A famous document, kept by a member of Vasco da Gama's first expedition round the Cape of Good Hope in 1497, and probably the most accurate record of the expedition. Little is known of the author, who was a sailor. The Roteiro was translated from Portuguese into English and published by the Hakluyt Society.

Rothman, Miem E. Afrikaans authoress. Born near Swellendam, Cape, 1875. Began writing and in 1922 joined the staff of *Die Burger* with whom she remained until 1928. Acquired national fame through her homely but well-told stories, signed 'M.E.R.' She was awarded a Honorary Doctorate at Stellenbosch University, 1950, and the Hertzog Prize for Afrikaans Literature in 1953.

Rotten Stomach. A disease afflicting ostriches, causing inflammation of the stomach, due to the presence of the Palisade Worm (*Strongylus douglasi*).

Roupell, Arabella. South African artist. Born in 1817 as Arabella Piggott, she married an official of the English East India Company, T. B. Roupell of Madras. During the 2 years (1843–5) they spent at the Cape, Mrs. Roupell produced a collection of magnificent colour plates, which were published in a large folio in 1849. She lived to the immense age of 97 and died as recently as 1914.

Roux, General Paul Hendrik. Clergyman and soldier. Born in Hopetown, Cape Province, in 1862, he was educated at Paarl and proceeded to Stellenbosch Theological Seminary in 1884. After completing his studies in Europe, he was appointed to the Dutch Reformed congregation at Senekal, O.F.S., in 1891, where he enjoyed great respect. During the South African War he decided to enlist as a burgher, instead of as a chaplain, and rose to be a general. He was taken prisoner in the O.F.S. in 1900, sent to Ceylon and remained in exile for some time after the peace. He returned to resume his work as a minister at Vredefort, moving to Beaufort West in 1905, where he died in 1911.

Rouxville: 1. Town in the Orange Free State, founded in 1863 and named after the Reverend Pieter Roux, the

earliest visiting minister of the Dutch Reformed Church. Farming centre. Scene of fighting in the South African War. Population: 3,228, including 1,000 Whites.
2. Northern suburb of Johannesburg.

Roworth, Edward. South African artist. Born in Lancashire on June 21, 1880, he settled in the Cape in 1902 and soon gained popularity on account of his representations of old homesteads, oak trees and many other characteristic local subjects. His most famous painting was done in 1909 and showed the members of the National Convention (q.v.). From 1937 to 1949 he was Professor of Fine Art at the Michaelis School in the University of Cape Town. In 1953 he retired entirely from his teaching work to concentrate on painting. He died in 1964.

Royal Durban Light Infantry. South African military unit, founded on April 10, 1873. Was on local defence in Zulu War, 1879, fought in the South African War, 1899–1902, the Zulu Rebellion of 1906, World War I in South West Africa and in World War II in North Africa, being part of the garrison captured by the enemy at Tobruk. It later served with the 6th South African Armoured Division in Italy.

Royal Natal Carbineers. South African military unit, founded on January 15, 1855. Fought against Bushmen in 1850's and 1860's, in Langalibalele Rebellion in 1873, in Zulu War, 1879, South African War, 1899–1902, Zulu Rebellion, 1906, World War I (South West Africa), in World War II (Abyssinia, North Africa and Italy). Sergeant G. M. Quentin Smythe won V.C. in 1942.

Royal Society of South Africa. Founded in 1877 as the South African Philosophical Society, and renamed in 1909. Its headquarters are in Cape Town. Membership is open only to professional scientists of standing. Transactions are regularly published.

R.P.K. Abbreviation for Regiment President Kruger (q.v.).

R.P.S. Abbreviation for Regiment President Steyn (q.v.).

R.S. Abbreviation for Regiment Smuts (q.v.).

R.S.W.D. Abbreviation for Regiment Suid-Westelike Distrikte (q.v.).

R.T.M. Abbreviation for Regiment Tobie Muller (q.v.).

Ruacana Falls. Large but little-known waterfall on the Cunene River (q.v.) on the border of South West Africa and Angola. The cataract, which is V-shaped, is 352 feet high and 760 feet wide at its crest.

Rubbervale. Hamlet in the Eastern Transvaal on railway from Messina to Komatipoort. Established about 1909 during the world rubber boom, when hopes were entertained of developing supplies of wild rubber in these parts. Farming and native labour recruiting centre.

Rubber Vine (*Landolphia kirkii* Dyer). Climbing shrub yielding excellent rubber. Delagoa Bay.

Rube, Charles Ernest. Diamond and gold mining magnate. Born in France in 1852. He reached Kimberley in 1876 and became manager of the French Diamond Mining Co. Later joined the firm of Wernher, Beit & Co. of whom he became a partner. He died in 1914.

Rubie, John Fonthill. South African lawyer. Born in England he was called to the Bar in 1883, and after the South African War began practice in the Transvaal. In 1902 he became a member of the special Criminal Court in Pretoria, which preceded the establishment of the Supreme Court. Later, in 1904, he was President of the Special Criminal Court for Swaziland and the legal member of the Swaziland Concessions Commission. He died on October 14, 1907.

Rubusana, Reverend Dr. Walter B. First Bantu member of the Cape Provincial Council. Born on February 21, 1858, at Mnandi near Somerset East, Cape Province, and educated at Lovedale. He became a teacher and acted as assistant to the Rev. R. Birt, at Peelton Mission Station before he was ordained as a Congregational Minister in 1884. In 1905 he joined the Native Deputation to His Majesty's Government, and he presided over the First Native Convention in 1909. He was elected as member of the Cape Provincial Council for Tembuland in 1910 and sat until 1914. He wrote a *History of South Africa from the Native Standpoint* for which he was awarded an honorary doctorate in Philosophy by McKinley University in the U.S.A. He was the first Bantu to serve as Moderator at the Midland Missionary Committee of the Congregational Union of South Africa. He died in 1936.

Rudd, Charles Dunell. Partner of Cecil John Rhodes. Born at Hanworth Hall, Norfolk, on October 22, 1844, he was educated at Harrow and Cambridge, being a distinguished athlete. At the age of 22 he reached the Cape, in 1866, and spent several years hunting with John Dunn (q.v.). One of the earliest comers to Kimberley, he met Cecil John Rhodes, and it was through each buying a quarter claim in the De Beers Mine that the partnership was originally established. That was the first step towards what became ultimately De Beers Consolidated Mines. In 1883 Rudd was elected to the Cape Parliament, where he represented Kimberley for five years and was largely responsible for the introduction of effective legislation to stop I.D.B. He had made his way to the Witwatersrand, and became one of the main figures in the foundation of the Goldfields of South Africa (later on the Consolidated Goldfields). On behalf of Cecil Rhodes, he proceeded to Matabeleland in 1888 and secured the concession from Lobengula on which the grant of the Charter to the British South Africa Company was based. Some time after, he retired from business and settled in England. He died in 1916.

Rudder Fish, Blue Fish or Butter Bream (*Kyphosus fuscus*). Found from False Bay to Zululand, and Indian Seas to Pacific. About 28 inches long.

It has a neat, compressed body and even scales. Brown back, silvery below. Good eating.

Ruff (*Philomachus pugnax*). A large wader, very like a Greenshank (q.v.) but for its medium, straight bill, stone-coloured plumage with darker markings, and chrome legs. Its ruff shows only in the European breeding season. *See* WADER.

RUGBY FOOTBALL IN SOUTH AFRICA

by

R. K. STENT

Cape Times, Cape Town

SOUTH Africa's place in rugby football is established. Not only have past Springbok teams, touring overseas, proved nearly invincible, but the type of game played has usually given pleasure to spectators. Yet in recent years there has been a falling off in the high standard set by such sides as the famous (original) 1906 Springboks, who toured the British Isles, and their successors—the 1912, 1931 and 1951 teams—and 1958 saw France win one and draw the other of two Test matches played in South Africa.

However, the Springbok side which toured the British Isles in 1960 was of an exceptionally high standard, and increased the great record: that of the 20 international matches played during the five tours of the British Isles, South Africa have won 18, drawn one and lost but one—the very first Test of all, against Scotland in 1906.

The origins of rugby in South Africa have been traced to matches played between regiments of the British Army engaged in the earlier Kaffir and Zulu Wars, but no details are known. It is generally accepted that rugby, as we know it, sprang from a near-relation called the 'Winchester Game' which was introduced to the Diocesan College, Rondebosch, by Canon G. Ogilvie, when he came from Winchester College to be headmaster of 'Bishops.'

Several old boys from this school helped to form the first two rugby clubs in the Cape Peninsula—Hamiltons (1875) and Villagers (1876) and these two old rivals recently played their 200th match! The only other claim to have started rugby in this country comes from Swellendam, in the South-West Cape, where the game is believed to have flourished in 1865. A great fire destroyed the documents which would have provided proof.

The arrival in South Africa in the early 1880's of the famous English international, W. H. Milton (later Sir William) gave the game a fillip. In 1883 the Western Province Rugby Union was formed, to be followed a few months later by the Eastern Province Union. The Griqualand West Union was formed in 1886 and the Transvaal in 1889. By this date the game was well under way in Natal.

When the first British team came to South Africa (W. E. Maclagan's 1891 side), the tour was regarded as mainly an 'educational' one. However, South Africa lost the first Test by only a goal and a try (which then totalled four points) to nil, so early aptitude was apparent.

In 1896, after another British side had won three of the four Tests, South Africa gained her first international victory—a 5-nil win at Newlands.

B. H. (Fairy) Heatlie captained South Africa that day, and today he is still remembered as one of the 'greats' of the game. In 1903 came the third British side to South Africa and, after two draws, they lost the third Test, to give South Africa her first 'rubber' win. The score was 8–nil.

In 1906 Paul Roos took the first Springboks to Britain, the 'characters' in this team being the four three-quarters from Stellenbosch—J. A. Loubser, Japie Krige, 'Boy' de Villiers and A. C. Stegmann, known as the Thin Red Line, because of their maroon Stellenbosch jerseys.

Meanwhile, the New Zealand All Blacks were also touring triumphantly, but the first trial of strength with the Springboks occurred only after World War I, when Theo Pienaar took a side to New Zealand that won one, drew one and lost the only other Test, so that honours were even.

They were even again, at two Tests all, in 1928 when Maurice Brownlie's All Black team came to South Africa, but the Springboks gained first blood in 1937, winning the second and third Tests after losing the first one.

The rivalry was renewed in 1949, after World War II, when the Springboks won all four Tests in South Africa, but New Zealand had her own back, with a 3–1 victory, in 1956. In the meantime, a British side (Robin Thompson's 1955 Lions) had shared the honours with two Tests both in South Africa. In 1958 came the sensational defeat by France.

South Africa regained the upper hand over their traditional rivals, New Zealand, by winning the 1960 series of Tests in South Africa by two matches to one, with one drawn. The games were dourly fought and full of interest, without providing much spectacle. The Springboks' strategy was less rigid than the steam-rolling methods of the All Black forwards. The position was all square and one to go and South

Africa won the last game at Port Elizabeth by 8 points to 3. A curious feature of the series was that South Africa dropped their full back captain, Roy Dryburgh, after the defeat at Newlands and replaced him with 23-year-old Avril Malan. Malan also captained the Springbok team that sailed for the British Isles later in the year. This team proved to be almost invincible for they beat Wales 3–0, Ireland 8–3, England 5–0, Scotland 12–5 and drew with France 0–0. In fact, during the whole tour they were defeated only once, by the Barbarians.

Following the defeat by France in 1958, South African Rugby was at the cross-roads. Frank Mellish, Chairman of Selectors, evolved an improved system of trials, which incorporated Junior Springbok games and short tours. In 1959 a Junior Springbok team visited the Argentine, winning all its games. The first team to come to South Africa on a short tour was Scotland in 1960, being defeated 18–10 at Port Elizabeth. The tour by the 1960 All Blacks followed, and South Africa avenged the defeat in the New Zealand Test series of 1956. This time the Springboks won two tests, drew one and lost one. South Africa was ready for the tour of Britain and France, and played 34 games in all.

They lost only one, to the Barbarians, and were held to a pointless draw by France in Paris. Two teams to arrive on short tours in 1961 were the Irish and the Australians. The Springboks won the Tests, and the series against the Lions in 1962 in the tour which followed. But in 1963 Australia made history on a Springbok tour by drawing a Test series for the first time.

In 1964 more rugby history was made. A Welsh team made the first overseas tour as an individual unit. It played four games in South Africa and lost the Test match to the Springboks in Durban by 29 points to 5 on May 23, 1964. The Welsh tour was followed by a second visit to South Africa by a

French team which arrived in July 1964 and played five games. This included a Test match at Springs on July 25, when, for the second time in French Rugby history, they beat the Springboks on South African soil—by 8 points to 6.

1965 will be remembered as a black year in South African rugby. The Springboks embarked on a short tour of Ireland and Scotland in the out-of-season period (for South Africa) of April, immediately after a long hot summer. They played five games, drawing one and losing four. These included the international games against Ireland and Scotland. Ireland beat South Africa for the first time in history 9–6, and Scotland defeated South Africa for the second time on Scottish soil 8–5. The points record for the short tour was: 37 for, 53 against.

There followed the major tour of Australia and New Zealand. For the first time in history Australia defeated South Africa on Australian soil. Australia won the first Test in Sydney 18–11 and the second in Brisbane 12–8.

Four Test matches were played in New Zealand, South Africa winning the third at Christchurch 19–16 after a great second half recovery. New Zealand won the remaining three, the first at Wellington 6–3, the second at Dunedin 13–0 and the fourth at Auckland 20–3.

For the first time in history a rugby team from the Argentine toured South Africa in 1965. They were called the Pumas and did well to beat Southern Universities and the Junior Springboks, but they lost heavily to S.A. Country Districts XV. South Africa reciprocated by sending a mixed team to South America in 1966. The team, which included seven Springboks, won all 13 games.

The Australian Wallabies' tour of South Africa in 1969 was a complete victory for South Africa, the scores of the four Test matches being 30-9, 16-9, 11-3 and 19-8.

Less successful, however, was the Springboks' 1969-70 tour of Britain, for, apart from anti-South African demonstrations, they were defeated by Scotland 6-3, and England 11-8, and they drew with Ireland 8-8 and Wales 6-6.

South Africa's record against the major rugby countries now reads:

	P	W	D	L	F	A
Scotland . .	8	5	0	3	104	38
Ireland . .	8	6	1	1	124	48
Wales . .	8	7	1	0	95	22
England . .	6	5	0	1	40	20
France . .	6	2	2	2	75	28
New Zealand .	26	13	2	11	222	222
Great Britain .	28	14	4	10	290	198
Australia . .	25	18	0	7	376	204

Ruggens. Literally backs or ridges. Closely-packed hills in rolling country, which occurs in various parts of the Cape, including Caledon and Bredasdorp. They are usually fertile. Area also known as Ruggensveld.

Ruigte Vallei. Site of major dam for Orange River Scheme (q.v.), five miles from Norvals Pont. A wall 200 feet high is to be capable of being raised to 390 feet.

Rundi Ruin (also known as **Lundi Ruin**). Ancient ruin on the left bank of the Lundi River, between Victoria and Tuli in Rhodesia. The building is 54 feet in diameter and stands on a granite hill.

Rupert, Dr. Anton Edward. South African industrialist. Born at Graaff-Reinet on October 4, 1916. Studied at the University of Pretoria and became a lecturer in Chemistry at the Pretoria Technical College. In 1939 he began manufacturing snuff in Johannesburg and started the Voorbrand Tobacco Co. Out of this developed the giant Rembrandt Tobacco Corporation (q.v.) with its world-wide activities. Also contributes greatly to the encouragement of art and education in South Africa. In 1966 became Honorary Industrial Adviser to the Lesotho Government.

Rusape (also spelt **Rusapi**). Town in Rhodesia, east of Salisbury. Headquarters of the Makone district. Farming and administrative centre. Population: 1,700, including 440 Whites.

Rusawi School. Public school for boys at Marandellas, Rhodesia.

Rusbank. Literally resting bench. Frequently found in old Dutch houses, the seat being made of interwoven thongs of leather or hide.

Russell, Sir Alexander Fraser. Chief Justice of Southern Rhodesia. Born in Cape Town, 1876, he was educated at the South African College, from where he went to Cambridge and was called to the Bar in 1901. Commencing practice in Cape Town, he gained considerable success, until in 1915 he became a judge of the Supreme Court of Southern Rhodesia. After the establishment of Responsible Government he rose to Chief Justice in 1931. He died in 1952.

Rustenburg: 1. Town in Transvaal, founded in 1850 and so called, according to the Rev. Lion Cachet, 'because the Boers had to suffer less here from the attacks of the natives,' i.e. it was a place of rest (Rust in Dutch). Near by President Kruger had his farm, and a monument testifies to his association with the place. During the first British occupation of the Transvaal in 1877, a fort was erected, within which the garrison was besieged during the 1880–1881 War, but withstood the attack. Some of the earliest sittings of the Transvaal Volksraad, as far back as 1852, took place in Rustenburg. Fighting occurred round there in the South African War. Today the town is noted for its large tobacco industry, citrus and other fruit production, and sub-tropical agriculture generally, which is aided by the extensive irrigation system. Population: 36,300, including 19,860 Whites.
2. Famous old Cape Town mansion in Rondebosch. Origins of the estate go back to the 17th century, when the forerunner of the present building was used by early governors as a country-house. Farm now forms part of Groote Schuur estate, but the house belongs to Rondebosch Girls' High School, which is usually called Rustenburg.

Rutile. Ore of Titanium found in South West Africa near Omaruru, formerly exploited. *See* ILMENITE.

Rysmier. *See* BUSHMAN RICE.

S

S.A.A. Abbreviation for South African Artillery (q.v.).

S.A.A.F. Abbreviation for South African Air Force (q.v.).

S.A.B.C. Abbreviation for South African Broadcasting Corporation (q.v.).

Saaidam. System of irrigation practised in parts of South Africa, particularly in the North-Western Cape along the Zak River (q.v.) and Fish River near Kotjeskolk. The rivers have narrow channels, overflow their banks and fill temporary dams which, when the waters recede, are planted with crops, particularly wheat. Very heavy crops are produced, the Zak River Estates being particularly successful.

Saasveld. Old Dutch homestead at Cape Town, originally erected in the 17th century and occupied by the Van Oudtshoorn family. Demolished in 1953, its façade and other important features being preserved and re-erected at Fransch Hoek 10 years later.

Sabi River (not to be confused with Sabie in the Transvaal). Important river in Rhodesia, 400 miles long, rising near Marandellas, its principal tributaries being the Mundi and Odzi Rivers. Flows southward through undeveloped but potentially rich country, makes a turn and enters Mozambique territory, where it is called the Save, entering the sea near Mambone. Irrigation and agricultural projects are under way in the Sabi River valley. Communications have been improved by the Birchenough Bridge, one of the largest of its kind in the world.

Sabie. Township in the Eastern Transvaal, in the Drakensberg foothills and overlooked by Mount Anderson, 7,651 feet, among the highest points in the Province. Name is derived from a native word meaning 'Sand.' Established as a gold mining camp in 1886, it still attracts prospectors. Hydroelectric power station set up there by the Electricity Supply Commission. Leading forestry centre. Population: 5,420, including 1,100 Whites.

Sable Antelope (*Hippotragus niger*). Known to the Afrikaner as the Swart Witpens, or 'Black-White-Stomach' on account of its markings. This antelope, one of the largest and handsomest of its species, can grow to a height at the shoulder of nearly 5 feet. It is found in the Kruger National Park, in Rhodesia and in Mozambique, where it usually grazes in herds of up to 50. The Sable Antelope can be very dangerous when wounded and is attacked by few animals except lions. A dark, reddish-brown coat and white rump, with magnificent back-curved horns in both male and female.

S.A.C.M. Abbreviation for South African Corps of Marines (q.v.).

S.A.C. of C. Abbreviation for South African Corps of Chaplains (q.v.).

S.A.C. of M.P. Abbreviation for South African Corps of Military Police (q.v.).

S.A.C. of S. Abbreviation for South African Corps of Signals (q.v.).

SACS. *See* SOUTH AFRICAN COLLEGE.

Saddle-Bill (*Ephippiorhynchus senegalensis*). A very handsome black-and-white tropical bird, rare in South Africa, found chiefly on the rivers in the Kruger Park, where it roosts in pairs on high trees, or flies with its great white wings slowly moving. The 'saddle' is a yellow plate overlying the top of the bill. *See* STORKS.

S.A.E.C. Abbreviation for South African Engineer Corps (q.v.).

Saffron-Wood or **Safraanhout** (*Eleodendron oroceum* D.C.). Tree up to 40 feet. Wood hard, suitable for furniture. Eastern districts of Cape Province.

Safmarine. Popular name given to the South African Marine Corporation Limited, a South African-owned shipping company, with its head office in Cape Town. Established in 1946 with the collaboration of the late Dr. H. J. van der Bijl (q.v.) and Henry D. Mercer, Chairman of the States Marine Corporation in the U.S.A., with 3 'Victory' ships, it began a monthly service to the Cape. Further capital was secured in 1959 from the Industrial Development Corporation (q.v.) and in 1961 Safmarine took over control of the Springbok Line from the British and Commonwealth Shipping Co. Ltd. Two of the largest ships of the Union Castle Line, the *Transvaal Castle* and *Bloemfontein Castle*, were taken over by Safmarine and renamed *S.A. Vaal* and *S.A. Oranje*. Safmarine today operates 30 modern ships, totalling 632,983 tons, with another 214,250 under construction, including two 203,000-ton tankers, making a total of 1,050,233 tons. Services are run to America, Europe, Japan and the Pacific.

Sail-Fish (*Histiophorus gladius*). One of the large sword-fish found in Indian seas. About 12½ feet long. Blue back and silver underneath, with long marlin, or spiked nose, and very high dorsal fin. Feeds on shoal fish, such as Mackerel, and is one of the anglers' 'big game.'

St. Aidan's College. Roman Catholic public school for boys in Grahamstown. Founded by Rt. Rev. Bishop Ricards in 1876; run by the Society of Jesus.

St. Andrew's College. Founded by Bishop Armstrong in Grahamstown, 1855, with high school and university department. The latter was given up upon the founding of Rhodes University College in 1904. Noted for its fine buildings. St. Andrew's is entitled to a special Rhodes Scholarship for its boys.

St. Augustine's. Mission station in Zululand, near Nqutu. Succeeded an early outpost of the Anglican Church, set up at Kwa Magwaza, and destroyed in 1879 during the Zulu War. Was built, at cost of £7,000, by Archdeacon Charles Johnson. The church holds 2,000, being one of the largest in Southern Africa. The name derived from the North African Saint Augustine of Hippo.

St. Croix Island. Named by Bartholomew Diaz, who landed there in 1486. Lies off the mouth of the Swartkops River, five miles north of Port Elizabeth. Rises to a height of 195 feet, consisting mostly of rock.

St. George's College. Boys' public school in Salisbury, Rhodesia, established by Jesuit Fathers in 1896.

St. John's College. Anglican school for boys in Johannesburg, founded in 1898, by the Reverend John T. Darragh, Vicar of St. Mary's. Buildings were in the centre of the city until 1906, when they were removed to Houghton Estate where preparatory and secondary departments were built, designed by Sir Herbert Baker.

St. John's River. *See* UMZIMVUBU RIVER.

St. Leger, Frederick York. Journalist and co-founder of the *Cape Times*. Born, 1836, in Limerick, Ireland, studied at Cambridge and reached the Cape in 1856, as headmaster of St. Andrew's College, Grahamstown. Worked on the Diamond Fields, then helped to found the *Cape Times* in 1876 and was editor until 1891. He

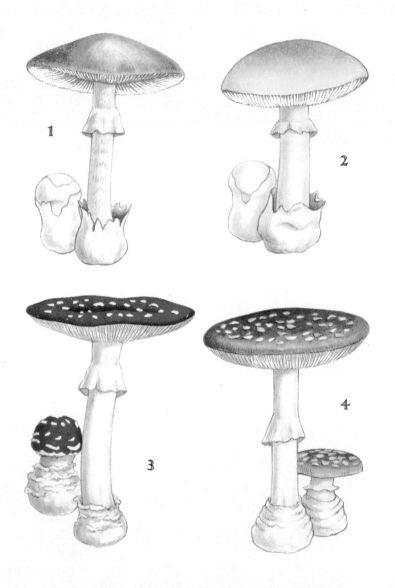

PLATE IX: FOUR POISONOUS SOUTH AFRICAN FUNGI

1. *Amanita phalloides* (Death Cup). 2. *Amanita capensis* (Cape Death Cup).
3. *Amanita muscaria* (Fly Agaric). 4. *Amanita pantherina* (Panther).
(For detailed caption see end of article 'Mushrooms and Fungi'.)

entered Parliament in 1898 and died in 1901.

St. Marks. Village in Eastern Cape Province. Population: 70, including 30 Whites.

Saint-Pierre, Jacques Henri Bernardin de. French traveller and author. Born in Le Havre in 1737, became a military engineer, served in Russia and France before retiring from the Army to write. In 1768 stationed in Mauritius (The Isle of France), and on the way there and back visited Cape Town. His *Voyage à l'Ile de France*, issued in 1773, contains a famous early account of the Cape. Also wrote the novel, *Paul et Virginie*, about Mauritius, which became a classic. Honoured by Napoleon, he died in 1814.

Sakabula

Sakabula, Kaffer Vink or Long-tailed Widow-Bird (*Diatropura progne*). One of the most famous South African birds, belonging to the Weaver family (q.v.). Males in breeding dress sail across the veld with their long tails streaming behind. Polygamous; common from Eastern Province northward, wherever there is long grass for nesting. The male of all widow-birds guards the nest conspicuously while his small brown wives conceal themselves. *See* WEAVERS.

Sak River. *See* ZAK RIVER.

Saldanha. Village on shores of Saldanha Bay (q.v.). Population: 3,630, including 1,000 Whites.

Saldanha, Antonio da. Portuguese navigator in command of a squadron of the fleet, sent from Lisbon to the East in 1503. He named Table Mountain and was probably the first white man to climb it. (He went by the Platteklip route.) Table Bay was called for over a century the 'Watering Place of Saldanha,' the name being transferred later to the present Saldanha Bay.

Saldanha Bay. Large inlet on the south-west coast of the Cape Province. Situated about 55 miles north of Table Bay, it is far safer and larger than the latter and but for the lack of water, only remedied in recent years, would probably have become the site of the first European settlement in South Africa. Efforts have been repeatedly made to develop it as a port, and at times of great pressure it has provided a valuable alternative to Table Bay docks. Because of its strategic importance Saldanha Bay has figured in many naval campaigns. The original Dutch outpost set up in 1666 was seized by the French in that year and again in 1670. In 1781 the French Admiral de Suffren planned its capture, and the Dutch fleet surrendered there after the British attack on the Cape in 1796. During the American

Civil War the famous Confederate raider *Alabama* (q.v.) used it for a short while as a base. Its convenience for berthing ships unable to enter overcrowded Table Bay led to the foundation of a company which planned a railway and further improvements. Development however, has been slow, although progress has been made at Langebaan and other centres of the fishing and whaling industries. In World War II Saldanha Bay was used as a place of assembly for convoys and since then a Naval Training Gymnasium has been set up there by the South African authorities.

Salem. Village in the Eastern Cape Province, established by 1820 settlers under Reverend William Shaw, who here set up the first Sunday School and Methodist Church in South Africa. Name in Hebrew means 'Peace.' Population: 900, including 150 Whites.

Salisbury. Capital and largest city of Rhodesia. Called after Lord Salisbury, Prime Minister of Britain. It was founded on September 12, 1890, the day the Pioneer Column (q.v.) arrived and hoisted the flag over present Cecil Square. It was intended to establish the city below Mount Hampden, but Harari Koppie was erroneously selected. Was known as Fort Salisbury, until in 1897 it became a municipality and was called Salisbury. Its altitude, 4,850 feet, gives Salisbury a healthy climate. Population (urban area) 324,800, including 88,000 Europeans and 230,000 Africans, 6,800 Asians and Coloured (figures include smaller communities in the neighbourhood, such as Greendale, Hatfield, Highlands, Mabelreign, Meyrick Park, Mount Pleasant, etc.). The University College of Rhodesia (opened in 1957 by the Queen Mother), the Archives, etc., are situated here, and it is the seat of the Government and the Rhodesian Parliament. It is the centre of the Rhodesian tobacco industry with a turnover of £20,000,000 a year, the sales floors being a popular attraction in normal times. Manufacturing industries include textiles, foodstuffs, fertilisers, flour-milling, radio, concrete, footwear, chemicals, etc.

Salisbury Island. Situated in Durban Bay and named after H.M.S. *Salisbury*, which brought the earliest British forces to Natal. As a South African naval base during World War II it was linked to the mainland by a causeway, and after the war was used to accommodate the University College for Indians (q.v.).

Salmon-Bass, Kabeljou, Cob or Cape Cod (*Otolinthus ruber*). Well-known fish found from Walvis Bay to Delagoa Bay, Mauritius and Madagascar. In England it is known as Meagre or Maigre, and as the Jew-fish (Jewel Fish) because of its shiny 'ear-bones.' Very good eating. South African angling record for length is well over 6 feet.

Salmon, Cape. *See* GEELBEK.

Salmon, Rock (*Lutianus gembra*). Fish found in Indian Seas, extending to Natal and East London. About 24 inches long. *See* SNAPPER.

Salt. Salt pans of Southern Africa have always been used as 'licks' by wild animals. Natives have sometimes even used salt as currency. The 'Panneveld' of the Northern Cape was developed by early settlers. Salt is produced commercially near Jacobsdal, O.F.S., Port Elizabeth, Vryburg, etc., and near Cape Cross in South West Africa.

Salting. A South African colloquial expression applied in two senses: (1) A salted horse is one that has survived horse-sickness and is therefore resistant to this disease. (2) Salting a mine is fraudulently introducing gold or other precious metals into barren rock by loading a gun with the metal and firing it against the ore, and in other ways.

Salting barren soil with diamonds is an equally serious legal offence.

Salt River, rises near Riebeek's Kasteel near Malmesbury, flows through that town, reaching the sea at Table Bay. Flow is today erratic. Also an industrial suburb of Cape Town, noted for its railway workshops. Oldest railway junction in South Africa, dating from 1860.

Salt River Railway Disaster. Accident on the electric railway line between Cape Town and Simonstown. On June 9, 1926, a crowded train to Simonstown, shortly after 5 o'clock, was derailed, striking the upright pillars of the bridge at Salt River Station. Heavy loss of life, deaths including Sir Malcolm Searle (q.v.) Judge-President of the Cape.

Salvia (Labiatae). Blue-flowered plant related to mint and sage. Large family chiefly of herbs, with leaves in opposite pairs and square stems. Four stamens. Petals usually two-lipped, tubular below and divided above. Among other members are Leonotis or wild Dagga, bearing axillary heads of tubular orange flowers, the dry sepals of which persist as a prickly ball; Wayside Stachys, pink and blue, lipped; and the bright Purple Banner (*Scutellaria paucifolia*) and Purple Top (*Hemizygia bracteosa*) of Rhodesia.

Samango Monkey (*Ceropithecus labiatus*). Like the Vervet Monkey (q.v.) found in wooded areas in the vicinity of water on the eastern side of South Africa, mainly in Zululand. Yellowish-black in colour, the head is very dark, the fur becoming lighter towards the hindquarters. Hands, feet and face are black, the tail shading from dark to light from root to tip. Feeds on practically all vegetable matter.

Sambal. Old Cape Malay seasoning made of vegetables, including cucumbers and onions shredded fine, to which are added quinces, spices, vinegar and other flavouring. Used as a condiment with meat.

S.A.M.C. Abbreviation for South African Medical Corps (q.v.).

S.A.M.N.S. Abbreviation for South African Military Nursing Service (q.v.).

Sampson, Henry William. Labour Leader and Cabinet Minister. Born in 1872 in London in a working-class environment. Qualified as a printer and came to South Africa in 1891. Helped to develop the South African Typographical Union, serving as General President for 25 years, and later Life President. In 1902 he went to Johannesburg, became chairman of the Witwatersrand Trades and Labour Council, opposing Chinese labour importation for the mines. In 1907 was elected to the Town Council for the new Labour Party, and in 1910 to Parliament. Took a leading part in securing adequate compensation for victims of Miners Phthisis. Under the Pact régime, joined the Hertzog Cabinet as Minister of Posts and Telegraphs and of Public Works from 1928 till 1933. Active in international negotiations for workers in South Africa. He died in 1938.

Sampson, Victor. Judge of the Cape Supreme Court and Attorney-General of Cape Colony. Born in Cape Town in 1855, entered the Civil Service in 1871, and was admitted to the Bar in 1881. Went to Grahamstown in 1885, where he continued to practise. Moving to Kimberley in 1898, he held a special retainer for De Beers, and in the same year was elected as Member for Albany for the Progressive Party. After the South African War in 1904, joined the Jameson ministry as Attorney-General until 1908. Returned to practise in Grahamstown until 1915, when he became a judge of the Eastern Districts Local Division. Retired in 1925, and died in Port Elizabeth in 1940.

Sanae. Abbreviation for South African National Antarctic Expedition, applied to its main base in Queen Maud Land established in 1960. *See* ANTARCTIC.

Sanderling (*Crocethia alba*). Medium-sized migratory bird with brownish-grey back and white rump. A whole line of Sanderlings can often be seen running back and forth with the tide, feeding on what it brings in. *See* WADERS.

Sandflats. Village near Alexandria, Eastern Cape Province. Population: 180, including 120 Whites.

Sandgrouse (family Pteroclididae). A family resembling the game birds in habit (*see* FRANCOLIN and PHEASANT), but belonging to the dry Kalahari. They are of medium size, and speckled brown, with a dark brown and white necklace. Except at breeding times, they fly in flocks, coming in swiftly to drink, and living on seeds and small bulbs.

Sandile. Xosa chief. Name derived from Alexander. Born near the eastern frontier of the Cape about 1823, became Chief about 1850, but fell out with Sir Harry Smith of the Cape. He was active in native wars of this decade, but his tenacity gradually subsided. In the 1877–1878 War at first neutral, but became involved and was attacked by the British troops. Retreating into the Pirie bush, was killed by two random bullets in 1878.

Sandpiper (sub-order Limicolae). Small member of the Wader family (q.v.) with a brown, speckled back and throat, white rump and long, straight bill. There are several kinds of Sandpipers, none as plentiful in South Africa as in England, mostly migrants that frequent dams, river mouths and margins.

Sandpipers. Of all migrant Waders (q.v.) the Curlew Sandpipers (*Erolia testicea*) are the commonest and most sociable, gathering on mud or sandy spits in grey-brown and white crowds, their coats often turning chestnut before they leave for the breeding season. They have rather long, curved bills. The Common Sandpipers of Europe are much less common in South Africa, have more brown in their colouring and have straight bills, and are seen only in two's and three's, sedately lifting their tails as they walk.

Sand River Convention. Agreement signed between representatives of the Boers, headed by Andries Pretorius, and of the British Government (W. S. Hogg and C. Mostyn Owen) on January 17, 1852, recognising the independence of the emigrant farmers north of the Vaal River, in what became the South African Republic. Met on the farm Boskop, near Ventersburg, O.F.S.

Sandton. Municipality north of Johannesburg, mostly residential, including Sandown, Bryanston and adjoining areas, established July 1, 1969. Population 20,000, mostly white.

Sand Snakes. *See* SKAAPSTEKERS.

Sandy Point. New fishing harbour on St. Helena Bay, on the west coast of Cape Province, built at cost of R2,250,000 and including a 2000-foot breakwater and 280-foot quay. Opened October 1969.

Sangiro. Pen name of A. A. Pienaar (q.v.).

Sani Pass. Leads from Natal to Basutoland and rises to 9,000 feet, beginning near Himeville, before reaching Mokhotlong (q.v.). A jeep transport service has been established on account of its steep gradient.

San Januario de Humpata. *See* HUMPATA.

Sannah's Post. Station near Bloemfontein, where General Christiaan de Wet (q.v.) gained a notable victory on March 30, 1900, taking over 400 prisoners and an enormous amount of war material.

Sannieshof. Village near Delareyville, Transvaal. Population: 1,915, including 649 Whites.

SANTA. *See* SOUTH AFRICAN NATIONAL TUBERCULOSIS ASSOCIATION.

Sappi. Popular name for South African Pulp and Paper Industries Limited, a company producing paper, pulp and chemical by-products, near Springs and Ngodwane (q.v.), Transvaal, and at Mandini on the Tugela River in Zululand. Started manufacturing paper from mealie and wheat straw, later using wood pulp. The plant at Tugela uses waste from sugar plantations. Newsprint and mechanical printing papers are now also turned out; imports have almost ceased.

Sardines. *See* PILCHARDS.

Saron. Mission station near Tulbagh, Cape Province. Population: 2,049, including 6 Whites.

Sasbank. *See* SUID AFRIKAANSE SPAAR-EN VOORSKOT BANK.

Sasolburg. Town in the Northern Orange Free State, established September 14, 1954, in conjunction with the founding of Sasol (Suidafrikaanse Steenkool Olie en Gas Korporasie —South African Coal, Oil and Gas Corporation) (q.v.). Population: over 28,000, including 16,000 Whites.

Sassaby (*Damaliscus lunatus*). Large antelope found in the Transvaal, Mozambique and Rhodesia. Grows to a height of nearly 5 feet, and is one of the fleetest among antelopes. The meat is highly esteemed by hunters. It is today protected game. Both male and female grow horns, wide, rather than long. A shiny, chocolate-brown coat.

Sassaties or **Cabobs.** Old Cape Malay dish, consisting of small pieces of mutton or pork, flavoured with curry and roasted on a skewer, preferably over a wood fire. The name is derived from the Malay sisate, meaning minced meat.

S.A.St.C. Abbreviation for South African Staff Corps (q.v.).

Satour. *See* SOUTH AFRICAN TOURIST CORPORATION.

Sauer, Dr. Hans. Rhodesian pioneer. Born in Smithfield, O.F.S., in 1857. In 1876 went to study medicine in London and Edinburgh, where he qualified in 1881. Returned and settled in Kimberley, where he became Medical Officer of Health and met his lifelong friend, Cecil Rhodes. During the Kimberley smallpox epidemic he quarrelled with Dr. L. S. Jameson, who declined to recognise the disease. After the discovery of gold, Sauer moved to the Rand, as Rhodes' representative and as M.O.H., remaining until 1889. Went to London in 1891 and read for the Bar, passed his examinations, but changed his plans, and in 1893 returned to Rhodesia as managing director of the Rhodesia Exploration and Development Co. Ltd. In the Matabele Rebellion of 1896 he accompanied Cecil Rhodes and a handful of others unarmed into the Matopos to make peace with the insurgent leaders. Was a member of the Reform Committee in the Jameson Raid, being fined £2,000 for his participation. Retired to England and died in 1939. His autobiography *Ex Africa* is a classic of its kind.

Sauer, Johannes Wilhelmus. South African statesman. Born in Burgersdorp in 1850, educated at the South African College. Became a solicitor in Aliwal North. Elected into the Colonial Parliament in 1876. A supporter of Sir Gordon Sprigg (q.v.), became Secretary for Native Affairs in the ministry of Sir Thomas Scanlen (q.v.) from 1881 to 1884, and was Colonial Secretary under Cecil Rhodes in 1893. In 1896 he led the Opposition in the House. Protagonist of the non-whites, describing himself as a 'philanthropical radical'; refused a knighthood. He died on July 24, 1913.

Sauer, Paul Oliver. South African Cabinet Minister. Born at Wynberg 1898, son of J. W. Sauer (q.v.). Joined the National Party and in 1929 was elected to Parliament. Became Minister of Transport in Cabinet of Dr. D. F. Malan (q.v.) in 1948 and later served as Minister of Lands and Water Affairs. Retired 1963.

Saulspoort. Village in the Transvaal, named after the native chief, Tsheole, the name being corrupted into Saul. Seat of the chieftain of the Bakhatla tribe, near to the Pilansberg (q.v.) on ground owned by President Kruger.

Sawmills. Village 57 miles north of Bulawayo in Rhodesia. Centre for teak industry in the Gwaai Forest.

Saxenburg. Island formerly believed to lie between the Cape of Good Hope and St. Helena. Appears on old maps, its topography being described in detail. Unusual cloud formations may account for legend.

Scab. Disease of livestock, particularly sheep, caused by a parasite of the mite or acari family. In Afrikaans it is referred to as Brandsiekte (burning sickness). Causes damage by ruining quality of the wool. Incurable until discovery in early 19th century of a successful dipping solution, applied first voluntarily, finally by compulsion. Opposition against the Scab Act was overcome. In 1893 the firm of William Cooper & Nephew offered to eradicate scab within a few years, for £735,000 cash, but the offer was rejected. Introduction of the dipping tank in 1890 has almost eradicated the disease. Scab Inspectors are employed by the Government to prevent any recurrence.

Scabbard-Fish, Kalkvis (*Lepidopus caudatus*). Fish found in Walvis Bay, Table Bay, False Bay, also eastern Atlantic Ocean, Mediterranean and off Australasia. About 5 to 6 feet. Body much elongated and compressed like a ribbon and without scales. Very good eating and known in New Zealand as Frost Fish.

Scandrett, Mrs. Charlotte Louise. Pioneer of women's franchise and other rights in South Africa. Born in Swellendam in 1865, daughter of Thomas Taylor, married Arthur William Scandrett, and was a foundation member of the League of British Women, later the Women's Unionist Association. From 1915 to 1925 she was President of the National Council of Women of South Africa, and a delegate to international conferences. She received the King's Jubilee Medal for her services to South African Social Welfare. Died in 1944.

Scanlen, Sir Thomas Charles. Premier of Cape Colony. Born in 1834 at the Cape; qualified as an attorney. Was M.L.A. for Cradock from 1870 to 1896, Prime Minister from 1881 to 1882 and legal adviser to the British South Africa Co., in 1894. Lived in Rhodesia, where his positions included that of Senior Member of the Executive Council in 1896, and Acting Administrator in 1898 and from 1903 to 1906. Retired in 1908, and died on May 15, 1912.

Schapera, Professor Isaac. South African anthropologist. Born on June 23, 1905, he attended the South African College and the University of Cape Town. In 1930 he joined the staff of the University of the Witwatersrand. For 15 years, from 1935 to 1950, he held the Chair of Social Anthropology in the University of Cape Town. His numerous learned publications won him international fame and in 1948 he was Visiting Professor in the University of Chicago, followed in 1950 by an appointment as Professor of Anthropology at the London School of Economics.

Scheepers, Commandant Gideon. Boer soldier. Born in 1878 near Middelburg, Transvaal; joined the

South African Republic State Artillery in 1894, as a heliograph operator, later being seconded to O.F.S. to organise a similar service there. Became a scout in the South African War and rose to Commandant. Associated with a group of Cape Rebels in 1901, was captured and charged with murder, attempted murder, flogging a British subject, placing prisoners in the firing line, etc. He was sentenced to death and shot at Graaff-Reinet in 1902 in distressing circumstances.

Schepel. Old Cape measure of capacity, equal to one and one-third of a bushel. Four schepels equalled one Muid or Sack.

Schermbrucker, Frederick Xavier. Soldier and Cabinet Minister, born in Schweinfurt-on-Main in Germany in 1833. He was invited to the Cape with the military settlers in 1857. In the Eastern Cape Province he soon attained prominence and was elected to Parliament in 1868. In 1875 he moved to the Orange Free State, and edited the *Bloemfontein Express*. Member of Legislative Council at the Cape in 1882, and from 1884 to 1890 was Minister of Public Works. Helped to develop colliery industry at Indwe, Cape. He died on April 27, 1904.

Schlenter. Name for spurious objects, particularly diamonds or bars of gold. Word dates from early days of Kimberley, possibly derived from German surname Schlenter.

Schlesinger, Isidore William. South African financier and industrialist. Born in New York in 1871, son of a Hungarian immigrant associated with the famous Labour leader, Samuel Gompertz. From youth I. W. Schlesinger displayed exceptional financial and administrative gifts, and came to the Transvaal in 1894, as a manufacturer's agent. Became an insurance salesman. After the South African War, founded the African Realty Trust, opening up townships in Port Eliza-

beth, Cape Town and Johannesburg. In 1904 he started the African Life Assurance Society, followed by the Colonial Banking and Trust Co. in 1910, and the African Guarantee and Indemnity Co. In 1914 Schlesinger established the African Theatres Trust, later African Consolidated Theatres. More enterprises followed—African Films and African Film Productions (the first successful locally made pictures). His *African Mirror* newsreel still exists. At Langholm, near Grahamstown, he established pineapple plantations, and canneries in Port Elizabeth. Through technical inadequacies of the catchment area his irrigation venture at Kendrew, near Graaff-Reinet, failed, but he created at Zebediela (q.v.) the largest orange orchard in the world, with 650,000 trees. Also interested in early talkies, owned theatres in Britain and attempted to introduce the American drug store to South Africa. Was the head of over 100 companies, including newspapers and department stores, employing tens of thousands of South Africans. He died in 1949.

Schlesinger, John. South African capitalist and industrialist, son of I. W. Schlesinger (q.v.). Born in Johannesburg, he was educated at Michaelhouse, Natal, and at Harvard University, U.S.A. He served in the American forces in World War II. Joining the organisation as a young man, he succeeded his father as chairman of his numerous companies in 1949.

Schmidt, George. German missionary, known as 'The Apostle of the Hottentots.' Arrived at the Cape in July 1737, the first missionary to settle for the purpose of converting the heathen. At Baviaanskloof started the mission station of Genadendal (q.v.), converted Hottentots, but was hampered by the Dutch authorities, forbidden to administer baptism and ordered to leave the country in 1744.

Genadendal was abandoned, but was later restarted and is still flourishing.

Schneider. French firm of armament makers at Le Creusot who produced famous 'Long Tom' field gun (q.v.). Not to be confused with Snider (q.v.).

Schoemansdal. Village in the Northern Transvaal. Founded by the Voortrekkers in 1849, on the outskirts of the Zoutpansberg, near the present town of Louis Trichardt; was the most northerly white settlement in South Africa, being prosperous as a point of departure for hunters and traders leaving for the interior. Name derived from the Voortrekker leader, Stefanus Schoeman. In 1867 was destroyed during a native war and never restored.

Schoeman, Stefanus. Early Transvaal statesman. Born in 1810 in the Cape Colony; joined the Great Trek, reaching the Transvaal with A. H. Potgieter (q.v.); was elected Commandant-General, but quarrelled with President M. W. Pretorius, for whom he deputised during his absence in the O.F.S. Disputes ended in a Civil War in 1862, in which he led the faction against the future President Kruger. Was defeated and banished to the O.F.S., but returned and, in 1867, became diplomatic agent in the Northern Transvaal. He died in 1890. The village of Schoemansdal (q.v.) was called after him.

Schoemansville. Residential township near Haartebeestpoort Dam near Pretoria, founded in 1925, named after the landowner, Johann Schoeman.

Schonland, Sir Basil F. J. South African physicist. Born at Grahamstown, February 5, 1890, the son of Professor S. Schonland (q.v.). After St. Aidan's College and Rhodes University he studied at Cambridge, and during World War I served as Signals Officer. From 1920 to 1922 he did physics research in the Cavendish

laboratory, Cambridge; he was then appointed Professor of Physics at Cape Town and in 1936 director of the Bernard Price Institute of Geophysics at the University of the Witwatersrand, doing important research on lightning discharge and radio. Schonland's work on aircraft detection methods, embodied in Radar, led to his appointment in Britain as Superintendent of the Army Operational Research Group, and later as Scientific Adviser to the Commander-in-Chief. Again in South Africa, he became first President of the Council for Scientific and Industrial Research, but returned to Britain in 1954, first as Deputy Director and in 1958 Director of the Atomic Energy Research establishment, Harwell. He retired in 1961 with many honours, including a Fellowship of the Royal Society.

Schonland, Dr. Selmar. South African botanist, born in Frankenhausen, Germany, in 1860. Coming to South Africa, he settled in Grahamstown and from 1889 to 1910 was director of the Albany Museum. Upon the founding of Rhodes University College in 1904, he became Professor of Botany, doing research work, especially on succulents. He died in 1940.

Schoombie. Village in the Eastern Cape Province, named after the farmer of the area, noted for its wool production, salt pans and stud farms.

Schoon, R. Early traveller in the Transvaal. In 1827 reached the source of the Marico River in the Western Transvaal, following it for 150 miles, to the kraal of Moselekatse. Explored Bechuanaland, met Moselekatse and in 1834 discovered Lake Chrissie in the Eastern Transvaal, being the first man to reach the Zoutpansberg after Coenraad Buys (q.v.).

Schreiner, Olive Emily Albertina. South African author. Born at Wittebergen Mission Station on March 24, 1855, daughter of the Rev. Gottlob

Schreiner, a German missionary, and of an English mother. Even as a small child she showed signs of an unusual imagination, but her early education was slight, mostly acquired on her own initiative. Best-known book, *The Story of an African Farm*, appeared in 1883, under the nom de plume of Ralph Iron, its true authorship not being revealed for some time. She went to England, was accepted among eminent figures of the day, developing a friendship with Havelock Ellis. She became an upholder of rights for women. A close friend of Cecil John Rhodes, until the Jameson Raid. Controversy was caused by her attacks on the methods of colonisation in Rhodesia, contained in *Trooper Halkett of Mashonaland*. During the South African War, she worked hard for the Afrikaner people and for the restoration of peace. Married Samuel Cronwright (who assumed her name) (q.v.), settled in Hanover and in De Aar, continuing her writing. Last years spent in England. She died in 1920 at Wynberg.

Schreiner, William Philip. Prime Minister of Cape Colony, and brother of Olive Schreiner (q.v.). Born in 1857 in the district of Herschel, C.P., where his father, the Rev. Gottlob Schreiner, was a German missionary. Studied at the South African College and read for the Bar at Cambridge. In 1882 he began a successful practice in Cape Town. Then, entering politics, he was at first a supporter of Cecil Rhodes, serving in his cabinet as Attorney-General, but after the Jameson Raid they quarrelled and Schreiner became one of the leaders of the Afrikander Bond (q.v.). From 1898 to 1900 he was Premier. Defended Dinizulu after the 1906 Zulu Rebellion, became a senator after Union, and from 1914 to his death in 1919 was High Commissioner in London.

Schwartz, Professor E. H. L. South African geologist. Born in 1873, came to South Africa in 1895, settling in Grahamstown. Worked for the Cape Geological Commission, attracting notice through his unorthodox views on certain aspects of South African geology and through sponsoring a scheme for changing the climate of the Kalahari, by diverting the Okavango and other rivers. This was put forward in his book *Thirstland Redemption*. He died in 1928.

Schweizer-Reneke. Town in the Western Transvaal. Established in 1885, replacing the native village, Mamusa. Named after Captain Schweizer and Field-Cornet Renecke, killed in 1885 during an expedition against the local tribe. Fighting took place there in the South African War. Farming centre; efforts at diamond washing have been made near by. Population: 7,380, including 2,100 Whites.

Scientia. Township outside Pretoria entirely composed of buildings and laboratories of the Council for Scientific and Industrial Research (q.v.).

Scientists of South Africa. The Nobel Prize, greatest of all international scientific honours, has been won by at least one South African, Dr. Max Theiler, born at Pretoria, the son of the famous veterinary researcher, Sir Arnold Theiler (q.v.). Dr. Theiler received the award for medicine in 1951, for development of a vaccine against Yellow Fever. Botany, however, is the science in which a born South African first won distinction, in the person of Christian Hendrik Persoon (q.v.), who became the 'Father of Mycology,' or the study of fungi, in the 18th century. It was not until the 19th century, however, that other important researchers of local origin began to appear. Among them were the aeronautical pioneer, Goodman Household (q.v.), who did successful gliding in the 1870's, and the distinguished medical man Professor Emil Hoffa who at Würzburg and Berlin became the 'Father of Modern Orthopaedics.' Professor Edwin Goldman, senior assistant to Paul Ehrlich, one of the greatest pathologists of his age, is remembered for his 'classical researches on tissue-staining,' as the *British Medical Journal* put it, and as one of the first successful investigators of cancer. Dr. Harry Bolus was one of the most famous South African-born botanists, with an international reputation. In the field of chemistry, Professor P. D. Hahn worked on 'the phosphorescence of metals,' anticipating radio-activity.

Inspired by the mineral wealth of the country, South Africans made outstanding contributions to geology, among them Dr. David Draper (q.v.), Dr. Hans Merensky, Dr. Percy A. Wagner (q.v.) and Dr. A. L. du Toit (q.v.)—all well known overseas. Alpheus F. Williams (q.v.) did research on the origin of diamonds.

In physics the names of Dr. H. J. van der Bijl (q.v.), pioneer of radiotelephony, J. Jennings (inventor of wireless telegraphy independent of Marconi), Professor Athelstan Spilhaus, the meteorological and geophysical authority now in the U.S.A., Professor K. van der Merwe of New York University, the atomic physicist, along with Sir Basil Schonland, pioneer of radar and director of Harwell Atomic Research Establishment in Britain, deserve especial honour. Professor T. E. W. Schumann, formerly holder of a chair at the University of West Virginia in the United States, is a noted meteorologist.

Sir Solly Zuckerman, born in Cape Town, originally a zoologist, was Scientific Adviser to the British Government in World War II, particularly on matters connected with the effects of blast and bombing. Professor Geiling of Chicago, a South African, became a Senior Adviser on Malaria and other problems to the U.S.A. Government. Dr. T. J. Dry deserves mention because of his work

on cardiology at the Mayo Clinic for a period of 21 years. The now almost standard pregnancy test with the Xenopis Laevis frog was devised at Cape Town University by Dr. H. Zwarenstein and Dr. A. Zoond.

Professor J. L. B. Smith of Rhodes University at Grahamstown won distinction throughout the world through his identification of the first Coelacanth (q.v.) and later through his discovery of their breeding grounds in the Indian Ocean. Dr. Edna Plumstead of the Witwatersrand University, Johannesburg, made the epoch-making identification of the Glossopteris (q.v.), the earliest form of flowering plant. Archaeologists of renown born in South Africa were Professor Claude van Riet Louw and Professor A. J. H. Goodwin, both of whom revolutionised thinking on the prehistoric past of this continent.

Technical inventions by born South Africans used in other lands include the Konimeter, devised by the former Government Mining Engineer Sir Robert N. Kotze (q.v.) for measuring the dust content of air underground, and the Tellurometer, evolved by the staff of the Council for Scientific and Industrial Research (q.v.) for accurate surveying with the aid of short radio waves. This apparatus is exported all over the world and manufactured under licence in the United States and elsewhere.

In the humanistic sciences, South Africans of international standing include General J. C. Smuts (q.v.), for his work as a philosopher and his authorship of the doctrine of Holism, Professor C. T. Loram of the Chair of Education at Yale, Professor Sydney Raubenheimer, holder of the same post at the University of California, Professor C. W. de Kiewit, the historian, now head of the University of Minnesota, U.S.A., Professor S. Herbert Frenkel, the distinguished economist and holder of a chair at Nuffield College, Oxford, and many others.

The foregoing takes no account of the vast number of scientists, born overseas, who achieved fame through their work in Southern Africa. *See also* HEART TRANSPLANTS and PROFESSOR C. BARNARD.

Scimitar-Bill (*Rhinopomastus cyanomelas*). Bird partial to Thorn-veld from Orange River and Northern Natal northward. Very similar to Kakelaar (q.v.) but much smaller and black all over.

Scorpion-Fish (*Scorpaena natalensis*). Fish caught off False Bay to Natal. About 12 inches long. Reddish, spotted with black. All members of this family have heads armed with ridges or spines, very long fins and bright colours, mimicking surrounding objects.

Scotchman (*Polysteganus praeorbitalis*). Fish found from Algoa Bay to Natal. About 20 inches long.

Scott, Rev. Guthrie Michael. Clergyman and politician. Born on July 30, 1907, he was educated at Taunton and, having moved to South Africa, at Grahamstown. Entering the ministry he was ordained in 1930 and from 1935 to 1939 worked in India. During World War II he joined the Royal Air Force but in 1943 returned to South Africa, being attached to St. Alban's Colonial Mission and to St. Joseph's Orphanage at Johannesburg. A strong critic of many aspects of South African policy, he left the Union in 1950 to work at Chichester in England. Regarding himself as a champion of the black African, he appeared before the United Nations Organisation in 1947 to make complaints of conditions in South West Africa. He wrote books and helped to set up the Africa Bureau, of which he became director, aimed at attacking the Union, etc.

Scott, Colonel Jack. South African mining industrialist. Born in the Transvaal May 23, 1903, and educated at Potchefstroom and City and Guilds

College, London, he showed an early interest in the gold-mining possibilities of the Klerksdorp district, and was largely responsible for establishing the Strathmore Investment group of companies. Upon their merger with the General Mining and Finance Corporation (q.v.), he became Vice-Chairman. He retired in 1962.

Scott, Sir John. Lieutenant-Governor of Natal from 1856 to 1864. Born in 1814. During his period of office first Indian labourers introduced and first railway constructed. Coming into conflict with the colonists on many matters he was transferred as Governor to British Guiana. Died in Chislehurst, Kent, on June 29, 1898.

Scottburgh. Seaside resort on the Natal South Coast, 38 miles from Durban. Named after Lieutenant-Governor John Scott (1856–1864). Became popular during the present century. Noted for its fine golf course. Population: 1,800, including 1,020 Whites.

Scully, William Charles. South African author. Born in Dublin, Ireland, on October 29, 1855; came to South Africa in 1867 and lived in the Eastern Province. Was an early digger on the Diamond Fields, then was attracted to the Transvaal by gold discoveries and spent some years around Pilgrims Rest. In 1876 entered Cape Civil Service, becoming magistrate in the Eastern Province, Namaqualand, etc. Began to write, particularly about the native races, his best-known books being *Twixt Sun and Sand* and *Daniel Vananda*. He died in 1943.

Sculpture. The first South African sculptor to attain distinction was Anton Anreith (q.v.) in the 18th century, many of whose works may still be admired at the Cape. Little of merit was done during the 19th century, most sculpture being imported from abroad. Although himself of Dutch origin, Anton von Wouw evolved a distinctively South African style, his studies of Boers and natives being particularly striking. More recently a valuable contribution has been made by the late E. Meyerowitz, an outstanding wood-carver, as well as by Moses Kottler and Lippy Lipschitz, who use a variety of media, both in stone and in wood. Kottler's work varies from the tenderly accurate to the modernistic, while that of Lipschitz is essentially modern. Another distinguished South African sculptor is I. Mitford Barberton. Immigrant artists who have settled in South Africa, including Ernest Ullman, Zoltan Barborecki and F. Cuairan, have been responsible for striking and beautiful studies of South African subjects.

Sea-Bat (*Platax teira*). Fish found off Natal and Indo-Pacific Ocean. About 20 inches long, yellowish-brown with dark stripes in the young. One of the Butterfly-fish (q.v.).

Sea-Bream (**Ray's Sea-Bream, Black Sea-Bream, Pomfret** or **Cheese-Fish**) (*Brama raii*). Found in Atlantic, Mediterranean and Pacific Oceans, and not uncommonly in Table Bay and on the Agulhas Bank. About 28 inches long, and excellent for eating. Named after John Ray, 17th century naturalist.

Sea-Horse (*Hippocampus capensis*). Belongs to the family of Flute-mouths, all of which have long snouts, ending in a little mouth. They are mainly tropical, shore fish. The Cape Sea-Horse has been found only in the Knysna estuary and lagoon. It is about 5 inches long, its head turned at a sharp angle, its scales arranged in ridges round the short body and long curly tail. The male carries the eggs in a pouch attached to his body.

Sea Lion (*Actocephalus pusilus*). Amphibious, sociable and polygamous mammal, found on small islands from Saldanha Bay to Algoa Bay. Owing to its round shape, flippers and finned feet, it is specially equipped for sea life, and hunts for fish as far south as the Polar Ice. It has long teeth and powerful shoulders. The skin of the female and young male is an article of commerce controlled by Government, but not as valuable as that of the true Northern seal. The Sea Lion differs from the latter in having small ears and something of a neck, and hind flippers turned forwards for walking. (The Seal moves on its body on land, its flippers sticking out backwards for swimming.) A 7-foot herd leader, having won a score of small, 4-foot mates in battle, will guard each of their two young for weeks without daring even to eat.

Searle, Sir Malcolm William. Judge-President of the Cape. Born in London, 1855; came to South Africa at age of five; educated at Diocesan College, and from 1875 at Cambridge. Called to Inner Temple in 1882 and began practice in Cape Town. After Union, in 1910, was appointed Judge of the Cape Provincial Division. Served University of the Cape of Good Hope from 1897 until 1918. Was Judge President of the Cape of Good Hope from 1922 until his death on June 9, 1926, in the Salt River railway disaster (q.v.).

Sebele. Succeeded Sechele (q.v.) in 1863 as Bakwena Chief. Visited England with Khama in 1895, and was received by Queen Victoria.

Sechele. Chief of Bakwena, occupying a territory now part of Bechuanaland. Successfully defied Moselekatse and his Matabele, allowing the introduction of Christianity under David Livingstone in 1843. Developed leprosy in 1860 and died in 1863.

Secretary Bird (*Sagittarius serpentarius*). One of the best-known and characteristic birds of South Africa, in many ways related to the Eagles. Has a great reputation as a snake-killer.

Commonest in South-West Cape, but occurs in open country in all parts. So called on account of the feathers at the back of its head, reminiscent of a clerk with a pen behind his ear. *See* BIRDS.

Secunde. A rank in the service of the Dutch East India Company, signifying 'Second in Authority.' The first holder of this post at the Cape of Good Hope was Jacob Ryniers, who took office in 1653, under Commander Jan van Riebeeck. The last was Johan Isaac Rhenius, who held the office from August 1786 until September 1795, when the first British régime began.

Sedgefield. Village in the Cape Province, near Knysna, on the edge of Swartvlei (part of a chain of lakes). It is a holiday resort, founded early in the present century, and named after Sedgefield in County Durham, England, home of its founder, Henry Barrington.

Seed-Eater (Fringillidae). Small singing bird common over much of South Africa. It belongs to the Finch family, all members of which have stout, short bills, and good voices. One of the loveliest singers is the Black-throated Seed-Eater of the dry country north of the Orange River. Small yellow rump and black ruff, but, in general effect, grey-green, with speckled wings like most of the other Seed-Eaters. *See* CANARY, BUNTING.

Seeheim. Village in South West Africa, at junction of railway to Luderitzbucht.

Segal, Abraham (Abe). South African tennis champion. Born in Johannesburg, October 23, 1930, and educated at the Johannesburg Trade School. Began serious play in 1947 and in 1955 appeared for the first time in the South African Davis Cup team.

Seifsa. Abbreviation for Steel and Engineering Industrie's Federation of South Africa. Established in 1943.

Seitz, Dr. Theodor. Last German Governor of South West Africa, born 1863 in Seckenheim, Germany. He joined the colonial service, and in 1895 became a District Officer in the Cameroons. In 1900 he was appointed to the Colonial Office in Berlin, and in 1907 was made Governor of the Cameroons. From 1910 to 1915 he was Governor of South West Africa, until its surrender to the South African forces. He died in 1949. Several books from his pen provide a record of his career.

Sekukuni. Chief of the Bapedi (q.v.), son of Sekwati, founder of this tribe, whom he succeeded in September 1861. A man of considerable ability and strong personality, he gave the South African Republic a great deal of trouble. In 1876 he rebelled and drove the farmers of Lydenburg into lager at Krugers Post. By February 1877 he was forced to submit and was fined, but failed to pay. Costly military operations organised by President T. F. Burgers proved unavailing. The British took over the Transvaal and tried again to enforce their authority. Sekukuni attacked certain pro-Government clans, refused the terms offered by General Sir S. Wolseley and, only at heavy cost of life and treasure, was defeated by British troops on November 28, 1879. He surrendered to Commandant Ferreira on December 2, was sent as a prisoner to Pretoria, but was set free after the First Boer War in 1881, when the Convention of Pretoria was signed. He was murdered in August 1882 by Mampoer, his half-brother.

Selborne, Lord (William Waldegrave Palmer). Governor and Statesman. Born in England in 1859, he was educated at Winchester and Oxford, entering Parliament as a Liberal in 1885. After serving as Under-Secretary for the Colonies from 1895–1900, and First Lord of the Admiralty from 1900, he became Governor of the

Transvaal and Orange River Colony and High Commissioner in 1905. His tact and personal charm greatly helped the establishment of the Union. His famous 'Selborne Memorandum', issued on January 7, 1907, served as the basis for the National Convention (q.v.). Returning to England in 1910 he died in 1942.

Selous, Frederick Courtney. Rhodesian hunter and explorer, born in London, 1851, and educated at Rugby. He sailed for Africa in 1871, landed at Port Elizabeth, made his way to Kimberley and from there started his first expedition into the Matabele country. He soon became a well-known figure, and was much respected by the Matabele king Lobengula and his subjects. Between 1876 and 1878 he traded far beyond the Zambesi into the Kafue country, and in 1879 to the Mashukulumbwe. His first book aroused great interest in big game hunting, and after a visit to Britain he returned in 1881, intending to settle down as an ostrich farmer. Instead he travelled into Barotseland. In 1889 he met Cecil John Rhodes, in connection with his plan for the establishment of the Chartered Company, and the occupation of Mashonaland. Selous undertook to act as guide for the proposed expedition in 1890. He gained great renown but little monetary reward. After fighting in the Matabele War, he went back to England. He was killed in action in East Africa in 1917.

Selukwe. Town in the south of Rhodesia, established in 1904 on Selukwe goldfield started in the 1890's. It is mainly an administrative centre, with an important chrome industry near by. Population: 2,500, including 500 Whites.

Sena. Settlement in Mozambique on the Zambesi River, and centre for the Sena Sugar Estates Ltd., which produces approximately 100.000 tons of sugar yearly, owning plants at Marromeu and Luabo.

Senecio. See DAISY.

Senekal. Town in the Eastern Orange Free State, named after Frederick Senekal, Commandant-General of the Orange Free State burghers in the Basuto War of 1858. It was founded in 1879 and has grown into a dairying and wool-growing centre. Population: 10,600, including 2,010 Whites. Original name was De Put.

Serang. Malay name (originated by the slaves) for the foreman of a gang working at the Cape Town Docks.

Seretse Khama. See KHAMA, SIR SERETSE.

Seringa (*Kirkia acuminata*). One of the most graceful trees in the Low Veld, Bechuanaland, Rhodesia and across Central Africa. Round-topped, leafy, growing up to 30 feet, with a smooth grey bark. Unlike most South African trees it is deciduous, with beautiful yellow and orange autumn tints. The small white flowers grow in slender sprays. Fruit a hard four-angled capsule. Although the wood, a mottled light and dark brown, is much used for furniture, it is not durable. See TREES.

Serowe. Seat of Bamangwato chiefs in East Botswana, 38 miles from Palapye (q.v.). Population 34,182.

Serpa Pinto, Alexandre Alberto de la Rocha. Governor of Mozambique and Portuguese explorer, born in Portugal on April 10, 1846. He began a military career and gained world fame through his crossing of Africa between 1877 and 1879, in which he rivalled H. M. Stanley. Later Serpa Pinto traced the source of the Zambesi, and was awarded the Gold Medal of the Paris Geographical Society in 1881. His appointment as Governor of Mozambique in 1889 coincided with the diplomatic troubles with Britain about the Portuguese frontier and the Massekessi Incident (q.v.). He died in 1900.

Sesheke. Village in Zambia, on Zambesi River. Administrative centre for Barotseland.

Seshogo. Village near Pietersburg, Northern Transvaal, seat of the Lebowa (North Sotho) Territorial Authority, established in 1969.

Sestigers. Literary movement in Afrikaans, taking its name from the fact that it began in the 1960's. Supported by younger novelists and poets anxious to get away from conventional ideas. Its members include André Brink, Breyten Breytenbach, W. A. De Klerk, Jan Rabie, Etienne Le Roux, Bartho Smit, Ingrid Jonker, Adam Small and others.

Settlers. Village on the Springbok Flats in the Northern Transvaal. Established in 1908. Farming centre.

Settlers' Bible. Jocular name given to the *Grahamstown Journal* (q.v.).

Sevenoaks. Wattle-growing centre in Natal, near Greytown, called after town in England.

Seventy-Four (*Polysteganus undulosus*). Fish found in Table Bay, False Bay to Natal. About 40 inches long. So called because of its banded markings which give it a supposed resemblance to the hull of an old 74-gun warship. *See* BREAM.

Seymour. Village in the Eastern Cape Province named after Lieutenant-Colonel Seymour, military secretary to Governor Sir George Cathcart. Founded in 1853 as a centre for the Kat River Settlement of the Hottentots (q.v.), it grew into a flourishing wool and general farming community. Population: 930, including 126 Whites.

Sezela. Sugar milling centre on the south coast of Natal, near Umzinto. Population: 2,708, including 240 Whites.

Shabani. Township founded about 1913 in the south of Rhodesia, adjoining the Shabani Asbestos mine.

Its growth dates from after World War I. Population: 15,900, including 1,700 Whites.

Shakaskraal. *See* CHAKASKRAAL.

Shamva. Township north of Salisbury, Rhodesia, dating to about 1910. Gold mining and tobacco centre.

Shangaan. Tribe of Zulu origin living in the valley of the Limpopo River in Mozambique, also found in Rhodesia and in the Republic. They are noted dancers and possess considerable artistic ability. Large numbers emigrate yearly to the Witwatersrand, on contract for the mines.

Shangani Patrol. Group of 33 troopers under Major Allan Wilson (q.v.). During the Matabele War of 1893 they went in pursuit of the Matabele king Lobengula and crossed the Shangani river, which came down in flood, cutting off their return. On December 4, at a point 84 miles north-west of Shiloh, they were attacked by overwhelming forces of Matabele. They refused to surrender and, singing 'God Save the Queen,' went on fighting until the last man was killed. Temporarily buried near Zimbabwe, they were finally laid to rest at World's View in the Matopos (the Rhodesian Pantheon) where a monument commemorates their heroism.

Shank End. Jocular name given to the Cape Peninsula.

Shannon. Settlement near Bloemfontein, Orange Free State. Population: 1,823, including 871 Whites.

Sharks. Many varieties, all differing from ordinary fish in having cartilage in place of bones; skin covered, not with scales, but with rough denticles; teeth usually numerous; 5 to 7 gill-slits on each side; cigar-shaped body and high upper lobe of tail-fin. Length ranges between 5 and 50 feet. Most species are viviparous but the Zebra Shark (*Stegostoma fasceatum*) lays a few large eggs, each enclosed in a horny case (sometimes found along the sea margin). The young are born or hatched looking like the adult. Sharks can be recognised from afar by the high tail-fin and by the fact that, because the mouth is greatly underhung, they turn over to attack and expose their light underside. Although seen scavenging round Cape harbours, they are much more plentiful off the Natal coast. The majority are dangerous. Authenticated attacks on man have mostly been traced to the 5-foot Durban Grey Shark (*Carcharinus melanopterus*) and the larger Black Fin Shark (*C. limoatus*) rather than to the 30–40-foot man-eater (*Cachasodon carcharias*). The 15-foot Tiger Shark (*Galeocerdo articus*) is aggressive but in the main an offal-eater. A 289-pounder has been caught in Natal with a rod and line.

Of the harmless species, the 40-foot Basking Shark (*Cetorhinus maximus*) appears to be a Cape summer visitor, which has been seen surfacing off Simonstown and Hout Bay. Its numerous teeth are small and it lives on tiny organisms strained by its long gill-rakers. Very similar to this and the largest known is the 50-foot Whale Shark (*Rhincodon typus*). The first South African specimen, washed up in Table Bay in 1829, is preserved in the Paris Museum. Cape Town Museum contains a 20-foot specimen found at Noordhoek in 1934.

The shark of economic importance to South Africa is the 6-foot Vaalhaai (*Galerhinus galeus*), hunted for its liver oil. In Australia the fins are dried and exported to China for shark fin soup. The skin is sold for smoothing wood, for leather and for covering ornamental boxes. *See* MARINE RESOURCES.

Sharpeville. Bantu township at Vereeniging, Transvaal, the scene of serious inter-racial disturbances on March 21, 1960. According to an official report a mob of 20,000 attacked the police station. The police fired and 69 persons were killed. A judicial enquiry afterwards took place.

Shaw, Louise Flora (Lady Lugard). British journalist, born in Ireland in the 1850's, the daughter of General Shaw; joined the staff of the London *Times* and became head of its Colonial Department. As such she came into close contact with Cecil Rhodes, with whose ambitions she had much sympathy and for whom she carried out missions behind the scenes in Whitehall. She visited South Africa as special correspondent and met President Kruger. In 1902 she married the famous British explorer and Colonial Governor, Sir Frederick Lugard (later Lord Lugard). She wrote several books and died on January 25, 1929.

Shawbury. Large Methodist mission station and training college in Transkei, near Qumbu, named after the Reverend William Shaw.

Shearwater (*Tubinares*). Medium-sized ocean bird of the Petrel group (q.v.) nesting in the Antarctic during the summer and coming to the Cape for the winter. The Great Shearwater is a mottled-brown colour, with a dark cap. The Sooty Shearwater is more slenderly built and black all over. *See* BIRDS.

Sheep. *See* WOOL.

Sheikh Joseph (more correctly **Sjeg Yussuf**). Moslem saint, whose tomb or Kramat (q.v.) is one of the places of pilgrimage among the orthodox Cape Malays. A prince on the island of Bantam in the Dutch East Indies, and a direct descendant of the prophet Mahommed, he came into conflict with the Dutch East India Company, and was banished to the Cape in 1694. With him were several wives and a retinue of courtiers. He was treated with great respect by the Governor, W. A. van der Stel, and when he died, in 1699, was buried near the present

1. *Strelitzia nicolai* (wild banana). 2. *Aloe candelabrum* (candelabra aloe).
3. *Albizzia adianthifolia* (flat-crown). 4. *Adansonia digitata* (baobab).
5. *Euphorbia ingens* (naboom).

village of Faure, adjoining Somerset West.

Sheil, John Devonshire. Judge of the Cape Supreme Court, born near Dublin in 1855. He began his career as a soldier in the Royal Dublin Fusiliers and came to South Africa in the Gun War of 1880–1881. He then studied for the Bar and was called in 1889. Settling at the Cape, he was appointed to the Bench of the Eastern Districts Court in 1902, from which he retired in 1913. He died in 1935.

Shelduck (*Casarca cana*). Large, striking-looking duck, found in dams and pans on the Karroo and Highveld, less commonly at the Cape. Lavender head of male and white face of female conspicuous. Resembles Egyptian Goose in flight (q.v.). Nests in burrows. *See* DUCK.

Shelly Beach. Seaside resort, south of Port Shepstone, on the South Coast of Natal. Noted for its wealth of beautiful seashells.

Shepstone, Sir Theophilus. South African statesman, born in England on January 8, 1817. He arrived at the Cape with his parents in 1820, served as interpreter in the war against the Xosas in 1835, and in 1839 became British Resident in Kaffraria. His skill in handling the Africans led in 1845 to his appointment as Agent for Native Affairs in Natal. In 1856 he was promoted to Secretary for Native Affairs in Pietermaritzburg, and in 1872 successfully arranged the complicated succession to the Zulu throne and the formal coronation of Cetewayo (q.v.). He was sent to England to consult with the Colonial Office in 1874, and in 1877 was responsible for the occupation and annexation of the Transvaal to the British Crown. He remained in Pretoria until 1879. In 1880 he retired, but was appointed Administrator of Zululand in 1884. He finally retired to Pietermaritzburg, where he was venerated by every non-European. Died June 23, 1893. His native nickname was 'Somtseu,' signifying 'Mighty Hunter.'

Shepstone's Hen. Egg money set aside for payment of Government tax and so named in honour of Sir Theophilus Shepstone (q.v.), who was in charge of revenue in Natal.

Shiloh. Moravian (q.v.) mission station in the Eastern Cape Province, near the Kat River; destroyed during the rising of 1851.

Shimian (also **Tshimyane**). Drink concocted by natives, particularly in Natal, from treacle and water left to ferment in the sun.

Shippard, Sir Sidney Godolphin Alexander. South African diplomat and lawyer. Born in England, 1838; educated at Kings College School and Oxford; called to the Bar in 1867. Three years later he emigrated to the Cape, where he settled in Kimberley, and from 1873 to 1877 was Attorney-General for the colony of Griqualand West. His first judicial experience was as Acting Recorder for the High Court of Griqualand in 1877. From 1880 to 1885 he was a judge of the Supreme Court of the Cape Colony. He also served as British Commissioner in the joint Anglo-German commission to investigate the claims of the two countries to the coast of South-West Africa. Upon the establishment of the first courts in Bechuanaland, he was appointed Chief Magistrate and President of the Land Commission. He was Deputy High Commissioner for the Bechuanaland Protectorate and the Kalahari Desert from 1885 to 1895. He wrote much on legal subjects, including a report of the famous case of Bishop of Grahamstown *v.* Williams in 1879. He was a man of great charm and learning. Died in England in 1902.

Famous South African Shipwrecks

Date	Name of Ship	Place
1552	*Sao Joao*	Pondoland Coast
1553	*Sao Bento*	Pondoland Coast

Date	Name of Ship	Place
1585	Santiago	Near Quilimane
1589	Sao Thome	Off Madagascar
1593	Santo Alberto	Pondoland Coast
1622	Sao Joao Baptista	Eastern Cape
1630	Sao Goncalo	Plettenberg Bay
1635	Nossa Senhora de Belem	Pondoland Coast
1647	Haarlem	Table Bay
1660	Marichal	Table Bay
1673	Zoetendal	Cape Agulhas
1682	Joanna	Cape Agulhas
1685	Good Hope	Port Natal
1686	Stavenisse	Natal South Coast
1702	Merestyn	Jutten Island
1713	Bennebroek	Natal Coast
1722	Schoonberg	Cape Agulhas
1729	Saxenburg	Cape Agulhas
1740	Visch	Table Bay
1755	Doddington	Bird Island, Algoa Bay
1756	Schuylenburg	Near Simons Bay
1773	Jonge Thomas	Table Bay
1776	Ceres	Table Bay
1778	Colebrooke	False Bay
1780	Hoop	Table Bay
1782	Grosvenor	Pondoland Coast
1782	Victor	Table Bay
1784	Severe	Table Bay
1788	Maria	Plettenberg Bay
1794	Sao Jose	Camps Bay
1796	Hercules	Coast of Kaffraria
1799	Sceptre	Table Bay
1805	Napoleon	Hout Bay
1813	William Pitt	Cape Receife
1815	Arniston	Cape Agulhas
1825	Mary	Port Natal
1829	Eole	Coast of Kaffraria
1840	Hope	Cape St. Francis
1842	Sabina	Cape Receife
1844	St. Mungo	Cape Agulhas
1846	Catherine	Waterloo Bay
1847	Thunderbolt	Cape Receife
1850	British Settler	St. Helena Bay
1852	Birkenhead	Danger Point
1854	Charlotte	Algoa Bay
1856	Zalt Bommel	Table Bay
1861	Bernicia	Robben Island
1862	Waldensian	Struys Point
1864	Eastern Province	Ratel River Mouth
1865	Athens	Table Bay
1865	City of Peterborough and 30 other ships	Table Bay
1865	Dane	Cape Receife

Date	Name of Ship	Place
1867	Bosphorus	Cape St. Francis
1868	Borderer	Table Bay
1870	Queen of the Thames	Struys Point
1871	Gambia	Algoa Bay
1872	Quanza and 6 others	East London
1872	Princess Alice and 3 others	Port Natal
1873	Bismarck	Near Keiskama River Mouth
1875	Celt	Near Danger Point
1875	Kafir	Near Cape Point
1876	Windsor Castle	Near Dassen Island
1876	Namaqua	Near Hondeklip
1879	Clyde	Near Danger Point
1880	Surprise	Durban
1880	Lancastria	Table Bay
1880	American	Near Cape Palmas
1881	Calcutta	Near Bashee River Mouth
1881	Teuton	Quoin Point
1886	Finland	Near Port Alfred
1891	Wallarah	Dassen Island
1895	Fascadale	Natal South Coast
1896	Drummond Castle	Cape Ushant
1896	Greystoke	Cape Agulhas
1896	Queen Victoria	Near Port Elizabeth
1898	Dorothea	Zululand Coast
1899	Thermopylae	Table Bay
1900	Sybille	Lambert's Bay
1900	Kikapo	Hout Bay
1901	Hermes	Table Bay
1901	Ismore	St. Helena Bay
1901	Tantallon Castle	Robben Island
1902	Newmark Castle	Off Zululand Coast
1902	City of Lincoln	Table Bay
1903	Gertrude Woermann (1)	Near Port Nolloth
1903	Gertrude Woermann (2)	Near Swakopmund, S.W.A.
1906	Oakburn	Hout Bay
1906	Oakburn	Danger Point
1907	Heraclides	Near Luderitzbucht
1908	Newmark Castle	Zululand Coast
1909	Waratah	Off the Natal Coast
1909	Maori	Duiker Point
1909	Umhlali	Near Kommetjie

Date	Name of Ship	Place
1910	*Lisboa*	Saldanha Bay
1910	*Eduard Bohlen*	Conception Bay, S.W.A.
1911	*Lusitania*	Off Cape Point
1911	*Balli*	Near Luderitzbucht
1911	*Itzehoe*	Cape Receife
1913	*Haddon Hall*	Hoetjes Bay
1914	*Clan Stuart*	Simonstown
1915	*Rangatira*	Robben Island
1919	*Nautilus*	Possession Island
1923	*Mossamedes*	Cape Frio
1925	*King Bleddyn*	Cape Frio
1926	*Cawdor Castle*	Conception Bay, S.W.A.
1928	*Cariboo*	South of East London
1929	*Western Knight*	Near Port Elizabeth
1931	*King Cadwallon*	Near East London
1931	*Rosandra*	Walvis Bay
1932	*Ovington Court*	Walvis Bay
1939	*Stuart Star*	Near East London
1946	*City of Lincoln*	Quoin Point
1948	*Basuto Coast*	Table Bay
1966	*South African Seafarer*	Table Bay

Note: this list does not take account of war-time sinkings

Shrews, Jumping or **Elephant** (Macroscelididae). Small, mouse-like animals with long trunk noses, large ears and such elongated ankles that they appear to be balanced on their toes. They progress in a series of bounds. Although found in moist areas, they seem to prefer districts like Namaqualand and South West Africa.

Elephant Shrew

They are timid, harmless and live entirely on a useful diet of insects.

Shrews or **Shrew-mice** (Saticidae). Small insectivorous mammals, with flat ears, tiny eyes and a keen sense of smell. They are timid and harmless, their defence being the emission of a musky odour. Sometimes they come into gardens for cockroaches, beetles and snails.

Shrikes (Laniidae and Prionopidae). The Butcher-bird family of strongly-built birds with hooked and toothed bills. Real Butcher Birds impale their prey on thorns until ready for eating, and feed on lizards, mice, young birds, etc. Smaller shrikes eat locusts and beetles. Most varieties have loud scolding voices; some, like the Bokmakierie (q.v.), sing well. The Fiscal Shrike or Jacky Hangman (*Lanius collaris*) is the best known of the smaller birds of prey all over South Africa as it sits conspicuously on telegraph wires. Dull black with white chest. A harsh note, but quite a good song. Several varieties. The Boubou Shrike or Waterfiskaal of the Cape belongs to thick bush and is seldom seen. Male and female sing a duet like that of the Bokmakierie. Various types, brown to black and white. Down the coast from Natal live the many coloured Shrikes. *See* BIRDS.

Shrimps. *See* MARINE RESOURCES.

Sibasa. Administrative centre in the Northern Transvaal, for the reserves occupied by the Bavenda tribe. In beautiful mountain country.

Sickle-Fish, Concertina-Fish (*Drepane punctata*). Found off Natal and in the Indo-Pacific Ocean, also on the west coast of Africa as far south as Angola. About 15 inches long, and nearly as deep. Silvery, with golden sheen, and black bars or spots supposedly like the stops on a concertina keyboard. Not much relished by Europeans.

Sidvokodvo. Village in Swaziland, administrative centre of the new Swaziland Railway (q.v.).

Sigcau (also known as **Sigcawu**). Pondo chief and son of Umquikela. On February 15, 1888, succeeded the latter, but, proving incapable and weak, allowed chaotic conditions to develop in his still independent territory. The Cape Government, under Cecil John Rhodes, decided to intervene and on March 17, 1894, Sigcau agreed to become a British subject and place Pondoland under the Crown. After the annexation Sigcau took legal proceedings against the Colonial Government, which culminated in a trial before the Privy Council in London, the case being argued by the late H. H. Asquith, afterwards British Prime Minister. Sigcau was successful in vindicating his rights. He died in 1905.

Sillimanite. Refractory mineral exploited in North-Western Cape Province.

Silveira, Dom Gonzalo da. Portuguese missionary and saint, born of a noble family in Almeirim, on the River Tagus. He joined the Jesuit Order in 1543, and in 1556 was posted to Goa, where he did outstanding work in spreading the Catholic faith. In 1560 he extended his work to Mozambique, which still fell under the jurisdiction of Portuguese India. Both he and his companion, a lay-brother, André da Costa, were charged with the conversion of the local tribes to Christianity. He penetrated far into the interior, and set up a mission with the Monomotapa and the Makalanga. Exciting the hostility of the local chief by baptising 50 natives, he was strangled on March 16, 1561, and his body cast into the river. His martyrdom later won him canonisation.

Silverfish, Kapenaar (*Polysteganus argyrozona*). Fish found from Table Bay to Natal. About 30 inches long Good eating. *See* BREAM.

Silver Tree (*Leucadendron argenteum*). A beautiful, much-branched tree, up to 50 feet high. Indigenous only in the Cape Peninsula, preferring damp, loamy soil with a southern aspect and an altitude of 600 to 900 feet. Much prized for the sheen of its long silky leaves. The old farm Wittebomen and the modern station Wittebome in the Cape Peninsula were named in its honour. (It was known formerly as 'Witte Boom' or 'White Tree.') *See* PROTEA.

Silvie or **Blinkvis** (*Austrosparus tricuspidens*). One of Silver Bream fishes found in the Breede River mouth, and very common from Mossel Bay eastwards. About 14 inches long. *See* BREAM.

Simonstown. Naval base 20 miles from Cape Town, on Simon's Bay, an inlet on False Bay. Its name is derived from Governor Simon van der Stel, as is that of the Simonsberg, at the foot of which it lies. The chief value of the port was its protection against the winter gales which made Cape Town dangerous before docks were built. Although previously used, it was not until 1742 that Simonstown became an official harbour, and that a village began to spring up. By the end of the 18th century it already possessed military and naval installations. Under the British occupation its strategic value was recognised to the full. It was used as a naval base during the first régime, from 1795 to 1802, and was the scene of a naval mutiny, an echo of the one at Spithead in 1797. In 1806 large developments began. Admiralty House was built in 1814 when the Navy decided to station a squadron there permanently. It has remained the most important naval station in the southern hemisphere. The town maintained a certain amount of commercial traffic until 1899, when the Admiralty took almost complete control. Work on the new dockyard, begun in 1899, was finished in 1910 at a cost of £2,500,000. With the establishment of a South African Navy a demand for a change developed and in April, 1957, Simonstown was handed over to the Union Department of Defence, though the United Kingdom retained the right to use it as needed, in war and peace. The town is picturesque and full of quaint old buildings. Population: 9,000, including 4,000 Whites.

Simon van der Stel Foundation. Named after Governor Simon van der Stel (q.v.). Established on April 9, 1959, for the protection of historical buildings and other antiquities in South Africa.

Sink-Holes. Underground cavities in certain parts of the Southern Transvaal, particularly in the Dolomite formation. Believed to be due mainly to pumping out vast quantities of water for gold-mining operations. Serious accidents in recent years include the collapse of ground occupied by much of the surface equipment of the West Driefontein Mine in December 1962, with the loss of 29 lives; and the engulfment on August 3, 1964, of five houses on the Blyvooruitzicht mine, with the loss of another six lives. Intensive research has followed and a new technique of filling the underground cavities with slimes and other material is being developed. Much of the township of Carltonville (q.v.) has been endangered by sink-holes.

Sinkins. Afrikaans name for rheumatism.

Sinoia. Village in Rhodesia. Tobacco and gold mining centre. Chiefly noted for its proximity to the famous Sinoia Caves, containing a deep blue pool, the level of which never varies. Population: 2,000, including 600 Whites.

Sipolilo. Administrative station in Rhodesia, noted for its view of the Zambesi Escarpment.

Sir Lowry's Pass. Village near Somerset West, Cape Province. Population: 880, including 40 Whites. Named after Governor Sir Lowry Cole.

Sishen. Mining centre near Kuruman, Bechuanaland, in the north of Cape Province, a major source of iron ore for Iscor (q.v.). It is linked by rail to the main line at Kimberley.

Siskin or **Pietjie Kanarie** (Fringillidae). Singing bird of the Canary family (q.v.) found along the Cape mountain ranges, from Cape Town to the borders of the Eastern Cape Province and in the Drakensberg mountains of Natal. Easily distinguished by its chocolate back and olive-green underparts. *See* BIRDS.

Situtunga (*Tragelaphus specei selousi*). Antelope found in swampy country, north of the Zambesi, and in tropical Africa. To the old Boers it was known as the Water Kudu, or the Water Skaap (Water Sheep). Its elongated hoofs enable the Situtunga to make its way without difficulty through marshes, though it is slow and clumsy on land. It is not good eating. Concealed in reeds or nearly submerged, it is difficult to find, and was first reported in 1852, by David

Situtunga

Livingstone. Height about 4 feet at the shoulder. The male alone has rather thick horns.

Sjambok. Whip, usually made of a strip of rhinoceros, hippopotamus or giraffe hide. The word is derived from the Persian 'chabuk,' meaning a whip.

Skaapstekers, Sand Snakes and Grass Snakes (Colubridae). Are typical back-fanged snakes, i.e. they have certain hollow, or ridged, back teeth through which poison flows. None is particularly dangerous to man. They are common over most of the veld, and in sheep kraals where there are lizards, beetles, etc. Many varieties have stripes or spots, and some of the Sand Snakes are slender to a degree. The Hissing Sand Snakes (or Whip Snakes) get their name from the fact that, while snakes normally breathe very slowly to match their sluggish life, in moments of anger they take a deep breath and hiss it out rapidly. *See* SNAKES.

Skaapwagter. Afrikaans name for Capped Wheatear. Literally 'Shepherd.' *See* WHEATEAR.

Skaife, Dr. Stacy Harold. South African naturalist. Born in London on December 12, 1890, and educated at the Universities of Redding and of Leipzig. At the age of 23 he came to South Africa to take up a teaching career at Rondebosch Boys' High School, but already showing his lifelong interest in Natural History, he joined the Department of Agriculture in 1916 as an entomologist and was on the staff of the Cedara Agricultural College in Natal. From here he transferred in 1920 as Organising Inspector of Agricultural and Scientific Education. During these years he began writing books which gained great popularity, several of them being addressed to children. At the request of the Government, Dr. Skaife in 1935 organised a radio educational service for schools. Under the pen-name of

Hendrik Brand, Dr. Skaife in 1929 began writing thrillers and detective stories, which appeared in Afrikaans, most of them featuring the detective, Adriaan Hugo. They achieved national popularity. International fame, however, came to him on account of his epoch-making researches into the life and characteristics of termites and ants, as well as on insects generally, on which he published standard treatises. In 1944 he was appointed Chairman of the Fisheries Development Corporation, a post he continued to hold until 1948.

Skans. A form of redoubt, thrown up by Boers in the field for protection and usually made of earth and stones. Skanses were widely used in the South African War.

Skans

Skelm (a rogue). A word widely used in South Africa, derived from the Dutch 'schelm.' (Compare German Schelm.) The word is also used by Robert Burns in 'Tam-o'-Shanter.'

Skerm. Protective screen of thorn branches and tree trunks made by hunters and travellers in parts of South Africa to prevent attacks by wild animals.

Skerm

Skilling. Coin in circulation at the Cape until the British occupation; equal to twopence farthing.

Skilpadbessie, 'Tortoise Berry' or Duinebos (*Mundia spinosa* D.C.). Prickly shrub up to 3 feet. Berries eaten by birds. South coastal areas in Cape Province.

Skilpad Trek. Old Afrikaner game in which two players (usually children) are fastened together by means of a thong round their waists or necks, and, going down on all fours, indulge in a tug-of-war with the thong between their legs.

Skimmel. A white or grey horse; an old expression also found in German (Schimmel).

Skipper or **Saury** (*Scombresox saurus*). Member of the Flying-Fish family, with long body and very long jaws, dark blue above and silvery below, 18 inches long. Found from St. Helena Bay to Mossel Bay, as well as in North Atlantic and near Australia. Swims in large shoals near the surface, and when chased, leaps out of the water or skims the surface. The Flying-Fish (q.v.) have obviously evolved from this type by a pectoral-fin development.

Skipskop. Village near Bredasdorp, Cape Province. Population: 120, including 60 Whites.

Skokiaan. Drink brewed by Africans, particularly on the Witwatersrand. The basis is generally yeast, which is allowed to ferment, but extra ingredients, including carbide, are sometimes added to give it a 'kick.'

Skoongesig. Village near Middelburg, Transvaal. Population: 380, including 120 Whites.

Sks. Abbreviation for skillings (q.v.).

Skua (family Laridae). Seabird common about Table Bay and off the west and south-west coasts. It differs from a gull in being largely brown, with a strongly hooked beak. It lives by robbing gulls and tern of their fish. A dashing, hawk-like flight. *See* GULL.

Skyscrapers. *See* ARCHITECTURE.

Slagter's Nek Rebellion. Insurrection in 1815 which arose from the prosecution of a farmer, Frederik Cornelius Bezuidenhout, on the Baviaan's River in the Eastern Cape Province. He was charged with ill-treating a native servant and summoned to court. When he ignored this and other warnings, Lt. Frans Rossouw and 12 Hottentot soldiers were sent to arrest him. He resisted and was killed. His companions were brought to trial, found guilty and sentenced to death. The sentence was carried out publicly with considerable clumsiness, a rope breaking, and death resulting only on the second attempt. The whole affair caused great indignation among the settlers, and after more than a century has not been forgotten.

Slamse Mense. Name applied to the Cape Malays, derived from the word Islam. They also refer to themselves as such. *See* CAPE MALAYS.

Slangbos, 'Snake bush' (*Stoebe cinerea* Thunb.). Much-branched low shrub. Widespread in Cape Province, Orange Free State and Natal.

Slangkop (*Ornithoglossom glaucum*). Poisonous Cape plant, particularly dangerous to cattle. A different plant, equally poisonous, is found in the Transvaal and carries the same name.

Slangrivier. Coloured settlement near Heidelberg, Cape. Population: 1,040.

Slangverklikker. Afrikaans name for Cape Ground-Robin. *See* ROBIN.

Slangwyster. Afrikaans name for Grey Tit. *See* TIT.

Slave Pits. Mysterious excavations in the eastern mountains of Rhodesia, the purpose of which has never been explained. They average 20 feet in diameter and are 6 or 7 feet deep, too shallow to be used as effective places of confinement for slaves or cattle, as was originally thought. They have a peculiar tunnel approach, usually only a foot or two wide. Some of these slave pits are said to be covered with roofs. They are particularly common around Inyanga (q.v.).

Slave Pit

Slavery. Slave-trading and slavery had been practised in Africa from time immemorial, and the introduction of slaves to the Cape by Europeans dates from the earliest days of settlement. At first they were few in number, the return under van Riebeeck in 1657 showing three males and eight females. Larger imports began from the west coast of Africa in 1658, and were reinforced by numerous Malays and other Easterners from 1667 onwards, many of whom were skilled craftsmen. From them originated the Cape Malay community. Legislation was introduced to regulate the rights of slaves, who in certain circumstances were permitted to purchase their freedom. Later a Protector of Slaves was appointed. Mortgages could be passed on their security. Largely through such British humanitarians as Clarkson, Wilberforce and the Quaker community, the slave trade was forbidden in all British possessions in 1807, by which time the Cape had already become British territory. A slave rebellion in 1808 was suppressed with severity, but an easing of the position followed, and the 1820 settlers were forbidden to hold slaves. In 1833 the House of Commons passed an Act forbidding slavery throughout the King's possessions, and voted the very considerable sum of £20,000,000 as compensation to owners. Of the 770,280 slaves liberated, the Cape possessed 39,021, of whom more than half, namely 21,613, were males, and over 5,000 were under six years old. Their value was estimated at £3,041,290, but the compensation granted came to £1,247,401 0s. 7d. The method of paying this by means of 3½ Government stock, stamp duties, etc., mystified the farmers, produced much embitterment, and was one cause of the Great Trek (q.v.). Slavery of a different kind was found along the entire East African coast and lasted almost to the end of the 19th century, thousands of victims being captured, in what is today the Federation of Central Africa, by Arab and other traders. Final steps for the extermination of this traffic were carried out during the first decade of the present century. *See* MIXED COMMISSION.

Sleeman, Sister Lucy. Pioneer Rhodesian nurse, born in England. She joined a party to South Africa, 1890, and on board the *Spartan* gained the friendship of Sister Rose Blennerhassett (q.v.), with whom she went to Rhodesia and set up the first hospital in Umtali. She later married Granville Vines, a Kimberley engineer.

Slegtkamp, Captain Henri Frederick. Boer guerilla fighter. Born in Holland in 1873, came to South Africa as a young man and won distinction in native warfare and in the South African War, particularly in association with Captain 'Jack' Hindon (q.v.) at Spion Kop. He retired to Middelburg, Transvaal, and died on February 2, 1951.

Slimies (*Lioganthus equula*). A group of smallish fish belonging to tropical or sub-tropical waters, with compressed bodies, a slimy covering to their scales, spines on their bodies and mouths that can be protruded. Scavengers belong to the same group.

Sloley, Sir Herbert Cecil. Resident Commissioner of Basutoland, and expert on Native Affairs. Born in Calcutta, 1855, he was educated in England and began his career in a London bank. At the age of 22 he came to South Africa to join the Cape Mounted Rifles, in which he distinguished himself repeatedly. He transferred to the Cape Police in 1883, and then to the Basutoland Mounted Police, of which he became Assistant Commissioner in 1889. He was Government Secretary of Basutoland in 1898 and from 1916 Resident Commissioner there. He died in 1937.

Slurry. Village in the Western Transvaal, noted for its large cement factory. The name is derived from a mixture produced in the making of cement. Population: 1,135, including 317 Whites.

Sluysken, Abraham Josias. Last Governor of the Cape under the Dutch East India Company. Born in Holland, he entered the service of the Company at an early age and was Director of Trade at Surat when, in 1793, he was sent to the Cape. Arriving during the stay of Nederbergh and Frijkenius (q.v.) he took over a colony on the verge of collapse, deep in debt, and was soon confronted with a rising by the Boers in Graaff-Reinet and Swellendam. In the circumstances he acted with tact, and when news came of an impending British attack, he did his best to improve the slender defences of the Colony. Refusing to surrender voluntarily, he gave way to the inevitable in 1795 and was repatriated in a neutral 'cartel' ship to Holland. There he was exonerated by the National Assembly at The Hague. Sluysken published in 1797 a book on his experiences, *Verhaal gehouden by den Commissaris van de Caap de Goede Hoop* (Narrative of the Commissary of the Cape of Good Hope).

Smartt, Sir Thomas William. Cabinet Minister and Leader of the former Unionist Party. Born, 1858, in Ireland, he studied medicine in Dublin and came to South Africa in 1880, making his home in Britstown in the Karroo. There he became interested in farming and established the famous Smartt Syndicate, which erected one of the largest dams in the country at Houwater near Britstown. In 1895 he was elected to the Cape Parliament and was immediately appointed Colonial Secretary by Sir Gordon Sprigg. He was besieged with Rhodes in Kimberley during the South African War. In 1900 he became Commissioner of Public Works, and held a similar post in the Jameson Ministry from 1904 to 1908. After taking part in the National Convention, he became leader of the new Unionist Party, and successor to Sir L. S. Jameson (q.v.). He was in the Opposition until the merger of the South African and the Unionist Party in 1921 brought him back into office, as Minister of Agriculture. He held this post until 1924 and died in 1929.

Smee-Eend. Afrikaans name for Red-bill (q.v.).

Smelling Out. Procedure followed by African witchdoctors to detect alleged offenders. The Xosa word is 'uku Nuka.' In former times anybody 'smelt out' was immediately killed.

Smit, Erasmus. First Minister to the Voortrekkers, born in Amsterdam on August 2, 1778. He was the son of the steersman on a ship trading to the Indies, and spent his childhood in an orphanage. In 1801 he became a missionary, first in America and in 1804 at the Cape, where he worked with Dr. J. Vanderkemp at Bethelsdorp (q.v.). Since the Dutch Reformed Church at the Cape refused to ordain him, Smit became a schoolmaster, and, having married the sister of the Voortrekker leader, Gerrit Maritz, he joined the emigrants in 1836. He became their unofficial chaplain, taking regular services, performing marriages and accompanying the Trekkers to Natal. He settled in Pietermaritzburg, where he died in 1863.

Smit, Jacobus Stephanus. Administrator of the Transvaal and South African High Commissioner in London. Born on October 9, 1878, near Pretoria, he qualified for the Bar, and was elected to Parliament in 1920. He was High Commissioner for the Union in London from 1925 to 1929, as well as South African delegate to the League of Nations and to the Disarmament Conference in Geneva. This was followed by his appointment as Administrator of the Transvaal from 1929 to 1934, and by his membership of the Diamond Board. He died in 1960.

Smit, Nicolas Jacobus. Vice-President of the South African Republic, born in Graaff-Reinet, 1837. He emigrated as a child to the Transvaal and took part in the early campaigns against the natives, notably the chiefs Sechele and Makapan. Settling at Potchefstroom, he became Field-Cornet in 1864. In 1876 he fought in the Sekukuni War. He retired to his farm in 1880 until the outbreak of the First Boer War, in which he distinguished himself at the Battle of Ingogo. Upon the restoration of peace he was elected to the Volksraad for Middelburg, and in 1883 appointed a member of the Independence Delegation. In 1886 he became Vice-President of the South African Republic. He died in 1896.

Smith, Sir Abercrombie. South African statesman, civil servant and administrator. Born on May 12, 1834, at St. Cyrus in Scotland, he studied at Glasgow University and was among early research workers on heat and electricity under Lord Kelvin. In 1860 he came to the Cape for reasons of health, began practice as land surveyor and entered Parliament as Member for King William's Town in 1865. Sir John Molteno appointed him Minister of Crown Lands in his first Cabinet in 1872. The rapid development of the Cape Government Railways was largely due to his efforts. Later he became Auditor-General and Public Debt Commissioner. He died in 1919.

Smith, Alfred Aloysius. Adventurer, known as Trader Horn. Born in 1854 near Glasgow, he came to Africa in 1871 and spent many years prospecting and trading in different parts of the continent. In the 1920's he was reduced to selling mouse traps from door to door in Johannesburg. While doing so he attracted the attention of Mrs. Ethelreda Lewis (q.v.), the South African novelist, who recorded his story in book form. This proved a sensational success, not only in England, but in the United States, where it was filmed as *Trader Horn*. Other books followed, including *Harold the Webbed*, from which he benefited financially. How many of Trader Horn's adventures were true remains a question. He died in 1931.

Smith, Sir Andrew. Explorer and botanist. Born in Scotland, 1797, he qualified in medicine and joined the British Army as a surgeon. He was sent to the Cape in 1820 and encouraged local scientific research, founding, in 1825, the South African Museum. When sent as a Government delegate to visit the chief Gaika on the Eastern Border, became interested in exploration, and in 1833, on behalf of the 'Association for the Exploration of Central South Africa,' he began a series of journeys, which took him through the present Transvaal and into Matabeleland. His diaries and numerous botanical observations are classics of their kind. He retired from the Army in 1857 and died in England in 1872. In 1939 his journals were published in two volumes by the Van Riebeeck Society.

Smith, Charles Thomas. Judge of the Cape Supreme Court and Chancellor of the University of the Cape of Good Hope. Born in England, 1823, and educated in Germany and at Cambridge. Beginning work as a legal tutor, he was called to the Bar in Britain and practised until 1869, when he became a judge of the Eastern Districts Court at the Cape. After 11 years in Grahamstown, he moved to Cape Town in 1880, where he became prominent in educational matters. In 1889 he was appointed Vice-Chancellor of the University of the Cape of Good Hope. He retired in 1892, and died in Cape Town in 1901.

Smithfield. Town in the Southern Orange Free State, founded in 1848 and named in honour of Governor Sir Harry Smith of the Cape. It saw much fighting with the Basutos, but in 1855 a Treaty of Friendship was signed there. between the Orange Free State and Moshesh. Further fighting took place near by in the South African War. It has grown into a prosperous irrigation and wool-growing centre. Population: 3,000, including 970 Whites.

Smith, Sir Harry George Wakelyn. Governor of the Cape of Good Hope. Born at Whittlesea in Cambridgeshire, England, in 1787. Joined the Army at 17 and in 1805 took part in the siege of Montevideo and campaign in South America. Distinguished himself in Peninsular War, in 1812 War against U.S.A. and in Waterloo campaign. First came to Cape to play important part in Native War of 1836. His victories in India, especially over the Sikhs at Aliwal in 1846, brought him promotion to Major-General and a baronetcy. He was appointed Governor of the Cape in 1847. There he showed great military ability, in dealing with both the frontier tribes and the emigrant Boers from the Cape, whom he defeated at Boomplaats (q.v.), in the Orange Free State, in 1848. Despite an irascible temper, he was not unsuccessful as a governor, and his historic ride of 600 miles from Cape Town to Grahamstown to face a war-time crisis made him a popular hero as did his sympathy with the Colonists in opposing the introduction of convicts. He returned to England in 1852, and was placed in command of the Northern and Midland Military Districts and died in 1860. His autobiography was published in 1901.

Smith, Ian Douglas. Prime Minister of Rhodesia. Born at Selukwe, 1919, he was the first Rhodesian to achieve this position. Educated at Chaplin School, Gwelo, and Rhodes University, Grahamstown, he joined up as a R.A.F. pilot in 1941 during World War II, and while flying with the Rhodesia Squadron (No. 237) was shot down over Italy. Discharged in 1946 he returned to Rhodesia and was elected Member for Selukwe,

1948. In 1953 he became Member for Midlands in the Federal Parliament. As leader of the Rhodesian Front Party he became Prime Minister in 1964, with the policy of achieving Rhodesian independence. This was proclaimed unilaterally on November 11, 1965. *See* RHODESIA.

Smith, Professor Johannes Jacobus. South African philologist and first editor of the official Afrikaans Dictionary. Born on October 5, 1881, near Tulbagh, he was educated in Paarl and Stellenbosch before continuing his studies overseas, where he specialised in Germanic languages. While in London he was called to the Bar and gained top marks for England. In 1914 he was appointed to the Chair of German and French at Victoria College and, after it had become the University of Stellenbosch in 1919, he became the first Professor of Afrikaans. Meanwhile from 1917 to 1924 he was editor, first of *Ons Moedertaal*, and then of *Die Huisgenoot*. A leading member of the S.A. Akademie, he took a deep interest in the Afrikaans language, helped to standardise spelling rules and from 1925 to 1943 was editor of the Afrikaans Dictionary, doing a vast amount of work. He was involved in a dispute with the Akademie on spelling rules, which ended in a compromise in 1932. He was also a member of the Place Names Commission and of the Joint Matriculation Board and a Trustee of the South African National Gallery. He retired from his dictionary editorship in 1943 and died on June 18, 1949.

Smith, Pauline. South African novelist and short story writer. Daughter of a former District Surgeon of the Oudtshoorn area, she grew up in the Little Karroo, which remained a favourite background for her books. After the death of her family, she made her permanent home in England, but continued to write on South Africa. Her most famous book is *The Little Karroo*, published in 1925, and containing a number of short stories of classical merit, notably *The Pain*. Her output was small but of a very high standard. She died in 1957.

Smith Pommer. Leader of a Griqua Rebellion. Of Hottentot origin, he came from the Kat River settlement in the Eastern Province, and became an official under Adam Kok III, when the latter was still independent. Gaining the friendship of the Pondo chief, Umquikela, he roused a section of the Griqua people in Griqualand East during the Native War of 1878 to support the Xosas. Assisted by a Hottentot leader named Adam Muis, he looted European stores. He was killed and his rebellion quashed by a force under Captain Blyth.

Smith's Coasters. Small shipping line set up by the firm of C. G. Smith & Co. of Durban, and engaged mainly in sugar traffic between South African ports. Now part of Unicorn line (q.v.).

Smith, Sir William James. Judge of the Transvaal Supreme Court. Born at Cheltenham in 1853, he went to school there and in 1875 was called to the Bar at Lincoln's Inn. After practising for five years in London, he became a judge of the Gold Coast, but soon resigned, and in 1882 was appointed a judge in Cyprus. There he rose to be Chief Justice in 1892. In 1897 he was appointed to a similar post in British Guiana. Because Roman-Dutch Law was in use in that Colony he was selected in 1902 for an appointment on the Transvaal Bench, which he filled with distinction until his death in 1912.

Smoorvis. Braised fish: an old Cape Malay dish.

Smouse. Traditional South African name for a hawker, particularly one who goes from farm to farm selling goods of all kinds. The business of the smouse is a very old established one and is referred to as early as the 18th century when François Le Vaillant (q.v.) visited the Cape. There were two kinds of smouses, those who travelled with a wagon, and those who were content with the so-called 'penswinkel' (stomach shop), or tray. Many famous South Africans began their careers as smouses, one of those proud to refer to the fact being Samuel Marks (q.v.). The origin of the word is uncertain.

Smuts, Field-Marshal Jan Christian. Premier of the Union of South Africa. Born on the farm Bovenplaats outside Riebeek West, Cape Colony, on May 24, 1870, and son of Jacobus Abraham Smuts, a farmer and Member of the Colonial Parliament. Like hundreds of other Boer children, it was not until the age of 12 that he was sent to school, although he had received some teaching from his mother. He was intended for the ministry of the Dutch Reformed Church. After attending the school of T. C. Stofberg (afterwards Senator Stofberg), where one of his fellow-pupils was the future Dr. D. F. Malan (q.v.), Smuts went to Victoria College in Stellenbosch, 1886, forerunner of the present University. There he met his wife-to-be, the gifted student Sibella Margaretha (nicknamed Isie) Krige. Fate brought him into personal touch with Cecil John Rhodes when the statesman visited the college. After a brilliant career at Stellenbosch, Smuts went to Cambridge, 1891, where he read for the Bar, and where he wrote a book, never published, on the work and poetry of Walt Whitman. In 1895 he returned to South Africa and began practice in 1896 in Johannesburg. His ability brought him to the notice of President Kruger, who appointed him State Attorney in 1898. Upon the outbreak of the Boer War Smuts took an important, though not exclusive part in the production of *A Century of Wrong*, putting the case of

the Republics against Britain. Within a short while of joining the Boer forces, his ability and gifts as a guerrilla leader brought him into prominence. His historic raid far into the Cape Colony carried him close to Malmesbury and within sight of Table Mountain. The end of the South African War found him in the field. He took a leading part in the Peace negotiations at Vereeniging, after which he decided that the only hope for his people was to accept the new British Crown Colony régime. He became one of the leaders of the 'Het Volk' movement (q.v.) and was elected into the newly-established Parliament. As Cabinet Minister his personality soon brought him into prominence. He enjoyed the close friendship of General Louis Botha (q.v.) but was regarded as being the more reserved and intellectual. A ruthless streak in him was shown in the way he handled the struggle waged by the Indian community, led by M. K. Gandhi. Upon the establishment of Union, Smuts became Minister of Defence, Mines and the Interior. He created the Union Defence Force. As Minister of Mines he was involved in violent labour disputes of 1913 and 1914, which were only subdued by calling up the armed forces and the Imperial Garrison. For what was regarded as high-handed action, he incurred much odium. By this time General Hertzog (q.v.) had seceded from Botha's Cabinet and founded what became the National Party. Upon the outbreak of World War I, Smuts resumed his rôle as a soldier, and took charge of the campaign in East Africa. His intellectual stature had impressed the British Government, and in 1917 he left the East African theatre to take part in the Imperial War Conference in London. He joined the War Cabinet, became a Privy Councillor and was largely responsible, amongst other things, for the establishment of the Royal Air Force. Besides being frequently on the Western Front, he took part in an early attempt to make peace with Austria in 1917. His advice on the campaign against the Turks in Palestine led to victory in those parts. Already he had conceived the idea of founding the League of Nations, and he paid a visit for the Allied authorities to Hungary during the 1918 revolution. After attending the Peace Conference at Versailles in 1919, Smuts returned to South Africa to become Prime Minister, following the death of General Louis Botha. He found himself weighed down with post-war problems and, although he won the 1920 election, his severity during the 1922 Rand Revolt ultimately led to his defeat at the hands of General Hertzog. Outside politics he wrote an important philosophical work, *Holism and Evolution*, in 1926. In 1930 he became a Fellow of the Royal Society and the following year Rector of St. Andrew's University. For nine years he was leader of the Opposition, until the Gold Standard Crisis of 1933 led to the reunion of the parties and to his acceptance of office under Hertzog. Smuts was Deputy Prime Minister until 1939. Upon the outbreak of World War II he again became Prime Minister. As intimate collaborator of Winston Churchill and others, his rôle in this struggle was almost greater than during World War I. At the same time he had to deal with many internal difficulties. One of his major achievements was drafting the Covenant of the United Nations. He received the greatest honours both in Europe and the United States. In 1948 he was defeated in the General Election. He continued his political activities until his death in 1950.

Smuts House. Building erected at University of Witwatersrand to accommodate South African Institute of International Affairs. It contains a complete replica of General J. C. Smuts's study.

Smythe, Charles John. Prime Minister of Natal. Born in Scotland, 1852, he came to Natal in 1872, where he farmed cattle near Nottingham Road in 1876. Upon the grant of Responsible Government he was elected to the Legislative Assembly, in 1893, and from 1897 to 1899 was Speaker. This led to his appointment as Colonial Secretary from 1899 to 1903. From 1905 to 1906 he was Prime Minister of Natal, and later a delegate to the National Convention. He died in May 1918.

Snake. An expression used by the early diamond diggers to describe a curling dyke of barren rock occurring in the diamond pipes.

Snake-Bird or **Darter** (*Anhinga rufa*). A relative of the Duikers (q.v.), but with a long snaky neck, very small head and long stiff tail. The neck has a curious kink, which results in a sudden thrust forward of the head. It swims low with only head and neck visible, ready to spear a fish. It is found on the larger rivers and on other inland waters in South Africa. A sociable bird that flies with others of its kind to nest at the top of tall trees.

Snakebite Serum. Was developed under the initiative of the late F. W. FitzSimons (q.v.) at the Port Elizabeth Museum, where it has been marketed for nearly half a century. Also produced under the auspices of the South African Institute of Medical Research in Johannesburg. Special outfits are manufactured for the use of travellers and farmers.

Snake, Blind. A very small, non-poisonous, burrowing species, with practically no eyes. The closeness of the vent to the blunt tail has given this family the name 'Two-headed Snake.' The rudimentary pelvis on their skeletons show the lizard ancestry of snakes. Like all non-poisonous snakes, Blind Snakes have sharp solid teeth, one group, **Typhlopidae**, having none in the lower jaw, and the other, Leptotyphlopidae (often called worm-snakes) having none in the upper. Both groups live under dead leaves or stones, and burrow for worms, ants and other insects. They never climb trees. *See* SNAKES.

Snake, Egg-Eating (*Dasypeltis scabra*). Group: Colubridae. One of the harmless snakes, found everywhere in South Africa, but nowhere common. In its mouth are only rudimentary teeth, their place being taken by little bony projections from the neck bone, coated with enamel for holding, and sawing through, egg shells. The contents are swallowed and the shell thrown out. An expert climber, this snake traces birds' nests by their smell and will take only fresh eggs. *See* SNAKES.

Snake, Garter. *See* ROUSBANDJIE.

Snake, Grass. *See* SKAAPSTEKERS.

Snake, Herald or **Red-Lipped** (*Leptodira hotanbaeia*). One of the best-known, back-fanged snakes of the Colubridae (not very poisonous) group (*see* SKAAPSTEKER). It is widespread throughout Africa. It frequents gardens, hiding under rubbish, comes out at night, and will bite fiercely if captured. It eats toads, mice and other small creatures. Average length 2 feet. Olive-brown in colour, back flecked with white dots. It has a bright red upper lip. It was named in honour of the *Eastern Province Herald*. *See* SNAKES.

Snake, Mole (*Pseudaspis cana*). (Group: Colubridae). Non-poisonous species found in sandy scrub in all parts of South Africa. It lives on rats, moles, lizards, round which (as does every non-poisonous snake) it coils its body before swallowing them. The fur usually is cast out some hours later, but the bones are often digested by powerful juices. Uninterested in climb ing trees. It gives birth to its young

alive—40 or more at a time. The colour varies—shiny black, brick red or brown with black spots. *See* SNAKES.

Snake, Night (*Lamprophis aurora*). (Group: Colubridae). Non-poisonous snake found, but infrequently, in the Cape Province and the Transvaal. It is a pale olive-brown, sometimes specked with black, with a line of yellow down its back. It feeds on mice, and is an excellent tree-climber.

Snake, Sand. *See* SKAAPSTEKERS.

Snake Stone. Alleged remedy against snakebite, consisting of a piece of bone rubbed to an oval, burnt at the edges and applied to the wound. Its medical efficacy is nil.

Snake, Three-Cornered or **Vylslang** (*Simocephalus*). (Group: Colubridae). Found in Natal, Mozambique and Rhodesia. So called because of its three-cornered section. Non-poisonous. Average length 3 feet.

Snake, Water (Group: Colubridae). Non-poisonous species found commonly in many parts of South Africa, particularly in swampy ground and near rivers. It grows to a length of about 2 feet. There are two varieties, Olive-brown and Green, the latter with a long tapering body and very large eyes. Both are expert swimmers and divers for frogs and fish, which they carry to land and then crush in their coils, if too large to swallow. *See* SNAKES.

Snake, House (Boodon). (Group: Colubridae). Non-poisonous species useful in keeping down mice and other vermin. These snakes are among the few that do not climb trees. They vary in length from 1 foot to 2 feet 6 inches, and (by those who wish to examine them!) will be noticed often to have odd-coloured eyes and (like most innocent snakes) small, solid teeth, two rows in the top and one in the lower jaw. Contrast Skaapstekers and *see* SNAKES.

SNAKES OF SOUTHERN AFRICA

by

DR. J. A. PRINGLE

Natal Museum, Pietermaritzburg

SNAKES are generally recognised by the absence of limbs, but this is not a distinguishing characteristic, for the Pythons and related groups have rudimentary limbs while certain lizards are legless.

A curious feature of snake anatomy is that the two halves of the lower jaw are separated in the front, and connected by an elastic ligament, so that their mouths can stretch to swallow very large prey. Some of them kill their prey by venom, some by crushing, and many simply swallow it alive.

Most snakes live on the ground but the Boomslang and Bird Snake are expert climbers; some, such as the Shield Snake, Black-Natal and the Blind Snakes, live underground; others, like the Water Snakes, are good swimmers. Pythons spend much of their time in water while Sea Snakes are so completely adapted to marine life that they cannot live on land.

When they feed, snakes like to feast and then retire to digest the meal. Muscle, bone, teeth all disappear and the only undigested parts are hair or feathers. They feed ravenously during the summer, lay up a store of fat and stop feeding entirely at the onset of winter. Some are fastidious about their food: the Night Adder eats only frogs, the Egg-eater only eggs; others have a wide range of diet which includes rodents, birds, lizards and frogs, while others again are cannibals. They invariably swallow their prey head first to prevent the limbs from obstructing passage into the mouth. The process of swallowing is a slow and at times a painful one. The snake literally walks over its prey by moving its jaws forwards alternately and thus slowly drawing it into its mouth, pausing frequently to rest and breathe. Once the prey passes into the throat it is forced down by constricting the gullet in rhythmic wave-like motions.

Snakes usually emerge in the late afternoon and evening to hunt for food; they find it by sight, by taste, by waiting patiently in suitable areas or accidentally by prowling around. They have indifferent sight and cannot clearly distinguish a stationary object, but any movement will at once attract their attention. The eyes are placed on the sides of the head and the main field of vision is thus lateral. For several inches in front of the nose there is a blind area. Ahead of this is a zone where the field of vision of the two eyes overlaps and this is the area of optimum stereoscopic vision.

Certain snakes, such as the Night Adder, Boomslang, Cobra, House Snake and Python, lay eggs, while in others, such as the Ringhals, Puff Adder and Mole Snake, the young are born alive. The Python protects and incubates her eggs, but other snakes lay them in holes underground and leave them to incubate. Snakes take no paternal interest in their progeny and the young soon scatter and fend for themselves. The eggs require a high humidity for incubation, but temperature is not of great importance, although eggs hatch more quickly in a warm atmosphere.

Snakes slough their skins at intervals during their entire life, in some cases several times a year. At the first signs of sloughing, the eyes turn blue and the snake becomes sluggish and refuses food. As the snake rubs its lips against stones or branches, so the skin peels off and is rolled gradually inside out. The skin is cast from the tip of the nose to the end of the tail, including the eye scales, and the emerging snake reveals all its colours in their resplendent hues.

The following are the main groups of snakes:

Viperidae: Puff Adder, Gaboon Adder, Night Adder, Berg Adder, Horned Adder and Burrowing Adder.

Hydrophidae: Black-and-yellow Sea Snake.

Elapidae: Black and Green Mambas, Banded Cobra, Yellow Cobra, Mfesi, Ringhals.

Colubridae: Boomslang, Bird Snake, Skaapsteker, Water Snakes, Sand Snakes, Egg-eaters, Red-lipped Snake, Mole Snake, Bush Snake, File Snake, House Snake.

Boidae: Python.

Leptotyphlopidae: Worm Snakes.

Typhlopidae: Blind Snakes.

The majority of snakes are not poisonous, some are slightly venomous and only a limited number are fatal to man.

Note on Snake Groups

Viperidae: Long, hinged front poison fangs, thick, short bodies, heads usually triangular.

Hydrophidae: Solid (non-poisonous) teeth in front; deeply grooved nearly hollow fangs behind. Marine dwellers.

Elapidae: Fixed, hollow front fangs.

Colubridae: Large mixed group, none with hinged poison fangs. Some have only solid teeth (harmless); some are back-fanged and some front-fanged.

Boidae: No fangs. Victim is crushed.

Leptotyphlopidae: Solid (non-poisonous) teeth in lower jaw alone.

Typhlopidae: Solid teeth in top jaw alone.

Snakes, Sea (Hydrophidae). A very poisonous family of snakes with deeply-grooved fangs in the front of the upper jaw. They differ from all other snakes in having a flat, propeller tail. They produce their young alive (Viviparous) and shed their skins frequently, but in small pieces. The Black-and-yellow Sea Snake, the only South African species—about 2 feet 6 inches long—is found in rock pools all round the coast, and will attack viciously if provoked. *See* SNAKES.

Snapper. A large family of chiefly warm-water fishes, most of them good eating, although some are suspected of being poisonous. None is of much economic importance. *See* JOHNNY and SALMON, ROCK.

Sneeze Hottentots. This is a corruption of 'Sjienies,' Dutch and Afrikaans for 'Chinese.' This tribe, which lived north of the Great Fish River in the Eastern Province, was so called from their appearance. The name has been preserved in the Sneeze Flats.

Sneezewood or **Nieshout** (*Ptaeroxylon utile*, E. & L.). Tree up to 50 feet, 2 feet in diameter. Very important timber, having great durability as fencing posts in constantly damp, heavy soil. Grows in eastern coastal areas of Cape Province, Natal and Transvaal.

Snider. A type of early firearm. The name is derived from Jacob Snider, an American of Dutch descent who devised a way of converting the British Enfield rifle musket into a breech-loading weapon to take a metal cartridge. Not to be confused with Schneider (q.v.). The Snider was widely used in South Africa 1877–81.

Snipe. Bird of the Wader group, found in marshy land everywhere in South Africa. The Ethiopian Snipe (*Capella nigripennis*) is much like the European bird, with brown spotted coat and long, rather flat bill. It has, too, the habit of circling over the nest, and diving down suddenly. The larger migratory species from Europe is the Solitary or Double Snipe (*Capella media*). The Painted

Snipe (*Rostratula benghalensis*) is a beautiful variety, found also in Asia. Both male and female have bright buff spots on their wings, the female having a reddish throat. She is believed, like the Button-Quail (q.v.), to lay her eggs in a succession of nests for her many plainer husbands to incubate and rear.

Snoek (*Thyrsites atun*). Fish found from Mossamedes to Table Bay, False Bay to Mossel Bay and sometimes as far as Algoa Bay; also off Tristan da Cunha, Southern Australia, New Zealand and Chile. About 3½ feet long. Occurs in great migratory shoals and was formerly the staple food of the Coloured community at the Cape from about September to June. Exported to England after World War II, it fell into undeserved disfavour owing to bad canning. It is noted for its fine flavour when fresh or salted. *See* MARINE RESOURCES.

Snotsiekte. A cattle disease characterised by a discharge from the mouth and nostrils. It also occurs in certain wild game, including wildebeest.

Snowdrop, Cape. *See* CRASSULA.

Snysel. Old Cape dish, somewhat resembling macaroni and made of strips of dough, cut into short pieces. It is used to thicken soup.

Sobantu. Zulu name for Bishop John William Colenso (q.v.), meaning 'Father of his People.'

Sobhuza II. King of the Swazis. Born in 1898, son of Bhunu, whom he succeeded in 1899 with his grandmother, Nabotsibeni, as Queen Regent. Educated at Lovedale (q.v.), proclaimed Ingwengama, or King of the Swazis, 1922, and visited England, where he met King George V. In 1923 he appealed unsuccessfully to the Privy Council in an important land case concerning the validity of concessions granted to early White settlers by his grandfather, Umbandine.

He has worked consistently for the benefit and development of his country.

Sobosobo (*Solanum nigrum*). Wild fruit found in South Africa, which produces berries in clusters. Sometimes made into jam.

Soccer in Southern Africa. Although the achievements of South Africans in Rugby football have gained greater prominence, the Association game has always enjoyed popularity. It was played by members of the garrison in the early days, but the first serious efforts to establish it systematically were made in 1881 at Port Elizabeth by a Scottish player, formerly of Queen's Park. His death put an end to the attempt. Natal, however, in June 1882 established its own Football Association, comprising 5 clubs. Both on the Diamond Fields and on the Rand the game secured an early hold, but it was Sir Donald Currie (q.v.) who provided the first major encouragement when in 1892 he included it in the yearly Currie Cup Tournament. Soccer also gained a widespread vogue in schools, only challenged in recent years by the rise of Rugby.

The Griqualand West Football Association dates from 1890, the Western Province Football Association from 1896 and the Transvaal Football Association from 1899. The first overseas visitors arrived in 1897, when, warmly encouraged by the Rand, a team of Corinthians from Britain toured South Africa, defeated the local sides and gave a vast stimulus to the game. South Africa sent her first team abroad in 1906, when Harry N. Heeley led his men against the Argentinians. No further effort was made until 1924, when a side toured the United Kingdom.

Professionalism was introduced by the National Football League in 1959, and has gone from strength to strength, with crowds of over 20,000 not unusual at games between the better teams. Many professionals from England, Scotland and Greece have been imported by various clubs. As a result amateur soccer attracts smaller crowds.

Visitors include Tottenham Hotspur in 1963 and Arsenal, Eintracht (West Germany) and Real Madrid in 1964, bringing Soccer still further into prominence.

Social Welfare. As in Europe and America, the beginnings of social services in South Africa were in the hands of the Church, but it was not until 1808 that, thanks to the generosity of the Widow Moller, the first local 'Orphan Asylum' ('Zuid-Afrikaansche Weeshuis') was established in the Cape. Opening its doors on September 26, 1815, and controlled by an inter-denominational board of Dutch Reformed Church members and Lutherans, this became the forerunner of a network of privately administered institutions, and it was not until the 20th century that the State began to play a serious part.

Today the Department of Social Welfare, with its headquarters in Pretoria, co-ordinates and administers most activities as far as the Government is concerned. One of the earlier measures falling under its aegis is the Probation Act of 1911, followed by a supplementary measure in 1917. The Blind Persons Act No. 11 of 1936 and the Children's Act No. 31 of 1937 are also administered by the Department. The former covers the payment of grants, through associations, to aid the blind, the augmentation of earnings of blind persons, the registration of approved associations for caring for the blind and the activities of the National Council for the Blind; while the latter not only safeguards children but covers adoptions, the supervision of homes and places of safety, probation services, children's courts, family allowances and maintenance grants. The Department of Social Welfare also attends to the registration of welfare organisations under Act No. 40 of 1947, and controls collections for approved charities and institutions. On behalf of the Prisons Department, it conducts investigations in terms of the Disability Grants Act No. 36 of 1946, and of the Work Colonies Act of 1949, whose purposes are indicated by their titles.

Government policy is to allow freedom for private and Church enterprise wherever possible, but to reduce overlapping. Large subsidies are paid towards many good causes. Approved private welfare organisations registered under the Act are estimated to number over 1,800. The Department of Social Welfare also assists in the training of social workers at universities and other institutions. The rehabilitation of delinquent children (the word child being defined as anyone under the age of 19) is now carried out under the Social Welfare Department and no longer under that of Prisons.

Many Social Welfare activities are, however, still handled by other departments, including those of Education, Labour, Arts and Sciences, Native Affairs, Coloured Affairs, Pensions, Health, etc. Unemployment Insurance, Maternity Benefits, the provision of sheltered employment for handicapped persons, etc., fall under the Department of Labour, while pensions for non-Whites come under the Department of Bantu Affairs. Among other important bodies must be mentioned the South African National Council for the Deaf, the National Council for the Care of Cripples, the South African Merchant Seamen's Trust Fund and the Legal Aid Bureaux, conducted in conjunction with the Law Society. Courses in Social Welfare are given at most South African universities, and are encouraged by the State.

In Rhodesia and Zambia, Social Welfare activities are divided among several departments, including those of Health, Education and Law.

Soekmekaar. *See* ZOEKMEKAAR.

Soekor. *See* SOUTHERN OIL EXPLORATION CORPORATION.

Soetgras 'Sweet Grass' (*Eragrostis lehmannia* Nees). Good cattle feed. Griqualand West, Orange Free State, Transvaal.

Sofala. Ancient settlement in Northern Mozambique, founded in 1505 by Pedro d'Anhaya, a Portuguese navigator, who put up the original fort. Long before that it was known as a trading centre for East Africa, carrying on a large export of slaves. Sofala is mentioned in Milton's *Paradise Lost*, and has been identified by many scholars with the Ophir from which the gold for Solomon's temple was secured. A traffic certainly was carried on between there and the settlements at Zimbabwe (q.v.). Dhows are today built there by the Africans.

Soga, Rev. Tiyo. First ordained minister of African origin in South Africa. Born in 1829 at Gwali on the Tyumie River, Eastern Province. He was the seventh child of one of the chief counsellors of Gaika. His mother having become a Christian, he went to school and was befriended by the Rev. William Chalmers of the Glasgow Missionary Society. At the age of 15 he was sent to Lovedale for further education, and two years later, in 1846, went to Scotland to study for the ministry. He completed his studies in 1856 and was ordained in the same year. His wife was a Scotch girl, Janet Burnside. Returning to South Africa in 1857, he became a member of the staff of the London Missionary Society and was soon well known not only as a preacher, but as a composer of hymns in his own language and as a writer. He died in 1871.

Soil Erosion. Although the menace of soil erosion in South Africa was recognised by a few botanists over a century ago, and although a few enterprising farmers such as Eugene Cloete, near Molteno, attempted measures against it, concerted action on a national scale is of very recent date, largely the result of the propaganda of C. J. J. van Rensburg (q.v.). The Veld Trust, established in 1942, regards as its main task the spreading of information about the danger.

Soil erosion is due to a variety of causes, among them over-stocking the land, particularly with goats, which gnaw down the young vegetation that holds the soil together, the downhill ploughing of land and the making of footpaths and tracks that catch water. The result is the formation of dongas and sluits or, worst of all, sheet erosion —removal of all soil down to bedrock.

Remedies include contour ploughing, grass leys, adequate cattle feeds and dams to catch the run-off. Through the Land Bank, Government funds are now available for fighting soil erosion. Some of the worst cases— such as at Vlekpoort in the Eastern Province—have been successfully treated, but even now millions of tons of South Africa's most valuable humus and topsoil are annually lost. Twenty miles out to sea the red soil brought down by the Orange River can still be recognised. The unwillingness of the African, who regards all cattle, irrespective of quality, as wealth, to allow reductions in their number remains a major obstacle to success, but progress is being made. *See* GRASSES and NATIONAL VELD TRUST.

Solder. The word originally meant a loft but is now also applied to the upper storeys of old houses. *See* BRANDSOLDER.

Soldier. *See* WITVIS.

Soles. Fish of the Heterosomata ('odd-body') division, having one side plain, one side coloured and both eyes on the same side. They swim horizontally, with undulating body movements, but spend most of their time on the bottom, covered with sand or gravel. The young are normally shaped and swim vertically, but as their bodies deepen they lie flat, the skull bones twist and one eye (there is no rule as to which) moves across the face. Although in the northern hemisphere this is one of the most important groups (containing halibut, plaice, turbot, sole, flounder, etc.); in the southern seas only two species are valuable: the Mud Sole (*Austroglossus pectoralis*), 20 inches, from False Bay to Natal, and the Small Scaled Sole (*A. microlepis*), 80 inches and up to 9 lb. in weight, caught only from Table Bay north to Walvis Bay. *See* MARINE RESOURCES.

Solf, Dr. Wilhelm. German statesman and colonial expert, born on October 5, 1862, in Berlin. He became Colonial Secretary for the German Empire in 1911, exercising a great influence on the progress of South West Africa and German East Africa. He continued to hold this position until the Peace of Versailles in 1919. The following year he became Ambassador in Tokyo. He died in 1926.

Solly, Mrs. Julia Frances. Pioneer of women's rights, born at Seaforth Hall near Liverpool in 1862. She married H. L. V. Solly, a mining engineer, with whom she came to South Africa in 1890. From 1895 onwards she was active in the move to secure the vote for women. Settling near Cape Town at Knorhoek, Sir Lowry's Pass, in 1901, she concentrated on this cause as far as South Africa was concerned. The close friend of Olive Schreiner, she was one of the chief personalities in the National Council of Women in South Africa. She helped to set up the South African Botanical Society and several other scientific bodies. On the occasion of the Silver Jubilee of King George V she was one of five women awarded a special medal. She died in 1953.

Solomon, Saul. Cape statesman, printer and publisher. Born in St. Helena of Jewish parents, in 1817, he came to the Cape as a small child, attended the South African College, as its most brilliant pupil, and was apprenticed to the printing trade. In 1840 he founded the famous firm of Saul Solomon and Co., who soon became Government printers, and in 1853 was elected to the first Cape Parliament, where his ability gained him the nickname of the 'Cape Disraeli.' In 1857 he became interested in the *Cape Argus*, founded by B. H. Darnell and R. W. Murray (q.v.), and in 1863 became its sole owner, soon exercising great influence throughout South Africa. When in 1871 the Cape received Responsible Government he was offered, but refused, the Prime Ministership. His politics were Liberal and he was a strong champion of the non-European, also State aid for Church finance and other reforms. A family tragedy—the loss of a small daughter by drowning—decided him to retire to Scotland, in 1883. He left his business in incompetent hands, with the result that it went insolvent in 1885 but was reconstructed in 1886 as the still existent and flourishing Argus Printing and Publishing Company. In 1892 he died at his home in Argyllshire. Saul Solomon's career is doubly remarkable because through an illness as a small child his growth was permanently stunted. Although his head and trunk were of normal size, his legs were so small that he had to stand on a box when addressing Parliament and had to be lifted into a cab. His home, Clarensville, Sea Point, was the recognised haunt of leading citizens.

Solomon, Saul (Junior). Judge of the Supreme Court. Born in Cape Town in 1875, the son of the statesman Saul Solomon (q.v.), he was educated at Bedford Grammar School in England before proceeding to Oxford. In 1900 he was admitted to the Cape Bar, but moved to Johannesburg in 1902. In 1906 he decided to take Holy Orders, and was ordained in 1908. After a

spell in a London slum Solomon returned to South Africa, where he
worked at Johannesburg and Cape
Town, but, following his conversion
to Catholicism in 1916, returned to the
Bar on the Rand, where he soon
attained high distinction. In 1927 he
became a judge. He died in 1960.

Solomon, Sir William Henry. Chief
Justice of the Union of South Africa.
Born at Bedford, Cape, in 1852, he
was educated at Lovedale as well as
at the South African College and
at Cambridge. In 1877 he was called
to the Bar at the Inner Temple and
the following year began practice at
the Cape. He was for a while also in
Kimberley, where, in 1887, he was
appointed to the Bench. Nine years
later he was transferred to the Eastern
Districts Court at Grahamstown.
After the South African War he became
a judge in the newly-established
Supreme Court of the Transvaal, and
in 1910 one of the original judges of
the Appellate Division in Bloemfontein. He was promoted to Chief
Justice in 1927, and retired in October,
1929. He died in Wales on June 13,
1930. For learning and ability he is
recognised as one of the greatest
lawyers South Africa has produced.

Somabula. Village between Bulawayo
and Gwelo in Rhodesia. Diamonds
were discovered in the Somabula
Forest, 1906, and were worked for
a number of years.

Somerset, Lord Charles Henry.
Governor of the Cape of Good Hope.
Born in 1768, the second son of the
Duke of Beaufort and grandson of the
famous Admiral Boscawen. He arrived
at the Cape on April 5, 1814. His
period of office was on the whole a
stormy one, chiefly because of his
authoritarian disposition. The charge
of extravagance and financial incom-
petence was repeatedly discussed in
the House of Commons. On the other
hand he showed a keen interest in the
advancement of agriculture, and was

a good friend to the 1820 settlers in
their times of trouble. Several towns
were founded during his régime, including Beaufort West, Somerset East,
Somerset West and Fort Beaufort, all
named after his family. His major
dispute on the Freedom of the Press
brought him into conflict with Thomas
Pringle and John Fairbairn (qq.v.)
whose *South African Commercial
Advertiser* he suppressed. After being
recalled to England to give an explanation of his actions, he resigned office
in April 1827, and died in Brighton on
February 20, 1831.

Somerset East. Town in the Eastern
Cape Province, founded in 1825, and
named after Governor Lord Charles
Somerset (q v.). It was repeatedly
involved in frontier wars against the
natives, but is now chiefly noted as a
wool and farming centre, as well as for
its famous school, Gill College (q.v.).
Population: 9,779, including 2,314
Whites.

Somerset Strand. Seaside resort on
the northern side of False Bay in
particular favour with the Afrikaner
section of the community. It was
originally called Van Ryneveld's Dorp,
and developed at the start of the 19th
century as a fishing village. The rise
of Somerset West (q.v.), three miles
off, brought it into popularity as a
holiday spot, many farmers coming
there to camp. Since 1897 it has been
a municipality on its own account,
though linked with Somerset West by
an almost continuous line of houses.
Population: 22,250, including 11,000
Whites. It is now usually referred to as
'The Strand.'

Somerset West. Town in the Western
Cape Province 31 miles from Cape
Town, founded in 1822 and named
after Governor Lord Charles Somerset
(q.v.). It lies at the foot of the Hottentots Holland Mountains, surrounded
by vineyards and orchards. Many
people retire there, including well-
known personalities from overseas,

like the author H. V. Morton. Some of the early houses are still standing. Through the efforts of Cecil Rhodes, one of the largest explosives factories in the world, also producing fertilisers and chemicals, was established at Firgrove near by in 1902. Population: 12,000, including 8,000 Whites.

Somerville Estate. Game reserve set up in the Winburg district of the Orange Free State in 1924. It covers about 24,000 acres and includes many species of antelopes, wildebeest, etc. Administered by the Provincial Council.

Somkele. Village in Zululand, named after a former chief. It attained prominence early in the present century, when a coal mine was opened up near by, and a railway built. The seams proved a disappointment, and the venture was abandoned. Today it is a trading centre.

Somtseu. Nickname given by the Zulus to Sir Theophilus Shepstone (q.v.), signifying a 'great hunter.'

Songalolo. From the Xosa word meaning 'to roll up.' Popular name in the Eastern Cape for *Julus terristris*, the large, dark millipede.

Sonop. Village near Brits, Transvaal. Population 730, including 630 Whites.

Sordwana Bay. Inlet on the coast of Zululand. *See* KOSI BAY.

Sore Eye Flower. *See* AMARYLLIS.

Sorrel. *See* OXALIS.

Sour-Fig, Hottentot Fig, Vygie (Aizoaceae). Larger member of the vast Mesembryanthemum group, with white, yellow or pink flowers and long fleshy leaves. Planted extensively to bind sandy soil on slopes. The astringent juice is used medicinally; the fruit makes delicious jam. The family consists entirely of succulent plants, many with brilliant flowers. Mainly sandveld, Karroo and semi-desert. *See* SUCCULENTS.

Sour Plum or **Suurpruim** (*Ximenia caffra* Sond). Shrub with short spines on the stems. Fruit about an inch long, fleshy, edible.

Sour Veld. Areas of poor soil covered with coarse, dry grass indigestible to cattle.

South Africa. *See* REPUBLIC OF SOUTH AFRICA and UNION OF SOUTH AFRICA.

SOUTH AFRICA—CHRONOLOGY

1488 Bartholomew Diaz, a Portuguese navigator, rounds the Cape of Good Hope and lands at Algoa Bay (St. Croix).

1497 Vasco da Gama, a Portuguese, lands at St. Helena Bay and Mossel Bay, and reaches Natal on Christmas Day, hence the name.

1503 Antonio de Saldanha lands at Table Bay and explores Table Mountain.

1580 Sir Francis Drake rounds the Cape.

1601 The first fleet of the English East India Company calls at Table Bay.

1648 Wreck of the *Haarlem* on Blaauwberg Beach, the crew remaining on shore for five months.

1650 The Dutch East India Company decide on Table Bay as a victualling station.

1652 Jan van Riebeeck and his party arrive at the Cape.

1655 Building of Cape Town Castle commenced.

1679 Simon van der Stel appointed Governor. Foundation of Stellenbosch.

1688 First Huguenot settlers arrive.

1699 Wilhelm Adriaan van der Stel appointed Governor.

1706 Protest by Adam Tas and other burghers against the Governor.
1751 Founding of Swellendam.
1754 Census taken showing number of Europeans 5,510, slaves 6,279.
1760 The Orange River crossed by the hunter, Jacobus Coetsee.
1778 Fish River fixed as a boundary of Cape Colony.
1779 First Kaffir War.
1782 Kaffirs defeated by Boer Commandos. The *Grosvenor* wrecked.
1786 Graaff-Reinet founded, and six burghers appointed as councillors.
1787 Second Kaffir War.
1795 The Cape surrendered to the English. General Craig appointed first English governor. Government of Dutch East India Co. ceases. Risings at Graaff-Reinet and Swellendam.
1798 Great Fire at Cape Town. Post Office begun.
1800 First newspaper founded at Cape Town.
1803 The Cape restored to Holland under the peace of Amiens in 1801.
1804 Founding of Uitenhage.
1805 Cape again under British rule.
1806 British forces under General Baird conquer the Cape.
1812 Foundation of Cradock and Grahamstown.
1814 Lord Charles Henry Somerset appointed Governor.
1815 Slagter's Nek Rebellion.
1818 Fifth Kaffir War. Foundation of Beaufort West and Worcester.
1820 5,000 British immigrants (1820 settlers) arrive at Algoa Bay; Port Elizabeth first so named.
1824 First Synod of the Dutch Reformed Church.
Farewell, King and Fynn secure land in Natal from Tshaka, the Zulu chief. Moshesh founds the Basuto.
1825 Birth of Paul Kruger. Cape Colony extended to Orange River. Foundation of Somerset East.

1828 English settlers in Natal dispersed. Foundation of Malmesbury. Tshaka killed and succeeded by his younger brother, Dingaan.
1830 Kaffraria opened up for commerce.
1833 Decision to abolish slavery by the British Government, against cash compensation.
1834 Sir Benjamin D'Urban appointed Governor. Slaves emancipated.
1835 Town of Durban laid out. Trichardt's Trek.
1836 Great Boer Trek from Cape Colony begun.
First Volksraad north of Orange River.
1838 Massacre of Boers at Weenen by Dingaan, the Zulu Chief. Pretorius defeats Dingaan. Boers establish a republic in Natal.
1842 Dick King's ride to the Cape Colony for assistance for the British. Boers trek from Natal.
1843 Natal officially declared British. Griqualand and Basutoland created treaty states.
1844 Natal annexed to Cape Colony. Later separated again.
1846 Seventh Kaffir War.
1848 Territory between Orange and Vaal Rivers proclaimed Orange River Sovereignty under British control.
1851 Defeat of British and Boer forces at Viervoet by Moshesh.
1852 Sand River Convention acknowledges independence of the Transvaal.
1854 First Parliament under Representative Government meets at Cape Town. Orange Free State Republic formed with J. P. Hoffman as President.
1855 Foundation of Pretoria.
1859 Construction commenced of first railway from Cape Town to Wellington.
1860 Table Bay Docks begun.
1864 J. H. Brand President of the Orange Free State. Paul Kruger elected Commandant-General.

1867 Discovery of diamonds near Vaal River.
1870 Founding of Kimberley.
1872 Responsible Government granted to Cape Colony.
1876 Sir Theophilus Shepstone appointed Administrator of the Transvaal; he occupies South African Republic.
1879 Zulu War. Defeat of British at Isandhlwana. Victory at Ulundi. Prince Imperial of France killed.
1880 First Boer War. Battle of Majuba.
1883 Paul Kruger elected President of the South African Republic.
1884 Barberton goldfields opened.
1885 Railway to Kimberley opened.
1886 Proclamation of the Witwatersrand goldfields. Town of Johannesburg laid out.
1890 First Rhodes Ministry at the Cape.
1894 Railway line between Johannesburg and Lourenço Marques opened.
1895 Railway traffic opened between Durban and Johannesburg.
1896 Jameson Raid.
1899 The South African War begun.
1902 Peace of Vereeniging signed. Death of Cecil John Rhodes.
1904 Death of Paul Kruger in Switzerland.
1905 Discovery of the Cullinan Diamond.
1907 Transvaal Ministry under General Botha.
1908 National Convention.
1909 South Africa Act passed by British Parliament.
1910 On the 31st of May the Act of Union comes into force. First Union Cabinet under General Botha. First Union Parliament meets in November.
1913 Miners' strike and riots on the Witwatersrand.
1914 South Africa at war with Germany and her allies. Rebellion breaks out.
1915 Invasion of South West Africa.
1916 General Smuts in command of 50,000 South African soldiers in

German East Africa (now Tanganyika).
1919 Death of General Botha.
1922 Rand Revolt.
1924 'Pact' Government under General Hertzog.
1926 Imperial Conference recognises Dominion Status.
1931 Statute of Westminster passed by Imperial Government.
1932 Gold Standard crisis.
1933 'Fusion' Government of Hertzog and Smuts; birth of the United Party.
1939 Second World War. Split between General Hertzog and General Smuts. General Smuts becomes Prime Minister. South Africa declares war on Germany on September 6.
1940 South African forces under General Pienaar help defeat Italian armies in Abyssinia.
1942 Death of General Hertzog. South African troops participate in victory at the battle of Alamein.
1945 Germany and Japan surrender unconditionally.
1946 Boom in Orange Free State gold shares. Odendaalsrus centre of new goldfields.
1948 Nationalist Party win general election. Dr. D. F. Malan Prime Minister.
1949 Death of several prominent South Africans: J. H. Hofmeyr, scholar, politician, Deputy Prime Minister in Smuts Cabinet; Dr. H. J. van der Bijl, industrialist, chairman of Escom, Iscor and other concerns; I. W. Schlesinger, financier and industrialist.
1950 Death of Field-Marshal the Right Honourable J. C. Smuts (September 11). War starts in Korea. South Africa sends air squadron to assist UNO forces.
1951 Act abolishing existing form of Coloured franchise.
1952 Appeal Court Judgment upholding Coloured franchise.

Legislators removed from office under Suppression of Communism Act.

300th Anniversary Celebrations of Landing of Jan van Riebeeck. High Court of Parliament declared illegal by Appellate Division of Supreme Court.

1953 Dr. D. F. Malan attends Commonwealth Conference. Foundation of Liberal Party.

1954 Johannes Gerhardus Strijdom succeeds Dr. D. F. Malan as Prime Minister.

1955 Resettlement of Natives in Western Johannesburg suburbs, including Sophiatown.
Report by Holloway Commission on University facilities.

1956 Enlarged Senate and changes in Coloured vote.
Tomlinson Report issued.
Treason Arrests.
Sir David Graaff becomes leader of United Party.

1957 Simonstown handed over by Royal Navy to South African Navy.
Death of Sir Ernest Oppenheimer.

1958 General Election.
Death of J. G. Strijdom.
Dr. H. F. Verwoerd becomes Prime Minister.
Commencement of Treason Trial.

1959 Death of Dr. D. F. Malan.
Decimal Coinage Act passed.
Bantu Authorities introduced.
South African Expedition to Antarctic.

1960 Celebration of Union's 50th Jubilee.
Mining disaster at Coalbrook.
Riots at Sharpeville.
Union Referendum decides in favour of Republic.

1961 Introduction of decimal coinage.
Commonwealth Conference in London attended by Dr. H. F. Verwoerd, who applies for continued membership, but, in the face of attacks by other Premiers, withdraws application.

Republic Act passed by Union Parliament with effect from May 31, 1961.

1962 Expansion of military forces.
Removal of legal restrictions on sale of liquor to Bantu.
Orange River project authorised.

1963 Transkei receives self-government. Voters' roll prepared.
Orange River project construction begun.

1964 29 Rhodesian chiefs tour South Africa.
Sinkhole accidents on West Rand.
South Africa sends medical supplies to Congo on request of Government there.

1965 Opening of first Nuclear Research Station at Pelindaba, Transvaal.

1966 South African success against Liberia and Abyssinia in action brought by the latter on South-West Africa in the World Court at The Hague.
Dr. H. F. Verwoerd assassinated and succeeded as Premier by B. J. Vorster.

1967 Final withdrawal of British Navy from Simonstown.
South African Police in action against Rhodesian terrorists.

1968 Diplomatic relations established with Malawi. South African Indian Council receives statutory powers. Tswana and Ciskei Territorial authorities established. Death of Dr. T. E. Dönges and inauguration of President J. Fouche.

1969 Telephone Cable to Europe opened. Air service to South America and U.S.A. opened by South African Airways.

South Africa Foundation. Non-governmental organisation established in 1960, with headquarters in Johannesburg, for the purpose of answering overseas misrepresentations about South Africa. Responsible for bringing out important visitors, distributing authoritative information, etc.

South African Air Force. Founded on February 5, 1915, as the South African Flying Corps. Took part in the German South West African Campaign of 1915. During the German East African Campaign operated as a squadron of the R.F.C. In March, 1922, was in action during the Rand Revolt and sent two planes to South West Africa during the Bondelswart Hottentot Rebellion, 1922, and again in 1925. Expanded during World War II, when there were more than 50 squadrons in Italy. In 1950–53 a squadron served in Korea with forces of United Nations.

South African Airways. See TRANS-PORT IN THE REPUBLIC OF SOUTH AFRICA.

South African Artillery. See TRANSVAAL HORSE ARTILLERY.

South African Association for the Administration and Settlement of Estates. Trust Company established in Cape Town in 1836 and still in existence, the oldest of its kind in South Africa.

South African Association for the Advancement of Science. Founded in Cape Town, 1903, it is open to membership of both professional scientists and private individuals interested in science. It is modelled on the British Association, with separate sections for different branches of science, and has twice held joint meetings with that body in South Africa, in 1905 and in 1929. Meetings for reading papers occur in different cities of the Republic, Rhodesia, South West Africa and Mozambique every year. Its highest award is the South African Medal. The headquarters are in Johannesburg. A journal and annual report are issued.

South African Broadcasting Corporation. Statutory body established in 1936, to conduct broadcasting services in the Union and South West Africa. It is largely modelled on the British Broadcasting Corporation, and took over the services previously carried on by the African Broadcasting Company, a privately-owned concern established by the late I. W. Schlesinger. The headquarters of the South African Broadcasting Corporation are in Johannesburg. It is controlled by a Board of governors, appointed by the State President. Licences are collected through the Post Office, and there are studios in Johannesburg, Pretoria, Pietermaritzburg, Bloemfontein, King William's Town, Grahamstown, Port Elizabeth, East London, Cape Town, Durban and Windhoek, apart from a national short-wave installation at Paradys, near Bloemfontein. Programmes are provided under three services—English, or A Programme; Afrikaans, or B Programme; and Springbok (advertising), C Programme. The latter first opened on May 1, 1950. These three services operate on a country-wide basis. Radio Bantu serves and is mainly staffed by Non-Whites, with seven programme services in six languages. Rediffusion services have begun in Johannesburg Bantu townships. Special Indian language services operate in Natal. In addition to Springbok, there are two regional advertising services—Radio Highveld from Johannesburg and Radio Good Hope from Cape Town. An external service—Radio South Africa—transmitting to all parts of the world, started operating full-scale in 9 languages on May 1, 1966.

Also offering programmes is the Lourenço Marques commercial station, established by the Radio Club of Mozambique and serving both the Republic and Rhodesia. See also BROADCASTING, RHODESIAN BROADCASTING CORPORATION and WIRELESS TELEGRAPHY.

South African Coal, Oil and Gas Corporation (Sasol). Government-backed corporation established under the Companies Act, September 26, 1950, to construct plant for producing oil and petrol from coal. As work began in the Northern Orange Free State, a new town came into existence, known as Sasolburg (q.v.). The plant has been built in 2 sections, partly under German and partly under American auspices. On November 1, 1955, the sales of Sasol began, at first only in the Transvaal. Many difficulties delayed the intended output of the 71,000,000 gallons of petrol and oil a year, but these have been overcome. The building of the plant cost over £70,000,000 (R140,000,000). Production of artificial rubber began in 1963. Allied to Sasol is Gaskor, which supplies industrial gas in bulk by pipeline to the Rand.

South African College (SACS). High School and Preparatory School for Boys in Cape Town. Oldest institution of its kind in Southern Africa. Founded in 1829 as 'Het Zuid Afrikaansch Atheneum,' to provide both ordinary and higher education for Colonists. Maintained degree classes after establishment of University of Cape of Good Hope in 1873, which were gradually separated from the South African College and ultimately merged into the University of Cape Town, established in 1918. The original establishment became South African College High School, and continued to occupy the old buildings in the Cape Town suburb of the Gardens. There it remained until 1955, when the first of a large new series of buildings in Newlands was occupied.

South African Constabulary. Semi-military force established under the command of Major-General Sir Robert Baden-Powell during the South African War, in 1900, and used for the pacification and control of the former Boer Republics. It was ultimately merged into the Transvaal Police.

South African Corps of Chaplains. South African military unit, founded on October 18, 1946.

South African Corps of Marines. South African military unit, founded on July 1, 1951.

South African Corps of Military Police. South African military unit, founded on November 10, 1939.

South African Corps of Signals. South African military unit, founded on November 1, 1923, with sections in Cape Town, Durban, Johannesburg, Pretoria, Bloemfontein, Port Elizabeth and East London. During World War II served with South African Air Force at various stations, also all round the coast of the Union and outside Cairo.

South African Engineer Corps. South African military unit, founded on July 1, 1914, stationed in Durban, Uitenhage, Cape Town, Bloemfontein, Johannesburg and Pretoria. Expanded enormously during World War II, when every type of engineering work was undertaken, including the manufacture of poison gas. Served in Abyssinia, North Africa and Italy.

South African Flying Corps. Original name of South African Air Force (q.v.).

South African Indian Council. Established under an Act of Parliament in 1968, with 25 members and an executive of 5, the chairman being appointed by the Minister of Indian Affairs. See INDIANS and NATIONAL INDIAN COUNCIL.

South African Irish. South African military unit, officially 22nd Field Regiment, South African Artillery. Founded as South African Irish in November, 1939. Served in East Africa and Abyssinia in World War II then in Egypt as part of 1st South African Division. In 1941 fought at Sidi Rezegh, losing over 50 per cent killed, wounded and prisoners, and then with 4th Field Regiment, South African Artillery at Alamein. Motto: 'Faugh a Ballagh' (Here's the Lad).

South African Iron and Steel Industrial Corporation. Popularly known as Iscor. Principal producer of iron and steel in the Republic, and one of its major industries. After several previous attempts to set up a steel industry in Pretoria through private enterprise, particularly through the efforts of C. F. Delfos (q.v.) and Samuel Marks (q.v.), the Union Government decided to g ive its official backing and to supply the major part of the funds. Iscor came into existence on June 5, 1928, under the Iron and Steel Industry Act No. 11 of that year. Its original capital was £3,500,000 of which £500,000 was subscribed by the Union Government and the rest offered to the public. Later the Government increased its proportion of the holdings substantially; it has always had control of the directorate. Work began on the construction of the plant at Pretoria West with great vigour, largely owing to the energy and ability of the late Dr. H. J. van der Bijl (q.v.), who was the first chairman. Very large ore bodies were opened up at Thabazimbi in the Rustenburg district, while coke was secured from a blend of Natal and Transvaal coal. Dolomite and limestone required for flux were close to the building site. Clearing of ground commenced at the beginning of 1931, and on December 4, 1933, the coke ovens were fired. The first blast furnace was blown in on March 7, 1934, and the first pig iron produced on March 20 of the same year. The first Iscor pig iron was tapped on April 5, 1934. Since then Iscor has grown enormously, and after World War II the original plant near Pretoria was more than doubled by the construction of similar works in Vanderbijl Park (q.v.) on the Vaal River, 35 miles south of Johannesburg. In 1969 it was announced that a third major plant would be erected at Newcastle, Natal. The combined production today is about 4,000,000 tons a year. Iscor has large interests in the Union Steel Corporation at Vereeniging, African Metals Corporation (Amcor) (qq.v.), as well as in collieries in Natal, etc. Its staff today is in excess of 20,000 of all races. Large deposits of manganese are exploited at Sishen, near Kuruman. Apart from making all types of steel sections and rails, Iscor produces reinforcements, billets of many kinds, plates, material for wire manufacturing, shafting, and many types of tar and coal products. During World War II it was of enormous importance to South Africa, and produced quantities of armaments, including ordnance. A very large programme of expansion, to cost about R1,500,000,000, is in progress and will raise output capacity to 4,500,000 tons by 1973, and to over 8,000,000 tons a year before 1980. *See also* NEWCASTLE

South African League. Political organisation formed in the Cape as a counterblast to the Afrikander Bond. It was avowedly pro-British and though not founded by him, presently gained the support of Cecil John Rhodes. It came into prominence agout 1894, but faded away after the South African War.

South African Marine Corporation Limited. *See* SAFMARINE.

South African Medical Corps. South African military unit, founded on April 1, 1913.

South African Military Nursing Service. South African military unit, founded on September 8, 1915.

South African National Tuberculosis Association. Popularly known as SANTA. Organisation set up in 1947 to fight tuberculosis in South Africa, and absorbing several earlier organisations. By 1952 it had raised £700,000. By means of settlements and hospitalisation, SANTA has succeeded in providing valuable facilities for the poorer population in many parts of the country. It receives substantial contributions from the Government, but is dependent to a large extent on the generosity of the public.

South African Nautical College. *See* GRANGER BAY.

South African Paper and Pulp Industries. *See* SAPPI.

South African Party. Formed on the establishment of the Union of South Africa in 1910, through the merger of the Afrikander Bond, Orangia Union, Het Volk and a number of English-speaking elements. It lasted in this form until 1913, when the National Party (q.v.), under General J. B. M. Hertzog, seceded, but preserved its name and identity, being reinforced in 1920 by the Unionist Party (q.v.). Until his death in 1919 the South African Party was led by General Louis Botha and thereafter by General J. C. Smuts. It became part of the present United Party in 1933.

South African Police. Established on April 1, 1913, as a merger of existing forces of the four provinces. Until 1926 certain semi-military duties, particularly in native territories, were performed by the South African Mounted Rifles, which were then absorbed into the South African Police. Left over from pre-Union days were the police forces in Durban and Pietermaritzburg, controlled by the Borough authorities, whose work was finally taken over in 1937; in 1939 the South West African Police were also merged in the main organisation. The South African Police consists of approximately 22,000 men, of whom about one half are white. There are about 1,000 police stations in the Republic and South West Africa, the entire territory being divided into nine divisions. Headquarters and training centre are in Pretoria, which is also the seat of the South African Criminal Bureau, the Finger Print Organisation, etc.

South African Railways and Harbours. *See* TRANSPORT IN THE REPUBLIC OF SOUTH AFRICA.

South African Reserve Bank. Official central bank of the Republic of South Africa. Largely under the inspiration of the late Sir Henry Strakosch, it came into existence under the terms of the Currency and Banking Act of 1920, with effect from December 17 of that year, and opened its doors on June 30, 1921. It has the sole statutory right of issuing bank notes, handles the accounts for the Government and serves the needs of commercial banks in its area. The head office is in Pretoria, but branches exist in Johannesburg, Cape Town and other important centres. Its capital is R2,000,000, but its assets are about R200,000,000. The South African Reserve Bank handles the sales of the gold output of South Africa, fixes the discount rate, and plays a large part in the running of the National Finance Corporation of South Africa (q.v.).

South African Staff Corps. South African military unit, founded on February 1, 1923.

South African Tourist Corporation. Statutory body set up by the Union Government to encourage tourist traffic to the Union. Established in 1947, with head office in Pretoria, and branches in London, New York, Salisbury, Nairobi and elsewhere. Its functions are to supply information, but not to handle traffic.

South African War. Although the British Army had been ordered to mobilise on October 7, 1899, it was not until October 10 that the final Boer ultimatum was received. Fighting began on the following day, October 11. On October 12 Mr. Conyngham Greene, the British Agent, left Pretoria and the Boers invaded Natal. The first victory was the capture of a British armoured train at Kraaipan in Bechuanaland. The early stage of the war was an almost continuous series of disasters for the British, culminating in the 'Black Week' (q.v.). The forces of the Republics reached Mafeking, besieged it and penetrated far into the Cape, also besieging Kimberley. Although offers of help from various units of the British Commonwealth, including Canada, had come previously, it was only in December, when General Buller asked for heavy reinforcements, that the true seriousness of the position was recognised in Britain. On December 18, 1899, Lord Roberts became Commander-in-Chief, with Lord Kitchener as Chief of Staff. The arrival of large British reinforcements brought on a reversal of the Boer fortunes, with the result that on February 7, 1900, General Piet Cronje was obliged to surrender with 4,000 prisoners at Paardeberg. Barely a fortnight later Bloemfontein was captured. Mr. Joseph Chamberlain announced, on May 11, 1900, the intention of the British Government to annex the two Boer Republics. Despite the Boers' gallant and skilful fighting, the main force of the British crossed the Vaal at Vereeniging on May 27, 1900, and took Pretoria on June 5. Efforts to end the campaign proved fruitless when General Louis Botha, now the supreme commander of the Boers, refused to accept the terms of surrender offered by General Buller. With the Boer administration moving into the Eastern Transvaal, the campaign began to take on a guerrilla character, in which the genius of General Christiaan de Wet (q.v.) brought him international fame. The annexation of the Boer Republics, the Orange Free State on May 24, 1900, and the Transvaal on September 1, did nothing to reduce the severity of the war. While the Boer representatives, headed by President Kruger, did their best to secure intervention overseas, most of the other nations continued to maintain a policy of neutrality. General de Wet invaded Cape Colony during 1900 and was effectively supported by other expeditions under General J. B. M. Hertzog and General J. C. Smuts. To end the

costly and difficult campaign, Lord Kitchener, who had replaced Lord Roberts as Commander-in-Chief, established his system of blockhouses (q.v.) but the fighting continued, and even the internment of tens of thousands of Boer women and children and other non-combatants in concentration camps (q.v.) did not bring the contest to an end. Renewed efforts were made to end the struggle, and, on February 13, 1901, Kitchener proposed an interview with Botha to discuss a settlement. Unfortunately Botha refused the terms offered and the contest was resumed. The Boers were now in desperate straits, but still carried on, using supplies taken from the British and inflicting heavy damage. Efforts made by the Netherlands Government to mediate were turned down by the British in January, 1902, but in March the first successful contacts were made by the opposing sides. Some Boer delegates met in Klerksdorp on April 9 and others in Pretoria on April 12. The final discussions began on May 15, 1902, and were agreed to three days later. Peace was signed in George Hey's house in Pretoria on May 31, 1902. According to official figures, 448,725 men of all ranks fought on the British side in South Africa, of whom 52,414 were raised in that country itself and 30,000 were contributed by other parts of the British Commonwealth. Exact figures of the numbers on the Boer side are difficult to determine, but the overall total is estimated at around 60,000. The actual number who surrendered at close of the struggle was 21,256, including 11,166 in the Transvaal, 6,455 in the O.F.S. and 3,635 in Cape Colony. British casualties totalled 97,477, of whom 5,774 were killed, 2,018 died of wounds, 198 died from accidents and 13,350 died from disease, a number considerably larger than those killed in action. Boer losses were estimated at about 6,000 men killed, apart from deaths in the concentration camps. The total financial cost of the War is given as £205,000,000.

Southern Brubru (*Nilaus brubru*). Small insectivorous bird of the Shrike family (q.v.), found in the Kalahari, on the Orange River and in Natal. It is black and white like the Fiscal Shrike, but smaller, and has a flute-like voice.

Southern Cross Steel Works. Large plant at Middelburg, Transvaal, controlled by Rand Mines (q.v.) and American interests. First producers of stainless steel in South Africa. Output of 10,000 tons a year. Opened 1967.

Southern Oil Exploration Corporation. (Soekor). Statutory body established in 1965 to carry out exploration for oil in South Africa and adjoining waters. Its head office is in Johannesburg. *See* OIL.

Southern Picarel (*Marsis australis*). Fish of the Grunter type, found off Natal coast. About 10 inches long. The name is Spanish, from a similar Mediterranean fish.

Southern Rhodesia. *See* RHODESIA.

Southport. Seaside resort in Natal, on the south coast, near Port Shepstone. It has a golf-course near the water's edge. Population: 400, including 250 Whites.

South West Africa. Territory administered by the Republic of South Africa. Its 317,887 sq. miles make it considerably larger than any single province in the Republic. From north to south it measures 1,300 miles. For reasons of convenience, Walvis Bay and its environs, covering 374 sq. miles, though actually part of the Cape Province, are administered along with the rest of the territory. Save for a barren coastal zone, mainly occupied by sandhills, South West Africa comprises a series of great plateaux, and desert conditions prevail over considerable areas. The principal rivers are the Orange (q.v.), which forms the southern boundary, the Cunene (q.v.), on the northern boundary, the Zambesi, on which South West Africa abuts along the Caprivi Zipfel (q.v.), the Okavango, the Chobe or Linyanti and the Kwando. There are also relatively small rivers like the Swakop and Kuisep. Colonisation of South West Africa began with the advent of early white traders from the Cape in the 18th and early 19th centuries, who were followed (about 1840) by missionaries, mainly from Germany. Several of their stations have since become towns, including Keetmanshoop and the capital, Windhoek. In 1884 Adolf Lüderitz (q.v.), with the approval of Bismarck, established German authority first at Angra Pequena, then renamed Lüderitzbucht, and soon afterwards inland. During the ensuing years the difficulty in subduing the native tribes culminated in the Herero War (q.v.). The discovery of diamonds in 1908 gave a great impetus to prosperity, and substantially added to the number of white settlers, who, by the time the First World War broke out, numbered about 20,000. Railways were built, towns laid out and wireless installations provided. During World War I forces from the Union defeated the German troops in South West Africa, who surrendered at Korab in 1915. The country remained under military administration until 1919, when under the Treaty of Versailles Germany renounced the ownership of her colonies, which were placed under the League of Nations. The latter in its turn entrusted the mandate over South West Africa to the Union, which formally accepted it on September 12, 1919. From January 1, 1921, civil administration began under an Administrator, and in 1925 South West Africa received its own Legislative Assembly. Since 1949 the territory has been represented in the Union Parliament by 4 Senators and 6 Members in the House of Assembly. The

PLATE XI: SOUTH AFRICAN SNAKES

1. *Dispholidus typus* (green boomslang). 2. *Psammophylax rhombeatus* (spotted skaapstekker). 3. *Haemachatus haemachates* (ringhals). 4. *Dendroaspis polylepis* (black mamba). 5. *Pseudoapis cana* (mole snake). 6. *Naja nivea* (Cape cobra or geelslang). 7. *Bitis arietans* (puff adder). 8. *Python sebae* (python).

population is estimated as about 620,000, of which about 100,000 are Whites. Rehoboth (q.v.) possesses certain traditional rights of self-government, while most of the native tribes are under their own chiefs in reserves. Following the establishment of United Nations, the rights of the former League of Nations were taken over, and the Union began submitting annual reports, as it had done to the League of Nations. Criticism and attacks on the Union policy led to their suspension. The principal industries of South West Africa are: the production of diamonds (q.v.), most of which come from the semi-desert coastal zone, and the cultivation of karakul skins, which have created a market of international importance. Among the metals, the most important are found at Tsumeb (q.v.). The former German port of Swakopmund has become a seaside resort, and great development has taken place at Walvis Bay (q.v.), which is growing rapidly. South West Africa has 1,890 miles of railways, administered by the South African Railways and Harbours, besides airlines serving the more important centres. Among the white population the predominating language is Afrikaans, followed by German and then English.

SOUTH WEST AFRICA—CHRONOLOGY

1482 Diago Cam (Cão) first reaches Cape Cross on coast of South West Africa.

1488 Angra Pequena (now Lüderitz Bay) discovered by Bartholomew Diaz.

1685 Simon van der Stel's expedition to the Namaquas.

1760 Jacobus Coetzee, on a hunting expedition, finds springs of Warmbad.

1761 Hendrik Hop's expedition to Herero country.

1792 Willem van Reenen reaches neighbourhood of Rehoboth.

1792 Pieter Pienaar lands at Walvis Bay and explores Swakop Valley.

1805 The Albrecht brothers settle as missionaries at Warmbad.

1811 Warmbad destroyed by Natives.

1815 The Rev. J. H. Schmelen establishes Bethanien mission station in Namaqualand.

1821 Death of Jager Afrikaner.

1824 Rev. J. H. Schmelen reaches Walvis Bay overland.

1825 Rev. J. H. Schmelen penetrates to neighbourhood of Windhoek.

1836 Sir James Alexander explores Namaqualand and south-west.

1840 Jonker Afrikaner settles at Windhoek.

1842 Rhenish Mission Station founded at Windhoek.

1844 Foundation of Barmen.

1845 Foundation of Rehoboth and Walvis Bay.

1849 Foundation of Otjimbingwe.

1850 Massacre at Okahandja.

1850-1 Francis Galton and C. J. Andersson explore Herero and Ovambo country.

1855 C. J. Andersson reaches Lake Ngami from Gobabis.

1861 Thomas Baines and James Chapman cross from Bechuanaland to Walvis Bay.

1863 War begins between Namaquas and Hereros. Rhenish missionaries ask for German protection.

1866 Keetmanshoop founded.

1870 Peace between Hereros and Namaquas made at Okahandja.

1874 Transvaal Boers under Gert Alberts trek to Rietfontein near Gobabis.

1876 W. C. Palgrave visits South West Africa and annexes Walvis Bay.

1878 Union Jack hoisted at Walvis Bay.

1880 Foundation of Berseba.
Ten Year War begins between Hereros and Namaquas.
Departure of W. C. Palgrave.

1883 Adolf Lüderitz sets up settlement at Angra Pequena.

1884 German Protectorate declared.

1885 Hereros submit to Germans.
Concessions granted to companies.

1886 Border with Angola defined.

1888 Rising of Hereros.

1890 Death of Maherero.
Boundary with British territory settled.
Caprivi Strip defined.

1892 German Imperial Commissioner appointed (Dr. H. Goering).

1893 Rising under Witbooi.

1894 First Governor (von Leutwein) appointed.

1898 Work begun on Swakopmund harbour.
Railway to Windhoek started.

1904 Outbreak of Herero War and Bondelswarts rebellion.

1906 Compulsory education introduced for White children.

1907 Karakul farming commenced.

1908 End of Herero War.
Discovery of diamonds.

1911 Walvis Bay boundary arbitration by King Alphonso of Spain.

1913 Large wireless station built at Windhoek.

1914 Outbreak of World War I.
Invasion of German South West by Union troops under General Louis Botha.
Railways linked with those of South Africa at De Aar.

1915 Surrender of German forces at Korab under Col. V. Francke.

1920 South West Africa becomes Mandated Territory of Union of South Africa.
G. R. Hofmeyr becomes first Administrator.

1922 Bondelswarts Rebellion.

1924 Unrest among Rehoboths.

1926 First Legislative Council for South West Africa established.

1929 Settlement of Angola Boers in South West Africa.

1939 South West African Police merged with South African Police.

Caprivi Strip administration taken over by Union.

1946 United Nations refuses request for incorporation of South West Africa in the Union.

1949 South West Africa receives six seats in Union House of Assembly.

1955 Trade returns of South West Africa incorporated in those of Union.
United Nations debate on South-West Africa.
Union called on to submit reports.

1956 Rev. M. Scott and others submit evidence to United Nations.

1958 U.N. 'Good Offices' Committee visits South West Africa.

1960 South West Africa takes part in Union Republic Referendum.

1961 Proceedings begun before International Court of Justice regarding annual reports by South Africa on South West Africa.

1962 Visit by U.N. delegates, Dr. V. Carpio and Dr. S. M. De Alva.

1963 Successful offshore diamond mining begun.

1964 Odendaal Committee reports on development of South West African resources and territories.

1966 World Court decides that Liberia and Abyssinia are not entitled to bring action for revocation of South African mandate over South West Africa.
U.N. declares South African mandate to be terminated. Rejected by Republic.

1967 5-Year Plan introduced in South West Africa.

1968 U.N. delegation attempts to enter South West Africa and fails.
Self-government for Ovambos.
Terrorist attempts on northern boundary.

1969 U.N. orders South Africa to evacuate South West Africa.
Britain, U.S.A. and other powers abstain from vote. Ignored by Government.

South West Africa Company. Anglo-German company, established in 1892, to develop large land holdings in Damaraland. These originally covered 4,500 sq. miles of farms, mineral rights over 22,000 sq. miles, also mining and freehold rights along a six-mile strip on either side of any railway built by it north of the Tropic of Capricorn. This company sponsored the Otavi Minen und Eisenbahn-Gesellschaft (see OTAVI MINE). Recently it has engaged largely in prospecting and has exploited vanadium occurrences. Its German associations terminated after World War I. The head office is in London.

South West Africa Infantry. South African military unit, founded in 1939. Served in North Africa in World War II.

Soutpan. Village near Brandfort, Orange Free State. Population: 1,424, including 209 Whites.

Soutpansberg. Mountain range in the Northern Transvaal, named after the saltpan discovered there by the Voortrekkers. The local tribes held out among their fastnesses till near the end of the 19th century. The Blaauberg reaches a height of 6,734 feet.

Soweto. Complex of new Bantu residential areas named from the first syllables of the words South Western Townships. The population already exceeds 600,000.

Spaanspek (*Melo hispanicus*). A popular Cape sweet melon, with a rough rind. The name (literally 'Spanish bacon') is believed to have been derived from the rich colour of the flesh.

Space Research. South Africa's participation in Space Research began in 1958 with the installation near Esselen Park, Transvaal, between Pretoria and Johannesburg, of a Minitrack station to follow the movements of the first United States artificial satellite *Explorer I*. Work is carried on in conjunc-

tion with the National Institute of Telecommunications Research at Johannesburg. Another station was set up in 1958 at Haartebeesthoek. During the journey by the American satellite *Mariner II* past the planet Venus, the South African 'Deep Space Information Facility' was the first in the world successfully to transmit a command to the satellite, and it set up a record for long-distance communication at 54,000,000 miles. From here, too, the instruction was transmitted to the U.S.A. satellite that took the first close-up photographs of Mars in 1965. In 1964 the French Government set up a further Tracking Station at Pienaars River near Pretoria, which began operations in 1965. Under Professor L. Ahrens, the Department of Geochemistry of the University of Cape Town has carried out work of fundamental importance on ' stony meteorites ' (chondrites), of special value in studying geology of the moon. *See also* HAARTEBEESTHOEK.

Spadonas. A type of ostrich feather, the first year's pluckings from a young bird.

Spandau Kop. Prominent mountain outside Graaff-Reinet, belonging to the Sneeuwberg. The name, believed to have been derived from the German town of Spandau near Berlin, was given by an early German settler named Werner.

Sparrman, Andreas. Swedish naturalist and traveller at the Cape, born in 1747. He studied medicine and, through his friendship with Captain Ekeberg of the Royal Swedish East India Company, secured a post of tutor to Sub-Governor M. Kerst of the Cape of Good Hope. Arriving in 1772, he became an interpreter and was granted leave by Governor van Plettenberg to practise medicine. On the arrival of Captain James Cook's first expedition to Australia that year, he joined its staff, but returned in 1775 and trekked as far as the modern

Eastern Province. He went back to Sweden in 1776 and issued the first part of his *Voyage to the Cape of Good Hope*, which was soon translated into English (1782 and 1785). He was one of the first visitors to undertake a serious study of South African botany. He died in Stockholm, 1820.

Sparrow (family Ploceidae). A bird needing little description, classed with the Weavers (q.v.) though its rough, untidy nest belies the connection. The Cape Sparrow or Mossie is much handsomer than the English *Passer domesticus*, which has been introduced to Durban.

Sparrow-Hawk (family Falconidae). *See* EAGLES.

Spear-Fish. *See* MARLIN.

Special Service Battalion. South African military unit for men between 17 and 22, founded on May 1, 1933. Headquarters at Roberts Heights (q.v.), with detachments in Durban and Cape Town. It was formed for rehabilitating poor and physically defective boys. Now part of the Permanent Force.

Spekbossie, 'Bacon Bush' (*Zygophyllum flexuosum* E. & Z.). Shrub with angular branches. Leaves flat, fleshy. Flowers yellowish. Cape Division and northwards to Clanwilliam Division.

Spekvreter. Afrikaans name for Familiar Chat. *See* CHAT.

Spelonken. Area in the Northern Transvaal noted for its many caves. (Afrikaans 'spelonke,' Latin *spelunca*.)

Spencer-Jones, Sir Harold. British astronomer. Born in 1890 and joined the Royal Observatory at Greenwich in 1913. From 1923 to 1933 he was His Majesty's Astronomer at the Cape and from 1933 to 1955 Astronomer Royal at Greenwich. Among his achievements was the most accurate determination of the distance of the Earth from the Sun. He died in 1960.

Sperrgebiet ('Prohibited Area' in German). Zone in South West Africa, mainly along the coast, access to which was prohibited without special permission, owing to its wealth in diamonds. The Sperrgebiet was established during the German régime, and has been maintained since then by the South African Government.

Spider. Four-wheeled vehicle very popular in South Africa in pre-motor car days for its lightness and its high wheels, which allowed it to pass over obstacles.

Spider

SPIDERS OF SOUTHERN AFRICA
by
DR. R. F. LAWRENCE
Natal Museum, Pietermaritzburg

THE southern end of the African continent is as rich in spiders as in their relatives, the scorpions, solifugids, whip-scorpions and harvest-men, which make up the class Arachnida. The Cape Peninsula alone probably contains as many species as Western Europe.

Spiders can be divided into two large groups according to how they exploit their environment. The true trapdoor spiders and the large hairy 'baboon' spiders or 'tarantulas,' as these Harpactirae are erroneously called, are among the world's largest, easily covering a large saucer with their outspread legs. Both these types have four lungs and mandibles moving downwards in a vertical plane, while all other spiders have two lungs and mandibles (poison jaws) moving sideways pincer-fashion in a horizontal plane. All these four-lunged trapdoor spiders live in silk-lined tubes underground, those of the true trapdoors being closed by a stopper-like door which can be opened and pulled shut; the false trapdoors merely making a rather crude tube about an inch in diameter and more than a foot deep, its opening covered by a thin sheet of web.

All the remaining spiders (about 25 families) form a vast army rivalling the insects in the diversity of their structure and the variety of their habits. Spiders have explored every part of the earth's surface, except the polar deserts. We find them motionless in webs slung between trees and shrubs, or leaping like minute apes through grass; running on water like the most practised pond-skater, carried long distances by it, or plunging beneath it in pursuit of prey; living on bark, under fallen logs or, in South West Africa, even burrowing through loose dune sand. The flower or crab-spiders are almost entirely adapted for a sedentary life on flowers or grass, the two very long front legs, armed with powerful spines, forming pincers for snapping up a visiting bee or fly; they are slow and ungainly, walking sideways, or depending for concealment on immobility and colour. They favour beautiful arrangements of white, pink, yellow and green, or a decorative pattern of rich chocolate brown. *Thomisus*, the commonest crab-spider, is usually entirely white or yellow, matching the Cape chincherinchee it inhabits. Another flower-spider, *Synaema*, is vivid green with a large leaf-like chocolate marking on the abdomen.

The enormous Argyopidae family, which make a wheel-patterned web, produce such strange variations of shape and size that some do not look like spiders at all. They range in size from the huge cylindrical *Nephila*, widespread in Africa and Madagascar, where its web of tough golden strands sometimes clogs the telegraph wires, to minute cave dwellers in eternal darkness, whose web is smaller than a penny. Between these come bizarre forms like the forest-dwelling *Gasteracantha* which mounts one pair of sharp powerful spines, usually red-tipped, fore and aft, and another at each side; or *Pycnacantha* encircled with sharp spines like a hedgehog. These fiercely armoured types are always females, the males beside them looking like apologetic and insignificant dwarfs. Another odd member of this family is *Tetragnatha*, which folds its long limbs against the narrow body to resemble a stick, building the web above and parallel to the streams which it always haunts.

Another large family with a bad reputation contains the Lycosidae or wolf-spiders. These are strongly built, keen-eyed rovers who leap upon their prey. Of these one genus is named *Tarantula*, perhaps after the town Tarentum in Italy.

The bite of only one species in South Africa is dangerous to man, the 'button-spider' *Latrodectus*, and serum against its poison is prepared in most of the tropical and semi-tropical countries it inhabits.

To illustrate the almost embarrassing richness of our spider life, let us in imagination visit some of their recognised types of habitat. In our garden is the banded garden spider *Argyope*; further afield between young trees or in plantations, *Gasteracantha* and the large bark-spider *Caerostris* with a corrugated back difficult to see against a rough tree trunk; all these spiders make large wheel webs. *Hersilia*, a flattened quick-moving spider, with greatly elongated spinners, inhabits only the bark of trees.

Near water we shall find *Tetragnatha*, as well as a lovely silver, red and green spider called *Leucage*; the large agile water-spider *Thalassius* fishes by grasping the bank with its hind legs, resting the fore ones lightly on the skin of the water, and diving for small fish or tadpoles passing below. Along the banks of the streams will be seen the *Lycosas*.

In thick creepers lurks the powerful *Palystes* with banded legs, a wandering type often found on the walls of lamplit rooms. There also are found Oxyopidae, small agile spiders which rival the crab-spider in beauty of colour patterns, many of them due to irridescent scales like those of the Lepidoptera. A larger vivid-green species lives only in the everlasting, *Helichrysum cooperi*, of the Drakensberg, where it feeds on insects caught by the bright green, sticky leaves.

In open spaces with tufted grass, one can sometimes start a number of small spiders, each with a small white bag bouncing merrily behind; these are the mothers of *Pardosa*, a small form of Lycosid. Half hidden beneath tufts of bushes are the funnel-shaped nests of other wolf-spiders.

Another habitat consists of our dwelling houses, where hang the terraced webs of the domesticated daddy-long-legs or *Smeringopus*, a spider with a weakness for dark corners and caves.

Jumping spiders are numerous and found everywhere. Small, stronglybuilt, with enormous eyes like searchlights at the front of the head, they are the longest sighted of all spiders, being able to focus 2 to 3 inches. They circle their prey, stalk it and finally leap upon it, much as a lion strikes down a zebra.

Spilhaus, Arnold Wilhelm. South African centenarian and commercial pioneer. Born at Lubeck in Germany on December 1, 1845. He came to the Cape in 1869, traded on the East Coast and was later connected with the start of the diamond industry. He went into business in 1876, became a prominent figure in the Chamber of Commerce, and died on October 12, 1946, at the age of 101.

Spion Kop. Battle in Boer War on January 24, 1900, with the heaviest casualties in the campaign—2,053, including 383 British and 50 Boers killed. The British attack, although resulting in the capture of the hill, was called off.

Spitzkop. Name applied to pointed mountains in several parts of Southern Africa. One of these, in the vicinity of Pilgrim's Rest, was the site of one of the gold diggings about 1872. There is a Spitzkop in South West Africa, noted for its inaccessibility, which was climbed shortly before World War II.

Sponssiekte. Cattle disease, which derives its name from swellings on the body of the animal. 'Spons' is Dutch for sponge.

Spookvoël. Afrikaans name for Greyheaded Bush Shrike. *See* SHRIKES.

Spoonbill (*Platalea alba*). Bird found beside fresh waters in South Africa. It is closely related to the Ibis, except for bare red face and peculiar red bill. Bears a crest on back of head. Usually in small parties among herons and Ibises, but rare.

Spoor. Literally a track or trace. There are many kinds of spoors, including those left by animals and vehicles. Bushmen are famed as trackers, as are several other African races.

Spoorbond. Organisation of Afrikaansspeaking railway workers, recognised in 1948.

Spreeu. Afrikaans name for Starling (q.v.).

Sprigg, Sir John Gordon. Prime Minister of Cape Colony. Born at

Ipswich in 1830, he was originally a shorthand writer with the well-known old firm of Gurney, attached to the Houses of Parliament in London, but in 1858 visited the Cape and was so attracted that he remained permanently. Settling near King William's Town he became a successful dairy and sheep farmer and in 1876 was elected Member for East London in the House of Assembly. Attaining prominence in the House, he was asked by Governor Sir Bartle Frere in 1878 to form a Cabinet in succession to that of Sir John Molteno, and remained in office as Prime Minister and Colonial Secretary until 1881. From 1884 to 1886 he was Colonial Treasurer, from 1886 to 1890 Prime Minister and Treasurer. Further periods of office followed, as Treasurer from 1893 to 1896 and as Prime Minister from 1896 to 1898, again from 1900 to 1904. A strong supporter of British connections, he took the lead in 1897 when he visited London in connection with Queen Victoria's Diamond Jubilee, offering to contribute, on behalf of the Cape, a battleship to the Royal Navy. Although it was accepted with gratitude, the proposition was later altered to an annual contribution of £30,000 towards the Admiralty. He died in Cape Town on February 4, 1913.

Springbok. Originally known as Springbokfontein. Town in the North-Western Cape Province and chief administrative centre of Namaqualand. Founded in 1862, it became a municipality in 1933. Picturesquely located among granite koppies, it serves the needs of the nearby copper mines, and is much visited during the spring by tourists in quest of the famous Namaqualand wild flowers. During the South African War it was besieged and captured by General S. G. Maritz (q.v.). Population: 3,400, including 1,700 Whites.

Springbok or **Pronkbok** (*Antidorcas marsubialis*). Once the most common

of all Southern African antelopes, now limited mainly to a few reserves. They derive their name from their habit of characteristic display-leaping or 'pronking' (q.v.). At one time vast herds stampeded through the veld across the Karroo, even into villages, doing great damage. Today they can be shot only under authority. The flesh makes very good eating. Springbok are particularly graceful and both sexes carry small horns. The reddish-brown of the back is separated by a dark line from the pure white of the underparts. Height about 30 inches, to the shoulder.

Springbok Flats. Rich agricultural area in the Northern Transvaal, about 50 miles across, opened up after South African War; large producer of grain, peanuts, etc.

Springbok Legion. Organisation of ex-service men and women in South Africa, established at the end of World War II, originally to protect the interests of those who had been at the Front. Later it acquired a strongly political and 'Left' complexion.

Springfontein. Railway junction and village in the southern Orange Free State, of considerable strategic importance in the South African War. It is a dairying centre. Population: 3,260, including 800 Whites.

Spring-Hare (*Pedetes caffer*). Small timid rodent found in many parts of Southern Africa, from the Cape Province to Angola. Takes its name from its way of leaping nine or ten feet when chased. Its body measures about 2 feet and its tail about 20 inches. In habit it is nocturnal and sociable. It is widely hunted on account of its damage to crops. A moderate speed is its only defence. It can easily be tamed. *See* HARE.

Springs. Town on the East Rand in the Transvaal established as a colliery centre on a farm called 'The Springs,' because of its many fountains. It was already in existence in the 1890's as a source of coal supplies for the Netherlands South African Railway Company, but became a township only in 1902. Since then the opening of the Far East Rand goldfields has made it one of the principal centres on the fields, not only for mining but for manufactures. Population: 143,179, including 48,102 Whites, 91,894 Bantu, 1,238 Asiatics and 1,945 Coloureds.

Square-Face. Nickname for gin, because of the square bottles in which it is usually sold.

Square Hill. Battle in World War I, in which the Cape Corps (q.v.) specially distinguished itself. Square Hill, situated near the road from Jerusalem to Nablus, was captured by Cape Corps and other units, September 18, 1918, and successfully held for two days, despite heavy losses. Of one group of 400 men in action, 152 were casualties.

Squatting. The practice of occupying land—often farm land—without permission. The term is applied most frequently to Africans.

Squirrels. Group of small rodents widely distributed in Southern Africa. Of these the best known are the Grey Squirrels (*Sciurus carolinensis*) introduced to Groote Schuur by Cecil John Rhodes during the 1890's. They have grown to a larger size than their European counterparts and are extremely tame, particularly in the public gardens in Cape Town. The Cape Ground Squirrel (*Xerus inauris*) flourishes in the barren parts of the Karroo and has remarkable powers of adaptation to unfavourable surroundings. It lives in underground colonies. Other varieties are the Red-headed Squirrel, the Western Striped Squirrel, particularly common in South West Africa, and the Grey-footed Squirrel, which prefers the bush country of the Transvaal and Rhodesia.

S.S.B. Abbreviation for Special Service Battalion (q.v.).

Staatsartillerie (State Artillery). Only standing forces in the two Boer republics, the Orange Free State and Transvaal (S.A. Republic). That in the O.F.S. was the older, having been formed in 1880, under Major R.

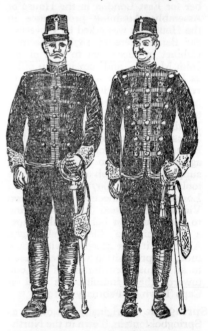

Staatsartillerie Uniforms

Albrecht, a German officer, with a total wartime strength of 400 men. The State Artillery of the S.A. Republic dated from 1890, two of its officers, Maj. J. F. Wolmarans and Maj. P. E. Erasmus, being sent to Europe for training. It was built up with the aid of German and Austrian officers and equipped with Krupp and French (Schneider) guns. At the time of the South African War it numbered 800 men. Both units distinguished themselves for efficiency and gallantry.

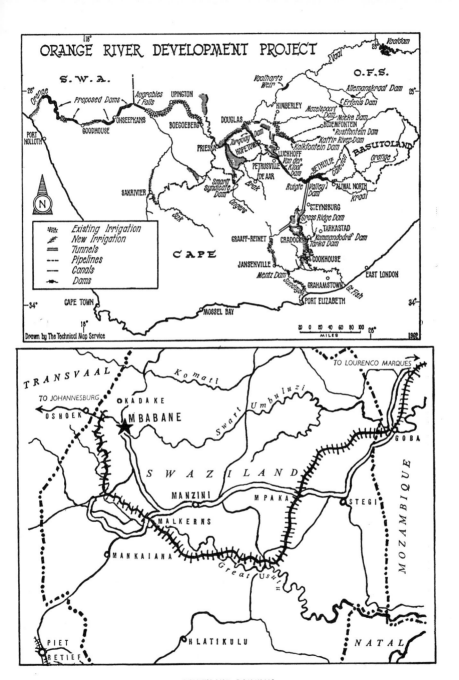

ORANGE RIVER DEVELOPMENT PROJECT

SWAZILAND RAILWAY

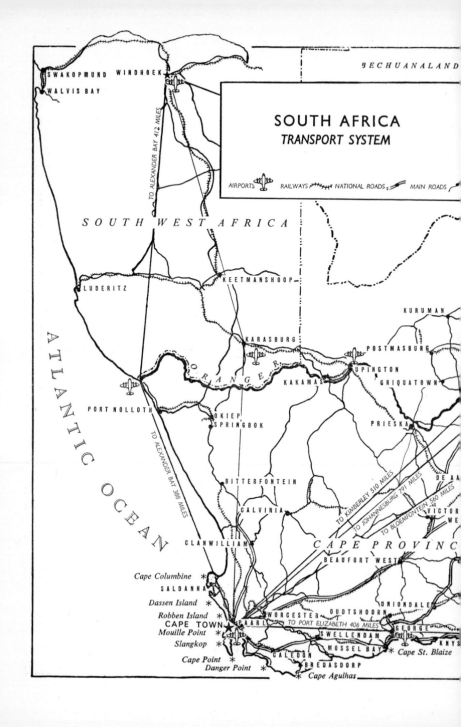

SOUTH AFRICA
TRANSPORT SYSTEM

AIRPORTS ✈   RAILWAYS ▪▪▪▪   NATIONAL ROADS ⬍   MAIN ROADS ⬍

BECHUANALAND

SWAKOPMUND WINDHOEK
WALVIS BAY

SOUTH WEST AFRICA

TO ALEXANDER BAY 412 MILES

LUDERITZ

KEETMANSHOOP

KURUMAN

KARASBURG

POSTMASBURG

ORANGE

UPINGTON

KAKAMAS

GRIQUATOWN

PORT NOLLOTH

OKIEP
SPRINGBOK

PRIESKA

TO ALEXANDER BAY 388 MILES

ATLANTIC OCEAN

BITTERFONTEIN

TO KIMBERLEY 510 MILES

TO JOHANNESBURG 791 MILES

TO BLOEMFONTEIN 560 MILES

DE AA

CALVINIA

VICTOR
WE

CLANWILLIAM

CAPE PROVINC

BEAUFORT WEST

Cape Columbine *
SALDANHA
Dassen Island *
Robben Island *
CAPE TOWN
Mouille Point *
Slangkop *
Cape Point *
Danger Point *

WORCESTER

OUDTSHOORN

UNIONDALE

PAARL

TO PORT ELIZABETH 406 MILES

GEORGE

SWELLENDAM

KNYS

CALEDON

MOSSEL BAY

Cape St. Blaize *

BREDASDORP

Cape Agulhas

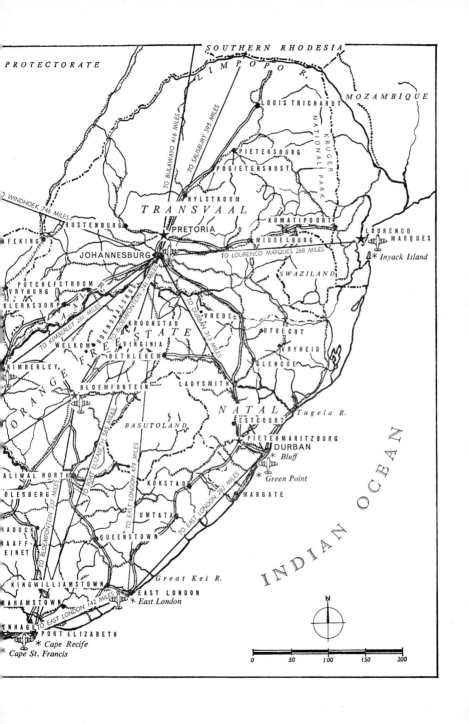

SOUTHERN RHODESIA

PROTECTORATE

LIMPOPO R.

MOZAMBIQUE

LOUIS TRICHARDT

PIETERSBURG

POGIETERSRUST

NYLSTROOM

TRANSVAAL

KRUGER NATIONAL PARK

KOMATIPOORT

RUSTENBURG

PRETORIA

MIDDELBURG

LOURENCO MARQUES

JOHANNESBURG

Inyack Island

SWAZILAND

POTCHEFSTROOM

VRYBURG

KLERKSDORP

VREDE

UTRECHT

KROONSTAD

VRYHEID

WELKOM

VIRGINIA

GLENCOE

BETHLEHEM

KIMBERLEY

FREE STATE

ORANGE

BLOEMFONTEIN

LADYSMITH

NATAL

Tugela R.

BASUTOLAND

ESTCOURT

PIETERMARITZBURG

DURBAN

Bluff

ALIWAL NORTH

* Green Point

KOKSTAD

OLESBERG

MARGATE

UMTATA

RADOCK

RAAFF-EINET

QUEENSTOWN

KINGWILLIAMSTOWN

Great Kei R.

RAHAMSTOWN

EAST LONDON

* East London

ENHAGE

PORT ELIZABETH

* Cape Recife

Cape St. Francis

INDIAN OCEAN

TO BULAWAYO 416 MILES
TO SALISBURY 595 MILES
WINDHOEK 746 MILES
AFEKING
TO LOURENCO MARQUES 268 MILES
TO KIMBERLEY 281 MILES
TO ODENDAALSRUST
TO BLOEMFONTEIN 247 MILES
TO DURBAN 313 MILES
TO FORT ELIZABETH 585 MILES
TO EAST LONDON 479 MILES
TO EAST LONDON 287 MILES
TO BLOEMFONTEIN 337 MILES
TO EAST LONDON 142 MILES

N

0   50   100   150   200

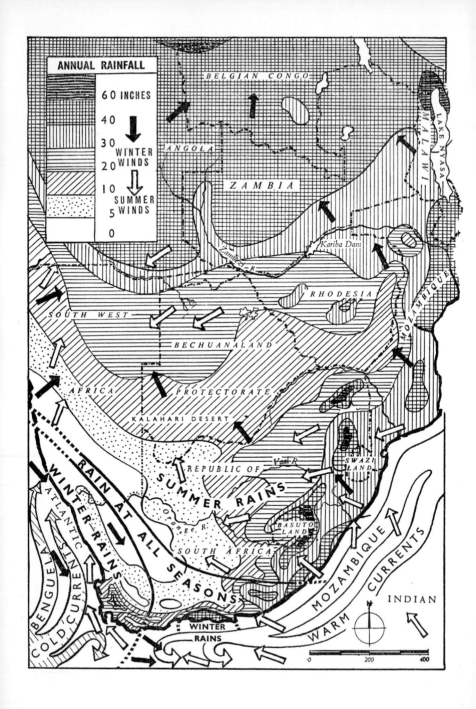

Stachys. *See* SALVIA.

Stad. Dutch word meaning 'town.' Spelt 'stat' when applied to an African village.

Staggers. Disease developed by horses, usually through eating Senecio or Ragwort. *See* DAISY.

Stals, Dr. Albert Jacobus. South African cabinet minister, born in Tulbagh, 1880. He was educated at Stellenbosch, Dublin and Berlin, qualifying in law and in medicine, and gaining distinction in both. He entered Parliament as member for Hopetown, and also served as a member of the South African Medical Council, the Board of Trade and Industry and the Shipping Board, of which last he was Chairman. Upon the coming to power of Dr. D. F. Malan in 1948, he became Minister of Health and Social Welfare. He died in 1951.

Stampriet. Irrigation settlement in south of South West Africa, noted for its large artesian wells.

Stand. Originally Standplaas, or Standing-place. Land title on the Witwatersrand and in other mining districts. Originated in Pilgrim's Rest among the diggers, who were in the habit, on the early goldfields in the 1870's, of securing plots or pieces of ground to deposit their tools and tents next to claims they were washing for alluvial in the river. For this they paid a usual fee of 10/- a month. Later townships of stands were laid out, both in Barberton and in Johannesburg. Thus arose a system of leasehold, to some extent still in operation. Since the Township Act of 1908, facilities have been provided for the conversion of leasehold into freehold, against the payment, under a fixed tariff, of compensation to the owner.

Standard and Diggers News. Daily newspaper in Johannesburg, established 1887 as the *Standard*, and shortly afterwards merged with the independent *Diggers News*. It continued to appear until the outbreak of the South African War.

Standard Bank of South Africa Ltd. The main credit for founding this institution goes to John Paterson (q.v.) of Port Elizabeth, whose first efforts were made in 1857. Failing to secure support in the Cape, he took advantage of the new English Companies Act and registered the Standard Bank of British South Africa (to use its original name) as one of the earliest concerns under that law in 1862. Commencing with a capital of £1,000,000, it grew rapidly, its progress stimulated by the discovery of the Diamond Fields. In 1863 it absorbed the Commercial Bank of Port Elizabeth, the Colesberg Bank, the British Kaffrarian Bank and the Fauresmith Bank in the Orange Free State. The Beaufort West Bank was taken over in 1864, the Fort Victoria and Fort Beaufort Bank in 1873, the Albert Bank in 1874, the Swellendam Bank and the London and South African Bank in 1877, the Malmesbury Agricultural Bank and the Caledon Agricultural Bank in 1878, the Wellington Bank in 1890, the Kaffrarian Colonial Bank and the Western Province Bank in 1891 and the Worcester Commercial Bank in 1892. The African Banking Corporation was acquired in 1920. Apart from operating in all parts of the Republic, the Standard Bank has a chain of branches throughout South West Africa, Mozambique, Rhodesia and Central and East Africa, with representation in most important overseas centres. Its head office is in London. In 1965 a close liaison was established with the well-known Chase National Bank, whose South African network was merged into the Standard.

Standerton. Town in the Transvaal, on the Vaal River. Established in 1879 and named after the original farmer, Adriaan Stander. A large bridge built there by the Republican government was blown up during the South African War, and much fighting took place in the vicinity. After the return of peace it was, until World War I, a garrison town for the Imperial forces. Today Standerton is noted for its cattle trade, milling and other industries. Population: 23,000, including 8,000 Whites.

Stanford. Fishing centre near Hermanus, Cape Province. Population: 730, including 420 Whites.

Stanger. Town on the north coast of Natal, named after Dr. William Stanger, first Surveyor-General of Natal, and established about 1850. Important centre for sugar production and general farming. Tea was formerly produced near by at Kearsney (q.v.). A monument to the Zulu king, Tshaka (q.v.), stands in the town. On the site of the present Stanger stood Dukuza, principal kraal of Tshaka, a fact still well remembered by the Zulus. Population: 13,200, including 2,000 Whites, 6,800 Indians and 4,000 Bantu.

Stapelia. See SUCCULENTS.

Star. Evening newspaper in Johannesburg. Established as the *Eastern Star or Grahamstown Advertiser and Anglo-African* in Grahamstown on January 6, 1871. Founded by a printer named O'Brien, it passed into the hands of the brothers Thomas and George Sheffield, appearing weekly. Following the death of its main financial supporter, Dean Williams, in 1887, it was moved to the newly-discovered Witwatersrand and made its first appearance in Johannesburg on October 17 of that year. For a while it continued to be called the *Eastern Star*, coming out twice weekly. On April 1, 1889, it became the *Star* and began to appear daily. Brought into conflict with the government of President Kruger in 1897, it was temporarily closed down and appeared for a while under the name

of *The Comet*. It ceased publication during the South African War, but reappeared in January 1902. Since then it has been published regularly.

Starling or **Spreeu** (Sturnidae). Family of birds strongly represented in South Africa, of three very different types. (1) Ox-Peckers (q.v.); (2) Glossy Starlings, of which all, including the large Red-winged Starling that haunts the Cape rooikrantz and fruit trees, have a metallic sheen; and (3) less well-groomed varieties like the Speckled European Starling and the Wattled Starling. The last is a fawn-grey bird, so called from the male's appearance at breeding time; known too as the Locust-bird from its habit of following swarms of locusts and nesting in crowds where they settle.

State Artillery. See STAATSARTILLERIE.

Stavenisse. Dutch East Indiaman wrecked on the coast of Natal on February 16, 1686, between the mouths of the Umzinto and Umzimkulu rivers. About 60 survivors came ashore, under Captain Willem Knyff, and built a smaller vessel out of the wreckage, in which 20 of them set sail for the Cape of Good Hope. The *Centaurus*, as she was called, duly arrived, and later returned for those who had stayed behind. The *Noord* was also sent and saved several others. Her commander later purchased (for £50) the Bay of Natal from local chiefs, a deal not ratified by the Dutch East India Company.

Stead, William Thomas. English journalist. Born 1849, he became famous as editor of the *Pall Mall Gazette*, and of the *Review of Reviews*. An intimate friend of Cecil John Rhodes, he later became a strong pro-Boer, and exercised much influence in their favour. He visited South Africa on several occasions. He was drowned in the *Titanic* in 1912.

Steelpoort. Mining village in Eastern Transvaal. Centre of vanadium production at Kennedy's Vale.

Steenberg's Cove. Fishing centre near Hopefield, Cape Province. Population: 550, including 30 Whites.

Steenbok (*Rhachiceros campestris*). Literally 'Stone Buck.' Very small and beautiful antelope, with white under parts, the male carrying short horns. Solitary except at breeding time, but found over most of Southern Africa. It is still widely hunted for its delicate meat. Steenbok have the habit of standing still, in order to blend with the landscape. A special variety, known as Sharpe's Steenbok (*Raphiceros sharpei*), occurs in North-Eastern Transvaal, Swaziland and Rhodesia.

Steenbras, Red (*Petrus rupestris*). Fish found in Table Bay, False Bay and up to Natal. About 5 feet long.

Steenbras, White (*Lithognathus lithognathus*). Fish found off west coast of South Africa and False Bay to Natal. About 58 inches long. *See* BREAM.

Steer, Captain George Lowther. War correspondent and author. Born in East London, 1909; educated at Grahamstown and Oxford. He served as war correspondent for the London *Times* in the Abyssinian war against Mussolini and again in the Spanish Civil War. The *Daily Telegraph* sent him to the Russo-Finnish front in 1940. He wrote a number of books on his experiences, and died in 1945.

Stegi. Village in Swaziland, founded officially in 1927. Administrative centre in Lebombo Mountains. Population: 3,600, including 100 Whites.

Steinkopf. Village in Namaqualand, established early in the 19th century by the London Missionary Society under the name of Kookfontein. It was given its new name in 1842, when it became a German Lutheran mission station under Dr. Steinkopf.

Stella. Village near Vryheid, Natal. Population: 800, including 540 Whites.

Stellaland. Miniature republic formed by Boer adventurers of portion of present-day Botswana in July 1882. The territory was granted to Gerrit Jacobus Van Niekerk and his followers, who had backed the chief Massouw in a war against his rival Mankoroane. Stellaland, which comprised 416 farms of 3,000 morgen each, was so called after a comet (the Latin word for star being *stella*) visible at the time. Its capital was Vryburg (q.v.) and its president G. J. Van Niekerk. It was absorbed into Bechuanaland in 1884. *See also* GOSHEN.

Stellenbosch. Town in the Western Cape Province, the second oldest in South Africa, founded in 1679 by Governor Simon Van der Stel (q.v.). A major centre of the wine and fruit industry, it stands in beautiful mountain country beside the Eerste River. From the start the town was noted for its stately houses, many of which are still in existence, and for its avenues of oaks, the first of which were established by Governor Van der Stel himself. Outbreaks of fire destroyed many of the thatch-roofed buildings in 1710, again in 1803 and in Victorian times. The town has been a leading educational centre since the first school was opened in 1683. A theological seminary and a 'Gymnasium' were set up in 1859 by the Dutch Reformed Church. In 1866 the latter became Stellenbosch College and in 1887 was renamed Victoria College, in honour of Queen Victoria's Golden Jubilee. Many of South Africa's leading figures, including General Smuts, General J. B. M. Hertzog and Dr. D. F. Malan, studied there. In 1918 Victoria College became the University of Stellenbosch (q.v.) by special Act of Parliament. Population: 26,000, including 12,000 Whites, 12,000 Coloured, 145 Asiatics and 1,769 Bantu.

Stellenbosch District Bank. Last survivor of the once numerous local banks in South Africa. Established in September 1882, it encountered considerable difficulties in its early years, and for a short while in 1889 actually closed its doors. Fortunately it recovered and is today a very prosperous concern, handling a large share of the Stellenbosch business. Its deposits are nearly R10,000,000.

'Stellenbosched.' Jocular expression invented during the South African War, referring to those officers who had not proved sufficiently competent, and were therefore sent to Stellenbosch away from the fighting.

'Stem van Suid-Afrika, Die' (The Voice of South Africa). Official South African national anthem. The words were written in Afrikaans by C. J. Langenhoven on October 26, 1918 and the music by M. L. de Villiers (qq.v.). Despite efforts by the authorities to secure an approved translation into English, the anthem is usually sung in Afrikaans.

Stent, Vere Palgrave. South African journalist and writer, born in South Africa in 1872. He was educated at St. Andrew's College in Grahamstown and in England. As a very young man he came to Kimberley, where he met Cecil John Rhodes, and, through this friendship, trekked to Rhodesia. As correspondent of the *Cape Times*, he was present at the Matabele Rebellion in 1896, and at the famous indaba to which Cecil Rhodes and a handful of companions went unarmed to meet the leaders of the insurgent Matabele. Stent was also in the siege of Mafeking and saw much active service in the South African War. He became editor of the *Pretoria News* and gave it a strongly pro-Imperialist line. He died in 1941.

Sterkfontein. Site of a cave in the Transvaal near Krugersdorp, noted for limestone occurrences, in which numerous prehistoric remains of early man have been recovered over years, particularly by the late Dr. Robert Broom (q.v.). In former times Sterkfontein was considerably damaged

through careless or ignorant exploitation of the limestone, and many valuable remains were lost.

Sterkspruit. Village near Herschel, Cape Province. Population: 240, including 80 Whites.

Sterkstroom. Village in the Eastern Cape Province, so named because of the strong (sterk) stream running past. It was founded in 1875 and, in the days before Natal and the Transvaal dominated the markets, a certain amount of coal mining was carried on near by. Today it is noted for its sheep. Population: 5,250, including 1,000 Whites.

Stern, Irma. South African painter. Born at Schweizer-Renecke, Transvaal, on October 2, 1894, she studied in Germany at Berlin and Weimar, gaining international recognition through the strength, novelty and strongly African note in her paintings. Besides figuring at exhibitions in Paris, Amsterdam, Berlin and elsewhere, Irma Stern's work has been acclaimed at such famous shows as the Biennale at Venice, and another display at São Paulo in Brazil. She also wrote illustrated books on the Congo and Zanzibar. Died at Cape Town in August 1966.

Sterretjie. *See* AMARYLLIS.

Stertriem. Literally a tail thong. Strip of hide worn over their buttocks by the Hereros and other African tribes in South West Africa.

Stevenson-Hamilton, Lt.-Col. James. South African zoologist and game conservationist, first curator of the Kruger National Park. Born in Dublin, 1867; educated at Rugby and entered the Royal Military College at Sandhurst. He was commissioned as a lieutenant in the 6th Royal Dragoons in 1888 and first saw service in South Africa during the Zulu Rebellion of that year. He accompanied Major St. Hill Gibbons on his Cape to Cairo Expedition in 1898 and on the exploration of the watershed between the Congo and Zambesi in 1898–1899. After serving in the South African War, he was appointed Warden of the Transvaal Government Game Reserves in 1902, a position he held until 1926 when the Sabi Game Reserve, of which he was virtually the creator, was converted into the Kruger National Park. He remained curator of this until his retirement in 1946. Many honours came his way, including membership of the King's Bodyguard for Scotland (Royal Company of Archers). He wrote books which are regarded as standard works, *Animal Life in Africa*, *The Lowveld*, *African Eden*, etc. He died in 1957.

Stewart, The Rev. Dr. James. Missionary and educationist. Born in Edinburgh on February 14, 1831, he was educated in that city and at the University of St. Andrew's, securing doctorates both in medicine and theology. After considerable travelling in Europe and America, he joined David Livingstone's expedition to the Zambesi in 1862, and in 1866 reached the Cape, where he became the Principal of Lovedale. Although he intended to return to his explorations, he remained there permanently, raising the institution to great importance and prosperity. One of his most important other achievements was the establishment of the Church of Scotland Mission in Livingstonia, in what is now Zambia, in 1875. In 1899 he was the first missionary to become Moderator of the Free Church of Scotland. He died in 1905.

Steyn, Hermanus. President of the Swellendam Republic, born in 1743 near Bruintjes River on what was then the frontier of the Cape Colony. After his marriage in 1765 to Margaretha van Staden he settled near Swellendam, and soon gained the esteem of his neighbours. The advent of the 'Patriot Movement' at the Cape in the 1770's interested

him greatly, and when the Dutch East India Co.'s régime collapsed in 1795 and the Swellendam burghers decided to set up their own Republic, he was chosen President. After a few months the arrival of the British put an end to this experiment. He died about 1804.

Steyn, Lucas Cornelius. Chief Justice of the Republic of South Africa. Born near Viljoenskroon, O.F.S., December 21, 1903, and educated at Stellenbosch University. In 1931 became Attorney-General for South West Africa and Senior Law Adviser to South African Government, 1944. After promotion to Transvaal Bench, August 1951, was appointed Judge of Appeal, March 1955.

Steyn, President Marthinus Theunis. Born on the farm Rietfontein, near Winburg, O.F.S., in 1857, and educated at Grey College, Bloemfontein. He then went to Leyden and the Inner Temple, London, to study law. Admitted as an advocate he began practice in Bloemfontein in 1882, became State Attorney in 1889, and judge in the same year. In 1896 he was elected State President, and despite poor health exercised a moderating influence in the dispute between the South African Republic and Britain, arranging the meetings in Bloemfontein between Lord Milner and President Kruger which were the final attempt to prevent hostilities. Once the war began he joined his burghers in the field, completely shattering his constitution. He worked ceaselessly to rebuild the fortunes of his people, by whom he and his wife (born Tibbie Fraser) were idolised. Wise, moderate and tactful, he did inestimable service in founding the Union. During the 1914 Rebellion crisis he again tried to prevent hostilities. In 1916, while addressing a meeting in Bloemfontein, he collapsed and died.

Steynberg, Coert Laurens. South African sculptor. Born at Pretoria in

1905 and educated at Bethal, Transvaal, Rhodes University, and in England, in 1933 he received the commission to take part in decorating South Africa House in London. Commissions for numerous monuments followed, including those to the Huguenots at French Hoek and to General De Wet at Bloemfontein. He received an overseas award for his design for a memorial to 'the Unknown Political Prisoner.' His sculpture for a monument to the peace negotiations at Vereeniging gave rise to much controversy as did his plan for a giant head of President Kruger in the Kruger National Park.

Steynsburg. Town in the Eastern Cape Province, named after Douw Steyn of Bulhoek, grandfather of President Kruger, who is believed to have been born on the neighbouring farm. It was founded in 1873 and attained municipal status in 1892. Fighting took place near by in the South African War, during the Boer invasion of the Cape. Today it is a leading wool centre. Population: 4,330, including 1,000 Whites.

Steynsdorp. Village in the Eastern Transvaal, formerly the centre of the Komati Goldfield, established in 1887, and named after President M. T. Steyn of the Orange Free State. After the fields (which were regarded as an extension of the De Kaap formation) were abandoned about 1904, the population dwindled and today the old camp has almost disappeared.

Steynsrus. Village near Lindley in the Orange Free State, named after President M. T. Steyn. Farming centre. Population: 2,255, including 695 Whites.

Steytler, Abraham Isaac. Cape clergyman, nicknamed the 'Dutch Reformed Pope' on account of his great influence. Born at Sea Point, Cape Town, on February 5, 1840, he attended the school of the well-known

Dr. Changuion, later proceeding to England and Holland and returning with a Divinity degree from the University of Utrecht. In 1863 he became minister at Uitenhage, where he showed his strong personality and gifts of organisation. A portion of his parish was cut off and a new village established under the name of Steytlerville (q.v.). In 1881 he received a call to Cape Town, where he spent the rest of his career, being prominent not only in the affairs of his own church but in education. He was elected Moderator of the Cape Synod of the Dutch Reformed Church, retired in October 1915 and died on December 17, 1922.

Steytlerville. Town in the Cape Province Midlands, established in 1876 by the Dutch Reformed Church, with the proviso that no liquor should ever be sold there. Its name is derived from that of the Reverend A. I. Steytler (q.v.). The production of mohair for which it was noted has been gradually replaced by wool. Population: 2,164, including 600 Whites.

Stick Insects (Phasmidae). A name given to a group of mostly wingless insects of different sizes that mimic stalks and twigs. *See* HOTTENTOT GODS.

Stilfontein. Gold mining town near Klerksdorp, Transvaal, founded 1949. Population: 30,000, including 14,000 Whites.

Stilt, Black-Winged (*Himantopus himantopus*). Bird of Wader family (q.v.), usually found in loose flocks, near weedy river margins or vleis, over most of South Africa. It is pure white, with black wings and very long, pink legs.

Stinkblaar. *See* TOBACCO, WILD.

Stinker. Common name for Giant Petrel. *See* PETREL.

Stinkwood, Black, or Stinkhout (*Ocotea bullata* E. Mey). Large evergreen tree up to 80 feet. Wood regarded as one of the best timbers in the Re-

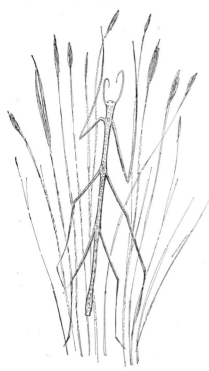

Stick Insect

ancestry in Graaff-Reinet in 1844, he went at an early age to London and to Germany, being called to the Bar in 1865. The following year he began practice in Cape Town, but shortly after moved to the Eastern Province. In 1877 he was made Attorney-General of the Cape Colony, and two years later a judge of the Supreme Court. He died in 1880.

Stockenstrom, Sir Andries. Lieutenant-Governor of the Eastern Province of the Cape Colony, born at the Cape on July 6, 1792. He was of Swedish descent and son of another Andries Stockenstrom, Landdrost of Graaff-Reinet, murdered in 1811 by the Xosas. He began his career as a soldier, being commissioned as an ensign in the Cape Regiment, and distinguished himself in the wars against the frontier tribes. From 1822 to 1824 he was engaged in marking the boundary of the Colony. Through

public, taking a natural polish. Knysna and Natal forests. Its unattractive name originates from the fact that for a short while after being cut it has a strong smell. Production today is under state control and no method of growing it from seed has yet been found. *See* PLANTS.

Stints (*Erolia minuta*). Next to the Curlew Sandpipers (q.v.), among which they are usually found, these are the most plentiful of South African migratory Waders. They are small, with rather warm brown coats and bills only slightly curved at the tip.

Stiver. *See* STUIVER.

Stockenstrom, Andries. Judge and Attorney-General. Born of Swedish

Stinkblaar

his achievements there he became in 1828 Commissioner-General of the Eastern Province and a member of the Governor's Council of Advice. In 1829 he was entrusted with the task of settling a large number of Hottentots on the Kat River, which gave rise to much criticism. During a visit to Europe in 1833 pressure was successfully brought to bear upon him to retire on pension. He caused great offence by giving hostile evidence about the colonists' behaviour before a committee of the House of Commons. Even greater protests were aroused when he was made Lieutenant-Governor of the Eastern Districts in 1836, and immediately restored the province of Queen Adelaide (q.v.) to the local tribes. He was ordered by a mass meeting in Grahamstown to explain his hostile behaviour in England. Undeterred, he proceeded to make the best possible peace with the local chiefs. Because of the feeling against him he became involved in a libel action, which he lost. He became a strong opponent of the Voortrekkers, whom he tried to force to return to the Cape. There was fresh unpleasantness in England, where he first renounced his office, then withdrew his resignation, and finally accepted a baronetcy and pension. A stormy petrel of South African politics, he remained a figure of controversy until his death in 1864.

Stock Exchange, Johannesburg. Although the Cape was founded by the Dutch East India Company, whose shares were in demand in many lands, and although small companies were formed in the colony in the 18th century for mining and other purposes, it was not until about 1820 that shares were dealt in on the Commercial Exchange in Cape Town, most deals being by public auction. The discovery of copper in Namaqualand in the 1850's led to the first South African share boom, but the first stock exchange was set up in Kimberley in 1880.

Further exchanges were opened in Barberton in 1884. The Johannesburg Stock Exchange, founded in 1887, was at first rivalled by others in Klerksdorp, Durban, Pietermaritzburg, Cape Town, Port Elizabeth, Potchefstroom and Pretoria, but all these ultimately closed again. Today it is the only institution of its kind in South Africa, with wide international connections, and members in most other local cities. Over 1,400 stocks are listed, representing an issued capital of over R8,000,000,000. There are 233 members. Proprietary rights cost up to R8,500. *See also* UNIT TRUSTS.

Stockfish (Hake) (*Mercuccius capensis*). One of the Cod-fish group, of which haddock, whiting and hake are well-known European members. In spite of the name there is some doubt as to whether it is identical with the last. Stockfish is a deep-water variety, 40 inches long, with small, silvery-grey scales. It has become the mainstay of the South African fishing industry from Walvis Bay to Natal, but chiefly north and north-west of Table Bay. Caught, chiefly by trawlers, down to 300 or more fathoms. The flesh has an unfortunate tendency to become soft and milky. *See* MARINE RESOURCES.

Stockley, Cynthia. Rhodesian novelist. Born in England in 1877 as Lilian Julia Webb, came to Rhodesia in 1896 and first married Captain P. G. W. Stockley of the Rhodesian Police and later Colonel Pelham-Browne. The publication in 1903 of her novel, *Virginia of the Rhodesians*, brought her prominence. *Poppy*, which followed, drew much comment for its outspokenness. She died in 1936.

Stompneus Bay. Fishing village near Hopefield, Cape Province. Population: 590, including 110 Whites.

Stomstertjie. Alternative name for Krombek (q.v.).

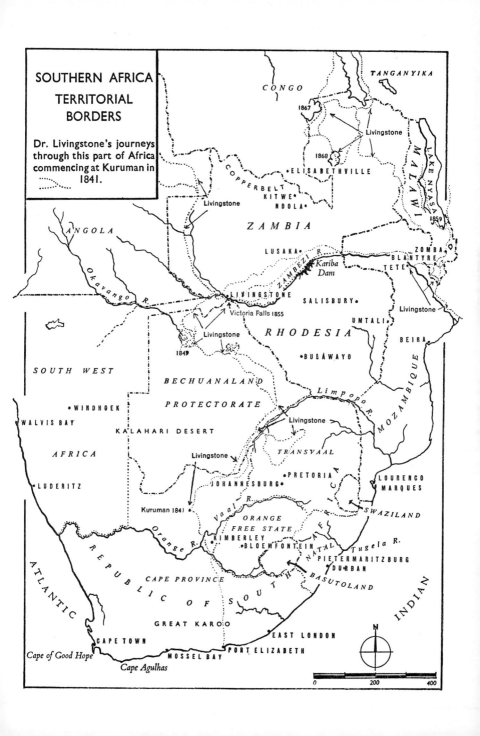

SOUTHERN AFRICA
TERRITORIAL
BORDERS

Dr. Livingstone's journeys
through this part of Africa
commencing at Kuruman in
1841.

CONGO
TANGANYIKA
1867
Livingstone
1868
•ELISABETHVILLE
LAKE NYASA
COPPERBELT
KITWE•
NDOLA•
1859
Livingstone
ZAMBIA
LUSAKA•
ZAMBEZI R.
ZOMBA
BLANTYRE
TETE
ANGOLA
Okavango R.
Kariba
Dam
LIVINGSTONE
SALISBURY•
Livingstone
Victoria Falls 1855
Livingstone
UMTALI
R.
BEIRA
MOZAMBIQUE
1849
RHODESIA
•BULAWAYO
SOUTH WEST
BECHUANALAND
PROTECTORATE
Limpopo R.
•WINDHOEK
WALVIS BAY
KALAHARI DESERT
Livingstone
TRANSVAAL
AFRICA
Livingstone
•PRETORIA
LOURENCO
MARQUES
•LUDERITZ
JOHANNESBURG•
Vaal R.
Kuruman 1841
SWAZILAND
ORANGE
FREE STATE
Orange R.
KIMBERLEY
•BLOEMFONTEIN
NATAL
Tugela R.
PIETERMARITZBURG
DURBAN
REPUBLIC OF SOUTH AFRICA
CAPE PROVINCE
BASUTOLAND
INDIAN
ATLANTIC
GREAT KAROO
CAPE TOWN
Cape of Good Hope
MOSSEL BAY
Cape Agulhas
EAST LONDON
PORT ELIZABETH
N
0   200   400

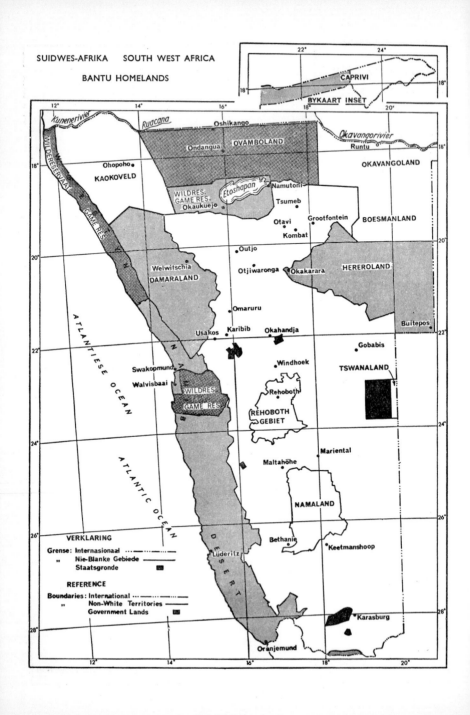

SUIDWES-AFRIKA   SOUTH WEST AFRICA

BANTU HOMELANDS

CAPRIVI

BYKAART INSET

Kunenerivier   *Rucana*   Oshikango

Ondangua   OVAMBOLAND   *Okavangorivier*

Runtu

Ohopoho•   OKAVANGOLAND

KAOKOVELD

WILDRES.   *Etoshapan*   Namutoni

GAME RES.

Okaukuejo   Tsumeb

BOESMANLAND

Otavi   Grootfontein

Kombat

•Outjo

Welwitschia   Otjiwaronga   •Okakarara   HEREROLAND

DAMARALAND

•Omaruru

Karibib   Okahandja   Buitepos

Usakos

Gobabis

•Windhoek   TSWANALAND

Swakopmund

Walvisbaai   WILDRES.

GAME RES.   •Rehoboth

REHOBOTH

GEBIET

ATLANTIESE OCEAN

Mariental

Maltahöhe

NAMALAND

ATLANTIC OCEAN

VERKLARING   Bethanie

Grense: Internasionaal ·····————·   •Keetmanshoop

  „   Nie-Blanke Gebiede ————   Lüderitz

     Staatsgronde   ▪

REFERENCE

Boundaries: International ·····————·

  „   Non-White Territories ————

     Government Lands   ▪   Karasburg

Oranjemund

Stonechat (*Saxicola torquata*). *See* CHAT.

Stoneman, Dr. Bertha. South African botanist. Born in Jamestown, New York State, and educated at Cornell University, she came to South Africa in 1897 as lecturer in botany at Huguenot College (q.v.). She soon attained distinction in her science, on which she published a number of works. Honorary degrees were conferred upon her, and she became Principal of Huguenot College in 1920. She retired from this post in 1932 and died in 1943.

Stone Pine or **Umbrella Pine** (*Pinus pinea*). Mediterranean species much cultivated in the Cape Peninsula, to which it lends singular beauty. Tall, with umbrella-shaped branching. *See* DANNEBOL.

Storks (family Ciconiidae). Long-billed, long-necked and long-legged birds, found chiefly in the Eastern Cape, Natal and the Highveld, but occasionally in other parts of the country. Most are migrants from Europe and Asia, very few nesting in South Africa. The only well-known variety is the *White Stork*, which has red legs and black wings. It is a locust-eater that usually sleeps in large trees. Storks resemble Herons, but fly with necks outstretched. *See* MARABOU and SADDLE-BILL.

Stormberg. Mountain range near Wodehouse, Cape Province; a continuation of the Drakensberg, rising to about 6,000 feet, noted for bleak but majestic scenery and for the deposits of coal discovered there by a pioneer named North in 1878. The coal, of poor grade, was for a long time the sole local supply, until the opening of the Natal and Transvaal fields. During the South African War the British sustained a heavy defeat near Stormberg Junction on December 10, 1899, General Gatacre losing over 700 men.

Stormjaers. Jocular name given by the Boers in the field to a large indigestible dumpling dipped in fat. The name was also applied during World War II to members representing the active branch of the Ossewa Brandwag (q.v.).

'Stormvogel.' South African ocean racing craft, built at Stellenbosch by Cornelis Bruynzeel and launched in April 1961. A 74-foot ketch, she has been successful in many international contests in South African, European and American waters.

Stow, George William. South African geologist and ethnologist. Born at Nuneaton, Warwickshire, England, on February 2, 1822. Studied engineering and then medicine, without qualifying. Emigrating to the eastern Cape in 1843, he became interested in geology, particularly phosphates, and in Bushman paintings, of which little was then known. Largely self-educated, he was among the first geologists to study the diamond fields, and in 1878 reported on coal in the Orange Free State and near Vereeniging. He died on March 17, 1882, leaving important geological and ethnological material, much of it unpublished.

Strakosch, Sir Henry. South African economist and capitalist. Born in 1871, he began his banking career in London, and in 1895 came to South Africa, where his major interests were henceforth to be found. His career was largely associated with the firm of Goerz & Co., later the Union Corporation (q.v.). His international reputation as an economist made him adviser to the Union Government on drafting the South African Currency and Banking Act of 1920, which led to the establishment of the South African Reserve Bank. In the same year and on several later occasions he represented South Africa at international financial conferences, and in 1923–1924 was likewise South African delegate to the League of Nations. The

Indian Government retained him to advise on currency and finance, and he took part in the Imperial Economic Conference in Ottawa, 1932. Amongst his other activities was membership of the committee dealing with the prospects of the Channel Tunnel. He wrote a number of works on economics. He died in 1943.

Strand. Usual name of Somerset Strand (q.v.).

Strandfontein. New seaside resort for Coloured people on False Bay, near Muizenberg.

Strandlopers. Hottentots formerly found on the shores of the Western Cape and encountered by Van Riebeeck and other early settlers. Most of their food consisted of shellfish and other marine produce. A few survivors of these primitive tribes have been reported on the coast of South West Africa.

Strandveld. Coastal region in the south of the Cape Province between Cape Agulhas and Mossel Bay, and including the districts of Bredasdorp and Riversdale.

Strand Wolf (*Hyaena brunnea*). Species of Hyena, known to frequent the sea coast. (*See* HYAENA.)

Stratford, James. Chief Justice of the Union of South Africa. Born in the Eastern Province, 1869, and educated at St. Aidan's College, Grahamstown. He began work as a land surveyor in the service of the Transvaal Government, then went to Oxford, studied law, and was called to the Bar in 1898. From 1901 to 1902 he practised in Cape Town, then in the Transvaal. In 1921 he was appointed to the Transvaal Bench, being promoted to the Appellate Division in 1927 and made Chief Justice in 1938. He retired in 1939 and died in 1952.

Strauss, Jacobus Gideon Nel. South African political leader. Born at Calvinia, Cape Province, in 1900, he qualified for the Bar but first served as

private secretary to General J. C. Smuts from 1923 to 1924. Elected to Parliament in 1932, he became Minister of Agriculture and Forestry in 1944 and in 1950 succeeded General Smuts as leader of the United Party and of the Parliamentary opposition, a position from which he retired in 1956.

Streepkoppie. Afrikaans name for Cape Bunting. *See* BUNTING.

Street-Keeper. An official appointed by many smaller South African towns to supervise the condition of the thoroughfares, the operation of the water furrows, the disposal of rubbish, the collection of stray animals and the like.

Strelitzia (Musaceae). Name from Princess Catharine of Mecklenburg-Strelitz. A group of plants belonging to the banana family including the Crane Flower (*Strelitzia reginae*), a herb 2 or 3 feet high, with strange orange and mauve flowers, resembling a bird's head; and the much larger Wild Banana or Wit Piesang (*Strelitzia augusta* Thunb.), which has unbranched stems up to 18 feet, leaves up to 4 feet and flowers in a claret-coloured spathe. Both belong to the coastal areas in Natal and North-East Cape Province.

Strelitzia (*Crane Flower*)

Strijdom, Johannes Gerhardus. Prime Minister of the Union of South Africa. Born on July 14, 1893, near Willowmore, Cape Province, on the farm Sandvlakte. He was educated in Fransch Hoek and at Stellenbosch, where he became greatly interested in the rights of the Afrikaner community. After taking his legal degree, he joined the Civil Service in Pretoria, but was admitted to the Bar in 1918. He set up in practice as an attorney in Nylstroom, Transvaal, and while there began to take an active part in politics. Elected as member for Waterberg in 1929, he soon attracted attention by his uncompromising views. After the reconciliation of General Smuts and Hertzog in 1933, Strijdom was for a while the only Transvaal supporter of Dr. D. F. Malan's National Party. When Dr. Malan came into power in 1948, Strijdom, who had meanwhile acquired the nickname of 'The Lion of Waterberg,' became Minister of Lands and Irrigation, and when Dr. Malan retired in 1954, he succeeded him as Prime Minister. As such he strongly maintained the National policy of apartheid and all that it involved. His health began to fail, and he died in 1958.

Struben, Frederick P. Theophilus. Founder of the first successful gold-mining company on the Rand. Born in Pietermaritzburg on June 14, 1851, he came to Kimberley in 1870 and prospected on the Witwatersrand in 1883. In February 1884, in conjunction with his brother H. W. Struben (q.v.), he purchased the farms Sterkfontein, Swartkrans and Wilgespruit. In March 1884 the Sterkfontein Junction Syndicate was established on the Rand. In September 1884 the famous Confidence Reef was struck there and announced in Pretoria the following June. Crushing with the five-stamp battery began in December 1885. Struben retired in 1888 to live in England and died in Devonshire on September 7, 1931.

Struben, Hendrik Wilhelm. Brother of F.P.T. (q.v.), born while his family, resident in England, were visiting Germany, on October 9, 1840. He came to South Africa in 1850, grew up in Pietermaritzburg and for a while lived in Kimberley. He joined his brother in establishing himself on the Rand at Wilgespruit. After the discovery of gold he withdrew and in 1890 settled in Rosebank, Cape Town, where he died in 1915.

Strydenburg. Village in the Karroo, so called because of the disputes (stryd) attending its foundation in 1893. Wool production centre. Population: 1,300, including 542 Whites.

Sts. Abbreviation for Stuivers (q.v.).

Stuart, Henri George. Judge of the Orange Free State Republic. Born in 1863, and educated at Grey College, Bloemfontein, the South African College, Stellenbosch, and in Holland. In 1887 he began practice as a barrister in Bloemfontein, being promoted to the Bench of the Republic in 1896. He was in the field as a Commandant during the South African War, became a member of the Union Senate in 1910 and later retired to farm. He died in Ladismith, Cape, in 1939.

Stuart, Jacobus. Writer on the Transvaal. Of Scottish descent, he was born in Holland in 1803, became a civil servant and emigrated to Natal in 1851. From Pietermaritzburg he trekked up-country and went trading in the Transvaal among the Boers, for whom he developed a great liking. His book *De Hollandsche Afrikanen en hunne Republiek*, issued in 1854, was the earliest reliable account of the country. In 1857 he helped to draft the original Republican constitution. He also put forward the first scheme to encourage immigration to the Transvaal from Holland. He died in 1878.

Stuartstown. Early name for Ixopo, Natal (q.v.)—still sometimes used.

Stuiver. Coin formerly in circulation at the Cape and abolished after British occupation. Nearly equivalent to a penny, but later valued at a half-penny.

Stumpnose, Red (*Chrysoblephus gibbiceps*). Fish found off Table Bay (rare), False Bay to Natal. About 26 inches long. Excellent eating.

Stumpnose, White (*Austrosparus globiceps*). Fish found off South-West Africa to the Cape, and False Bay to Natal. About 20 inches long.

Stumptail. Alternative name for Krombek (q.v.).

Sturgess, Eric William. South African tennis champion. Born in Johannesburg 1920, and educated at Parktown Boys' High School. Won his first title at 15 years, and was South African singles champion at 19. He was South African National singles champion 11 times and won the doubles championship 8 times. After serving during World War II in the South African Air Force, he captained the South African Davis Cup team in 1947, 1949 and 1951.

Stuttaford, Richard. South African merchant and Cabinet Minister. Born in Cape Town, 1870, he was educated in England and France, and joined the retail firm established by his father, S. R. Stuttaford (q.v.). Except as a member of the Cape Town City Council, and of the Cape Town Chamber of Commerce, he at first took no prominent part in public affairs, but in 1924, at the age of 54, he entered Parliament as member for Newlands. There his knowledge of commerce proved of great value, and he was invited by General Smuts to take part in negotiations with British commercial authorities in Ottawa. In 1942 he became Minister of Commerce and Industries in the Cabinet of General Smuts. In an entirely different field he also made his name in South Africa, being responsible for the establishment in 1921 of the first Garden City in the country. *See also* PINELANDS. He died in 1945.

Stuttaford, Sampson Rickard. Department store owner, born in England in 1833. He emigrated to the Cape after receiving his training in commerce in London. In the business of A. W. Fletcher he met his lifelong associate, William (afterwards Sir William) Thorne, and in 1857 established Plymouth House, which soon became known as Thorne, Stuttaford & Co. The business moved to Adderley Street in 1871 and branches were later established in Johannesburg (1892) and in Durban (1924). He died in 1915.

Stutterheim. Town in the Eastern Cape Province named after Major-General Richard von Stutterheim, commander of the German Legion (q.v.) in the Crimean War, a body rewarded for its services to the British by being settled near there in 1858. The place lies picturesquely at the foot of the Amatolas, on the Kubusie River, with forests near by. Farming and saw-milling centre. Population: 10,560, including 2,200 Whites.

Styfsiekte (literally 'Stiff Sickness,' also known in Afrikaans as Lamsiekte). Form of paralysis occurring in cattle, sheep and goats, and occasionally horses. It was formerly prevalent in Southern Africa.

Succulents. The desert and semi-desert conditions of a large part of South Africa provide a vast array of succulents of all shapes and sizes. To the family Asclepiadaceae belong the Aasblom or Carrion Flowers (*Stapelia*), low, prickly, fleshy plants with a single dark open trumpet flower, as well as many creepers with succulent stems or leaves, such as the Hanging Milkwort (*Ceropegia*) and the Wax Creeper Kannetjies (*Microloma*). *See* EUPHORBIA, SOUR FIG, LILY, MELON and PLANTS.

Sugar. Efforts to grow sugar cane were made at the Cape of Good Hope as early as 1672, but proved a failure, and it was not until the start of colonisation in Natal that any success was achieved. None the less sugar—called Umoba—had already been grown there by the Zulus before the first settlers arrived. The first successful white grower was George Morewood, who in 1852 started a mill at Compensation. In 1855 H. Milner and J. B. Miller of Redcliffe introduced the crushing of cane by steam power. Shortage of labour handicapped progress until 1860, when the first Indian immigrants reached the Colony. From that day a gradual advance began. For many years output was negligible, and even by 1891 the yield was only 11,235 tons. By 1898 production stood at 32,493 tons. The opening of new areas in Zululand, largely through the efforts of Sir Liege Hulett (q.v.), stimulated the output considerably, so that in 1909 production was 86,790 tons. Only in 1914, however, was the 100,000-ton mark passed, at 102,653 tons. Since then modernisation of the mills, improved fertilisation and the substitution of more productive varieties for the Uba type of cane preferred in the past have enormously added to the output, which has now passed 1,400,000 tons a year. Apart from the Natal Sugar Belt, which extends along the Coastal Belt from the vicinity of Port Shepstone for nearly 200 miles into the heart of Zululand, sugar production has been successfully established in the Pongola area of the Transvaal, in Swaziland and at Triangle in Rhodesia. The amount of sugar needed by the Republic is estimated at about 800,000 tons, the balance being exported.

Sugarbird (family Nectariniidae). *See* SUNBIRDS.

Sugar Bush. *See* PROTEA.

Suid-Afrikaanse Akademie vir Wetenskap en Kuns (South African Academy for Science and Art). Founded in 1909 for the encouragement of the Afrikaans language under the name of the S.A. Akademie vir Taal, Lettere en Kuns. Membership is secured by election, and proceedings are published. The Academy was incorporated by Act of Parliament in 1921, and amended in 1942. The headquarters are in Pretoria.

Suid-Afrikaanse Noodhulpliga (South African Emergency League). Afrikaner organisation closely resembling the Red Cross and the St. John Ambulance Brigade, founded at Pretoria by the Afrikaanse Taal en Kultuurvereeniging on April 16, 1935. It operates on a national basis and has sections for first aid, home nursing, etc.

Suid-Afrikaanse Spaar- En Voorskot Bank (South African Savings and Loan Bank). Co-operative bank established in January 1922, with an original capital of £200. Its head office is in Johannesburg.

Suid-Afrikaanse Taalbond. *See* TAALBOND (SUID AFRIKAANSE).

Suikerbekkie. *See* SUNBIRDS.

'Suikerbos. *See* PROTEA.

Suikerbosrand'. Range with large nature reserve between Heidelberg (Transvaal) and Meyerton.

Suikerbossie. Popular South African song, composed about 1935 by Frederick S. Michel (1898-1969).

Sumptuary Laws. Legislation introduced by Governor Tulbagh in 1754 to prevent settlers living excessively luxurious lives. Similar laws had been introduced in India, and in 1755 these were amended to suit conditions at the Cape. Among the subjects touched on were the use of coaches, the employment of liveried servants, the use of large sunshades by persons of low rank, etc.

Sunbirds or **Suikerbekkies** (Nectariniidae). A tropical family of which many varieties are distributed over Southern Africa. They are small birds, all with long, curved bills for drinking nectar; the females plain, the males decked nearly always with a metallic sheen. Perhaps the most beautiful is the Malachite Sunbird, or Jan Groentjie, with his long straight tail and blue-green sheen. Only one relative, the Long-tailed Sugarbird (*Promerops cafer*), has quiet colouring, offset by an immensely long tail, to be seen blowing among the proteas of the Western Cape.

Sunday Houses. Were those owned by farmers in neighbouring dorps, for use during the weekends while attending church or nagmaal.

Sundays River. Probably called after a Boer family named Zondag living near by in the 18th century. Rises near the Compassberg, flows through Graaff-Reinet and Jansenville, through the Zuurberg and into Algoa Bay. Chief tributary is the Great Riet River. Largely used for irrigation (Lake Mentz, etc.) near Kirkwood, Addo, etc. Total length 300 miles.

Sunday Times. Sunday newspaper established in Johannesburg in 1906 by George Kingswell. It immediately attained enormous popularity and today enjoys the largest circulation in South Africa, over 450,000.

Sundra. Settlement near Delmas, Transvaal. Population: 1,786, including 1,241 Whites.

Sun-Fish, Ocean (*Mola*). A family of rare and curious fish, most of which are between 6 and 10 feet long. They are round and flat (mola, a millstone), beaked, their heads and bodies appearing as one, their tail-fins sticking out from top and bottom surfaces. They appear to start life shaped normally, become round and spiked all over and, as a third stage, take their adult shape. The Ocean Sun-fish

(*Mola mola*) is found fairly frequently swimming lazily on the surface of Cape waters from December to March. A hump-back variety, first reported in Alexandria in 1839 (*Mola alexandrini*), has also been met at Kommetjie (Cape) in 1934 and at Sea Point, Cape Town, 1942. Much smaller Truncate Sunfish (*Ranzania truncata*), 28 inches long, have also been found some half a dozen times at the Cape.

Suni. Species of very small and graceful antelope found in the warmer parts of Southern Africa, between Zululand and Malawi. There are two varieties, Livingstone's Suni (*Nesotragus livingstonianus*), under 18 inches high, and the slightly larger Zululand Suni (*Nesotragus zuluensis*). They are nocturnal except in dull or rainy weather, and seldom venture out of the thick scrub, apparently having no need to drink. Their colour and their speed make them almost impossible to see. The males have small horns.

Sunwich Port. Township on the south coast of Natal, near Port Shepstone, established after World War I. Population: 100, including 70 Whites.

Surmullet. A small group of good eating fish (the head said to be poisonous) caught mostly off Natal and Indo-Pacific coasts, but occasionally in False Bay. They are often called Red Mullet on account of their brilliant colours, and, in Australia, Goat-Fish, because of the barbels on their chins. They were an ornamental pond fish in Ancient Rome.

Susan, Hendrik. South African musician. Born 1903, he began in the Civil Service, but soon turned to orchestral music, specialising in Boer melodies and composing. His orchestra became nationally famous and widely copied. He retired in 1954.

Sutherland. Village in the Karroo, founded in 1855 and named after the Reverend Henry Sutherland. Noted for its cold winter climate, and for its wool production. Population: 1,809, including 681 Whites.

Suurbraak. Mission station near Swellendam, Cape Province. Population: 1,491, including 137 Whites.

Suurkaree (*Rhus ciliata* Licht). Shrub or tree up to 30 feet. Leaves aromatic. Good stock feed. Griqualand West and Orange Free State. *See* KAREEBOOM and KRAAIBOS.

Suzman, Mrs. Helen. Progressive Party Member of South African Parliament. Born Helen Gavronsky, educated at University of the Witwatersrand. Served with War Supplies Board 1941-4, became a prominent worker for South African Institute of Race Relations and Lecturer in Economic History at the University of the Witwatersrand. Elected for the United Party to Parliament in 1953, she joined the Progressive Party upon its foundation and was elected as its sole representative in 1958.

S.W.A.I. Abbreviation for South West African Infantry (q.v.).

Swakopmund. Town in South West Africa, at the mouth of the Swakop River, which rarely flows. It was established under the German régime in 1892, when great efforts were made to develop it as a seaport and a pier was built to protect shipping. Unfortunately these proved a failure, through silting up and the rivalry of the more convenient Walvis Bay. Since World War I, when it was among the first towns to be occupied by the Union troops, it has become a seaside resort for the Territory. Population: 6,040, including 2,775 Whites.

Swakop River. In South West Africa, 250 miles long. Enters sea near Swakopmund. Rises east of Damara highlands in Waterberg district. (Not to be confused with the Waterberg, Transvaal.) Flow very irregular but water is obtainable by digging in its bed.

Swallow (family Hirundinidae). Small bird with deeply forked tail, generally distributed through South Africa, except in the driest regions. Migrants from the European winter. All Swallows, Martins (q.v.) and Swifts (q.v.) are long-winged, insectivorous birds, spending most of their lives in the air. Their bills are short, with wide gapes, their feet and legs feeble. Their mud nests are usually feather-lined. Most varieties have steel-blue backs, and white, chestnut or black underparts.

Swan (*Cygnus alor*). A pair is said to have survived a shipwreck on the Humansdorp coast. They have established a colony near by on the Kromme River.

Swapo. Abbreviation for South West Africa People's Organisation. Political body of Bantu declared illegal in the territory. *See* SOUTH WEST AFRICA.

Swart, Charles Robberts. First President of the Republic of South Africa. Born in the Orange Free State in 1894, he studied in his own country and in the United States, where he spent several years, his experience there including work as a journalist and as a minor actor in Hollywood. Returning to South Africa he became secretary in 1921 of the National Party in the Orange Free State. As a supporter of General Hertzog (q.v.) he was elected to Parliament for Ladybrand in 1923. In 1948 he became Minister of Justice under Dr. D. F. Malan, and on the death of Dr. E. G. Jansen in 1960 succeeded him as governor-general. He retired from the Presidency in 1967.

Swart Eend. Afrikaans name for Black Duck. *See* DUCK.

Swartkop. Afrikaans name for Black-headed Oriole. *See* ORIOLE.

Swartkops: 1. Military aerodrome near Pretoria (not to be confused with Zwartkoppies, q.v.) established by the South African Air Force during World War I.

2. Suburb of Port Elizabeth on the Swartkops River. Attempts at drilling for oil, about 1908, resulted in the discovery of a valuable mineral spring, now exploited by a sanatorium. There is also a large yacht club.

Swart Piek. Afrikaans name for Ant-eater Chat. *See* CHAT.

Swartruggens. Village near Rustenburg, Transvaal. Population: 2,325, including 691 Whites.

Swart Witpens. Name for the Sable Antelope (q.v.), so called because of its contrasting skin pattern of black and white.

Swartz, Marthinus. Boer hunter. His early career is obscure but in 1857 he was hunting in present-day Rhodesia in the company of William Charles Baldwin (q.v.). One of the earliest white visitors to the Victoria Falls, having been there in 1861, he also visited Barotseland in 1863. Little is known of his later years.

Swartz, Thomas R. (Tom). Political leader of Coloured People, in South Africa. Born in Transkei in October 1905, his father being a trader. Became a writer and for 30 years worked on *Territorial News* at Umtata. Interested in the advancement of his people he moved to Cape Town, where he became an estate agent. As leader of the Federal Coloured People's Party he gained prominence and in 1959 was appointed chairman of the Coloured Affairs Council. In 1969 he was elected to the Coloured People's Representative Council as Chairman. *See* COLOURED AFFAIRS.

Swaziland. Bantu kingdom, on the east of the Transvaal. Its area is 6,704 sq. miles, and it is governed by the Ingwenyama or King, Sobhuza II (q.v.). Mbabane is the capital. Parliament consists of a Lower House of 24 members and a Senate of 12, of whom 6 are nominated by the King. The west of Swaziland is very mountainous, abutting on the Barberton district, but the remainder is to a large extent low lying, hot, and in places infested with malaria. Swaziland is recognised as excellent cattle country. Since the 1880's it has been a producer of gold and more recently of tin and asbestos, the latter derived from the Havelock Mine in the west, which contains one of the largest cableway installations in Southern Africa, running across the mountains. Large iron deposits are being opened up at Bomvu Ridge, and the first railway from Kadake to Goba on the Mozambique border came into operation in 1964. With the assistance of the Colonial Development Corporation, large areas have been placed under timber in the Pigg's Peak district and elsewhere, while tropical agriculture has received much assistance. The population is: Africans 390,000, Europeans 5,919, Coloureds 1,378. Area 6,705 square miles.

Swaziland Railway. Although efforts to build a railway from Lourenço Marques (q.v.) to the Transvaal went back to Victorian times, and although a company with this object was founded in 1902 by Major W. Karri-Davis, its only success was the laying of a line by the Portuguese to their border village of Goba. Nothing happened till 1959 when, as a result of an order to the Anglo-American Corporation of South Africa (q.v.) for the supply of 12,000,000 tons of Swaziland iron ore to Japan over a period of years, the first railway in the country was approved. Begun in 1962 and opened for traffic in October 1964, it runs for 137 miles from the mines at Kadake, near the Transvaal border, to Mozambique. *See also* NGWENYA IRON ORE MINES, KADAKE *and* SIDVOKODVO.

Swazis. African tribe also known as the Amangwane, and related to the Zulus, using virtually the same language. They inhabit the territory between Natal and Mozambique known as Swaziland (q.v.). The origins of the kings can be traced to the 16th century,

Swazis

when Mswazi gave his name to the tribe. For a while the Swazis were under the jurisdiction of Tshaka (q.v.), but their king, Sobhuza I, quarrelled with him and settled near the present town of Bremersdorp. Later, however, the friendship was restored. Sobhuza I was succeeded in 1839 by Mswazi II, who first contacted the Boers at Lydenburg. Both Mswazi and his successors, Umbandine and Bunu, gave concessions to any who applied for them, spreading inextricable confusion, which Sir Theophilus Shepstone, during the first British occupation of the Transvaal, vainly tried to remedy. One result was the establishment of the Klein Vrystaat (q.v.), merged in 1889 in the South African Republic. The British authorities agreed to recognise the independence of the Swazis, subject to the existence of a joint administration by white settlers. This state of affairs lasted until the South African War, after which Swaziland became a High Commission Territory. The Swazis are still governed by their own king, Sobhuza II, but the discovery of gold and tin has brought a number of European settlers into the country, where a considerable area is in European hands. The Swazis have

their own courts, under the Paramount Chief, whose headquarters are at Lozitehlzi. Missions from various churches are active in the territory.

Swellendam. Town in the Western Cape Province, founded in 1745 and named after Governor Hendrik Swellengrebel and his wife Engela ten Damme, whom he married in 1728. In South African history it is also notable in having seen the establishment of the first local Boer republic, in 1795, under Hermanus Steyn, the landdrost, ancestor of President M. T. Steyn (q.v.). Later a Swellendam commando fought at the Battle of Muizenberg against the British, as the first republican military unit in the country. Many attractive old buildings survive from the early days, notably the Drostdy, which has become a museum and a national monument. The town lies near the Breede River and the Langeberg mountains. It is the centre of a rich wheat-producing and general farming area. For many years it was the centre of the commercial empire of Barry and Nephews, who dominated the countryside in Victorian times up to the 1870's, issued their own banknotes, and traded with their own ships at Port Beaufort (q.v.). Population: 5,000, including 2,511 Whites.

Swellengrebel, Hendrik. First South African-born Governor of the Cape. Son of a Russian, Jan Swellengrebel, from Moscow, in the service of the Dutch East India Company, and of Johanna Cruse, who was South African born. He was born at the beginning of the 18th century, joined the Company's service, rose to Secunde in 1737 and to Governor in April 1739. He was well liked and only his voluntary resignation in 1749 ended his term of office. In March 1751 he went to Europe for the first time, because his sons were living there and he had lost his wife some time earlier. He died in Utrecht, 1763.

Swempi (*Francolinus coqui*). *See* FRANCOLIN.

Swift (family Micropodidae). A bird of very similar build and habits to the Swallow (q.v.), but classified differently because of its larger size. South Africa is rich in Swifts, although it has few varieties. The birds spend their lives wheeling thousands of feet above the ground and uttering a cry like a high scream. Even the young show perfect mastery of the air in their first flight. Most Swifts build in colonies on mountain precipices, some being migratory.

Swinburne. Village in Harrismith district of Orange Free State, on railway line to Natal. Formerly known as Albertina.

Sword-Fish (*Xiphias gladius*). About 12 feet long with a sword or rostrum elongated about 3 feet, with which it has been known to attack boats. Belongs to warm seas and not known for certain ever to have been caught at the Cape. The South African Museum at Cape Town has a model, part of which is the head of a real specimen, probably exhibited in the first South African Museum of 1825.

Sydney-on-Vaal. Village near Barkly West, Cape Province. Population: 130, including 90 Whites. Named after Sydney Mendelssohn, the famous book collector and diamond pioneer, who established a remarkable public library there. Alluvial diamond centre.

Syfret, Edward Ridge. South African accountant and financier. Born in Cape Town, 1860, the son of Edward John Maynard Syfret, who in 1851 founded the firm today known as Syfret's Trust. E. R. Syfret began his career in the drapery business of A. W. Fletcher, but on the death of his father in 1885 he took over his accountancy, and, largely through his close friendship with Cecil John Rhodes, raised the business to great heights of influence and success. He died in 1937.

Syfret's Trust Co. Ltd. Large financial house, with its headquarters in Cape Town, established as a private firm by Edward John Maynard Syfret in 1851, and greatly developed by his son, Edward Ridge Syfret, who was a close associate of Cecil John Rhodes and many other well-known personalities of the day. Syfret's Trust, which has many allied concerns, has approximately R500,000,000 of funds under administration.

Symons, Major-General Sir William Penn. British soldier, born in Cornwall in 1843. He joined the 24th Regiment of Foot in 1863, and took part in the Galeka Campaign of 1877 in the Eastern Cape, and in the Zulu War of 1879. After many years of service in Burma, India and elsewhere in the East, he rose to be major-general just before the outbreak of the South African War, and was posted to Natal. A few days after the start of hostilities he was mortally wounded at Talana Hill, and died on October 20 1899.

Sysie. Afrikaans name for Seed-eater. *See* CANARY.

T

TAAIBOS

Taaibos. Township near Sasolburg, Orange Free State, noted for large power station. Population: 2,188, including 1,268 Whites.

Taaipit. Literally 'tough kernel.' A species of yellow or white peach, difficult to separate from its stone. Also called Clingstone.

Taalbond (Suid-Afrikaanse). Society formed in 1890 for the purpose of encouraging the use of the Dutch, and later of the Afrikaans, language. It holds examinations recognised by the authorities as a standard of proficiency, drawing a considerable number of candidates each year.

Tabankulu. Village in the Transkei, near the Insizwa Mountains of Pondoland; administrative, trading and native labour recruiting centre; established in 1894. The name means 'Big Mountain.' Population: 650, including 150 Whites.

Tablecloth. Notable cloud formation covering the summit of Table Mountain, and rolling down the precipices above Cape Town. It is caused by the moisture-laden south-easter striking the mountain.

Table Mountain. Although there are several Table Mountains in South Africa, where this type of geological formation is common, the most famous one is undoubtedly Table Mountain on Table Bay, which was first so called in 1503 by Antonio da Saldanha (q.v.), who was also the first European to reach the top. At its highest point, Maclear's Beacon, it measures 3,550 feet above sea-level. The almost vertical face on the Central Cape Town side is about 2 miles long, and on its longest side, from the Eastern Table to the end of the 12 Apostles, it measures 6 miles. Since 1929 a cableway

TAIT

has operated to the summit on the Kloof Nek side. Table Mountain in Natal is 3,151 feet high.

Tachard, Father Guy. Priest and traveller, born in France in 1650. Entering the Society of Jesus, he became an eminent scholar and was chosen in 1685 to lead a party of four others to the East, on a mission to the King of Siam. At the Cape they received hospitality from Governor Simon van der Stel. Some years later he passed that way again on a second voyage. His *Voyage de Siam* gives valuable details about life in early Cape Colony, but brought upon the Governor the censure of the Company for being too friendly to a Catholic. He died in Bengal in 1712.

Tafelboom. *See* ACACIA.

Tagati. Zulu word meaning 'magic,' particularly applied to male and female witches. Under African custom, punishment for practising Tagati was death.

Tailings Wheel. Device formerly used on the Rand gold mines for the discharge of slimes and other waste products from the metallurgical plant on to the dump. It was 40 to 50 feet in diameter.

Tailor-Bird. Common name for Green-backed Bush-Warbler (*Camaroptera brachura*), a small bird with olive-green back, dark head and grey underparts. The male cocks his tail or performs a dance round a branch, singing a stirring little song. Common in thick bush from Knysna to the Eastern Transvaal. *See* WARBLER.

Tait, Admiral Sir William Eric Campbell. Governor of Southern Rhodesia. Born in Plymouth, 1886, he

Tailings Wheel

entered the Navy, served in World War I, and was in the crew of the royal yacht *Victoria and Albert* from 1919 to 1921. After service in the China, Mediterranean and West Indies stations he became Commander-in-Chief, South Atlantic, at Simonstown, and in November 1944 Governor of Southern Rhodesia. He died on July 17, 1946.

Takhaar. Name applied to unsophisticated Boers. The word means 'tacked hair,' and is derived from the former custom in the rural areas of cutting

Takhaar

hair by placing a basin over the head of the customer and cutting off what protruded below.

Talana. Hill near Glencoe, Natal. Scene of Boer reverse in South African War on October 20, 1899. The neighbouring village is now the site of a large glass-works. The name in Zulu means 'The Little Shelf.' Population: 1,213, including 228 Whites.

Tamboekie. Tribe living in the Eastern Cape Province, originating from the intermarriage of Bushmen with the Amatembu, a Bantu group. This appears to have taken place during the 18th century. They came into conflict with the Korannas (q.v.) and later made their home in the vicinity of Queenstown. Their language indicates their mixed origin.

Tamboekie Grass (*Cymbopogon validus*). Wild grass found in the Eastern Cape Province and Swaziland, growing from 6 to 12 feet high. Its name is derived from the tribe (q.v.).

Tampan (*Ornithorus savignyi*). An insect related to the tick and frequently found in fowl-runs. It is very difficult to eradicate.

Tanner, Brigadier-General William Ernest Collins. South African soldier, born in Fort Jackson on November 16, 1875. He was educated at Hilton and at Pietermaritzburg College before joining the Natal Carbineers, with which regiment as well as with the Scottish Horse he served in the South African War. Thereafter he was sent to the Royal Staff College, and was a member of the permanent staff of the Natal Militia. Upon the establishment of Union, Tanner was foundation member of the South African Permanent Force. During World War I he commanded the Second South African Infantry, the 8th Infantry Brigade and the First South African Infantry. He served in South West Africa, France, Flanders and Egypt. He died in 1943.

Tarantula or **Baboon Spider.** *See* SPIDERS.

Tarentaal. Afrikaans name for Guinea-fowl (q.v.).

Tarka River. Tributary of Great Fish River (q.v.).

Tarkastad. Town in the Eastern Cape Province, established in 1874, the name being derived from a Hottentot word meaning 'The River of Women.' Wool-growing centre. Population: 4,530, including 900 Whites.

Tas, Adam. Early Cape political leader, born in Amsterdam in 1668. Received a commercial education and reached the Cape of Good Hope before 1691. There he became a free burgher living with and working for his well-to-do uncle, Henning Huising. At the age of 31 he was appointed an ensign in the Burgher Infantry, and in 1703 married a rich widow, Elizabeth van Brakel. Established on his estate, Adam Tas took the lead among the settlers in objecting to the extravagances and dictatorial methods of Governor Willem Adriaan van der Stel (q.v.). Arrested in 1706, Tas was kept in gaol for 13 months. Complaints had meanwhile reached Amsterdam and in 1707 the Governor was called to account and Adam Tas was set free. He renamed his home Libertas, as a pun on his own name. He died in 1722. The family, which is of Jewish origin and spells its name Tasch, is still living in Holland.

Tati. Territory of about 2,000 sq. miles, originally granted by Lobengula to S. H. Edwards (q.v.), now part of Botswana. Capital, Francistown.

Taung. Village in Botswana, which existed long before the arrival of the white man. Its name (originally written Taungs) means 'Home of Lions.' After the occupation of Bechuanaland in 1884 it became an administrative centre. It was captured by the Boers during the South African War. Produces lime and is a centre for the nearby Vaal-Hartz irrigation areas (q.v.), but its chief claim to fame is through the 'Taungs Skull' (q.v.). Population: 1,600, including 400 Whites.

Taung Skull. Prehistoric skull found in 1924 in the quarries of the Northern Lime Company at Taung (q.v.) and passed on by Mr. E. G. Izod, one of the directors, to Miss J. Salmons of Witwatersrand University, who showed it to Professor Raymond A. Dart of the same institution. The skull, at first regarded as that of a fossil baboon, caused a scientific stir when Professor Dart recognised it as one of the earliest human relics. Known officially as *Australopithecus africanus* Dart, it has become the subject of an extensive literature.

Taxation. Under the Dutch East India Company (q.v.) in the 17th and 18th centuries, taxation usually took the form of payments for monopolies, farmed out to the highest bidder by public auction, and of duties on the transfer of land. With effect from 1711, tithes had to be paid by all farmers on grain harvested, a measure which caused offence and much fraudulent evasion. In 1751 the States General in Holland ordered every European in the Cape, as in all other overseas Dutch possessions, to pay the '50th penny,' equal to 2 per cent on the value of all his property, as a contribution to the expenses of a war. Towards the end of the Dutch East India Company's régime in 1792, two Special Commissioners sent out from Holland. Nederburgh and Frykenius adopted a further series of heavy taxes, including a duty on every slave imported, as well as one on all goods shipped into or away from the colony. The transfer duties on land were raised from 2½ to 4 per cent. A new charge was made on all carriages and vehicles for pleasure, on ships arriving in Table Bay, on brandy brought to Cape Town, on the property of persons leaving the colony, on auction sales, etc. A stamp duty was also exacted on a wide variety of transactions.

Poll Tax, the size of which was not defined by law, was long collected in the more settled districts of Cape Town, Stellenbosch and Swellendam, where so-called 'Lion and Tiger Money' was also collected to aid in keeping down wild animals. House Tax (or Watch Tax) was only collected in Cape Town, being used to pay for the night-watchmen. Sheep and black cattle were taxed in Stellenbosch, Swellendam and Graaff-Reinet.

After the first British occupation in 1795 the system of monopolies was abolished, and licences were substituted, while a tariff of market charges was substituted for tithes; Stamp Duties, Auction Duties and Customs Duties were retained. The 19th century witnessed the development of the excise system and the abolition of most export duties. Both the Transvaal and the Orange Free State introduced their own customs tariffs, mainly for revenue purposes. Income Tax made its appearance in Cape Town in 1840, but disappeared again, and was only reintroduced during the Depression in 1904. The Union Income Tax dates from 1914, being introduced to provide revenue for World War I.

With the discovery of South Africa's mineral wealth came a new series of taxes, particularly Claim Licences, Diggers' Licences, etc., but with the evolution of the industry a far more scientific system developed, based on the fact that the right to precious metals was inherently vested in the State. This resulted in the system of Mining Leases, begun about 1902, which today provides a very large portion of the Republic revenue. Other characteristically South African taxes were the Quit-rent on farms and the Poll Tax on natives, both of special importance in Victorian times.

Today by far the largest source of revenue for the Republic is Income Tax, which accounts for over half the total.

Customs and Posts and Telegraphs follow in that order.

Apart from the Republic Income Tax there is also the Personal Tax, calculated on income and collected by the individual provinces. In the protectorates, Income Tax is paid only by Europeans, but Poll Tax is due from Bantu inhabitants. For the first time a Sales Tax was introduced in 1969. Income Tax was introduced in Southern Rhodesia in 1918. In South West Africa taxation is similar to that in the Republic.

Tchagra (*Tchagra tchagra*). Insectivorous bird, one of the Redwing Shrikes. Found from Hermanus along Southern Cape, up Natal coastal region and in Eastern Transvaal. Greyish colouring, with dull chestnut wings. Its name is an imitation of its scolding voice, but it has a beautiful whistle. It is short-winged and keeps to dense bush. There are a number of very similar Redwings in the more tropical areas, more striking but all with fine voices. *See* SHRIKE.

Tea. Owing to its sub-tropical climate the cultivation of tea was attempted in Natal in the 1850's, but success was only achieved after Sir J. L. Hulett (q.v.) and some fellow settlers on the North Coast imported tea plants and seeds from Assam in 1879. The industry developed till an output of 3,000,000 lb. was achieved in 1907, while efforts were also made in the Northern Transvaal and in the Eastern Cape. Overseas competition, however, led to the gradual abandonment of the estates. Since 1960 production on a substantial scale has begun again in the Transvaal and Natal.

Teak, or Kajatehout, Bloodwood, Sealing-wax Tree (*Pterocarpus erinaceus* Lam.). Up to 60 feet. Timber strong, very durable and easily worked. Natal and Transvaal.

Teak, Cape (*Adinia galpinii* D. Oliver). Swaziland. Tree 30–90 feet. Excellent timber resembling teak.

Teak (Rhodesian). Important variety of timber grown in Rhodesia and Zambia, and used for building as well as for furniture-making. Though not identical botanically with Asiatic teak (*Tectona grandis*), it has formed the foundation of an industry which extends from the Khami River to north of the Gwaai River, and through the Shangani and Umgusa Valleys. Altogether this forest covers over 2,000 sq. miles.

Teal (family Anatidae). Name usually applied in South Africa to the Red-billed Teal (*see* REDBILL). The Cape Teal is Cape Wigeon (*see* DUCK).

Technical Services Corps. South African military unit, founded February 1, 1923.

Telegraphs. The first telegraph line in Southern Africa was opened in 1860 between Cape Town and Simonstown, being operated by a private company. An extension was carried to Port Elizabeth and Grahamstown, and in 1873 came into use in Natal. After the first British occupation of the Transvaal in 1876, a line was carried from Newcastle to Pretoria. From then on the network rapidly covered the whole of South Africa. Simultaneously with the occupation of Southern Rhodesia by the Pioneer Column, a telegraph line was pushed forward from Vryburg first to Tuli and later to 'Fort Salisbury.' Cecil Rhodes had the ambition of carrying the African transcontinental telegraph line across to Cairo, and secured the necessary facilities from Kaiser Wilhelm II of Germany, authorising a link-up through the then German colony of East Africa. Telegraph lines have been linked up, but cables, radio and telephone communication have in a large measure superseded this scheme.

Telephones. As early as 1878, soon after their introduction into the United States, the first telephone instruments were installed at the Cape of Good Hope, but for communication only on a direct line. The first telephone exchange was established among a group of merchants and business people in Port Elizabeth in 1882. The first exchange in Cape Town followed in 1884. Telephone lines were first used in the Transvaal about 1889. In 1891 Pretoria received an exchange. Johannesburg began a service about 1893, the Natal Telephone Company was formed in 1896 and Bulawayo followed in 1898. Since then the network has grown rapidly. Public call boxes came into use about the time of the South African War, when the first trunk lines were also laid down. Automatic telephones date from 1922, when the first exchange was opened in Camps Bay, Cape Town. Overseas connections began in July 1931 by radio between Cape Town and within a 300 mile radius of that city and the United Kingdom. The service was officially opened on February 1, 1932. The Republic today has over 1,500,000 telephones in use. In 1969 a 360-channel coaxial submarine telephone cable from Cape Town to Lisbon was put in use, linking South Africa with Europe, America and most other countries overseas. Direct dialling between Johannesburg and Cape Town and covering most of the Republic and South West Africa is in operation.

Television. Demonstrations of television by the Baird system were given at the Empire Exhibition at Milner Park, Johannesburg, in 1936, but despite occasional freak reception from overseas and experimental work by amateurs on closed circuit installations, the Republic Government has hitherto declined to authorise general television in South Africa. Closed circuit television, including production of videotape features is increasing, training of SABC staff in television techniques is in progress and in 1969 a Television Commission was appointed to make recommendations. The first station in Rhodesia, largely backed by South African capital and operated on a commercial basis, was opened in 1960.

Tellurometer. Instrument invented in South Africa in 1956 by Dr. T. L. Wadley in association with the Council for Scientific and Industrial Research (q.v.). Based on the application of short-wave radio transmission to land surveying and map-making. Widely used by the military and other authorities. Now also manufactured under licence in the United States and elsewhere.

Tembisa. Large Bantu township near Kempton Park, Transvaal. Population: 75,000.

Tembu. Tribe in the Eastern Cape Province, which came into prominence during the Frontier War of 1835. After giving much trouble, a section settled in what became known as Emigrant Tembuland, with its headquarters in Cala. This was annexed by conquest in 1858 to the Cape Colony, and resettled in 1865. After further unrest, Tembuland proper was ceded by the ruling Chief Gangelizwe in 1875. Umtata is today the most important centre of this area.

Tembuland. Portion of the Transkei, its principal places being Umtata, Mqanduli, Engcobo and Emjanyana. It must be distinguished from Emigrant Tembuland (q.v.).

Tendega. Village in Northern Natal, noted as a colliery centre. The name in Zulu means 'to be lazy.'

Tennis. *See* LAWN TENNIS.

Tercentenary Foundation. *See* CAPE TERCENTENARY FOUNDATION.

Terns (family Laridae). Gregarious sea-birds common around all the coasts of South Africa. Smaller than gulls (q.v.) and with many more varieties, including migrants from far north and south. They are mostly grey-and-white birds, with a black breeding cap. Their very long wings and forked tails (origin of the name Sea Swallows) make them graceful flyers. They live on fish, swooping to spear them with a sudden thrust.

Terry, Edward. English traveller and author, born in 1590. He left one of the earliest English accounts of conditions at Table Bay before European settlement. His *Voyage to East India* appeared in 1655. He died in 1660.

Tete. Oldest white town in Southern Africa; situated on the Zambesi in Mozambique, approximately 300 miles from the coast. Established 1531 as a mission station of the Dominican Fathers, and associated with the saint Gonzalo da Silveira (q.v.). Still surviving is the cathedral erected in 1563. In 1763 Tete became a municipality. It was always an important trading centre and was visited by David Livingstone. Today it benefits from the proximity of important coal mines. Population: 2,500, including 400 Whites.

Teyateyaneng. Township in Basutoland, referred to locally as 'T.Y.' The name means 'The Little Winding River.' Administrative and trading community.

T.H.A. Abbreviation for Transvaal Horse Artillery (q.v.).

Thaba Bosigo (also written Thaba Bosiu). Flat-topped mountain in Basutoland on which the great chief Moshesh (q.v.) established his headquarters in 1832. Attacked by Zulus and other tribes, it remained an impregnable stronghold. In the Basuto War of 1865 the burghers of the Orange Free State, under Louw Wepener (q.v.), attempted to storm the mountain, but were beaten off, Wepener being killed. Most of the Basuto chiefs are buried on Thaba Bosigo, the name of which means 'The Mountain of Night.'

Thaba Induna. Hill near Bulawayo, used as a place of execution by the Matabele king, Lobengula (q.v.). The

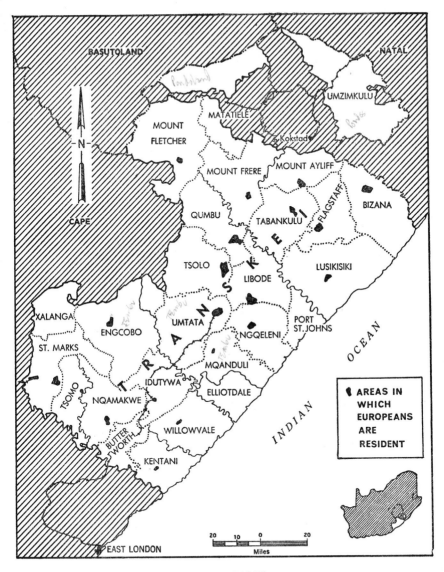

BASUTOLAND

NATAL

UMZIMKULU

MATATIELE

MOUNT
FLETCHER

Kokstad

MOUNT FRERE   MOUNT AYLIFF

CAPE

QUMBU   TABANKULU   FLAGSTAFF   BIZANA

TSOLO   LIBODE   LUSIKISIKI

XALANGA   UMTATA   PORT
                                         ST. JOHNS
ENGCOBO   NGQELENI

ST. MARKS

TSOMO   IDUTYWA   MQANDULI

NQAMAKWE   ELLIOTDALE

BUTTER
WORTH   WILLOWVALE

KENTANI

OCEAN

INDIAN

AREAS IN
WHICH
EUROPEANS
ARE
RESIDENT

20   10   0   20

Miles

EAST LONDON

TRANSKEI

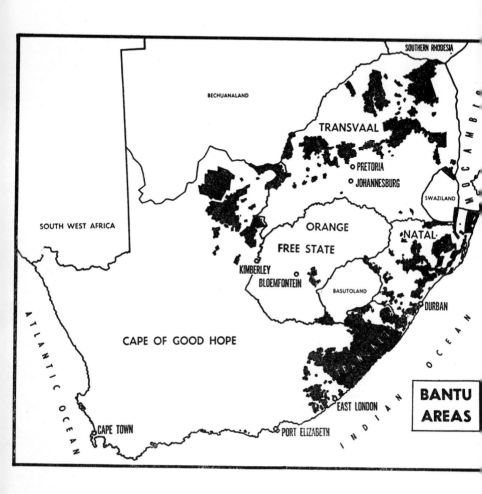

SOUTHERN RHODESIA

BECHUANALAND

TRANSVAAL

PRETORIA
JOHANNESBURG

SWAZILAND

SOUTH WEST AFRICA

ORANGE

FREE STATE

NATAL

KIMBERLEY

BLOEMFONTEIN

BASUTOLAND

DURBAN

CAPE OF GOOD HOPE

EAST LONDON

CAPE TOWN

PORT ELIZABETH

ATLANTIC OCEAN

INDIAN OCEAN

MOÇAMBIQUE

BANTU
AREAS

name means 'The Hill of the Counsellors.'

Thaba Nchu ('Black Mountain'). Town in the Orange Free State, once independent native territory inhabited by the Baralong tribe, under their chief Moroka. Because of his co-operative attitude the Boers did not interfere with his powers, but after his son Sepinare in 1880 attempted to make war, the area was annexed to the Republic. Fighting took place there during the South African War. Today it is a farming centre, but there is a native reserve near by. Population: 1,000, including 800 Whites.

Thaba 'Ndoda. Literally 'The Hill of Men.' A peak in the Amatola range near King William's Town, which figured in many early battles on the Cape eastern frontier.

Thabazimbi. Township near Rustenburg, Transvaal, belonging to Iscor Steel Works (q.v.), and used to supply its needs of iron ore. The reserves are estimated to exceed 100,000,000 tons. Population: 6,900, including 2,750 Whites.

Theal, Dr. George McCall. South African historian, born in New Brunswick, Canada, in 1837. He came to South Africa in 1870 to join the staff of the Lovedale Mission in the Eastern Province. There he remained until 1877, when he joined the Cape Civil Service in the Native Affairs Department and was sent as agent to the Gaika chief, Oba. Such was his success in handling the tribesmen that in 1878 he was put in charge of a large area in the Eastern Province. Already greatly interested in the history both of the Europeans and the Natives, he began writing school books, which were later expanded into something far more ambitious. In March 1879 he was appointed to the position of Keeper of the Colonial Archives and started writing the famous books on South African history as well as those

on Native life. For this purpose he was sent by the Government to examine archives in Lisbon, London, Amsterdam, Rome and other centres of the Continent. His most important work, a History of South Africa in eight volumes, occupied him most of his life. He also contributed a volume on South Africa to the well-known series, 'The Story of the Nations.' His other major works include the set of 35 volumes, 'Records of Cape Colony,' which contains a mass of documents transcribed from Continental archives. A further series, 'Records of South-East Africa,' in nine volumes, did a similar service for historians working on Portuguese records. In 1891 the Cape Government created for him the post of Colonial Historiographer, which he occupied for the rest of his career. Various overseas bodies, including the Dutch Royal Academy of Arts and Sciences, elected him to honorary membership. Despite ill health, he continued his work until his death in 1919.

Theatre. Stage performances in South Africa can be traced back even before the first European settlement, for in 1635 the survivors of the Portuguese ship *Nossa Senhora de Belem*, wrecked on the coast of Natal north of the Umzimvubu River, are known to have passed the time by arranging a bullfight in an enclosure specially constructed for the purpose, and by producing a comedy and other pieces.

In 1695 the early Dutch traveller the Rev. François Valentyn mentions seeing 'players' on board English Indiamen putting in at the Cape, while Peter Kolbe (q.v.) also mentions plays acted during a voyage to the colony. Occasional references appear in other 18th-century accounts, including the books of O. F. Mentzel (1733–41), but it was not until the arrival of a French garrison in 1780 that an organised stage was established, on which the newcomers, to pass the time, produced various plays in their own language. There is reason to believe that the classic *Marriage of Figaro* was acted at the Cape as early as 1783, a year before it was done in Paris! These activities came to an end with the departure of the French troops, and it was not until 1795, with the first British occupation, that there was a revival. Amateur societies, largely patronised by the officers, which held their activities in English, were soon joined by a rival organisation using the Dutch language. In 1800 the 'African Theatre'—the oldest in South Africa and still standing, though no longer used for its original purpose—was erected on what is now Riebeek Square, Cape Town. Great interest was shown in the stage, productions also taking place again in French. By 1829 amateur acting had begun in Stellenbosch; Grahamstown followed suit in 1837, Pietermaritzburg in 1846, Port Elizabeth in 1853 and King William's Town in 1854.

The first attempts at local dramatic authorship may be traced to Charles Etienne Boniface, who after translating French pieces followed with compositions of his own, including *De Nieuwe Ridderorde* (*The New Order of Knighthood*), printed in Cape Town in 1832. Joseph Suasso de Lima also tried his hand and received a certain amount of support.

Professionals from overseas made their appearance in 1848, when a French company had a season in Cape Town. In the same year James Lycett from England started as a producer. It was not, however, until 1855 that Sefton Parry, father of the modern South African stage, arrived to begin a series of productions with his own company; he remained until 1863. From then on overseas companies and producers appeared in growing numbers, encouraged by the prosperous and open-handed digger community on the Diamond Fields. In November

1873 Captain Disney Roebuck landed at the Cape with his own company, where he played several seasons and attracted a number of rivals. The first Gilbert and Sullivan opera, *The Pirates of Penzance*, was produced at Cape Town in 1885 by 'Bonomi's Juvenile Opera Company.'

Important theatrical figures in South Africa towards the end of the 19th century were Luscombe Searelle, Leonard Rayne (q.v.), Frank de Jong, Sass and Nelson, Rosenthal and Hyman, etc., etc. The rise of the Witwatersrand Gold Fields produced sufficiently profitable houses to attract London stars. Among the earliest was Genevieve Ward, the great Shakespearian actress, who toured the country in 1891 and was followed the next year by Mrs. Brown Potter and Kyrle Bellew. With the new century the distinguished visitors became more frequent, including Lily Langtry in 1906, Frank Benson, who repeated the tour many years later, Seymour Hicks, Marie Lloyd in 1911, Marie Tempest, H. B. Irving, Alfred Paumier, Matheson Lang in 1912, Clara Butt, Maud Allen and a host of others.

A remarkable incident was the production in 1910 of the *Pageant of South Africa* by Frank Lascelles, as part of the celebrations attending the establishment of the Union. This took place at the foot of Adderley Street, Cape Town, with a cast of several thousand, and attracted enormous audiences. In the same year a South African writer, Stephen Black (q.v.), had a real stage success with his series of local plays, including *Love and the Hyphen* and *Helena's Hope*.

On the eve of World War I the first revues were produced on the South African stage, and retained their vogue for nearly a generation. The outbreak of hostilities added, if anything, to the popularity of the theatre, and visiting companies, such as those of Alan Doone, played for several years. After the war, the inflow of stars was resumed, including Harry Lauder, George Robey, Irene Vanbrugh, the Macdona Players with their Bernard Shaw specialities, Arthur Boucher, Owen Nares, Sybil Thorndike, Lewis Casson, Maurice Moscovitch, Olga Lindo, Julian Rose, Herschel Henlere and many others. The music hall, however, which had flourished since Victorian times, was overshadowed by revue.

With the advent of talking pictures in 1929 the theatre in South Africa suffered a blow from which it took years to recover, though during this period two important developments occurred: the beginning of the repertory movement at Cape Town, Johannesburg and elsewhere, and the birth of the Afrikaans stage, of which the Belgian, Paul de Groot, may be regarded as the pioneer. Visits by overseas celebrities became rare, but never completely stopped, and there was a distinct revival shortly before World War II. Even that conflict brought celebrities to South Africa's shores, including Noel Coward and others who were working for E.N.S.A.

Since World War II South Africa has witnessed a gratifying revival of the stage, including particularly the Brian Brooke Company, which began in a modest way in Cape Town in 1947 and has lasted down to the present day, now having its own theatre in Johannesburg. That city also possesses the Alexander Theatre, owned by the Repertory Society, and sundry smaller houses. In Cape Town, with its Leonard Schach Company, are the Little Theatre, owned by the university, the Labia and the Hofmeyr, to testify to the vitality of the South African stage. (*See also* EOAN GROUP.) It is estimated that in 1960 there were over 100 professional actors in the country. Rhodesia likewise has made progress, now having repertory societies in Salisbury, Bulawayo, Umtali and other major centres. Particularly generous help has been given to the stage in the Central African Federation by Sir Stephen and Lady Courtauld.

A striking tribute to the achievement of the South African stage was the successful London run in 1961 of a Bantu company from Johannesburg in the musical *King Kong*. South African actors who have attained fame abroad include Laurence Harvey, Basil Rathbone and Moira Lister. *See also* NATIONAL THEATRE ORGANISATION, ATHOL FUGARD and H. W. D. MANSON.

Theiler, Sir Arnold. South African bacteriologist and founder of Onderstepoort Veterinary Laboratory. Born at Frick in Switzerland on March 26, 1867, and educated at Aarau, Berne and Zurich. He came to South Africa in 1891 as Consulting Veterinary Surgeon to the Johannesburg Sanitary Board. From there he was promoted to Veterinary Surgeon to the South African Republic in 1893, and, on the outbreak of the rinderpest epidemic, he was seconded for duty in that connection, in conjunction with the famous German bacteriologist, Dr. Robert Koch (q.v.). The first Veterinary Research Laboratory in the country was set up first at Daspoort, north of Pretoria, and then at Onderstepoort near by. *See* ONDERSTEPOORT. In 1902, after the South African War, Theiler was reappointed Veterinary Bacteriologist. During the following years he did research on gallamsiekte (q.v.) and many other subjects. He was appointed Director of Veterinary Research in 1910, and Director of Veterinary Education and Research in 1920, as well as Professor of Veterinary Science at the Transvaal University College (later the University of Pretoria). In 1907 he was knighted. After retiring in 1927 he continued to be sent on scientific missions overseas. Decorations and distinctions came to him from all over the world. He died in Pretoria in 1936.

Theiler, Dr. Max. South African Nobel Prize winner and medical researcher. Son of Sir Arnold Theiler (q.v.). Born at Pretoria in 1899, studied medicine and specialised in microbiology. Settling in the United States, he became associated with the Rockefeller Institute and in 1930 made his major discovery, the virus of Yellow Fever and a vaccine to counteract it. For this he received the Nobel Prize in 1951.

Theron, Daniel. Boer scout, born in the Cape in 1870. He settled about 1891 in the Transvaal and practised in Krugersdorp as a law agent. Came into the news for assaulting W. F. Monypenny, editor of the *Star* (q.v.), for certain allusions in his pages, allegedly insulting to womanhood. He was fined, but the money was promptly collected from sympathisers. He joined the Boer forces in the South African War as a captain in the Transvaal Cyclist Corps. After the battle of Colenso he was placed in charge of a special group of scouts, among whom his feats became a legend. He was killed in action in 1900.

Thesen Line. South African shipping company, founded by A. L. Thesen, a Norwegian, who reached South Africa in 1869. Intending to emigrate to New Zealand, he was blown out of his course and made his home in Knysna, where he set up the firm of Thesen & Co. In 1895 his sailing vessels were replaced by a steamer. Others were later added. The Thesen Line was taken over by the Houston Line of Liverpool in 1921, and later by the Unicorn Shipping Lines (q.v.). Vessels trade between ports in the Republic and as far north as the Congo.

Theunissen. Town in the Northern Orange Free State, named after Helgaard Theunissen, original land owner. It was established in 1907. Farming and wool-growing are the chief occupations. There was fighting near by in the South African War.

Population: 7,340, including 1,600 Whites. Noted for 870-foot high mast forming part of Frequency Modulation network of South Africa Broadcasting Corporation (q.v.), the highest structure in the Southern Hemisphere.

Thibault, Louis-Michel. South African architect, inventor and artist, born in France in 1750. He came to the Cape as a military engineer for the Dutch East India Company in 1783. Two years later he was appointed Government Architect and put up numbers of magnificent buildings. Among the masterpieces which remain as his monument are the balcony in the courtyard of the Castle in Cape Town, known as 'The Kat'; the Drostdy at Tulbagh; the Government buildings in Caledon Square and the old Supreme Court Building in Adderley Street. Thibault died in 1815.

Third Field Regiment (South African Artillery). *See* TRANSVAAL HORSE ARTILLERY.

Third Transvaal Scottish. Original name of Seventh Medium Regiment, South African Artillery (q.v.).

Thirstland. Area in the north of Bechuanaland, notorious for its lack of water. *See* THIRSTLAND TREK.

Thirstland Trek. Emigration of Boers from the South African Republic during the 1870's. Inspired by religious differences, a group of burghers emigrated in May 1874, and were followed in 1875 by a larger group, comprising 128 wagons, with about 480 people inclusive of servants. Travelling in easy stages, they entered the Thirstland region (q.v.). Survivors of the terrible hardships eventually reached the Okavango River and crossed over into Angola, where they were given land by the Portuguese at San Januario de Humpata. They and their descendants remained there until about 1926, when it was arranged by the Union Government to settle them in South West Africa chiefly around Gobabis.

Thompson, 'Matabele.' *See* MATABELE THOMPSON.

Thomson, Sir Francis Vernon. Shipping magnate and chairman of the Union-Castle Line. Born in 1881; entered the shipping business in London, and was Assistant Director of the Ship Management Branch of the Ministry of Shipping at the end of World War I, also Vice-Chairman of the Ship Licensing Committee. He became Chairman of the London Ship Owners' Society, Chairman of the Baltic Exchange and of many other important bodies. During World War II he was principal Shipping Adviser to the Government. He died in 1953.

Thrush (family Turdidae). Singing bird widely distributed in South Africa. Of the Rock Thrushes there are two distinct types: the Cape Rock Thrush (*Monticola rupestris*) has grey-blue head and neck; the Sentinel (*Monticola explorator*) is a smaller bird, grey-blue except on its tail parts. Both have light chestnut Robin-like tails. The Cape or Olive Thrush has a dark back, yellow beak and orange-yellow underparts, and is a much shyer bird. All thrushes have a partiality for snails and fruit. *See* ROBIN.

Thunberg, Carl Peter. Swedish botanist and traveller at the Cape, born in 1743. From 1770 to 1776 he travelled in Europe, Africa and the East, spending a considerable time at the Cape. His *Travels* appeared in Latin but was translated into English in 1795. He wrote on the flora of the Cape and of Japan, and died in 1828.

Tick. Primitive insect of the Acari family. Ticks of various kinds are responsible for Scab in sheep and for East Coast Fever (q.v.). The only effective way of freeing sheep of them is by dipping in an arsenic solution,

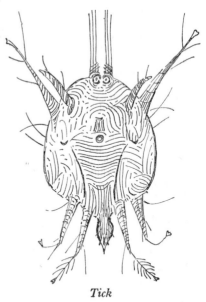

Tick

although in modern times an arsenic-resistant species has developed.

Tick Bird. *See* OX-PECKER and EGRET.

Tickey. A threepenny piece. Word introduced by the Cape Malays (q.v.) from 'Tiga' meaning three.

Tiger. *See* LEOPARD.

Tiger. South African fish. *See* GRUNTER.

Timlin, William H. South African artist. Born in 1896, he qualified as an architect and made his home in Kimberley, where he soon became known for his distinctive style. Apart from very attractive landscapes, he was responsible for several fanciful works, reminiscent of Arthur Rackham, notably *The Ship that Sailed to Mars*, which was filmed in the United States, and *The Building of a Fairy City*. He died in 1943.

Timmins, Howard Benson. South African publisher. Born in Kimberley June 16, 1904, and educated there and in England. After a five-year practical training with the London publishing firm George Allen & Unwin Ltd, he returned to South Africa as a publisher's representative, and in 1944 commenced publishing on his own account. His efforts opened a large market for South African writers on history, biography, travel, art, etc., the sales aggregating several million copies.

Tin. Already exploited at Rooiberg, Transvaal, by the Ancients. Finds caused a considerable share boom in 1905–1906. Workings were established at Rooiberg and Zaaiplaats, which, though never large, have been profitable. Important fields have been opened up in recent years at Kamativi, Rhodesia; the Erongo Range in South West Africa and the Macready Mine in Swaziland have both been productive.

Tinker-Birds (family Capitonidae). A group of small Barbets (q.v.) named after their 'anvil-tapping' calls. They have short, strong bills with which they bore into old trees. The Red-fronted Tinker Bird has a scarlet forehead, and is a fairly common insect-eater in bush country from the Eastern Cape to Zululand. More northerly varieties have yellow on forehead or rump.

Tinktinkie. Afrikaans name for Cape Wren-Warbler. *See* WARBLER.

Tintenpalast (German 'Ink Palace'). Nickname for original German Government Buildings at Windhoek; still in use.

Tit (Paridae). Small bird found in the drier parts of South Africa, preferring treeless country with scrub vegetation. Less plentiful than in Europe and Asia. A short, strong bill and hairy plumage. A little tree acrobat, it eats fruit, seeds and insects. The most interesting South African member is the Penduline Tit or Kapokvoël (*Anthroscopus minutus*), with its woven nest of down or wool. A short tube in this nest leads to some dozen tiny eggs. Below is the 'flat' for the father bird.

Tit-Babbler (family Muscicapidae). A small bird of the Flycatcher family (q.v.), found in open, bushy country from the Cape to the Transvaal, Namaqualand and Zululand. It has very beautiful singing and call notes. Active and easily seen, it has a blue-grey coat, strongly striped throat, and a tail tipped with white above and chestnut underneath.

Tobacco. Tobacco was used by colonists as a popular object of barter with the Hottentots and other tribes from the time of Van Riebeeck, but its cultivation began in Southern Africa in 1719, when an expert, Cornelis Hendriks, was sent to the Cape from Amsterdam. The first plantings took place at Rondebosch, but failed. Later attempts were successful and by 1752 the Xosas were also producers. Tobacco was planted by the Voortrekkers in Natal, the O.F.S. and the Transvaal, where the Magaliesberg valley proved specially suitable. It was one of the first crops to be cultivated by settlers in Rhodesia, though the industry did not become important until about 1910. Cigarette manufacture, by hand, began in Port Elizabeth about 1875 and was later extended to Cape Town. Mechanisation followed in the 1890's, and large factories appeared after the South African War. Scientific research and improved methods of cultivation were introduced and co-operative societies formed in the Transvaal before Union, under the Crown Colony régime. By far the largest producing areas in Southern Africa today are in Rhodesia, Zambia and Malawi, which specialise in Virginia leaf for export to England and elsewhere. Buyers from many countries attend the sales in Salisbury, where the trade is concentrated. In the Republic, production of Virginia leaf is mainly in the Magaliesberg district of the Transvaal

and in the Oudtshoorn and neighbouring districts of the Cape. Smaller
quantities of Turkish leaf are grown
near Fransch Hoek and elsewhere in the
Western Province. Growers are organised into powerful co-operatives, of
which the Magaliesberg one is the
leader. Most of the consumption is in
the Republic; exports are on a limited
scale. Cigarette manufacture is mainly
concentrated in Johannesburg, Durban
and Cape Town. *See also* RHODESIA.

Tobacco, Wild (*Nicotiana glauca*)
(Solanaceae). Small Rhodesian tree
with terminal clusters of narrow
yellow tubular flowers. To the same
family belong the cultivated potato
(*Solanum tuberosum*), tomato (*Solanum
lycopersicum*) and tobacco (*Nicotiana
tabacum*). All members of the family
have four/five stamens, four/five lobes
to the tubular flower, and alternate
leaves. Stinkblaar (*Datura stramonium*)
is a coarse plant two feet high, with
large shiny serrated leaves and trum-
pet-shaped white flowers. Although
poisonous it is used medicinally.
Apple of Sodom or Bitterappel (*Solanum panduriforme*) has a very poisonous bright yellow fruit, like tomato,
and mauve flowers of Nightshade
type. *See* CAPE GOOSEBERRY.

Toby (Tetrodon). Natal name for a small
fish known as Blaasop (q.v.) at the
Cape and Puffer in England. There are
a number of varieties, all with a
remarkable capacity for puffing themselves up. Their flesh is poisonous.

Todd, Reginald Stephen Garfield.
Former Premier of Southern Rhodesia.
Born at Invercargill, New Zealand,
July 13, 1908, and educated in theology
at Otago University, the University of
the Witwatersrand and in the United
States. Settling in Rhodesia in 1934 as
Superintendent of the Dadaya Mission,
he was elected to Parliament in 1946
and was Prime Minister of Southern
Rhodesia from 1953 to 1958. After
retirement he became leader of the
Central Africa Party.

Toering

Toering (Malay—'tudung'). A conical
straw hat worn by Malays, particularly
by coachmen on festive occasions. (See
illustration.)

Tog-Boys. Africans working in Natal
towns, who are licensed as labourers
and messengers, their status being
guaranteed by a badge and number.

Togryer. An old-fashioned expression
for a transport rider.

Tokolosh (Tokeloshe, and other spell-
ings). Supernatural creature in native
folklore, reputed to resemble a man
but to be of smaller stature; to have a
tail covered with hair; to lurk in
rivers where young people pass, and
to drag them into the water.

Tollie. South African expression for a
young male calf. The word is derived
from the Xosa 'intole.'

Tomlinson Report. Important survey
of the position of the Bantu community in South Africa, carried out
under the Chairmanship of Professor
F. R. Tomlinson, of the Chair of
Agricultural Economics at the University of Pretoria. A Commission on
the Socio-Economic Development of
the Bantu Areas was appointed in 1951
and produced a report in 17 volumes,
together with 63 detailed maps. Of

these only a limited number were deposited in important reference libraries and similar institutions, shorter versions being issued to the public. The Tomlinson Report envisaged the establishment of a number of more or less self-governing Bantu communities, based on the existence of native reserves, to which further zones were to be added. It proposed intensive development of industry in the Bantu areas, but recognised the fact that several million Bantu would continue to remain in the European cities and other portions of the country earmarked for the White population. The total expense proposed for the development of the Bantu areas was approximately R200,000,000.

Tongaat. Town on the north coast of Natal, a sugar-milling centre. The name means 'twisting,' and is taken from the character of the river which passes there. Founded by the Byrne Settlers (q.v.) of 1849 as Victoria, its name was changed to Tongaat shortly after the South African War. Population: 8,839, including 540 Whites, 6,001 Indians and 2,289 Bantu.

Tongaland. *See* AMATONGALAND.

Toorbos. An expression used by early settlers for forests in which the natives practised their magic rites. Literally a 'magic forest.'

Topnaars. A tribe of Hottentots living in South West Africa.

Toppie. Afrikaans name for Layard's Bulbul. *See* BULBUL.

Torch Commando. Political organisation established, largely with the support of ex-servicemen, in April 1951, its leaders including A. G. ('Sailor') Malan, the famous South African fighter pilot in the R.A.F. It took its name from the torches carried by participants in its spectacular early processions. The objects of the Torch Commando were largely those of the United Party (q.v.). Its activities came to an end about 1953.

Torquay. Site of large diversion dam for Orange River Scheme (q.v.). Situated between Hopetown and Douglas.

Tortelduif. Afrikaans name for Turtledove. *See* DOVE.

Totius. Pen name of J. D. du Toit (q.v.).

Tourism. Efforts to attract visitors to South Africa go back to the 1890's when steamship excursions from Europe were first advertised. In 1911 the *Empress of Asia*, the first cruise liner, called. Natal set up a publicity department of her railways in 1906, and following Union in 1910 the South African Railways expanded this work through an office in London. After World War I a regular publicity budget, including the use of overseas press and of films, was introduced. Thomas Cook and Son, who had opened in South Africa in 1900, were joined by other firms. From 1926 there was a fairly frequent flow of cruise ships from the U.S.A. Efforts were also begun to stimulate tourist visits from Rhodesia and other African countries. Since World War II, thanks to the founding of the South African Tourist Corporation (q.v.), there has been a steady rise in traffic, helped by air lines. Of 275,538 visitors in 1967, 185,749 came from Africa (mostly Rhodesia), 65,862 from Europe (38,780 from Britain) and 16,170 from America.

Touws River. Railway camp, owned departmentally by the South African Railways; on the edge of the Karroo, north of the Hex River Mountains. Became municipality, 1959. Population: 7,520, including 4,000 Whites.

Toweel, Victor. South African boxing champion. Born at Benoni, Transvaal, in 1928 and educated at Christian Brothers' College, Boksburg, he began boxing at nine years old, and won 298 of his first 300 amateur fights. As a bantam-weight he won the first world title for a South African, against

Manuel Ortiz on March 31, 1950. He lost to Jimmy Carruthers on March 21, 1953.

Toweel, William. South African boxer. Born at Benoni, Transvaal, 1934, he won 84 out of 90 amateur contests and drew with Robert Cohen for the World Bantamweight Championship on December 3, 1955. Changing over to Lightweight, he successfully defended the British Empire title four times against Johnnie van Rensburg.

Trade. South Africa's largest single export is gold, most of which finds its way to the London Bullion Market and thence to the treasuries at Fort Knox, U.S.A., and other financial centres of the world. In recent years a large market has also developed in Switzerland, France and elsewhere. Diamonds, too, mainly go to Britain before being cut, the ' sights ' to the trade being arranged at Hatton Garden, but the largest ultimate purchaser is the United States. India and the Continent of Europe are also valuable customers. Cutting is carried out in the Netherlands, America, Israel, and to some extent in the Republic itself.

The major purchaser of South African wool is the United Kingdom, though, owing to the vast re-exports from that country, it is not easy to determine the exact consumption by the U.S.A., Western Germany, France, Belgium, Czechoslovakia, Switzerland, Italy, Russia and most other states possessing textile industries. Coal is shipped to South America, the Middle and Far East, and copper, tin, asbestos, chrome, etc., to Europe and the U.S.A. Grain and sugar go to the United Kingdom as well as to the Continent, while France and the U.S.A. have a traditional liking for South African crayfish, and canned fish (pilchards, etc.) have secured a large market in Europe and Australia. South Africa is one of the main exporters of fresh fruit,

both citrus and deciduous, Britain and the Continent of Europe, notably Scandinavia and Germany, being large consumers. For wines and spirits (brandy and liqueurs) the main outlets are in Britain, Canada and Scandinavia.

Nearly every kind of South African manufactured article enjoys a market in Rhodesia, and to a lesser extent in Mozambique and elsewhere in many parts of the African continent. A demand has also developed in other parts of the world, as illustrated by the export of Rand-built lifts to Peru, of Cape Town-made men's suits to the U.S.A., and of the remarkable scientific instrument known as the Tellurometer, invented and developed in South Africa, to America and many other places.

In the field of imports, though many of these, particularly textiles, have declined owing to the growth of locally owned and operated works, Britain still holds her own, with Japan, Italy, the U.S.A., France, Switzerland and Austria as rivals. Motor vehicles are imported from the United Kingdom, the U.S.A., Germany, Canada, France, Italy and several other countries, recent entrants in the ranks being Australia and Japan. Though South Africa herself already figures as an exporter of machinery and parts, she continues to import substantially from Britain, the U.S.A., France, Western Germany, Italy and many other countries.

Since 1955 the trade figures for South West Africa have been merged in those of the Union (now the Republic), yet it is still possible to indicate the main trends there. The largest export is diamond, followed by karakul skins, wool and meat, dairy products and hides. Base metals (lead, copper and zinc) are mostly from the Tsumeb workings, with manganese also a substantial item.

Exports from Zambia are dominated by copper, zinc and cobalt; those from Rhodesia by asbestos, tobacco, chrome ore, tea, maize, clothing, hides, ground-nuts, lead, radios, etc. The principal market for Rhodesian exports is the United Kingdom, which takes over 48 per cent, followed by Western Germany, the Republic of South Africa, the United States, the Netherlands, India, Sweden, Italy, France, Australia, Japan, Belgium and the U.S.S.R. The main supplier of goods to Rhodesia is also the United Kingdom, with the Republic of South Africa second. At a considerable distance follow the United States, Western Germany, the Congo, the Netherlands, Australia, Canada, Iran and Sweden.

The chief export of Mozambique (apart from its large transit trade with South Africa and the Federation) is cotton, followed by sugar, cashew nuts, sisal, tea and vegetable oils. Most of these go to Portugal. Imports include textiles, coal (from the Republic of South Africa), railway material, machinery, iron and steel, motor cars, oil, grain, footwear and liquor.

Note. Owing to the speed with which statistics go out of date, no figures are given here.

Trade Unions. Apart from a Guild of Silversmiths, founded at the Cape in 1715, the earliest South African trade union was the Printers' and Bookbinders' Mutual Benefit Society, set up in Cape Town in 1857, replaced in 1881 by the Cape Town Typographical Society, with counterparts in other centres, and in 1898 by the South African Typographical Union. As in most other parts of the Commonwealth, immigrants accustomed to trade unionism in Britain were responsible for the first efforts on local soil. The diamond mines of Kimberley witnessed the formation of several craft unions in the 1880's, and an early strike of miners in 1885 was suppressed by force of arms. After the discovery of gold on the Witwatersrand several overseas unions, including the Amalgamated Society of Engineers,

formed offshoots in the Transvaal. The first Miners' Union was formed in 1892, its growth aided by the presence of many Australian working men. After the South African War there was a strong revival, to which visits by Keir Hardie, Tom Mann and other famous figures from overseas contributed. All unions were white, as were the bodies involved in the first big mining strike on the Witwatersrand in 1907.

Unionisation spread, and there were further serious mining strikes in June 1913, involving violence and the mobilisation of troops and police, as well as in January 1914. An attempt at a General Strike was quashed by General J. C. Smuts, who summarily deported to England most of the trade union and labour leaders.

During the ensuing years a movement developed for the linking up of unions into the South African Industrial Federation, largely through the efforts of the late Archie Crawford. A major strike on the coal and gold mines, brought on by an effort to reduce wages to compensate for the disappearance of the wartime premium on the price of gold, began in January 1922 and culminated early in March in the Rand Revolt (q.v.), suppressed by troops and police after heavy fighting. Profiting by the painful lessons thus learnt, the Government introduced Conciliation Laws, Wage Boards and other benefits. Trade unions in the Republic now have a combined membership of over 490,000, official registration being required. The largest group is the South African Confederation of Labour, founded in 1957 and reconstructed in 1968, with 200,000 members. The Trade Union Council of South Africa (Tucsa), has 62 unions and over 142,000 members, the South African Federation of Trade Unions 56,000, and the Koordinerende Raad van Suid-Afrikaanse Vakverenigings 72,000. On a more specialised basis are the Federal Consultative Council of the South African Railways and Harbours Staff Association (83,164), the Mechanics' Unions Joint Executive (45,000) and sundry smaller ones. In 1964-65 South African Trade Unions owned assets valued at R10,624,661 and had a revenue of R3,857,545.

Coloured unions exist, but trade unions for the Bantu are not recognised, alternative machinery for negotiation being provided.

Trader Horn. *See* SMITH, ALFRED ALOYSIUS.

Transalloys. Name of plant erected at Witbank, 1962, jointly by the Anglo-American Corporation of South Africa (q.v.) and the Avesta Jernverks Aktiebolaget, a leading Swedish company, for the manufacture of low-carbon ferrochrome by the Avesta process. The installation cost over R7,000,000.

Transkei. Region of the eastern Cape Province between River Kei (q.v.) and Natal border, excluding the districts of Maclear and Elliot, and comprising Tembuland, of which Bomvanaland forms a portion, Pondoland, Fingoland, Galekaland, the Idutywa Reserve and Griqualand East. Area 16,554 square miles. The latest estimated population figures are 1,500,000, including 16,000 Whites. Over many years an administrative system developed under distinguished chief magistrates in the capital town, Umtata (q.v.), supported by recognised chiefs and headmen. In May 1957 the Bunga (q.v.) was replaced by a new Transkeian Territorial Authority. This in turn was replaced under Act 48 of 1963, when self-government was adopted with effect from 1964 and all Bantu inhabitants given the vote, including those outside the Transkei borders. Under the first electoral law 880,425 voters were registered in 1963. Large sums, advanced by the South African Government, have been invested in development, including an irrigation scheme, the Lubisi Dam, costing R6,000,000, also plantations of fibre, tea, coffee and other products, the construction of reclamation works, forestry, education etc.

The Transkei Legislative Assembly consists of the four Paramount Chiefs, 60 chiefs, and 45 members elected by registered voters, who can also be members of the Transkeian tribes living elsewhere in South Africa. There is a Cabinet, elected by the Assembly, consisting of a Chief Minister and five Ministers, namely of Justice, Education, Interior, Agriculture and Forestry, and Roads and Works.

There is power of direct taxation, and control of local police, inferior courts, Justices of the Peace, local public works and roads, Bantu municipal institutions, the local Civil Service, labour matters and welfare services. Bills passed by the Assembly require the assent of the State President.

Members of the Cabinet may be removed by the State President after a petition by the Assembly. The Assembly must sit at least once a year and it shall be dissolved five years from the date of its first meeting, or earlier on the recommendation of the Cabinet or by the proclamation of the State President.

Excluded from the jurisdiction of the Assembly are military matters and the movement of South African troops in the territories, control of arms factories, the appointment of diplomatic representatives and the making of treaties or international agreements, police, Post Office and radio, national roads, railways, harbours and aviation, entry of non-Transkeians into the territory, the Transkeian High Court (to be established), currency, banking and public loans, customs and excise and the amendment of the Transkeian Constitution Act itself.

Provision is made for a Transkeian flag and national anthem. Xosa is an additional official language, and Sesotho may be used for official purposes.

The Transkei is the first of the 'Separate Development Self-Governing Areas' under the Government's policy with regard to the Bantu.

Transkei Democratic Party. Opposition party established in 1964 under the leadership of Paramount Chief Victor Poto (q.v.).

Transkei National Independence Party. Governing party in the Transkei under Chief Kaiser Matanzima (q.v.).

TRANSPORT IN THE REPUBLIC OF SOUTH AFRICA

THE Railways, as well as the Harbours, the Airways and a network of Road Services which covers the whole of the Republic and South-West Africa, are State owned and controlled. By the South Africa Act, dated March 1910, the South African Railways and Harbours Administration was established under the following operative clause: 'The railways, ports and harbours of the Union of South Africa shall be administered on business principles, due regard being had to agricultural and industrial population in the inland portions of the provinces of the Union.' The policy of the whole organisation is directed by the Minister of Transport, a member of the Cabinet. He is advised by a Railways and Harbours Board of three members, but actual management is vested in a General Manager. The total invested capital on March 31, 1968, was R2,303,824,438 The Administration has never failed to meet its interest commitments on this investment.

In South Africa, the term Railways and Harbours Administration is used in an inclusive sense, since the Administration is responsible also for the harbours, South African Airways, the railway-owned road transport system and a host of subsidiary services such as lighthouses and shore radio beacons, the railway police force (which is not part of the South African Police) and catering services.

Although the South African Railways as at present constituted date only from 1910, railway history in South Africa goes back 100 years. The first railway line was in Natal, a 2-mile stretch between the Point and Durban, opened on June 26, 1860. Cape Province followed with the line from Cape Town to Eerste River, 21 miles long, on February 13, 1862. Port Elizabeth and East London came later, but in the Transvaal a line was started in 1888 from Johannesburg, the present Braamfontein Station, to Boksburg. Opened on March 17, 1890, it was not called a railway because of public prejudice, but the 'Rand Tram.'

In 1910, three separate railways were operating in South Africa—the Natal Government Railways, the Cape Government Railways and the Central South African Railways. These were merged when the four provinces, the Cape, Transvaal, Natal and the Orange Free State, joined to form the Union of South Africa. The total capital of the new organisation on May 30, 1910, was £87,263,366.

After Union, development was rapid. Today, the railway system remains by far the most important section of transport, covering the 790,246 sq. miles of the Republic and South West Africa. The capital account of the railways, as distinct from other transport services, stood at R1,924,763,886 at the end of March, 1968.

The railways are operated over a route mileage of 13,706 miles with 19,160 track miles. While steam traction is still extensively used, South

Africa has 2,334 miles of electrified track (5,031 track miles) and work is in progress on the electrification of a further 526 route miles. Electrification is primary policy.

Diesel-electric traction was introduced in 1958. The first major order for units was placed in the United States of America at a cost of R5,743,461. The intention is to use diesel traction on sections remote from coal supplies and where water problems recur. In some parts the water is not suitable for locomotive purposes while in regions such as South West Africa, which is more than 1,000 miles from the nearest coal mines, water supplies decrease almost to vanishing point during certain times of the year. Diesel traction is used mainly in South West Africa.

The South African Railway gauge is 3′ 6″ but 121 miles between Port Elizabeth and Avontuur in the Cape Midlands, as well as a few minor lines in Natal, still have narrow gauge (two feet) lines. The whole of South West Africa was converted to the 3′ 6″ gauge in 1960 at an estimated cost of nearly R13,000,000.

South Africa has four major harbours, Cape Town, Durban, Port Elizabeth and East London, while Walvis Bay in South West Africa and Mossel Bay, between Cape Town and Port Elizabeth, are rapidly developing ports. The capital account of the harbours on March 31, 1968, stood at R127,077,626. Buffalo Harbour, East London, is the only river port in the Republic. All the other harbours are man-made.

South African ports handle more than 42 million tons of import and export traffic a year. Durban is South Africa's busiest port and the major port in tonnage on the African continent.

The principal ports are equipped with all possible facilities from cranes to mechanised handling equipment. The Sturrock Graving Dock at Cape Town is 1149½ feet long and the largest dry-dock in the southern hemisphere. Graving docks are also available at Durban and East London. Nearly 1,000 miles of oil pipeline are operated by the Railways, one from Durban to the Rand (over 400 miles) and the other from Durban to Oogies, Transvaal, later to serve Richards Bay (520 miles).

The third arm of transport controlled by the South African Railways is the network of road services, operating over nearly 31,793 route miles. Passengers, goods and livestock are carried; more than R32,215,164 is invested in vehicles and equipment.

Initially the road services were introduced to feed the railway system and to bring areas not served by public transport into the national economy. Extended in response to public demand, they have partially lost their essential characteristic as feeders of the railways. More recently, tourist road services have been developed with excellent results, especially in South West Africa.

In March, 1968, South African Airways celebrated its thirty-fourth birthday. The first public air services were provided by a private company, Union Airways, for parcels and mails rather than passengers. In 1934 South African Airways were started as part of the Railways and Harbours Organisation, and all assets of Union Airways were taken over. The development of air transport in South Africa has been remarkable. On March 31, 1968 South African Airways operated 24 aircraft of different types, including six Boeing 707 Inter-Continental Jets and seven 727s. During the year ended March 31, 1968, South African Airways carried 976,587 passengers and 12,468 tons of freight and 3,197 tons of mail.

Apart from domestic and regional services, South African Airways carry out trunk services to Europe via the west coast of Africa, regional services to neighbouring territories, a network of domestic services and a service between Johannesburg and Sydney (Australia), in partnership with Qantas Airways. A new service to South America and the U.S.A. was also introduced in 1969.

Transvaal. Second largest province of the Republic, area 110,450 sq. miles, representing 23 per cent of the total area. The name is derived from the fact that the country lay across the River Vaal. The population according to the 1960 census was 6,225,052, of whom 1,455,372 were Whites, 4,601,545 Bantu, 62,918 Asiatics and 105,217 Coloured. White population in 1966, 1,657,000. The number of voters was 657,407 in 1955.

Transvaal Horse Artillery. South African military unit, part of 3rd Field Unit, South African Artillery. Founded on March 17, 1904. Served in the action of Sandfontein in 1914 and in German South West Africa. Contributed three batteries to the 3rd Field Brigade in 1940 and was also attached to the 5th South African Brigade. Saw action at Sidi Rezegh in 1941 and elsewhere.

Transvaal Leader. Morning newspaper established at Johannesburg on April 10, 1899, and finally merged in the *Rand Daily Mail* in May 1915.

Transvaal Scottish. South African military unit, founded on December 12, 1902. In 1914 it sent two battalions to German South West Africa and in 1916 men of the 1st Battalion formed the B Company of the 4th South African Infantry and those of the 2nd Battalion formed the C Company. Saw action at Sidi Rezegh in 1941. Motto: 'Alba Nam Buadh.'

Transvaler, Die. Morning newspaper established in Johannesburg on October 1, 1937. Strong supporter of the National Party, the editors including Dr. H. F. Verwoerd. A previous paper, *De Transvaler* ('De' and not 'Die'), was published in Johannesburg in 1904 by Fred Horak.

Tredgold, Sir Clarkson Henry. Judge of the Supreme Court of Southern Rhodesia. Born in Cape Town in 1865 and educated at the South African College, he was called to the Bar in 1889. In 1897 he moved to Bulawayo, where he became Public Prosecutor. In 1900 he was made Solicitor-General and in 1903 Attorney-General. Sixteen years later he became a judge, retiring in 1925. He died in East London in 1938.

Tree Fern or **Boomvaring** (*Hemitelia capensis*). Belongs to the same family (Cyantheaceae) as the Cycads (q.v.), its rough brown stem surmounted by a crown of long pinnate leaves. Coastal region, among thick undergrowth.

Tree Mouse (Dendromyinae). Small arboreal rodent found in Southern Africa, often making its home in birds' nests and eating chiefly vegetation, insects and small reptiles. There are several varieties, including the Grey Tree Mouse, the Small Tree Mouse and the Chestnut Tree Mouse, ranging in size up to about 3 inches.

Trees. While much of the Republic of South Africa is covered with thornbush (*see* ACACIA), natural forest, on account of fires and indiscriminate felling, is largely limited to sheltered kloofs, the mountain ranges parallel with the south and east coasts (notably the Knysna and Tsitzikama, q.v., forests and the Drakensberg escarpment of Natal) and the Transvaal. (*See also* ADDO BUSH.) Most of the forest trees—the Seringa (q.v.) being among the notable exceptions—are evergreen, and have smooth, leathery leaves. Woody climbers ('Monkey Ropes') festoon these forest trees, grey streamers of lichen crown the giant Yellowwoods (q.v.). Ferns and Tree Ferns (q.v.), mosses and orchids are plentiful wherever the rainfall is adequate. Unique to Table Mountain and its environs are the lovely Silver trees (q.v.). European trees, such as the Stone Pines (q.v.), oaks (q.v.), poplars and willows, imported centuries ago, grow freely, though often not so grandly as in their moister homes. In the 19th century Australian Wattles and Flowering Gums (q.v.) were introduced, primarily to bind the sand of the Cape Flats.

That much of South Africa, now relatively bare, was once forest-clad is shown by such names as Hout Bay. (*See* IRONWOOD, STINKWOOD, CAPE MAHOGANY, SNEEZEWOOD, HUILBOS, ACACIA, KAFFIRBOOM, EUPHORBIA, FLAMBOYANT, KEI-APPLE, OLIVE, ROOIELS and WITGAT.) Today extensive afforestation schemes are reclothing slopes both for commercial purposes and for water conservation. (*See* FORESTRY.)

South West Africa is not rich in trees. The Namib is generally bare of vegetation except for an occasional Kokerboom (*Aloe dichotonia*) (q.v.), bearing yellow winter clusters of flowers; and round the Walvis Bay area the strange Welwitschia (q.v.). The Upper Kuisip Zone has a fairly abundant vegetation, with camelthorns (*Acacia giraffae*), ebony trees, wild figs and the handsome Ana tree (*Acacia celbida*). The central plateau (Ovamboland) has a richer flora, with many acacias, baobabs (qq.v.), palms and wild figs. Great Namaqualand, drier than Damaraland, grows chiefly Kokerboom, Acacia and Camelthorn.

Rhodesia's wet summers and dry winters produce, over the greater part of that vast territory, open woodland or savannah. In the former the dominant trees are leguminous Brachystegia (*see* PEA), with their attractive russet spring colouring. These trees vary in height according to rainfall from 12 to 100 feet, their light foliage allowing the long grass and flowering bushes to grow freely below. In the hot, dry river valleys the characteristic trees are the beautiful 40-foot Mopane (q.v.), the Baobab with its grotesquely swollen trunk (q.v.), tall Fan Palms (*Borassus aethiopum* and *Hypnaene ventricosa*), along with the many acacias (q.v.), euphorbias (q.v.) and bauhinias (q.v.). Zambia compensates for its paucity in general flora by immense forests of Rhodesian Teak (q.v.).

Trek, Great. *See* GREAT TREK.

Trek Airways. Unscheduled air line operating between South Africa and Europe, particularly Germany.

Trek Wagon. As developed in South Africa, the trek wagon differs in certain respects from its counterpart in Europe, and from the famous 'Covered Wagon' of early America. Built by local craftsmen, many of them slaves, the original 'kakebeenwa' (jawbone wagon) of the first trekkers was considerably lighter than its modern successor. It measured 12 to 15 feet long and 3 to 3½ feet wide. Local Stinkwood, Yellowwood and Ironwood were used, great care being taken that the wood was completely dry. The 'onderstel' or under-carriage, which carried the wheels and axle-trees, was divided into the 'voorstel' and 'agterstel,' while above each axle-tree lay a heavy piece of timber, or 'skamel,' upon which rested the 2-inch-thick 'buikplank,' or wagon-platform. The beam or 'langwa' (long wagon) which connected the two axle-trees was specially

Trek Wagon (kakebeenwa)

reinforced with a piece of iron. To hold the 'disselboom' (the 10-foot pole to which the oxen were harnessed) a strong piece of timber, called the 'tang,' was pinned through the centre of the front axle-tree. A 'trektou' or draw-rope of twisted rawhide was attached to the 'disselboom.' Each ox carried its yoke or 'jukskei' with two pairs of mortices for the pegs holding the 'nekstrop.' The brake, which was applied to the iron-tyred wheels and known as the 'remskoen,' was originally made of wood, though metal was later substituted. Modifications were adopted in the design of the 'kakebeenwa,' making it lower, longer and heavier. The principal centres of the wagon-building industry, which at one time was of great importance, were Wellington (with its settlement at Wagonmakers Vlei), Oudtshoorn, Grahamstown, King William's Town, Pietermaritzburg, Potchefstroom and Pretoria, but there were few towns without their craftsmen. A well-built ox-wagon in the 19th century cost £300.

Tretchikoff, Vladimir. Artist. Born in Russia, December 13, 1913, but owing to the outbreak of Revolution brought up in Manchuria. Showed his artistic gifts at an early age. During World War II he worked for the British Information Office in Singapore, Malaya, before its capture by the Japanese. After 23 days in a lifeboat, he was imprisoned in Java by the Japanese and then released on parole. During these years he already achieved popularity as a painter but not until coming to South Africa in 1946 did he attain sensational success. Within a short while his originals fetched record prices and his reproductions sold in thousands. Highly successful shows in Cape Town and elsewhere in South Africa were followed by others in the United States, Canada and London.

Trew, Anthony Francis. South African author. Born in Pretoria June 5, 1906, and educated at Diocesan College, Cape Town. During World War II served in the South African and Royal Navies and took part in guarding Russian convoys. Became Secretary-General of the Automobile Association of South Africa. In 1961 wrote *Two Hours to Darkness,* a novel which achieved worldwide success.

Triangle. Large sugar-growing centre in Low Veld of Rhodesia.

Trichardt. Village in the Transvaal founded in 1906 and named after the Voortrekker Carel Trichardt (q.v.); a flourishing farming centre. Population: 500, including 400 Whites. (Not to be confused with *Louis* Trichardt, q.v.)

Trichardt, Carel (also known as Carolus Trigardt). Voortrekker hunter and explorer. Son of the famous Louis Trichardt (q.v.), he was born in Graaff-Reinet in 1810, and accompanied his father on his trek north in 1835, to the Zoutpansberg and then to Lourenço Marques. Arriving there in 1838, he was asked by his father to find out the settlement possibilities in the north. He trekked alone to the town of Mozambique, went inland a good distance, and even penetrated to East Africa. There is evidence of his having reached Abyssinia. He eventually returned to Lourenço Marques on foot, to find his father and most of the party dead. The few survivors had been removed to Natal. Karel followed them again on foot. He later settled in the Transvaal, where he lived near Middelburg. He died about 1903. Many people thought that it was he who discovered the Victoria Falls, 20 years before Livingstone, but Servaas le Roux, the Rhodesian writer, who devoted much time to an investigation, declared it to be unproven.

Trichardt, Louis. Voortrekker leader, of Swedish ancestry, the youngest son of Carel Johannes Trichardt. Born near Stellenbosch in 1783. The family

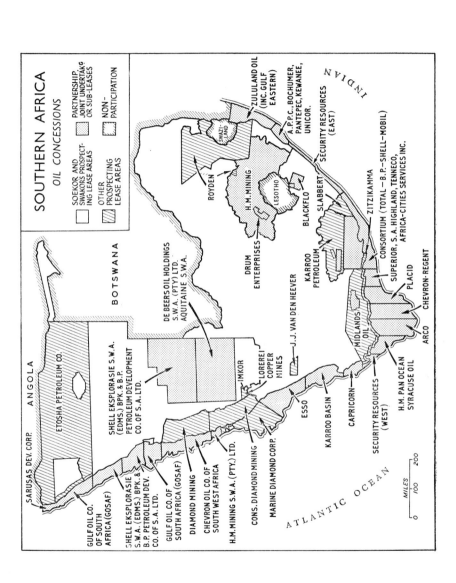

SOUTHERN AFRICA
OIL CONCESSIONS

SOEKOR AND
SWAKORS PROSPECT-
ING LEASE AREAS

OTHER
PROSPECTING
LEASE AREAS

PARTNERSHIP,
JOINT UNDERTAKG
OR SUB-LEASES

NON-
PARTICIPATION

ANGOLA

BOTSWANA

SWAZI-
LAND

LESOTHO

INDIAN

ATLANTIC OCEAN

MILES
0   100   200

SARUSAS DEV. CORP.

GULF OIL CO.
OF SOUTH
AFRICA (GOSAF)

SHELL EKSPLORASIE
S.W.A. (EDMS.) BPK. &
B.P. PETROLEUM DEV.
CO. OF S.A. LTD.

GULF OIL CO. OF
SOUTH AFRICA (GOSAF)

DIAMOND MINING

CHEVRON OIL CO. OF
SOUTH WEST AFRICA

H.M. MINING S.W.A. (PTY.) LTD.

CONS. DIAMOND MINING

MARINE DIAMOND CORP.

ESSO

KARROO BASIN

CAPRICORN

SECURITY RESOURCES
(WEST)

H.M. PAN OCEAN
SYRACUSE OIL

ARCO

CHEVRON-REGENT

PLACID

SUPERIOR, S. A. HIGHLAND, TENNECO,
AFRICA-CITIES SERVICES INC.

CONSORTIUM (TOTAL—B.P.—SHELL—MOBIL)

ZITZIKAMMA

SLABBERT

BLACKFLO

KARROO
PETROLEUM

MIDLANDS
OIL

J.J. VAN DEN HEEVER

LORERE!
COPPER
MINES

IMKOR

DRUM
ENTERPRISES

H.M. MINING

ROYDEN

ETOSHA PETROLEUM CO.

SHELL EKSPLORASIE S.W.A.
(EDMS.) BPK. & B.P.
PETROLEUM DEVELOPMENT
CO. OF S.A. LTD.

DE BEERS OIL HOLDINGS
S.W.A. (PTY.) LTD.
AQUITAINE S.W.A.

SECURITY RESOURCES
(EAST)

A.P.P.C., BOCHUMER,
PANTEPEC, KEWANEE,
UNICOR.

ZULULAND OIL
(INC. GULF
EASTERN)

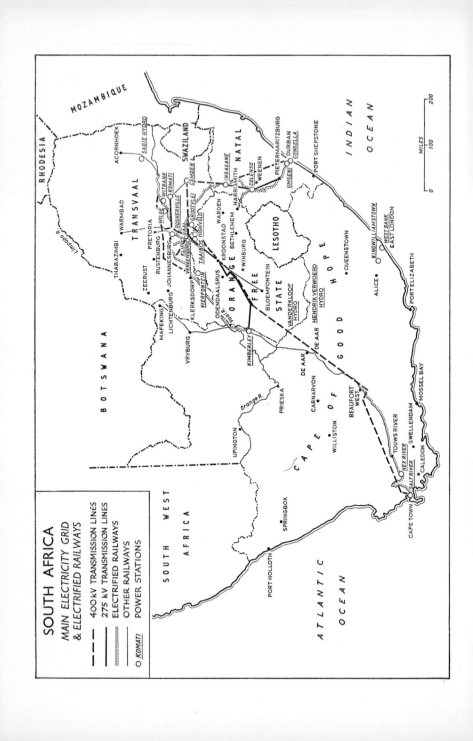

soon moved to Graaff-Reinet and then near Uitenhage. Because of losses sustained through Kaffir Wars, Louis Trichardt, who farmed first near the present site of Somerset East and then near the Great Fish River, decided to trek. Accompanied by his son, Carel, he crossed the Orange River, where he was joined by five families and later encountered another party of trekkers under Johannes van Rensburg, likewise on their way north. Trichardt's expedition penetrated as far as the Zoutpansberg in the Northern Transvaal, where he expected to be joined by a party under Hendrik Potgieter. After waiting in vain for a year, he found himself in a grave plight, and led his party to the coast across the Drakensberg, reaching Lourenço Marques after fearful hardships on April 13, 1838. He and his party were kindly received by the Portuguese but contracted fever, and more than half of them died. Trichardt was one of the victims, and died on October 25, 1838. The survivors were brought to the then republican Natal by ship. Trichardt's *Diary*, a unique record of Voortrekker days, was edited by Gustav S. Preller (q.v.) and published in 1917.

Trigger-Fish. A group of brightly-coloured fish, many of them poisonous, with compressed bodies covered with small rough or spiny scales. Abundant in warm seas, especially among coral reefs. Name derived from peculiar back spines. When first spine is erected it becomes locked and impossible to move by external force.

Trimen, Roland. South African naturalist, born in England. He came to the Cape in the 1860's and devoted a year to studying and collecting butterflies. His discoveries were published by the British Museum. He was appointed Curator to the South African Museum, and wrote extensively on insects.

Tripple. Mode of very steady trotting, something between a rapid walk and a

canter, the horse alternately moving both legs on each side together. An accomplishment peculiar to South African horses, which increases their value.

Tristan Da Cunha. Volcanic island in South Atlantic, 1,500 miles from Cape Town. Discovered in 1506 by Portuguese navigator Admiral Tristao da Cunha (q.v.). Occupied by a Cape garrison in Napoleonic times and ever after maintained contact with South Africa, some of the inhabitants of mixed origin settling there. For many years it was visited annually by a British warship from Simonstown. The Cape Government in 1904 ordered one of its officials, J. Hammond Tooke, to prepare a report on evacuation of the islanders (which was not, however, carried out). A South African company began rock-lobster canning there in 1950; weather observations are also made. The outbreak of a volcano, dormant since historic times, led to the evacuation, on October 10, 1961, of the entire Tristan population of over 100. Brought first to the Cape and then to England, they could not adapt themselves to the life, and, given the 'all clear' by a research expedition, returned in 1963.

Triumvirate. Also known in Afrikaans as Driemanskap. Group of three leaders appointed by the Volksraad of the Transvaal in 1880 on the initiative of Paul Kruger, to administer the country during the British régime, until the restoration of the Republic. It comprised Paul Kruger as Vice-President, Piet Joubert as Commandant-General and Martinus Wessels Pretorius. It continued to function until the election of Kruger as President in 1883. Another Triumvirate or Driemanskap was established later in the Klein Vrystaat (q.v.).

Trogon (family Trogonidae). *See* NARINA TROGON.

Trompsburg. Town in the Orange Free State. The first settlement was called Jagersfontein Road, and later Hamilton, after Governor Sir Hamilton Goold-Adams (q.v.). A town was founded there in 1898, and named after Bastian Tromp, owner of the original farm. Wool centre. Population: 2,087, including 682 Whites.

Tropsluiters (literally 'Procession-Enders'). Persons engaged in the early days of settlement at the Cape to walk at the end of funeral processions to lengthen them. A curious superstition existed that the last person in a funeral cortège would be the next to die, so it was usual for the tropsluiters frequently to change their position so as to minimise this possible risk!

Trotha, General Lothar Von. *See* VON TROTHA.

Trotter, Mrs. Alys Fane. South African writer and artist, born in 1863. She came to South Africa in the 1890's with her husband, the first Consulting Electrical Engineer employed by the Cape Colonial Government. Attracted by the beauty of the old Cape Dutch houses, she began studying them systematically. The result was a series of newspaper articles illustrated by herself, later collected and published under the title of *Old Cape Colony*. Mrs. Trotter returned to England, where she wrote poetry. She died in 1962, aged 99.

Trust Bank of Africa. Commercial bank founded on June 23, 1954, by Johannes Stephanus (Jan) Marais (q.v.) with the collaboration of the Federale Volksbeleggings group of companies (q.v.). Its head office is in Cape Town. Originally specialising in small loans, it became a fully-fledged commercial bank in 1963.

Trustfeed. Bantu settlement near New Hanover, Natal. Population: 1,187.

Truter, Sir John Andries. More correctly Johannes Andreas Truter. First Chief Justice of Cape Colony. Born in Cape Town in 1763, he studied law at Leyden and, taking his doctorate in 1787, returned to Cape Colony two years later to find a post with the Dutch East India Company. In 1793 he was made Secretary of the Court of Justice and in 1803, during the régime of the Batavian Republic, he became Secretary to the Council of Policy. Deciding to establish himself as an advocate, he began practice in 1806, was made Fiscal (q.v.) in 1809 and Chief Justice in 1812. He held office until 1827, when he retired. He died in 1845.

Truter, Pieter Jan. Early traveller in the Western Cape. He led a party in 1801 across the Orange River eastward into the Kalahari desert, hoping to find a supply of cattle from the local natives. They were the first party of Europeans to reach the site of Kuruman. They went on to Lattakoo, and on their homeward journey followed the course of the Orange River.

T.S. Abbreviation for Transvaal Scottish (q.v.).

T.S.C. Abbreviation for Technical Services Corps (q.v.).

Tsamma or **Kaffir Watermelon.** Common South African name for *Citrullus vulgaris*. Wild melon found in the Kalahari desert. The pulp when sweet forms a staple food of the Bushmen.

Tsetse Fly (*Glossina morsitans*). Insect carrying the parasite known as *Trypanosoma brucei*, causing Sleeping Sickness. It has depopulated very large parts of Central Africa. In cattle the Tsetse Fly is responsible for Nagana (q.v.). In Southern Africa it is now hardly to be found, except in Malawi and certain parts of Zambia.

Tshaka (also written **Chaka**). King and founder of the Zulu nation, born in 1787. He was the son of Senzangkona, who belonged to a group known as the Mhlongos. On the death of Dingiswayo he made himself chief, and this group came to be known as the Zulus. He then revolutionised the mechanism of war in Southern Africa, introducing the stabbing assegai instead of the older throwing type, and developing the horn system of tactics, by which his enemies were surrounded and annihilated. Within a short time he had complete control of the present territory of Natal. He is reputed to have slain over a million men, sparing the women as wives for his warriors. With the European settlers, who had just reached Natal in 1823, Tshaka maintained friendly relations and even gave a generous grant of land to Nathaniel Isaacs (q.v.). Despite his barbarity and sadism, Tshaka was a man of great ability and in some ways an attractive personality. He was finally murdered by his brother Dingaan (q.v.) and a group of other conspirators. A monument to Tshaka still stands in Stanger, erected by the Zulu people.

Tshimyane. *See* SHIMIAN.

Tsitsikama Forest. Natural forest near the south coast of the Cape Province, between Knysna and Humansdorp. It includes large stands of hardwoods and is a favourite holiday resort. The name is derived from the Hottentot and means 'bright and clear.'

Tsitsikama National Park. Established in 1966 near Storm's River mouth, it extends along the coast from Humansdorp to Groot River and Nature's Valley.

Tsitza Falls. Famous waterfall near Shawbury Mission Station, in the Transkei, 40 miles from Umtata. Height 375 feet. *See* UMZIMVUBU RIVER.

Tsolo. Village in Transkei, established in 1876, and taking its name, which means 'pointed,' from the shape of a neighbouring hill. During the rising of 1880 the magistrate and his staff were besieged there, and for reasons of safety the settlement was moved from its original site to its present position beside a small river, the Xokonxa. It is now an administrative and trading centre. Population: 900, including 250 Whites.

Tsomo. Village in the Transkei, named after a local chief and established in 1877. Administrative and trading station. Population: 500, including 140 Whites.

Tsumeb. Township in the north of South West Africa, headquarters of the Otavi mine, now associated with interests of the O'okiep Copper Company (q.v.). It produces zinc, lead and copper, being linked by one of the longest narrow-gauge lines in Africa with the rest of the country's railway system; established about 1903. Population: 7,796, including 3,987 Whites.

Tube Mills. Revolving drums used on the gold-mines of the Rand for crushing ore. They were introduced about 1903, the design being based on mills used for preparing cement. Owing to the difficulty of finding sufficiently resistant material, their perfection was delayed until the invention of the manganese steel liner by R. Hadfield of Sheffield.

Tuberculosis. Because of its sunshine and its dry climate, Southern Africa, particularly the Karroo, was from early days recognised as a haven for sufferers from tuberculosis, thousands of whom found health in this country. In recent times a ban has been imposed upon the entry of tuberculous sufferers without special authority. Among Europeans the tuberculosis rate in the Republic—15 per 100,000—is comparable with the best overseas, but among non-Europeans the position, though considerably improved, is by no means satisfactory. The worst conditions prevail among the Cape Coloureds, among whom the death rate fell from 446 per 100,000 in 1946 to 319 per 100,000 in 1952. Accurate figures are not available for Bantu, but are believed to be less bad. Health propaganda is largely handled by the South African National Tuberculosis Association.

Tucsa. Abbreviation for Trade Union Council of South Africa. *See* TRADE UNIONS.

Tugela River. Rises on eastern side of the Mont-aux-Sources in the Drakensberg and falls almost vertically for 1,800 feet in one of the most spectacular waterfalls of Southern Africa. It is 200 miles long and enters the sea north of Durban. Until the Zulu War it formed the northern boundary of Natal. Tributaries are the Klip, Sundays, Buffalo (or Umzinyati) on the north and the Mnweni, Umlambonja, Little Tugela, Bloukrans, Bushmans, Mooi and Inadi on the south. Tugela means 'startling.'

Tulbagh. Town in the Western Cape Province, named after Governor Ryk Tulbagh (q.v.). It was founded in an area previously known as 'Het Land van Waveren,' first explored in 1699. The church was built in 1743 and the village laid out in 1795. Several fine old buildings survive, including this church and the original Drostdy, now a private home. Apart from its attraction to tourists, Tulbagh is famous for its fruit and wine. Population: 1,938, including 797 Whites.

Tulbagh, Rijk. Governor of the Cape, born in Utrecht, Holland, 1699. He arrived at the Cape in 1716 in the *Terhorst*, and attracted the attention of Governor De Chavonnes by his studious ways. In 1722 he became Clerk to the Council of Policy, and in 1725 Fiscal. Further promotion to Secunde followed in 1739, and in 1751 he was made Governor. His régime was one of progress, though memorable for austerity legislation against what he regarded as needless frivolity. His popularity is indicated by his nickname of 'Vader Tulbagh.' He died in Cape Town in August 1771 and is buried in the Groote Kerk.

Tuli. Township in the south of Rhodesia, on the Shashi River in the Gwanda district, and one of the oldest in the colony, established in 1890. It was of strategic importance in the operations of the Pioneer Column (q.v.), and later as a stop for the mail coaches from the south, but gradually declined in prosperity.

Tulp (Dutch for **Tulip**) (Iridaceae). Familiar name applied to various wild bulbous plants of the Homeria group, with yellow or salmon flowers and sword-shaped leaves. They are deadly to cattle and sheep. *See* IRIS.

Tuna. *See* TUNNY.

Tungsten (also known as **Wolfram**). Mineral used in steel production, in making electric filaments, etc. Mined in Namaqualand, in South West Africa and in Rhodesia. Usually found as scheelite ore. Deposits also exist in Zululand, in the Murchison Range, near Potgietersrust and elsewhere. During World War II there was an enormous overseas demand for tungsten owing to the cutting off of supplies by enemy action.

Tunny (*Thunnus thynnus*). A big game-fish belonging to the Mediterranean and sub-tropical seas, but caught in Table Bay and Hout Bay occasionally. Average 10 feet long. Most members of this family—mackerels, bonitos and katonkels (*see under separate heads*)—have a good commercial value, the flesh being reddish, firm and oily.

On January 31, 1964, the late Dr. Verwoerd (q.v.), Prime Minister of the Republic of South Africa, caught a 468-pound blue fin tunny off Fish Hoek in False Bay in the boat *Speranza* belonging to Desmond Hare.

Turfloop. University college for Bantu students, situated 12 miles from Pietersburg in the Northern Transvaal, and established in 1959. Certain traditional features of African architecture have been embodied in the design of the buildings, which, when the Teachers' College, Agricultural College, Hospital and Medical School have been completed, are likely to cost over R5,000,000. *See also* UNIVERSITIES.

Turnbull, John William. Judge of the Natal Supreme Court. Born in Edinburgh in 1829, he studied at Cambridge and was called to the Bar at Lincoln's Inn in 1855. Four years later he began practice at Pietermaritzburg, where in 1869 he was elected to the Legislative Assembly. He became a judge in 1888 and died in 1902.

Turnstone (Limicolae). One of the Arctic-breeding waders (q.v.), common in inland waters and on seaweedy rocks in South Africa between November and April. A dull little bird most of the year, recognisable by its upturned bill and orange legs, shortly before its migration the head and underparts become white with black bands, and the back black and chestnut. See BIRDS.

Turpentine Tree. See MOPANE.

Turtle-Dove, Cape (*Streptopelia capicola*). See PIGEON.

Twain, Mark. Famous American humorist. Visited South Africa from 1895 to 1896 on a lecture tour around the world, during which time he called on the Reform Prisoners in Pretoria Gaol. He describes this journey in *Following the Equator*.

Tweedie. Village near Lions River, Natal. Population: 110.

Tweed, John. British sculptor, born in Glasgow in 1869. His famous figure of Van Riebeeck was erected in 1900 at the foot of Adderley Street, Cape Town, as a gift from Cecil John Rhodes. Later Tweed was responsible for the statue of Rhodes at Bulawayo, as well as for others of him at Salisbury and Mafeking, and for the statue in Salisbury of Alfred Beit. One of his best-known works was the monument to the patrol under Major Allan Wilson (q.v.) which perished in the Matabele War. He also did a very fine bust of the Bechuana King Khama. Tweed died on November 12, 1933.

Tweekop (*Typhlops bibronii*). See SNAKE, BLIND.

Tweeling. Village near Frankfort, Orange Free State. Population: 1,311, including 432 Whites.

Tweespruit. Village in the Orange Free State, established after the South African War for a number of ex-soldier British settlers. It is noted for its large dairy installations and cattle breeding. Population: 2,275, including 248 Whites.

Twelve Apostles. Part of Table Mountain Range overlooking Camp's Bay; includes St. Peter's Peak (above Slangolie Kloof), St. Paul's Peak, St. Luke's Peak, Judas Peak.

Tygerpoort Dam. Large irrigation scheme on the Kaffir River, 22 miles south of Bloemfontein. Begun in 1922 as an earthen dam with reinforced concrete core wall, 395 feet long and 65 feet high (95 feet above foundations). When full, the water area is 4 sq. miles and the irrigable area about 2,700 acres.

Tylden. Village in the Eastern Cape Province, named after Captain G. Tylden of the Royal Engineers, who was in command there in 1851 during a campaign against the Tambookie tribe. Population: 150, including 40 Whites.

Tyson, Thomas Gilbee. Kimberley pioneer, born in Kent in 1849. He arrived on the Diamond Diggings in 1872, served in several campaigns and became Secretary of the Kimberley Club. He was a close friend of Cecil Rhodes, a director of De Beers and a dominant figure in public affairs. He died in 1912.

Tyumie River. Tributary of Keiskama River (q.v.).

Tzaneen. Town in the Northern Transvaal, founded as an experimental farm by the administration of Lord Milner after the South African War. Laid out as a village in 1924. Noted for its sub-tropical agriculture and forestry. Population: 10,200, including 4,200 Whites.

U

UBOMBO

Ubombo. Administrative station near Nongoma, Zululand, scene of a fight between the Zulus and the Mandhlakasi tribe in 1888. Boers who helped the Zulus were granted farms, which are still occupied by their descendants. Population: 280, including 50 Whites.

U.D.I. Abbreviation for Unilateral Declaration of Independence. *See* RHODESIA.

Ugie. Village in the Eastern Cape Province, named after his birthplace in Scotland by an early missionary, the Rev. Newnay. Large undenominational orphanages were established there by the Rev. T. M. R. Smit after the Spanish influenza epidemic in 1918, to care for children left destitute. Population: 2,423, including 707 Whites.

Uglies. A construction of wire fixed to their bonnets by the wives and daughters of the 1820 settlers, in order to provide themselves with extra shade while at work.

Uintjie (*Moraea edulis*). The name, 'little onion,' is applied to a wild edible bulb, which can be made into an attractive dish by an old Cape recipe. Another species, known as Water Uintjie, is a water lily, the roots of which resemble asparagus when roasted. *See* IRIS.

Uitenhage. Town in the Eastern Cape Province, 21 miles from Port Elizabeth. Founded in 1804 and named after J. A. Uitenhage de Mist, the Commissary-General sent to the Cape by the government of the Batavian Republic. It lies on the Zwartkops River, and is an important industrial centre, with railway workshops, wool-washeries, textile mills, motor assembling plants, tyre factories, etc. It is also a farming centre of importance. During its early days the entire eastern frontier was administered from Uitenhage, under its famous Landdrost J. G. Cuyler (q.v.). Population: 65,500, including 22,000 Whites, 13,000 Coloureds, and 30,000 Bantu.

Uitlander. Name given by the Boers to the immigrant settlers of other nationalities in the Transvaal after the discovery of gold. The grievances of the Uitlanders were largely responsible for the Boer War.

Uitvalgrond. Literally surplus ground. Pieces of land which, owing to bad surveying, were found to be ownerless. The old Republics' law declared these to be the property of the State. Some were of considerable extent. The most famous piece of Uitvalgrond was the farm Randjeslaagte on which the city of Johannesburg was laid out. Allied to this institution was that of the Inkruip Plaas (creeping-in farm) (q.v.).

Ukoanyama. Language spoken by tribe in Ovamboland in extreme north of South West Africa.

Ulco. Village near Barkly West, Cape Province. Large lime works. Population: 2,202, including 598 Whites.

Ulundi. Main kraal of Cetewayo (q.v.), the Zulu king in Zululand, near Mahlabatini. It was the scene of his final defeat in the Zulu War, on July 4, 1879, and was burnt down in the fighting.

Umbogintwini. Township 15 miles south of Durban, on the Natal south coast. Site of the great explosives and chemical works established in 1908 by the British firm of Kynoch, and now owned by African Explosives and Chemical Industries. Today production is concentrated on fertilisers and many kinds of chemicals, plastics, etc.,

590

the making of dynamite being carried on at other plants of the company. The name Umbogintwini means 'Place of Stones.' Population: 2,112, including 524 Whites.

Umbumbulu. Village near Umlazi, Natal. Population: 60, including 30 Whites.

Umdoni Park. A 350-acre estate on the south coast of Natal, left to the nation by Sir Frank Reynolds (q.v.) in 1930, with R120,000 for its upkeep. The mansion, Botha House, occupied by the widow of General Louis Botha (q.v.) until her death in 1937, is now the seaside home of the Prime Minister.

Umfaan. Zulu name for a small boy, also used in Natal for a very junior male servant.

Umfazi. Xosa word for a married woman.

Umgeni River. Rises near Impendle, Natal, and enters the sea at Durban. Tributaries are the Lion, Karkloof, Impolweni, Umqeku and Umsunduzi. Chief attraction of the Umgeni are the two famous waterfalls, the Howick, 350 feet high, and the Albert, 70 feet high, 12 miles downstream.

Umhlali. Seaside resort on the Natal north coast, 35 miles from Durban.

Umhlanga Rocks. Seaside resort in Natal, 12 miles north of Durban. The name is the Zulu word for a species of reed found there. Population: 1,995, including 1,255 Whites.

Umkomaas. Seaside resort on the Natal south coast, at the mouth of the river of that name (q.v.). Noted for its fine golf course and as the site of a pulp production plant. Population: 1,740, including 1,100 Whites.

Umkomaas River. Rises in the Drakensberg and enters the sea south of Durban. Its name means in Zulu 'Gatherer of the Waters.' The upper reaches are very wild. Tributaries include the Uzani, Eland, Umkobeni

and the Ixopo (or Inhlaveni). Before reaching Kimberley, Cecil Rhodes and his brother in the early 1870's tried to grow cotton in the upper Umkomaas Valley.

Umkonto Wa Swize. Literally 'Spear of the Nation.' Illegal Bantu organisation, which came into prominence in South Africa in 1962 on account of outrages and attempts at terrorism, including sabotage of public services, etc. Heavy sentences were imposed on members caught by the police.

Umlungu. Xosa word for a white man.

Umpanda. *See* PANDA.

U.M.R. Abbreviation for Umvoti Mounted Rifles (q.v.).

Umtali. Town in Rhodesia, in the Eastern Highlands. Founded in 1890 on a site about 14 miles away, but removed in 1896 close to the railway. Today it is the third town in the Colony, and a popular tourist resort with beautiful mountain scenery and streets lined with blossoming trees. There are a growing number of industries, and the amenities include a fine library. Near by is a monument on a koppie, erected at the instance of Colonel Methuen to African troops killed in World War I. On the summit of the Christmas Pass, through which the Pioneers approached Umtali, stands another memorial, to Kingsley Fairbridge (q.v.), the local land-surveyor's son who started the famous Child Emigration Scheme. It was unveiled by the Queen Mother on her visit in 1953. Population: 50,000, including 9,200 Whites.

Umtali Murder Case. Constitutional crisis which arose in 1911, through the action of Lord Gladstone, first Governor-General of the Union and High Commissioner for South Africa, in reprieving the accused in the case of Rex versus Alukuleta. He had been charged with rape committed in Umtali, and had been found guilty. In his capacity as High Commissioner,

Lord Gladstone, relying on the view of the judge, acted against the finding of the jury and without any recommendation by the Administrator of Southern Rhodesia. The reprieve created much excitement in legal and other circles, and nearly led to the resignation of the Administrator.

Umtamvuma River. In extreme south of Natal, forms the boundary between that province and the Cape.

Umtasa (also known as **Mutasa**). Chief of the Manicas. In 1890, when Rhodesia was occupied, he was much pressed by both Portuguese and British to grant concessions over his territory, which lay in a strategic position on the northern frontier of Mozambique. Umtasa granted certain rights to the Portuguese, which gave rise to the Massekessi incident (q.v.).

Umtata. Capital of the Transkei, founded in 1860, when a group of Europeans settled there to keep apart two warring chiefs, Nquiliso of the Pondos and Gangelizwe of the Tembus. Fighting took place near by during the Tambookie War of 1878 and a squadron of Cape Mounted Police was stationed there. It developed into the main administrative centre for the Transkei and meeting place of the Bunga (q.v.) or Transkeian Territories General Council. It is the seat of an Anglican bishop and possesses a cathedral. The name is derived from the Bantu name for a local species of Sneezewood. Population: 17,800, including 4,100 Whites.

Umtentweni. Seaside resort on the Natal south coast. Population: 1,400, including 800 Whites.

Umtiza (*Umtiza listeri* Sim). Much-branched evergreen tree up to 25 feet. Wood very hard and heavy, regarded as excellent for bearings.

Umvoti Mounted Rifles. South African military unit, founded in September 1865. Served in the Zulu War of 1879, in 1899 with Buller's Natal Force during the Relief of Ladysmith and again in the Zululand Rebellion of 1906 and 1907. It was mobilised in 1914, serving in German South West Africa with the Central Force. In World War II it served with the 4th South African Infantry Brigade in North Africa and was taken prisoner in Tobruk in 1942. Motto: 'Toujours Prêt.'

Umvoti River. Rises in the Karkloof Mountains near Mt. Gilboa and reaches the Indian Ocean near Stanger on the Natal north coast. Its main tributary is the Ihlimbitwa.

Umvuma. Township in Rhodesia, 54 miles from Gwelo on the line to Fort Victoria. It lies 4,540 feet above sea-level and has a population of 110 Europeans, 300 Africans and 60 of other races. Founded in 1902 as a mining centre, Umvuma flourished from 1912 to 1924 owing to the nearby Falcon Copper Mine. Since its closing, the main importance of the place has been through farming.

Umzimkulu. Village in Cape Province, on boundary of Natal. Population: 960, including 140 Whites.

Umzimkulu River. The second largest in Natal, rises in the Drakensberg and reaches the sea at Port Shepstone. At one time efforts were made to open it to navigation. Total length 120 miles. Tributaries are Ipolela, Ingwangwani and Umzimkulwana. The name in Zulu means 'Great River.'

Umzimvubu River (also known as the **St. John's River**) rises in the Drakensberg and flows into the Indian Ocean at Port St. John's, breaking through two great masses of rock, known as the Gates of St. John. The name Umzimvubu means Hippopotamus. Chief tributary is the Tsitsa River, renowned for its 375-feet falls, among the highest in South Africa. Small coasters formerly crossed the bar of the Umzimvubu.

Umzinto. Village in the south of Natal, noted as a sugar milling centre. It is 47 miles south of Durban. The name means: 'The Kraal of Achievement.' Population: 6,000, including 400 Whites.

Underberg. Village on the Natal side of the Drakensberg, noted for its trout fishing. Population: 500, including 200 Whites.

Unemployment. Benefits for unemployed persons in the Republic of South Africa are regulated by the Unemployment Insurance Act of 1946, with its amendments. Replacing an earlier measure in 1937, it lays down a scale of contributions by employers, employees and the State. Domestic and farm workers are not included in the provisions of the law. Owing to favourable economic conditions prevailing since its establishment, the calls on the Unemployment Insurance Fund have been small and it has accumulated resources exceeding £100,000,000. Periods of major unemployment in South Africa occurred after the South African War, especially in the Cape Colony and Natal, between 1904 and 1908, and during the World Depression, between 1929 and 1932.

Unicorn Shipping Lines. South African shipping company, specialising in coaster trade. Associated with Union Corporation (q.v.), and incorporating Smith's Coasters, Thesen Line and Grindrod, Gersigny & Co.'s fleets. Has over 25 ships. Headquarters in Durban.

Union Bank. Early Cape financial institution with unlimited liability. Established in 1847, it attained prosperity but through mismanagement suspended payments in 1890, ruining most of its shareholders. All its debts, amounting to nearly £900,000, were paid.

Union Buildings. The seat of the Government in Pretoria. Its construction was approved by the Transvaal Colonial government, which earmarked the necessary funds. Building began in 1910, when the foundation stone was laid by the Duke of Connaught, and was completed in 1913. The design, embodying many old Dutch architectural motifs, was by Sir Herbert Baker, and the cost £1,130,000. Dominating the summit of Meintjes Kop, the building, with its great amphitheatre, can house over 1,500 officials. In its basement are the Government Archives of the Transvaal and of the Union.

Union-Castle Line. Established in 1900 as a result of the amalgamation of the Union and the Castle Lines (qq.v.). At first the management remained in the hands of the firm of Donald Currie and Co., but in April 1912 control was bought by the Royal Mail Steam Packet Company, of which Sir Owen Phillips (later Lord Kylsant) was the head. This arrangement came to an end in 1932, when the Union-Castle Mail Steamship Company resumed its independence. In 1956 control passed to the Cayzer, Irvine group, headed by Lord Rotherwick, which is also linked with the Clan Line, the British and Commonwealth Co., etc. The Company's fleet measures nearly 500,000 tons. *See also* SAFMARINE.

Union Corporation Limited (not to be confused with Union Steel Corporation Ltd. (q.v.)). Rand mining group, established in 1897 as A. Goerz Co. Ltd., succeeding the private German firm of Adolf Goerz Co. It received its present name during World War I. Has large gold and industrial holdings, mainly in South Africa but also in Mexico and elsewhere.

Uniondale. Town in the southern Cape Province, established in 1856 through the union of two rival villages, Lyon and Hopedale. The place was noted for its wagon-building and ostrich feather industries. Both died away, and it is now maintained by general farming operations, including tobacco, wheat and fruit. Population: 3,000, including 1,200 Whites.

Unionist Party. Founded at the time of Union and representing strongly pro-British elements. Its leaders included Sir Thomas Smartt, Sir James Fitzpatrick, Sir George Farrar, Sir Lionel Phillips (qq.v.). and others. In 1920 it merged with the South African Party (q.v.).

Union Line. First regular South African steamship service to England, established as the 'Union Steam Collier Co.' in 1853, but converted to passenger service in 1857, when the first vessel, the *Dane*, arrived at the Cape. Thereafter it secured the mail contract, which from 1876 it shared with the Castle Line (q.v.), the ships sailing during alternate weeks. The two companies were amalgamated in 1900 into the Union-Castle Line (q.v.). At the time the Union Line had 19 ships, totalling 104,107 tons.

Union of South Africa. Former member state of the British Commonwealth of Nations. It came into existence on May 31, 1910, in terms of the South Africa Act, passed by Parliament in 1909. On May 31, 1961, after a Referendum, it became the Republic of South Africa (q.v.).

Union Steel Corporation of South Africa Ltd. Pioneer steel manufacturing company, established in 1911 by the late Samuel Marks (q.v.). It began operations at Vereeniging in 1913, using scrap metal as its raw material for rails, billets, etc. Later it manufactured drill-steel and other specialities. It now operates two plants and has large interests in the production of nuts and bolts. Usco is associated with Iscor (q.v.).

United Federal Party. Founded May 10, 1953, at Johannesburg, and developed from the Torch Commando (q.v.) particularly to encourage federation with neighbouring territories. Among its founders was Senator G. Heaton Nicholls.

United Party. Officially the United South African National Party. Established in 1934 as a result of the coalition between General J. B. M. Hertzog (q.v.) and General J. C. Smuts (q.v.), as the leader and his deputy respectively. Its foundation was the result of a compromise, whereby the former South African Party conceded to members of the former National Party the right to continue their propaganda for a republic. Though it had powerful support, from both the English and the Afrikaans side, it almost immediately suffered a serious loss through the withdrawal of the 'purified' National Party, under the late Dr. D. F. Malan (q.v.).

The official birthday of the United Party was December 5, 1934, when it commanded four-fifths of the seats in the House of Assembly. With the passing of the years, however, considerable setbacks were sustained, and on the outbreak of World War II the split between General Hertzog and General Smuts left the latter in command. The United Party remained in power until the General Election of 1948, since when it has been the principal opposition. Several groups, including the Liberals and Progressives, have in their turn seceded from the United Party.

Unit Trusts. Although 'closed-end' trusts made their appearance in South Africa with the establishment on May 14, 1934 of the Units Securities and Trust Co. Ltd. at Johannesburg, it was not until 1959, when an amendment in the law, sponsored by the late Dr. T. E. Dönges (q.v.), made possible the operation of 'open-end' trusts, that the principle of the 'Growth Fund' could be introduced. The big development, however, is far more recent. Between 1965 and 1969 the assets of such institutions in South

Africa have risen from R600,000 to over R600,000,000. *See also* STOCK EXCHANGE.

Universities. The first attempts at university education in Southern Africa go back to 1829, when the South African College came into existence in Cape Town. It made provision in its syllabus for teaching boys such subjects as the classics, philosophy, mathematics and theology. Out of this developed several similar institutions, including the Diocesan College (q.v.) in Cape Town, Gill College (q.v.) in Somerset East, etc. The need for local training of young lawyers and other professional men caused a 'Board of Examiners' to be established in 1858, which set papers and which, in 1874, became the University of the Cape of Good Hope. The latter remained a purely examining body, leaving the actual tuition to the South African College, which added a steadily-increasing range of subjects to its curriculum. In 1859 the first efforts were made to train ministers of the Dutch Reformed Church in Stellenbosch. These led in 1866 to the founding of the Gymnasium in that town, and in 1881 to the starting of Stellenbosch College. This was re-named Victoria College in 1887. Under the influence of Cecil John Rhodes, plans were laid, towards the end of the century, for establishing a teaching university at Groote Schuur to serve the whole of South Africa, to which the few existing institutions were to be affiliated. A School of Mines had already been opened in 1896 in Kimberley, in conjunction with the South African College. This school presently extended its activities to the Witwatersrand, where, after the South African War, the Transvaal Technical Institute was founded to serve both Johannesburg and Pretoria. In due course this split up into the South African School of Mines and Technology in Johannesburg and the

Transvaal University College in Pretoria. Facilities for higher education were meanwhile under way in Bloemfontein, through the Grey College (originally founded by Governor Sir George Grey in 1855), and in Burgersdorp, Cape, where in 1869 a theological seminary was begun. This was removed in 1905 to Potchefstroom. In Durban technical classes were begun shortly after the Boer War. In 1904, Rhodes University College in Grahamstown succeeded the original higher department of St. Andrew's College. The bequest for university purposes of sums totalling several hundred thousand pounds by Cecil John Rhodes, Alfred Beit and Sir Julius Wernher led to confusion and rivalry between institutions at the start of the present century. After the establishment of Union, inquiries were conducted by the Government, and in 1918 the South African College became the University of Cape Town, Victoria College the University of Stellenbosch, the remaining institutions being affiliated to a new University of South Africa. (The University of the Cape of Good Hope went out of existence.) A new institution was also set up in 1916 at Fort Hare, known as the South African Native College. Since then separate universities have been set up in Johannesburg (University of the Witwatersrand) in 1922, Pretoria in 1930, Durban and Pietermaritzburg (University of Natal) in 1949 and Bloemfontein (University of the Orange Free State) in 1950. In 1951 the Potchefstroom Universiteit vir Christelike Hoër Onderwys and Rhodes University in Grahamstown (to which was attached the University College of Fort Hare) were likewise inaugurated. The University of Port Elizabeth was established in 1963 and the Rand Afrikaans University in October 1966. The older University of South Africa continued to operate, with its headquarters in Pretoria, though it concentrated mainly on extra-mural studies. Universities in the Republic have today over 62,000 students, of whom about 5,000 are non-white, and a full-time teaching staff of around 3,000. Their revenue exceeds R28,000,000. Following the decision of the Government to terminate the system of 'mixed universities,' separate university colleges have been established in the Cape, Transvaal and Natal for non-Europeans. A university college established, under the auspices of the Roman Catholic Church, in Roma in Lesotho has become independent. To serve the Central African Federation, the University College of Rhodesia and Nyasaland was established in 1955 in association with the University of London, which awards its degrees. This institution maintains no colour bar, and now functions for Rhodesia alone, Zambia having taken steps to set up its own university at Lusaka. Since 1963 Mozambique has had a university of its own at Lourenço Marques, associated with the famous old University of Coimbra in Portugal.

University College for Indians. Established with 100 students in temporary premises on Salisbury Island, Durban, in 1961, and within four years grown to nearly 1,000. In addition to the usual Arts and Sciences, the College has the only courses in South Africa in Hindi, Arabic and Oriental Studies. Large new buildings are under construction near Westville.

University College of the Western Province. College for Coloured students, established near Bellville, near Cape Town, in 1959. *See also* UNI-VERSITIES.

Upington. Town on the Orange River in the North-West Cape Province. It was originally called Olyvenhoutdrift, but renamed in 1885 after Sir Thomas Upington, Prime Minister of Cape Colony. It owes its prosperity mainly to the development of irrigation on the

Orange, combined with its strategic situation on the borders of the Republic and South West Africa. The building of a railway there in 1914 from De Aar, the existing railhead, carried out at the rate of over one mile per day, was a preliminary to the invasion of South West Africa. Population: 26,840, including 7,500 Whites, 14,000 Coloureds and 5,000 Bantu.

Upington, Beauclerk. South African lawyer, son of Sir Thomas Upington (q.v.); born in Dublin in 1872 and educated at the South African College and at Trinity College, Dublin. Settling at the Cape, he soon became one of the most distinguished criminal lawyers in South Africa, many stories being told about his achievements in court. He died in 1938.

Upington, Sir Thomas. Prime Minister of the Cape and judge of the Supreme Court. Born near Cork, Ireland, in 1844; studied at Trinity College, Dublin, and was admitted there to the Bar in 1867. Owing to poor health he came to South Africa in 1874 and began practice. He became prominent and in 1878 was appointed Attorney-General. From 1884 to 1886 he was Prime Minister. Returning to practice, he became a judge in 1892 and remained on the bench until 1896, when he resigned in order to resume a political career. In the cabinet of Sir Gordon Sprigg, Upington again became Attorney-General. He died on September 10, 1898.

Upper Kubusi. Settlement near Stutterheim, Cape Province. Population: 2,737, including 246 Whites.

Uranium. South Africa's uranium industry began after the Second World War. In 1944 and 1945 scientific surveys indicated the extent of the uranium-bearing ores on the goldfields and were followed by a visit to South Africa of a joint mission from the United States and Great Britain to arrange details for the production of uranium oxide. Uranium plants were built rapidly on a number of mines, and the first shipments of uranium oxide left South Africa early in 1953. Estimated reserves are given at 370,000 tons of uranium oxide in 1,100 million tons of ore.

In the first quarter of 1964, there were 14 mines, members of the Chamber of Mines, listed as uranium producers. In 1964, South Africa's production of uranium oxide totalled 4,445 tons. This included relatively small quantities to countries other than the United States, to which the bulk of production is sold. Shipments in 1962 amounted to 4,598 tons and the falling off conforms to the pattern established by the agreement negotiated in 1960 with the United Kingdom Atomic Energy Authority for a deferment of deliveries of uranium oxide to Britain over the longer period ending 1970.

At the request of the Authority a further deferment of deliveries to Britain, involving 2,724 tons, was arranged early in 1963. In effect, the total deliveries of uranium oxide to the United States and Britain from the beginning of 1963 remain unaltered at 19,918 tons but the British proportion, amounting to 8,985 tons, will now be spread out until 1973.

Monazite concentrates containing thorium are produced near Van Rhynsdorp, Cape Province, and from titaniferous beach sands at Umgababa, Natal.

On Rand mines producing uranium as well as gold, the process of extraction begins after the gold has been extracted. Slimes are conveyed to the adjacent uranium extraction plant, some of which treat slimes from more than one mine. There the slimes, mixed with water and dilute sulphuric acid, are agitated by air until the uranium is dissolved. This uranium-bearing solution is removed on rotary filters. Clarified and passed to the ion-exchange section of the plant for precipitation, the final product emerges as a bright yellow substance, looking like freshly made mustard.

This product is sent by road tankers to Calcined Products (Pty.) Ltd., a central plant, where the uranium oxide is sampled, dried, calcined and packed in metal drums for shipment overseas.

Usakos. Village in South West Africa, noted for its railway workshops, established under the German régime. Population: 4,244, including 1,606 Whites.

Utixo. Xosa name for God.

Utrecht. Town in the north of Natal, founded in 1853, and named after the city in Holland. The neighbourhood originally was an independent Boer republic, merging into the Transvaal in 1860 and remaining part of it until 1902. Along with the Vryheid (q.v.) district, Utrecht was then handed to Natal. In both the Zulu War and the South African War Utrecht was in the thick of the fighting. It is now a colliery and agricultural centre. Population: 7,200, including 1,420 Whites.

Uvongo. Seaside resort on the south coast of Natal, established 1920, and noted for the picturesque waterfall near the mouth of the Uvongo River. The name means 'Rumbling.' Population: 3,280, including 2,000 Whites.

Uys, Jamie (Jacobus Johannes). South African film producer. Born at Boksburg, Transvaal, on May 30, 1921, originally trained as a teacher, but after 3 years at a school, he went farming. He then founded his own production house, specialising in Afrikaans feature films, as well as in bilingual versions. Among his most successful were *Hans en die Rooinek, Rip Van Wyk, The Fox has Four Eyes*.

Uys, Pieter Lafras. Voortrekker leader, born near Uitenhage in 1797.

Having spent most of his earlier life farming on the frontier, he joined a family party of 150 Trekkers in 1837, led by his father, Jacobus Uys. Later Pieter Uys took a prominent part in planning the early government of the emigrants, and in swaying their decision to enter Natal. While fighting the Zulus after the murder of Piet Retief, on April 11, 1838, he and his companions were ambushed at Italeni. His son, Dirk, saw him surrounded and went back to his aid. Both were killed.

V

VAALBOS

Vaalbos (*Tarchonanthus camphoratus* Linn.). Large balsam-scented shrub, the young leaves of which are grey and velvety on upper surface. Found in Cape Province and Griqualand West.

Vaaldam. On the Vaal River, constructed 18 miles from Vereeniging and the largest dam of its kind in the Southern Hemisphere. It was built in 1935, and cost R3,264,000. The dam was long used as a landing place for flying boats in the Overseas Airways service. Capacity 512,560 million gallons. *See* VAAL-HARTZ IRRIGATION SCHEME.

Vaal-Hartz Irrigation Scheme. Largest enterprise of its kind south of the Equator, situated 50 miles north of Kimberley at the junction of the Vaal (q.v.) and the Hartz rivers. The scheme was envisaged by Cecil John Rhodes before the end of the 19th century, but was not taken in hand until 1934, when the enabling act was passed. It has an upper storage dam 14 miles below the confluence of the Vaal and Wilge rivers capable of holding about 700,000 acre-feet, submerging about 50 sq. miles. The main diversion is about 3 miles above Warrenton. The total waterway impounded extends over 300 miles. Nearly 90,000 acres are under irrigation and about 200,000 acres are used by the 1,200 settlers for grazing. So successful has the enterprise been that the average gross annual income of each settler is approximately R2,600. Groundnuts and wheat are among the chief crops.

Vaalpens. Nickname applied to Transvalers. It was also used as a description of a type of Bushman in the Southern Kalahari. The name means

VANADIUM

'Tawny Stomach' (cf. American 'Yellow-Belly').

Vaal River. Major tributary of the Orange River. It rises in the South-Eastern Transvaal near the Klipstapelberg, and measures about 700 miles. The name is derived from its yellowish-brown colour. It is of great industrial importance, meeting the needs of the entire Witwatersrand, a large part of the Orange Free State and many other areas. The Vaal River is a major source of water for irrigation (*see* VAAL-HARTZ IRRIGATION SCHEME). Among its tributaries are the Wilge, Rhenoster, Vals, Vet, Riet, Hartz, Mooi, Sand and Waterval rivers. The original name given by the Hottentots was Ki-Gariep, meaning Yellow River.

Vadoek. Cloth used in old-fashioned farmhouses for miscellaneous wiping-up.

Valanculos. Small harbour in Mozambique, near Inhambane.

Valley of a Thousand Hills. Valley between Durban and Pietermaritzburg noted for its magnificent vistas, especially from Botha's Hill and Drummond.

Valley of Desolation. Spectacular valley near Graaff-Reinet, an extreme example of erosion, and largely visited by tourists.

Valspan. Non-White settlement near Warrenton, Cape Province. Population: 4,610, including 324 Coloured and 4,286 Bantu.

Vanadium. Metal used in steel industry. Extensive titaniferous iron ore deposits in the Transvaal and Natal contain vanadium pentoxide. Recently a plant was erected at Witbank to treat ore mined near Middelburg for the production of fused pentoxide for export. Vanadium is also mined in South-West Africa at Aukas and Abenab and in Zambia.

Van Blokland, Jonkheer Gerard Theodoor Beelaerts. Transvaal diplomat, born 1843; descended from an old Dutch noble family. His father, F. A. W. Beelaerts van Blokland, was one of the early friends of the Voortrekkers. Van Blokland Jnr. became a lawyer and a member of a committee for collecting funds to help the Boers in the South African Republic. He met the delegates who came to London to revise the Pretoria Convention in 1883, and assisted them as legal adviser. In return he was appointed Minister for the South African Republic to Germany, France and Portugal from 1884 onwards, and held this post unpaid until the end of his life. In 1887 he became Government Commissioner in Europe on the Board of the Netherlands South Africa Railway Company. He died in 1897.

Van Bruggen, Jochem. Afrikaans novelist, born on September 29, 1881, in Groede, Holland. His family came to South Africa and settled in Johannesburg in 1892. After being educated at the Pretoria Gymnasium School, he served in the South African War and for a while was a teacher. He took up writing, producing poetry, dramas and novels. His most famous work is *Ampie*, a study of a Poor White; he also attained considerable success with other books. He died on February 22, 1957.

Van de Graaff, Cornelis Jacob. Governor of the Cape, born in Holland. He arrived with his family in 1785, in succession to Van Plettenberg (q.v.). Despite his military reputation Van de Graaff proved extravagant and tactless, which was particularly inappropriate in view of the financial difficulties prevailing. Complaints became numerous, he was recalled in 1791 and

but for his friendship with the Stadholder would have been dismissed. He is chiefly remembered because, in his honour and in that of his wife, Reinet, a new district and village in the east of the Colony was in 1785 called Graaff-Reinet (q.v.).

Vandeleur, General Sir John Ormsby. British soldier. Born in England, 1763, of Dutch ancestry. He joined the British Army in 1781 and served in Flanders before reaching the Cape in 1791. Some years later he was transferred to India, held a command in the cavalry at Waterloo, and became a general in 1838. He died in 1849.

Van Den Bos, Dr. Willem Hendrik. South African astronomer. Born at Rotterdam, Holland, September 25, 1895, he secured his doctorate at Leyden in 1925 and went straight to the Union Observatory, Johannesburg. In 1927 was appointed Chief Assistant and in 1941 Union Astronomer, a post he held until his retirement. One of the world's leading authorities on double stars, he was President of the Commission appointed for their study by the International Astronomical Union.

Van Den Heever, Christian Maurits. Afrikaans novelist, poet and linguist, born at Norvals Pont, Cape Province, in 1902. He went to school in Bloemfontein and Utrecht, Holland. For a while he was a teacher, then entered the Civil Service, and served in the editorial department of the *Landbouweekblad* and *Die Volksblad* (q.v.) in Bloemfontein. After taking his degree in Holland, he became a lecturer in Nederlands and Afrikaans at Grey University College, Bloemfontein. He then became Professor of Afrikaans at the University of the Witwatersrand. His literary work included some of the best novels written in Afrikaans, notably *Somer*, also poems and the standard biography of General J. B. M. Hertzog. He died in 1957.

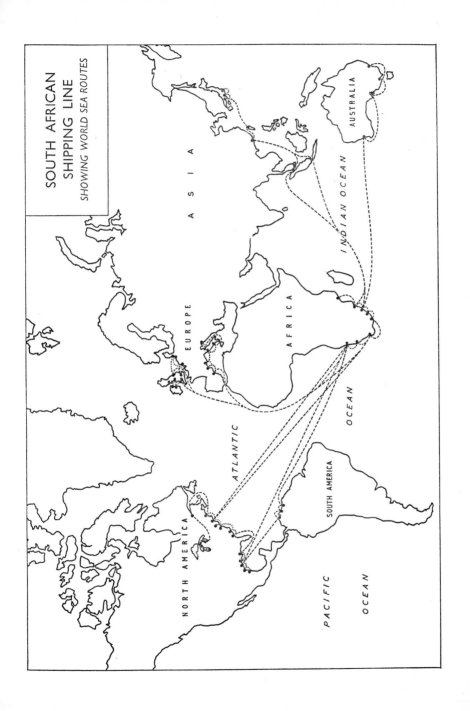

SOUTH AFRICAN
SHIPPING LINE
SHOWING WORLD SEA ROUTES

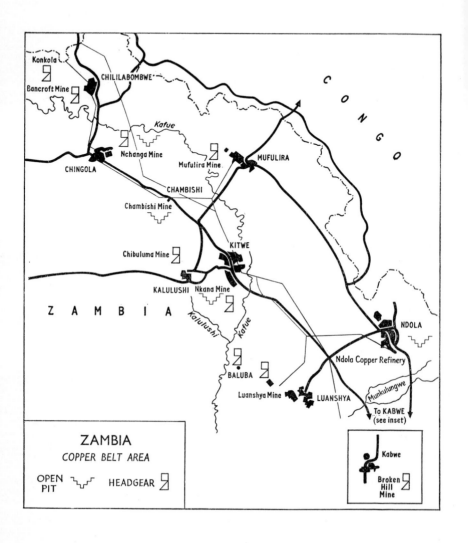

Konkola

Bancroft Mine

CHILILABOMBWE

Katue

Nchanga Mine

CHINGOLA

Mufulira Mine

MUFULIRA

CHAMBISHI

Chambishi Mine

KITWE

Chibuluma Mine

KALULUSHI Nkana Mine

Z A M B I A

Kalulushi *Katue*

BALUBA

Luanshya Mine LUANSHYA

NDOLA

Ndola Copper Refinery

Munkulungwe

To KABWE
(see inset)

C O N G O

ZAMBIA

COPPER BELT AREA

OPEN
PIT

HEADGEAR

Kabwe

Broken
Hill
Mine

Van der Bijl, Dr. Hendrik Johannes.
South African engineer, inventor and industrialist, born in Pretoria on November 23, 1887. After being educated at Stellenbosch, where he specialised in science, he went to Germany in 1909 and gained his doctorate of philosophy at the University of Leipzig by research on ionised liquids. In 1912 he became lecturer in physics at the Technical University in Dresden, proceeding in 1913 to the United States as Research Physicist for the American Telephone and Telegraph Company and the Western Electric Company. During his stay in America he was partly responsible for the installation of the first trans-continental telephone across the U.S.A. from the Atlantic to the Pacific. He did work of great importance on the thermionic valve, on which he wrote the standard textbook. In 1920, on the invitation of the Union Government to become Technical Adviser on Industrial Development, he returned to South Africa. His first task was to organise the Electricity Supply Commission, of which he became Chairman. He was entrusted with the organisation of the S.A. Iron and Steel Industrial Corporation (Iscor) (q.v.) and was its Chairman for many years. During World War II he was Director-General of War Supplies. He did much original research and wrote extensively on scientific subjects. He died on December 2, 1948.

Vanderbijlpark. Town on the Vaal River, near Vereeniging, named after the late Dr. H. J. van der Bijl (q.v.). It came into existence in 1942, primarily for the purpose of housing a duplicate of the Iscor steel plant in Pretoria. Designed on ambitious lines and on a unified plan, it grew rapidly. Population: 70,000, including 42,000 Whites and 27,000 Bantu. It has large metal and other subsidiary industries.

Van der Hoff, Reverend Dirk. Pioneer Dutch Reformed minister in

the Transvaal, born in Dordrecht, Holland, in 1814. He studied at the University of Leyden and was ordained in 1840. Making the acquaintance of Professor Lauts, the early friend of the Boers, he was persuaded to emigrate to the South African Republic. He arrived in 1853 at Potchefstroom, later became the first minister in Pretoria, invented its original name, Pretoria-Philadelphia, designed the Republican flag and did much to establish the new state. He died in 1881.

Van der Hum. Liqueur made of naartjies (tangerines) and originating at the Cape. It is now sold not only throughout South Africa but in England and on the Continent.

Vanderkemp, Doctor Johannes Theodorus. Missionary. Born in Rotterdam, Holland, in 1747, he began his career in the Army as a lieutenant of the Dragoons, but took his discharge in 1780. Moving to England he suffered a severe family loss and underwent a religious conversion which resulted, in 1799, in his being sent to the Cape as a worker for the London Missionary Society. Failing to establish himself in the Xosa country, he settled near Port Elizabeth, and set up a station named Bethelsdorp. As a matter of religious principle he married a Hottentot woman. He died in 1812.

Van der Kloof. Site of major dam in Orange River Scheme (q.v.). Situated between Petrusville and Luckhoff, Orange Free State. A wall 270 feet high will control water for 70,000 acres.

Van der Post, Colonel Laurens. South African author. Born in the Orange Free State in 1906, he became a journalist and gradually took to literature. His first novel, *In a Province*, appeared in 1934, but real fame did not come to him till after World War II. He served in Abyssinia, the Middle East and the Far East, where he was taken prisoner by the Japanese. *Venture to the Interior*, published in 1952, became an international best-seller. It was followed by *Flamingo Feather*. Working for the British Colonial Office in Bechuanaland and elsewhere, he gathered material which was embodied in *The Lost World of the Kalahari* issued in 1958.

Van der Riet, Frederick John Werendly. Judge of the Eastern Districts Court, born in Swellendam, 1868. He was educated at Stellenbosch, began a career in the Civil Service of Cape Colony, but was admitted to the Bar in 1894. From 1897 to 1899 he practised in the Transvaal, then returned to Grahamstown, where he lived many years. He was elected to Parliament in 1912 and was made a judge in 1923. He died in 1929.

Van der Ross, Dr. Richard Ernest. Cape Coloured leader and educationalist. Born at Cape Town November 17, 1921, he qualified as a teacher at the University of Cape Town and joined the staff of Battswood Training College there. He visited America in 1947 on a Carnegie Foundation Scholarship and secured his Doctorate in Philosophy in 1952. He has written extensively on the problems of his race.

Van Der Spuy, Johannes Petrus. South African cabinet minister and diplomat. Born at Reitz, Orange Free State on November 24, 1912 and educated at the Universities of Stellenbosch and the Orange Free State. Became a lecturer at the Pretoria Technical College and at the Goudstadse Onderwys Kollege. Sat in Parliament from 1961 to 1967, when he became Ambassador to Austria. He joined the Cabinet as Minister of Education, Arts and Sciences in 1969.

Van der Stel, Simon (more correctly spelt **Symon**). First Governor of the Cape of Good Hope. Son of Commander Adriaen van der Stel, a prominent official of the Dutch East India Company, and of Maria Lievens, who was partly of Malay origin. Born in Mauritius on October 14, 1639, he was in 1679 made Commander at the Cape, where he soon displayed an interest in the country unequalled by any of his predecessors. This showed itself in the founding of the town of Stellenbosch in 1680, in the opening of the Drakenstein district in 1684, in prospecting for copper in Namaqualand in 1685, in the vigorous help given to the Huguenot settlers who arrived in 1688, in his attempt to colonise Natal, in his encouragement of tree-planting, of the wine industry and of schools, and in many other ways. In appreciation of his work the Dutch East India Company promoted him to the rank of Governor in 1691. To this title was added in 1692 that of Extraordinary Counsellor of India. Van der Stel found time to develop his beautiful estate of Constantia, where he retired in 1699 upon handing over the Governorship to his son, Willem Adriaan (q.v.). He died there in June 1712.

Van der Stel, Willem Adriaan (more correctly **Adriaen**). Governor of the Cape of Good Hope, eldest son of Simon van der Stel (q.v.). Born in Amsterdam in 1664, and at the age of 15 accompanied his father to the Cape. His first post there was as cashier for the Dutch East India Co. He succeeded his father as Governor in 1699. His taste for farming was given free rein and he set up a magnificent estate at Vergelegen, near the Hottentots-Holland. The scale of his operations and his personality gave rise to complaints, which culminated in a petition sent by a group of 63 burghers to Holland in 1705. Van der Stel handled the situation badly and imprisoned Adam Tas and several other leaders. He was recalled to Holland for an inquiry. Despite his lengthy written defence, the verdict went against him—Vergelegen was confiscated and sold and he was dismissed from the service of the Company. He died in Amsterdam in 1723.

Van der Walt, Tjaart. Boer commandant on the Eastern Cape frontier, born in 1749. He distinguished himself as a daring leader in the incessant fighting against the Hottentot and other marauders, particularly during the campaign of 1802, when he was elected Commandant-General. He was killed in action on August 8, 1802.

Van Deventer, Lieutenant-General Sir Louis Jacob. South African soldier, born in the O.F.S. in 1877. He fought in the South African War, and as a commandant, second-in-command under General J. C. Smuts, took a prominent part in his famous raid into Cape Colony. Later he joined the Union Defence Force and was Commander-in-Chief during the East African Campaign from 1917 to 1919. He died on August 27, 1922.

Van Diggelen, Hendrik Cornelis Tromp. South African physical culture pioneer. Born in Dewetsdorp, Orange Free State in 1886. He originally qualified as a mining engineer in Germany, but made his name as a professional strong man, wrestler and ultimately teacher of physical culture. He also wrote extensively on the subject. Died January 9, 1967.

Van Eck, Dr. Hendrik Johannes. South African engineer and industrialist. Born near Kimberley on April 27, 1902, he studied at Stellenbosch as well as in Germany, at Leipzig and Charlottenburg (Berlin), specialising in chemical engineering. He joined the South African Iron and Steel Industrial Corporation (Iscor), becoming Works Manager. Upon the establishment in 1940 of the Industrial Development Corporation (q.v.) he was one of its original executives, and he succeeded Dr. H. J. van der Bijl (q.v.) as chairman. Under him the

I.D.C. attained great success and substantial prosperity.

Van Essche, Maurice. South African artist. Born in Antwerp, Belgium, October 4, 1906, and studied in Paris under Henri Matisse. Sent by the Belgium Government to the Congo to paint studies of the tribes there in 1939, he later exhibited widely in Europe. In 1943 he came to South Africa as lecturer in Fine Arts at the Witwatersrand Technical College and in 1946 moved to Cape Town. In 1952 was appointed Senior Lecturer in Fine Art at the Michaelis School of the University of Cape Town. Since then he has exhibited regularly at the Biennale Exhibition, Venice, and at other important overseas shows.

Van Hunks. Legendary Cape character whose smoking match with the Devil produced the 'Tablecloth' overhanging Table Mountain when the south-east wind blows.

Van Niekerk, Gerrit Jacobus. Boer freebooter, born about 1840 near Fauresmith, O.F.S. He settled near the present town of Christiana in the Transvaal, on the farm Kromellenboog, now the centre of a famous irrigation scheme. During the intertribal wars on the Western Transvaal frontier, between Mankoroane and Massouw, he brought a party of volunteers to support the latter. In gratitude Massouw gave him a piece of land, on which he set up the miniature republic of Stellaland (q.v.) in 1883. He later became Chief of Police in Pretoria and died in 1896.

Van Pittius, Jan Hendrik Frederik Eduard Rudolf Claudius Gey. Judge of the Supreme Court of the Transvaal, born in Ventersdorp, Transvaal, in 1879. He was educated in Pretoria and took his doctorate in law at Leyden, Holland, in 1906. After being called to the Bar in Britain, he began practice in Pretoria in 1907 and was soon recognised as a learned lawyer. In 1926 he was appointed to the Bench. He died five years later.

Van Reenen. Village near Klip River, Natal. Population: 240, including 100 Whites.

Van Reenen, Jacobus. Early Cape political leader, born in 1727. He became a farmer and in 1778 took the lead in the despatch of a deputation to Holland on behalf of the 'Kaapse Patriote,' who demanded self-government for the settlers. As a man of wealth and a former burgher counsellor, he was asked to accompany the deputation in 1779 to Amsterdam. They received little satisfaction there, but had at least taken a first step towards self-determination.

Van Reenen, Willem. Early Cape explorer. First heard of in 1791 when he led a party of four who aimed at surpassing the record of Hendrik Hop (q.v.) made 29 years earlier. They crossed the Orange River and penetrated into what is now South-West Africa, somewhere in the vicinity of Walvis Bay.

Van Rees, Catharina Felicia. Writer of the 'Volkslied' (q.v.) of the South African Republic. Born in Holland, she gained the friendship of President T. F. Burgers (q.v.) when he was a student there. She met him again in 1875 on his later visit, when she was moved to write the song, which at the time of the South African War was translated into many languages. She died at Velp near Arnhem on April 1, 1915, aged 83.

Van Rensburg, C. J. Janse. Pioneer in combating soil erosion in South Africa. Born in 1907; entered the Department of Agriculture and for years waged a lonely fight endeavouring to arouse interest in saving the soil, until the Government eventually recognised the importance of his warnings and set up a department devoted to this work. He died in 1958.

Van Rensburg, Dr. Johannes Frederik Janse. South African political leader. Born at Winburg, O.F.S., on September 24, 1898, he studied at Stellenbosch and Pretoria, becoming Law Adviser to the Government. Appointed Secretary of Justice in 1931, he became Administrator of the Orange Free State in 1936. Visiting Europe in that year he was attracted in Germany by the Nazi Party and resigned his post. In 1941 he became Commandant-General of the Ossewabrandwag (q.v.), but later retired to go farming. Died 1966.

Van Rensburg, Niklaas. Boer prophet and visionary, born near Ottosdal in the Transvaal in 1862. He attracted attention at an early age through his gifts as a seer. During several native campaigns and in the South African War, he fought as a burgher. His success in foretelling moves by the opposing forces gained him the confidence of distinguished Boer leaders such as De Wet. After the return of peace he settled on his farm near Lichtenburg, where he continued to make forecasts. These gained special significance during the political crisis attending the outbreak of World War I, and he played a considerable part in the preliminaries of the 1914 rebellion. He died in 1926.

Vanrhynsdorp. Town in the North-Western Cape Province, on road to Namaqualand. It takes its name from the Hon. P. B. van Rhyn, on whose farm the place was sited in 1887. Apart from serving the needs of important irrigation settlements on the Olifants River, the town draws prosperity from the recently-developed deposits of monazite (radio-active mineral) at Knersvlakte. Population: 2,129, including 777 Whites.

Van Riebeeck, Johan (Jan). First Dutch Commander of the Cape of Good Hope and founder of colonisation in South Africa. Born in April 1618 in Culemborg, Holland, of a good family. He served in one of the ships that took off the castaways from the *Haarlem*, wrecked in Table Bay in 1649. His comment on the report submitted by the two leaders of the castaways, Leendert Janssen and Nicholas Proot, displayed such sense and logic that he was selected by the Dutch East India Company as commander of the proposed trading outpost on Table Bay. On December 24, 1651, he sailed for the Cape, arriving at Table Bay on April 6, 1652. There he constructed the first fort, planted vegetables and erected a hospital. After many difficulties he managed to create a successful settlement, but he did not regard this appointment as a permanency, and petitioned repeatedly for a transfer. This was not granted until he had been at the Cape for 10 years. He died on January 18, 1677.

Van Riebeeck Society. Organisation established in Cape Town in 1918, under the chairmanship of the late Rt. Hon. John X. Merriman, 'for the publication of South African Historical Documents.' Since then it has published a volume of important material almost every year, including reprints of rare books. These are supplied to members at reduced prices. To coincide with the 300th anniversary of the landing of Jan Van Riebeeck at Table Bay, the Society undertook the issue of the first fully annotated reprint and English translation of his diary.

Van Ryneveld, General Sir Pierre. South African airman and soldier. Born in the Orange Free State on May 2, 1891, and educated at Grey College, Bloemfontein, and University of London. Entering the newly established Union Defence Force, he studied at the Imperial Staff College in England and in World War I served in France and the Middle East, first with the Royal North Lancashire Regiment and, from April 1915, with the Royal Flying Corps. Famed for the historic flight from London to Cape Town via

Cairo in 1920, accompanied by Sir C. J. Quinton Brand (q.v.). (*See also* AVIATION.) Became Director of Air Services for South Africa in 1920, Commandant of the South African Military College in 1929, Chairman of the Civil Air Board in 1931. During World War II he was Chief of the General Staff under General Smuts (q.v.). He retired in May 1949.

Van Ryneveld's Pass Dam. Large irrigation works on the Sundays River (q.v.) overlooking Graaff-Reinet. Begun in July 1920 and completed about three years later, they included a wall 1,160 feet long and 106 feet high above the river bed (141 feet above lowest foundation). The original capacity of the dam has been much reduced by silting and the irrigable area cut from 20,000 acres to 7,000, mostly under fruit and lucerne. The main settlement is at Kendrew, 18 miles distant.

Van Ryneveld, Willem Stephanus. Early agricultural expert and lawyer, born in Cape Colony in 1765. He joined the service of the Dutch East India Company and was President of the Court of Justice from 1809 to 1812. He was a friend of Lady Anne Barnard (q.v.), who drew his portrait. In 1804 he produced the first book on the improvement of cattle to be issued in South Africa.

Vanstadensrus. Village near Wepener, Orange Free State. Population: 480, including 136 Whites.

Van Wouw, Anton. South African sculptor, born near Utrecht in Holland in 1862. He intended to become a teacher, but his outstanding gifts as an artist soon indicated his true career. He studied sculpture in Holland and Italy before following his parents to the Transvaal in 1889. In Pretoria he could find no work as an artist and first served in a gunsmith's shop, but presently began drawing advertisements and modelling decorations in plaster. The decision of 'Sammy'

Marks (q.v.) to erect a monument to President Kruger gave him his chance, and after many delays it was placed in Church Square, Pretoria. During the South African War he worked in Holland on the Kruger statue, and was inspired to do many other beautiful and moving bronzes, which were to make him famous, notably 'Kruger in Exile' and 'Bad News.' He also did outstanding work on native subjects. A number of statues of famous South Africans, including those of J. H. Hofmeyr in Cape Town and of General Louis Botha, preserve his memory. He died in Johannesburg in 1945.

Van Wyksdorp. Village near Ladismith, Cape Province. Established in 1904. Population: 600, including 480 Whites.

Vanwyksvlei. Irrigation settlement in the North-Western Cape Province, near Carnarvon, noted for its production of wheat. Named after a local farmer. Founded 1882. Population: 1,460, including 322 Whites.

Van Zyl, Major Gideon Brand. First South African-born Governor-General. Born in Cape Town in 1873, he qualified as an attorney, served in World War I and in 1916 was elected to the Cape Provincial Council. A strong supporter of General J. C. Smuts (q.v.), he was appointed Deputy-Speaker in 1934 and Administrator of the Cape Province in 1942. From 1945 to 1950 he was Governor-General. Died in 1956.

Van Zyl, Hendrik Stephanus. Judge-President of the Cape, born near Clanwilliam, Cape, in 1876. He went to school at the age of 13, studied at Stellenbosch and joined the Cape Civil Service in 1897. After showing interest in politics he went to Cambridge, where he became President of the Cambridge Union, despite his pro-Boer views. He was admitted to the Bar in 1903, became Adviser of the National Convention in 1908 and

judge of the Cape Provincial Division in 1920. In 1935 he was made Judge-President. He died in 1955.

Van Zyl, Jacobus Wilhelmus. Judge of the Cape Supreme Court. Born at Cape Town on December 22, 1909, and educated at Rondebosch Boys' High School and University of Stellenbosch. Admitted to the Bar in 1933, he was appointed to the Bench in 1950. In 1950 he was appointed Chairman of the Press Commission (q.v.).

Vardon, Frank. Elephant hunter. In 1845 he accompanied William Cotton Oswell (q.v.) and gained a place in scientific history by his earliest report to scientists on the Tsetse Fly (q.v.).

Vastrap. Popular country dance, originating from the Hottentots. The name means 'to tread firmly.'

Vatjie. A small barrel used on trek for drinking-water and usually slung under the ox-wagon.

Veld (Dutch Field). A term loosely applied by early settlers to flat open country in Southern and Central Africa (often wrongly spelt 'Veldt'). Also used in a geographical sense, as in Bushveld (q.v.), Highveld (in the Southern Transvaal, above a height of 4,000 feet), Middelveld, between 2,000 and 4,000 feet, and Lowveld, below 2,000 feet (especially in the Transvaal and Swaziland). In the Cape Province are found the Roggeveld (literally Ryeveld) in the Fraserburg and Sutherland Districts of the north-west; Nieuwveld near Beaufort West; Bokkeveld (literally Buck-veld) in the Western Karroo, divided into the Warm and Cold Bokkeveld; Trekveld, north of Calvinia; Winterveld, between Victoria West and Hanover; Middelveld, near Hope Town; Kaapenveld, south of Prieska; Panneveld, noted for its saltpans, near Kenhardt and in Gordonia; Hardeveld, on the west coast in South Namaqualand; Richterveld (q.v.), near the Orange River mouth ;

Koudeveld (Cold Veld), near Graaff-Reinet; Noorsveld (Harsh Veld), near Jansenville; and Suurveld, formerly spelt Zuurveld (q.v.), near Grahamstown; also the Achterveld, near Victoria West. In South West Africa are the Hukweveld (q.v.) and Kaokoveld (q.v.).

Velddrif. Fishing centre near mouth of Berg River, Cape Province. Population: 4,000, including 1,900 Whites. Original settlement known as Laaiplek (literally 'Loading Place').

Veld Rat. *See* OTOMYS.

Veldsingers. A literary movement started in South Africa about 1910 to encourage local poetry, particularly in English. It attracted several dozen members, and secured the influential support, amongst others, of Olive Schreiner, who wrote an introduction to a *Veldsingers Verse*, published in 1912. So little of the work was of literary quality that the movement gradually died.

Veld Sores. Skin eruptions forming shallow ulcers and occurring both in animals and human beings. They are of microbic origin, aggravated if not caused by dirt. Antibiotics are today an effective cure.

Veld Trust. *See* NATIONAL VELD TRUST.

Velskoen (wrongly spelt **Veldskoen**). Shoes made of soft hide and noted for their comfort. They were originally manufactured by the Hottentots and copied by the early settlers. The making of velskoens was an industry of some importance until the rise of modern shoe manufacture in the Union.

Velskoen

Venda. *See* BAVENDA.

Ventersburg. Town in the Northern Orange Free State, founded in 1864 and named after B. G. Venter, the original farm owner. Farming centre. The Sand River Convention (q.v.) was signed near there in 1852. Population: 3,560, including 1,500 Whites.

Ventersdorp. Town in the Western Transvaal, on the Schoonspruit, founded in 1887 and named after J. H. Venter, who owned the original farm. Diamond diggings formerly operated in the neighbourhood, but latterly industries have developed, including several factories and a lime works. During the South African War the town was of strategic importance and the scene of a meeting between President M. T. Steyn and General Christiaan de Wet. During his visit in 1903 Joseph Chamberlain met General Delarey there. Population: 4,414, including 1,566 Whites.

Venterskroon. Village on the Vaal River in the Potchefstroom district. Named after the original farm owner. Farming centre.

Venterspost. Mining centre in the Western Transvaal, named after the large Venterspost Gold Mine, opened up in 1932. Population: 20,000, including 4,500 Whites.

Venterstad. Village near the Orange River, not far from Aliwal North. Founded 1882, and named Ventersburg after the farmer on whose ground it was established. To avoid confusion with another Ventersburg in the O.F.S. it was given its present name. Noted for wool and cattle production. Population: 2,300, including 600 Whites.

Vereeniging. Town in the Southern Transvaal on the Vaal River. Founded in 1892 and named after the original owners, the 'Suid Afrikaanse en Oranje Vrijstaatse Kolen en Mineralen Myn Vereeniging' (South African and

Orange Free State Coal and Mineral Mining Association). The name has no reference to attempts at political union between the South African Republic and O.F.S. Beginning as a colliery centre, sponsored by Samuel Marks (q.v.), the town soon gained importance from its situation on the Transvaal frontier. The completion of the railway to the Cape further stimulated its growth. Vereeniging acquired world prominence at the end of the South African War, during May 1902, when the peace negotiations took place there, though the actual Treaty of Vereeniging was signed in the house of Mr. George Heys in Pretoria. In the new century the town developed as a coal, milling, tile manufacturing and general farming centre, the last particularly helped by Samuel Marks' great Maccauvlei Estate near by. The establishment of the large power station of the Victoria Falls and Transvaal Power Co. in 1909 was followed in 1913 by the opening of the first full-scale steel works in South Africa, the Union Steel Corporation (q.v.). This marked the beginning of Vereeniging as a centre of heavy industry, and led to the opening of Stewart and Lloyd's pipe works and many other plants. Today Vereeniging is one of the largest manufacturing centres in South Africa. The Vaal River near by, besides supplying the needs of the Rand, has been developed as a pleasure resort. Population: 88,700, including 28,000 Whites.

Vergunning. Literally a grant. Right granted under the Gold Law of the South African Republic, by which the holder of a farm which had been proclaimed a goldfield was entitled to make over, to whomever he wished, a certain number of claims. These carried certain privileges.

Verkeerdevlei. Village near Brandfort, Orange Free State. Population: 550, including 200 Whites. The name means 'Wrong Vlei.'

Verkleurmannetjie. Popular name for Chameleon (q.v.), literally 'Little Man who changes Colour.'

Verkramptes. Expression in Afrikaans, introduced in 1967 by Professor W. J. de Klerk of Potchefstroom University, and first used in speech at Warmbath, Transvaal, to describe an unduly rigid and narrow-minded clique. Derived from the German *Verkrampft*. The word immediately acquired nation-wide popularity in English and Afrikaans. *See* VERLIGTES.

Verligtes. Opposite of Verkramptes (q.v.). Literally 'enlightened ones' in Afrikaans.

Verlorenvlei. Shallow lake near Clanwilliam, Cape Province, 11 miles long and about a mile wide.

Vermiculite. Flaky mineral used for insulation, etc. Large deposits of vermiculite are being exploited in the Eastern Transvaal. The quality of the material is good, and most of the production is exported. Other deposits in the Pietersburg and Zoutpansberg districts are exploited sporadically. The quality varies from an exfoliation rate of 1:12 times to 1:30 times.

Verneuk Pan. Large salt pan in the north-west of the Cape Province, so called because of the mirages which mislead (verneuk) the traveller. It measures approximately 12 miles by 26 miles. It was chosen in 1929 by Sir Malcolm Campbell for his attempt on the world land speed record in his famous car, the 'Bluebird.' He reached 254 miles per hour on it, but broke the record later at Daytona Beach in the United States.

Versfeld, Robert Loftus Owen. South African rugby player and administrator, born in Cape Town, 1862. He attended Green Point Grammar School and qualified as an attorney, practising in the Eastern Cape Province. Moving to Pretoria in 1890, he played rugby for Hamiltons and the

Transvaal. Henceforth he was a dominant figure in the game and, after his retirement from play in 1897, in its administration. He died on May 4, 1932. In his honour the principal rugby field in Pretoria is named the Loftus Versfeld Ground.

Verster, Lieutenant General Jacobus Pieter. Chief of the South African Air Force. Born at Boksburg, Transvaal on May 22, 1919 and educated at Pretoria University. He joined the S.A.A.F. in 1938 as a pilot, served in Bomber Command in World War II, being twice shot down and then taken prisoner. Appointed Chief of the Air Force on December 1, 1967.

Verulam. Sugar milling centre near Inanda, Natal north coast. Population: 2,626, including 257 Whites.

Vervet Monkey or Blue Ape (*Cercopithecus pygerythrus*). Known to the Zulus and Amaxosa as Inkau, to the Swazis as Ingobiyana and Basutos as Inkalatshana. Found mainly in the east, from Swellendam to the Transvaal, favouring forests and bush in the vicinity of water. Timid but cunning, it runs in troops and is a menace to crops of all kinds. In addition it feeds on bulbs, roots, seeds and birds' eggs, thus indirectly doing a great deal of harm. Natural enemies are snakes, leopards and the larger birds of prey, who contribute towards keeping the numbers down to a reasonable level.

Verwoerd, Dr. Hendrik Frensch. Prime Minister of the Republic of South Africa. Born in Holland on September 8, 1901, he came to South Africa as a small child, receiving his education at Wynberg Boys' High School, Milton High School, Bulawayo, and Stellenbosch University. After further work in Germany, Holland and the United States he received the appointment of Professor of Applied Psychology at Stellenbosch in 1927, changing to the Chair of Sociology and Social Work in 1933. In 1936 organ-

ised National Conference at Kimberley on Poor White problem. Upon the founding of the National newspaper *Die Transvaler* in 1937 he became editor, a post he held till the victory of his party in 1948 led to his appointment as senator. He was Minister of Bantu Affairs from 1950 to 1958, when he succeeded the late J. G. Strijdom as Prime Minister. In 1960 he entertained Mr. Harold Macmillan, the British Prime Minister, as his guest during his visit to South Africa. In the same year an attempt was made on his life and in 1961 he attended the Premiers' Conference in London that led to South Africa's withdrawal from the Commonwealth. Assassinated in Parliament by a temporary messenger, Demetrios Tsafenas, on September 6, 1966.

Verwoerdburg (formerly Lyttelton). Town near Pretoria, named after the Honble. Alfred Lyttelton, Colonial Secretary at the time of its foundation (1906). It became well known as an Air Force training centre and camp in World War II. Population 26,650, including 19,000 Whites.

Victoria (Natal). *See* TONGAAT.

Victoria Cross. Since the establishment of the V.C. in 1856, 119 V.C.s have been won in Southern Africa, 21 of them by South Africans. The first occasion was in the Battle of Draaibosch in the Cape Native War of 1877, when it was awarded to Major Moore. During World War I, 13 V.C.s were won by South Africans, namely: Capt. A. W. Beauchamp-Proctor, R.A.F.; Capt. W. A. Bloomfield, S.A. Mounted Brigade; Sgt. F. C. Booth, Rhodesia Native Regiment; Pvt. W. F. Faulds, S.A. Infantry; Lt. R. V. Gorle, Royal Field Artillery; Col. H. Greenwood, Yorkshire Light Infantry; Capt. P. H. Hansen, Lincolnshire Regiment; Capt. R. F. J. Hayward, Wiltshire Regiment; Lance-Corporal Hewett, S.A. Infantry; Capt. A. M. Lascelles, Durham Light Infantry; Capt. O. A. Reid,

Liverpool Regiment; Col. J. Sherwood-Kelly, Royal Inniskilling Fusiliers; Col. R. A. West, Tank Corps. In World War II, V.C.s were awarded to Squadron-Leader J. R. Nettleton, S.A.A.F. (1942); Sgt. Q. Smythe, Royal Natal Carbineers (1942); Lt. G. R. Norton, Kaffrarian Rifles (1944); Lt. Edwin Swales, S.A.A.F. (1945) (posthumously).

Victoria East. Division of the Eastern Province of the Cape, established in 1847, its main centre being Alice (q.v.).

Victoria Falls. Largest, though not highest, waterfall in Africa, situated on the Zambesi River, 1,635 miles from Cape Town. Although it has been claimed that the early Boer hunters saw the Falls, there is no definite evidence of the fact, and the honour still goes to Dr. David Livingstone, who sighted them on November 16, 1855. The Bantu name is Mosioatunya, meaning 'The Smoke that Thunders.' The Zambesi above the Falls is approximately a mile wide and plunges into a series of zigzagging gorges, which extend for many miles. In every respect the Victoria Falls are larger than their great American rival, the Niagara, their height being 347 feet as against 158 feet for Niagara, while the width is 1,900 yards as against about 800 for Niagara Falls. The Victoria Falls are still completely unspoilt, the natural beauty having been carefully preserved. The main divisions of the Falls are: the Devil's Cataract (also known as Leaping Waters), the Main Falls, the Rainbow Falls and the Eastern Cataract. A large hotel has been built by the Rhodesia Railways. The whole area is a national park. A certain amount of power is used for local purposes but the scheme for supplying the Witwatersrand has never been carried out. On the initiative of Cecil John Rhodes, the railway bridge was carried over the Victoria Falls within reach of the spray. Since its completion in 1904, the place has been in direct touch with the outer world.

Victoria West. Town in the Karroo, founded in 1844 and named after Queen Victoria. Large wool centre. Population: 4,060, including 1,100 Whites.

Vierfontein. Village and site of large Escom power station near Viljoenskroon, O.F.S. Population: 4,590, including 1,179 Whites.

Vierkleur: 1. The flag of the old South African Republic, comprising red, white, blue and green stripes. The three former colours ran horizontally and the last vertically.
2. Flag of Orange Free State adopted in 1856, with red, white and blue canton in top left-hand corner against alternate horizontal stripes, three orange and four white.

Viervoet. The name of a hill in the Orange Free State, where a British force commanded by Major H. D. Warden was defeated by the Basuto under Moshesh (q.v.) on June 20, 1851.

Vigiti Magna. Legendary city of the African empire of Monomotapa (q.v.), which early travellers believed to exist in the centre of the continent. Van Riebeeck actually sent an expedition to find the city in 1660.

Vila Cabral. Town in Northern Mozambique, east of Lake Nyasa, centre of settlement in healthy Highland country, 4,000 feet above sea-level.

Vila de João Belo (formerly known as **Chai-Chai**—'**Kill-Kill**'). Town in Mozambique, near the mouth of the Limpopo River, which is navigable for more than 30 miles inland from there. As the capital of the Gaza district, it is bounded by large areas of intensely developed tropical farms, mostly operated by Africans. A light railway inland was built from there in 1895.

Vilakazi, Dr. Benedict (1906–1948). Zulu poet and philologist. Born of a Protestant family in Natal, he was converted to Catholicism. Educated at Mariannhill (q.v.), he came largely under the influence of Father Bernhard Huss (q.v.). He qualified as a teacher and in 1930 was appointed lecturer in Zulu in the Department of Bantu Studies, University of the Witwatersrand, the first of such appointments in the country. A fine writer of Zulu and English, he collaborated with Dr. C. M. Doke in compiling the new Zulu Dictionary and was the author of several books. He died when 42 years old.

Vila Luiza. *See* MARRACUENE.

Viljoen, General Ben. Born in Cape Colony in 1868. He settled in the Transvaal as a youth, served as a policeman in Krugersdorp and helped in 1896 to bring in the Jameson Raiders. In the South African War he repeatedly distinguished himself by dashing exploits, helping to capture the famous gun 'Lady Roberts,' waging a guerrilla campaign in the Transvaal and escaping from British imprisonment. Ultimately he was captured and sent to St. Helena, where he wrote his reminiscences. After the war he settled with a number of his followers in Mexico, and died in the U.S.A. in 1917.

Viljoen, Jan. Boer pioneer and hunter, born in the Eastern Province of the Cape in 1822. He fought in the Battle of Boomplaats (q.v.) in 1848 and later settled near the present town of Zeerust in the Transvaal. He undertook many journeys into the far interior, claiming to have discovered the Victoria Falls ahead of Livingstone. Although this has never been proved, he certainly penetrated far inland and had a remarkable hunting record. He died in 1904.

Viljoen, Dr. Willem Jacobus. Educationist and pioneer of the Afri-kaans language. Born in Richmond, Cape Colony, in 1869, he was educated in South Africa, at the University of Leyden and at Strasbourg, where he was responsible for an early thesis on the origin of the Afrikaans language. In 1894 he was appointed Professor of Modern Languages at Victoria College, now the University of Stellenbosch, and remained there until 1910. He was one of the principal personalities of the Afrikaanse Taalbond from 1897 onwards, and helped to simplify the spelling of Dutch in South Africa. Together with Hubertus Elffers he edited an English-Dutch and Dutch-English dictionary. In 1910 he became Director of Education for the Orange Free State, followed by a similar appointment at the Cape in 1918, when he was also made Vice-Chancellor of the University of South Africa. The next year he became Chairman of the Native Education Commission. He died in 1929.

Viljoensdrift. Town on the Vaal River, on the Orange Free State side, facing Vereeniging and noted for its collieries. It began in 1857, through the opening there of a ferry by J. H. Viljoen across the shallow 'drift.' When, in 1895, President Kruger closed the drifts against merchandise going through to the Rand, thereby bringing Britain and the South African Republic to the verge of war, Viljoensdrift was greatly in the news. It saw fighting in the South African War. Population: 5,000, including 1,500 Whites.

Viljoenskroon. Town in the Northern Orange Free State, in the heart of the maize-producing area. Named after the original owner of the farm. Population: 5,000, including 1,500 Whites.

Villagers. Second oldest rugby football club in South Africa, after Hamiltons (q.v.) Founded in Cape Town in 1876, with J. P. Cloete as captain. It is still flourishing.

Villiers. Village in the Northern Orange Free State, on the Vaal River, named after the original farm owner, De Villiers; founded in 1907. Farming and irrigation centre. Population: 2,800, including 1,000 Whites.

Villiersdorp. Town in the Western Cape Province. Founded in 1841 and named after a farmer who built the first church. The most important local institution is the De Villiers Graaff High School, founded in 1907 by Sir David de Villiers Graaff, who contributed £50,000 towards its funds. The town is also noted for its fruit and wine trade, and for its scenery. Population: 1,800, including 1,100 Whites.

Vines. *See* WINE.

Vingerpol ('Finger Shrub'). Common South African name for *Euphorbia truncata*. So called because of its likeness to a human hand. Grows in the Karroo and is used for stockfeed.

Vink. Afrikaans name for Weaver (q.v.).

Vintcent, Sir Joseph. Judge of the High Court of Southern Rhodesia. Born at Mossel Bay in 1861 and educated at Diocesan College, Charterhouse and Cambridge. He was called to the Bar in 1885, became Crown Prosecutor in British Bechuanaland and in 1894 first judge of the High Court of Matabeleland. He was promoted to judge of the High Court of Southern Rhodesia in 1898, and held this post until his death in 1914.

Vioolsdrift. Ford on the lower reaches of the Orange River. The origin of the name, which means Violin's Drift, is obscure.

Vipya. Plateau in Northern Malawi, centre of large forestry scheme.

Virginia. Town on the Orange Free State goldfields. Figured in the fighting in the Boer War, but at that time was scarcely a hamlet. Owing to the development of several large goldmines near by it is growing fast and has a population of 48,300, including 14,000 Whites.

Visvanger. Afrikaans name for Kingfisher (q.v.).

Vlei Muis. *See* OTOMYS.

Voetgangers. *See* LOCUSTS.

Voetsak. South African expletive to chase away a dog. Reputed to be an abbreviation for 'Voort se ek' (Away, I say). It is claimed that dogs in other countries will also react to it.

Volk (Het). Party in the Transvaal under the Crown Colony régime, established in January 1905, its leaders including General Louis Botha, General Schalk Burger, General J. C. Smuts, General Delarey and others. Establishing an alliance with the Johannesburg Responsible Government Association, it came into power in 1907, under the new constitution. When the Union was formed in 1910 it was merged in the South African Party (q.v.). The name 'Het Volk' is Dutch for 'The Nation.'

Volksblad, Die. Afrikaans evening paper issued in Bloemfontein, established on March 26, 1915, in continuation of *Het Westen* of Potchefstroom. It is a strong supporter of the National Party. An earlier journal of the same name, *Het Volksblad*, was issued in Cape Town during 1849, and another one from 1856 to 1886.

Volkskas. Commercial bank founded by Joseph Jacobus Bosman and a small group of Afrikaans-speaking South Africans in Pretoria on February 1, 1935. It now has a nation-wide system of branches and ranks as the third largest bank in the Republic.

Volkslied: 1. National Anthem of the South African Republic, words by the Dutch writer Catharina Felicia van Rees (q.v.), with music by Richard Hol. Written and composed in 1875. It commences 'Kent Gij dat Volk van Heldenmoed.'

2. National Anthem of the Orange Free State Republic. Words by H. A. L. Hamelberg (q.v.), with music by M. F. G. Nicolai (q.v.). Written and composed in 1865. Begins: 'Hef Burgers, 't Lied des Vryheid aan.'

Volksraad. Literally 'Council of the Nation.' Name of the legislature of the former Boer Republics, still used in Afrikaans to describe the House of Assembly. The first Volksraad was set up by the Voortrekkers on December 2, 1836, soon after they had crossed the Orange River. It consisted of seven men, who also sat as a Court of Justice. On June 6, 1837, a further Volksraad was elected at Winburg. After the crossing of the Drakensberg, the emigrants set up the Republic of Natalia, where in March, 1839, another Volksraad, consisting of 24 members, was established. In 1840 the first Transvaal burghers set up a Volksraad at Potchefstroom. Others were established at Rustenburg, Lydenburg and elsewhere. The powers of the Volksraad were defined in the Transvaal under the Constitution of 1857, and in the Orange Free State under that of 1854. Various amendments were made and in 1889 the Second Volksraad, with limited powers, was established to satisfy the demands of the Uitlanders (q.v.). Before the outbreak of the South African War each of the two Transvaal Volksraads numbered 27 members, while that of the Orange Free State, which had only a single legislature, numbered 60.

Volksrust. Town in the Eastern Transvaal, near the Natal border, established in 1885, and so called because the Boer people (Volk) had rested on the original farm, named Llanwarne, after the Battle of Majuba (q.v.) in 1881. The town was the scene of an important conference between Lord Loch and President Kruger, held in a railway coach parked half-way across the frontier. Today Volksrust is a dairying centre with a general agricultural background. The town is often jocularly referred to as 'Vonderful Volksrust,' because of many stories about record cabbages, etc., grown there. Population: 10,000, including 4,300 Whites.

Volkstem, Die. Afrikaans daily newspaper published in Pretoria, established as *De Volkstem* and issued in Nederlands in August 1873. During the 1880's it appeared both in English and Nederlands for a short while. Publication was interrupted during the South African War. In 1949 it was transferred to Johannesburg and it ceased publication in 1950.

Volschenck, Jan Ernst Abraham. South African artist, born in 1853 near Riversdale, of Dutch descent. After studying in Europe, he made his home near the place of his birth, and specialised in landscapes, which strikingly conveyed the hazy air of the Cape mountains. He died in 1936.

Von François. *See* FRANÇOIS.

Von Lettow-Vorbeck, General Paul Emil. German soldier. Born at Saarlouis in the Saar on March 20, 1870, he joined the Artillery, serving in South-West Africa and the Cameroons. In June 1914 he was placed in charge of the German troops in German East Africa, with the rank of colonel. During the East African campaign in World War I his skill and resourcefulness became a byword, and the Allied forces completely failed to hold him down, even after General Smuts took over command of the forces in 1916. He ultimately crossed over into Mozambique in 1917 and remained undefeated until the armistice in 1918, only surrendering on November 13, when he heard of the capitulation of Germany. He visited South Africa in 1954 and received a great welcome from his former opponents. Died in 1964.

Von Trotha, General Lothar. Military commander in German South-West Africa. Born at Magdeburg, Germany, in 1848; became a professional soldier, and in 1894 was placed in command of the German forces in East Africa. Promoted to brigadier, he commanded a German detachment in the Boxer Rising in China in 1900. Was appointed Governor in South West Africa and commander of the troops during the Herero War in 1904, but aroused much criticism by his ruthlessness. He retired in 1906, was promoted to general and died at Bonn in 1920.

Von Veltheim, Curt (real name, **Ludwig Kurtze**). German adventurer, born in 1857 in the Hartz mountains. He began his career as a sailor, led an adventurous life in the East, Australia and South America, and arrived in Johannesburg in 1895. He approached several leading members of the Uitlander movement with schemes for kidnapping President Kruger. Wolf Joel (q.v.), one of the heads of the firm of Barnato Brothers, refused to have anything to do with his project. A quarrel developed, Von Veltheim drew a revolver and shot him dead. He was tried for murder and acquitted, but was deported by order of President Kruger. Some years later, Von Veltheim was again in trouble in England for attempting to blackmail S. B. Joel (q.v.). He was found guilty and given a long prison sentence. He made a fresh attempt to return to South Africa in 1930, but was recognised and deported. He died the same year.

Voorkamer. Literally a 'front room.' Name given to the drawing-room of old Cape Dutch houses.

Voorkis. Box on the front of an ox-wagon, literally 'front box.'

Voorloper. A person, usually a small African, who walks at the head of a team of oxen.

Voorkis

'**Voortrekker**'. A 50-foot ketch, built by Thesens of Knysna in 1967, participating in the 1968 Transatlantic Race, in which it came second, and first in handicap. *See* BRUCE T. DALLING.

Voortrekkerhoogte. Cantonments outside Pretoria, established under the name of Roberts Heights after Field-Marshal Lord Roberts (q.v.) at the close of the South African War. Occupied at first by the Imperial garrison, they became in 1913 the headquarters of the newly-founded Union Defence Force, and were renamed Voortrekkerhoogte in 1938, to coincide with the centenary of the Voortrekkers. The South African Military College and other establishments are also to be found there.

Voortrekker Monument. *See* PRETORIA.

Voortrekker Movement. Youth movement for young Afrikaners, launched in 1913, but formally established in Bloemfontein on September 30, 1931, mainly through the efforts of the late Dr. N. J. van der Merwe. It has sections for both boys and girls, and is run on lines resembling Scouts and Guides. *See* YOUTH MOVEMENTS.

Vorster, Balthazar Johannes. South African Prime Minister. Born in Jamestown, Cape Province, December 1915 and educated at Stellenbosch University. He strongly opposed South Africa's participation in World War II, for which reason he was interned. After qualifying as an attorney, he went to the Bar, practised at Johannesburg and entered Parliament. Appointed Minister of Justice in August 1961, he introduced the Sabotage Act and other measures against subversion. Succeeded Dr. H. F. Verwoerd (q.v.) as Premier in September 1966.

Vosburg. Village in the northern part of the Karroo, established in 1895, and named after the Vos family, which was well known there. In 1948, Vosburg attracted attention on account of alleged gold discoveries. The 'strike' was a set of cattle bones found in the veld, carrying in the teeth a gold-like substance. This was later found to be a form of tartar, but not before a number of optimists had tried to peg claims. Population: 800, including 200 Whites.

Vrede. Town in the Northern Orange Free State, founded in 1874, and so called because the committee charged with the survey put an end to its arguments by making peace (Vrede). After the evacuation of Bloemfontein in 1900 the town for a while was the seat of the fugitive Orange Free State republican government, and even issued an official newspaper, now very rare. Vrede was one of the earliest centres of revolt in the 1914 Rebellion (q.v.). Farming centre. Population: 7,300, including 2,300 Whites.

Vredefort. Town in the Northern Orange Free State. Founded in 1877 and so called because it brought peace (vrede) for many farmers, who previously had been complaining about the long journey to church in Kroonstad. It was a centre of gold prospecting long before the present O.F.S. mining began there. The nearby koppie is geologically important. Population: 2,780, including 780 Whites.

Vredefort Crater (also known as **Vredefort Mountain Land**). Remarkable geological formation in Northern Orange Free State near Vredefort, of disputed origin. A crater 30

miles long and 10 miles deep produced, according to some recent views, by an immense meteorite and later "plugged" by granite intrusion from below.

Vredenburg. Village in the Western Cape Province near Saldanha Bay, originally called 'Prosesfontein' or the Fountain of Lawsuits. Wheat-growing centre. Population: 3,500, including 1,500 Whites.

Vredendal. Village near Vanrhynsdorp, Cape Province. Population: 3,560, including 1,500 Whites.

Vryburg. Town in Botwsana, founded in 1882 as the capital of the Republic of Stellaland (q.v.). Trading centre and base for the Pioneer Column before their march into Mashonaland in 1890. The town was captured by the Boers in the South African War, when it saw a good deal of fighting. In 1915, after the Rebellion, General Christiaan de Wet (q.v.) was captured near by. Population: 19,600, including 5,500 Whites.

Vryheid. Town in the north of Natal, capital of the 'New Republic,' set up by a group of Boers in 1884 on land granted by the Zulu chieftain Dinizulu. When this was incorporated into the South African Republic in 1888, the rôle of Vryheid (Freedom) as a capital came to an end. It remained important as a farming centre and in the South African War saw much fighting. Because of its link with Zululand, the town, along with the district of Utrecht, was handed to Natal in 1903, after the return of peace. For a time it became a colliery centre, and attempts were made to start an iron industry. Population: 14,710, including 6,550 Whites.

Vulture (Aegypidae). Bird of prey, with bare head and neck and powerful hooked beak adapted to its work of tearing at carcases. Below the neck lies a soft ruff of feathers, on which the bird can rest its head. Its wings are magnificent. South Africa boasts six kinds of Vulture, of which the commonest in the south is the Cape Vulture or Kolbe's Griffon, with blue neck, brown back and darker wing-tips and tail. In the Transvaal and northward it is replaced by the smaller White-Backed Vulture. In the Kruger Park, but rarer and more aloof, is the hideous Black or Lappet-faced Vulture bearing folds of crimson flesh round its neck. In the same area lives the White-Headed Vulture. There are two smaller, rarer types, one, the Witkraai, with a white neck, the other, the Southern Hooded Vulture, with a brown ruff, white hood and pink face.

Vumba. Mountain range in the east of Rhodesia, rising over 5,000 feet. It is a popular health resort because of its beautiful scenery and cool air. It was visited by the Queen Mother and Princess Margaret in 1953.

Vundhla, Philip Q. Bantu leader. Born in Eastern Cape at the beginning of the century, he settled on the Rand and became active in trade unionism. Organised the Bantu mine workers' strike after World War II. A man of great influence, he was elected Chairman of the Advisory Board for the Soweto Townships of Johannesburg (q.v.). Becoming convinced of the uselessness of extreme measures, he began a policy of conciliation, with impressive results. In recent years has been active in the Moral Rearmament movement.

Vyebos (*Mesembrianthemum spinosum* L.). Low bush with wiry branches becoming spiny after flowering. Karroid areas in Cape Province.

Vygie. *See* SOUR-FIG.

W

Waders (sub-order Limicolae). A large group of long-legged, short-tailed birds of the sea-shore, with long, slender bills. All are strong fliers, many of them breeding in the Arctic. Of those that nest in South Africa the chicks are born ready to run, and covered with down. Waders from the far north are dull-coloured during their months in South Africa, but sometimes show traces of breeding colours. Among Waders can be classed Plovers, Lapwings, the large Oyster Catchers, Stilts, Stints, Sanderlings, Ruffs, Avocets, Sandpipers, Curlews, Turnstones and Phalaropes. *See under separate headings.*

Wadley, Dr. Trevor Lloyd. South African physicist and inventor. Born in 1920. Joined staff of Council for Scientific and Industrial Research and became head of its Telecommunications Research Institute. Among his major achievements was the development of the Tellurometer (q.v.), now in world-wide use, also the crystal-controlled variable frequency radio receiver and generator. This is built under C.S.I.R. licence in England, where over 10,000 sets, representing a value of £5,000,000, have been produced.

Wagenaar, Zacharias (more correctly Wagner). Born in Dresden, Germany, in 1614. Early commander of the Cape. Had served the Dutch East India Company for many years, and was already in poor health and growing old when he was appointed to succeed Jan van Riebeeck in 1662. Under his régime the building of the Castle in Cape Town was begun in 1665. He was transferred to Batavia in 1666. Upon his death in 1668 he left money to the poor of the Cape. He was also an artist of considerable ability.

Wages. Wages in the Republic of South Africa are governed by the Wage Act of 1937, administered by the Department of Labour, in conjunction with the Industrial Conciliation Act, adopted in the same year. It gave powers of compulsion to Wage Boards, whose determinations, based on official surveys and statistics, as well as on information placed before them, are binding on both employers and employees. Separate investigations have been carried out on a very large number of industries and various branches of commerce, there being special powers to restrict different scales to particular areas. Under the law, wage determinations are automatically suspended while the terms of the Industrial Conciliation Act are invoked. Under wartime legislation cost-of-living allowances were also introduced, many being subsequently embodied in permanent scales of wages. As part of the general movement towards improving the economic position of the Bantu, large numbers of employers have in recent years voluntarily raised the rates paid by them beyond the figures officially laid down.

Wag-'n-Bietjie (Wait-a-Bit). Name variously applied in different localities. Sometimes it refers to species of thorned Asparagus, more often to thorn trees, such as Haakdoring, near Queenstown to *Erythrina acanthocarpa* and in the Eastern Cape to *Zizyphus mucronata.*

Wagner, Dr. Percy Albert. Eminent South African geologist, born in Richmond, Cape Colony, in 1885, educated at the South African College, the School of Mines in Johannesburg, and overseas. He produced a standard work, *The Diamond Fields of Southern*

Africa, in 1913, and did much research for the Union Geological Survey. He died in 1929.

Wagon. *See* TREK WAGON.

Wagon-building. Formerly important industry in South Africa, producing a large number of different types, trek wagons, Cape carts, Scotch carts and many other varieties. The main centres of the industry were at Wellington (where one area had the name of Wagonmaker's Valley), Paarl, Oudtshoorn, King William's Town, Queenstown and Pietermaritzburg. Most wagon-builders used local timbers, particularly the hard woods, and showed a high degree of skill and ingenuity. With the advent of the motor car, wagon-building gradually declined, though certain firms became constructors of bus and truck bodies, and as such still survive.

Wagtail, Cape, or Kwikstertjie. Little bird of Pipit family (q.v.), very familiar both in gardens and on the sea-shore. It has a dipping flight and an up-and-down movement of its long tail. A more striking variety is the black-and-white Pied Wagtail of Natal and the Victoria Falls.

Wahlberg, Professor A. J. A. Swedish naturalist. He travelled through South Africa in the 1830's, particularly in the Eastern Province, and made extensive collections of butterflies and other insects. In 1855 he undertook a trek to Lake Ngami, accompanied by F. Green. He was killed in 1856 by an elephant while hunting in Matabeleland.

Wahlenbergia. *See* LOBELIA.

Wakkerstroom. Town in the South-Eastern Transvaal, established by President Martinus Wessel Pretorius, in whose honour it was called Martinus Wesselstroom, in 1859. Soon afterwards the simpler name, Wakkerstroom, was chosen (from the lively Umzinyati River). Fighting took place there in the South African War.

Deposits of oil shale (torbanite) have been exploited. Population: 2,663, including 500 Whites.

Walker Bay. Large bay on which Hermanus is situated. Named after early navigator, Captain Walker, R.N.

Walker, George. One of the alleged discoverers of the Witwatersrand Main Reef. Born in Wigan, Lancashire, in 1853, he came to South Africa as a young man and worked as a brick-layer. In 1886 he was employed by the Struben brothers at Wilgespruit and, according to tradition, found the Main Reef one Sunday in 1886, while walking on the farm Langlaagte. Walker never derived any appreciable financial benefit and was found living in poverty as an old man. He died as a pensioner of the Chamber of Mines at Krugersdorp on December 18, 1924.

Wallace, Edgar. English novelist and journalist, first editor of the *Rand Daily Mail.* Born in London, 1875, he grew up in great poverty, selling newspapers as a boy. In 1896 he joined the Army, was sent to the Cape and was stationed at Simonstown. He began writing imitations of Rudyard Kipling's poems, which were published in the *Cape Times* and appeared as *Writ in Barracks.* His first story to attract notice was *The Mission that Failed,* issued at the Cape in 1898. Leaving the Army, he became a Reuter correspondent and after the outbreak of the South African War served the *Daily News* (1900) and the *Daily Mail* (1901–1902) in the field. One of his famous 'scoops' was the exclusive news of the signing of the Peace of Vereeniging. From 1902 to 1903 he was editor of the *Rand Daily Mail.* He then returned to England and began writing the thrillers and detective stories which made him world-famous. He died in 1932.

Walmer. Town in the Eastern Cape Province, largely a residential area. Merged in Port Elizabeth on January 1, 1967. It was laid out in 1853 and named after one of the titles of the Duke of Wellington. Population: 28,000, including 11,000 Whites.

Walvis Bay (also **Walfisch Bay**). Seaport on the coast of South West Africa administered, as a matter of convenience, with that territory, though legally a part of the Cape Province. Known to the early Portuguese navigators as almost the only good natural harbour between Angola and Saldanha Bay, it was frequented by Dutch, English and American whalers in the 19th century and in 1876 occupied for the Cape Colony by the explorer W. C. Palgrave (q.v.). In 1884 Germany laid claim to the rest of South West Africa, and the following year it was decided to annex the bay. A magistrate and staff were stationed there, but hardly any development took place until World War I, although an arbitration, in 1912, carried out by King Alphonso of Spain, defined the boundaries of British and German territory. With the decision of the Union in 1914 to invade German South West Africa, Walvis Bay became an important strategic point and troops were landed there. From that time it rapidly overshadowed the nearby German port of Swakopmund, and is today the largest harbour in South West Africa. Meat-packing works were erected there in 1926 and the fishing industry rapidly developed. The construction of wharves brought a large increase in shipping. Today Walvis Bay has many industries and, despite its desert setting, is growing fast. Population: 19,500, including 8,000 Whites, 3,500 Coloureds and 8,000 Bantu.

Wanderers Club. Large sporting club in Johannesburg. One of the oldest on the Rand, it was established in 1887, in grounds officially known as 'Kruger Park,' adjoining the centre of the city. Removed in recent years to northern side, near Melrose. Has 11,000 members, a golf-course, cricket fields, tennis courts and large club-house.

Wankie. Colliery centre in Rhodesia, founded in 1903, at the railhead from the south to the Victoria Falls. The name is that of a former Bantu chief. Enormous coal deposits, first located in 1895 by A. Giese, led to the opening of the mine in 1900. The production today serves both Rhodesia and Zambia, and has reached over 4,000,000 tons a year. Population: 23,300, including 2,000 Whites.

Waratah. Passenger steamer of Lund's Blue Anchor Line, trading between Australia and Britain via South Africa, and the subject of the greatest maritime mystery connected with this country. On July 26, 1909, the *Waratah* (9,339 tons), with 211 souls on board—including 92 passengers—left Durban for East London. She never arrived and her fate still remains unknown.

Warblers (Sylviidae). A large family of plainly-dressed little birds, both sexes alike. Some are migrants from Europe, like the Garden and Willow Warblers, and others permanently live in South Africa, like the shy Babbling Reed-Warbler, with its glorious notes of song. The commonest at the Cape among bushes is the Cape Wren-Warbler, or Tinktinkie, a noisy and conspicuous little bird with spotted chest and long tail and many ringing notes.

Ward, Charles George. Transvaal judge, born near King William's Town in 1864. He was educated at Cambridge and was called to the Bar in 1890. After practising in Kimberley he moved in 1898 to Rhodesia, returned to the Transvaal after the signing of peace, and was appointed to the Transvaal Bench in 1910. He died in 1923.

Ward, Daniel. South African lawyer, born in Ireland in 1848. He was called to the Bar in 1881, and wrote a standard book on income tax and another on parliamentary elections. Coming in the course of his work to South Africa in 1894 he became Crown Prosecutor of British Bechuanaland. Thereafter he practised at the Cape, and became Government Law Adviser. He was strongly in favour of codifying South African law. In 1904 he became a judge in the Orange River Colony. He retired in 1923 and died in Cape Town in 1926.

Warden. Village in the Eastern Orange Free State, established in 1913, and named after Major Charles Warden, British resident of the Orange River Sovereignty, in 1848. Farming centre. Population: 3,650, including 1,232 Whites.

War, First World. *See* WORLD WAR I.

Warmbad. Village in South-West Africa, in the south, so called because of its warm springs. The Rhenish Mission Society started a station there in 1805, but it was not until 1890 that it became a White settlement. During the invasion of South-West Africa by the Union troops in 1914 an action was fought there. Farming centre. Population: 177, including 133 Whites.

Warmbaths. Health resort north of Pretoria in the Transvaal, called after the warm springs which attract thousands of visitors. Its virtues were known from Voortrekker times, but it was not until the 1880's that a township developed, named Hartingsburg after Professor Harting, a great friend of the Boer cause in Holland during the Majuba Campaign. The place became Warmbaths soon afterwards. Population: 6,975, including 2,550 Whites.

Warner Beach. Seaside resort on the Natal south coast, now part of the municipality of Kingsburgh (q.v.); 20 miles from Durban. Founded about 1910 and named after a land surveyor.

War of the Axe. Popular name for the Seventh Kaffir War, and so called by the Xosas because it was caused by the

arrest of a native accused of stealing an axe from a frontier store in Fort Beaufort. While he was being taken for trial in Grahamstown, a party of armed Xosas under their chief, Tola, attempted a rescue on March 16, 1846. The resultant costly war lasted for nearly two years and brought the extension of British authority over a considerable new area on the frontier. *See* SMITH, SIR HARRY.

Warren, General Sir Charles. British soldier. Born in Bangor, Wales, in 1840 and educated at Cheltenham College and Bridgnorth. He then trained at Sandhurst and Woolwich, before entering the Royal Engineers in 1857. His first post took him on a survey to Gibraltar, and after serving as an instructor he was posted to Palestine on archaeological work. In 1876 he was sent to the Cape to define the much disputed frontiers between the Griqualand West Diamond Fields and the O.F.S., about which he later wrote an amusing book called *On the Veld in the '70's*. During the Griqualand West Rebellion of 1878 he commanded the Diamond Fields Horse and fought against the Bechuanas. As Administrator and Commander-in-Chief of Griqualand West he led the Northern Border Expedition in 1879. Recalled overseas, he did work in the Middle East, but in 1884 was back in South Africa as major-general to occupy Bechuanaland ahead of the South African Republic. Entered English politics, and, after being Commissioner of the Metropolitan Police in London, held a post in Malaya. On the outbreak of the South African War he was made Lieutenant-General of the Fifth Division, South African Field Force. He became involved in disputes with the War Office, and was criticised for alleged excessive caution. His policy at Spion Kop was much disputed. After carrying on operations in the North-West Cape he returned to England in 1900. He died in 1927.

Warrenton. Village in the north of the Cape Province, named after General Sir Charles Warren, commander of the Bechuanaland expedition in 1885. Captured by the Boer forces in the South African War, and of considerable importance in preventing the relief of Mafeking, further north. Now chiefly noted as a dairy centre. Population: 10,800, including 2,800 Whites.

War, Second World. *See* WORLD WAR II.

Wartburg. German settlement near New Hanover, Natal. Population: 450, including 280 Whites.

Wart Hog (*Phacochaerus aethiopicus*). Wild animal found over a large part of Southern Africa north of the Orange River, including Natal, the Kruger National Park, Rhodesia, Bechuanaland and Mozambique. Unlike the Bush Pig (q.v.) it prefers comparatively thinly-grown areas, but also likes muddy ground. It is largely nocturnal in habit and lives in holes in the ground. Normally the Wart Hog grows to a height of 2 feet 6 inches. It takes its name from large growths between the tusks and below the eyes. Can be dangerous when hunted. The meat makes moderately good eating.

Washbank. Village near Dundee, Natal. Population: 2,374, including 89 Whites.

Washkansky, Louis. *See* HEART TRANSPLANTS.

Water Buck (*Cobus ellipsiprymnus*). Heavily-built antelope found in small herds in sub-tropical country such as Eastern Transvaal, Zululand and Rhodesia, and keeping within range of marshy ground and banks of rivers. A Waterbuck stands about 4 feet at the shoulder. It has great powers of survival and will defend itself in midstream with its long, twisted horns. A good climber and swimmer, with a noble carriage.

Water Court. Court of law established early in 20th century to deal with the numerous disputes over irrigation rights because the volume of litigation on this head threatened to hold up other legal business. The Cape Colony led the way to the establishment of Water Courts, which were regulated under the Irrigation Law of 1906, and were adopted in the Transvaal under its own Irrigation Act in 1908. The position for the whole Union was regularised under the Irrigation Act of 1930, which, with various amendments, is still the basic law. Water Courts comprise a judge and two assessors, who go on circuit hearing disputes falling within their purview. Altogether the country is divided into 22 Water Court districts. There are also Water Courts in Rhodesia.

Waterfalls. Township to the south of Salisbury, chiefly residential, established in 1948, with its own Town Management Board. There are a fair number of industries. The population is 3,000 Europeans, 2,600 Africans and 470 of other races.

Waterfiskaal. *See* SHRIKES.

Waterford. Village near Jansenville, Cape Province. Population: 420, including 140 Whites.

Waterkloof: 1. Suburb of Pretoria, and a fashionable residential area. **2.** Small village in the Orange Free State, near Philippolis, established by the Dutch Reformed Church and taken over by a Village Management Board in 1922. Farming centre. Population: 180, including 100 Whites.

Water Lily, Blue (*Nymphaea capensis*). Aquatic plant with floating leaves and thick rhizomes in mud. South African species has only blue or mauve flowers. Found rarely today in permanent vleis at low altitude in the Cape, from Piquetberg to Bredasdorp. Extinct in Cape Peninsula during last 30 years.

Watermeyer, Egidius Benedictus. South African writer and judge, born in Cape Town in 1824. He received his doctorate at Leyden, Holland, in 1843, then proceeded to London, where he worked under Samuel Warren, author of *Ten Thousand A Year*. Returning to South Africa in 1847, he began practising in Cape Town, and in 1855 became a judge. Noted for his learning and for his excellent literary style, he was one of the most popular figures in the Colony. He died at the early age of 43 years in 1867. His writings were published in book form.

Watermeyer, Ernest Frederick. Chief Justice of the Union of South Africa, born in 1880 at Graaff-Reinet. He was educated at Stellenbosch, Bath in England, Cambridge, and in 1905 began practising at the Cape. In 1920 he became Chairman of the special Income Tax Court and in 1922 a member of the bench of the Cape Provincial Division. Fifteen years later, in 1937, he was made Judge of Appeal and in 1943 Chief Justice. He died in 1958.

Watermeyer, John Philip Fairbairn. Judge of the High Court of Southern Rhodesia. Born in Cape Town in 1861 and educated at the South African College and Cambridge. He began practice in the Cape in 1885, became a judge of the High Court of Matabeleland in 1896 and judge of the High Court of Southern Rhodesia two years later. He died in 1914.

Waterpoort. Village in the Magato Mountains, Northern Transvaal, noted for its quarries, from which many important buildings in Pretoria and elsewhere have been constructed.

Waterston, Dr. Jane Elizabeth. Pioneer woman doctor of South Africa, born in 1845 in Inverness, Scotland. She reached the Cape in 1867 to join the staff of Lovedale as a teacher. Six years later she went to Britain to qualify first as a nurse and then as a doctor. Unable to secure her degree there, she took it in Brussels, though she later gained several qualifications in the land of her birth. She returned to Cape Town in 1883, the first woman doctor in the country, and built up a very large practice. Her charity and strong pro-British political views made her famous. She took a considerable part in the affairs of the medical profession, and did a great deal to relieve suffering during the South African War. She died in 1932.

Waterval Boven (also known as **Waterval Bo**). Railway camp in the Eastern Transvaal on the line to Lourenço Marques. Established during the construction of the railway about 1894, and called after the picturesque waterfall near by. During the South African War it was used by the Boers as a prisoner-of-war camp. The place formerly possessed the only rack-railway in South Africa, to overcome a very steep gradient, but through diverting the route this has become unnecessary. A monument commemorates the many deaths from fever during the railway construction. Population: 6,500, including 2,500 Whites.

Waterval Onder. Village in the Eastern Transvaal, near the Elands River waterfall, five miles from Waterval Boven (q.v.). Noted for its beautiful scenery; it is a trout-fishing resort. During the South African War President Kruger spent some time there, before finally leaving the Transvaal in August 1900.

Watsonias (Iridaceae). A group of hillside plants with grassy stems and leaves, most commonly found within the cloud belt of the Cape mountains. There are red, pink and orange varieties. They have sessile flowers, well-spaced and tubular, on long stems, the upper ones opening slowly. The pink *Watsonia densiflora* stands up well to Natal grass fires. *See* IRIS.

Watt, Sir Thomas. South African politician, born in Shawlands near Glasgow, Scotland, in 1857. He studied at Glasgow University and became a solicitor. In 1883 he reached Natal and settled in Dundee. After serving in the

South African War he was elected to the Natal Parliament and became Minister of Justice and Education, and then a member of the National Convention. After Union he became Minister of Posts and of Public Works. Served under Botha and Smuts until 1924 as Minister of Public Health, Interior and Railways. He died, aged 90, in 1947.

Wattle and Daub. Primitive form of construction, much used by early South African settlers, and based on the system used by many Africans in building their huts. A framework of poles is set up, between which saplings and branches are threaded. When this is sufficiently rigid the whole is covered with thick layers of mud or 'daub' (clay). Such huts have the advantage of being very quickly erected, but are liable to be infested by insects and to give way in heavy rain.

Wattle, Black. See ACACIA.

Wauchope, Major-General Andrew Gilbert. British soldier, born in 1846 at Niddrie Marischal in Scotland. He began his career in the Navy as a midshipman in 1860, securing his discharge two years later. He joined the Army and in 1865 received his first commission in the 42nd Regiment. After service in Cyprus (1878–1880), in Egypt and the Sudan, he was promoted to major-general and given command of the Highland Brigade on the outbreak of the South African War. Within a few weeks of his arrival he was killed at the head of his men at Magersfontein. Though buried on the battlefield, a monument to him was erected, by a curious misunderstanding, at Matjesfontein, hundreds of miles away.

Waveren. Name originally given to the Tulbagh district of the Cape, honouring a family named Oetgens van Waveren in Holland.

Waxbills (family Ploceidae). Small weaver family, well represented in South Africa, particularly in the Eastern Province, Natal and Transvaal. Male and female usually alike and brightly coloured. Nest sometimes on the ground, sometimes in trees, not suspended in colonies like other weavers. Varieties include Common Waxbill (Rooibekkie), the Black-cheeked, Blue-breasted, Orange-breasted, Ruddy, Swee, Violet-eared and Zebra Waxbill.

Wax Creeper. See SUCCULENTS.

Way, William Archer. South African poet and educationist. Born in Devonshire in 1869, he was educated at Christ's Hospital and at Oxford. At the age of 22 he came to Cape Colony and in 1891 became first Vice-Principal of Dale College in King William's Town, then Principal of Graaff-Reinet College (1897–1910) and lastly Principal of the Grey High School in Port Elizabeth. Though his main contribution was as a teacher, he was a writer of considerable merit, with a limited output. He died on February 9, 1928.

Wayfarers. Youth movement for Coloured girls. See also YOUTH MOVEMENTS.

Weavers (Ploceidae). Very large and interesting family, including Waxbills, Bishop Birds (qq.v.) and Widowbirds. Nests are usually suspended in colonies from branches or reeds. Stout little birds, male and female very different. The White-browed Weaver is abundant near Victoria Falls, and has a big, untidy nest, with opening each side. The Social Weaver builds in enormous communal nests, usually in camel-thorn tree of Griqualand West, Transvaal and South West Africa. The Scaly Weaver (name from black feathers on head and throat) is common in dry areas. The Buffalo Weaver is larger and black, flecked with white, often seen on the ground, half a dozen pairs building a communal stick nest. Common only in Transvaal. The yellow-chested Black-backed Weaver (or Bos-Musikant) builds a suspended nest in forest or dense bush. Eastern Province to Zululand. Unlike other weavers, this bird is not sociable. Spotted-backed Weaver (or Bontrug Vink) is abundant in colonies along the coastal belt of the Eastern Province to Natal, and in the Transvaal. The Cape Weaver (or Geelvink) is a common type at the Cape, like the Olive Weaver of the Eastern Province. The Spectacled or Bottle Weaver of the Eastern Province, Natal and the Transvaal has a black streak through its eye and builds an exceptionally beautiful nest, with a long funnel. The male of the Red-headed Weaver (north of Swaziland into Eastern Transvaal) is unusually handsome, its nest neat and strong, with a long spout. Equally

Social Weaver

striking is the male Southern Pink-billed Weaver (Quelea Finch), his black face halved with pink. Flocks invade areas of the Free State and Transvaal from their Karroo breeding places. *See* Birds.

Weenen. Village in Natal, one of the oldest in the province, founded in 1839 by the Voortrekkers; so named because of their weeping (*weenen*) after the massacre by the Zulus at Bloukrans (q.v.) and elsewhere. Farming and irrigation centre. Population: 3,668, including 487 Whites.

Weeskindertjies (Literally "Little Orphan Children" in Afrikaans). *See* Nemesia.

Weights and Measures (Cape). Cape measures, used in land surveying as an alternative to the English kind and unofficially in many branches of trade, were in use in Holland and over most of Central Europe at the time of Van Riebeeck's first settlement. Now superseded by the Metric System (q.v.).

LENGTH:
12 Cape inches = 1 Cape foot
12 Cape feet = 1 Cape rood
426 Cape roods = 1 English mile
(1,000 Cape feet = 1,033 English feet).

AREA:
144 Cape square feet = 1 Cape square rood
600 Cape square roods = 1 morgen
1 morgen = 2·11654 acres
1 square mile = 302·38 morgen.

CAPACITY:
4 schepels = 1 muid or sack (3 bushels).

See also Anker, Half-Aum *and* Leaguer.

Weinthal, Leo. South African journalist, born in Graaff-Reinet in 1865. He was associated with newspapers in early Johannesburg and Pretoria, editing the pro-Kruger English journal, *Press*, and serving as correspondent for *The Times*, *Daily Telegraph* and Reuter. He was an intimate friend of President Kruger. Settling in England after the South African War, he founded the *African World* in 1902. He published *The Story of the Cape to Cairo Rail and River Route* in five volumes in 1923 and he died in 1930.

Welch, Rev. Dr. Sidney Read.
Historian and Catholic priest. Born in
Cape Town on July 4, 1871, he attended the Marist Brothers College
there before proceeding to Rome,
where he was ordained on May 19,
1894, and given his Doctorate in
Divinity. Apart from his duties as a
priest in Cape Town, where he spent
almost his whole life, he became a
writer of note and for some years
edited the *Catholic Magazine*. With a
special grant from the Union Government he carried out historical research
in the Vatican archives on the early
history of South African exploration,
particularly on the Portuguese navigators. Further investigations in the
Portuguese archives at Lisbon yielded
a great amount of new material and
resulted in the publication of six books
on South and East African history,
covering the period from the 15th
century to 1806. The Portuguese
Government showed their appreciation by conferring special honours
upon him. He died on September 2,
1956.

Welensky, Sir Raphael (Roy).
Former Prime Minister of the Central
African Federation. Born in Salisbury
on January 20, 1907, he worked as an
engine driver and first came into prominence as a prize fighter and a trade
unionist, making his home at Broken
Hill. For twenty years, from 1933 to
1953, he was chairman of the Rhodesian Railway Workers' Union. Elected
to the Legislative Council of Northern
Rhodesia in 1938, he was promoted to
the Executive Council in 1946. After
the founding of the Central African
Federation he became Minister of
Transport in 1954 and in 1956 Prime
Minister of the Federation. Retired in
1963.

Welkom. Town on the Orange Free
State goldfields. Founded as recently
as 1947, it is already the second largest
centre in the province, on account of
the enormous development of the

neighbouring gold mines. It has been
laid out on scientific lines. Population: 124,000, including 34,000 Whites.

Wellington. Town in the Western
Cape Province, founded in 1840, and
named after the Duke of Wellington.
It has beautiful surroundings. Originally called Wagenmakers Vlei, it remained one of South Africa's chief
wagon-building centres until the coming of the motor car. It has always
been a centre for wine, wheat and
fruit and has important fruit drying
and preserving works. Pieter Retief and
General J. B. M. Hertzog were both
born there. In 1874 the Huguenot
Seminary (later the Huguenot University College (q.v.)) was established at
Wellington, the first institution of
higher learning for women in South
Africa. This has now become a training institution for social workers of the
Dutch Reformed Church. Population:
14,200, including 4,340 Whites.

Welverdiend: 1. Village near Potchefstroom, Transvaal. Population: 630,
including 480 Whites. Mining centre.
2. Diamond digging centre near
Lichtenburg, Transvaal. Population:
340, including 130 Whites.

Welwitsch, Friedrich Martin Josef.
Austrian botanist and explorer. Born
in Carinthia in 1807, he qualified as a
medical man at Vienna in 1836 and
then moved to Portugal, where in 1839
he was made Curator of the Botanical
Gardens at Coimbra and Lisbon. In
1853 he began his travels in Angola,
where he succeeded in making a very
fine botanical collection, and where in
1854 he met David Livingstone. These
journeys continued until 1860; three
years later Welwitsch settled in
London. One of his most remarkable
discoveries was the plant named after
him, *Welwitschia mirabilis* (q.v.). He
wrote extensively in Portuguese and
his herbarium is partly in the British
Museum and partly in Lisbon. He
died in 1872.

Welwitschia Mirabilis. Unique plant found in the semi-desert Namib region of the coast of South West Africa. Although long known to the local tribes, who used it as fuel and made stools from its woody stem, it became known to science only in 1858 when the traveller Friedrich Martin Josef Welwitsch first reported it in Europe. Adapted to survival in conditions where rainfall is under one inch yearly, it depends on a thick tap-root which penetrates to a depth of over 60 feet. The most striking features on the surface are two 6-foot, leathery, dull-

Welwitschia Mirabilis

green leaves, usually torn into numberless strips by the wind. The central stem is hollow, partly underground, and up to 3 inches thick. The Welwitschia belongs to the Gymnospermia family. Its seeds grow within a pointed cone like that of a pine tree, to which the plant has certain remarkable resemblances. In January every year a circle of cones forms around the crown. Male and female cones grow on separate plants, the male dark salmon in colour and the female greenish. By May the seeds ripen and are carried away by the wind, only those moistened by rain ever germinating. Protected by law, the Welwitschia has been cultivated successfully at Stellenbosch University and Montreal. The plant is believed to reach an age of several centuries.

Wendt, Theophil. South African musician, born in London in 1874, and educated in England and Germany. He came to Grahamstown at the age of 22 as music master for the Diocesan School for Girls and St. Andrew's College. He composed a special song for the Grahamstown Exhibition of 1898, and in 1899 returned to England. From 1900 to 1903 he was back in South Africa, then spent a year in Argentina, returning to London in 1904. There he established a reputation as a musician of ability, and in 1912 accompanied the Wheeler-Edwards Light Opera Company to South Africa as its conductor. Upon the establishment of the Cape Town Orchestra in 1914, he was appointed conductor, holding this position until his resignation in 1924, when he became Musical Director of the recently-established Johannesburg Broadcasting Studio. He resigned, again spending several years in England, but returned to South Africa shortly before his death in 1951.

Wenela. Abbreviation for Witwatersrand Native Labour Association (q.v.).

Wenning, Pieter. South African artist, born in Holland in 1874 and brought to South Africa at an early age for health reasons. He worked in De Bussy's bookshop in Johannesburg, but his urge was always to paint, and his outstanding gifts attracted the attention of D. C. Boonzaier (q.v.), who persuaded him in 1916 to settle at the Cape. Struggling with poverty and ill-health, he sold his pictures at very low prices. They were recognised even then to be entirely original in their style, though under Impressionist influence. He died in Pretoria in 1921, aged 47. Today his pictures, owing to their beauty and scarcity, fetch high prices.

Wepener. Town in the Eastern Orange Free State, named after Commandant Louw Wepener, who led the burghers in their assault on Thaba Bosigo (q.v.) in the Basuto War of 1865. The town was besieged by the Boers during April

1900, but relieved after 16 days. It is now important for its flour-milling, wheat production and general farming. Population: 4,150, including 1,200 Whites.

Wepener, Lourens Jacobus. Military leader in the Orange Free State Republic. Of Swedish descent, he was born on July 21, 1812, near Graaff-Reinet and settled on a farm between Aliwal North and Dordrecht. His military experience dated from the Native War of 1850–1851, soon after which he moved into the Orange Free State, where he spent the rest of his life. During the campaign against the Basutos he gained distinction for his gallantry and ability, and was chosen to lead the historic attack on the Basuto stronghold at Thaba Bosigo. On August 15, 1865, he was killed while leading a party of volunteers to the top. His body was recovered later.

Wernher, Sir Julius Charles. Mining magnate, born 1850 in Darmstadt, Germany, where his father was attached to the Grand-Ducal court. He entered a London bank as a learner, served in the Prussian cavalry in the Franco-German War of 1870–1871, and, like Alfred Beit (q.v.), took a post in Paris with Jules Porges (q.v.). Porges sent him in 1871 as his representative to Kimberley, where he was elected to the Mining Board and soon gained wealth and prominence. After the discovery of the Rand he extended his operations to the Transvaal. In 1888 he became one of the four original 'Life Governors' of De Beers Consolidated Mines. He settled in London as Porges' partner and, when the latter retired in 1889, continued operations under the name of Wernher, Beit & Co., the largest mining house in South Africa, if not in the world, controlling the Rand Mines group and other huge interests. Apart from occasional visits to South Africa, he spent the rest of his life in England. A noted art collector, he died in 1912,

leaving the largest South African fortune on record—over £11,000,000. *See also* CORNER HOUSE.

Werth, Albertus Johannes. Administrator of South-West Africa, born in Malmesbury in 1880. He was educated at Stellenbosch, and became one of the early supporters of the National Party under General Hertzog. In 1920 he was elected Member of Parliament for Kroonstad, for which he sat until 1926, when he became Administrator of South West Africa. This post he held until 1933. In 1938 he became Member of Parliament for George. He was particularly interested in industry and finance. Died in 1948.

Wesleyan Methodist Church of South Africa. Although individual Methodists were to be found among the British troops which occupied the Cape from 1795 onwards, it was not until 1816 that the first minister, the Rev. Barnabas Shaw, landed, with the purpose of serving them and of carrying on mission work. Large numbers of Methodists were among the 1820 settlers (q.v.), including, amongst others, the Rev. William Shaw, who soon gained great prominence in the Eastern Province. Grahamstown became one of the principal centres of Methodism, but the 'mother church' was erected in the village of Salem. Vigorous missionary activities were carried far inland, while important Methodist communities sprang up in Natal, the Orange Free State and the Transvaal. By 1883 the parent organisation in Britain decided that control through mission organisation was no longer desirable, and the first South African Conference took over all churches and missions south of the Vaal River. This relation with Britain continued until 1927, when a private Act gave the South African Conference jurisdiction over the Transvaal, Swaziland, Bechuanaland and Mozambique. The Methodist Church has set up a Chair of Divinity at Rhodes

University in Grahamstown, jointly with the Church of the Province of South Africa and the Congregationalist Church. A large number of schools, orphanages and other institutions are also maintained. Today there are about 3,038 churches and 3,800 'preaching places' in Southern Africa. Number of adherents (1963): 269,825 Whites, 11,903 Coloured, 1,313,129 Bantu.

Wessels, Cecilia (Mrs. E. E. Beecroft). South African singer. Born in the Orange Free State, daughter of Sir Cornelius Wessels, the Administrator, and educated in Bloemfontein and Cape Town. Studied music at the South African College of Music under Professor Bell and at the Royal Academy of Music, London. During her long career overseas as a singer, she performed under Sir Henry Wood, Sir Malcolm Sargent and many other famous conductors, and appeared in opera at Sadler's Wells, Bayreuth and Berlin, specialising in Wagner roles. She retired to Cape Town.

Wessels, Sir Johannes Wilhelmus. Chief Justice of the Union of South Africa, born in 1862 in Cape Town, and educated at the South African College and Cambridge. Admitted to the Cape Bar in 1886, he was recognised as an outstanding lawyer and, moving to the Transvaal, became leader of the Bar there. One of his most famous cases was the defence of the Jameson Raiders in 1896. In 1902 he was appointed to the Bench of the Transvaal Supreme Court, becoming Judge-President in 1920, Judge of Appeal in 1923 and Chief Justice in 1932. He died in Pretoria on September 6, 1936. He was one of the most learned South African lawyers and the author of the famous *History of Roman Dutch Law* and a standard work on the Law of Contract.

Wesselsbron. Village in the Orange Free State, laid out in 1920, and named after Commandant C. Wessels. Maize growing and general farming centre.

Population: 4,400, including 1,200 Whites.

Wesselton. Suburb of Kimberley, famed for the Wesselton Mine, discovered in 1890 on the farm Benauwdheidsfontein, which belonged to the Wessels family. It was later taken over by H. A. Ward, who worked it successfully for a number of years. After a dispute with De Beers Consolidated Mines, Ward, by order of court, was allowed to wash 5,000,000 loads of diamonds before the property passed to that company in 1896.

Western Province Rugby Club. The third oldest in South Africa, after Hamiltons and Villagers (qq.v.). Founded in 1877, and no longer in existence. Not to be confused with the Western Province Rugby Union, formed in 1883.

West London (now **Crawford**). Original name of township on Cape Flats, near Cape Town, so named in contrast to East London (q.v.).

West, Martin. Lieutenant-Governor of Natal and first civilian administrator of that colony. Born in England, the son of a civil servant in the Treasury, he studied at Balliol College, Oxford, before he joined the East India Company's service. He served in Bombay but had to retire on grounds of ill-health and became Resident Magistrate in Grahamstown. From this post he was in 1845 appointed Lieutenant-Governor of the recently annexed territory of Natal, still a dependency of the Cape. As such he was not very successful, and retired in 1849, dying the same year.

Westminster. Settlement of British ex-soldiers, set up in the Orange Free State by the Duke of Westminster after the South African War. Many of the original colonists had been his tenants. It has attained prosperity, particularly through dairying, horse-breeding, and vegetable growing.

West Nicholson. Township in the south of Rhodesia. It was founded in 1898 and takes its name from a gold mine which had developed from the earlier Nicholson Reef. Although now mainly a farming and prospecting centre, West Nicholson has frequently come into the news as the southernmost terminal of the Rhodesia Railways, whence it is expected that a line will be continued to join the South African Railways at Messina (q.v.) about 100 miles away. The famous Liebig Ranch (q.v.) is near by.

Westonaria. Town named after the Western Areas gold mine on the far west Rand. Population: 35,000, including 9,500 Whites. It was established in 1943.

Westrup, William. South African novelist, born in England in 1881. He came to South Africa during the Boer War and later settled in Johannesburg, becoming secretary of important mining groups. In 1908 he began writing short stories and novels. One of his most popular creations was the prospector known as 'Old McBein.' He died in 1943.

Westville. Residential township near Durban, Natal. Population: 20,550, including 12,400 Whites.

Whale. Ocean-dwelling mammal, occurring on a large scale in the waters surrounding South Africa and hunted since the days of Van Riebeeck. Today whaling is conducted mainly from large factory ships, attended by smaller catcher vessels, but a certain amount of shore-based whaling is still carried on, particularly from Natal. The killing of whales is regulated by international agreement. The harpoon has now been replaced by the whale gun, which was invented towards the end of the last century by the Norwegian, Sven Foyn. South Africa has several whaling companies, and has made a substantial contribution to world oil products. A collection of whale skeletons is on exhibition in the grounds of the Cape Town Museum.

Four types are hunted in the South African seas:

Whalebone or *Right Whales.* These are toothless but furnished with two plates of dark, horny 'baleen,' which strain the water from the myriads of minute crustaceans on which they live. To this group belong the Southern Black Right Whale (*Balaena australis*), 70 feet, and the Hump-backed Whale (*Megaptera longimana*), 50 feet, both hunted for their blubber and whalebone.

Sperm Whales. These have permanent teeth in their lower jaws only and feed at great depths on squids, octopuses, etc. They are rich in blubber, spermaceti oil (from their skulls) and ambergris (from their intestines). Of this group the 60-foot Cachalot (*Physeter macrocephalus*) is the best known.

Beaked Whales. These have two pairs of large teeth and an elongated skull. Among this type are Cuvier's Whale (30 feet) and the rare Layard's Beaked Whale (20 feet), which has enormous teeth protruding from the lower jaw.

Killer or *Grampus* (20 feet). This is the most voracious of all. Equipped with numerous small teeth, and hunting in small parties, it devours whales, seals and fishes of all sorts. To the same group belongs the playful porpoise (q.v.).

Whale-Bird (*Heteroprion desolatus*). Small petrel found off the coasts of South Africa (*see* PETREL), sometimes very plentifully. Blue-grey with dark bands across back and tip of tail, the bill boat-shaped and containing a 'strainer.' The tail ends in a wedge. Can be recognised by a less steady flight than that of the larger petrels.

Wheat. For climatic reasons South Africa, despite efforts at growing wheat going back to the beginning of settlement, has had limited production which has always had to be supplemented by imports. Cultivation is concentrated in the Western Cape Province, the Eastern Orange Free State (*see* CONQUERED TERRITORY) and restricted parts of other provinces. Production in 1966-67 was 5,614,000 bags (about 9,000,000 bushels.) For the first time South Africa produced enough for her own requirements in 1968. Hard wheat is grown in Lesotho. *See* AGRICULTURE.

Wheatear, Capped (*Oenanthe pileata*). Small bird of the Robin family, fairly common near Cape Town, and abundant in grain country near Malmesbury. Known in Little Namaqualand as Koggelaar, a comedian, from its antics and song in the breeding season, when it appears to imitate every other bird. Nests on the ground, often in a deserted burrow.

Whelan, Archbishop William Patrick. Catholic prelate. Born at Wakkerstroom, Transvaal, April 29, 1907, and educated at St. Aidan's College, Grahamstown, Natal University College, and in Dublin. After editing the *Catholic Times of South Africa* from 1934 to 1938, he was made Bishop of Johannesburg in 1951 and in 1954 Archbishop of Bloemfontein. In February 1964 his statement, as Director of the Press Division of the South African Bishops' Conference, on the theory and practice of Apartheid (q.v.) and the positive achievements of the Government in power, drew widespread attention and official opposition from other members of the local Church hierarchy.

White-Eye (Zosteropidae). A family of greenish-yellow birds with a circle of white feathers round their eyes, found in most districts of South Africa. Like Tits in their habits, feeding on insects, nectar and fruit, and probably more useful than harmful to farmers.

White-eyes go about in small parties, in and out of trees, cheeping excitedly.

White, Field-Marshal Sir George Stuart. British soldier, born in 1835 in County Antrim, Ireland. He studied at Sandhurst and joined the Army in 1853. After service in the Indian Mutiny in 1857 he spent many years in the East, winning the V.C. in Afghanistan in 1879, and rising to Commander-in-Chief in India in 1889, a post he held until 1897 when he was made Quartermaster-General in London. On the outbreak of the South African War he became Commander-in-Chief in Natal, where he was responsible for the successful defence of Ladysmith. In 1900 he became Governor of Gibraltar, and in 1903 Field-Marshal. He died in 1912.

Whitehead, Sir Edgar Cuthbert Fremantle. Prime Minister of Southern Rhodesia. Born in Berlin, the son of a British diplomat, on February 8, 1905, he studied at Oxford and reached Rhodesia in 1928. Entering politics in 1939, he served as Acting High Commissioner in London from 1945 to 1946. In the latter year he became Minister of Finance, Posts and Telegraphs and held office till 1953. He was minister representing the Federation in Washington, U.S.A., in 1957 was Prime Minister from 1958 to 1962.

White River. Village in the Eastern Transvaal, founded about 1904 as a centre for an irrigation settlement set up by the government of Lord Milner for demobilised British soldiers. Since then it has become one of the most important citrus-growing centres in the country and also handles a large traffic of visitors to the Kruger National Park. Sub-tropical crops of various kinds are grown there. Population: 1,825, including 1,800 Whites.

Whites. Grade of ostrich feather; the long, pure white wing feathers from the male.

Whites. Centre of cement industry near Ventersburg, Orange Free State. Population: 1,538, including 313 Whites.

Whittlesea. Village in the Eastern Cape Province named after the birthplace in England of Governor Sir Harry Smith (q.v.). It was founded in 1849 and became an important defence outpost in the native war of 1850–1853. Some of the old fortifications are still in existence. Farming centre. Population: 650, including 130 Whites.

Wichgraf, Fritz. German artist. Born in Potsdam May 9, 1853. He was a pupil of the well-known artists, Albert Bauer of Weimar and H. Von Angeli of Vienna. Came to the Transvaal 1896 and painted many celebrities, including Dr. W. Schulz, Captain Carl von Brandis (1897) and Paul Kruger (1899), whose Government requested it for display at the Paris Exhibition in 1900. His best-known picture is 'The Boer Deputation,' now in Pretoria.

Widow-Bird (family Ploceidae). *See* SAKABULA and WEAVERS.

Widow-Finch, Black (*Hypochera funerea*). Small bird found in parts of the Eastern Province, through the Transkei and Natal to the Eastern Transvaal. Male is black only in mating season.

Wielewaal. Afrikaans name for Black-headed Oriole (q.v.).

Wiener, Ludwig. Business man and legislator. Born in Berlin in 1838, he spent his younger years in the United States, came back to Europe and reached South Africa as a lad of 17. At first he traded in the Tulbagh district, where he was in business until 1870, and then joined a firm of merchants in Cape Town, of which he became the senior partner. In 1883 he was elected a Member of Parliament for Cape Town City and sat in the House for many years. He did a great deal for the promotion of commerce and maintained the doctrine of free trade. He is chiefly remembered on account of the holiday which he introduced to the Cape, known jocularly as St. Wiener's Day. He died in 1921.

Wigeon, Cape. *See* DUCK.

Wild Almond (*Brabeium stellatifolium*). Also known as Kaffir Chestnut. Although poisonous when raw, the fruit can be used as cocoa after being roasted.

Wild Cat. *See* CAT, AFRICAN WILD.

Wild Coast. Name given to the section of the Pondoland coast between the mouth of the River Kei and the border of Natal. It is noted for its camping sites and unspoiled bathing beaches.

Wildebeest or **Gnu** (a Hottentot word). Large antelope notable for its speed and tenacity. It is about 4 feet high and dark brown in colour. The Black Wildebeest (*Connochaetes gnu*) is a curious-looking animal, his face like that of an ox, with fierce up-turned antelope horns and a long white tail, like that of a horse. He performs strange antics in flight. The Blue Wildebeest (*Connochaetes taurinus*) is a heavier animal, with short, thick horns, no neck and a more stolid nature. Both are found plentifully in the Game Reserves.

Wildeperd (literally **Wild Horse**). South African fish. *See* ZEBRA (fish).

Wilderness. Seaside resort on the southern coast of the Cape Province, between Cape Town and Port Elizabeth. It lies near the mouth of the Kaaiman's River and is noted for its beautiful scenery. Originally a fishing settlement, it has become a fashionable holiday and golfing resort. The lagoon there is known as 'The Ebb and Flow.' Population: 350, including 220 Whites.

Willemsmit. Township in the Karroo adjoining Philipstown (q.v.).

Williams, Alpheus Fuller. Son of Gardner F. Williams (q.v.). Mining engineer and General Manager of De Beers. He was born in San Francisco in

1874 and studied at the University of California. Shortly before the South African War he came to Kimberley to join the staff of De Beers under his father, whom he succeeded as General Manager in 1905. He retired in 1932 and became the founder of a large civil engineering concern. He wrote a standard book, *The Genesis of the Diamond*, and *Some Dreams Come True*. He died in 1953.

Williams, Frederick Condé. Judge of the Natal Supreme Court, born in England in 1844. He began his career as a newspaper man and was admitted to the Bar in 1873. After a spell in Jamaica, he was appointed to the Supreme Court of Natal in 1881 and remained there until 1884. He died about 1902.

Williams, Gardner Fuller. American mining engineer, and first General Manager of De Beers Consolidated Mines. He was born in 1842 in California, where his father was already established as an engineer at the time of the 1849 gold rush. He studied at the Mining College in Freiberg in Germany, and in the United States. After gaining widespread experience in California, Nevada, Mexico and elsewhere, he came to South Africa in 1884 to take up an appointment on the Barberton Goldfields, but, making the acquaintance of Cecil John Rhodes, he went to Kimberley, where he became the trusted adviser of the empire builder. As such he played an important part in the early development of the Rand and of Rhodesia, where he helped to draft the Mining Laws. Upon the establishment of De Beers Consolidated Mines in 1888, he was appointed General Manager and was responsible for the evolution of much of the modern technique of mining and recovering stones. During the South African War his rôle in the defence of Kimberley was an important one, and in 1902 he produced a standard work, *The Diamond Mines of South Africa*,

on the history and geology of the Fields. He retired in 1905 and spent most of his later years in the United States, where he died in 1922.

Williams, Sir Robert. Engineer and railway pioneer. Born in Aberdeen in 1860, son of William Williams, he studied engineering in his native city, and reached Kimberley in 1881. There he became closely associated with Cecil John Rhodes, who sent him north. With Rhodes he established the Zambesi Exploring Company Ltd. and Tanganyika Concessions Ltd., becoming Managing Director of both. Through his efforts the railway was carried through Northern Rhodesia to the Congo border in 1909. Gaining the confidence of the Belgian and Portuguese authorities he fathered the Rhodesia–Katanga Junction Railway and Mineral Company, and helped to create the copper industry of the Congo. He was elected Vice-President of the famous Union Minière, as well as of the Katanga Railway Company. But his greatest ambition was to build a railway from Lobito Bay in Angola to link up with the systems of the Congo and Rhodesia. Work began in 1906 on a concession granted to Williams and, after interruptions due to World War I, was completed in 1928. The line runs for over 820 miles inland from the west coast. He died in 1938.

Williston. Village in the northwestern Cape, founded in 1845 as a mission station called Amandelboom (Almond Tree), because of a fine old tree that grew there. It was given its present name, in honour of the Colonial Secretary, Hampden Willis, in 1883. Wheat growing on the nearby Zak River and sheep farming are the chief industries. Population: 3,400, including 1,000 Whites.

Willoughby's Consolidated Company Limited. Rhodesian mining and land company, founded in 1894 and named after Sir John C. Willoughby (q.v.), its first Chairman. It owns over 1,000,000 acres and operates four ranches with nearly 40,000 head of cattle.

Willoughby, Major Sir John Christopher. Rhodesian soldier and pioneer. Born in England February 20, 1859, and educated at Eton and Cambridge. Entered the Army in 1879 and served in Egypt. In 1890 appointed second-in-command of the Pioneer Column (q.v.). Served in the Matabele War (q.v.) and took leading part in the Jameson Raid (q.v.), for which he received a sentence from the British courts. In the South African War he had charge of transport for the Flying Column for the Relief of Mafeking. He served in World War I and died on April 16, 1918.

Willowmore. Town in the Cape Province, established in 1862 by the landowner, a farmer called Lehmkuhl, who combined his wife's maiden name, More, with that of a large willow tree growing near by. There was fighting there in the South African War during the Boer raids on Cape Colony. The town was formerly a centre of ostrich-feather production, but is now noted for wool and mohair. Population: 3,930, including 1,100 Whites.

Willowvale. Village in Cape Province, near Idutywa. Founded in 1879 as a military outpost and noted for attractive scenery. Population: 490, including 160 Whites.

Wilson, Major Allan. Rhodesian soldier, born in Ross-shire, Scotland, in 1856. He went to school at Kirkwall in the Orkneys and at Fochabers, Morayshire. As a young man he joined the Cape Mounted Rifles, served in Basutoland, then in Bechuanaland, and on the outbreak of the Matabele War of 1893 became major in command of the Victoria Column. He took charge of the ill-fated Shangani Patrol (q.v.), and was killed at the head of his men on December 4, 1893.

Wilson, J. H. Early hunter and trader. He first reached Kolobeng, in the Bechuana district, about 1846, having emigrated from the vicinity of Grahamstown. He went into partnership with Samuel H. Edwards (q.v.), with whom he made many journeys into the Kalahari desert and even explored beyond Lake Ngami. Wilson's later career is obscure, though he is known to have been on the Diamond Fields after their discovery, during the 1870's.

Wilson, 'Matabele.' See MATABELE WILSON.

Wilson Patrol. See SHANGANI PATROL.

Winburg. Original capital of the Orange Free State, established by the Voortrekkers in 1836. First spelt Wenburg, the origin of the name is still disputed, being traced by some authorities to the Boer victory over the local Matabele and by others to the victory won in a legal dispute about the site selected. It figured in several other native wars, and saw fighting in the South African War and in the 1914 Rebellion. Wheat and wool centre. Population: 5,000, including 1,454 Whites.

Windhoek. Capital of South West Africa. It began in 1870 as a station of the Rhenish Mission, and took its name from a Nama word meaning 'The Place of Smoke,' which was put into Dutch by early transport riders. The present town was founded by Captain Kurt von François in October 1890. Large sums were spent on its development by the German authorities, and in 1897 the construction of a railway from Swakopmund was begun. Because of its elevation above the sea —5,600 feet—it became popular for its bracing climate. It had just been equipped with one of the most powerful wireless stations in the world, capable of direct communication with Berlin, when World War I broke out. Windhoek was evacuated by the

Germans, and occupied by the Union forces on May 13, 1915. Since then it has grown steadily, and has become the seat of the Legislative Council. It is the centre for the karakul skin trade, which attracts buyers from overseas. The number of industries is increasing. Population: 64,700, including 35,700 Whites, 23,000 Bantu and 6,000 Coloureds.

Windsorton. Village in the north of the Cape Province, on the Vaal River. Originally known as Hebron, it was founded in 1869 as one of the earliest camps on the River Diggings, and renamed towards the end of the century in honour of P. E. Windsor, a well-known pioneer. It is a holiday resort for the district, where occasional diamond-washing occurs. Population: 2,011, including 223 Whites.

Wine. Similarity of climate and soil to those of the Mediterranean countries prompted the cultivation of grapes and attempts at wine-making at the Cape of Good Hope in 1655, but no serious progress was made until the arrival of the first Huguenot settlers in 1687–8, some of whom had experience from their native France. From that date progress was so rapid that by the beginning of the 18th century a flourishing export trade had begun, particularly in the famous sweet wines of Constantia, which for generations enjoyed a vogue even at the courts of Europe and were referred to in French, German, English and other literature. This traffic reached its peak in the 1820's, after which changes of taste, coupled with the imposition of heavy customs tariffs overseas, caused the industry to decline. A further set-back was caused by Britain's trade agreement with Portugal in 1860, and the outbreak of the vine diseases Oidium and Phylloxera (qq.v.). The latter, which ravaged the Cape vineyards at the end of the 18th century, made necessary their complete replanting with insect-resistant stocks. While

wine and brandy production for the local market never stopped, exports had dwindled so seriously that repeated efforts were made with Government help to revive them. Measures taken included the establishment of a Government Wine Farm at Constantia and the importation of the overseas expert, Baron von Babo. The fortunes of the industry were revolutionised after the founding of the K.W.V. (q.v.) in 1917. After World War I the traffic was further revived with the aid of the British house of Burgoyne and others. Today the South African product enjoys a market in Britain, Canada, Scandinavia and many other countries, while the despatch, during a period of shortage, of a tanker full of Cape wine to France itself in 1959 shows how times have changed. For climatic reasons production is concentrated in the western districts of the Cape Province, where nearly 180,000 acres are under cultivation, with about 200,000,000 vines. A large export in high-class table grapes and a large raisin industry are also maintained.

Winkelspruit. Seaside resort on the Natal south coast, 21 miles from Durban, now part of the municipality of Kingsburgh.

Winsloe, Colonel Richard William. British soldier. Born in Somersetshire in 1835 and joined the Army in 1853. Served in the Crimea and the Zulu War and, after being severely wounded in the Battle of Ulundi, was promoted to lieutenant-colonel. During the 1880 War he commanded the besieged British troops in the fort at Potchefstroom, for which he was appointed Aide-de-Camp to the Queen. In later years he served in Burma and wrote an account of the Siege of Potchefstroom. He died on June 5, 1917.

Wireless Telegraphy. *See also* SOUTH AFRICAN BROADCASTING CORPORATION. Successful experiments in wireless transmission were carried out in Port

Elizabeth in 1897, where a Post Office engineer named Edward Jennings invented wireless telegraphy independently of Marconi, but received no encouragement. German wireless sets were also imported by the Boers for use at the time of the South African War, but were captured by the British. Attempts at wireless communication were made, but did not prove of practical value. After the war wireless telegraphy was introduced for naval ships at Simonstown in 1904 and steps were taken by the Natal Colonial Government in 1908 for the erection of a transmitting station. This came into existence at Jacobs, near Durban, in 1910 when the first ships regularly trading with South Africa were also equipped. In 1911 the first wireless station was ordered for use at Slangkop, and the Germans decided to set up a high-power transmitter at Windhoek, then still in German South-West Africa. Considerable progress in wireless was made during World War I and in 1921, when the first wireless telephony was introduced at Port Elizabeth, on Bird Island.

By agreement with the Imperial Government, Beam Wireless was opened in 1927 between Klipheuvel Station, near Cape Town, and London. The system was removed from private hands and taken over by the Union Post Office in 1948. Overseas telephone services began on February 1, 1932, and have since been extended to cover almost the whole world. *See also* BROADCASTING and SOUTH AFRICAN BROADCASTING CORPORATION.

Witbank. Town in the Transvaal, the main centre of the coalfields of that province. It was founded in 1890 and has become an important industrial centre, containing one of the main stations of the Electricity Supply Commission, erected in 1923; also works for the production of carbide and cyanide of potassium (for use in the reduction works of the gold mines).

During the South African War Witbank acquired fame through the fact that, after his escape from a P.O.W. camp in Pretoria, Winston Churchill hid in the workings of a local colliery, on his way to Lourenço Marques. Population: 40,000, including 23,000 Whites.

Witbooi, Hendrik. Chief of the Witbooi Hottentots in South West Africa. (So called on account of the white cloth they wore round their heads.) He first came into prominence in 1884, when he succeeded his father Moses as head of the tribe at Gibeon, and began a war against the Hereros which lasted until 1892. After making peace he settled at Hoornkrans near Rehoboth, where he came into conflict with the new Acroman régime. He was attacked by Major Von François (q.v.) on April 12, 1893, but escaped. After a hard struggle he surrendered on September 15, 1894, and lived peacefully at Gibeon until 1904. On the outbreak of the Herero War, he broke his promise and went into rebellion. After treacherously killing many settlers he was brought to bay near Keetmanshoop, where he died of wounds on October 29, 1905. He had a certain amount of education and kept a diary, which was published in 1929 by the Van Riebeeck Society.

Witchwood. *See* NEMESIA.

Witgat (*Boscia albitrunca* Gilg. & Ben.). Shrub or small tree. Good stock feed. Seeds edible. Portions of roots used by natives for coffee or porridge. Widely distributed in Griqualand West.

Witkraai. Afrikaans name for Egyptian Vulture. *See* VULTURE.

Witkruis. Afrikaans name for Black Eagle. *See* EAGLES.

Witogie. Afrikaans name for Cape White-Eye. *See* WHITE-EYE.

Wit Ooievaar. Afrikaans name for White Stork. *See* STORKS.

Witvis (Cape), Soldier (Natal) (*Cheimerius nufar*). Fish found in Table Bay, off Agulhas Bank and Natal. About 24 inches long. *See* BREAM.

Witwatersrand. Literally the 'Ridge of the White Waters.' Largest goldfield in the world and principal industrial area of Southern Africa. The original Witwatersrand extended from Randfontein to Springs (qq.v.) a distance of approximately 60 miles, but discoveries since 1932 have carried its limits to the vicinity of Potchefstroom and Klerksdorp. The original Witwatersrand carries an area of approximately 1,200 sq. miles, and comprises the towns of Westonaria, Randfontein, Krugersdorp, Roodepoort, Maraisburg, Johannesburg, Germiston, Boksburg, Benoni, Brakpan, Springs and Nigel. This is estimated to contain a population of nearly 3,000,000, including about 800,000 Whites. The climate is healthy and bracing, largely because of the elevation above sealevel of between 5,000 and 6,000 feet.

Witwatersrand Native Labour Association. Large organisation associated with the Transvaal and O.F.S. Chamber of Mines for the recruitment of Bantu workers outside the Republic. Operations extend to Malawi and beyond. (*See* GOLD MINING INDUSTRY and NATIVE RECRUITING CORPORATION).

Witwatersrand Rifles. South African military unit, founded in December 1899. Served in the South African War and in the German South West Africa Campaign of 1915. During the rest of World War I some 94 per cent of the officers and 80 per cent other ranks served overseas in other units. In World War II served with 6th Armoured Division. Motto: 'Pro Deo Rege Patria.'

Witzieshoek. Native reserve in the north-eastern Orange Free State, in the Drakensberg, named after an early chief, Witzie, who was defeated there by the burghers of the Republic in 1857. The present reserve was set up in 1867, for the Mopeli tribe. The area is noted for its fine mountain scenery.

W.N.L.A. *See* WITWATERSRAND NATIVE LABOUR ASSOCIATION.

Woburn. Military village on the former Eastern frontier of the Cape, founded in 1848 and destroyed on Christmas Day 1850, during the Native invasion. All the men living there were killed (*see also* AUCKLAND, ELY and JUANASBURG). Woburn in England is associated with the career of Governor Sir Harry Smith (q.v.).

Wodehouse. District in the Cape Province, named after Governor Sir Philip Wodehouse (q.v.).

Wodehouse, Sir Philip Edmond. Governor of Cape Colony, born in England in 1811. Began his career as a 'Writer' in the Civil Service of Ceylon in 1828, and rose to be Government Agent for the Western Province of that island in 1843. Eight years later he was made 'Superintendent' of British Honduras, followed by promotion, in 1854, to Governor of British Guiana. In 1861 he succeeded Sir George Grey (q.v.) as Governor of the Cape. During his term the country passed through a serious depression, but also witnessed the discovery of diamonds in 1867. A pleasant, gentlemanly figure, he may claim the credit for having brought the long series of wars with the Basutos to a close by allowing Moshesh, in 1865, to 'come under the Queen's blanket' as a British subject. He fought a hard battle to prevent the grant of Responsible Government to the Colony, for which he did not consider it ripe. In 1870 he returned to England and in 1872 became Governor of Bombay, where he remained for five years. He died in 1887.

Woermann, Adolf. German shipowner and Colonial pioneer, born at

Hamburg in 1847. On behalf of the family business he helped to develop trading stations on the west coast of Africa, which ultimately became the German colonies there. In 1880 he started his own steamship company, the Woermann Line, which extended operations to German South West Africa and South Africa after 1884. From 1884 to 1890 he sat in the Reichstag. He died in May 1911 at Hamburg.

Woermann Line. German steamship line trading with South Africa, founded by Adolf Woermann (q.v.). From 1896 it ran a coasting service from Cape Town to South West Africa, and from 1898 a regular monthly service to the Cape. The Company became associated with the Hamburg-America Line in 1907 and was embodied in their German 'Round Africa' service. Since World War I the Woermann Line has been part of the German East Africa organisation.

Wolfram. *See* TUNGSTEN.

Wolhuter, Harry. Game ranger and author, born in Beaufort West in 1877. He worked on the early Witwatersrand, fought in the South African War and in 1902 joined Colonel J. Stevenson-Hamilton (q.v.) as his assistant warden for the Sabie Game Reserve, later the Kruger National Park. Wolhuter's most celebrated achievement was killing a lion with a pocket knife. He wrote an excellent book of reminiscences, *Memories of a Game Ranger*, and retired in 1946.

Wolkberg (Cloud Mountain). Mountain range 50 miles from Pietersburg, in the Northern Transvaal. Noted for its vast spectacular cave, over 3,000 feet long and with underground lakes.

Wolmarans, Senator Andries Daniel Wynand. Boer statesman, son of F. G. A. Wolmarans. He was born in Potchefstroom on September 19,

1857, became a member of the first Republican forces during the South African War, and joined a delegation sent to Europe by the Republic to secure intervention in the struggle by foreign powers. Upon the grant of Responsible Government in the Transvaal, he was elected to the Legislative Council. After Union he became a senator. He died in 1928.

Wolmaranstad. Town in the Western Transvaal, established in 1890 and named after Jacobus M. A. Wolmarans, Volksraad member, on whose farms, Rooderand and Vlakfontein, the place was laid out. Diamond digging is carried on near by. During the South African War it was in the midst of the fighting. Population: 5,872, including 2,500 Whites.

Wolseley. Village in the western Cape Province, originally known as Ceres Road. Founded in 1875 when the railway arrived there, but renamed soon after in honour of Field-Marshal Lord Wolseley, who took command in the Zulu War in 1879. The place first gained attention through its woolwashing industry. Since then canneries and mills have grown up. Population: 2,323, including 1,016 Whites.

Wolseley, Field-Marshal Viscount (Garnet Joseph Wolseley). Born in Ireland in 1833, and joined the British Army at the age of 19. After service in Burma, the Crimea, the Indian Mutiny and China, he was posted to Canada, where in 1870 he suppressed the Red River Rebellion. In 1873 he took charge of an expedition against the Ashantis on the African West Coast, and in 1875, as general, he was placed in command in Natal. Transferred to Cyprus as first Administrator, Wolseley was recalled to South Africa to replace Lord Chelmsford after the early British defeats in the Zulu War of 1879. Though the position had been restored before his arrival, he closed off the campaign and captured Cetewayo, the Zulu king. He became

Governor of Natal and set up a new system of government in Zululand under a number of lesser chiefs. Meanwhile the Transvaal had been annexed for the first time and Wolseley was appointed its Governor on September 29, 1879. He put an end to the long-drawn-out Sekukuni War, and set up a new constitution for the Transvaal as a Crown Colony. After his return to England Wolseley played a major part in reforming the British Army, overcoming much opposition. He successfully fought in Egypt in 1882 at Tel-el-Kebir but in 1884 failed in his efforts to relieve General Gordon at Khartoum. In later years he was Commander-in-Chief in Ireland from 1890 and of the British Army from 1895 to 1899. He wrote a number of books, including a Life of the Duke of Marlborough, and died in Mentone on the Riviera in 1913.

Woltemade, Wolraad. Early Cape hero and humanitarian. A dairyman of German origin, who on June 1, 1773, in a heavy north-west gale, saw the Indiaman *Jonge Thomas* driven ashore near the mouth of the Salt River. The officials of the East India Company, preoccupied with saving cargo, were leaving the ship's crew to perish, when Woltemade came past on horseback. He rode into the waves, bringing back two men holding to the animal's tail. This act he repeated until he had saved 14 of the crew. He went in once more, but was overcome by the waves and drowned. The Dutch East India Company honoured his memory by naming a ship *Die Held Woltemade* (The Hero Woltemade). In modern times several stations outside Cape Town have been named Woltemade, and a statue by I. Mitford-Barberton stands in the grounds of the South African Mutual Head Office in Pinelands.

Wonderboom. Famous tree north of Pretoria, belonging to the wild fig family. It is known to be many cen-

turies old and, with its numerous branches and other ramifications, covers nearly an acre. It is 67 feet high.

Wonderboom

Wondergat. Natural formation in Bechuanaland, 18 miles from Mafeking. A remarkable hole (gat) cut by Nature in the limestone rock, about 250 feet across. Although the area is extremely dry, the hole is always filled, below the sheer white 50-feet walls, with clear, deep-blue water. Six miles distant, at Grootfontein, is a similar pool. Underground rivers connect these formations, the level of which hardly varies. Grootfontein supplies Mafeking with over 5,000,000 gallons of water daily, far beyond its needs. Another, smaller Wondergat is found near Lichtenburg, Transvaal.

Wood, Field-Marshal Sir Henry Evelyn. British soldier, born at Braintree, Essex, on February 9, 1838. He was the son of the Reverend Sir John Page Wood, Bart. He went to school at Marlborough and entered the Navy—not the Army. Joining as a midshipman in 1852 he served with the Naval Brigade in the Crimean War, was severely wounded and distinguished himself for gallantry at Sebastopol. In 1855 he changed over to the Light Dragoons, with whom he served in India and won the V.C. in 1859. He saw African service in 1879 in Ashanti and in the Zulu War. After the defeat of Majuba he was appointed successor to Sir George Colley (q.v.) as commander in the field, but before he was able to take effective measures an armistice had been concluded. He later served in the commission that negotiated the restoration of Transvaal independence. From 1893 to 1897 he became Quartermaster-General and from 1897 to 1901, during the South African War, Adjutant-General. He wrote a number of books, including his autobiography, *From Midshipman to Field Marshal*, and died on December 21, 1919.

Wood, George. Early hunter. He arrived in Natal about 1865 and in 1866 trekked to Lake Ngami, where he started a trading store. Three years later he trekked across the present Rhodesia, and was among the earliest white men to visit Zimbabwe. In 1873 he hunted in company with F. C. Selous (q.v.). In 1882, while trekking in Barotseland, he and all the members of his party perished.

Wood, Dr. John Medley. South African botanist. Born at Mansfield, Nottinghamshire, in 1827, he spent 7 years at sea before he settled in Natal in 1852. After 30 years' farming he was appointed in 1882 Director of the Durban Botanic Gardens as well as Curator of the Colonial Herbarium. He edited *Natal Plants* and wrote extensively. Besides his eminence as a scientist, which gained him an honorary doctorate, he was a keen athlete and sportsman. He died in 1912.

Woodpeckers (family Picidae). Medium-sized birds with an interesting adaptation to their life of climbing trees and hunting for insects. They have two strong claws turned backwards, and two forwards, unusually strong, straight bills for drilling and extracting insects, sticky tongues and tail feathers as a prop for climbing. They have loud calls as well as a method of tapping signals. Most have grey-green backs, wings striped with yellow—the male—and crimson caps.

The most widely-spread is the Cardinal. One member of the family, the Crowned Woodpecker (*Geopolaptes olivacens*), has chosen a different habitat in open country, preferably among rocks, and is usually seen in small parties, getting its food entirely from the ground, and boring a tunnel nest in a bank.

Wool. The original sheep at the Cape produced a hairy growth, which could not be dignified by the name of wool, and it was not until the importation of the first merinos by Colonel Robert Jacob Gordon (q.v.) that the wool industry of the country may be said to have begun seriously. Its advance was largely due to the enterprise of the Van Bredas, Van der Bijls and other early breeders of the Western Cape Province. The native stock was gradually improved and superseded as the settlement extended first across the Karroo and then into the Orange Free State and beyond. Although the Cape was responsible for the first wool sheep in Australia, the country continued to suffer right through the 19th century from the inferior grades produced by local farmers. Prices on the whole were low and quality poor, progress being handicapped by the widespread prevalence of scab. Only very gradually was it possible for the Government to enforce a policy of dipping, which ultimately eradicated the disease. Drought and other plagues also caused the output of wool to fluctuate

Merinos

enormously. In the 20th century the policy of importing high-grade breeding rams from abroad, particularly from Australia, was intensified. Research was undertaken (particularly at Grootfontein, Cape Province) and, by joining the International Wool Organisation, South Africa succeeded in participating in the world-wide prosperity created by wool. The Cape Province is by far the largest producer in Southern Africa, followed by the Orange Free State. According to the most recent figures, the Republic has approximately 40,000,000 sheep, of which over 23,000,000 are in Cape Province, over 19,000,000 in the Orange Free State, 4,500,000 in the Transvaal, and about 1,500,000 in Natal.

Wooldridge. Village near Peddie, Cape Province. Population: 360, including 30 Whites.

Worcester. Town in the Western Cape Province, established in February 1820 and named after the brother of Governor Lord Charles Somerset, the Marquess of Worcester. Standing on the edge of the Hex River Mountains, it is one of the most attractively situated towns in South Africa. Besides its numerous industries, including distilleries, canneries and woollen-mills, Worcester has a large power station erected by the Electricity Supply Commission since World War II, to operate the electrified sections of the main railway line through the Hex River Mountains to Touws River. Winter sports, including ski-ing, are carried on near by during the season. Worcester is also noted for its large Schools for the Blind and for the Deaf and Dumb. Population: 37,500, including 12,750 Whites.

World's View. Site in the Matopo Hills of Rhodesia, selected by Cecil John Rhodes as his burial place. He described it as 'A View of the World.' Since then a number of other Rhodesians have been laid to rest there, including Sir L. S. Jameson, Sir C. P. Coghlan, and the Shangani Patrol.

World War I. The view still prevailed in 1914 that when the King, as head of the British Empire, declared war, South Africa was automatically involved (a circumstance that largely contributed to the Rebellion, q.v., of that year), and the Union, though only 4 years old, played an independent rôle from an early stage. At the start of hostilities in August 1914, General Louis Botha, the Prime Minister, offered to replace the Imperial garrison with local troops, and a few days later the last British forces departed. The Union Defence Force, established as recently as 1912 and now the mainstay of the country's military activities, first had to devote its energies to the suppression of the Rebellion, and despite landings at Lüderitzbucht in September 1914, it was not until 1915 that its major move began against German South West Africa. The fact that enemy territory directly adjoined the Union was a source of anxiety to the authorities, especially after reports of alleged frontier violation at Nakob.

Because of the ill-feeling generated by the Rebellion, only volunteers were employed in the invasion of German South West Africa, a policy continued throughout the war. A double attack was made—overland from the Upington side, the railway from De Aar being laid at the rate of a mile a day, and from the sea, in January 1915, at Walvis Bay and Swakopmund. As the Union troops advanced the German troops withdrew, though there were actions at Gibeon, Rietfontein and elsewhere. On May 11 Windhoek was captured, and the enemy, driven back north, surrendered at Khorab on July 9, 1915.

Meanwhile preparations were afoot for the despatch of a South African brigade to France and of other forces to German East Africa and Egypt. The first troops reached the Western Front on April 23, 1916, winning much glory but suffering heavy casualties in the battle of Delville Wood (q.v.). Operations by South African troops in East Africa began in December 1915; owing to the unsatisfactory results achieved, the original commander, General Sir Horace Smith-Dorrien, was in 1916 followed by General J. C. Smuts (q.v.), aided by L. J. van Deventer (q.v.). Sickness, particularly malaria, made heavy inroads on the South Africans and, thanks to the exceptional skill and resourcefulness of General Paul Von Lettow-Vorbeck, the campaign there dragged on until the 1918 Armistice, the surrender of the Germans, still undefeated, taking place on the soil of Northern Rhodesia. Apart from this South African units served in the Middle East theatre, including Egypt and Libya early in 1916. Total enlistments by South Africans were 231,591, of all races, including 146,515 White troops, 382 White nurses, 1,925 Coloured troops and 82,769 in the Native Labour Contingent. Casualties (nearly all White) totalled 18,642—of whom 6,606 were deaths (4,632 killed or died of wounds) and 12,036 were wounded—and 2,400 were taken prisoner. Service in the different campaigns was as follows:

Whites

Rebellion	30,000
German South West Africa	67,237
France	30,880
German East Africa and Central Africa	47,521
do. (Road and Military Labour Corps)	1,044
Service in Union	5,180

Bantu

German South West Africa (non-combatant)	35,000
France (non-combatant) ..	5,823
East and Central Africa ..	18,000

In addition 25,090 served in the South African Native Labour Corps in France. Many thousands also joined Imperial units, the Royal Navy and Royal Air Force (and its predecessors, the Royal Flying Corps and Royal Naval Air Service).

Munition production on a small scale took place in the workshops of the South African Railways, besides which cordite from local explosives factories was supplied to Britain. Many South African experts went to Britain to serve in war factories, and the services of K. B. Quinan, manager of the Cape Explosives Works, lent to the British Government during the 1914–15 'Shell Crisis' to build the giant explosives works at Gretna, Queensferry and elsewhere, were publicly acknowledged by the Cabinet in the House of Commons.

During World War I Rhodesia enjoyed the distinction of contributing the highest proportion of her White man-power of any member of the British Commonwealth, enlistments being estimated at 6,831 out of a total population of 25,000, and of these 732 gave their lives. Detachments of the B.S.A. Police and other units supported Botha's invasion of German South West by attacks on the Caprivi Zipfel (q.v.). Rhodesians also fought along with the South Africans in East Africa and in France.

World War II. The outbreak of World War II brought a major political crisis to South Africa, General J. B. M. Hertzog (q.v.), the Prime Minister, refusing to join Britain in breaking off relations with Germany and attempting to proclaim the neutrality of the Union. Defeated on this issue in Parliament, he gave way to General J. C. Smuts (q.v.), and on September 6, 1939, 3 days after the United Kingdom, South Africa also declared war. Beyond the setting up of a War Supplies Organisation under Dr. H. J. van der Bijl (q.v.), for which preparations had been made in time of peace, and the mobilising of certain units, little change occurred in the Union until the fall of France and the entry of Italy as the ally of Germany in June 1940 brought the war to African soil. The existence of a large section of the populace still opposed to the Union's participation, coupled with attempts at sabotage on the Home Front, prompted the Government to do without conscription. In spite of this the enlistments by volunteers compared favourably with those in other units of the Commonwealth, totalling 345,049. Among them were many women, who did excellent service as combatants, while tens of thousands of Bantu were employed as guards, drivers and in similar capacities. As in World War I, Coloured men served in the Middle East.

To avoid difficulties, a system was adopted with South African troops under which all those willing to serve outside Africa took a special oath, those who did so being distinguished by the wearing on their shoulders of the famous 'Red Tab.'

During the latter part of 1940 the first units from the Union proceeded to East Africa, large base camps being set up in Kenya—at Gilgil and elsewhere. The first action against the enemy occurred at El Wak on the border of Italian Somaliland on December 14, 1940, followed by the successive invasions of that country and of Abyssinia. In both these campaigns South Africans played an outstanding rôle, largely owing to the remarkable military gifts of General Dan Pienaar (q.v.). Over 80,000 Italian prisoners were sent to the Union during the war, most of them confined at Sonderwater near Pretoria.

After the victory in Italian East Africa South African units were transferred to the Middle East theatre, where they fought gallantly and suffered heavy losses in the Western Desert fighting. The worst single disaster was the capture at Tobruk on June 21, 1942, of almost 10,000 South African troops under General Klopper, who was confronted with an impossible strategic situation. South Africans played a notable part in the Battle of El Alamein, and in the advance that finally drove the Axis troops out of North Africa. With reorganisation of Allied forces the South Africans became part of the Sixth Division. Continuing their service in Europe, the South Africans shared in the entire Italian campaign, besides which, as in World War I, large numbers served in the Imperial units in Europe and the East. With the entry of Japan into the war in 1941 and her victories in the Indian Ocean, a grave danger arose of her occupying Madagascar. To forestall this South African troops played a leading part in the seizing of that island in 1942. Many South Africans also served in the Burma campaign and in many other theatres.

Apart from this the small South African Navy, reorganised during World War II, took part in operations in North Africa (including Tobruk) and elsewhere. On the industrial side the Union contributed impressively to the Allied cause, building up valuable munition works, supplying innumerable kinds of stores, handling repairs, and provisioning thousands of ships in convoy. The South African Air Force underwent great expansion and fought in East Africa, the Middle East and Europe, including some of the famous long-distance raids on German-occupied Poland and Rumania. Large numbers of Royal Air Force recruits were trained in the Union.

Rhodesia rivalled her recruiting achievements in World War I, though this time she adopted conscription. Out of 67,000 Whites enlistments numbered 8,000, units often being brigaded with those from the Union. They fought with much gallantry in Italian East Africa, the Middle East and Burma, where the King's African Rifles (q.v.) and other African regiments were in action. Rhodesia was a major training centre for the Royal Air Force, as part of its overseas dispersal scheme, thousands of men receiving their 'wings' there. Large contributions in man-power were also made by the High Commission Territories, notably Basutoland and Swaziland, which raised labour contingents, and Bechuanaland, which provided substantial numbers of troops.

Worsfold, William Basil. South African writer, born in 1858 in Yorkshire, England, and educated at Wakefield School. He studied at University College, Oxford, and qualified for the Bar. After lecturing at his university, he became interested in South Africa and in 1895 wrote an account of that country. This was followed by a history in 1898 and by a further book on Portuguese Nyasaland in 1899. During 1900 he wrote another history; he edited an account of Lord Milner's work in South Africa from 1897 to 1902. From 1904 to 1905 he was editor of the *Star* in Johannesburg. Even after his return to England he continued an interest in the country and wrote an account of the Union in 1912, a life of Sir Bartle Frere in 1923 and a large number of other books. He died in 1939.

W.R. Abbreviation for Witwatersrand Rifles (q.v.).

Wragge, Walter Thomas. Judge of the Natal Supreme Court. Born in 1842, he studied at Oxford and began his career in the Indian Civil Service. He was called to the Bar in 1879 and became a judge of the Natal Supreme

Court in 1883. Retiring in 1898 he died in 1913.

Wrasses. A large family of brightly-coloured fish, many of them small, belonging to temperate and tropical waters, especially among rocks and coral reefs. Natal and Indian seas. Most, but not all, are edible. Some have the curious habit of building sea-weed nests in rock crevices. Among them are the Beaked Wrasse (*Gomphosus coeruleus*) (10 inches) and the tiny 4-inch Sea Swallow (*Lambroides diminiatus*), with its black, lengthwise band. Several varieties have ornamental bars and stripes.

Wulp. Afrikaans name for Curlew (q.v.).

Wuppertal. German mission station near Clanwilliam, Cape Province. Population: 740, including 30 Whites.

Wylde, Sir John. Chief Justice of the Cape Supreme Court and brother of Lord Chancellor Wylde. Born in London in 1781, he was educated at St. Paul's School and Cambridge, and was called to the Bar at the Middle Temple in 1805. After serving as Judge-Advocate of New South Wales from 1815 to 1825, he became first Chief Justice of the Cape in 1827 and remained in office until 1855. He died in Cape Town in 1859.

Wynberg. Suburb of Cape Town, and until 1927 an independent municipality. It was founded in the 17th century, and took its name from the surrounding wine farms. Later a beautiful residential area grew up on Wynberg Hill. The second railway in the Cape, taking off from the Cape Town–Wellington line at Salt River, was built to Wynberg in 1862.

X

Xalanga. District in the Transkei, of which Cala (q.v.) is chief town. Name is derived from a Xosa word meaning 'a vulture.'

Xanthium Spinosum. Also known as Burweed or Boetebossie. Plant accidentally introduced into South Africa in 1859. It was found near Simonstown, and soon spread throughout the country, its burs—or prickly fruits—causing heavy loss to sheep farmers. Legislation was later introduced to ensure its extermination, but it is still to be found.

Xesibe. Tribe in the Eastern Cape Province, inhabiting an area on the eastern part of the Umzimvubu River basin.

Xesibe District. Portion of the Transkei, the main centre of which is Mount Ayliff (q.v.).

Xinavane. Settlement in Mozambique near Lourenço Marques, and centre for the Incomati Sugar Estates.

Xosa (more correctly **Amaxosa**, also spelt **Xhosa**). African tribe with its home in the Eastern Cape Province. Originally known as the Aba-nguni, after an early ruler named Mnguni, of whom virtually nothing is known. A successor of his, at some late date, was known as Xosa, from whom the tribe has taken its more common designation. According to J. H. Soga, the tribe probably originated in East Africa, being divided into a number of clans. These moved into Southern Africa some time in the 17th century, and after internecine wars two parties, the Gaikas and Galekas, separated about 1750. They were established beyond the Fish River when the first white settlers made contact with them

about 1752. From that time there were frequent wars between the two races, and the Great Fish River came to be accepted as the southern boundary. Governor Sir Benjamin D'Urban in 1835 set up the 'Province of Queen Adelaide' (q.v.) as a buffer territory, but received orders from London to return it to the Xosas. The chief cause of trouble was the theft of cattle in raids across the frontier. After the Battle of Grahamstown in 1819 their offensive power was considerably reduced, but despite the fact that certain sections like the Galekas were normally friendly, they continued to be a menace until 1856 when, through the calamity of the Cattle Killing Delusion (q.v.), they broke their own military power. Henceforth the Xosas lived in peace with the European settlers, largely through the efforts of Governor Sir George Grey, who did his utmost to encourage the spread of education and civilisation. In 1877 they were, however, once more involved in what proved to be the last serious native war on the eastern frontier. In their culture and language the Xosas are closely related to the Zulus (q.v.). They practise circumcision, which is carried out on young men at puberty. Polygamy is recognised by their own law, and most of the agricultural work is left to the women. Since the discovery of the Witwatersrand the Xosas have contributed a considerable percentage of the labour force of the Witwatersrand and other gold mines, as well as of the non-European population of South African cities. It is estimated that there are about 2,500,000 Xosas in South Africa.

Y-Z

Yachting in South Africa. Individual owners began yachting early in the 19th century, but it was not until 1857 that the first regatta took place in Table Bay, followed in 1858 by the first one at Durban and by the foundation of the Durban Regatta Club which became the still flourishing Royal Natal Yacht Club. Since then the sport has achieved enormous popularity, and not only at the coast. Of more than 120 yacht clubs in South Africa, nearly one-third operate on inland waters in the Transvaal, with large numbers in the Orange Free State and in Rhodesia. The total membership is over 25,000. *See also* BRUCE DALLING, ' VOORTREKKER ' and ' STORMVOGEL '.

Yao. Tribe scattered in Malawi and Mozambique.

Yates, Dornford. *See* MERCER, C. W.

Yellow Ground. Characteristic geological formation occurring in the diamond pipes at Kimberley, where it overlies the Blue Ground (q.v.). It was first thought that only Yellow Ground carried the stones.

Yellowtail (*Seriola lalandii*). Albacore (corrupted to Half-cord). A highly-esteemed food fish, up to 6 feet long, arriving in shoals from October throughout the Cape summer, off Port Nolloth, Cape Agulhas and especially in False Bay. Strong and graceful, it has an olive-green back and yellow-green tail. The Latin name honours the French naturalist, Delalande, who visited the Cape in 1820.

Yellow-Wood (*Podocarpus falcatus*). Magnificent tree with massive trunk and wide, spreading crown. Slow-growing and found chiefly in Tzitsikama Forest (gigantic specimens known to be two thousand years old).

Several varieties elsewhere east of Table Mountain. Wood: light yellow and of even grain; valuable for furniture and flooring. *See* PLANTS.

Yeta II. King of the Barotse (q.v.) and son of Lewanika (q.v.).

York. Village near New Hanover, Natal, founded by the Byrne Settlers in 1849. Population: 40, including 10 Whites.

Young, Professor Andrew. South African geologist, born in Perthshire in 1873. He studied at Edinburgh and was appointed to the Chair of Mineralogy and Geology at the South African College in 1902. He attained considerable distinction in his researches, notably on inland tides. He died in 1937.

Young, Francis Brett. English writer on South Africa. Born at Halesowen, Worcestershire, in 1884 and qualified in medicine at the University of Birmingham. Passed through South Africa as army doctor 1915 on the way to East Africa. Well known as a novelist in England before revisiting South Africa in 1936. *They Seek a Country*, a story of the Great Trek, appeared in 1937, followed in 1939 by *The City of Gold*, based on the story of the Rand. In 1945 he settled in St. James, Cape Town, where he wrote *In South Africa*. Failing health took him in 1949 to Montagu, where he died March 28, 1954.

Young, Sir Hubert Winthrop. Governor of Northern Rhodesia, born in 1885. In 1932 he became Governor of Nyasaland, where he remained for two years, and he was Governor of Northern Rhodesia from 1934 to 1938. During this period his wife, Lady Margaret Mary Rose Young, who had qualified as an air pilot, was lost and found again in dramatic circumstances in the Rhodesian bush. He died in 1950.

Young, Professor Robert Burns. South African geologist and brother of Professor Andrew Young (q.v.). Born in Scotland in 1874, he was educated at the Universities of Glasgow and Edinburgh. In 1903 he came to South Africa and joined the staff of the South African College, but soon changed over to the School of Mines in Johannesburg. Apart from his important researches on the formation of the Witwatersrand, he was considerably interested in archaeology, and became President of the Geological Society of South Africa. He died in 1949.

Youth Movements. South Africa occupies a unique position as the place where the most famous of all Youth Movements, that of the Boy Scouts, had its origin. During the Boer War General Robert Baden-Powell (q.v.), while in command of the garrison besieged in Mafeking (q.v.), used boys as runners and messengers. This gave him the idea of an organisation which in 1907 came into existence in England as the Boy Scouts. As early as 1908 the movement started in the Transvaal, and in 1910 the Union's first Governor-General, Lord Gladstone (q.v.), became its first Chief Scout. In 1923 the various provincial Boy Scout Associations were merged. Girl Guides began in South Africa in 1910 and were fully organised in 1920. Efforts to start Scouting for Non-Whites began in 1911. 'Trackers' were established in 1919, but were replaced in 1922 by the Pathfinders. The African Boy Scouts Association was started in 1950. In 1931 the first Indian Boy Scouts were established in Natal, and in 1936 the Paladins were set up in the Transvaal for Coloured boys. Although the Scout Movement has always been non-racial, a number of Afrikaners preferred to set up their own organisations. Of these the most important was the

Voortrekkers. Dr. C. F. Visser of Bloemfontein made his first attempts in this direction in 1918, but in 1929 a new beginning was made, and largely through the efforts of Dr. Nicholas Johannes van der Merwe, who became their leader, the Voortrekkers began to grow rapidly. Today they are found in most parts of the Republic, with separate sections for boys and girls.

Yule, Major-General Sir James Herbert. British soldier, born in 1847 and entered the Army in 1865. Served in Burma, Afghanistan and India. As colonel he was placed in charge, first of infantry reinforcements sent from India on the outbreak of the South African War, and afterwards of an infantry brigade in Natal. He was in action at Talana Hill, tried to intercept the Boer retreat from Elandslaagte and commanded the retreat to Ladysmith. He died in 1920.

Yutar, Dr. Percy. Deputy Attorney-General for the Transvaal. Born in Cape Town, July 29, 1911, and educated at the University of Cape Town. Joined Civil Service in 1934 in the Telephone Department, but three years later transferred to the Department of Justice, becoming Public Prosecutor in Johannesburg in 1940. Well-known for handling many important criminal cases, including several connected with subversion.

Zak River. River in the North-Western Cape, noted for its irrigation scheme and large wheat production by means of Saaidams (q.v.). Now usually spelt 'Sak.'

Zambesi (also written **Zambezi**). Largest river in Southern Africa; rises in Eastern Angola, and in its earlier reaches is known as the Liba or Liambui. The name Zambesi is believed to be a corruption of the word Ambei, signifying 'Great Waters,' the 'Z' having been added as an expression of emphasis. Starting at an altitude of 5,000 feet above sea-level in latitude 11 degrees 21 minutes South and

Zambesi River Stern Wheeler

longitude 24 degrees 4 minutes East, the Zambesi flows through the Lobale, Barotse and Mambunda country, and along the Caprivi Zipfel (q.v.), which forms the extreme north-eastern frontier of South West Africa. After passing such cataracts as the Katima and Motilo Falls, and being fed by a series of rivers, including the Chobe (Lunyanti), Longo, Loeti, Nengo, Luanginga, Luampa, Kabompo and others, the Zambesi reaches the Victoria Falls (q.v.), below which there are further tributaries, notably the Gwaai, Sengwe, Sanyati, Angwa, Hunyani, Kafue, Luangwa and Shire. The last brings down the waters of Lake Nyasa and greatly adds to the size of the Zambesi. After a number of rapids the Zambesi enters the Kariba Gorge (q.v.), where the greatest storage and water power scheme in Africa has been constructed. For about 120 miles towards its mouth, the Zambesi is navigable for shallow-draught steamers. It forms a delta, covering about 4,000 sq. miles, and enters the sea in Northern Mozambique The length of the river is approximately 1,600 miles, and the area drained is about 520,000 sq. miles. Towards the end of the 19th century the British Navy maintained a number of gunboats at the mouth of the Zambesi, by special arrangement with the Portuguese authorities.

Zambesi Nicator. Alternative name for Yellow-spotted Shrike. *See* SHRIKES.

Zambia (formerly **Northern Rhodesia**). Independent Commonwealth republic, formerly part of Federation of Rhodesia and Nyasaland. Its area of 291,000 square miles is nearly twice that of the former Southern Rhodesia; its population is far smaller: 3,780,000 according to the 1966 estimate, comprising 3,700,000 Africans, 70,000 Whites, 10,000 Asian and 2,600 Coloured. The capital is Lusaka (q.v.). The republic is headed by a President, with wide powers, who is elected at the same time as the National Assembly or Parliament of 75 members. He appoints the Vice-President, as well as the Cabinet. Ten of the Assembly seats are reserved for representatives of the White community, while the traditional rulers of the various tribes have a 'House of Chiefs', whose functions, however, are only advisory.

By far the most important part economically is the Copperbelt in the north near the Congo border, where are the greatest sources of wealth and the major population centres. Copper mining and refining, of which Zambia is one of the world's chief operators, is the main industry, with an output in 1968 of 804,134 tons (refined) valued at over £358,161,000. At Kabwe, too, large quantities of zinc (44,600 tons) and lead (16,300 tons) are recovered. Further mining development is in progress. Total value of mineral output in 1967 was £236,000,000.

Manufactures are still in the early stages, with 297 establishments in 1961 employing 17,894 people, and output worth £11,400,000. Building construction in 1962 stood at £2,702,000. Foreign trade figures in recent years are impossible to separate from those of the whole Central African Federation. *See also* RHODESIA RAILWAYS, KARIBA and individual towns.

Farming, mainly African, includes tobacco, maize and cattle; experiments are being made with rice and other tropical crops. Fish are being cultivated in Lake Kariba and other waters. Currency: Kwachas and Ngwees (q.v.).

Crops in Zambia, 1966–67

Maize, 4,163,000 bags.
Groundnuts, 188,000 bags.
Tobacco, 12,000,000 lb.

ZAMBIA—CHRONOLOGY

1798 Dr. Francisco José de Lacerda and J. Pinto, Portuguese explorers, follow the Zambesi beyond Tete to Cazembe, 780 miles from the sea, where de Lacerda dies.

1802–11 Pedro Baptista and Amaro José, Portuguese half-castes, cross Africa from Angola to the Zambesi and traverse the present Zambia.

1831 Captain Gamito, a Portuguese, reaches Cazembe from Mozambique.

1850 David Livingstone reaches the Zambesi from the south.

1855 Livingstone discovers the Victoria Falls.

1858 Livingstone explores the Shire River, Lake Nyasa and the Zambesi River.

1860–3 British expedition on the Zambesi.

1875 Dr. Emil Holub reaches the Zambesi.

1877 Colonel A. A. Serpa Pinto crosses Africa.

1883–7 Dr. Emil Holub visits the Mashukulumbwe country.

1889 Northern Rhodesia brought under African Order-in-Council. British South Africa Company receives its charter.

1890 Elliott Lochner signs treaty with King Lewanika of Barotseland.

1891 Mr. (later Sir) Harry Johnson becomes Her Majesty's Commissioner and Consul-General for Central Africa.

1896 Northern Rhodesia divided into North-Eastern and North-Western Rhodesia.

1897 Robert Coryndon appointed first British Resident in Barotseland.

1898 Chartered company secures sole mineral rights in Barotseland from King Lewanika.

1902 Roan Antelope and Bwana Mkubwa copper mines found.

1903 Final suppression of slave trade.

1904 Angoni tribe submits to British authority.
Victoria Falls Bridge opened.
Railway crosses Zambesi.

1905 Livingstone becomes capital of North-Western Rhodesia.

1906 Railway carried to Broken Hill.

1908 Kansanshi Mine produces first copper.

1910 Nkana Mine discovered by Moffat Thompson.

1911 North-Eastern and North-Western Rhodesia united.

1912 Copper production begun at Bwana Mkubwa Mine.

1917 Proposal to merge Northern and Southern Rhodesia approved in Legislative Council at Salisbury, but taken no further because of disagreement of elected members. Advisory Council established in Northern Rhodesia.

1918 German forces under General von Lettow-Vorbeck surrender near Fort Rosebery.

1923 Exclusive right of prospecting over 52,000 square miles granted by chartered company to Rhodesian Congo Border Development Company Limited.

1924 Protectorate established over Northern Rhodesia. First Governor, Sir Herbert Stanley.

fact that his uncle was Head Gardener to the Grand Duke Theodor of Baden. In the latter's park at Schwetzingen he met a well-known botanist, Theodor Hartweg, whom in 1822 he accompanied on a voyage to Mauritius. Disembarking at the Cape, he decided to go no further and began making large collections in conjunction with C. F. Ecklon (q.v.). An outstanding botanist but a bad business man, he struggled for years to make a precarious living by exporting plants from the Colony. Forced to sell his own precious herbarium to Dr. K. W. L. Pappe (q.v.), he finally took a post as an ordinary gardener. He died from smallpox in December 1858.

Ziekentrooster. Literally 'Sick Comforter.' A chaplain employed by the Dutch East India Company, usually of very slight academic attainments. He was not expected to preach but merely to read out passages from the Scriptures.

Zietsman, Paul. Early Boer hunter in Rhodesia, where he is known to have done a great deal of game shooting between 1868 and 1870.

Zimbabwe Creeper (*Podranea bryesi* Sprague) (Bignoniaceae). Conspicuous and attractive Rhodesian climber with terminal clusters of pink tubular flowers, opening into five petals; five sepals and four stamens. Fruit a long capsule (pod) with many winged seeds. Bignoniaceae is a family chiefly of shrubs and trees, and containing also Cape (or Kaffir) Honeysuckle (*Tecomaria capensis*), a straggling shrub 6 to 8 feet, found in bushy country of Eastern Cape and Natal; autumn flowering; bright orange tubular flowers with prominent pistil and stamens; cultivated as a hedge. *See* JACARANDA.

Zimbabwe Ruins. Most famous of ancient relics in Rhodesia. They are located approximately 17 miles from Fort Victoria, and were dis-

covered in 1867 by Adam Renders (q.v.), who was followed in 1870 by Carl Mauch (q.v.). Opinions as to their age range from the time of biblical King Solomon to a few centuries ago. Gertrude Caton-Thompson held that they were not more than about 800 years old, but this view has been disproved by radio-activity tests, which make the age nearly 1,000 years. The ruins are divided into three groups. The Acropolis occupies the summit of a koppie and is in the nature of a fortification. In the neighbouring valley is the Elliptical Temple, with great cyclopean walls and an overall length of about 265 feet. These walls rise to a height of about 30 feet, and are up to 15 feet thick, a characteristic feature being the chevron pattern in the stonework. The third landmark is the Conical Tower, regarded by many, but not all, as a phallic symbol. Between the Elliptical Temple and the Acropolis are a large number of broken-down walls, extending for nearly a mile, which occupy a space known as The Valley of the Ruins. A good deal of damage was done in the past by prospectors and amateur archaeologists, but the ruins today are carefully guarded by the Government. *See also* ARCHAEOLOGY.

Zinc. Metal found in the Transvaal and in Zambia, where it is commercially produced at Kabwe.

Zoar. Mission station near Ladismith, Cape Province. Population: 1,673, including 10 Whites.

Zoekmekaar. Village in the Northern Transvaal, established 1916. The name is derived from the incident when, according to tradition, the surveyors became separated in the mist, and had to seek each other (Zoek Mekaar). Cattle-breeding and general farming are carried on near by. Population: 2,000, including 400 Whites.

Zomba. Township in Malawi, established in September 1900, 42 miles north-east of Blantyre and 37 miles from Limbe. It is now chiefly used for housing government officials. The population is 800 Europeans, 5,300 Africans and 530 of other races.

Zonderwater. Farm near Pretoria, on which is located a large part of the Premier Mine (q.v.). During World War II it was used as an Army training centre, as well as a prisoner-of-war camp for as many as 80,000 Italians.

Zoutpansberg. *See* SOUTPANSBERG.

Zuid-Afrikaansche Republiek Polisie. Police force of the former South African Republic, established in 1881. Its detective section was known as 'Geheime Speurders.' At the outbreak of the Boer War they numbered perhaps 1,400 men, of whom all but 200 were white. Apart from duties within the Transvaal, they also kept order in Swaziland. During the Boer War the 'Zarps' maintained a very gallant record in the field and suffered heavy casualties.

Zulu Cattle. Breed developed in Zululand, very tough, though small in build.

Zulus. African tribe numbering approximately 2,500,000. Their main home is in northern Natal, in the territory now known as Zululand. Associated races and clans are found throughout a large part of Natal and into the Cape Province. The Matabele of Rhodesia and the Angoni (q.v.) of Malawi are also related. The Zulus are believed to have emigrated from the vicinity of the great Central African lakes about the 15th century, and were a group of little importance until about the 18th century, when, through the organising power and warlike gifts first of Dingiswayo and later of Tshaka (q.v.), they developed from an obscure and allegedly timid clan into a name of terror throughout Southern Africa. After the murder of Tshaka and the fruitless attempt of Dingaan (q.v.) to halt the entry into his country of the Voortrekkers, the

majority of the Zulus withdrew north of the Tugela River, which became the accepted boundary between them and the Whites, although large numbers of Zulus settled in Natal proper. There was comparative peace under Panda (q.v.), but disputes came to a crisis during the reign of Cetewayo (q.v.), who was defeated in the Zulu War (q.v.), deposed, and ultimately reinstated with very limited powers. During the 1880's Zululand became the scene of great turmoil and inter-tribal wars between a number of minor chiefs. British authority was established, but it was not until 1897 that the country finally became part of Natal. Among the African people the Zulus are regarded as aristocrats. They have a high moral standard, a fine language, handsome appearance and natural dignity. Many of them have found employment in the police, but they have an aversion to mining. In 1906 there was a further rising in Zululand (*see* BAMBATA REBELLION), since when the country has been at peace. Despite the development of a considerable sugar industry in Zululand, the country remains under the traditional style of tribal exploitation and there is still a Paramount Chief, recognised by the Government. Large numbers of Zulus are today to be found in Durban and other cities.

Zulu War. Relations between the Natal Colonial authorities and the Zulu people steadily deteriorated after the death of Panda (q.v.) in 1872, largely on account of the tyrannical system of government still enforced by his successor, Cetewayo (q.v.). Periodic representations by the Natal Government and the tactful efforts of Sir Theophilus Shepstone (q.v.), who in 1873 carried out a formal 'coronation' of the Zulu king, failed to stop Cetewayo's attempts to assert his authority over fugitives from his country into Natal. Matters came to a head in December 1878 over a disputed boundary with the Transvaal. Extra British troops had been imported and on January 10, 1879, a British force invaded Zululand. Incompetent leadership was responsible for the disaster of Isandhlwana (q.v.) on January 22, when more than 800 lives were lost. Immediately after came the Zulu onslaught on Rorke's Drift (q.v.), in which a handful of defenders beat off the attack that might have subdued Natal. Upon the receipt of news of these defeats in Britain, which was delayed owing to the absence of cable links, a large number of reinforcements were despatched to Natal, where Lord Chelmsford had been replaced by Sir Evelyn Wood. The renewed invasion of Zululand began on March 29, 1879, and was followed by the capture of Eshowe and the final defeat of the Zulu forces, first at Kambula and then at Ulundi, the Zulu army being variously estimated at between 12,000 and 25,000. Cetewayo was captured on August 28. Among the casualties was the Prince Imperial, Louis Napoleon of France (q.v.). About 30,000 British troops were involved in the campaign, the cost of which was over £5,000,000.

Zuurbekom. Pumping station of the Rand Water Board (q.v.) south of Johannesburg, noted for its plentiful dolomite springs, which at one time provided a large part of the Johannesburg water supply.

Zuurbraak. Village in the Cape Province, established as a station by the London Missionary Society in 1812 by the Reverend Seidenfaden. It lies between Swellendam and Heidelberg and is noted for the beauty of its scenery and for the fertility of its soil.

Zuurveld (Sout Veld). Original name of the district of Albany (q.v.).

Zwartkoppies. Farm on the east of Pretoria where Senator Samuel (Sammy) Marks lived for many years. He moved there during the early 1880's and carried out many of the first experiments in modern agriculture, including ploughing, silage and dairying, in the Transvaal. Zwartkoppies Hall, the homestead, was enlarged until it had over 40 rooms, where many visiting celebrities were entertained. The estate has been entailed for several generations under the will of Mr. Marks and is still in the hands of the family.

Zwartkops: 1. Township seven miles out of Port Elizabeth, on the river of the same name. Popular as a residential and yachting centre.
2. Station of the South African Air Force outside Pretoria, established during World War I, and used for training purposes.

Zwartkops River (also written **Swartkops**). Rises in Winterhoek Mountains and flows through Uitenhage, where it is largely used in the woolwashing industry. Near the mouth it becomes a popular resort for yachtsmen and fishermen from Port Elizabeth. Enters the sea at Algoa Bay.

Zwartruggens. Settlement in the Transvaal, near Rustenburg, established early in the present century. Its name is derived from the black ridges (ruggens) in the neighbourhood. Diamonds have been exploited near by.

Zwelitsha. Bantu township near King William's Town, established in connection with a large textile mill catering particularly for the needs of the native population, and employing over 1,000 hands. Large cotton interests in Britain collaborated in the project, which was set up with Government assistance. Population: 6,237, including 7 Whites.

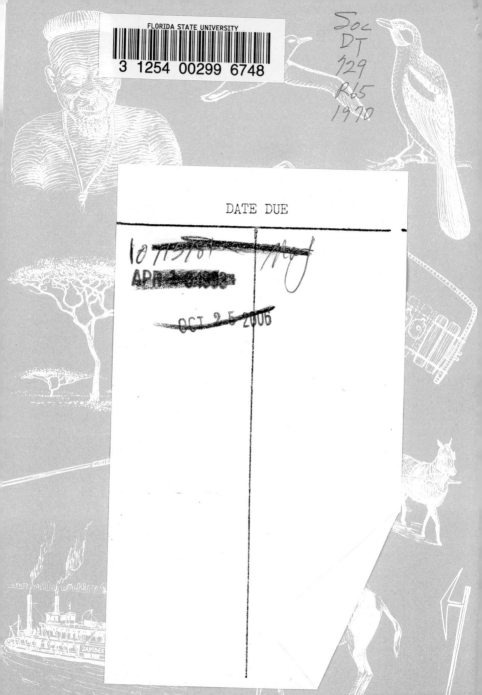